W9-AJQ-009

ALSO BY DORIS KEARNS GOODWIN

THE BULLY PULPIT

TEAM OF RIVALS

WAIT TILL NEXT YEAR

THE FITZGERALDS AND THE KENNEDYS

LYNDON JOHNSON AND THE AMERICAN DREAM

No Ordinary Time has won the following awards:

Pulitzer Prize for History
Harold Washington Literary Award
New England Bookseller Association Award
The Ambassador Book Award
The Washington Monthly Political Book Award

NO ORDINARY TIME

Franklin and Eleanor Roosevelt:
The Home Front in World War II

Doris Kearns Goodwin

SIMON & SCHUSTER
New York   London   Toronto   Sydney   New Delhi

Simon & Schuster
1230 Avenue of the Americas
New York, NY 10020

This Simon & Schuster hardcover edition November 2013

SIMON & SCHUSTER and colophon are registered trademarks of Simon & Schuster, Inc.

For information about special discounts for bulk purchases, please contact Simon & Schuster Special Sales at 1-866-506-1949 or business@simonandschuster.com.

The Simon & Schuster Speakers Bureau can bring authors to your live event. For more information or to book an event contact the Simon & Schuster Speakers Bureau at 1-866-248-3049 or visit our website at www.simonspeakers.com.

Designed by Levavi & Levavi
Jacket design by Jackie Seow
Jacket photograph courtesy of the Franklin D. Roosevelt Library and Museum, Hyde Park, New York

Manufactured in the United States of America

10 9 8 7 6 5 4 3 2 1

Library of Congress Cataloging-in-Publication Data

Goodwin, Doris Kearns.
  No ordinary time : Franklin and Eleanor Roosevelt :
the home front in World War II / Doris Kearns Goodwin.
    p.   cm.
  Includes bibliographical references and index.
  1. Roosevelt, Franklin D. (Franklin Delano), 1882–1945. 2. Roosevelt, Eleanor, 1884–1962. 3. World War, 1939–1945—United States. 4. United States—History—1933–1945. 5. Presidents—United States—Biography. 6. Presidents' spouses—United States—Biography. I. Title.
E807.G66   1994
973.917'092'2 b—dc20   94-28565

ISBN 978-1-4767-5057-6
ISBN 978-1-4391-2619-6 (ebook)

To my sons,

Richard, Michael, and Joseph

CONTENTS

PREFACE

On May 10, 1940, Hitler invaded Holland, Luxembourg, Belgium, and France, bringing the "phony war" to an end, and initiating a series of events which led, almost inevitably, to America's involvement in history's greatest armed conflict. The titanic battles of that war, the movement of armies across half the surface of the globe, have been abundantly described. Less understood is how the American home front affected the course of the war, and how the war, in turn, altered the face of American life. This book is the story of that home front, told through the lives of Franklin and Eleanor Roosevelt and the circle of friends and associates who lived with them in the family quarters of the White House during World War II.

The Roosevelt White House during the war resembled a small, intimate hotel. The residential floors of the mansion were occupied by a series of houseguests, some of whom stayed for years. The permanent guests occasionally had private visitors of their own for cocktails or for meals, but for the most part their lives revolved around the president and first lady, who occupied adjoining suites in the southwest quarter of the second floor. On the third floor, in a cheerful room with slanted ceilings, lived Missy LeHand, the president's personal secretary and longtime friend. The president's alter ego, Harry Hopkins, occupied the Lincoln Suite, two doors away from the president's suite. Anna Boettiger, the president's daughter, moved into Hopkins' suite when Hopkins moved out. Lorena Hickok, Eleanor's great friend, occupied a corner room across from Eleanor's bedroom. This group of houseguests was continually augmented by a stream of visitors—Winston Churchill, who often stayed for two or three weeks at a time; the president's mother, Sara Delano Roosevelt; Eleanor's young friend Joe Lash; and Crown Princess Martha of Norway.

These unusual living arrangements reflected the president's need to have people around him constantly, friends and associates with whom he could work, relax, and conduct much of the nation's business. Through these continual houseguests, Roosevelt defied the limitations of his paralysis. If he could not go out into the world, the world could come to him. The extended White House family also permitted Franklin and Eleanor to heal, or at least conceal, the incompletions of their marriage, which had been irrevocably altered by Eleanor's discovery of Franklin's affair with Lucy Mercer in 1918. There were areas of estrangement, untended needs that only others could fill.

Encompassed by this small society, Franklin Roosevelt led his nation through the war. Although his role as commander-in-chief has been studied at length, less attention has been paid to the way he led his people at home. Yet his leadership of the home front was the essential condition of military victory. Through four years of war, despite strikes and riots, overcrowding and confusion, profiteering, black markets, prejudice, and racism, he kept the American people united in a single cause. There were indeed many times, as those who worked with him observed, when it seemed that he could truly see it all—the relationship of the home front to the war front; of the factories to the soldiers; of speeches to morale; of the government to the people; of war aims to the shape of the peace to come. To understand Roosevelt and his leadership is to understand the nation whose strengths and weaknesses he mirrored and magnified.

At a time when her husband was preoccupied with winning the war, Eleanor Roosevelt insisted that the struggle would not be worth winning if the old order of things prevailed. Unless democracy were renewed at home, she repeatedly said, there was little merit in fighting for democracy abroad. To be sure, she did not act single-handedly—civil-rights leaders, labor leaders, and liberal spokesmen provided critical leverage in the search for social justice—but, without her consistent voice at the upper levels of decision, the tendency to put first things first, to focus on winning the war before exerting effort on anything else, might well have prevailed. She shattered the ceremonial mold in which the role of the first lady had traditionally been fashioned, and reshaped it around her own skills and commitments to social reform. She was the first president's wife to hold—and lose—a government job, the first to testify before a congressional committee, the first to hold press conferences, to speak before a national party convention, to write a syndicated column, to be a radio commentator, to earn money as a lecturer. She was able to use the office of first lady on behalf of causes she believed in rather than letting it use her, and in so doing she became, in the words of columnist Raymond Clapper, "the most influential woman of her time."

The two stories—that of the Roosevelts and that of America—are woven, in this book, as in reality, into a single narrative, beginning in May 1940 and ending in December 1945. This has required the tools of both history and biography: the effort to illuminate the qualities of Franklin and Eleanor Roosevelt has demanded occasional departures from chronology. Yet the spine of this work is narrative. Most studies of the home front have been arranged topically—production, civil rights, rationing, women, Japanese Americans, etc. But a president does not deal with issues topically. He deals with events and problems as they arise. By following the sequence of events ourselves, it is easier to see the connections between the home front and the war, between the level of production at a particular time and the decisions about where and when to fight, between the private qualities of leadership and the public acts.

And there is also a quality to this period which can only be conveyed through narrative—the sense of a cause successfully pursued through great difficulties, a theme common to America itself and to the family which guided it. "This is no ordinary time," Eleanor Roosevelt told the Democratic Convention of 1940, "and no time for weighing anything except what we can best do for the country as a whole." Guided by this conviction, the nation and its first family would move together through painful adversities toward undreamed-of achievements.

SECOND FLOOR FAMILY QUARTERS*

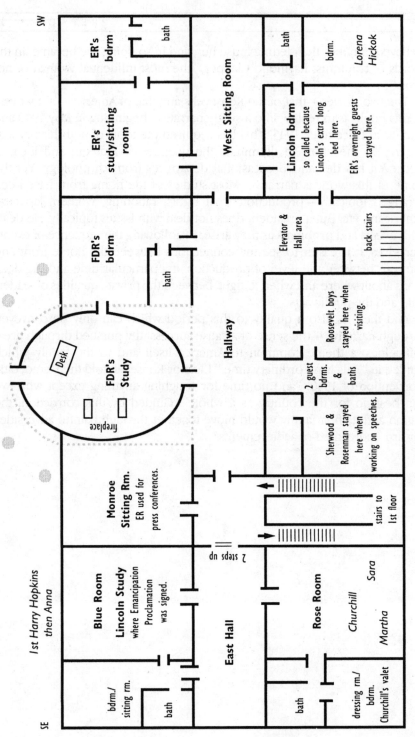

ER's bdrm

bath

ER's study/sitting room

West Sitting Room

bath

Lincoln bdrm
so called because Lincoln's extra long bed here.
ER's overnight guests stayed here.

bdrm.

Lorena Hickok

FDR's bdrm

bath

Elevator & Hall area

back stairs

Desk

FDR's Study

fireplace

Hallway

Roosevelt boys stayed here when visiting.

2 guest bdrms. & baths

Sherwood & Rosenman stayed here when working on speeches.

1st Harry Hopkins then Anna

Monroe Sitting Rm.
ER used for press conferences.

stairs to 1st floor

2 steps up

Blue Room
Lincoln Study
where Emancipation Proclamation was signed.

East Hall

Rose Room

Churchill

Sara

Martha

bdrm./ sitting rm.

bath

bath

dressing rm./ bdrm.
Churchill's valet

SW

NW

SE

NE

*Missy LeHand's suite was located on the third floor.

CHAPTER 1

"THE DECISIVE HOUR

HAS COME"

On nights filled with tension and concern, Franklin Roosevelt performed a ritual that helped him to fall asleep. He would close his eyes and imagine himself at Hyde Park as a boy, standing with his sled in the snow atop the steep hill that stretched from the south porch of his home to the wooded bluffs of the Hudson River far below. As he accelerated down the hill, he maneuvered each familiar curve with perfect skill until he reached the bottom, whereupon, pulling his sled behind him, he started slowly back up until he reached the top, where he would once more begin his descent. Again and again he replayed this remembered scene in his mind, obliterating his awareness of the shrunken legs inert beneath the sheets, undoing the knowledge that he would never climb a hill or even walk on his own power again. Thus liberating himself from his paralysis through an act of imaginative will, the president of the United States would fall asleep.

The evening of May 9, 1940, was one of these nights. At 11 p.m., as

Roosevelt sat in his comfortable study on the second floor of the White House, the long-apprehended phone call had come. Resting against the high back of his favorite red leather chair, a precise reproduction of one Thomas Jefferson had designed for work, the president listened as his ambassador to Belgium, John Cudahy, told him that Hitler's armies were simultaneously attacking Holland, Luxembourg, Belgium, and France. The period of relative calm—the "phony war" that had settled over Europe since the German attack on Poland in September of 1939—was over.

For days, rumors of a planned Nazi invasion had spread through the capitals of Western Europe. Now, listening to Ambassador Cudahy's frantic report that German planes were in the air over the Low Countries and France, Roosevelt knew that the all-out war he feared had finally begun. In a single night, the tacit agreement that, for eight months, had kept the belligerents from attacking each other's territory had been shattered.

As he summoned his military aide and appointments secretary, General Edwin "Pa" Watson, on this spring evening of the last year of his second term, Franklin Roosevelt looked younger than his fifty-eight years. Though his hair was threaded with gray, the skin on his handsome face was clear, and the blue eyes, beneath his pince-nez glasses, were those of a man at the peak of his vitality. His chest was so broad, his neck so thick, that when seated he appeared larger than he was. Only when he was moved from his chair would the eye be drawn to the withered legs, paralyzed by polio almost two decades earlier.

At 12:40 a.m., the president's press secretary, Stephen Early, arrived to monitor incoming messages. Bombs had begun to fall on Brussels, Amsterdam, and Rotterdam, killing hundreds of civilians and destroying thousands of homes. In dozens of old European neighborhoods, fires illuminated the night sky. Stunned Belgians stood in their nightclothes in the streets of Brussels, watching bursts of anti-aircraft fire as military cars and motorcycles dashed through the streets. A thirteen-year-old schoolboy, Guy de Liederkirche, was Brussels' first child to die. His body would later be carried to his school for a memorial service with his classmates. On every radio station throughout Belgium, broadcasts summoned all soldiers to join their units at once.

In Amsterdam the roads leading out of the city were crowded with people and automobiles as residents fled in fear of the bombing. Bombs were also falling at Dunkirk, Calais, and Metz in France, and at Chilham, near Canterbury, in England. The initial reports were confusing—border clashes had begun, parachute troops were being dropped to seize Dutch and Belgian airports, the government of Luxembourg had already fled to France, and there was some reason to believe the Germans were also landing troops by sea.

After speaking again to Ambassador Cudahy and scanning the incoming news reports, Roosevelt called his secretary of the Treasury, Henry Morgenthau, Jr., and ordered him to freeze all assets held by Belgium, the Netherlands, and Luxembourg before the market opened in the morning, to keep any resources of the invaded countries from falling into German hands.

The official German explanation for the sweeping invasion of the neutral lowlands was given by Germany's foreign minister, Joachim von Ribbentrop. Germany, he claimed, had received "proof" that the Allies were engineering an imminent attack through the Low Countries into the German Ruhr district. In a belligerent tone, von Ribbentrop said the time had come for settling the final account with the French and British leaders. Just before midnight, Adolf Hitler, having boarded a special train to the front, had issued the fateful order to his troops: "The decisive hour has come for the fight today decides the fate of the German nation for the next 1000 years."

There was little that could be done that night—phone calls to Paris and Brussels could rarely be completed, and the Hague wire was barely working —but, as one State Department official said, "in times of crisis the key men should be at hand and the public should know it." Finally, at 2:40 a.m., Roosevelt decided to go to bed. After shifting his body to his armless wheel chair, he rolled through a door near his desk into his bedroom.

As usual when the president's day came to an end, he called for his valet, Irvin McDuffie, to lift him into his bed. McDuffie, a Southern Negro, born the same year as his boss, had been a barber by trade when Roosevelt met him in Warm Springs, Georgia, in 1927. Roosevelt quickly developed a liking for the talkative man and offered him the job of valet. Now he and his wife lived in a room on the third floor of the White House. In recent months, McDuffie's hard drinking had become a problem: on several occasions Eleanor had found him so drunk that "he couldn't help Franklin to bed." Fearing that her husband might be abandoned at a bad time, Eleanor urged him to fire McDuffie, but the president was unable to bring himself to let his old friend go, even though he shared Eleanor's fear.

McDuffie was at his post in the early hours of May 10 when the president called for help. He lifted the president from his wheelchair onto the narrow bed, reminiscent of the kind used in a boy's boarding school, straightened his legs to their full length, and then undressed him and put on his pajamas. Beside the bed was a white-painted table; on its top, a jumble of pencils, notepaper, a glass of water, a package of cigarettes, a couple of phones, a bottle of nose drops. On the floor beside the table stood a small basket —the Eleanor basket—in which the first lady regularly left memoranda, communications, and reports for the president to read—a sort of private post office between husband and wife. In the corner sat an old-fashioned rocking chair, and next to it a heavy wardrobe filled with the president's clothes. On the marble mantelpiece above the fireplace was an assortment of family photos and a collection of miniature pigs. "Like every room in any Roosevelt house," historian Arthur Schlesinger has written, "the presidential bedroom was hopelessly Victorian—old-fashioned and indiscriminate in its furnishings, cluttered in its decor, ugly and comfortable."

Outside Roosevelt's door, which he refused to lock at night as previous presidents had done, Secret Service men patrolled the corridor, alerting the guardroom to the slightest hint of movement. The refusal to lock his door was related to the president's dread of fire, which surpassed his fear of assassination or of anything else. The fear seems to have been rooted in his childhood, when, as a small boy, he had seen his young aunt, Laura, race down the stairs, screaming, her body and clothes aflame from an accident with an alcohol lamp. Her life was ended at nineteen. The fear grew when he became a paraplegic, to the point where, for hours at a time, he would practice dropping from his bed or chair to the floor and then crawling to the door so that he could escape from a fire on his own. "We assured him he would never be alone," his eldest son, Jimmy, recalled, "but he could not be sure, and furthermore found the idea depressing that he could not be left alone, as if he were an infant."

Roosevelt's nightly rituals tell us something about his deepest feelings—the desire for freedom, the quest for movement, and the significance, despite all his attempts to downplay it, of the paralysis in his life. In 1940, Roosevelt had been president of the United States for seven years, but he had been paralyzed from the waist down for nearly three times that long. Before he was stricken at thirty-nine, Roosevelt was a man who flourished on activity. He had served in the New York legislature for two years, been assistant secretary of the navy for seven years, and his party's candidate for vice-president in 1920. He loved to swim and to sail, to play tennis and golf; to run in the woods and ride horseback in the fields. To his daughter, Anna, he was always "very active physically," "a wonderful playmate who took long walks with you, sailed with you, could out-jump you and do a lot of things," while Jimmy saw him quite simply as "the handsomest, strongest, most glamorous, vigorous physical father in the world."

All that vigor and athleticism ended in August 1921 at Campobello, his family's summer home in New Brunswick, Canada, when he returned home from swimming in the pond with his children and felt too tired even to remove his wet bathing suit. The morning after his swim, his temperature was 102 degrees and he had trouble moving his left leg. By afternoon, the power to move his right leg was also gone, and soon he was paralyzed from the waist down. The paralysis had set in so swiftly that no one understood at first that it was polio. But once the diagnosis was made, the battle was joined. For years he fought to walk on his own power, practicing for hours at a time, drenched with sweat, as he tried unsuccessfully to move one leg in front of the other without the aid of a pair of crutches or a helping hand. That consuming and futile effort had to be abandoned once he became governor of New York in 1929 and then president in 1933. He was permanently crippled.

Yet the paralysis that crippled his body expanded his mind and his sensibilities. After what Eleanor called his "trial by fire," he seemed less arrogant, less smug, less superficial, more focused, more complex, more interesting. He returned from his ordeal with greater powers of concentration and greater self-knowledge. "There had been a plowing up of his nature," Labor

Secretary Frances Perkins observed. "The man emerged completely warm-hearted, with new humility of spirit and a firmer understanding of profound philosophical concepts."

He had always taken great pleasure in people. But now they became what one historian has called "his vital links with life." Far more intensely than before, he reached out to know them, to understand them, to pick up their emotions, to put himself into their shoes. No longer belonging to his old world in the same way, he came to empathize with the poor and underprivileged, with people to whom fate had dealt a difficult hand. Once, after a lecture in Akron, Ohio, Eleanor was asked how her husband's illness had affected him. "Anyone who has gone through great suffering," she said, "is bound to have a greater sympathy and understanding of the problems of mankind."

Through his presidency, the mere act of standing up with his heavy metal leg-braces locked into place was an ordeal. The journalist Eliot Janeway remembers being behind Roosevelt once when he was in his chair in the Oval Office. "He was smiling as he talked. His face and hand muscles were totally relaxed. But then, when he had to stand up, his jaws went absolutely rigid. The effort of getting what was left of his body up was so great his face changed dramatically. It was as if he braced his body for a bullet."

Little wonder, then, that, in falling asleep at night, Roosevelt took comfort in the thought of physical freedom.

• • •

The morning sun of Washington's belated spring was streaming through the president's windows on May 10, 1940. Despite the tumult of the night before, which had kept him up until nearly 3 a.m., he awoke at his usual hour of eight o'clock. Pivoting to the edge of the bed, he pressed the button for his valet, who helped him into the bathroom. Then, as he had done every morning for the past seven years, he threw his old blue cape over his pajamas and started his day with breakfast in bed—orange juice, eggs, coffee, and buttered toast—and the morning papers: *The New York Times* and the *Herald Tribune,* the *Baltimore Sun,* the *Washington Post* and the *Washington Herald.*

Headlines recounted the grim events he had heard at 11 p.m. the evening before. From Paris, Ambassador William Bullitt confirmed that the Germans had launched violent attacks on a half-dozen French military bases. Bombs had also fallen on the main railway connections between Paris and the border in an attempt to stop troop movements.

Before finishing the morning papers, the president held a meeting with Steve Early and "Pa" Watson, to review his crowded schedule. He instructed them to convene an emergency meeting at ten-thirty with the chiefs of the army and the navy, the secretaries of state and Treasury, and the attorney general. In addition, Roosevelt was scheduled to meet the press in the morning and the Cabinet in the afternoon, as he had done every Friday morning and afternoon for seven years. Later that night, he was supposed to deliver a keynote address at the Pan American Scientific Congress. After asking Early to delay the press conference an hour and to have the State Department draft a new speech, Roosevelt called his valet to help him dress.

• • •

While Franklin Roosevelt was being dressed in his bedroom, Eleanor was in New York, having spent the past few days in the apartment she kept in Greenwich Village, in a small house owned by her friends Esther Lape and Elizabeth Read. The Village apartment on East 11th Street, five blocks north of Washington Square, provided Eleanor with a welcome escape from the demands of the White House, a secret refuge whenever her crowded calendar brought her to New York. For decades, the Village, with its winding streets, modest brick houses, bookshops, tearooms, little theaters, and cheap rents, had been home to political, artistic, and literary rebels, giving it a colorful Old World character.

The object of Eleanor's visit to the city—her second in ten days—was a meeting that day at the Choate School in Connecticut, where she was scheduled to speak with teachers and students. Along the way, she had sandwiched in a banquet for the National League of Women Voters, a meeting for the fund for Polish relief, a visit to her mother-in-law, Sara Delano Roosevelt, a radio broadcast, lunch with her friend the young student activist Joe Lash, and dinner with Democratic leader Edward Flynn and his wife.

The week before, at the Astor Hotel, Eleanor had been honored by *The Nation* magazine for her work in behalf of civil rights and poverty. More than a thousand people had filled the tables and the balcony of the cavernous ballroom to watch her receive a bronze plaque for "distinguished service in the cause of American social progress." Among the many speakers that night, Stuart Chase lauded the first lady's concentrated focus on the problems at home. "I suppose she worries about Europe like the rest of us," he began, "but she does not allow this worry to divert her attention from the homefront. She goes around America, looking at America, thinking about America . . . helping day and night with the problems of America." For, he concluded, "the New Deal is supposed to be fighting a war, too, a war against depression."

"What is an institution?" author John Gunther had asked when his turn to speak came. "An institution," he asserted, is "something that had fixity, permanence, and importance . . . something that people like to depend on, something benevolent as a rule, something we like." And by that definition, he concluded, the woman being honored that night was as great an institution as her husband, who was already being talked about for an unprecedented third term. Echoing Gunther's sentiments, NAACP head Walter White turned to Mrs. Roosevelt and said: "My dear, I don't care if the President runs for the third or fourth term as long as he lets you run the bases, keep the score and win the game."

For her part, Eleanor was slightly embarrassed by all the fuss. "It never seems quite real to me to sit at a table and have people whom I have always looked upon with respect . . . explain why they are granting me an honor," she wrote in her column describing the evening. "Somehow I always feel they ought to be talking about someone else." Yet, as she stood to speak that night at the Astor ballroom, rising nearly six feet, her wavy brown hair slightly touched by gray, her wide mouth marred by large buck teeth, her brilliant blue eyes offset by an unfortunate chin, she dominated the room as no one before her had done. "I will do my best to do what is right," she began, forcing her high voice to a lower range, "not with a sense of my own adequacy but with the feeling that the country must go on, that we must keep democracy and must make it mean a reality to more people. . . . We should constantly be reminded of what we owe in return for what we have."

It was this tireless commitment to democracy's unfinished agenda that led Americans in a Gallup poll taken that spring to rate Mrs. Roosevelt even higher than her husband, with 67 percent of those interviewed well disposed toward her activities. "Mrs. Roosevelt's incessant goings and comings," the survey suggested, "have been accepted as a rather welcome part of the national life. Women especially feel this way. But even men betray relatively small masculine impatience with the work and opinions of a very articulate lady. . . . The rich, who generally disapprove of Mrs. Roosevelt's husband, seem just as friendly toward her as the poor. . . . Even among those extremely anti-Roosevelt citizens who would regard a third term as a national disaster there is a generous minority . . . who want Mrs. Roosevelt to remain in the public eye."

The path to this position of independent power and respect had not been easy. Eleanor's distinguished career had been forged from a painful discovery when she was thirty-four. After a period of suspicion, she realized that her husband, who was then assistant secretary of the navy, had fallen in love with another woman, Lucy Page Mercer.

Tall, beautiful, and well bred, with a low throaty voice and an incomparably winning smile, Lucy Mercer was working as Eleanor's social secretary when the love affair began. For months, perhaps even years, Franklin kept his romance a secret from Eleanor. Her shattering discovery took place in September 1918. Franklin had just returned from a visit to the European front. Unpacking his suitcase, she discovered a packet of love letters from Lucy. At this moment, Eleanor later admitted, "the bottom dropped out of my own particular world & I faced myself, my surroundings, my world, honestly for the first time."

Eleanor told her husband that she would grant him a divorce. But this was not what he wanted, or at least not what he was able to put himself through, particularly when his mother, Sara, was said to have threatened him with disinheritance if he left his marriage. If her son insisted on leaving his wife and five children for another woman, visiting scandal upon the Roosevelt name, she could not stop him. But he should know that she would not give him another dollar and he could no longer expect to inherit the family estate at Hyde Park. Franklin's trusted political adviser, Louis Howe, weighed in as well, warning Franklin that divorce would bring his political career to an abrupt end. There was also the problem of Lucy's Catholicism, which would prevent her from marrying a divorced man.

Franklin promised never to see Lucy again and agreed, so the Roosevelt children suggest, to Eleanor's demand for separate bedrooms, bringing their marital relations to an end. Eleanor would later admit to her daughter, Anna, that sex was "an ordeal to be borne." Something in her childhood had locked her up, she said, making her fear the loss of control that comes with abandoning oneself to one's passions, giving her "an exaggerated idea of the necessity of keeping all one's desires under complete subjugation." Now, supposedly, she was free of her "ordeal."

The marriage resumed. But for Eleanor, a path had opened, a possibility of standing apart from Franklin. No longer did she need to define herself solely in terms of his wants and his needs. Before the crisis, though marriage had never fulfilled her prodigious energies, she had no way of breaking through the habits and expectations of a proper young woman's role. To explore her independent needs, to journey outside her home for happiness, was perceived as dangerous and wrong.

With the discovery of the affair, however, she was free to define a new and different partnership with her husband, free to seek new avenues of fulfillment. It was a gradual process, a gradual casting away, a gradual gaining of confidence—and it was by no means complete—but the fifty-six-year-old woman who was being fêted in New York was a different person from the shy, betrayed wife of 1918.

• • •

Above the president's bedroom, in a snug third-floor suite, his personal secretary, Marguerite "Missy" LeHand, was already dressed, though she, too, had stayed up late the night before.

A tall, handsome woman of forty-one with large blue eyes and prematurely gray, once luxuriant black hair fastened by hairpins to the nape of her neck, Missy was in love with her boss and regarded herself as his other wife. Nor was she alone in her imaginings. "There's no doubt," White House aide Raymond Moley said, "that Missy was as close to being a wife as he ever had —or could have." White House maid Lillian Parks agreed. "When Missy gave an order, we responded as if it had come from the First Lady. We knew that FDR would always back up Missy."

Missy had come a long way from the working-class neighborhood in Somerville, Massachusetts, where she had grown up. Her father was an alcoholic who lived apart from the family. Her mother, with five children to raise, took in a revolving group of Harvard students as tenants. Yet, even when she was young, Missy's childhood friend Barbara Curtis recalled, "she had a certain class to her. I remember one time watching her go around the corner—our houses weren't too far apart—and my mother looked out the window and called my attention to her. She said, 'she certainly looks smart.' She had a dark suit on to go to high school. She stood out for having a better appearance and being smarter than most."

After secretarial school, Missy had gone to New York, where she became involved in Roosevelt's vice-presidential campaign in 1920. Impressed by Missy's efficiency, Eleanor asked her to come to Hyde Park after the election to help Franklin clean up his correspondence. From the start, Missy proved herself indispensable. When asked later to explain her astonishing secretarial skill, she said simply, "The first thing for a private secretary to do is to study her employer. After I went to work for Mr. Roosevelt, for months I read carefully all the letters he dictated. . . . I learned what letters he wanted to see and which ones it was not necessary to show him. . . . I came to know exactly how Mr. Roosevelt would answer some of his letters, how he would couch his thoughts. When he discovered that I had learned these things it took a load off his shoulders, for instead of having to dictate the answers to many letters he could just say yes or no and I knew what to say and how to say it."

A year later, when Franklin contracted polio, Missy's duties expanded. Both Franklin and Eleanor understood that it was critical for Franklin to keep active in politics even as he struggled unsuccessfully day after day, month after month, to walk again. To that end, Eleanor adhered to a rigorous daily schedule as the stand-in for her husband, journeying from one political meeting to the next to ensure that the Roosevelt name was not forgotten. With Eleanor busily occupied away from home, Missy did all the chores a housewife might do, writing Franklin's personal checks, paying the monthly bills, giving the children their allowances, supervising the menus, sending the rugs and draperies for cleaning.

When Roosevelt was elected governor in 1928, Missy moved with the Roosevelt family to Albany, occupying a large bedroom suite on the second floor of the Governor's Mansion. "Albany was the hardest work I ever did," she said, recalling the huge load she carried for the activist governor without the help of the three assistants she would later enjoy in the White House. By the time Roosevelt was president, she had become totally absorbed in his life—learning his favorite games, sharing his hobbies, reading the same books, even adopting his characteristic accent and patterns of speech. Whereas Eleanor was so opposed to gambling that she refused to play poker with Franklin's friends if even the smallest amount of money changed hands, Missy became an avid player, challenging Roosevelt at every turn, always ready to raise the ante. Whereas Eleanor never evinced any interest in her husband's treasured stamp collection, Missy was an enthusiastic partner, spending hours by his side as he organized and reorganized his stamps into one or another of his thick leather books. "In terms of companionship," Eliot Janeway observed, "Missy was the real wife. She understood his nature perfectly, as they would say in a nineteenth-century novel."

• • •

At 10:30 a.m., May 10, 1940, pushed along in his wheelchair by Mr. Crim, the usher on duty, and accompanied by his usual detail of Secret Service men, the president headed for the Oval Office. A bell announced his arrival to the small crowd already assembled in the Cabinet Room—Army Chief of Staff George Marshall, Navy Chief Admiral Harold Stark, Attorney General Robert Jackson, Secretary of Treasury Henry Morgenthau, Secretary of State Cordell Hull, and Undersecretary Sumner Welles. But first, as he did every day, the president poked his head into Missy's office, giving her a wave and a smile which, Missy told a friend, was all she needed to replenish the energies lost from too little sleep.

Of all the men assembled in the big white-walled Cabinet Room that morning, General George Catlett Marshall possessed the clearest awareness of how woefully unprepared America was to fight a major war against Nazi Germany. The fifty-nine-year-old Marshall, chief of operations of the First Army in World War I, had been elevated to the position of army chief of staff the previous year. The story is told of a meeting in the president's office not long before the appointment during which the president outlined a pet proposal. Everyone nodded in approval except Marshall. "Don't you think so, George?" the president asked. Marshall replied: "I am sorry, Mr. President, but I don't agree with that at all." The president looked stunned, the conference was stopped, and Marshall's friends predicted that his tour of duty would soon come to an end. A few months later, reaching thirty-four names down the list of senior generals, the president asked the straight-speaking Marshall to be chief of staff of the U.S. Army.

The army Marshall headed, however, was scarcely worthy of the name, having languished in skeletal form since World War I, starved for funds and manpower by an administration focused on coping with the Great Depression and an isolationist Congress. Determined never again to be trapped by the corruptions of the Old World, the isolationists insisted that the United States was protected from harm by its oceans and could best lead by sustaining democracy at home. Responding to the overwhelming strength of isolationist sentiment in the country at large, the Congress had passed a series of Neutrality Acts in the mid-1930s banning the shipment of arms and munitions to all belligerents, prohibiting the extension of credits and loans, and forbidding the arming of merchant ships.

Roosevelt had tried on occasion to shift the prevailing opinion. In 1937, he had delivered a major speech in Chicago calling for a "quarantine" of aggressor nations. The speech was hailed by interventionists committed to collective security, but when the press evinced shock at what they termed a radical shift in foreign policy and isolationist congressmen threatened impeachment, Roosevelt had pulled back. "It's a terrible thing," he told his aide Sam Rosenman, "to look over your shoulder when you are trying to lead—and find no one there." He had resolved at that point to move one step at a time, to nurse the country along to a more sophisticated view of the world, to keep from getting too far ahead of the electorate, as Woodrow Wilson had done. The task was not easy. Even the outbreak of war in September had not led to a significant expansion of the army, since the president's first priority was to revise the Neutrality Laws so that he could sell weapons to the Allies. Fearing that larger appropriations for the ground forces would rouse the isolationists and kill his chances to reform neutrality policy, the president had turned a deaf ear to the army's appeals for expansion.

As a result, in 1940, the U.S. Army stood only eighteenth in the world, trailing not only Germany, France, Britain, Russia, Italy, Japan, and China but also Belgium, the Netherlands, Portugal, Spain, Sweden, and Switzerland. With the fall of Holland, the United States would rise to seventeenth! And, in contrast to Germany, where after years of compulsory military training nearly 10 percent of the population (6.8 million) were trained and ready for war, less than .5 percent of the American population (504,000) were on active duty or in the trained reserves. The offensive Germany had launched the morning of May 10 along the Western front was supported by 136 divisions; the United States could, if necessary, muster merely five fully equipped divisions.

In the spring of 1940, the United States possessed almost no munitions industry at all. So strong had been the recoil from war after 1918 that both the government and the private sector had backed away from making weapons. The result was that, while the United States led the world in the mass production of automobiles, washing machines, and other household appliances, the techniques of producing weapons of war had badly atrophied.

All through the winter and spring, Marshall had been trying to get Secretary of War Henry Woodring to understand the dire nature of this unpreparedness. But the former governor of Kansas was an isolationist who refused to contemplate even the possibility of American involvement in the European war. Woodring had been named assistant secretary of war in 1933 and then promoted to the top job three years later, when the price of corn and the high unemployment rate worried Washington far more than foreign affairs. As the European situation heated up, Roosevelt recognized that Woodring was the wrong man to head the War Department. But, try as he might, he could not bring himself to fire his secretary of war—or anyone else, for that matter.

Roosevelt's inability to get rid of anybody, even the hopelessly incompetent, was a chief source of the disorderliness of his administration, of his double-dealing and his tendency to procrastinate. "His real weakness," Eleanor Roosevelt observed, "was that—it came out of the strength really, or out of a quality—he had great sympathy for people and great understanding, and he couldn't bear to be disagreeable to someone he liked . . . and he just couldn't bring himself to really do the unkind thing that had to be done unless he got angry."

Earlier that spring, on at least two occasions, Secretary of the Interior Harold Ickes had brought up the Woodring problem with Roosevelt, suggesting an appointment as ambassador to Ireland as a face-saving gesture. The president did not think this would satisfy Woodring. "If I were you, Mr. President," Ickes replied, "I would send for Harry Woodring and I would say to him, 'Harry, it is either Dublin, Ireland for you or Topeka, Kansas.' The President looked at me somewhat abashed. Reading his mind, I said, 'You can't do that sort of thing, can you, Mr. President?' 'No, Harold, I can't,' he replied."

The confusion multiplied when Roosevelt selected a staunch interventionist, Louis Johnson, the former national commander of the American Legion, as assistant secretary of war. Outspoken, bold, and ambitious, Johnson fought openly with Woodring, bringing relations to the sorry point where neither man spoke to the other. Paralyzed and frustrated, General Marshall found it incomprehensible that Roosevelt had allowed such a mess to develop simply because he disliked firing anyone. Years earlier, when Marshall had been told by his aide that a friend whom he had ordered overseas had said he could not leave because his wife was away and his furniture was not packed, Marshall had called the man himself. The friend explained that he was sorry. "I'm sorry, too," Marshall replied, "but you will be retired tomorrow."

Marshall failed to understand that there was a method behind the president's disorderly style. Though divided authority and built-in competition created insecurity and confusion within the administration, it gave Roosevelt the benefit of conflicting opinions. "I think he knew exactly what he was doing all the time," administrative assistant James Rowe observed. "He liked conflict, and he was a believer in resolving problems through conflict." With different administrators telling him different things, he got a better feel for what his problems were.

Their attitude toward subordinates was not the only point of dissimilarity between Roosevelt and Marshall. Roosevelt loved to laugh and play, closing the space between people by familiarity, calling everyone, even Winston Churchill, by his first name. In contrast, Marshall was rarely seen to smile or laugh on the job and was never familiar with anyone. "I never heard him call anyone by his first name," Robert Cutler recalled. "He would use the rank or the last name or both: 'Colonel' or 'Colonel Cutler.' Only occasionally in wartime did he use the last name alone. . . . It was a reward for something he thought well done."

As army chief of staff, Marshall remained wary of Roosevelt's relaxed style. "Informal conversation with the President could get you into trouble," Marshall later wrote. "He would talk over something informally at the dinner table and you had trouble disagreeing without embarrassment. So I never went. I was in Hyde Park for the first time at his funeral."

As the officials sat in the Cabinet Room, at the great mahogany table under the stern, pinch-lipped stare of Woodrow Wilson, whose portrait hung above the fireplace, their primary reason for gathering together was to share the incoming information from Europe and to plan the American response. Ambassador John Cudahy in Brussels wired that he had almost been knocked down by the force of a bomb which fell three hundred feet from the embassy. From London, Ambassador Joseph P. Kennedy reported that the British had called off their Whitsun holiday, the long weekend on which Londoners traditionally acquired the tan that had to last until their August vacation—"tangible evidence," Kennedy concluded, "that the situation is serious."

Plans were set in motion for the army and navy to submit new estimates to the White House of what they would need to accomplish the seemingly insurmountable task of catching up with Germany's modern war machine. For, as Marshall had recently explained to the Congress, Germany was in a unique position. "After the World War practically everything was taken away from Germany in the way of materiel. So when Germany rearmed, it was necessary to produce a complete set of materiel for all the troops. As a result, Germany has an Army equipped throughout with the most modern weapons that could be turned out and that is a situation that has never occurred before in the history of the world."

•   •   •

While the president was conducting his meeting in the Cabinet Room, the men and women of the press were standing around in small groups, talking and smoking behind a red cord in a large anteroom, waiting for the signal that the press conference in the Oval Office was about to begin. The reporters had also been up late the night before, so "some were a little drawn eyed," the *Tribune*'s Mark Sullivan observed. "We grouped about talking of—do I need to say? I felt that . . . for many a day and month and year there will be talk about the effect of today's events upon the United States. We shall talk it and write it and live it, and our children's children, too."

The meeting concluded, the president returned to his desk, the red cord was withdrawn, and the reporters began filing in. In the front row, by tradition, stood the men representing the wire services: Douglas Cornell of Associated Press, Merriman Smith of United Press, and George Durno of the International News Service. Directly behind them stood the representatives of the New York and Washington papers. "Glancing around the room," a contemporary wrote, "one sees white-haired Mark Sullivan; dark Raymond Clapper; tall Ernest Lindley . . . and husky Paul Mallon." Farther back were the veterans of the out-of-town newspapers, the radio commentators, and the magazine men, led by *Time*'s Felix Belair. And then the women reporters in flat heels, among them Doris Fleeson of the *New York Daily News* and May Craig, representing several Maine newspapers.

Seated at his desk with his back to the windows, Roosevelt faced the crowd that was now spilling into the Oval Office for his largest press conference ever. Behind him, set in standards, were the blue presidential flag and the American flag. "Like an opera singer about to go on the stage," Roosevelt invariably appeared nervous before a conference began, fidgeting with his cigarette holder, fingering the trinkets on his desk, exchanging self-conscious jokes with the reporters in the front row. Once the action started, however, with the doorkeeper's shout of "all-in," the president seemed to relax, conducting the flow of questions and conversation with such professional skill that the columnist Heywood Broun once called him "the best newspaperman who has ever been President of the United States."

For seven years, twice a week, the president had sat down with these reporters, explaining legislation, announcing appointments, establishing friendly contact, calling them by their first names, teasing them about their hangovers, exuding warmth and accessibility. Once, when a correspondent narrowly missed getting on Roosevelt's train, the president covered for him by writing his copy until he could catch up. Another time, when the mother of a bachelor correspondent died, Eleanor Roosevelt attended the funeral services, and then she and the president invited him for their Sunday family supper of scrambled eggs. These acts of friendship—repeated many times over—helped to explain the paradox that, though 80 to 85 percent of the newspaper publishers regularly opposed Roosevelt, the president maintained excellent relations with the working reporters, and his coverage was generally full and fair. "By the brilliant but simple trick of making news and *being* news," historian Arthur Schlesinger observed, "Roosevelt outwitted the open hostility of the publishers and converted the press into one of the most effective channels of his public leadership."

"History will like to say the scene [on May 10] was tense," Mark Sullivan wrote. "It was not. . . . On the President's part there was consciousness of high events, yet also complete coolness. . . . The whole atmosphere was one of serious matter-of-factness."

"Good morning," the president said, and then paused as still more reporters filed in. "I hope you had more sleep than I did," he joked, drawing them into the shared experience of the crisis. "I guess most of you were pretty busy all night."

"There isn't much I can say about the situation. . . . I can say, personally, that I am in full sympathy with the very excellent statement that was given out, the proclamation, by the Queen of the Netherlands." In that statement, issued earlier that morning, Queen Wilhelmina had directed "a flaming protest against this unprecedented violation of good faith and all that is decent in relations between cultured states."

Asked if he would say what he thought the chances were that the United States could stay out of the war, the president replied as he had been replying for months to similar questions. "I think that would be speculative. In other words, don't for heaven's sake, say that means we may get in. That would be again writing yourself off on the limb and sawing it off." Asked if his speech that night would touch on the international situation, Roosevelt evoked a round of laughter by responding: "I do not know because I have not written it."

On and on he went, his tone in the course of fifteen minutes shifting from weariness to feistiness to playfulness. Yet, in the end, preserving his options in this delicate moment, he *said* almost nothing, skillfully deflecting every question about America's future actions. Asked at one point to compare Japanese aggression with German aggression, he said he counted seven ifs in the question, which meant he could not provide an answer. Still, by the time the senior wire-service man brought the conference to an early close, "partly in consideration of the tired newspaper men and partly in consideration of the President," the reporters went away with the stories they needed for the next day's news.

• • •

While the president was holding his press conference, Eleanor was in a car with her secretary, Malvina Thompson, heading toward the Choate School near the village of Wallingford, Connecticut. Built in the middle of three hundred acres of farm and woodland, with rolling hills stretching for many miles beyond, Choate was a preparatory school for young boys. The students were mostly Protestant, though in recent years a few Catholics had been admitted, including the two sons of Ambassador Joseph Kennedy, Joe Jr. and John Fitzgerald Kennedy.

Like Missy, Malvina Thompson, known to her friends as Tommy, was a fixture in the Roosevelt household, as critical to Eleanor's life as Missy was to Franklin's. Short and stocky, with brown hair and a continual wrinkle in the bridge of her nose, the forty-eight-year-old Tommy had started working for Eleanor when Franklin was governor of New York. She had married Frank Scheider, a teacher in the New York public schools, in 1921 and divorced him in 1939. She had no children. She had her own room in every Roosevelt house: a sitting room and bedroom in the White House, a bedroom in Eleanor's Greenwich Village apartment, and a suite of rooms at Val-Kill, Eleanor's cottage at Hyde Park.

Born of "good old Vermont granite stock," Tommy was smart and tough with a wry sense of humor. "When she walked," a relative recalled, " she gave the impression of saying 'You'd better get out of my way or else.' " Tommy was the person, Eleanor said in 1938, "who makes life possible for me."

During the past seven years in the White House, Eleanor and Tommy traveled more than 280,000 miles around the United States, the equivalent of nearly a hundred cross-country trips. Franklin called Eleanor his "will o' the wisp" wife. But it was Franklin who had encouraged her to become his "eyes and ears," to gather the grass-roots knowledge he needed to understand the people he governed. Unable to travel easily on his own because of his paralysis, he had started by teaching Eleanor how to inspect state institutions in 1929, during his first term as governor.

"It was the best education I ever had," she later said. Traveling across the state to inspect institutions for the insane, the blind, and the aged, visiting state prisons and reform schools, she had learned, slowly and painfully, through Franklin's tough, detailed questions upon her return, how to become an investigative reporter.

Her first inspection was an insane asylum. "All right," Franklin told her, "go in and look around and let me know what's going on there. Tell me how the inmates are being treated." When Eleanor returned, she brought with her a printed copy of the day's menu. "Did you look to see whether they were actually getting this food?" Franklin asked. "Did you lift a pot cover on the stove to check whether the contents corresponded with this menu?" Eleanor shook her head. Her untrained mind had taken in a general picture of the place but missed all the human details that would have brought it to life. "But these are what I need," Franklin said. "I never remembered things until Franklin taught me," Eleanor told a reporter. "His memory is really prodigious. Once he has checked something he never needs to look at it again."

"One time," she recalled, "he asked me to go and look at the state's tree shelter-belt plantings. I noticed there were five rows of graduated size. . . . When I came back and described it, Franklin said: 'Tell me exactly what was in the first five rows. What did they plant first?' And he was so desperately disappointed when I couldn't tell him, that I put my best efforts after that into missing nothing and remembering everything."

In time, Eleanor became so thorough in her inspections, observing the attitudes of patients toward the staff, judging facial expressions as well as the words, looking in closets and behind doors, that Franklin set great value on her reports. "She saw many things the President could never see," Labor Secretary Frances Perkins said. "Much of what she learned and what she understood about the life of the people of this country rubbed off onto FDR. It could not have helped to do so because she had a poignant understanding. . . . Her mere reporting of the facts was full of a sensitive quality that could never be escaped. . . . Much of his seemingly intuitive understanding—about labor situations . . . about girls who worked in sweatshops—came from his recollections of what she had told him."

During Eleanor's first summer as first lady, Franklin had asked her to investigate the economic situation in Appalachia. The Quakers had reported terrible conditions of poverty there, and the president wanted to check these reports. "Watch the people's faces," he told her. "Look at the conditions of the clothes on the wash lines. You can tell a lot from that." Going even further, Eleanor descended the mine shafts, dressed in a miner's outfit, to absorb for herself the physical conditions in which the miners worked. It was this journey that later provoked the celebrated cartoon showing two miners in a shaft looking up: "Here Comes Mrs. Roosevelt!"

At Scott's Run, near Morgantown, West Virginia, Eleanor had seen children who "did not know what it was to sit down at a table and eat a proper meal." In one shack, she found a boy clutching his pet rabbit, which his sister had just told him was all there was left to eat. So moved was the president by his wife's report that he acted at once to create an Appalachian resettlement project.

The following year, Franklin had sent Eleanor to Puerto Rico to investigate reports that a great portion of the fancy embroidered linens that were coming into the United States from Puerto Rico were being made under terrible conditions. To the fury of the rich American colony in San Juan, Eleanor took reporters and photographers through muddy alleys and swamps to hundreds of foul-smelling hovels with no plumbing and no electricity, where women sat in the midst of filth embroidering cloth for minimal wages. Publicizing these findings, Eleanor called for American women to stop purchasing Puerto Rico's embroidered goods.

Later, Eleanor journeyed to the deep South and the "Dustbowl." Before long, her inspection trips had become as important to her as to her husband. "I realized," she said in a radio interview, "that if I remained in the White House all the time I would lose touch with the rest of the world. . . . I might have had a less crowded life, but I would begin to think that my life in Washington was representative of the rest of the country and that is a dangerous point of view." So much did Eleanor travel, in fact, that the *Washington Star* once printed a humorous headline: "Mrs. Roosevelt Spends Night at White House."

So it was not unusual that, on May 10, 1940, Eleanor found herself away from home, driving along a country road in central Connecticut. Months earlier, she had accepted the invitation of the headmaster, George St. John, to address the student body. Now, in the tense atmosphere generated by the Nazi invasion of Western Europe, her speech assumed an added measure of importance. As she entered the Chapel and faced the young men sitting in neat rows before her, she was filled with emotion.

"There is something very touching in the contact with these youngsters," she admitted, "so full of fire and promise and curiosity about life. One cannot help dreading what life may do to them. . . . All these young things knowing so little of life and so little of what the future may hold."

Eleanor's forebodings were not without foundation. Near the Chapel stood the Memorial House, a dormitory built in memory of the eighty-five Choate boys who had lost their lives in the Great War. Now, as she looked at the eager faces in the crowd and worried about a European war spreading once again to the United States, she wondered how many of them would be called to give their lives for their country.

For several days, Eleanor's mind had been preoccupied by old wars. "I wonder," she wrote in her column earlier that week, "that the time does not come when young men facing each other with intent to kill do not suddenly think of their homes and their loved ones and realizing that those on the other side must have the same thoughts, throw away their weapons of murder."

Talking with her young friend Joe Lash that week at lunch, Eleanor admitted she was having a difficult time sorting out her feelings about the war. On the one hand, she was fully alert to the magnitude of Hitler's threat. On the other hand, she agreed with the views of the American Youth Congress, a group of young liberals and radicals whom Eleanor had defended over the years, that the money spent on arms would be much better spent on education and medical care. Her deepest fear, Lash recorded in his diary, was that nothing would come out of this war different from the last war, that history would repeat itself. And because of this sinking feeling, she could not put her heart into the war.

Building on these feelings in her speech to the boys of Choate, Eleanor stressed the importance of renewing democracy at home in order to make the fight for democracy abroad worthwhile. This argument would become her theme in the years ahead, as she strove to give positive meaning to the terrible war. "How to preserve the freedoms of democracy in the world. How really to make democracy work at home and prove it is worth preserving.... These are the questions the youth of today must face and we who are older must face them too."

•   •   •

Eleanor's philosophical questions about democracy were not the questions on the president's mind when he met with his Cabinet at two that afternoon. His concerns as he looked at the familiar faces around the table were much more immediate: how to get a new and expanded military budget through the Congress, how to provide aid to the Allies as quickly as possible, how to stock up on strategic materials; in other words, how to start the complex process of mobilizing for war.

The president opened the proceedings, as usual, by turning to Cordell Hull, his aging secretary of state, for the latest news from abroad. A symbol of dependability, respected by liberals and conservatives alike, the tall gaunt Tennessean, with thick white hair and bright dark eyes, had headed the department since 1933. Hull spoke slowly and softly as he shared the latest bulletins from his embassies in Europe, his slumped shoulders and downcast eyes concealing the stubborn determination that had characterized his long and successful career in the Congress as a representative and senator from Tennessee. In Holland, it was reported with a tone of optimism that later proved unfounded, the Dutch were beginning to recapture the airports taken by the Germans the night before. In Belgium, too, it was said, the Allied armies were holding fast against the German thrusts. But the mood in the room darkened quickly as the next round of bulletins confirmed devastating tales of defeat at the hands of the Germans.

After hearing Hull, the president traditionally called on Henry Morgenthau, his longtime friend and secretary of the Treasury. Just before the Cabinet meeting had convened, Morgenthau had received word that the Belgian gold reserves had been safely evacuated to France, and that much of the Dutch gold was also safe. But this was the extent of the good news Morgenthau had to report. All morning long, Morgenthau had been huddled in meetings with his aides, looking at the dismal figures on America's preparedness, wondering how America could ever catch up to Germany, since it would take eighteen months to deliver the modern weapons of war even if the country went into full-scale mobilization that very day.

Labor Secretary Frances Perkins, the only woman in the Cabinet, tended to talk a great deal at these meetings, "as though she had swallowed a press release." But on this occasion she remained silent as the conversation was carried by Harry Hopkins, the secretary of commerce, who was present at his first Cabinet meeting in months.

For the past year and a half, Hopkins had been in and out of hospitals while doctors tried to fix his body's lethal inability to absorb proteins and fats. His health had begun to deteriorate in the summer of 1939, when, at the height of his power as director of the Works Progress Administration, he was told that he had stomach cancer. A ghastly operation followed which removed the cancer along with three-quarters of his stomach, leaving him with a severe form of malnutrition. Told in the fall of 1939 that Hopkins had only four weeks to live, Roosevelt took control of the case himself and flew in a team of experts, whose experiments with plasma transfusions arrested the fatal decline. Then, to give Hopkins breathing space from the turbulence of the WPA, Roosevelt appointed him secretary of commerce. Even that job had proved too much, however: Hopkins had been able to work only one or two days in the past ten months.

Yet, on this critical day, the fifty-year-old Hopkins was sitting in the Cabinet meeting in the midst of the unfolding crisis. "He was to all intents and purposes," Hopkins' biographer Robert Sherwood wrote, "a finished man who might drag out his life for a few years of relative inactivity or who might collapse and die at any time." His face was sallow and heavy-lined; journalist George Creel once likened his weary, melancholy look to that of "an ill-fed horse at the end of a hard day," while Churchill's former daughter-in-law, Pamela Churchill Harriman, compared him to "a very sad dog." Given his appearance—smoking one cigarette after another, his brown hair thinning, his shoulders sagging, his frayed suit baggy at the knees—"you wouldn't think," a contemporary reporter wrote, "he could possibly be important to a President."

But when he spoke, as he did at length this day on the subject of the raw materials needed for war, his sickly face vanished and a very different face appeared, intelligent, good-humored, animated. His eyes, which seconds before had seemed beady and suspicious, now gleamed with light. Sensing the urgency of the situation, Hopkins spoke so rapidly that he did not finish half of his words, as though, after being long held back, he wanted to make up for lost time. It was as if the crisis had given him a renewed reason for living; it seemed, in reporter Marquis Childs' judgment at the time, "to galvanize him into life." From then on, Childs observed, "while he would still be an ailing man, he was to ignore his health." The curative impact of Hopkins' increasingly crucial role in the war effort was to postpone the sentence of death the doctors had given him for five more years.

Even Hopkins' old nemesis, Harold Ickes, felt compelled to pay attention when Hopkins reported that the United States had "only a five or six months supply of both rubber and tin, both of which are absolutely essential for purposes of defense." The shortage of rubber was particularly worrisome, since rubber was indispensable to modern warfare if armies were to march, ships sail, and planes fly. Hitler's armies were rolling along on rubber-tired trucks and rubber-tracked tanks; they were flying in rubber-lined high-altitude suits in planes equipped with rubber de-icers, rubber tires, and rubber life-preserver rafts. From stethoscopes and blood-plasma tubing to gas masks and adhesive tape, the demand for rubber was endless. And with Holland under attack and 90 percent of America's supply of rubber coming from the Dutch East Indies, something had to be done.

Becoming more and more spirited as he went on, Hopkins outlined a plan of action, starting with the creation of a new corporation, to be financed by the Reconstruction Finance Corporation, whose purpose would be to go into the market and buy at least a year's supply of rubber and tin. This step would be only the first, followed by the building of synthetic-rubber plants and an effort to bring into production new sources of natural rubber in South America. Hopkins' plan of action met with hearty approval.

While Hopkins was speaking, word came from London that Neville Chamberlain had resigned his post as prime minister. This dramatic event had its source in the tumultuous debate in the Parliament over the shameful retreat of the British Expeditionary Force from Norway three weeks earlier. Responding to clamorous cries for his resignation, Chamberlain had stumbled badly by personalizing the issue and calling for a division to show the strength of his support. "I welcome it, indeed," he had said. "At least we shall see who is with and who is against us and I will call on my friends to support me in the lobby tonight."

But the division had not turned out as Chamberlain expected: Tory officers in uniform, feeling the brunt of Britain's lack of preparedness, surged into the Opposition lobby to vote against the government. In all, over thirty Conservatives deserted Chamberlain, and a further sixty abstained, reducing the government's margin from two hundred to eighty-one. Stunned and disoriented, Chamberlain recognized he could no longer continue to lead unless he could draw Labour into a coalition government. For a moment earlier that day, the German invasion of the Low Countries threatened to freeze Chamberlain in place, but the Labour Party refused his appeals for a national government. "Prime Minister," Lord Privy Seal Clement Attlee bluntly replied, "our party won't have you and I think I am right in saying that the country won't have you either." The seventy-one-year-old prime minister had little choice but to step down.

Then, when the king's first choice, Lord Halifax, refused to consider the post on the grounds that his position as a peer would make it difficult to discharge his duties, the door was opened for Winston Churchill, the complex Edwardian man with his fat cigars, his gold-knobbed cane, and his vital understanding of what risks should be taken and what kind of adversary the Allies were up against. For nearly four decades, Churchill had been a major figure in public life. The son of a lord, he had been elected to Parliament in 1900 and had served in an astonishing array of Cabinet posts, including undersecretary for the colonies, privy councillor, home secretary, first lord of the admiralty, minister of munitions, and chancellor of the Exchequer. He had survived financial embarrassment, prolonged fits of depression, and political defeat to become the most eloquent spokesman against Nazi Germany. From the time Hitler first came to power, he had repeatedly warned against British efforts to appease him, but no one had listened. Now, finally, his voice would be heard. "Looking backward," a British writer observed, "it almost seems as though the transition from peace to war began on that day when Churchill became Prime Minister."

Responding warmly to the news of Churchill's appointment, Roosevelt told his Cabinet he believed "Churchill was the best man that England had." From a distance, the two leaders had come to admire each other: for years, Churchill had applauded Roosevelt's "valiant effort" to end the depression, while Roosevelt had listened with increasing respect to Churchill's lonely warnings against the menace of Adolf Hitler. In September 1939, soon after the outbreak of the war, when Churchill was brought into the government as head of the admiralty, Roosevelt had initiated the first in what would become an extraordinary series of wartime letters between the two men. Writing in a friendly but respectful tone, Roosevelt had told Churchill: "I shall at all times welcome it if you will keep me in touch personally with everything you want me to know about. You can always send sealed letters through your pouch or my pouch." Though relatively few messages had been exchanged in the first nine months of the war, the seeds had been planted of an exuberant friendship, which would flourish in the years to come.

• • •

Once the Cabinet adjourned, Roosevelt had a short meeting with the minister of Belgium, who was left with only $35 since an order to freeze all credit held by Belgium, the Netherlands, and Luxembourg had gone into effect, earlier that morning. After arrangements were made to help him out, there began a working session on the speech Roosevelt was to deliver that night to a scientific meeting.

Then Roosevelt, not departing from his regular routine, went into his study for the cocktail hour, the most relaxed time of his day. The second-floor study, crowded with maritime pictures, models of ships, and stacks of paper, was the president's favorite room in the White House. It was here that he read, played poker, sorted his beloved stamps, and conducted most of the important business of his presidency. The tall mahogany bookcases were stuffed with books, and the leather sofas and chairs had acquired a rich glow. Any room Roosevelt spent time in, Frances Perkins observed, "invariably got that lived-in and overcrowded look which indicated the complexity and variety of his interests and intentions." Missy and Harry Hopkins were there, along with Pa Watson and Eleanor's houseguest, the beautiful actress Helen Gahagan Douglas. The cocktail hour, begun during Roosevelt's years in Albany, had become an institution in Roosevelt's official family, a time for reviewing events in an informal atmosphere, a time for swapping the day's best laughs. The president always mixed the drinks himself, experimenting with strange concoctions of gin and rum, vermouth and fruit juice.

During the cocktail hour, no more was said of politics or war; instead the conversation turned to subjects of lighter weight—to gossip, funny stories, and reminiscences. With Missy generally presiding as hostess, distributing the drinks to the guests, Roosevelt seemed to find complete relaxation in telling his favorite stories over and over again. Some of these stories Missy must have heard more than twenty or thirty times, but, like the "good wife," she never let her face betray boredom, only delight at the knowledge that her boss was having such a good time. And with his instinct for the dramatic and his fine ability to mimic, Roosevelt managed to tell each story a little differently each time, adding new details or insights.

On this evening, there was a delicious story to tell. In the Congress there was a Republican representative from Auburn, New York, John Taber, who tended to get into shouting fits whenever the subject of the hated New Deal came up. In a recent debate on the Wage and Hour amendments, he had bellowed so loudly that he nearly swallowed the microphone. On the floor at the time was Representative Leonard Schultz of Chicago, who had been deaf in his left ear since birth. As Mr. Taber's shriek was amplified through the loudspeakers, something happened to Mr. Schultz. Shaking convulsively, he staggered to the cloakroom, where he collapsed onto a couch, thinking he'd been hit in an air raid. He suddenly realized that he could hear with his left ear—for the first time in his life—and better than with his right. When doctors confirmed that Mr. Schultz's hearing was excellent, Mr. Taber claimed it was proof from God that the New Deal should be shouted down!

Harry Hopkins was no stranger to these intimate gatherings. Before his illness, he had been one of Roosevelt's favorite companions. Like Roosevelt, he was a great storyteller, sprinkling his tales with period slang and occasional profanity. Also like Roosevelt, he saw the humor in almost any situation, enjoying gags, wisecracks, and witticisms. "I didn't realize how smart Harry was," White House secretary Toi Bachelder later remarked, "because he was such a tease and would make a joke of everything."

Missy was undoubtedly as delighted as her boss to see Harry back at the White House, though her playful spirit most likely masked the genuine pleasure she took in the company of this unusual man. Once upon a time, after Hopkins' second wife, Barbara, died of cancer, there had been talk of a romance between Missy and Harry. In a diary entry for March 1939, Harold Ickes reported a conversation with presidential adviser Tommy Corcoran in which Corcoran had said "he would not be surprised if Harry should marry Missy." In that same entry, Ickes recorded a dinner conversation between his wife, Jane Ickes, and Harry Hopkins in which they "got to talking about women—a favorite subject with Harry. He told Jane that Missy had a great appeal for him."

Among Hopkins' personal papers, there are many affectionate notes to Missy. During a spring weekend in 1939 when Missy was at the St. Regis in New York, Hopkins sent her a telegram. "Vic and I arriving Penn Station 8. Going direct to St. Regis. Make any plans you want but include us." On another occasion, when Hopkins was in the hospital for a series of tests, he wrote her a long, newsy letter but admitted that "the real purpose of this letter is to tell you not to forget me. . . . Within a day or two I expect to be out riding in the country for an hour or so each day and only wish you were with me."

The president, Harry, and Missy had journeyed together to Warm Springs in the spring of 1938. "There is no one here but Missy—the President and me—so life is simple—ever so informal and altogether pleasant," Hopkins recorded. "Lunch has usually been FDR with Missy and me—these are the pleasantest because he is under no restraint and personal and public business is discussed with the utmost frankness. . . . After dinner the President retreats to his stamps—magazines and the evening paper. Missy and I will play Chinese checkers—occasionally the three of us played but more often we read—a little conversation—important or not—depending on the mood."

But if over the years their familiarity had brought Harry and Missy to the point of intimacy, Missy had probably cut it short, as she had cut short every other relationship in her life that might subordinate her great love for FDR. No invitation was accepted by Missy if it meant leaving the president alone. "Even the most ardent swain," Newsweek reported, "is chilled at the thought that, to invite her to a movie he must call up the White House, which is her home." At the end of her working day, Missy preferred to retire to her little suite on the third floor, where, more often than not, she would pick up her phone to hear the president on the line, asking her to come to his study and sit by his side as he sorted his stamps or went through his mail.

If this behavior seemed mistaken in the eyes of her friends, who could not imagine how someone so young and attractive, who "should have been off somewhere cool and gay on a happy weekend," would give up "date after date, month after month, year after year," Missy had no other wish than to be with Roosevelt, her eager eyes watching every movement of his face, marveling at his overwhelming personality, his facility for dealing with people of every sort, his exceptional memory, his unvarying good humor. "Gosh, it will be good to get my eyes on you again," Missy wrote Roosevelt once when he was on a trip. "This place is horrible when you are away."

While Franklin was mixing cocktails, Eleanor was on a train back to Washington from New York. For many of her fellow riders, the time on the train was a time to ease up, to gaze through the windows at the passing countryside, to close their eyes and unwind. But for Eleanor, who considered train rides her best working hours, there was little time to relax. The pile of mail, still unanswered, was huge, and there was a column to be written for the following day. Franklin's cousin Margaret "Daisy" Suckley recalls traveling with Eleanor once on the New York–to–Washington train. "She was working away the whole time with Malvina, and I was sitting there like a dumbbell looking out the window, and suddenly Mrs. Roosevelt said to Malvina, 'Now I'm going to sleep for fifteen minutes,' and she put her head back on the seat. I looked at my watch, and just as it hit fifteen minutes, she woke up and said, 'Now Tommy, let's go on.' It was amazing. I was stunned."

Even if Eleanor had reached the White House that evening in time for the cocktail hour, she would probably not have joined. Try as she might over the years, Eleanor had never felt comfortable at these relaxed gatherings. Part of her discomfort was toward alcohol itself, the legacy of an alcoholic father who continually failed to live up to the expectations and trust of his adoring daughter. One Christmas, Eleanor's daughter, Anna, and her good friend Lorena Hickok had chipped in to buy some cocktail glasses for Eleanor's Greenwich Village apartment in the hopes she would begin inviting friends in for drinks. "In a funny way," Anna wrote "Hick," as Miss Hickok was called, "I think she has always wanted to feel included in such parties, but so many old inhibitions have kept her from it."

But, despite Anna's best hopes, Eleanor's discomfort at the cocktail hour persisted, suggesting that beyond her fear of alcohol lay a deeper fear of letting herself go, of slackening off the work that had become so central to her sense of self. "Work had become for Eleanor almost as addictive as alcohol," her niece Eleanor Wotkyns once observed. "Even when she thought she was relaxing she was really working. Small talk horrified her. Even at New Year's, when everyone else relaxed with drinks, she would work until ten minutes of twelve, come in for a round of toasts, and then disappear to her room to work until two or three a.m. Always at the back of her mind were the letters she had to write, the things she had to do."

"She could be a crashing bore," Anna's son Curtis Dall Roosevelt admitted. "She was very judgmental even when she tried not to be. The human irregularities, the off-color jokes he loved, she couldn't take. He would tell his stories, many of them made to fit a point, and she would say, 'No, no, Franklin, that's not how it happened.'"

"If only Mother could have learned to ease up," her son Elliott observed, "things would have been so different with Father, for he needed relaxation more than anything in the world. But since she simply could not bring herself to unwind, he turned instead to Missy, building with her an exuberant, laughing relationship, full of jokes, silliness, and gossip."

• • •

"Stay for dinner. I'm lonely," Roosevelt urged Harry Hopkins when the cocktail hour came to an end. There were few others at this stage of his life that the president enjoyed as much as Hopkins. With the death in 1936 of Louis Howe, the shriveled ex-newspaperman who had fastened his star to Roosevelt in the early Albany days, helped him conquer his polio, and guided him through the political storms to the White House, the president had turned to Hopkins for companionship. "There was a temperamental sympathy between Roosevelt and Hopkins," Frances Perkins observed. Though widely different in birth and breeding, they both possessed unconquerable confidence, great courage, and good humor; they both enjoyed the society of the rich, the gay, and the well-born, while sharing an abiding concern for the average man. Hopkins had an almost "feminine sensitivity" to Roosevelt's moods, Sherwood observed. Like Missy, he seemed to know when the president wanted to consider affairs of state and when he wanted to escape from business; he had an uncanny instinct for knowing when to introduce a serious subject and when to tell a joke, when to talk and when to listen. He was, in short, a great dinner companion.

As soon as dinner was finished, Roosevelt had to return to work. In less than an hour, he was due to deliver a speech, and he knew that every word he said would be scrutinized for the light it might shed on the crisis at hand. Taking leave of Hopkins, Roosevelt noticed that his friend looked even more sallow and miserable now than he had looked earlier in the day. "Stay the night," the President insisted. So Hopkins borrowed a pair of pajamas and settled into a bedroom suite on the second floor. There he remained, not simply for one night but for the next three and a half years, as Roosevelt, exhibiting his genius for using people in new and unexpected ways, converted him from the number-one relief worker to the number-one adviser on the war. Later, Missy liked to tease: "It was Harry Hopkins who gave George S. Kaufman and Moss Hart the idea for that play of theirs, 'The Man Who Came to Dinner.'"

As the president was preparing to leave for Constitution Hall, he remembered something he had meant to ask Helen Gahagan Douglas during the cocktail hour. There was no time to discuss it now, but, stopping by her room, he told her he had an important question for her and asked if she would meet him in his study when he returned. "Certainly," she replied, and he left to address several thousand scientists and scholars at the Pan American Scientific Congress.

"We come here tonight with heavy hearts," he began, looking out at the packed auditorium. "This very day, the tenth of May, three more independent nations have been cruelly invaded by force of arms. . . . I am glad that we are shocked and angered by the tragic news." Declaring that it was no accident that this scientific meeting was taking place in the New World, since elsewhere war and politics had compelled teachers and scholars to leave their callings and become the agents of destruction, Roosevelt warned against an undue sense of security based on the false teachings of geography: in terms of the moving of men and guns and planes and bombs, he argued, every acre of American territory was closer to Europe than was ever the case before. "In modern times it is a shorter distance from Europe to San Francisco, California than it was for the ships and legions of Julius Caesar to move from Rome to Spain or Rome to Britain."

"I am a pacifist," he concluded, winding up with a pledge that was greeted by a great burst of cheers and applause, "but I believe that by overwhelming majorities . . . you and I, in the long run if it be necessary, will act together to protect and defend by every means at our command our science, our culture, our American freedom and our civilization."

Buoyed by his thunderous reception, Roosevelt was in excellent humor when he returned to his study to find Helen Gahagan Douglas waiting for him. Just as he was settling in, however, word came that Winston Churchill was on the telephone. Earlier that evening, Churchill had driven to Buckingham Palace, where King George VI had asked him to form a government. Even as Churchill agreed to accept the seals of office, British troops were pouring into Belgium, wildly cheered by smiling Belgians, who welcomed them with flowers. The change was made official at 9 p.m., when Chamberlain, his voice breaking with emotion, resigned. It had been a long and fateful day for Britain, but now, though it was nearly 3 a.m. in London, Churchill apparently wanted to touch base with his old letter-writing companion before going to sleep.

Though there is no record of the content of this first conversation between the new prime minister of England and the president of the United States, Churchill did reveal that when he went to bed that night, after the extraordinary events of an extraordinary day, he was conscious of "a profound sense of relief. At last I had the authority to give directions over the whole scene. I felt as if I were walking with Destiny, and that all my past life had been but a preparation for this hour and this trial."

"Therefore," Churchill concluded, "although impatient for morning, I slept soundly and had no need for cheering dreams. Facts are better than dreams." He had achieved the very position he had imagined for himself for so many years.

While Roosevelt was talking with Churchill, Helen Douglas tried to prepare herself for the important question the president wanted to ask her. Perhaps, she thought, it was related to her work with the farm-security program, or the National Youth Administration. Both Helen and her husband, fellow actor Melvyn Douglas, were ardent New Dealers, members of the National Advisory Commission for the Works Progress Administration and the California Advisory Commission for the NYA. Earlier that year, they had hosted Mrs. Roosevelt's visit to Los Angeles, accompanying her to the migrant-labor camps in the San Joaquin Valley.

"The day was unforgettable," Helen later recalled. "Soon after we started,

Mrs. Roosevelt spotted a cluster of makeshift shacks constructed of old boards, tarpaper and tin cans pounded flat, one of the ditch bank communities that were commonplace in California then." She asked to stop the car and walked across the field toward some migrants. "One of the bent figures straightened to see who was approaching and recognized her at once. 'Oh, Mrs. Roosevelt, you've come to see us,' he said. He seemed to accept as a natural event of American life that the wife of the President of the United States would be standing in a mucky field chatting with him."

Perhaps the president's question related to something his wife had told him about her journey. To be sure, Helen knew that Roosevelt loved movies and movie people, but not even that knowledge prepared her for the whimsical nature of the question the president posed to her that night.

"OK, Helen," Roosevelt began, his eyes flashing with good humor. "Now, I want you to tell me exactly what happened under the table at Ciro's between Paulette Goddard and Anatole Litvak." The juicy gossip Roosevelt wanted to hear involved the Russian-born director Anatole Litvak and Paulette Goddard, the vivacious brunette actress who was married first to the filmmaker Hal Roach and then to Charlie Chaplin. As Helen Douglas told the story, Goddard and Litvak were having dinner at the elegant nightclub, where the men had to wear tuxedos and the women long dresses, when the urge to make love became so strong that they eased themselves onto the floor under the table. As the moans were heard across the restaurant floor, waiters rushed to the scene with extra tablecloths to cover the sides of the table. Or so the story was told. "I love it, I love it," Roosevelt responded.

Returning to the White House from Union Station just as Helen was finishing her tale, Eleanor heard her husband's laughter and assumed that, as usual, he was with Missy, relaxing at the end of the day. At such times, she later admitted to her son Elliott, she felt terribly left out, wishing that she could let herself go and simply join in the frivolity. But as it was, she knew that if she opened the door she would be driven to talk business, to share the information and insights she had gleaned from her recent trip. Then, if her husband was tired and unresponsive, she would feel hurt and rejected. It had happened this way before. Better to go to her own bedroom and wait until morning to see her husband. "All her life," her niece Eleanor Wotkyns observed, "Eleanor yearned to be more spontaneous, to relax more readily, but in the end how can one force oneself to be spontaneous?"

At ten after eleven that evening, according to the White House usher diary, both Eleanor and Franklin went to bed—Franklin settling into his small bedroom off his study, Eleanor into her own suite of rooms, next to her husband's, in the southwest corner of the mansion. But the separation by night belied the partnership by day—a partnership that would help change the face of the country in the years ahead.

CHAPTER 2

"A FEW NICE BOYS
WITH BB GUNS"

At 1 p.m. on May 16, 1940, President Roosevelt was scheduled to address a joint session of Congress. It was the president's first appearance in the House Chamber since the war in Western Europe had begun. Despite the blinding rain falling steadily since early morning, a huge audience had gathered to hear him.

Here, on the floor of the House of Representatives, all the contending forces of American life had gathered over the years to argue their causes—abolitionists versus slaveowners, liberals versus conservatives, unions versus management, farmers versus city-dwellers. On a number of occasions, particularly in the nineteenth century, the debates had descended into physical violence as members brandished pistols, smashed one another's heads with tongs, canes, and brass spittoons, and pummeled each other with fists. The very size of the House Chamber, with large numbers of legislators, clerks, and page boys running from place to place, conspired to produce confusion and chaos.

As one o'clock neared, there was a stir among the audience, an air of expectation. Every face, not knowing for sure where the country was going, wore a look of nervousness. In the Congress in 1940, there were 526 men and five women, nearly three hundred lawyers, two dozen schoolteachers, sixty merchants, twenty bankers and insurance agents, nine newspaper publishers, five dentists, a half-dozen preachers, the owner of the largest cattle ranch in the world, an amateur magician, and a half-dozen or more aspirants to the presidency. There was one Negro.

At 12:59 p.m. the assistant doorkeeper announced the members of the Cabinet. The spectators responded with warm applause. But when the audience caught sight of the president himself, his right hand holding a cane, his left hand grasping the forearm of a Secret Service man, they jumped to their feet, applauding and cheering him as he had never been cheered in the Capitol before, a bipartisan ovation that could only be interpreted as a demonstration of national unity in a time of crisis.

It had been a week no one in the Western world would forget. After only five days of fighting, Holland, with tens of thousands of her citizens said to be dead, had surrendered; the Belgian army was almost totally destroyed, and France, reputed to possess the best army in all of Europe, was being overrun. The Germans seemed to have discovered a radically new style of air-ground warfare that was somehow free from ordinary constraints of time and distance. The speed and destructiveness of Germany's powerful tanks —able to cross rivers and canals as if they were paved boulevards, resisting all fire at normal ranges—were almost incomprehensible. Against these metal mastodons, French Premier Paul Reynaud lamented, the French defenses were like "walls of sand that a child puts up against waves on the seashore." Equally hard to fathom was the effectiveness of Germany's air force, roaring in ahead of advancing columns, bombing communication lines, strafing and terrorizing ground troops to the point of an almost total Allied collapse.

For many in the audience, Roosevelt's dramatic journey to the Hill awakened memories of Woodrow Wilson's appearance before Congress in the spring of 1917, when America entered the Great War. Now, once again, Europe was engaged in an expanding war that threatened to engulf the entire world, and emotions were running high. As the applause continued to swell, the president slowly maneuvered his body up the long ramp from the well of the House to the rostrum.

Standing at the podium, his leg braces firmly locked into place, the president looked at his audience, and an uncharacteristic wave of nervousness came upon him. Absent were both his conspicuous smile and the swaggering way he usually held his head; in their place, a slight slump of the shoulders and a grim expression that matched the gray day. Reporters seated behind the podium detected anxiety in his trembling hands and in the faltering way he tried and failed, not once but twice, to put on his glasses. From the center of the visitors' gallery, where she was seated between Missy and Tommy, Eleanor looked down anxiously, a flush on her cheeks.

The president had cause to feel apprehensive. He knew that both Britain and France were looking to the United States for help. Alone among the democratic nations, the United States possessed the potential resources— the abundance of raw materials, the oil fields, the bauxite mines, the assembly lines, the production equipment, the idle manpower, the entrepreneurial skills, the engineering know-how—necessary to wage technological war on a scale equal to that of Nazi Germany. "I trust you realize, Mr. President," Churchill had written earlier that week, "that the voice and force of the United States may count for nothing if they are withheld too long."

But, as much as Roosevelt wanted to help, he recognized all too well—in a way neither Churchill nor French Premier Paul Reynaud could possibly have imagined—how unprepared America was, both mentally and physically, for war. In Europe, the vision of the New World coming to the rescue of the Old was so alluring that dreams were confused with realities, the boundary between potential and actual production erased, a mobilization that had not even begun considered a *fait accompli.* To harness a nation's economic potential for war was a complex process at any time, but, given the realities of American life in 1940, it seemed an almost impossible task.

•   •   •

The America over which Roosevelt presided in 1940 was in its eleventh year of depression. No decline in American history had been so deep, so lasting, so far-reaching. "The great knife of the depression," wrote Robert S. and Helen Merrill Lynd in their classic study, *Middletown in Transition,* "had cut down impartially through the entire population, cleaving open lives and hopes of rich as well as poor. The experience had been more nearly universal than any prolonged recent emotional experience in [America's] history. It had approached in its elemental shock the primary experiences of birth and death."

To be sure, the worst days were over—the days when breadlines and soup kitchens were forming in every city, when evicted families were shivering in makeshift tents in the dead of winter and jobless men were bivouacking around wood fires at the railroad tracks. The massive relief programs of the New Deal had stopped the precipitous slide of the first three and a half years, providing an economic floor for tens of millions of Americans.

But the economy had not yet recovered; business was still not producing well enough on its own to silence the growing doubts about capitalism and democracy. Almost ten million Americans, 17 percent of the work force, were without jobs; about two and a half million found their only source of income in government programs. Of those who worked, one-half of the men and two-thirds of the women earned less than $1,000 a year. Only forty-eight thousand taxpayers in a population of 132 million earned more than $2,500 a year.

In his second inaugural, Roosevelt had proclaimed that he saw "one-third of a nation ill-housed, ill-clad, ill-nourished." On this spring day three years later, he could still see abundant evidence of serious deprivation. Thirty-one percent of thirty-five million dwelling units did not have running water; 32 percent had no indoor toilet; 39 percent lacked a bathtub or shower; 58

percent had no central heating. Of seventy-four million Americans twenty-five years old or older, only two of five had gone beyond eighth grade; one of four had graduated from high school; one of twenty had completed college.

Though equal opportunity in a classless society still dominated the rhetoric of the day, the reality was a pyramidal society, a fortunate few at the top and the great mass of citizens stuck at the bottom with few opportunities to move upward on the economic ladder. America was then a predominantly small-town nation, with the majority of citizens living in towns of fewer than twenty-five thousand people. Within these towns, as in the neighborhoods of larger cities, society was stratified along class, racial, and ethnic lines.

"Class membership," historian Richard Polenberg has written of this period, "determined virtually every aspect of an individual's life: the subjects one studied in high school, the church one attended, the person one married, the clubs one joined, the magazines one read, the doctor one visited, the way one was treated by the law, and even the choice of an undertaker."

The American nation had been formed by the continual movement of people from Europe to the New World and then across a hostile continent in a restless, unflagging quest for new opportunity. But now, with the Western frontier closed and every section of America afflicted by depression, most Americans seemed frozen in place, rarely venturing to cross the lines of their county, much less their state.

To be sure, the New Deal, particularly in its exhilarating early days, had profoundly altered the relationship between the government and the people, giving the state final responsibility for the well-being of its citizens. Rejecting the traditional notion that government was the handmaiden of business, the New Deal Congress had enacted an unprecedented series of laws which regulated the securities market, established a minimum wage, originated a new system of social security, guaranteed labor's right to collective bargaining, and established control over the nation's money supply. "It is hard to think of another period in the whole history of the republic that was so fruitful," historian William Leuchtenberg has written, "or of a crisis that was met with as much imagination."

But by 1940, the New Deal revolution had sputtered to an end. The country was weary of reform, and Congress was in full rebellion against the administration's domestic agenda. A bipartisan coalition of conservative Southern Democrats and Republicans had seized the initiative, crushing the president's housing program, slashing appropriations for relief, killing the federal theater project, and eliminating the administration's undistributed-profits tax.

To complicate the situation further, the president's enemies on domestic issues were his friends in foreign policy, and vice versa. Since 1939, most conservative Democrats had supported the president's moves to aid the Allies, while many liberals and Midwestern progressives, fearing that the pull toward war would bring an end to social reform, had joined the isolationist cause.

For the president, there was perhaps additional anxiety in the recognition that the end of the "phony war" defined the beginning of a new presidency for him, one that would be judged by different standards. Roosevelt's old hero Woodrow Wilson was a painful memory in this regard. Wilson, too, had been cheered as never before on that April day in 1917 when he had come to Congress to ask for a declaration of war against Germany. Yet, two years later, after his bruising battle with the Senate over the League of Nations, the cheers had turned to jeers, and his presidency had been destroyed.

· · ·

The leadership of the House and Senate—Speaker William Bankhead, House Majority Leader Sam Rayburn, and Senate Majority Leader Alben Barkley—sat behind the president on a marble dais, facing the semicircular rows of seats. In the front row sat the Cabinet—Secretary Woodring gripping the edge of his chair, Secretary Hull holding his chin in his hand, Harry Hopkins slumped in a tense silence. Across the chamber, buddy poppies could be seen on hundreds of lapels, a tribute to the soldiers of World War I who had fought on Flanders Field.

"These are ominous days," the President began in a low, solemn tone, facing a battery of microphones that would carry his words to the world, "days whose swift and shocking developments force every neutral nation to look to its defenses in the light of new factors. . . . No old defense is so strong that it requires no further strengthening and no attack is so unlikely or impossible that it may be ignored."

Nearly a third of the president's address was devoted to a skillful schoolmasterly description of the flying times from Greenland, the Azores, and the Caribbean Islands to key American cities, to show that, in an age of air warfare, despite the claims of the isolationists, the natural barriers of the Atlantic and Pacific oceans no longer afforded the same protection they had in the past. Deriving strength from the positive reaction to his words, Roosevelt's voice swelled as he warned that Nazi Germany not only had more planes than all its opponents combined, but appeared to have a weekly productive capacity that was far greater than that of its opponents.

How could America respond to this alarming situation? Roosevelt's answer was bold. He asked for appropriations to recruit an additional half-million men for the army, to purchase guns and equipment, to build modern tanks, and to construct naval ships. Then he made a dramatic call for a staggering productive capacity of fifty thousand planes a year, which would in only twelve months put America ahead of Germany, creating an aerial armada second to none in the world. How Roosevelt arrived at the fifty-thousand figure, way beyond the best hopes of his army and navy combined, is still not clear. Some say the giant number—more than ten times the current capacity—was put forth in a conversation with newspaper owner Lord Beaverbrook; others point to a conversation with Secretary Hull. Whatever the source, army historian Irving Holley concludes, "the President's big round number was a psychological target to lift sights and accustom planners in military and industrial circles alike to thinking big."

Speaking later about the fifty-thousand figure, U. S. Steel Chairman Edward Stettinius said it seemed at first "like an utterly impossible goal; but it caught the imagination of Americans, who had always believed they could accomplish the impossible." By laying down the gauntlet in such a sensational way, by projecting on his audience his own faith in the ability of the American people to respond to crisis, Roosevelt seemed to cast a spell upon the members of the House and the Senate, who sprang to their feet and began applauding wildly.

"There are some," Roosevelt concluded, "who say that democracy cannot cope with the new technique of government developed in recent years by a few countries—by a few countries which deny the freedoms which we maintain are essential to our democratic way of life. This I reject." To cope with present dangers, he admitted, the nation requires "a toughness of moral and physical fiber," but these are precisely "the characteristics of a free people, a people devoted to the institutions they themselves have built."

In times of crisis, presidential scholar Grant McConnell has written, the nation, which seemed only an abstraction the day before, suddenly becomes a vivid reality. A mysterious process unfolds as the president and the flag become rallying points for all Americans. At such moments, if the president is able to meet the challenge, he is able to give shape, to organize, to create and recreate the nation.

On May 16, 1940, President Roosevelt met this challenge. When he finished his speech, the voices of the senators and representatives rose in a ringing shout, a sustained ovation whose echoes remained in the chamber after the president had left.

The rain was over, but drops of water still dripped from the trees when the president emerged from the Capitol. At the bottom of the steps, Eleanor took leave of her husband to join a group of young people for lunch at the Powhatan Hotel. The president returned directly to his office, buoyed not simply by the tremendous reception he had received, but even more by his own expression of faith in the dormant powers of democracy, his unalterable belief in the American people.

• • •

Roosevelt "believed that with enough energy and spirit anything could be achieved by man," the philosopher Isaiah Berlin wrote in an essay comparing Roosevelt and Churchill. "So passionate a faith in the future," Berlin went on, "implies an exceptionally sensitive awareness, conscious or self-conscious, of the tendencies of one's milieu, of the desires, hopes, fears, loves, hatreds, of the human beings who compose it, of what are described as 'trends.' " This uncanny awareness, Berlin argued, was the source of Roosevelt's genius. It was almost as if the "inner currents [and] tremors" of human society were registering themselves within his nervous system, "with a kind of seismographical accuracy."

In his imagination on this grim May day, Roosevelt could already envision the construction of hundreds of new factories, fueled by new public-private partnerships, producing planes and tanks and guns, humming with the energies of millions of citizens. On the nation's roads he pictured tens of thousands of American families, their life's possessions in their automobiles, willing to go to wherever the opportunity for work would take them. Little matter that the economy was still depressed and that millions of workers had lost their skills. To the man whose ebullient energy had overcome paralysis, it was natural to believe that the American people, once aroused, would transform the nation, pitching into the work at hand with spirit and resilience. But even Roosevelt could not have imagined that he stood that day on the verge of the most profound transformation in American history.

"There's something that he's got," Harry Hopkins once told Frances Perkins. "It seems unreasonable at times, but he falls back on something that gives him complete assurance that everything is going to be all right that I can't even grasp, that he isn't able . . . to explain to me. I'm just left feeling that it's a ridiculous position he's taken. Why should he be sure that it will be all right?"

No factor was more important to Roosevelt's leadership than his confidence in himself and in the American people. "His most outstanding characteristic is an air of supreme self-confidence," journalist W. M. Kiplinger wrote as the crisis of the European war deepened. "He always gives the impression that to him nothing is impossible, that everything will turn out all right."

The president had a remarkable capacity to transmit this cheerful strength to others, to allow, White House Counsel Sam Rosenman observed, "those who hear it to begin to feel it and take part in it, to rejoice in it—and to return it tenfold by their own confidence." Frances Perkins claimed that "his capacity to inspire and encourage those who had to do tough, confused and practically impossible jobs was beyond dispute." Like everyone else, she said, she "came away from an interview with the President feeling better, not because he had solved any problems . . . but because he had made me feel more cheerful, stronger, more determined."

So it had been in 1933, when, in the midst of the worst days of the Depression, the new president was able to communicate his own strength and assurances to a badly frightened people. Speaking of his first inaugural address, *Collier's* observed that "the new President does not delude himself as to the difficulties that lie before him, and yet he was serenely confident as to the ultimate outcome." By this single speech, Rosenman wrote, Roosevelt accomplished one of the most significant achievements of his presidency: "the renewal of the courage and hope and faith of the American people.

Within a week, more than half a million letters and telegrams were on their way to the White House, expressing faith in him and in his leadership."

Such serenity and strength were precisely the qualities called for in the spring of 1940, as America faced a second national crisis, even more fearful than the first. His belief that dormant energies of democracy could mobilize the nation to meet the Nazi threat was matched only by his own faith in himself. To be optimistic had become his stance in life, so much that, even when he had no reason to be so, he acted upbeat, so as not to disappoint the expectations of everyone around him.

• • •

In the afterglow of the president's triumphant speech, all the leading Republicans—Kansas governor and Republican presidential candidate in 1936, Alf Landon; newspaper publisher Colonel Frank Knox; and New York Governor Tom Dewey—fell into line. Even former President Herbert Hoover was forced to admit, "the President is right." What made this united front more striking was that the president had made no mention in his speech of how the government was going to pay for the new defense program. When reporters queried him, he used the metaphor of "a four alarm fire up the street" which must be extinguished immediately, without worrying about cost. His homely figure of speech evaded the issue and achieved his end. The main thing was to arouse the public to the Nazi threat, and then worry about how to raise the cash.

But the unified alarm about American security, as *Time* magazine pointed out, "was quickly succeeded by alarm over the fate of the GOP in 1940." On second thought, Tom Dewey proclaimed, the fifty-thousand figure was ridiculous. On second thought, Alf Landon stated, the president's message was "tragically late." On second thought, newspaper publisher Frank Gannett said, the message dramatized "the failure of the New Deal to meet and solve the basic problems facing the country."

The expected Republican criticism assumed a darker tone that Sunday night, May 18, when Colonel Charles Lindbergh, the famed aviator, in a nationwide radio address accused the administration of creating "a defense hysteria" and insisted that the United States was not threatened by foreign invasion unless "American peoples bring it on through their own quarreling and meddling with affairs abroad." The only reason we are in danger of becoming involved, he concluded, "is because there are powerful elements in America who desire us to take part. They represent a small minority of the American people, but they control much of the machinery of influence and propaganda. They seize every opportunity to push us closer to the edge."

The isolationists had found their champion. Senator Bennett Clark of Missouri termed Lindbergh's speech "magnificent," and Representative John Rankin of Mississippi called it "the finest advice I have heard in many a day." Senator Gerald P. Nye of North Dakota was glad, he said, "to hear a voice like

Lindbergh's raised in the cause of sanity at this wild moment—a moment engineered by the President."

Lindbergh's scathing critique legitimized congressional fault-finding with the president's popular speech. "During the present Administration," Senator Clark argued, "we have spent in excess of $6 billion on building up the Army and the Navy, and now we are told that we are pitifully unprepared. Simply because an emergency has developed abroad, are we going to turn over lump sums to the same outfit of bunglers that apparently wasted the $6 billion we spent." Two days later, Clark took the floor again. "[Are we going] to pour another billion dollars down the same rat hole?" he asked. (In fact, spread over the years of the Roosevelt administration the $6 billion amounted to less than three-quarters of a billion a year, hardly enough to keep a small army in existence.)

"If I should die tomorrow," Roosevelt told Henry Morgenthau at lunch in a rare moment of blind fury the day after Lindbergh's speech, "I want you to know this. I am convinced Lindbergh is a Nazi." Roosevelt did not anger easily, Eleanor later observed, "but when he did get angry, he was like an iceberg and . . . he could say things that would finish a relationship forever." On the issue of Lindbergh, however, Roosevelt was not alone. "When I read Lindbergh's speech," President Herbert Hoover's Secretary of State Henry Stimson wrote Roosevelt, "I felt it could not have been better put if it had been written by Goebbels himself. What a pity that this youngster had completely abandoned his belief in our form of government and has accepted Nazi methods because apparently they are efficient." Speaking in a more tempered voice, Eleanor told a newspaper reporter she thought the first part of Lindbergh's speech, which analyzed the position of America in the air, was "excellent," but "the last three paragraphs," referring to the sinister elements in America, seemed to her "unfortunate."

Despite the discordant note provided by Lindbergh's blast, the president's skillful speech achieved exactly what he wanted. Before the week was over, the Congress had voted to raise the debt ceiling and to authorize even more monies than the administration had requested. To the army would go a half-billion to train new troops, expedite munitions, and build new tanks and new planes. The navy would receive a quarter-billion to step up its ship-building program and to provide all vessels with the latest equipment. Also included in the congressional appropriations was the establishment of additional aviation schools and an increase in the number of pilots from twelve hundred to seven thousand a year.

•   •   •

Even the most lavish appropriations, however, could not shorten the waiting period of eighteen months projected for the actual delivery of the new tanks, planes, and weapons. The president's optimism about the future was one thing; the reality of America's present state of preparedness—as evidenced by the army's sorry maneuvers currently under way in Louisiana—was quite another.

Under a hot May sun, "on russet roads of sand and clay," the army's "Blue" forces, forty-thousand strong, were on the march in the biggest peacetime maneuver in the history of the United States. The Blues were heading west from Fort Benning, Georgia, to the Sabine Forest in Louisiana to defend their "mythical nation" against a lightning attack by thirty thousand "Red" forces moving east from Texas. (The defenders were given the benefit of more troops.) The war games were intended to serve as a field test of the new triangular divisions, to evaluate the use of horse cavalry against mechanized forces, and to provide practice in advancing large units under danger of air attack.

Through nine months of strenuous training, the soldiers had been living in the field and sleeping on the ground in rain and freezing weather to harden them for this first great maneuver. The supply officers had been preparing nearly as long to accumulate the 177 freightcar-loads of food, 190 tankloads of gas, 10,000 pieces of artillery, 3,500 horses, 1,600 observer stations, and 9,000 civilian volunteers. The games were scheduled to last two weeks and to cost more than a million dollars a day.

The announcement of the war games conjured an image of mock battles with long columns of soldiers running toward each other through the woods, waving flags, shooting blanks, hurling sham explosives into the air. In this glorified image, victory would be accorded to the side that reached a certain goal line first. Anticipating an exciting display of action, men, women, and children lined the Louisiana streets and the Gulf Coast highways to cheer the men on.

In reality, the maneuvers comprised a series of discrete and often invisible exercises—such as penetrating a line, crossing a river, bringing down a plane, or establishing a machine-gun nest on a knoll. At every point, an umpire, with a distinguishing badge on his arm, would determine which side had achieved the advantage. If, for instance, a squadron of Red airplanes came upon a line of Blue trucks moving along the highway in broad daylight, the penalty assessed against the Blues for leaving themselves exposed to "aerial attack" would be severe. Or, if the Blues reached a particular bridge first and could prove they had sufficient explosives to blow it up, then the Reds, upon reaching the "blown-up bridge," would be forced to stay in place until their engineers were able to improvise a new bridge in the same spot. In each instance, an umpire would be on top of the action, record his scores in a small book, and compare with the other umpires that evening to create a pattern of all the advances and losses during the entire day's actions.

"Consider the task," a *Times-Picayune* reporter observed, "faced by the men who shall umpire the war games." Whereas football referees must be on top of every play and watch the movements of twenty-two players on a level playing field, the field of play in the war games included muddy swamps, thick forests, and steep hills, nearly a hundred miles long and fifty miles wide, encompassing nearly seventy thousand players moving an average of 150 miles a day.

On May 10, the first day of the maneuvers, the Red forces, under General Walter Krueger, gained the advantage by surprising the Blues with an early-morning attack. At 4:30 a.m., a column of big armored trucks, their headlights "drilling bright tunnels through the blackness," roared down the back roads of Louisiana, awakening farmers and setting their dogs to howl. At the same time, a squadron of Red bombers attacked the Blue airport at McComb, Mississippi, causing damage to scores of Blue planes. The advance guard of the Blues, led by General Walter Short, had just arrived in the Sabine Forest when the Reds attacked. Exhausted from an overland march from Georgia covering more than six hundred miles, the Blues were no match for the Reds, who won the first encounter decisively. But two days later, the Blue reinforcements arrived at the scene, and the Blues succeeded in penetrating the Red line of resistance. And so it continued for two weeks, as first one side, then the other gained the advantage.

Before the maneuvers officially started, a series of landing accidents destroyed three pursuit planes and so completely damaged the undercarriage of a transport plane that twelve soldiers had to parachute out before it spiraled to the ground. One of the twelve became entangled in his parachute and drowned in the Pearl River. Two days later, Private Harold Vanderbilt of Cove, Arkansas, was killed when he slipped off a log and was crushed under a heavy army truck. That same day, Private Marion Caudell was electrocuted when the radio antennae on his scout car came in contact with a high-tension wire. By week's end, twelve soldiers were dead and nearly four hundred had been admitted to the hospital for injuries and diseases. As the war games progressed, the death toll rose. In a related maneuver, two entire flight crews, eleven men in all, were killed when two army bombers crashed to the earth in the middle of a suburban development.

But the accidents were not the only problem. It was the antiquated equipment, measured against the backdrop of the fast-moving war in Europe, that turned the gigantic maneuvers into a farce. In every critique, inside the army and out, lack of equipment was cited as *the* major problem. Though the morale of the American soldiers was universally praised, it was clear from the shape of the European struggle that courage and daring mattered less than the heavy power of the Germans' revolutionary form of attack—with dive-bombers, artillery, and heavy tanks all tied into one consolidated force. The most glaring weakness the maneuvers revealed was a stunning lack of combat planes. Though the assembly of planes at Barksdale Field was billed as "the greatest concentration of combat planes" ever brought together in the United States, virtually "a sea of planes," the actual total was only four hundred, a mere one day's supply in the current war. Until their opinion was undercut by Germany's shocking use of its air force as the spearhead of its blitzkrieg, the American generals had maintained that the air force was merely an auxiliary force. Consequently, the American army had almost no warplanes. At the end of the maneuvers, General Short admitted that, of the thirty-four missions he had requested of the air corps, only two were accomplished.

Nor were the American ground troops accustomed to shaping their behavior in response to air power. "Too frequently," *The Army & Navy Journal* observed in its critique of the maneuvers, "roads were jammed with motor vehicles closed up bumper to bumper, thus affording excellent targets, not only for artillery fire and air bombing, but also giving the enemy excellent information regarding locations and movements. The occasions when attempt was made to hide vehicles at halts, even in this wooded country, were rare."

Lack of tanks posed a problem almost as troubling as lack of planes. For too many years, high-ranking traditionalists, still believing in the superiority of the horse, had opposed action to upgrade the armored forces. As late as February 1940, even though the Polish cavalry had been dismembered by the German panzers in a matter of minutes, the *Cavalry Journal* was still arguing for the supremacy of the horse. "It is a mistake to persuade the public to attach exaggerated importance to motorization and mechanization," the *Cavalry Journal* contended, "because these can only play a small part in static warfare, which would seem to be the only sort of warfare probable in Western Europe. . . . The idea of huge armies rolling along roads at a fast pace is a dream. Apart from all questions of space and capacity of roads and bridges, rivers and mountains hamper the mass employment of motor vehicles." Besides, "men can keep animals in health and work for indefinite periods without difficulty or outside assistance, but oil and tires cannot like forage be obtained locally."

As a result of such attitudes, though there were acres and acres of land literally covered with the thirty-five hundred horses available for the maneuvers, only 450 tanks participated. And these tanks, Senator Henry Cabot Lodge, Jr., pointed out, were virtually all the tanks the United States had, or about "one finger of the fan-like German advance." When these few tanks were put into action, the results were electrifying. As townspeople watched from porches and roofs, two hundred horses galloped through the streets to their "deaths" in a futile effort to fend off the "slashing, onrushing mechanized brigade." In another exercise, witnesses watched in amazement as a tank brigade roared down an overgrown hill through briars, sumac, and bushes, over ravines where no horse could have crossed. "They were hit on all sides by these red hot bullets but the tanks were immune to rifle fire and small machine gun fire," one observer noted. "I wonder what would have been the effect if we had had on the hillside a unit of horse cavalry, where those red-hot bullets were shooting through the air."

Though cavalry leaders adamantly denied that the motor had made the horse obsolete, General Brees acknowledged that during the maneuvers the infantry and the horse cavalry had tended to become "road-bound"; the infantry was reluctant to detruck and the cavalry stuck to the roads, even when the muddy terrain made forward movement all but impossible.

In addition to numerical superiority, the German tanks were far superior to the American tanks in quality. Whereas the German soldiers sat in comfort and convenience in their heavy vehicles, complete with upholstered seats, shock absorbers, and bumpers, the driver of an American tank, buttoned up in fifteen tons of steel, with virtually no windows, was dependent for sight and direction on signals from the car commander, who sat above him in the turret. And since the clatter of the tank was like "the noise of ten robots tap dancing inside a cement mixer," the business of signaling was no easy matter. Amid such din, the commander in the turret had to rely on foot signals to the driver's shoulder and back. Two kicks meant "Go straight ahead." One kick on the right or left shoulder called for a right or left turn. If the soldier on top was shot, the driver was completely blind. Not surprisingly, soldiers dubbed the American machines "hell buggies."

"The gravity of this situation," Senator Lodge told his colleagues, "consists in the fact that it is almost as difficult to produce tanks as it is to produce planes." To manufacture even one light tank, more than half a dozen time-consuming steps had to be taken, with each part made in a different place: the motor by Continental Aircraft, the armor plate by Diebold Company in Ohio, rubber treads by Goodyear, weapons by Browning, special gears by a variety of firms. Then all the parts had to be sent to Rock Island Arsenal in Illinois to be assembled.

In recognition of the weaknesses revealed by the games, a secret meeting took place in the basement of Alexandria High School on the day the maneuvers ended. At this meeting, Generals Adna Chaffee and John Magruder, commanders of the army's sole tank brigade, and other officers committed to tanks, such as Colonel George Patton, presented their case for an independent armored force. Up to this moment, the tank brigade was under the calvary and infantry divisions, which had deliberately reduced the number of tanks. Pointedly, the chiefs of cavalry and infantry were not invited to the meeting, though they were nearby at the time. The basement conspirators sent their recommendation for an independent branch to Washington. General Marshall responded positively. He withdrew all armor from Cavalry and Infantry and placed it in a new, independent armored force.

American arrogance died during the maneuvers. "Overnight, the pleasant doings in Louisiana became old-fashioned nonsense," Time reported. "Against Europe's total war, the U.S. Army looked like a few nice boys with BB guns."

"The fact remains," Senator Lodge asserted, "that our Army today is not what it ought to be." For, if these troops were the cream of the U.S. Army, the best-trained, the most fully equipped, and if they evidenced such great problems, then one could only begin to imagine the situation in the rest of the army.

This was the desolate backdrop to the president's call for arms in his address to the Congress. "What smoldered beneath his words," *Time* observed, "was the warning that the U.S. will have to arm with all its might and main, because the world that is closing in on it is no longer safe for democracy."

•   •   •

Encouraged by the generally positive reaction to his congressional speech, Roosevelt turned his attention next to the difficult task of translating the idea of preparedness into reality. So complex were the demands of modern warfare, requiring the conversion of existing plants and the creation of new facilities, compelling the transfer of scientific research from objects of peace to weapons of war, demanding new accommodations between business, government, and labor, that dozens of critical policy decisions had to be made.

It was Roosevelt's primary strength that he saw how one decision related to another. The way the government was organized to meet the crisis, for example, would influence the cooperation of industry, the allocation of manpower, and the control of scarce resources. "There were evidently many times when he could truly see it all," Frances Perkins' biographer George Martin wrote, "men, guns, ships, food, the enemy, the Allies."

The first undertaking was to mobilize the business community behind the drive for preparedness. The Congress could provide the money, but it could not build the planes, design the tanks, or assemble the weapons. Without the cooperation of private industry, Roosevelt believed, the massive production effort needed for defense would never get off the ground. The fundamental challenge, as Roosevelt saw the situation that spring, was to bring the proprietors of the nation's chief economic assets—the men who ran the steel mills, the coal mines, the factories, and the automobile plants —into the defense effort as active participants.

It would not be an easy task. For years, business had been driven by an almost primitive hostility to Roosevelt, viewing his zealous support for the welfare state and organized labor as an act of betrayal to his class. Indeed, so incoherent were most businessmen in their rage at Roosevelt that they refused even to say the president's name, referring to him simply as "that man in the White House." The story is told of Howland Spencer, one of Roosevelt's wealthy neighbors, whose anger at the president was so fierce that he exiled himself to the Bahamas through the thirties and forties and only came back after Roosevelt's death.

The hostility had begun in the early days of the New Deal, when business felt steadily encroached upon by the never-ending series of laws which set minimum wages, regulated working conditions, and bolstered unionization. The ill-will had crystallized in 1935, when the Chamber of Commerce formally broke with the president, issuing a vicious denunciation of the New Deal. Roosevelt was wounded by the ferocity of the attack. As he looked back on his first term, he believed he had saved capitalism from itself by tempering its harshest effects. Without the New Deal, he believed, capitalism in America would have been overcome, as it was in Europe, by fascism or communism. Yet, Roosevelt complained, the U.S. Chamber of Commerce appreciated none of this, preferring to castigate him as a traitor to his class.

Roosevelt had responded in kind, lashing out at businessmen as "economic royalists" who were using their economic power to block equality of opportunity for the ordinary citizen in the same way the English Tories had sought to control the lives of the colonists. In the months that followed this outburst, the president's split with business deepened. Indeed, Roosevelt had found in class divisions an important source of political strength. The forces "of organized money are unanimous in their hatred of me," the president told a tumultuous working-class crowd during the 1936 campaign, "and I welcome their hatred. I should like to have it said of my first Administration that in it the forces of selfishness and of lust for power met their match. . . . I should like to have it said of my second Administration that in it these forces met their master."

As the situation in Europe darkened, the fears of business blazed into hysteria at the prospect of the increased power war would bring to the president. If war came, the president of the American Iron & Steel Institute said, "as certain as night follows day," while we are fighting "to crush dictatorship abroad," we will be "extending one at home." Some businessmen went so far as to suggest that Roosevelt was maneuvering the country into war in order to accomplish his Machiavellian design to install a permanent form of socialism in the United States.

But now, with thousands of people dying at the hands of Hitler every day, Roosevelt decided that the time had come to bring an end to his private war with business, to change his tack and give business a piece of the action, a chance to show whether or not it could truly deliver. "It was a political necessity on the eve of war," the Washington correspondent for *The Nation,* I. F. Stone, wrote at the time, "for a left-centered government in the United States to conciliate the Right by taking some of its representatives into the government. The same process, in reverse, occurred in England, whereby a Conservative government under Churchill conciliated Labor by taking the Bevins and the Morrisons into the Cabinet."

The scheme Roosevelt devised—a seven-member advisory board to be known as the National Defense Advisory Commission (NDAC)—was ingenious. Roosevelt's clever formula was to combine businessmen and New Dealers in equal measure, hopeful that the businessmen would thereby strengthen the faith of the right, while the New Dealers would keep the liberals in line.

For the critical job of directing the actual production process itself, Roosevelt chose millionaire businessman William Knudsen, head of General Motors, a classic example of the self-made man. Born in Copenhagen, Knudsen had come to America at the age of twenty, barely speaking a word of English. He had begun his career in the auto industry as an installer of assembly plants and then moved up the organization to become Henry Ford's production manager. A dispute with Ford led to his becoming vice-president of General Motors, with the task of building a Chevrolet to outsell Ford's Model T. He did this so successfully that he was appointed president of General Motors in 1937, commanding a salary of more than $350,000 a year.

"To many a citizen tired of New Deal–Business baiting," *Time* observed, "Knudsen was a symbol of the hope that business and the New Deal would work together." For his part, Knudsen was thrilled at the chance to serve the country that had served him so well. "I am most happy," he wrote the president after his appointment, "you've made it possible for me to show my gratitude to my country for the opportunity it has given me to acquire home, family and happiness in abundant measure."

In addition to Knudsen, Roosevelt brought in Edward Stettinius, chairman of U.S. Steel, to supervise the production and delivery of raw materials, and Ralph Budd, chairman of the Chicago, Burlington & Quincy, to handle transportation. For seven years, Washington observer Constance Green recorded, these men had formed the core of resistance to the New Deal; "now the captains of industry whom General Hugh Johnson in early NRA days had called 'Corporals of Disaster,' were again honored in Washington." Before the end of the summer, hundreds of businessmen found themselves at the very center of government action, and once they were there, their attitudes toward government control underwent a remarkable change.

Responding to the president's olive branch, the National Association of Manufacturers took out a full-page advertisement in June, pledging its knowledge, skill, and resources to the task of national defense, calling for national unity in the midst of crisis. "In the field of national defense," well-informed sources had been telling business all along, "Roosevelt is a conservative." Now, with Roosevelt's stress on cooperation rather than coercion, business began to believe that maybe this was so, that perhaps, if they put aside their hatred for the regime in power, there just might be "a little something in this saving the world for democracy again."

But, of course, Roosevelt never moved in only one direction at a time. The complex problem he faced was how to reawaken support on the right without instilling anger and discontent on the left. To this end, he gave the New Dealers four of the seven appointments. To handle labor, he brought in labor leader Sidney Hillman. A short, spare man who peered through bifocals and spoke with a marked Lithuanian accent, Hillman had come to America at twenty, the same age as Knudsen, landing in Chicago. He had become a cutter of men's garments at a time when conditions in the clothing industry were intolerable. Leading a revolt among the tailors, Hillman had created the Amalgamated Clothing Workers of America, and then, from the strength of this base, had become John Lewis' right-hand man in building the CIO.

Even more reassuring to the left, the President put Leon Henderson, a noisy New Dealer, in charge of prices. People said of the overweight Henderson that he looked like a Sunday-supplement caricature of a radical, with his wrinkled suits, his curly hair, and his nickel cigar stuck in the corner of his mouth. Born in Millville, New Jersey, and educated at Swarthmore on an athletic scholarship, Henderson had come to Washington to work for the Works Progress Administration. After moving on from there to the Securities and Exchange Commission, he had become a leader in the New Deal attack on business abuse.

To round out this strange amalgam of a commission, Roosevelt brought in University of North Carolina Dean Harriet Elliott to represent consumers, and Federal Reserve Board member Chester Davis to supervise farm products.

Within the NDAC in the months ahead, a fierce battle would rage between the businessmen, who argued that production was best served by industries working freely under the profit system, and the liberals, who believed that a democracy at war should forge wholly new connections between government, business, and labor, moving more in the direction of socialism. "If you are going to war in a capitalist country," Henry Stimson wrote, "you have to let business make money out of the process or business won't work." To the contrary, historian Bruce Catton argued, suppose that liberal bureaucrats instead of industrialists were running the program; perhaps then an entirely different kind of war effort would emerge, one that vested power and responsibility more directly in the workers themselves.

"The conflict was enduring," New Deal economist John Kenneth Galbraith recalled. "My memory of wartime Washington by no means excludes the menace of Hitler and the Japanese. But almost as poignantly it is of the New Dealers' battle with the reluctant business spokesman. . . . At times it seemed that our war with business took precedence over the war in Europe and Asia. There were weeks when Hitler scarcely entered our minds compared with the business types in Washington."

No sooner had the president announced his seven-member advisory commission than the conservative press began demanding that it be given real power and that Knudsen be appointed its "czar." "In private life," the *Kennebunk Journal* observed, "even a peanut stand has to have one boss." It was all voiced in the guise of needing to centralize power for efficiency, but, as liberal commentators pointed out, "the cry for a czar sprang from the desire of big business to take full control of defense and to use defense for its own purposes." In other words, the *New Republic* wryly observed, "let democratic processes abdicate in favor of a business dictatorship. If the lack of a chairman becomes a real problem," the *New Republic* continued, then Leon Henderson "would be the excellent choice."

But the president was not about to abdicate his own leadership of the defense effort to anyone—businessman or New Dealer, conservative or liberal. Spreading power among contending forces allowed Roosevelt to retain undisputed authority in his own hands. When, at the end of the first meeting of the NDAC, Knudsen asked, "Who is my boss?" the president instantly replied, "I guess I am." This reply, more than anything, Budget Director Harold Smith recorded in his diary, "helped to clear the atmosphere." "So long as Roosevelt held the final power over defense," I. F. Stone wrote, "he remained an obstacle to big business attempts to use defense as an excuse for repealing the social reform legislation of the New Deal and weakening the labor movement."

Yet, by refusing to grant Knudsen power proportionate to his responsibility, Roosevelt hobbled the mobilization effort in 1940. The task Roosevelt set for the NDAC was nothing less than the conversion of a peacetime economy to war production, but Knudsen was never given the tools to operate effectively. Roosevelt was being truthful and not truthful at the same time. While claiming that the American people would do anything asked of them provided they fully understood what they were being asked, Roosevelt was afraid of asking too much. Despite the swelling demand for preparedness, he did not trust the people's willingness at this juncture to make sacrifices in order to speed up the mobilization process.

On the contrary, at his press conference announcing the NDAC, he deliberately sought to assure the public that consumer goods would not be restricted. "I think people should realize," he said in answer to a question by Doris Fleeson, "that we are not going to upset, any more than we have to, a great many of the normal processes of life. . . . This delightful young lady will not have to forego cosmetics, lipsticks, ice cream sodas. . . . In other words, we do not want to upset the normal trend of things any more than we possibly can help."

• • •

Even as Roosevelt nursed the relationship between business and government along, he understood clearly that the marriage was "an uneasy one, with both parties meditating extensive infidelities." By playing the role of matchmaker, he risked incurring displeasure from both sides, but since the whole basis of the nation's war-production program depended on cooperation by industry, he was willing to assume that risk.

On Sunday evening, May 26, 1940, Roosevelt carried his appeal for the new partnership to the American people in a special "fireside chat." During his seven years in the White House, Roosevelt had delivered thirteen fireside chats. The first four talks, in the spring and summer of 1933, had focused on the banking crisis, the currency situation, the New Deal program, and the National Recovery Act. Averaging fewer than two chats a year since then, on the belief that less is more, he had delivered his last nationwide radio address on September 3, 1939, on the outbreak of the European war.

The term "fireside chat" had been inspired by Press Secretary Steve Early's statement that the president liked to think of the audience as being "a few people around his fireside." The public could then picture the president relaxing in his study in front of the fireplace and imagine that they were sitting beside him. "You felt he was talking to you," correspondent Richard Strout recalled, "not to 50 million others but to you personally."

In talking on the radio, Roosevelt used simple words, concrete examples, and everyday analogies to make his points. In contrast to the dramatic oratory suitable when speaking to a crowd, Rosenman recalled, "he looked for words that he would use in an informal conversation with one or two of his friends," words the average American could easily understand. Each speech was the product of extensive preparation, having gone through perhaps a dozen drafts before the president was satisfied that he had the talk he wanted.

Roosevelt also paid careful attention to his delivery and to the sound of his voice. When he discovered that the separation between his front two lower teeth was producing a slight whistle on the air, he had a removable bridge made, which he kept in his bedroom in a heart-shaped silver box. On more than one occasion, White House secretary Grace Tully recalled, he forgot to bring the box with him, and "there was a last minute dash" to retrieve the false tooth from his bedroom.

On the evening of this Sunday's broadcast, the president assembled his usual group for cocktails and dinner. Missy was there, along with Hopkins and Rosenman. It was not a relaxed occasion. "There was no levity," Rosenman recalled. "There was no small talk." As the president mechanically mixed drinks, his mind "thousands of miles away," he was reading a series of the most recent dispatches from Europe, all of them depicting a complete rout of the Allied armies. "All bad, all bad," he muttered as he read one report after another.

"The President was worried," Rosenman observed. Everyone was worried. "It was a dejected dinner group." But once the president settled himself in the Diplomatic Cloak Room on the first floor, sitting behind a desk crowded with three microphones, a reading light, and a pitcher of water, his old spirit returned. As the hour of ten o'clock approached, the peak listening hour, he put out his cigarette, arranged his reading copy, and then, on signal, began to speak.

In his mind's eye, Frances Perkins observed, he could actually see the people gathered in their kitchen, their living rooms, their parlors. "He was conscious of their faces and hands, their clothes and homes. . . . As he talked his head would nod and his hands would move in simple, natural, comfortable gestures. His face would smile and light up as though he were actually sitting on the front porch or in the parlor with them. People felt this, and it bound them to him in affection."

"My friends," he began, "at this moment of sadness throughout most of the world I want to talk with you about a number of subjects that directly affect the future of the U.S." He then went on to assure the nation that whatever needed to be done to keep the U.S. secure would be done. We shall build our defenses, he said, "to whatever heights the future may require. We shall build them swiftly, as the methods of warfare swiftly change.

"It is whispered by some," the familiar voice continued, "that only by abandoning our freedom, our ideals, our way of life, can we build our defenses adequately, can we match the strength of the aggressors. . . . I do not share these fears."

On the contrary, though fascism had a tremendous head start in mobilizing for war, Roosevelt had no doubt that American democracy, with its free-enterprise system and its reservoir of mass energy, would win the struggle in the long run. As long as a new relationship between business and government could be forged, success was assured.

Reaching first to the business community, Roosevelt extended an extraordinary promise of governmental cooperation and support. "I know that private business cannot be expected to make all of the capital investments required for expansion of plants and factories and personnel which this program calls for at once. It would be unfair to expect industrial corporations or their investors to do this, when there is a chance that a change in international affairs may stop or curtail orders a year or two hence. Therefore, the Government of the United States stands ready to advance the necessary money to help provide for the enlargement of factories, of necessary workers, the development of new sources of supply for the hundreds of raw materials required, the development of quick mass transportation of supplies. And the details of this are now being worked out in Washington, day and night."

Indeed, even as Roosevelt spoke, officials in the War Department were drafting legislation that would sanction a new "cost plus fixed fee" contract which would allow the government to defray all costs essential to the execution of defense contracts and guarantee the contractor a profit through a fixed fee determined in advance. In other words, the government would assume primary financial responsibility for the mobilization process. At the same time, legislation was being drafted to permit the government to make advance payments of up to 30 percent of the contract price, and to allow defense contracts to be let without the cumbersome procedure of lowest bids. Where private capital was unable to finance expansion because the facilities involved had no demand in peacetime—powder plants, high explosives, bombs—the government would be authorized to construct and operate the plants on its own.

After reaching out to business, Roosevelt turned his attention to his basic constituency—the people at large. "We must make sure in all that we do that there be no breakdown or cancellation of any of the great social gains which we have made in these past years. We have carried on an offensive on a broad front against social and economic inequalities, against abuses which had made our society weak. That offensive should not now be broken down by the pincers movement of those who would use the present needs of physical military defense to destroy it."

There was nothing in the present emergency, he went on, to justify lowering the standards of employment, reducing the minimum wage, making workers toil longer hours without due compensation, or breaking down the old-age pensions. Though businessmen were already arguing for a suspension of New Deal regulations that bore on labor, working conditions, and minimum wages on the grounds that such legislation restricted speedy mobilization, Roosevelt took the opposite tack. "While our navy and our airplanes and our guns may be our first lines of defense, it is still clear that way down at the bottom, underlying them all, giving them their strength, sustenance and power, are the spirit and morale of a free people."

When the president reached this part of his speech, Eleanor, listening from the living room of her Greenwich Village apartment, must have breathed a sigh of relief. She trusted that in her husband's heart he intended, even in the face of war, to preserve the social and economic reforms of the New Deal, but she worried that all the businessmen now swarming around the White House would demand an end to the hated New Deal as the price for their support.

Over the years, Eleanor had come to a distrust of business far deeper than her husband's equivocal attitude. Believing that business inevitably placed priority on the bottom line, she regularly excoriated the blindness of the let-business-alone people whose philosophy was "Take from the bottom, add to the top." "One can't be sure of any corporation," she once wrote, "if a huge sum of money should be placed before it."

When the president's fireside chat came to an end, Eleanor called Joe Lash, who announced that he had liked the last part of the speech, about safeguarding the social advances, best. Chuckling appreciatively, she said she, too, was "glad [the president] had said it—so that it was definitely there."

But the underlying tone of the speech reflected a subtle shift in the president's attitude toward business—a new willingness on the part of government to meet business on its own terms. Beyond the agreement to permit companies to expand their plants at the government's expense, Roosevelt was also considering a variety of alternative measures urged upon him by the business community, including legislation to remove the profit limitations on defense contracts, and new rulings to ease the rigid requirements of antitrust laws.

As each of these issues came to the fore in the months ahead, Eleanor found herself on the side of the New Dealers against her husband. Though she appreciated the president's need to consolidate forces within the United States in order to win the war, she insisted that the war would not be worth winning if the old order of things prevailed.

CHAPTER 3

"BACK TO THE HUDSON"

As the days of May wound to a close, Franklin Roosevelt was faced with one of the most controversial decisions of his presidency: a choice between rearmament at home and aid to the Allies. With France on the verge of defeat, United States military leaders were unanimous in urging Roosevelt to stop supplying the Allies and to focus instead on rearming at home. If the U.S. should later be drawn into a conflict without sufficient munitions on hand, General Marshall warned, "the War Department would naturally and rightfully be subject to the most serious adverse criticism." From London, Ambassador Joseph Kennedy weighed in with a similar analysis, saying it seemed to him that the struggle for England and France was hopeless and "if we had to fight to protect our lives we would do better to fight in our own backyard."

Sobered by the critical reports of the army maneuvers in May, Roosevelt understood only too well how little Americans had in the way of weapons to send to the Allies. But he was determined nonetheless to send whatever he could, even if it meant putting America's own short-term security in jeopardy. "If Great Britain goes down," Roosevelt reasoned, "all of us in the Americas would be living at the point of a gun." The only answer, he believed, in direct contrast to the opinion of his military chiefs, was to bet on the prospect that, if the U.S. did everything in its power to help, the Allies would somehow survive until such time as America could get itself into shape to enter the war.

It was a daring decision. At lunch with Harold Ickes, Roosevelt admitted that he might be wrong in his estimate of Allied strength. "And if I should guess wrong," he said, "the results might be serious." If Britain and France were to fall, the precious American supplies would be taken over by Germany, and the U.S. would be even further diminished in strength. On the other hand, he agreed with the Allied High Command that "one airplane sent to the Allies now will be worth more than ten sent in six weeks and more than 100 sent in six months."

With each day, as the Germans continued their triumphant march through France, the president's bet looked worse and worse. The daily telegrams from Ambassador William Bullitt in Paris reflected an almost hysterical state of mind. "At this moment there is nothing between those German tanks and Paris," Bullitt reported, predicting that there would be communist uprisings and mass butcheries in the city of Paris as the German army drew near. "The Paris police have no weapons except antiquated single shot rifles," he advised on May 28. "Incidentally, we have exactly two revolvers in this entire Mission with only 40 bullets and I should like a few for ourselves."

"This may be the last letter that I shall have a chance to send you," Bullitt wrote Roosevelt on May 30. "In case I should get blown up before I see you again, I want you to know that it has been marvelous to work for you and that I thank you from the bottom of my heart for your friendship."

Bullitt tended by nature to pessimism, but his fears in this instance were fully warranted. After only two weeks of fighting, the French army was disintegrating before the eyes of the British. More than ninety-two thousand soldiers were already dead, and it was clear that the French could not stay in the fight much longer. Meanwhile, the British Expeditionary Force, considered by Churchill "the whole root and core and brain of the British army," was trapped on the beaches at Dunkirk in northern France, its back to the sea. More than sixty thousand British soldiers lay dead, captured, or wounded, and the remaining 350,000, many of them dying from starvation, appeared doomed.

By the morning of May 24, German panzer units were only fifteen miles from Dunkirk. The towering belfry of St. Eloi Church, in the center of the city, was already visible to the German troops. Dunkirk, and the British Expeditionary Force, appeared to be Hitler's for the asking. But then, before the final blow could be struck, the advance of the German panzer troops was suddenly called off. This strange, totally unexpected halt remains incomprehensible—Hitler's first great mistake of the war. Believing it would be best to recover and regroup before bringing the campaign to a final victory, Hitler ordered a three-day rest, just enough time for the Allies to put in place the massive evacuation that became known as the "miracle of Dunkirk."

From Harwich and Margate, from the Narrow Seas to North Foreland, from dozens of little ports on the southern coast of England, a singular armada, made up of every ship known to man, including yachts and trawlers, gunboats and destroyers, motorboats and lifeboats, sailed across the strait to Dunkirk. From there, over a nine-day period, amid blazing ruins, firebombs, and high seas, nearly 340,000 men escaped to England.

As the last of the Allied troops reached the safety of British soil, Churchill delivered a fervent speech to the British Parliament that stirred the souls of the British people and excited the admiration and support of all their Allies. "We shall not flag or fail," Churchill promised. "We shall go on to the end, we shall fight in France, we shall fight in the seas and oceans . . . we shall defend our island, whatever the cost may be, we shall fight on the beaches, we shall fight on the landing grounds, we shall fight in the fields and in the streets, we shall fight in the hills; we shall never surrender, and even if, which I do not for a moment believe, this island or a large part of it were subjugated and starving, then our Empire beyond the seas, armed and guarded by the British Fleet, would carry on the struggle until, in God's good time, the new world, with all its power and might, steps forth to the rescue and the liberation of the old."

Churchill's rousing words bestowed a mythical meaning on Dunkirk that would live in the hearts of Englishmen for generations to come. "So hypnotic was the force of his words," British philosopher Isaiah Berlin has written, "so strong his faith, that by the sheer intensity of his eloquence he bound his spell upon [the British people] until it seemed to them that he was indeed speaking what was in their hearts and minds." If they possessed the courage and determination he perpetually saw in them, it was because he had helped to create it by the intensity of his belief in their qualities. "They conceived a new idea of themselves. They went forward into battle transformed by his words."

The miraculous evacuation produced an upsurge of hope in the American people as well, a renewal of belief that Britain, with the aid of American supplies, might yet defeat Germany. An opinion poll taken the week after Churchill's speech revealed a 43-percent increase in the numbers who favored the sale of planes to the Allies.

But the prime minister understood that wars were not won by evacuations. The nation's gratitude for the army's stunning escape, he cautioned, "must not blind us to the fact that what has happened in France and Belgium is a colossal military disaster." Indeed, the men who returned to England were scarcely an army. In the chaos of the retreat, the BEF had been forced to leave virtually all its heavy equipment behind, including 680 of the 700 tanks it had sent to France, 82,000 scout cars and motorcycles, 8,000 field telephones, 90,000 rifles, and an even greater number of machine guns. In the 9 days of the evacuation, 10 of the nation's 74 destroyers had been sunk and 177 RAF planes had been downed, leaving only 238 aircraft in all of England.

Left in ruins, with a thousand civilians killed, the town of Dunkirk had become a junkyard, with wrecked vehicles, discarded weapons, and abandoned bodies everywhere. A reporter for the *Herald Tribune* described the gruesome scene: "Over a distance of several miles the highway was lined with thousands of Allied trucks and other motorized vehicles. Immense numbers of these had been driven into ditches to prevent their use by the enemy." Along the quays, the chaos was even greater, as motorcycles and trucks and cars were jammed together in every conceivable fashion. "The final jam was completely impossible to disentangle."

These had been Britain's best troops. To these troops, Churchill observed, "all the first fruits of our factories had hitherto been given"—the product of hundreds of thousands of men and women working round the clock. The loss was so calamitous for Britain that it was almost like starting all over again. At that moment, in all of Britain, there were only 600,000 rifles and 500 cannons, many of them borrowed from museums—nowhere near enough to mount an adequate defense against the expected German invasion, much less a second attempt to push the Germans back. "Never," Churchill admitted, "has a nation been so naked before her foes."

• • •

In all the world, only the United States had the ability to resupply the British military. In the middle of May, Churchill sent a "most secret" letter to Roosevelt, promising that, no matter what happened in France, Britain would continue the war alone, and "we are not afraid of that." But in order to keep going, Britain needed help. His immediate needs, Churchill outlined, were forty or fifty destroyers, several hundred airplanes, anti-aircraft equipment, ammunition, and steel.

Roosevelt responded the following day, promising Churchill that he was doing everything in his power to make it possible for the Allied governments to obtain all the munitions on his list, including "the latest type of aircraft." Only the destroyers presented a significant problem, Roosevelt advised, for "a step of that kind could not be taken except with the specific authorization of the Congress," and this was not the right time to make such a move.

In the days that followed, Roosevelt directed his military chiefs to examine Churchill's list of urgent needs and do whatever was needed to send Britain everything they possibly could. He justified his decision on the basis of his own six-month scenario. In this remarkably prescient document, Roosevelt predicted against all odds that by the winter of 1940–41, with the help of the U.S. in supplying munitions, Britain would still be intact, the French government would be resisting in North Africa, and Russia and Japan would still be inactive.

On each of these points, the army and navy chiefs violently disagreed. They doubted that France could survive past the summer; they feared the French could not put up much opposition in North Africa; and they foresaw an invasion of Great Britain in the near future. To their minds, the only answer for the United States was to admit its inability to furnish weapons in quantity sufficient to alter the situation, acknowledge that we were next on the list of victims of the Axis powers, and devote every means to preparing to meet that threat at home.

The army chiefs were particularly disturbed by the president's intention to furnish planes to Britain. Considering the sorry state of the army air force, they believed that virtually anything sent abroad would jeopardize America's national security. "I regret to tell you," Marshall told Morgenthau, whom the president had designated as his representative in securing aid for the Allies, "I do not think we can afford . . . to accommodate the British government." To send even a hundred planes to the Allies, Marshall argued, a mere three days' supply, would set the pilot-training program in America back at least six months. "We have a school at Shreveport," General George H. Brett noted cynically, "instructors, schedules, students, everything except planes."

An even more serious strain was created when the president agreed to send twelve B-17 bombers to Britain. Without mincing words, Marshall pointed out that the B-17 was the only efficient bomber the United States possessed and that we had on hand only fifty-two of them. Releasing twelve would mean losing nearly one-quarter of the United States' supply and "would be seriously prejudicial to our own defensive situation."

Allied requests for guns and ammunition provoked another round of opposition. No further 75mm guns should be released, the chief of army intelligence cautioned. "It would take two years for production to catch up with requirements." Speaking more bluntly, General Walter Bedell Smith warned that if we were required to mobilize after having released guns necessary to this mobilization "and were found to be short in artillery materiel," then "everyone who was a party to the deal might hope to be found hanging from a lamp post."

Still, Roosevelt insisted on sending munitions to Britain, standing firm against the unanimous opinion of his military advisers, key legislative leaders, and his own secretary of war, who continued "to absolutely disapprove of the sale of *any* US military property." On the Senate floor, Senator Nye of North Dakota called for the president's resignation, charging that the Roosevelt policy of aid to the Allies was "nothing but the most dangerous adventurism." That same week, Navy Secretary Charles Edison reported to Roosevelt that Senator David I. Walsh of Massachusetts was "in a towering rage about the sale of Navy stuff to allies. He is threatening to force legislation prohibiting sale of anything. . . . Whole committee in a lather."

"I say it is too risky," Walsh told his colleagues, "too dangerous, to try to determine how far we can go in tapping the resources of our own Government and furnishing naval vessels, airplanes, powder and bombs. It is trampling on dangerous ground. It is moving toward the edge of a precipice—a precipice of stupendous and horrifying depths. . . . I do not want our forces deprived of one gun, or one bomb or one ship which can aid that American boy whom you and I may some day have to draft. I want every instrument. I want every bomb, I want every shell, I want every plane, I want every boat ready and available, so that I can say when and if it becomes necessary to draft him, 'Young man, you have every possible weapon of defense your Government can give you.' "

• • •

"All of Mr. Roosevelt's authority was needed to bludgeon the army officers into quiescence," *The New Republic* reported. At the president's insistence, the War Department searched long-forgotten statutes and determined that, so long as the arms were considered "surplus," it would be legal to sell them to a private corporation, which in turn could sell them to the British. Once this legal device was figured out, and once U.S. Steel was selected as the middleman, Marshall reluctantly agreed, under intense presidential pressure, to approve a long list of equipment for transfer, including 93 bomber planes, 500,000 Enfield rifles, 184 tanks, 76,000 machine guns, 25,000 Browning automatic rifles, 895 75mm guns, and 100 million rounds of ammunition. As he initialed the list, Marshall somewhat righteously observed that he could only define these weapons as surplus after going to church to pray for forgiveness. "It was the only time that I recall that I did something that there was a certain amount of duplicity in it."

At every step, the president's intervention was needed. "I am delighted to have that list of surplus materials," Roosevelt told Morgenthau on June 6. "Give it an extra push every morning and every night until it is on the ships." Since the equipment was scattered in army depots and arsenals across the country, with some tanks and guns at Rock Island, Illinois, others at Schenectady, New York, and still others at San Francisco, California, emergency telegrams had to be dispatched to each of these places, telling the commanding officers to move the selected equipment to a central loading station in Raritan, New Jersey.

Working night and day under strict secrecy, soldiers at each arsenal loaded huge crates of rifles and guns into more than six hundred freight cars headed for Raritan. All along the line, word was flashed to give these freight trains the right of way. In the meantime, a dozen empty British freighters were standing by at Raritan, waiting to take the precious cargo home. By June 11, everything was ready to be loaded, but the transfer could not take place until the contracts had been signed, and Secretary Woodring refused to sign them. Only when the president directly ordered him to sign did Woodring finally execute the documents. Five minutes later, army headquarters called Raritan to say the transfer had been made. "Go ahead and load."

All through that night, hundreds of longshoremen, three huge derricks, and more than twenty barges worked to unload the trains and put the cargo aboard the British ships. The next day, the first British ship, *The Eastern Prince*, sailed to England. So hurried had the loading process been, with stores of weapons simply dumped wherever they could fit, that the unloading process was a nightmare. But Britain assigned its best technical workers to match the right handbooks, and the right range tables to the right field guns, to link the 75mm's with the correct horse poles and straps, to unite the spares with the guns to which they belonged. By the end of June, all twelve ships had sailed to England, carrying seventy thousand tons of equipment which, when new, had been worth over $300 million.

"For weeks," Edward Stettinius later observed, "while England's war factories worked night and day to make up the losses . . . there were few guns in all of Britain that could stop a tank besides the 900 75's from America. The 80,000 Lewis, Marlin, Browning and Vickers machine guns strengthened the defenses of every threatened beachhead and every road leading in from the coast. . . . They went to men who almost literally had no arms at all in the most critical hour of Britain's history since the Spanish armada sailed into the English Channel."

• • •

Surely the negotiations involving the shipment of such massive amounts of equipment could not actually be kept secret, but since nothing had been said officially, no one knew exactly what was going on. The time had come for the president to tell the American people what he was doing. By good fortune, Roosevelt had received an invitation to speak at the commencement exercises at the University of Virginia in Charlottesville on June 10. Since his son FDR, Jr., was graduating from the Virginia Law School that day, the school officials hoped that the president might be enticed to accept their offer. Roosevelt had said he could make no commitment until the last minute, but now, at midnight the night before, he accepted their invitation, intending to use the forum to discuss his commitment to aid the Allies.

As Franklin and Eleanor were getting ready to leave for the train that would take them to Charlottesville that Monday, June 10, the news reached the White House that Italy was entering the war on the side of the Germans. After a week of tense maneuvering in which Roosevelt had tried to keep Italy's dictator, Benito Mussolini, from this explosive expansion of the war, Mussolini had taken the impetuous plunge. If he waited any longer, the Italian dictator feared, France would surrender without his help, and he would lose his chance to share in the spoils.

As Roosevelt perused the State Department's draft of his commencement address, he added a caustic phrase he had seen in a letter from French Premier Paul Reynaud about stabbing one's neighbor in the back. To Roosevelt, it seemed an accurate description of Italy's action. But undersecretary of State Sumner Welles, who had been trying to keep Italy out of the war, argued against using the stab-in-the-back metaphor, claiming it was inflammatory. The president finally agreed; the colorful phrase was deleted from the draft.

But, talking with Eleanor on the three-hour train ride to Charlottesville, the president began to reconsider. He understood the wisdom of the State Department's advice, he told her, but he wanted for once to speak candidly, without holding back out of diplomatic courtesy. Eleanor fully supported him in his desire, encouraging him to reinstate the controversial phrase. "If your conscience won't be satisfied unless you put it in I would put it in," she advised. When the train pulled into Charlottesville, the sentence was back in the text. Feeling altogether satisfied with the speech now, the president waved and smiled at the crowd gathered at the station. A reporter who had traveled with the president's party observed a marked change in Roosevelt's demeanor: whereas he had looked "grave and pale" when he boarded the train in Washington, he now appeared wholly relaxed; "the decision that he had made seemed to strengthen him."

Several thousand persons crowded the Memorial Gymnasium and applauded loudly as the president, in traditional cap and gown, stood at the podium. Speaking slowly and forcefully, Roosevelt uttered the words that would stick in public memory long after the rest of the speech was forgotten. "On this tenth day of June, 1940, the hand that held the dagger has struck it into the back of its neighbor."

Churchill was listening to the president's speech with a group of his officers in the Admiralty War Room at midnight his time. When they heard Roosevelt's angry charge against Italy, Churchill recalled, "a deep growl of satisfaction" spread across the room. "I wondered about the Italian vote in the approaching presidential election; but I knew that Roosevelt was a most experienced American party politician, although never afraid to run risks for the sake of his resolves."

The President's stiff denunciation of Italy captured the imagination of the crowd, but far more important was Roosevelt's ringing public confirmation of America's policy of aiding the Allies. Placing aid to the Allies and America's own military buildup on an equal basis, he told his audience: "We will extend to the opponents of force the material resources of this nation," and at the same time, "we will harness and speed up those resources in order that we ourselves in the Americas may have the equipment and training equal to the task of any emergency and every defense. . . . We will not slow down or detour. Signs and signals call for speed: full speed ahead." There were no disclaimers in Roosevelt's pledge, no qualifying adjectives to diminish the force of his promise to extend "the material resources of this nation" to the Allies.

"We all listened to you," Churchill cabled Roosevelt, "and were fortified by the grand scope of your declaration. Your statement that the material aid of the United States will be given to the Allies in their struggle is a strong encouragement in a dark but not unhopeful hour." Though the amounts involved, in terms of the supplies needed in modern war, were small, they were tremendously important from a strategic and political point of view. For, with the president's pledge at Charlottesville, the British had gained their chief objective—a share in America's vast industrial potential.

The president's pledge, army historians suggest, reflected his "determined faith, not fully shared by the Army staff nor even by General Marshall," that American industry could produce munitions for the Allies in ever-increasing volumes without "seriously retarding" the rearmament program at home. While he appreciated the enormous task involved in converting factory production from household items to weapons of war; while he understood the complications involved in teaching those without the proper experience and skill how to build tanks and planes; while he recognized that millions of people would have to move from locales in which they had long been settled, he believed that, in the end, American industry would come through.

The president returned to the White House that night, "full of the elan of his Charlottesville speech," Assistant Secretary of State Adolf Berle recorded. "He had said for once, what really was on his mind, and what everybody knew; and he could speak frankly, and had done so." It was a liberating feeling. It was "holiday time" for FDR, Jr., as well, who had brought two of his classmates with him back to the White House. At midnight, as Eleanor readied herself for the night train to New York, she found all of them involved in a fiery discussion with Harry Hopkins about world economics. "Though I mildly suggested that a little sleep would do them all good, I left them convinced that the discussion had just begun."

The media were quick to recognize the significance of Roosevelt's talk. "It was a fighting speech," *Time* reported, "more powerful and more determined than any he had delivered since the war began." With this speech, *Time* concluded, "the U.S. had taken sides. Ended was the myth of U.S. neutrality. . . . Ended was the vacillating talk of aiding the Allies; nothing remained now but to get on with the job." Writing in a similar vein, the *New York Post* maintained that Roosevelt "rose to the occasion and gave to the country the pronouncement for which it has waited. . . . The most productive nation in the world has thrown its productive capacity into the scales."

•   •   •

But when all was said and done, there was nothing "the most productive nation in the world" could do to save France. At dawn on the morning of June 14, German troops entered Paris. Parisians awakened to the sound of German loudspeakers warning that any demonstrations or hostile acts against the troops would be punishable by death. At every street corner decrees were posted: all radio stations were now in the hands of the Germans, all newspapers suspended, all banks closed.

Here and there knots of people stood and watched as thousands of Nazi troops marched in goosestep toward the Arc de Triomphe. Women wept and crossed themselves; the men were grim. At Napoleon's tomb the German soldiers methodically searched the battle flags to remove every German flag they could find—each one symbolizing a lost German battle in the Great War. The German troops swept down the Champs-Elysées, from the Tomb of the Unknown Soldier; past the Gardens of the Tuileries, past the Louvre to the Hôtel de Ville, where they made their headquarters. As the German national anthem blared from every corner, Dr. Thierry de Martel, director of the prestigious American Hospital and a good friend of Ambassador Bullitt's, decided that life under the German occupation would be intolerable. He plunged a hypodermic needle filled with a fatal dose of strychnine into his arm.

When the parade was over, jubilant Nazi soldiers photographed each other before the Arc de Triomphe, at the Tomb of the Unknown Soldier, and in the Gardens of the Tuileries. Racing one another to the top of the Eiffel Tower, a group hauled down the French flag that had flown on the mast atop the tower and replaced it with the German swastika. After the 9 p.m. curfew, Paris, save for the tread of Nazi guards patrolling the city's old cobblestones, fell silent.

A week later, Hitler laid down his terms for an armistice, and, in the same railroad car in a clearing in the woods at Compiègne where the Germans had capitulated to the Allies in 1918, a defeated and humiliated France concluded a truce. After the signing, Hitler ordered that the historic carriage and the monument celebrating the original French victory be conveyed to Berlin. Then, in an attempt to obliterate even the slightest physical memory of Germany's earlier defeat, he ordered that the pedestal of the carriage and the stones marking the site be destroyed. With the French surrender, Adolf Hitler was now the master of Austria, Czechoslovakia, Poland, Luxembourg, Belgium, Denmark, the Netherlands, Norway, and France.

The French collapse produced a sharp drop in American hopes for an Allied victory. By the end of June, only a third of the American people believed Britain would win the war. Though a majority still continued to favor sending aid to the Allies, the level of support was dropping. General Marshall and Admiral Stark were now convinced that they had been right all along. Five days after the surrender, they urged the president to discontinue all aid to Britain at once and transfer most of the fleet from the Pacific to the Atlantic. The president flatly rejected both proposals. In what is considered "one of his most decisive prewar moves," he decreed that aid to Britain would proceed and that the fleet would stay at Pearl Harbor. The positioning of the fleet was of great importance to Churchill, who had told Roosevelt privately he was looking to him "to keep that Japanese dog quiet in the Pacific."

In backing Churchill that critical spring despite the opposition of his military, Roosevelt was placing his faith in the American people. Though he had seen support for the Allies fluctuate with news from abroad, he sensed a significant shift in the public mood. Isolationism still remained a powerful force, but a majority of Americans were beginning to understand that they could no longer escape from commitment, that they had a role to play in the world. For the moment, they were willing to extend themselves only so far; their chief goal in aiding the Allies was to keep the U.S. out of the war. But for now, that was as far as Roosevelt needed or even wanted to go.

• • •

On June 20, after weeks of hesitation, Roosevelt finally resolved the continuing public feud in the War Department. He fired Secretary of War Woodring and announced a sweeping reorganization of his Cabinet. "When the President did decide to get rid of anybody," author John Gunther has written, "he could usually only bear to do so after deliberately picking a quarrel, so that he could provoke anger and then claim that he himself was not to blame." In this case, the quarrel was ready-made in Woodring's refusal to agree to the president's requests for releasing munitions to England.

Woodring's departure was the moment Assistant Secretary Louis Johnson, FDR's faithful ally, had been dreaming of for years. Surely, now, the president would make good on his long-standing promise to elevate Johnson to the high post of war secretary. But, unbeknownst to Johnson, the president had conceived a brilliant plan which left the assistant secretary out in the cold.

The plan called for a reorganization of both the War Department and the Navy Department to make possible a coalition Cabinet. For secretary of war, Roosevelt selected Republican conservative Henry Stimson, the patron saint of the Eastern establishment. At seventy-three, his gray hair cut straight across his broad brow, Stimson had served under every president since William McKinley, working for William Howard Taft as secretary of war and for Herbert Hoover as secretary of state. A graduate of Phillips Academy, Andover; Yale, Skull and Bones, and Harvard Law School, Stimson was as deeply connected to the upper strata of American government and society as any man alive. He was a curious mixture of conservatism and liberalism, known as an excellent manager with an unusual ability to bring out the best in those around him. "Even if I had had any hope that the President would make me Secretary of War," Interior Secretary Harold Ickes recorded in his diary, "I would have had to admit... that the Stimson appointment was excellent."

As navy secretary, the President chose Colonel Frank Knox, the *Chicago Daily News* publisher who had been Alf Landon's running mate on the Republican ticket in 1936. Unlike Stimson, Knox had come up the hard way, moving from grocery clerk to gym teacher, from cub reporter to publisher. A colorful figure at sixty-seven, with an open, pleasant face and reddish hair, Knox still cherished the memory of charging up San Juan Hill with Teddy Roosevelt's Rough Riders. As conservative on domestic issues as Stimson, Knox was a forceful speaker, an unsparing critic of the New Deal. Taken together, historian Bruce Catton observed, the appointments were further evidence of "a truce between the New Deal and big business... a bit of assurance that the defense effort was not to be a straight New Deal program."

But the domestic views of Stimson and Knox were of secondary importance to the president compared with the fact that both men were ardent interventionists, willing to take their stand against the isolationist tendencies of their own party. Time and again, both men had expressed themselves in support of generous aid to the Allies, on the theory that Nazism and all its implications must be destroyed. And their devotion to public service made them ideal choices for the Cabinet. While some Republicans vigorously protested Roosevelt's "double cross" on the eve of the Republican convention and demanded that Stimson and Knox be read out of the Republican Party, the announcement was generally greeted with approval. "Abroad, these nominations will serve to emphasize the essential unity of America," the *Washington Post* editorialized. "At home, this infusion of new blood should help accelerate the preparedness program."

Vastly pleased by the reactions to his surprise appointments, the president decided to spend the weekend of June 21 at his Hyde Park estate. It was the first time he had been able to enjoy his childhood home since early May. Traveling with Missy and Hopkins and a phalanx of reporters, he boarded his special train at midnight, Friday, at the railroad siding under the Bureau of Engraving and Printing, on 14th Street.

Although the overnight journey to Hyde Park took less than ten hours, hundreds, even thousands of people were involved. For six hours before the president's departure, all rail traffic was deflected from the tracks to be used, so that responsible railroad men could walk every yard of track, inspecting for cracks or broken switches. In the areas adjacent to the tracks, all parked cars were removed, lest they prove hiding places for conspirators. Security agents tested the food and drinks as they were loaded into the dining car. In the Pullman car in front of the president's private car, typewriters and mimeograph machines were installed for his staff. The swirl of activity never stopped, with reporters gathering in the club car until the wee hours of morning, but in the president's compartment the blinds were closed and all was quiet. Roosevelt was sound asleep.

• • •

That same weekend, Hitler decided to celebrate his victory over France with a visit to Paris, his first journey to the city which had enchanted him since his early years as an art student. So closely had he dreamed of Paris that he was certain he could find his way anywhere solely from his knowledge of the buildings and the monuments. Accompanied by a small group of architects and photographers, including Albert Speer, Hitler arrived at Le Bourget before dawn and drove straight to the Opéra, his favorite building. A white-haired French attendant led Hitler's party through the sumptuous foyer and up the great ornamental stairway. When they reached the part of the stage in front of the curtain, Hitler, looking puzzled, told the attendant that in his mind's eye he was certain a salon was supposed to be to the right. The attendant confirmed Hitler's memory; the salon had been eliminated in a recent renovation. "There, you see how well I know my way about," Hitler remarked in triumph to his entourage.

From the Opéra, Hitler was driven down the Champs-Elysées and taken to the Eiffel Tower, the Arc de Triomphe, and Napoleon's tomb. In the tomb, he trembled with excitement and ordered that the remains of Napoleon's son, which rested in Vienna, be transferred to Paris and placed beside those of his father. Minutes later, his mood having shifted, he ordered the destruction of two World War I monuments: the statue of General Charles Mangin, leader of the colonial troops, whose memorial included an honor guard of four Negro soldiers, and the monument to Edith Cavell, the English nurse who became a popular heroine and was executed in 1915 for aiding over two hundred Allied soldiers to escape from a Red Cross hospital in German-occupied Belgium.

As the three-hour tour came to an end, an exhilarated Hitler told Speer: "It was the dream of my life to be permitted to see Paris. I cannot say how happy I am to have that dream fulfilled." That evening, Hitler ordered Speer to resume at once his architectural renovations of Berlin. However beautiful Paris was, Berlin must, in the end, be made far more beautiful. "In the past I often considered whether we would not have to destroy Paris," he confided to Speer. "But when we are finished in Berlin, Paris will only be a shadow. So why should we destroy it?"

•   •   •

The weather in Hyde Park was "delightfully cool and brilliant" when the president's train pulled into Highland Station that Saturday morning. From the train station it was an easy ride over country roads to Springwood, the president's thirty-five-room estate on the Hudson River. This was the place to which Roosevelt would regularly return when he needed sustenance and peace, the place where he could always relax, no matter what was going on in the world.

Today, as for so many days throughout his fifty-eight years, the president's mother, Sara Delano Roosevelt, was at the door to greet him. Her waist had thickened over the years, but at eighty-five, she was still a handsome woman, with her high forehead, her thick white hair, and her gold lorgnette. Exquisitely dressed in white or black, the only two colors she regularly wore, Sara moved with great distinctness, embodying in her carriage the impression of superiority. But there was warmth in her eyes, and her smile was so startlingly similar to her son's that audiences at movie theaters broke into spontaneous applause when they saw her face.

As the president kissed his mother at the door, reporters recollected that it was just a year ago at the same doorway that Sara Roosevelt had greeted the British monarchs, King George VI and Queen Elizabeth, during their royal visit to Hyde Park. "The weather was much the same as it was on that historic week end last year," one reporter observed, "and the hills across the Hudson River stood out as clearly against the backdrop of the Catskill Mountains to the north but there remained only a memory of the peace which existed in the world at that time."

It is said that, in the weeks before the king and queen arrived, Sara's neighbors along the Hudson had asked her if she was going to redecorate the house. "Of course not," she responded, in her best starchy manner, "they're not coming to see a redecorated house, they're coming to see *my* house."

On the day of the visit, Sara had waited in the library with Franklin and Eleanor for the king and queen. Much to her displeasure, Franklin had prepared a tray of cocktails for the royal visitors. For years, the question of serving alcohol in the Big House had been a point of contention between mother and son—so much so that Franklin had simply gone around his mother by moving his cocktail hour to a secret hiding place in the cloak-room beneath the stairs. The secrecy lent a mischievous air to the gatherings, as journalist Martha Gellhorn recalled. "Shrieks of laughter" would erupt from the cloakroom, she said, "as if we were all bad children having a feast in the dorm at night."

But on this occasion, Franklin had proved as stubborn as his mother, insisting that the alcohol remain in open and ready condition. When the king came into the library, Franklin greeted him with a twinkle in his eye: "My mother does not approve of cocktails and thinks you should have a cup of tea." The king reflected for a moment and then observed, "Neither does my mother." Whereupon the president and the king raised their glasses to one another in an unspoken bond and proceeded to drink their martinis.

There were occasions when Sara's strength failed, when she was tormented by stomach pains or suffered keenly from the heat. At such times, she told her son, she wondered, "Perhaps I have lived too long, but when I think of you and hear your voice I do not ever want to leave you." She thought of him almost all the time, Sara had written Franklin right after his May 16 address to the Congress, "and realize a little of the feelings of responsibility you have, with all the horror of what is going on and the wish to help. I am very proud of the way you keep your head."

There was an extraordinary bond between mother and son. "Nothing," Eleanor observed, "ever seemed to disturb the deep, underlying affection they had for each other."

The president had no special plans for this June weekend beyond rest and relaxation. In the mornings, he slept late; at lunchtime, he lingered longer than usual at the table; and in the afternoons, he took long leisurely rides through his estate and through the surrounding countryside. The unhurried pace was just what he needed to regenerate his energies and refocus his brain. Time and again, Roosevelt confounded his staff by the ease with which, even in the darkest hours, he managed to shake off the burdens of the presidency upon his arrival at Hyde Park, and emerged stronger and more confident in a matter of days.

• • •

"All that is in me goes back to the Hudson," Roosevelt liked to say, meaning not simply the peaceful, slow-moving river and the big, comfortable clapboard house but the ambience of boundless devotion that encompassed him as a child. As the adored only son of a young mother and an aging patriarch, Roosevelt grew up in an atmosphere where affection and respect were plentiful, where the discipline was fair and loving, and the opportunities for self-expression abundant. The sense of being loved wholeheartedly by his parents taught Roosevelt to trust that the world was basically a friendly and agreeable place.

Photographs of Sara Delano, twenty-six years old at the time of his birth, reveal a young woman conscious of her beauty, with lustrous upswept hair, high cheekbones, a long, sleek neck, and large brown eyes. She had spent most of her childhood in a forty-room country estate, Algonac, high above the Hudson River, near Newburgh, New York. There, under the protective wing of her autocratic but loving father, Warren Delano II, she had led a life of elegance and ease, with private tutors, dancing lessons, and trips to the Orient. Her summer days were spent in the country, rowing on the river, riding horseback through the woods, and picnicking on the shore; her winters were divided between social life in Manhattan and the outdoor life of Algonac, complete with sleighrides in the fields and skating on the ponds. It was a tranquil life, producing within Sara the deep sense of privilege and place which she passed on to her son.

Years later, Sara recognized that her parents had deliberately kept from their children "all traces of sadness or trouble or the news of anything alarming." So highly did the Delanos value the outward appearance of tranquillity, Sara proudly recalled, that no one was ever allowed to complain or to cry, even if there was something terribly wrong. At age four, Sara had fallen on the sharp corner of a cabinet. The deep wound was sewed shut with needle and thread. That Sara never flinched or cried drew her father's praise. But in casting a positive light on this aspect of her childhood, Sara failed to appreciate, as her great-grandson John Boettiger, Jr., later put it, that "pain-killing can itself be a lethal act." When she married, she would strive to shelter her son in the same way as her father had sheltered her. "If there remained in Franklin Roosevelt throughout his life," Boettiger, Jr., observed, "an insensitivity towards and discomfort with profound and vividly expressed feelings, it may have been in part the lengthened shadow of his early sheltering from ugliness and jealousy and conflicting interests."

Franklin's father, known as "Mr. James," was nearly twice Sara's age when she married him. Tall and slender with full muttonchop whiskers, he, too, had grown up in an environment of wealth and privilege. Like the Delanos, the Roosevelts defined themselves primarily as country gentlemen, adopting the habits, the hobbies, and the love of the outdoors that characterized the English gentry. Mount Hope, the country estate on which James was born, was twenty miles upstream from Algonac. The Roosevelt family money had been made years before in dry goods, real estate, and trade, primarily the West Indies sugar trade. As a young man, James, after graduating from Harvard Law School, had taken an interest in coal and the railroads, but never was he more content than when he was in the country, hunting, fishing, or riding. At the age of twenty-five, he had married a second cousin,

Rebecca Howland, and the following year a son, James Roosevelt Roosevelt, known as "Rosy," was born. It was, from all accounts, a peaceful marriage, which lasted for nearly twenty-five years, until Rebecca suffered a fatal heart attack.

Four years later, Mr. James was introduced to Sara Delano at a small dinner party hosted by the family of his fourth cousin Theodore Roosevelt. Both James and Sara knew at once that they wanted to marry; the courtship lasted just ten weeks. On October 7, 1880, as the autumn sun was just beginning to set, James took his new bride to Springwood, the rambling house in Hyde Park he had bought two decades earlier, when Mount Hope burned to the ground.

There, at Springwood, in a bedroom overlooking the snow-covered lawn, Franklin Delano Roosevelt was born on January 30, 1882. It was a difficult birth, so difficult that the doctors advised Sara not to have any more children. Unable to produce a large family, Sara focused her prodigious energies on shaping the life of her healthy, handsome son.

"No moment of Franklin's day was unscheduled," Roosevelt biographer Geoffrey Ward has written. "His mother oversaw everything, followed him everywhere. . . . Hers was a loving even adoring autocracy but an autocracy nonetheless," in which the boy's natural longing for a bit of privacy was felt by his mother to be a deliberate shunning of her company. Once, when Franklin was only five years old, his mother noticed that he seemed melancholy. When she asked him why he was sad, he did not answer at first, so she repeated her question. "Then," Sara recalled, "with a curious little gesture that combined entreaty with a suggestion of impatience, he clasped his hands in front of him and exclaimed, 'Oh, for freedom!' "

The incident made Sara wonder if perhaps she was regulating her son's life too closely, but after a short experiment in which he was given no rules for an entire day and allowed to roam at will with absolutely no attention from his mother, Sara reported, he "of his own accord went contentedly back to his routine."

Everything about the boy's childhood seemed structured to make him feel that he was the center of his parents' world. In the early years, Mr. James spent hours every day with his son, teaching him how to row and sail, and skate and sled. Wherever his parents went—whether to visit friends in their carriage or for long walks along the river or to Europe for vacations—Franklin went with them. Surrounded by older people, the young boy developed early on a remarkable ease with adults, an unusual poise, an excellent set of manners which earned him much praise. Relatives consistently remarked on what a "nice child" he was, so adaptable, so uncomplaining, so "bright and pleasant and happy."

Relaxed relationships with children his own age were harder to come by. Most of Franklin's boyhood friends were the children of other River families who were brought to his house to play at scheduled hours and then taken back home. Only with the children of families who worked on his parents' estate did he have what approached spontaneous relationships, and even then everyone involved always knew that the young Roosevelt was ultimately in charge.

An intuitive child, Franklin learned to anticipate the desires of his parents even before he was told what to do. "It never occurred to me," Sara wrote, "to caution him against hazardous undertakings.... Franklin had proved himself such a responsible little boy that I never for a moment believed he would undertake anything he was not fully equipped to handle." The mother's confidence built confidence in the son; he rarely disappointed his parents' high expectations. "We never were strict merely for the sake of being strict. We took secret pride in the fact that Franklin instinctively never seemed to require that kind of handling."

Yet one consequence of early adaptation to a parent's wishes is the fear that all the love captured with so much effort is simply admiration for the good manners and the achievements and the good nature, not truly love for the child as he really is. What would happen, the precocious child wonders, if I appeared on the outside as I really am on the inside—sad, angry, rude, jealous, scared? Where would my parents' love be then? The child's fear of exposure can remain in the adult. This would explain Franklin Roosevelt's lifelong tendency to guard his weaknesses and shortcomings as if they were scars, making it difficult for him to share his true feelings with anyone.

As the boy's world widened beyond his house, his sense of confidence deepened. Accompanying Mr. James on daily rounds of his estate, walking with him in the tiny village of Hyde Park, sitting next to him at St. James Church, the boy could not help observing the deferential treatment his father received, the respect accorded the Roosevelts almost as a matter of right. So, too, when he rode in the carriage with his mother as she dispatched food and clothing to the sick and poor, he recognized at once that his family was in the position of having more than enough for themselves so they could give to others. These early observations instilled in the boy the confident belief that the Roosevelts were special people, inheritors of a proud tradition.

When Franklin was eight, his father suffered a serious heart attack that would leave him essentially an invalid for the remaining ten years of his life, unable to play tennis, ride horseback, or even enjoy the long walks in the woods he had once loved so much. More than any other event in Franklin's childhood, his father's heart attack had an indelible impact on the development of his personality. From that point on, the boy's built-in desire to please his parents by being a "nice little boy" was amplified by the fear that if he ever appeared other than bright and happy it might damage his father's already weakened heart. The story is told of a ghastly injury the young boy received when a steel rod fell on his head, leaving an ugly gash in his forehead. Refusing to worry his father, Franklin found a cap to cover the wound and insisted that Mr. James never be told.

In later years, Roosevelt's anxiety to please would become so finely tuned that he would be able to win the hearts and minds of almost everyone he met. "By the warmth of his greeting," Sam Rosenman wrote, "he could make a casual visitor believe that nothing was so important to him that day as this particular visit, and that he had been waiting all day for this hour to arrive. Only a person who really loved human beings could give that impression." It seemed at times as if he possessed invisible antennae that allowed him to understand what his fellow citizens were thinking and feeling, so that he could craft his own responses to meet their deepest needs.

But the desire to please became a two-edged sword in the White House, when the president's lack of candor led to confusion. Wanting to set each caller at ease, he had a habit of nodding his head in agreement. The visitor would leave, mistakenly assuming he had garnered the president's support. "Perhaps in the long run," New Deal adviser Raymond Moley argued, "fewer friends would have been lost by bluntness than by the misunderstandings that arose from engaging ambiguity."

Mr. James' illness brought Sara even closer to her only son, so close that she could not bear to part with him when the time came for him to go to boarding school at Groton. Instead, she kept him home two additional years, not letting him go until he was fourteen. The day before Franklin finally left for school, Sara and he spent many hours together. "We dusted his birds," she wrote in her diary, "and he had a swim in the river. I looked on with a heavy heart." For weeks afterward, Sara could not pass his empty bedroom without breaking down in tears.

Because he started school two years later than most of his classmates, Franklin was always set apart from the rest of the boys. "They knew things he didn't," Eleanor said later. "He felt left out." Unaccustomed to the ordinary give and take of schoolmates, Franklin put his fellow students off. The studied charm that impressed his parents' friends and delighted the faculty at Groton seemed affected to boys his own age. "They didn't like him," Eleanor once said. "They had to give him a certain recognition because of his intellectual ability. But he was never of the inner clique." Resentful at his lack of popularity, yearning to be at center stage as he had been all his life, Franklin turned at times to sarcasm, an unfeeling ribbing of his schoolmates, which only made things worse.

Never once, however, did Franklin admit to his mother, as he would later confess to his wife, that something had gone "sadly wrong" at Groton. On the contrary, blurring the distinction between things as they were and things as he wished them to be, his ever-cheerful letters convinced her that his career at Groton was a great success. "Almost overnight," Sara recorded, "he became sociable and gregarious and entered with the frankest enjoyment into every kind of social activity."

At Harvard College, Franklin faced rejection once more when he was blackballed from the exclusive Porcellian Club, but there was such a variety of things at the college to claim his attention—the rowing crew, the debutante dances, the Hasty Pudding Club, the Fly Club, the student newspaper —that the hurt was less visible. What is more, Franklin was beginning to learn from his success at the *Crimson*—where he was made managing editor and then president—that, if he wanted to assume center stage, he had to create situations where he was the best person to handle a particular job.

During the fall of Franklin's freshman year, his father died. Unable to bear the loneliness of Hyde Park, Sara took an apartment in Boston for the winter so that she could be near Franklin. "She was an indulgent mother," a family friend observed, "but would not let her son call his soul his own." Early on, Franklin had sensed the competition between his interest in other girls and his mother's love. Now it seemed even more important to keep his girlfriends a secret lest his mother feel betrayed. The only way he knew how to fend her off was to become evasive and vague, sharing with her all the unimportant details about his girls while reserving for himself the feelings that really mattered.

Over time, Franklin's evasiveness became a pattern he could never break. "The effort to become his own man without wounding his mother," Ward observed, "fostered in him much of the guile and easy charm, love of secrecy and skill at maneuver he brought to the White House." On occasion, when his deviousness seemed to go beyond the bounds of necessity, it seemed as if he were enjoying subterfuge for its own sake.

So successful was the young Franklin at hiding his emotions that he took his mother and close friends totally by surprise when he announced that he had fallen in love with his fifth cousin Eleanor and intended to marry her. Though Sara had seen Franklin with Eleanor on numerous occasions, she had absolutely no idea the relationship was heading toward marriage.

"I know what pain I must have caused you," Franklin wrote his mother after he told her the shocking news, "and you know I wouldn't do it if I really could have helped it. . . . I know my mind, have known it for a long time and know that I could never think otherwise . . . and you, dear Mummy, you know that nothing can ever change what we have always been and always will be to each other—only now you have two children to love and love you—and Eleanor as you know will always be a daughter to you in every true way."

Sara was not so easily assuaged. Reminding Franklin that at twenty-one he was much too young to marry, she exacted a promise from him to postpone the official announcement for a year. In the meantime, she tried to engage his interests elsewhere: first by securing a job for him in London; then, after that failed, by taking him on a Caribbean cruise. But when the trip was over, he was still in love with Eleanor. Sara was desolate. "I am feeling pretty blue. . . . The journey is over & I feel as if the time were not likely to come again when I shall take a trip with my dear boy. . . ." Sara wrote. "Oh how still the house is. . . ." With unerring intuition, Eleanor apprehended Sara's pain. "Don't let her feel that the last trip with you is over," Eleanor advised Franklin. "We three must take them together in the future. . . ."

As the waiting period drew to a close, Franklin selected an engagement ring at Tiffany's, which he gave to Eleanor on her twentieth birthday. The official announcement, made a few weeks later, produced a round of congratulatory notes. "I have more respect and admiration for Eleanor than any girl I have ever met," Franklin's cousin Lyman Delano wrote. "You are mighty lucky," one of Eleanor's previous suitors told Franklin. "Your future wife is such as it is the privilege of few men to have." But perhaps the letter both Franklin and Eleanor treasured the most was the affectionate note from President Theodore Roosevelt, who offered to give his niece away in marriage.

•   •   •

If Franklin thought that marriage represented an escape from his mother, he was wrong, for she was unable to back off and he was unable to make her go. Instead, he allowed her to compete with Eleanor for his devotion, build a town house in New York that adjoined his and Eleanor's, retain the purse strings for the family, and share with Eleanor in the task of raising their children.

Over the years, Franklin's failure to separate from his mother would play a major role in undermining his marriage, but for now, as we seek to understand the wellspring of the president's equanimity as he faced the Nazi threat in June 1940, it must be recognized that his mother's unequivocal love for him remained a powerful source of strength all the days of his life. "Reasonable it is to assume," the *Ladies' Home Journal* correctly surmised shortly after Roosevelt moved into the White House, "that much of the President's strength in facing incredible obstacles [was] planted in a childhood presided over by a mother whose broad viewpoint encompasses the art of living."

To be sure, other factors contributed to the president's sublime confidence, chief among them his mental victory over polio, which strikingly confirmed his native optimism. "I think," Eleanor said, "probably the thing that took most courage in his life was his meeting of polio and I never heard him complain. . . . He just accepted it as one of those things that was given you as discipline in life. . . . And with each victory, as everyone knows, you are stronger than you were before."

But in the end, no factor was more important in laying the foundation of the president's confident temperament than his mother's early love. So it was that, as Hitler journeyed triumphantly to Paris, Roosevelt returned quietly to Hyde Park, the locus of his earliest memories, the nest in which his expansive personality unfolded most freely.

CHAPTER 4

"LIVING HERE IS
VERY OPPRESSIVE"

As the White House geared the country for war in the spring of 1940, Eleanor became increasingly depressed. For seven years, through days that began at 6 a.m. and ended long after midnight, she had carved out a significant role for herself as her husband's partner in social reform. She believed in what she was doing and knew that her work was respected by millions of people, including, most crucially, her husband. "The President was enormously proud of her ability...," Frances Perkins confirmed. "He said more than once, 'You know, Eleanor really does put it over. She's got great talent with people.' In cabinet meetings, he would say, 'You know my Missus gets around a lot ... my missus says they have typhoid fever in that district ... my Missus says that people are working for wages way below the minimum set by NRA in the town she visited last week.' "

Now, however, with the president concerned about little but munitions and maneuvers, Eleanor felt a sense of remoteness, a lack of connection to both her husband and the major issue of the day. Robbed of desire, she moved mechanically through her duties; all sense of challenge seemed to have fled. "All that she had worked for over so many years was now in jeopardy," Eleanor's grandson Curtis Roosevelt observed. "She feared that everything would be taken away from her—her value, her usefulness, her role."

"Living here is very oppressive," she confessed to her daughter, Anna, "because Pa visualizes all the possibilities, as of course he must and you feel very impotent to help. What you think or feel seems of no use or value so I'd rather be away and let the important people make their plans and someday I suppose they will get around to telling us plain citizens if they want us to do anything."

Eleanor had an intriguing idea: she would see if she could go to Europe with the Red Cross to help organize the relief effort for refugees. It seemed to her the perfect solution—the chance to relieve suffering and dislocation while at the same time to be right in the thick of things, delivering clothing, blankets, and medical supplies to shelters in bombed-out cities, organizing hot meals for children in schools and canteens, giving first-aid instruction to civilians.

Eleanor had worked with the Red Cross before. While she and Franklin were in Washington during World War I, she had run a canteen at Union Station. Clad in the familiar khaki uniform, she and her fellow volunteers had handed out cups of coffee, newspapers, sandwiches, candy, and cigarettes to trainloads of soldiers en route to army camps and ports of embarkation. "I loved it," she said later. "I simply ate it up." Freed by the war from the social duties she detested, she was able, for the first time in her married life, to spend her days doing work she truly enjoyed.

Indeed, so much had Eleanor loved her work with the Red Cross that summer of 1918 that she had offered her services to go overseas. Many women she knew were working in canteens near the front in France, and she felt that their work was more central to the war. "Yet," she lamented in her memoirs, "I knew no one would help me to get permission to go, and I had not acquired sufficient independence to go about getting it for myself."

Now, twenty-two years later, she was the first lady and she had a plan. On May 12, she was scheduled to accompany her husband on a cruise down the Potomac River on the presidential yacht, U.S.S. *Potomac*. Included in the president's party were Missy, Attorney General and Mrs. Robert Jackson, and the object of Eleanor's campaign, the chairman of the Red Cross, Norman Davis, a white-haired, ruddy-complexioned man of sixty years.

For the president, the *Potomac* offered the perfect escape from both the heat of Washington and the persistent ring of the telephone. Having loved the water since he was a child, he enjoyed nothing more than sitting on the deck, an old hat shading his head from the sun, a fishing rod in his hands. The *Potomac* was not a luxury liner, but a converted Coast Guard patrol boat, rough and ready, tending to roll with the waves, a sailor's boat, with a fair top speed of sixteen knots.

It was a brilliant afternoon, with blue skies and a strong breeze, but even the most perfect day for cruising could not still the anxiety Eleanor felt, the legacy of a frightful childhood experience during a trip to Europe with her parents, when their ship, the *Britannica,* was hit by another ship. The collision beheaded a child and killed a number of other passengers. Amid the "cries of terror," the two-and-one-half-year-old Eleanor clung frantically to the men who were attempting to throw her over the side of the ship into the arms of her father, standing in a lifeboat below. The transfer was eventually accomplished, but a fear of the sea was ingrained in the small child which the adult woman could never fully shake. In the early days of her marriage, knowing how much Franklin loved to sail, Eleanor had made a concentrated effort to conquer her panic, but in recent years, except on special occasions such as this particular cruise, she generally stepped aside and allowed Missy to take her place.

On deck, the president's party gathered in a circular lounge equipped with heavy cushions, easy chairs, and tables. There, as the president relaxed with his fishing rod, Eleanor zeroed in on the chairman of the Red Cross. Davis, a peace-minded idealist who had been appointed to the chairmanship by Roosevelt in 1938 after serving under two previous presidential administrations, listened with genuine interest to Mrs. Roosevelt's proposal, but knew he could not say yes until he talked it over with his fellow Tennessean, Secretary of State Cordell Hull. So the matter rested while the *Potomac* continued its lazy cruise down the river, returning to the Washington Navy Yard after ten o'clock that night.

The following day, Davis discussed Eleanor's proposal with Secretary Hull. The spring of 1940 was a critical period for the American Red Cross. For months, while Germany marched into Czechoslovakia and Poland, Davis had maintained a policy of "extreme circumspection," trying to keep a neutral attitude in the tradition of the International Red Cross. But with the German invasion of Western Europe, all pretense to neutrality was cast aside. At the moment of Eleanor's request, the Red Cross was focusing all its relief efforts entirely on those nations that were being overrun by Germany. If Eleanor were to join the Red Cross in Europe now, she would be placing herself in a dangerous situation.

At another moment, Eleanor was told, it might have worked, but now, because of "the imminence and possibility of a Hitler victory" and because "the capture of a President's wife would be a serious matter," her request was denied.

• • •

Two weeks later, Eleanor suffered an additional disappointment when her young friends in the American Youth Congress turned on her for supporting her husband's call for rearmament. Throughout the 1930s, Eleanor had developed a special bond with the young activists involved with the AYC, an umbrella organization including members of the YMCA, the American League for Peace and Democracy, and the Popular Front. Though she knew that some of the young people belonged to the Communist League, she trusted that the majority were liberals like herself, committed to social reform and collective security. In recent months, her trust had been tested as the AYC, following the flip-flop of Soviet policy in the wake of the Nazi-Soviet pact, had abruptly shifted its stance from pro–New Deal collective security to antiwar isolationism. Still, she refused to give up on her young friends, believing that with her support the liberals would win out.

To this end, she agreed to address the closing session of the Youth Congress at the Mecca Temple on West 56th Street in New York on May 26, 1940. Reaching out to the antiwar crowd, she admitted that she knew all too well how futile war was as a means of solving problems. "You don't want to go to war," she said simply. "I don't want to go to war. But war may come to us." Declaring that England had long "been asleep" and therefore totally surprised by Hitler's onslaught, she told the delegates it was necessary to arm in order to avoid the same crisis. "I think occasionally in the world, you are faced with events over which you have no control." However, she added, her definition of a defense program included, in addition to arms, more and better housing, expansion of the health program, and continuation of work relief until everyone had a job.

The delegates listened in sullen silence, extending only polite applause when she finished. Harlem Representative Vito Marcantonio, who cast the only vote in Congress against the president's defense program, received a standing ovation far exceeding in volume and length that accorded to Mrs. Roosevelt. Describing what he called a "war hysteria" in Congress, Marcantonio charged that the president's defense program was bound to "take us right into the meat-grinder of European battlefields." The only purpose of the war, he went on, as the delegates jumped to their feet, cheering, whistling, and stomping, was to "defend the American dollar and the British pound."

"Poor Mrs. Roosevelt!" *The New York Times* editorialized after her Mecca Temple speech. "After mothering this brood of youngsters . . . harboring them under her wing at White House teas, she suddenly discovers them to be ducklings taking to the water of Communist propaganda as to their natural element. Her scolding did no good. . . . They refused to reconsider their resolution against preparedness."

When Eleanor reached her Village apartment that night, she called Joe Lash, who had been in the audience, to see what he thought of her speech. He answered honestly, saying he didn't feel she had convinced anyone, that even their polite applause "was to demonstrate their views to her rather than to appreciate what she had to say to them." Normally, Eleanor was able to accept criticism as a matter of course, but on this night, gloom crowded in on her. The many small struggles of political life suddenly became too much, and she felt terribly weary.

In the days that followed, emptiness and exhaustion set in. Eleanor's mood became unpredictable, shifting from placid to sullen to stern in a matter of hours. "I really think," a worried Tommy confided to Anna in mid-June, "and this is strictly between you and me, that your mother is quite uncontented. . . . She has wanted desperately to be given something really concrete and worth while to do in this emergency and no one has found anything for her. They are all afraid of political implications etc. and I think she is discouraged and a bit annoyed about it. She spoke to your father and to H[arry] H[opkins] and Norman Davis. Outside of making two radio speeches for the Red Cross she has not been asked to do anything. She works like Hell all the time and we are busier than ever, but . . . she wants to feel she is doing something worthwhile and it makes me mad, because she has so much organizing and executive ability she could do a swell job on anything she undertook. . . . I hate to see her not visibly happy and I feel powerless to do anything about it. She would probably dismember me if she knew I wrote this to you, but I know you are about the only one to whom I could write like this and have it end with you."

Eleanor's dark mood was barely visible to the outside world. To rant or rave, to create a scene, was not her way. Believing that her best recourse was to escape from Washington—"anything that makes me forget the war clouds," she confessed, "is a blessing these days"—she embarked on a series of journeys in late May and early June—a week in New York, an expedition to Appalachia, and then a return trip to New York.

In traveling to Arthurdale, the small homestead community in the hills of West Virginia that she had vigorously supported over the years, Eleanor hoped to buoy her spirits. Considered "Eleanor's baby," Arthurdale was a product of the imagination of the early New Deal, an attempt to relieve the desolation of the hundreds of miners and their families who had been stranded in Scott's Run, West Virginia, when the mines were permanently closed. With Eleanor's backing, the government had advanced the capital for the construction of a school, a community center, and fifty farmhouses, hoping to see under what conditions part-time farming and industrial employment could be combined. Once the structures were completed, fifty families were invited in, on the promise that they would repay the government in thirty years.

But the key to whether the transplanted miners could make a living and repay the government was the successful establishment of an industry within the community to go along with the subsistence farming, and that task had proved more difficult than anyone had anticipated. Fearing that a government-subsidized factory would destroy private industry, Congress had refused to appropriate the funds for the factory, forcing the homesteaders to rely solely on their farms for their livelihood. Eleanor would not be defeated, however, and over the years she had managed to help the homesteaders in a hundred ways: a special grant here, a WPA project there, a government-subsidized nursery school here, a craft shop there.

But during this visit, her energies already depleted, Eleanor came to see the price of her continued support. So dependent on her had the homesteaders become that when their school bus broke down they sent it to the White House garage for repairs. "Deeply disillusioned" at the sight of what she now recognized as a frightful loss of initiative, she admitted to Joe Lash when she returned to New York that "they seemed to feel the solution to all their problems was to turn to government."

In New York, the days were more pleasant. Speaking to an overflowing audience of students at City College, she received a standing ovation. Touring the exhibits at the New York World's Fair, she was met everywhere she went by a huge, friendly crowd, waving to her, throwing out kisses, calling out, "God Bless You." The lights, the attention, the universal murmurs of support were still there, but as soon as she returned to the White House, it all disappeared. The problem was not simply, as she wrote, "the anxiety which hangs over everybody," the exhaustion that comes from "the state of apprehension in which we are living," but, rather, her sense of being cut off from her husband at this critical time.

In the past, Eleanor's trips around the country had been a source of fascination and pleasure to the president, who delighted in the thought-provoking stories she invariably carried back. Over the years, a cherished tradition had evolved. The first night of Eleanor's return, he would clear his calendar so the two of them could sit alone at dinner and talk, so he could hear her impressions while they were still fresh. These long, relaxing talks had become *the* bond between husband and wife, a source of continued enjoyment in one another.

But when Eleanor returned to the White House after her trips to Arthurdale and New York, she was told the president had no time for their traditional dinner. She could join him in his study for a meal, but Harry Hopkins would also be there. At dinner, she tried to engage her husband in a conversation about Arthurdale, but it was clear from the start that his thoughts were following a train of their own. The conversation quickly turned to the war, with Hopkins holding forth at great length. As Eleanor listened to Harry talk, it became obvious that he was far better acquainted with the subject than she was, though how he had learned so much about military matters in such a short time she simply could not fathom. Having little to add, she sat in silence, feeling unwanted and irrelevant.

But Franklin, perhaps feeling the difficulty of Eleanor's position on a night meant for the two of them alone, returned the conversation to domestic affairs and the New Deal. Eleanor took the opening and proceeded to pour out all her worries about the domestic situation, the recent cut in the food allowance for unemployed mothers, a new study on the spread of illiteracy, the civil-liberties questions involved in fingerprinting aliens, the need for greater housing programs and more old-age pensions.

The next day, Eleanor felt, in her own words, "terribly guilty," confessing to Joe Lash that she shouldn't have distracted the president with stuff that didn't relate directly to the international crisis, that he had listened to her late into the night and then worried about all the issues she raised until all hours of the morning.

As guilt and sadness overwhelmed her, Eleanor's feelings of loss focused on Harry Hopkins. Of all the people in the administration, Eleanor felt most closely connected to Hopkins. Indeed, it was her appreciation, back in 1928, for the work this impassioned young social worker had done in New York that had brought Harry to the president's attention in the first place, setting in motion his remarkable career as head of the largest work-relief program in the history of the country, a program that at one point employed more than 30 percent of the unemployed at a cost of $6 billion.

From the start, Eleanor shared with Harry an abiding faith in the unemployed, a belief that they were decent, honest people suffering through no fault of their own, totally deserving of government help. "Both Harry Hopkins and Mrs. Roosevelt were driven during the depression by a sense of urgency," WPA Administrator Elizabeth Wickenden recalled. "They never forgot there were these millions of people who had absolutely nothing, who had once held a steady job and had a sense of self-respect. From their wide travels across the country, they kept in their minds a vivid picture of the lives of these people, and that image drove them to push the government to create as many jobs for as many people as it possibly could."

Under Hopkins' resourceful leadership, the WPA employed two million people a month. It built thousands of schools, libraries, parks, sidewalks, and hospitals. It sponsored murals for the walls of public buildings, and hot lunches for the children of the poor; it put writers to work preparing tourist guides to American cities and states; it supported plays and playwrights and actors and directors. These were the programs that captured Eleanor's heart; it was the WPA sites Eleanor visited most frequently in her tireless trips round the country, bringing back an unrivaled knowledge of the mood of the American people.

To Harold Ickes' criticism that the jobs the WPA created were not permanent, that the only way to relieve unemployment in the long run was to prime the pump by subsidizing private enterprise, Hopkins replied, "people don't eat in the long run. They eat every day. . . . " Regularly attacked in the press as a reckless waster of the taxpayers' money, Hopkins countered: "If I deserve any criticism, it is that I didn't do enough when I had the chance."

Hopkins, Eleanor wrote in her column, "My Day," in 1938, "is one of the few people in the world who gives me the feeling of being entirely absorbed in doing his job well. He seems to work because he has an inner conviction that his job needs to be done and that he must do it. I think he would be that way about any job he undertook." If Eleanor loved someone, a relative of hers once said, she lost her critical faculty entirely and was bound to be disappointed when reality set in. But until that moment, she was able to give herself wholly to love. When Harry's wife, Barbara, was dying of cancer, Eleanor was there. When Harry himself was in the hospital for months at a stretch, Eleanor was there. When Harry's six-year-old daughter, Diana, needed comfort and care, Eleanor brought her to live at the White House, installing her in a bedroom on the third floor, near the sky parlor, and offered to be her guardian should anything happen to her father.

Eleanor's closeness to Hopkins inevitably generated gossip. "Around the White House," the maid Lillian Parks recalled, "there was some talk that Eleanor was romantically inclined toward the gaunt Harry." In journalistic circles, according to Eliot Janeway, the talk took a meaner tone. "In the days before Hopkins discovered Churchill and became resident lapdog he did whatever he could to get in with Roosevelt. Among the fellows in our poker game the great joke was that he even did his duty by Eleanor."

Whatever truth there might be to the gossip, there is little doubt that the bond between Harry and Eleanor was shaped above all by their shared pledge to the poor and the unemployed and their shared belief in the New Deal's restorative powers.

"It was strange," Eleanor later told her son Elliott, "but when I came back from New York that first night of the German invasion, I felt a great sense of foreboding, a fear that the war would get in the way of all the domestic progress we were making. But then, when I saw Harry back in the White House, I felt better, for I knew that he had never been interested in military affairs and that he'd stick with me no matter what happened."

Eleanor was correct in suggesting that Hopkins had little interest in military matters. Rejected from the army in World War I because of a blind eye, he had never fired a gun or fixed a bayonet in infantry drill. His only war experience was welfare work with the Red Cross in Mississippi and Alabama. Furthermore, Robert Sherwood observed, "his New Deal pacifism inclined him emotionally toward a kind of isolationism." Writing to Eleanor on August 31, 1939, the day before the war broke out, Hopkins had said: "The war news is disquieting, but I hope and pray there will be no war. It would seem as though all of civilization were crumbling right under our very eyes."

But now, to Eleanor's mind, Harry had made a devastating turn of 180 degrees in his interests and concerns. He had suddenly transformed himself into an expert on foreign affairs, as if the problems of the sick and the unemployed were no longer of any consequence to him. His total shift from domestic to international concerns was inexplicable to her, suggesting to Eleanor that all along he had been more allied to her husband's concerns than to hers, that their friendship had never meant as much to him as it did to her.

Indeed, Harry Hopkins was so close to the president at this point, Frances Perkins recalled, that he was almost admitted—but not really, since no one ever was—to "a total friendship" with him. Situated in the best guest room in the White House—the large suite that had once been Abraham Lincoln's study, in the southwest corner of the second floor, consisting of one large bedroom with a four-poster bed, a small sitting room, and a bath—Hopkins was available to talk with the president at any hour about anything and everything, about consequential matters and "ordinary fooling," as Hopkins once put it, "passing the time of day and the small talk of people who are living in the same house."

Tommy alluded to Harry's changed position in the White House in a letter to Eleanor's daughter, Anna. "Harry and Missy are thicker than the well-known thieves at the moment," Tommy wrote; "he is staying here and has gone completely over to the other side of the house. If your father does not eat with your mother and any guests, Harry eats with him and Missy and it makes me mad and ready to smack him because your mother was so darn faithful about going to see him when he was sick, agreeing to take Diana if anything happened to him, etc. It seems to me if he had a lick of sense or appreciation, he would make it a real point to spend time with your mother."

During this period, Frances Perkins noticed that Eleanor seemed to be away from the White House even more than usual. She was always going somewhere, Perkins recalled. "It had begun to cause grumbling around, such as 'Where's Mrs. Roosevelt? Why doesn't she stay home? Why doesn't she take care of her husband?' " At one point, Perkins went to see Eleanor. "I really think you ought to be here in the White House more. I say it to you in the warmest kind of friendship. I think it would be better for you and better for the President. The President needs you and needs you here."

Eleanor looked at Perkins and, "with the sweetest smile, sort of twisting her eyes and smiling sweetly, she shook her head and said, 'Oh, no Frances, he doesn't need me any more. He has Harry. . . . He doesn't need my advice any more. He doesn't ask it. Harry tells him everything he needs to know!' "

In the past, Eleanor had been able to work for long stretches without tiring, sleeping only four or five hours a night. But now, as the world around her turned hostile and cold, she had periods of such exhaustion that she found it difficult to get up in the morning. "One day," Tommy reported to Anna, "she didn't come down to breakfast until nearly ten a.m. and I nearly had a fit. I could contain myself no longer, so at 9:30 I went up to see what was wrong. She just decided to stay in bed. I told her to please send out advance notices in the future when she was going to do something so unheard of."

•   •   •

Eleanor was no stranger to depression. In the months surrounding her husband's first inauguration, in 1933, she had experienced a period of turmoil and loss similar to what she was feeling in the spring of 1940. What she feared then, as she feared now, was the loss of the unique partnership she had forged with Franklin since his paralysis, a partnership that allowed her both an independent existence and the chance to contribute in important ways to his fame and power. As the first lady of New York, she had been able to spend three days a week away from Albany, teaching literature, drama, and American history to the young girls at Todhunter, a private school in Manhattan, while still managing to be her husband's "eyes and ears" in the State Capitol the rest of the week.

But with her husband's nomination to the presidency, she was concerned that her dual existence would come to an end, that she would become a prisoner in the White House, a slave to the superficial, symbolic duties of the first lady. As she saw it, the move to the White House would destroy her working partnership with Franklin and bring an end to any personal life of her own.

She couldn't bear it, she told her friend Nancy Cook in a long letter written on the eve of Franklin's victory at the convention, she just "could not live in the White House." When Nancy showed the indiscreet letter to Louis Howe, his "pale face darkened ... his lips drew into a thin line, and when he had finished he ripped the letter into shreds, tiny shreds, and dropped these into a wastebasket." Then, according to historian Kenneth Davis, he ordered sternly, "You are not to breathe a word of this to anyone, understand? Not to anyone."

Howe's injunction was respected. The public was never aware of the dismal mood that accompanied Eleanor's journey to the nation's capital. Only a few friends knew how deadened she felt inside, as if all the elements that had rooted her in life and given her a sense of identity were being torn away from her. An accurate gauge of her confusion is her admission in her memoirs that just before the inauguration she tentatively suggested to her husband that, beyond being hostess at the necessary functions, he might like her to do a real job and take on some of his mail. "He looked at me quizzically and said he did not think that would do, that Missy, who had been handling his mail for a long time, would feel I was interfering. I knew he was right and that it would not work, but it was a last effort to keep in close touch and to feel that I had a real job to do."

It was, in retrospect, a terrible idea. Eleanor was much too independent and strong-willed to spend her time simply reflecting her husband's thinking in answering the mail, but at the time Eleanor interpreted Franklin's negative response as a personal rejection. The downward spiral escalated.

"My zest in life is rather gone for the time being," Eleanor had confessed to her friend Lorena Hickok in a grim letter written in the spring of 1933, soon after she had become first lady. "If anyone looks at me, I want to weep ... ," she continued. "I get like this sometimes. It makes me feel like a dead weight & my mind goes round & round like a squirrel in a cage. I want to run, & I can't, & I despise myself. I can't get away from thinking about myself. Even though I know I'm a fool, I can't help it!"

By the summer of 1933, Eleanor's melancholy had passed. "The times of depression are very often felt as gaps," a psychologist has written, "temporary losses of certainty or identity which leave us feeling empty." Seen in this light, Eleanor's despondency was the intervening period of chaos between the breakup of her old identity as teacher and political activist in New

York State and the establishment of a new identity in the White House. In a remarkably short period of time, with the help of her friends Louis Howe and Lorena Hickok, Eleanor was able to forge a new role for herself, as a new kind of first lady, an activist role never practiced or even imagined before. "Within a few months," one historian has written, "she was more firmly established in the public mind than she had ever been in her native state as a sharply defined personality, a forceful mind, an acutely sensitive conscience, a remarkably strong moral character."

Though Eleanor was able to surmount her particular unhappiness in 1933 by carving out a new role for herself as first lady, the storm which had swept her up in 1933 and again in 1940 had a deeper origin, in the devastating losses she had experienced as a child.

•   •   •

The story of Eleanor's recurring depressions must begin with her alcoholic father, Elliott Roosevelt. The third of four children born to Theodore Roosevelt, Sr., and Martha "Mittie" Bulloch, Elliott had grown up in a world of privilege: a fashionable town house in Manhattan, a country estate in Oyster Bay, Long Island, private tutors and private schools. In a remarkable household that would produce a president of the United States in the eldest son, Teddy, Elliott was considered the best-looking, the most athletic, the most gregarious, and in many ways the most endearing of them all. But, for reasons that are not easy to understand, Elliott was never able to hold his own in the unrelenting competition that governed everyday life among the talented Roosevelts.

At the age of fourteen, upset by his failure to keep up with his brother Teddy academically, Elliott began having mysterious seizures. "Yesterday during my Latin lesson . . . ," he wrote his father from St. Paul's, "I had a bad rush of blood to my head, it hurt me so that I can't remember what happened." There was some talk of epilepsy, but the attacks were most likely an unconscious mechanism of escape from competitive struggles he could not otherwise endure. An earlier problem with German had produced a similar fainting spell along with a plaintive letter to his father: "Teedee is a much quicker and more sure kind of boy, though I will try my best and try to be good as you if [it] is in me, but it is hard."

Incapable of putting forth the concerted effort needed to stay in school, Elliott wandered off to the Himalayas. Upon his return to New York, he courted Anna Hall, a debutante of such great beauty that her image remained for years in the minds of those who saw her. The stories are legion. The poet Robert Browning was so struck by Anna's looks that he asked if he could sit and gaze at her while she had her portrait painted. Eleanor's cousin Corinne Robinson was so entranced by the sight of Anna, "dressed in some blue gray shimmering material," that the vision stayed with her for the rest of her childhood. But the deepest imprint was on her daughter, Eleanor, who opened her memoirs, written at the age of fifty-five, with the comment that her mother was "one of the most beautiful women" she had ever seen. As a little girl, she added, she was "grateful to be allowed to touch her [mother's] dress or her jewels or anything that was part of the vision."

Elliott Roosevelt and Anna Hall made a dazzling couple. They were invited everywhere, and Anna fell in love. Like so many others, she, too, was affected by Elliott's radiant smile and charming personality. She was nineteen and he was twenty-three when they married. Their happiness was short-lived. The responsibility of marriage and the birth of three children—Eleanor, Elliott Jr., and Hall—served to increase Elliott's anxiety to the point where his casual drinking became heavier and heavier.

When he was not drinking, he was loving and warm, everything Eleanor wanted in a father. "[My father] dominated my life as long as he lived and was the love of my life for many years after he died," Eleanor wrote in her memoirs. One of her earliest recollections is of being dressed up and allowed to come down and dance for a group of her father's friends, who enthusiastically applauded her performance. Then, when she finished, her father would pick her up and hold her high in the air, a moment of triumph for both the father and the little girl. "With my father I was perfectly happy," she recalled. "He would take me into his dressing room in the mornings or when he was dressing for dinner and let me watch each thing he did."

When he was drinking, however, everything changed. The routine of everyday life became impossible to maintain. The household was filled with recrimination. Night after night he would show up too late for dinner, and many nights he failed to show up at all. At one point, he made a servant girl pregnant and a scandal erupted in the newspapers. At times, his drinking led to a melancholy so deep that he threatened suicide. In such moods, he would totally forget the promises he had made to his wife and his daughter only the day before. One afternoon, Eleanor recalled, her father took her and three of their dogs for a walk. As they came up to the door of the Knickerbocker Club, he told Eleanor to wait for a moment with the dogs and he would be right back. An hour passed, and then another, and then four more, and still Eleanor remained at the door, patiently holding the dogs. Finally, her father came out, but so drunk that he had to be carried in the arms of several men. The doorman took Eleanor home.

Still, Eleanor preferred her warm and affectionate father to her cold and self-absorbed mother. At least with her father, she said, she never doubted that she "stood first in his heart," whereas for as long as she could remember she felt that her beautiful mother was bitterly disappointed, almost repelled, by the plainness and the ungainliness of her only daughter. Forced to wear a brace for several years for curvature of the spine, Eleanor recalled that even at the age of two she was "a shy solemn child," completely "lacking in the spontaneous joy or mirth of youth." Moreover, she knew, "as a child senses those things," that her mother was trying to compensate for her lack of beauty by teaching her excellent manners, but "her efforts only made me more keenly conscious of my shortcomings."

Perhaps Anna, having been taught to value beauty and charm as the most important attributes in a woman, did instinctively recoil from her daughter's unattractive looks. But, though Eleanor could never admit it, her father's erratic behavior was the more likely cause of the distance between mother and daughter. Feeling the weight of the world on her shoulders, Anna had little energy left for a stubborn and precocious little girl who kept her father on a pedestal and blamed her mother when her father had to be sent away on various "cures" to various sanitariums. Perhaps, in rejecting Eleanor's fervent love for her father, Anna was rejecting that part of herself that had fallen in love with such an untrustworthy man.

Eleanor slept in her mother's room while her father was away and could hear her mother talking with her aunts about the problem with her father. "I acquired a strange and garbled idea of the troubles which were going on around me. Something was wrong with my father." Eleanor was only seven at the time, too young to understand the intolerable strain on her twenty-eight-year-old mother, a strain that produced in Anna very bad recurring headaches. "I would sit at the head of her bed and stroke her head," Eleanor recalled. "The feeling that I was useful was perhaps the greatest joy I had experienced."

But aside from these dreamy moments serving her mother, Eleanor felt most of the time "a curious barrier" between herself and the rest of her little family. In the late afternoons, she recalled, her mother sat in the parlor with her two brothers. "Little Ellie adored her, the baby [Hall] sat on her lap. . . . [I can] still remember standing in the door, very often with my finger in my mouth—which was, of course, forbidden and I can see the look in her eyes and hear the tone of her voice as she said, 'Come in, Granny.' If a visitor was there she might turn and say: 'She is such a funny child, so old-fashioned, we always call her Granny.' I wanted to sink through the floor in shame, and I felt I was apart from the boys." The painful memory of these afternoons in the parlor remained with Eleanor, reappearing thirty years later in a fictional composition in which she wrote of "a blue eyed rather ugly little girl standing in the door of a cozy library looking in at a very beautiful woman holding, oh so lovingly, in her lap a little fair haired boy."

For most of Eleanor's eighth year, her father remained in exile in Abingdon, Virginia, where her mother and her uncle Theodore had sent him in the hope that the forced separation from his family would motivate him to take hold of himself. "A child stood at a window . . . ," Eleanor wrote in her composition book. "Her father [was] the only person in the world she loved, others called her hard & cold but to him she was everything lavishing on him all the quiet love which the others could not understand. And now he had gone she did not know for how long but he had said 'what ever happens little girl some day I will come back' & she had smiled. He never knew what the smile cost."

On her eighth birthday, Eleanor received a long and loving letter from Abingdon, addressed to "My darling little Daughter." "Because Father is not with you is not because he doesn't love you," he wrote. "For I love you tenderly and dearly. And maybe soon I'll come back all well and strong and we will have such good times together, like we used to have. I have to tell all the little children here often about you and all that I remember of you when you were a little bit of a girl and you used to call yourself Father's little 'Golden Hair'—and how you used to come into my dressing room and dress me in the morning and frighten me by saying I'd be late for breakfast."

These letters, filled only with love for her, Eleanor later wrote, were the letters she loved and kissed before she went to bed. But there were other letters, filled with news of the life he was leading in Abingdon, that inadvertently brought her pain and reinforced her feeling of being an outsider. In these newsy letters he often spoke of riding horseback with a group of little children near where he lived. "I was always longing to join the group," Eleanor later wrote. "One child in particular I remember. I envied her very much because he was so very fond of her."

A month after Eleanor's eighth birthday, her mother contracted a fatal case of diphtheria. Her father was told to return from his exile in Virginia, but Anna died before he was able to get home. "I can remember standing by a window when Cousin Susie told me that my mother was dead," Eleanor later wrote. "Death meant nothing to me, and one fact wiped out everything else—my father was back and I would see him very soon."

When Elliott finally arrived, Eleanor recorded, "he held out his arms and gathered me to him. In a little while he began to talk, to explain to me that my mother was gone, that she had been all the world to him and now he only had my brothers and myself, that my brothers were very young and that he and I must keep close together. Some day I would make a home for him again, we would travel together and do many things. Somehow it was always he and I. I did not understand whether my brothers were to be our children or whether he felt that they would be at school and college and later independent. There started that day a feeling which never left me—that he and I were very close together and some day would have a life of our own together. . . . When he left, I was all alone to keep our secret of mutual understanding."

The decision was made to send Eleanor and her brothers to their grandmother Hall's while Elliott returned to Virginia. From then on, Eleanor admitted, "subconsciously I must have been waiting always for his visits. They were irregular and he rarely sent word before he arrived, but never was I in the house even in my room two long flights of stairs above the entrance door that I did not hear his voice the minute he entered the front door." During these precious visits, Elliott painted a picture for his daughter of the valiant, gifted, upright little girl he expected her to be, and Eleanor did her best, she later wrote, despite her consciousness of her ugly looks and her many deficiencies, to make herself into "a fairly good copy of the picture he had painted."

The year after her mother died, Eleanor's four-year-old brother, Ellie, also fell ill with diphtheria and died. Though she was a child herself, Eleanor tried to comfort her father. "We must remember," she wrote him, "Ellie is going to be safe in heaven and to be with Mother who is waiting there. . . ."

But then, when Eleanor was ten, the visits and the letters from her father stopped. The years of heavy drinking took their final toll. Suffering from delirium tremens, Elliott tried to jump out of the window of his house, had a seizure and died, at the age of thirty-four. "My aunts told me," Eleanor recalled, "but I simply refused to believe it, and while I wept long . . . I finally went to sleep and began the next day living in my dream world as usual. My grandmother decided we children should not go to the funeral and so I had no tangible thing to make death real to me. From that time on . . . I lived with him more closely, probably, than I had when he was alive."

From the melancholy lives of both her parents, as she would learn again in her own marriage, Eleanor had come to understand that promises were made to be broken, and that no one's love for her was meant to last. The legacy of repeated loss as a child left her prey to the recurring depressions she suffered as an adult. Always waiting in the wings, depression was for Eleanor a dark companion that strode to center stage whenever there were turnabouts in the established pattern of her life.

• • •

But the legacy of Eleanor's childhood also produced resilient strength. No matter how many times her father disappointed her, Eleanor knew, at bottom, that he loved her profoundly, that he had chosen her as his favorite child. And this knowledge was something that neither alcoholism nor death could destroy. "It was her father who acquainted Eleanor with grief," Joe Lash has written. "But he also gave her the ideals that she tried to live up to all her life by presenting her with the picture of what he wanted her to be —noble, studious, religious, loving and good."

"We do not have to become heroes overnight," Eleanor once wrote. "Just a step at a time, meeting each thing that comes up, seeing it is not as dreadful as it appears, discovering that we have the strength to stare it down." So, step by step, Eleanor willed herself to become the accomplished daughter her father had decreed her to be, the fearless woman that would make him proud. Every inch of her journey was filled with peril and anxiety, but she never stopped moving forward. "The thing always to remember," she said, is that "you must do the thing you think you cannot do."

As a young girl trapped in the austere household of her grandmother after her parents died, Eleanor used to hide books under her mattress so she could wake up in the middle of the night to read them, defying her grandmother's edict that she be allowed to read only at set times and in set places. Her passionate reading of Dickens and Scott awakened within her a romantic belief that, no matter how grim everything seemed, there was always some way out.

Hers came when her grandmother sent her away to a boarding school in

London run by an inspired teacher, Mademoiselle Souvestre. From the moment Eleanor arrived at Allenswood and looked into the smiling eyes of the seventy-year-old headmistress, she felt that she was starting "a new life," free from all her earlier troubles. In Mademoiselle Souvestre, Eleanor found the maternal love she had never enjoyed as a child, and in the power of that love, the young girl blossomed. Excelling at everything she did—at her lessons in every subject, at poetry recitations, even at field hockey—Eleanor quickly became "everything" at the school, the most respected student among faculty and students alike. Step by step, Eleanor later said, Allenswood "started me on my way to self confidence." Her three years there, she said, were "the happiest of my life."

Not long after her return to New York, Eleanor began seeing her cousin Franklin at parties and dances. They had first met when they were two and four, but now, fifteen years later, a special bond developed between them. Eleanor was unlike any girl Franklin had met. She was serious and intelligent, free from affectation, and wholly uninterested in the world of debutante balls. Though her interest in philosophy and ethics seemed ridiculous to her cousin Alice Roosevelt, Teddy's daughter, who noted sarcastically that Eleanor "always wanted to discuss things like whether contentment was better than happiness," Franklin was intrigued. He enjoyed her company immensely. He invited her to Campobello in the summer, to dances and football games at Harvard in the fall, and to Hyde Park in the spring, where they rode together in the woods and sat on the porch at twilight reading poetry to one another.

While Franklin completed his studies at Harvard, Eleanor was happily ensconced at the Rivington Street settlement house in New York, where she supervised a class of immigrant children in exercise and dance. From her early childhood, when her father had taken her to a newsboy clubhouse which his father, Theodore Roosevelt, Sr., had started, Eleanor found herself "tremendously interested in all these ragged little boys and in the fact which my father explained, that many of them had no homes and lived in wooden shanties." Her work at the settlement house was tremendously stimulating to her, and she was delighted to feel that she could be of some help.

One afternoon when Franklin was in New York, she asked him to pick her up at the settlement house. Just before they were ready to leave, a young girl suddenly fell ill, and Eleanor enlisted Franklin's help to take the child home. Nothing in Franklin's sheltered life had prepared him for the grating sounds and sour smells of the dilapidated tenement where the young girl lived. "My God," he told Eleanor, "I didn't know anyone lived like that."

How easy Eleanor felt in Franklin's presence! Her awkwardness seemed suddenly to disappear, her old dejection passed away. The inferiority she had always experienced in the presence of men vanished as she came to trust that he thought her better and more interesting than all the other young women in the world. The letters she wrote during the first months of their romance reveal an absolute delight at the experience of falling in love, combined with a fervent wish to be with her lover every moment of the day.

"Though I only wrote last night," she told him one autumn day when she was seventeen, "I must write you just a line this morning to tell you that I miss you every moment & that you are never out of my thoughts dear for one moment. . . . I am so happy. Oh! so happy & I love you *so* dearly."

And she knew that he loved her as she loved him. "It is impossible to tell you what these last two days have been to me," Eleanor wrote after a weekend together at Hyde Park, "but I know they have meant the same to you so that you will understand that I love you dearest and I hope that I shall always prove worthy of the love which you have given me. I have never before known what it was to be absolutely happy."

As the days and months passed, Eleanor recalled, she came to realize that the hours they were together meant the most to her. She was happiest when she was with him. Though she was only nineteen when he asked her to marry him, she was absolutely sure that it was right. "When he told me that he loved me and asked me to marry him, I did not hesitate to say yes, for I knew that I loved him too." A week later, Eleanor was still filled with joy. "I was thinking last night of the difference which one short week can make in one's life. Everything is changed for me now. . . . I am so happy."

Franklin's letters from this period no longer exist. Eleanor burned them —most likely in 1937, Joe Lash speculates, when she was working on her autobiography and found his youthful avowals of constancy unto death too painful and uncomfortable to reread. Yet there is no doubt that he, too, had been caught in the tide of a powerful love. "I am the happiest man just now in the world," he told his mother after Eleanor accepted his proposal, "likewise the luckiest."

•   •   •

When Eleanor married Franklin, she traded the chance for deeper involvement in social work for the hope of finding happiness as a wife and mother. Six children quickly followed (one of the six died at twenty months). "For ten years I was always just getting over having a baby or about to have another one, and so my occupations were considerably restricted." At one point, she expressed a desire to return to the settlement house, but her mother-in-law dissuaded her on the grounds that she would be coming home with germs that would contaminate her own children.

Forced to remain at home while her husband went to work, Eleanor found her old insecurities returning. So painful was the memory of her own tormented childhood that she approached the task of mothering with little joy. She worried constantly about nutrition, illness, and discipline. Her lack of confidence caught Franklin by surprise. "He had always been secure in every way, you see," Eleanor later said, "and then he discovered that I was perfectly insecure."

It was only after her last child was born, in 1916, and after the crisis provoked by Lucy Mercer, that Eleanor found her identity. Free to define a new role for herself beyond her family, she poured all her pent-up energies into a variety of reformist organizations dedicated to the abolition of child labor, the establishment of a minimum wage, and the passage of protective legislation for women workers. In the process, she discovered she had real talents for organization, leadership, and public life. Her political activities expanded still further after Franklin's paralysis, when he turned to her to keep the Roosevelt name in the public eye while he concentrated on regaining his health. "The polio was very instrumental in bringing them much closer into a very real partnership," Anna observed. "They were finding mutual interests on a totally different level than they had been before."

During Franklin's years as governor and president, the Roosevelts became so deeply involved with one another that they seemed like two halves of a single whole whose lives, as New Deal economist Rexford Tugwell put it, "were joined in a common cause." Her astonishing travels, her strong convictions, her curiosity about almost every phase of the nation's life, from slum clearance to experimental beehives, from rural electrification to country dances, provided fascinating material for endless conversations, arguments, and debates.

Their working partnership involved the creation of a shared emotional territory in which they could relate to each other with abiding love and respect. To be sure, on some occasions, she irritated and even exasperated him, but he never ceased to respect and admire her. Nor did she ever stop loving him. "I hated to see you go . . . ," Eleanor wrote Franklin in the 1930s as he set out on a journey overseas. "We are really very dependent on each other though we do see so little of each other."

Understanding the nature of their relationship, it is not surprising, then, that Eleanor anguished so much in the spring of 1940 over the fear that her partnership would break apart. The husband who had been her close friend would now be more remote, his attention directed to international concerns. The man who loved nothing more than the detailed stories of her travels, now had little time and less inclination to listen to her.

But just as she had surmounted her unhappiness in 1933 and managed to etch a role for the first lady in domestic affairs never before practiced, so now, as the imperatives of war propelled a conversion of the nation, she would slowly come to grips with her depression, rallying her forces once more to effect a transformation of her role to fit the changing times.

• • •

By the end of June, Eleanor had found her first wartime cause in the movement to open America's doors to the refugee children of Europe. With the entire continent under Nazi control, and England living in fear of imminent invasion, the public cry for evacuating as many European children as possible reached a crescendo.

The chance to work on a project that mattered both to her and to the world was a tonic to Eleanor. Into her Greenwich Village apartment she brought together representatives of various relief and charitable agencies —including the American Friends Service Committee, the German-Jewish Children's Aide, and the Committee for Catholic Refugees—to determine what could be done. The refugee crisis seemed the perfect focus for Eleanor's abilities, combining her humanitarian zeal with her organizational skill. Clearly, there was no time to lose.

On the morning of June 20, at a hastily arranged conference at New York's Gramercy Park Hotel, a new umbrella organization was born with Eleanor as honorary chair—the U.S. Committee for the Care of European Children. The purpose of the new committee was to coordinate all the different agencies and resources available in the United States for the care of refugee children. The first goal was to get the State Department to relax its restrictions on the granting of visas; the second, to establish a network of families in the United States willing to care for the children once they arrived.

That evening at Eleanor's apartment, the new committee held its first meeting. A number of members were anxious to have the Republican banker Winthrop Aldrich as chairman. Before endorsing him, Eleanor excused herself and called the president to see what he thought of Aldrich. Roosevelt, who was in his study when she reached him, having dinner with Harry Hopkins, was appalled at the idea. "You know, darling," he told her, wildly overstating his case to make his opposition clear, "he would be the first to welcome Hitler with open arms." Placed in a delicate situation by her husband's sharp reaction, Eleanor quickly composed herself, walked back into the living room, and said in her most disarming manner, "It was kind of Mr. Aldrich to offer to be chairman, but is it not better from the point of view of geography to have someone from the Middle West?" At that, she turned immediately to the Chicago philanthropist and New Deal loyalist Marshall Field; she knew it would be a bother for him, but could he accept? Though caught somewhat off guard, Field gave his assent, and a troublesome problem was averted.

The plight of the refugees, particularly the British children, touched such a responsive chord in the American public that within two days the committee was flooded with thousands of offers of homes. All of these offers had to be confirmed and evaluated, a laborious task which Eleanor willingly shouldered. "I think men are worse than women on committees," Eleanor confided in a letter to her daughter, Anna, "and they do think more of their importance. I hope I'll never think I am of any importance, it makes one so stuffy!"

Moreover, as Eleanor quickly recognized, the task of "finding homes into which to put children when they arrive" was delightfully simple compared with "the horrid legal details" involved in having the children admitted to the country in the first place. From the start, Eleanor understood that visitor visas were the only way to get around the low monthly quotas for immigration which had been set by a xenophobic Congress in the late 1920s. In a radio program on CBS, Eleanor argued for an administrative ruling that would permit refugee children to enter the United States as temporary visitors rather than as immigrants. "The children are not immigrants," she said. "The parents of these children will recall them when the war is over. ... Therefore [they] should be classified as temporary visitors and not as immigrants. ... Red tape must not be used to trip up little children on their way to safety."

Since visitor visas were not subject to numerical limitations, the change Eleanor advocated promised to open America's doors to tens of thousands of refugees, and simultaneously to provide an invaluable precedent for saving countless lives in the years ahead. The principal obstacle was the head of the State Department's visa section, Breckinridge Long. A Southerner who proudly traced his roots to the Breckinridges of Kentucky and the Longs of North Carolina, Long was adamantly opposed to the admission of refugees under any circumstances. In a diary filled with invectives against Jews, Catholics, New Yorkers, liberals, and in fact everybody who was not of his own particular background, Long interpreted the widespread desire to admit the British refugee children as "an enormous psychosis" on the part of the American people. "I attribute it to repressed emotion about the war," he recorded in his diary, "the chance finally to DO something, however wrongheaded it may be."

Long had first met FDR during the Wilson administration, when they were both assistant secretaries, Long at State, Roosevelt at Navy. A successful international lawyer, Long had made a sizable contribution to the Democratic campaign fund in 1932 and was rewarded with an ambassadorship to Italy. There, Mussolini and the fascist regime captured his heart until Mussolini's foreign adventures and Italy's invasion of Ethiopia changed his mind. Resigning from the ambassadorship, he returned to the United States, where in January 1940 he was made head of a Special War Problems Division in the State Department, which included the visa section.

Long had come to the unshakable conviction that the admission of refugees would endanger national security, since the Germans were using visitor visas to send spies and foreign agents abroad. Every single one of the now defeated countries, according to Long, had been honeycombed with spies and fifth-column activities. There was some truth to his claims.

But not even Long, whose skill at carrying the security gambit to an illogical extreme boggled the mind, was able to argue that British children were German spies. Moreover, in the summer of 1940, the tide of support for letting the British children into America was so strong, running through every class in American society, that it promised, for a time, to overwhelm the more general antirefugee sentiment that had been prevalent for so many years.

Capitalizing on the moment at hand, Eleanor appealed directly to Franklin, patiently explaining why it was necessary to go over Breckinridge Long's head. For days and weeks, she said, she had been arguing with Long to no avail. The president assured her he would do his utmost, and the next day, in a signal victory for the refugee advocates, Roosevelt ordered Long's boss, Secretary of State Hull, to simplify the procedure so that the British children could come in. A new ruling was issued the following day whereby visitor visas would be issued to British refugee children "upon a showing of intention they shall return home upon the termination of hostilities."

Eleanor was delighted. "I think your mother is really enjoying her work with the refugee committee," Tommy told Anna. "She looks very well and of course, is always happier when she feels she is doing something constructive."

One pressing problem remained: how to get the children here. "The English," Harold Ickes recorded in his diary, "cannot spare warships to convoy bottoms [unarmed merchant ships] bringing in refugee children and it isn't safe to send them except under convoy." Nor was it safe to send American mercy ships into the sub-infested waters. "The very surest way to get America into the war," Long argued, "would be to send an American ship to England and put 2000 babies on it and then have it sunk by a German torpedo." Roosevelt shared Long's fear about sending American ships, but when the pressure to save the British children refused to abate, the Congress took matters into its own hands, passing an amendment to the Neutrality Act which permitted unarmed, unescorted ships to sail to Britain to evacuate British children provided safe conduct was granted by all belligerents.

• • •

While Americans fretted over the plight of British children who were not yet in danger, the people who most urgently needed help were the Jewish refugees from Germany who were trapped in Vichy France. One of the provisions in the French armistice agreement required the Vichy government to return on demand all German citizens named by the German government. As American ships crossed the Atlantic to save the British children, Gestapo agents were on their way to France to round up every German Jewish man, woman, and child they could find. But when Congressman William Schulte of Indiana tried to broaden the use of the visitor visas to any European child under sixteen, his bill was killed before it even reached the floor. The crucial difference, in terms of American public opinion, between the British and the German children was that the British boys and girls were mostly Christian, the German children mostly Jewish.

Throughout the 1930s, as tens of thousands of Jews fled Nazi Germany, Roosevelt worked behind the scenes to let more people in. Estimates show that, in the years between 1933 and 1940, nearly 105,000 refugees from Nazism reached safety in the United States, a record, though limited, that went beyond that of any other country. Only Palestine, which took in 55,000 during these same years, approached the American figure.

But those who were granted refuge were pitifully few compared with those who were trying to flee. "The long pathetic list of refugee ships, unable to find harbors open to them," historian David Wyman argues, "testifies to the fact the world of the late 30s and early 40s was a world without room for the Jews of . . . Europe." The sad saga of the *St. Louis,* which set out from Germany for Cuba in May 1939 with 930 Jewish refugees aboard, was a dramatic case in point. On reaching Havana, the passengers were not allowed to disembark and the ship was turned away. For weeks, as the ship hovered close enough to Miami for the refugees to see the lights of the city, negotiators tried without success to get the U.S. government to provide temporary sanctuary. A telegram to FDR from a committee of the passengers received no reply. The *St. Louis,* memorialized in the movie *Voyage of the Damned,* was forced to sail back to Europe, where many of its passengers eventually died in concentration camps.

Roosevelt was not unsympathetic to the plight of the Jewish refugees. Though anti-Semitism had been part and parcel of the cloistered world in which he and Eleanor had grown up—"The Jew party [was] appalling," Eleanor had written her mother-in-law in 1918 after an evening with Bernard Baruch. "I never wish to hear money, jewels or sables mentioned again"— politics had broadened their attitudes and expanded their sensibilities. During the Roosevelt presidency, though Jews constituted only 3 percent of the U.S. population, they represented nearly 15 percent of Roosevelt's top appointments. Indeed, so prominent were Jews in the Roosevelt administration that bigots routinely referred to the New Deal as the Jew Deal and charged that Roosevelt was himself a Jew. "In the dim distant past," Roosevelt had replied, "[my ancestors] may have been Jews or Catholics or Protestants. What I am interested in is whether they were good citizens and believers in God. I hope they were both."

But it was one thing to sympathize with the plight of the Jewish refugees and quite another to pit his presidency against the xenophobic, anti-Semitic mood of his country in the late 1930s and early '40s. This Roosevelt was unwilling to do. Roper polls confirmed that, though people disapproved of Hitler's treatment of Jews in Germany, the majority of Americans were manifestly unwilling to assist the Jews in practical ways, especially if it meant allowing more Jewish immigration into the U.S. In answer to a question posed in 1938, "What kinds of people do you object to?," Jews were mentioned by 35 percent of the respondents; the next-highest category, at 27 percent, were "noisy, cheap, boisterous and loud people," followed by "uncultured, unrefined, dumb people" at 14 percent and then all other types. The following year, another Roper poll found that 53 percent of the Americans asked believed Jews were different from everyone else and that these differences should lead to restrictions in business and social life.

The desperate situation of the refugees stranded in Europe was brought to Eleanor's attention on June 24, when she hosted a small dinner at her village apartment for her friend Joe Lash and two members of the European underground, Karl Frank and Joseph Buttinger. Buttinger had been head of the underground socialist movement in Austria while Frank had been organizing in Germany. The question was whether Mrs. Roosevelt could do anything for the leading people of the various socialist parties—German, Austrian, Spanish, and Polish. All these people had fought Hitler for years and were now in mortal danger. Buttinger's group had lists of the people who'd been stranded in France and the ones who had moved on to Spain or Portugal. Could she help?

Agreeing at once that she would do what she could, she rose from the table to put in a call to her husband. But if Eleanor expected public support from her husband at this juncture, she was mistaken. For weeks, ever since the Nazi invasion of the Low Countries, the president had been hearing tales of the great success of the Nazis' various infiltration schemes. In Norway, it was said, thousands of Nazi agents, camouflaged as lecturers, refugees, newspapermen, and diplomatic attachés, had infiltrated the country in the months before the invasion. Then, six weeks before the actual seizure, Norway was flooded with German "tourists" who remained on the scene to help the German troops. In Holland, fifth columnists were said to have figured prominently in the Germans' successful parachute landings, signaling to the planes from the ground and then providing the sky troops with Dutch military and police uniforms when they landed.

Addressing the joint session of Congress on May 16, the president had condemned "the treacherous use of the fifth column by which persons supposed to be peaceful visitors were actually a part of an enemy unit of occupation." Ten days later, in his fireside chat, he had used even more forceful language to warn that "today's threat to our national security is not a matter of military weapons alone. We know of new methods of attack, the Trojan horse, the fifth column that betrays a nation unprepared for treachery. Spies, saboteurs and traitors are all the actors in the new strategy. With all that we must and will deal vigorously."

Thus, while Eleanor and other refugee advocates were fighting to liberalize immigration, Roosevelt was moving in the opposite direction. Preoccupied with the question of subversion, he put the State Department to work on tightening restrictions to prevent infiltration of Nazi agents into the United States. Though it was absurd to believe that Jewish refugees, Hitler's principal victims, would somehow become his principal weapons against the United States, the widespread paranoia about foreigners combined with anti-Semitism to cast a net so wide that everyone except the British children was caught in it.

Eleanor reached Franklin in his study, where he was relaxing with Hopkins at the end of a long workday. "He was somewhat impatient and irritated," Lash recorded in his diary, "that it wasn't taken for granted he was already doing all that was possible. He kept bringing up the difficulties while Mrs. Roosevelt tenaciously kept pointing out the possibilities. 'Congress wouldn't let them in. Quotas are filled. We have tried to get Cuba and other Latin American countries to admit them but so far without success. . . . Can't locate people in France. Spain won't admit even American refugees.' Mrs. Roosevelt interrupted to remind FDR he had always said we could bribe the Spanish and Portuguese governments." There the conversation came to an unsatisfactory end.

When she hung up the phone, Eleanor voiced her inability to understand what had happened to America—the traditional land of asylum, unwilling to admit political refugees. But she said she would take the lists herself and send them to her friend Sumner Welles in the State Department. The European underground should understand it now had a friend at court. In her letter to the State Department the next day, Eleanor said she hoped "the list could be put into the hands of our people in Europe with the request that they do everything they can to protect these refugees. I do not know what Congress will be willing to do, but they might be allowed to come here and be sent to a camp while we are waiting for legislation."

Eleanor's protracted conversation with her husband that evening established the basic pattern their relationship would follow in the years to come. Whereas in the 1930s they had worked side by side in common pursuit of the same goals, now, more and more, she would find herself in the role of the agitator while he remained the politician. On a variety of fronts, she would put pressure on the president when he was tired and would have preferred not to have pressure put upon him. But, as Eleanor's friend Trude Pratt Lash observed, "she had this sense of having to do whatever was humanly possible to do in a difficult time," and nothing, not even her husband, could stop her from trying.

In response to the persistent urgings of Eleanor's committee and other refugee groups, the State Department finally agreed to establish a special procedure to expedite the issuance of visitor visas to political, intellectual, and other refugees in special peril in Spain, Portugal, and southern France. Under this procedure, the President's Advisory Committee on Political Refugees (PAC) would take the first crack at evaluating the lists of names, satisfying themselves as to the purpose for which the refugees sought entry and the manner of their departure from the U.S. at the conclusion of the emergency period. Once the list was approved by the PAC, the consuls abroad were supposed to issue the visas automatically.

It was a summer of high hopes. As long as America and other countries were willing to open their doors to the Jews, the Nazis, at this juncture, were still willing to let them go. Liberal use of visitor visas seemed the ideal solution. "I know it is due to your interest," Karl Frank wrote Eleanor the day after the emergency procedure had been put into operation. Already "many hundreds of people have been granted visitors visas."

"We all know," a grateful Joseph Buttinger told Eleanor, "how decisive your protective word was at a time when it looked as if the rescue action would come to a standstill."

Though still without a sure sense of the shape or direction of her new role in a world torn by war, Eleanor was on her way, beginning once more to believe she still had important tasks to accomplish and that her work would still be acknowledged by others. The depression of that spring was, in fact, part of a healing process, a mourning for the loss of her old relationship with her husband, and the birth pangs of a difficult and ultimately more influential partnership.

CHAPTER 5

"NO ORDINARY

TIME"

The president's second term was coming to an end. Ever since George Washington refused a third term, no man had even tried to achieve the office of the Presidency more than twice.

All spring long, Eleanor had tried to push Franklin to make a definite effort to prepare a successor. "Franklin always smiled and said he thought people had to prepare themselves, that all he could do was to give them opportunities and see how they worked out. I felt that he, without intending to do so, dominated the people around him and that so long as he was in the picture, it was very hard for anyone to rise to a position of prominence."

Roosevelt "really meant to develop somebody" who would be a natural successor, Frances Perkins believed, but never quite got around to it. At one point, before Hopkins' health deteriorated, the president did seem to be grooming him for the presidency. Then there was South Carolina Senator Jimmy Byrnes, whom the president liked immensely, but who, Roosevelt felt, would be forever scarred politically by his conversion from Catholicism to Protestantism so that he could marry a wealthy Southern girl. At various times, the president emboldened the hopes of sixty-nine-year-old Secretary of State Cordell Hull, Attorney General Robert Jackson, Federal Security Agency Chief Paul McNutt, and Postmaster General James Farley, the big bald-headed chairman of the Democratic National Committee, who had more friends in more places across the country than any other person in public life. But in the end, he committed himself to no one.

"Perhaps," Perkins admitted, "it wasn't in his nature to do it, so that he was working at cross-purposes with himself, when he was trying to do it." For, at bottom, "he obviously did like being President. It was a full time occupation for all of his energies and talents and anybody is happy and content when fully functioning. Even when the problems are very great, full functioning is such a rare experience that it's quite pleasing."

But the two-term limitation had become a cherished tradition, and Roosevelt knew, as 1940 opened, that he would be asking for trouble if he tried to buck it. In political circles in the winter and early spring, the dominant opinion was that Roosevelt should not run for a third term. "This is a government of law, and not of one man, however popular," Democratic Senator Patrick McCarran said. "No President should seek a third term," West Virginia Senator Rush Holt maintained, "that is, if he believes in the continuation of democracy in this country. Has it come to the place in the glorious history of our great country that we have exhausted all leadership until today our existence depends upon one man in 130 million?"

Coupled with the uncertainties of a bid for re-election, Roosevelt nourished a genuine desire to return to Hyde Park. In a conversation with Senator George Norris, he expressed his weariness. "George, I am chained to this chair from morning till night. People come in here day after day, most of them trying to get something from me, most of them things I can't give them, and wouldn't if I could. You sit in your chair in your office too, but if something goes wrong or you get irritated or tired, you can get up and walk around, or you can go into another room. But I can't, I am tied down to this chair day after day, week after week, and month after month. And I can't stand it any longer. I can't go on with it."

Roosevelt had signed a contract with *Collier's* in January to write a series of articles at an annual salary equal to the $75,000 he received as president. "The role of elder statesman appealed to him," Eleanor said. Throughout much of the winter, his mind had been happily occupied with two building projects at Hyde Park. For years, Roosevelt had wanted a small place of his own where he could write and think in peace away from the bustle of the Big House. At the far end of his property, on a hilltop overlooking the Hudson Valley, he had found the perfect spot to build a small stone cottage, a simple place with a cozy living room, a small kitchen, three bedrooms, and a magnificent porch overlooking the Catskills to the north and rolling wooded fields to the south. "It's perfect, just perfect," he would often say, as he and Missy gradually furnished the place to his own liking, hung the pictures he wanted to see, and chose the books he wanted to read. Some day in the future, Roosevelt imagined, he might even want to live full-time at Top Cottage. So hurt was his mother by his plans for a home away from home, however, that he solemnly promised never to spend a full night there so long as she was alive.

At the same time, he was deeply involved with plans for a presidential library on the grounds of his estate, to house the White House papers and all the other documents of his public life since he first went to the New York State Senate in 1910. Having collected things—stamps, coins, stuffed birds, prints, and books—since he was a child, he took great pleasure in the process of sorting his papers, spending hours at a time with his Hyde Park neighbor Margaret Suckley, whom he had brought on the staff to supervise the transfer. "Every time he came to Hyde Park in the winter and spring of 1940," Miss Suckley recalled, "he brought large gobs of stuff—papers, documents, statues, presents—to be taken to the attic and sorted out for the library." All through the spring, housekeeper Henrietta Nesbitt confirmed, "we were clearing out storerooms, packing and shipping to Hyde Park; in fact, the Roosevelts were closing up."

But after the fall of France, the third-term dialogue shifted. "If times were normal," Senator Elmer Thomas told reporters, "I would not favor a third term for President Roosevelt, [but] I consider 1940 an abnormal year." Arguing along similar lines, Representative Charles Kramer noted that "a speeding car simply cannot change drivers without losing control. No one in the United States is better informed on world affairs than President Roosevelt or so capably qualified to guide us through this critical period. Whether it be the first, second, third or fourth term is not as important as competent leadership."

"I think my husband was torn," Eleanor told an interviewer years later. "He would often talk about the reasons against a third term," but "there was a great sense of responsibility for what was happening. And the great feeling that possibly he was the only one who was equipped and trained and cognizant not only of the people who were involved in the future, and in what was going to happen, but of every phase of the situation."

Candidly, she concluded: "Now, whether that was purely a sense of responsibility, whether there was some feeling of not wanting to leave the center of history . . . no one, I think, could really assess. . . . When you are in the center of world affairs, there is something so fascinating about it that you can hardly see how you are going to live any other way. In his mind, I think, there was a great seesaw: on one end, the weariness which had already begun, and the desire to be at home and his own master; on the other end, the overwhelming interest which was the culmination of a lifetime of preparation and work, and the desire to see and to have a hand in the affairs of the world in that critical period."

While the president was grappling with the perplexing question of whether he should run again or not, Eleanor carefully avoided asking him what he was going to do. She felt she had no right to put pressure on him by saying what she wished he would do. "It was a position of such terrific responsibility," Eleanor explained, "involving the fates of millions where the final decisions always had to be made alone, that the decision of whether or not to run again had to be made by the President himself, uninfluenced."

Eleanor's habitual reluctance to give advice, which extended to her children as well as her husband, had its roots in her sense that "one never knows, one can never be certain that one's advice is correct." At one point, before the German blitzkrieg, she had suggested that "the President might have served his purpose in history and that . . . new leadership was required for the next step ahead." Unless, she cautioned, "the international crisis made him indispensable."

All through her married life, Eleanor had suffered under the domination of her mother-in-law's strong opinions about everything, her haughty inclination to declare what she considered "the straight path," the best and proper thing to do in any situation. Once, after a long evening with Sara and her two sisters, Eleanor remarked to Franklin, "They all in their serene assurances and absolute judgments on people and affairs going on in the world make me want to squirm and turn bolshevik." Determined not to follow in Sara's footsteps, she generally held back her counsel.

"Will the President seek a third term?" reporters asked her repeatedly. "I don't know," she could honestly respond. "I haven't asked him." When reporters tried to get the answer in a different way, by inquiring where she thought she would be after 1940, she replied, "When you have been married as long as I have to a man who has been in public office a long time, you will learn never to think ahead and you will make up your mind to accept what comes along."

But of course she did think ahead, and when she did, she admitted to her old friend Isabella Greenway, she "would not look forward to four years more in the White House with joy." Too much of her day, she felt, was still taken up with the superficial aspects of the first lady's job. Despite her best efforts to focus her energies on a few important issues, "there was no end to the appointments, teas, social obligations." Indeed, in 1939, her secretary recorded that Eleanor received 9,211 tea guests, 4,729 dinner guests, and 323 house guests. It was particularly hard in the busy winter months, when her day was so filled with routine obligations that she couldn't even start working on her mail until after midnight. Staying up regularly until 3 or 4 a.m., she still had to arise at 7 or 8 to begin another long day. If only she could do some work of her own, she remarked, "take on a job and see it through to a conclusion."

There was, however, no room in a world at war for such personal desires.

"At the present moment," Eleanor concluded her letter to Greenway, "what anyone likes or dislikes does not seem very important."

•   •   •

By refusing to say whether or not he would seek a third term, Roosevelt had effectively paralyzed the political process. By July, leading Democrats were beginning to panic. Believing the time for a decision had come, Democratic National Committee (DNC) Chairman James Farley drove up to Hyde Park on July 9.

Whatever the president decided, Farley was determined not to retreat from the decision he had already taken: to have his own name placed in nomination for the presidency. Though he understood that his candidacy was a long shot at best, he believed someone in the party had to take a principled stand against the third term. The problem with the third term, as Farley saw it, even beyond the risk of shattered tradition, was the fact that having the same man run for president again and again created an inflexible political situation in which ordinary people, particularly younger men and women scattered all around the country, lost interest in politics. When a president is satisfied with the work of the people he's got, he tends not to change them; the turnover is slight and there is little chance for aspiring outsiders to get experience. The young people who ought to be hustling for votes feel everything has already been arranged, and, over time, passion diminishes. Farley was hoping to get Roosevelt to commit himself against running again once and for all.

The journey to Hyde Park took Farley through Rockland County, where he was born and grew to manhood, evoking memories of his parents, his Catholic boyhood, and his years of work in the family's bricklaying business before he entered politics and achieved, as he put it, "greater success than I had dreamed of." Rising steadily through the ranks of the Democratic Party, Farley was in 1928 and 1930 elected secretary and then chairman of the New York State Democratic Committee, where he played a major role in organizing the successful gubernatorial campaigns for FDR. Recognizing Farley's charm and great organizing talent, Roosevelt had chosen him to direct his presidential campaign in 1932 and then had appointed him postmaster general. In 1936, Farley once again directed Roosevelt's tremendously successful campaign, and increased his reputation as a political genius by correctly predicting that the president would carry all but two states. In the past year, however, primarily because of Farley's known opposition to the idea of a third term, relations had cooled to the point where, that very morning, the newspapers had carried a story that Farley would soon resign his Cabinet post to go into private business.

The temperature was ninety-five degrees when Farley reached the president's home. There, still playing the role of the gracious hostess, the president's mother was waiting for him on the broad front porch. Dressed in black lace, she grasped Farley's hand in a warm welcome and then lost no time in asking him if there was any truth to the story that he was thinking of leaving the Roosevelt administration to head the New York Yankees.

"You know," she said, using her hands to emphasize what she was saying in the same way her son did, "I would hate to think of Franklin running for the Presidency if you were not around. I want you to be sure to help my boy."

"Mrs. Roosevelt, you just have to let these things take their course," Farley answered.

But letting things take their course was not in Sara's character. If her son wanted a third term, then everything should be done to make it happen. As Sara and Farley were talking, Harry Hopkins and Missy LeHand came downstairs, and the small party moved into the entrance hall, bordered on one side by a large glass case containing a collection of birds Franklin had shot and stuffed as a boy, on the other by the young man's collection of early-nineteenth-century naval prints.

Since the president was not home from church, Sara led her guests into the spacious living room, which she and her son had designed as a showcase for the family's fifteen thousand leather-bound books, the president's rare coins, and his treasured stamp collection. At the center of the elegant room, flanking the stone fireplace, stood two highback chairs—the one to the left was Sara's; the one to the right, Franklin's; Eleanor was forced to find a chair wherever she could. After all these years, Sara was still the mistress of the house.

Half an hour before lunch, a Chinese gong was tapped, and it was rung once again five minutes before the food reached the table. At the second ring, the banter stopped as Sara led her guests into the dining room, with its heavily carved dark sideboards, and chairs whose leather seats were too well worn for comfort.

At that moment, Eleanor came downstairs. Greeting Farley in the hallway on the way in, she told him she was "both pleased and shocked by the news" in the morning papers that he was leaving politics and going into business. "Of course, I am pleased to have anything happen to you which would be personally beneficial, but I am shocked at the thought you may not direct things in the coming campaign," she said.

Eleanor liked Farley. The jovial party chief was as forthright and simple as Franklin was labyrinthine and complex. Furthermore, she believed her husband was largely to blame for the rift that had grown between the two. Eleanor was still talking with Farley when the president returned from church. Guiding everyone into the dining room, Franklin sat at one end of the table and Sara at the other. In the dining room as in the living room, Eleanor had no seat of her own but simply found a place as best she could —on this occasion, next to Harry Hopkins. "There was a lot of good-natured conversation during the meal," Farley recalled. "Somehow a discussion of Andrew Jackson was raised, during which the President recalled how the hero of New Orleans was attacked on the question of the legality of his wife's divorce. The President's mother pricked up her ears at the mention of divorce, and after listening for a moment or two, turned to me and said: 'My heavens! I didn't know they had such bad things as divorce so long ago.' "

Having had her own way for so many years, Sara tended to say exactly what she thought, speaking in a straightforward, undiplomatic manner. Once, in the middle of a lunch at Hyde Park, a young visitor turned to Eleanor and said, "Mrs. Roosevelt, what is the President going to do about the budget?" Eleanor stopped to think for a moment and at the end of the table Sara suddenly spoke up. "Budget, Budget? What does the child mean? . . . Franklin knows nothing about the budget. I always make the budget." On another occasion, when the flamboyant governor of Louisiana, Huey Long, was monopolizing the luncheon conversation, Sara glanced at him from head to foot, taking in his striped suit and his polka-dotted tie. Then, in a loud stage whisper, she said to the guest beside her: "That's the reason why I didn't want Franklin to go into politics. He has to deal with such dreadful people."

After lunch, the president asked Farley to join him in his study, a narrow room off the back hall that had been his school room as a boy. The room was small but it contained all the president needed: a comfortable old chair, a big desk, a few mementos of his earlier career, including the placard he had carried for Woodrow Wilson at the Democratic convention in 1916 and the books he wanted near by. "Everything right within reach," he liked to say. From this cluttered room, so unsatisfactory for press conferences that reporters tumbled onto the porch outside, forced to relay the questions and answers back and forth, the president directed the affairs of the nation during the nearly two hundred visits he made to Hyde Park during his presidency. Over the years, Sara had begged him to let her fashion a study befitting his high political office. But he liked the tiny room exactly as it was, the perfect size for his crippled body to maneuver in and manipulate the movements of others.

The midday sun was so hot that before settling down to talk both the president and Farley took off their coats and ties. For the first ten minutes, pictures were taken of the two men smiling and laughing. As soon as the photographers left, however, there was a heavy silence, until the president approached the unpleasant task of admitting to Farley—indirectly, of course —that if the convention nominated him for a third term he would indeed run.

"Jim," the president began, starting off, typically, at the opposite end of what he meant to say, "I don't want to run and I'm going to tell the convention so. You see I want to come up here," he added with a smile, directing his eyes through the open window of his study toward the woods and the Hudson River far below. The house at Hyde Park was at its most beautiful on summer afternoons. It was there under the blossoming trees that he had read as a child, there in the woods that he had first learned to ride a pony, and everything today was just as he remembered it from his boyhood.

Now, Farley was as sentimental as any politician, but, having promised himself that he would not succumb to the president's charm, he cut Roosevelt short. If the president made his wish not to run specific, Farley asserted, the convention would not nominate him. All that was needed was Roosevelt's word. Farley went on to enumerate the reasons he believed a third term would be devastating to the Democratic Party. The president, Farley said, was making it impossible for anyone else to be nominated by refusing to declare his intentions one way or the other.

Mopping his face with a handkerchief, Roosevelt finally asked what Farley would do if he were in the president's place. "In your position," Farley bluntly responded, "I would do exactly what General Sherman did many years ago—issue a statement saying I would refuse to run if nominated and would not serve if elected."

" 'Jim,' Roosevelt said, his right hand clasping the arm of his chair as he leaned back, his left bent at the elbow to hold his cigarette and his face and eyes deadly earnest, 'if nominated and elected, I could *not* in these times refuse to take the inaugural oath, even if I knew I would be dead within thirty days.' "

With this statement, Farley had the information he had come for—Roosevelt was definitely planning to run for a third term. There was a pause, and then Farley resumed the conversation. "Now I am going to say something else you won't like. . . . I am going to allow my name to go before the convention. . . . I feel I owe it to my party."

On hearing the unwelcome news, which smashed his hope to be drafted by acclamation, the president simply nodded, making no attempt to change Farley's mind. When it was clear the discussion was exhausted, Roosevelt thrust out his hand to Farley and said, "Jim, no matter what happens, I don't want anything to spoil our long friendship."

•   •   •

The weekend before the Democratic convention was set to open in Chicago, the president invited Missy, Dr. Ross McIntire, White House speechwriter Sam Rosenman, and two friends of Missy's, the Bartletts, for an overnight cruise on the *Potomac,* announcing to anyone who would listen that he had absolutely no plans to attend the convention. Despite Farley's intention to "fight" him for the nomination, the president refused to ask the delegates to vote for him, believing that, at the very least, he deserved a spontaneous draft as a show of warmth and affection from the party he had led so well for so many years. At the same time, he knew that he would be stronger in the general election the less anxious he seemed for a third term, which both Washington and Jefferson had refused.

Never leaving anything to chance, the president sent Harry Hopkins to

Chicago. In the troublesome days to come, Roosevelt would insist that Hopkins had been given no authority to act on the president's behalf, that he was simply there to listen and report back to the White House. But once Hopkins got to Chicago and installed himself in a third-floor suite in the Blackstone Hotel with an open wire to Roosevelt in his bathroom, everyone assumed that Hopkins was acting for the president.

From the outset, Harry Hopkins found himself in an untenable position, as bewildered delegates, looking for some word, any word, from FDR, came knocking on his door at every hour of the day. "There was a great deal of news emphasis laid upon the appearance of anybody at Hopkins' headquarters," Frances Perkins recalled. "If anybody turned up there, that was news and in the papers, whereas the regular officers of the convention, even [FDR fund-raiser Frank] Walker and [Bronx boss Ed] Flynn, didn't have as many newspapermen watching their door as watched Hopkins' door." The most glaring contrast was provided by the Farley offices across the street in the Stevens Hotel. DNC Chairman Farley's suite normally would have been the hub of the convention, but so large was Roosevelt's shadow even without an announced intention to run that Farley's rooms remained, in his own words, "as deserted as a church at the setting of the sun." A few delegates came to pay their respects to the big party chief, but even these few, Farley noted, seemed "timidly ill-at-ease."

Since the delegates did not dare to criticize the president directly, "the man who got all the dead cats and overripe tomatoes was Harry Hopkins," reporter Marquis Childs observed. "There was bitterness among the organization leaders at [Hopkins'] presence there," Ed Flynn admitted. "While they had nothing against him personally, in fact a great many of them were fond of him, they felt that he, representing the President, distinctly lowered their prestige. . . . They considered [Hopkins] an amateur."

To be sure, Hopkins' lack of experience did produce mistakes. A seasoned political hand would have called on Farley at once, but Hopkins let several days go by before sending word through a whispered message that he would like the chief to come to his suite. "If Harry Hopkins wants to see me," the proud Farley exploded, "he can see me in the office of the Democratic National Committee where everybody else sees me." The next morning, Hopkins came to call on Farley, but by then Farley was so hurt and angry that nothing was accomplished.

"He threw one leg over the arm of a chair at my desk," Farley recalled. "He looked tired; his eyes were sunk deep in his pallid face; his scanty hair looked as though it had been combed with his fingers. He was restless, constantly fingering a cigarette." The haggard look was familiar, but the difficulty with words was not. "Well," Hopkins finally blurted out, "what I want to say is that whatever you may hear, the Boss wants you to run the campaign."

"Be that as it may," Farley replied, making it clear that he was still determined to have his own name placed in nomination, "I can't discuss it with you."

• • •

The weekend cruise of the *Potomac* might have seemed a rest from the hubbub in Chicago, but on July 13, with Sam Rosenman aboard, it was obvious that the president was intending to work on a message to be delivered to the convention.

During both of the previous conventions, in 1932 and 1936, Roosevelt had relied on Rosenman, a graceful writer and a clear thinker, for help with both the party platform and the acceptance speech. The task at hand now, as Roosevelt explained it to Rosenman on the quiet journey down the river, was a statement to the delegates confirming that he was not actively seeking a third term and that he wanted them to feel free and clear to vote for whomever they wanted. Though Hopkins and Jimmy Byrnes feared that the president's posturing might open the door for someone else to receive the nomination, Roosevelt stubbornly insisted that, unless the convention came to him with an overwhelming show of support, he would refuse the nomination.

As Rosenman set to work on the statement, the president read the newspapers, fished, perused his stamps. "One would never imagine that significant political history was being made," Rosenman observed, "by the calm, thoughtful man" sitting in the stern relaxing with his hobbies. In the evening, after dinner, to his great delight, the president caught a rock bass and an eel. Then, while Missy and her friends adjourned to an upper deck, he rolled up his shirtsleeves and got to work on the brief message that Rosenman had drafted.

Missy tried to turn her mind from the distressing business of the convention. More and more, she saw, her boss was leaning toward a third term. For months, Missy had been living with the happy thought that, when the president's second term was over, she would accompany him to Hyde Park. In Missy's eyes, a friend observed, "Top Cottage was the most cherished spot in all the world, the first home that could truly be hers as well as his." Though she relished the excitement and prestige of her position in the White House, she loved Franklin more. Her whole existence was wrapped up in him, and she knew that, once they were back at Hyde Park, she would have much more time to spend with him alone.

It was now sixteen years since the languid days Missy and Franklin had spent together on the *Larooco* (the seventy-one-foot houseboat he had purchased in 1924, during his convalescence from polio) so he could sun, bathe, and fish in the warm waters off the Florida coast. Four months each winter for three years, Missy had served as Franklin's hostess on the boat, sharing conversations with the guests who regularly came aboard, sitting by his side as he fished off the deck, providing warmth and understanding when the frustrations of his paralysis broke through his cheerful exterior. "There were days on the *Larooco*," Missy later admitted to Frances Perkins, "when it was noon before he could pull himself out of depression and greet his guests wearing his light-hearted facade."

Eleanor had accompanied Franklin for two weeks during the first winter's cruise, but the aimless days drove her crazy and she hated every minute of the trip. "I tried fishing but had no skill and no luck," she recalled. "When we anchored at night and the wind blew, it all seemed eerie and menacing to me." Far better for everyone concerned, she decided, if Missy stayed aboard while she returned to New York, where she could keep Franklin's name alive by attending meetings, making speeches, and talking with political leaders. Franklin's mother had objected at first to this curious arrangement in which Missy was clearly the "wife" for months at a time, but Eleanor was thankful for the freedom it afforded her to shape her days as *she* wanted them.

The desultory pattern of the years from 1924 to 1927 was such that, after the winter's cruise came to an end, Franklin and Missy moved directly to Warm Springs, Georgia, a resort community where spring water came out of the ground at a soothing eighty-six degrees, winter and summer alike, providing therapy for crippled patients and relaxation for wealthy vacationers. Still searching for the elusive cure that would restore power to his legs, Roosevelt had first journeyed to the little community on the side of a mountain in the autumn of 1924, after hearing that the healing waters had made it possible for a fellow polio victim to walk again.

"Warm Springs was not much beyond the horse-and-buggy stage in those days," recalled Egbert Curtis, manager of the Warm Springs property. "The little whitewashed cottages were dilapidated, and the single hotel in town was pretty run-down, but Roosevelt loved the place the moment he saw it, so much so that he decided to invest money in it, with the idea of sprucing it up and turning it into a national resort."

Eleanor accompanied Franklin on his first visit to Warm Springs, but her reaction to the small Southern town was as negative as her husband's was positive. It was later said that Eleanor began asking questions about the plight of the poor blacks in the town as she rode from the train station the first night; and that once she started asking questions, she never stopped. "We didn't like her one bit," one Southern lady admitted. Between the harsh segregation, the suffocating poverty, the Spanish moss, which she hated, and the sound of the Southern drawl, which grated on her ears, Eleanor could not wait to get away.

It was Missy who stayed by Franklin's side in Warm Springs, as elsewhere, cheering him on as he underwent a daily regimen of exercise in the healing waters, hoping against hope to strengthen his legs to the point where he could walk on his own power again. "I can still remember the day he almost made it," Egbert Curtis recalled. "We had a substitute head nurse that day, a large woman. He braced himself against one wall in the living room, and the nurse walked backward in front of him. Slowly, ever so slowly, he forced his body across the room—one inch at a time, it seemed. He was so drenched with sweat that I was afraid he would collapse from exhaustion. I've always believed that something happened that day, that, while he pretended it was a triumph, the effort to simply inch his way forward was so monumental that this was the moment he knew he would never really walk again. It was not long after this, in fact, that he decided to return to New York and get back into politics, a decision that effectively brought an end to his physical recovery. I remember looking at Missy's face while he was trying to walk. She was in tears."

In the spring of 1927, Roosevelt decided that he had had enough of the pleasant but purposeless existence on the houseboat. The *Larooco,* damaged by a hurricane the previous winter, was sold for junk. "So ended a good old craft with a personality," Roosevelt wrote.

Missy was devastated by the sale of the *Larooco.* The pattern of her life with the man she loved was being disrupted, and there was absolutely nothing she could do about it. That June, she collapsed in her cottage at Warm Springs. It was thought at first to be a mild heart attack, a consequence of the rheumatic fever she had suffered as a child, but though her "heart action quickly improved," as Roosevelt noted in a letter to his mother, she began experiencing alarming bouts of delirium and depression. It was "a little crack-up," secretary Grace Tully later admitted; "a nervous breakdown," in the words of Missy's high-school friend Barbara Curtis.

So severe was Missy's disorientation that the doctor at Warm Springs, Dr. LeRoy Hubbard, ordered her hospitalized and had removed from her hospital room every object that she could use to harm herself. For weeks, while Roosevelt returned to Hyde Park for the summer, Missy remained under the doctor's care. In early July, her brother Bernard LeHand found her greatly improved. "I had a most enjoyable afternoon with Missy on the lawn," he wrote Roosevelt. "She of course has not regained the strength—therefore moves and acts very deliberately and calmly but such an improvement. Just herself—that's all ... [She] can read. ... Remembers everything—in detail except for the first eleven day period at the hospital during which time she is hazy on happenings except perfectly conscious of her deliriums. Since the 28 of June has been normal—and it was her own suggestion that visitors be excluded until such time as she was convinced that she had "arrived." Conscious of her own condition ... She would like her fountain pen. A pencil does not appeal to her, although a pen is really considered a dangerous 'weapon.' I am confident that you will decide to take her to Hyde Park for August."

By November 1927, Missy's strength had returned and she was able to go back to work. The storm had passed. "Except for a few intervals, I never thought of her as unhealthy," Egbert Curtis confirmed. "She was always so cheerful and so vigorous that she made everyone else feel good. What amazed me always was the amount of wit and laughter that flew around in her presence."

But the following autumn, the pattern of Missy's life was jolted again when Roosevelt yielded to pressure and agreed to run for governor of New York. It was October 1928; Roosevelt was in Warm Springs, and the Democratic State Convention was about to convene. New York Governor Al Smith, the Democratic incumbent, had received his party's nomination for president, so the governor's race was up for grabs. Believing that the magic Roosevelt name would generate a large turnout, the Democratic leaders pleaded with Roosevelt to run.

From the beginning, Missy was opposed to his running for governor, believing it would end forever his chances to recover and cut short the time she was able to spend with him. "Don't you dare. Don't you dare," she told him again and again. He seemed at first to agree with her, reckoning that he still needed another year of therapy on his legs.

For days, Roosevelt deliberately stayed out of touch with the party leaders in New York, stealing away for long picnics far out of the reach of the single telephone which stood in the lobby of the old hotel. In desperation, Smith called Eleanor at Hyde Park, imploring her to reach her husband and persuade him to accept the nomination. Eleanor agreed to communicate with Franklin and see if she could get him to talk to Smith. Her message reached him while he was giving a speech in a small town ten minutes from Warm Springs. Franklin returned at once to Warm Springs, where, assisted by Egbert Curtis, he made his way into the phone booth at the old hotel to call Smith. "He was in there a long time," Curtis recalled. "When he finally came out he looked very agitated and was wringing with sweat. 'They want me to run for Governor and that is the last thing I want to do,' he said. I asked if he had accepted. 'Curt, when you're in politics you have to play the game,' he replied."

Roosevelt's decision to run for governor represented a final victory for Eleanor in the long struggle with her mother-in-law provoked by Franklin's polio. Sara was convinced that Franklin should preserve his remaining strength by giving up all thought of a career and settling down at Hyde Park as a gentleman farmer, while both Eleanor and Louis Howe felt strongly that he should resume his political activities and continue to lead a useful life. "My mother-in-law thought we were tiring my husband and that he should be kept completely quiet," Eleanor recalled. "She always thought that she understood what was best particularly where her child was concerned."

"I hated the arguments," Eleanor later admitted, "but they had to happen. I had to make a stand." The struggle over Father's recovery was *the* big issue, Anna observed, against which everything else paled into insignificance. "Father sympathized with mother," Jimmy observed; he was determined to ignore his disability and carry on where he left off. "Ultimately," Jimmy concluded, "he came to admire his wife more than he did his mother."

Within days of Roosevelt's decision, Missy fell ill once again, suffering what was probably a second nervous breakdown. The collapse prevented her from taking part in his successful campaign, but by January she had recovered sufficiently to move into the Governor's Mansion, where, with Eleanor's full support, she was allocated a bedroom of her own on the second floor, right next to FDR's master suite.

• • •

Missy went on to become the most celebrated private secretary in the country. "Marguerite LeHand is the President's Super-Secretary," *Newsweek* announced in an adulatory article written five months after Roosevelt became president. Missy's genius was not simply in doing everything she was asked to do with exceptional skill, but in anticipating the wants and needs of her boss before he knew them himself. She was known to interrupt the most statesmanlike conference on occasion to announce that the time had come for him to take his cough medicine, or to advise him to put on his jacket because of the draft.

"If she thought he was getting pretty tired or stale" from the strain of daily work, Sam Rosenman recalled, "she would arrange a poker game, or invite some guests in whom he liked. He wouldn't know anything about it until maybe six that night. Had she asked he would have said, 'No, I have too much to do.' Acutely sensitive to his moods and feelings, she would know when to bring out the stamps so he could work with them. She would know when to arrange picnics. She was, all in all, fairly indispensable."

"We loved Missy," White House maid Lillian Parks recalled, "because she was so much fun. She could always find the humor in things. They always had bets going and FDR would get up pools and cheat to win before he was found out and had to pay up. She made every day exciting for FDR."

One of the president's sweetest pleasures was to get behind the wheel of his special automobile, which had been designed for him by Ford so that it could be operated by hand levers instead of foot pedals. From all accounts, however, Roosevelt was a dreadful driver, so bad that many of his friends and relatives, including Eleanor, refused to ride with him. But Missy loved nothing more than to accompany him on a late-afternoon spin, sharing his delight as he revved up the motor and left his handicap behind.

At dinner, if Eleanor was away, Missy presided as the president's hostess. "She always did it the right way," the president's cousin Margaret Suckley recalled. "She had great tact. She knew when to escort people in, how to seat a table, and how to keep the conversation going with charm and ease. She was very gracious in handling people." She could get along with anybody, her friend Barbara Curtis remarked, from the king and queen to the butlers and the maids. "Without making a point of it, she had absorbed certain upper-class mannerisms over time."

Though Missy would often have only minutes to change from her secretarial attire to her evening clothes, she took great pride in her appearance.

Her closet was filled with elegant clothes, including, one of her relatives recalled, a few fabulous nightgowns which she liked to wear as evening gowns. "Missy could be the most glamorous woman in the room," Lillian Parks observed, "her chandelier earrings swaying."

But to list all the things Missy did, numerous as they were, is to circumscribe her value in the White House. "Missy was an operator," journalist Eliot Janeway observed. "She was on terms of absolute equality with all the figures she dealt with—[press secretary] Steve Early, [appointments secretary] Marvin McIntyre, [adviser] Sam Rosenman, [speechwriter] Robert Sherwood." Because her judgment of people was so "instinctively sound," the president valued her reactions on everything. Her shrewd observation that a sarcastic passage in a letter "didn't sound like him" smoothed many a ruffled temper. "She was one of the few people who could say 'No' to the President and say it in a way he could take," Rosenman said.

During the 1936 campaign, a turgid speech on finance had been prepared for the president to deliver at Forbes Field. With the speechwriters present, the president started reading the draft aloud. Before he reached the end of the second page, Missy stood up and announced: "By this time the bleachers are empty and the folks are beginning to walk out of the grandstand." As she walked out of the room, everyone burst into laughter. The draft was discarded.

Over the years, Eleanor had come to terms with Missy's primacy in Franklin's working life. "For some reason," Anna's son Curtis Roosevelt mused, "perhaps because Missy came from a lower social class, Eleanor was not threatened by her the way she was with Lucy Mercer."

At the same time, Eleanor knew that, without Missy to attend to Franklin's personal needs, the independent life she had labored to create for herself would be impossible to maintain. "Missy alleviated Mother's guilt," Elliott Roosevelt observed; "knowing Missy was always there allowed Mother to come and go as she pleased without worrying about Father or feeling she was neglecting her wifely duties."

For her part, Missy was ever mindful of the importance of staying close to Eleanor. "This is where Missy was a very, very astute little gal," Eleanor's daughter, Anna, later said. "Dearest ER," Missy wrote Eleanor one Christmas in the mid-1930s, "I have had such a happy year and I hope you know how very much I appreciate being with you—not because of the White House—but because I'm with you. I love you so much. I never can tell you how very much."

Still, there were moments of annoyance and resentment on both sides of this tangled relationship. Nor could it have been otherwise, since both women loved the same man. When Doris Fleeson wrote a long and flattering piece on Missy for *The Saturday Evening Post* which revealed the centrality of Missy's position in the White House, Eleanor resolutely refused to acknowledge that Missy had the slightest influence on the president politically. Only if Eleanor could tell herself that Missy simply did unquestioningly what the president asked her to do, could she accept Missy's role without feeling it intruded on her own role as the president's number-one adviser.

The question whether Missy's love for the president was a physical one has been the subject of many conversations within the circle of Roosevelt's family and friends, and opinion varies widely.

Though physicians examining Roosevelt after his polio attack specifically noted that he had not been rendered impotent by the disease, his son Jimmy believed that "it would have been difficult for him to function sexually after he became crippled," since the sensation in his lower body was "extremely limited." Further, Jimmy argued, he would have been "too embarrassed" to have sex, too vulnerable to humiliation.

Elliott disagreed with his brother's assessment. In a co-authored book written long after both his parents were dead, he alleged that Missy and his father had been lovers. "Everyone in the closely knit inner circle of father's friends accepted it as a matter of course. I remember being only mildly stirred to see him with Missy on his lap as he sat in a wicker chair in the main stateroom [of the *Larooco*] holding her in his sun-browned arms, whose clasp we children knew so well.... He made no attempt to conceal his feelings about Missy." From that point on, Elliott claimed, "it was no great shock to discover that Missy shared a familiar life in all its aspects with father."

"I suppose father had a romance of sorts with Missy," Jimmy countered in his own book five years later, "and I suppose you could say they came to love one another but it was not a physical love.... Elliott makes a lot of Missy being seen entering or leaving father's room in her nightclothes but was she supposed to dress to the teeth every time she was summoned at midnight? This had become her home, too and ... none of us thought anything about it at the time. Besides," Jimmy added, "if it had been a physical love, I believe mother would have known—she was very intuitive, you know —and had she thought it was, she would never have accepted the situation as fully as she did. The whole thing was pretty confusing and pretty complex."

Beneath the complexity, however, it is absolutely clear that Franklin was the love of Missy's life, and that he adored her and depended on her for affection and support as well as for work. In Missy's White House papers at the FDR Library, there is preserved a sweet note that captures the warmth and pleasure in their relationship. "From FDR to MAL: 'Can I dine with you? Or will you dine with me?' "

Despite these good times, Missy was ready for a change after eight years in Washington. "I think by 1940 Missy was tired of sharing the president with so many people," a friend observed. At Hyde Park, an ideal existence stretched before her, closer in kind to the happy days on the *Larooco*. Only a few months earlier, it had all seemed possible, but now everything seemed to be pointing to another term in the White House.

The presidential party returned to the White House late Sunday afternoon. The convention was scheduled to open the following day, but the heat in Washington that evening was so oppressive that it was impossible to work. Even the president, who rarely seemed to mind the heat, was so uncomfortable that he decided to watch a movie and retire early, postponing the final editing of his convention statement until morning.

•   •   •

While her husband sweltered in the heat of the capital, Eleanor was spending the week at Val-Kill, the fieldstone cottage Franklin had built for her on the grounds of the Hyde Park estate, enjoying "the most delightful July weather" she could ever remember, "warm enough in the sun to enjoy drying off after a swim, but cool enough so that even a good walk is not too exhausting."

It was a week Eleanor would long remember, for it marked the beginning of her intimate friendship with Joe Lash, a friendship that would endure until the end of her life, "as close a relationship as I ever knew Mother to have," Eleanor's daughter, Anna, observed. Though they had known each other for six months, the happy days they spent together that week in July, sitting for hours by the pool with their legs dangling in the water, walking through the woods in the late afternoons, and talking on the porch until long past midnight, put their friendship in a new light. From that moment on, the thirty-year-old Lash, young enough to be her son, became part of every plan Eleanor made for the future.

An intense, moody intellectual with brown eyes and black hair, Lash had been swept up by the revolutionary fervor of the 1930s. While still at City College, he had joined the Socialist Party. After receiving a graduate degree in English at Columbia, he had served as national secretary of the American Student Union, a militant popular-front organization committed to radical change in the economic and social order.

Eleanor first met the young student leader in November 1939, when he was called upon to testify before the House Un-American Activities Committee. "It was a confusing time for Joe," his college friend Lewis Feuer recalled. On the one hand, he was still committed to the radical program of change which united liberals, socialists, and communists in the popular front. But with the signing of the Nazi-Soviet pact, which gave Hitler a green light to invade Poland, he had lost his fervor for the popular front and had become increasingly disenchanted with his communist colleagues in the American Student Union, who were, he believed, mindlessly following the Soviet line in calling for an isolationist policy at home. The conflict in loyalties and the ideological crosscurrents revealed in his statement to the committee struck a responsive chord in Eleanor, who sat through the entire proceedings to assure the young people of her moral support. When the testimony was completed, she invited Lash and five of his friends back to the White House for dinner.

"It is funny how quickly one knows about people," Eleanor wrote Lash the following November. "I think I knew we were going to be friends . . . when I looked across the table at you about a year ago!" In the months that followed the hearing, Eleanor kept in touch with Lash, who resigned his position at the American Student Union in early 1940 and was trying unsuccessfully to find another job. "Joe was pretty vulnerable at that point in his life," Feuer recalled. "For ten years he had been a leader in the student movement and now, even though he believed he had done the right thing, he was isolated from his friends and colleagues."

Drifting aimlessly during the spring of 1940, Lash had trouble understanding why someone as powerful and strong as Eleanor would claim a special kinship with him. He recognized they were both fighting for the same goals, for a better order of things to emerge after the war. He shared the belief that the struggle for freedom must be carried on at home as well as abroad, but he could not imagine, in his depressed state, why she enjoyed having him around so much.

But as Eleanor opened up her heart to him that July week at Val-Kill, and shared with him the story of her own private melancholy and the deep convictions of inadequacy she had lived with all her life, Lash came to understand that it was precisely because he was having difficulty that she was drawn to him. "Perhaps . . . my miseries reminded her of her own when she was young. Insecurity, shyness, lack of social grace, she had had to conquer them all and helping someone she cared about do the same filled a deep unquenchable longing to feel needed and useful. Her children had grown up and moved away. The President was immersed in public affairs. She had a compelling need to have people who were close, who in a sense were hers and upon whom she could lavish help, attention, tenderness. Without such friends, she feared she would dry up and die."

There was a simplicity to the days at Val-Kill that Lash found delightful. When he arrived on Sunday, Eleanor met him at the train station in her riding habit. The management of the household was much less formal than the regime at the Big House. "There wasn't a lampshade that wasn't askew," one guest remembered, "and nobody cared if the cups and plates matched." What mattered was the cheerful atmosphere that pervaded every room of the only real home Eleanor had ever known. In the living room by the fire, she finally had a chair of her own, surrounded by a sofa, a set of easy chairs, a piano, and little tables covered with family photographs.

After an informal lunch served family-style, as all meals in the cottage were served, Eleanor led Joe outside for an afternoon swim in the big pool that stood to the left of the cottage, flanked by flowers and surrounded by lawn. At poolside they were joined by Eleanor's friend and former bodyguard from the Albany days, the handsome state trooper Earl Miller, and his fiancée, Simone von Haven.

After dinner, Eleanor and Joe sat together on the porch in the gathering dark and talked till midnight. Had Joe been close to his father? Eleanor wanted to know. The answer was no. His parents were Russian Jews who had ended up in New York City, in a small grocery store in Morningside Heights which kept them so busy that there was little time for family life. Joe was only nine when his father died. She talked with him about philosophy and his plans for the future. She gave him advice. Here was a perceptive and intelligent young man with whom it was easy and pleasant to talk, a sympathetic soul.

In the early days of her marriage, Eleanor had come to understand how absolutely Franklin guarded his weaknesses and vulnerabilities. Sensing this, she had gradually retreated from intimacy. With Lash, however, she felt free to expose her own vulnerabilities. Indeed, it seemed, at times, as if Eleanor were driven to tell her new friend the entire list of her inadequacies, describing in embarrassing detail the stories of her anguished past, sharing with him the terrors of the year she came out into society and had to attend all the balls, admitting that she had never felt comfortable in the Big House and that Mrs. James *still* did not approve of her public activities, on the grounds that she was not doing for Franklin what a wife ought to be doing.

Clearly, the young intellectual filled an emotional need in Eleanor's life. "She was entranced by discussing ideas without worrying about political consequences," Lewis Feuer suggested. "Joe Lash had a strong streak of idealism and a kind of romantic melancholy which she adored. I believe she sort of fell in love with him that summer and began to feel like a young woman again." In a letter written to Joe not long after convention week, Eleanor said: "I'd like you to feel you had a *right* to my love & interest & that my home was always yours when you needed it or anything else which I have. . . ."

For his part, Lash loved Eleanor, needed her, and idealized her as mentor, friend, and soul mate. "She personifies my belief and faith in the possibility of the social democratic way instead of the communist," he wrote in his diary. "At times there is a haunting beauty about her expression and profile," he observed. "Very much like the picture of her mother that adorns the hall." During one conversation, Lash hazarded that a hundred years from then her personal imprint on the nation would be as great as the president's. "Nonsense," Eleanor replied laughingly, "the function of women is to ease things along; smooth them over."

•   •   •

So it was that the president and his wife were hundreds of miles apart as the delegates assembled in Chicago's sprawling stadium on Monday, July 15. At the White House that evening, Missy played hostess in Eleanor's absence as the president and a small group of guests gathered in the upstairs study to listen to the live radio broadcast of Speaker Bankhead's opening address. At Val-Kill, Eleanor was similarly occupied in her own study, huddled by her radio with Tommy and Joe Lash by her side.

The mood at the convention, commentators noticed, was "strangely subdued." The delegates, so lively and expansive only four years before, had become irritable at the president's refusal to declare himself. They were worried about the popularity of the Republican presidential nominee, liberal businessman Wendell Willkie. They were worried about breaking the tradition of the third term. But there was no one else they could trust to steer the Democrats to victory.

Still, they muttered, if the president wanted a third term, why couldn't he simply come out and say so? "The President could have had anything on God's earth he wanted if he had the guts to ask for it in the open," a group of liberal newspapermen observed. "The people trust him and the people want to follow him; nobody, no matter how whole-souled, can follow a man who will not lead, who will not stand up and be counted, who will not say openly what we all know he thinks privately."

The ugly mood on the floor sent startled convention leaders back to their smoke-filled rooms to figure out what to do. From his private suite, Harry Hopkins placed a series of frantic calls to the president, advising him to drop his coy routine and to tear up the statement he had prepared insisting he did not want to be a candidate. "This convention is bleeding to death," Harold Ickes wired the president, "and your reputation and prestige may bleed to death with it." The only solution, Ickes counseled, with nine hundred "leaderless delegates milling around like worried sheep," was "a personal appearance" by the president.

The president flatly rejected both Ickes' and Hopkins' advice, insistent on "acting out his curious role to the last scene," determined, for the sake of the general election and for the historical record, to make it clear he was not actively seeking an unprecedented third term, demanding that the convention come to him of its own free will. "I have never seen the President more stubborn," Sam Rosenman recalled, "although stubbornness was one of his well-known characteristics."

The president's statement was given to Senator Alben Barkley to read, at the end of the keynote address, on Tuesday night. Barkley was originally scheduled to speak in the early evening, but the proceedings ran so late that it was nearly midnight in Washington before the senator from Kentucky approached the podium. When the president received final confirmation that Barkley was about to speak, he called Eleanor at Val-Kill. Could she listen to the statement and let him know what she thought? Taken by surprise at the whole idea of a statement, Eleanor roused Joe Lash from his bedroom to join her on the porch, where they set up her portable radio.

Alben Barkley was an orator of the old Southern school. He flailed his arms and his face grew red as he worked himself into an oratorical frenzy recapitulating the great achievements of the New Deal. Finally, he came to the climactic moment. "And now, my friends, I have an additional statement to make on behalf of the President of the United States." The president, Barkley said, wished to make clear to the convention that he had "no wish to be a candidate again" and that "all the delegates to this convention are free to vote for any candidate."

There was a moment of uncomprehending silence. In the end, the statement said neither yes nor no. Yet it was what the statement did *not* say that counted: nowhere did the president say that he would refuse to serve if nominated, nor did he officially recognize the power of the two-term tradition. Clearly, Roosevelt was in the hunt. Or was he? The delegates sat for a moment in their seats, uncertain what they were supposed to do. Then, from some loudspeaker not in view, a single booming voice shouted, "We want Roosevelt!" This was all that was needed to ignite the crowd, which picked up the chant and made it their own. "We want Roosevelt." "New York wants Roosevelt." "California wants Roosevelt."

The mysterious voice was later traced to the basement, where Edward Kelly, Chicago's mayor, had planted his "leather-lunged, pot-bellied" superintendent of sewers with a powerful microphone and detailed instructions to begin the stampede as soon as Barkley finished reading the president's statement. However contrived its beginning, the demonstration took on a life of its own. With state banners held aloft, the delegates formed a long parade which wound its way through the aisles, knocking down chairs, surging, singing, screaming. After a short struggle with the Farley contingent, the Massachusetts banner was seized from its holder and carried into the parade. Watching the wild scene from the stage, Farley's eyes were dimmed with tears. A similar struggle with Vice-President John Garner's supporters in the Texas contingent resulted in scores of men rolling on the floor in quest of the banner. And still the demonstration raged.

In the president's moment of triumph, Eleanor shook her head resignedly, knowing now that his nomination was a certainty. She did not see why the presidential statement had had to be made. Naïvely, she had never considered that the delegates to the convention did not feel entirely free to make their own choices regardless of what the president said. But, she admitted when she talked with her husband after the convention finally adjourned, there are times when "even obvious things may have to be said."

•   •   •

Despite the tumultuous demonstration, the delegates awoke on Wednesday morning feeling rightly that they had been used to serve the president's political purposes. If they were willing to shatter a tradition as old as the country and go down the line for Roosevelt, then, they felt, they deserved at the very least a personal appearance from the president.

"The President has got to come," Frances Perkins was told. "This thing is going to blow up." No matter if the president won the nomination, "he won't have the party back of him." With no prospect of the president's coming to Chicago, the leaderless crowd resembled a restless audience at the performance of a play without its leading man. The mood was definitely sour, Perkins agreed, as she picked up the phone to call the president and urge him to come, "to make a speech, receive a number of delegates and go away—that is, spread light and sweetness over it."

"Absolutely no," the president replied. "I wouldn't think of doing such a thing. I've said I won't go and I won't go. . . . Too many promises will be extracted from me if I go. They'll begin to trade with me. I can't do it."

When Perkins persisted, the president shifted the conversation. "How would it be if Eleanor [came]?" he asked Perkins. "You know Eleanor always makes people feel right. She has a fine way with her." Perkins thought that was an excellent idea. "Call her up and ask her," the president told Perkins. "She's pretty good about this kind of thing. . . . If she says no, tell her what I say, talk with me about it, but I don't want you to tell her that you've talked with me. Don't let Eleanor know that I'm putting any pressure on her."

Perkins reached Eleanor at dinnertime. "Things look black here," she told Eleanor; "the temper of the convention is very ugly. . . . I think you should come." When Eleanor demurred, Perkins insisted, telling her that things were getting worse by the moment, that the delegates would be reassured by her presence and "comforted if she thought what they were doing was right." Still Eleanor balked, although she agreed that she would call the president to talk it over with him.

Listening only to Eleanor's side of the conversation, Tommy thought it would be a terrible move for Eleanor to go. Never before had a first lady addressed a convention; at a time when the sacred two-term tradition was about to be broken, it made little sense, Tommy thought, to break another tradition as well. "I thought it was extremely dangerous," Tommy admitted later to Lorena Hickok. "I did not want to see Mrs. Roosevelt sacrificed on the altar of hysteria."

For his part, Joe Lash could not understand Eleanor's reluctance to go, just as he found it impossible to fathom her hesitancy about another four years in the White House. "For someone like me who loves politics so much," he admitted in his diary, "it is incomprehensible that she wouldn't want to be in Washington much less the White House." Patiently Eleanor explained her reluctance. Suppose she went and gave a speech and said some things the president later said. Immediately "the cry of 'petticoat government' would go up. She would be accused of making up the President's mind and it could get under the President's skin. It would get under anyone's skin."

"Well, would you like to go?" Roosevelt cheerfully inquired, when Eleanor called him, not wanting to ask for help directly if he didn't have to. "No," Eleanor replied, "I wouldn't *like* to go! I'm very busy and I wouldn't like to go at all."

"Well," Roosevelt responded, quickly shifting gears, "they seem to think it might be well if you came out." Then Eleanor asked, "Do you really want me to go?" And so, finally acknowledging that he needed her, he said, yes, "perhaps it would be a good idea."

So, like a good soldier, Eleanor agreed, on the condition that she could call Farley first and see how he felt about it. Knowing there was bad feeling, she later wrote in her memoirs, because "Harry Hopkins has been more or less running things and perhaps has not been very tactful," she was "not going to add to the hard feelings." When Farley heard Eleanor was calling, he was so "overcome with emotion" he was unable at first to speak. At last, he told her it was perfectly all right with him if she came and, from the president's point of view, it was essential. They would delay the vice-presidential nomination until after she had spoken. "Thanks, Jim, I appreciate this. I'll come," she said.

That night, Roosevelt's name was placed in nomination, along with the token candidacies of Farley, Vice-President Garner, Maryland Senator Millard Tydings, and Cordell Hull. The vote was a foregone conclusion: the president received an overwhelming majority of 946 votes on the first ballot. Only 150 votes were cast for all the other candidates. Yet, though the victory was Roosevelt's, the delegates reserved their emotions for the defeated Farley, who mounted the rostrum to speak. "Never had the delegates cheered more heartily," the *Washington Post* observed. "My name has been placed in nomination for the Presidency by a great and noble American," Farley began, referring to the frail but widely respected Virginia Senator Carter Glass, who had risen from his sickbed to deliver the nominating speech. "As long as I live I shall be grateful to [him]." But the time has come, Farley went on, to suspend the rules and declare Roosevelt the candidate by acclamation. The audience cheered and cried as the band struck up "When Irish Eyes Are Smiling" in tribute to the party chief. In her sitting room at Val-Kill, Eleanor sang along in a low voice.

In a revealing statement, Eleanor said that when she heard her husband nominated by acclamation she "felt as though it were somebody else's excitement and that it had very little to do with me." Eleanor was not alone in her sense of alienation. Because of the way the convention had been structured, because Hopkins had pressured the delegates to vote for the president without the presence of the president's assuaging charm, many of the delegates saw their vote as a command rather than a choice. They saw nothing else they could do. And they were right. But they didn't feel good about it.

Though the nomination had not come in the exact form Roosevelt wanted —the "draft" would never be able to shake off the quotation marks surrounding it, since votes had been cast for other candidates—it had been achieved nonetheless, and without the kind of party split that might have hurt the chances for victory in November. All in all, Rosenman recalled, the mood in the president's study that night was one of "general satisfaction and relief."

His nomination secured, Roosevelt turned at once to the vice-presidency. Though it was nearly 3 a.m., he told Chicago Mayor Edward Kelly that his choice was Agriculture Secretary Henry Wallace. Wallace, Roosevelt believed, was a dependable liberal, a good administrator, a deep thinker, and a fervent supporter of aid to the Allies. The response from Boss Kelly was not enthusiastic. To the party leaders in Chicago, Wallace was a babe in the political woods. He had started life as a Republican and only recently switched to the Democratic Party. "The party longs to promote its own," Frances Perkins observed, "and Henry Wallace was not its own. He wasn't born a Democrat. . . . They would have liked to have had somebody that came right up through the Democratic machine, who owed his whole life to them." But Roosevelt was adamant. Wallace was the man he wanted, he told Kelly, and then he went to bed.

Thursday morning, while the president was having breakfast, Harry Hopkins called to report that things looked bad for Wallace. The opposition was growing by the minute—already there were ten candidates with more votes than Wallace. It would be a cat-and-dog fight, Hopkins warned. "Well, damn it to hell," the president angrily replied, "they will go for Wallace or I won't run and you can jolly well tell them so." Then, turning to Rosenman, he said, "I suppose all the conservatives in America are going to bring pressure on the convention to beat Henry." Well—"I won't deliver that acceptance speech until we see whom they nominate."

By Thursday afternoon, July 18, as Eleanor was in the plane heading for Chicago, the convention had spun out of control. The galleries were packed with placards for a dozen different candidates, including Federal Loan Administrator Jesse Jones, Federal Security Agency head Paul McNutt, Jimmy Byrnes, and Speaker of the House William Bankhead. Everywhere one went, the name of Henry Wallace was met by jeers and catcalls. As Perkins interpreted the unruly situation, the ugliness was the result of Roosevelt's months of silence and the seeming hauteur involved in his failure to appear. "He not only wants to be nominated himself," the delegates seemed to be saying, "he wants to pick his own man. He doesn't want to leave that to the convention. He doesn't want to let us have a runoff here between our political racehorses." But since nobody could afford to show their resentment to the President, it was deflected onto Wallace.

By early evening, as Eleanor's plane was coming in for a landing in Chicago, the president was beginning to get "quite concerned," as Sam Rosenman put it, "about what might happen that night at the Convention." Jim Farley was the first to greet Mrs. Roosevelt as she stepped from the plane in a soft crepe dress and a navy cloth coat. The first lady paused to take some questions from reporters, and then followed Farley into a large sedan, complete with a motorcycle escort and a Chicago police guard of about fifty men.

On the way to the Stevens Hotel, Eleanor told Farley that she would miss him terribly in the upcoming campaign. She said she felt as though she had known him all her life and that she could always turn to him for advice. Thus reassured, Farley confided in her the slights he had experienced at Hopkins' impolitic maneuvers. Having been wounded by Hopkins herself in recent months, Eleanor understood Farley's pain.

Eleanor was brought into the convention hall on Farley's arm, "which was just the way it ought to be," Frances Perkins noted. "They were smiling at each other like obviously close friends." At the sight of the first lady, the entire convention rose to its feet in a rousing cheer. Acknowledging her warm welcome with a smile and a wave of her hand, Eleanor took a seat beside Mrs. Wallace on the platform just as the evening session was about to get under way.

Trouble began immediately. The first lady was scheduled to speak as soon as the nominating speeches for vice-president were finished. From the opening address for Speaker Bankhead, which evoked a demonstration far exceeding the expectations of a "symbolic candidacy," it was clear that the president's nomination of Henry Wallace faced an uphill climb. The situation worsened as names of other candidates were placed in nomination, each to loud, sustained applause. "The rebel yells grew in intensity," *The New York Times* reported, "and there seemed to be a determination, coming out of nowhere, to demonstrate for anybody not picked by the White House."

When the name of Henry Wallace was presented to the convention, the shouts and boos outnumbered the cheers as the delegates rose in rebellion against their president's choice. "It was agony," Frances Perkins recalled. "I shall never forget Henry Wallace's face as he sat there. . . . It was a dreadful thing to go through, terrible. There were catcalls, hisses, all the more vulgar and outward manifestations of dislike and disappointment. I never lived through anything worse. . . . He was listening . . . but his eyes were way off. . . . I remember thinking that his face and posture depicted the kind of suffering that a man in the Middle Ages being tried for some heresy which he couldn't understand might show. The storm was rolling over him and he had to take it. This was certainly nothing he had anticipated."

For Mrs. Wallace, attending her first national convention, the situation was incomprehensible. "Poor Mrs. Wallace was almost out of her mind," Perkins observed. "Her brain was reeling around inside her head. The antagonism and the ill will was a crushing thing, a very hard thing to bear. I remember seeing Mrs. Roosevelt take her hand."

"The noise in the room was deafening," Eleanor recalled. "You could hardly hear yourself or speak to your next door neighbor." At one point, Mrs. Wallace turned to Eleanor and said in understated fashion, "I don't know why they don't seem to like Henry."

How well Eleanor remembered her own discomfort at the first national convention she had ever attended, in Baltimore in 1912! Conventions, Eleanor thought at the time, should be seminars to debate ideas and policies, a "meeting ground of the nation's best minds." Instead, she found a raucous brawl, a fight between Woodrow Wilson and House Speaker Champ Clark that belonged in the gutter. When Clark's daughter was carried aloft through the aisles, arms and legs akimbo, in a procession of support for her father, Eleanor was "frankly appalled." Frustrated and uncomfortable, she left after only one day.

To be sure, Eleanor had traveled a long political road since 1912; the world of politics had become her world as well as her husband's. But the pandemonium at the 1940 convention was unlike any she had seen before. At this stage—as rumors spread that unless Wallace was nominated Roosevelt himself would not accept first place on the ticket—anything seemed possible.

•   •   •

The scene in the president's study was not a cheerful one. In silence, a large group of staffers listened to the disturbing reports on the radio. A card table had been set up in the middle of the room so the president could relax with a game of solitaire while awaiting his wife's speech and the vice-presidential balloting.

The president's figure, the expression on his face, and the tone of his voice all revealed fierce irascibility. The rebellion had captured the emotions of both the crowd and the commentators, who made it clear that the real target of the anger was not Wallace but the president's arrogance in forcing *his* man upon the delegates. "As the fight got more and more acrimonious," Sam Rosenman recalled, "the President asked Missy to give him a note pad and a pencil. Putting aside his cards he started to write. The rest of us sat around wondering what he was writing. We all felt a great desire to sneak around and read over his shoulders, but none of us succumbed to that temptation."

Finally, after writing in silence for five full pages, the president turned to Sam: "Put that in shape Sam," he said, a strained expression on his face. "Go on Sam, and do as I've told you. . . . I did not want to run and now some of the very people who urged me the most are putting me in the position of an office-hungry politician, scheming and plotting to keep his job. I'm through." He then returned to his game of solitaire.

As Sam walked out of the room into the corridor with the handwritten sheets in his hand, Missy, Steve Early, Pa Watson, and Dr. McIntire followed behind him, demanding to know what it said. At one point, Watson reached out his "hamlike paw and snatched the sheet of paper away from Sam," but Sam got it back and brought it over to a small lamp in the hallway. With Missy and Watson bent over his shoulder, he began to read.

It was a stunning document—a statement to the convention declining the presidential nomination—which he intended to deliver if Wallace lost. Interpreting the battle over Wallace as the conservatives' struggle for the direction of the Democratic Party, Roosevelt's statement argued that "until the Democratic party makes clear its overwhelming stand in favor of liberalism, and shakes off *all* the shackles of control by conservatism and reaction, it will not continue its march of victory." From the beginning of the convention, it claimed, the forces of reaction had been busily engaged in the promotion of discord. Now it was no longer possible to straddle the issue. The time for a fight to the finish had come. Therefore, "I give the Democratic Party the opportunity to make that historic decision by declining the honor of the nomination."

Pa Watson was apoplectic. "Sam, give that damned piece of paper to me —let's tear it up.... He's all excited in there now—and he'll be sorry about it in the morning. Besides, the country needs him. I don't give a damn who's Vice-President and neither does the country. The only thing that's important to the country is that fellow in there."

In trying to keep the president from doing something he would soon come to regret, Watson was playing the role normally assigned to Missy. Over the years, she had held up dozens of letters the president had written in anger and pleaded with him the next morning not to follow through. Most of the time, the president's fury had subsided and the letter was thrown away, but if his bad humor remained, she simply put the letter in the drawer of her desk and tried again in another day or two.

This time, however, Missy was absolutely delighted by the sudden turn of events. The poisonous atmosphere at the convention only reinforced her case. It was difficult enough for the president to lead with the country divided on foreign policy; it was impossible without the steadfast support of his own party. She had already seen the toll exacted on Roosevelt by the stress of the eight years; she feared a third term would deplete his energy and destroy his health.

"Fine, I'm glad," she said; the president was doing "the only thing he could do."

In the hallway, Watson continued to argue his case for tearing the paper up, but Rosenman refused. "Pa, I hope he never has to read this speech, but if I know that man inside," if Wallace loses, Roosevelt is going to read it, "and nobody on earth is going to be able to stop him." With this, Rosenman picked up the draft and went to his room to polish it.

When Rosenman returned fifteen minutes later, the president was still playing solitaire. "Pa Watson was almost in tears and looked at me angrily for bringing the sheets back," Sam recalled. "I suppose he had hoped I would run off with them and hide." By now, everyone in the room knew what was happening, and everyone, except Missy, told the president he was making a fatal mistake. But Rosenman knew it was hopeless to try to change his mind, for "if I ever saw him with his mind made up it was that night."

We will never know for sure if Roosevelt truly intended to withdraw or if his statement was simply a ploy. But one thing is certain: once the statement was delivered, events were likely to take on a life of their own, making it difficult for the president to turn things around.

• • •

It was 10:30 p.m. before the state delegates finished their nominating speeches. The plan was to have Mrs. Roosevelt speak first and then proceed with the balloting. But at the last minute, Frances Perkins and Lorena Hickok, the two women most instrumental in getting the first lady to come to Chicago, were overcome with panic. "Oh, she *can't* go now," Eleanor heard the two of them shouting just as FDR fund-raiser Frank Walker reached her chair to escort her to the rostrum. "It's a terrible thing to make her do." By now, the delegates were totally out of control, surging madly up and down the aisles, yelling and screaming. Surely this was not the moment to make history by inviting the wife of a presidential nominee, for the first time ever, to address a major political party conclave.

But Eleanor quietly rose from her chair, and when she reached the rostrum, a majestic silence fell over the tumultuous convention, perhaps the most heartfelt expression of respect and admiration the entire week. She knew before she started that the only hope lay in persuading the delegates to put their personal interests aside at a time when the country was facing one of the most severe challenges in its entire history.

Her words were simple and brief, but the stillness of the listeners testified to their eloquence. She began with an expression of thanks for Jim Farley. "Nobody could appreciate more what he has done for the party, what he has given in work and loyalty." She then moved directly into her message, which pleaded with the delegates to recognize that this was not "an ordinary nomination in an ordinary time," that the president could not campaign as he usually did, because he had to be on the job every minute of every hour. "This is no ordinary time," she repeated, "no time for weighing anything except what we can best do for the country as a whole."

"No man who is a candidate or who is President can carry this situation alone. This responsibility is only carried by a united people who love their country and who will live for it ... to the fullest of their ability." Without mentioning Wallace, she was reminding the delegates that, if the president felt that the strain of a third term might be too much for any man, and if he believed a particular person was the person best equipped to give him help, then they, in asking him to run again, must respect his judgment.

By the time she finished, the prevailing emotion of the crowd had been transformed. Genuine applause erupted from every corner of the room. Trivial hurts and jealousies subsided as the delegates recalled why they had chosen Roosevelt in the first place. All along, they had simply wanted some sign of appreciation for what they were doing, and now the first lady was giving it to them.

Eleanor's remarkable speech gave the delegates a chance to get their second wind, Alben Barkley said, and it put them in a much better frame of mind. Sam Rosenman agreed. Speaking for the admiring group in the president's study, he said the speech seemed to lift everything "above the petty political trading that was going on and place it on a different level, far removed."

As soon as Eleanor sat down, the balloting began. In the study, the president laid aside his cards and tallied the votes himself. The atmosphere was tense at first, as Bankhead took an early lead, but, with each state that was called, support for the president's choice grew, and by the end of the first ballot, Wallace had garnered a majority of the votes to become the vice-presidential nominee.

The mood in the president's study lightened perceptibly as Roosevelt phoned the convention and announced that he would deliver his acceptance speech within fifteen minutes. But first he asked to be taken into his bedroom to wash his face and change his shirt. The ordeal had taken its toll on the fifty-eight-year-old man, who, Rosenman noted, looked "weary and bedraggled, his shirt wilted from the intense heat." It took him only a few minutes to freshen up, however, and when he came out he was smiling and "looking his usual, jaunty, imperturbable self."

Excepting Missy, the entire group happily accompanied the president to the radio-broadcasting room in the basement. There, at 1:20 a.m. East Coast time, he finally told the convention and the entire nation that he would break the precedent of 175 years and run for a third term. Throughout his entire speech, which would take twenty minutes, Missy was in tears.

Seated before a battery of microphones, in a melancholy voice that sometimes grew emotional, the president gave his reasons both for accepting the nomination and for having kept silent for so long. When he was elected in 1936, he told the delegates, it was his firm intention to turn over the reins of government at the end of his second term. That intention remained firm when the war broke out in 1939. But "it soon became evident" that a public statement at that time announcing that he would not run again "would be unwise from the point of view of sheer public interest." So he waited, and then the German conquest of Europe occurred, and "the normal conditions under which I would have made public a declaration of my personal desires was gone."

"Lying awake, as I have on many nights, I have asked myself whether I have the right, as Commander-in-Chief of the Army and Navy, to call on men and women to serve their country or to train themselves to serve and, at the same time, decline to serve my country in my own personal capacity if I am called upon to do so by the people of my country. . . . Like most men of my age, I had made plans for myself, plans for a private life of my own choice and for my own satisfactions to begin in January 1941. These plans, like so many other plans, had been made in a world which now seems as distant as another planet."

Remarking later on the "painful humbuggery" of this passage, Hedley Donovan, a young *Washington Post* reporter, wrote: "Being highly eligible myself for the other draft, I couldn't grieve too much for FDR's lost private plans." But the speech was just right for the crowd that night, and when it came to the end, the cheering delegates rose as one.

Eleanor was seated on the platform throughout the speech, watching blue searchlights shed their glare on a huge drawing of the president's face hung on the west wall, listening along with everyone else. When her husband's last words came across the loudspeaker, she rose and cheered as the band played "Hail to the Chief." Then, as the weary delegates wandered home to bed, she was driven to the airport to return to Hyde Park.

As the plane began to taxi down the runway, a man came running frantically across the field. The president was on the phone in the hangar, wanting to thank his wife for the excellent job she had done. He was not effusive, Eleanor later recalled. That was not his way, though on several occasions he said to others: " 'Her speech was just right.' I think he thought that people should know by their own feelings when they had done well."

Harry Hopkins was on a second line, also filled with gratitude. When he volunteered that he knew he had made many mistakes, Eleanor frankly agreed. She had seen the hurt on Farley's face. "You young things don't know politics," she said. Then the plane took off.

The next morning, Roosevelt slept soundly until eleven o'clock, but Eleanor, feeling as if "it had all been a dream with a somewhat nightmarish tinge," was up for an early breakfast, though she had slept only a few hours on the flight. "What a schedule she has kept," Joe Lash marveled in his diary. "She was up til 3 a.m. Thursday, had breakfast at 9 a.m., took a plane to Chicago after her broadcast, spent a hot constantly on the go eight hours in Chicago, back to the plane and here for breakfast at 9:30. Now she's taking a bath and will be ready for a full day again which includes a swim, a column, letters, picnic with 30 Hudson Shore Labor School people and dinner with Mrs. James."

In the days that followed, Eleanor was, Tommy told Hick, "swamped with wires and letters of approval" for her speech. "Mrs. Roosevelt stills the Tumult of 50,000," one headline read. But perhaps the letter that meant the most came from Seattle, from her daughter, Anna. "Your speech practically finished me," Anna wrote. "By that I mean you did a wonderful job." She went on to say that the president's speech was very moving, too, although he sounded weary at first, but the point of her letter was to tell her mother how proud she was to be the daughter of such an extraordinary woman. Three days later, Anna wrote again. That morning, Anna related, she had received a letter from Eddie Roddan, a friend who had been at the convention. The letter asserted that "Mrs. Roosevelt *saved* the situation." "We could sense that you had done much more than make a speech, darling, but Eddie's letter makes us very curious to hear the story."

Only one sour note spoiled Eleanor's triumph. Apparently Harry Hopkins was so angry and hurt at what Mrs. Roosevelt had said to him that, Tommy reported, "he is sulking and will not come to Hyde Park." At a luncheon with Jim Farley a week after the convention, Eleanor explained the situation. "Jim, I'm going to tell you something I have discussed with no one but Franklin. Hopkins has complained to Franklin that he didn't like the way I talked to him in Chicago. You will remember I went directly to the Stevens with you and then to the convention, so that I didn't see him. From the Stadium I went directly to the airport. He called me at the airport to say how sorry he was that he did not get to see me. I told him that I was sorry that I didn't get to see him because there were some things I wanted to talk to him about. . . . I told him quite frankly I did not think he had political judgment and that he had helped create an unfavorable situation."

But the final word was Tommy's. "Gosh," she remarked, noting Harry's estrangement, "it seems hard to believe that adults can be so self-centered in a time like this."

For her part, Eleanor deliberately underplayed what she had accomplished. In a remarkably disingenuous column, she reported that the atmosphere in Chicago "was much like the atmosphere one always finds on these occasions. To me, there is something very contagious about the friendly atmosphere brought about by meeting old friends. I was delighted when Mrs. Henry Wallace arrived to sit beside me."

But the delegates at the convention and the people in the White House knew and appreciated the perilous task Eleanor had accomplished. "She is truly a magnificent person," Tommy wrote Hick, "and while you and I have always known that and admitted it, it takes a dramatic thing once in a while to recharge us. . . . Being too close to the picture very often dulls one's appreciation."

CHAPTER 6

"I AM A

JUGGLER"

"I am a juggler," Roosevelt once said. "I never let my right hand know what my left hand does." Throughout his presidency, he repeatedly displayed an uncanny ability to toss a number of balls up in the air and keep them afloat. Whereas critics decried his clever tricks as evidence of manipulation and deception, admirers considered such sleight of hand the mark of a master politician. Never would his juggling act be put to a more severe test than in the summer of 1940, when he had to deal with Britain's urgent request for destroyers, passage of a selective-service bill, the drafting of a controversial tax law, and, influencing all of them, a presidential election.

Almost no one, it seemed, had anything positive to say about life in the nation's capital that summer. Under the strain of a record heat wave which clung to the area for six weeks, flowers wilted, tempers flared, and a general mood of irritation settled over the city. The Capitol building was air-conditioned, but most federal offices and most residential homes in Washington were not. Under normal circumstances, particularly in an election year, when time for campaigning was needed, the politicians would have fled and the wheels of government would have ground to a halt. But this summer, with most of Europe at Hitler's feet, the usual flight from the capital was barred. "I shudder for the future of a country," one congressman commented, "whose destiny must be decided in the dog days."

Air conditioning had recently been installed in six of the White House rooms, including the president's study and bedroom, the first lady's suite, Hopkins' quarters, and Missy LeHand's bedroom on the third floor. But the president's chronic sinus problems were such that he could not work or sleep in an air-conditioned room. Even electric fans seemed to bother him, Sam Rosenman observed, so he would simply take off his coat and tie, roll up his sleeves, and perspire freely.

As he suffocated in the heat, Roosevelt was struggling to find a legal way to make the transfer of the fifty destroyers Churchill had requested in May. There was nothing America could do that would be of greater help to England, Churchill repeatedly emphasized during the summer. More than half the British fleet of destroyers had been sunk or damaged at Dunkirk; eleven more had been damaged in July. Without destroyers to protect its merchant ships from submarines, an island nation which imported every gallon of its oil and half its food could not survive.

Destroyers were also needed, Churchill told Roosevelt, to repel the expected German invasion. On July 16, Hitler had directed his generals to begin a massive air offensive against England with the goal of driving the Royal Air Force out of the skies in preparation for an invasion in mid-September. Night after night, German planes pounded the southern coasts of England, damaging airfields, dockyards, communication lines, and radar stations. (In a single night, the Luftwaffe hit six radar stations, but, not realizing how critical radar was to Britain's defense, the Germans did not pursue the attack.) Meanwhile, hundreds of German barges were moving down the coasts of Europe, convoys were passing through the Straits of Dover, and tens of thousands of German troops were gathering along the northern coasts of France. The Battle of Britain was under way.

The next three or four months would be vital, Churchill cabled Roosevelt on the last day of July. Britain had a large construction program in progress which would produce new destroyers by late fall or early winter. But until that time, only American destroyers could fill the gap. "Mr. President," Churchill concluded, "with great respect I must tell you that in the long history of the world, this is a thing to do now."

Roosevelt agreed. He told his Cabinet on August 2 that "the survival of the British Isles under German attack might very possibly depend on their getting these destroyers.'' But he faced what seemed an insurmountable obstacle. On June 30, when the Congress adopted the Munitions Program of 1940, which expanded the monies available to national defense beyond the fiscal-year appropriation, Senator David Walsh had attached an amendment stipulating that nothing could be delivered to a foreign government without the certification by Congress that it was surplus material unnecessary to American defense. The stipulation posed a special problem for the transfer of the destroyers Churchill wanted: five months earlier, in an attempt to ward off consigning these same destroyers to a junk heap, Navy Chief Admiral Stark had testified to Congress that they were truly essential to American defense.

During the discussion at the Cabinet meeting, Navy Secretary Frank Knox brought up the possibility of exchanging the destroyers for access to British bases in the Americas, in Newfoundland, Trinidad, Bermuda, and other places. The Cabinet responded enthusiastically to the idea of an exchange, but everyone still assumed, Roosevelt noted after the meeting, that this could not be accomplished without congressional authorization, and that ''in all probability the legislation would fail.'' A majority could be fashioned if members of the Republican minority were brought along, but that seemed unlikely given the bitter divisions that had paralyzed the Congress all summer long over the question of compulsory selective service.

• • •

A bill to create the first peacetime draft in American history had been introduced in both the House and Senate in June. Though no one familiar with the American military situation doubted the necessity of conscription, Roosevelt had been reluctant at first to take a strong stand, believing that aid to Britain had to be given first priority. ''It would have been too encouraging to the Axis,'' he explained to one of his advisers, ''too disheartening to Britain, too harmful to our own prestige to make selective service a matter of personal contest with Congress and be defeated.''

Arrayed against the draft was a potent combination of isolationists, pacifists, liberals, gold-star mothers, educators, and youth groups. Day after day, black-veiled matrons who called themselves the Mothers of the USA marched in front of the Capitol, vowing to hold a ''death watch'' against conscription. By the end of July, the opposition had grown so vocal, reporter Mark Sullivan wrote, that ''it was said the whole idea of conscription might die, unless Mr. Roosevelt comes to the rescue.'' War Secretary Stimson agreed: ''The President has taken no very striking lead,'' he recorded in his diary, ''and that is reflected in Congress.'' Indeed, so nervous was Stimson about the military weakness of his country that he found himself waking up at night in a cold sweat.

Finally, on the first Friday of August, Mark Sullivan reported, Mr. Roosevelt the president took precedence over Mr. Roosevelt the candidate. At his weekly press conference, the president endorsed selective service publicly for the first time. Typically, he began the conference by saying he had nothing important to announce. He talked good-humoredly about going to Hyde Park that weekend, then paused, as if this were all he had to say. Instantly the questions began, with a planted inquiry from Fred Essary of the *Baltimore Sun.* "Mr. President," he said, "there is a very definite feeling in Congressional circles that you are not very hot about this conscription legislation and as a result, it really is languishing."

In reply, Roosevelt unequivocally endorsed selective service and urged adoption of the legislation as "essential to national defense." Endorsement of the draft seemed on the surface a risky move for Roosevelt in an election year. "It may very easily defeat the Democratic national ticket—Wallace and myself," Roosevelt predicted in a private letter to a Democratic editor in Illinois. But Roosevelt could sense that public opinion was shifting and that the country was ready to be moved.

While Roosevelt backed the draft, Eleanor continued to argue for a wider form of national service available to both men and women through an expanded National Youth Administration and Civilian Conservation Corps. "To tie it up with military training alone," she wrote in her column in midsummer, "[is to miss] the point of the situation we face today. Democracy requires service from each and every one of us." In Eleanor's view, real national defense meant the mobilization of the country as a whole, so that every individual could receive training to help end poverty and make the community a better place in which to live. When Eleanor told Franklin's friend Harry Hooker this, he said he couldn't believe what he was hearing; that she was a dreamer to believe that either war or poverty could ever be eliminated. Undaunted, Eleanor took the subject up again in a column a few days later, trying to explain why so many young people were in opposition to the draft.

"The way it was written," columnist May Craig warned Eleanor, "it looked as though you shared their views against the draft. Reporters commented you were bucking the old man."

"I am not bucking the President," Eleanor replied, "but would like to see a wider service." Nonetheless, after receiving a memo from her husband telling her in no uncertain terms why the draft was essential, Eleanor made it clear in her next column that her desire for wider service did not mean she was against the draft. The question of selective service, she wrote, "is simply a question of whether or not we are going to get adequate defense against overseas attack. . . . We won't get it if we don't get selective service."

Once she understood how important the draft legislation was to her husband, Eleanor never wavered in her public support for his position. When her pet organization, the American Youth Congress, came out with a sweeping statement against the draft, she characterized it as "stupid beyond belief," and told *The New York Times* it would play "into the hands of the people who would like to see us as unprepared as possible." In reply, AYC head Joseph Cadden, who had spent many evenings at the White House talking with Eleanor, said, "We are all sorry to see Mrs. Roosevelt use angry invective instead of reasoned arguments. . . . We do not feel as Mrs. Roosevelt evidently does, that the supporters of conscription have a monopoly on wisdom when the fate of our democratic insititutions are concerned."

With White House backing, the draft legislation slowly began to move forward in the Congress in early August. But victory was by no means assured. Most observers agreed that the ultimate fate of the bill rested on the stance Republican nominee Wendell Willkie took toward it in his formal acceptance speech, which was scheduled to be delivered in Elwood, Indiana, on August 17. (Though the Republican convention had nominated Willkie in June, he had deliberately waited until August to deliver his acceptance speech, so that it could mark the official beginning of his campaign.) If Willkie came out in opposition to selective service and decided to lead the charge against it, there was little hope for passage. If he endorsed the bill, Senator Hiram Johnson of California predicted, "a dozen timid Democratic Senators and 50 election-conscious Congressmen will be free to support it, since it will no longer be a campaign issue."

"What Wendell Willkie thinks of conscription," the Scripps-Howard Washington correspondent reported in mid-August, "is becoming as much a Washington puzzle as was . . . Mr. Roosevelt's third term intentions."

The man whose views on the draft were so eagerly sought in Washington that summer was one of the most unconventional presidential candidates in the nation's history. A successful businessman, Willkie had no political experience. He had no organization. He had never been a candidate for public office before. He had been a Democrat for most of his life. And his internationalist views were in direct opposition to the powerful isolationist wing of the Republican Party. He had come into the convention with the support of only 3 percent of Republican voters, compared with 67 percent for the odds-on favorite, New York's District Attorney Thomas E. Dewey. But once the delegates came together in Philadelphia, his candidacy took on a life of its own, developing an unstoppable momentum, the *Washington Post* observed, "like nothing a Republican gathering has seen before." From an initial vote of 105 out of 999, Willkie climbed to a stunning victory on the sixth ballot.

Described by journalists as a "shaggy bear," Willkie stood over six feet tall and weighed 220 pounds. After graduating from Elwood High and Indiana University, he had developed an outstanding reputation as a courtroom lawyer for General Tire in Akron, Ohio, and then moved on to New York to become president of a billion-dollar utilities corporation, Commonwealth and Southern. Although in his early years he had been a progressive Democrat, a spirited supporter of Woodrow Wilson's New Freedom, as president of a giant utility company he found himself at fundamental odds with the New Deal's Tennessee Valley Authority. Possessed of charm, wit, and intelligence, he gradually emerged as a supersalesman for business in its fight against governmental interference.

"Nothing so extraordinary has ever happened in American politics," a dazed Harold Ickes wrote. "Here was a man—a Democrat until a couple of years ago—who, without any organization went into a Republican National Convention and ran away with the nomination for President. . . . No one doubts Willkie's ability. He is an attractive, colorful character, bold and resourceful. . . . He will be no easy candidate to defeat." The president agreed with Ickes' assessment, believing that the liberal Willkie was "the most formidable candidate for himself that the Republicans could have named."

* * *

It must have been frustrating for Roosevelt, who was accustomed to being the center of the country's attention, to realize that all action on the draft was stalled until Willkie delivered his speech. But with one door closed, Roosevelt managed to open another. On August 13, he convened what Stimson later called "a momentous conference" in the Oval Office with Stimson, Knox, Morgenthau, and Undersecretary of State Welles at which he announced that he had decided to go ahead with the destroyer deal without congressional approval. Though he knew he was opening himself to powerful criticism, he felt he had no other choice. His attempts to reach the Republican minority had failed, and Senator Claude Pepper, who had agreed to sponsor the destroyer bill, had told him the day before that the legislation had "no chance of passing." No one spoke against the president's decision, Stimson recorded in his diary, though "everyone felt it was a desperate situation and a very serious step to take."

In making this extraordinary decision to bypass Congress with an executive agreement, Roosevelt was fortified by a lengthy legal brief which attorney Dean Acheson had published in *The New York Times* on August 11. Acheson argued that the commander-in-chief had the authority to exchange destroyers for bases without congressional approval as long as the net result of the deal produced an increase in America's national security. And the president was the one who kept the accounts. Attorney General Robert Jackson confirmed Acheson's opinion. Referring to the president's twin powers as commander-in-chief of the army and the navy and head of state in relations with foreign countries, Jackson advised Roosevelt that the sweep of these combined powers provided adequate constitutional authority for the president to negotiate the destroyer deal without Congress.

On the basis of this advice, which was what Roosevelt wanted to hear, he decided to complete the deal, and then and only then tell Congress. Later that day, he cabled Churchill the good news that he was ready to transfer the destroyers provided Britain agreed to lease its island bases for ninety-nine years. Churchill accepted the proposal immediately. While the agreement was being negotiated, Roosevelt arranged a hasty summit meeting for August 17 with Canada's Prime Minister Mackenzie King. Roosevelt liked King and knew the Canadian leader would be helpful in working out the details of the transfer. Arrangements were made to hold the meeting in upstate New York so that Roosevelt could inspect the First Army maneuvers in Ogdensburg on the same trip.

But Roosevelt also had a little mischief in mind. By scheduling the summit for the same day as Willkie's acceptance speech, he hoped, he later joked, that he would "steal half the show." He did.

The president arrived in Ogdensburg at noon, accompanied by Secretary of War Henry Stimson. Immediately upon their arrival, a motorcade was formed, consisting of the president's car, five cars for guests, six buses for journalists, and nine trucks for photographers. Wearing a seersucker suit and a Panama hat, the president rode for five hours over a distance of seventy miles to inspect ninety-four thousand soldiers assembled in six divisions. At every crossroad in every hamlet, reporters observed, the presidential motorcade was met by scores of cheering residents, "girls in their prettiest dresses and men in their Sunday suits."

As the motorcade halted before the first of the six divisions massed to greet their commander-in-chief, ten thousand officers and men stood at attention in perfectly formed lines and squares, their field guns slanting skyward under brightly colored regimental banners that had once flown at such historic places as Gettysburg, Big Horn, and Meuse-Argonne. Twenty-one guns sounded a tremendous salute, and the division band played the presidential ruffles and flourishes. "The weather was beautiful, bright and clear and it made a fine sight," the seventy-two-year-old Stimson recorded in his diary. "I wished very much that I was . . . working with the troops instead of sitting in a motor car all day and watching them."

Beneath the impressive show, however, the situation remained desperate. During these exercises, as in the maneuvers the previous May, the troops were so handicapped by lack of equipment that they were drilling with broomsticks instead of machine guns, and driving trucks instead of tanks. More alarming was the condition of the men. Five of the six divisions assembled for these August maneuvers were undertrained, overweight National Guard units from New England, New York, and Pennsylvania. "They haven't got the bodies soldiers must have," one military observer reported. "They haven't got the psychology of the soldier. . . . Just because mechanized divisions race into battle with soldiers jammed into trucks, it doesn't mean that the soldiers are any good if they get out of the trucks with fat under their belts, short-winded and with legs that won't stand up for a hard march."

These troops were volunteers, Lieutenant General Hugh Drum explained to the president during a picnic lunch in the shade of the woods. Many of them had never fired a gun. During the daily marches, they were falling to the ground in great numbers from heat and exhaustion. During a maneuver the previous day, an inexperienced road-construction crew had inadvertently left fifteen dynamite sticks under a roadbed over which the president's train was scheduled to pass a few hours later. Fortunately, the mistake was quickly discovered.

The only answer, General Drum stressed, was conscription. "The voluntary system must be replaced by a national conscription system if we are to succeed. We are wasting our time and ignoring basic lessons of history by discussing volunteers vs. conscription systems. Let us not be blind to the realities. . . . The day when we could put guns into the hands of citizen soldiers, teach the manual of arms and send them to match their spirit and brawn against that of an enemy has passed."

The president could not have asked for better evidence of the need for conscription than the sight of these paunchy National Guardsmen, unaccustomed to life in the open, inexperienced at firing a gun. "The men themselves were soft—fifteen miles a day was about all they could stand and many dropped out," Roosevelt admitted to his newspaper friend L. B. Sheley. "Anybody who knows anything about the German methods of warfare would know that the army would have been licked by thoroughly trained and organized forces of a similar size within a day or two."

As the hour of Willkie's speech approached, an air of anticipation surrounded the presidential party. But in spite of the importance of the speech for the future of the draft, the president stubbornly made a point of being too busy to listen. At 3 p.m., as the broadcast began, one reporter observed, "the radio in the President's car was silent" and Roosevelt listened intently to a lecture by first army officers on the goals of the maneuvers. By not listening to the broadcast, the president was able to tell reporters searching for a reaction that he would have to read the speech first before commenting.

Willkie's speech, delivered under a broiling sun which had sent the mercury well above the hundred-degree mark before noon, was heard by a vast crowd of over two hundred thousand, assembled at Callaway Park, about two miles from the center of Elwood. From all over the Midwest these people had come, in sixty-three special trains, three hundred Pullmans, twelve hundred buses, and sixty thousand cars. By 5 a.m. the day of the speech, the surrounding cornfields looked like a refugee camp, with tens of thousands of men and women camped out on blankets or sleeping in their cars. A majority of the homes of Elwood had been turned into boarding houses, and the one hotel in town was long since filled. Along the main street of the town, storefronts were converted into hot-dog stands and souvenir shops hawking Willkie stamps, license plates, playing cards, bats, pillow cases, and glass tumblers.

As Willkie stepped to the front of the platform, facing a grove of trees under which thirty-five thousand people were sitting, with four times that number standing behind the seats, he received a tremendous ovation. Smiling broadly, sweat dripping from his forehead, he waited for the applause to subside. Then he began. "Today we meet in a typical American town. The quiet streets, the pleasant fields that lie outside, the people going casually about their business, seem far removed from the shattered cities, the gutted buildings and the stricken people of Europe. Instinctively we turn aside from the recurring conflicts over there.... Yet ... instinctively also ... we know that we are not isolated from those suffering people. We live in the same world as they and we are created in the same image.... Try as we will, we cannot brush the pitiless picture of their destruction from our eyes or escape the profound effects of it upon the world in which we live."

With these opening words, Willkie cast his lot against the isolationist sentiment so prevalent in the Midwest. He then went on to say he could not ask the American people to put their faith in him "without recording my conviction that some form of selective service is the only democratic way in which to assure the trained and competent manpower we need in our national defense."

This was exactly what the Roosevelt administration wanted to hear. "Willkie for Draft Training," the headlines would read. But Willkie went even further down the line with the administration, stating that he was in full agreement with the president's policy enunciated at Charlottesville of extending the full material resources of America to the opponents of force.

Even in the domestic section of his speech, where he criticized the New Deal's attack on business, Willkie emphasized that he agreed with the New Deal's minimum wages and maximum hours, with federal regulation of banks and the securities market, and with unemployment insurance and old-age benefits. It was only at the end, when he challenged Roosevelt to a series of debates, that the speech took on a partisan tone.

Listening with May Craig on a car radio, driving back to Hyde Park from New York City, Eleanor was impressed. "He has a good voice and speaks well over the radio," Eleanor observed. "It was a brave speech," Craig agreed. "Willkie is a strong man and he spoke strongly. One thing is certain. We have two unusual men from whom to choose our next leader."

By late afternoon, Roosevelt and Stimson were heading back to the president's train for the summit meeting with Canada's prime minister. The original plan called for the conference to take place in the two small vestibules in Roosevelt's car (one equipped for dining, the other for sitting) while the train remained in the yards at Ogdensburg. But at the last minute Ed Starling, chief of the White House Secret Service detail, noticed two huge gas tanks between the train and the river. Uncomfortable with the situation, Starling had the train moved to the quiet village of Heuvelton, where the president and the prime minister could talk undisturbed late into the night. Along the tracks, fifty National Guardsmen with fixed bayonets patrolled the area, while an army patrol boat stood watch on the St. Lawrence River. Outside the train, as the sun beat down, dozens of laborers worked round the clock, stuffing huge chunks of ice into the train's air-conditioning system.

When MacKenzie King and Jay Moffat, the American minister to Canada, arrived, a round of cooling drinks was served. The president, Moffat noted, was tired but exhilarated from his long drive across the hot country roads inspecting the troops. He wished, he said, that everyone who opposed the draft could see with their own eyes what he had seen that day—the proof that voluntary enlistments would not suffice. "He talked at random about whatever came into his head," Moffat recalled. "His talk on the whole was brilliant and the charm of the man, a happy blend of Chief of State, man of the world, and host, was never more vivid." He was anxious to get the full text of the Willkie speech, for the first reports were fragmentary.

At dinner, Stimson joined the president's party. In the middle of the meal, the text of Willkie's speech came in over the wire. All conversation stopped as the president read the speech. A broad smile came over his face when he reached Willkie's endorsement of both the draft and aid to the Allies. If this was true, the master politician declared, if Willkie was agreeing with the administration on all these issues, then "Willkie is lost." Historians in later years would agree with Roosevelt's instant analysis, considering Willkie's failure to delineate how he differed from the president a fatal blunder. But the men on the train that night were thrilled. Stimson described the speech as "able and courageous," and Moffat called it "a godsend."

The remainder of the evening, Stimson recorded, passed in a happy discussion of the destroyer deal. The president told the Canadian prime minister that he "had originally felt he would require the action of Congress in order to release the destroyers," but that he had decided to go ahead on his own. The two heads of state agreed that, once the agreement was signed, American crews should bring the destroyers to some place in Canada where they could officially be turned over to Britain. "Almost with tears in his eyes," King thanked the president and agreed to telegraph Churchill that night to send British crews to Canada at once to man the ships. Time was of the essence, for, even as Roosevelt and King were meeting, the sky in southern England had become "a place of terror, raining blazing planes, shell splinters, parachutes, even flying boots." And with each passing day, the RAF losses were mounting.

Roosevelt's discussion with King and Stimson lasted late into the night, after which the president and King went to sleep in adjoining compartments. The next morning, at breakfast, Stimson told Moffat that he had gone to sleep much easier as a result of the late-night talks. Indeed, so important was the destroyer deal in Stimson's mind that he dared to profess that "perhaps today would mark the turn of the tide of the war." In talking with Stimson that morning, Moffat observed in the old man a new energy: "the old war horse smelled the smell of battle, and rejoiced. It had given him a new zest in life."

In the days that followed, however, an unexpected obstacle arose when Churchill balked at the idea of announcing the trade publicly. He had no problem turning over his bases for destroyers, but he preferred to see the two transactions as two friends in danger helping each other with gifts rather than "anything in the nature of a contract, bargain or sale." If the bases were seen as payment for the destroyers, he told Roosevelt, "people will contrast on each side what is given and received," and since there was no comparison between the questionable value of the antiquated craft and the permanent strategic security afforded to the U.S. by the island bases, the prime minister would look foolish.

Roosevelt appreciated Churchill's predicament, but he also understood that the only way to win popular approval in America for the deal was to present it as a shrewd Yankee bargain. So Churchill was told that the U.S. Constitution made it impossible for the president to send essential weapons as a gift; the destroyers could only come as a *quid pro quo* in an exchange which added to the security of the United States. With no way out, Churchill agreed to the exchange.

•   •   •

There remained the problem of announcing the agreement to the Congress and the American public. "Congress is going to raise hell over this," Roosevelt predicted. He had hoped to keep the deal under wraps until the Selective Service Act passed the Congress, but by early September Great Britain's need for the ships was so urgent that he could no longer afford to wait.

The date he chose for the startling announcement was September 3; the place, the tiny vestibule of his private car on the Roosevelt train, forty-five minutes after he had departed from South Charleston, West Virginia, where he was inspecting restoration work being done on a long-abandoned ordnance plant. With no knowledge of the stunning announcement the president was about to make, *New York Daily News* correspondent Doris Fleeson observed that morning that Roosevelt's face had a yellowish tint and that he was irritable, which she interpreted as a sign of fatigue in a man of his genial temperament. After luncheon with the president on the first day out, financier Bernard Baruch confided in TVA head David Lilienthal that the president seemed to be "brooding about something"; his mind wasn't on what they were talking about, and twice he said that "he might get impeached for what he was about to do."

The mystery was solved at noon, when the president called a press conference in the sitting room of his private car. The room comfortably accommodated seven, the *Time* correspondent observed, but "twenty odd jammed in, jostling each other as the train rolled along." He did not have much to tell them, the president announced half-apologetically, his face unable to hide a smile at the enormity of the secret he was about to reveal. What he was going to relate, the president suggested, was "the most important event in the defense of the U.S. since Thomas Jefferson's Louisiana Purchase." He then went on to explain that in return for fifty destroyers he had acquired from the British the right to nine strategic bases. When the president was asked if the Senate needed to ratify the agreement, he said no. "It is all over. It is done." As the reporters raced from the room to file their stories, the drawn shade of the window revealed FDR, "massive-gray-headed; smiling," relieved that the thing was done.

As Roosevelt expected, the news of the deal provoked harsh criticism in Washington. While approving the trade in principle, Wendell Willkie denounced Roosevelt's decision to bypass Congress as "the most dictatorial and arbitrary of any President in the history of the U.S." The *St. Louis Post Dispatch* agreed, noting that Roosevelt had merely informed Congress of the agreement. "Note well the word 'informed.' The President is not asking Congress—the elected representatives of the people—to ratify the deal. He is telling them that it has already been ratified by him. Mr. Roosevelt today committed an act of war. He also becomes America's first dictator."

The news reached the House of Representatives just as the final debate was to begin on the draft legislation. The president's timing stunned even his staunchest supporters. "If Mr. Roosevelt can do what he likes with our destroyers without consulting Congress," Representative Frances Bolton argued in her maiden speech on the floor, "and we give him our boys, God alone knows what he will do with them." When she finished she received a standing ovation.

But as far as Roosevelt was concerned, the end justified the means. If fifty old destroyers which had been collecting rust and barnacles helped turn the tide of battle in Britain's favor, then the risk was worth taking. Churchill agreed, understanding as he did that, beyond the transfer of the ships, the deal represented "a decidedly unneutral act by the U.S." According to every standard of history, Churchill later wrote, the German government would have been justified in declaring war upon the U.S. for the destroyer deal. Explaining the deal to the Parliament, Churchill predicted that, from this moment on, the affairs of the British Empire and the U.S. would inevitably be mixed together, rolling along unstoppably like the Mississippi River. "Let it roll on," he cried, "full flood, inexorable, benignant, to broader lands and developments."

Even as Churchill spoke, the American destroyers, one reporter observed, "their four tunnels raking sharply, canvas caps laced over the black muzzles of anti-aircraft guns on deck, sleek brass-nosed torpedoes nursing dynamite death below decks," were arriving at the entrance to Halifax Harbor, where, "by the long arm of coincidence," Churchill joked, they were met by a British ship, carrying the first batch of British crews.

For days, American sailors had worked to give the ships a fresh coat of paint and stock them with every necessary piece of equipment. The British captains, weary from battle, were overwhelmed by the immaculate condition of the ships and the lavishness of the provisions. "There were coffee makers, china, silver and table cloths in the wardroom," author Philip Goodhart reported, "pencil sharpeners in the cabins while such unaccustomed luxuries as tinned asparagus, corn, chipped beef, clams, instant coffee, tomato juice and pumpkins bulged out of the store cupboards." At ten o'clock on the morning of September 9, the ships were decommissioned by the U.S. Army in a simple ceremony. Before noon, they were on their way to do battle in the Atlantic.

Fortunately for the president, the initial attacks against the destroyer deal were more than balanced by expressions of approval as the advantages to America in gaining the bases became clear. Though his technique was occasionally deplored, Roosevelt was universally praised for his skill in getting the better end of the deal. "We haven't had a better bargain," the *Louisville Courier Journal* exulted, "since the Indians sold Manhattan Island for $24 in wampum and a demi john of hard liquor." "The President's bargain," the *Washington Post* gleefully noted, "was the first major expansion of the American frontier since the Spanish American War."

Popular approval for the destroyer deal strengthened the hand of the president's supporters on conscription, as did rising approval of the draft in the polls, and when the vote was finally taken, first in the Senate and then in the House, the historic legislation passed by a comfortable margin.

• • •

Thus reassured on the twin issues of the destroyers and the draft, a confident and composed president headed for a weekend rest at Hyde Park. The old house was charged with excitement when the president arrived on the morning of September 7. The cause of the excitement was the presence of Crown Princess Martha of Norway. Tall and willowy, full of light and gaiety, the thirty-nine-year-old Martha looked, in the words of reporter Bess Furman, "exactly as a princess should look." Everything in her appearance, from her gray dress and her gold jewelry to her high cheekbones and chiseled mouth, bespoke good breeding. A handsome woman with large brown eyes, long lashes, and a clear complexion, Princess Martha was to become one of the president's most intimate companions.

Martha's birth, in Stockholm, had occasioned a twenty-one-gun salute in both Norway and Sweden to mark the arrival of the granddaughter of Oscar II, king of the combined union of Norway and Sweden. By the time Martha grew up, Norway and Sweden had ended their union, but the blood ties between the dynasties of the two countries remained strong. Martha's father was a Swedish prince, the younger brother of the Swedish King Gustav V. Her mother was a Danish princess, the younger sister of the Norwegian King Haakon VII. Martha was only a child when she met her first cousin and future husband, Prince Olav. As the only son of King Haakon, Olav was Norway's adored "little prince." Songs and poems were written in his honor, and his picture hung on every schoolroom wall. When Olav and Martha became engaged in 1929, Norway went wild with excitement. As the couple rode through the streets of Oslo on their wedding day, they were cheered by tens of thousands of jubilant spectators. The marriage soon produced two princesses, Ragnhild and Astrid, and a prince, Harald, destined one day to follow his father to the throne.

The royal family's reign had been brought to an abrupt end when the Nazis invaded Norway in early April 1940. For two months, the king and the members of the Parliament had bravely resisted German demands for surrender, moving deeper and deeper into the north woods to avoid capture. "I cannot accept the German demands," Haakon told his nation as the infuriated Germans tried to kill him. "It would conflict with all that I have considered to be my duty as King of Norway. . . ." When advancing German troops made it impossible for Haakon to hold out any longer, he and his son fled to London to set up a government in exile, while Princess Martha, concerned about the safety of her children, accepted an offer of asylum from President Roosevelt.

Roosevelt had met both Olav and Martha in the spring of 1939, when the royal couple traveled to the United States to dedicate the Norwegian exhibit at the World's Fair. From the first moment the president saw Martha, dressed in her favorite shades of gray, he was entranced by her good looks and her lively manner. No sooner had they exchanged greetings than the princess asked the president what he thought of the speech Hitler had delivered that morning. All day long, Roosevelt had avoided comment on the speech, claiming that he had not heard it, but now, confronted with a direct question by the princess, he was forced to reply. "It left the door about an inch open," he told Martha in an offhand judgment that would make headlines the following day. To the delight of both Franklin and his mother, the royal couple spent a weekend that spring at Hyde Park, enjoying a festive picnic, a concert by the Vassar College Choir, and a large country dinner.

These carefree days seemed far removed in August 1940, when Martha and her children joined eight hundred American refugees aboard the army transport ship the *American Legion* for the perilous voyage to the United States. Troubled by rumors of a Nazi plan to kidnap the princess and her son, the ship was forced to take a circuitous route from the Arctic port of Petsamo, Finland, down the Norwegian coast, through the mined waters of the North Atlantic into New York. When the ship landed safely, Martha spoke to the press, denouncing Hitler in "brave words" that impressed Eleanor. From the docks in New York, the princess journeyed to Hyde Park, accompanied by her children, her lady-in-waiting, the court chamberlain, and a retinue of servants.

It was clear at once that the president regarded the effervescent princess as a superlative addition to his household. At breakfast, lunch, or dinner, she sat upright in her chair, a never-failing smile on her face, and when the president spoke, she gazed into his face in a girlish, good-humored way. It was amusing to watch her flirt, one witness reported. "Martha would sit and simper and tell him how wonderful and beautiful he was." She would bat her eyes and put on "a little girl act," and the president "seemed to eat it up."

"Nothing is more pleasing to the eye," Roosevelt once observed, "than a good-looking lady, nothing more refreshing to the spirit than the company of one, nothing more flattering to the ego than the affection of one." Roosevelt was a ladies' man by temperament, Jimmy Roosevelt explained, "at his sparkling best when his audience included a few admiring and attractive ladies." Little wonder, then, that the president developed such strong feelings of affection for Martha, who sat by his side, giggling and looking "adoringly" at him. "He seems to like it tremendously," one guest reported, "and there is a growing flirtatious intimacy. . . ."

Anna's daughter, Eleanor Seagraves, a teenager at the time, recalls the spark Martha provided to the Roosevelt household. "She was a lot of fun, and not at all stiff or stuffy. I remember that her lady-in-waiting had a tattoo on her arm." Down-to-earth, practical, and unassuming, Martha had an open, vivacious personality which served her well.

On Saturday evening, September 7, the entire Roosevelt household, including Martha, Sara, Eleanor, and Missy, journeyed to nearby Peekskill for an end-of-summer clambake at the home of the Morgenthaus. "It became a kind of annual event," Henry Morgenthau III explained. "There was beer and brandy and singing. FDR would join in the singing. It was that kind of free, relaxed evening with good food that FDR enjoyed." It was cold that night, Eleanor wrote in her column, "but the big bonfire looked warm and we all wore plenty of warm garments." After dinner, the entire party went into the living room for a square dance. "Mrs. Roosevelt loved to square dance," Morgenthau recalled.

While the Roosevelt party was enjoying the festivities at the Morgenthaus', over six hundred German bombers were coming down in long shallow dives over London, the heaviest attack ever delivered on a single city. More than four hundred people were killed in a matter of minutes, and fourteen hundred were seriously injured. Buses and trains stopped running, the lights went out, and large fires sprang up all over the city. "The London that we knew was burning," one horrified Londoner later wrote—"the London which had taken thirty generations of men a thousand years to build . . . and the Nazis had done that in thirty seconds."

Earlier that week, in what would later prove to be a great tactical error, German Air Marshal Hermann Goering had decided to shift his priorities from daylight attacks on the RAF in southern England to massive night bombings of London. The decision was in part an emotional one, reflecting a desire to retaliate against the British people for the recent bombing of Berlin, which, unbeknownst to the Germans, had resulted from a minor navigational error. Goering also hoped to destroy the will of the British people by disrupting the daily life of their capital.

Goering's shift in tactics came at just the wrong moment. After a month of heavy fighting in the air, the battered RAF Fighter Command was on the verge of exhaustion. The German superiority of numbers was beginning to tell. "A few more weeks of this," journalist William Shirer has written, "and Britain would have no organized defense of its skies. The invasion could almost certainly succeed." The raids on London, which would continue for fifty-seven consecutive nights, gave the RAF a chance to recover, regroup, and regain the upper hand. By mid-October, long after Goering had promised Hitler that the RAF would be driven from the skies, the British Fighter

Command was still in control. The prerequisite for the invasion had not been met, forcing Hitler on October 12 to postpone the preparations for "Sea Lion" until the following spring.

Of course, no one in Britain realized this at the time. On the contrary, the furious attacks on London that began on September 7 and became known as the Blitz seemed to signal just the opposite: that the Nazi invasion was about to begin. Throughout the country, church bells rang and military units were told to be ready to move at an hour's notice. From this night on, *New Yorker* correspondent Molly Panter-Downes has written, there were "no longer such things as good nights. There [were] only bad nights, worse nights and better nights," as Londoners learned to adapt to an entirely new way of life—lining up in the evenings for public shelters, carrying blankets and babies to the vast dormitories in the underground tubes, shifting their sleeping quarters to their basements.

"The amazing part of it," Panter-Downes marveled, "is the cheerfulness and fortitude with which ordinary individuals are doing their jobs under nerve-wracking conditions." Small shopkeepers whose windows had been totally blown apart would hang up "Business as Usual" stickers in the open spaces and exchange jokes and stories with their customers. And everywhere one looked, in the heaps of rubble that had once been homes, offices, and churches, were paper Union Jacks stuck defiantly to the sides of crumbling walls. Londoners suddenly came to realize, reported Ben Robertson, correspondent for the liberal daily, *PM,* that "human character can stand up to anything" if it has to. For the British people, this was indeed, as Churchill had predicted, "their finest hour."

•   •   •

Sunday morning, September 8, as "a vast smoky pall" hung over London and exhausted firemen struggled to bring the fires under control, President Roosevelt proclaimed a nationwide day of prayer. Accompanied by Mrs. Roosevelt, Princess Martha, and the Countess Ragni Ostgaard, Martha's lady-in-waiting, Roosevelt drove to his family church, the St. James Episcopal Church, an ivy-covered stone building set in a peaceful grove of trees. There, seated between Eleanor and Martha, he heard the minister proclaim: "We are on the brink of the greatest catastrophe of all times. Can the hand of the oppressor be stayed? The President of the United States believes that it can, with God's help. That is why he has called upon us to join today in prayer."

Luncheon that afternoon was a royal affair, as the President brought Martha together with the former empress of the Austro-Hungarian Empire, Zita, and her two young sons, the Archduke Otto of Hapsburg and Archduke Felix. The former empress, who had been safely exiled in Belgium until the German bombs destroyed her asylum, had arrived in the United States in mid-July.

Seated at the head of the table, holding herself erect, the president's mother reveled in the presence of her royal guests. There was something in

Sara's demeanor that suggested her own form of majesty. "Sara was known in some circles as 'The Duchess,' " one family friend explained, "not because she gave orders, but because she had an unconscious air of being considered above all other people. I don't think that she felt anyone was her social equal, except maybe the queen of England, and she wasn't sure about that."

When Sara talked, she spoke with great slowness and distinctness, pronouncing every syllable of every word. Keeping a vigilant watch on the table at large, she was particularly taken with the composure of Martha's children, whose excellent manners reminded her of Franklin's when he was a boy. The children were all fair-haired and good-looking with regular features. Turning her gaze from Martha's children to her own child, his head so like hers, Sara smiled broadly. This was her house, her family, her world, and she was perfectly at ease.

•   •   •

When Martha left at the end of the weekend the president issued an open invitation to the princess to live at the White House until she found a proper residence for herself and her children. Martha took him up on his generous offer, settling herself into the Rose Suite, on the second floor of the family quarters. There she remained for weeks, joining the president for tea in the late afternoons, sharing his cocktail hour at night, accompanying him on his weekend cruises on the *Potomac.* "She was a special character," Secret Service Agent Milton Lipson recalled, "a real beauty."

"I don't think I will ever be able to express my gratitude for your kindness toward me and my children," Martha wrote the president. "The way you talk to my three little children and make them happy by collecting and finding stamps also makes me very happy."

"There was no question," Jimmy Roosevelt recalled, "that Martha was an important figure in Father's life during the war." Indeed, Jimmy observed, "although historians have never really looked into it, there is a real possibility that a true romantic relationship developed between the president and the princess. Father obviously enjoyed her company. He would kiss her hello when she arrived and goodbye when she left and good night if she stayed over." Martha's ubiquitousness became a source of teasing among the president's aides, who took to describing her as "the president's girlfriend."

Teasing within the White House was one thing, but when reporter Walter Trohan wrote a series of suggestive articles about Princess Martha in the *Chicago Tribune,* Steve Early was furious. "Early tried every way he could to get me to stop writing about Martha," Trohan later recalled, "but I was having too much fun so I just kept doing it. For example, I'd count the number of times Martha had been to Hyde Park in the space of four and five weeks. Then I'd describe her descending the steps of the train in high heels and black silk hose. If you read between the lines, the drift was clear. 'Goddamn it,' Early would say, 'after Eleanor, isn't the president entitled to some feminine interest?' I'd say, 'Isn't Missy enough?' and that would end the conversation, but I'd never ever write anything negative about Missy. I liked her too much."

Eventually, with the help of the president, who drove with her to scout out possible choices, Martha found a magnificent estate to rent, Pook's Hill, a rambling twenty-four-room stone house on 105 acres of wooded land in Bethesda, Maryland. "Martha and her lady-in-waiting were very much elated when we met at tea time," Eleanor reported on September 26, "because they found a comfortable house." Still, Martha continued to visit the White House regularly, often staying overnight, and on a number of occasions the president drove out to Pook's Hill to visit her.

For the most part, Eleanor regarded Martha's flirtatiousness with wry detachment, explaining to a friend that "there always was a Martha for relaxation and for the nonending pleasure of having an admiring audience for every breath." After three decades of watching her husband bask in the glow of admiring females, Eleanor was rather accustomed to the situation Martha created. Knowing that she was unable to play so casually at love, Eleanor looked with both disdain and longing at Martha's coquettishness. "I can't imagine Mrs. Roosevelt even thinking of flirting," Betsey Whitney, Jimmy Roosevelt's first wife, said. Yet, near the end of her life, speaking in a wistful tone, Eleanor told a friend that flirting was the one thing she wished she had learned how to do when she was young.

• • •

If Eleanor managed to take her husband's fondness for Martha in stride, Missy was distraught. Keeping an anxious watch on the president whenever the princess was around, Missy could not help noticing how his spirits soared the moment Martha entered the room. In the past, Missy was the one who had always sat in the place of honor next to the president in his car, a lap robe tucked around them. Now, when the President took his long rides in the afternoon for relaxation, it was Martha who sat by his side.

Once, when Missy was in her late twenties, she was asked by a friend if she ever regretted not being married. "Absolutely not," Missy laughingly replied. "How could anyone ever come up to FDR?" To be sure, there had been a few romances in her life, a dalliance with Eleanor's bodyguard, the handsome state trooper Earl Miller, in the early 1930s, and a more serious romance with William Bullitt a few years later.

It is not clear how these romances started or ended. Earl Miller claims that he deliberately played up to Missy because he could see that Eleanor, whom he loved, was being hurt by Missy's closeness with Franklin. For two years, Miller says, he squired Missy around, taking her out to dinner or the movies in their free time. "Missy had me put on night duty so that I could come to her room [at Warm Springs]," Miller recalls. But the carefree Miller had not counted on Missy's becoming emotionally involved. When she discovered he was simultaneously "playing around with one of the girls in the Executive Office," she took to her bed and cried for three days.

Missy's involvement with Bullitt was more significant. Born into a wealthy old-line Philadelphia family, Bullitt had distinguished himself at Yale as editor of the *Yale Daily News* before embarking on a successful career as a newspaper correspondent and foreign diplomat. In 1933, Roosevelt appointed him ambassador to Russia; three years later, he was made ambassador to France. Outgoing and opinionated, Bullitt had married and divorced two women—Ernesta Drinker, a Philadelphia socialite, and Louise Bryant Reed, widow of the writer John Reed.

The people closest to Missy believed that Bullitt was very much in love with her. The gossip in Missy's home town was that something big was going on. Suddenly the young secretary was sporting beautiful jewelry, all courtesy of Bullitt. "He used to telephone her all the time from Russia, and when he'd come to Washington he'd take her out," Missy's friend Barbara Curtis recalled. "Indeed, at one point he wanted to marry her, but her attraction to Roosevelt was simply too overpowering." This was, Jimmy Roosevelt confirmed, "the one real romance" in Missy's life. "Father encouraged it, feeling, I think she had devoted a lot of her life to him and was entitled to a life of her own."

Others saw Bullitt's interest in Missy in darker tones. "I think Bullitt used Missy as a way of getting access to FDR," Morgenthau's son, Henry III, observed. "He was a great operator, and he led Missy to believe he would marry her when he never intended to." In his diary, Henry Morgenthau, Jr., records a meeting with the president to discuss various candidates for director of the budget. "I was very much amused at Miss LeHand seriously suggesting Bill Bullitt and the President said, quite curtly, 'No, no, he is all wrapped up in international diplomacy and knows nothing about this' to which Miss LeHand answered, 'But he would like to. . . .' "

When Bullitt was in Russia, Dorothy Rosenman recalled, Missy traveled to Moscow to see him, only to find on arriving there that he was involved with a ballet dancer. "I don't know why the engagement ended," Jimmy Roosevelt wrote. "I believe Bill treated her badly. . . ." And from then on, "Missy devoted the rest of her life to father."

The second week of September, Missy celebrated her forty-second birthday at a White House dinner with a half-dozen friends and colleagues, including the president, Harry Hopkins, Grace Tully, and Roberta Barrows. "I remember that she was uncharacteristically quiet that night," Roberta Barrows recalled. "She seemed sad and lonely, as if she were brooding about something." Perhaps, taking stock of her life as she began her forty-third year, Missy was forced to admit to herself that her chances for marriage and children were all but gone.

Over the years, Missy had enjoyed warm relations with the five Roosevelt children. "Nearer my age than Father's," Jimmy Roosevelt remarked, "Missy was a wonderful go-between. I often relied on her judgment as to the best times to approach Father on some delicate matter." In Missy's files at the Roosevelt Library, there are scores of affectionate letters to and from Roosevelt's daughter, Anna, suggesting an almost sisterly relationship. But, as close as Missy was to the Roosevelt children, it was not the same as having a husband and family of her own. In later years, Anna admitted that she hated driving in a car with her father and Missy because Missy automatically took the preferred seat next to him, so that she had to find a seat wherever she could. FDR, Jr., also admitted that he had resented Missy terribly when he was younger. At one point the anger tumbled out. "Are you always so agreeable?" he asked her. "Don't you ever get mad and flare up?" She looked at that moment, FDR, Jr., recalled, "as if she were going to cry."

•   •   •

There remained one unfinished piece of business before the Congress adjourned in 1940—tax legislation. Though the Congress had imposed new taxes in June in order to raise part of the revenue needed for the defense effort, a more comprehensive tax program was required. Despite the promise of the cost-plus-fixed-fee contracts, private enterprise remained reluctant to convert its plants to defense production until a new tax structure had been put into place.

In mid-July, Roosevelt told business what it wanted to hear. He called for legislation that would permit companies building new plants and equipment to amortize their capital expenses within five years or less. This meant that companies could deduct 20 percent of their capital costs before arriving at the net income on which taxes were paid. At the same time, he proposed repeal of the Vinson-Trammell Act, which held aircraft and shipbuilding manufacturers to a flat 8-and-12 percent profit rate. In its place, he recommended a steeply graduated "excess profits tax" that would apply to all companies, not just airplane manufacturers and shipbuilders.

Liberals were dismayed, believing that Roosevelt was surrendering to what amounted to a strike by capital instead of labor, a deliberate refusal by business to sign any defense contracts until it got the precise tax legislation it wanted. There was truth to these claims. At the August 2 Cabinet meeting where the destroyer deal was discussed at length, Stimson warned Roosevelt that "delay in enacting legislation covering the amortization question was holding up many contracts." Yet, unlike the scattered labor strikes that summer at the Kearney Shipyard, Vultee Aircraft, and the Boeing Company, where the demand for a raise of 10 cents was greeted on Capitol Hill with the cry of "treason," *Nation* columnist I. F. Stone noted, "no such harsh accusation has been made against the aviation companies, though plane contracts to the value of 85 million have been held up by their recalcitrance."

As the probusiness legislation emerged from the House Ways and Means Committee, liberal opposition heightened. It was "a lousy bill," Morgenthau told Roosevelt. Drafted by a lawyer from the Chamber of Commerce, it sponsored "the very kinds of discrimination that the President, and the

Treasury have for so many years opposed." First, Morgenthau warned, the wording of the excess-profits tax would place "a grave handicap on growing business, would give established corporations a near monopoly in their industries." Second, the final version of the amortization scheme was so generous that, in effect, government would be fully responsible for building the plants and equipping them at its own expense, while permitting corporations to make huge profits at practically no risk.

"This is abandoning advanced New Deal ground with a vengeance," Harold Ickes recorded in his diary. "It seems to me intolerable to allow private people to use public capital in order to make a guaranteed profit for themselves. . . . If private citizens won't supply munitions of war at a reasonable profit and take pot luck with the rest of the citizens in the matter of taxation, then the government ought to build its own plants and conscript the necessary managers to run them."

Eleanor agreed wholeheartedly with Morgenthau and Ickes. For months, Joe Lash had been telling her that the administration's defense program evoked no enthusiasm because "there was no clearcut vision of the kind of world that was wanted." What was so discouraging to Lash about the fight of the manufacturers to lift the profit margin of 8 percent was that it meant "we still had the old order of things." If only, Lash urged Eleanor, the president were willing to carry a fight against monopoly, promising that something different would emerge out of the war, then young people would go enthusiastically into battle. Youth wants "battle cries," Lash said, "with which it can go to death exultantly—something worth dying for."

Taking up Lash's hope that a new economic system would emerge out of the war that would place the forces of production at the disposal of all, Eleanor suggested in her column that, while the government was drafting men, it should also "draft such capital as may be lying idle for investment in ways which may be deemed necessary for defense." The best minds in the country, she said, should be occupied with "determining how it can be made equally certain that capital, wherever possible, is drafted for the use of the country in just the way that lives are drafted." In a follow-up column written two weeks later, Eleanor endorsed the controversial Russell-Overton amendment to the September Selective Service Act, which allowed the president to take over uncooperative factories. Responding to Willkie's charge that this provision would "sovietize" American industry, Eleanor wrote: "I, for one, am glad to see some consideration is being given to a draft of industry as well as men."

Eleanor's economic musings provoked a sharp rebuttal from business writer Ralph Robey in *Newsweek*. Claiming that she had been led astray in her thinking, Robey warned that, should her ideas be followed, "that is, should the government start taking over our accumulated supplies of wealth," then "our system of private enterprise will necessarily come to an absolute dead end. There will be no supply of private savings with which to go ahead—no private wealth out of which to make the investment necessary to create jobs—Everything, from top to bottom, will have to be government."

Robey need not have worried, for on the revenue issue the president was listening to Stimson, the War Department, and the conservatives in Congress rather than to Morgenthau, Ickes, or his wife. Stimson, never having been a New Dealer, shared none of Morgenthau's suspicions of big business, nor his urgent desire to protect the principles of tax reform. As Stimson and the War Department saw the situation, the need for production was so great that nothing must be placed in the way of getting started. The War Department was not in the business of social reform; its goal was not to change the nation's industrial pattern but to procure munitions as quickly as possible. "There are a great many people in Congress who think that they can tax business out of all proportion and still have businessmen work diligently and quickly," Stimson wrote. "This is not human nature."

Though Roosevelt did not share Stimson's unqualified enthusiasm for business, he did agree that the primary task at hand was to convert industries of peace into industries of war, and to this end he was willing to give business what it wanted even if it meant capitulating on the tax bill. "I regret to say," Ickes recorded in his diary, "the President is willing to take what Congress will give him and Congress will give him only what big business is willing that he should have."

During a heated session over the legislation on the president's back porch at Hyde Park that summer, Morgenthau reported that Roosevelt sat in his rocker and repeated over and over, "I want a tax bill; I want one damned quick; I don't care what is in it; I don't want to know. . . . The contracts are being held up and I want a tax bill." When Eleanor gamely offered to continue the fight, Morgenthau advised her to back off. "Leave the President alone," he warned. "He is in one of those moods."

But Eleanor was constitutionally incapable of leaving the president alone. On a Sunday night in September, with FDR's economic adviser Charles Taussig as her dinner guest, she renewed her arguments against the tax bill, charging that manufacturers were placing profits before patriotism. The president listened sympathetically, nodding his head in his usual manner, but he remained absolutely firm in his conviction that it was necessary to accept an imperfect law in order to encourage the defense program. Once the legislation went through, he predicted, the mobilization program would get under way. In this prediction Roosevelt was correct, for, when the revenue bill finally passed later that fall, the capital strike came to an end and war contracts began to clear with speed.

Army historians contend that passage of the amortization law was a major turning point in the mobilization process. The rapid-write-off provision converted high tax rates from "a liability into an asset," inducing business "to retain its earnings in the form of expanded plant and equipment." With tax rates at their peak, the historians argue, the success of the amortization privilege "shattered conventional beliefs that high tax rates would inevitably lead to drying up of capital."

But liberals were correct in suggesting that small business would be hurt by the way the tax legislation was structured. As the defense program got under way, military-procurement agencies turned more and more to big business. A study released the following summer indicated that in the first year of the mobilization fifty-six large corporations accounted for three-fourths of the dollar value of all prime contracts. "We had to take industrial America as we found it," War Department Undersecretary Robert Patterson explained. "For steel we went to the established steel mills. For autos we went to Detroit." Large firms had the facilities and experience to handle large orders. "It would have been folly to have ignored the great productive facilities of these concerns and to have placed our business with companies that could not produce."

In the months ahead, as the cries of small businessmen began to be heard on Capitol Hill, new legislation would be enacted to try to increase the relative share of small business in total army procurement. But by then, the basic pattern—the link between big business and the military establishment, a link that would last long into the postwar era and lead a future president to warn against the "military-industrial complex"—was already set. Eager for action—too eager, liberals thought—the president made war production his overriding concern. He could fight only one war at a time. If this priority produced negative consequences for small business, that was a price he was willing to pay.

The 76th Congress had been a tumultuous gathering. So trying were the conditions, observers noted, that, just after the final House vote on conscription, Speaker William B. Bankhead died of a stroke. (He was replaced by Sam Rayburn of Texas.) But in the end, despite the blunders, divisions, and dillydallying, the Congress had granted the president the legislation he needed to begin the process of mobilization, and with it the revitalization of the American economy after a decade of depression.

It was the president's custom each year on the night that Congress was due to adjourn to host a poker game in his study. The game would begin in the early evening, and then whoever was ahead at the moment the Speaker called to say that Congress had officially adjourned would be declared the winner. On this night, Morgenthau was far ahead when the Speaker phoned, but Roosevelt pretended that the call was from someone else and the game continued until midnight, when Roosevelt finally pulled ahead. At this point, Roosevelt whispered to an aide to go into another office and call the study. When the phone rang, he pretended it was the Speaker and declared himself the winner. Everyone was in high spirits until the next morning, when Morgenthau read in the paper that the Congress had officially adjourned at

9 p.m. He was so angry that he handed in his resignation. Only when the president called and convinced him that it was all in good fun did Morgenthau agree to stay. Morgenthau should have realized that Roosevelt was not above a little deception if it helped him win his bets!

CHAPTER 7

"I CAN'T DO
ANYTHING ABOUT HER"

When Eleanor accepted A. Philip Randolph's invitation to speak at the Convention of Sleeping Car Porters on September 16, 1940, she set in motion a chain of events that would carry her into the center of a convulsive battle for racial equality in the armed forces. Although few recognized it at the time, this battle would prove a turning point in American race relations. It would stimulate a new spirit of militancy in the black community, a new willingness to protest. The civil-rights movement that would flower in later decades was struggling to be born.

A. Philip Randolph, the man who would lead the movement in the 1940s, was a commanding figure with a handsome face and a voice so resonant that he once considered a career in acting. When he was still in his twenties and living in Harlem, he had founded an independent journal, *The Messenger,* which became an influential voice for radical action among Negroes in America. In 1925, he was asked to organize the overworked Pullman porters, who had been trying without success to form a union since 1900. The odds against the union were great; it took a leader of Randolph's intelligence and ability to counter the Pullman Company's propaganda, threats, and spies. When Randolph succeeded in creating the powerful Brotherhood of Sleeping Car Porters, he became, almost overnight, the most important Negro leader in America.

Eleanor was joined at the dais by Negro leaders Mary McCleod Bethune and Walter White.

The daughter of an illiterate South Carolina sharecropper, the youngest of seventeen children, Bethune was the only one in her family to receive an education. At fifteen, after taking every subject taught at the little missionary school near her home, she was given a scholarship to attend Scotia Seminary in North Carolina. There she became inspired with the vision of founding a school to help other Negroes. Her purpose was realized when she founded a Negro primary school in Florida and then built it into Bethune-Cookman College.

Walter White, by contrast, was born into a middle-class family, the son of a postman in Atlanta. Slender in build with fair skin, blue eyes, and blond hair, White was only one-sixty-fourth Negro. But when his father died from an injury which his son believed was brought about "by his being a colored man," White became a leader of the Negro cause. After graduating from Atlanta University, he wrote for the Negro publication *The Crisis,* conducted investigations of race riots and lynchings, and assumed a permanent position with the NAACP.

Eleanor's presence that evening was a testament to the long journey she had taken from the insulated days of her childhood when she listened to her Southern relatives reminisce about the slaves they had owned on their plantation in Georgia. "I quite understand the southern point of view," she later wrote, "because my grandmother [Martha Bulloch] was a Southerner . . . and her sister had a great deal to do with bringing us up when we were small children. . . ." When Eleanor first moved to the segregated city of Washington, D.C., with her young husband, her primary contact was with black household staff members, whom she persisted then in calling darkies and pickaninnies. Her sympathetic comprehension of the Negro situation in America had been a gradual awakening, a product of her exhaustive travels around the country and her developing friendships with Negro leaders, which, one black historian has written, "began to resemble a crash course on the struggle of blacks against oppression."

Though the New Deal never succeeded in giving full justice to the economic needs of black Americans, Eleanor was largely responsible for the steady increase over the years in the numbers of Negroes on public relief and in the funds they earned. When she first began inspecting New Deal programs in the South, she was stunned to find that Negroes were being systematically discriminated against at every turn. Under the Agricultural Adjustment Act (AAA), Negro tenant farmers were the first to be cast off in the wake of the crop-reduction program. Under the National Recovery Act (NRA), Negroes either had to accept less money for the same work performed by whites or risk replacement. Even Eleanor's favorite program, the WPA, was guilty of discrimination. "Is it true," Eleanor queried Harry Hopkins, "that wages for Negroes in regions 3 and 4 (the southern regions) under work relief are lower than those established for white people? It is all wrong to discriminate between white and black men!"

Largely because of Eleanor Roosevelt, black complaints against New Deal programs received a hearing at the White House, and in 1935 the president agreed to sign an executive order barring discrimination in the administration of WPA projects. From that point on, the Negro's share in the New Deal expanded. By the end of the thirties, the WPA was providing basic earnings for one million black families; three hundred thousand black youths were involved in NYA training programs, and another quarter-million were serving in the CCC. Though the Negro's proportionate share in state activity was never as large as it should have been, the cumulative effect of the New Deal programs provided an economic floor for the entire black community. "For the first time," commented a delegation of Negro social workers visiting Hyde Park in the summer of 1939, "Negro men and women have reason to believe that their government does care."

During the thirties, Eleanor's public identification with black causes encouraged the hopes of the black community. In 1938, when confronted with a segregation ordinance in Birmingham, Alabama, that required her to sit in the white section of an auditorium, apart from Mrs. Bethune and her other black friends, she had captured public attention by placing her chair in the center aisle between the two sections. In 1939, she had resigned from the Daughters of the American Revolution (DAR) after it barred the Negro singer Marian Anderson from its auditorium. Over the years, she invited hundreds of Negroes to the White House, had her picture taken with them, and held fund-raising events for Negro schools and organizations. Although these actions may seem purely symbolic now, they must be evaluated in the context of their times. "Blacks in the thirties found them impressive," historian Nancy Weiss has written, "because there had been nothing like them in anyone's memory."

The president was far more cautious than his wife. While Eleanor thought in terms of what *should* be done, Franklin thought in terms of what *could* be done. "I did not choose the tools with which I must work," he told Walter White in the mid-thirties, explaining his refusal to endorse a federal antilynching campaign. "Had I been permitted to choose them I would have selected quite different ones. But I've got to get legislation passed by Congress to save America. The southerners by reason of the seniority rule in Congress are chairmen or occupy strategic places on most of the Senate and House committees. If I come out for the anti-lynching bill, they will block every bill I ask Congress to pass to keep America from collapsing. I just can't take that risk."

Yet, without a federal law, the U.S. government was powerless to intervene against lynchings in individual states. Eleanor refused to give up. Much to the dismay of the president's Southern-born secretaries, Steve Early and Marvin McIntyre, she continued to speak out in favor of an antilynching law.

"They were afraid," Eleanor later explained, "that I would hurt my husband politically and socially, and I imagine they thought I was doing many things without Franklin's knowledge and agreement. On occasion they blew up to him and to other people." During the antilynching campaign, Early complained in writing that Eleanor's friend Walter White had been bombarding the president with telegrams and, "Frankly, some of his messages to the President have been decidedly insulting." Mrs. Roosevelt must understand, Early went on, that, even before President Roosevelt came to the White House, Walter White was "one of the worst and most continuous troublemakers." Undeterred, Eleanor penned a personal note to Early: "If I were colored," she stated, "I think I should have about the same obsession that he [White] has. . . . If you ever talked to him, and knew him, I think you would feel as I do. He really is a very fine person with the sorrows of his people close to his heart."

Across the country, Eleanor's activism in behalf of blacks engendered scathing comments. "If you have any influence with the President," a New Jersey woman wrote Missy LeHand, "will you please urge him to muzzle Eleanor Roosevelt and it might not be a bad idea to chain her up—she talks too damn much." Throughout the South, she became a symbol of everything wrong with the attitudes of white Northerners toward Southern society. "The South is sick and tired of being treated as a conquered province," Georgia Representative George Cox warned his fellow Democrats, "and if the party which it has cradled and nurtured and supported all these years permits itself to be used as an instrument for its complete undoing then you may depend upon its people finding some other means of protection."

Never once, however, did the president move to curb his wife's activities in behalf of the Negroes. Do you mind if I say what I think, she once asked her husband. "No, certainly not," he replied. "You can say anything you want. I can always say, 'Well, that is my wife; I can't do anything about her.' "

In part, Franklin tolerated Eleanor because she represented the more generous, idealistic side of his own nature, the humanitarian values he himself held but felt unable to act upon in the context of the Southern-dominated Congress. But it was also good politics. While he kept the party intact in the South, Eleanor was building new allies in the North among tens of thousands of migrating blacks who were gaining access to the ballot in urban areas such as New York, Chicago, and Detroit. In the Northern precincts, the same photographs of Eleanor entertaining various black figures that had been circulated throughout the South as proof of White House treachery contributed to a historic shift in the political allegiance of Negroes. Before the Roosevelts came into power, Negroes, still loyal to the party of Lincoln, had consistently voted the Republican ticket. In 1936, blacks swung decisively into the Roosevelt coalition. "I'm not for the Democrats," explained one black who had voted Democratic for the first time in 1936, "but I am for the man." Though the president had taken no specific initiatives in behalf of the Negroes, and had failed to support the antilynching campaign, he had managed, with Eleanor's substantial help, to convey to blacks that the administration was on their side. "When you start from a position of zero," civil-rights leader Clarence Mitchell, Jr., later observed, "even if you move up to the point of two on a scale of 12, it looks like a big improvement."

• • •

By the time of the porters' convention, however, a new and explosive issue —the elimination of discrimination and segregation in the armed forces— had replaced lynching as the dominant concern among Negro Americans.

When the U.S. began to rearm in the summer of 1940, Negro citizens had flocked to recruiting stations by the thousands, only to be met by a series of obstacles. In the regular army of close to a half-million men, there were only forty-seven hundred Negroes, two Negro officers, and three Negro chaplains. There were only four Negro units, the Ninth and Tenth Cavalry and the 24th and 25th Infantry regiments, and only one was receiving combat training. There was not a single Negro in the Marine Corps, the Tank Corps, the Signal Corps, or the Army Air Corps.

As stories of discrimination began surfacing in different parts of the country, the *Pittsburgh Courier* provided front-page coverage and launched a national drive for equal participation in the armed forces. The NAACP followed suit, resolving at its national convention to devote its full energies to the elimination of Jim Crow in the military. Discrimination in the military became for many blacks a symbol of the entire order of racial separation in the South. The struggle for "the right to fight," as it came to be called, mobilized thousands of Negroes who had not been previously involved in civil rights, expanding the ranks of the NAACP and the circulation of the Negro press.

The new mood contrasted sharply with the "close-ranks" strategy articulated by W. E. B. Du Bois during World War I, which had called on Negroes to "forget our special grievances and close ranks shoulder to shoulder with our white fellow-citizens." This time, feeling it was the psychological moment to strike out for their rightful place in American society, Negro leaders were taking an openly aggressive stance.

Through her talks with civil-rights leaders and her correspondence with Negro citizens, Eleanor had achieved a vague understanding of the new mood in the Negro community. In early September, she had received a disturbing letter from a Negro doctor, Henry Davis. "At a time when everyone is excited about increasing the size of the army," he told her, he had been refused an active commission simply because of his dark skin. "I am greatly disappointed and am very much depressed," he admitted, "gradually losing faith, ambition and confidence in myself."

It was not until the porters' convention, however, when she talked at great length with Randolph, that Eleanor came to appreciate the full dimensions of the situation. The discrimination Dr. Davis had experienced, Eleanor was told, was widespread. In Charlotte, North Carolina, a Negro high-school teacher holding a master's degree from Columbia had been severely beaten by white soldiers stationed at a recruiting office when he sought information for his pupils. At the University of Minnesota, Walter Robinson had successfully completed the Civil Aeronautics Authority flight-training program, finishing thirteenth in a class of three hundred. But when he applied for enlistment in the Army Air Corps, he was told that it was useless to complete the application. "There is no place for a Negro in the Air Corps," the lieutenant in charge said. Dr. Winston Willoughby, a Negro dentist, had received an equally peremptory response when he sought a commission in the Dental Corps. "Hell, if you said you were colored I would have saved you a trip," he was told. "There are no colored dentists in the Dental Corps."

The situation in the navy, where four thousand Negroes served, was even more hypocritical. To the extent the navy had opened its doors to Negroes, it was strictly as mess men, assigned to make the officers' beds, serve their meals, clean their rooms, shine their shoes, and check their laundry. Unaware of this depressing situation, many Negroes had been drawn into the navy by false promises, only to find, once they were in, that there was no room for advancement.

The same week as the porters' banquet, fifteen navy mess men aboard the U.S.S. *Philadelphia* had come to a determination to speak up against the intolerable conditions. Led by twenty-five-year-old Byron Johnson, who had joined the navy in 1937 on the promise he would be taught a trade, the fifteen sailors wrote an open letter to the *Pittsburgh Courier*. "Our main reason for writing," the letter began, "is to let all our colored mothers and fathers know how their sons are treated after taking an oath pledging allegiance and loyalty to their flag and country. . . . We sincerely hope to discourage any other colored boys who might have planned to join the Navy and make the same mistake we did. All they would become is seagoing bell hops, chambermaids and dishwashers. We take it upon ourselves to write this letter regardless of any action the Navy authorities may take. We know it could not possibly surpass the mental cruelty inflicted upon us on this ship." Signed Byron Johnson, Floyd Owens, Otto Robinson, Shannon Goodwin, et al.

The navy's reaction to the published letter was swift and severe. The signers were placed in the brig, indicted for conduct prejudicial to good order, and given dishonorable discharges for "unfitness." "I am still 100 percent a loyal American," Byron Johnson stated. "If necessary I'd gladly fight for my country. However, I don't feel we 15 fellows have received a fair deal. Not given an opportunity to defend ourselves at any sort of a trial, we are kicked out of the Navy because we dared express our convictions to the *Pittsburgh Courier*—in a country where free speech is supposed to be every man's privilege."

Despite the punishment exacted, the courageous action of the fifteen mess men, like a small rock tumbling over the side of a mountain, initiated an avalanche of protest that would eventually change the face of the navy. With cynicism and hope existing side by side under the charged conditions of impending war, hundreds of Negro mess men in dozens of ships began to speak up. "Since other mess attendants . . . are putting up such a stiff fight for equality," three Negro sailors wrote from the U.S.S. *Davis* in San Diego, "we feel it only right for us . . . to do our share. . . . Before now, we were afraid of the consequences if we fought naval discrimination, but now that we have outside help which has given us new hope, we are prepared and determined to do our part on the inside to the last man." Signed Jim Pelk, L. Latimore, Raymond Brown. "I understand the plight of these colored sailors," another mess man wrote, "for I am one myself, having quit college to join the Navy. You may publish my name if you feel it necessary to do so. That, of course, would probably mean that I would meet the same fate Byron Johnson and his friends met. But I am fanatical enough about it all to allow that to happen to me, if necessary."

Conditions in the Navy remained unrelievedly bleak, but the new conscription law provided a small ray of hope for the army. During the congressional debate, in response to public pressure about the use of Negro troops, language had been added to the bill, pledging to increase Negro participation in the army to a figure equivalent to the percentage of Negroes in the population, about 10 percent. "In the selection and training of men under this act," the amendment further provided, "there shall be no discrimination against any person on account of race or color." The problem, Negro leaders recognized, was the next sentence in the bill, which promised that "no man shall be inducted for training and service unless he is acceptable" to the army and "until adequate provision shall have been made for shelter, sanitary facilities, water supplies, heating and lighting arrangements, medical care and hospital accommodations." Would the army ever deem large numbers of Negroes acceptable? Could lack of separate shelter and facilities for Negroes preclude their induction?

To obtain answers to these questions, Randolph and White had requested a meeting with the president in early September. Just before she was to speak to the porters, Eleanor learned that the president's secretaries Early and Watson had failed to respond to the request. Making a note to herself to see what she could do, Eleanor walked to the podium. She delivered a passionate pledge to the Negro audience to give her "faith, cooperation and energy" in order to make America a better place, a place where everyone, Negro and white, could live in equality and opportunity. When she finished, her face expressing genuine affection and concern, she received a standing ovation.

Later that evening, from her apartment in Greenwich Village, Eleanor dictated a note to her husband, telling him she had just heard that no conference was ever held on the subject of "how the colored people can participate" in the armed forces. "There is a growing feeling amongst the colored people . . . [that] they should be allowed to participate in any training that is going on, in the aviation, army, navy. . . . I would suggest that a conference be held with the attitude of the gentlemen: these are our difficulties, how do you suggest that we make a beginning to change the situation? There is no use of going into a conference unless they have the intention of doing something. This is going to be very bad politically besides being intrinsically wrong and I think you should ask that a meeting be held."

When Eleanor returned to Washington two days later, she bypassed Early and Watson and confronted the president directly. "She has already spoken to the President," Early informed Watson; "a meeting is to be arranged for next week," with the secretaries of war and navy; Arnold Hill, former secretary of the Urban League; and Walter White and Philip Randolph, Negro leaders. Unable to contain his scorn, Early went on to tell Watson that Mrs. Roosevelt would telegraph the addresses of Hill and Randolph, though the address of Walter White, because he came so frequently to visit Mrs. Roosevelt, was "altogether too well known to [White House usher] Rudolph Forster and others here about."

The president's meeting with the three civil-rights leaders took place at twelve-thirty on Friday, September 27. Navy Secretary Frank Knox and Assistant Secretary of War Robert Patterson were also present. Randolph opened the discussion. "The Negro people . . . feel they are not wanted in the armed forces of the country. They feel they have earned their right to participate in every phase of the government by virtue of their record in past wars since the Revolution, [but] they are feeling . . . they are not wanted now."

The president responded by referring to the War Department's recent pledge to recruit and place Negroes in all branches of the armed forces. "Of course," he emphasized, "the main point to get across is . . . that we are not [as we did] in the World War, confining the Negro to the non combat services. We're putting them right in, proportionately, into the combat services. . . . Which is *something.*"

"We feel that is fine," Randolph countered, but only a beginning. Earlier that morning, the three Negro leaders had met in the NAACP office to draw up a memo outlining the steps that would have to be taken to integrate Negroes into the defense program. These actions included selecting officers for army units regardless of race, integrating specialized personnel such as Negro doctors and dentists into the services, broadening opportunities for Negroes in the navy beyond menial services, appointing Negroes to local selective-service boards, designating centers where Negroes could be trained for work in aviation, and appointing Negro civilians as assistants to the secretaries of the navy and war.

Although there might be problems in putting white and Negro soldiers together in Southern regiments, the Negro leaders admitted, there was no reason to anticipate insurmountable difficulties in the North. Roosevelt nodded his head in agreement and suggested backing into the formation of mixed units by mixing up replacements. "The thing is we've got to work into this," the president said. "Now, suppose you have a Negro regiment . . .

here, and right over here on my right in line, would be a white regiment. . . . Now what happens after a while, in case of war? Those people get shifted from one to the other. The thing gets sort of backed into.''

Encouraged by the president's open-mindedness about the army, Randolph turned to Knox and asked about the prospects for integrating the navy. The secretary spoke bluntly, suggesting that the problem in the navy was almost insoluble. ''We have a factor in the Navy that is not so in the Army, and that is that these men live aboard ship. And in our history we don't take Negroes into a ship's company.''

''If you could have a Northern ship and a Southern ship it would be different,'' Roosevelt laughingly observed, ''but you can't *do* that.'' He then went on to suggest putting Negro bands on white ships to accustom white sailors to the presence of Negroes on ships.

At the conclusion of the meeting, the president promised to confer with Cabinet officers and other government officials about the problem and then to talk with the civil-rights leaders again. Vastly encouraged, the Negro leaders awaited further word from the president. Beneath the cordiality of the meeting, however, the armed forces remained unyielding in their opposition to the idea of integration. At this crucial moment in America's history, General Marshall argued, there is no time ''for critical experiments which would have a highly destructive effect on morale.'' Secretary Knox agreed, telling Roosevelt that, if he were asked to desegregate the navy at the same time that he was supposed to create a two-ocean navy, he would have to resign. In his diary that evening, Stimson deplored the strain a ''rambunctious'' president was putting on the War Department by attempting ''to satisfy the Negro politicians who are trying to get the Army committed to colored officers and various other things which they ought not to do.''

''I sent [Undersecretary Robert] Patterson to this meeting, because I really had so much else to do,'' Stimson recorded. ''According to him it was a rather amusing affair—the President's gymnastics as to politics. I saw the same thing happen 23 years ago when Woodrow Wilson yielded to the same sort of a demand and appointed colored officers to several of the Divisions that went over to France, and the poor fellows made perfect fools of themselves. . . . Leadership is not embedded in the Negro race yet and to try to make commissioned officers to lead the men into battle is only to work disaster to both. Colored troops do very well under white officers but every time we try to lift them a little beyond where they can go, disaster and confusion follow. . . . I hope for heaven's sake they won't mix the white and colored troops together in the same units for then we shall certainly have trouble.''

Stimson's disparaging opinion of the performance of colored troops in previous wars mirrored the official conclusions of the Army War College Report on ''Negro Manpower'' issued in 1925. ''In the process of evolution,'' the report observed, ''the American negro has not progressed as far as other sub species of the human family. . . . The cranial cavity of the negro is smaller than whites. . . . The psychology of the negro, based on heredity derived from mediocre African ancestors, cultivated by generations of slavery, is one from which we cannot expect to draw leadership material. . . . In general the negro is jolly, docile, tractable, and lively but with harsh or unkind treatment can become stubborn, sullen and unruly. In physical courage [he] falls well back of whites. . . . He is most susceptible to 'Crowd Psychology.' He cannot control himself in fear of danger. . . . He is a rank coward in the dark."

In World War I, the report went on, the Negro officer was a failure in combat. "Negro troops are efficient and dependable only so long as led by capable white officers. Under Negro officers they have displayed entire inaptitude for modern battle. Their natural racial characteristics, lack of initiative and tendency to become panic stricken, can only be overcome when they have confidence in their leaders."

Negroes saw a different reality. Proud of the many awards garnered by the few colored regiments that actually did see combat in World War I, Negroes laid the blame on the army for improperly training and equipping the colored troops. "Soldiers who were asked to submit like lambs to segregated training facilities," black opinion held, "could not be expected to perform like lions on the battlefield." If Negroes were given half a chance, civil-rights leaders maintained, their performance would bring glory to both their race and their country.

For seven days, Randolph and White anxiously awaited an affirmative response from the White House, but nothing came. When follow-up telegrams and telephone calls were not returned, White turned in despair to Eleanor, explaining that not getting a reply from the White House put him in a most difficult position with his people. "We did not want to violate the unwritten rule about revealing what had taken place in the conference with the President until the White House had given us authority to do so." With his note to Eleanor, White enclosed the draft of a statement to be issued jointly by the White House and the civil-rights leaders, describing the positive nature of the discussions on September 27. Eleanor promised to get the draft statement into the hands of the proper people, eliciting appreciation from White for her "usual prompt and vigorous action."

Eleanor's intervention prodded the War Department into action, but the resulting statement was not what Eleanor and the civil-rights leaders wanted to hear. Measured against the heightened expectations of the civil-rights leaders, the actual concessions that were granted—the promise that Negro units would be formed in each major branch of the service and the announcement of plans for training Negroes in aviation—seemed minor indeed. Beyond this the War Department would not go, flatly refusing to consider the possibility that Negro officers could lead white troops or that selected Northern regiments could be integrated. "The policy of the War Department," the statement concluded, "is not to intermingle colored and white enlisted personnel in the same regimental organizations. This policy has been proven satisfactory over a long period of years and to make changes would produce situations destructive to morale and detrimental to the preparation for national defense."

The policy statement was disappointing enough in itself, but disappointment turned to fury when, in presenting it to the press, Steve Early gave the false impression that the three Negro leaders had agreed with the wording and countenanced the policy of segregation. This put the three men in an impossible situation; their seeming acquiescence was condemned as betrayal by their own groups. Under the circumstances, they had no choice but to strike back. In a joint public statement of their own, they vigorously repudiated the White House press release as trickery and characterized Roosevelt's official approval of the policy as "a stab in the back of democracy . . . a blow at the patriotism of twelve million Negro citizens." Of all the shabby dealings, *The Crisis* commented, "none is more shameful or indefensible than the refusal to give Negroes a fair chance in the armed forces."

"I am sorry we were forced to take this step," Walter White explained to Eleanor in a personal note. "But the White House announcement left no other alternative." Saddened by the turn of events, Eleanor appealed to her husband to rectify the situation. Roosevelt, appreciating the predicament of the Negro leaders, agreed to issue a statement of his own, deeply regretting the misinterpretation of the earlier statement which had led to the faulty assumption that the Negro leaders had approved a policy of segregation. The president reassured the Negro community that, despite the War Department's affirmation of the status quo regarding the use of Negro officers in current units, there was "no fixed policy" regarding future units. In approving the statement as written, the president explained, he was simply saying that, "at this time and this time only," in the present emergency, "we dare not confuse the issue of prompt preparedness with a new social experiment, however important and desirable it may be."

"Rest assured," Roosevelt told White in a separate letter, "further developments of policy will be forthcoming to ensure fair treatment on a nondiscriminatory basis." Though White and Randolph found Roosevelt's response most reassuring and encouraging, the Negro press continued to pound away at the White House. "We are inexpressibly shocked," the *Crisis* editorialized, "that a President at a time of national peril should surrender so completely to enemies of democracy who would destroy national unity by advocating segregation." In Harlem, thousands of Negroes attended a mass meeting to protest the War Department policy. The White House was besieged with angry letters. "The Negro situation has become more difficult," White House aide Jim Rowe warned the president in the weeks before the election. "Never before has the power of the Negro vote loomed so portentous," the *Pittsburgh Courier* observed, reporting a tremendous growth of pro-Willkie sentiment among Negroes. "It looks as though they are all going against him," Harry Hopkins confided to Farm Security Administrator Will Alexander; "tell me what to do."

What the Negroes wanted at that moment, Hopkins was told, was the promotion of Colonel Benjamin Davis, grandson of a slave, to brigadier general, and the appointment of William Hastie, dean of Howard Law School, as a civilian aide to Secretary Stimson. Change in the structure of the military would only come, Negroes now believed, if strong black men were placed in positions of leadership.

Roosevelt heard the cry of his political advisers. Moving quickly to repair the damage that had been done, he announced the promotion of Colonel Benjamin Davis, commander of the 369th National Guard Regiment in New York, to brigadier general, and the appointment of Dean William Hastie to the War Department. Stimson considered both appointments a terrible mistake. In his diary, he decried the fact that "the Negroes are taking advantage of this period just before the election to try to get everything they can in the way of recognition from the army" and blamed the situation on "Mrs. Roosevelt's intrusive and impulsive folly." And in a letter to Knox the following day, he noted sarcastically that, when he called on the Navy Department the next time with his colored brigadier general, he "fully expected to be met with a colored Admiral."

Stimson's negative attitude was reflected in the president's mail. "Are you crazy appointing a nigger as General in the U.S Army?" an angry man from West Virginia wrote. "It is incomprehensible to normal Americans," an Illinois couple wrote, "for you to appoint a member of the red, yellow or black race to the high rank of Brigadier General." But the Negro press was pleased, calling the twin appointments a major victory "in the fight for equitable participation of colored people in the national defense program." Sending a personal word to the president on the eve of the election, Walter White expressed his thanks "for all you did to insure a square deal for Negroes in the defense of our country."

The irony of the situation was not lost on Eleanor. Had it not been for the inept way the War Department and the White House press office handled the original statement, the appointments that so delighted the Negro community would probably not have been made. Up until this time, Eleanor had believed that, as long as segregated facilities were provided equally to blacks and whites alike, there was no issue of discrimination. But now she was coming to understand that things were not that simple, that "the basic fact of segregation which warps and twists the lives of our Negro population" was itself discriminatory.

• • •

No sooner had the commotion over the president's meeting with the civil-rights leaders begun to subside than Eleanor became embroiled in a fiery argument with the State Department over its refugee rescue operation. In mid-September, she learned from friends on the President's Advisory Committee that the visa arrangements entered into with such high hopes in July had completely broken down. After working indefatigably all summer long, sifting the lists, negotiating with various agencies, and examining affidavits, the PAC had submitted 567 carefully selected names, supported by all the necessary documents, to the State Department. The visa procedure was supposed to move forward automatically from that point on. But somewhere along the line, something had gone wrong; more than three months had passed and only fifteen visas had been issued.

A deliberate policy of obstruction was under way, directed from the top of the State Department, from the man in charge of refugee matters, Breckinridge Long. Working with what one refugee scholar has called "a singleness of purpose and a formidable arsenal of political weapons," Long had successfully devised a series of obstructive tactics that walled out any applicant the State Department wished to exclude. In a secret memo addressed to State Department officials James Dunn and Adolf Berle, Jr., early in the summer, Long had spelled out his plans: "We can delay and effectively stop for a temporary period of indefinite length the number of immigrants into the United States. We could do this by simply advising our consuls to put every obstacle in the way and to require additional evidence and to resort to various administrative advices which would postpone and postpone and postpone the granting of the visas."

On September 28, the day after the president's meeting with Randolph, White, and Hill, Eleanor penned an indignant note to her husband describing the unhappy situation. "Mr. [James] McDonald [chairman of the PAC] is so wrought up about it, he wants to talk to you for about 15 minutes. He would come to Washington, and I promised to help him. Because he feels that their good faith has been impugned and because he also feels that there is something he ought to tell you which makes him extremely uncomfortable [most likely she is referring here to the perceived anti-Semitism of Breckinridge Long] and about which he does not wish to write, he is asking for an appointment. I am thinking about these poor people who may die at any time and who are asking only to come here on transit visas and I do hope you can get this cleared up quickly."

Eleanor's note stirred Franklin to contact Undersecretary Sumner Welles. "Please tell me about this," the president wrote. "There does seem to be a mix-up. I think I must see McDonald." In reply, Welles suggested that the president talk first with Breckinridge Long. A meeting was set for noon, October 3. Long was well armed, carrying fearsome stories purporting to prove that many of the refugees Eleanor and her friends wanted to bring into the country were not refugees at all, but German agents trying to use America's hospitality for their own dark purposes. By playing on the president's fears that spies had infiltrated the refugee stream, Long managed to persuade Roosevelt that the State Department's cautious policy was the only way to go.

"I found that he [Roosevelt] was 100% in accord with my ideas," Long recorded triumphantly in his diary. "The President expressed himself as in entire accord with the policy which would exclude persons about whom there was any suspicion that they would be inimical to the welfare of the

United States no matter who had vouchsafed for them. I left him with the satisfactory thought that he was wholeheartedly in support of the policy which would resolve in favor of the United States any doubts about admissibility of any individual."

When the president met with McDonald the following week, the battle was already lost. Refusing to face the situation head on, Roosevelt spun one diverting story after another until the half-hour was up. When McDonald started condemning and criticizing Long, the president warned him not to "pull any sob stuff." The meeting ended with nothing accomplished.

Still Eleanor refused to give up, bombarding the president with requests for action, but Franklin, preoccupied with the question of Britain's survival, was unwilling to listen. "Something does seem wrong," she insisted in one note. *"What* does seem wrong?" Franklin replied, manifestly annoyed.

• • •

Eleanor's sole triumph during this period was her successful intervention in behalf of eighty-three Jewish refugees who had sailed to America aboard the Portuguese freighter the S.S. *Quanza.* Filled to capacity with 317 passengers, the *Quanza* had steamed into New York Harbor in late August. All those in possession of American visas were allowed to debark. The remaining passengers, refugees who had escaped from occupied France, pleaded with authorities to let them come ashore, too. "Impossible," said the officials, "no one can step onto America soil without the proper papers." The *Quanza* sailed on to Veracruz, hoping to find a more receptive port, but the Mexican authorities ordered the ship to return to Europe. "Complete despair overwhelmed the passengers," one young woman traveling with her parents recalled: Europe to them was "a German concentration camp." Preparing for the return trip, the *Quanza* docked at Norfolk, Virginia, to load up with coal. While the ship remained in the harbor, Jewish organizations appealed to Mrs. Roosevelt for help.

Eleanor was at Hyde Park when she received word of the situation. Convinced that something should be done, she appealed to her husband directly. He agreed to send Patrick Malin, representing the PAC, to Norfolk to see what he could do to secure visas for children, for aliens holding visas from other countries, and for bona-fide political refugees. Working quickly, Malin certified all the documents that were presented to him and construed everybody else to be a political refugee so that the entire ship could disembark.

Long was furious. "I remonstrated violently," he recorded in his diary, "said that I thought it was a violation of the Law . . . that I would not be party to it, that I would not give my consent, that I would have no responsibility for it." But Malin refused to back down. "When he [Long] told me that he felt he could not take responsibility for them," Malin wrote, "I informed him that they were already landing."

"Mrs. Roosevelt saved my life," one passenger affirmed.

• • •

But Eleanor's success was short-lived. Long was soon back in the saddle, cleverer and more treacherous than ever. "The department does not refuse visas," Freda Kirchwey explained in *The Nation.* "It merely sets up a line of obstacles stretching from Washington to Lisbon and on around to Shanghai. . . . It is as if we were to examine laboriously the curricula vitae of flood victims clinging to a piece of floating wreckage and finally to decide that, no matter what their virtues, all but a few had better be allowed to drown." The resulting "record," she concluded, "is one which must sicken any person of ordinary humane instincts."

On November 15, refugee advocate Joseph Buttinger appealed again to Eleanor. Remembering how she had helped in June, he sent her a long memo detailing the various obstacles that were keeping refugees from getting their visas. "It looks again," he pleaded, "as if only your word could once more help us to overcome the barricades and hindrances in this ghastly situation."

Attached to the memo was a chilling two-page letter from a Jewish doctor which detailed a story that would become all too familiar in the years ahead. On Tuesday, October 22, a police officer had appeared at his home in the province of Baden, Germany, and told him he had an hour to pack up whatever could fit in a single suitcase. When the doctor and his family reached the designated assembly point, he learned that "all Jews, not only of the town but of all Baden and the Palatinate had been hit by the same fate." There was a moment of relief when they learned they were not being taken "to dreaded Poland," but conditions in the refugee camp in France where they ended up were far worse than anything they had imagined. Thirteen thousand refugees were living "like criminals behind barbed wire in dark, cold, wet, unhealthy barracks without beds, table or chair." In the first seven weeks, he reported, more than five hundred refugees had died.

At the end of his letter, which somehow made its way to the White House, the doctor pleaded for help. "For us here there only exists one solution, the quick emigration from Europe. All our appeals in that respect have been in vain so far. If the United States continues to work so slowly the number of dead here is going to increase in a most deplorable manner."

When Eleanor sent the material on to her husband, she attached a personal note of her own. "FDR, Can't something be done?" There is no evidence that Roosevelt ever replied to Eleanor's note. "The President's overriding concern was the war," Eleanor's friend Justine Polier explained, "and he probably didn't like to be urged as much as he was in regard to refugees."

At one point, as continued reports of Long's intransigence filtered in, Eleanor flared up angrily at her husband. "Franklin, you *know* he's a fascist," she said over lunch. "I've told you, Eleanor, you must not say that," the president replied, cutting her short with an "unusually cross" tone. "Well, maybe I shouldn't say it," Eleanor countered, "but he is!"

So the battle to save lives by bringing large numbers of refugees into America was lost during the crucial months of 1940, when Germany was still willing to grant exit permits to the Jews. "True, the Nazis wished to be rid of the Jews," historian David Wyman has written, "but until 1941 this end was to be accomplished by emigration, not extermination. The shift to extermination came only after the emigration method had failed, a failure in large part due to lack of countries open to refugees."

Eleanor's failure to force her husband to admit more refugees remained, her son Jimmy later said, "her deepest regret at the end of her life."

•   •   •

Through the months of September and October, while Willkie was conducting a vigorous campaign in thirty states, traveling by train for 17,300 miles, the president insisted on limiting his trips to war plants and shipyards. In his acceptance speech, he had contended that, with the war raging in Europe, he would have neither the time nor the inclination to campaign for re-election. Yet one look at the crowded schedule the president kept that autumn suggests that under the guise of nonpolitical inspection trips the old politician was alive and well.

On the last day of September, Roosevelt telescoped three "inspections" into six hours. He began his tour at Aberdeen Proving Ground in Maryland, where all guns and their carriages were fully proofed before being issued to troops and all powders, shells, and bombs were tested to check quality and performance. During the previous fifteen months, employment at the proving ground had nearly tripled, and a six-day work week was now in force. Facilities of this nature, designed for use in the actual operation of the army, were known as command facilities. To carry out their expansion— including airfields, army posts, artillery ranges, camps, forts, hospitals, research labs, and a new Pentagon building—the War Department had to acquire unprecedented quantities of land. (Over the next five years, the U.S. government would purchase more than five million acres of land for these command facilities, an area larger than the commonwealth of Massachusetts.)

Seated in an open touring car, the president saw at close range the new types of ordnance, including the new Garand automatic rifle and a new railway howitzer. He witnessed an impressive display of mobile artillery, ranging from eight-inch guns to the antitank cannon, and saw a completely mechanized company exercise over a field with steep hillocks and quagmires. Though the army would continue to experiment with new weapons, he told reporters traveling with him, the point had been reached where the current models could be standardized and carried into mass production.

Driving southward to the Glenn Martin plant in Baltimore, Maryland, where the B-26 twin-engine bomber, "said to be the fastest bomber in the world," was being built, the president saw construction under way for a new building that would eventually accommodate forty thousand workers. The Glenn Martin Company, America's oldest builder of bomber planes, had come close to bankruptcy only a few years earlier, but now, with $400 million worth of orders, it was flourishing. Construction was also under way at Fort Meade, Maryland, which Roosevelt visited after a picnic lunch. Then housing two thousand men, Fort Meade was being enlarged, by an $11-million building program, to serve as a gathering center for twenty-five thousand men at a time.

Everywhere Roosevelt looked, there were signs of a rapidly improving economy. With new army camps and defense plants appearing all across the country, with textile mills running double shifts to fill orders for uniforms and blankets, with shipyards working round the clock, the unemployment rolls were swiftly shrinking—by four hundred thousand in August, by five hundred thousand in September. The eleven-year depression was, at last, coming to an end.

Returning to the White House in an ebullient mood, Roosevelt penned a letter to his son-in-law, John Boettiger. "The main point of these trips which has never yet appeared in print is that the places visited by me—arsenals, Navy yards, private plants, etc.—get a real enthusiasm and speed up production during the days following my visit. It does seem to help."

The following week, the president journeyed to the Midwest to inspect steel plants in Pittsburgh and Youngstown, a government housing project for defense workers at Terrace Valley, and the Wright Field in Dayton, Ohio, where he saw new types of planes, "one knifing through the air and another moving so unbelievably slowly that it seemed to be hung on a wire." Everywhere he went, he was greeted with all the fervor and trappings of an old-fashioned campaign. Schools were dismissed, and more than a quarter-million people lined his route. Still, he refused to acknowledge that he was campaigning. "I have come here today very informally," he said, " on what is essentially a trip to educate myself, to learn about what is happening for national defense."

While the president reveled in the cheering crowds, Eleanor headed to the West Coast to visit her oldest son, Jimmy, who had just been ordered to active duty at Marine headquarters in San Diego, California. Tall, thin, and prematurely balding, Jimmy had married Boston debutante Betsey Cushing soon after his graduation from Harvard. In 1937, after working in the insurance business for seven years, he had joined the White House staff as his father's secretary. He was generally credited with excellent work, but after two years, the stress of the position, coupled with charges in the press that he had used his public office for private gain, proved too much. He suffered a perforated ulcer, had two-thirds of his stomach removed, and was forced to resign. That fall, he moved to Los Angeles to become a film executive with Samuel Goldwyn Productions. The move coincided with the breakup of his marriage and the start of a new romance with Romelle Schneider, the nurse who had cared for him when he was in the hospital.

Twenty-six-year-old FDR, Jr., an officer in the navy reserve, was also affected by the standing order to report to duty. Considered the "golden boy" of the family, with his father's good looks and outgoing personality, FDR, Jr., had distinguished himself in both academics and athletics at Harvard. His marriage to heiress Ethel du Pont was labeled the wedding of the decade. After Harvard, on the advice of his father, he had chosen law in preparation for a career in politics, but now, like so many thousands of young Americans, he had his plans interrupted by the war.

Soon all four of the Roosevelt boys would be in the armed forces: thirty-year-old Elliott would accept a captain's commission in the Army Air Corps, and twenty-four-year-old John would join the navy. Of all the boys, Eleanor was closest to Elliott. "Elliott was the most like her father and brother," Minnewa Bell, his fourth wife, observed. "She had the feeling that Elliott was going to be a drinker. She was closer to Elliott because she worried about him more." Like all the Roosevelt boys, Elliott had gone to Groton, but when the time came to apply to Harvard he had willfully flunked his entrance exams. Unable to get his feet on the ground, he had moved from one career to another and from one woman to another. In 1940, his second marriage was already in trouble.

The youngest son, John, was quieter and more reserved than his older brothers. When he entered Harvard, his father warned the freshman dean that "he has to study to get things done" and "will not be good at assuming or seeking leadership." The only one of the four boys who would never run for political office, John once worked under a pseudonym to avoid the favoritism that was attached to the Roosevelt name. Married at twenty-two to socialite Anne Lindsay Clark, he was a manager at Filene's department store in Boston when he entered active duty with the navy.

The boys' disappointing careers and broken relationships (between the four of them there would be eighteen marriages) devastated Eleanor. "None of them really lived up to the name," Eleanor's friend Abram Sacher observed, "and some of them, in fact, demeaned it" by exhibiting an astonishing lack of sensitivity about using their father's influence to make money. "She didn't know what to do with her sons," Anna's son Curtis Roosevelt admitted. "They were often very rude to their father. At dinner, arguing about politics, particularly FDR, Jr., and Elliott, they were so extraordinarily arrogant with FDR."

Characteristically, and perhaps not without some cause, Eleanor blamed no one but herself. "I don't seem to be able to shake the feeling of responsibility . . . ," Eleanor wrote Hick in the mid-thirties, at the time of Elliott's first divorce. "I guess I was a pretty unwise teacher as to how to go about living. Too late to do anything now, however, & I'm rather disgusted with myself. I feel soiled. . . ."

"She felt that the guilt was all hers," Elliott later wrote, "because she had been unable to extend to us in our nursery days the warmth of love that the young find as necessary as food or drink." Eleanor believed she had failed as a mother because "she was so unsure of herself in the early days." Lacking confidence in her mothering skills, she allowed her ever-confident mother-in-law to take charge of hiring the nurses and setting up the nursery, accepting Sara's intervention both grudgingly and gratefully, cowed by inexperience and fear. "I was not allowed to take care of the children," Eleanor recalled, "nor had I any sense of how to do it."

"At a visceral level," Curtis Roosevelt recalled, "a kid can sense lack of confidence in a parent. My mother, Anna, lacked it. ER lacked it. Sara had it. She was the grande dame. She knew who she was and what she wanted." Even as a great-grandchild, Curtis recalled, he was drawn to that supreme confidence, "like a moth to the flame."

The struggle between the two women was no mere skirmish; it was war. Since Sara was unable to prevent her son's marriage, Eleanor observed in an unpublished article, "she determined to bend the marriage to the way she wanted it to be. What she wanted was to hold onto Franklin and his children; she wanted them to grow as she wished. As it turned out, Franklin's children were more my mother-in-law's children than they were mine."

Granny referred to them as *her* children, Jimmy recalled. She told them, "your mother only bore you, I am more your mother than your mother is." Even as a young boy, Jimmy recognized that this was a cruel thing for his grandmother to say, but he loved her and needed her too much to condemn her: "She was sort of a fairy godmother."

The children remembered Eleanor as a dutiful but preoccupied mother who read to them in bed, heard their prayers, and tried to teach them right from wrong. "It did not come naturally to me to understand little children or to enjoy them," Eleanor confessed. "Playing with children was difficult for me because play had not been an important part of my own childhood."

In contrast to their tangled feelings about their mother, the children would remember for the rest of their lives the adventures they shared with their father. "Franklin loved his small children," Eleanor recalled. "They were a great joy to him; he loved to play with them and I think he took great pleasure in their health and good looks and in their companionship. He made the children feel that he really was their age." On Saturday afternoons, he would "play the most ridiculous baseball games with them and go on paper chases and do all the things that . . . children enjoy." In later years, when their father had less and less time for them, the children tended to romanticize their playful romps, setting their father's spontaneity against their mother's stiffness.

Discipline was always a source of trouble in the Roosevelt household. "I was the disciplinarian, I'm afraid," Eleanor recalled. "[Franklin] found punishing a child almost an impossibility. He just couldn't do it. I remember distinctly once telling Johnny to go upstairs to his room, and just having a feeling that he hadn't gone. I went into my husband's study at Hyde Park and found Johnny sitting in his lap, weeping his heart out on his father's shirt front, and both of them looking equally guilty when I discovered them."

• • •

Although Eleanor anguished over her inability to communicate easily with her sons, she derived priceless comfort from her close relationship with her only daughter, Anna. When Anna was small, however, Eleanor was no more at ease with *her* than with the boys. Anna later told her third husband, James Halsted, that her mother was "very unpredictable and inconsistent in bringing up her children. Inconsistent in her feelings—sweet and lovely one hour and the next hour very critical, very demanding, and very difficult to be with. You could never tell what she really meant." Until Anna entered adolescence, she was closer to her father than to her mother. All the happiest moments of her childhood revolved around him, riding with him on the front of his horse to "the most unexpected spots in peaceful deserted glens deep in the woods," coasting with him down the steep hill behind the house at Hyde Park, where there were sudden bumps and the sled "would take off into the air," walking the mile and a half or so with him to her school in Washington, talking about "all sorts of things I liked to hear about—books I was reading, a cruise we might be going to take. . . ."

Anna was fifteen the summer her father contracted polio. Suddenly the wonderful playmate who had taken long walks with her and sailed with her and done so many physical things was now struggling to walk with heavy steel braces, the sweat pouring down his face. It was "traumatic," Anna later admitted. The situation was aggravated by the fact that Anna was in a new school in New York, much larger than her previous school, and was having trouble making friends. Meanwhile, Eleanor was so consumed in helping Franklin recover that she "did not realize that Anna was in difficulty." Interpreting her daughter's sullenness as typical adolescent behavior, Eleanor failed to appreciate that, with all the focus on Franklin, Anna had become convinced that she no longer mattered to either her mother or her father. "It never occurred to me," Eleanor later admitted, "to take her into my confidence and consult with her about our difficulties or tell her just what her father was going through."

The tension between mother and daughter was finally released late one afternoon that fall. Eleanor was reading a story to her youngest boys when the strain of trying both to nurse her husband and to mother her children suddenly overwhelmed her. She began to cry and she could not stop. Emancipated for the moment from the felt need of remaining in control (the only time in her life she remembered having gone to pieces in this manner), Eleanor flung herself on her bed and sobbed shamelessly for hours. "This outburst of mine had a good result so far as Anna and I were concerned," Eleanor later recognized. "She saw that I was not cold and unfeeling after all. And she poured out her troubles to me, saying she knew she had been wrong in thinking I did not love her. It was the start of an understanding between us.''

From that day forward, Eleanor gave Anna her best hours. When Anna returned from her first round of debutante dances, Eleanor waited up for her in case she wanted to talk. Though Anna was blonde and beautiful with marvelous long legs, Eleanor recognized some of her own insecurities in her daughter's awkward presence. One night, they talked until dawn. During these intimate exchanges, Eleanor shared with Anna the sorrows of her own childhood, the buried anger at her mother, the disillusionment with her father.

And then, one night, in the most memorable talk of all, Eleanor told her daughter about Franklin's love affair with Lucy Mercer. "I felt very strongly on Mother's side," Anna recalled. "I was mad—mad at Father" for his having hurt her mother so deeply. "Emotionally from then on I was always closer to my mother than I was to my father."

When Anna's youthful marriage to New York stockbroker Curtis Dall began to fall apart only a few years after they were wed, it was Eleanor who provided understanding and support. Then, when Anna fell in love with John Boettiger, the *Chicago Tribune* correspondent, during the 1932 campaign, Eleanor watched over and protected their love. In the forbidden phase of the romance, while both lovers were still married, Eleanor provided empathy, sanction, and encompassing love. "Eleanor saw in John the nice son she might have had," Anna's son Curtis observed. "He was smart, very good-looking, and knowledgeable about the issues. At the same time, he was very responsive to her, calling her Lovely Lady and flirting with her. It was nice for Anna that her mother and John got along so well."

On the eve of Anna's marriage to John in 1935, Eleanor sent a private letter to John. "I love Anna so dearly that I don't need to tell you that my willingness to let her go speaks much for my trust and love of you," she wrote. She would never interfere, she promised, but she had one last word of motherly advice: "Remember that Anna is I think rather like me, she'd always rather have the truth even if it is painful and never let a doubt or suspicion grow up between you two which honest facing can dispel."

The following year, Anna and John moved to Seattle, Washington, where they had an unusual opportunity to work together on a major West Coast daily—the *Seattle Post-Intelligencer*. At William Randolph Hearst's invitation, John was made publisher and Anna became associate editor of the women's pages. "The Northwest welcomed the Boettigers with bands and fireworks," a reporter from *The Saturday Evening Post* noted. "Crowds met the train at hinterland stations. Seattle threw a big banquet." It was a happy time for the young couple. Under their leadership the *Post-Intelligencer* expanded its circulation, and the two of them became the toast of the town. Glowing features portrayed John, with his "jovial manner, resonant voice and big physique" as a natural-born politician while Anna was likened to movie star

Katharine Hepburn, with her long legs, her figure "as slim and boyish as a schoolgirl," her careless clothes, and her manner of speaking directly.

Eleanor was despondent when Anna left Washington. "Perhaps I needed to have you away...," she wrote, "to realize just how much it means to have you.... I have felt sad every time we passed your door." But she was determined not to let the distance diminish their relationship. She wrote to her daughter several times a week, talked to her frequently on the phone, and scheduled her lecture tours so that she could spend a week in Seattle every spring and fall. So, this October, after watching Jimmy drill with his battalion on the evening of October 16, Eleanor flew to Seattle, where she spent the rest of the week with Anna and John in their new home, a sprawling white house on Lake Washington with ten bedrooms and five baths. "I begin to feel really at home in Seattle," a relaxed Eleanor told her readers. "There seems to be an endless flow of conversation that can fill up long hours of time." With the boys, Eleanor confided to Hick, she felt only tolerated, but with her daughter, she felt wanted and needed. "I suppose that is why I enjoy being with Anna and John so often."

•   •   •

Everything Eleanor heard on her cross-country trip convinced her that the Willkie campaign was gaining momentum. His crowds were growing with each passing day; his polls were steadily rising, and his message was gaining strength and substance. In late September, the Republican challenger had shifted his strategy, adopting a more strident tone. If Roosevelt continued in office, he shouted to audiences at every stop, "you can count on our men being on transports for Europe six months from now." The specter of American boys fighting in Europe opened what one historian has described as a "wide crack in a dam holding back floodwaters of popular emotion." Willkie's polls began to move upward; Roosevelt's victory margin began to shrink.

Eleanor sensed this change in sentiment and predicted that the president would lose unless he took to the road himself in a full-scale campaign. Though she conceded that he was coming into contact with thousands of people through his "inspection trips," she believed there was something fundamentally deceptive about his insistence that these forays to factories and arsenals were not campaign stops. The American people, she argued, did not want to be taken for granted. The president's responsibility was to go to them directly, to outline his positions, to counter Willkie's charges, and to ask for their support.

"Dearest Franklin," she wrote in mid-October. "I hope you will make a few more speeches. It seems to me pretty essential that you make them now as political speeches. The people have a right to hear your say in opposition to Willkie between now and the election."

Harold Ickes agreed with Eleanor. After presenting his arguments to Steve Early, Ickes went in to see Missy. Knowing that Missy had no fear of speaking honestly to the president, Ickes shared with her his worries about the campaign. "I painted her a pretty dark picture," Ickes recorded in his diary. "I asked her frankly whether the President wanted to win and suggested that the way he had been acting I was disposed to doubt whether he did or not. She said that he did . . . but he didn't like to put himself in a position of making it possible for Willkie, to say that he, Willkie, had smoked him out. I told Missy that in his speech of acceptance the President had said in effect that he would feel free at any time to correct any misrepresentations or misstatements and that certainly Willkie had given him a sufficient basis on this ground to justify his going out on the stump."

Under pressure from both Eleanor and Ickes, the president finally announced on October 11 that he would make five major campaign speeches in the weeks ahead. Following Ickes' suggestion, he justified his departure from his convention pledge by referring to the gross misrepresentations of the Willkie campaign, which required him to counter falsifications with facts. "I will not pretend that I find this an unpleasant duty," he told a cheering crowd at his first speech, in Philadelphia on October 23. "I am an old campaigner and I love a good fight."

The president may have spoken the truth when he said he loved a good fight, but two days later, when CIO chief John L. Lewis delivered a vitriolic personal attack against him in a speech that was broadcast on national radio, he was perceptibly disturbed. The isolationist labor leader had been criticizing the administration for months; he had denounced the creation of the NDAC as a turn to the right and had fought against conscription on the ground that it would deprive labor of all its gains under the New Deal. But few observers predicted that he would actually break with Roosevelt and support Willkie.

At 9 p.m., as Lewis moved up to the microphones to speak, the president was sitting by his radio in his study, accompanied by Harry Hopkins and Grace Tully. Eleanor was at the Olney Inn for dinner with a group of female journalists, including Ruby Black, Martha Strayer, Emma Bugbee, and Bess Furman. It had been a busy day for Roosevelt, starting with a press conference in the morning, various appointments, lunch with Eleanor, a meeting with the Cabinet, a brief appearance at a tea Eleanor had arranged for the National Conference of Negro Women, and a visit to the doctor. He was tired, but with only ten days left before the election and thirty million Americans tuned in to the event, the Lewis speech was too important to miss.

Delivered in a deep baritone voice, rich in rhetoric, Lewis' speech was perhaps the most vigorous attack ever launched against the popular president. He denounced the president as a man whose motivation and objective was *war.* "His every act leads me to this inescapable conclusion. The President has said that he hates war and will work for peace but his acts do not match his words." Indeed, Lewis argued, "the President has been scheming for years to involve us in war."

"Are we," Lewis asked, "to yield to the appetite for power and the vaunting ambitions of a man who plays with the lives of human beings for a pastime? I say no. I think the reelection of President Roosevelt for a third term would be a national evil of the first magnitude.... It is time for the manhood and the womanhood of America to assert themselves. Tomorrow may be too late. If not Roosevelt whom do I recommend?

"... Why, Wendell Willkie, of course ... a gallant American," a man with a common touch, a man "born in the briar and not to the purple," a man who "has worked with his hands and has known the pangs of hunger." Then Lewis issued a surprising ultimatum. Convinced that the division between Roosevelt and Willkie was so close that labor's vote would carry the election, he told his immense constituency that if Roosevelt was re-elected it would mean that labor had rejected his advice. If that were so, he would have no choice but to resign as president of the CIO. In other words, "sustain me now, or repudiate me." The choice was the public's: a vote for Roosevelt would be a vote against Lewis.

Both Roosevelt and Hopkins were "sad and low" after the speech. Visiting the White House the following morning, labor leader Sidney Hillman said that he had never seen either of them "so thoroughly scared." For Roosevelt, the depth of the hatred so evident in the speech was hard to comprehend. Though the president could understand and accept opposition to his domestic and foreign policies, Lewis' anger ran so deep that it could not be categorized in ordinary terms.

In private conversation, Willkie conceded that Lewis' dislike of Roosevelt was so profound that it was almost pathological. "John never can forget that he came up the hard way," Willkie observed. "The President is very genteel and he is patronizing to John without meaning to be and this drives John wild." Nor could Lewis forget the time he had received an invitation to bring his wife to tea with the president and the first lady. Eleanor was out of town, so Missy served, as she often did, as the president's hostess, but Lewis interpreted Eleanor's absence as a deliberate slight.

Hundreds of telegrams poured into the White House the day after the Lewis speech. In some mysterious way, Lewis' attack had created a powerful counterforce. "We take the liberty of assuring you that John L. Lewis did not speak for us," the New York local of the Amalgamated Clothing Workers wrote; "the attack made by Lewis is a betrayal of the interests and cause of labor." "Paducah labor is for you 100 percent," another telegram read. "Our shirtworkers starved on a dollar a day under Republican rule. Now we have 13 dollar forty hour week and a union. We are all talking and working and voting for you." "Don't let Lewis' speech weaken you," UMW Local #6082 wired. "We are behind you 100 percent." Sensing for the first time that the president might be in trouble, Roosevelt's supporters rallied to his side with passion and conviction. "John L. Lewis has kicked his mother after he had milked her dry," Alex Tunis wrote from West 97th Street in New York. "You are the only President that ever done anything for the miners," a miner's wife wrote from Barnabus, West Virginia. "I don't want to go back to the day before you took office. Them were terrible days for the miners. I hope you and Mrs. Roosevelt continue in the White House as long as you live and I hope you live a long time." Writing in a similar vein, a Minnesota home-maker assured the president that she would never forget that because of him her aged mother's last days were made comfortable, mentally as well as physically. "Old age pensions is only one thing for which you are to be eternally thanked."

Buoyed by stacks of similar telegrams, the president took to the road with a lift in his heart. "I am an old campaigner," he repeated with increasing conviction before every crowd, "and I love a good fight." On October 28, before a capacity crowd of twenty-two thousand at Madison Square Garden, Roosevelt set out to answer the Republican charge that he had been slow in preparing the U.S. for defense. Every seat in the Garden was filled; another thirty thousand people were gathered outside, trying to get in. For seven years, the president began, Republican leaders had blocked every effort to strengthen America's defenses, shouting from the rooftops that our armed strength was sufficient for any enemy. "Great Britain would never have received an ounce of help from us if the decision had been left to [Congressman Joseph] Martin, [Congressman Bruce] Barton and [Congressman Hamilton] Fish." At the first use of the rhythmic sequence "Martin, Barton and Fish," the crowd roared with laughter. When he used it again, they were ready to join in, yelling "Barton" and "Fish" as soon as he said "Martin." By the end of the speech, the crowd was on its feet, yelling, screaming, and laughing.

"The way of the man with his crowds," one reporter wrote, "very great and responsive, roused them as much as anything he said. In every toss of his head, in every lift of a jutting chin, in every crackling, twitting jibe at his opponents, in every gesture and fillip of his speaking, he was as cocky a candidate" as one could imagine. "I have just come from one of the most remarkable experiences of my life," David Lilienthal recorded in his diary at midnight that night. "I sat on the platform not ten feet from the President and heard him deliver a really great speech." When the president first arrived, Lilienthal observed, "his face was gray under the lights and showed the strain of that awful walking. Nothing I have ever seen was like the next few minutes. The President's voice as he spoke was strong, there wasn't a trace of weariness at any time. He seemed to be in fine fettle."

The masterly speech came at the climax of a fourteen-hour day of strenuous campaigning. It was nearly midnight when the president returned to Penn Station to board his special train to Washington. In the confusion of the large crowd that had gathered at the track, Roosevelt's press secretary, Steve Early, was stopped by two policemen, one Irish, the other Negro. They were under orders to keep everyone away from the train. Early tried to push his way through but was shoved back. In the melee, he kicked the Negro policeman, James Sloan, in the groin. When Sloan, a decorated patrolman and father of five who had just returned to duty after an operation for a hernia, had to be taken to the hospital for treatment, the incident became a front-page story in the Negro press. Republicans quickly capitalized on it. Pictures of Sloan recuperating in his bed were handed out in black neighborhoods. "Negroes," the caption read, "if you want your President to be surrounded by Southern influences of this kind, vote for Roosevelt. If you want to be treated with respect, vote for Wendell Willkie!"

Early was reportedly inconsolable, fearing he might have lost the election for the president, but when reporters interviewed Patrolman Sloan at his bedside, the controversy came to an end. "I am a Democrat," Sloan said. "If anybody thinks they can turn me against our great President who has done so much for our race because of this thing, they are mistaken."

• • •

On the 29th of October, the president set in motion the first peacetime conscription in history with a drawing of draft numbers to determine the order of induction. Two weeks earlier, on registration day, all males between twenty-one and thirty-five had been required to present themselves at their local draft boards, where they were each assigned a serial number. Now, on lottery day, the chance selection of numbers stirred in the big fishbowl with a big wooden dipper would determine which of the young men who had registered would be called to leave civilian life for a year's military training, and in what order they would be called.

A number of Roosevelt's advisers had strongly urged him to postpone the lottery until after the election, but he refused. The timing was so bad, Sam Rosenman observed, that "any old-time politician would have said [it] could never take place." It was a brave decision on the president's part to let it happen at this time, Stimson recorded in his diary, "when there is a very bitter campaign being made against it on account of his support of the Draft." But after it was over, Stimson came to believe that the solemn nature of the historic ceremony "served to change the event . . . into a great asset in his favor."

The president's expression was serious as he sat beside Secretary Stimson on the stage of Washington's Departmental Auditorium. Both the large glass fishbowl and the long ladle used to stir the cobalt capsules had been used in World War I to select the men who would go into battle. The strip of yellow linen used to blindfold Secretary Stimson was cut from the covering of the chair used at the signing of the Declaration of Independence. After putting his blindfold in place, Stimson reached his left hand into the large jar, picked up the first capsule he touched, and handed it to the president. "The first number," Roosevelt announced, reading into a battery of microphones carrying his voice across all three radio networks, "is one-fifty-eight."

No sooner had the president spoken then a woman's scream was heard. Seated in the middle of the crowded auditorium, Mrs. Mildred Bell gasped. Her twenty-one-year-old son, Harry, who was supposed to be married the following week, held number 158. Now, suddenly, his future was linked to that of his country. Number 158 was held by some six thousand registrants in different precincts throughout the country, including Cleveland welder Michael Thomson, father of three children; Jack Clardy, a one-armed Negro banjo picker from Charlotte, North Carolina; and unemployed James Cody of Long Island City. In New York, the surnames of those bearing number 158 told a story in themselves: Farrugia, Chan, Re, Weisblum, Tsatsarones, Stoller, Clement. Some were pleased and proud to be the first number called, others said they'd make the best of it, still others were upset at their bad fortune. "This is the first lottery I ever won in my life," several jokingly complained. It took seventeen hours to draw the remaining nine thousand capsules, but when the bowl was finally empty, the order of induction for more than sixteen million men had been established.

Eleanor was in Maine delivering a speech at Colby College while the lottery was taking place. "As I listened to the radio," she wrote Joe Lash, "and heard the draft numbers read, I found myself thinking of you and hoping that your number would not come up. I want you so much to get started along lines which you can follow and develop into great influence and use to others of the younger generation and I would hate to see you packed off for a year of army training. . . . I don't feel the same about my boys, except FDR Jr. whom I would like to see take his bar exam in March."

• • •

Roosevelt was anxious and testy on the day after the drawing. Riding to Boston in his special train for a speech to be delivered that night at the Boston Garden, he was bombarded by messages from frightened Democrats who feared he would lose the election unless he guaranteed to American mothers that their sons were being sent to army camps only to be trained, that they would never have to fight. Seeking to allay these concerns, he decided to include in his speech a pledge that would haunt him again and again in the years ahead. "Very simply and honestly," he said, "I can give assurance to the mothers and to the fathers of America that each and every one of their boys in training will be well housed and well fed. . . . And while I am talking to you fathers and mothers I give one more assurance. I have said this before, but I shall say it again, and again, and again. Your boys are not going to be sent into any foreign wars." In all his previous speeches, he had qualified the pledge that American boys would not fight in foreign wars by adding the phrase "except in cases of attack." The speechwriters had inserted a similar qualification in the draft of the Boston speech, but the president insisted on removing the words. "It's not necessary," he argued. "It's implied clearly. If we're attacked, it's no longer a foreign war."

The president's impulsiveness, Rosenman observed, was to cause him "a lot of headaches later," for his opponents took great pleasure in quoting the categorical pledge he had made in Boston. In her column two days later, Eleanor gently took issue with the disingenuousness of her husband's promise. "Today," she told her readers, "no one can honestly promise you peace at home or abroad. All any human being can do is to promise that he will do his utmost to prevent this country from being involved in war."

•   •   •

The day was warm for the 5th of November; in the Roosevelt home at Hyde Park, the family was getting ready for the short journey into town to vote in the presidential election. As he always did on election day, Roosevelt stopped to chat with his Hyde Park neighbors before entering the little town hall. Reporters observed nothing in the president's demeanor to indicate concern over the outcome of the election; on the contrary, he seemed "extraordinarily jovial," joking with staff and journalists alike. Yet, underneath his cheery manner, Roosevelt was fully aware that in the latest Gallup poll Willkie's support was almost even with his, making the election too close to call.

Inside the town hall, photographers waited in the balcony overhead to snap a picture of the president as he emerged from behind the green curtains of the voting booth. Standing next to her son in line, Sara stepped up to the table. "What name please?" the election clerk inquired. "Sara Delano Roosevelt," she answered firmly, "and it's been my name for a good many years." In the confusion created by the photographer, Eleanor started to leave the building before she had recorded her vote. Reminded by her husband, she hastily returned to the booth.

During the afternoon, the president made a halfhearted attempt to work on his stamp collection in his study, while Eleanor and Joe Lash went on a long walk through the woods. Eleanor told Lash she hoped that, if the president were re-elected to an unprecedented third term, he "would do all the things he had wanted to do and knew had to be done but had not done because of political considerations."

At six o'clock, Eleanor welcomed about forty family members and friends, including Harry Hopkins, Frances Perkins, and Helen Gahagan, to a buffet supper at her cottage. With a wood fire on the hearth, she moved from one guest to another, putting everyone at ease. Toward nine o'clock, the guests wandered back to the Big House, where they chatted nervously, listened to the radio, and awaited the returns.

Seated apart from all the guests, alone at the mahogany dining table with large tally sheets and a long row of freshly sharpened pencils before him, the president of the United States charted the election results. Occasionally, the door slid open to admit Missy LeHand, carrying the latest totals for the president to add to his tally. As the early returns filtered in, the president's face darkened. In almost every state Willkie was doing far better than Alf Landon had done. Sweating profusely, Roosevelt called Mike Reilly, his Secret Service guard. "Mike, I don't want to see anybody in here," he said. "Including your family?" Reilly asked. "I said anybody," Roosevelt repeated, as he closed the door. It appeared to Reilly that the president had lost his nerve.

By 11 p.m., however, as the votes in the big states of New York, Illinois, Ohio, and Pennsylvania began to come in, showing heavy Democratic majorities, the tide turned toward the president. Nationwide, the votes of labor, Negroes, and the foreign-born were holding up. In the lowest-income districts, the president was winning nearly 75 percent of the votes. The tension in the house began to dissipate. At midnight, a smiling president emerged to greet a jubilant crowd of local Democrats parading across the lawn with torchlights. "It looks all right," the president told his cheering neighbors. "We, of course, face difficult days in this country. But I think you will find me in the future just the same Franklin Roosevelt you have known a great many years. My heart has always been here. It always will be."

Behind the president, as he spoke from the balcony, stood his mother, his wife, and his sons FDR, Jr., and John. Farther back, standing by himself, Harry Hopkins did "a little jig and clapped his fist into the open palm of his left hand as if to say 'we did it.' " When the president finished speaking, the family turned toward the house. "We want Eleanor," the crowd shouted. "We want Eleanor." But Eleanor gestured them away. "What have I to do with it? It's the President they want to hear—not me."

As the president fell asleep that night in his childhood home, he had reached the highest peak of his career. In numbers, it was not a great victory. He had won 54.7 percent to 44.8 percent for Willkie, the smallest plurality since the election of 1916. But he had won, despite the hatred of conservatives and isolationists, despite the attacks of John L. Lewis. He had won something that neither Washington nor Jefferson nor Jackson had ever achieved—a third term as president of the United States.

CHAPTER 8

"ARSENAL OF

DEMOCRACY"

"Just how does the President think?" reporter John Gunther once asked Eleanor Roosevelt. "My dear Mr. Gunther," Eleanor replied. "The President never thinks. He decides."

Mr. Gunther's question was on the minds of several Cabinet members in mid-November 1940, when the president seemed unable and unwilling to concentrate his thoughts on a new and disturbing crisis: Great Britain was on the verge of bankruptcy.

The cash reserves of the British treasury, the U.S. was told after the election, were no longer sufficient to pay for the munitions and supplies that Britain had ordered from the U.S.—supplies needed now more than ever. Though Britain's success in repulsing the Luftwaffe had postponed the threatened invasion until spring, the German advantage in war materials was growing and would continue to grow as Germany increasingly moved to supplement its own vast production with that of the industrial countries it had conquered—Holland, Belgium, France, Czechoslovakia. Without American supplies to close the gap, Britain would be defeated in a matter of months.

What to do? The idea of loaning the money to Britain was raised in the Cabinet, but no one believed that Congress would go along, given America's experience with unpaid debts in World War I. During the discussion, the president, Frances Perkins recalled, threw out "a question here and a hint there." Perkins had the feeling that "he was thinking about something, about some way in which the people of the U.S. could assist the British," but he had nothing concrete to offer. The problem seemed insoluble.

In the midst of the crisis, as administration officials were frantically scurrying from one meeting to another, the president suddenly announced that he was leaving Washington for a ten-day sail through the Caribbean on the navy cruiser the U.S.S. *Tuscaloosa*. He told his stunned Cabinet, "All of you use your imaginations" to come up with an answer. To be sure, the exhausted president needed to rest after the wearying campaign. "The more I sleep, the more I want to sleep," he was heard to say. But the timing of the pleasure trip was profoundly disturbing to those who worried about Britain's survival.

"Hope you have a grand trip," Eleanor wired Franklin from Abilene, Texas, as she set forth on a trip of her own—a rigorous lecture tour through the South and the Midwest. Everywhere she went, she kept her eye on the economic and social weaknesses of the nation preparing for war. Driving through the rural sections of Texas, she was saddened to see that, despite the New Deal's housing program, people were still living in shacks, "made of scraps apparently, bits of corrugated iron, even heavy cardboard is used. . . . I cannot help feeling that there should be a better way of meeting this problem." Hearing reports that, of the first million men selected for the draft, almost 40 percent were found physically unfit for military service, Eleanor hoped the sorry figures would "give impetus to the movement for a comprehensive and nationwide health program." And as always, there remained the plight of the Negro, particularly visible in the slums of Chicago and Detroit.

"In every place," Tommy reported to Anna, "the audiences have been capacity audiences and the attention and interest excellent. There is no question that your mother is an idol to the people of this country." Looking over Tommy's shoulder at this point, Eleanor observed, with a flash of self-deprecatory humor, that instead of saying, "your mother is an idol," Tommy should say, "your mother isn't idle."

•   •   •

Hundreds of people were standing on the dock at Miami when the president, accompanied by a handful of his closest aides, including Harry Hopkins, Pa Watson, and Dr. Ross McIntire, arrived to board the ship. With a happy smile on his face, he waved his hat to the applauding crowd and stood by the rail while the national anthem was played. Horns began to blow as the ship was cast off and continued until the vessel was out of the harbor and steaming into the Atlantic.

The president spent his days with his white shirtsleeves rolled up over his wrestler's arms, talking, fishing and basking in the sun. From the beginning of the trip to the end, the newspapermen who followed faithfully behind on a convoy destroyer had no idea where they were going or how long they would be gone. At Guantanamo Bay the cruiser pulled into the dock for an hour's stop so that a large stock of Cuban cigars could be carried on board. At Jamaica, St. Lucia, and Antigua, the president hosted British colonial officials and their wives at lunch. At Eleuthera Island he was joined by the duke of Windsor. Relaxing evenings were spent on deck cheering boxing matches between black mess attendants, listening to drummer contests between sailors and marines, playing poker, and watching movies— including *Tin Pan Alley,* starring Betty Grable, and *Northwest Mounted Police,* with Gary Cooper and Paulette Goddard.

At designated points along the way, navy seaplanes circled the presidential flotilla and landed alongside the *Tuscaloosa* to deliver the White House mail. Several chatty letters from Eleanor arrived. She was enjoying her trip, she told him, though she was growing weary of the Southern voice. "I think of you as sleeping and eating and I hope getting a rest from the world."

But the world would not go away. From daily news dispatches Roosevelt learned that heavy raids on London had devastated the House of Commons, and that massive bombings of Coventry, Birmingham, and Bristol had so severely damaged dozens of war factories that vital production would be halted for months. At the same time, it was reported that the severity of German submarine sinkings had escalated; in a matter of weeks, seven merchant vessels carrying tons of needed supplies had been sunk. And from Washington came news of the unexpected death of Lord Lothian, British ambassador to the U.S., who had worked unremittingly to strengthen his country's bond with the United States. A Christian Scientist, Lothian had refused treatment for a simple infection that turned toxic.

On the morning of December 9, a seaplane touched down with a letter from Winston Churchill. Having composed it over a period of weeks, Churchill regarded the letter as "one of the most important" he had ever written. "My dear Mr. President," Churchill began. "As we reach the end of this year I feel you will expect me to lay before you the prospects for 1941. I do so strongly and confidently." At the outset, he wanted the president to understand that while Britain could endure "the shattering of our dwellings and the slaughter of our civil population by indiscriminate air attacks," she was facing "a less sudden and less spectacular but equally deadly danger"— economic strangulation. "Unless we can establish our ability to feed this Island, to import the munitions of all kinds which we need, we may fall by the way, and the time needed by the U.S. to complete her defensive preparations may not be forthcoming." He went on to catalogue in detail the losses in production and shipping Britain had sustained from the bombing raids and the U-boat attacks. "Only the United States," he wrote, "could supply the additional shipping capacity so urgently needed as well as the crucial weapons of war."

Last of all, he came to the knotty problem that was on everyone's mind— the problem of finances. "The moment approaches where we shall no longer be able to pay cash for shipping and other supplies. While we will do our utmost and shrink from no proper sacrifices to make payments across the exchange, I believe you will agree that it would be wrong in principle and mutually disadvantageous in effect if, at the height of this struggle Great Britain were to be divested of all saleable assets so that after the victory was won with our blood, civilization saved and the time gained for the United States to be fully armed against all eventualities, we should stand stripped to the bone. Such a course would not be in the moral or economic interests of either of our countries. . . .

"You may be assured that we shall prove ourselves ready to suffer and sacrifice to the utmost for the Cause, and that we glory in being its champions. The rest we leave with confidence to you and to your people, being sure that ways and means will be found which future generations on both sides of the Atlantic will approve and admire."

Churchill's letter had a profound effect on the president, though he said little about it at first. "I didn't know for quite a while what he was thinking about, if anything," Hopkins said later. "But then—I began to get the idea that he was refueling, the way he so often does when he seems to be resting and carefree. So I didn't ask him any questions. Then, one evening, he suddenly came out with it—the whole program. He didn't seem to have any clear idea how it could be done legally. But there wasn't a doubt in his mind that he'd find a way to do it."

The president's "whole program," later to be known as "lend-lease," was the unconventional idea that the United States could send Britain weapons and supplies without charge and then, after the war, be repaid not in dollars but in kind. How Roosevelt arrived at this ingenious idea, which cut through all the stale debates in Washington about loans and gifts, is not clear. "Nobody that I know of," White House speechwriter Robert Sherwood has written, "has been able to give any convincing idea" of how the refueling process worked. "He did not seem to talk much about the subject in hand, or to consult the advice of others, or to 'read up' on it. . . . One can only say that FDR, a creative artist in politics, had put in his time on this cruise evolving the pattern of a masterpiece."

Frances Perkins later described the president's idea for lend-lease as a "flash of almost clairvoyant knowledge and understanding." He would have one of these flashes every now and then, she observed, much like those that musicians get when "they see or hear the structure of an entire symphony or opera." He couldn't always hold on to it or verbalize it, but when it came, he suddenly understood how all kinds of disparate things fit together. Though Stimson could justly complain that trying to follow the president's intuitive thought processes as he moved from one idea to the next in no logical order was "very much like chasing a vagrant beam of sunshine around a vacant room," Roosevelt made up for the defects of an undisciplined mind with a profound ability to integrate a vast multitude of details into a larger pattern that gave shape and direction to the stream of events.

• • •

The president returned to Washington Monday afternoon, December 16, tanned, rested, and in excellent humor. The following day, at his press conference, he puffed hard on his cigarette and then revealed his startling plan. He had heard a great deal of nonsense about finances in the past few days, he began, by people who could think only in traditional terms. Whereas banal minds assumed that either the Neutrality Acts of the late 1930s or the Johnson Act, barring loans to defaulters on World War I debts, would have to be repealed in order to allow loans or gifts to England, he had a much simpler notion in mind—a gentlemen's agreement that eliminated the foolish dollar sign entirely, and allowed England to make repayment in kind after the war.

"Well, let me give you an illustration: Suppose my neighbor's home catches on fire, and I have a length of garden hose four or five hundred feet away. If he can take my garden hose and connect it up with his hydrant, I may help to put out his fire. Now what do I do? I don't say to him before that operation, 'Neighbor, my garden hose cost me $15; you have to pay me $15 for it.' What is the transaction that goes on? I don't want $15—I want my garden hose back after the fire is over. All right. If it goes through the fire all right, intact, without any damage to it, he gives it back to me and thanks me very much for the use of it." And if the hose was damaged by the fire, he could simply replace it.

The president's idea, Frances Perkins observed, "was really based upon very old, primitive and countrified ways of doing things. . . . He could draw very large deductions and large plans from such simple operations which he had observed in his childhood and youth, which were common in the country and seemed natural, like lending hoses or ladders to a neighbor when his house was on fire, and the neighbor would reciprocate when he could." Even if the ladder burned and the neighbor was unable to repay the actual money it cost, then, "the next potato crop he gets, he comes around with a few barrels of potatoes for you." The moral of the story was clear: by sending supplies to the British now, the U. S. would be abundantly repaid by the increase to its own security.

• • •

The following week, the president took his argument for lend-lease to the American people in a fireside chat that would later become known as the "arsenal for democracy" speech. A fierce debate over aid to England was engulfing the nation, on street corners and college campuses, in labor halls and country stores, in corporate boardrooms and family living rooms. In September, a powerful noninterventionist organization, the America First Committee, had been formed. Sixty thousand citizens were already on board, and it was said to be gaining members "like a house afire." America Firsters were convinced that extensive aid to Britain would inevitably drag

America into the war. It was important for the president to find the words that would undercut the opposition and set the tone for the congressional debate that would follow the introduction of the lend-lease bill.

The speech went through seven drafts. Speechwriters Sam Rosenman and Robert Sherwood came to live at the White House for the week. It was Harry Hopkins who suggested the key phrase "arsenal of democracy." Roosevelt, Sherwood recalled, "really enjoyed working on this speech for, with the political campaign over, it was the first chance he had had in months and even years to speak his mind with comparative freedom."

As the appointed hour of 9 p.m. approached, theater owners in New York noted a decided drop in attendance: thousands of people who would otherwise have gone to the movies stayed home to listen to the president's speech. Roosevelt began by telling the nation that there was no hope of a negotiated peace with Germany. "No man can tame a tiger into a kitten by stroking it. There can be no appeasement with ruthlessness." If Britain fell, the "unholy alliance," which now included Japan as well as Germany and Italy, would continue its drive to conquer the world, and then "all of us in all the Americas would be living at the point of a gun."

Next he summoned the American people to become "the great arsenal of democracy" by showing "the same resolution, the same sense of urgency, the same spirit of patriotism and sacrifice as we would show were we at war." This job, he emphasized, "cannot be done merely by superimposing on the existing productive facilities the added requirements for defense." Americans must discard the notion of "business as usual." He admitted that "there is risk in any course we may take," but he insisted that there was less chance of getting into war if the U.S. did all it could to support the nations fighting the Axis.

In arguing for aid to Britain as an alternative to war, Roosevelt crystallized what a large number of his fellow citizens were thinking and feeling. A recent Gallup poll revealed that a clear majority of Americans favored military aid to Britain but 88 percent of those polled said they would vote against American entrance into the war. As long as lend-lease was positioned as a substitute for war, it would gather wide support. "I call for this national effort," the president concluded, "in the name of this nation which we love and honor and which we are privileged and proud to serve. I call upon our people with absolute confidence that our common cause will greatly succeed."

On the night of the fireside chat, the Germans subjected London to the heaviest bombing attack of the war, hoping to counter the effect that Roosevelt's words might produce on British morale. A large part of the old city was destroyed. The ancient Guildhall, seat of the city's municipal government since the days of William the Conqueror, was reduced to a blackened shell, as was the historic house off Fleet Street where Dr. Samuel Johnson had written many of his famous works. Eight Christopher Wren churches and the Central Criminal Court, better known as Old Bailey, were also hit and burned. "The havoc," one reporter wrote, "was comparable only to that wrought in the Great Fire of 1666."

"London has nothing to smile about at the moment," Germany's propaganda minister, Joseph Goebbels, recorded in his diary. The Reichminister was mistaken. At 3:30 a.m., thousands of Londoners were crowded around their radios listening to the president's broadcast. His words, Churchill told Roosevelt the next day, stirred hope and confidence. "When I visited the still-burning ruins today, the spirit of the Londoners was as high as in the first days of the indiscriminate bombing in September, four months ago.

"I thank you for testifying before all the world that the future safety and greatness of the American Union are intimately concerned with the upholding and the effective arming of that indomitable spirit."

• • •

Labor leader Walter Reuther, architect of the historic sit-down strikes in Detroit in the mid-thirties, answered the president's call for an end to "business as usual" with a provocative plan to manufacture war planes in automobile plants. Production of planes, he pointed out, was 30 percent behind schedule and would continue to lag as long as the aircraft industry continued to rely on the "slow and costly methods of hand-tooled custom made production." Though Detroit had mass-produced four million cars the previous year, the combined production of all the airplane manufacturers in 1939 was eighteen hundred planes. "Conventional methods will never bring results in unconventional warfare," Reuther argued.

Reuther's plan was based on the theory that plane- and auto-making were alike at many steps. Instead of building entirely new aircraft plants which could not be put into operation for eighteen months, he proposed adapting existing automotive machinery to aircraft manufacture. "We propose to transform the entire unused capacity of the auto industry into one huge plane production unit."

The plan called for the president to appoint an aviation production board of nine members, three each representing government, management, and labor. The board would have complete authority to supervise and coordinate the mass production of airplanes in the auto industry. Each auto plant would be asked the make the parts it could best manufacture—Buick might put out the crank shafts, Dodge the cylinders, and Hudson the valves—and then two central plants would be used to assemble the planes.

The announcement of the Reuther plan created a sensation in the press. Columnist Dorothy Thompson called it "the most important event" in weeks, and columnist Walter Lippmann claimed the proposal held historic importance because it represented "the first great plan which organized labor had offered in its status not of a hired man but of the responsible partner."

Roosevelt's immediate response was equally positive. "It is well worth our while," he wrote William Knudsen, "to give a good deal of attention to this program." But even before a meeting between Knudsen and Reuther was arranged, the attacks from both the aircraft and the automobile industries began. Though planes and autos were alike to a point, the industrialists argued, the higher degree of precision required to produce a delicately balanced plane demanded special skills, special equipment, and hand-held operations. There was some truth to this argument, but the problem was not insurmountable, as was evidenced by the fact that, under contracts let earlier in the year, the Cadillac plant in Detroit was already at work manufacturing the most precise parts of the Allison engine, while Murray & Briggs were stamping wing parts for Douglas bombers. What was insurmountable was the reluctance of the aircraft industry to cheapen production methods and lower prices at a time when the government was prepared to pay any price for the planes it so desperately needed. A similar reluctance affected the auto industry, which was enjoying its most profitable season in years as the reviving economy allowed Americans to buy some of the comforts they had been unable to afford for so long.

Under the weight of industry's attacks, the excitement about the Reuther plan faded. By the time Knudsen finally sat down to talk with Reuther, the plan was already dead. "Mr. Knudsen and I had met previously on opposite sides of the table," a bitter Reuther told the press after the fruitless meeting. "I thought on this matter of national defense we might sit on the same side. I was mistaken."

The hostile reaction to the Reuther plan had deeper roots than the fear of losing profits. "The fear," correspondent I. F. Stone concluded, "was a fear of losing power, a fear of democracy in industry as instinctive as the fear and hatred kings felt for parliament." Historian Bruce Catton reached a similar conclusion. The problem, he wrote, was that "labor had grown up and had ideas. This wasn't going be be like the last war, with the trade associations running industry and [Samuel] Gompers exhorting the boys not to strike. . . . Labor was coming up to the quarter deck just as if it had a right to be there, making suggestions about how the ship ought to be handled." Treasury Secretary Henry Morgenthau expressed the same sentiment in more succinct terms: "There is only one thing wrong with this proposal," he warned Roosevelt. "It comes from the wrong source."

It would take the attack on Pearl Harbor and American entry into the war to create a receptive audience for Reuther's vision of mass-producing airplanes in automobile plants. But in the meantime, precious time was lost.

• • •

The Christmas holidays found the White House in a state of cheerful confusion, with dozens of houseguests coming and going—some staying only for the night, some for a few days, others for longer stretches. There was Sara Roosevelt, the president's mother, who brought her maid and took up residence in the Rose Suite, the principal guest quarters on the second floor, which the queen of England had occupied during the royal visit in 1939.

There was Crown Princess Juliana of the Netherlands, who arrived with her two little daughters and a retinue of servants. There were Elliott Roosevelt and FDR, Jr., with his wife, infant son, and nursemaid. There was an odd assortment of single men occupying various bedrooms on the third floor, including Eleanor's younger brother, Hall; Franklin's old friend Harry Hooker; and Eleanor's new friend Joe Lash.

Despite the full household, Eleanor managed to slip away for several days to New York, where she lunched with author Ernest Hemingway, whose book *For Whom the Bell Tolls* was currently on the best-seller list; saw Ethel Barrymore in *The Corn Is Green;* enjoyed an excellent production of the opera *Tristan and Isolde;* and finished her Christmas shopping at Arnold Constable, where she bought eighteen dozen pairs of nylon-silk hose and fourteen sets of matching ties and handkerchiefs. In her customary fashion, Eleanor had begun shopping for this Christmas the day after the previous Christmas; she couldn't bear the anxiety of waiting until the last minute, she once told a friend, but preferred to stretch the process over the entire year, taking comfort in the gifts that were accumulating month by month in her special Christmas closet.

The president, White House housekeeper Henrietta Nesbitt reported, was in a happy mood when Eleanor returned. "He was just bursting with news." For weeks, he had been trying to make arrangements to bring Prince Olav to Washington from London as a surprise Christmas present for Princess Martha and the children, and finally everything had been worked out. How was he getting here? Eleanor asked, knowing how difficult it was to secure any form of transportation from Europe. "By clipper," Roosevelt announced. "I arranged it."

Eleanor spent the morning after she returned going over menus with Mrs. Nesbitt. The week before Christmas was a trying time for the household staff. Besides the houseful of guests, there was a special round of parties—a formal reception for the members of the judiciary, a state dinner in honor of Crown Princess Juliana, and a large reception for White House employees and their families. Mrs. Nesbitt did not deal well with added stress. A plain, unimaginative woman of German stock with a stern face and a dark bun pulled tightly at the nape of her neck, Mrs. Nesbitt supervised a staff of twenty-six, including cooks, butlers, ladies' maids, and chambermaids. She was not a professional housekeeper—Eleanor had originally hired her in the mid-twenties to bake pies and strudels for large parties at Hyde Park— but she was thrifty, and Eleanor was determined to keep a tight rein on expenses at the White House.

For years, the president had pleaded with Eleanor to find a new house-keeper to replace Mrs. Nesbitt. All his life, he had loved good food—he was especially fond of quail and pheasant cooked so rare as to be bloody. He loved oyster crabs, out-of-the-way country cheeses, and peach cobbler. But Mrs. Nesbitt maintained that a proper diet consisted of "plain foods, plainly prepared." She served the same simple meals over and over again, to the point where White House guests could predict by the day of the week what they would have for dinner—tongue with caper sauce on Mondays, boiled beef on Tuesdays, roast beef and mashed potatoes on Wednesdays. The word was out that the White House cuisine was impossibly drab, dull, and overcooked.

For the president, who rarely had a chance to eat out in restaurants because of his paralysis, Mrs. Nesbitt was a unique cross to bear. But, true to form, he could not bring himself to fire her. So Mrs. Nesbitt—or "Fluffy," as she was called behind her back—remained at her post, month after month, year after year. Elliott Roosevelt recalled various dinners at the White House when Missy, "always handsome in a dinner gown," would catch the president's eye as some overcooked dish appeared. They would smile knowingly at one another, proceed to eat as much as they could bear, and then rummage up egg sandwiches in the little kitchen off the president's study.

As long as Mrs. Nesbitt remained in charge of the kitchen, her concept of what should be eaten prevailed. She insisted, for instance, on serving Roosevelt broccoli even though he let everyone know that he didn't like it. "Fix it anyhow," she told the cooks; "he *should* like it." Once, when royal guests were dining with the president, the call came to the kitchen for hot coffee. Mrs. Nesbitt sent iced tea instead. "It was better for them," she said.

The housekeeper's personal tastes governed breakfasts as well. "My God!" the president exclaimed one morning to Grace Tully. "Doesn't Mrs. Nesbitt know that there are breakfast foods besides oatmeal? It's been served to me morning in and morning out for months and months now and I'm sick and tired of it!" Later that day, he called Tully in for dictation. Leaning back in his chair, he held in his hand an advertisement for various cereals he had torn from the morning paper. "Corn Flakes! 13 ounce package, 19 cents! Post Toasties! 13 ounce package, 19 cents! Cream of Wheat! two for 27 cents! . . . Now take this gentle reminder to Mrs. Nesbitt."

When Mrs. Nesbitt failed to respond to his gentle reminders, Roosevelt turned to Eleanor. "Do you remember," he asked her in a memo, "that about a month ago I got sick of chicken because I got it (between lunch and dinner) at least six times a week? The chicken situation has definitely improved, but 'they' have substituted sweetbreads, and for the past month I have been getting sweetbreads about six times a week. I am getting to the point where my stomach positively rebels and this does not help my relations with foreign powers. I bit two of them today." Eleanor must have relayed the message, but the sweetbreads kept coming until the president sent Mrs. Nesbitt an ultimatum, telling her he did not want to see sweetbreads again for at least two months!

Unfortunately for the president, Eleanor had absolutely no taste for fine food. Her own cooking was limited to scrambling eggs, and she never thought about what she was eating. To her mind, good conversation created a good meal; the food was secondary. Though she tried to respond to the president's specific requests, the White House food remained, "to put it mildly," frequent visitor John Gunther observed, "undistinguished."

If the food was undistinguished, the company was not. The president loved the bustle of Christmas, the festive atmosphere, the holly that decked the mansion, and the gay conversations. Whether greeting guests on a receiving line or sharing a dinner, he was a genial host, charming and attentive. If the conversation flagged, he could always get it going by asking a question, telling a story, or exchanging a piece of gossip. Clever company and bright conversation stimulated him; talk was his favorite form of relaxation.

This Christmas, the president took added pleasure in the arrival of a new puppy named Fala, a gift from his cousin Margaret Suckley. He had longed for a puppy for years, he told his cousin as he lifted the little Scottish terrier into his arms, but Eleanor did not consider the White House a proper place to bring up a dog. Roosevelt had had pets before, but Fala became his friend in a way no other pet had been. Fala accompanied the president everywhere, eating his meals in Roosevelt's study, sleeping in a chair at the foot of his bed. Within a few weeks of his arrival, the puppy was sent to the hospital with a serious intestinal disturbance. He had discovered the White House kitchen, and everyone was feeding him. When he came home, Roosevelt issued a stern order to the entire White House staff: "Not even one crumb will be fed to Fala except by the President." From then on, Fala was in perfect health.

"In years to come," author William Klingaman has written, "many Americans would remember December 25, 1940, as one of the happiest Christmases of their lives." Though there were terrible problems abroad, the economy at home was showing signs of prosperity for the first time in more than a decade. Factories were working double shifts; the railroads were adding personnel and equipment, steel production was on the rise. Unemployment had fallen by nearly two million since the previous year. People had money now and were spending it. Automobile manufacturers were looking to their biggest year since 1929. Restaurant operators were enjoying a marked increase in business; people were ordering prime steak for the first time in years. Gift buying in department stores that December, *The New York Times* reported, approached "an orgy of spending as if customers were determined to show there was at least one country that enjoyed peace and good will."

For her part, Eleanor seemed more driven than usual, racing from one event to the next, helping Santa Claus hand out toys to seven hundred needy children from the stage of a local theater, attending the annual Christmas party for the Salvation Army, greeting a community chorus of Negro carolers and looking in on a neighborhood celebration at Green's Court, a squalid alley dwelling within sight of the Capitol building. "Here life is not so pleasant," she conceded, "but for another year we may hope for fewer alleys and better places to live in."

• • •

On January 6, 1941, the president was scheduled to present his lend-lease program to Congress in his annual State of the Union Address. While the speech was being drafted, Eleanor was reading *And Beacons Burn Again,* a new book by a British author. It would not be the landed gentry that would save England, the book argued, but the miners and the workers and the people from the slums. "Here is something to make us swell with pride," Eleanor wrote in her column on New Year's Day, "for it proves that our American conception of equality . . . is putting faith in the place it should be, in the strength and capacity of the average human being. Justice for all, security in certain living standards, a recognition of the dignity and the right of an individual human being without regard to his race, creed or color— these are the things for which vast numbers of our citizens will willingly sacrifice themselves."

"Eleanor was forever discussing how the world would look after the war," her friend Trude Pratt Lash later observed, "and finally her ideas took hold in the president's call for four freedoms in his State of the Union." The speech had gone through three or four drafts, Sam Rosenman recalled, when the president suddenly announced "he had an idea for a peroration." He paused, gazed at the ceiling, and then told his secretary to take down his words. As his speechwriters listened, he slowly dictated what would turn out to be the most memorable part of the speech—a call for a world based on "four essential human freedoms": freedom of speech, freedom of worship, freedom from want, and freedom from fear. Eleanor never claimed credit for anything her husband did or said, and there is no way of tracing the direct connection between Eleanor's ruminations about democracy and Franklin's concept of four freedoms, but the link seems obvious.

Eleanor was seated in the president's box next to Missy, Lorena Hickok, and Princess Martha, who was elegantly dressed, reporters noted, in a black coat and silver fox, when Roosevelt entered the House chamber at 2:03 p.m. The speech began on a somber note: "As your President, performing my constitutional duty to 'give to the Congress information of the state of the union,' I find it unhappily necessary to report that the future and the safety of our country and of our democracy are overwhelmingly involved in events far beyond our borders." Because American security depended on defeat of the Axis, he explained, he was asking Congress for authority and funds to continue sending aid to England and other democracies fighting the Axis powers even if these nations could no longer pay with ready cash. "Let us say to the democracies: We Americans are vitally concerned in your defense of freedom."

As the country committed itself to national defense, he went on, it must never forget the goals for which it was fighting: equality of opportunity, jobs for those who could work, security for the needy, the ending of special privilege for the few, the preservation of civil liberties for all. Leaning forward in her seat, Eleanor smiled broadly as she heard these words, and the smile remained on her face as the president presented his vision of a new world founded on four freedoms. Since the beginning of the war, she had challenged her husband to recognize that the concept of a genuine national defense also encompassed better housing, work training, equal opportunity, and expanded health programs. Now, as the president gave eloquent voice to the ideas about democracy that were uppermost in her mind, she was elated.

Curiously, Eleanor's gratification led to a rare lapse of judgment. In the column she wrote the afternoon of the speech, she angrily observed that the Republicans had failed to applaud the president's address. "It looked to me as though those men were saying to the country as a whole, 'we are Republicans first. We represent you here in Congress not as citizens of the U.S. in a period of crisis, but as members of a political party which seeks primarily to promote its own partisan interests.' This is to me shocking and terrifying. There was running through my mind as I watched them, in what would have been an act of childish spite, if it had not been such a serious moment in history, the lines of a song which was popular when I was young: 'I don't want to play in your yard. I don't love you any more.'"

Reaction to Eleanor's comments was swift and savage. Republican Representative Edith Nourse told the House that Mrs. Roosevelt's suggestion that all members applaud "presents a new concept in American constitutional theory. Under our form of government, members of Congress are not elected to applaud the official utterances of the White House, but to frame legislation. The suggestion of a duty to applaud appears to me a dangerous and unwholesome manifestation of war hysteria." Representative Hoffman of Michigan took the argument even further, charging that "the Roosevelts apparently have in some way gotten the idea they are entitled to receive homage and applause as our King and Queen."

•   •   •

As Roosevelt approached his third inaugural, critics lamented his deviousness, his lack of candor, his capricious experimentation, his tendency to ingratitude. His character flaws were widely discussed—his stubbornness, his vanity, his occasional vindictiveness, his habit of yessing callers just to be amiable. Former aide Raymond Moley believed he had succumbed over the years to the "intensifying and exhilarating effect of power," to the unlovely habit of "telling, not asking," to an "irritable certitude" that led him to ascribe "self-interest or cowardice or subtle corruption or stupidity" to people who questioned his decisions.

But the critics' complaints were submerged by the wave of favorable publicity that accompanied Franklin Roosevelt's historic third term. His hair was thinner and grayer, reporters noted, his face heavier and more deeply lined; yet there was the same captivating smile in his eyes and on his lips, the same bright forehead, the same mannerism of tossing his head before replying to a question. His physical condition, his doctor said, was "the best in many years." As always, he ate heartily and enjoyed a nightly cocktail. His weight was a perfect 187½ pounds, and thrice weekly he continued to swim in the White House pool. Crises, wars, campaigns notwithstanding, he generally managed to sleep eight hours a night, from midnight to eight. "One of the grand things about him is that he can relax," Dr. Ross McIntire said. "In the main he has the ability to put his troubles aside when he shouldn't carry them with him."

The day before the inauguration, *The New York Times Magazine* painted a glowing portrait of a president who still retained an astonishing buoyancy despite the strenuous times. The challenge of war, it was suggested, had added a new dimension to his vitality. "Serious but not grim, concerned but not worried," reporter Charles Hurd wrote, "in confidence and vigor of assurance he is the same man who told the American people, 'The only thing we have to fear is fear itself.' " The article went on to describe the long hours the president worked, the voluminous correspondence he handled, the variety of newspapers he read, and the numbers of conferences he held.

"The Presidency and its problems have nevertheless left their mark on Mr. Roosevelt," the *Times* concluded. "Though he gives the impression of cheerfulness, it is cheerfulness without all the spontaneity associated with the first flush of the New Deal," and though he appears optimistic, "after nearly eight years correspondents have learned that the President does not always reveal his true feelings."

With this concluding assessment Eleanor heartily agreed. Still puzzled, after nearly thirty-five years of marriage, by her husband's inability to share himself openly with anyone, Eleanor remarked to Joe Lash that those final paragraphs of the *Times* piece perfectly captured the frame of mind of the president in the days before his fifty-ninth birthday. He had kept his own counsel for so long, she observed, that it had become "part of his nature not to talk to anyone of intimate matters."

Over the years, many tried to penetrate the president's reticence, but few succeeded. "The President talked so much," Frances Perkins recalled, "and yet, all through this talkativeness, there ran a kind of reserve. I saw him often: he dropped the curtain over himself. He never told you, or anyone else, just what was going on inside his mind—inside his emotions—inside his real intentions in life. . . . I think he never intended to reveal himself."

A week before the inauguration, Supreme Court Justice Felix Frankfurter begged Stimson to see more of the president and seek out opportunities for more talks alone with him. Stimson told Frankfurter he had been keeping away because he did not like to bother him. "Frankfurter said that was wrong," Stimson recorded in his diary, "that he was a very lonely man and that he was rather proud and didn't like to ask people to come to him but that he was sure that he would welcome my approaches, if I would make them."

To be sure, Harry Hopkins provided a companionship that comforted many lonely hours. Night after night, Roosevelt sat in his study with Harry, talking about the war, sharing a meal, exchanging gossip. There were times, Hopkins told the president, when he thought it might be easier if he found a place of his own. But Roosevelt always insisted he stay. "He seems to want to have someone around he can talk to when he wants to," Hopkins recognized, "or not talk to."

But even Harry Hopkins was replaceable. "Each imagines he is indispensable to the President," Eleanor once remarked. "All would be surprised at their dispensability. The President uses those who suit his purposes. He makes up his own mind and discards people when they no longer fulfill a purpose of his."

Still, it must be borne in mind that the president never seemed bothered by the loneliness ascribed to him by others. "He had more serenity than any man I have ever seen," Attorney General Francis Biddle said. "One felt that nothing ultimately would upset him." If friends and family were frustrated by his lack of capacity for intimacy, he regarded it as a strength.

• • •

"Bright-eyed and smiling," Eleanor was "just about the most composed person" during the inaugural festivities, the *Washington Post* observed. Not a trace of the fear so palpable in her at the time of the first inaugural remained. On the contrary, she seemed radiant, full of life, good-humored. Her eight years as first lady had opened up to her a new and irresistible world, filled with extraordinary accomplishment, pride, and prestige. Her old fear of failure, her melancholy, though not entirely disappearing, had substantially abated. In support of her belief that the position of first lady could be used as a power for good, she had committed herself to an astonishing range of activities which had earned her the lasting gratitude of millions of citizens.

Her years as first lady had also brought a positive change in her appearance. She had removed from her hair the ugly black hairnet that had accompanied her for too long in public life. Dressed by day in simple, tailored clothes and by night in elegant gowns, she walked with a more confident step, her naturally high complexion enhanced by a small amount of rouge.

To be sure, the first lady had her own share of critics. The hectic travel and honest talk that made her a heroine in some quarters rendered her vulnerable to attack in others. Columnist Westbrook Pegler called her "Madam President," "Empress Eleanor," and "The Gab." Why couldn't she stay home with her husband, she was frequently asked, "and tend to her knitting as an example for other women to follow"? After visiting the White House on a tour, one woman gave Eleanor unsolicited advice. "Instead of tearing around the country, I think you should stay at home and personally see that the White House is clean. I soiled my white gloves yesterday morning on the stair-railing. It is disgraceful." All these resentments came together in the 1940 campaign in a prominent button: "We don't want Eleanor, either."

Eleanor appeared unruffled by most of her critics. "If I could be worried about mud-slinging, I would have been dead long ago," she said. "Almost any woman in the White House during these years of need would have done what I have done"—become a voice for the poor, the migrants, the Negroes. Though this was certainly not true, Eleanor's insistence that she was only trying to do what others would have done, and did not deserve all the attention she received, only added to her charm.

"She is the President's Number One Adviser on sociological problems," *U.S. News* proclaimed. Many people assumed that the New Deal's domestic program would be abandoned as Roosevelt shifted his focus to war and defense, but "they reckoned without the President's wife.... She never lets the President or his administrators think that all is well, that there is time to rest from advancing their liberal objectives. She backs the President's most courageous self.... No matter how deeply absorbed he may become in international affairs, she will keep him from forgetting the New Deal."

• • •

A family reunion was arranged at Hyde Park for the weekend before the inauguration. Anna and John had flown in from from Seattle; Elliott was en route from Texas; and FDR, Jr., and Ethel had come up from Washington. "The nearer I draw to Hyde Park, the more excited I become," Eleanor wrote in her column, admitting a particular pleasure at the thought of seeing Anna. "With my daughter I feel the bond that exists with any child, but in addition there has grown between us the deepest understanding such as exists with an intimate friend. John is not just my son-in-law, but one of my dearest friends. I can be serious or I can be gay with Anna and John without any thought of age or generation to divide us."

"It was wonderful to have two full days in the country," Eleanor wrote. "We walked and talked, ate too much, and slept too little which is always the way of family reunions for once conversation starts time slips by unnoticed!"

Sara, too, was in her element, delighted to have her son at home, surrounded by family and friends before the White House claimed him for another four years. For every one of the guests she had a gay smile, but most of her attention, as always, was focused on her brilliant son. "I always have been proud of him and still am," she said.

The dinner table looked resplendent on Saturday night, January 11, 1941, with the president at one end and Sara at the other. In the course of the conversation, Eleanor raised the troubling question of housing under the defense program. During her last trip to the West Coast, she had seen the devastating effects of overcrowding in Washington State, where the navy yard and shipbuilding construction had attracted thousands of workers from all over the country, part of the first wave of what would be the greatest internal immigration in American history. In Bremerton, she noted, every habitable shack and shed had been rented, scores of families were crowded into unsanitary trailer camps, and two thousand children were without schools. "I think we are going to have to be a nuisance about these questions if we are going to be fair to people all over this country," she believed. "What we do now must be with an eye to the well-being of the people who are going to do the work essential to our defense. We have no right to ask them to sacrifice their home life to live in a way not compatible to our way."

In response, the president said he had just appointed Charles Palmer, an Atlanta real-estate man, to head the new Division of Defense Housing, with broad powers to assure speedy construction in connection with rearmament and military-training programs. This was not the response Eleanor wanted to hear. From her own sources she had learned that Palmer's interest in public housing "arose from his desire to rid Atlanta of slums that were depreciating his own holdings." In contrast to Eleanor's belief that "in the long run all housing is defense housing," Palmer had declared that "sociology was no part of his job, that overcrowding would remain the private builder's opportunity." For weeks, Palmer had been under fire in the liberal paper *PM* for his belief that government construction was not needed since the overwhelming percentage of defense housing could be handled by private firms. Now, this was the man the president had chosen to coordinate the government's housing program!

"Would he be sensitive to problems of low-cost housing, schools and the like in defense areas," Eleanor wanted to know. The president became restless, impatient. But, despite the uneasy glances flung at her by Sara, Eleanor persisted, saying "she had heard that Palmer was partial to real estate people." Clearly annoyed at this point, the president agreed to "appoint someone with Palmer to watch for these things." But, Eleanor countered, would that person "have any authority?"

While Franklin and Eleanor were arguing, Sara motioned to the butler to bring the president's wheelchair to the table. Furious at Eleanor's hectoring, Sara stood behind her son and had him shifted to the other end of the table. In the past, Sara's obvious reproof would have left Eleanor distraught—at a parallel family dinner two decades before, Eleanor had collapsed in tears when Sara turned on her about something—but at this point in her life, Eleanor had enough confidence to confront both her husband and her mother-in-law on an issue she considered important. After dinner, Anna, John, and FDR, Jr., all congratulated her on having stuck to her guns.

"My mother-in-law belonged to the established world of the last century," Eleanor once wrote. "She accepted its shibboleths without questioning." To her, "there were certain obligations she as a privileged person must fulfill. She fed the poor, assisted them with money, helped them with medical expenses. This was a form of charity required of her." She simply could not accept the idea that "human beings had rights as human beings"—a right to a decent house, a job, education, human dignity.

The next day, Sara invited the son of Arnulfo Arias, the president of Panama, to dine with the family. He was "a dandyish" young man, Lash observed, whom Sara affectionately called "Robertito." When it was learned that young Arias had bragged to reporters that he was lunching privately with the president, FDR, Jr., told his grandmother she was being taken in. Refusing to acknowledge this, Sara announced that she wanted to invite him to the White House for the inaugural festivities. "It fell to Mrs. Roosevelt," Lash recorded in his diary, "to tell her it could not be done. [Mrs. James] complained that she was never allowed to have any of *her* friends, an obvious dig at the kind of friends Mrs. R. invited."

How far off seemed the early days, when Eleanor had first started to work for the League of Women Voters. At that time, in 1921, she had entered a world of feminist women whose values and behavior were totally foreign to Sara—women who lived with other women; active, accomplished women who did things outside the home; independent women, well satisfied with their lives and convinced that they could not possibly live in any other way.

The apprenticeship of Eleanor Roosevelt had begun with two remarkable League women, Elizabeth Read and Esther Lape. Read, an honors graduate of Smith College, was an accomplished lawyer; Lape, a Wellesley graduate, had taught English at Swarthmore and Barnard and then achieved prominence as a publicist. Brilliant, hardworking, and ambitious, they had found in their love for one another the freedom from conventional marriage that allowed them to live according to their own desires, surrounded by music and books. Eleanor was immediately entranced by the stimulating lives these women led, with discussions of politics and public policy at dinner, and poetry readings after dessert. Their book-lined house in Greenwich Village reminded her of the happy days she had spent at Mademoiselle Souvestre's school in England.

When Eleanor first met Read and Lape, she was still suffering the effects of having discovered her husband's love affair with Lucy Mercer. She sorely lacked confidence. She needed appreciation and she was lonely. She found in Elizabeth and Esther's community of women the strength and encouragement to do things on her own, to explore her own talents, to become a person in her own right. Over the years, the friendships deepened into an intimacy which would continue for the rest of Eleanor's life.

Through her work with the League, Eleanor met two other lifelong friends, Nancy Cook and Marion Dickerman. Cook, a vital, tough-looking young woman, was the director of the Women's Division of the New York State Democratic Party. Dickerman, a tall, soft-spoken scholar whose grim countenance hid a dry wit, was a teacher and vice-principal at Todhunter, an exclusive girls school in Manhattan. Like Elizabeth and Esther, Nancy and Marion lived together in what has been described as a "Boston marriage." Over the years, both women had been actively involved in the long struggle for women's suffrage, the movement to abolish child labor, and the efforts to establish maximum working hours.

There is every evidence that the four women, along with half a dozen others (including Elinor Morgenthau and Caroline O'Day, members of the Women's Division of the New York Democratic State Committee, social worker Molly Dewson, and AP reporter Lorena Hickok), played a substantial role in the education of Eleanor Roosevelt, tutoring her in politics, strategy, and public policy, encouraging her to open up emotionally, building her sense of confidence and self-esteem. In contrast to the distant relationship she had with most of the males in her life at this juncture, her relationship with her female friends was warm and open, frolicsome and relaxed. They kissed and hugged each other when they met; they had pillow fights at night; they wrote long and loving letters when they were apart; they challenged the traditional sense of what was possible.

When Eleanor first came into contact with these bold and successful women, she found herself in awe of the professional status they had acquired. "If I had to go out and earn my own living," she conceded, "I doubt if I'd even make a very good cleaning woman. I have no talents, no experience, no training for anything." But all this would change as Eleanor, encouraged by her friends, began to discover a range of abilities she never knew she had—remarkable organizing skills, superb judgment, practical insight, and astonishing endurance. In the space of two years, with the guidance of her female colleagues, Eleanor emerged as a major force in New York public life, speaking out in behalf of political reform, worker's rights, and children's issues, sought after for statements in newspapers, chosen to serve on all manner of committees. At the same time, she began teaching three days a week at Todhunter, organizing courses in literature, drama, and American history. "She loved it," Marion Dickerman recalled. "The girls worshiped her."

Though Franklin and Louis Howe sometimes joked about Eleanor's "squaws" and "she-men," they both recognized that she was becoming an excellent politician and that her tireless work around the state would inevitably redound to Franklin's credit. Even before polio had crippled Franklin, Howe had encouraged Eleanor to become actively involved in politics. Once the polio struck, Eleanor's ability to stand in for her husband became critical. Moreover, both Franklin and Louis genuinely liked Elizabeth and Esther, Nan and Marion, and found their conversation stimulating and absorbing.

For Sara, Eleanor's transformation was harder to accept. Sara was appalled at the idea of a well-bred woman's spending so much time away from home in the public eye. A woman's place was with her husband and her children. "My generation did not do those things," Sara explained. The more involved Eleanor became in politics, the less time she had to take Sara out to lunch or to pour tea for Sara's friends. "My mother-in-law was distressed and felt that I was not available, as I had been," Eleanor recalled.

Sara often displaced her criticisms onto Eleanor's friends, making them feel uncomfortable whenever they came to visit at Hyde Park, scanning their mannish suits and oxford shoes with disapproving eyes, glaring in bewilderment at their close-cropped hair. To Sara, they all looked alike: unkempt, unconventional, unnatural. Understanding the situation, Franklin suggested that Eleanor and her friends Nan and Marion build a cottage for themselves in the woods so they could have a place of their own to pursue their interests apart from Sara's. "My Missus and some of her female political friends want to build a shack on a stream in the back woods," Franklin explained to Elliott Brown, whom he asked to supervise the project. He then became actively involved in the building of the "shack"—a fieldstone house which eventually grew to accommodate twenty-two rooms.

"The peace of it is divine," a grateful Eleanor told her husband the first summer she spent at Val-Kill, in 1925. From that time forward, though she stayed at the Big House whenever Franklin and the children were at Hyde Park, Val-Kill became Eleanor's home—the first home of her own she had ever had. "Can you tell me *why* Eleanor wants to go over to Val-Kill cottage to sleep every night?" a perplexed Sara once asked one of Eleanor's friends. "Why doesn't she sleep here? This is her home. She belongs here."

The woman who in 1925 had been frightened by the prospect of earning her own living was in 1941 among the highest-paid lecturers in the country, pulling in $1,000 a lecture. Her syndicated column, "My Day," was printed in 135 newspapers, placing her on a par for circulation with Dorothy Thompson, Westbrook Pegler, and Raymond Clapper. And in 1938, the first installment of her autobiography, *This Is My Story,* had been published to widespread popular and critical acclaim. To be sure, as Eleanor recognized better than anyone, her success was due in no small part to the fact that she was the president's wife. Nonetheless, in April 1940, when it was not at all certain that Roosevelt would run for a third term, United Features had renewed her column for five additional years, a clear recognition that she had established herself in her own right.

So, in January 1941, when it fell to Eleanor, seated at the table in Sara's house, to tell her mother-in-law that her young Latin American friend was not welcome in *her* house, the big white house on Pennsylvania Avenue, it was clear that the balance of power between the two dominant women in the president's life had shifted.

• • •

The president was in high spirits on January 20, 1941, as he headed toward the Capitol for his inaugural. The sky was clear, the sun shining, and the Gallup poll showed that his public support had reached a new high of 71 percent. Seated in an open-air car, he flashed his familiar smile and waved his top hat to the thousands of well-wishers who waited for him at every point along the way.

At high noon, the president stood before a cheering crowd on Capitol Plaza and took the oath of office for a third time. Nineteen members of the Roosevelt family witnessed the historic moment, including Sara, Eleanor, and all five children. When he began to speak, the raking winter sun lit up the right side of his face like a cameo. His voice was clear; his gestures were strong; his speech was a summons to the spirit of democracy.

"There are men who believe that democracy . . . is limited as measured by a kind of mystical and artificial fate—that for some unexplained reason, tyranny and slavery have become the surging wave of the future—and that freedom is an ebbing tide. But we Americans know that is not true.

"A nation, like a person," he went on, "has a body which must be housed and fed and clad and a mind which must be educated and informed but it also has something deeper, something more permanent, something larger than the sum of its parts. It is that something which matters most to its future —which calls forth the most sacred guarding of its present. It is a thing for which we find it difficult—even impossible—to hit upon a single, simple word. And yet, we all understand what it is—the spirit—the faith of America."

•   •   •

The first problem facing Roosevelt after his inauguration was getting the Congress to pass the lend-lease bill. Introduced in the House as H.R. 1776, the controversial legislation authorized the president to transfer munitions and supplies for which Congress had appropriated money to "the government of any country whose defense the President deems vital to the defense of the U.S."

Opponents attacked the bill on two grounds: first, that it granted the president dictatorial powers, "to carry on," in Senator Robert Taft's words, "a kind of undeclared war all over the world"; second, that it would lead America inexorably into war. Administration spokesmen took the opposite tack. By allowing Britain to continue the fight against Germany, they argued, the bill was the last best hope for keeping America out of the war.

The situation the administration faced was tricky: debate was essential to develop a mass base of support, but every day taken up in discussion was another day lost in Britain's desperate struggle to ready itself for the expected invasion. "The lend-lease bill will furnish a bigger test than the merits of the bill itself," Washington correspondent David Lawrence wrote. "It is whether America can make a military decision of tremendous interest to her national safety without taking weeks and weeks to debate the issue."

The hearings began in the House Committee on Foreign Affairs in January, before an overflowing crowd of reporters and spectators. By noontime, all the seats in the high-ceilinged committee room had been taken, and still the curious kept coming; they stood in the corners, sat on the windowsills, and waited in long lines in the corridor outside. The first witness to testify against the bill was the recently resigned ambassador to Great Britain, Joseph Kennedy. For weeks, after an indiscreet interview with *Boston Globe* columnist Louis Lyons which lost him his ambassadorship, Kennedy had been flirting with the isolationists, tantalizing them with the prospect that he would make an open break with the administration and join their crusade against the war. But Roosevelt, knowing his man better than his opponents, had invited Kennedy to the White House for an early-morning talk in mid-January. Relaxing in his bedroom, the president allowed Kennedy to pour out his heart about the miserable treatment he had received from "the boys in the State Department" and "the President's hatchet men." Kennedy told the president he didn't think it was fair to wind up seven years of service in his administration with a bad record. He had gone in for everything the president wanted, and now the time had come to do something for the Kennedy family.

Nodding sympathetically, the president reminisced about the good times the two of them had had together over the years, and told Kennedy that once the lend-lease bill got through he would make sure the country recognized how valuable a public servant Joe Kennedy had been. Disarmed as always by Roosevelt's charm, Kennedy shifted the tone of the statement he had prepared for Congress so substantially that his isolationist friends felt betrayed. Though he said he opposed lend-lease in its present form because the powers of Congress in foreign affairs should be preserved, he came out for complete aid to Britain, parroting the administration's line that aid to Britain was the best means of avoiding war. It was a confusing statement, neither for nor against, exposing Kennedy to criticism from both sides. But Roosevelt, who had feared his former ambassador to England might lead the isolationist charge, was greatly relieved.

A few days after the ambassador's testimony, Anna Roosevelt's husband, John Boettiger, sent Kennedy a friendly note. "Somehow or other," Boettiger wrote, "I feel sure we are all thinking along the same lines and that the Roosevelts, the Kennedys and the Boettigers will be struggling shoulder to shoulder first to keep America out of war, but always to keep America free!" In a somewhat self-pitying reply, Kennedy told Boettiger, "if my statements and my position means that, outside of the ever loyal Boettigers I am to be a social outcast by the administration, well so be it. . . . At any rate, I am delighted that you and Anna were sweet enough to send a note and I appreciate it more than I can tell you."

Kennedy's delight would have been diminished had he seen the subsequent exchange of letters between Boettiger and the president, occasioned by Boettiger's decision to send his father-in-law a copy of Kennedy's note.

After thanking his son-in-law for sending Kennedy's note, Roosevelt wrote in unusually candid terms: "It is, I think a little pathetic that he worries about being, with his family, social outcasts. As a matter of fact, he ought to realize of course that he has only himself to blame for the country's opinion as to his testimony before the Committees. Most people and most papers got the feeling that he was blowing hot and blowing cold at the same time—trying to carry water on both shoulders.

"The truth of the matter is that Joe is and always has been a temperamental Irish boy, terrifically spoiled at an early age by huge financial success; thoroughly patriotic, thoroughly selfish and thoroughly obsessed with the idea that he must leave each of his nine children with a million dollars apiece when he dies (he has told me that often). He has a positive horror of any change in the present methods of life in America. To him, the future of a small capitalistic class is safer under a Hitler than under a Churchill. This is sub-conscious on his part and he does not admit it. . . . Sometimes I think I am 200 years older than he is!"

Despite the setback of Kennedy's ambivalent statement, the opposition continued its relentless attack against the bill, culminating in a powerful warning from Charles Lindbergh that H.R. 1776 was "another step away from democracy and another step closer to war." Fully expecting this line of attack, the president had two weapons waiting in reserve—Harry Hopkins and Wendell Willkie.

In early January, Roosevelt had sent Hopkins to London to meet with Churchill and obtain a firsthand impression of Britain's resolve and Britain's needs. The journey to London, aboard a Pan American Clipper, had taken five days over a circuitous route. When Hopkins arrived, he was "sick and shrunken and too tired even to unfasten his safety belt." Years later, Churchill's daughter-in-law, Pamela Churchill Harriman, recalled her shock at her first sight of the ill Hopkins, a dead cigarette in his mouth, a weary man in a large overcoat which he never took off.

But the thrill of his mission soon served to revive Hopkins' health. At the welcoming dinner in his honor, the story is told, Churchill, knowing that Hopkins was a social worker with no military background, deliberately directed the conversation to issues of economic and social reform, emphasizing that after the war he planned to modernize Britain's slum cottages with electricity and plumbing. "Mr. Churchill," Hopkins interrupted, "I don't give a damn about your cottagers. I've come over here to find out how we can help you beat this fellow Hitler." When he heard this, Churchill's face lit up; he straightened his shoulders and got up from the table. "Mr. Hopkins, come with me," he said, leading Hopkins to his study.

For the next four hours, Churchill confided the entire direction of his nation's affairs to the president's envoy. "And from this hour," Churchill wrote in his memoirs, "began a friendship between us which sailed serenely over all earthquakes and convulsions. He was the most faithful and perfect channel of communication between the President and me. . . . There he sat, slim, frail, ill, but absolutely glowing with refined comprehension of the Cause. It was to be the defeat, ruin, and slaughter of Hitler, to the exclusion of all other purposes, loyalties, or aims. . . . He was a crumbling lighthouse from which there shone the beams that led great fleets to harbour."

While Hopkins was in England, he spent almost every waking hour with Churchill—journeying with him to Scapa Flow, Scotland; dining together night after night; relaxing at Chequers, Churchill's country home. Proximity to the great man had its effect; Hopkins became an ardent admirer of Churchill and an absolute partisan of Britain's cause. At a small dinner party one evening, Hopkins rose to his feet. "I suppose you wish to know what I am going to say to President Roosevelt on my return. Well, I'm going to quote you one verse from that Book of Books. . . . 'Whither thou goest, I will go and where thou lodgest, I will lodge, thy people shall be my people, and thy God my God!' " Then, in his own words, he added, "Even to the end." When Hopkins sat down, Churchill's doctor, Lord Moran, looked over at Churchill and saw tears streaming down his face.

With their friendship sealed, Hopkins moved to elicit Churchill's help in the lend-lease debate. In early February, Churchill was working on a major speech to be broadcast throughout the world. At Roosevelt's request, Hopkins asked Churchill to skew the speech to American public opinion by promising that lend-lease was the best means to keep the Americans out of the war. Churchill readily complied, weaving Hopkins' suggestions together with a personal note he had just received from the president in the hands of a second envoy—Wendell Willkie. Just before Willkie left for London, Roosevelt, with shrewd insight, had asked him to come to the White House. He gave Willkie a letter of introduction to the prime minister with a verse from Longfellow in his own handwriting. In his speech on February 9, Churchill put the verse to brilliant use.

"In the last war," Churchill began, "the U.S. sent two million men across the Atlantic. But this is not a war of vast armies firing immense masses of shells at one another. We do not need the gallant armies which are forming throughout the American Union. We do not need them this year, nor next year, nor any year; that I can foresee."

"The other day," Churchill continued, Roosevelt had sent him a verse from Longfellow, which he said "applies to you people as it does to us. . . .

> "Sail On, O Ship of State!
> Sail On, O Union Strong and great!
> Humanity with all its fears,
> With all the hopes of future years,
> Is hanging breathless on thy fate!

"What is the answer that I shall give in your name to this great man, the thrice-chosen head of a nation of 130 million. Here is the answer I will give to Mr. Roosevelt. Put your confidence in us. . . . We shall not fail or falter. . . . Give us the tools and we will finish the job."

When Willkie returned to the States on February 11, he went directly to the Hill to testify in behalf of the lend-lease bill. It was the most important testimony in six weeks of hearings. In a blue suit rumpled from the plane ride, with his hair drooping over one eye and his voice as hoarse as ever, Willkie declared that if we sat back and withdrew within ourselves there was no telling where "the madmen who are loose in the world" might strike next. With flashbulbs popping and twelve hundred people crowded against the marble walls, Willkie predicted that, "if the Republican party makes a blind opposition to the bill and allows itself to be presented to the American people as the isolationist party, it will never again gain control of the American government."

Repeatedly, Willkie found himself at odds with isolationists on the committee, who insisted on going over one by one the critical comments Willkie had made about Roosevelt during the campaign. "He was elected President," Willkie replied. "He is *my* President now." When asked about his prediction that if Roosevelt were elected America would be in the war by April 1941, Willkie smiled and said, "It was a bit of campaign oratory." The chamber burst into goodhearted laughter.

Eleanor, in her column that day, said she was "thankful beyond words" for Willkie's testimony. Her gratitude was not misplaced. The bill sailed through both houses with substantial majorities, and at ten minutes of four on the afternoon of March 11, a smiling Roosevelt signed lend-lease into law. Three hours later, the president declared the defense of Britain vital to the U.S. and authorized the navy to turn over to Britain thousands of naval guns and ammunition, three thousand charges for bombs, and two dozen PT boats. Full of confidence, the president told reporters he had already begun work on a supplemental request of $7 billion to implement lend-lease.

That night, as Big Ben struck midnight, Churchill stood up in Parliament to voice the gratitude of his people toward America for passing what he called "the most unsordid act in the history of any nation." With this act, he declared, "the most powerful democracy has, in effect, declared in a solemn statute that they will devote their overwhelming industrial and financial strength to insuring the defeat of Nazism." Put in simpler terms, a Londoner told journalist Molly Panter-Downes, "Thank God! The tanks are coming."

When Hopkins returned from England, a grateful Roosevelt designated him administrator of the lend-lease program, with a staff of thirty-five. While seventeen rooms were hastily cleared for Hopkins and his staff in the Federal Reserve Building, Hopkins continued to work out of his big bedroom on the second floor of the White House. There, from a card table set in the middle of his room, with documents and papers spilling off chairs and tables, he threw himself into what Pamela Churchill Harriman later called "one of the most massive undertakings in U.S. history."

The appointment provoked mixed reaction within the Cabinet. "The blind side of the President, when his personal friends are involved, seems to be growing blinder," Ickes lamented. "Hopkins has not the ability from any point of view intellectual or physical to carry such a job as this...." Morgenthau, too, had his doubts. "I am just worried sick over it, because Hopkins isn't well enough." But Stimson held a more positive view. "The more I think of it," he recorded in his diary after listening to Hopkins' "thrilling" descriptions of Churchill's leadership and the situation in Britain, "the more I think it is a godsend that he should be at the White House and that the President should have sent him to Great Britain where he has gotten on such intimate terms with the people there. It's a real connection that helps and Hopkins himself is a man that I have grown to appreciate and to respect more and more the more I see him."

In the days that followed Hopkins' return, the president spent many hours with him, soaking up the information Hopkins had gathered while he was in England. In the course of his sojourn, Hopkins had talked with more than three hundred men and women, including all the important leaders of Parliament; he had visited defenses, soldiers, and air forces; he had seen Churchill in action with British crowds. He knew more about Britain's problems than any American. And with Hopkins, as with Eleanor, Roosevelt knew he was receiving a straightforward picture of the situation, an honest and unbiased account, filled with insight, intuition, and human detail.

"Upon his return from England," Marquis Childs wrote in *The Saturday Evening Post,* "Hopkins' friends sensed a change in him. He was more serious, and at the same time more detached, as though he were relieved, happy almost at having found something in which he could abandon his own personal destiny, submerging himself in a task of immeasurable magnitude and immeasurable risk." Reporters began comparing Hopkins to Woodrow Wilson's intimate envoy, Colonel Edward House, and soon, Childs noted, "a spate of invitations fell upon him—to write for syndicates at astronomical rates, to lecture, to talk on the record and off the record, to attend little intimate dinners of important people."

"It tore Eleanor's heart up," Eleanor's friend Martha Gellhorn later said, "that Harry could forget the hungry and unemployed. . . . In the New Deal he had been Eleanor's protégé; now he was FDR's. He was wittier and brighter in the second period but much nicer in the first."

For Roosevelt, the lend-lease triumph was not simply the passage of the bill but the successful education of the American public. When the hearings started, the country was divided down the middle on lend-lease, with 50 percent in favor, 50 percent against. By the time the bill passed, those in favor had risen to 61 percent.

"Yes," Roosevelt prophetically remarked a few days after the bill passed, "the decisions of our democracy may be slowly arrived at. But when that decision is made, it is proclaimed not with the voice of one man but with the voice of 130 million."

With the passage of lend-lease, Goebbels recorded in his diary, "the Führer finally gave his propagandists permission to attack America. It was high time. Now we shall let rip. Mrs. Roosevelt is shooting her mouth off around the country. If she were my wife, it would be a different story."

CHAPTER 9

"BUSINESS AS USUAL"

In celebration of the passage of lend-lease, Roosevelt set off on a ten-day fishing trip to Florida with his usual group of friends—Hopkins, Watson, and Dr. McIntire. Eleanor accompanied him to the train station, kissed him goodbye, and then promptly headed for New York, where she dined at the Lafayette Hotel with friends, went to see the play *The Doctor's Dilemma,* and met with the British War Relief Society. After returning to Washington the next morning, she entertained eighty people in the State Dining Room, visited with financier Bernard Baruch, attended a concert, delivered a lecture on race relations, and spent two hours with a group of Negro pilots who were training at the Tuskegee Institute.

"This house is seething," Mrs. Nesbitt wearily recorded in her diary. "ER back for breakfast, out for dinner, here for supper. In the house she always goes at a dog trot, so fast she bends forward. Somebody said she can give you enough work in five minutes to keep you busy for two weeks. But she drives herself hardest of all."

Eleanor finally joined Franklin at the tail end of his trip, meeting him at Fort Bragg, in the sandy hills of eastern North Carolina. They had only a few minutes together on the train before the motorcade arrived to take them on a three-hour inspection tour of the immense camp, which had originally been designed for twenty thousand men but now held more than sixty-seven thousand.

For nine months, a labor force of 28,500 had worked 24-hour days to triple the size of the camp. They had built a road that stretched 74 miles, a reception center capable of handling 1,000 men at a time, 20 63-men barracks, and a new hospital with 99 interconnected buildings and beds for 1,680 soldiers. When a critical shortage of furnaces threatened to halt construction of the hospital, four railroad locomotives had been brought into the camp on temporary sidings to pump steam into the building. And still the ringing of hammers could be heard everywhere the Roosevelts went.

Eleanor found the 25-mile drive through Fort Bragg "extraordinarily interesting." She heard a general say that "they put up a building of some kind every 32 minutes." She was pleased with the range of activities available to the soldiers—the athletic programs, the recreation centers, the football fields, and the theaters—though she worried about the strain on the small city of Fayetteville, and took note, as always, of the lack of housing for workmen, who were sleeping in trailers, in the back seats of cars, in makeshift tents on the hillsides.

The hurried pace at Fort Bragg could have been seen at any number of spots across the country. In order to train and equip the army of 1.4 million that conscription had decreed, 46 new army camps had to be built. The camps were concentrated along the Eastern Seaboard, in the states of the Old Confederacy, and along the California coast. Ideally, the construction would have been finished before the draftees were inducted, but because funds were not available until the passage of the Selective Service Act in September, the army was struggling to complete the camps even as the troops arrived. The job was monumental: land had to be cleared, hills leveled, valleys filled, trees uprooted, roads surfaced, and drainage systems installed before the construction of barracks, laundries, officers' quarters, and rifle ranges could begin. The building of the new camps required 400,000 men, 908,000 gallons of paint, 3,500 carloads of nails, and 10 million square feet of wallboard.

The frantic schedule had resulted in scores of mistakes. Lacking proper engineering surveys, camps had been built on rocky terrains and swampy soil. "We're building this camp in a sponge," workmen at Camp Blanding in Florida complained. One camp had been located 16 miles from "the worst malaria area in the southeastern United States." Another lacked adequate water supplies and had to be moved. In some cases, confused orders had gone out to put up barracks before roads had been built. In other cases, men were brought in before even the most rudimentary facilities—latrines and kitchens—were available. "If our plans for military campaigns are no more extensive and no better than these constructions," Senator Harry Truman's special committee to investigate the national defense program later concluded, "we are indeed in a deplorable situation."

Each camp was a little city, with a population ranging in size from 40,000 to 80,000, with its own police force, fire department, water sewerage, and transportation system. "But to the new soldier," Lee Kennett has written in his study of the American soldier in World War II, "the camp that would be his home for the next few months was like no city he had known in civilian life." The buildings were all so similar, made with the same "bare, angular, institutional look of the Quartermasters' 700 Series plans," that it was almost impossible to tell them apart. All the intersections looked the same as well; the relentless rectangular layout made it easy to get lost. In the early days of the planning, Eleanor had suggested that "curved streets might make the camps more pleasant places," but the rectangular orthodoxy prevailed. The original intention was to leave the buildings unpainted, but here Eleanor achieved partial success—the structures were painted but the same drab color was used throughout. Whether in Louisiana, Florida, Mississippi, or New Jersey, the camp presented an unwelcoming aspect to the new arrival.

But all these problems paled beside the magnificent achievement of the Quartermaster Corps under General Brehon Somervell. By the spring of 1941, despite the waste and the bungling, despite the obstacles of weather and terrain, all 46 camps were open and functioning, ready to receive the new American army. And when they were finished, Geoffrey Perrett has written in his study of the American army during the war, "they were the best run, most comfortable, most efficient posts [the army] had ever possessed."

Roosevelt was delighted with his inspection tour. Reporters noted his high spirits and suggested that he seemed to be "sitting on the top of the world." Returning to his train, he passed a group of children from a Negro school in Fayetteville. His appearance made a lasting impression. Twelve months later, the school's principal, Edwin Martin, wrote him that the children still recalled "that wave of the hand and that broad smile."

As the train pulled away from the station, the army fired the president's 21-gun salute. "Fala stood with his paws on the window," Eleanor noted in her column, "and as each gun went off, he sniffed the air," a bewildered expression on his face.

•   •   •

On the night of their return to the White House, the president dined with Missy while Eleanor attended a dinner party at the Women's National Press Club. Special guests included Margaret Mitchell, author of *Gone with the Wind,* which had inspired the biggest movie of the year, and Marjorie Rawlings, author of *The Yearling.* In Eleanor's honor, the women journalists had devised a humorous skit depicting the curious assortment of houseguests Eleanor was constantly inviting to the White House, with members of the club impersonating the president and the first lady. At one point in the make-believe party, which sported a wildly clashing group of guests, an annoyed Franklin approached Eleanor. "You do have the damndest people at the White House, Eleanor," he told her. "Now, Franklin," she replied, "you know I had all the royalties you like, and besides . . ." Eleanor enjoyed every moment, leading the applause.

But even as the members of the press club teased Eleanor about her eclectic guest list, they had no idea that the newest addition to the Roosevelts' unorthodox "family" was one of their own—former AP reporter Lorena Hickok. Miss Hickok, known to everyone as Hick, had moved from New York to Washington in January to become executive secretary to the Women's Division of the Democratic National Committee. Leaving behind a rented apartment in Manhattan and a country house on Long Island, she could not afford to rent an apartment in Washington. Eleanor, understanding Hick's predicament, invited her to stay at the White House until she could sublet her New York apartment.

Hick ended up living in the White House for four years. The little room she occupied was part of the northwest corner suite on the second floor. Two hundred feet from the president's bedroom, this was the room where Louis Howe had once lived. It was originally designed as the dressing room for the larger bedroom next door, but it contained a bed, a dressing table, a desk that jiggled, an old-fashioned commode that served as a night table, and a fireplace. "I never knew any greater comfort or luxury," Hick later said, "than lying in bed and looking into that fire. It was wonderful not to have to carry in logs for it. Twice a day a man came in with logs, poked up the fire, and swept up the ashes."

Eleanor's generosity allowed Hick to keep her beloved country house in Mastic, Long Island. "But that was not the only reason why I stayed at the White House," Hick later admitted. "Although I never told Mrs. Roosevelt I couldn't bear the idea of being in Washington and hardly ever seeing her."

When Hick and Eleanor first became friends in the fall of 1932, the thirty-nine-year-old Hick was at the top of her profession as a journalist. Having worked at the Associated Press in New York for a dozen years, she was the most widely known female reporter in the country, respected for her political savvy, her passionate convictions, and her superb writing style. At poker games with her colleagues, she looked and acted like one of the boys, with her flannel shirt and trousers loosely covering her two-hundred-pound frame, and a cigar hanging from her mouth.

Eleanor that fall was at one of the lowest moments in her life, filled with terror at the thought of moving to Washington and becoming first lady, fearing that everything she had built in the previous decade with the help of her female colleagues would be destroyed.

Now, eight years later, the tables were turned. As Hick was moving into the White House, it was Eleanor who had transformed the position of first lady into one perfectly suited to her remarkable skills, while Hick was depressed and emotionally unstable.

To understand this reversal, one must understand their relationship in the days after Eleanor and Hick first became acquainted. During the last weeks of the 1932 campaign, Hick was assigned to cover Eleanor on a regular basis. "You'd better watch out for that Hickok woman," Franklin had warned his wife. "She's smart." But, the more time they spent together—sharing a drawing room on the presidential train, riding together in an automobile from one event to the next—the more Eleanor began to grasp the vulnerability and need that lay beneath Hick's hard-boiled exterior—a vulnerability that found an answering chord in Eleanor's own sense of weariness and pain.

In the time they spent in each other's company, Hick told Eleanor the story of her childhood days on a poor dairy farm in Wisconsin. Her father was an abusive man who beat her regularly, killed her dog, and crushed her mother's kitten against the house. "There must have been times when he was not angry," Hick later wrote, "times when he was gay, affectionate, perhaps even indulgent with his children, but I do not remember them." After leaving home as soon as she could, Hick put herself through high school by working as a servant in a number of rooming houses. She won every school prize that was offered, then spent two years at Lawrence University before quitting to become a cub reporter.

Her rise through the world of journalism was exceptional. She went from cub reporter at the *Battle Creek Journal* to society editor of the *Milwaukee Sentinel* within the space of a year. From there she moved on to the *Minneapolis Tribune,* where she became the first woman sports reporter and a star feature writer.

In her personal life, Hick had achieved less success. When she was twenty-five, she had fallen in love with a wealthy young woman named Ellie Morse, who was taking English courses at the university and trying to write poetry. For six years, Hick and Ellie lived together in what seemed to be a serene and happy relationship. Then, one day, without warning, Ellie eloped with an old boyfriend, leaving Hick in a ravaged state, certain she would never fall in love again.

Hick's story touched Eleanor profoundly, prompting her to share with the reporter the story of her own wretched childhood. "I am *not* unhappy," Eleanor assured Hick. "Life may be somewhat negative with me, but that is nothing new. I think it was when I was a child & is now a habit. . . ." Eleanor further confided in Hick the catastrophe of her husband's affair with Lucy Mercer and the slow, painful process of reconstructing herself through her work with the League of Women Voters and a dozen other organizations in her home state. But with her husband's move to the White House, she would be forced to leave all her friends behind, forced to invent herself all over again. It was a daunting prospect.

Hick empathized with Eleanor's fears of becoming first lady in a way that other friends did not. And she had the professional experience and political sophistication to help Eleanor figure out how to make the job she feared into one she wanted. It was Hick who suggested that Eleanor consider holding her own press conferences, restricted to female reporters so as to encourage the papers to employ more women. It was Hick who suggested that Eleanor publish a running account of her daily experiences in the form of a column, a suggestion that led directly to Eleanor's enormously popular syndicated column, "My Day." It was Hick who encouraged Eleanor to write frequent magazine pieces and spent hours editing her early drafts. But, far more important, it was Hick who fell madly in love with Eleanor, pursuing her in a way she had never been pursued before.

"Every woman wants to be first to someone in her life," Eleanor later explained to Joe Lash, "and that desire is the explanation for many strange things women do." When Franklin was inaugurated on March 4, 1933, Eleanor was wearing a sapphire ring which Hick had given her just before she left New York. "Hick, darling," Eleanor wrote Hick after the inauguration. "I want to put my arms around you . . . to hold you close. Your ring is a great comfort. I look at it and I think she does love me, or I wouldn't be wearing it!"

Every night of that first week in the White House, as Franklin summoned the Congress into special session and prepared his first fireside chat on the banking crisis, Eleanor had sat in her room writing to Hick, whose work had taken her back to New York immediately after the festivities. "I felt a little as though a part of me was leaving tonight. You have grown so much to be a part of my life that it is empty without you even though I'm busy every minute. . . . My love enfolds thee all the night through."

Hick called Eleanor at the White House the following day. "Oh! how good it was to hear your voice," Eleanor wrote later; "it was so inadequate to try and tell you what it meant. Jimmy was near and I couldn't say Je t'aime and je t'adore. . . . I go to sleep thinking of you and repeating our little saying.

"The nicest time of day is when I write to you," Eleanor assured Hick, pledging that she would kiss Hick's picture since she couldn't kiss her. "Remember one thing always, no one is just what you are to me. I'd rather be with you this minute than anyone else. . . . I've never enjoyed being with anyone the way I enjoy being with you."

For her part, Hick counted the days until she and Eleanor could be together again. Having found the love she had been seeking all her life, she was miserable without Eleanor. "Funny," Hick wrote, "how even the dearest face will fade away in time. Most clearly I remember your eyes, with a kind of teasing smile in them and the feeling of that soft spot just northeast of the corner of your mouth against my lips."

What are we to make of these intimate letters? "While they seem at first glance to be the letters of one lover to another," historian and former Roosevelt Library Director William Emerson observes, "the passionate words were more likely a substitute for the expressions of love Eleanor needed so desperately." Eleanor's friend Trude Lash agrees. "Eleanor had so many emotions stored up inside, that when Hick came along, it was almost like a volcanic explosion. But does that mean that Eleanor acted on her words, that she had a lesbian relationship with Hick? I do not think so."

Hick's biographer, Doris Faber, concedes the amorous phrases but reminds us that personal letters can be terribly misleading unless they are placed in the context of their time. In a ground-breaking study of correspondence between women in Victorian America, the world into which Eleanor was born, Carroll Smith-Rosenberg argues that women routinely used romantic, even sensual rhetoric to communicate with their female friends. At a time when relationships between men and women frequently lacked ease and spontaneity, women opened their hearts more freely to other women, exchanging secrets, sharing desires, admitting fears.

To be sure, the letters possess an emotional intensity and a sensual explicitness that is hard to disregard. Hick longed to kiss the soft spot at the corner of Eleanor's mouth; Eleanor yearned to hold Hick close; Hick despaired at being away from Eleanor; Eleanor wished she could lie down beside Hick and take her in her arms. Day after day, month after month, the tone in the letters on both sides remains fervent and loving.

Yet the essential question for the biographer is not whether Hick and Eleanor went beyond kisses and hugs, a question there is absolutely no way we can answer with certainty. The far more absorbing question, and the one that *can* be answered, is what role the precious friendship played in each of their lives at that particular juncture.

There is every evidence that Hick's love for Eleanor came at a critical moment in Eleanor's life, providing a mix of tenderness, loyalty, confidence, and courage that sustained her in her struggle to redefine her sense of self and her position in the world. For Eleanor, Hick's love was a positive force, allowing her to grow and take wing, write the story of her life the way *she* wanted it to be, even in the White House. Secure in the knowledge that she was loved by the most important woman in her life, Eleanor was able to create a public persona that was to earn the love of millions. "You taught me more than you know & it brought me happiness . . . ," Eleanor later told Hick. "You've made of me so much more of a person just to be worthy of you."

For Hick, the love that had made her so euphoric at the start soon left her wretched and sulking. When she was separated from Eleanor, she felt restless and miserable, able only with the greatest difficulty to concentrate on the work that had once given her such pleasure and prestige. What is more, in drawing so close to Eleanor, Hick had compromised her position as a journalist. "A reporter," Louis Howe once warned Hick, "should never get too close to a news source." Through her friendship with Eleanor, Hick found herself smack in the middle of some of the biggest stories of the First Hundred Days, but it never once occurred to her to share what she was hearing with her office. Her days as a reporter had come to an end before she recognized it.

Willing to submit to anything as long as she could spend time with Eleanor without feeling guilty, Hick resigned her position at AP in the summer of 1933. It was a major miscalculation. Though Eleanor found her a good

Franklin and Eleanor Roosevelt in a rare moment of relaxation on the south porch of the Roosevelt home at Hyde Park (1).

Eleanor was unlike any girl Franklin had met. She was serious and intelligent, free from affectation, and wholly uninterested in the world of debutante balls. The young couple is shown here on the beach at Campobello shortly after their marriage (2) and with their first child, Anna (3).

4

When Eleanor discovered a packet of love letters from Lucy Mercer (4) in 1918, the bottom, she said, dropped out of her world. Three years later, Franklin contracted polio. During his convalescence he lived for months at a time on a houseboat in Florida with his secretary, Missy LeHand, here to his left along with Maunsell Crosby and Frances Dana De Rahm (5), while Eleanor remained in New York.

5

Three generations of Roosevelt women: Anna, Eleanor, and Sara listen to Roosevelt accept the Democratic nomination for a second term (6).

6

7

8

Roosevelt with Harry Hopkins in the second-floor study, the president's favorite room in the White House (7). It was here that he read, played poker, sorted his beloved stamps, and conducted most of the business of the presidency. A door at the rear of the study led to the president's bedroom next door (8). After breakfast, pushed along in his wheelchair by the White House usher, the president headed for the Oval Office (9).

9

10

11

Eleanor occupied a second-floor suite adjacent to the
president's bedroom. Keeping the smaller room as her
bedroom (10), she turned the larger room into a sitting
room, where she greeted guests and handled her voluminous correspondence (11).

12

The Roosevelt White House during the war resembled a small, intimate hotel. The residential floors were occupied by a series of houseguests, some of whom stayed for years. Harry Hopkins, here with his daughter, Diana, and his wife, Louise (12), occupied a suite in the southeast corner of the second floor. Missy LeHand, pictured here with Roosevelt (13), lived in a cheerful room with slanted ceilings on the third floor.

13

From the first moment the president saw Martha, the crown princess of Norway, he was entranced by her good looks and her lively manner. Here Martha is shown with Eleanor, her husband, Crown Prince Olav, Sara and Franklin at Hyde Park (14), and in a procession with Franklin shortly after her arrival in the United States, where she remained throughout the war (16). Her son, Prince Harald, who is now the king of Norway, plays with Fala (15).

15

16

Eleanor had her own entourage, including her secretary, Malvina Thompson, here with Eleanor in England (17), and her friend Lorena Hickok, who lived in the White House for four years during the war, occupying a room across the hall from Eleanor's suite. Hick, as she was called, is shown below with Eleanor and Governor Paul Pearson of the U.S. Virgin Islands (18).

17

18

Knowing that his mother disapproved of his wife's women friends, Franklin built Eleanor a fieldstone cottage of her own on the grounds of the Hyde Park estate. Though Eleanor stayed at the Big House whenever Franklin and the children were at Hyde Park, she considered Val-Kill, here the site of a National Youth Administration Conference, the only real home she had ever known (19).

One friend recalled that whenever the president's daughter, Anna, here with her father and her second husband, John Boettiger (20), walked into her father's study, the president's whole face lighted up. The world's problems stopped for a few minutes; he just adored her.

All four Roosevelt boys were in the service during the war. Elliott, top left, was in the Army Air Corps; James, top right, was in the marines; while FDR, Jr., bottom left, and John, bottom right, were in the navy (21).

22

23

24

There was an extraordinary bond between the president and his mother. "Nothing," Eleanor observed, "ever seemed to disturb the deep underlying affection they had for each other." Here Sara is driving with Eleanor to Campobello in the summer of 1941 (22), accompanying Franklin after a speech in the U.S. Capitol (23), and standing between Franklin and Eleanor at St. John's Church in 1940 (24).

"All that is in me goes back to the Hudson," Roosevelt liked to say. Time and again Roosevelt confounded his staff by the ease with which, even in the darkest hours, he managed to shake off the burdens of the presidency upon his arrival at Hyde Park. Here are Franklin and Eleanor on the porch of Eleanor's house Val-Kill in 1943 (25); the front of the big house in winter (26); Roosevelt speaking to the Roosevelt Home Club at the home of his tenant farmer, Moses Smith, while Eleanor holds their grandchild, Elliott Jr., and Harry Hopkins listens (27).

27

After he had polio, Franklin built a cottage in Warm Springs, Georgia, where spring water came out of the ground at a soothing eighty-six degrees, winter and summer, providing therapy for crippled patients and relaxation for vacationers. The simple cottage became known as the Little White House (28).

28

Although it was difficult for Roosevelt to maneuver his leg braces in the narrow pews, he still attended church whenever he could. Franklin and Eleanor leave church after Easter services, April 13, 1941 (29).

job with Harry Hopkins that made use of her writing skills in evaluating WPA projects, Hick reproached herself bitterly for giving up her career, her colleagues, her daily by-lines, her life. "Unwittingly," Eleanor's granddaughter Eleanor Seagraves said, "Hick let herself slip into a role where she lost her old identity and became dependent on my grandmother." No longer a nationally recognized reporter, she found it degrading and hateful to be identified in pictures as Eleanor's secretary or bodyguard. Yet, even if she had wanted to get rid of the love that obsessed her, she could not.

Ironically, as Eleanor, with Hick's considerable help, grew into her role as first lady, the ardor of the friendship diminished. "No question that Hick helped Eleanor get her wings," a Roosevelt relative observed, "but once Eleanor began to fly she didn't need Hick the same way." Surrounded by the love and admiration of thousands, Eleanor no longer required the private reassurances from Hick that had bolstered her in the anxious days before she left New York for Washington. In the beginning of the relationship, it was Eleanor who was jealous of Hick's job and Hick's accomplishments—"I should work as you do, but I can't. I am more apt to disappoint you, dear, than you are to disappoint me"—but before long the lines of jealousy ran the opposite way. Sensing that she needed Eleanor more than Eleanor needed her, Hick became moody and sullen, demanding time with Eleanor alone, apart from Eleanor's family and friends.

Eleanor tried to accommodate Hick's desire for time alone, but, more often than not, she found herself apologizing to Hick for including other people in their plans. First it was Louis Howe. "I know you will be disappointed . . . ," she warned Hick, "but Louis seems so miserable I would feel horrible to tell him I wouldn't look after him that evening. You know I'd rather be with you." Then it was Anna. "I'd rather go alone with you but I can't hurt her feelings. . . ." There were so many others—Nan, Marion, Earl, Esther, Elizabeth. They all needed her, too, and though she understood Hick's "cry from the heart for something all her own," she couldn't turn her back on her old friends.

After each confrontation with Hick, Eleanor felt miserable. "I went to sleep saying a little prayer," Eleanor told Hick. "God give me depth enough not to hurt Hick again. Darling I know I'm not up to you in many ways but I love you dearly."

"I know you have a feeling for me which for one reason or another I may not return in kind, but I feel I love you just the same," Eleanor wrote Hick on another occasion. "You think some one thing could make you happy. I know it never does. We may want something, and when we have it, it is not what we dreamed it would be, the thing lies in oneself."

But over time, Hick's possessiveness wore Eleanor down. "I could shake you for your letter . . . ," Eleanor scolded Hick after Hick had complained of a change of plans. "I know you felt badly & are tired, but I'd give an awful lot if you weren't so sensitive."

The low point came during a trip to Yosemite, when Hick became so jealous of the attention the park rangers were showing Eleanor that she "shouted and stalked like a wild animal." When the trip was over, Hick bemoaned her conduct. "I hope you are having a happy, restful time . . . a happier, more peaceful time than you had with me. Oh, I'm bad, my dear, but I love you so, at times life becomes just one long, dreary ache for you. But I'm trying to be happy and contented."

Driven by Hick's behavior to a pitch of exasperation, Eleanor offered a piece of unthinking advice. "Of course you should have had a husband & children & it would have made you happy if you loved him & in any case it would have satisfied certain cravings & given you someone on whom to lavish the love & devotion you have to keep down all the time."

What exactly did Eleanor mean by suggesting to Hick that if she loved a man her frustrated cravings might have been satisfied? Cravings for what? For women instead of men? Was Eleanor unable to accept that Hick was a lesbian? Was she speaking from ignorance, prejudice, or fear?

For her part, Hick cursed the fate that bound her obsessively to Eleanor and hoped that someday she would be free of it. "It would be so much better, wouldn't it," she repeatedly asked Eleanor, "if I didn't love you so much sometimes. It makes it trying for you."

As Eleanor's passion diminished, her guilt increased. "Of course dear, I never meant to hurt you in any way," Eleanor told Hick in 1937, "but that is no excuse for having done it. It won't help you any but . . . I'm pulling myself back in all my contacts now. I've always done it with my children & why I didn't know I couldn't give you (or anyone else who wanted or needed what you did) any real food, I can't now understand. Such cruelty & stupidity is unpardonable when you reach my age."

Hick's melancholy was still evident in a long letter she wrote Eleanor shortly after the 1940 election. "I'd never have believed it possible for a woman to develop after fifty as you have in the last six years. My God, you've learned to do surprisingly well two of the most difficult things in the world —to write and speak. My trouble I suspect has always been that I've been so much more interested in the person than in the personage. I resented the personage and fought for years an anguished and losing fight against the development of the person into the personage. I still prefer the person but I admire and respect the personage with all my heart. . . . I can think of only one other person who undoubtedly felt about this as I have—or would have felt so, increasingly, had he lived, Louis Howe."

"You are wrong about Louis," Eleanor replied. "He always wanted to make me President when FDR was thro' & insisted he could do it. You see he was interested in his power to create personages more than in a person, tho' I think he probably cared more for me as a person as much as he cared for anyone & more than anyone else ever has! Sheer need on his part I imagine!"

How the words "he probably cared more for me . . . than anyone else ever has" must have hurt Hick, who knew in her heart that no one had ever loved Eleanor more than she. But at this point in the relationship, there was nothing Hick could do.

By the time Hick moved into the White House in 1941, a permanent pain had settled in her heart. Though she had come to accept that she could never mean to Eleanor what Eleanor meant to her, the yearning in her soul was still too powerful to allow her to break away. Accepting Eleanor's invitation was in some ways a self-destructive act, but, by living so close, she rationalized, she would at least have the chance to share an occasional breakfast with Eleanor in the morning or talk with her late at night. It was not enough, but it was better than nothing.

•   •   •

"A more discouraging agenda could not have been imagined," *U.S. News* suggested, than that which faced the president in early April, when he "settled down in his swivel chair" upon his return from Fort Bragg: "urgent proposals for more aid to Britain"; Allied defeats in the Middle East; "seizure of Axis ships in American ports; expulsion of the Italian naval attaché"; and, perhaps most discouraging of all, news of lagging production and record numbers of strikes.

Though 1940 had been relatively quiet on the strike front, with only 2.3 percent of the workers in the country involved—the lowest percentage since 1932—1941 became a banner year for strikes. One of every twelve workers, the highest percentage since 1919, would go out on strike in 1941, and the number of strikes would be exceeded in history only by 1937 and 1919.

The most severe strains that spring were in the aircraft industry, which was still in the process of being unionized, still fighting a rearguard action against the rights labor had gained in much of the automotive industry. But strikes were also being fought over wages, work conditions, work loads, and jurisdictional disputes. "Some friends of labor are very deeply troubled," columnist Raymond Clapper wrote, "over the fact that labor is working itself into a role of irresponsible obstruction to war production."

Believing that legislation was necessary to prevent strikes altogether, the War Department sought to use the strike statistics as a public-relations weapon. Every week in March and April, the War Department printed bulletins showing how many man days had been lost as a result of the various strikes at Allis Chalmers, Vultee Air, American Car and Foundry, and Motor Wheel. The bulletins also contained a list of critical items affected—light tanks, landing wheels for the P-40 plane, ammunition, blankets, generators, bombs, zinc. The public-relations effort worked. At theaters across the country, audiences loudly booed whenever pictures of strikers were shown on the newsreels.

Eleanor took a different tack, arguing that business caution, not labor excess, was the root of lagging production. She contended that the fear of being left with surplus capacity after the war was still operating as a brake on plans for expansion. As long as the defense agencies were weighted down with wealthy businessmen (dollar-a-year men, as they were called), there was little hope for change. "All these men will be returning to business," Eleanor told Bernard Baruch at lunch. "How can they be expected to crack down on people with whom they will have to do business in the future?"

"I cannot escape the feeling," Eleanor told the readers of her column, "that the tendency so far has been to say that labor must make sacrifices of wages and hours because of necessities of national defense. I have yet to see anywhere a statement that manufacturers and business concerns . . . shall make this same type of sacrifice by cutting profits and reducing the salaries of executives."

Amid these charges and countercharges came the news that the Ford employees in Dearborn, Michigan, had struck for the first time in the thirty-eight-year history of the River Rouge plant, the largest auto plant in the world. The Rouge plant was the capital of the Ford empire. An entirely self-contained twelve-hundred-acre unit, the plant generated enough power to light all the homes in Chicago, used enough water to supply all the families of Detroit, Cincinnati, and Washington combined, and wore out seven thousand mops a month to keep itself clean.

The strike had begun during the night shift in response to the firing of eleven union workers. As word of the firing spread, the men in one department after another began a spontaneous walkout. At midnight, with the strike officially authorized by the UAW-CIO, squads of union members roamed the plant urging workers to leave their jobs. By 3 a.m., almost all the night workers, eight thousand or more, were out in front of the plant, cheering and singing the union song, "Solidarity Forever." In the meantime, union members from the day shift began to arrive by the thousands to barricade the roads leading into the plant.

Ever since 1936, *Newsweek* reported, the UAW-CIO had awaited the chance to crack Ford, "the last unconquered citadel in its campaign to organize the auto industry." In the wake of the sit-down strikes in the mid-thirties, General Motors, Chrysler, Studebaker, Nash, Packard, and Willy had all come to terms with the union. In moments of vanity, owner Henry Ford liked to believe that he was different from all his colleagues, that they had brought their troubles on themselves whereas he had been an ideal employer, so ideal that his employees didn't need a union.

In truth, fear had been the operating force behind the reluctance of the Ford employees to join the union. Over the years, Ford Service Department head Harry Bennett had built a powerful goon squad of three thousand ex-pugilists, ex-jailbirds, fired policemen, and small-time gangsters, whose primary function was to spy on the employees, taking names of any workmen who accepted union leaflets, tearing union buttons off the caps of employees, physically assaulting union organizers. Little wonder that for so many years the union drive at Ford had stalled.

Ford's miserable labor relations complicated the government's position in the defense crisis. The War Department believed that Ford's immense facilities were essential to rapid munitions production, but labor's vociferous complaints were hard to ignore. In the end, the need for mass production won out; on November 7, 1940, the army had awarded Ford a $122-million contract for the production of four thousand plane engines—the largest such order of the arms program. A week later, a second contract had followed, for a mosquito fleet of four-wheel-drive midget cars, able to go anywhere and get there fast.

Labor spokesmen were horrified at the government's decision to reward "union enemy number one." In liberal circles, the Ford contracts were considered a grievous setback which threatened to take away all the rights working people had achieved through a decade of bitter struggle. "Ford is the country's foremost violator of the Wagner Act," *The Nation* decried, referring to the National Labor Relations Act of 1935, which guaranteed collective-bargaining rights and outlawed such management practices as blacklisting union organizers and spying on union members, "a symbol of the determination of big business to remain above the law," and yet the government had chosen to award the company with not one but two contracts.

The first lady shared labor's discontent, telling delegates at an American Student Union Convention that she thought it was "a bad thing to give contracts to uncooperative people." For his part, the president fully appreciated the complexity of the situation, but his first impulse, he told Henry Stimson, was "to let bygone issues go and concentrate on getting Ford to play fair with labor in the future." It was Roosevelt's belief that once Ford accepted large defense contracts change was inevitable; the dynamics of the situation would eventually force Ford into accepting the union. It was with similar reasoning that Roosevelt had expressed the naïve hope to Negro leader A. Philip Randolph that, by putting white and black regiments side by side in the fluid situation of war, the armed forces would eventually back into integration.

In February 1941, Ford's refusal to "play fair" took its toll on the company. Though Ford was the lowest bidder on a large government order for airplanes, the War Department, under strong pressure from labor, felt compelled to reject the bid because management refused even to sign a clause pledging future compliance with the labor laws. "Best news in a long time," I. F. Stone wrote. The decision gave heart to union organizers at Ford, who began a new drive. Emboldened further by a Supreme Court decision that fixed responsibility on Ford for violating the Wagner Act, union leaders succeeded in signing up thousands of workers. The stage was set for the strike that began on the first of April, when Ford fired the union's key organizers.

From the beginning, the historic strike was complicated by racial conflict. Though the overwhelming majority of the workers stood behind the strike, there remained within the plant nearly two thousand nonstriking Negroes who claimed loyalty to Ford and refused to join the union. Stationing themselves on the roof of the main plant, hundreds of Negro employees hurled metal buckets into the crowd of picketers marching peacefully below. At one point in the struggle, two hundred Negroes armed with steel bars and crudely fashioned swords rushed the main gate, engaging in hand-to-hand combat with the strikers. By the second day of the strike, with company agents busily stirring up racial hatred in the streets, the situation had escalated out of control, threatening to produce a full-scale race war. If the violence continued, the Ford Company argued, the government would have to issue an injunction and send troops to end the strike. Ford also claimed to have evidence of a direct connection between the CIO and the Communist Party. The strike, Ford alleged, was part of the communist program to impede America's mobilization.

Fortunately for the strikers, Roosevelt's lines of intelligence stretched beyond Ford's assessment of the situation. From Hyde Park, where she had gone for the weekend, Eleanor sent Franklin a copy of a long memo she had received from civil-rights leader Mary McCleod Bethune. In this memo, Bethune explained that, though it was true that Ford had earned the loyalty of Negroes by employing "more Negroes in skilled and semi-skilled capacities than any other auto manufacturer in the company," the policy was rooted in opposition to the union. Over time, Bethune explained, "the Ford Negro workers have been propagandized very strongly against trade unionism of any kind and it was expected that in any labor dispute these workers would form the backbone of the Ford anti-union forces." Ford's immediate plan, Bethune had learned, was to use these Negro workers as the vanguard of a back-to-work movement sometime after the weekend. If this was attempted, Bethune predicted, it would result in "one of the bloodiest race riots in the history of the country." Bethune closed by saying she was sending this confidential information to Eleanor in the hope that Eleanor would use her influence to prevent an occurrence "which would set race relations back a quarter of a century."

Armed with the information Bethune provided, Roosevelt appreciated the terrible bind in which the Negro workers found themselves, caught between their past loyalty to Ford and their hopes for the future. "It will be a bitter blow to those who look to the future of the Negro in trade union organizations," the *Pittsburgh Courier* observed, "if this most crucial strike is lost by use of Negro scabs."

Refusing to be drawn into the situation on Ford's side, the president articulated a policy of "watching and waiting and watching," intended to give the mediation machinery a full chance to work. Republicans in the Congress had a field day with the Ford strike. "With the help of the President of the U.S., Hitler has closed the Ford plant," Congressman George Dondero argued. "The dictators in Europe ought to be celebrating today." Representative George Shafer of Battle Creek agreed: "I am convinced the President and his utterly incompetent Secretary of Labor have purposely remained inert and silent while the defense program has been sabotaged."

While the Republicans railed against the president for failing to issue an injunction, he was working behind the scenes to bring about a peaceful settlement. With Roosevelt's approval, NAACP head Walter White journeyed to Detroit to address the Negroes in the plant. Speaking from a union car, White urged the Negro workers to reject their role as strikebreakers, to evacuate the plant and stand shoulder to shoulder with their fellow workers. After several tense days, the Negro workers finally agreed to come out of the plant, clearing the way for the negotiations between labor and management to begin.

The fate of the strikers now rested in the hands of two men, the seventy-seven-year-old founder of the company, Henry Ford, and his only son, Edsel. The elder Ford, stooped and diminished by a series of small strokes, had begun to show unmistakable signs of failing powers: forgetfulness, stubbornness, episodes of inattention and drowsiness. His eyes, one Ford employee said, looked as if someone had "dimmed the power behind them." Two decades earlier, Edsel had replaced his father as president of the company. When the old man came into the plant, however, his word was still law. In June 1940, Edsel had committed Ford to build nine thousand Rolls-Royce engines for British Spitfire planes. Henry agreed at first, but when he realized that the company was expected to deal directly with the British, he changed his mind. It was against his isolationist principles to provide war materials to a foreign power. Edsel was humiliated by the sudden turnabout; when William Knudsen asked him to explain, he could only say that his father had made him do it.

On the central issue of the strike, however, Edsel stood his ground against his father. Whereas the elder Ford believed he could bring the fledgling union to its knees by simply refusing to accept its existence, Edsel argued strongly that negotiating with labor was the only path to the future. It was Edsel who convinced his father to allow Ford officials, for the first time in the history of the company, to sit across a conference table from union representatives. "Mr. Ford gave in to Edsel's wishes," Harry Bennett conceded. The union would never have won "if it hadn't been for Edsel's attitude."

As part of the agreement, preparations were made for a company-wide election to determine whom the workers wanted to represent them. Both the CIO and its conservative rival, the AFL, were on the ballot, along with the option of remaining a nonunion shop. When the votes were counted, the CIO had won a smashing victory, taking 70 percent of the vote to 27 percent for the AFL. A mere 2.6 percent had voted to keep Ford a nonunion shop.

The results took Henry Ford totally by surprise. "It was a measure of Henry Ford's contact with reality," his biographer Robert Lacey observed, that he actually cherished the expectation that his men, "in a gesture of confidence and gratitude for his lifetime of laboring on their behalf," would reject both union options and decide to keep Ford a nonunion shop. "It was perhaps the greatest disappointment he had in all his business experience," Ford's production chief, Charles Sorensen, recalled.

After the election, Henry Ford was never the same again. His zest seemed to vanish. When the time came to sit down with the CIO and work out a new contract, he simply caved in—granting the union virtually everything it asked, including wages equal to the highest in the industry, the abolition of the infamous spy system, and reinstatement of all employees dismissed for union activities. Union leaders pronounced the settlement the greatest of all labor victories in their generation.

• • •

Labor's victory at Ford vindicated Roosevelt's faith that the mobilization process would be an agent of positive change. But he also knew that every delay in the defense program was deadly, and that the public was turning against unions with a vengeance. In the House, a bill was introduced providing "treason" penalties for strikes on defense work; in Georgia, the draft board announced it would furnish no more men for the army until the government moved to stop strikes. Trying to steer a middle course, the president promised to take action against unjustified strikes in the defense industry.

Eleanor, unconstrained by her husband's need for balancing opposing sides, became even more emphatic in her support of labor, arguing that the bill to provide the death penalty for strikers was "perfect nonsense." "We ought not to behave as though this question were a case of patriotism," she said. "The strike situation is not so bad. If we take all the hours of man hours lost from the defense program we find there is a loss of only one-tenth of one percent man labor hours in the year so far."

At her press conference on April 7, Eleanor conceded that she had received a great many letters from mothers of service trainees demanding that labor be forced to produce the arms their sons were called to bear. But in the long run, Eleanor argued, maximum productivity could only be attained if the workers were satisfied that their rights and interests were fully respected. Seen in this light, the strike at Ford was not a sinister act to be feared but, rather, an affirmation of the vitality of democracy.

Eleanor's support for labor became more difficult to maintain in the weeks ahead, when a wildcat strike at the North American Aviation plant in Inglewood, California, halted production on desperately needed twin-engine bombers. This time, in contrast to the situation at Ford, a small splinter group with admitted ties to the Communist Party had arrogantly defied both the federal government and the CIO by walking out in the middle of negotiations. "The infamous hand" of the Communist Party "is apparent," UAW labor leader Richard Frankensteen warned. "This is not just a charge on the part of the company management."

With the North American strike, *Time* observed, "Franklin Roosevelt reached a worm-turning point. Having tolerated strikes in defense industry for many months—until the public was fed up and Congress indignant—he either had to put up or curl up."

In a tense mood, Roosevelt signed an executive order directing the secretary of war, with the help of twenty-five hundred federal troops, to take possession of the plant and break the strike. As the uniformed troops marched into the area, the local strike leader, Joe Freitag, issued a defiant call. "The armed forces will not break our strike. Bombers can't be made with bayonets." Freitag was wrong. Only two hours after the army battalions took over, the workers returned, streaming through the gates by the thousands. The strike was over.

• • •

Spring had come to Washington. The cherry blossoms were in bloom. Yet the glacial mood of the capital refused to melt. Accusations filled the air as the mobilization process faltered. Production of planes was 30 percent behind schedule. "Washington rarely ever has been in such confusion as today," Washington correspondent David Lawrence wrote. "The internal situation is becoming almost as grave as the external." Though the president had replaced the NDAC in December with a stronger organization, the Office of Production Management (OPM), headed jointly by former NDAC members William Knudsen and Sidney Hillman, he had not yet developed an organization that could run without him. When he was indisposed or preoccupied with other matters, the wheels seemed to stop moving. "What has not yet been realized," Lawrence continued, "is that it is impossible for the President through the normal peacetime type of organization to carry on war preparations which amount to the same thing as if America were actually at war."

"It took Hitler more than five years to get ready for this war," observed Leon Henderson, the rumpled chief of yet another new organization, the Office of Price Administration and Civilian Supply (OPACS), designed to prevent profiteering and undue price rises. "We've got months, not years in which to prepare." And the battle could only be won "if this nation produces more and faster than any nation has ever produced before."

New Dealers argued that business was intentionally holding down defense production in order to profit from the tantalizing rise in consumer demand for civilian products that was accompanying the military buildup. Business countered that it was doing all it could to expand its defense production in an atmosphere poisoned by labor strife and social-welfare concerns.

The struggle focused that spring on the automobile industry, which was producing new cars in record numbers, "gobbling an intolerable share of scarce raw materials"—80 percent of all rubber, 49 percent of strip steel, 44 percent of sheet steel, 34 percent of lead. While the War Department agonized over America's limited supply of steel, aluminum, and rubber, auto dealers were proudly displaying their shiny new models in showrooms. The new Packard boasted a streamlined shape with fenders integral to the body and a high radiator grill; Willys announced a new price leader, the American Blue Streak Coupe; Chevrolet introduced a new "get away" gear or second speed.

As the new head of OPACS, Leon Henderson was at the center of the controversy. For months he had argued for a sharp curtailment in the production of passenger cars in order to force the industry to divert its men, management, and raw materials from civilian to defense needs. "You can't have 500 bombers a month *and* business as usual," declared Henderson. "We cannot fight a war with convertible coupes," I. F. Stone added, "or overawe a Panzer division with a brigade of statistics on automobile sales."

But Henderson's call for a 50-percent cut in the production of automobiles met unrelenting resistance at the top of the administration, from William Knudsen. The OPM chief argued that a cut of 50 percent would throw the entire industry into chaos, resulting in widespread unemployment and tremendous distress. Moving quickly to outflank Henderson, Knudsen called a press conference on April 17, and announced with great fanfare that he had just concluded a meeting with the leaders of the auto industry. "The entire industry willingly accepted an initial 20 percent reduction in the production of motor vehicles for the model year beginning August 1," Knudsen proudly announced.

It sounded swell, I. F. Stone noted in *The Nation,* but it was in fact a ruse, given that production for the banner year of 1941 was already running more than 20 percent ahead of the previous year, so a cut of 20 percent would merely bring it back to normal. "The problem," Stone continued, "is to turn existing mass-production facilities as rapidly as possible to the production of armament. We are fumbling that problem, and we have no time to fumble." The time had come, Stone concluded, for Knudsen to turn in his resignation. Stimson agreed. "I am afraid," the secretary of war recorded in his diary, "that Knudsen is too soft and slow because of his connection with the auto industry."

Eleanor was in full agreement with Henderson and Stimson; she had argued all along that Knudsen was fatally biased toward industry. Entering the fray, she approached the problem from a different angle, calling on the American people "to begin thinking about doing without various commodities such as new automobiles and aluminum kitchen utensils when present stocks are exhausted." Instead of competing for various articles now, she urged Americans to save their money for the future, for the abundant new cars and refrigerators that would become readily available after the emergency ended. Echoing Eleanor's sentiments, Henderson predicted that Americans would "cheerfully forego the luxury of new automobiles in order to assure adequate mechanized equipment for defense."

Henderson was wrong. In truth, just the opposite phenomenon developed that spring, whereby anxious consumers, afraid that the supply of cars would eventually be curtailed, rushed to the showrooms in greater numbers than ever before. It would take the attack on Pearl Harbor to create the patriotic mood that, along with rationing and a limited supply of civilian goods, stimulated Americans to do precisely as Eleanor suggested—to put their money in government bonds, which could be cashed in for houses and cars and washing machines as soon as the war ended. Indeed, during the war, personal savings would rise to unprecedented levels, laying the foundation for the postwar boom.

But for the time being, in the fractious mood that characterized a still-divided America in the spring of 1941, Eleanor's pleas fell on deaf ears, and the struggle between Henderson and Knudsen continued unabated.

• • •

By the end of April, a tone of weariness and irritation had crept into the president's voice as he tried to juggle the cries of isolationists with Britain's struggle to survive. "The President has on his hands at the present time," Admiral Harold Stark observed, "about as difficult a situation as ever confronted any man anywhere in public life."

With the coming of spring, the Germans had resumed their offensive, and the results were devastating. The first week of April witnessed the invasion of Yugoslavia, heralded by the killing of seventeen thousand civilians in Belgrade within the first twenty-four hours. Eleven days later, the overwhelmed Yugoslavians signed an act of surrender. After Yugoslavia, it took the Germans less than four weeks to conquer neighboring Greece, and to drive British forces in Libya back to the Egyptian border.

While British armies were meeting disaster abroad, Britain's home economy was on the verge of strangulation and collapse. In March and April, German submarines seemed to be roaming the North Atlantic at will; British ships were being sunk at the terrifying rate of three times their capacity to replace them. Imports into Britain had fallen to a volume less than needed to feed the British people or to keep the factories going. Unless the Battle of the Atlantic could be won, there was little hope that the country could survive.

For months, Stimson and Knox had been pressuring the president to ask the Congress for the power to convoy British ships across the Atlantic. Without American intervention "to forcibly stop the German submarines," Stimson told Roosevelt, "the dispatch of additional supplies to Britain was like pouring water into a leaky bathtub." The navy plans called for transferring three battleships, four cruisers, and one aircraft carrier from the Pacific fleet to the Atlantic to serve as escorts for the merchant ships.

Roosevelt knew that everyone was waiting for him to cross the line, and he knew that sooner or later he would cross it. But, for the moment, he refused to take the lead, convinced that convoys would lead to shooting, and shooting would lead to war. Believing that his broad consensus for lend-lease had been forged on the assumption that aid to Britain would prevent, rather than instigate, American entry into war, Roosevelt feared that convoys would shatter the national agreement and force him to carry a divided nation into war. A national poll on the 8th of April confirmed the president's fears. When asked if they supported convoys, 41 percent of the American people were in favor, 50 percent opposed.

The president proposed instead a more limited action—the establishment of an extended patrol system to detect German subs and report their locations to British ships. When it was suggested by the press that these patrols, which the president likened to those used by the pioneers to scout Indians, might in effect be convoys, an aggravated Roosevelt remarked that "one could not turn a cow into a horse by calling it a horse." Yet FDR, Jr., in a confidential letter to his sister, Anna, on April 2, did precisely that when he told her that his destroyer, the U.S.S. *Mayrant,* was going to be part of the new "escort patrol" squadron, "which is the cutest name I can imagine for what I think will be actual convoying before long."

From the German perspective, there was little doubt, as Goebbels wrote in his diary in April, that "the U.S.A. is preparing to make the leap to war. If Roosevelt were not so chary of public opinion, he would have declared war on us long ago."

On Tuesday morning, April 22, a discouraged Stimson went to see the president. Stimson warned his boss from the outset that he was going to speak very frankly and hoped Roosevelt wouldn't question his loyalty and affection. "He reassured me on that point and then I went over the whole situation of the deterioration in the American political situation toward the war that has taken place since nothing happened immediately after the lend-lease victory. I cautioned him on the necessity of his taking the lead and that without a lead on his part it was useless to expect the people would voluntarily take the initiative."

Though Stimson was delighted by the "intimate" nature of his conversation with the president, he remained apprehensive about Roosevelt's lack of leadership. "I am worried," he recorded in his diary, "because the President shows evidence of waiting for the accidental shot of some irresponsible captain on either side to be the occasion for his going to war. I think he ought to consider the deep principles which underlie the issue in the world and [have] divided the world into two camps, [of] one of which he is the leader."

At the very moment when Stimson was talking frankly with the president, Interior Secretary Harold Ickes was baring his own disgruntled soul to Missy LeHand. Ickes was so concerned about the president's lack of leadership that he was considering resigning from the Cabinet. "Knudsen simply is not delivering the goods," he recorded in his diary. "Big business is having altogether too much say about our preparedness program. We are talking about asking working men to give 24 hour service in shifts, but we listen to businessmen talk about 'business as usual.' " In every direction, Ickes believed, there was a growing discontent with the president's leadership. "He still has the country if he will take it and lead it." But people were starting to say, "I am tired of words; I want action."

"I turn to Missy," Ickes wrote in his diary on April 22, "when I feel deeply about how things are going because I not only trust her discretion but have confidence in her wisdom, even if I mistrust her on the subject of Harry Hopkins. I took my hair down and told her exactly how I felt about the situation. I found that she had the same thoughts and the same apprehensions. She knows that he is tired and she appreciates as keenly as anyone the fact that he is relying more and more on the people in his immediate entourage. I told her that I would be perfectly satisfied if he fired everyone else and relied solely on her. She agreed with me that no one could hope to get in from the outside as Felix Frankfurter had suggested. . . . She realizes that something ought to be done to build up public sentiment in the country and remarked caustically that, while we were doing nothing, Senator Wheeler and others were going about making speeches and creating an adverse sentiment."

On Friday, May 2, the president journeyed to Staunton, Virginia, to dedicate the home in which Woodrow Wilson had been born. With Eleanor on the West Coast, Missy accompanied him as the official hostess. It was a rough day for Roosevelt. His stomach was in turmoil, he was running a temperature, and all the color from his face was gone. "FDR looked as bad as a man can look and still be about," the *Time* reporter observed. Though he managed to get through his brief address, the accompanying pleasantries were canceled.

That evening, Dr. McIntire found the president suffering from an intestinal disturbance and severe anemia. His red-blood-cell count, which should have been at five million, had dropped suddenly to 2.8 million. The immediate therapy involved iron injections, two transfusions, and complete rest.

Unaware of her husband's illness, Eleanor was cheerfully ensconced with Anna and John at their home in Seattle. Curiously, when Eleanor had first arrived on the West Coast the week before, she had had a premonition that something was wrong. In her mailbox at the Ambassador Hotel in Los Angeles was a message saying that Washington was calling. "My heart sank," she admitted. "But in a few minutes my husband's calm and reassuring voice announced that he was just calling to give me a little conversation."

The president's illness kept him away from his desk for nearly two weeks. Canceling all appointments, he spent most of his time in his bedroom, accompanied only by Harry and Missy. To be sure, for at least half of that period he was truly sick, but even after his temperature was normal and his intestinal disturbance had cleared itself up, he remained in bed, inaccessible to all but Harry and Missy. At one point during this period of isolation, Robert Sherwood was invited in to talk. Surprised at how healthy Roosevelt seemed, never once coughing or sneezing, Sherwood asked Missy what was going on. Missy smiled and said, "What he's suffering from most of all is a case of sheer exasperation."

Missy knew her man. Frustrated by the contradictory impulses of public attitudes toward the struggle, dismayed at the prospect of carrying a divided country into war, the president was "waiting to be pushed into the situation." Throughout his long political career, Roosevelt had worked hard to fathom the unfathomable force of public opinion. From long experience, he had learned that in a democracy one man alone cannot guide tens of millions of people without following (and shaping, as far as one could) that intangible force called the spirit of the country. He had seen at first hand President Woodrow Wilson's failure to reinforce his foreign policy with public and congressional backing. He had, in effect, made what historian Eric Larrabee has called "a compact with the electorate which he had every reason for wishing to keep." Yet so confused and so volatile was public opinion in the spring of 1941 that Roosevelt was like a man staring into a fog.

By the middle of May, the percentage of people supporting convoys had risen from 41 percent to 55 percent, even though three-quarters of the population believed convoying would eventually put the country into war. At the same time, 79 percent of the people expressed the strong desire to stay out of the fighting; and 70 percent felt the president had either gone too far or was already doing enough to help Britain. Roosevelt recognized that with education he could command a national majority on convoys and even on direct involvement in the war, but he feared that his consensus would quickly vanish if a substantial portion of the people felt that he, rather than a recognized threat to national security, had compelled involvement.

So Roosevelt's bed became the escape he needed to avoid action and deflate pressure. "Missy was exactly right," journalist Eliot Janeway affirmed. "Simply put, the President was in bed because he was in a funk, feeling there was nothing he could do except let the tides fall."

• • •

Eleanor returned from the West Coast on the evening of May 7 in good spirits. Her trip had been a fruitful one, and there was much to tell the president. She had lectured in a dozen places, often following Charles Lindbergh. The questions she received, she believed, reflected his arguments and gave her an insight into the isolationists' frame of mind. She had spent a morning touring one of the new housing projects built under the U.S. Housing Authority; she had talked with a lively group of young men and women involved in a defense-training program sponsored by the NYA; she had spent an afternoon with a group of Negroes at a WPA center for Negro art. And, perhaps of greatest potential interest to the president, she had been taken on a tour of the Boeing Aircraft plant in Seattle, where she witnessed the completion of the first four motor bombers. "Since defense is now the key thing," Lash observed in his diary, "she is determined to learn as much as she can in her detailed human being interest sort of way, just as she had with WPA etc."

But before seeing her husband, Eleanor journeyed to Hyde Park for the weekend. That Sunday was Mother's Day, and Sara needed Eleanor's help in preparing her traditional Mother's Day broadcast to the nation. Speaking from her living room at exactly noon, the president's eight-six-year-old mother characterized 1941 as a year marked with great suffering, "probably the most crucial year in history." Watching Sara's stalwart performance, Eleanor could not help admiring the old lady. "There is no one I know who sets a greater value on the duties and pleasures of motherhood," Eleanor wrote in her column. That same week, Sara traveled to Toronto to raise money for one of her charities. "Isn't she amazing?" Eleanor commented to Anna.

Franklin and Eleanor talked together on the phone several times that weekend, and Eleanor was relieved to discover that he was in good humor, responsive and cheerful, "on the way to being quite well." Anxious to know whether his young trees had survived the early-spring drought, he asked her to make an inspection and report back as soon as she could. Hyde Park in the spring was one of the most delightful places in the world. Eleanor reveled in the sight of the river tumbling past and the sounds of the birds in the woods. When she reported that everything not newly planted seemed unharmed, he was delighted.

Yet no sooner had Eleanor arrived at the White House than the old tensions resumed. Impatient to disclose what she had discovered in her cross-country trip—delays in defense housing, inequities in recreational facilities provided for whites and Negroes, the refusal of certain industries to hire Italians and Germans—she found her husband "very tired and very edgy." What is more, she felt unable to break in on Harry and Missy's territory.

"The situation with Harry, Missy and Pa is funny," Eleanor admitted in a long letter to Anna. "It is a very closed corporation just now. So far I've told him nothing as I didn't think he was well enough to accept any disagreeable facts." But as long as she was away so often, it was inevitable that her husband would turn to others for companionship. It was, after all, Missy and Harry, not Eleanor, who had sat with Roosevelt in his bedroom night after night when he was sick, talking with him, playing cards with him, soothing his frustration.

In the third week of May, the president's energy returned; lethargy gave way to action. "Franklin is much better," Eleanor told Esther Lape, "really looks very well and is now working very hard to catch up with what he missed while he was ill." In the Oval Office, where silence had reigned for more than a fortnight, there was now a welcoming air, with lights burning until well after midnight and a steady stream of visitors.

After weeks of avoiding the press, the president announced that he would deliver a major speech to the nation on May 27. It seemed that everyone was asked to contribute to the draft—Hopkins, Stimson, Welles, Knox, Hull, Berle, Sherwood, and Rosenman. In the meantime, the White House received some twelve thousand letters from all over the country advising the president what to say. It fell to Sherwood and Rosenman, as usual, to collect all the suggestions and then sit with the president to hear what *he* wanted to say. Generally, Roosevelt would dictate his thoughts at the end of the day, until it was time to go to bed. Then the speechwriters would retire to the large table in the Cabinet Room, where, with scissors and paste, they would begin the task of assembling a coherent speech. The following night, after reading the draft, the president would dictate some more, and then his aides would return to the Cabinet Room to start a second draft.

These drafting sessions often lasted most of the night. During the preparations for the May 27 speech, Eleanor told Sherwood and Rosenman that she had seen their lights in the Cabinet Room at 3 a.m., and gently scolded them for working so hard and staying up so late. "If I máy say so, Mrs. Roosevelt," Sherwood countered, "you were up rather late yourself." Unperturbed, Eleanor replied, "I was working on my mail," failing to understand why everyone laughed.

The major thrust of the speech concerned the president's decision to declare an unlimited national emergency, a step which, under the law, the chief executive could take only when he believed war to be imminent. With this proclamation came a variety of domestic and international powers which a peacetime president did not possess—including the power to increase the size of the regular army or navy, to place compulsory defense orders in factories or plants, and to assign priority rating to producers and suppliers, directing them to fill defense orders ahead of private orders. In the last hours before the speech, the president began to waver. "There's only a small number of rounds of ammunition left to use," he explained, "unless Congress is willing to give me more. This declaration is one of those few rounds, and a very important one. Is this the right time to use it or should we wait until things get worse—as they surely will?" Ultimately, he decided this *was* the right time.

Just before the president began to speak at 10:30 p.m., the electric meters in power stations across the country began jumping skyward as people everywhere, in cities and remote towns, in mountains and valleys, in mansions and tenements, turned on their radios. "For almost an hour," *The New York Times* reported, "a whole nation here stilled itself to listen to his words."

Speaking in the oppressive heat of the East Room into a bank of microphones before a gathering of representatives of the Pan American Union, the president began by recalling that he had promised the people he would not send their boys to war except in case of attack, then went on to define what was meant by the word "attack." "Some people seem to think that we are not attacked until bombs actually drop in the streets of New York or San Francisco or New Orleans or Chicago. But they are simply shutting their eyes to the lesson that we must learn from the fate of every nation that the Nazis have conquered. The attack on Czechoslovakia began with the conquest of Austria. The attack on Norway began with the occupation of Denmark . . . and the attack on the U.S. can begin with the domination of any base which menaces our security—North or South. . . . We know enough by now to realize that it would be suicide to wait until they are in our front yard. When your enemy comes at you in a tank or a bombing plane, if you hold your fire until you see the whites of his eyes, you will never know what hit you. Our Bunker Hill of tomorrow may be several thousand miles from Boston.''

With this broadened definition of "attack," the president justified his decision to add more ships and planes to the American patrols. And beyond that, he promised that "all additional measures necessary to deliver the goods will be taken. Any and all further methods or combination of methods . . . are being devised."

Finally, "I have tonight issued a proclamation that an unlimited national emergency exists and requires the strengthening of our defense to the extreme limit of our national power and authority." In justifying his proclamation, he said that a succession of events had made it clear that "what started as a European war" had developed into "a war for world domination." Indifference to this fundamental fact would "place the nation at peril."

Eleanor was seated in the front row as the president spoke, surrounded on all sides by flags and representatives of all the nations of South and North America. "The atmosphere in the room was one of suppressed and intense excitement," she wrote. "Diplomats are trained to observe the amenities, no matter what they feel, but everybody's face showed some emotion as the evening progressed. I felt strangely detached, as though I were outside, a part of the general public. I represented no nation, carried no responsibility."

But then she looked at her husband's face and, "like an oncoming wave, the thought rolled over me. What a weight of responsibility this one man at the desk, facing the rest of the people, has to carry. Not just for this hemisphere alone but for the world as a whole! Great Britain can be gallant beyond belief, China can suffer and defend herself in equally heroic fashion, but in the end the decisive factor in this whole business, may perhaps be . . . the President of the United States. In my capacity of objective citizen, sitting in the gathering, I felt that I wanted to accept my responsibility and do my particular job whatever it might be to the extent of my ability. I think that will be the answer of every individual citizen of the U.S.A."

Harry Hopkins was in his bedroom, listening to the speech in his old bathrobe. According to Robert Sherwood, Hopkins always preferred to listen to the president's speeches on the radio, so he could imagine himself in the living room of an ordinary family. After the diplomats left, Eleanor came into Harry's room to invite him to join the president in the Monroe Room, where a small group of friends, including songwriter Irving Berlin, were gathered to enjoy a midnight snack. The president seemed completely at ease, laughing and smiling as he listened to Berlin play the piano and sing some of his favorite songs.

This transition from a grim speech to an intimate party with popular music, Rosenman observed, "would have been difficult for most men. For the President, however, those who knew him thought it nothing unusual. It was not callousness or indifference. It was the kind of relaxation that helped him to meet the terrible problems and burdens of the next day, and to live through twelve years of nerve-racking decisions."

The response to the speech was overwhelmingly favorable. More than a thousand telegrams were delivered to the White House that night. "They're 95 percent favorable," the president remarked. "And I figured I'd be lucky to get an even break on this speech."

On the whole, Henry Stimson was pleased with the speech. Though the final draft was not as strong as he had hoped—at the last minute, the president elected not to disclose his plans for transferring part of the fleet to the Atlantic—the proclamation of emergency promised to create a receptive atmosphere down the line, when more drastic steps were needed.

"We listened to father's speech on the train and were greatly thrilled," Anna wrote her mother. "The speech came over beautifully and he sounded well and strong, thank goodness." Listener polls published the next day revealed that the president's speech had set an all-time record in the history of radio. It was estimated that more than sixty-five million people in twenty million homes had heard the talk—70 percent of the total home audience in the U.S. The second-highest rating was also held by the president—his fireside chat on December 29 had been heard by 59 percent of the radio audience. Only one other broadcast had come even close to these figures: the second Louis-Schmeling fight at Yankee Stadium in 1938 had achieved a rating of 57.2 percent. To understand the magnitude of the interest in Roosevelt's words, one need only realize that America's top-ranking radio comedy shows—*Jack Benny, Bob Hope, Fibber McGee and Molly, The Goldbergs, Ma Perkins, Amos 'n' Andy*—were currently garnering what were considered fabulous ratings of 30 to 35 percent.

The speech was heard round the world as well. Goebbels lambasted it in his diary as "demagogic and aggressive." Roosevelt's talk, the propaganda minister believed, was nothing but "beer-hall bragging" that should not be taken seriously. "What can the USA do faced with our arms capacity? They can do us no harm. He will never be able to produce as much as we, who have the entire economic capacity of Europe at our disposal." Nonetheless, Goebbels admitted, Roosevelt's "reckless accusations" against Germany were irritating. "The USA stands poised between peace and war. Roosevelt wants war, the people want peace. . . . We must wait and see what he does next."

CHAPTER 10

"A GREAT HOUR
TO LIVE"

T he president's return to health at the end of May signaled an end to the hours Missy had enjoyed with him isolated from the world at large. Indeed, no sooner was Roosevelt's vigor restored than he motored to Pook's Hill to spend an afternoon with Princess Martha. Missy was under no illusion that the president fully reciprocated her devotion. She knew, however, that she had been a central presence in his life for twenty years, someone to whom he could always turn for undivided comfort and support. It was most unsettling to watch herself being supplanted by another woman.

As the felt injustice of her position accumulated, "she may have begun," Roosevelt's grandson Curtis Roosevelt surmised, "to face him with emotional demands: Why don't you respond to me, acknowledge me more, give me what I give you? She may have been getting too protective, making demands he couldn't meet. He could never cope with people who started making emotional demands. He didn't like weepy women. He was turned off by people who couldn't fit into his game."

Part of the problem, Elliott Roosevelt observed, was that "Missy was not as relaxing for the President as she used to be." She had become so influential in the Washington community, representing so many people to the president, that she could no longer simply "sit and simper" the way Martha did. For Jim Rowe, Felix Frankfurter, Harold Ickes, and untold others, Missy had become *the* conduit to the president, advising them "when to approach FDR and when to put off a vexing matter until another day." In Missy's files there are numerous requests for her to intervene on behalf of one person or another.

"Some of the people who worked closely in the administration with my husband . . . ," Eleanor Roosevelt later noted, "were brought in through Missy's efforts . . . [presidential adviser] Tom Corcoran, [Ambassador] William Bullitt. . . .

"I think none of them ever meant a great deal to Franklin. I also think they exploited Missy's friendship, believing her more interested in them personally than in what they could contribute to Franklin's work. In that they were mistaken; . . . though occasionally someone fooled her for a time, I always waited for enlightenment to come, with confidence born of long experience."

To make matters worse, Missy was afflicted that spring with insomnia, and the opiates she was taking to combat it were having a bad effect. More and more, her benign temper was punctuated by outbursts of irascibility. The pressure of her job began to get to her. "The president would work night after night," Missy's friend Barbara Curtis remarked, "and she was always right there working with him. He could take it, but I think her strength just didn't hold out to take all that."

"She said quietly one time that he had no idea of the demands he put upon people who were close to him," Barbara's husband, Egbert Curtis, recalled. "Would you do this? Would you do that? And it went beyond some of their powers to keep up."

On June 4, 1941, the dam burst. At six-thirty that evening, the president was relaxing with the members of his White House staff, including Missy, Harry Hopkins, Grace Tully, and Pa Watson, at a party hosted by Harry Somerville, the manager of the Willard Hotel. Mr. Somerville's party, an annual tradition, was normally held at the Willard, but on this evening the event was held at the White House so the president could attend. A piano was rolled in, and Marvin McIntyre played all the songs FDR loved.

Near the end of the dinner, Grace Tully recalled, Missy arose from her chair, saying she felt ill and very tired. Tully urged her to excuse herself and retire to her room, but she insisted on staying until the president left. He did so at 9:30 p.m. and, moments later, Missy let out a piercing scream, wavered, and fell to the floor unconscious. Dr. Ross McIntire and Commander George Fox, the president's physical therapist, took her to her room on the third floor and sedated her.

The doctors seemed to think at first it was some sort of heart trouble or a kind of nervous collapse, much like the ones she had experienced before, brought about in this case by a combination of sleeplessness and overwork. "It was very secret," White House secretary Toi Bachelder remembered. "The fact that she was ill was kept very quiet. Nobody said anything."

The next morning, when White House maid Lillian Parks arrived at the third-floor sewing room across from Missy's bedroom, a distraught nurse was in the hallway just outside Missy's door. "She's gotten up and I can't get her back in bed," the nurse said, asking for help. Parks walked into the room. "Come on, Miss LeHand," she said sternly. "Come get into bed." Responding to the tone of Parks' voice, Missy climbed meekly back into bed, where she remained, stroking Parks' arm, until Dr. McIntire and a second doctor arrived. McIntire told Parks that Missy was utterly exhausted, that she had been working too hard and needed complete rest. Her speech was slightly slurred, but this was attributed to the opiates and the sleeplessness.

Eleanor was in Hyde Park the night Missy collapsed, but as soon as she heard about the situation, she called Maggie Parks, Lillian Parks' mother, who had retired from the White House two years earlier. "Missy loved you," she told Maggie; "would you come back and sit with her at night? She is so lonely."

So Maggie sat through the nights with Missy, listening to her ramblings, her wild callings for FDR, her worries that her work was piling up and that her boss would suffer as a result. "It's sad to love a man so much," Maggie commented to her daughter, believing that "the strain of loving and knowing nothing could come of it" had helped bring about Missy's illness.

Eleanor did not know what to make of Missy's collapse. "Missy is very ill again," she confided to Anna on June 12. "She's been taking opiates and had a heart attack and then her mind went as it does, so now we have three nurses and the prospect of some weeks of illness before we get her straightened out." The following week, Eleanor suggested to Anna that Missy's problem was complicated by "change of life."

In 1941, the superstitions of past ages still retained a firm hold on popular attitudes toward menopause. "Too many women," Maxine Davis wrote in *Good Housekeeping*, "attribute all sorts of ailments—headaches, backaches, worries, depression, bad temper—to the menopause. . . . Other women nourish the gnawing fear that they'll lose their minds. They can remember Aunt Ida and Mother's horror stories of cousin Edith, who finally had to be committed to an institution."

In Missy's case, the loss of the childbearing function that accompanied menopause may have been the hardest to bear, providing dread confirmation of her failure to marry and build a family of her own. Though she was only forty-three, a monumental door was closing behind her, never to be opened again.

As Missy's feelings of desolation and uncertainty intensified, she began to write a series of agitated, scarcely decipherable letters to people who had been close to her over the years. Passages in these tormented letters were manic descriptions of her love life, fantasies of a world she had never entered. "The letters told of this one being in love with her, and that one wanting to marry her," Anna confided years later to the writer Bernard Asbell. "Everyone realized that she could no longer be trusted with important information. These friends and the family drew together to get the letters out of sight, to hush up Missy's lapse."

For the president, Missy's breakdown was a catastrophe. Day after day he visited her third-floor apartment. As time went by, she seemed to get worse, not better. How many hours Roosevelt had spent with Missy in this comfortable suite, escaping from official guests. There stood the familiar chair and the wooden bookcase he had carved for her years before as a special present; there the familiar desk and the four-poster bed. Nonetheless, everything had changed. On the bed, her head propped high on the pillows, Missy looked like a frightened stranger. Anguished eyes peered at him, instead of the gaze of love he had found for twenty years.

Unable to grieve, unable to accept the fact that Missy was not getting better as she always had before, Roosevelt developed an illness of his own; his throat became infected and he began to run a temperature. Worried about her husband's fever, Eleanor begged him to see an outside doctor. But in a letter to Anna, she admitted that Missy's collapse was the most likely cause of Franklin's illness. "Missy has been worse for the last few days," Eleanor confided, "and that may be at the bottom of much of Pa's trouble."

In retrospect, it is clear that Missy's condition was caused by neither insomnia nor the change of life; her collapse on the evening of June 4 was most likely a small stroke, an undiagnosed warning signal for the major stroke she suffered two weeks later. The naval ambulance arrived at the White House at 9:30 p.m. on Saturday, June 21. The president had spent the afternoon with Princess Martha and had worked through dinner clearing up his correspondence with Grace Tully. He was still at work when Missy was carried out on a stretcher to the ambulance and taken to Doctors Hospital at 35th and I streets.

Since Missy had suffered from rheumatic heart disease as a child—the dread disease which "licks the joints and bites the heart"—it is most likely that her stroke was caused by a cerebral embolism, a clot that was formed in her heart and carried by her blood to her brain. When it reached the narrow blood vessels of the brain, it got stuck, cutting off the blood flow to the brain cells on her left side. The result was the loss of movement in her right arm and leg, and the loss of her ability to speak coherently.

Word of Missy's illness gradually slipped out. "I was distressed to hear from Mother that you have been miserable," Anna wrote Missy. "Please, do be a good girl and get well quickly. Even thinking of the pressure of responsibility and work on you all makes one shudder and the importance of watching one's health becomes greater than ever. Being sick is never any fun—and it's not natural to think of you that way."

"My dear Missy," Sara Roosevelt wrote from Campobello, "I do not like to think of you still in bed, but I believe you and I are cases for bed. I for old age and you for rest to an overworked rather delicate organ. For the autumn perhaps you will come to Hyde Park and rest with me."

For her part, Missy must have been horrified by the breakdown of her body, overwhelmed by a sense of solitude. The doctors held out hope that over time she would be able to relearn the movements necessary for standing and walking, but she was particularly sensitive to the effect of her illness on her speech. She refused most visits, except those of the Roosevelts, who came to see her at Doctors Hospital nearly every week all summer long.

For the president, the visits were unbearable. All his life, he had steeled himself to ignore illness and unpleasantness of any kind, to maintain an attitude of perpetual cheer. So now he would wheel himself into her room, his face set in a wide smile, a series of amusing anecdotes on his lips. But the president's cheery monologues were not what Missy needed to hear. Tired and bewildered, filled with dread and foreboding, she frequently broke into tears. Suddenly Roosevelt had no more stories to tell. He would look at her, smile another smile, and say goodbye.

For Eleanor, who was more accustomed to vulnerability and loss, the visits were easier to handle. She went to see Missy as often as she could, sending her flowers, fruit, presents, and letters. "The strange thing," Elliott Roosevelt observed, "was that Mother was more protective and upset about Missy's illness than Father. He seemed to accept it and go through the loss without its affecting him nearly as much as I would have thought it would have affected him."

To outside observers, Roosevelt's equanimity in the face of Missy's illness seemed disturbingly coldhearted. "Roosevelt had absolutely no moral reaction to Missy's tragedy," Eliot Janeway remarked. "It seemed only that he resented her for getting sick and leaving him in the lurch. This was proof that he had ceased to be a person; he was simply the president. If something was good for him as president, it was good; if it had no function for him as president, it didn't exist."

In a moment of anger at the president after a bitter political fight that summer, Harold Ickes made a similar observation. "As I sat at the Cabinet table yesterday looking at the President," he recorded in his diary, "I felt a clear conviction that I had lost my affection for him . . . despite his very pleasant and friendly personality, he is as cold as ice inside. He has certain conventional family affections for his children and probably for Missy LeHand and Harry Hopkins, but nothing else. Missy, who has been desperately ill for several weeks, might pass out of his life and he would miss her. The same might be true as to Harry, but I doubt whether he would miss either of them greatly or for a long period. When Louis Howe died, so far as appearances, the President was not noticeably affected, although no one has ever had a more devoted friend than Louis Howe."

That Roosevelt made no outward display of his feelings did not mean, however, that he was indifferent to Missy's distress. Indeed, his actions tell a different story. While Missy was in the hospital, he ordered round-the-clock care, absorbed every expense, and wrote each of her doctors personal notes. "No words will ever be able to express to you," he wrote Dr. John Harper, "my very deep feeling of appreciation and gratitude for the outstanding and unselfish services you have rendered in looking after my secretary, Miss LeHand."

In the months that followed the stroke, Missy's condition improved, but ever so slightly. With the help of daily physical therapy, movement began to return to her right leg, and after many weeks of practice she was ready, with the help of a heavy brace and crutches, to start walking again. "The case has been a difficult one, indeed," Dr. Winfred Overholser wrote the president, "but I am encouraged by the progress made in the last few weeks." But such are the mysteries of rehabilitation that the right hand and arm stubbornly resisted any improvement at all, as did the function of speech. Though she was able to understand both spoken and written language, she was unable to speak herself except in simple phrases.

Recognizing that Missy's therapy would take months, if not years (and even when it was completed, there was scant hope that she could return to her demanding job in the White House), Roosevelt worried about what would happen to her if he should die. The only money Missy ever had was her annual salary, which at its peak of $5,000 was half that of the male secretaries. With no savings in the bank and no family money to back her up, there was no guarantee that her medical expenses would be covered.

With this in mind, Roosevelt took a decisive act. He arranged a luncheon with his old friend and legal adviser, Basil O'Connor. At the lunch, he told O'Connor that he wished to alter his will in order to leave half of his estate to Missy. O'Connor fiercely opposed the change, for it involved removing the Roosevelt children as beneficiaries. But Roosevelt insisted. He argued that "the children could care for themselves, but this faithful aide could not."

The new provision was incorporated into Roosevelt's will five months after Missy's stroke. After first directing that half of his estate (which was eventually probated at more than $3 million) be left to his wife, he directed that the remaining half be left "for the account of my friend Marguerite LeHand" in order to cover all expenses for "medical attention, care and treatment during her lifetime." Upon Missy's death, the trustees were instructed to distribute the remaining income in equal shares to his five children.

"I owed her that much," Roosevelt later explained to his son Jimmy. "She served me so well for so long and asked so little in return."

• • •

That June of 1941, a storm was gathering in the black community. Though some progress had been made in opening doors to blacks in the armed forces, discrimination in the mushrooming defense industry continued unabated. All over the country, the new war plants were refusing to hire blacks. "Negroes will be considered only as janitors," the general manager of North American Aviation publicly asserted. "It is the company policy not to employ them as mechanics and aircraft workers." In Kansas City, Standard Steel told the Urban League: "We have not had a Negro working in 25 years and do not plan to start now." And from Vultee Air in California a blanket statement was issued: "It is not the policy of this company to employ other than of the Caucasian race."

The black press abounded with stories of flagrant discrimination. In early 1941, a hundred NYA trainees were sent to Quoddy Village to work in an aircraft factory near Buffalo. One of the hundred was black, and he was the only one not hired, even though he had the best grades of the group. "Negroes who are experienced machinists are being refused employment," the *Pittsburgh Courier* observed, "while white men and boys who have had no training in this work are being hired and trained later."

"What happens," Walter White asked in a long letter to the *New York Post*, "when a Negro who has had excellent training at one of NYC's technical or trade schools applies for one of the thousands of new jobs opening up? He finds the jobs segregated even in New York City. 'Wanted—white Mechanics, tool and die makers, sheet metal workers.' Far less frequently he finds, 'Wanted—colored. Porters, cleaners, janitors.' " Or perhaps, White went on, "the colored applicant is told that he can get a job only if he is a member of the AFL aeronautical workers union, chartered by the International Association of Machinists, whose constitution bans all but white persons from membership."

The fundamental unfairness of the situation led A. Philip Randolph to a radical change in thinking. For years, he and other civil-rights leaders had relied on decorous middle-class pressure applied through letters, telegrams, and conferences with government-department heads. But now, as Randolph witnessed Negroes being "shunted from pillar to post, given the run-around and oft-times insulted when they applied for war jobs to help make our country an arsenal of democracy," he concluded that all these established methods were simply "chloroform for the masses. When the chloroform wears off, the passions of the beast of race prejudice flare up again."

The time had come, Randolph argued, setting the strategic stage for the civil-rights movement of later decades, to mobilize the power and pressure that resided, not in the few, not in the intelligentsia, but in the masses, the organized masses. "Only power," he observed, "can effect the enforcement and adoption of a given policy, however meritorious it may be."

Randolph's shift in strategy had taken concrete form in early 1941. Traveling with his friend and colleague Milton Webster on a long train ride through the deep south to visit the Sleeping Car Brotherhood Divisions, Randolph had suddenly declared that "we ought to get 10,000 Negroes and march down Pennsylvania Avenue and protest against the discriminatory practices in this rapidly expanding economy." There was silence; then Webster asked: "And where are you going to get 10,000 Negroes?" "We can get them," Randolph promised softly.

As the two civil-rights leaders continued their journey through the South, they proposed the idea of a Negro march on Washington at every stop where they could find an audience. "I think the first place we talked was Savannah," Webster recalled. "It scared everybody to death. The head colored man in Savannah opened up the meeting and introduced me and ran off the platform to the last seat in the last row." But as the word began to spread through the Brotherhood, thousands of voices joined in the refrain. For the first time, Randolph later recalled, "the voiceless and helpless 'little men' became articulate. In meeting after meeting, the 'forgotten black man' could rise and tell an eager and earnest crowd about jobs he had sought but never got, about the business agent of the union giving him the brush-off, how he had gone to the gates of the defense plants only to be kept out while white workers walked in, how he cooled his heels in an office and finally was told with a cold stare 'no more workers wanted.'"

Encouraged by the enthusiastic response, Randolph formed a national March on Washington Committee with branches in eighteen cities. Within days, the Sleeping Car Brotherhood was out on the streets, approaching people in churches and schools, shops, and bars, publicizing the march, and raising money to finance the movement. Black newspapers printed Randolph's call to march in banner headlines. "Be not dismayed in these terrible times," Randolph exhorted the black community. "You possess power, great power. The Negro stake in national defense is big. It consists of jobs, thousands of jobs. It consists of new industrial opportunities and hope. This is worth fighting for.... To this end we propose that 10,000 Negroes march on Washington.... We call upon President Roosevelt ... to follow in the footsteps of his noble and illustrious predecessor [Lincoln] and take the second decisive step to free America—an executive order to abolish discrimination in the work place. One thing is certain and that is if Negroes are going to get anything out of this National defense, we must fight for it and fight for it with gloves off."

By June, there was every indication that, on the first of July, not ten thousand but perhaps twenty-five thousand Negroes would be streaming into Washington, reporter Murray Kempton wrote, "crying for their rights, to the boundless embarrassment not merely of politicians but of the arsenal of democracy which had forgotten them." Reports of a phenomenal surge of support were beginning to reach the White House—dozens of trains had already been hired from Chicago, Memphis, and Cleveland; thousands of dollars had been raised. "Let the Negro masses speak," Randolph proclaimed. "It will wake up Negro as well as white America."

In the White House, the reaction to the news that the march was gathering force was one of fear and anxiety. All spring long, the president had denied repeated requests from Walter White to discuss the exclusion of Negroes from employment in defense. "The pressures of matters of great importance," Pa Watson had informed White, "is such that it does not seem probable he will be able to comply with your request for a personal conference."

Fortunately, the president had Eleanor to keep him at least somewhat informed about the volatile situation. Her exhaustive travels that spring, which had taken her to various Negro projects, homes, and colleges—including Virginia College for Negroes and Tuskegee Institute, where she had addressed five thousand blacks in the chapel, had brought her to a clear understanding of why the idea of the march had so fully captured the heart and soul of the black community. Speaking to a crowd of nine thousand in early June at St. Paul Auditorium in Minnesota, with hecklers and placards in the audience proclaiming, "Who is President? Eleanor or Franklin?" and "My Day is not your day," she had spurred the black members of the audience to great cheers when she expressed her fervent hope for the time "when there would be no such thing as discrimination against any person in this country."

"Mrs. Roosevelt's coming will be a never to be forgotten event," one of those present, Joseph Albright, wrote the president's secretary Steve Early after her speech in St. Paul. "The praiseworthy manner in which she flayed racial discrimination before the large audience made a profound impression upon us all. . . . Will you express to the President that the opportunity for Negroes out here to see and hear Mrs. Roosevelt has only served to endear him more deeply in our regard and to strengthen our loyalty to his cause."

Eleanor returned to Washington armed with stories about blacks with Ph.D.'s and law degrees finding it impossible to secure work in defense plants except as janitors and cleaners. The stories had an effect upon the president. This was not how a democracy was supposed to work, and he knew it. Nor could he justify the position of the Naval Academy earlier that spring, when it refused to allow its lacrosse team to play against Harvard if a black member of Harvard's team appeared on the field.

On a Sunday in late May, Roosevelt sent a handwritten note to William Knudsen and Sidney Hillman containing a radical suggestion that may well be the first official call for what later became known as affirmative action. "To order taking Negroes up to a certain percentage in factory order work. Judge them on *quality*—the 1st class Negroes are turned down for 3rd class white boys." Two days later, Knudsen replied: "I have talked with Mr. Hillman and we will quietly get manufacturers to increase the number of Negroes for defense work. If we set a percentage it will immediately be open to dispute; quiet work with the contractors and the unions will bring better results."

It was precisely the realization that "quiet work" with contractors would never do the job that had led Randolph to the idea of direct action and mass appeal in the first place. But, however sympathetic the president was to the substance of Randolph's quest, he was vehemently opposed to the idea of tens of thousands of Negroes converging on the streets of Washington. He feared that people would be hurt or killed and that the march itself would set a bad precedent for other groups.

Recognizing that his wife enjoyed much deeper trust and support within the black community than he did, the president turned to her for help, asking her to share his concerns with the black leaders. Eleanor agreed, and wrote a thoughtful letter to Randolph. "I have talked with the President," she began, "and I feel very strongly that your group is making a very grave mistake at the present time to allow this march to take place. I am afraid it will set back the progress which is being made, in the Army at least, towards better opportunities and less segregation. I feel if any incident occurs as a result of this, it may engender so much bitterness that it will create in Congress even more solid opposition from certain groups than we have had in the past.... You know that I am deeply concerned about the rights of Negro people, but I think one must face situations as they are and not as one wishes them to be. I think this is a very serious decision for you to take."

Understanding the spirit in which Eleanor's letter was written, Randolph released it to the *Pittsburgh Courier*. "I am submitting the letter received from Eleanor Roosevelt," he explained, "which expresses an important point of view from not only an influential person but a strong and definite friend of the Negro. There is no question that can rise in the minds of the Negroes about the fact that she is a real and genuine friend of the race."

But Randolph was unable to accept Eleanor's advice, believing as he did that nothing had arisen in the life of Negroes since the Emancipation that had "gripped their heart and caught their interest and quickened their imagination more than the girding of our country for national defense without according them the recognition and opportunity as citizens, consumers and workers they felt justified in expecting." Nothing short of the president's commitment to issue an executive order abolishing discrimination in national defense would warrant calling off the march.

Feeling besieged on every side, Roosevelt called on Aubrey Williams, the liberal head of the National Youth Administration, for help. "When I got into the President's office," Williams recalled, "I saw that he was tired and irritable. I said nothing waiting for him to speak.... He rubbed his eyes and leaned over towards me and said: 'Aubrey, I want you to go to New York and get White and Randolph to call off the march.... The missus is up there and you can get in touch with her....'" "Get the missus and Fiorello [LaGuardia] and Anna [Rosenberg, regional director of New York City's Social Security Board] and get it stopped.'"

The meeting took place at City Hall on the morning of June 13. "Mrs. Roosevelt reminded me of her sympathy for the cause of racial justice," Randolph recalled, "and assured me she intended to continue pressuring the President. But the march was something else. Had I considered the problems? Where would all those thousands sleep and eat?" Randolph answered that they would go to hotels and order dinner. "But the attitude of the Washington police, most of them Southerners," Eleanor went on, "and the general feeling of Washington itself are such that I fear that there may be trouble if the march occurs." Randolph listened to Eleanor's concerns but insisted that the movement for the march had touched a chord so deep that he "could not think of calling it off." Furthermore, Walter White added, they had tried all spring to see the president, but each time had been rebuffed. Eleanor assured White and Randolph that "she was definitely in favor of definite action to be taken now," and that she would get in touch with the president immediately, "because I think you are right."

After the meeting, Anna Rosenberg called Pa Watson to report that both Eleanor and LaGuardia agreed strongly that nothing would stop the march "except the President's pressure and direction." It was their joint recommendation that the president invite Randolph and White and the relevant government officials to a meeting in his office.

Roosevelt agreed. He scheduled a White House conference for Wednesday afternoon, June 18. Besides the two civil-rights leaders, he invited Secretary of War Stimson, Secretary of the Navy Knox, OPM heads Knudsen and Hillman, Aubrey Williams, and Anna Rosenberg. Eleanor was unable to attend: she and Joe Lash were on their way to Campobello to get the house in order for the arrival of thirty students for a Student Leadership Institute which Lash was running at the Roosevelt cottage in July.

The president opened the meeting with small talk and then, in typical fashion, turned raconteur, entertaining his audience with political anecdotes. To Roosevelt it seemed so natural that everyone should be fond of hearing his charming stories that he was somewhat taken aback when Randolph broke in. "Mr. President, time is running out. You are quite busy, I know. But what we want to talk with you about is the problem of jobs for Negroes in defense industries."

"Well, Phil, what do you want me to do?"

"Mr. President, we want you to issue an Executive Order making it mandatory that Negroes be permitted to work in these plants."

"Well, Phil, you know I can't do that. . . . In any event I couldn't do anything unless you called off this march of yours. Questions like this can't be settled with a sledge hammer. . . . What would happen if Irish and Jewish people were to march on Washington? It would create resentment among the American people because such a march would be considered as an effort to coerce the government and make it do certain things."

"I'm sorry Mr. President, the march cannot be called off."

"How many people do you plan to bring?"

"One hundred thousand, Mr. President."

The astronomical figure staggered belief. Perhaps Randolph was bluffing. Turning to White, Roosevelt asked, "Walter, how many people will really march?" White's eyes did not blink. "One hundred thousand, Mr. President," he affirmed.

Years later, NAACP leader Roy Wilkins suggested that it may well have been a bluff on Randolph's part, but what an extraordinary bluff it was. "A tall courtly black man with Shakespearean diction and the stare of an eagle had looked the patrician FDR in the eye—and made him back down."

Mayor LaGuardia broke the impasse. "Gentleman," he said, "it is clear that Mr. Randolph is not going to call off the march and I suggest we all begin to seek a formula." The president agreed, asking the black leaders to adjourn to the Cabinet Room with the government officials and come up with the kind of order they thought he should issue. Stimson was clearly annoyed. He considered the meeting "one of those rather harassing interruptions with the main business with which the Secretary of War ought to be engaged—namely, in preparing the Army for defense." Knudsen took the position that an executive order was unnecessary; it was his experience that "more can be done through persuasion and education than by force." But Randolph stood firm: "It was not enough to depend on persuasion and education since the process had been proved to be ineffective so far."

The next morning, Joe Rauh, a young government lawyer, was called in by presidential assistant Wayne Coy to draft the actual language of the order. "As Coy was leaving," Rauh recalled, he said: " 'Hey, Joe, if we're doing this don't forget the Poles.' The Roosevelt administration had been under fire for discriminating against the Poles in Buffalo. So Coy wanted me to throw them in as well, which I did, changing the phrase to read forbidding discrimination on grounds of 'race, color, creed or national origin.' "

When Rauh completed his work, the draft was sent to LaGuardia and Randolph, but Randolph was still not satisfied, arguing it was not strong enough. Back it came and back it went, and still Randolph wanted more. "Who is this guy Randolph," Rauh wondered. "What the hell has he got over the President of the U.S.?" Finally, Rauh said, "We've got every piece of constitutional power in this, there's nothing more I can do, but I've got an idea. I'll change it around one more time and then we should send it to Mrs. Roosevelt. Let her read it to Randolph and say: 'Now, I don't want a general critique that this is not strong enough; tell me what should be done.' "

Communicating with Eleanor on the remote island of Campobello was not easy. There was no phone in the cottage, so Eleanor had to walk a half-mile down the road to the home of the island's lone telegrapher, and sit on the steps until a call came through. But at last Eleanor spoke to Randolph, who agreed that the last draft was just great. The struggle was over. In later years, Rauh would come to believe that Randolph was "one of the greatest and most dignified men" he had ever known.

The president signed Executive Order 8802 on June 25. The order called upon both employers and labor unions "to provide for the full and equitable participation of all workers in defense industries, without discrimination because of race, creed, color or national origin." In addition, a five-member commission was set up, the Fair Employment Practices Commission, soon to be known as the FEPC. Chaired by Mark Ethridge, a liberal newspaperman from the South, the FEPC was empowered to investigate grievances, monitor compliance, and publicize its findings.

Randolph was thrilled. "The President has just drafted the Executive Order," he telegraphed Eleanor. "I therefore consider that the proposed Negro March on Washington is unnecessary at this time." The telegram went on to express his warmest thanks for her "fine spirit of cooperation and help in securing this action on the part of the President." There had grown between Randolph and Eleanor a strong bond of affection and respect. Even at the height of the tensions, Randolph had assured Eleanor that "the Negro people have the utmost faith in your great spirit and purity of heart on their question, and we know that whatever position you take is a result of your convictions that it is in the interest of the Negro people."

Rejoicing in the news, Eleanor telegraphed Randolph immediately that she was "very glad that the march has been postponed and delighted that the President is issuing an Executive Order on defense industries. I hope from this first step, we may go on to others."

The response of the black community to the executive order was overwhelmingly positive. It was greeted, the *Negro Handbook* noted, "as the most significant move on the part of the Government since the Emancipation Proclamation." The *Amsterdam News* called it "epochal to say the least," suggesting that, if Lincoln's proclamation had been designed to end physical slavery, Roosevelt's was designed "to end, or at least curb, economic slavery." To be sure, there remained serious concerns about the inadequate budget, the small staff, and the meager enforcement penalties provided, but it was, the National Negro Congress said, "a great step forward" nonetheless.

"Never before in the history of the nation," the *Chicago Defender* observed, had Negroes, from illiterate sharecroppers in Arkansas to college students in Chicago, "ever been so united in an objective and so insistent upon an action being taken." When the President signed the executive order, "faith in a democracy which Negroes had begun to feel had strayed from its course was renewed throughout the nation."

• • •

At dawn of June 22, 1941, in a stunning move that would prove to be a great turning point of the war, Germany invaded Russia. "Now the guns will be thundering," Goebbels recorded in his diary at 3:30 a.m. "May God bless our weapons."

The idea of invading Russia had been an integral part of Hitler's imperial dream for decades. "When we speak of new territory in Europe today, we must think principally of Russia and her border vassal states," he had written in *Mein Kampf* in 1925. "Destiny itself seems to wish to point out the way to us here. This colossal empire in the East is ripe for dissolution. The end of Jewish domination will also be the end of Russia as a state." The Nazi-Soviet pact of 1939 had not changed but simply postponed Hitler's plans.

"The novelty," Hitler's biographer Alan Bullock has written, "lay not so much in the decision to turn east as in the decision to drop the provision he had hitherto regarded as indispensable, a settlement with Britain first." Since the beginning of the war, the Nazi leader had insisted that he could oppose Russia only when he was free in the West. A two-front war had been the nightmare of German generals for a century. But in the last month of 1940, while the struggle in England was still unfinished, Hitler had committed himself to what would turn out to be an irrevocable decision to invade Russia in the spring. The war against Russia, he convinced himself, would be over quickly—in three months at most—and then the final attack on England could begin. "We have only to kick in the door," Hitler told General Alfried Jodl, "and the whole rotten structure will come crashing down."

On the eve of the attack, Hitler dispatched a letter to Mussolini. "Since I struggled through to this decision, I again feel spiritually free," he claimed. "The partnership with the Soviet Union . . . seemed to me a break with my whole origin, my concepts and my former obligations. I am happy now to be delivered from this torment."

"Everything is well prepared. The biggest concentration of forces in the history of the world," Goebbels noted in the last hours before the attack. The propaganda chief was not exaggerating. The Germans had amassed 150 divisions on the Russian border—more than three million men supported by twenty-seven hundred planes, thirty-three hundred tanks and six hundred thousand motor vehicles. "The Führer seems to lose his fear as the decision comes nearer. All the exhaustion seems to drop away."

For months, Britain and the U.S. had sought to warn Soviet leader Joseph Stalin that Allied intelligence reports indicated large numbers of German troops massing in the east. But nothing could shake the Russian dictator's blind hope that his country would somehow escape Hitler's vengeance. Thus the attack, when it came, took the Soviet Union by surprise, catching a large portion of the Soviet air force on the ground, destroying thousands of planes before they could get up into the air. "War is mainly a catalogue of blunders," Churchill observed in his memoirs, "but it may be doubted whether any mistake in history has equaled that of which Stalin and the Communist Chiefs were guilty when they . . . supinely awaited or were incapable of realizing, the fearful onslaught which impended upon Russia."

The Germans invaded Russia on a wide front, driving simultaneously toward Kiev and the Dnieper River in the south and toward the Baltic States and Leningrad in the north. Then the two armies were to make a junction and press on to Moscow. The opening days of the campaign seemed to justify Hitler's optimism. In two weeks' time, German troops had reached the Dnieper, and by mid-July they were in Smolensk, only two hundred miles from Moscow. Hundreds of thousands of Russians were killed in those first few weeks, and over six hundred thousand were taken prisoner. The German troops seemed unstoppable.

The president was asleep when news of the invasion reached Washington, but before the sun rose, lights were on at the State Department. At Chequers, Churchill was also asleep, having given strict orders never to be awakened before eight unless Britain herself had been invaded. At exactly eight, the prime minister's secretary John Colville knocked on Churchill's door. "Tell the B.B.C. I will broadcast at nine tonight," Churchill said. Minutes later, the prime minister's valet, Frank Sawyers, walked from room to room breaking the news. Anthony Eden, Churchill's foreign secretary, who had spent the weekend at Chequers, recalled that when he answered Sawyer's knock he was handed a large cigar on a silver salver. "The Prime Minister's compliments," Sawyers said, "and the German armies have invaded Russia."

Churchill spent the rest of the day preparing for his speech. He wanted his countrymen and the entire world to know that he was absolutely committed to Russia's cause. "I have only one purpose, the destruction of Hitler," Churchill explained to Colville before the speech, "and my life is much simplified thereby. If Hitler invaded Hell I would make at least a favourable reference to the Devil in the House of Commons."

Finished only twenty minutes before delivery, the speech was vintage Churchill—full of passion and conviction. "No one has been a more consistent opponent of Communism than I have for the last twenty-five years. I will unsay no word that I have spoken about it. But all this fades away before the spectacle which is now unfolding.... Can you doubt what our policy will be?... We are resolved to destroy Hitler and every vestige of the Nazi regime. From this nothing will turn us—nothing.... Any man or state who fights on against Nazidom will have our aid.... It follows, therefore, that we shall give whatever help we can to Russia and the Russian people...."

Roosevelt, in contrast, exercised a cautious policy of making haste slowly, keeping in touch with the unfolding events but maintaining a public silence. Indeed, that Sunday evening, he escaped the press by motoring to Princess Martha's estate in Maryland for a long and leisurely dinner. "Perhaps," an irritated Ickes mused, "he was not able to make up his mind as to what our attitude should be. It would be just like him to wait for some expression of public opinion instead of giving direction to that public opinion."

But, in spite of Harold Ickes' impatience, Roosevelt had good reason to move slowly. For one thing, his Cabinet was divided on how to respond to the Russian invasion. Whereas Ickes and Hull believed in giving Russia all possible aid, Stimson and Knox, along with General Marshall and the entire General Staff, were convinced that Russia would be unable to contain Hitler. Scarce American equipment sent in haste to the Soviet Union would simply fall into Germany's hands. Better, Stimson argued, to use "this precious and unforeseen period of respite" to redouble our aid to England and push "with the utmost vigor our movements in the Atlantic theater of operations."

Across the United States, opinion was equally divided. For the isolationists, the Russian invasion simply confirmed the wisdom of keeping America out of the war. The struggle between Nazism and communism is "a case of dog eat dog," Missouri Democrat Bennett Clark argued. "Stalin is as bloody-handed as Hitler. I don't think we should help either one." America should rejoice, isolationist opinion held, in watching two hated dictatorships bleed each other to death. For Catholics, who felt bound by a recent papal encyclical which stated that communism was "intrinsically wrong" and that "no one who would save Christian civilization may give it assistance on any understanding whatsoever," the best action was to do nothing.

On the political left, confusion reigned. For months, following the Nazi-

Soviet pact, communist-leaning organizations had been busily engaged in marching for peace, provoking strikes, and opposing aid to England. With Russia under attack, however, these same forces began to cry out for immediate intervention and massive aid for Russia. Robert Sherwood recalled attending an interventionist rally in Harlem on the Sunday afternoon of the Russian invasion. When he entered the Golden Gate Ballroom, there was a communist picket line in front with placards condemning the Fight for Freedom supporters as "tools of British and U.S. Imperialism." By the end of the rally, the picket line had totally disappeared. "Within that short space of time," Sherwood marveled, "the Communist party line had reached all the way from Moscow to Harlem and had completely reversed itself."

That same day, in a different part of the city, Michael Quill, the left-leaning head of the Transport Workers of New York, was delivering an angry speech denouncing the imperialist war, arguing that the American worker should have absolutely nothing to do with it. In the middle of his speech, he was handed a note informing him that the Nazis had invaded the Soviet Union. Without missing a beat, Quill totally changed direction, arguing that "we must all unite and fight for democracy."

In Campobello, where she sat by her portable radio with her friend Joe Lash and the reporter May Craig, Eleanor was unsure what to make of the news. "Will it be good or bad?" she kept asking. It all depended "on whether the Russians can hold out." But then "where will our Catholics go?" For his part, Lash felt immensely relieved. "It's the event I've been waiting for since the Nazi-Soviet Pact," he admitted in his diary. For two years, Lash had been caught in the crossfire between his peace-oriented leftist friends and his own belief that Hitler had to be fought. But now all those divisions were suddenly healed. Still, Lash worried. "I couldn't believe that Hitler would attack if he wasn't sure of victory."

From morning to night, Eleanor and her friends listened to the radio. Finally, with a little persuasion, Eleanor agreed to call her husband to get more information, using the island's single telephone connection. "He said he thought it would be helpful," Eleanor repeated to Lash, "except for the Catholics." He said "Hitler expected to defeat Russia in two months. . . . We asked whether he would go on radio. Said he wouldn't. Said it was too damn hot.'"

Yet, when the president finally met with the press in his office on June 24, he made it all sound easy. "Of course we are going to give all the aid we possibly can to Russia," he declared with a smile, never for a moment betraying the anxiety he must have felt in deciding to overrule his military advisers and stake everything on the chance that the Red Army could hold out until the onset of winter, much longer than anyone was predicting it could at the time. His only problem, he said, was that he had absolutely no idea what the Soviet government actually needed. Indeed, so scant were the diplomatic reports from Russia that he "probably knew less of what was going on in Moscow at this time than any desk man in a newspaper office."

And even after a specific list was obtained, he emphasized, " we can't simply go to Mr. Garfinkel's [department store] to fill the order."

Still thirsting for firsthand knowledge three weeks later, Roosevelt sent Hopkins on an arduous double mission to London and Moscow. The first leg of his circuitous journey took him to Montreal, to Gander, Newfoundland, and from there to Prestwick, Scotland. By the time he reached Britain, he was seriously ill, but, as usual, he refused to rest, insisting that he be taken immediately to see Churchill. The two men discussed the new landscape created by the Russian invasion. Hopkins assured Churchill that the president wanted Britain to have first lien on all planes, tanks, and munitions, but he needed to know in detail how the British and Russian requests could fit together. When Hopkins left Chequers, he asked Churchill if there was anything he wanted to tell Stalin. "Tell him, tell him," Churchill said, "tell him that he can depend on us. . . . Goodbye—God bless you, Harry."

After a difficult journey seated on a machine gunner's stool near the tail of an unheated PBY plane, the ailing envoy arrived in Moscow and was taken inside the Kremlin through a series of long corridors to meet Joseph Stalin. Hopkins later wrote: "No man could forget the picture of the dictator of Russia . . . an austere, rugged determined figure in boots that shone like mirrors, stout baggy trousers and snug fitting blouse. He wore no ornament, military or civilian. He's built close to the ground, like a football coach's dream of a tackle. He's about five feet six, about a hundred and ninety pounds. His hands are huge, as hard as his mind. His voice is harsh but ever under control. He's a chain smoker, probably accounting for the harshness of his carefully controlled voice. He laughs often enough, but it's a short laugh, somewhat sardonic, perhaps. There is no small talk in him."

Hopkins was elated by his intimate conversation with Stalin. He found the Russian leader intelligent, courteous, and direct. "Not once did he repeat himself. He talked as he knew his troops were shooting—straight and hard. . . . He smiled warmly. There was no waste of word, gesture, nor mannerism. . . . Joseph Stalin knew what he wanted, knew what Roosevelt wanted, and he assumed that you knew."

In four hours of conversation, Hopkins saw no signs of the cruel and ruthless temperament that lay behind Stalin's mask of politeness. Like so many other Americans who met Stalin during the war, Hopkins came away impressed. "There was little in Stalin's demeanor in the presence of foreigners," Russian envoy Charles Bohlen later admitted, "that gave any clue of the real nature and character of the man." Yet this son of an alcoholic who began working as a troubleshooter for Lenin, organizing a series of bank robberies to fill the revolutionary coffers, and eventually rose to the top of the Communist Party, was directly responsible for the deaths of millions of his own countrymen. Through his forced collectivization of the Russian peasants in the twenties and his purge trials of the thirties, which resulted in the execution of every rival Bolshevik figure, Stalin had spread a reign of terror through the entire Russian nation. Hopkins must have had some sense of these events, but Russia was still so embroiled in mystery that he was able, like Churchill, to let the past fade away before the unfolding spectacle of the Nazi invasion.

As Hopkins listened to Stalin talk, even with the thunder of the German army rumbling in the distance, he came away convinced that Russia could and would hold out. However many Russian troops were killed, there were always more to take their place. "I feel ever so confident about this front," Hopkins cabled Roosevelt. "The morale of the population is exceptionally good. There is unbounded determination to win." Stalin admitted that the Soviets had been taken by surprise and that the German army was "of the very best," with "large reserves of food, men, supplies and fuel," but he argued that the Red Army had superiority in numbers of divisions. Moreover, the Germans were already finding that moving mechanized forces through the vast plains and thick forests of Russia was "very different than moving them over the boulevards of Belgium and France."

The primary need of the Russian army, Stalin told Hopkins, was for vast quantities of light anti-aircraft guns to give protection against low-flying planes. The second need was aluminum, to be used in the construction of airplanes. It was this request that convinced Hopkins that Stalin was viewing the war on a long-range basis. "A man who feared immediate defeat would not put aluminum so high on the list of priorities." The third need was machine guns. "The outcome of the war in Russia," Stalin told Hopkins, "would largely depend on . . . adequate equipment, particularly in aircraft, tanks and anti-aircraft." In short, the Soviet Union, like Britain, was depending on America's miraculous mass production to produce the weapons and material needed to win the war.

•   •   •

Though this sublime faith in America's productive capacity would ultimately be justified, the mobilization effort in the summer of 1941 remained disappointing. There were growing signs of forward movement in a number of different areas, but overall production was still lagging. In July, *Life* devoted a special issue to analyzing America's progress in national defense over the previous year. "The country is awake," *Life* concluded, "though not yet aroused." More than $30 billion had been set aside for defense, yet there was still not a lot to show, since a high proportion of the funds had gone into plant expansion and tooling up.

Among the crucial instruments of war, planes were still a major problem. Though a bottleneck in engines had been cleared up, propellers were now in short supply, and the production process as a whole was nowhere near as fast as it would have to be for the U.S. to catch up with Germany. Production of medium tanks had made excellent progress in 1941—Chrysler's new twenty-eight-ton tank was two months ahead of schedule—but the army still had no heavy tanks. The "brightest spot" in defense was smokeless-powder production, which had been almost nonexistent two years before and was now moving so rapidly that cutbacks might soon be possible. Pride could also be taken in General Motors' AC Spark Plug factory, which had turned from spark plugs to .50-caliber machine guns and was now rifling forty barrels in the time it used to take to rifle one, but production of armor plate was behind schedule, as was production of antitank guns. Surely, *Life* concluded, the defense situation in 1941 was better than it had been in 1940, but, considering the urgency of the crisis, things "should be a lot better."

The president's men refused to acknowledge failure. They defined the first year of the mobilization process as an "educational phase." They likened the president to a baseball promoter who had built a new stadium and a new team from the bottom up and was now waiting to get the rest of the county into the grandstands. Then the game of total defense could really begin.

To be sure, a tooling-up period of six to twelve months was inevitable in the production of complex munitions, but the president could not escape the charge that he lost precious time in 1940 by failing to push business harder toward all-out war production. He had had an election to win and needed to make peace with business in order to win it, but a price had been paid.

Aluminum was a case in point. The previous November, Edward Stettinius, NDAC commissioner for industrial materials, had assured the country that there was more than enough aluminum for everything in sight. For forty-eight years, one monopoly, ALCOA, had been supplying America with 100 percent of all the aluminum it needed, and now, Stettinius claimed, this "good' monopoly was gearing up for the peak load required for the airplane defense program.

Not everyone agreed that ALCOA was a good monopoly. For two years, Thurman Arnold's antitrust division in the Justice Department, "the battered citadel of a romantic lost cause," to use I. F. Stone's words, had been waging war against ALCOA. Arnold's antitrust suit, which had generated thousands of pages of testimony but was still to be decided, had the fervent support of Eleanor Roosevelt, who saw in the struggle the old fighting spirit of the New Deal.

"There never was a monopoly as tight and as agile as ALCOA," observed Arthur Goldschmidt, who was working for Harold Ickes at the time. "First they had patent control, then they moved to control power, then mining. Everything they did was calculated to keep supply down and prices up. They even kept the auto industry—no mean feat—from having scrap, fearing it would lower prices."

Limited supply was damaging enough in peacetime; in wartime, it was catastrophic, for, even as Stettinius was heaping praise on ALCOA's unlimited capacity, ALCOA was unable to fill the defense orders already on its books. "As soon as Roosevelt made his speech calling for fifty thousand planes," Goldschmidt recalled, "I took out a yellow pad and figured out how much aluminum was necessary for each plane, recognizing that bombers take more than fighters. When I totaled up the figures, it was clear that the astronomical amount needed was way beyond what ALCOA was producing." Worse still, since no one at ALCOA was willing to admit this fact in public, the OPM was still discouraging others from entering the field.

It took the creation of the Truman Committee, charged in April 1941 with responsibility for investigating the national defense program, to spur new companies into the field. As one airplane company after another testified at hearings to delays in manufacturing as a result of the shortages of aluminum, the ALCOA men finally had to admit that they simply could not keep up with demand. The government responded to the admission by bringing Reynolds Metal Company into the aluminum business with a generous Reconstruction Finance Corporation loan to finance construction of a large new plant. But invaluable time had been lost. "When the story of the war comes to be written," Harold Ickes testified at the hearings, "if it has to be written that it was lost, it may be because of the recalcitrance of ALCOA."

In July, while Hopkins was in Russia discussing Russia's desperate need for aluminum, the OPM announced a two-week nationwide scrap drive to collect worn-out pots and pans for remelting and reuse. It was estimated that five thousand dishpans, ten thousand coffee percolators, two thousand roasters, and twenty-five hundred double boilers would make one plane. All told, it was hoped that the aluminum gathered from American housewives would make about two thousand planes.

The response was overwhelming. Enthusiastic householders, delighted at the call for service, hauled an astonishing collection of aluminum wares to their village greens—Uncle Mike's coffeepot, Aunt Margaret's frying pan, the baby's milk dish, skillets, stew pots, cocktail shakers, ice-cube forms, artificial legs, cigar tubes, watch cases, and radio parts. Great piles of the precious metal accumulated.

All along, Roosevelt had argued that, once the energies and passions of the American people were aroused, America's home front would win the war. The aluminum drive was the first test of the president's belief, and the people came through with spectacular ingenuity and imagination. In Cleveland, a popular dairy promised one free ice-cream cone to every child who turned in a piece of aluminum. In Tacoma, a police judge declared that every fine assessed during the scrap drive would have added to it one piece of aluminum. In Lubbock, Texas, a likeness of Adolf Hitler was placed in the middle of the courthouse square as a target for the pots and pans hurled by the citizens. In Albany, Mrs. Lehman, wife of the governor, turned in two dozen pieces of kitchenware, including an ice-cream mold. "Many a good dessert has it molded for this family," she said.

But popular success was not matched at the administrative level. In the midst of the drive, Undersecretary of War Patterson discovered to his horror that some quartermaster had ordered dozens of aluminum chairs and brass cuspidors. "He laughed over this," David Lilienthal recorded in his diary, "saying that if you didn't take it as a joke, it would be awful." Worse still, the authorities eventually determined that, though scrap could be remelted for peacetime purposes, only virgin aluminum could be used in the making of planes. Nonetheless, what Roosevelt had stirred up with the great aluminum-scrap drive was nothing less than an exhibition of the dormant energies of a patriotic democracy.

• • •

By the middle of the summer, heartened by the reports Hopkins had cabled from Moscow, the president was fully committed to sending Russia everything she needed as quickly as possible. "I am sick and tired of hearing that they are going to get this and they are going to get that," he told his Cabinet during a forty-five-minute outburst on Friday afternoon, August 1; "the only answer I want to hear is that it is under way."

The president directed his fire mainly at Stimson, who looked "thoroughly miserable," Morgenthau observed. It was, Ickes wrote, "one of the most complete dressings down that I have witnessed." The Russian war had been going on for six weeks, Roosevelt pointed out, and, despite our initial promises, we had done nothing for them. He believed that the War Department and the State Department were giving the Russians a runaround. "Get the planes off with a bang next week," Roosevelt insisted, specifying that 150 pursuit planes be sent along with a smaller number of four-engine bombers. "I want to do all of this at once," he declared, "in order to help their morale."

Stimson thought the attack "highly unfair," arguing that the delay was "due largely to the uncorrelated organization which the President had set up." He had never seen a list of Russian wants, nor had the War Department. The slip-up was not the fault of the War Department, he countered, but of Harry Hopkins' organization. With Hopkins away, there was no one with authority to cover sales to other countries. Furthermore, Stimson insisted, even if the administrative snafus were straightened out, the United States simply did not have the equipment to supply both Britain and Russia. "All of these other people are just hellbent to satisfy a passing impulse or emotion," Stimson remarked in his diary, "and they have no responsibility over whether or not our own army and our own forces are going to be left unarmed or not."

General Marshall heartily agreed with this sentiment. "In the first place," Marshall wrote Stimson, "our entire Air Corps is suffering from a severe shortage. . . . If any criticism is to be made in this matter, in my opinion it is that we have been too generous to our own disadvantage and I seriously question the advisability of our action in releasing the P-40s at this particular time."

But the president refused to back down, saying that "we must get 'em, even if it was necessary to take them from the troops." He was really in a "hoity-toity humor," Stimson wrote, "and wouldn't listen to argument." Ickes was delighted: for the first time in months, he observed, the president seemed tough, alert, and "very much on the ball," finally recognizing that "this was a time to take some risks." Ickes' own view of the Russian aid situation was that "we ought to come pretty close to stripping ourselves, if necessary, to supply England and Russia, because if these two countries between them can defeat Hitler, we will save immeasurably in men and money."

As soon as the Cabinet meeting was over, the president designated Wayne Coy, whom he considered one of his best administrators, to take charge of Russian orders. "We have done practically nothing to get any of the materials they asked for on their actual way to delivery in Siberia," Roosevelt wrote Coy the next morning. "Please get the list and please with my full authority, use a heavy hand—act as a burr under the saddle and get things moving!"

Even with the president's order, it was not easy to get things moving. "Our own Army and Navy were impoverished," Coy later explained. "Congress and the American press were demanding more supplies for the Army then in training." It was only "little by little," Coy wrote, that "there came to be an understanding that Russia's ability to hold off the German hordes gave us greater time to train and equip an Army and Navy and build up military production. As that opinion grew, the Russian supply program grew."

With the signing of the first Moscow protocol in the fall, the U.S. committed itself to a long list of supplies, including trucks, tanks, submachine guns, fighter planes, light bombers, enough food to keep the Russian soldiers from starving, and enough cotton, blankets, shoes, and boots to clothe and bed the entire Russian army. A few weeks later, the president formally declared the defense of the Soviet Union vital to the United States, bringing Russia under lend-lease. A massive aid program, second in size only to the British, was finally under way.

• • •

On August 3, Roosevelt left Washington, supposedly for a midsummer fishing trip in the waters of Cape Cod. "My husband, after many mysterious consultations," Eleanor recalled, "told me that he was going to take a little trip up through the Cape Cod Canal. . . . Then he smiled and I knew he was not telling me all that he was going to do."

"There was nothing about the start of the trip to make us think that it was other than the usual thing," Dr. McIntire recalled. The party consisted only of Pa Watson, naval aide Captain John Beardall, and McIntire—"all tried and true fishermen." To be sure, McIntire noted that Roosevelt seemed particularly excited, but the doctor attributed his lightened mood "to the lift that a vacation at sea always gave him."

"I hope to be gone ten days," Roosevelt wrote his mother in Campobello. "The heat in Washington has been fairly steady and I long to sleep under a blanket for the first time since May. But I am feeling really well and the progress of the war is more conducive to my peace of mind—in spite of the deceits and wiles of the Japs. Do take care of yourself and you will read shortly daily reports from the Potomac."

Before he left, the president made plans to join Princess Martha for a sail in Buzzards Bay, along the coast of Massachusetts, where she was vacationing with her children for the month of August. "I hope this map will be sufficient for you to find us on the cross marked," the princess wrote the president. "It is the second small pier on the right hand side when entering the bay. It belongs to the New Bedford Yacht Club which is a square house with a bright green roof. I am very much looking forward to your visit."

On the morning of the 4th, a clear and sunny day, the president's yacht found the spot, picking up Princess Martha and her brother Prince Carl of Sweden. Nearly twelve months had passed since Martha's arrival in the U.S., and in that time Roosevelt had seen more of this good-natured, pretty woman than of any other person beyond his immediate White House circle. The little party fished, ate lunch on the dock, and fished some more. People sailing small boats that day swore they had seen the president of the United States at the edge of the yacht, dressed in a sport shirt and slacks. "They came back and told their friends," Frances Perkins recalled. "People said they were absolutely crazy and they had dreamed something." At the end of the relaxing day, the *Potomac* headed back to South Dartmouth. As the yacht neared the harbor, the president loaded his royal guests onto a speedboat and personally escorted them to the dock. Then, under a bright moon, the *Potomac* sailed to Martha's Vineyard.

The real adventure began as the *Potomac* came upon a flotilla of American warships—including the heavy cruiser the U.S.S. *Augusta* and five destroyers. On the decks of the *Augusta* were all the principal officers of the U.S. Armed Forces—General George Marshall; Admiral Harold Stark; General Henry Arnold, commander of the U.S. Army Air Force; and Admiral Ernest King, commander-in-chief of naval forces. Transferring to the *Augusta,* the president prepared to begin a secret journey through treacherous seas to a conference off the coast of Newfoundland with Winston Churchill.

On the other side of the Atlantic, Churchill was readying himself for his part of the historic voyage on board a new British battleship, the *Prince of Wales.* On the morning of his departure, Churchill's aide-de-camp found him as excited as a schoolboy. "Churchill probably never had shown so much exuberance and excitement since Harrow," Commander W. H. Thompson wrote. "He bumped over the grass of his country place like a balloon dragged by a hurrying child. He was all smiles and mystic gestures, quick lurches of the head, whispers." Three times that morning, Churchill asked Thompson when they were due to depart, and when the appointed hour finally arrived, he jumped into the waiting car and "flashed his most bewitching smile."

"We are just off," Churchill cabled Roosevelt as the *Prince of Wales* put out to sea. "It is 27 years ago today that the Huns began their last war. We must make good job of it this time. Twice ought to be enough. Look forward so much to our meeting."

Harry Hopkins had flown thirty hours in rough weather from Moscow to the airfield at Archangel, on the White Sea, to the British airbase at Scapa Flow, Scotland, so that he could meet up with the *Prince of Wales* and journey with Churchill to the Atlantic Conference. In the middle of his flight, he realized he had left his satchel of life-sustaining medicines in Moscow, but he refused to turn back, knowing that if he did he would miss his connections with Churchill. Without his daily injections, he became desperately ill. By the time he arrived aboard the *Prince of Wales,* he seemed, Robert Sherwood has written, "at the end of the last filament of the spider's web by which he was hanging on to life." But after eighteen hours of sleep and emergency transfusions, he miraculously revived. In the mornings, he worked on his Russian report; in the afternoons, he sat with Churchill on the deck talking; in the evenings, he and Churchill spent hours playing backgammon for a shilling a game.

Through the entire seven-day trip, Churchill was irrepressibly cheerful. He sang merrily, walked informally about the ship, and for the first time in months read books for pleasure. He was about to meet the legendary president of the United States, and he could no longer contain his excitement. "You'd have thought Winston was being carried up to the heavens to meet God!" Hopkins later said. In his conversations with Hopkins, Churchill struggled to find out what kind of man Roosevelt was underneath. What did the New Deal really mean to him? What did he really think of Germany? Across the Atlantic, Roosevelt was asking Frances Perkins, who had known Churchill as a young man before World War I, a similar set of questions. What kind of fellow was he? Would he keep his word? Was he angry at anybody? Did anger becloud his judgment at times?

Hopkins understood how important it was for the future of both Britain and the U.S. that these two men get along. Knowing both personalities, he could see that they had much in common. They had both learned through long experience, one reporter wrote, that "the longest way around is sometimes the shortest way home. Both had a gift for rhetoric, an instinct for the telling phrase. They were both students of politics and history." But there were differences—Roosevelt, Hopkins believed, was more of an idealist in international affairs; Churchill was still an old-style imperialist. Roosevelt was almost always charming, enjoying gossip and small talk, whereas Churchill tended to be gruff, wasting little time on pleasantries. On the other hand, Churchill was more forthright and open with people than Roosevelt. Hopkins' main concern was that both men, accustomed to being the focus of attention, would continually try to take center stage. He feared their formidable egos would clash. "I suppose you could say," he told CBS correspondent Edward R. Murrow when he first arrived in London to meet Churchill, "that I've come here to try to find a way to be a catalytic agent between two prima donnas." But Hopkins' worries would soon be put to rest. From the moment the two men met, it was clear that they were destined to be not only allies in a common cause but special friends.

On Saturday morning, August 9, the *Prince of Wales,* with her flags flying and her band playing the Sousa march "Stars and Stripes Forever," came within sight of the *Augusta.* "Around us were numerous units big and small from the U.S. Navy," Churchill's aide-de-camp Lieutenant Thompson recalled. "How hungrily Winston Churchill looked over their firepower. How we needed it!" With the naked eye, the figure of Franklin Delano Roosevelt could be discerned standing on the upper deck, supported by his son Elliott. As Churchill boarded the *Augusta,* the crowd stirred and the navy band struck up "God Save the King." Roosevelt remained still for several instants. Then a smile began to run over his face like a rippling wave and his whole expression turned into one of radiant warmth. "I have never seen such a smile," Thompson said. "At last, we've gotten together," Roosevelt said, with that gay and brotherly cordiality which could not help charming the prime minister. "Yes," Churchill nodded, with an equally agreeable elegance of intonation. "We have."

The opening discussion centered on what to do about Japan's increasingly aggressive stance in the Pacific. For more than a year, Roosevelt had been trying to avoid a showdown with Japan, whose expansionist policies under Premier Fumimaro Konoye threatened American interests in the Pacific. To the president's mind, a détente with Japan was essential to gain the time he needed to train the armed forces and mobilize the factories to accomplish the real end of American foreign policy—the destruction of the Hitler menace. Roosevelt believed an early war with Japan would mean "the wrong war in the wrong ocean at the wrong time."

In recent months, an intense struggle had broken out within the Cabinet. Stimson, Morgenthau, and Ickes were convinced that stronger measures—including a total embargo on oil shipments—were required, while Hull insisted that stopping oil would inevitably lead to war. In June, the debate over the oil embargo had assumed political significance at home when Ickes, in his capacity as fuel administrator, was forced to ration oil in New England. "It's marvelous," Morgenthau taunted the president, describing a cartoon just published in the *Washington Star.* "It's got you leaning up against the gas tanks saying sorry, no gas today and . . . it's got a car driving up with a Japanese as a chauffeur and Hull filling the gas tank . . . and Sumner Welles saying, any oil, sir, today?"

Despite the urgings of Morgenthau and Ickes, the president continued to hold out against imposing an embargo, fearing it would simply drive Japan to the Dutch East Indies and that would mean war in the Pacific. "It is terribly important for the control of the Atlantic," Roosevelt told Ickes on the first of July, "for us to help keep peace in the Pacific. I simply have not got enough Navy to go around—and every little episode in the Pacific means fewer ships in the Atlantic."

"The Japanese are having a real drag-down and knock-out fight among themselves," Roosevelt further explained, "and have been for the past week —trying to decide which way they are going to jump—attack Russia, attack the South Seas (thus throwing in their lot definitely with Germany) or whether they will sit on the fence and be more friendly with us. No one knows what their decision will be."

But in mid-July, when forty thousand Japanese troops invaded rubber-rich Indochina and quickly took over the country, the president finally agreed to take retaliatory action. He froze all Japanese assets in the U.S., notified Japan that the Panama Canal would be closed for repairs, and announced that he was cutting off all high-octane, gasoline. Whereas Stimson and Ickes believed that all gasoline—not just high-octane, suitable for airplanes—should be embargoed, Roosevelt preferred to move one step at a time, "to slip the noose around Japan's neck, and give it a jerk now and then."

Churchill was ready at the Atlantic Conference to take a tough line against Japan. He pleaded with Roosevelt to sign a joint declaration warning Japan that any future encroachment in the South Pacific would produce a situation in which the U.S. and Great Britain "would be compelled to take counter measures even though this might lead to war." Roosevelt seriously considered Churchill's proposal, but in the end he settled on a softer, unilateral message, fearing that the strong language of the joint declaration would guarantee war.

Turning to the other side of the world, the two leaders forged a concrete arrangement which finally committed American envoys to escort both British and American ships as far as Iceland. Though Churchill had hoped for more dramatic evidence of American support, he came away convinced that Roosevelt "would wage war, but not declare it and that he would become more and more provocative" in the Atlantic, including forcing an incident at sea with Germany.

But the Atlantic Conference would be remembered by posterity not so much for the strategic commitments that were made as for the Atlantic Charter, a stirring declaration of principles for the world peace to follow "the final destruction of the Nazi tyranny." For some time, Roosevelt had been anxious to lay down a set of broad principles which would guide Allied policy during and after the war. Churchill readily agreed to the idea, eager for any means to identify the policies of the United States and Great Britain. The resulting declaration pledged the two countries to seek no territorial aggrandizement, pursue no territorial changes which did not accord with the wishes of the people concerned, respect the rights of all peoples to choose the form of government under which they would live, commit themselves to free trade, and work for both disarmament and a permanent system of general security.

For both Roosevelt and Churchill, the emotional peak of the conference came on Sunday morning, as Roosevelt boarded the *Prince of Wales* for a religious service, complete with the singing of a dozen common hymns.

Supported by his son Elliott, Roosevelt crossed the narrow gangway from the *Augusta* to the *Wales* and then walked the entire length of the ship to his designated place beside Churchill on the quarterdeck. "One got the impression of great courage and strength of character," *Prince of Wales* Captain W. M. Yool recalled. "It was obvious to everybody that he was making a tremendous effort and that he was determined to walk along the deck if it killed him." Holding hymnbooks in their hands, the two leaders joined in song, with hundreds of British and American sailors crowded together side by side, sharing the same books. "The same language, the same hymns and more or less the same ideals," Churchill mused that evening. "I have an idea that something really big may be happening—something really big."

"If nothing else had happened while we were here," Roosevelt later said, the joint service that sunlit morning "would have cemented us." For one brief moment, human togetherness gained ascendancy. Over the vast ship, so bright and gay with its glittering colors, there was a unity of faith of two people. "Every word seemed to stir the heart," Churchill attested, "and none who took part in it will forget the spectacle presented . . . It was a great hour to live."

• • •

The mood of good cheer at Argentia was dispelled temporarily on the last day of the conference with the arrival of disagreeable news from Washington. Extension of the draft, which most observers assumed would be easily accomplished, had passed the House of Representatives by the razor-edged vote of 203 to 202. The Selective Service Act of 1940 had obligated draftees for a period of only twelve months; the extension called for an additional eighteen. Had a single vote gone the other way, the new army would have melted away, nullifying everything that had been accomplished in the last year.

Opponents castigated the extension as a breach of contract with the draftees, who had been told they would only have to serve one year. General Marshall acknowledged the limiting language of the original bill, but to demobilize now, he argued, would be "to court disaster." In the past two years, the U. S. Army had grown eight times its initial size. It was just now "reaching the point where it could provide the country with an adequate defense." Wholesale release of men would destroy "the battle worthiness of nearly every American division."

At the height of the debate in Congress, while a million draftees in camps across the nation were wondering whether they would be allowed to return to civilian life in a matter of weeks or be forced to remain in the service for another eighteen months, *Life* magazine sent a reporter to Fort McClellan, Alabama, to sample soldier sentiment. After talking to some four hundred privates from five different regiments, the *Life* reporter concluded that morale in the camp was very low.

The most important reason for the low morale was the general sense of uncertainty. "As far as the men can see, the Army has no goal. It does not know whether it is going to fight, or when or where." Lack of equipment was also producing a rising tide of discontent. Whereas draftees had been content to train with stovepipe rifles and cardboard tanks in the early months, they were losing patience with the lack of real weapons. "We came here to learn how to fight a blitzkrieg. Instead, we get close-order drill and kitchen police."

Everywhere one looked, the reporter observed, on walls of latrines, on trucks, on field-artillery pieces, the word "OHIO" could be seen. It stood for "Over the Hill in October," a code name for the massive desertion that was planned for October, once the year's service was up. Most of the citizen soldiers would do nothing so drastic, but their palpable resentment was communicated in letters to their parents, and the parents relayed their sons' sentiments to their congressmen. Stimson acknowledged that morale was slipping. "The absence of any concrete war objective," he explained to the president in mid-August, "coupled with delays in getting their weapons and lack of energy and imagination here and there among their instructors, are being reflected in the spirit of the men and I am seeing letters on the subject."

The rumbles from the army camps undoubtedly contributed to the close margin in the Congress. "Mindful of next year's election," Marshall's biographer Forrest Pogue observed, "members from strongly isolationist areas of the country were weighing their desire to back the Army against their chances of returning to Washington. In most cases, Washington won."

The vote on August 12 came after a long day of fiery debate. The overhead galleries were packed. As soon as the voting began, it became clear that Democrats as well as Republicans were deserting the administration. After the first tally, the House rules allowed those who wanted to change their votes to approach the well below the rostrum and gain recognition from the Speaker, Sam Rayburn of Texas. This continued for some time until Rayburn saw the total become 203 for and 202 against, at which point he quickly proclaimed victory. "On this vote," he shouted, "203 members have voted 'Aye,' 202 members have voted 'No,' and the bill is passed!" A great protest was lodged by Republicans who claimed that the voting was not finished, that there were still changes and additions to be made. But Rayburn said it was too late: the totals had already been announced.

The news of the paper-thin margin, Hopkins recalled, had "a decidedly chilling effect" upon everyone at Argentia, particularly the British. Accustomed to the parliamentary way of thinking, the British regarded the division within the Democratic Party on an issue of such critical importance as a signal of "No Confidence" that would, in their country, result in the fall of a Cabinet. "The Americans are a curious people," a British man in the street commented. "I can't make them out. One day they're announcing they'll guarantee freedom and fair play for everybody in the world. The next day they're deciding by only one vote that they'll go on having an Army.''

But Roosevelt was not discouraged. Though it was not a pretty victory, it was a victory nonetheless, and it meant that he could keep the soldiers on duty for another eighteen months. A near catastrophe had been averted. The army was saved.

CHAPTER 11

"A COMPLETELY

CHANGED WORLD"

As American relations with Japan moved to a thunderous climax during the fall of 1941, the Roosevelt family suffered a pair of personal losses. In the space of three weeks in September, both the president's mother, Sara, and Eleanor's brother, Hall, died.

At Campobello that summer, Eleanor could see that her mother-in-law was failing. She had suffered a stroke in June and, aside from a few appearances at lunch, had remained in her bedroom all summer long. "I should not be surprised if this were the start of a more restricted life for her," Eleanor had written Anna. Watching Sara's steady decline, Eleanor begged her to engage a trained nurse. Sara stubbornly refused until Franklin wired her, asking if, for his "peace of mind," she would allow a nurse to be hired. "Of course, you are right to have a nurse," Sara quickly replied. "I am sorry you got alarmed. I wish you were here looking out of my window. I am taking off two days in my room, don't be anxious and do keep well, my one and only."

The presence of the nurse buoyed Sara's spirits, and her condition seemed to improve. When the time came for her to close up the cottage, she insisted on walking down the front steps herself. She had to stop halfway down to lean on the banister and catch her breath, but she made it to the back seat of her automobile without assistance.

Eleanor flew to New York in early September to meet Sara upon her return from Campobello and help her get settled at Hyde Park. As the two women sat together at breakfast, Eleanor noticed Sara's pale face and labored breathing. Struck by a sudden premonition that death was imminent, she called Franklin at the White House and told him to come to Hyde Park. As a young child, Eleanor had suffered miserably from not being told that her father was ill until after he died; for years, she had been unable to accept that he was really dead. Now she wanted to spare Franklin such pain.

Impressed by the tone of Eleanor's voice, Roosevelt decided to leave for Hyde Park on the overnight train. Sara was lying quietly in her bedroom with her brother Fred and her sister Kassie at her side when she received word that her son was on his way. "A telegram has just come from the President," the butler announced. "He will be here tomorrow morning at 9:30." Sara brightened perceptibly. "I will be downstairs on the porch to meet him," she said. But when morning came, Sara was too weak to venture downstairs. She did insist, however, on dressing up for her son—she put on an elegant bed jacket edged with lace, and had her hair wound into a braid with a bright-blue ribbon.

Sara's bedroom was in the two-story wing that had been added in 1916, when the house was enlarged to thirty-five rooms. From her window she could see her beloved trees and glimpse arrivals to her house. How delighted she had been over the years to greet the many distinguished men and women who had journeyed to Hyde Park to see her son! To be sure, she was irritated at times, when her unfailing eye discerned cigarette butts in her rose garden or small holes in her Oriental rugs, but she had long since decided that "a mother should be friends with her children's friends," even if some of them were overweight, grubby, chain-smoking newspapermen.

It gave her great comfort to know how much the old house still meant to her son and his children. More than any recent birthday gift, she had enjoyed the scroll presented to her from her grandchildren when she turned eighty. "Although we are now scattered in different places, Hyde Park has been and always will be, our real home, and Hyde Park means you and all the fun you give us there."

During the summer, as her body had begun to fail her, Sara had made herself happy by simply thinking about her son and remembering all the good times they had shared together. "I lie on my bed or sit in a comfortable armchair all day," she told Franklin, but "you are constantly in my thoughts and always in my heart." Sitting in her sunny window, writing little notes to family and friends, she admitted: "I think of you night and day." Indeed, so successful was Sara in conjuring up her son's image that even when they were apart she could picture him with different people in different situations. No sooner, for instance, had she heard the first rumors about the president and the prime minister meeting somewhere on the Atlantic than she could see them in her mind's eye walking up her lawn.

At 9:30 a.m. on Saturday, September 6, just as he had promised, the president pulled into the gravel driveway. Sara was lying on her chaise longue, propped up with pillows, when her son appeared in the doorway. He rolled swiftly toward her, kissed her cheek, and touched her hand with the same warmth he had shown her all his life. "Now that he is back, everything is changed," Sara had written nearly forty years earlier, when Franklin had returned from a trip to Europe. "Such happiness to be together again."

Franklin spent the rest of the morning and most of the afternoon giving his mother the details of his summit meeting with Winston Churchill, telling her what was going on in Washington, talking of old times. At the family dinner that night, everyone agreed that Sara seemed better; it was hoped that the crisis had passed. But at 9:30 p.m., she lapsed into a deep state of unconsciousness from which the doctors were unable to rouse her. A blood clot had lodged in her lung, and her circulatory system collapsed. Franklin returned to her room and sat with her through most of the night, while Eleanor called family and friends to tell them that the end was near.

As dawn came, the dying woman lay motionless. Her face, with its broad brow and high cheekbones, its beautiful mouth and aristocratic lines, was not disfigured by the proximity of death. Finally, just before noon, two weeks before her eighty-seventh birthday, with her son by her side, Sara Delano Roosevelt died.

Less than five minutes later, with no storm, wind, or lightning to prompt it, the largest oak tree on the estate simply toppled to the ground. "The President went out and looked at it," his bodyguard Mike Reilly recalled, "struck, as we all were, by the obvious symbolism." Geologists later explained that, because of the thin layer of earth over the rocky base that surrounded the Hyde Park area, such occurrences were not out of the ordinary. For anyone who had known the president's mother, however, that was never the true explanation.

• • •

In the days that followed Sara's death, *The New York Times* reported, the president "shut himself off from the world more completely than at any time since he assumed his present post." Canceling all appointments, he withdrew into the seclusion of his Hyde Park home. For a time at least, the events of the war were pushed into the background.

"I am so weary, I cannot write," Eleanor scribbled to Hick the day after

Sara's death. "I was up most of last night and I've been seeing relatives all day."

Eleanor was "of course attending to everything," Franklin's half-niece, Helen Robinson, noted in her diary. It was Eleanor who called the undertakers and had the body carried from the second-floor bedroom to the spacious book-lined library, where it would lie in a mahogany coffin beneath the portraits of various Roosevelt ancestors. It was she who met with the Reverend Frank Wilson, the rector at the country church where Sara had worshiped for more than half a century, to plan the burial. "The endless details," Eleanor wearily confessed to her aunt Maude Gray, "clothes to go through, checks, books, papers."

"The funeral was nice and simple," Eleanor wrote. While Reverend Wilson performed the Episcopal rites, Sara's family and friends, servants and tenants sat in the library amid the fine paintings, prints, and antique furniture she had collected over the years. The coffin was then transported in procession three miles north to the churchyard behind St. James. There some three dozen men and women assembled under the towering pines to watch as Sara's casket was lowered into the ground beside her husband, James. The president stood with one hand on the open sedan that had carried him to the church. "He never looked toward the grave," *Washington Post* reporter Amy Porter noted, "nor did he return an anxious glance cast his way by his wife." Finally, with a tolling of church bells and the familiar words "earth to earth, ashes to ashes, dust to dust," the solemn ceremony came to an end.

"I think Franklin will forget all the irritations & remember only pleasant things," Eleanor wrote Maude Gray, "which is just as well." To be sure, as in any parent-child relationship, the irritations were legion. "Don't you think you've had enough of your . . . cocktails for one evening?" Sara would frequently ask. "You promised me you would see [Hyde Park neighbor] Edith Eustis," she reminded Franklin in one of her last letters, "so please telephone her at once." Unable to accept that her son was a grown man even when he was president of the United States, Sara would pester him constantly to wear his rubbers and listen in on his phone calls. "Mama, will you *please* get off the line," a relative once heard the president telling her. "I can hear you breathing. Come on, now." On another occasion, when Sara was eighty-two and Franklin was fifty-six, Sara simply announced to newsmen at Hyde Park that she wasn't going to let her son go to church the next day because he was so far behind on his mail.

Yet, once Sara was gone, as Eleanor predicted, a surge of positive remembrances came to the fore, crowding any disagreeable memories from Franklin's mind. Long to be cherished was the memory of the time when he was quarantined in the Groton School infirmary with scarlet fever. Since no visitors were allowed to enter the quarantined room, Sara had climbed a tall rickety ladder several times a day so she could peer over the window ledge and talk with her son. "At first sight of me," Sara later wrote, "his pale, little face would break into a happy, albeit pathetic smile." Equally treasured was the memory of winter nights at Hyde Park, as he lay sprawled on the floor of the library before the fire, organizing and pasting his stamps while his mother read aloud to him.

The president managed to get through the days without breaking down until, late one afternoon, sorting through his mother's things with his secretary Grace Tully, he discovered a box he had never seen. Inside, with each item carefully labeled in her familiar writing, were his first pair of shoes, his christening dress, his baby toys, a lock of his baby hair, and an assortment of the little gifts he had made for her when he was young. Looking down with a tear-stained face, he quietly told Grace that he would like to be left alone. The tears were so unlike the president's habitual composure, and the dismay depicted on his face was so out of keeping with his usual cheerfulness, that she hurried from the room. "No one on his staff had ever seen Franklin Roosevelt weep," Geoffrey Ward observed. Nothing in his entire life had prepared him to deal with such crushing sorrow.

Eleanor's own emotions were more complex. On the one hand, as she looked at the peaceful expression on Sara's face, with "all the lines smoothed out, and the stark beauty of contour," she could not help respecting "the rich, full, confident life" Sara had led. "She loved her own home and her own place. . . . She had seen her only son inaugurated as President three times and still felt that her husband was the most wonderful man she had ever known. Her strongest trait was loyalty to the family. If anyone else in the world were to attack a member of her family she would rise to their defense like a tigress. . . . She had long contemplated this final resting place beside her husband."

Yet there were too many hurts over too many years to allow Eleanor to feel a deep sense of personal loss. "I kept being appalled at myself because I couldn't feel any real grief," Eleanor wrote to Anna, "and that seemed terrible after 36 years of fairly close association." In the early days of her marriage, Eleanor had spent more hours with her mother-in-law than with anyone else, lunching with her, riding with her to visit family friends, taking tea in the late afternoons, absorbing her ideas on everything from decorating to children. But this period was branded on Eleanor's memory as a time of humiliating dependence. "I had so much insecurity in my young life," she later explained. "At first the sense of security that my mother-in-law gave me made me very grateful." But before long, Eleanor felt oppressed by Sara's dominating personality.

The strain of accommodating herself to Sara's wishes finally proved too much for Eleanor. A few weeks after she and Franklin moved into the new house on East 65th Street that Sara had bought for them, Eleanor broke down. "I did not quite know what was the matter with me," she recalled years later, but "I sat in front of my dressing table and wept and when my bewildered young husband asked me what on earth was the matter with me, I said I did not like to live in a house which was not in any way mine, one that I had done nothing about and which did not represent the way I wanted to live. Being an eminently reasonable person, he thought I was quite mad and told me so gently, and said I would feel different in a little while and left me alone until I should become calmer.''

Eleanor pulled herself together in short order, but the tension with Sara failed to subside. When Eleanor decided to redecorate her half of the town house, Sara told her not to bother, for "she could make it attractive in half an hour," and, besides, everyone liked *her* house better than her daughter-in-law's. Again and again, Eleanor was stung by Sara's belittling jibes about her clothes, posture, and appearance. "If you'd just run a comb through your hair, dear," Sara would tell Eleanor in front of dinner guests, "you'd look so much nicer."

"What happened would never have happened," Anna mused years later, "if Mother had the self-assurance to stand up to Granny. There would have been separate houses, but Mother didn't know how to stand up at that period." Over the years, a blistering anger formed in Eleanor's heart—directed mainly toward herself, for having submitted for so long to everyone else's wishes but her own. Though she had long since ceased to be dependent on her mother-in-law, it was not until Sara's death that Eleanor fully comprehended how far she had journeyed from the early days of her marriage. "I looked at my mother-in-law's face . . . ," she told Joe Lash, "& understood so many things I had never seen before." Had Sara had her way, Eleanor realized, her daughter-in-law would have lived a quiet life along the Hudson, tending mainly to hearth and home. "She thought that the land was tied with the family forever."

Having achieved a measure of peace in her own feelings about Sara, Eleanor was able to reach out to Franklin in ways she never could before. "Mother went to father and consoled him," James recalled. "She stayed with him and was by his side at the funeral and through the difficult days immediately afterward. She showed him more affection during those days than at any other time I can recall. She was the kind you could count on in a crisis, and father knew that."

A renewed commitment to one another is evident in the communications between husband and wife in the weeks that followed. Knowing that her husband needed her, Eleanor canceled a long-awaited trip to the West Coast so that she could stay in Washington. "Can I have MacKenzie King at Hyde Park on the 31st," Franklin asked his wife, recognizing that, with Sara gone, Eleanor was now the mistress of the house. "Will you let me know?" Then, the following day, confronted with a long letter of sympathy from one of Sara's friends, Franklin sent it on to Eleanor with a personal note: "Do be an angel and answer this for me." Even Henrietta Nesbitt noticed that something was different when she approached Eleanor's bedroom one morning and discovered, to her surprise, that the president was having breakfast with her—"a rare treat for them both," Nesbitt remarked.

Still, Eleanor remained wary of letting herself get too close. "Pa sprang on me today that I had better take Granny's room [which was twice the size of her own Spartan cubbyhole], but I just can't and I told him so," she wrote Anna. "Of course, I know I've got to live there more, but only when he is there and I'm afraid he hasn't realized that and isn't going to like it or understand it. Will you and the boys understand or does it make you resentful?"

To Eleanor's mind, the Big House had taken on the old lady's forbidding personality. The only way to make it her home was to redecorate it. Her first thought was to turn Sara's snuggery into a study for herself. But, as she quickly discovered, the prospect of changing any of the rooms stirred deep anxiety in her husband. He wanted to keep the old house exactly as it was. The only change he supported in the fall of 1941 was a request Sara had made just before she died to rearrange the room in which he was born so that it looked as it had in 1882, the year of his birth. Franklin never flatly rejected Eleanor's plans; such a confrontation would be unthinkable for him. Instead, he waited until Anna came east and then let her know that he wanted absolutely no changes in the house. In other words, Eleanor said after Anna relayed Roosevelt's wishes to her, "Hyde Park is now to be a shrine and it will still not be a home to me."

●　●　●

The same week that Sara died, Eleanor's brother, Hall, collapsed in his home and was taken to Vassar Hospital in Poughkeepsie, New York. Years of chronic alcoholism had destroyed his liver, "as they told him it would," Eleanor wrote Maude Gray. When Eleanor arrived at her brother's bedside, he begged her to grant him two wishes: to have him moved to Walter Reed Hospital in Washington and to bring him a bottle of gin. The first was easy; with one telephone call, the transfer was arranged. The second was more difficult. Eleanor regarded liquor as her mortal enemy; it had killed her father and destroyed her uncles and her brother. But now that Hall was dying, she wanted to give him as much comfort as possible. Against everything she held dear, she took a bottle of gin from the house at Hyde Park and smuggled it into the hospital.

The boisterous Hall struck everyone as extraordinarily unlike his sister. His features were like hers—a large frame with dark hair and blue eyes— but his face wore the never-failing smile of irrepressible youth, whereas hers invariably wore a look of anxiety and fretfulness. With Eleanor's father, mother, and younger brother Elliott dead, Hall was all she had left of her family, and she loved him deeply, often treating him as a son instead of a brother. When she married, she kept a room for him in her New York town house so he would always feel he had a home.

But, the more responsibility Eleanor undertook, the more self-indulgent and irresponsible Hall became. While he was a dazzling student at Harvard, with an intellect which both Franklin and Eleanor recognized as superior to their own, he was never able to commit himself to a steady line of work, moving from engineering to banking to civil service. He began drinking when he was in his twenties and never stopped. By the time he was fifty, he had divorced twice and was drinking between three-quarters and a whole gallon of expensive wine a day, in addition to gin, rum, and whiskey.

When Hall drank, he became querulous and crude. Curtis Roosevelt, Anna's son, remembers being petrified of his great uncle. "The level of noise was so high," Curtis recalled, "the tone of voice so abrasive, the horseplay a little out of control. I was terrified he'd pick me up, throw me in the air, and then forget to catch me." At formal White House dinners, Elliott Roosevelt recalled, Hall "had a penchant for applying a playful squeeze to a person's knees on the nerve just above the joint. In the middle of the first course, a shriek from Missy rose above the conversation of the fourteen other guests, and she leaped from her chair. We knew that Hall had been up to his tricks again." From her end of the table, Eleanor said softly to her brother, "I wish you wouldn't do those things."

Yet there was no one who could make Eleanor laugh or smile as much as Hall. He radiated charm and seemed to have an inexhaustible talent for having a good time. "There was nothing that made Eleanor happier," Hall's daughter, Ellie Wotkyns, recalled, "than dancing with my father. He was such a wonderful dancer and she loved to waltz with him. When she saw happiness you could almost feel her touching it and liking the warmth of it. I believe both my aunt and my father were basically unhappy; he hid his unhappiness with a jolly demeanor, she hid hers with hard work. And in the end, she hung on to work as tightly as he hung on to drink."

Eleanor returned to Washington immediately after Sara's funeral so she could be with her brother. Though he was slipping in and out of consciousness and failed to recognize either his live-in companion, Zena Raset, or his daughter, Ellie, he seemed to know Eleanor and her presence served to quiet him. "This watching Hall die and seeing Zena suffer is a pretty trying business," Eleanor wearily confessed to Anna. "It is such an unattractive death, he's mahogany color, all distended, out of his head most of the time and his speech is almost impossible to understand. He moves insistently and involuntarily so you try to hold him quiet and it is really most distressing."

While Eleanor attended her dying brother, Franklin was readying a major speech for delivery to the nation on September 11. He had committed the United States to convoys at the Atlantic Conference, but he had not yet revealed the new policy to the American people. A submarine attack on the U.S.S. *Greer* gave him the incident he needed to mobilize public support behind convoys.

The events surrounding the *Greer* attack were not quite as the president described in his nationwide radio address. He said the German submarine had "fired first upon the American destroyer"; he claimed the *Greer*'s identity as an American ship was "unmistakable." In fact, the *Greer* had deliberately stalked the German sub, having been alerted to its presence by a British plane. The British plane had attacked the U-boat with depth charges while the *Greer* continued in pursuit. The sub fired a few torpedoes, the *Greer* responded with a few depth charges, and the chase came to an uneventful end. There was no positive evidence, the navy told the president, that the sub knew the nationality of the ship at which it was firing.

But the fact that German torpedoes had been fired on an American ship was all Roosevelt needed to reassert the principle of freedom of the seas. "No matter what it takes, no matter what it costs," the president warned the Axis powers, "we will keep open the line of legitimate commerce in these defensive waters. . . . Let this warning be clear. From now on, if German or Italian vessels of war enter the waters, the protection of which is necessary for American defense, they do so at their own peril. . . . When you see a rattlesnake poised to strike, you do not wait until he has struck before you crush him. These Nazi submarines and raiders are the rattlesnakes of the Atlantic."

To implement this warning, the president announced the final decision of the government to convoy British supplies, and a new policy by which the navy would shoot on sight any German raiders that came into our defensive zones. "It was," Stimson wrote, "the firmest statement and the most forward position yet taken by the President." Churchill was exultant. The shooting war in the North Atlantic had begun.

The president's "shoot on sight" policy won the solid support of 62 percent of the American people. "Sentiment on Capitol Hill has changed almost overnight," Washington correspondent David Lawrence reported. The news of the attack led "many a Congressman to say that the American people will not have their ships fired on and that defense of the freedom of seas will once again command substantial support in both houses."

Yet, for all the positive results that the president's depiction of the *Greer* attack produced, an unfortunate precedent was set that would return in later years to haunt the American republic. "Roosevelt's deviousness in a good cause," Senator William Fulbright said after the Gulf of Tonkin incident helped propel escalation in Vietnam, "made it easier for Lyndon Johnson to practice the same kind of deviousness in a bad cause."

• • •

The following weekend, the president brought a dozen guests to Hyde Park, including Crown Princess Martha and her three children, FDR, Jr.'s wife, Ethel, and two grandchildren. Though it was only two weeks since his mother's death, he wanted to fill the Big House with life and laughter once again. On Sunday, Hall's condition worsened. Hall had "suddenly gone very bad," Dr. McIntire informed the president at Hyde Park. "He may not last throughout the afternoon." While Eleanor, who had remained in Washington, hurried to the hospital, the president headed for Highland Station to catch the overnight train to Washington. Hall's condition was so bad when Eleanor reached the hospital that she decided to stay with him through the night. Sleeping fitfully in her clothes, she awoke to find him emitting ghastly noises as he struggled for breath.

This had been a bad day, she admitted to Joe Lash, who had been staying with her at the White House. "My idea of hell, if I believed in it, would be to sit or stand & watch someone breathing hard, struggling for words when a gleam of consciousness returns & thinking 'this was once the little boy I played with & scolded, he could have been so much & this is what he is.' It is a bitter thing & in spite of everything I've loved Hall, perhaps somewhat remissedly [sic] of late, but he is part of me."

"The President returned this morning," Tommy told Anna, "with the Crown Princess and Mme. Ostgaard and Jimmy has the Maurice Benjamins staying here. If anything happens to Hall today or tomorrow, I wonder if they will have the sense to leave. I doubt it."

The end came at 5 a.m. on Thursday morning, September 25. Eleanor was by her brother's side when he died. Exhausted, she returned to the White House before breakfast and went straight to her husband's bedroom. Jimmy was with his father when his mother arrived and was so struck by the intimacy of the scene that followed that he remembered every detail years later. " 'Hall has died,' Eleanor told Franklin simply. Father struggled to her side and put his arms around her. 'Sit down,' he said, so tenderly I can still hear it. And he sank down beside her and hugged her and kissed her and held her head on his chest. I do not think she cried. I think Mother had forgotten how to cry. She spent her hurt in Father's embrace. . . . For all they were apart both physically and spiritually much of their married life, there remained between them a bond that others could not break."

Though Eleanor was grateful that Hall's agony had finally ended, she felt as if she had lost a child, and grieved terribly over the waste of a potentially brilliant life. "My mother-in-law was 86 and she had a great life, full of rich experience," Eleanor observed to her journalist friend Martha Gellhorn. "Hall was just 51 and could have had much more out of life." What bothered her most, Tommy observed, was "the terrible waste of a promising life. If he had some illness from a natural cause, I think she could bear it better."

For hours that night, Tommy recalled, Eleanor dug out old photos and letters from Hall and talked about their childhood. Among the photos was a picture of Hall as a toddler, with blond curls and a little round face. In one of the folders, she found a letter from her father to her grandmother at a sad period of his life, as well as a batch of letters from Hall to her. Reading the letters made her so unhappy that Tommy suggested she burn the entire correspondence and get it out of her life. Eleanor agreed; she lit a fire and slowly fed one letter after another into the flames.

"The loss of someone whom you love is hard to bear," Eleanor observed years later in her memoirs, "but when sorrow is mixed with regret and a consciousness of waste there is added a touch of bitterness which is even more difficult to carry day in and day out. I think it was in an attempt to numb this feeling that I worked so hard at the Office of Civilian Defense that fall."

•   •   •

The president had created the OCD the previous spring with a broad mandate to enlist men, women, and children as defense volunteers. When her friend Mayor LaGuardia was named director, Eleanor thought she had won her battle for including social service in defense. But in the months that followed, as the OCD remained narrowly intent on signing up air-raid wardens, aircraft spotters, and volunteer fire brigades, Eleanor was disappointed.

At a press conference the week before Sara died, Eleanor had indirectly charged the OCD with failing its mission, declaring that "no government agency as yet had given civilian volunteers an adequate opportunity to participate in the defense effort." Her comments were construed by the press as criticism of LaGuardia's leadership. "There are 135,000,000 people in this country," LaGuardia wrote Eleanor. "The criticism of 134,999,999 wouldn't touch me. Yours did." The mayor went on to suggest that if she really wanted to implement her ideas she should come to work at the OCD as assistant director.

Eleanor was tantalized by LaGuardia's offer. Since her first days in Washington, she had longed for a specific job of her own to focus her energies. With a defined job, she believed, she would finally be able to follow through on her ideas and see the end results of her efforts. Yet, on the eve of accepting the unpaid assistant-directorship, she was overcome with apprehension. This would be the first government job ever held by a first lady; what if she ended up as a target for everyone who wanted to get at the president? What if she and LaGuardia clashed? "I'm worried about the civilian defense job," she confided to a friend, "because I don't want to do it & . . . at this moment I feel very low."

In spite of her fears, Eleanor accepted the offer and promised to report for work at the end of September. She then threw herself wholeheartedly into familiarizing herself with the organization. "I honestly think your mother is going to get a tremendous amount of interest out of the civilian defense job," Tommy wrote Anna. "When she talks about it, there is a gleam in her eye and a sparkle which has been absent for a long time." Indeed, during the black days of watching Hall die, the prospect of the OCD job was the one sustaining hope that kept Eleanor going.

After Hall's burial on Saturday, September 27, at Tivoli, New York, in the Hall family vault, Franklin and Eleanor drove to Hyde Park for the weekend. Unable to sleep, Eleanor came downstairs at 3 a.m. and spent the next three hours mentally organizing the OCD work. At dawn, she began making notes which detailed the goals she hoped to accomplish in her first month on the job. "If I feel depressed," she once said, "I go to work. Work is always an antidote for depression."

For her first day on the job, Monday, September 29, the first lady chose a trim black silk dress with a touch of white at the collar and several strings of pearls. The early-morning air was crisp as she set forth on foot from the White House to the OCD offices at Dupont Circle. It took a good half-hour, even at Eleanor's long-legged pace, but since she did not think she would get exercise any other way, she was determined to walk to and from work. En route, a young woman came up beside her and said: "You are Mrs. Roosevelt and I am from California and I have always wanted to shake hands with you." The encounter buoyed Eleanor's spirits as she approached her ninth-floor office.

Eleanor's office, which she shared with her friend Elinor Morgenthau, who served as her assistant, contained a pair of desks, a gray fireplace, and a red carpet. At a brief press conference that morning, Eleanor pledged that she would be on the job at nine every morning and remain as long as possible. As for the work she would do, she outlined three goals: to give every person wishing to volunteer an opportunity to train for work; to provide meaningful jobs that would be of benefit to the community, such as work in nursery schools, recreational facilities, housing projects, and homes for the aged; and to prepare citizens to meet emergency calls.

Though Eleanor's broad definition of defense would eventually bring her into conflict with the Congress, her early months on the job were productive. She was hard-pressed at times to stay on top of everything, since she was still responsible for a daily column, a weekly radio broadcast, a semi-annual lecture tour, and a vast personal correspondence, but she gloried in the feeling that the OCD job was hers and hers alone. "I am ridiculously busy," Eleanor wrote to Martha Gellhorn, but the tone of the letter suggested that she loved every minute of her frenetic activity.

For his part, Franklin was delighted to see Eleanor so happy and absorbed. "He was glad," Social Security Regional Director Anna Rosenberg laughingly remarked, "to channel her energies into one area so that she would leave him alone in other areas. He knew that she felt frustrated because many of the liberal programs had to be put aside."

"What's this I hear?" Franklin teased Eleanor one morning. "You didn't go to bed at all last night?" Eleanor nodded her head. "I had been working on my mail without regard to the time, and when suddenly it began to get light, I decided it was not worth while going to bed."

With Eleanor abundantly fulfilled by her work, the tensions with her husband eased. Lash records an enjoyable evening in the president's study on the last day of September. Franklin and Harry Hopkins were already sitting down to supper when Eleanor, Lash in tow, dashed in with profuse apologies for being late. To Eleanor's delight, the president had not even noticed the delay. "There is an advantage to a household where everybody is busy," she later observed. The conversation centered for a while on Mayor LaGuardia, with a good deal of spoofing about his childlike fascination with fire engines. From LaGuardia, the conversation shifted to Benjamin Franklin, whose bust by Houdon the president urged Eleanor to take into her bed-room. "You can always say, 'I have Franklin with me,'" he cracked. The president then asked everyone to name four outstanding leaders, including Ben Franklin. His choices, he said, were Franklin, Jefferson, Teddy Roosevelt, and the earl of Orrery, a confidential adviser of Oliver Cromwell, "concerning whose life he knew the most intimate details." Eleanor countered with her choices: Anne Hutchinson, Harriet Beecher Stowe, Emily Dickinson, and Carrie Chapman Catt. All told, Lash concluded, it was "a jolly party."

Two weeks later, on Eleanor's fifty-seventh birthday, the president persuaded her to join him on a cruise down the river. For the occasion, he had invited a small group of her friends, including Tommy, Joe Lash, ballroom dancer Mayris Chaney, and Helen Gahagan. "We all had a very pleasant time," Lash recorded in his diary, "and I think she had a good time in spite of not wanting anyone to mention her birthday." In the afternoon, Eleanor sat in a deck chair and worked on her mail while the president relaxed with his stamps and the guests sat around chatting. But at six-thirty everyone came together for a grand dinner with champagne and a special toast to Eleanor. It was the first time in more than a year, the president affectionately pointed out in his toast, that he had been able to get his wife on his boat, so the occasion merited a special round of applause.

• • •

During the months of September and October, the president was preoccupied with U-boat sinkings in the Atlantic. On the 19th of September, the *Pink Star*, an American cargo vessel, was sunk off Greenland. Included in the lost cargo was enough cheddar cheese to feed more than three and a half million laborers in Britain for an entire week; a supply of evaporated milk which represented a year's production for three hundred cows; and crates of machine tools which required the labor of three hundred workers for four months. Three weeks later, the *Kearney*, one of America's newest destroyers, built in New Jersey at a cost of $5 million, was torpedoed while on patrol near Iceland; and two weeks after that, the destroyer *Reuben James* was sunk, with the loss of over a hundred American sailors.

"I think the Navy are thoroughly scared about their inability to stamp out the submarine menace," Stimson confessed in his diary. "The Germans have adopted new methods of hunting in packs and shooting under water without showing themselves and it is a new deal and it is pretty hard to handle."

Roosevelt understood that lend-lease would fail unless the United States could keep the sea-lanes open. The time had come, he decided, to take the next step—to ask Congress to remove Neutrality Act restrictions that prevented merchant ships from being armed. He had considered going to Congress in July, but when he was warned that a request for revision would provoke a filibuster and jeopardize extension of the draft, he backed off. Opinion was changing, however. In April, only 30 percent of the American people thought that American ships should be armed; by the end of September, the figure had risen to 46 percent; and now, in the wake of the recent sinkings, an overwhelming majority of 72 percent favored arming merchant ships.

Still, it was not easy to get the Congress to act. The revision passed the House by a close margin and then stalled in the Senate, where critics argued that the U.S. was provoking incidents at sea in order to arouse the American public. "If we continue to look for trouble," Senator Robert Reynolds warned, "the probabilities are that we will eventually find it." Was anyone surprised that American ships were being fired on? America Firster John Flynn asked. "American war vessels, under orders of war-like Knox, are hunting down German subs. . . . The American people must realize that . . . they are the victims of a conspiracy to hurry them into the war."

It took eleven days of acrimonious debate before the Senate finally agreed, on November 8, to amend the Neutrality Act to arm merchant ships. The thirteen-vote margin was the smallest the administration had received on any major foreign-policy initiative since the beginning of the war. The closeness of the vote made it clear to Roosevelt that, short of some dramatic event, there was no chance of getting Congress to vote a declaration of war against Germany. "He had no more tricks left," Robert Sherwood observed. "The bag from which he had pulled so many rabbits was empty." His only recourse was to wait on events.

•   •   •

He did not have to wait for long. The Japanese attack on Pearl Harbor on the 7th of December provided the answer to the president's dilemma.

After Japan's invasion of Indochina in July, Roosevelt had agreed to a policy of sanctions, including an embargo of high-octane oil. Implemented by subordinates while he was away at the Atlantic Conference with Churchill, the limited embargo he had sanctioned had become full-scale. By the time Roosevelt realized that all types of oil had been closed to Japan, it was too late—without seeming weak—to turn back.

Japan could not tolerate the embargo on oil. The crisis strengthened the hand of the military. On October 16, War Minister General Hideki Tojo replaced Fumimaro Konoye as premier, and gave Japanese diplomats until the last day of November to arrange a satisfactory settlement with the United States that would end sanctions; if they failed, war would begin in early December. In the meantime, active preparations were under way for a massive air strike against Pearl Harbor.

The stumbling block in the negotiations was China. Whereas Japan was willing to remove its troops from Indochina and promise not to advance beyond current positions in return for America's lifting of the embargo, she refused to withdraw completely from China. For a time, it seemed that Roosevelt would accept a partial withdrawal of Japanese troops from China, but strong protests from Nationalist Chinese leader Chiang Kai-shek hardened the U.S. position.

While the negotiations dragged on, the president adhered to his customary routine. The weekend that Tojo assumed power in Japan, Roosevelt was at Hyde Park with Princess Martha and Harry Hopkins. Anna and John Boettiger were also there, having flown east from Seattle for a short visit. The weather was crisp and autumnal, and, as always, Roosevelt found an agreeable sense of repose among the familiar surroundings. Driving through the countryside during the day or lying down in the clean linen of his bed at night, with his dog, Fala, at his feet, he must have felt, for a few moments at least, as though the war were far away.

The following weekend, while Eleanor was in New York on OCD business, the president invited Princess Martha to join him for a leisurely cruise on the *Potomac*. The nature of his relationship with Martha at this point is not clear. Neither of the principals ever talked openly about their friendship. The White House usher diaries during this period, however, testify to her frequent presence: Thursday night, November 6, 7:30 to 11:45, dinner with Crown Princess Martha; Saturday, November 15, 1:17, lunch in study with Martha followed by a special showing for the two of them of Walt Disney's new movie, *Dumbo*; Sunday, November 16, 6:20 to 10:50, to Pook's Hill for dinner with Martha; Thursday, November 20, 4:30, swim with Martha, her lady-in-waiting, and her kids, followed by tea in the West Hall and dinner; Tuesday, November 25, 7:30 to 12:00, dinner with Martha. On most of these occasions, Eleanor was traveling on OCD business. Her job was taking her out of town more than she had originally assumed it would, but she felt more fulfilled than she had in years.

At a Cabinet meeting on November 14, Secretary of State Cordell Hull told the president that negotiations with Japan had reached an impasse. The tone of Hull's voice, Frances Perkins later recalled, was "very discouraged and cynical." Hull said he had come to believe that the Japanese diplomats were hypocrities; "they were always being so superficially, excessively polite, showing him such respect, that it made him angry to think that they thought he didn't see through their little ploy." According to Perkins, Hull had "a quaint way of saying quite rough things," which, when added to his inability of saying the "cr" sound because of his lisp, produced a most humorous effect. "If Cordell Hull says Oh Chwist again," Roosevelt confided in Perkins, "I'm going to scream with laughter. I can't stand profanity with a lisp."

In late November, as he had done for nearly two decades, the president planned a journey to Warm Springs to celebrate Thanksgiving with the patients and staff of the polio foundation. This particular trip held special meaning, since Missy LeHand would also be there, having left Doctor's Hospital in early November to continue her convalescence at the rehabilitation center at Warm Springs. The physical condition of her legs had been steadily improving. It was hoped that a return to the little Georgia community she loved would stimulate the return of her speech.

"Just as you move out of one hospital I move into another," Hopkins wrote Missy on November 12, as he entered the Naval Hospital for a round of diagnostic tests to determine why he was experiencing difficulty in walking. "But Harper tells me you are a model patient compared with me. I complain about the food, the nurses and in general leave the impression that I know much more about running the hospital than Navy doctors do. At least now I am relaxed and reading some books. . . . I am delighted at the reports I hear from you and just as soon as I can push my way out of the hospital I am coming down to see you."

When Missy arrived at Warm Springs, she was installed with a private nurse in a little cottage that stood at the top of the hill across from the main complex of the foundation—a cluster of buildings which included a hospital, rehab center, dining hall, auditorium, and treatment pools. To the polio patients who had known Missy over the years, "so quick and full of fun . . . so often running errands for the boss that her path and theirs had many points of intersection," it must have seemed strange to see her now, tired and bewildered from her long train ride, unable to walk, unable to talk. If Warm Springs had brought life and hope back to Roosevelt, perhaps it could do the same for her.

The president was scheduled to leave Washington for Warm Springs on November 19, but the situation at home was so tense—with striking miners paralyzing the entire steel industry—that the trip was postponed. Earlier in the month, on the orders of John L. Lewis, fifty-three thousand United Mine Workers, representing 95 percent of all the men who worked in captive mines owned by steel companies, had gone on strike when the National Defense Mediation Board refused to grant Lewis' request for a union shop, which would have compelled the remaining 5 percent to join the UMW. (Although, true to his word, Lewis had resigned as president of the CIO after FDR's victory, he had remained as president of the UMW.)

"I must say," FDR, Jr., had written Eleanor from the navy, "it's a pretty discouraging and disgusting sight to see a great country blackmailed by a bull-headed rascal like Lewis. . . . I know Pa's knowledge and judgment of not only public opinion but the whole cross-word puzzle show is thoroughly sound. But still, sometimes I wish he'd leave his kind nature in his bunk some morning and roll up his sleeves and really get tough—it would be a wonderful show to watch."

Young Franklin got his wish, for this time the president did get tough, threatening to send in the troops if the miners refused to return to work. "I tell you frankly," Roosevelt pledged, "the government will never compel this 5 percent to join the union by a government decree. That would be too much like Hitler's methods toward labor." Though Roosevelt was not opposed in principle to the idea of a union shop, he believed it had to come about through negotiations between labor and management, not through a government decree. The president's hard line paid off. On November 22, Lewis agreed to compulsory arbitration and the miners went back to work. "We felt a weight off our minds and hearts," Eleanor wrote, "when we knew the coal strike was to be arbitrated. I know what a relief it is for men to go back to work."

With the settlement of the coal strike, the president rescheduled his trip to Warm Springs for November 27. But then, the day before he was set to go, he received word that, in the midst of the continuing negotiations, a Japanese expedition was heading south from Japan. He "fairly blew up," Stimson recorded in his diary, "jumped up in the air, so to speak, and said ... that changed the whole situation because it was evidence of bad faith on the part of the Japanese."

November 27 was "a very tense, long day," Stimson reported, as news of the Japanese expedition kept coming in. "I have washed my hands of it," Secretary Hull told Stimson. "It is now in the hands of you and Knox." Still, there was no clear understanding of where the expeditionary force was headed. "If the current negotiations end without agreement," Admiral Stark warned the president later that day, "Japan may attack: the Burma Road, Thailand, Malaya, the Netherlands East Indies, the Philippines, the Russian Maritime Provinces. ... The most essential thing now from United States viewpoint, is to gain time. Considerable Navy and Army reinforcements have been rushed to Philippines but desirable strength not yet been reached. Precipitance of military action on our part should be avoided so long as consistent with national policy. The longer the delay, the more positive becomes the assurance of retention of these Islands as a naval and air base."

The president agreed with Stark about the importance of playing for time. Though he had little hope now that an agreement could be reached, he instructed Hull to send a proposal to the Japanese demanding that Japan leave China and Indochina in return for an American promise to negotiate new trade and raw-materials agreements. The note reiterated what the United States had been saying for months: that Japan could at any moment put an end to the exploding situation by embracing a peaceful course, and that once she did this her fears of encirclement would come to an immediate end.

The following day, the president left for Warm Springs, where he hoped to remain for ten days so that he could celebrate Thanksgiving with the polio patients. Stimson was "very sorry that he went but nobody spoke out and warned him." The presidential train reached the village of Newman, Georgia, about noon on Saturday, November 29. Welcomed by sunny skies and a friendly crowd, Roosevelt decided to ride the remaining forty miles to Warm Springs in an open automobile, waving to the crowds gathered along the way. The newspapermen, arriving at Warm Springs, settled themselves in two cottages, then "had a few drinks and entered into the spirit of a much-needed holiday."

While the others relaxed, the president drove directly to Missy's cottage to say hello, bringing Grace Tully with him. "You had to have at least two people," Egbert Curtis once explained, "so you could talk across Missy to the other person. Suppose I could only say yes, yes, it would be very difficult for you or anybody else to talk with me."

Tully hoped the visit would bolster Missy's spirits, but the president was ill at ease and distracted, too tired and worn, writer Bernard Asbell suggests, to "endure the ordeal of trying to cheer Missy—the old, cheery, talkative, loyal Missy—who could now say without great effort only a single word." He stayed only fifteen minutes before telling Missy he had to return to his own cottage.

No sooner had the president reached the "little White House," as his unpretentious cottage on the edge of a ravine was called, than Secretary Hull phoned to say "the Far East picture was darkening and that the talks in Washington were in such brittle state that they might be broken at any time." The president told Hull to call again after dinner; if things were no better, he would return to Washington.

When Hull called at 9 p.m., he told Roosevelt that he had just finished reading an explosive speech which Premier Tojo was scheduled to deliver the following day. The speech called on Japan, "for the honor and pride of mankind," to take immediate steps to wipe out U.S. and British "exploitation" in the Far East. Hull was convinced that a Japanese attack was imminent; he advised Roosevelt to return to Washington as soon as possible. The president agreed to leave the following day.

On Sunday morning, Grace Tully accompanied the president as he paid a short farewell call on Missy. She was "nearly in tears at losing us so soon," Grace recalled. Accustomed for decades to being at the center of the whirling action, she could only sit back and watch as the presidential party pulled away, leaving her alone in a small cottage in a tiny community in the middle of Georgia.

• • •

Eleanor was in the midst of a press conference on Monday morning, December 1, when the presidential party returned. She had just announced some appointments to the OCD when Franklin's dog, Fala, came running into the room. "That means the President is here," she told reporters, a smile on her face as she leaned down to pat Fala's head.

Tensions with Japan continued to escalate through the first week of December, as the United States awaited Japan's reply to Secretary Hull's note. By Friday's Cabinet meeting, on December 5, Secretary Knox was so agitated, Frances Perkins recalled, that you could see "the blood rush up to his neck and face." Still, the president insisted that the United States keep the option of peace alive. "We must strain every nerve to satisfy and keep on good relations with this group of Japanese negotiators," he told Hull. "Don't let it deteriorate and break up if you can possibly help it."

Toward the end of the meeting, the discussion turned to the whereabouts of the Japanese fleet. "We've got our sources of communication in pretty good shape," Knox assured the president, "and we expect within the next week to get some indication of where they are going."

On Saturday afternoon, December 6, intelligence experts at the War and Navy departments, who had broken the secret Japanese code in July, intercepted a message from Tokyo informing the Japanese ambassador that a fourteen-part response to Hull's ten-point document was on its way. By early evening, the first thirteen parts had been transmitted; the fourteenth part, Tokyo said, would be sent the following morning. When the first thirteen parts were deciphered, a feeling of dread filled the air. It was obvious from the point-by-point rejection of each and every one of Hull's proposals that Japan was refusing all reconciliation; only one glimmer of hope remained— nowhere in the thirteen points had Japan formally broken off negotiations.

The improbable hope of Saturday night was crushed on Sunday morning, December 7, when the fourteenth part of the Japanese message, terminating diplomatic negotiations, arrived. Within minutes, a second message came through, instructing Ambassador Kichisaburo Nomura to deliver the entire fourteen-part reply to Secretary Hull at precisely one o'clock. To Colonel Rufus Bratton, chief of the Far Eastern Section of the War Department, the timing of the 1 p.m. deadline seemed significant. With a sinking heart, he told General Marshall that he feared it might coincide with an early-morning attack somewhere in the Pacific. Marshall acted swiftly, writing a priority dispatch to the various American commanders in the Pacific. "The Japanese are presenting at 1 p.m. EST today what amounts to an ultimatum. Just what significance the hour set may have we do not know, but be on the alert." Uncertain of the security of the scrambler phone, Marshall opted to send his warning by the slower method of commercial telegraph. In order of priority, the warning was to go first to Manila, then to Panama, and finally to Hawaii. By the time the message reached the telegraph station in Honolulu, the attack on Pearl Harbor had already begun.

• • •

Shortly after 7:30 a.m., local time, while sailors were sleeping, eating breakfast, and reading the Sunday papers, the first wave of 189 Japanese planes descended upon Pearl Harbor, dropping clusters of torpedo bombs on the unsuspecting fleet. Half the fleet, by fortunate coincidence, was elsewhere, including all three aircraft carriers, but the ships that remained were tied up to the docks so "snugly side by side," Harold Ickes later observed, "that they presented a target that none could miss. A bomber could be pretty sure that he would hit a ship even if not the one he aimed at." Within minutes— before any anti-aircraft fire could be activated, and before a single fighter plane could get up into the air—all eight of the American battleships in Pearl Harbor, including the *West Virginia*, the *Arizona*, and the *California*, had been hit, along with three destroyers and three light cruisers.

Bodies were everywhere—trapped in the holds of sinking ships, strewn in the burning waters, scattered on the smoke-covered ground. Before the third wave of Japanese planes completed its final run, thirty-five hundred sailors, soldiers, and civilians had lost their lives. It was the worst naval disaster in American history.

Knox relayed the horrifying news to the president shortly after 1:30 p.m. Roosevelt was sitting in his study with Harry Hopkins when the call came. "Mr. President," Knox said, "it looks like the Japanese have attacked Pearl Harbor." Hopkins said there must be some mistake; the Japanese would never attack Pearl Harbor. But the president reckoned it was probably true —it was just the kind of thing the Japanese would do at the very moment they were discussing peace in the Pacific. All doubt was settled a few minutes later, when Admiral Stark called to confirm the attack. With bloody certainty, the United States had finally discovered the whereabouts of the Japanese fleet.

While the president was on the phone with Stark, Eleanor was bidding luncheon guests goodbye. Heading back toward her sitting room on the second floor, she knew by one glance in her husband's study that something had happened. "All the secretaries were there, two telephones were in use, the senior military aides were on their way with messages. I said nothing because the words I heard over the telephone were quite sufficient to tell me that finally the blow had fallen and we had been attacked." Realizing at once that this was no time to disturb her husband with questions, Eleanor returned to work in her room. Earlier that morning, she had begun a chatty letter to Anna which spoke of her plans to come to California for a visit in early January. When she resumed writing after lunch, she told Anna, "the news of the war has just come and I've put in a call for you and Johnny as you may want to send the children East." In the confusion of the first news of Pearl Harbor, it was thought that Japan might attack the West Coast as well. Finally, she drew the letter to a close. "I must go dear and talk to Father."

The first thing Eleanor noticed when she went into her husband's study was his "deadly calm" composure. While his aides and Cabinet members were running in and out in a state of excitement, panic, and irritation, he was sitting quietly at his desk, absorbing the news from Hawaii as it continued to flow in—"each report more terrible than the last." Though he looked strained and tired, Eleanor observed, "he was completely calm. His reaction to any event was always to be calm. If it was something that was bad, he just became almost like an iceberg, and there was never the slightest emotion that was allowed to show." Sumner Welles agreed with Eleanor's assessment. In all the situations over the years in which he had seen the president, he "had never had such reason to admire him."

Beneath the president's imperturbable demeanor, however, Eleanor detected great bitterness and anger toward Japan for the treachery involved in carrying out the surprise attack while the envoys of the two countries were still talking. "I never wanted to have to fight this war on two fronts," Franklin told Eleanor. "We haven't got the Navy to fight in both the Atlantic and the

Pacific ... so we will have to build up the Navy and the Air Force and that will mean that we will have to take a good many defeats before we can have a victory."

At Jimmy Roosevelt's home in Washington, the phone rang. The White House operator was on the line telling him his father wanted to talk with him. Jimmy had not yet heard the news of Pearl Harbor. "Hi, Old Man, what can I do for you?" Jimmy asked. "I don't have time to talk right now but could you come right away?" "Pa, it's Sunday afternoon," Jimmy said, laughing, but then, sensing there was something wrong from the tone of his father's voice, he agreed to come at once. "He was sitting at his desk," Jimmy recalled. "He didn't even look up. I knew right away we were in deep trouble. Then he told me. He showed no signs of excitement, he simply and calmly discussed who had to be notified and what the media campaign should be for the next forty-eight hours."

"Within the first hour," Grace Tully recalled, "it was evident that the Navy was dangerously crippled." And there was no way of knowing where the Japanese would stop. The president's butler Alonzo Fields recalls overhearing snatches of a remarkable conversation between Harry Hopkins and the president that afternoon in which they imagined the possibility of the invading Japanese armies' driving inland from the West Coast as far as Chicago. At that point, the president figured, since the United States was a country much like Russia in the vastness of its terrain, we could make the Japanese overextend their communication and supply lines and begin to force them back.

Meanwhile, a little bit at a time, the public at large was learning the news. "No American who lived through that Sunday will ever forget it," reporter Marquis Childs later wrote. "It seared deeply into the national consciousness," creating in all a permanent memory of where they were when they first heard the news.

• • •

Churchill was sitting at Chequers with envoy Averell Harriman and Ambassador John Winant when news of the Japanese attack came over the wireless. Unable to contain his excitement, he bounded to his feet and placed a call to the White House. "Mr. President, what's this about Japan?" "It's quite true," Roosevelt replied. "They have attacked us at Pearl Harbour. We are all in the same boat now."

"To have the United States at our side," Churchill later wrote, "was to me the greatest joy." After seventeen months of lonely fighting, he now believed the war would be won. "England would live; Britain would live; the Commonwealth of Nations and the Empire would live." The history of England would not come to an end. "Silly people—and there were many ... ," Churchill mused, "—might discount the force of the United States," believing the Americans were soft, divided, paralyzed, averse to bloodshed. He knew better; he had studied the Civil War, the bloodiest war in history, fought to the last inch. Saturated with emotion, Churchill thought of a remark British politician Sir Edward Grey had made to him more than 30 years before. The U.S. was like "a gigantic boiler. Once the fire is lighted under it there is no limit to the power it can generate."

Shortly before 5 p.m., the president called Grace Tully to his study. "He was alone," Tully recalled, with two or three neat piles of notes stacked on his desk containing all the information he had been receiving during the afternoon. "Sit down, Grace. I'm going before Congress tomorrow. I'd like to dictate my message. It will be short."

He began to speak in the same steady tone in which he dictated his mail, but the pace was slower than usual as he spoke each word incisively, specifying every punctuation mark. "Yesterday comma December 7th comma 1941 dash a day which will live in world history..."

While the president worked on his speech, Eleanor was across the hall, rewriting the script for her weekly radio broadcast. When she reached the NBC studios at 6:30 p.m., she was joined by a young corporal, Jimmy Cannon, who was scheduled to follow her with a report on morale in the army. Astonished to be in the presence of the first lady, the young soldier fumbled with the clasp on his script. "She leaned over," he later wrote, "gently took it from me and broke the clasp."

"For months now," Eleanor began, "the knowledge that something of this kind might happen has been hanging over our heads.... That is all over now and there is no more uncertainty. We know what we have to face and we know we are ready to face it.... Whatever is asked of us, I am sure we can accomplish it; we are the free and unconquerable people of the U.S.A."

Corporal Cannon listened to the first lady's cultured voice and then delivered his own message. As she arose to go, he later told a *PM* reporter, she turned to him and said suddenly, as though it had been on her mind all the time she had been there, "The Japanese Ambassador was with my husband today. That little man was so polite to me. I had to get something. That little man arose when I entered the room." Apparently, Eleanor could not get out of her mind the fact the Japanese ambassador was talking to her husband at the very moment when Japan's airplanes were bombing Pearl Harbor.

It is a curious story, for there is no evidence that the Japanese ambassador was at the White House that Sunday. The only explanation is that Eleanor mistook the Chinese ambassador, who had stopped by to see the president shortly after noon, for the Japanese ambassador. Indeed, in the weeks to follow, the inability to tell a Chinese from a Japanese proved so widespread that Chinese consulates took steps to tag their nationals with signs and buttons: "Chinese, not Japanese, please." As angry citizens mistakenly victimized their Chinese allies, *Life* magazine marched into the fray with a rule-of-thumb guide to distinguish "friendly Chinese from enemy alien Japs." The typical Chinese, *Life* argued, "is relatively tall and slenderly built. His complexion is parchment yellow, his face long and delicately boned, his nose more finely bridged." In contrast, the typical Japanese "betrays aboriginal antecedents in a squat, long-torsoed build, a broader, more massively boned head and face, flat, often pug nose, yellow-ocher skin and heavier beard."

At eight-thirty on Sunday night, the Cabinet began to gather in the president's study. A ring of extra chairs had been brought in to accommodate the overflow. The president, Perkins noted later, was sitting silently at his desk; he was preoccupied, seemed not to be seeing or hearing what was going on around him. "It was very interesting," Perkins observed, "because he was always a very friendly and outgoing man on the personal side. He never overlooked people. . . . But I don't think he spoke to anyone who came in that night. He was living off in another area. He wasn't noticing what went on on the other side of the desk. He was very serious. His face and lips were pulled down, looking quite gray. His complexion didn't have that pink and white look that it had when he was himself. It had a queer gray, drawn look."

Finally, he turned around and said, "I'm thankful you all got here." He went on to say this was probably the most serious crisis any Cabinet had confronted since the outbreak of the Civil War. Then he told them what he knew. "I remember," Perkins later said, "the President could hardly bring himself" to describe the devastation. "His pride in the Navy was so terrific that he was having actual physical difficulty in getting out the words that put him on record as knowing that the Navy was caught unawares. . . . I remember that he said twice to Knox, 'Find out, for God's sake, why the ships were tied up in rows.' Knox said, 'That's the way they berth them!' It was obvious to me that Roosevelt was having a dreadful time just accepting the idea that the Navy could be caught off guard."

By 10 p.m., congressional leaders had joined the Cabinet in the over-crowded study. The president told the gathering that he had prepared a short message to be presented at a joint session of Congress the following day. The message called for a declaration by Congress that a state of war had existed between Japan and the United States from the moment of the attack Sunday morning. He then went on to describe the attack itself, repeating much of what he had told his Cabinet, including new information that Japanese bombs had also hit American airfields in Hawaii, destroying more than half the planes in the Pacific fleet. Apparently, the planes had been an easy mark, since they were grouped together on the ground, wing tip to wing tip, to guard against subversive action by Japanese agents. "On the ground, by God, on the ground," Roosevelt groaned.

"The effect on the Congressmen was tremendous," Stimson recorded. "They sat in dead silence and even after the recital was over they had very few words." Finally, Senator Tom Connally of Texas spoke up, voicing the question that was on everyone's mind. "How did it happen that our warships were caught like tame ducks in Pearl Harbor?" he shouted, banging the desk with his fist, his face purple. "How did they catch us with our pants down? Where were our patrols? They knew these negotiations were going on. They were all asleep."

"I don't know, Tom," the president muttered, his head bowed, "I just don't know."

Historians have focused substantial time and attention trying to determine who knew what and when before the 7th of December—on the theory that Roosevelt was aware of the Japanese plans to attack Pearl Harbor but deliberately concealed his knowledge from the commanders in Hawaii in order to bring the United States into hostilities through the back door. Unable to swing Congress and the public toward a declaration of war against Germany, critics contend, the president provoked Japan into firing the first shot and then watched with delight as the attack created a united America.

To be sure, Roosevelt was concerned that, if war came, the Japanese should be the ones to initiate hostilities. Stimson records a conversation on November 25 in which the president raised the possibility that Japan might attack without warning. The question Roosevelt asked "was how we should maneuver them into the position of firing the first shot without allowing too much danger to ourselves." But in the discussion, as in all others preceding Pearl Harbor, the reigning assumption was that Japan would attack from the south. Though Pearl Harbor was mentioned once, the previous January, in a report from the U.S. ambassador to Japan, Joseph Grew, to the State Department, it was assumed, again and again, right up to December 7, that the Philippines was the most likely target for Japanese aggression.

Moreover, "without allowing too much danger to ourselves," is the important phrase in the president's conversation with Stimson. Common sense suggests that, if the president had known beforehand about Pearl Harbor, he would have done everything he could to reposition the fleet and disperse the airplanes to ensure minimal damage. For the purposes of mobilizing the American people, one American ship torpedoed by the Japanese at Pearl Harbor would have sufficed. It is inconceivable that Roosevelt, who loved the navy with a passion, would have intentionally sacrificed the heart of its fleet, much less the lives of thirty-five hundred American sailors and soldiers, without lifting a finger to reduce the risk. It is an inquiry that obscures the more important question that Senator Connally posed: "How did it happen that our warships were caught like tame ducks in Pearl Harbor?"

It happened because the U.S. forces at Pearl Harbor were fatally unprepared for war on the morning of December 7. "Neither Army or Navy Commandants in Oahu regarded such an attack as at all likely," Secretary Knox explained to Roosevelt. "Both [General Walter Short and Admiral Husband Kimmel] felt certain that such an attack would take place nearer Japan's base of operations, that is, in the Far East." Lack of readiness characterized every aspect of the base—from the unmanned aircraft batteries to the radar station whose sentries went off duty at 7 a.m. that morning.

A great military base, historian William Emerson explains, takes years of planning and coordination. "The anti-aircraft artillery must be tied into the central command post. The ground observer corps must fill in where the radar system leaves off. People must react to each other with the speed of

Las Vegas croupiers." None of this had yet come together at Pearl Harbor, which had been only a minor naval base until the early summer of 1940, when the decision was made to base the fleet there. "We are operating on a shoestring," Rear Admiral Patrick Bellinger had warned in January 1941, with great deficiencies in planes, equipment, materiel, personnel, and facilities. It was estimated that one effective patrol through 360 degrees, at a distance of eight hundred miles, with necessary relief in planes and pilots, required at least 180 reconnaissance planes. Nowhere near this number was available at Pearl Harbor, nor was there manpower to operate them. Nor, once the attack came, was there adequate anti-aircraft artillery or an adequate number of fighter planes.

But this was not the time for recriminations. "The damage was done," Dr. McIntire said, "and the thing to do was to repair it." Not the least of Roosevelt's strength as a leader was his ability to close his mind against the setbacks of the past and focus instead on making plans. Relief came in action: in perusing troop dispositions with General Marshall, in getting Stimson and Knox to mount guards around defense plants, in placing the Japanese Embassy under surveillance, in putting the final touches on his speech to the Congress.

At a little past 10 p.m., in the middle of the president's meeting with Cabinet and congressional leaders, Missy telephoned from Warm Springs. She wanted to talk with the president. Grace Tully took the call, heard the distress in Missy's voice as her old friend struggled desperately to make herself intelligible. But there was no way Grace could interrupt the president to ask him to speak with Missy. Instead, she typed out a message. "Missy telephoned and wanted to talk with you. She is thinking about you and much disturbed about the news. She would like you to call her tonight. I told her you would if the conference broke up at a reasonable hour— otherwise you would call her in the morning."

Toward midnight, the meeting in the president's study drew to a close; and while every face wore an expression of regret and reproach, there was also relief. For Stimson, it was in the knowledge "that the indecision was over and that a crisis had come in a way which would unite our people." No matter how great the damage, at least, the matter was settled. "You know," Frank Knox whispered to Frances Perkins, "I think the boss must have a great load off his mind. I thought the load on his mind was just going to kill him, going to break him down. This must be a great sense of relief to him. At least we know what to do now."

• • •

"Monday was almost worse than Sunday," Marquis Childs observed. "A merciful kind of shock prevailed under the first impact and now as that wore off, the truth was inescapable." In Washington, the rumors of damage "hovered like a low-hanging gas, spreading the panic that seemed to infect the capital." On the same day as Pearl Harbor, the Japanese had attacked the Philippines, Malaya, Wake Island, Guam, and Hong Kong.

At noon, under heavy security, the president motored from the East Gate of the White House to the Capitol, where, to deafening applause, he delivered a brief but powerful speech. From his first words, commemorating the day that would "live in infamy," to his call upon Congress to declare that, since "the unprovoked and dastardly attack by Japan on Sunday, December 7th, a state of war has existed between the United States and the Japanese Empire," the president's anger and indignation burned through. His head held high, his chin thrust out, Roosevelt roused his audience to a standing ovation when he pledged that "this form of treachery shall never endanger us again. The American people in their righteous might will win through to absolute victory." The Congress responded unambiguously to the president's call; both chambers approved a declaration of war, with only one dissenting vote—that of white-haired Representative Jeanette Rankin of Montana.

Isolationism collapsed overnight. "American soil has been treacherously attacked by Japan," former President Herbert Hoover stated. "Our decision is clear. It is forced upon us. We must fight with everything we have." Senator Arthur Vandenberg of Michigan, who had struggled long and hard against American involvement in the war, phoned the White House to tell the president that "he would support him without reservation." Even Representative Hamilton Fish of New York, one of Roosevelt's severest critics, urged the American people "to present a united front in support of the President." After months of vacillation, confusion, and hesitation, the United States was committed at last to a common course of action.

Amid the surge of patriotism that suddenly enveloped the country, union leaders hastily agreed that there would be "no strikes or lockouts" for the duration of the war. All disputes would be peacefully settled by a new War Labor Board, to be created by the president. "Labor's response to the Axis attack has been splendid and spontaneous," Sidney Hillman reported to the president five days after Pearl Harbor. After a series of conferences with representatives of the CIO and the AFL, Hillman was able to promise Roosevelt "that the outlook for constructive participation by labor in the victory effort is good."

Eleanor had accompanied her husband to the Capitol when he made his speech, but as soon as he was finished, she rushed back to the White House to prepare for an overnight trip to the West Coast. Amid reports that Los Angeles and San Francisco might soon be attacked, she and Fiorello LaGuardia felt the need to strengthen civilian-defense organization and morale. At present, the OCD had a total of 950,000 people enrolled as air-raid wardens, fire-fighting auxiliaries, and medical corpsmen. Now the time had come to assign specific people to specific posts in order to translate plans into action. "Hell, this isn't a pinochle party we're having," LaGuardia said, "It's war."

En route to Los Angeles, the pilot brought Eleanor a wire report that San Francisco was being bombed by the Japanese. When she awakened LaGuardia to tell him the news, he put his head out of the curtains, "looking for all the world like a Kewpie," Eleanor recalled. If the report was true, he said, "we will go direct to San Francisco." The mayor's instantaneous response was so characteristic of him that Eleanor "glowed inwardly." When the report proved erroneous, the mayor and the first lady proceeded as planned to Los Angeles. There they met with the governor of California, the mayor of the city, and the State Counsel of Defense. "I am not here to give you any message," Eleanor said. "I am here to get down to work. I came here to find out from you what are the most helpful things we in Washington can do to help you. Tell me what you found lacking and what you want."

As Eleanor traveled up and down the coast, she bore witness to the growing hysteria directed against aliens and citizens of Japanese descent. Within two hours of Pearl Harbor, FBI agents had begun taking key Japanese leaders into custody. California is "a zone of danger," the *LA Times* proclaimed the day after the attack. It is the duty of alert citizens "to cooperate with the military authorities against spies, saboteurs and 5th columnists." As the panic spread, government officials swooped down upon Japanese banks, department stores, produce houses, and newspapers, locking their doors with giant padlocks. Houses where aliens lived were searched for pictures or documents that might suggest loyalty to the emperor of Japan; drawers and closets were rummaged for anything that might conceivably be used as a weapon. In the process, thousands of radios and cameras were confiscated.

"Rumors were everywhere," recalled Jiro Ishihara, a young Japanese American who was in high school in East Los Angeles at the time. "We'd hear that the person down the street had been picked up for having feudal dolls and that a neighbor had been taken away for having Japanese recordings. So my father burned everything that had the slightest connection to Japan. When you contributed to the Japanese relief fund, you got these magnificent certificates, but they had the imperial seal on them, so we threw them into the fire along with everything else. The hardest problem was a small sword my father had been given when he first came to the States by an old swordmaster in his family. That sword meant a lot to him, so we asked a Jewish friend of ours to hold it for us. It was a terrible time."

Swimming against the rising tide of prejudice and fear, Eleanor had her picture taken with a group of American-born Japanese in Tacoma, Washington. In the statement that accompanied the picture, she warned of unwarranted suspicions against loyal citizens. "Let's be honest," she said. "There is a chance now for great hysteria against minority groups—loyal American born Japanese and Germans. If we treat them unfairly and make them unhappy we may shake their loyalty which should be built up. If you see something suspicious, report it to the right authorities, but don't try to be the FBI yourself."

"We know," Eleanor wrote in her column, "there are German and Italian agents, Japanese as well, who are here to be helpful to their own nations. But the great mass of people, stemming from these various national ties, must not feel they have suddenly ceased to be Americans.''

Eleanor's call for tolerance antagonized many Californians. ''When she starts bemoaning the plight of the treacherous snakes we call Japanese, with apologies to all snakes,'' the *Los Angeles Times* proclaimed, ''she has reached the point where she should be forced to retire from public life.'' Undeterred, she continued to speak out: ''I think almost the biggest obligation we have today is to prove that in a time of stress we can still live up to our beliefs and maintain the civil liberties we have established as the rights of human beings everywhere.''

While Eleanor was on the West Coast, Franklin delivered a fireside chat in which he outlined a program for doubling and quadrupling war production by increasing working hours, establishing factories, and using more available materials for war production. Later that night, Sam Rosenman stopped by to see if the president was still up. As he entered the oval study, he found Roosevelt sitting at his desk, at work on his stamps, smoking a cigarette. ''He was all alone,'' Rosenman remarked. ''If Missy had been well she would have been sitting up with him in the study that night. She always did in times of great stress to see whether there was anyone he wanted to call or talk to. . . . The President looked up as I came in and smiled . . . a sad and tired smile.''

To be sure, Princess Martha was still available for pleasant companionship —she had dinner with the president two of the six nights Eleanor was on the West Coast—but in moments of crisis like this, calling for work round the clock, there was no substitute for the devoted love and loyalty of Missy LeHand.

•   •   •

In the days that followed Pearl Harbor, Roosevelt found himself in an awkward situation. He had been telling his countrymen for more than a year that Hitler's Germany was the real enemy. He had expected that Germany would join Japan in declaring war against the United States. But time was passing and still nothing was heard from Berlin. ''Was it possible,'' political scientist James MacGregor Burns has written, ''after all Washington's elaborate efforts to fight first in Europe, with only a holding action in the Pacific, that the United States would be left with only a war in the Far East?''

The answer came on December 11, when Adolf Hitler, who viewed America as a decadent democracy incapable of making a sustained commitment to war, delivered a vitriolic speech against Roosevelt and declared war against the United States. ''A world-wide distance separates Roosevelt's ideas and my ideas,'' he began. ''Roosevelt comes from a rich family and belongs to the class whose path is smoothed in the democracies. I was only the child of a small, poor family and had to fight my way by work and industry.'' Whereas National Socialism had led to an unprecedented economic revival in Germany, Hitler claimed, Roosevelt's New Deal had not succeeded in bringing about even the slightest improvement. "This is not surprising if one bears in mind that the men he had called to support him, or rather, the men who had called him, belonged to the Jewish element, whose interests are all for disintegration and never for order." And then, Hitler contended, Roosevelt had provoked war in order to cover up the failures of his New Deal. "This man alone," he thundered, "was responsible for the Second World War," and under the circumstances, Germany "considers herself to be at war with the United States, as from today."

The next day, in response to a written request from the president, the United States Congress unanimously recognized that "a state of war exists between the United States, Germany and Italy."

• • •

When Eleanor returned to Washington on December 15, the capital had moved to a wartime footing. "It seems like a completely changed world," she noted sadly. Previously, casual visitors had been allowed to stroll around the White House grounds during the day. But now sentry boxes, staffed with Secret Service and White House guards, were set up at all the external gates. Only those with official appointments were allowed inside, and only after careful scrutiny. "No more Congressional constituents," Lorena Hickok remarked, "no more government clerks hurrying through the grounds . . . no more Sunday tourists feeding the squirrels, taking snapshots and hanging around the portico hoping someone interesting would come out."

Eleanor chafed at the new restrictions; she particularly disliked the long blackout curtains, "gloomy in winter and hot in the summer," that had been fitted on all the windows. Fires were no longer allowed in the fireplaces, Hick noted wistfully. It was feared that smoke rising from the chimneys would attract enemy bombers. "The house was chill and silent, as though it had died. Even Fala did not bark."

The week after Pearl Harbor, the Secret Service presented the president with a long report of recommended changes to improve White House security. It proposed covering the skylights with sand and tin, camouflaging the house, painting the colonnade windows black, setting up machine-gun emplacements on the roof, and building an air-raid shelter in a subbasement area of the new East Wing. The president rejected most of the suggestions, "with not a little annoyance," though he finally agreed to the construction of a temporary shelter in the Treasury Department, which would be accessed by a tunnel that would run under the street from the White House to the Treasury.

Secret Service agent Milton Lipson recalls sleeping in the shelter at night with a group of fellow agents as they practiced dry runs in the event of a bombing raid. "One of the Secret Service men would sit in a wheelchair, and then we would use our stopwatches to see how long it would take to get the president from the White House to the shelter. We got it down to under a minute." When Morgenthau tried to get the president to visit the shelter, Roosevelt told the Treasury secretary, "Henry, I will not go down into the shelter unless you allow me to play poker with all the gold in your vaults."

Though Eleanor understood the need for protection against a bombing attack, she insisted that the doors of the White House remain open to the American people. "Mrs. Roosevelt is very much annoyed today with Secret Service and indirectly with Morgenthau," Tommy wrote Esther Lape on December 16, "because they insisted she could not have 350 foreign students in the White House for tea. Also because civilian defense counsel here does not want to have the usual lighted community Xmas tree across the street in Lafayette Park because it is so close to White House. In exasperation, Mrs. Roosevelt asked if they were going to take down the Washington monument because an enemy could measure the distance between it and the White House."

CHAPTER 12

"TWO LITTLE BOYS PLAYING SOLDIER"

About 9 a.m. on Monday, December 22, the president's chief butler, Alonzo Fields, was summoned to the president's bedroom. As he reached the door he heard a heated argument. "You should have told me," Eleanor was saying. "Why didn't you tell me? I can't find Mrs. Nesbitt anywhere. If only I had known." At this juncture, the president noticed Fields standing at the door. "Now, Eleanor, all that little woman would do even if she were here is to tell Fields what we can tell him ourselves right now. Fields, at eight tonight we have to have dinner ready for twenty. Mr. Churchill and his party are coming to stay with us for a few days."

"It had not occurred to him," Eleanor bluntly observed in her column, unaccountably venting her anger before the entire country, "that this might require certain moving of furniture to adapt rooms to the purposes for which the Prime Minister wished to use them. Before all the orders were finally given, it was 10 a.m. and I was half an hour late for my press conference."

In point of fact, although the president had known for nearly two weeks that Churchill was coming to Washington, he was not expecting the prime minister until the following day. The original schedule had called for the prime minister, after ten days at sea, to anchor in Chesapeake Bay and then cruise up the Potomac River to Washington. But once he arrived on American soil, Churchill's doctor, Lord Moran, explained, "he was like a child in his impatience to meet the President. He spoke as if every minute counted. It was absurd to waste time; he must fly."

The flight to Washington made a lasting impression on Churchill's aide-de-camp Commander C. R. (Tommy) Thompson. "It was night time. Those in the plane were transfixed with delight to look down from the windows and see the amazing spectacle of a whole city lighted up." Though blackout restrictions had been issued for Washington, they were not yet fully in force; compared with London, the city seemed ablaze with light. "Washington represented something immensely precious. Freedom, hope, strength. We had not seen an illuminated city for five years. My heart filled."

The president was waiting at the airport, propped against a big car, when Churchill's plane landed. Churchill clasped Roosevelt's hand and then introduced him to Lord Moran. "Even in the half-light," Moran later recalled, "I was struck by the size of his head. I suppose that is why Winston thinks of him as majestic and statuesque, for he has no legs to speak of."

Eleanor greeted her guests as they stepped off the elevator on the second floor, inviting Churchill and his aides for a cup of tea. "The President was in his wheelchair," Eleanor's houseguest—an old friend, Mrs. Charles Hamlin —recalled, "and all were laughing and talking and in excellent spirits." Shorter by almost a head than Roosevelt, Churchill wore a knee-length double-breasted coat, buttoned high, in seaman fashion. He gripped a walking stick to which was attached a flashlight for the purpose of navigating London blackouts. "He reminded me of a big English bulldog who had been taught to give his paw," Mrs. Hamlin observed.

At dinner that first night, as at all subsequent dinners, the conversation sparkled, Roosevelt and Churchill vying with one another to assume center stage. Surrounded by guests, including Minister of Aircraft Production Lord Beaverbrook, British Ambassador to the United States Lord Halifax, Secretary and Mrs. Hull, and Undersecretary and Mrs. Welles, the president looked sublimely self-confident. The conversation turned to the president's first meeting with the prime minister, at Argentia. Roosevelt laughingly recalled that the news of the secret meeting had leaked from the British side, not the American. It must have been the British Cabinet, Roosevelt suggested, since, unlike the American president, the prime minister had to get permission to leave the country from his Cabinet. No, Churchill retorted, twinkling his eyes, "It must have been the women."

Over the course of the evening, the conversation developed into a peculiar tug of war. When Roosevelt was at center stage, gaily holding forth, Churchill would slump into silence, his chubby face petulant. Then, after five minutes of surly biding, Churchill would enter the conversation with an unforgettable quip that turned all eyes toward him—at which point the president would once again begin to talk. Finally, just before dinner ended, the president held up his glass of champagne. "I have a toast to offer—it has been in my head and on my heart for a long time—now it is on the tip of my tongue—'To the Common Cause.' "

"At ten o'clock," Eleanor recorded, "the gentlemen left us to consult together, while the ladies made conversation until after midnight, when their husbands returned a bit shamefaced to take them home. . . . I still remember that as time wore on that evening I suddenly caught myself falling asleep as I sat trying to talk to my guests." It is little wonder that Eleanor's head occasionally nodded. In addition to preparing for Churchill's arrival and conducting a press conference at the OCD, her fifteen-hour day found her attending a half-dozen Christmas celebrations for various alley dwellers, putting in an appearance at the headquarters of the Salvation Army, sitting in on a meeting of the American committee for British Catholic relief, and looking in on the Washington premiere of *Adeste Fideles*, a film of Christmas in wartime Britain.

Churchill was installed in the Rose Suite, on the second floor of the family quarters. His valet slept in the adjoining dressing room, and his two secretaries were given the Lincoln study, across the hall. The White House staff had worked all day shifting beds around to accommodate Churchill and his staff. The quiet upstairs hall was turned into the headquarters of the British government, with a flow of messengers carrying secret documents in the old red leather dispatch cases so characteristic of the British Empire. The Monroe Room was emptied of its furniture and transformed into a map room to provide a place for Churchill to hang the large maps that had come with him from England, representing the present strategic situation on land, sea, and air.

Despite the last-minute arrangements, Eleanor lamented, she was unable to give the prime minister all the things he liked to have. In the morning, Churchill confronted the President's butler Alonzo Fields. "Now, Fields," Churchill began, his bare feet sticking out below his long underwear, his crumpled bedclothes scattered on the bed, the floor strewn with British and American newspapers, "we had a lovely dinner last night but I have a few orders for you. We want to leave here as friends, right? So I need you to listen. One, I don't like talking outside my quarters; two, I hate whistling in the corridors; and three, I must have a tumbler of sherry in my room before breakfast, a couple glasses of scotch and soda before lunch and French champagne and 90 year old brandy before I go to sleep at night."

"Yes, sir." Fields nodded, not offended in the least by the prime minister's gruff, straight-talking manner.

In the days that followed, the president and prime minister stayed up talking, drinking brandy, and smoking cigars until 2 or 3 a.m. Accustomed to late hours, Churchill managed to disappear every afternoon for a long nap. "I'll be back," he would suddenly say in the midst of a conversation with Roosevelt. After two hours, during which Roosevelt had remained at his desk in the Oval Office, Churchill would reappear, reinvigorated.

Several times during these late nights, Roosevelt's head nodded. But soon a remark of Churchill's would rouse him, the conversation would resume, and there would be peals of merry laughter. "There is no question," Eleanor observed, "when you are deeply interested it is possible to go on working til all hours of the night. But for the people who have to wait up til you are through it is a deadly performance."

For the better part of three weeks, despite Eleanor's efforts, the late nights continued. "Mother would just fume," Elliott recorded, "and go in and out of the room making hints about bed, and still Churchill would sit there." It almost seemed, Elliott believed, as if Churchill were deliberately goading Eleanor by keeping Franklin up drinking brandy and smoking cigars. Repulsed by the abundant trays of liquor that accompanied Churchill wherever he went, Eleanor went to Franklin, White House maid Lillian Parks recalled, and told him "that she worried about Churchill's influence on him because of all the drinking. FDR retorted she needn't worry because it wasn't his side of the family that had a drinking problem."

On the second day of his visit, the prime minister had joined the president in an extraordinary dual press conference. Wearing a polka-dot bow tie, a short black coat, and striped trousers, he stared imperturbably into space, his long cigar between his compressed lips, as Roosevelt spoke. When the time came for him to speak, reporters in the back of the crowded room called out that they could not see him. Asked to stand, he not only complied, but scrambled atop his chair. "There was a wild burst of applause and then cheering," *The New York Times* reported, "as the visitor stood there before them, somewhat shorter than many had expected, but with confidence and determination written on the countenance so familiar to the world." In answer to questions, Churchill said the most immediate problem was allocating scarce materials to the forces fighting Hitler in various theaters of the world. However, once the great productive power of the United States was turned loose, he predicted, the problem of choosing where and when war supplies should be sent would be eliminated.

In the course of the Arcadia Conference, as the Christmas talks came to be known, the president and prime minister reaffirmed the commitment they had made at Argentia to a strategy of dealing with Germany first. This was now made more difficult for Roosevelt by the overwhelming desire of the American people—strengthened with each new defeat in the Pacific—to take revenge upon Japan. "The news around us is pretty gloomy," Stimson recorded in his diary during Churchill's visit. The Japanese were sweeping through Malaya and the Philippines with astonishing ferocity. On December 12, a force of three thousand Japanese had come ashore on the coast of Luzon, in the Philippines; twelve days later, seven thousand Japanese troops had landed at Lamon Bay; the main Japanese force struck at Lingayen Gulf on the day Churchill arrived in Washington. Within a matter of days, Guam, Wake, and Hong Kong had fallen. In the Philippines, General Douglas MacArthur, General Jonathan Wainwright, and their troops were trapped on the southern tip of the Bataan Peninsula and the rock of Corregidor. These were the battles that held the attention of the American people. It was American territory that was being invaded, and American men who were dying. Nonetheless, Roosevelt never wavered from his resolve to defeat Germany first.

Roosevelt also reaffirmed America's commitment to lend-lease. In an emergency action on the night of Pearl Harbor, the army had stopped the movement of all supplies to Britain and Russia in order to ensure that its own needs would be met. Hitler's propagandists triumphantly announced to the world that America's supply line had been cut off. But at the Arcadia Conference, Roosevelt declared that America's entry into the war would bring an increase, not a decrease, in lend-lease supplies.

In the Soviet Union, the struggle for survival had reached a crucial stage. During seven months of fighting, the Russians had lost more territory than the whole of France, and more people than all the other combatants combined. In September, German troops had reached the outskirts of Leningrad and had cut the city off from communications and supplies. By the end of December, as the siege of Leningrad entered its seventeenth week, more than three thousand Russians were dying of starvation every day. "Even daily air raids no longer make any special impression," survivor Elena Skrjabina recalled. "Everyone is occupied with only one thought; where to get something edible so as not to starve to death."

As the death rate in Leningrad grew, there weren't enough coffins to contain the bodies. "When you leave the house in the morning," Skrjabina recorded in her diary, "you come upon corpses lying in the streets. The corpses lie around for a long time since there is no one to take them away." The first week of January, a friend of Skrjabina's dropped by. "He was always a gay, lively, young man but now he is unrecognizable. He came to find out if the large gray cat which belonged to an actress living in our apartment house was still alive. He was in hopes that the cat had not been eaten since he knew how much the actress adored it. I had to disappoint him. All animals have been eaten, either by occupants of our house or by our agile neighbors."

More than one million people would die in Leningrad before the nine-hundred-day siege came to an end, but in late December 1941, the tide of war in Russia was beginning to turn. As the Russian winter set in, the Red Army unleashed a massive counterattack against the thinly clad German soldiers. (Hitler had refused to issue sufficient winter coats or boots on the ground that the war in Russia was supposed to be over by winter.) In the extreme cold, which reached temperatures of minus forty degrees Fahrenheit, even minor wounds could lead to shock and death. In a single day in December, more than fourteen thousand German soldiers had to undergo amputation as a result of frostbite. Now it was Germany's turn to experience the desperate suffering of war.

While the president and prime minister continued their discussions, the chiefs of staff of both countries met in order to establish a method of unified command. On the American side, the Joint Chiefs were represented by Chief of Staff General George Marshall; Commander General, U.S. Army Air Force, Henry Arnold; Commander in Chief of Naval Forces Ernest King; and Roosevelt's personal military representative, Admiral William Leahy; on the British side by Field Marshal Sir John Dill, Chief of the Imperial General Staff; Chief of Air Staff Sir Charles Portal; Admiral of the Fleet Sir Dudley Pound; and Lord Beaverbrook. The British wanted to create two committees—one in London, the other in Washington—but Roosevelt wanted a single structure, and after what Hopkins called "a hell of a row," he got what he wanted. The war would be run from Washington. A Combined Chiefs of Staff organization was set up, along with a Combined Munitions Board to pool resources and move them from spot to spot around the world.

"Our people are very unhappy about the decision," Lord Moran noted, "and the most they will agree to is to try it out for a month. They were, however, brought back to good humor by the final figures of the production estimates (45,000 aircraft in 1942, 100,000 in 1943; 45,000 tanks in 1942, 75,000 in 1943). I think Winston, more than anyone here, visualizes in detail what this programme means to the actual conduct of the war. He is drunk with the figures."

"We live here as a big family," Churchill telegraphed Labour Party leader Clement Attlee, "in the greatest intimacy and informality, and I have formed the very highest regard and admiration for the President. His breadth of view, resolution and his loyalty to the common cause are beyond all praise."

On Christmas Eve, the prime minister joined the president in the traditional Christmas-tree lighting ceremonies. The president had insisted on having the tree, despite the worries of the Secret Service, though he had agreed to relocate it from Lafayette Park to the southern grounds of the White House. Though the lights would still bring danger, historian William Seale observed in *The President's House*, the Secret Service "could at least better protect the President this way; only those people invited as spectators would pass through the iron fence, while thousands of uninvited would remain outside." For the fifteen thousand citizens who gathered in the clear twilight to hear the two leaders speak, it was a night to remember. A crescent moon hung overhead. In the distance loomed the Washington Monument, its red light burning, and farther south the monuments to Jefferson and Lincoln. Standing at the president's right on the South Portico with the Marine Band playing "Joy to the World," the prime minister smiled broadly as the president pressed the button which set the colored lights of the Christmas tree twinkling. As the crowd roared its approval, the president introduced his "old and good friend" to say a word to the people of America.

The great orator did not disappoint. "Let the children have their night of fun and laughter," he began. "Let the gifts of Father Christmas delight their thoughts, let us share to the full in their unstinted pleasure before we turn again to the stern tasks in the year that lies before us. But now, by our sacrifice and daring, these same children shall not be robbed of their inheritance or denied their right to live in a free and decent world."

For Eleanor, the Christmas holidays were distressing. For the first time in years, not a single Roosevelt child was home for the holidays: all four boys were in the service, and Anna was in Seattle. Joe Lash records in his diary a worrisome telephone conversation with Eleanor during this period. "Her voice did not have the customary ring to it, so I asked her how she was. There was a period of silence. . . . Then we both mumbled something inconsequential and hung up." Sensing something was seriously wrong, Lash jumped into a taxi. "She started to scold me for having come," Lash wrote, "and then confessed she had a hard day and burst into tears. I thought bad things had happened at OCD which shows how little I understand her." She told Lash her melancholy was rooted in the loss of her four boys to the war. "She knew they had to do it, but it was hard. By the laws of chance not all four would return. Again she lost control and wept."

Only one sock hung on the mantel in the president's room. Eleanor had put it there, labeled it for Fala, and filled it with rubber bones and toys. Ten-year-old Diana Hopkins also had a stocking, but it was hung by the fireplace in her father's room. In the absence of children and grandchildren, the president decided to dispense with his traditional reading of Dickens' *Christmas Carol*.

After the Christmas-tree lighting ceremony, the president invited Martha and her husband, Crown Prince Olav (whom the president had once again brought over from England as a present for Martha), to the Red Parlor for tea with Churchill, Lord Beaverbrook, Lord Moran, and Harry Hopkins. In the midst of this festive gathering, Eleanor asked Franklin if he had called Missy in Warm Springs to wish her a merry Christmas. He replied that he had not called her and wasn't planning to. This apparent callousness was something she simply couldn't understand, she told Lash. "She could never get accustomed to his lack of real attachment to people,'" Lash recorded in his diary. "Could never conceive of him doing a reckless thing for a friend because of personal attachment. Said she had to have contact with people she loved to get refreshment and strength for her duties and work. President seemed to have no bond to people. Not even his children. Completely political person."

Yet, though Roosevelt's remoteness was difficult for those who loved him, Eleanor understood that "it kept him from making mistakes," it gave him an inner independence which freed him to make the right decisions for the right reasons, to be "the kind of person the times required."

Surely Missy understood Roosevelt's temperament as well as Eleanor. "He was really incapable of a personal friendship with anyone," she once confided in her friend, writer Fulton Oursler. But it was one thing to accept his remoteness while she herself was a vital participant in his world. It was quite another to sit in her cottage at Warm Springs, waiting for a phone call that never came. Among the possessions she treasured the most was a maroon box containing hundreds of engraved invitations to Marguerite A. LeHand— requests for the pleasure of her company at White House lunches, receptions, dinners; blue ribbons to admit the bearer to the presidential platform at the inaugural ceremonies; special passes to the 1932 Olympic games at Lake Placid; tickets to the Water Carnival at the U.S. Naval Academy; a seasonal pass from the New York State Racing Commission for entry to the Saratoga racetrack. But now the busy and fevered life these mementos represented had been replaced by monastic stillness as Missy sat in her wheelchair, desperately trying to make sense of her ruined life.

Five Christmases earlier, Missy had sent Franklin and Eleanor a sparkling letter, which thanked her boss for giving her such a happy year but ended on an ominous note: "I guess I'm usually too flippant to tell you 'Well done' but it sounds so inadequate somehow. However, you must know how proud I am every time you get something accomplished—which is all the time— just being with you is a joy I can't explain.

"Please let me do things for you—you are the ones who have my love and only real devotion—without that I would have little reason for taking up space, don't you think?"

Unable now to do things for the man she loved, Missy apparently lost faith in her reason for "taking up space." One night, during the 1941–42 holidays, the telephone rang in the home of Dr. C. E. Irwin, medical director of the Warm Springs foundation. It was after midnight, but he dressed and left immediately for Missy's cottage. As the sun was coming up, he returned, frazzled and confused. "I don't know what I'm going to do about Missy," he told his wife, Mabel, shaking his head in disbelief and sadness. "I think she tried to kill herself tonight."

There is no evidence that Franklin and Eleanor were ever told of this suicide attempt in Missy's cottage that night. Not a word was said in the chatty letter Missy's sister Ann Rochon wrote to Eleanor after visiting Missy over the holidays. "Missy and I had a lovely Christmas together and I want you to know how much she enjoyed all the wonderful presents that you and the President sent to her."

• • •

"Xmas was a very sad day for me," Eleanor admitted to her daughter. "I think Pa enjoyed all the officialdom and he did know that much of importance was being accomplished. I wish I could be less personal. It just didn't seem as though anywhere around there was much personal feeling. We didn't bother about stockings and nothing seems to have much zest but I suppose life must be like this till we return to peace!"

Churchill, too, was out of sorts on Christmas Day. Though he was his usual animated self through the afternoon working session, he retreated into silence at the formal dinner. Guests included Martha and Olav, Lord and Lady Halifax, Henry and Elinor Morgenthau. If the president seemed "jolly and care free" to Lord Moran, the prime minister was "silent and preoccupied" as he turned over in his restless mind the speech he was scheduled to deliver the following day before a joint session of Congress.

"He just wasn't having a good time," Morgenthau observed. "You see him on one side of Mrs. Roosevelt and Beaverbrook on the other, and Beaverbrook's face is a map of life, but in Churchill's face there is absolutely nothing. . . . He asked three times to be excused after dinner so, he says, 'I can prepare these impromptu remarks for tomorrow.' "

Of course, the remarks were anything but impromptu. As Churchill fully appreciated, the invitation to a foreigner to speak before a joint session of Congress was "a tremendous occasion." He could remember "nothing quite like it in his time," he told Moran. "The two democracies were to be joined together and he had been chosen to give out the banns. . . . He knew, of course, that some of the senators were not all friendly to the British. Would they perhaps show it? This morning he decided that what he was going to say to them was all wrong. At any rate, he had to finish his speech before he went to bed. He yawned wearily. He would be glad when it was all over. . . . He got up and asked the President to excuse him."

When Churchill left, sheets of music were handed out to the sixty-odd guests, and the president led everyone in singing carols. So astonishing was Roosevelt's appetite for life that evening, Moran marveled, that "it was difficult to believe that this was the man who was taking his nation into a vast conflict."

The prime minister's methods of preparing a speech fascinated Hopkins. Trained by years of vigorous debate in the House of Commons, Churchill liked to think on his feet, dictating his speeches as he paced up and down the room, imagining that a large crowd had already assembled. At various times, he would refer to notes he had made in the preceding days, but most of the phrasing and imagery emerged from his head and his heart, a product, Isaiah Berlin once observed, of his capacity "for sustained introspective brooding, great depth and constancy of feeling—in particular, feeling for and fidelity to the great tradition for which he assumes a personal responsibility." This peculiar pride in the British people had assumed a major role in Churchill's speeches in the dark days of 1940.

Hopkins told Moran, during a long conversation in his bedroom one evening, that it was interesting to hear two great orators with such different methods. When Roosevelt prepared a speech, Hopkins observed, he "wastes little time in turning phrases; he tries to say what is in his mind in the shortest and simplest words. All the time he gives to that particular speech is spent in working out what each individual in his audience will think about it; he always thinks of individuals, never of a crowd."

In contrast, though Churchill had learned by long experience the feel of an audience as a whole, he knew little about their individual lives, their experiences, their aspirations. Churchill, Isaiah Berlin observed, in contrast to Roosevelt, "does not reflect a social or moral world in an intense and concentrated fashion; rather, he creates one of such power and coherence that it becomes a reality and alters the external world by being imposed upon it with irresistible force."

At noon on the 26th, Churchill was still working on his speech when the motorcade arrived at the back entrance of the White House to take him to the Senate Chamber. "Churchill is always quiet before a speech," C. R. Thompson observed. "It is dangerous to speak to him. There is one little ritual between us. I must always ask him whether he has remembered to put his speech glasses in his pocket. He is forgetful of them, and has great difficulty reading typed notes without them. He patted his pocket. Yes, he had them."

Escorted to a small waiting room beside the Senate Chamber, Churchill paced rapidly up and down the room, mumbling whole sections of the speech to himself. Suddenly he stopped and looked directly at Moran, his eyes popping. "Do you realize we are making history?"

Minutes later, Churchill stood at the podium before the crowded chamber, his fingertips under the lapels of his coat, his heavy gold watch chain hanging from the pocket of his striped trousers. "I cannot help reflecting," he began, "that if my father had been American and my mother British, instead of the other way round, I might have got here on my own." The effect of these words was electric; cheers and laughter instantly overwhelmed the entire audience. Then, when the laughter died down, Churchill's voice quieted to a whisper as he spoke of the difficulties ahead in the struggle against the Axis powers.

He warned that the forces ranging against the Allies were powerful, bitter, and ruthless, and that "without doubt there is a time of tribulation before us during which ground will be lost which will be hard and costly to regain." But, with a magnificent confidence that contagiously echoed in repeated ovations, he drove home his central message that "the task which has been set is not above our strength, its pangs and trials are not beyond our endurance." In eighteen months, he pledged, American and British industry would produce results in war power "beyond anything that has been seen or foreseen in the dictator states."

His voice rising to a fury, he condemned Nazi tyrannies, heaped scorn on Mussolini, and questioned the sanity of the Japanese. "What sort of people do they think we are?" he shouted. "Is it possible they do not realize that we shall never cease to persevere against them until they have been taught a lesson which they and the world will never forget?"

At this juncture, David Lilienthal recorded in his diary, the place erupted, "the first sound of blood lust I have yet heard in the war." Overall, it was a masterpiece, Lilienthal concluded, "the color and the imagery of his style, the wonderful use of balance and alliteration and the way he used his voice to put emotions into his words. Why at one point he made a growling sound that sounded like the British lion!"

When Churchill finished, the *Washington Post* reported, there was a moment's silence, and then a mighty roar, as members of the House and Senate, the Cabinet, the Supreme Court, and the galleries were on their feet, clapping and cheering. "They had witnessed a magnificent drama. Now they wanted an encore." With a brilliant gesture, Churchill obliged. He turned, smiled, and then let his fingers shape the letter "V," the brave symbol captive peoples of Europe had engraved on history as a salute to victory. Throughout the chamber, hundreds of arms were raised in a return salute. It was a stunning climax to a speech which the *Post* ranked with Edmund Burke's defense of the American colonies.

When Churchill returned to the White House to join the president at a Cabinet meeting, he was sweating freely but a thrilling sense of mastery possessed him. "I hit the target all the time," he exulted to Moran. The laughter and applause had come just where he expected them. "It was a great weight off his chest," Moran noted in his dairy.

That evening, the president made up his mind that everyone had worked hard enough and needed relaxation, so he provided a movie in the upper hall, *The Maltese Falcon*. For two hours, the president and prime minister, Beaverbrook, and Canada's Prime Minister MacKenzie King watched as Humphrey Bogart's Sam Spade engaged in his memorable quest for a price-less statuette. Since Eleanor had retired to her study to catch up on her mail, her friend Mrs. Charles Hamlin sat in the front row between the president and prime minister. In the end, Mrs. Hamlin later remembered, when Bogart gave up Brigid O'Shaughnessy, the girl he loved, to justice, Mr. Churchill recalled that when he was home secretary a very similar case had come up to him. "It was a tragic case and the man did give up the girl." Churchill seemed very sad at the memory. When the picture was over, Eleanor re-joined the party and found "everyone completely restored to working capacity."

Eleanor watched the developing affection between the president and prime minister with a worried eye. "She saw in Churchill a male tendency to romanticize war," Eleanor's grandson Curtis Roosevelt observed. "She had a memory of Teddy Roosevelt caring about the environment and social progress but then getting totally caught up in the Spanish-American War. And she remembered FDR in Europe after the First World War, knowing he would have traded absolutely everything to be one of the heroic soldiers wounded in battle."

"Nobody enjoyed the war as much as Churchill did," Martha Gellhorn wryly observed. "He loved the derring-do and rushing around. He got Roo-sevelt steamed up in his boy's book of adventure."

No sooner, for instance, had Roosevelt seen Churchill's mobile map room than he wanted one of his own so that he, too, could visualize the progress of the war. Within days, a sophisticated map room was created on the ground floor of the White House in a low-ceilinged room that had previously been a coatroom for women. Located between the diplomatic reception room and Dr. McIntire's office, it provided easy access for the president when he visited the doctor for his daily massage. "The walls were covered with fiberboard," naval aide George Elsey recalled, "on which we pinned large-scale charts of the Atlantic and the Pacific. Updated two or three times a day, the charts displayed the constantly changing location of enemy and Allied forces. Different shape pins were used for different types of ships, a round-headed pin for destroyers, a square head for heavy cruisers. For the army we had a plastic cover with a grease pencil to change the battle lines as new dispatches came in."

The information was derived from the War and Navy Departments; it was hand-delivered by messenger several times a day and then transferred to the big maps. Special pins revealed the location of the leaders of the Big Three. Churchill's pin was shaped like a cigar, FDR's like a cigarette holder, Stalin's like a briar pipe. Since top-secret dispatches came in at all hours, the map room was manned around the clock by three shifts of officers taken from the navy, army, and air force. Beyond the map-room personnel, access was strictly limited to Roosevelt, Hopkins, Marshall, King, and Leahy.

There was one occasion, however, when Eleanor, passing the map room on her way down the hall, happened to glance inside. There, in front of the brightly colored charts, she saw her husband and Churchill engaged in animated conversation, pointing at different pins in various theaters of the war. "They looked like two little boys playing soldier," Eleanor observed. "They seemed to be having a wonderful time, too wonderful in fact. It made me a little sad somehow."

• • •

On New Year's Day, 1942, the president and the prime minister motored through the countryside of Virginia to lay a wreath on George Washington's tomb at Mount Vernon. On the way down, Eleanor later told her friend Justine Polier, Churchill kept saying, "After the war we've got to form an Anglo-American alliance to meet the problems of the world." And Franklin kept nodding his head and saying, "Yes, yes, yes!" Eleanor said nothing. Unlike Churchill, she did not believe that "we should stress the control of the English speaking people when peace comes." On the contrary, she thought that "all people who believe in democracy" should be included in whatever institution or organization controlled the peace. To focus on Anglo-American control was simply the "old British colonialism in a new form."

Ordinarily, Eleanor would have interrupted immediately, but she was intimidated by Churchill's dogmatic assertions. It seemed to her that once he gave his opinion the matter was concluded. So she sat in silence until she couldn't stand it anymore. "You know, Winston," she finally blurted out, "when Franklin says yes, yes, yes it doesn't mean he agrees with you. It means he's listening." Churchill listened to her stonily, a scowl on his face.

Churchill apparently did not comprehend the highly visible role Eleanor had been playing for nearly ten years as first lady—her public speeches, syndicated column, trips to slums, mines, factories. When Eleanor asked him at a luncheon a few days later what Mrs. Churchill was doing during the war, he puckishly expressed his delight that his wife, and indeed the wives of all his ministers, did not engage in any public activities but stayed at home—

failing to acknowledge the extensive role British women were already playing in the war effort. A strange silence fell on the table as all eyes turned toward Eleanor. But she never "batted an eyelash," according to Sam Rosenman, and the conversation resumed.

"Churchill wasn't very fond of Mother," Elliott Roosevelt recalled. "They were always very polite to each other but they were totally different personalities. She believed in the future and the expansion of democracy everywhere, while he was basically a monarchist at heart."

After lunch on New Year's Day, Lash, Tommy, and Eleanor gathered in Mrs. Roosevelt's sitting room and compared impressions of the president and prime minister. "The Prime Minister has the richer temperament," Lash began, "but the President is a more dependable, steadier man in a crisis." When Lash finished, Tommy clapped her hands and said she and Mrs. Roosevelt felt the same. The president was more hardheaded, they felt. He was less brilliant, but more likely to do the right thing. The president also gave the impression of being more under control, of never letting himself go.

"I like Mr. Churchill," Eleanor wrote Anna, "he's lovable and emotional and very human but I don't want him to write the peace or carry it out."

• • •

During the last week of December, twenty-six nations at war with the Axis had negotiated a declaration of unity and purpose. The document, entitled "A Declaration by the United Nations," pledged the full resources of each signing nation to the fight against the Axis, reiterated adherence to the principles of the Atlantic Charter, and pledged each country not to make a separate peace. It was Roosevelt who had come up with the phrase "United Nations" to express the common purpose that united the Allies.

Accounts vary as to how the president communicated his suggested title to the prime minister. By far the best story was told by Harry Hopkins, who claimed the president was so excited by his inspiration that he had himself wheeled into Churchill's bedroom early one morning, just as the prime minister was emerging from his bath, stark naked and gleaming pink. "Bathtubs," Churchill once said, "were a contrivance that America had foisted upon the British but there was nothing like a hot bath . . . lying back and kicking one's legs in the air—as at birth."

The president apologized and said he would come back at a better time. No need to go, Churchill said: "The Prime Minister of Great Britain has nothing to conceal from the President of the United States!"

The declaration was signed in the president's study at 10 p.m. As the invited guests gathered round, Mrs. Hamlin recalled, "It was as quiet as a church in the study—not a whisper, the only sound came from Fala who was stretched out sleeping heavily—oblivious of the momentous happenings."

The president signed first. Perhaps he should have used the title "commander-in-chief," he remarked. "President ought to do!" Hopkins said dryly.

Then the prime minister signed. Roosevelt looked at the signature. "Hey, ought you not to sign Great Britain and Ireland?" Churchill agreed, amending his signature. Foreign Minister Maxim Litvinov signed next for the Soviet Union, and finally Chinese Ambassador T. V. Soong for China. "Four-fifths of the human race," observed Churchill. "In the room," Lash recorded, "there was a sense of Hitler's doom being sealed."

As Churchill readied his return to England, Hopkins handed him a note to take to his wife, Clementine. "You would have been quite proud of your husband on this trip," Hopkins told Mrs. Churchill. "First because he was ever so good natured. I didn't see him take anybody's head off and he eats and drinks with his customary vigor. If he had half as good a time here as the President did having him about the White House he surely will carry pleasant memories of the past three weeks."

The hectic days and late nights took a toll on Hopkins, however. "His lips are blanched as if he had been bleeding internally," Lord Moran observed, "his skin yellow like stretched parchment and his eyelids contracted to a slit so that you can just see his eyes moving about restlessly, as if he was in pain." Living on sheer will and unquenchable spirit, Hopkins collapsed as soon as Churchill left, checking himself into the Naval Hospital in a state of nervous exhaustion.

When Churchill reached London, an affectionate message from the president awaited him. "It is fun," Roosevelt told Churchill, "to be in the same decade with you."

• • •

"We must raise our sights all along the production line," Roosevelt told the Congress in his State of the Union message on January 6, 1942. "Let no man say it cannot be done." He then proceeded to outline a staggering set of production goals for 1942: sixty thousand planes, forty-five thousand tanks, twenty thousand anti-aircraft guns, six million tons of merchant shipping. "The figures," *U.S. News* reported, "reached such astronomical proportions that human minds could not reach around them. Only by symbols could they be understood; a plane every four minutes in 1943; a tank every seven minutes; two seagoing ships a day." Thoroughly convinced that a dramatic announcement of spectacular goals would both rally the American public and serve notice on the Axis powers that America's vast industrial might would soon be producing munitions for all its Allies in every theater of war, the president had arbitrarily taken a pencil and revised the figures upward on the eve of his speech. When Hopkins questioned the wisdom of reaching so high, Roosevelt jauntily replied: "Oh—the production people can do it, if they really try."

Ironically, while the leaders of industry clung to a more or less static view of the American economy, rooted in prevailing notions of limited annual growth, it was Franklin Roosevelt and his impractical theorists, who never met a payroll, who held to a powerful vision of the country's latent potential, spurred by government spending, to produce more than anyone had ever dreamed possible.

"These figures," Roosevelt told a cheering Congress, "will give the Japanese and the Nazis a little idea of just what they accomplished at Pearl Harbor." Henceforth, Roosevelt said, workers must be prepared to work long and hard to turn out weapons twenty-four hours a day, seven days a week. Henceforth, every available tool, whether in the auto industry or the village machine shop, must be devoted to the production of munitions. "The militarists of Berlin and Tokyo started the war," he concluded, his voice rising."But the massed, angered forces of common humanity will finish it."

The automobile industry was the first to feel the force of the president's fighting words. The time for persuasion had passed; a complete ban was imposed on the retail sale of new passenger autos and of light and heavy trucks. The order froze all stock in the hands of dealers until January 15. On that date, a program of rationing the 450,000 cars and trucks on hand, plus the two hundred thousand currently on the assembly line, was announced. First call went to the government for lend-lease; the remainder was parceled out to doctors, police, and others whose operations were essential to public health and safety. The drastic action was necessary, Office of Price Administration chief Leon Henderson said, so the entire manufacturing facilities of the auto industry could be brought into the national armaments program.

"In the dealers' holiday-decorated showrooms," *Time* reported, "the stillness of death" prevailed, as forty-four thousand auto dealers and their four hundred thousand employees were laid off. To Eleanor's mind, this human hardship could have been avoided if the big automobile companies had accepted the necessity for conversion earlier. Instead, blindly insisting they could produce great quantities of both cars and planes, they had exposed the workers to a perilous situation.

Taking out her anger and frustration on OPM chief William Knudsen, Eleanor accosted him one afternoon to ask what he intended to do about all the people being thrown out of work. "Mr. Knudsen looked at me like a great big benevolent bear," Eleanor said, "as if to say, 'Now, Mrs. Roosevelt, don't let's get excited.' "

"I wonder if you know what hunger is?" Eleanor countered. "Has any member of your family ever gone hungry?"

Later, when called upon to explain her severity, Eleanor softened her attack. "I said nothing derogatory about anyone and nothing which I would not apply to myself," she argued. "None of us, whether we are government officials or private individuals, can afford to sit back and wait for the development of these problems without feeling the urgency that a group of hungry children in our homes would put upon us."

In truth, the auto industry's reluctance to convert before Pearl Harbor was part of a larger failure of will in the nation as a whole, but Knudsen was the man on the spot, and as a result he was the one to shoulder the blame.

Though Knudsen had been denied power commensurate with his responsibility, the president determined on January 13, 1942, that a shake-up was in order. He announced that former Sears, Roebuck executive Donald Nelson would head a powerful new organization, the War Production Board, which would have "final" decisions on procurement and production. It was the greatest delegation of power the president had ever made.

Knudsen was conducting a meeting when his secretary broke in to convey the news which had just come over the wire. "Look here," Knudsen told a colleague, holding a piece of paper torn from the ticker. "I've just been fired." Knudsen was stunned. The president who had called him Bill and treated him so warmly had not even had the courtesy to explain the shake-up face to face.

In the White House, Hopkins realized that the situation had been handled badly, but he knew from long experience that Roosevelt could never be made to tackle controversy head on. Securing the president's agreement to offer Knudsen a special commission in the army, Hopkins urged Federal Loan Administrator Jesse Jones to see Knudsen that night and persuade him to accept the post. "I have never seen a more disconsolate man," Jones reported. "After dinner he sat at the piano and played and hummed sad tunes as though his heart would break." Jones advised him to accept the presidential appointment, but Knudsen was so hurt he couldn't figure out what to do. Finally, Jones took matters into his own hands. He called the White House and asked for Hopkins. "Knudsen," Jones announced, "will accept a 3 star generalship in the Army," which put him in charge of "promoting production for war." When Knudsen failed to contradict him, Jones knew that the decision—which turned out to be an excellent one for everyone concerned—had been made.

The following day, with everything seemingly settled, the president invited Knudsen to the White House for lunch. At this point, wanting nothing so much as to leave the relationship on good terms, the old master set to work. His abundant charm was everywhere, in his warm greeting when Knudsen walked in, his generous praise of Knudsen's accomplishments, and his good-natured banter about Knudsen in a uniform. By the end of the luncheon, Knudsen said he would take any position the president offered. It was a triumph for Roosevelt. His ingenious maneuvering had produced a new director of war production without permanently alienating the old.

• • •

Gradually, one step at a time, the war was brought home to the American people. The tooling up period was over. The U.S. economy was finally prepared to swing into production on an unprecedented scale. "For more than a year," novelist Winston Estes observed in *Homefront*, "new defense factories and plants had been sprouting up from the landscape as though the ground underneath had been fertilized. And still they continued to appear, larger and more mysterious, turning out arms and munitions in unthinkable quantities." And while the new plants were being built, manufacturing concerns of every imaginable type were moving to convert their old plants to the production of weapons. A merry-go-round factory was using its plant to fashion gun mounts. A corset factory was making grenade belts. A manufacturer of stoves was producing lifeboats. A famous New York toy concern was making compasses. A pinball-machine maker was turning out armor-piercing shells. Despite continuing shortages of raw materials, 1942 would witness the greatest expansion of production in the nation's history.

On January 30, the President signed an Emergency Price Control Bill, which gave Henderson and the Office of Price Administration added, though still not sufficient, power to keep prices down. Under the new legislation, Henderson could impose ceilings on a selective range of consumer items from raw materials to finished goods; he could have violators imprisoned or fined, and he could fix maximum rents in defense areas. At the same time, a preliminary rationing system was established to hold the demand for goods to the available supply.

In the White House, Eleanor tried to set an example for housewives. When the need for parachutes put an end to silk stockings, she wore heavy black cotton stockings instead, announcing that she would do without just like everyone else. When a shortage of sugar was first contemplated, since the army and navy needed alcohol derived from sugar to make smokeless powder, Eleanor promised that the White House would be very careful in the use of sugar, relying on corn syrup and other substitutes wherever possible, replacing desserts with salads, if necessary. Eleanor's comments, Representative Emmanuel Celler of New York charged, provoked a run on sugar, which made sugar rationing inevitable. Without the hoarding brought about by the fear of loss which Eleanor incited, Celler argued, there would never have been a sugar shortage.

"It never crossed my mind," Eleanor rather naïvely said in self-defense, "that you couldn't tell the American people the truth and count on them to behave themselves accordingly. It is perfectly obvious that a housewife who goes out and buys 100 pounds of sugar for herself and puts it away is putting up the price of sugar for herself and her family. It is also obvious that she cannot buy enough pounds of sugar to last her through the war. . . . Sooner or later the hoarder is going to have to face the shortage and it is a lot more chummy to get into the boat with the rest of the citizenry from the start."

• • •

On the war front, everything was going badly. In the Far East, Japan's success was so complete that it surprised even the Japanese. In a matter of weeks, the Empire of the Rising Sun had seized what colonial powers had taken centuries to acquire. Nearly a million square miles of land—including Hong Kong, Thailand, Malaya, Burma, the Dutch East Indies—and a hundred million people had come under Japan's domain. In the Philippines,

General Jonathan Wainwright and his embattled troops were on the verge of defeat.

In the Atlantic, the United States was still losing its battle with the German submarine; merchant ships were still being sunk faster than new ships could be put into service. In the month of January alone, forty-three ships were sent to the bottom of the sea, with a loss of more than a thousand lives. By cutting off the supply line, Hitler was striking at the heart of the American war effort. "We are in a war of transportation," U.S. Maritime Commission Chairman Emory Land confirmed, "a war of ships. It's no damn sense making guns and tanks to be left in the U.S." General Eisenhower, deputy chief of the War Plans Division, admitted that tempers were short. "We've got to have ships and we need them now."

When the situation at sea was at its worst, Lord Moran found Churchill in his London map room. "He was standing with his back to me, staring at the huge chart with the little black beetles representing German submarines. 'Terrible,' he muttered. He knows that we may lose the war at sea in a few months and that he can do nothing about it. I wish to God I could put out the fires that seem to be consuming him."

On Sunday, February 15, the bottom seemed to drop out when Singapore, the symbol of Western power in the Far East, fell to the Japanese. "The news came to a great many people as a shock," Eleanor recorded in her column. "I had talked with the President and he said resignedly that of course, we had expected it, but I know a great many people did not." With food stocks running low and water supplies threatened, General Arthur Percival marched out under a white flag to surrender to the Japanese commander.

"Perhaps it is good for us," Eleanor mused, "to have to face disaster, because we have been so optimistic and almost arrogant in our expectation of constant success. Now we shall have to find within us the courage to meet defeat and fight right on to victory. That means a steadiness of purpose and of will, which is not one of our strong points. But somehow, I think we shall harden physically and mentally as the days go by."

At the center of the storm, the president remained, in presidential assistant William Hassett's recollection, "calm and serene, never impatient or irritable." Through all the bad news from the Far East, through the dark days of the submarine menace, there was "never a note of despair, chin up, full of fight." The years may have drawn lines around his eyes, *New York Times* reporter Anne O'Hare McCormick noted on the occasion of his sixtieth birthday, on January 30, 1942, but "neither time nor the hammer blows of defeat in the Pacific have shaken his steady self-assurance." On the contrary, despite the titanic tasks before him, he is "more at ease in all circumstances, more at home in his position, than any leader of his time. His nerves are stronger, his temper cooler and more even. If he worries, he gives no sign of it." Indeed, McCormick concluded, perhaps because "the uncertainties are resolved and the great debate is over, his mood seems brighter, if anything, than it was a few months ago."

•   •   •

If the fortunes of the war depended upon American shipping, then the only answer, Roosevelt reasoned, was to build ships and more ships, twice as many as the Germans could sink. In his State of the Union message, Roosevelt had set an incredibly high goal of eighteen million tons for 1942. Now, in the wake of the terrifying sinkings, he raised his sights even higher—to twenty-four million tons. "I realize that this is a terrible directive on my part," Roosevelt admitted to Emory Land, "but I feel certain that in this very great emergency we can attain it."

The crisis in shipping could not have occurred at a worse time. After years of neglect, the U.S. merchant fleet ranked only "fourth in tonnage in foreign trade, fifth in speed and eighth in number of new, first class ocean-going ships." From building fewer than a hundred ships a year, the U.S. Maritime Commission was now charged with building twenty-nine hundred ships right away; from dealing with forty-six shipways, it was now responsible for nearly three hundred; from thinking in terms of one hundred thousand men, it could soon count on more than seven hundred thousand. In peacetime, a shipfitter used to serve a four-year apprenticeship; the training period was now reduced to seven weeks. "It gives you a feeling like holding a hand grenade after removing the pin," Admiral H. L. Vickery admitted.

In attempting the impossible, the government turned to Henry Kaiser, an irrepressible sixty-year-old industrialist who had been involved in the building of Boulder Dam, Grand Coulee Dam, and the Oakland–San Francisco Bridge. Though new to the shipping business, Kaiser was an entrepreneurial genius who instinctively grasped Roosevelt's rule that "energy was more efficient than efficiency." He sent bulldozers to build his first yard in Richmond, California, across the bay from San Francisco on January 20, 1941. Eighty-five working days later, he laid his first keel.

Lavishly spending the government's money, building ships as fast as steel could be found, Kaiser reached for every crane, derrick, and bulldozer he could lay his hands on. He hired workers with little regard for qualifications on the theory that anyone could be trained on the job; he grafted the techniques of mass production to the art of building a ship, replacing riveters with welders to cut weight and save time, using prefabricated bulkheads, decks, and hulls to move the ships off the ways as quickly as possible.

Under Kaiser's leadership, the average time to deliver a ship was cut from 355 days in 1940 to 194 days in 1941 to 60 days in early 1942. With six new yards in operation after only one year in the business, Sir Launchalot, as he was dubbed, had become the pacesetter for the entire shipbuilding industry. The Maritime Commission translated each new record he set into a schedule increase for shipyards across the nation, from Bath and South Portland to Norfolk and Vancouver.

To be sure, the finished product—the Liberty Ship—was an ugly duckling which fell short of traditional shipbuilding standards. It was not fast and it tended on occasion to split in half. But Roosevelt reasoned it was better to have a lot of makeshift ships now—each one capable of carrying 2,840 jeeps, 440 light tanks and three million C-rations—than a fleet of faster, more graceful, more durable ships after the war was lost.

· · ·

As the dismal days of February drew to a close, Roosevelt decided to give a fireside chat, his first since Pearl Harbor. The speech was intended to involve the American people in the drama of the war, to lay out for them in the frankest terms the situation the Allies faced. At the same time, he hoped to reassure them that, despite the blackness of the present outlook, victory was bound to come. "No one," Robert Sherwood said, "is as good as the President in fixing the line between keeping up morale and confidence on the one hand and being too optimistic on the other."

Roosevelt told his speechwriters he was going to ask the American people to have a map of the world before them as they listened to him speak. "I'm going to speak about strange places that many of them never heard of—places that are now the battleground for civilization. . . . I want to explain to the people something about geography—what our problem is and what the overall strategy of the war has to be. I want to tell it to them in simple terms of ABC so that they will understand what is going on and how each battle fits into the picture. . . . If they understand the problem and what we are driving at, I am sure that they can take any kind of bad news right on the chin."

Responding enthusiastically to the president's request, American citizens by the thousands raced to their local stores to purchase maps. "The map business is booming," *The New York Times* reported. At C. S. Hammond & Co. on 43rd Street, E. O. Schmidt, the sales manager, had gone to the downtown warehouse on the Saturday morning before the speech and brought two thousand copies of their new atlas back to the store to augment their stock. By nightfall, the entire stock was completely sold. Mr. Schmidt said he had seen nothing like it in the twenty-four years he had been in the business. "Why even last night when I went home, my wife, who has never particularly cared about maps, asked me to put up on the wall a large commercial map I've had for years."

When the president spoke at 10 p.m. on February 23, more than sixty-one million adults (nearly 80 percent of the total possible adult audience) were by their radios, many with their maps spread before them. Speaking in a clear, confident tone, Roosevelt likened the present stage of the struggle to the early years of the Revolutionary War, when George Washington and his Continental Army were faced with formidable odds, recurring defeats, and limited supplies. "Selfish men, jealous men, fearful men proclaimed the situation hopeless." But Washington "held to his course" and a new country was born.

In similar fashion, Roosevelt said, the American people must be prepared to suffer more losses "before the turn of the tide." The months ahead would not be easy. But "your government has unmistakable confidence in your ability to hear the worst without flinching or losing heart." This war, he explained, was "a new kind of war," waged on "every continent, every island, every sea, every air-lane in the world. That is the reason why I have asked you to take out and spread before you a map of the whole earth, and to follow with me the references I shall make to the world-encircling battle lines of the war."

Revealing his own vast knowledge of geography, derived to a large extent from his beloved stamps, Roosevelt patiently described the Allied situation in every part of the world. In this new war, he explained, "the broad oceans which have been heralded in the past as our protection from attack have become endless battlefields." The road ahead would be difficult, but he was certain, he said, that it was only a matter of time until America's productive genius was fully mobilized, capable of giving the Allies "the overwhelming superiority of military material necessary for ultimate triumph."

"From Berlin, Rome and Tokyo we have been described as a nation of weakling-playboys," he concluded. "Let them tell that to General MacArthur and his men . . . Let them tell that to the boys in the flying fortresses. Let them tell that to the Marines!"

The speech was a great success, "even more effective," Sam Rosenman observed, "than the President's first fireside chat back in the dark days of 1933 during the banking crisis." *The New York Times* agreed, hailing the address as "one of the greatest of Roosevelt's career." Success bred the desire for more. Russell Leffingwell, an old friend and a partner at J. P. Morgan, advised Roosevelt that the only way to rouse the people was for him to speak more frequently on the radio.

"Sometimes," Roosevelt replied, revealing a subtle understanding of leadership, "I wish I could carry out your thought of more frequent talking on the air on my part but the one thing I dread is that my talks should be so frequent as to lose their effectiveness. . . . Every time I talk over the air it means four or five days of long, overtime work in the preparation of what I say. Actually, I cannot afford to take this time away from more vital things. I think we must avoid too much personal leadership—my good friend Winston Churchill has suffered a little from this. It must grow more slowly—remembering always that we have only been in the war for three months."

As always, Roosevelt's dominant instinct was to unify the nation. "No one understood better than he," historian Eric Larrabee has written, "the inner dynamics of American strength: how to mobilize it, how to draw on it, how to gauge its limits. Once mobilized, it did not need to be driven; it needed only to be steered."

•   •   •

If Roosevelt shrewdly understood the strength of America's democracy, he failed miserably to guard against democracy's weakness—the tyranny of an aroused public opinion. As attitudes toward Japanese Americans on the West Coast turned hostile, he made an ill-advised, brutal decision to uproot thousands of Japanese Americans from their homes, forcing them into incarceration camps located in the interior of the country.

The tortuous path to the president's tragic decision, considered by the American Civil Liberties Union "the worst single wholesale violation of civil rights of American citizens in our history," began with a false assessment by the military that the Japanese Americans were a substantial threat to national security. Though there was never any hard evidence brought forward to confirm sabotage on the part of the Japanese Americans, the rumors of shore-to-shore signaling and fifth-column treachery were so widespread that they became accepted as fact. "Two Japs with Maps and Alien Literature Seized," one report read. "Caps on Jap Tomato Point to Air Base," read another. Though the Army's West Coast commander, General John De Witt, admitted that nothing had actually been proved, he proceeded, in a tortured twist of logic, to argue that "the very fact that no sabotage has taken place is a disturbing and confirming indication that such action *will* be taken."

Racism fueled the claim of "military necessity." For fifty years, anti-Japanese sentiment had been embedded in the social structure of the West Coast, producing exclusionary laws and restrictions on alien citizenship. With the attack on Pearl Harbor and the humiliating defeats suffered by the Allies in the Pacific, the explosive force of this hostility was released. Day after day, newspapers headlined vilification against the Japanese, calling them "mad dogs, yellow vermin and nips." The atmosphere of hatred gave license to extremist elements. "California was given by God to a white people," the president of Native Sons and Daughters of the Golden West proclaimed, "and with God's strength we want to keep it as he gave it to us."

"These people were not convicted of any crime," Eleanor wrote years later in a draft of an unpublished article, "but emotions ran too high, too many people wanted to wreak vengeance on Oriental looking people. There was no time to investigate families or to adhere strictly to the American rule that a man is innocent until he is proved guilty."

Economic cupidity also played a significant role. "Originally," Eleanor wrote, the Japanese immigrants "were much needed on ranches and on large truck and fruit farms but as they came in greater numbers, people began to discover that they were not only convenient workers, they were competitors in the labor field, and the people of California began to be afraid." Though Japanese-owned farms occupied only 1 percent of the cultivated land in California, they produced nearly 40 percent of the total California crop. One pressure group, the Grower Shipper Association, blatantly admitted wanting to get rid of the Japanese for selfish reasons: "We might as well be honest," they said, openly coveting the rich farmland of the Japanese.

Had the Japanese Americans been politically organized, they might have countered these pressure groups, but since the first-generation parents, known as the Issei, were prevented by law from voting or becoming citizens, and since the great majority of American-born Nisei were still in school, they provided an easy target.

From every side, Roosevelt was exposed to pressure to act against the Japanese Americans. In California, the entire political establishment—including Governor Culbert Olson and Attorney General Earl Warren—were strongly on the side of evacuation. In the military, all the leading figures—General De Witt, Provost Marshal General Allen Gullion, Henry Stimson, and War Department official John McCloy—argued for internment. By the time the decision was made in mid-February, Francis Biddle, who had replaced Robert Jackson as attorney general in September, was the only significant hold-out, and because he was new to the Cabinet, his opinion held little weight.

In the absence of countervailing persuasive pressures, Roosevelt accepted the "military necessity" argument at face value, directing Stimson and McCloy to do whatever they thought necessary as long as they were as reasonable and as humane as possible. The War Department came back with a blanket order—Executive Order 9066—requiring the forced removal of all people of Japanese descent from any area designated as a military zone. Since the entire state of California, the western half of Washington and Oregon, and the southern part of Arizona were all designated as military zones, the order affected more than a hundred thousand citizens and aliens of Japanese descent.

Though Roosevelt later admitted that he regretted "the burdens of evacuation and detention which military necessity had imposed upon these people," he showed no qualms whatsoever when he signed the order on February 19. "I do not think he was much concerned with the gravity or implications of this step," Francis Biddle observed. "He was never theoretical about things. What must be done to defend the country must be done." Since everything depended, he believed, on winning the war, anything that threatened that prospect had to be dealt with boldly and harshly.

Told to bring only what they could carry, the evacuees were herded into sixteen hastily provided assembly centers at racetracks and athletic fields along the West Coast, while permanent centers further inland were being constructed by army engineers. "We are having quite a problem figuring out just what to take," twenty-six-year-old Charles Kikuchi wrote in his diary. "There is still so much junk around and you know how the Japanese like to hang on to old things. Anyway, we will have to store a lot of it since they will not allow us to take more than the barest of necessities."

In the assembly centers, Berkeley resident Mine Okubo has written, "there was a lack of privacy everywhere. The incomplete partitions in the stalls and the barracks made a single symphony of yours and your neighbor's loves, hates and joys. One had to get used to snores, baby cryings, family troubles." The older women could not bring themselves to stand in line for the communal shower; they bathed in tubs made from barrels instead; they pinned up curtains wherever they could.

"Can this be the same America we left a few weeks ago?" a young architectural draftsman named Ted Nakashima asked. "It all seems so futile, struggling to live our old lives under this useless, regimented life." Born in Seattle, Washington, Nakashima was the third son of Japanese parents who had been in the United States since 1901. His father was an editor, his oldest brother an architect, his middle brother a doctor. Yet all three brothers and their parents were forced to leave flourishing careers behind and spend their days amid the suffocating smell of horse manure in a stall that was only eighteen feet wide by twenty-one feet long.

"The senselessness of all of the inactive manpower," young Nakashima observed. "Electricians, plumbers, draftsmen, mechanics, carpenters, painters, farmers—every trade—men who are able and willing to do all they can to lick the Axis . . . Oddly enough I still have a bit of faith in army promises of good treatment and Mrs. Roosevelt's pledge of a future worthy of good American citizens. . . . What really hurts is the constant reference to we evacuees as 'Japs.' 'Japs' are the guys we are fighting. We're on this side and we want to help. Why won't America let us?"

When the news of Franklin's decision had reached Eleanor, she was shaken. She had witnessed the growing hysteria for weeks and had feared that something like this might happen. But so drastic was the president's order that it took her breath away. To her mind, the guarantees of the Bill of Rights must never be surrendered, even in the face of national disaster. When she tried to speak to her husband about his decision, however, he gave her a frigid reception and said he did not want her to mention it again.

Under ordinary circumstances, Eleanor would have argued her case relentlessly, regardless of the president's reaction, but the weeks that surrounded the evacuation decision found her in the midst of an all-consuming controversy of her own as the Office of Civilian Defense was exposed to irreparably damaging criticism.

•   •   •

With the coming of war, the activities of the OCD had moved to the forefront of public awareness, bringing Eleanor's philosophical differences with LaGuardia into the open. "I could not help realizing," Eleanor admitted, "that the mayor was more interested in the dramatic aspects of civilian defense—such as whether cities had good fire-fighting equipment—than in such things as building morale." To Eleanor's mind, the stresses and dislocations of war—such as migration, unemployment, housing, and health—were creating social problems as acute, if not so dramatic, as anything to be anticipated from bombing. But, try as she might, she could not turn LaGuardia's focus from the protective side. Eleanor saw that his work as mayor of New York "prevented him from giving his full time to organizing civilian defense. The few group meetings we had left me with an impression of great hurry and a feeling that decisions were taken which were not carefully thought out."

For the president, his desk piled high with somber reports from both the Atlantic and the Pacific, his wife's dispute with the mayor was irritating and disconcerting. "I can't take Eleanor and LaGuardia," he told Anna Rosenberg in confidence. "Each one comes with a story; each one is right; each one comes to me: I cannot cope with it and I want you to try and keep them away from me and reconcile their differences."

But there was no way that anyone could keep Eleanor away from Franklin when she had something to say. By mid-December 1941, she had become convinced that LaGuardia could not handle both the mayor's job and the OCD post. The time had come, she told her husband, for LaGuardia to step down from the OCD in favor of a full-time administrator. The president agreed with Eleanor. "I am brought to the realization by war," he diplomatically wrote LaGuardia, "that by acts of my own I have created for you an almost impossible situation." In the days and weeks before the war, Roosevelt went on, it had probably been possible for LaGuardia to carry both jobs. But as the war made each job more exacting, he realized he was asking something physically impossible of his good friend. Perhaps the best solution was to name a successor at the OCD who could administer the organization full-time. When it was put on this basis, LaGuardia agreed, albeit reluctantly, to step aside in favor of Harvard Law School Dean James Landis.

Rumors spread that Eleanor, too, was about to resign, but she denied them absolutely. The fact was that, with LaGuardia gone, she believed she had a fighting chance to realize her dream for the OCD. But on February 6, 1942, in the Chamber of the House of Representatives, Eleanor's wish was destroyed when two of her appointments to the OCD were subjected to a withering attack. "I rise today to utter a protest against 'boondoggling' in connection with the OCD," Representative Faddis began. "I want the members to take into consideration today the fact that we are paying Melvyn Douglas $8000 a year—as much as we are paying that matchless and heroic soldier, General MacArthur, when he is battling in the forests of the Philippines every day. . . . I call attention to the fact that we are paying this dancer, Miss Chaney, $4600 a year—almost twice as much as the base pay of Captain Colin Kelly [first hero of the war] and he gave his life in defense of this Nation."

When it was learned that both Melvyn Douglas and Mayris Chaney were close friends of Eleanor's, the criticism mounted. "The work of OCD concerns the safety and welfare of the people of this nation," columnist Raymond Clapper wrote. "Yet it has become a kind of personal parking lot for the pets and protégés of Mrs. Roosevelt. . . . How can you have any kind of morale with a subordinate employee, who happens to be the wife of the President, flitting in and out between lecture engagements to toss a few pets into nice jobs, some of them at salaries larger than a brigadier general and a rear admiral gets."

Had the high salaries been attached to work the country deemed essential, the flap would have quickly died down. But in the wake of war, Eleanor's noble ideas about mental health and physical fitness suddenly seemed luxuries, particularly since the real necessities of physical defense—gas masks and helmets—were not being provided in an organized way. Still, Marquis Childs observed, "the storm that burst out," particularly over Miss Chaney's assignment to teach dancing to children, "was far out of proportion to the cause. It became a witch hunt, and once Miss Chaney's status on the payroll was discovered, decency was out the window."

For days, while the men of Bataan were caught in a hopeless siege and Singapore was falling to the Japanese, one congressman after another rose to attack Eleanor Roosevelt and her friends. From both sides of the House, bitter assertions were launched that the country needed bombers, not dancers, and that "parasites and leeches" should be stricken from the payroll. "Mrs. Roosevelt," a woman from Kalamazoo wrote Eleanor, "you would be doing your country a great service if you would simply go home and sew for the Red Cross. Every time you open your mouth the people of this country dislike and mistrust you more."

"I am not in the least disturbed by the latest attack," Eleanor wrote her friend Paul Kellogg, editor of *Survey* magazine. "It is purely political and made by the same people who have fought NYA, CCC, WPA, Farm Security, etc." She would only be sorry, she said, if it lessened the effectiveness of the OCD or hurt the people involved.

But so violent was the newspaper frenzy that followed the congressional outburst that Eleanor found herself, for the first time in nearly ten years as first lady, a target of merciless criticism not only from conservatives but from people who counted themselves her supporters and friends. A woman writing from the Plaza Hotel in New York told Eleanor that she had always greatly admired her energy, ability, and accomplishments, but had now come to believe that, "in these troubled times, you should spend more time with the President. To us he seems a very lonely man, with heartbreaking burdens to carry."

The climax came when the House of Representatives took a direct slap at Eleanor by issuing a ban against the use of civilian-defense funds for "instruction in physical fitness by dancers." Eleanor realized that by staying in the job she was jeopardizing the survival of the OCD. The time had come to resign. "I still believe in all the things we started out to do," she wrote Florence Kerr, director of WPA Community Services Projects, explaining her resignation, "but I know if I stayed longer, I would bring more harm than good to the program."

Furthermore, Eleanor admitted, she had come to the reluctant conclusion that it was impossible for the wife of the president to have an official job with the government. Since no one could ever be sure if she was acting on her own behalf or in the name of the president (a circumstance she and her husband had often employed to great political advantage in an unofficial capacity), she was now, as a public official, being accorded a measure of influence and blame that went far beyond that of the ordinary public servant.

On the evening of February 20, Eleanor held a farewell party for all the people who had worked for her in the OCD. Looking back over her five months, she said, she felt no little pride in what she had accomplished, particularly in broadening the definition of defense to include nutrition, housing, recreation, and medical care. Now that everything was in place, she maintained, it was time to move on.

Yet, no matter what she said about the proper time to go, an aura of defeat clouded Eleanor's resignation. For she knew, and the press knew, that with her departure her dream of the OCD as a people's movement had come to a humiliating end.

• • •

No sooner had Eleanor resigned from the OCD than she became entangled in further controversy—a brutal battle between blacks and whites over the occupancy of a newly built federal housing project in Detroit. The two-hundred-unit development, named the Sojourner Truth project, had been developed for black defense workers by Eleanor's friend at the Federal Works Agency, Clark Foreman, a liberal Southerner who took the position that blacks were as entitled as whites to enjoy the benefits of the public-housing boom necessitated by the war.

Eleanor had repeatedly urged Franklin to use the defense emergency as a lever for replacing the slums of the city with permanent new housing that could still be used after the war ended. There was a chance, she believed, if new neighborhoods could be properly planned and designed, that blacks and whites could live together in peace. But Eleanor's ideas for the future were shattered at every turn by her old nemesis Charles Palmer, the housing coordinator she had vehemently opposed at the time of his appointment.

It was Palmer's position, backed by private real-estate interests, that the federal government should limit its role to the construction of temporary housing. As long as the workers had some sort of shelter while they produced for the war, it mattered little how long the buildings lasted. The Congress agreed. When the House approved a bill authorizing $300 million for new construction, it specified that none of it could be spent for slum clearance.

Even with these restrictions, Clark Foreman had managed to target money for the Sojourner Truth project. Everything proceeded according to plan until word of the project reached the white community in Detroit. Coming at a time when the majority of white workers were living in overcrowded, overpriced apartments, with three shifts to the same "hot" bed, the news provoked an emotional outburst.

The population of Detroit had exploded since 1940, as some three hundred thousand whites and fifty thousand blacks migrated from farmlands in Mississippi, Alabama, Tennessee, and Louisiana in search of employment in war plants. Thousands of workers were sleeping in boxcars, tents, church pews, and jails. Every habitable shed had been rented for all the traffic would bear, and new families were still pouring into Detroit at a rate of five thousand a month.

When white workers heard about the Sojourner Truth project, they demanded the units for themselves and enlisted the support of white residents in the neighborhood where the development was being built. Rudolph Tenerowicz, Detroit's congressman, carried the ball in Washington, successfully prevailing upon the members of the Conference Committee, consisting mostly of Southerners, to add a clause to the FWA's $300,000 appropriations bill specifying that "no money would be released unless the 'nigger lover' [Clark Foreman] was fired and the project converted to white occupancy." The FWA capitulated quickly and dishonorably. That same day, the Detroit housing committee was ordered to redirect its recruitment of prospective tenants from black to white. Minutes later, Clark Foreman "resigned."

Civil-rights leaders reacted with rage. Their first impulse was to contact Eleanor. "Surely you would not stand by and see the Sojourner Truth defense homes that were built for Negroes be taken away from us," Mrs. Charles Diggs wrote from Detroit. Calmly and directly, Eleanor approached the president, emphasizing that both blacks and whites, including Edward Jeffries, Detroit's mayor, and leaders of the UAW, were firmly committed to the position that the blacks should have the project.

Eleanor's intervention prevailed. "After a conference last night with many Negroes from Detroit," Palmer solicitously told her, "it looks as though we are going to get that project straightened out to their entire satisfaction." Two weeks later, the FWA directed the Detroit Housing Committee to begin its selection of black tenants, with occupancy set for the last day of February.

On Saturday morning, February 28, the first twenty-four Negro families, their household goods loaded on trucks and vans, began moving into their new homes. Overnight, seven hundred white pickets, armed with knives, guns, rifles, and clubs, gathered at the entrance to the project. A fiery cross was burning at the site. As the trucks, supported by a crowd of three hundred blacks, tried to cross the picket line, a battle erupted. Before it ended, many people, both black and white, were hospitalized, and 104 were arrested.

The disorder occasioned a great outpouring of Axis propaganda; newspapers in both Germany and Japan carried pictures of the bloody struggle. According to wire reports in Tokyo, Washington had arbitrarily ordered white Detroiters to take Negro war workers into their homes. "Many dead and wounded," Tokyo radio claimed.

Convinced that the government's vacillation had set the stage for the riot, Eleanor rushed headlong into the battle. From here on, she argued, the government must stay its course in behalf of the rights of black citizens. Her pleas did not go unheeded. On April 29, while eight hundred Michigan troops with fixed bayonets stood guard, black tenants were again moved into the Sojourner Truth project, this time without incident. With the situation happily resolved, Eleanor turned her attention to Clark Foreman. It was not fair, she told her husband, that Foreman was being blacklisted simply because he had exhibited the courage to stand up for the rights of black citizens. The president agreed. "What can we do for Foreman?" he wrote his Southern-born aide Marvin McIntyre. "He is not as bad as you think." A few weeks later, a job was found for Foreman in the manpower operation.

Even as Franklin acceded to some of Eleanor's specific requests, he refused to admit that, in so doing, he was planning for the future. When, shortly after the Sojourner Truth riot, Edwin Embree of the Rosenwald Fund pleaded with him to create a wide-ranging commission on race and color, he flatly refused. "Such a commission appears to me at this time premature," he explained. "We must start winning the war with all the brains, wisdom and experience we've got before we do much general or specific planning for the future. . . . I am not convinced that we can be realists about the war and planners for the future at this critical time."

For Eleanor, whose primary concern was the home front, not the war, the present and the future were inextricably linked. Speaking to a group of Washington church women shortly after Pearl Harbor, she had argued, "The nation cannot expect the colored people to feel that the U.S. is worth defending if they continue to be treated as they are treated now." These incendiary remarks, a man from Kentucky angrily wrote, "are probably the most dangerous ever uttered by a woman in your position. . . . Your quarrel in this respect seems to me to be with Providence."

"I am not agitating the race question," Eleanor replied. "The race question is agitated because people will not act justly and fairly toward each other as human beings."

Nowhere was this unjust treatment more obvious, Eleanor believed, than in the navy. The previous year, in response to the vigorous protest by civil-rights leaders against the relegation of Negroes to the position of mess men, the navy had created a committee to analyze the relationship between the "U.S. Navy and the Negro race." The committee held three short meetings before coming to the conclusion that "the enlistment of Negroes (other than as mess attendants) leads to disruptive and undermining conditions."

Pearl Harbor provoked a whole new round of protest. On December 9, the NAACP sent a telegram to Navy Secretary Frank Knox asking whether, "in view of the intensive recruiting campaign then underway, the Navy would accept colored recruits for other than the messman's branch." Answering for the Navy, the Bureau of Navigation (responsible for procurement and assignment of personnel) abruptly replied that "there had been no change in policy and that none was contemplated."

The navy's obstinate refusal to bend unleashed fierce pressure on the White House from black leaders and black newspapers across the land. The clamor and increasing political pressure convinced Roosevelt that something had to give. "I think," he wrote Knox on January 9, "that with all the

Navy activities the Bureau of Navigation might invent something that colored enlistees could do in addition to the rating of messman."

Responding to the president's tone, Knox asked the General Board to submit a plan for taking five thousand Negroes for billets other than as mess men. Two weeks later, the board reported back, concluding in no uncertain terms "that members of the colored race be accepted only in messman branch." The rationale once again was the intimate nature of life on a ship. "Men on board ship live in particularly close association; in their messes one man sits beside another, their hammocks or bunks are close together; in their common tasks they work side by side.... How many white men would choose that their closest associates in sleeping quarters, in mess be of another race? General Board believes that the answer is 'few if any' and further believes that if the issue were forced, there would be a lowering of contentment, teamwork and discipline in the service."

The president, much to Eleanor's satisfaction, refused to accept the board's report. In a blistering reply, Roosevelt told Knox that he regarded the report as (a) unsatisfactory and (b) insufficient. "Officers of the U.S. Navy are not officers only but are American citizens.... They should, therefore, be expected to recognize social and economic problems which are related to national welfare.... It is incumbent on all officers to recognize the fact that about 1/10th of the population of the United States is composed of members of the Negro race who are American citizens.... It is my considered opinion that there are additional tasks in the Naval establishment to which we could properly assign an additional number of enlisted men who are members of the Negro race.... I [ask] you to return the recommendations of the General Board to that Board for further study and report."

As the General Board reanalyzed the situation, the pressures for change continued to mount. Through February and March 1942, every black newspaper carried the story of black mess man Dorie Miller, whose heroic exploits on the bridge of his battleship at Pearl Harbor earned him the Navy Cross. The example of Miller's heroism became a principal weapon in the battle to end discrimination in the navy. Here was a high-school dropout who raced through flaming oil to carry his captain to safety. Seizing a machine gun left beside a dead gunner, Miller, without any weapons training, began to fire at the oncoming Japanese planes, downing one or maybe two of the enemy aircraft. Only after his ammunition was exhausted, the ship sinking rapidly, did he finally obey the order to abandon ship.

Although Miller's acts of heroism were mentioned in the first navy dispatches, he was referred to simply as "an unidentified Negro messman." The navy, it seems, did not want the first hero of the war to be a black man. That honor was reserved for West Point graduate Colin Kelly, who perished three days later. When Miller's name was finally released in March, the result of a determined effort by the *Pittsburgh Courier,* bills were introduced to accord him the Congressional Medal of Honor, and schools and parks were given his name. But "the greatest honor that could be paid mess attendant Dorie Miller," the NAACP argued, "would be for the U.S. Navy to abolish restrictions against Negro enlistments at once."

Now the navy's General Board had no choice but to capitulate. They issued a second report to Knox, agreeing that blacks could enlist for general service other than mess-man duty—as gunners, clerks, signalmen, radio operators, ammunition handlers, etc.—as long as the training and the units remained segregated. The change in policy was not as broad as civil-rights leaders had hoped for, but it was, the *Pittsburgh Courier* agreed, "a forward step." "Navy broke down a historic barrier," *The New York Times* reported. A door was now open, however slightly.

• • •

Some halting progress was also recorded in removing barriers against Negro labor in war industries. By early 1942, as a result of pressure from the Fair Employment Practices Commission, more than half the defense employees were committed to the principle of using Negro labor in production jobs. In hundreds of cases, Negroes were working in firms which had formerly banned them. In shipyards, Negro employment had risen from six thousand to fourteen thousand in twelve months. In the aircraft industry, which had employed no Negroes in 1940, five thousand were now employed. The gains were small but significant. "I look for an acceleration of this improvement," Roosevelt promised the Fraternal Council of Negro Churches, "as the demand for labor in our war industries increases."

Eleanor possessed less faith in the power of momentum. Without continual pressure, she feared, management would do all it could to shun its responsibility, either by keeping the numbers so small as to afford only token compliance, or by concentrating Negroes in unskilled jobs. And, beyond problems with management, there remained recalcitrant unions and prejudiced workers who threatened to strike when blacks were hired. Eleanor realized that the power of the FEPC was limited by the fact that its ultimate weapon—requesting cancellation of a defense contract—was no weapon at all, since the administration was loath to jeopardize war production. "For the government to terminate an important war contract by reason of the contractor's indulgence in discriminatory employment," one friend of the FEPC admitted, "would be highly impractical."

Still, Eleanor believed in the power of publicity generated by the hearings the FEPC held throughout the country in response to complaints of discrimination. Traveling from coast to coast, she engaged anyone who would listen, even at the risk of courting public displeasure, in a blunt dialogue about the role of the FEPC and the importance of bringing blacks into defense jobs. In the South, a mood of fury and indignation set in as Southern newspapers accused the FEPC "of trying to turn the South upside down under the clock of necessity brought on by the war emergency." With taunting sarcasm, the *Alabama Times* announced that "a bunch of snoopers, two of whom are

Negroes, will assemble in Birmingham to determine whether the South is doing right by Little Sambo.''

Believing that the existing Southern order was inherently harmonious, white Southerners rationalized away the rising dissatisfaction in the black community as the product of outside agitation. "Anyone who hears Delta Negroes singing at their work," a cotton trade journal in Tennessee intoned, "who sees them dancing in the streets, who listens to their rich laughter, knows that the Southern Negro is not mistreated. He has a carefree, child-like mentality and looks to the white man to solve his problems and take care of him."

"Don't you think there are enough difficulties," a woman from Winston-Salem wrote the president, "without Mrs. Roosevelt going around over the country stirring up strife between white and colored people? She can't realize the grave danger. . . . So see Mr. President if you can't put a stop to Mrs. Roosevelt stirring up trouble down here telling these people they are 'as good as the white people.' "

Resisting the mounting criticism of her progressive stance on civil rights, Eleanor continued to speak out, and without public objection from the president. Though his sense of what the country would accept on civil rights at particular moments was invariably more cautious, he refused to "put a stop to Mrs. Roosevelt's stirring up trouble." As long as he was persuaded that the advances she advocated corresponded to the general direction in which the American society was moving, and did not interfere with the conduct of the war, he was willing to bend with her current.

• • •

The differences between Franklin and Eleanor on the issue of compulsory national service were harder to reconcile. During the spring of 1942, a fierce debate divided Washington over how best to mobilize the labor force. Without government control in the form of civilian conscription for war work, the military argued, the organizational problems presented by the task of marshaling and directing seventy million people employed in fifteen hundred different trades and occupations in dozens of different defense centers would be insurmountable. In the absence of centralized control, the spontaneous movement of workers, wandering the country to the lure of premium wages, had resulted in too many workers in some areas, too few in others.

Convinced that the government's decentralized approach would never solve the manpower problem in a time of war, Eleanor came down strongly on the side of civilian conscription. "I've come to one very clear decision," she announced in mid-March, after a White House conference on man-power, "namely, that all of us—men in the services and women at home—should be drafted and told what is the job we are to do. So long as we are left to volunteer we are bound to waste our capacities and to do things which are not necessary."

Eleanor's call for civilian conscription provoked a violent outcry, directed to the idea of conscripting women. "This drive to Hitlerize women sets aside the civil and industrial gains of women won after centuries of struggle," the International Woodworkers of America resolved at their national convention. It "breaks down the American home and traditional family life, robs us of the power to safeguard the health and direct upbringing of our children." The press, assuming Eleanor was testing the wind for the administration, went after the plan with a vengeance. "If Mrs. Roosevelt's 'draft us all' plan becomes part of the law," Hugh Johnson wrote in the *New York World Telegram*, "we shall have here a complete Nazi pattern of forced labor."

When the president was asked about his wife's remarks, he noted pointedly that he had not participated in the conference she mentioned. What is more, he did not agree that civilian conscription was necessary. Wary of having the government assume too much power over something as sacred as man's right to a job, he chose instead to rely on indirect persuasion— giving draft deferments to skilled labor in war plants, giving the war industry first call on workers registered with the Employment Service, providing carrots and sticks for peacetime plants to convert to war production. Though admitting the possibility that this less centralized approach might not be sufficient, he wished to move one step at a time, trusting that democracy and momentum would carry the country where it needed to go.

The difference between Eleanor's call for conscription and Franklin's reliance on democratic incentives was deep, and signaled their incompatibility of outlook. The president was temperamentally opposed to the imposition of compulsory discipline upon the rich variety of human relations; Eleanor feared that, in the absence of imposed order and discipline, confusion would result. The confusion Eleanor feared, Roosevelt saw as the necessary price for democracy.

Indeed, the great voluntary migration that would irrevocably alter the face of American society had already begun. Since 1940, more than seven million Americans had moved across county and state lines in search of employment in the burgeoning war-production centers. By the end of the war, more than fifteen million civilians would have moved to different counties. The population patterns of the country would be permanently changed.

The greatest shift was from east to west, as millions of people, drawn by the shipyards and the aircraft plants on the West Coast, flocked to California, Oregon, and Washington. More than half the wartime shipbuilding and almost half the manufacture of airplanes were centered in these three coastal states, whose population would increase by over 34 percent during the war. "It wouldn't take any imagination at all," one migrant to the West Coast observed, "to think that you were going West on a covered wagon and were a pioneer again." California alone saw an enormous increase, of more than two million people. Here, journalist Richard Lingeman perceptively notes, "was the real gold rush in California's colorful history."

A second tide was carrying some six million whites and blacks from the country to the city and from the South to the North. In 1940, according to economists, there were far too many people on the nation's farms to allow a decent living for all. As the war drained the surplus to the cities—to Mobile and Charleston in the South, and Detroit and Chicago in the North —the agricultural depression of the thirties would finally be broken, and the profits of the farmers who remained on the land would reach record highs.

Though the mass exodus of blacks from the South to the North would create severe social problems in Northern cities, "by and large," economist Harold Vatter concludes, "and despite the hard, insecure, impoverished, and discriminating conditions of ghetto life the migration brought material improvement." Economist John Kenneth Galbraith agrees. "Before the war," he points out, "there were 1,466,701 black farm workers in the rural labor force of the Old Confederacy, all, virtually without exception, exceedingly poor. In 1970, there were 115,303."

The bustling movement of so many Americans was a tremendous relief to Roosevelt, coming as it did after the paralysis of the Depression years, when few people had either the psychic or the economic resources to get up and go. The great migrations confirmed his belief: if Americans were given opportunity, they would rise to the challenge.

CHAPTER 13

"WHAT CAN WE
DO TO HELP?"

Although public concerns dominated the thoughts and activities of the president and the first lady in the early months of 1942, the Roosevelt White House, where family and friends lived and worked in unusually close quarters, was also the site of the irrepressible renewal of love and desire. In the spring, Missy LeHand returned to her old room on the third floor in the hope of reclaiming her place in the president's heart; Harry Hopkins fell in love with socialite Louise Macy; Princess Martha visited the president again and again; Eleanor seemed obsessed by her relationship with Joe Lash; and the president, as always, seemed to be removed from everybody, in spite of his ever-tolerant, ever-cheerful manner.

In the second week of March, the president had Missy brought from Warm Springs to Washington. The hours she had put in with her therapists were beginning to pay off. Her right leg had improved so that she was able to walk with the use of a brace much like the one the president used. Her arm had not come back, however, nor had her throat condition much improved. Though she understood everything that was said to her, her speech remained almost impossible to understand. Still, there was hope that these faculties would eventually come back, and the doctors had decided that her recovery would be speeded up if she returned to the White House.

Missy reached the familiar gates shortly before 10 a.m. on March 18, and was taken immediately to her third-floor room, where Lillian Parks helped her unpack. Miss Parks recalls that Missy was depressed by the blackout curtains in her windows. White liners were fitted into the curtains so that she would not have to look at black windows.

While Missy was getting settled, the president arrived at the door to welcome her back. He stayed for ten minutes only; he was scheduled to see Admiral King in his office at eleven-fifteen. It was characteristic of Roosevelt to avoid conversation with a string of stories, but, no matter how much he talked, he could not help noticing the deep silences, the sudden shifts of expression, the dark and melancholy eyes. It must have been a somewhat strained meeting, more like a verification of the unbridgeable distance between them than a happy reunion.

For her part, nothing in the world mattered more to Missy than the understanding she had shared with the president. After four months apart, there was undoubtedly comfort in the simple sight of the familiar Roosevelt smile. During the last ten months, she had come to accept some of the inroads that her devastating stroke had made. But now, in the presence of the man she loved, her spirit seemed to gird itself for a renewed attempt to conquer her illness.

Missy's reappearance produced anxious moments for Grace Tully. Tully had replaced Missy as the number-one secretary, working directly with the president on much the same level of competence and reliability. Although she never enjoyed the intimacy, playfulness, and absolute trust Missy had, she had grown accustomed to her new and powerful position. At the same time, Missy was her close friend, and she felt she should involve Missy in the work of the White House as much as she possibly could. Knowing that Missy could read, for instance, Grace brought her the daily decoded messages from the State Department that described what was going on around the world. "I wanted her to feel that she was keeping up with things," Tully said.

The president provided nurses round the clock. They brought Missy her breakfast, wheeled her onto the sun porch for lunch, and kept her company at night. Now and then, Roosevelt would look in on her, but as the weeks went by, even these brief visits became less and less frequent. One night, the story is told, Missy eluded her nurse and made her way, with great difficulty, to the second floor. The door to the president's study was slightly ajar; inside, she saw Franklin laughing and smiling with Princess Martha. Just then, the nurse caught up with her patient and led her back to her room, where for several hours Missy wept.

As the weeks went by, Missy's anxiety increased. To be back in the White House, aware of the president's comings and goings but unable to participate in any real work, proved intolerable. She spent her days waiting for his visits, drifting about the White House like a wandering star in the president's constellation. "She felt there was nothing for her to do," Tully said; "she was getting depressed." Sometimes she had periods of such blackness, Lillian Parks recalled, that she seemed almost bent on destroying herself. At one point, she tried to set herself on fire.

The decision was made, with Missy's concurrence, to send her to Somerville, Massachusetts, to live with her sister, Ann Rochon. Perhaps there, in the shade of the old house on Orchard Street, she could better continue her recuperation. At seven o'clock on Saturday night, May 16, the president stopped by Missy's apartment to say goodbye. He stayed for less than ten minutes. In his study, Princess Martha and Harry Hopkins were waiting. The cocktail hour had begun, to be followed by dinner for three. At the stroke of ten, while the president was still relaxing over coffee with Martha and Harry, the car arrived to return Missy to the Somerville house she had left behind two decades earlier. She would never again return to the White House.

In Washington, Missy LeHand's absence from the president's inner circle was frequently lamented. At a dinner one night at the Rosenmans', Justice Felix Frankfurter noted, the talk turned to the "extraordinarily beneficent role" that Missy had played because of her "remarkable judgment, disinterestedness and pertinacity." Rosenman and Frankfurter agreed that her stroke was "a calamity of world dimensions." Missy, Rosenman said, was "one of the very, very few people who was not a yes-man, who crossed the President in the sense that she told him not what she knew to be his view or what he wanted to hear, but what were, in fact, her true views and convictions."

• • •

Roosevelt absorbed an additional loss that spring when he bade farewell to his mother's house on East 65th Street. The old house held many memories. It was here that he and Eleanor had come to live in the early years of their marriage; here that he had stayed during the first years of his recovery from polio; here that he had visited his mother for nearly four decades. When moving day arrived, Roosevelt drove to New York to go through the house one last time. "Knowing how deeply sentimental the President is," William Hassett recorded, "I felt that his heart was full as he separated himself from a place that held so many associations of life and birth and death, of joy and sorrow." Eleanor's memories of the place were far less positive than Franklin's, but she, too, felt a tug in her heart as she walked through the rooms, crowded with barrels and boxes, for the last time. "Many human emotions have been recorded by many people within the walls of these rooms," she wrote, "and if walls could talk, an interesting book might be written."

Earlier in the spring, Eleanor had found a new apartment at 29 Washington Square, which she intended to occupy whenever she was in New York. Only weeks before Sara died, she had given up her previous Greenwich Village apartment so that she could spend more time with her ailing mother-in-law at East 65th Street. Now that Sara was dead and the twin houses sold, she was free to purchase an apartment of her own.

The Washington Square apartment consisted of seven rooms—a high-ceilinged living room with a wood-burning fireplace and built-in bookcases beneath two windows facing the park's trees and lawns, a dining room, kitchen, three bedrooms, including a master bedroom with a connecting dressing room, a maid's room, and three baths. For Eleanor, who regularly spent a day or two a week in the city, it was a godsend to have a place of her own. "When I am in New York City," she once said, "I feel that I am an unofficial person leading a private life." Yet, even as she valued her independence, she had a private elevator installed just in case the president should ever want to visit. "At last I am settled here," she wrote her aunt Maude Gray on May 9. "It is a nice apartment with a lovely view and perfectly suited to Franklin if he ever comes!"

•   •   •

"Just a week from tonight you will be out of reach & starting on this new life that I dread so much for you," Eleanor wrote Joe Lash on April 6, as he was about to be inducted into the army. "A little bit of my heart seems to be with you always Joe. You'll carry it round wherever you go & in its place the thought of you will be with me wherever I go.... Sometimes I think if we have *chosen* to love someone, we love them even more than we do the children of our bodies...." Though she loved her own boys deeply, she explained, she had never enjoyed the secure relationship with them that she had with him. "With you I have that feeling of understanding & companionship. Now & then I have moments of that with the boys but it is not the same...."

On April 7, Eleanor threw a large going-away party for Lash at the Hotel Brevoort in New York. "It was a curious affair," Joe's friend Lewis Feuer recalled. "Suddenly a telegram arrived signed by ER saying there'd be a big dinner for Joe at this classy hotel. As the dishes were served, an orchestra of seven or eight came over and serenaded Joe. The dishes were ornate. We were at war. I thought it was in terrible taste. All this sentimentality about Joe going into the service."

On the third floor of the White House, Eleanor set aside a room for Lash to use whenever he was on leave. On her desk she placed an enlarged photo of Lash. "I want to be able to look at you all the time," she explained. In addition, Eleanor told Joe to call her collect at the White House whenever the president was away at Hyde Park, and to "know that her love was there for him always. No other engagement can't be given up, if there is a chance to see you!"

Before he left for his training camp in Miami, Lash gave Eleanor a miniature good-luck horseshoe, which she put on her chain "so it would be always with me as I like having something from you very near me always." Traveling on a train with a bunch of soldiers, she imagined for a moment she had seen his face. "Wouldn't it be fun sometime if you were in the crowd when I looked up?" In the White House, Eleanor waited anxiously for his letters and calls. "Your telegram came," she happily noted. "I could have kissed the telegram. I was so glad to have word from you."

Eleanor was not the central person in Joe's life that spring, however. For more than a year, he had been involved with a fellow worker at the International Student Service, Trude Pratt. The situation was complicated, since Trude was still married to Eliot Pratt, a wealthy man who was threatening to keep the children if she divorced him. During these months, Eleanor was close to Trude as well; indeed, she seemed to fall into the role of match-maker, much as she had done with her daughter, Anna, and John Boettiger in the heady days of their illicit romance, before their divorces were final. For hours on end, she counseled both Joe and Trude, offering advice, love, and support, providing safe cover for their meetings.

"Of one thing I am sure . . . ," she wrote Lash, perhaps reflecting her own experience, "don't accept a compromise. Trude must be all yours, otherwise you will never be happy.

"Someday I'll tell you why I'm sure that is so, but just now no corroborating history is of interest to you & all the contribution I can think of which is helpful, is to beg you not to accept ½ a loaf of love."

• • •

Perhaps only with Lorena Hickok had Eleanor ever felt the sense of being loved exclusively. In every one of her other relationships, it seemed, she was the third person in the triangle: the outsider looking in at her husband's intense relationship with his mother; the outsider looking in at the love between Esther Lape and Elizabeth Read, between Nancy Cook and Marion Dickerman, between Anna Roosevelt and John Boettiger, between Joe Lash and Trude Pratt, between Franklin and Missy and Martha and Lucy.

It was now more than a year since Hick had moved into the White House, and Eleanor remained intensely loyal to her old friend. "Our friend Hick is still here," Tommy complained to Esther Lape. "The ushers call her 'the enduring guest.'" "She can't pay rent and her income tax and her dentist bill," Tommy chided, "so she has cut out paying rent! . . . Elizabeth will be interested to know that one night when the Hickok was rather mellow and ranting on about how she adored Mrs. Roosevelt etc., etc. she said that if anything happened to her I was delegated to destroy all the letters which Mrs. R. had written her. I accepted the assignment but I did not add that I had already made up my mind on that score."

Whenever Eleanor was free for breakfast, she invited Hick to join her, in the West Hall in winter, on the South Veranda in summer. The two old friends would talk until breakfast was served, and then Eleanor would retire behind *The New York Times,* reading aloud an item here or there. Then, when Hick got home from her work at the Democratic National Committee, usually around 10:30 or 11 p.m., she would stop in Eleanor's sitting room so they could talk a bit while Eleanor was buried in mail. Sometimes, Hick recalled, "if she was out when I came in, she would come into my room and sit on the foot of my bed and talk for a little while." Though the intense feeling had cooled, there remained a strong bond between them; they enjoyed one another's company.

The same spring that Eleanor lost Joe Lash to the army, Hick became involved with Marion Janet Harron. Marion was ten years younger than Hick, a Phi Beta Kappa graduate from the University of California, a judge in the U.S. Tax Court. In the months that followed, her presence at the White House was so frequent that the guards at the gate no longer bothered to ask for her identification.

Eleanor experienced both relief and sorrow as she watched Hick fall in love with another woman. Knowing that her friend was happy lessened her guilt about the pain she had caused when she no longer needed Hick as Hick needed her. Yet, at the same time, there had undoubtedly remained a secret pleasure in knowing how passionately Hick loved her. And now that love had turned to someone else.

•　•　•

The war would be won, the president said again and again that spring, only if the incalculable force of American democracy could be let loose, if people scattered throughout the land came to feel that their individual skills and talents were an essential part of the common endeavor. A host of separate images prevailed: workers in aircraft factories assembling planes; welders at dockyards building ships; miners in West Virginia digging coal; farmers in Kansas planting crops; pilots at airfields learning to fly; sailors in the Atlantic dodging German submarines; soldiers in the Pacific fighting the Japanese. Roosevelt understood that the challenge was to find a way of binding these men and women together in the shared enterprise of total war.

To this end, he submitted to Congress in late April a seven-point economic program, including heavier taxes, war bonds, wage and price controls, and comprehensive rationing—designed to ensure, as he put it, "an equality of sacrifice." Explaining the program to the people in his second wartime fireside chat, he said that, though not everyone could have the privilege of "fighting our enemies in distant parts of the world," or "working in a munitions factory or a shipyard," there is "one front and one battle where everyone in the United States—every man, woman and child—is in action. . . . That front is right here at home, in our daily tasks.

"To build the factory, to buy the materials, to pay the labor, to provide the transportation, to equip and feed and house the soldiers and sailors and marines, and do all the thousands of things necessary in a war—all cost a lot of money, more money than has ever been spent by any nation at any time in the long history of the world." When the government spends such unprecedented sums, he explained, the money goes into the bank accounts of the people. "You do no have to be a professor of math or economics to see that if people with plenty of cash start bidding against each other for scarce goods, the price of these goods goes up." For that reason, a system of rationing and price control was needed. Henceforth, by the action of what came to be known as the "General Maximum Price Regulation," all prices would be effectively fixed for the duration of the war. The ceiling price of each item would be the highest price charged for that item in March 1942.

To bolster his call for shared sacrifice, he told the story of Captain Hewitt Wheless, a B-17 pilot who came from a small town in Texas with a population of 2,375. Wheless had just been awarded the Distinguished Service Cross for downing seven Japanese planes in a single mission that pitted him against eighteen Japanese zeros. During the lopsided attack, one engine on the American bomber was shut down, one gas tank was hit, the oxygen system was entirely destroyed, the radio operator was killed, the gunner was crippled, and the engineer's right hand was shot off. Still, the fight continued until the Japanese squadron ran out of gas and turned away. With both engines now gone and the plane practically out of control, the B-17 returned to its base and made an emergency landing. "As we sit here at home contemplating our own duties," he concluded, "let us think and think hard of the example which is being set for us by our fighting men."

Ten days later, Captain Wheless stood before a cheering crowd of eighteen thousand Boeing employees in the Seattle plant where the B-17 was produced. For an entire hour, not one rivet gun sounded; the deep boom of the drop hammer was stilled. It was the first time in months that work in the plant had come to a stop, as men in overalls and women in slacks heard a replay of the president's speech over the loudspeaker. When Wheless stepped to the microphone, he made it clear that he owed his life to the B-17, "the Queen of the Sky," and to the workers standing before him. "The men operating the planes don't want all the credit," he told the enthusiastic crowd. "I want to thank you for myself and a lot of other pilots who more or less owe their lives to your design and workmanship. Continue the good work and together we can't lose."

• • •

The continuing need to sustain national morale against the backdrop of military reverses in the Far East led Roosevelt that April to endorse a risky raid on Tokyo by a force of sixteen B-25s under the leadership of Lieutenant Colonel James H. Doolittle. Immediately after Pearl Harbor, the president had told his military chiefs that, despite the distances involved, a way had to be found to carry out a retaliatory raid on Japan. A much-needed lift to American spirits would be achieved, Roosevelt calculated, if a direct blow could be struck at the heart of Japan. Plans were drawn to launch a raid from a ship positioned some six hundred miles from the coast of Japan. It would be the first time heavily loaded bombers had ever taken off from a navy carrier. The question was whether the deck of the largest carrier was large enough to propel a fleet of B-25s.

On April 18, the day of the raid, the sea was rough. Doolittle was the first to take off. As he started his engines, heavy waves broke over the deck, sending cascades of spray along the sides of his twin-engine plane. If the plane was unable to get airborne, it would drop off the deck and be sliced in half by the sharp edge of the bow. At the far end of the carrier, carefully gauging the rise and fall of the deck, the flight-deck officer waved his checkered flag as a signal for takeoff to begin. Doolittle pushed his throttles forward, and the bomber waddled slowly down the deck. Standing nearby, a navy pilot shouted that the plane wasn't going to make it. But the wheels came off the deck just in time, and the plane took off without a hitch. Within an hour, the remaining fifteen planes were also in the air.

Doolittle and his squadron reached Tokyo shortly after noon; they dropped their bombs and then flew on to China. Though the physical damage from the raid was comparatively light, the psychological damage was enormous. The Japanese government had promised the people of Japan that their homeland would never be attacked. The Doolittle raid had shown that the empire was not invulnerable after all. When the news of the raid was broadcast throughout the world, everyone wanted to know where the planes had come from. Delighting in the mystery, Roosevelt smiled broadly. "They came from a secret base in Shangri-la," he said, referring to the mythical land in James Hilton's *Lost Horizon.*

It was the first good news from the Pacific theater. Telegrams of support flooded the White House. "I hope my two boys in the army have a similar opportunity," Mrs. T. J. Dykema of Pittsburgh wrote. "Give us more Doolittles and we will take our chances in the west," James Jordon of Oregon telegraphed. Even Stimson, who had been doubtful about this "pet project" of the president's, agreed the daring raid had had "a very good psychological effect in the country both here and abroad."

Moreover, through a series of strange twists and turns, the Doolittle raid led to the Battle of Midway. As the American bombs fell on Japanese soil, Admiral Isoroku Yamamoto, the commander-in-chief of the Japanese Combined Fleet, who had planned the attack of Pearl Harbor, strengthened his resolve to prevent any future penetration of Japan's perimeter. At his insistence, the decision was made to send an overwhelming force of ten battleships, four aircraft carriers, and seventy destroyers, 185 ships in all, to seize Midway Island, the farthest outpost of the Hawaiian chain.

Had the Japanese fleet been able to catch the much smaller American forces unawares, there is little doubt that Yamamoto would have achieved his aim. But because the navy had broken the Japanese code, Pacific Fleet Commander Admiral Chester Nimitz had an incalculable advantage, allowing him to concentrate his planes, carriers, and men at precisely the right points, waiting to pounce at precisely the right time. Nimitz launched his strike on June 4, 1942, just before the Japanese fleet reached Midway. Catching Yamamoto totally by surprise, the attack destroyed all four Japanese carriers, one heavy cruiser, three battleships, and 372 aircraft; thirty-five hundred Japanese sailors were killed.

The battle at Midway, Admiral King later observed, was a major turning point, "the first decisive defeat suffered by the Japanese Navy in 350 years. It put an end to the long period of Japanese offensive action and restored the balance of naval power in the Pacific." But victory at Midway was offset at Corregidor, where, on May 6, despite a valiant effort to hold out, American troops had been forced to surrender. "With broken heart and head bowed in sadness but not in shame," General Jonathan Wainwright wired the president, "I go to meet the Japanese commander."

The situation looked bleak on the Russian front as well. With the coming of spring, the Germans had launched a vast new offensive to defeat the Red Army. Refreshed and resupplied, the German army was pushing fast toward Leningrad in the north and Rostov and Stalingrad in the south. To ease the pressure, Stalin was demanding a second front in France; only simultaneous offensives in the East and the West, he argued, could vanquish Hitler.

By spring, officials in both Washington and London were engaged in daily discussions over the feasibility of a second front. That a massive concentrated force in Western Europe would be necessary to defeat Hitler was axiomatic to both General Marshall and the new War Plans Division chief, General Eisenhower. For weeks, with the strong backing of Henry Stimson, Marshall and Eisenhower had been arguing against a piecemeal scattering of Allied forces. "We've got to go to Europe and fight," Eisenhower urged, "and we've got to quit wasting resources all over the world—and still worse —wasting time. If we're going to keep Russia in, save the Middle East, India and Burma; we've got to begin slugging with air at West Europe; to be followed by a land attack as soon as possible."

Preliminary plans for a cross-Channel attack were presented to the president at the end of March. The plans called for a massive assault across the Channel by April 1943 (Operation Bolero). A more limited emergency operation (Operation Sledgehammer) was designed for the fall of 1942, to be employed if the Red Army was at the point of imminent collapse. Stimson feared that the president lacked "the hardness of heart" to commit himself wholly to this concentrated effort, which required resisting requests for troops in other theaters of the war. "The same qualities which endear him to his own countrymen," Stimson mused, "militate against the firmness of his execution at a time like this." Marshall, too, was concerned about the president's inability to reject appeals for other good purposes; he had a habit, Marshall observed, "his cigarette-holder gesture," of tossing out new operations in response to new information from troubled areas.

But when Marshall completed his presentation, the president not only endorsed the cross-Channel plan, but decided to send Marshall and Hopkins to London to secure Churchill's agreement. As Hopkins packed his bags, Roosevelt arranged for a naval doctor to accompany him to London to protect him from overexertion, and directed Marshall "to put Hopkins to bed and keep him there under 24-hour guard by army or marine corps" while he got some rest.

Churchill's wife, Clementine, was delighted to see Hopkins once again.

"Oh how glad I am that you are back once more," she told him, "to encourage, to cheer, to charm us. You can't think what a difference it makes to Winston. He is carrying a very heavy load and I can't bear his dear round face not to look cheerful and cherubic in the mornings, as up to now it has always done. What with Singapore and India . . . we are indeed walking through the Valley of Humiliation."

The discussions with Churchill went surprisingly well. For months, Churchill had been arguing against an all-out attack on Hitler's Europe, preferring a series of peripheral operations, in the Mediterranean, the Middle East, and North Africa. But now, as he listened to Marshall and Hopkins, Churchill knew that their arguments for a second front carried the weight of the president's convictions. "What Harry and George Marshall will tell you all about has my heart and mind in it," Roosevelt had wired Churchill. Before the first day's discussions were over, Hopkins had wired an optimistic report to Roosevelt. Churchill's conciliatory mood puzzled Canada's MacKenzie King. "It was not like him to agree, almost as it were, without a fight," King noted. "He may have decided that the time has not yet come to take the field as an out and out opponent of a second front."

Emboldened by Churchill's apparent support for the cross-Channel attack, Roosevelt cabled Stalin to ask if Foreign Minister Vyacheslav Molotov could come to Washington to discuss Allied plans for a second front to relieve the situation in Russia. A delighted Stalin replied that Molotov would come to Washington in three weeks.

While Hopkins was in London, Churchill received a report that Louis Johnson, Roosevelt's emissary to India, was trying, with Roosevelt's knowledge, to negotiate with Gandhi's Congress Party a military agreement that would commit the nationalist forces to join with British defenders to stop Japan's westward advance. In return, the nationalists were asking for some measure of immediate self-government to motivate the Indian people to feel they were defending their own freedom. On hearing the news, Churchill was furious. India was Britain's colony, and no one, not even his great friend Franklin Roosevelt, was going to tell Britain how to resolve the tangled situation. For two hours, Hopkins reported, Churchill walked around the room issuing a string of invectives.

At 3 a.m., long past the time when he was supposed to be in bed, Hopkins was still listening to Churchill. Churchill said that he would be ready to resign on the issue, but that if he did the War Cabinet would simply continue his policy. He then wrote to Roosevelt: "Anything like a serious difference between you and me would break my heart, and would surely deeply injure both our countries at the height of this terrible struggle." Once Roosevelt saw that pressing Churchill on India would do serious damage to Anglo-American relations, he dropped his efforts.

Molotov arrived at the White House on Friday afternoon, May 29. Since Eleanor was in West Virginia for a commencement at the school at Arthurdale, a stag dinner was prepared that evening for Molotov, Roosevelt, and

Hopkins. Two interpreters were also present. To the eyes of the president's butler, Alonzo Fields, Molotov had "an owlish, wise look" on his face, accentuated by his chubby cheeks, his stubby mustache, and his round glasses. On occasion, Fields noted, "his eyes would dart around with the glint of a fox waiting to spring on his prey." The need for continuous translation made conversation difficult, frustrating Roosevelt's desire to get to know Molotov. Moreover, whenever the conversation seemed about to open up, Molotov brought it back to the second front, insistent on securing a definite commitment from the Americans for the cross-Channel attack. So unswerving did Molotov prove, content to sit in his chair for hours on end sticking to his argument, that Roosevelt later nicknamed him "Stone Ass."

During the entire Molotov visit, one State Department official observed, the president and his advisers were "head-down in their desire to make the Soviets happy." Before Molotov arrived, Roosevelt had sent a memo to his Joint Chiefs, declaring that "at the present time, our principal objective is to help Russia. It must be constantly reiterated that Russian armies are killing more Germans and destroying more Axis material than all the 25 united nations put together."

"The fact that the Russians were carrying so heavy a load led to a guilt complex in our relations," Russian envoy Charles Bohlen observed. The guilt increased with the dark picture Molotov painted of the fighting on the Eastern front; in recent weeks, the Russians had suffered devastating defeats at Kharkov and Kerch, and it was clear that Sevastopol could not hold out much longer. The German army was now only eighty miles from Moscow.

Desiring to placate the courageous Russians, who were engaged every hour of every day with Hitler's finest troops, while American and British troops were fighting only on the periphery, Roosevelt asked Marshall, in Molotov's presence, whether "developments were clear enough so that we could say to Mr. Stalin that we were preparing a second front." When Marshall said yes, Roosevelt told Molotov to tell Stalin that "we expect the formation of a second front this year." Though Roosevelt's pledge did not specify when or where the second front would take place, Molotov was jubilant. The ice was broken. The president felt he was actually getting chummy with his Russian visitor.

Molotov was put up in the family quarters, in the room Churchill had occupied across the hall from Hopkins' room. Though Eleanor returned to the White House too late to join the Molotov party for dinner, she conversed with Molotov in her sitting room before going to bed. Earlier in the evening, Molotov had told Hopkins that he wanted to meet Mrs. Roosevelt, and though it was past midnight, Hopkins had brought him to Eleanor's room. Eleanor later remarked that she liked him immediately. She felt he was "an open, warm sort of person." They talked about women in Russia.

The following day, as Molotov greeted members of a Russian plane crew, Eleanor joined Franklin for a review of the Memorial Day parade. As the first soldiers passed, Roosevelt applauded with enthusiasm. Eleanor was glad to see the new types of equipment on exhibit, but in contrast to her husband, who enjoyed the spectacle immensely, she found it difficult to forget that killing was the object of the lavish weapons on display. Indeed, earlier in the month, she had taken public issue with her husband when he called for a series of parades to accompany different groups of draftees to camp. "American boys on their way to war don't love a parade," she had countered. "There's no glamour to this war."

As reports of Roosevelt's meeting with Molotov reached London, along with the implied promise of a "sacrificial landing" in 1942 if the Russians faced imminent collapse, Churchill decided to fly to the United States immediately. For, just as MacKenzie King had suspected, beneath his apparent support for a second front when he talked to Hopkins and Marshall in London, Churchill remained adamantly opposed to the idea of a direct assault on the Continent. Unable to fight off the ghosts of the Somme, where the British had lost sixty thousand men in a single day, he was determined "to go round the end rather than through the center." As he looked around him in the House of Commons, he once told special envoy Averell Harriman, "he could not help but think of all the faces that were not there," the faces of men destined to lead Britain who had never returned from the trenches. To order yet another direct assault on the Continent seemed to Churchill equivalent to consigning a new generation to death on the battlefield.

Churchill arrived at Bolling Field in Washington on June 18, and then flew to Hyde Park the next morning. "The President was on the local air-field," Churchill recalled in his memoirs, "and saw us make the roughest bump landing I have experienced. He welcomed me with great cordiality, and, driving the car himself, took me to the majestic bluffs over the Hudson River on which Hyde Park . . . stands."

For more than an hour, they drove together around the estate. With boyish enthusiasm, Roosevelt jerked the car forward and backward in an attempt to elude the Secret Service. "I confess," Churchill later admitted, "that when on several occasions the car poised and backed on the grass verges of the precipices over the Hudson I hoped the mechanical devices and brakes would show no defects." To reassure Churchill, Roosevelt invited him to "feel his biceps, saying that a famous prize-fighter had envied them." Much to Churchill's relief, the car finally came to a stop at the round drive-way in front of the president's house. Lunch was served, and then the two leaders ensconced themselves in Roosevelt's study for a long talk before taking tea at the house of his cousin Laura Delano and dinner at the Big House.

In Washington, Stimson was nervous. "I can't help feeling a little bit uneasy about the influence of the Prime Minister on him at this time. The trouble is WC and FDR are too much alike in their strong points and in their weak points. They are both penetrating in their thoughts but they lack the steadiness of balance that has got to go along with warfare." Stimson was right to worry. Churchill lost no time in expressing his anxiety about the potential bloodbath that a direct assault on the Continent would bring. The president listened carefully, though he stood firm on the need for some action to reduce the pressure on the Russians.

Churchill awakened early Saturday morning. "He surely is an informal house guest," Hassett noted. "He was out on the lawn barefoot and later was seen crossing the passage to Hopkins' room, still barefoot. The President calls him Winston. . . . The Boss has a knack for entertaining guests with a minimum of strain and fussiness both to him and to them. He always pursues the even tenor of his ways whether in the White House, on the train or here at Hyde Park. Never changes his routine; meets his guests at mealtime or when mutually convenient. Otherwise they and he are free to do as they please. If he did it differently, this steady stream of visitors would wear him to a frazzle."

In the morning, the president took the prime minister on a second tour of the estate, stopping first at the library and then at his beloved Top Cottage. After lunch, they settled down to talk in Roosevelt's small study on the ground floor. It was at this time, with Hopkins seated in the corner, that Churchill brought up the subject of "Tube Alloys," the English code name for the project to create an atomic bomb. "We knew what efforts the Germans were making to produce supplies of 'heavy water,' " Churchill recalled, "a sinister term, eerie, unnatural, which began to creep into our secret papers. What if the enemy should get an atomic bomb before we did! . . . I strongly urged that we should at once pool all our information, work together on equal terms, and share the results, if any, equally between us."

There was ample reason for concern. Three months earlier, German Propaganda Minister Joseph Goebbels had received an optimistic report about the latest developments in German science. "Research in the realm of atomic destruction," he recorded in his diary, "has now proceeded to a point where its results may possibly be made use of in the conduct of this war. Tremendous destruction, it is claimed, can be wrought with a minimum of effort. . . . Modern technique places in the hands of human beings means of destruction that are simply incredible. German science is at its peak in this matter. It is essential that we be ahead of everybody, for whoever introduces a revolutionary novelty into this war has the greater chance of winning it."

It was now nearly three years since the president's first discussion with economist and biologist Alexander Sachs about atomic developments. At that momentous meeting in October 1939, Sachs had delivered to the president a letter from Albert Einstein in which the celebrated physicist reported that scientists in Berlin had achieved the fission of uranium atoms and the release of colossal amounts of energy. On the basis of additional work done by Italian émigré Enrico Fermi and Hungarian physicist Leo Szilard, it was possible, Einstein predicted, to set up a nuclear chain reaction which could be harnessed into bombs so powerful that they could blow up entire ports. Though Roosevelt found the discussion interesting, he seemed to hesitate about committing government funds to such speculative research. But after Sachs reminded him of Napoleon's rejection of Fulton when the inventor tried to interest him in the idea of a steamship, Roosevelt agreed to move forward. "Alex, what you are after is to see that the Nazis don't blow us up," Roosevelt said. "This requires action."

Little progress had been made until after the fall of France, when substantial government funds were finally committed to atomic research. British scientists were also experimenting with atomic weaponry, Churchill told Roosevelt, but, with Britain under severe bombing, it was too risky to continue the research on the scale that was necessary. Churchill was delighted when the president said that the United States would assume the major responsibility for the development of the atomic bomb. Two months later, the Manhattan Project, directed by army engineer General Leslie Groves, was launched. By 1945, more than 120,000 people would be employed on the search for an atomic bomb, at a cost of $2 billion.

Atomic research would produce the most dramatic scientific development of the war, but the combined efforts of science, industry, and government would lead to a host of groundbreaking discoveries, including the large-scale production of penicillin to combat infections, the development of plasma, the use of synthetic drugs like Atabrine to substitute for scarce quinine, improved radar, proximity fuses for mines, and the jet engine.

•   •   •

After dinner at the Big House, where they were joined by Averell Harriman, the president and Churchill left for Highland Station to catch the overnight train to Washington. At the White House, Churchill was installed in the Rose Suite, in the family quarters. "There was something so intimate in their friendship," Churchill's aide Lord Ismay noted. "They used to stroll in and out of each other's rooms in the White House, as two subalterns occupying adjacent quarters might have done. Both of them had the spirit of eternal youth."

After an hour's respite for breakfast and the morning papers, Churchill joined the president and Hopkins in Roosevelt's study. They had just settled down when a secretary handed the president a telegram. It contained the devastating news that on June 21 the British garrison at Tobruk in Libya had surrendered to the Germans, with twenty-five thousand British soldiers taken prisoner. The president handed the telegram to Churchill without a word. "It was a bitter moment," Churchill conceded. For thirty-three weeks, Tobruk had withstood the German siege; now a garrison of twenty-five thousand had laid down their arms to perhaps one-half that number of Germans. "Defeat is one thing," Churchill wrote; "disgrace is another."

There was a moment of silence, and then Roosevelt turned to Churchill. "What can we do to help?" "Give us as many Sherman tanks as you can spare, and ship them to the Middle East as quickly as possible," Churchill replied. The president sent for General Marshall, and within days three hundred tanks and one hundred self-propelled guns were on their way to the Eighth Army in Alexandria. When Eleanor joined her husband and the prime minister at lunch, she was amazed at the spirits of the two men. Though they were obviously stricken by the news, their first reaction was to figure out what could be done. "To neither of those men," she marveled, "was there such a thing as not being able to meet a new situation. I never heard either of them say that ultimately we would not win the war. This attitude was contagious, and no one around either of them would ever have dared to say, 'I'm afraid.' "

In later years, Churchill admitted that the fall of Tobruk was "one of the heaviest blows" he could recall during the war. Not only was the military loss enormous, but the humiliating circumstances of the surrender had substantially damaged the reputation of the British army. Later that night, Lord Moran found him pacing his room, repeating over and over that Tobruk had fallen, crossing and recrossing the room with quick strides, a glowering look on his face. "What matters is that it should happen while I am here," he said. "I am ashamed. I cannot understand why Tobruk gave in. More than 30,000 of our men put their hands up. If they won't fight . . ." He stopped abruptly, fell into a chair, and seemed to pull himself together, recounting for Moran the generosity of the president's immediate response: "What can we do to help?"

The fall of Tobruk increased the importance of the Mediterranean theater in Churchill's mind and cemented his opposition to a cross-Channel attack in 1942. Though Marshall and Stimson continued to press their case, Roosevelt was unwilling to go ahead without the agreement of his friend and partner. The discussion turned instead to a project Roosevelt had been mulling over for weeks as an alternative to the attack on the Continent—an invasion of French North Africa. The smaller-scale invasion would pull German troops from the Eastern front, while at the same time helping to shore up the British position in the Middle East.

Relieved, Churchill threw his weight behind the operation, code-named Gymnast. "I am sure myself that Gymnast is by far the best chance for effective relief to the Russian front in 42," he told Roosevelt. "This has all along been in harmony with your idea. In fact it is your commanding idea. Here is the true second front in 42. Here is the safest and most fruitful stroke that can be delivered this autumn." There remained the unpleasant task of communicating the Gymnast decision to Stalin, who believed, on the basis of the fateful Molotov communiqué, that something much larger was in the works. Churchill volunteered to go to Moscow himself to break the news.

Marshall and Eisenhower remained adamant in their opposition to the president's "secret baby," as Stimson dubbed the plan to invade North Africa, in late October. To use up men and resources in a peripheral action when victory could only be won by a direct assault on the Continent seemed to their minds a fatal mistake. What is more, the operation itself seemed to them more risky than the president realized. Instead of an orderly buildup over many months, "we now had only weeks," Eisenhower wrote. "Instead of a massed attack across narrow waters, the proposed expedition would require movement across open ocean areas where enemy submarines would constitute a real menace. Our target was no longer a restricted front where we knew accurately terrain, facilities and people as they affected military operations, but the rim of a continent where no major military campaign had been conducted for centuries." Still, Roosevelt persisted in going forward, prompting Eisenhower to predict that the day the invasion order was signed would go down as "the blackest day in history."

When he issued the order, against the robust opposition of his advisers, Roosevelt was thinking not only of the negative effect on the Russians if another year were to pass without substantial action on the part of Anglo-American forces; he was also thinking of the negative effect on the American soldiers and the American people if there were no opportunity for U.S. ground troops to be brought into action against Germany in 1942. He had recently received a discouraged letter from FDR, Jr., written from an army base in Hawaii. The most depressing thing, his son had written, was the lack of action. "A lot of these guys aren't having any fun," he wrote, "just tense-ness and waiting our turn."

As the leader of a democracy, Roosevelt had to be concerned with the question of morale; the constant challenge he faced, through speeches and actions alike, was to figure out ways to sustain and strengthen the spirit of the people, without which the war could not be won. "We failed to see," George Marshall observed after the war, commenting on the army's opposition to the president's plan for North Africa, "that the leader in a democracy has to keep the people entertained. That may sound like the wrong word but it conveys the thought."

•   •   •

While Roosevelt and Churchill were together for these June meetings, Hopkins confided in them that he was engaged to be married to Louise Macy, the former Paris editor of *Harper's Bazaar,* a beautiful woman with dark hair worn in a long bob, bright-blue eyes, and a little gap between her two front teeth. She had graduated from the Madeira School in Washington, attended Smith College, and married and divorced a wealthy attorney. "In smart sets from Santa Barbara to Long Island, 'Louie' Macy is popular," *Time* reported. "She radiates good spirits, talks well, laughs easily." From the day Hopkins met her at the home of Averell and Marie Harriman, he seemed reborn emotionally and physically. "Looking better than he has for three or four years," William Hassett noted. "He's gained ten pounds," Eleanor told Anna, "and seems very perky."

There was still a great physical attractiveness in Hopkins—remarkable vitality came through his thinness and his pallor, conveying an image of a far younger, healthier man. Bill Hassett's diaries that spring are filled with references to the passion of Hopkins' romance. "Harry head over heels in love—52—and doesn't care who knows it," Hassett wrote after spending a long weekend with Harry and Louise at Hyde Park. A week later, Hassett noted that Louise had come again to Hyde Park for dinner, "to happiness of HH who languishes in love."

When Hopkins picked July for the wedding, the president suggested that the ceremony be held at the White House. Hopkins was delighted. "It is going to be done very quietly," he wrote Missy, apologizing for not having told her earlier, "and I only wish you could be here. Of all the people I know I should like to have you. When I see you I will tell you how nice she is."

To all outward appearances, the president was happy with the marriage. Louise was exactly the kind of woman he liked; she was gregarious and funny and she relished good-natured gossip. She was a gay addition to the White House "family." Still, Roosevelt must have feared that Hopkins' romance would make him less accessible for cocktails, meals, and conversation. It is unlikely that the president ever voiced these fears to his old friend. It was not his style to be open about his needs. Nor was it necessary, for Hopkins was equally impelled to make sure that his romance did not in any way undercut his friendship with Roosevelt. When the president asked him to continue living in the White House after the marriage, Hopkins never hesitated for a moment.

Plans were made, against Eleanor's better judgment, to rearrange Hopkins' suite to accommodate a wife. Eleanor's chief concern was for Harry's motherless daughter, ten-year-old Diana. "I'm worried about Harry's marriage & Diana's adjustment if they live at the White House," Eleanor admitted to Hick, "but F.D.R. & Harry seem to think it the only way out." In a letter to Esther Lape, Tommy recorded Eleanor's aggravation. "I imagine Mrs. Roosevelt told you about her reaction to the Hopkins family moving into the White House—bag and baggage," Tommy wrote. "This is with no consultation with Mrs. Roosevelt—just a statement of [Hopkins'] plans."

For more than four years, Eleanor had religiously kept the commitment she had made to Harry when his wife died that she would give Diana a home in the White House. "She did everything that you would normally do with a child as a mother," Diana gratefully recalled. "Everything—the manners, the clothes, the exposing one to literature, being sure the homework got done, the reading aloud, having the friends over, the laying on of the birthday party, the 'let your friends use my bathing suit'—and boy you should've seen some of those little 4th grade kids running around in ER's bathing suit—everything, everything except the arms around the body.

"I was a little kid," Diana went on. "I was dying for a mommy and if she had opened her arms and said, 'Come and hop on my lap,' I would've been there in a minute, hugging her around the neck." But Eleanor had told Harry at the start, Diana remembered, that she didn't want to become too close to Diana in a motherly way, because she felt that "someday he would remarry and she didn't want to step into this affection place where a new mother would come along one day and be able to fill it.''

Though Eleanor's relationship with Harry had cooled as a consequence of his absorption with the war, she knew she could count on his idealism at critical junctures. But now she feared the influence of Louise's lighter nature, her fascination with wealth and power, her delight in society. "Mrs. Roosevelt and Louise were polar opposites," Diana observed. "Mrs. Roosevelt was the most civic-minded person I have ever known. Politics and idealism controlled her life and everything she did. In contrast, Louie was absolutely apolitical. She was a more feminine, fluffy type of person. She didn't have a political cell in her body." Eleanor's fears were confirmed by the newspaper stories that accompanied Hopkins' engagement. Somewhere along the way, *Time* magazine reported, Hopkins had doffed the reformer's sackcloth and donned a sports jacket. "Hopkins is equally at home now in a relief office or at Newport, at a faculty dinner or in a rich friend's box at the races, with high minded old ladies or with glamour girls."

• • •

Nothing would prove more damaging to Eleanor and Harry's already troubled relationship than the tangled controversy surrounding Odell Waller, a young black sharecropper in Virginia who was convicted of killing his white landlord and sentenced to die at the end of June in the electric chair. Throughout his trial, Waller resolutely maintained that the killing was in self-defense. An all-white jury deliberated only twenty minutes before finding him guilty of first-degree murder. The defense argued that Waller had not received a fair trial since all the men on the jury were selected from a list of citizens who paid a yearly poll tax, a list that excluded almost without exception the poor white and the Negro sharecropper.

To Negroes across the country, Waller became a symbol of oppression, "of Negro toil in the white man's fields, of Negro fate in the white man's courts, of every black body which has swung at the end of a rope from barn or bridge." The injustice was made all the more conspicuous by comparison with a mirror-image case in the same county. R. G. Siddle, a white farmer, shot and killed an unarmed Negro sharecropper during a quarrel. Charged with murder, Siddle was acquitted by an all-white poll-paying jury in less than fifteen minutes.

As news of the Waller case spread, A. Philip Randolph formed a nationwide committee to pressure Virginia's Governor Colgate Darden to grant clemency. On June 16, a two-hour blackout was staged in Harlem; on every street, in every tavern and barbershop, the lights were turned out to protest the Waller verdict. Within a period of several weeks, seventeen thousand letters reached Darden's desk.

Eleanor became involved when Odell Waller sent her a handwritten note from his cell in the Richmond Prison: "I relize [sic] I'm a stranger to you, I have heard lots of people speak of what a nice lady you are and what I can hear is that you believe in helping the poor. . . . I was raised in Virginia on a farm. I never had a chance to make anything not even a good living. I always worked hard but I couldn't get anything out of it. I raised some wheat with a man named Oscar Davis an [sic] he took all of the wheat and I tried to get my share of it he wouldn't let me have the wheat. We got in a quarrel. And I shot him to keep him from hurting me not meaning to kill him. He carried a gun an [sic] I was afraid of him. . . . Please write to the Governor and get him to have mercy on me and allow me a chance. You will never regret it."

Moved by Waller's plea, Eleanor asked the president to intervene. Decisions on clemency were strictly the prerogative of the governor, and presidential action would be considered highly inappropriate. Roosevelt circumvented this dilemma with "a wholly personal and unofficial note" to the governor, signed by "an old friend who just happens to be President." In the note he described a similar case that had occurred when he was governor of New York. A man had shot his neighbor in the midst of an argument after the neighbor advanced against him in a threatening way. Though the jury convicted him of murder in the first degree, Roosevelt had the sentence commuted to life imprisonment and was always glad he had done so.

The president sent a copy of this letter to Eleanor with a covering note which reflected a poignant yearning for praise from his toughest critic. "Dearest Babs. Didn't I do good? Aren't you proud?" Eleanor was thrilled. "It's a grand letter. Thanks." she replied.

Despite the president's letter, Governor Darden decided, after ten hours of testimony at a clemency hearing, to refuse commutation. In desperation, Randolph and Walter White journeyed to Washington the day before the execution to see the president, unaware of the personal letter the president had already sent Governor Darden.

When Randolph's delegation arrived in Washington, Roosevelt was at Hyde Park, a fact that could not be disclosed since the president's comings and goings were kept secret in wartime. Told simply that an appointment was not possible, the group turned, as always, to Eleanor. With only eighteen hours left until the execution, Eleanor tried all day to reach Franklin at Hyde Park. Each time, Harry Hopkins told her the president was unavailable. Roosevelt knew why she was calling and, realizing there was nothing more he could do without making matters worse, was avoiding her calls.

As the hours passed, with Randolph's delegation waiting by the telephone at the NAACP headquarters, Eleanor became frantic. Between the late afternoon and the early evening, she called Hopkins four or five times, begging him to plead her case with the president. Still, the president refused to come to the phone, and Eleanor, Hopkins later remarked, "would not take 'No' for an answer." Finally, Hopkins realized that Eleanor was taking out her anger on him, that she had drawn the conclusion he was not pressing her case with the president adequately. "I felt that she would not be satisfied until the President told her himself, which he reluctantly but finally did . . . that under no circumstances would he intervene with the Governor and urged very strongly that she say nothing about it."

With a heavy heart, Eleanor placed a call to Randolph. She spoke simply and directly. "Mr. Randolph. I have done everything I can do. I have been to the President twice. And the President has said to me this is a matter of laws and not of men and if I go back to the President he will be displeased with me." A young black activist, Pauli Murray, was listening in to the conversation between Mrs. Roosevelt and Mr. Randolph. "There were five telephones in that office, and there were two of us glued to each telephone. I could hear tears in her voice."

The next day, at 8:35 a.m., Odell Waller was strapped into an electric chair at the Virginia penitentiary. "Have you ever thought," he wrote in a final statement, "about some people are allowed a chance over and over again then there are others allowed little chance, some no chance at all. I worked hard from sunup to sundown and it ended in death for me." At 8:45, the prison doctor declared, "Waller's debt to the community has been paid."

Waller's death had a powerful effect upon the Negro community. "We lost the fight to save his life," Randolph told his followers, "but even so we went a step forward. The Negroes are learning to use pressure. We didn't get quite enough pressure to crack this case but we almost did."

Predictably, Eleanor's public support of Waller drew a new round of criticism from white Southerners. "I cannot understand your sympathy for a Negro who murdered a white man," a resident of New Orleans wrote. A Virginian complained that she had watched the papers daily for accounts of Odell Waller. "I am very much disappointed that you do not devote more of your time to the Red Cross, the USO and help win the conflict rather than indulge in creating disorders among Americans. You are helping to make the Negroes uppish and forward."

During this same period, Eleanor received an angry letter from Pauli Murray. Writing in pain and disappointment, Murray suggested that the president had never been as forthright about race as his Republican rival Wendell Willkie, and that there were even times when she doubted that any white man had the capacity to solve the racial problem.

Eleanor was saddened and angry when she read Murray's letter. "I wonder if it ever occurred to you that Wendell Willkie has no responsibility whatsoever. He can say whatever he likes and do whatever he likes and nothing very serious will happen. If he were to be elected President, on that day, he would have to take into consideration the people who are heads of important committees in Congress . . . people on whom he must depend to pass vital legislation for the nation as a whole. For one who must really have a knowledge of the workings of our kind of government, your letter seems to me one of the most thoughtless I have ever read."

Knowing what Pauli Murray did not know and what she could not tell her, that the president *had* sent a letter to the Virginia governor in Waller's behalf, Eleanor judged her criticism totally unfair. Still, she held out her hand to the young militant with the suggestion of a personal meeting to talk things over. When Pauli arrived at the White House, Eleanor went over to her, hugged her, and mentioned Waller right away, saying what a terrible night it had been. "And this just removed all the anger," Murray recalled. "We met as two people—a bond of sympathy—we had been through a painful experience together." During this meeting, a friendship was born which lasted until Eleanor died.

•   •   •

In the weeks that followed, Eleanor could not shake the feeling that, on the critical night before the execution, Harry Hopkins had deserted her. One night she vented her frustration and anger directly at Hopkins. "She must've said a few very tough things," Diana Hopkins later suggested, and "he was a very frank guy and he must've really said something very tough to her." Eleanor took to her room for days. The White House staff assumed she was sick. "It's the first time I've ever known her to turn her face to the wall," Tommy told Esther Lape. "I was very disturbed." When Eleanor journeyed to New York the following week, she told Esther Lape, "Something happened to me. I have gotten used to people who say they care for me but are only interested in getting to Franklin. But there was one person of whom I thought this was not true, that his affection was for me and I found that this was not true and I couldn't take it." If their relationship had faltered before, it was now broken.

Outwardly, Eleanor's poise and dignity prevailed. She took it upon herself to plan Hopkins' wedding. The ceremony took place in front of the fireplace in the president's study on July 30, 1942. "A very nice affair," Hassett recorded. The fireplace was banked with greens, the president's desk was covered with white flowers, and vases of roses were everywhere. Franklin wore a white linen suit, Eleanor a blue-and-white polka-dot chiffon. "Harry trembled like an aspen leaf throughout the ceremony," Hassett observed, "but managed to fish the wedding ring out of his pants pocket at the proper time." A luncheon for one hundred guests followed.

"After Harry married Louise," Diana Hopkins recalled, "FDR was more lonely than ever before." Though Hopkins was still living at the White House, the relationship was not the same. Of course, Princess Martha was still available for conversation and companionship. Almost every weekend during the spring and early summer of 1942, the usher diaries reveal, the president spent the majority of his leisure time with Martha, either at her Pook's Hill estate, at the White House, or at Hyde Park.

It was a time of loneliness for Princess Martha as well. Though she filled her days with work for Norway—giving speeches about Norway's struggle for freedom, visiting Norwegian marine stations in the U.S.A. and Canada, entertaining Norwegian seamen posted on the East Coast, attending official banquets, hosting special events at the Norwegian Embassy—she was far away from her country, her husband, and her closest friends.

Both were in search of companionship, and they found it in each other. During this period, Diana Hopkins was told, the president would ask Louise Hopkins to chaperone for visits with Martha. "No sooner would Louise return to the White House from her volunteer work as a nurse at Columbia Hospital," Diana recalled, "than there would be a message that the president wanted her to join him for tea with Princess Martha immediately. There was no time even to get out of her uniform. She had to jump in the car and drive with the president to Martha's estate . . . Then they'd get there, and Princess Martha would say, 'Louise, why don't you go and see the children?' And so Louise would go and see the children, and the president and Martha would have tea, and this was one hell of a tough situation for [her]."

• • •

In the summer of 1942, the accustomed rhythms of daily life were disrupted in every factory, business, and home by the institution of rationing and price control. In his April address to the nation, the president had explained that rationing of scarce commodities was the only equitable solution to the shortages brought about by the war, since it prevented those who could pay the most from getting whatever was available and forced those in less fortunate circumstances to go without.

While the machinery for the rationing of consumer goods was being devised and set in motion, the government established a series of regulations at the manufacturing level. To ensure a sufficient amount of cotton and wool to supply the army with more than 64 million flannel shirts, 165 million coats, and 229 million pairs of trousers, the War Production Board mandated a new "Victory" suit for civilians, with cuffless trousers and narrower lapels. Reductions in the amount of cloth allowed also led to shorter, pleatless skirts, rising several inches above the knee, and to the creation of a new two-piece bathing suit.

Women took the loss of pleated skirts and one-piece bathing suits in stride, but when the rubber shortage threatened the continuing manufacture of girdles, a passionate outcry arose. Though government sources tried to suggest that "women grow their own muscular girdles, by exercising," woman argued that "neither exercise nor any other known remedy" could restore aging muscles to their original youthful tautness. Without "proper support from well-fitted foundation garments" to hold the abdomen in place, there was no way, journalist Marion Dixon argued in a contemporary health magazine, that a woman past thirty could keep her posture erect or do physical work without tiring. "Certainly," Dixon concluded, "Uncle Sam does not want American women to wear garments that would menace their health or hamper their efficiency, especially during wartime, when every ounce of energy and effort is needed."

The government heeded the women's cries. Not long after the first public discussion of curtailing girdles, the War Production Board announced that foundation garments were an essential part of a woman's wardrobe, and as such could continue to be manufactured, despite the precious rubber involved!

The first step in developing the rationing system was the creation of a list of essential items in short supply. Each item was then given a price in points, and each man, woman, and child in the country was given a book of stamps. The stamps in each ration book—worth forty-eight points each month, and good for six months—could be spent on any combination of goods, from meat, butter, and canned vegetables to sugar and shoes. When a sale was made, the retailer would collect the points and use them to replenish his stocks. Ration books were priceless possessions, as Mrs. Harold Calvert of Oklahoma City found out when her two children ate all the coupons from her first book and she had to present the damaged book before being issued a replacement.

By and large, American housewives accepted the system of rationing cheerfully. When butter became scarce, they added a yellow dye to margarine to make it look like butter. When sugar was cut back, they substituted corn syrup and saccharin in cakes and cookies. They planted Victory Gardens in their backyards. They saved kitchen fats and exchanged them at the butcher shop for points. There were also black markets in every city— places where scarce goods could be sold outside the normal channels of distribution. For a premium, almost anything could be bought—nylon hose for $5 a pair, cigarettes for 30 cents a pack, boneless ham for twice the ceiling price.

But nothing cut as deeply into the pattern of everyday life as the rationing of tires and gasoline. For millions of Americans who had known that "curious independence," as Marquis Childs put it, which ownership of a motorcar brings, "the untrammeled right to go as far and as fast, or almost as fast, as your money will permit," the most onerous restrictions were those on driving. A draconian order forbidding the sale of new tires anywhere in the country had been issued at the end of December, as Japan moved quickly toward the rubber-rich islands of Malaya and Indonesia. Since tire factories accounted for 75 percent of the country's annual consumption of crude rubber, it was essential to freeze the current supply while a rationing organization could be devised.

By early January 1942, a certificate program had been put into place; if an individual met certain standards of eligibility and could show genuine need, he was issued a one-time certificate that allowed him to buy a new set of tires. Determining who was eligible was a tricky process, as OPA Administrator John Kenneth Galbraith found out when he devised the list of people entitled to buy new tires. Galbraith's first list—which included physicians, war workers, public officials, and others rendering essential services, but failed to mention ministers—produced an immediate explosion, particularly in the rural South. "Roosevelt was outraged," Galbraith recalled, "that anyone could be so casual about both fundamentalist religion and the fundamentals of American politics. Ministers were promptly proclaimed essential."

Rationing of tires was followed by rationing of gasoline, which began on the Eastern Seaboard on the 15th of May, 1942. Though gasoline was not in short supply, the government believed that gas rationing was the only way to save rubber. The decision was made to start with the seventeen Eastern states and then extend the gas rationing westward. Consumers of gas were divided into different classes: the majority of drivers were granted A cards, which entitled them to five gallons a week; B cards were given to war workers, doctors, and others whose vocations required supplemental mileage; X cards were granted to those whose occupations required unlimited mileage.

The misrepresentation of one's status before the gas-rationing board carried a fine of $10,000 and a sentence of ten years in jail. Yet, within weeks, it became clear that thousands of motorists had wangled B or X cards when their work did not truly require them. Those who had willingly accepted A cards were bitter to find their neighbors in a privileged position. Public resentment grew when it became known that members of Congress had been automatically granted X cards. So angry was the outpouring of public sentiment that a resolution was introduced in the Senate requiring members to renounce their claim of special privilege. When the defiant senators defeated the resolution by a vote of sixty-six to two, the public mood darkened. "The very men to whom the whole country looks to set an example and to encourage the public to accept the personal inconvenience," Raymond Clapper wrote, "are doing exactly the reverse. Instead of trying to cooperate they are cackling like wet hens to hold their special privileges."

When Roosevelt realized how badly muddled the gas situation had become, he moved in several directions at once. In mid-June, he initiated a nationwide rubber drive, designed not only to gather precious tons of scrap, but also to instill in the American psyche a sympathetic understanding of the rubber shortage before the inevitable need for extending gas rationing to the country at large came into play. To kick off the drive, he gave a fireside chat. "I want to talk to you about rubber," he told the people, "about rubber and the war—about rubber and the American people." He then proceeded to describe the present shortage, along with the plans for building a new synthetic-rubber industry. "That takes time," he explained, "so we have an immediate need," which the American people could help to fill if they reached into their homes and their yards to recover old rubber tires dumped into basements or garages or still hanging from apple trees for kids to swing on, as well as old garden hoses, rubber shoes, and rubber raincoats. A two-week period from June 15 to June 30 was set aside during which filling-station operators were authorized to take the old rubber in and to pay for it at the rate of a penny a pound.

The response was overwhelming. In the course of two weeks, the nation's stockpile was increased by more than four hundred tons; the average contribution was almost seven pounds for each man, woman, or child. The White House itself was inundated with a motley assortment of rubber items. "Today I am mailing you my old rubber girdle I have cut and torn into strips," Mrs. Meta Kirkland wrote from Santa Ana, California. "I hope I may claim the privilege of being the first to donate personal wearing apparel for the good cause." From Ben Cohen in New York came a package of rubber balls and rubber bones. "On December 7th when the Japs bombed Pearl Harbor, my dog Snuffy went the way of all flesh, a tried and true pal," he wrote. "Our dog was all we had and I trust you don't think me a screwball after you receive my dog Snuffy's toys, these toys are the last of Snuffy's memory." And from the Sixteenth Ward Democratic Club of Reading, Pennsylvania, came a hundred thousand rubber bands collected and formed into a huge ball weighing more than seventy pounds.

Once the rubber drive was completed, the president turned to financier Bernard Baruch and asked him to head a committee to investigate the entire rubber question, to recommend such civilian actions as necessary to ensure an adequate supply of rubber for the armed forces. The choice of "Mr. Facts," as Baruch was dubbed during World War I because of his insistence on finding the facts before he approached any problem, was a master stroke. "The nation waits anxiously these days for the definite report on rubber," *The New York Times* observed in mid-August. "That report may mean the end of auto driving for leisure for the duration and thus drastically change the pattern of American life; but it is believed here that the man in the street will accept the sacrifice once the facts are laid before him. The confidence is due in no small measure to the character and reputation of the man whom the President has named to head the special investigating committee."

Baruch's report, made public in early September 1942, called for a new nationwide gas-rationing system. "Gas rationing is the only way of saving rubber," it concluded. "Every way of avoiding this method was explored, but it was found to be inescapable. The limitation on the use of gas is not due to a shortage of that commodity—it is wholly a measure of rubber saving. Any localized measure would be unfair and futile." The report also called for a reduction in the national speed limit to thirty-five miles per hour and the appointment of a "Rubber Director." "The Baruch report on rubber seems like the first really good job done in Washington since the war began," *The New Republic* noted. *Fortune* concurred. For all the initial confusion and public clamor over the first misguided attempt at rationing, *Fortune* observed, "the Baruch Committee report is supremely an example of the ability of a country and of a government to grow by its own criticism."

As nationwide gas rationing was put into place, pleasure driving virtually ceased. On Sundays, traffic shrunk to a trickle; red and green lights blinked mechanically on and off, but nothing stopped or started. Since Sunday drivers knew they were liable to be stopped by an OPA investigator and asked to explain why their trip was necessary, it was easier to leave the car at home. Citizens learned to walk again. In the months that followed, car pools multiplied, milk deliveries were cut to every other day, and auto deaths fell dramatically. Parties at homes and nightclubs generally broke up before midnight so that people could catch the last bus home.

All in all, pleasures became simpler and plainer as people spent more time going to the movies, entertaining at home, playing cards, doing cross-word puzzles, talking with friends, and reading. At the time of Pearl Harbor, William Shirer's *Berlin Diary* stood at the top of the best-seller lists. It was replaced the following spring by Elliot Paul's *The Last Time I Saw Paris* and John Steinbeck's *The Moon Is Down.* Then, in July, "a meteor burst across the publishing skies" as Marion Hargrove's memoir of training camp at Fort Bragg, *See Here, Private Hargrove,* became one of the best-selling books of all time. Americans liked to read, one observer noted, about what their boys were doing at that moment. When the boys went into action, books about the war itself, such as William White's *They Were Expendable,* took center stage.

Once the rubber mess was brought under control, the president turned his focus to the rising cost of living and the threat of inflation. The seven-point stabilization program he had called for in April had not yet passed the Congress. Fearful of constituent reaction in an election year, Congress was reluctant to impose price ceilings on farm products or to levy higher taxes. By summer's end, the entire stabilization program was in jeopardy, as food prices kept rising while wages were fixed. Labor was furious. "You cannot expect the laborer to maintain a fixed wage level if everything he wears and eats begins to go up drastically in price," Roosevelt said in a truculent address that ended with an ultimatum: if the Congress did not act by October 1 to stabilize farm prices, he would act on his own. His war powers enabled him to do so and he intended to use them.

Though Senator Robert La Follette of Wisconsin declared that the president had "placed a pistol at the head of Congress," the threat worked. The Congress passed the necessary legislation at 9 p.m. on October 2, only one day late. That same day, the president appointed Associate Justice James Byrnes of the Supreme Court to a powerful new position as director of economic stabilization. And later that week, the Congress agreed to increase personal and corporate income taxes. The fight against inflation was finally on track.

CHAPTER 14

"BY GOD,
IF IT AIN'T
OLD FRANK!"

On Thursday night, September 17, 1942, the president and first lady boarded the ten-car presidential train to begin a two-week inspection tour of factories, army camps, and navy yards. It had been a long day. The president had awakened early to bid farewell to Princess Martha, who had been a houseguest for several days. Then, from midmorning through dinner, he was caught in one meeting after another, with congressional leaders, economic advisers, and military men. Now, as he settled down in his oak-paneled private car, which held four staterooms, a comfortable living room, and a dining room large enough to seat twelve, the president was undoubtedly glad to relax.

Franklin Roosevelt was not a man who asked favors of a personal nature easily. Yet, on this occasion, he had made it clear to Eleanor that he wanted her to accompany him on his fortnight's train journey. She had agreed to go as far as Chicago with him; at that juncture, she would have to leave for previously arranged meetings in Washington. Later, perhaps, she could join him again, for the rest of the trip.

Roosevelt had been alone that summer in a way he had not been for years. Weekends at Martha's estate on Pook's Hill had offered him pleasant distraction from the war, but at the end of each working day, he was by himself. Harry Hopkins still lived in the White House, but while his devotion and energy had not wavered, his marriage had dramatically reduced the evenings he and Roosevelt could easily spend together. And, most important, it had become painfully apparent to Roosevelt that summer that he and Missy would never be able to restore their former relationship.

Against certain facts the president was helpless: against Missy's devastating illness; against his mother's death; against Harry Hopkins' falling in love. But with Eleanor, there was still a chance to alter the relationship so they could be together more often, perhaps a chance to open their hearts to one another again. He wanted her with him on the train.

As additional companions on the trip, the president had invited his two unmarried cousins, Laura Delano and Margaret Suckley. When Roosevelt was tired late at night and would see no one else, he enjoyed sitting with Laura and Margaret. "You're the only people I know," he told them once, "that I don't have to entertain." Like Franklin, both Laura and Margaret had been trained from early childhood to present a sunny face to the world, to be pleasant and gracious. "They were just very good company," Anna's daughter, Eleanor Seagraves, recalled. "They were charming, witty, intelligent, and full of fun. After Missy's stroke, they were around all the time."

At fifty-two, Laura Delano, known to family and friends as Polly, was still a beautiful woman. She had a thin face with high cheekbones and an exquisite widow's peak, which she accentuated by dying her hair a blue-white, almost purple shade. "She was the only person I knew on whom that purple hair looked wonderful," Eleanor Seagraves recalled. With her penchant for wearing red velvet slacks and adorning her wrists with five to six bracelets which rustled as she walked, she seemed to bring with her at 9 a.m. the brilliance of the late-night drawing room. Aware of the effect of her looks, she "flirted like mad," Eleanor's niece, Eleanor Wotkyns, recalled, bustling about the president with vivacious charm. The story was told that she had once been in love with the first secretary of the Japanese Embassy, Saburo Kurusu, the scion of a rich Japanese family. "It was quite a scandal," Anna's son Curtis Roosevelt observed, "totally unacceptable to the Delano family. The pressure was too great; the affair was ended, and Laura never married."

By contrast with the flamboyant Laura, Margaret Suckley was quiet and plain, free from the slightest shade of coquetry. Short and thin, with a wry sense of humor and a gentle demeanor, "Daisy" was an intelligent listener, a lover of birds, dogs, and books. It was Daisy who had given the president Fala, the beloved Scottish terrier who accompanied him everywhere. In 1940, the president had put Daisy in charge of sorting through his private papers for the library, a perfect job for this totally discreet woman.

Eleanor had mixed feelings about the Misses Delano and Suckley. Though she was glad to have them along since it gave her the freedom to leave the train at midpoint, as she wished, she had little patience with either the smiling homage they paid the president or the insubstantial nature of their conversation. "Evidently the P[resident] likes women who are not too serious," Tommy wrote Esther Lape. "Laura Delano is no fool, but she has the technique of so many women who appear to be just chatterers." What is more, Laura loved to gossip. "She had a compulsion to be the one who tells things before someone else," Curtis Roosevelt observed. "And while FDR delighted in gossip, Eleanor did not." Nor did Eleanor appreciate Laura's lighthearted humor. After Eleanor met Churchill, the only thing Laura wanted to know was whether he was sexy. Not knowing how to banter, Eleanor simply said, "I just don't know, Laura, I just don't know."

It was the president's wish, he had told his Secret Service aide Mike Reilly before the trip began, to see everything he could from coast to coast without pointless parades and fancy receptions that would only slow up production and prevent him from really absorbing what was going on. The only way to make this possible was to keep the trip "off the record," alerting the plant owners and the governors of all the states at the last possible moment, usually 3 a.m. the day of the president's arrival. Reporters were told they could only write about the trip after the fact.

The first stop was Detroit, where a transformation of historic proportions had taken place. In nine months, the entire capacity of the prolific automobile industry had been converted to the production of tanks, guns, planes, and bombs. Pearl Harbor had accomplished what UAW leader Walter Reuther had envisioned. General Motors was now making complete planes, anti-aircraft guns, aircraft engines, and diesel engines for submarines. Ford was now producing bombers, jeeps, armored cars, troop carriers, and gliders. Chrysler was building tanks, tank engines, army trucks, and mine exploders. The industry that had once built four million cars a year was now building three-fourths of the nation's aircraft engines, one-half of all tanks, and one-third of all machine guns.

Observers accustomed to the "swing-and-duck rivalry" that had existed in Detroit before Pearl Harbor were astonished to note that the Big Three were now "more or less loosely knit," dependent on one another for parts and subassemblies. "Ford is making all-important units for General Motors," journalist Walter Davenport reported in Collier's in the summer of 1942, "and the latter is loud in its praise of the lean, dry genius whom it used to pretend to ignore. It's just as if the Brooklyn Dodgers took a few days off and won a few games for the Phillies."

The first stop in Detroit was the Chrysler tank arsenal, the largest arsenal in the world devoted completely to the production of military tanks. Only a year ago, a cornfield had stretched across the site of the huge manufacturing plant, which measured five city blocks wide by two city blocks long, connected by a railroad track extending the full length of the building. As the president entered the plant in an open-top car, the startled workers whooped and whistled. "By God if it ain't old Frank!" one smudge-faced mill operator shouted. The president laughed with delight and waved his hat at the man. Accompanied by Eleanor, Governor Murray Van Waggoner of Michigan, and President K. T. Keller of Chrysler, Roosevelt proceeded to a testing ground where a new M-4 Sherman tank, heavier, faster, and safer than its predecessor, the Grant M-3, was experimenting with a half-dozen difficult maneuvers. An uneasy moment ensued when the powerful tank, after running through a series of muddy depressions, rumbled straight toward the president at considerable speed. Roosevelt's eyes bulged a bit as the driver brought the tank to a standstill about fifteen feet from his car. "A good drive!" the president laughingly remarked. "A good drive!"

At the time of the president's visit, tanks were rolling off the assembly lines at Chrysler, Cadillac, and fifteen other plants at the phenomenal rate of nearly four thousand a month. This extraordinary level of achievement can best be understood by recognizing that Germany, the previous world leader in tank production, was currently producing at a rate of four thousand a *year*. In September, Hitler announced a major expansion in Germany's tank production. The goal he set—eight hundred tanks per month—was less than 15 percent of Roosevelt's objective for 1943!

Later that afternoon, as a bright sun came out from under the clouds, the presidential party arrived at Ford's Willow Run, the big bomber factory named for the willow-lined stream which meandered through the woods and farmland on which the giant plant was built. Boasting "the most enormous room in the history of man," with a system of conveyors designed to bring the parts from manufacturing and subassembly into final assembly, Willow Run had captured the imagination of the public in the early months of 1942. "It is a promise of revenge for Pearl Harbor," exulted the *Detroit Free Press*. "Bring the Germans and Japs in to see it," Ford's production chief, Charles Sorenson, boasted; "hell, they'll blow their brains out." But it had taken longer than expected to build the $86-million plant, to design new fixtures for mass production, to train tool designers, engineers, production men. Only one bomber had come off the assembly line before the president's visit.

When the president and first lady arrived, Ford officials suddenly noticed that old Henry Ford was not in the welcoming lineup. The crusty chief was found in a far corner of the plant, playing with a new machine. Shrugging his shoulders, he reluctantly agreed to join the presidential party. But he was scrunched between the Roosevelts in the back seat, and his face wore a menacing look as he watched the enthusiastic response of his workmen to his old enemy. The president, as always, was enjoying himself thoroughly. Spotting two midgets working high up on the tail section of a half-assembled B-24, where persons of normal height would be unable to fit, he asked to say hello. The two men scrambled down immediately, thrilled at the chance to shake the president's hand.

As Eleanor cast her eyes about the huge L-shaped room, she took great pleasure in the sight of hundreds of women standing side by side with the men. For the first time in the history of the company, women were working on the assembly line as riveters, welders, blueprint readers, and inspectors. Only now, as the first anniversary of Pearl Harbor approached, were officials willing to admit what Eleanor had predicted many months before—that vast numbers of women would be needed as the men went off to war.

"I feel quite certain," Eleanor had insisted in 1941, long before anyone would listen, "that we will use women in many ways as England has done. I think it would save time if we registered women now and analyzed their capabilities and decided in advance where they could be used." The president had reacted positively at first to Eleanor's registration plan, but when he was told by War Manpower Commission chief Paul McNutt that large reserves of unemployed men were still available, he decided against it.

Attitudes toward female employment began changing when the dramatic increase in the armed forces substantially reduced the supply of male workers in war-production centers. The War Manpower Commission reflected this shift in a new statement of policy. "The present number of gainfully employed workers is inadequate to fill even the immediate requirements of the war production program," it stated. "In many areas the lack of adequate housing and transportation facilities compels full use of the local labor supply. These considerations require that substantially increased numbers of women be employed in gainful occupations in war production and essential civilian employment. The recruitment and training of women workers must be greatly expanded and intensified."

The first wave of women war workers had been drawn from women who were already working in lower-paid "feminized" jobs as maids and domestic workers, sewers of clothing, textiles, and shoes. These women needed little convincing to work in defense. Not only was the money substantially higher than anything they could earn elsewhere, but defense jobs were regarded by society as important and valuable. "Finally valued by others," Sherna Gluck observed in her study of women war workers, "they came to value themselves more." In the factory, moreover, there was a sense of sharing, of working together for a common goal.

The second pool of female war workers consisted of young girls, recent high-school graduates. This was the group targeted by the government in its patriotic ads calling on women to do their part in the war, to be "the woman behind the man behind the gun." In magazines and newsreels, Rosie the

Riveter was pictured as a blue-eyed, rosy-cheeked woman with a kerchief on her head, a rivet gun across her lap, and a powder puff in her coverall pocket, the perfect combination of health, strength, and femininity. "Actually what attracted me," Juanita Loveless explained, "was not the money and it was not the job because I didn't even know how much money I was going to make. But the ads . . . 'Do Your Part,' 'Uncle Sam Needs You,' 'V for Victory!' I got caught up in that patriotic 'Win the War, Help the Boys.' The patriotism that was so strong in everyone then."

Eleanor championed the movement of women into the factories. "I'm pretty old, 57 you know, to tell girls what to do with their lives," she said, "but if I were of a debutante age I would go into a factory—any factory where I could learn a skill and be useful." Cautioning girls not to marry too hastily from patriotic fervor, she advised them to get "every bit of preparation they could to expand their horizons and contribute to their country."

For years, there had remained in Eleanor's heart a feeling of sadness for having discarded too quickly, under the pressure of her mother-in-law's negative opinion, the settlement-house work she had loved as a young woman. Now, as new paths were opening up for millions of women who were just starting in life, she was delighted.

Though recruitment of recent students and women already in the work force before the war provided more than half of the women defense workers, the devouring need for war workers eventually led to the recruitment of full-time homemakers as well. For months, Paul McNutt had resisted the move—directing that "no woman with dependent children should be encouraged or compelled to seek employment until all other sources had been exhausted." By the fall of 1942, however, the point of exhaustion had been reached, and the recruitment of homemakers was beginning.

It was dusk when the presidential party left Willow Run. For all the hype, the president observed, Willow Run's production was nowhere near what Ford had promised. Ford's initial difficulties delighted North American Aviation's President J. H. Kindleberger. An outspoken critic of the government's decision to bring automobile companies into the business of building planes, Kindleberger consistently maintained that mass production of airplanes, each one requiring three hundred thousand rivets and one hundred thousand additional parts, was impossible. "You cannot expect blacksmiths to learn to make watches overnight," he sneered. But not long after the president's visit, Willow Run's production would begin to accelerate. By mid-1943, it would produce three hundred bombers a month, and by 1944, when the plant hit its stride, its monthly output would reach six hundred. Army historians argue further that, "if success is measured in terms of more airframe pounds produced with the least cost in dollars and man-hours," Willow Run held a decided margin of superiority over the industry average.

The following morning, Franklin and Eleanor inspected the Great Lakes Naval Training Station, where sixty-three thousand men, supervised by 550 officers, were learning to become radiomen, machinists' mates, aviation metalsmiths, torpedomen, and hospital corpsmen. At Eleanor's request, the president stopped at Camp Robert Small, where the first regiment of Negro naval recruits were being trained as gunners, signalmen, yeomen, and quartermasters. The school had been set up in response to Roosevelt's order the previous spring that Negroes must be trained for a variety of positions beyond that of mess men. As the president and first lady watched, the men went through an obstacle course designed to simulate a real battlefield.

The Negro service school at Camp Robert Small was separate from the main service school at the Great Lakes Naval Training Center, in Waukegan. The pattern of segregation required duplication of mess halls, sick bays, school instructors, housing and recreational facilities. "It was a luxury and a waste of manpower that the Navy could ill afford," Dennis Nelson wrote, but it remained in force, because the majority of white personnel desired it, and because the top officers of the navy still believed that abandoning segregation would at best "adversely affect morale, and at worst, result in serious racial conflict and bloodshed."

• • •

That night, as Eleanor flew back to the capital, the president's train reached the Twin Cities, where he visited the night shift of a cartridge plant that was producing six carloads of small-arms ammunition every day. On the walls, a number of striking posters could be seen. "Keep Sharp—We Have an Axis to Grind," "Fifty Caliber Zippers for Slant-Eyed Gyppers." The morale in the plant was infectious. Turning to General Brehon Somervell, the newly designated chief of the Army Service Forces, the president said, "Brehon, that was grand!"

The work of the Twin Cities cartridge plant had been compromised in recent months by a shortage of copper and brass. Years of experience suggested that brass was the only satisfactory material that could be used in the making of cartridge cases. Brass could be cleaned after firing and used over and over again; brass did not rust; brass was flexible. But so astronomical were the ammunition requirements for both the armed forces and lend-lease that by the summer of 1942 several ordnance plants were operating with less than one week's supply of brass. To alleviate the situation, ordnance plants were experimenting with steel cartridges. The problems at first seemed insurmountable—the inelasticity of steel caused the cases to expand and stick in the chamber after firing—but eventually steel proved a suitable substitute.

From Minnesota, the president's train passed through North Dakota and Montana en route to the West Coast. "Life on the train began to get a little cramped," journalist Merriman Smith reported. "The porters burned incense in the Pullmans as the dirty laundry piled up." But the president's spirits remained high as the train wended its way to Fort Lewis, Washington, an army post just outside Tacoma, and to the Bremerton Navy Yard.

When the president arrived at the Boeing plant in Seattle, he was joined by the Boettigers—Anna, John, and Anna's children, Sistie and Buzz. Roosevelt had not seen his daughter for nearly a year; her last visit to Washington had been in the fall of 1941, following Sara's death. Delighting in Anna's presence, the president was in the happiest frame of mind as his open car moved slowly past long lines of men and women engaged in the complex process of producing the B-17 bomber. Twelve months earlier, the first B-17 had rolled down the runway of Boeing Field. Hundreds of spectators had lined the fences and the roads that day to watch the birth of "The Flying Fortress," as the durable B-17 was named. Since that day, with women constituting nearly half of the work force, Boeing had turned out more aircraft per square foot of floor space than any other plant in the United States, earning the company a "joint Army-Navy E" award for excellence.

No single aircraft would contribute more to the American bombing offensive in Europe than the B-17. Between 1940 and 1945, 12,677 B-17s would be built, equipping thirty-three combat groups overseas. On the ground, the B-17 was a strange-looking creature, its sprouted machine guns extending like the quills of a porcupine. In the air, it commanded universal affection from its pilots. It had an excellent high-altitude capacity and the ability to absorb an exceptional amount of battle damage. "This was an airplane you could trust," B-17 pilots testified again and again. "To me," one bomber-group leader said, "the Flying Fortress was, and always will be, the Queen of the Sky. I owe my life to the Queen."

Standing on the Boeing assembly line that day was Inez Sauer, a married woman with two sons who had left behind her life of bridge parties, golf, and country-club luncheons to work in the factory. "My mother was horrified," she recalled. "She said no one in our family has ever worked in a factory. . . . You don't know what kind of people you're going to be associated with. . . . My father was horrified. He said no daughter of his could work in a factory. My husband thought it was utterly ridiculous."

Sauer's mother warned her that she would never go back to being a housewife, and she was right. Working at Boeing changed Sauer's outlook on life; she joined the union, marched in a labor demonstration, learned to respect people who worked with their hands, and came into contact with blacks for the first time in her life. When the war ended, she decided she could not go back to being a "club woman."

That night, the president had dinner with Anna and John; the next morning, Anna accompanied her father to the Kaiser shipyard in Portland, where she christened a new ship, the U.S.S. *Teal,* whose keel had been laid only ten days earlier, thereby breaking every shipbuilding record. The president sat in his open car at the top of the ramp while the hull plates were burned away with torches to free the ship from its berth. At that instant, Anna, remembering the lessons her father had given her in her youth on how to swing a baseball bat, pulled her arm back and swung the bottle. A resounding crack was heard when the bottle broke against the hull.

As the ship floated calmly in the waters of the river, the crowd of workers and dignitaries exploded in applause. "When we finished one of these beautiful ships," a female worker later recalled, "it was inspiring and thrilling. Once it . . . withstood the test of water your whole body thrilled because you'd done something worthwhile."

The U.S.S. *Teal* was the 576th ship build by the Kaiser shipyards in less than eighteen months, a remarkable record that inspired the president to tell the Kaiser employees that he wished "every man, woman and child" in the country could come to Portland to witness what "a wonderful piece of work" they were doing for their country. "With the help of God we are going to see this thing through together," he concluded, with a smile and a wave of his hand.

Standing beside the president, Henry Kaiser could hardly contain his pride. "Just look at those assembly lines," the heavily built man with the full face exclaimed, as he pointed to the ingenious methods which had allowed him to mass-produce cargo ships at a pace undreamed of before the war. The key to Kaiser's success, one of his associates said, was his imagination. "He can mentally visualize a whole vast, complex problem. He has enthusiasm, creative ability and the happy faculty of being unafraid to delegate responsibility. He will tackle anything he thinks is right and will do it without following any beaten path." When, for example, it was discovered that the largest cranes could not carry the immense superstructure of the ship off the assembly line, it was decided to cut the finished structure into four pieces, take each one off the line, and then weld them back together. It was faster to do it this way, even though it meant slicing the ship apart after it was built.

That afternoon, as the president's train headed south to California, Anna returned to her home in Seattle. "Your father missed you when you left," Margaret Suckley wrote her. "The rest of us were less entertaining." For Anna, the days with her father were filled with wonder. "It was almost too good to be true to have Father out here," she answered Margaret, "and we all felt that he was getting real rest despite the many inspection trips."

In California, the president journeyed to the Douglas Aircraft plant in Long Beach, where bombers and C-54 cargo planes, the largest transport ships currently in production, were being turned out at the phenomenal rate of four hundred per month. As his car entered the air-cooled building, a blackout structure with no windows, the Douglas executives gaped in amazement. Cheers and handclapping followed him through the plant as stunned men and women realized that the man in the green car was truly FDR.

The Douglas plant had been slow to hire women and slow to make them feel welcome when they first arrived. The women were "the lipsticks" or "the dollies" to the men. "The factory's no place for women," the new arrivals were told. "The happiest day of my life," one supervisor said, "will be when I say goodbye to each one of you women as I usher you out the front door." Every day for the first few weeks, as the women walked by the assembly line on their way to the washroom, the men whistled and hooted. When the catcalls continued despite repeated requests to stop, the women took matters into their own hands. As the men streamed out the door for lunch, the women were waiting. Every time a handsome young man walked by, they whistled and shouted. "Look at Tarzan! Isn't his body beautiful!" The men's antics ended abruptly. The women felt better, and production went up. "We may have thought a year ago we could never get along with them," one executive admitted. "Today we know we can never get along without them."

Eleanor rejoined Franklin in Fort Worth, Texas, and they journeyed together to the Consolidated plant, where the longest assembly line in the world was turning out B-24 Liberator planes. Produced in greater quantities than any other American plane, the B-24 would operate over more fronts for a longer period than any enemy bomber. Once again, Eleanor took special pleasure in hearing that women were "doing a swell job, better than they expected." Supervisors reported that women were more patient with detail, more capable of handling the repetitive jobs without losing interest, more eager to learn, less prone to hide their greenness, more willing to ask directions and take instruction. At Consolidated, one supervisor admitted, the production rate shot up immediately in the departments where they used large percentages of women. Mrs. Frances De Witt was one of Consolidated's best lathe operators. "I never did anything more mechanical than replace a blown-out fuse," she said. "But after the war broke out I wasn't satisfied with keeping house and playing bridge." After three weeks of craft school, she was hired by Consolidated. "The foreman asked if I could run a lathe. I said, 'I can, if you'll show me how.' He did, and I've been at it ever since."

"I'll deny it to the end of my days if you use my name," one male executive told a female reporter. "Listen, girl, I'll deny that I ever saw you. But if you want to know how I feel, I'll tell you. . . . If I had my way now, I'd say 'to hell with the men. Give me women.' "

Everywhere she went, Eleanor later reported, the plant managers wanted to know how and where they could get more women. "I hardly saw a man," she said, "who did not speak to me about the need for women in production." Her answer was always the same; she urged that special community services be established to alleviate the burdens on working mothers, and that companies make a firm commitment to the new policy of "equal pay for equal work" recently enunciated by the War Labor Board. In a letter to Joe Lash written from Fort Worth, Eleanor reported that "FDR seemed happy with his trip and much amazed at the increase in women workers. At last he is interested in nursery schools, family restaurants, etc."

For Negro women, the factory offered a respite from domestic servitude. "Had it not been for the war," a black riveter, Sybil Lewis, observed, "I would never have had the opportunity to work in different kinds of jobs and make the kind of money I made." Brought up in a segregated town in Oklahoma, Lewis had begun working at fourteen as a maid, the only job the women in her family had ever held. When the war came, she headed west, riding behind a curtain on a segregated train until she found a job at Douglas Aircraft. Though the jobs Negro women were given were all too often the most grueling and dangerous ones the factory had to offer—working with ammunition and gunpowder, poisonous plastics and acetone, sealing mud and nauseating glue—they relished the camaraderie and better wages of the factory in contrast to the loneliness and low pay of domestic work.

Within the factories and shipyards, prejudice against blacks abounded. The discrimination Sybil Lewis experienced, she later observed, was not "so much about being a woman," but about being a Negro. One white woman spoke for many when she said: "I still don't like to be near them, my mother is the same way. I can't say that the way I feel is right. I suppose it isn't, but I have been taught that way and that is the way I feel." Another woman told reporters she had tried to overcome her negative attitude but could not. "It don't make me no difference how hard I try, I just can't get used to working with niggers. I'll be so glad when this war is over and we don't have to do it no more."

In June, several thousand white workers at Hudson Naval Ordnance in Detroit had gone out on a wildcat strike, shutting down 60 percent of the plant's production, because eight Negro employees, in accordance with seniority rights, had been assigned to machines formerly operated by white men. "You can't expect the plant to adopt a missionary attitude concerning its colored employees," one plant manager said. "We can't buck the whole system. This is a plant and we are forced to produce. We can't produce if our employees are going to hold up production while they fight out the race question."

Still, Eleanor clung to the hope that, with daily contact, attitudes would change, and to some extent they did. "At first I thought I just couldn't do it," one female employee from Texas admitted, "but I wouldn't want to work with nicer people. If every white man could be as nice and polite as that colored man who works with me, he'd have something to be proud of. . . . I always thought colored people were not clean and smelled bad and weren't as good as white people, but these I have worked with at the plant are just as good as anybody." Another white woman, who could barely tolerate the idea of associating with Negroes at the start, found herself respecting and even liking a Negro colleague. "Alice," she told her supervisor in a tone of astonishment, "I said good night to Mary tonight when she left. I actually told a colored girl good night!"

As Eleanor traveled through the South with the president, she was besieged with angry charges from whites about the "Eleanor Clubs" that black servants were supposedly forming in her honor, demanding higher wages, more privileges, and fewer hours. In every town she had visited over the past year, she was told that an Eleanor Club had been formed soon thereafter, committing the Negro cooks and maids to a set of club rules which changed their relationship to their white employers. In Florida, Eleanor was told, a maid stopped bringing in wood for the fire because the other maids in the neighborhood had jumped on her and told her she could not belong to the Eleanor Club if she continued to do extra chores that were not part of the job. In South Carolina, a maid began coming in the front door instead of the back, telling her boss that this was the rule of the Eleanor Club.

"All the Negroes are getting so uppity they won't do a thing," one woman from North Carolina asserted. "I hear the cooks have been organizing Eleanor Clubs and their motto is 'A white woman in every kitchen by Christmas.'" In Louisiana, it was said, a white woman drove to her maid's house and asked her to come do the washing. The maid pointed to a mirror on the wall and said, "You look in that and you'll see your washerwoman. Now you get out of here!" In an army camp in the South, Eleanor was told, a Negro maid working for an officer and his wife had set an extra place for dinner. When she was asked who the place was for, she replied, "In the Eleanor Club, we always sit with the people we work for." In the midst of a fancy dinner party, another story went, the maid refused to continue serving when a derogatory remark about the president was made.

After hearing these stories from one end of the South to the other, Eleanor asked the FBI to investigate whether Eleanor Clubs truly existed, and if so, what they were doing. After a comprehensive field investigation, the FBI concluded definitively that, despite the great sweep of rumors, not a single Eleanor Club actually existed. The answer to the mystery, the FBI observed, lay in the troubles white women were experiencing retaining their Negro servants in the face of the higher-paying factory jobs the war had made available. "It was but logical that the blame was to be placed upon something or somebody," the FBI wrote. And that somebody was Eleanor, considered by many Southerners "the most dangerous individual in the United States today." Eleanor was relieved to receive the FBI report, fearing that such clubs would not advance the cause of the Negro maids. "Instead of forming clubs of that kind," she wrote, "they should enter a union and make their household work a profession."

• • •

While they were traveling together in the South, Franklin approached Eleanor with the idea that they should try once more to live as man and wife. As Jimmy Roosevelt later heard the story, Franklin turned to Eleanor late one night and asked her to stay home more; to commit herself, since civilian travel was restricted anyhow, to their life in the White House; to be his hostess at his cocktail hour, and do things with him on the weekends.

"I think he was really asking her to be his wife again in all aspects," Jimmy observed. "He had always said she was the most remarkable woman he had ever known, the smartest, the most intuitive, the most interesting, but because she was always going somewhere he never got to spend time with her. But now that Missy was gone and his mother was dead and Harry had Louise he was lonely and he needed her."

Franklin's request threw Eleanor into a tumult of conflicting emotions. For years, her most profound yearnings had centered on her husband; for years, there was nothing she would have cherished more than the prospect of intimacy, the chance to create a shared emotional territory in which each could depend on the other for love and support. But over the past decade, the experience of becoming a political force in her own right had brought with it a profoundly different sense of self—of independence, competence, and confidence. If joining her husband now meant giving up the life she had built for herself, it seemed a great deal to ask.

Eleanor told Franklin she would think over his request. She was leaving the train the next morning to fly to the West Coast to visit Anna and John, but when she returned to Washington, they would talk again.

• • •

From Texas, the presidential train turned east, stopping at Camp Shelby, near Hattiesburg, Mississippi, and Camp Jackson in South Carolina, where the president inspected the troops at huge parade grounds. For generations, the buttons on the uniform coats of the officers, as well as the distinctive military insignia, had been made of brass. Brass was considered ideal for ornamental purposes, because it resembled gold when it was polished. But as the supply of copper became inadequate to meet vital ammunition needs, the army was forced to replace its shiny bronze buttons with olive-drab plastic buttons. The shortage of silk, which had been largely imported from Japan, necessitated another change. Though silk had, because of its special weathering and draping qualities, long been the army's material of choice for banners and ribbons for decorations and medals, the army had to accept a rayon substitute.

But far more important than the ceremonial look of the officers was the striking increase in the size of the army. Almost four million men had been added to the army in 1942, bringing the total strength from 1.6 million to 5.4 million. Thirty-seven new divisions had been brought into being. The number of soldiers in the ground arms had doubled; the number in the service branches and the Air Corps had multiplied more than fourfold.

On Thursday, October 1, after traveling two weeks and nearly nine thousand miles, the president returned to Washington, where he reported on his trip at a special press conference. Seated in his shirtsleeves at his desk, smoking a cigarette from a long holder, he was in high spirits as he praised the morale of the American people. Reporters observed "no appearance of strain from the consecutive nights spent on the train." His voice was "smooth and unruffled" as he described his long trip in excellent detail.

The following week, he shared his impressions with the nation in a long, chatty radio address. The main thing, he observed, was that "the American people are united as never before in their determination to do a job and do it well.'' He went on to describe some of the places he had been, skillfully mingling praise for the positive things he had seen with criticism for employers who were still unwilling to hire women and blacks. ''I was impressed by the large proportion of women employed, doing skilled manual labor running machines,'' he said. ''Within less than a year from now, there will probably be as many women as men working in our war production plants.'' But in some communities, he charged, employers were still reluctant to hire women or blacks or older people. ''We can no longer afford to indulge such prejudices or practices,'' the president concluded. Eleanor could not have been more delighted had she written the speech herself.

True to her word, Eleanor arranged to have dinner alone with Franklin on Friday night, October 9. She recognized that, with Sara and Missy gone, Franklin needed her in ways he hadn't needed her in years. Even before their talk in Fort Worth, she had noted his more frequent invitations to join him for meals. It was clear that he was trying to forge anew the bond that had once held them so close. She, too, was at a peculiar crossroads. In recent months the nature of her relationships with three of her closest friends—Joe Lash, Harry Hopkins, Lorena Hickok—had been altered significantly, leaving her more alone than ever before.

Still, she could not accept her husband's proposal. Too much had happened over the years to allow her to begin again. There were too many hurts to forget.

It was now nearly four decades since their courtship, when Eleanor had believed their life together would be happy and untroubled. Things were much changed. Over the years, the very qualities that had first attracted Franklin and Eleanor to one another had become sources of conflict in their marriage. After initially valuing Franklin for his confidence, charm, and sociability, qualities that stood in contrast to her own insecurity and shyness, Eleanor had come to see these traits as shallow and duplicitous. After being drawn to Eleanor's sincerity, honesty, and high principles, Franklin had redefined these same attributes as stiffness and inflexibility. ''She bothered him because she had integrity,'' Anna Rosenberg observed. ''It is very hard to live with someone who is almost a saint. He had his tricks and evasions. Sometimes he had to ridicule her in order not to be troubled by her.''

If at first each had found in the other a complementary aspect of something lacking in his or her self, as time went by the tendency developed to disavow and demean the opposite qualities in the other, to be irritated rather than delighted by their differences. ''You couldn't find,'' Anna Boettiger mused, ''two such different people as Mother and Father.'' Whereas Franklin, Anna thought, had ''too much security and too much love,'' with parents and relatives and servants all doting on him, Eleanor seemed forever starved for love.

The hidden springs of Eleanor's insecurity had disrupted her marriage from the very beginning. The honeymoon trip to Europe was not easy. Though there were many good days, filled with marvelous sights and warm companionship, Eleanor found herself ill at ease in the presence of other young tourists. At Cortina, high in the Dolomites, Franklin decided to spend the day climbing a mountain. When Eleanor, having no confidence in her climbing ability, declined to join him, he invited a fellow guest at the hotel, a handsome young woman named Kitty Gandy, to go along.

"She was a few years his senior," Eleanor later explained, "but she could climb and I could not, and though I never said a word I was jealous beyond description." As the day wore on, Eleanor grew more and more restless. By the time the exuberant hikers returned to the hotel, filled with stories of all they had seen, Eleanor had lapsed into an irritable and aggrieved silence—a pattern of behavior that would be repeated hundreds of times in the years to come.

Fear of failure prompted Eleanor again and again to give up too soon on a variety of activities which would have allowed an easy companionship with her husband. After days of practicing golf on her own, she allowed Franklin's teasing remarks about her awkwardness to turn her away from trying to play again. A minor crash into a gatepost kept her from driving for more than a decade. The fear of losing control kept her from enjoying sledding or horseback riding. Terror of the water ruled out the pleasures of swimming and sailing. Nor, for reasons that even she did not understand, did Eleanor ever allow herself to learn enough about Franklin's stamp collection to share the fun of it. "If I had it to do over again," Eleanor confessed years later, "I would enter more fully into Franklin's collecting enthusiasm. I would learn all I could about stamps. Every collector appreciates the real interest of his family in what he is doing."

Even more troubling to the young couple's marriage was Eleanor's lack of ease in social situations. Though she was thoroughly comfortable in serious discussions with older people about politics or philosophy, she found herself incapable of casual conversation with people her own age. "I think I must have spoiled a good deal of the fun for Franklin because of this inability to feel at ease with a gay group," Eleanor admitted. The story is told of the evening she and Franklin went together to a large party. She was so impatient with the small talk that she left early and alone. Arriving at her doorstep without her key, she sat on the stoop, irritable and peevish, until Franklin sauntered in at three in the morning. Once again she had, by her own actions, made herself the wronged one.

Franklin tried on occasion to accommodate his wife's needs. Recognizing how much pleasure she received from her friendship with her aunt Maude Gray, he invited Maude to visit Campobello. "I know what a delight it is to Eleanor to have you," he told Maude, "and I am afraid I am sometimes a little selfish and have had her too much with me in past years and made life a trifle dull for her really brilliant mind and spirit." But on the whole, the ever-cheerful Franklin found Eleanor's manifold insecurities hopelessly bewildering, and though it troubled him to see her unhappy and depressed, he blithely assumed that if he left her alone everything would be all right.

Perhaps, as Franklin hoped, everything would have eventually worked out had Eleanor been able to derive confidence and comfort as a mother. But from the moment the children were born, the rivalry between her and Sara had been transformed into a battle over the children, a battle so fierce that the children ultimately became an additional force pulling Franklin and Eleanor apart.

This was the fertile soil that produced Franklin's affair with the young and beautiful Lucy Page Mercer. As is often the case, the affair was more a symptom of disturbance within the marriage than a disturbance itself. Franklin had married when he was "young and immature," Eleanor's cousin, Corinne Robinson observed, "and had a life sheltered by Mama. Eleanor and Franklin were both smart and had produced many children and on the whole it was a good marriage but it lacked the 'délicieux.' The affair with Lucy provided the danger and excitement that was missing from Franklin's life."

• • •

Lucy had first entered the Roosevelts' lives in the winter of 1914, when Franklin and Eleanor were living in Washington. Pregnant with her fourth child, Eleanor was overwhelmed by the voluminous social invitations to be sifted, accepted, and declined. The protocol was complicated; as assistant secretary of the navy, Franklin held an important social position which had to be maintained at all times. To help her with her correspondence, Eleanor hired Lucy Mercer to assist her three mornings a week.

Though she was only twenty-two, Lucy was well suited for the position. Her father, Carroll Mercer, was descended from a distinguished Catholic family which included the founders of Maryland. Her mother, Minnie, was rated by one social reporter "easily the most beautiful woman in Washington." As a young girl, Lucy was educated in elite private schools, but by 1914 the family had fallen on hard times. Carroll Mercer drank too much; the marriage was in trouble; and there was little money left. Lucy needed the income the job with Eleanor would provide. In return, she brought to her duties the intimate knowledge of Washington society which Eleanor lacked.

Lucy was tall and statuesque, with blue eyes, abundant brown hair, and a rich contralto voice that belonged in the best drawing rooms. The Roosevelt children welcomed the days Lucy came to work. "She was gay, smiling, and relaxed," Elliott recalled. "She had the same brand of charm as Father, and everybody who met her spoke of that—and there was a hint of fire in her warm dark eyes."

From the beginning, Lucy told her friend Elizabeth Shoumatoff, she and Franklin were drawn to one another. "Lucy was a wonderful listener," Anna later observed; "she knew the right questions" to ask; she had a gift of following the hidden meanings within conversations while appearing to be sailing on the surface. She was intelligent and responsive without being judgmental as Eleanor tended to be. Whereas Eleanor would invariably interrupt Franklin with "I think you are wrong, dear," Lucy saw no need to correct his stories, or to redirect the conversation. She enjoyed everything he had to say—light or lofty, silly or serious.

Almost imperceptibly, the story is told, the relationship slid from an affectionate friendship into an affair. Franklin was not by nature one to take great risks in his personal life, but at some point, it seems, he realized that his love for Eleanor and his children was not enough. "Of course he was in love with her," Lucy's close friend Eulalie Salley observed. "So was every man who ever knew Lucy." The need for camouflage gave ordinary conversations an air of mystery and romance which most likely increased Lucy's desirability to Franklin.

Fired by the intrigue, Franklin devised various stratagems to spend time with Lucy. In the late afternoons, they would meet in the hills of Virginia and motor together through the dirt roads and small hamlets of the countryside. Franklin's excursions did not escape the prying eyes of Theodore Roosevelt's daughter Alice Longworth. "I saw you 20 miles out in the country," she teased him. "You didn't see me. Your hands were on the wheel but your eyes were on that perfectly lovely lady." "Isn't she perfectly lovely?" a smitten Franklin replied. For the rest of their days, intimacy and country roads would be so joined that whenever Franklin and Lucy got together they set out for a long ride.

In the summers, with Eleanor and the children in Campobello, Franklin grew bolder; accompanied always by a circle of friends, he brought Lucy sailing with him on the river, to small dinner parties at night, to picnics in the woods. In love, he was determined to do what he wanted. As the months went by, Eleanor noticed the growing attraction between Franklin and Lucy. Nervous about leaving Franklin alone, she kept delaying her departure for Campobello in the summer of 1917. She finally left, but not without chiding Franklin that he seemed almost anxious to have her go. "You were a goosy girl to think or even pretend to think that I don't want you here *all* summer," Franklin wrote from Washington, "because you know I do! But honestly *you* ought to have six weeks straight at Campo, just as *I* ought to. . . ."

The next autumn, Eleanor's suspicions were confirmed. Franklin had returned from an inspection trip to Europe with pneumonia. It was then, while unpacking his trunks, that she came upon the devastating bundle of love letters from Lucy.

•   •   •

Shortly after the affair ended in 1918, Lucy left Washington to become a live-in governess for the six small children of a wealthy fifty-five-year-old widower, Winthrop Rutherfurd. Rutherfurd was a member of an old and distinguished family which included Peter Stuyvesant of New York and John Winthrop of Boston. An avid sportsman, Rutherfurd divided his days between an elegant town house in New York; an old estate at Allamuchy, New Jersey, surrounded by thousands of acres of deer park and mountain slopes;

and Ridgeley Hall, a winter home in Aiken, South Carolina, just across from the Palmetto Golf Club.

Lucy brought warmth and grace to the Rutherfurd household. Within weeks of her arrival, the children and the father alike had fallen in love with her. And the feeling was mutual; on February 13, 1920, Winthrop Rutherfurd and Lucy became man and wife. Two days later, Eleanor took note of the marriage in a letter to her mother-in-law. "Did you know Lucy Mercer married Mr. Wintie Rutherfurd . . . ?" she asked, in a chatty tone that gave no hint of the immense relief the news of the marriage must have brought.

With the removal of Lucy Mercer, Franklin and Eleanor made a renewed commitment to their marriage. For months thereafter, Franklin tried to do the things he knew would please Eleanor. He took to coming home earlier in the evenings, spending more time with the children, accompanying Eleanor to church. For her part, Eleanor made an effort to enjoy herself at parties, to be the gay companion he so desired her to be. Their life resumed. In appearance, everything was as it had been.

Beneath the surface, however, everything had changed, in both their individual lives and their relations to each other. Franklin's friends believed that his love affair had had a permanent effect upon his personality. "Up to the time that Lucy Mercer came into Franklin's life," Corinne Robinson Alsop observed, "he seemed to look at human relationships coolly, calmly, and without depth. He viewed his family dispassionately, and enjoyed them, but he had in my opinion a loveless quality as if he were incapable of emotion. . . . It is difficult to describe," Corinne said, "but to me it [the affair] seemed to release something in him." Corinne's husband, Joe Alsop, agreed, observing that Roosevelt's disappointment in this great love helped to banish the superficial aspects of his personality; "he emerged tougher and more resilient, wiser and more profound even before his struggle with polio."

Though the discovery of the affair had liberating dimensions for Eleanor, leading her to forge a new sense of herself in the world, the hurt would endure forever, finding expression in sudden flashes of anger, unpredictable changes of mood, immobilizing depressions. "I have the memory of an elephant," she once told a friend. "I can forgive but I cannot forget." Among the belongings on her bedside table when she died in her New York apartment in 1962, seventeen years after her husband had died, was a faded clipping of the poem "Psyche" by Virginia Moore.

> The soul that has believed
> And is deceived
> Thinks nothing for a while,
> All thoughts are vile.
>
> And then because the sun
> Is mute persuasion,
> And hope in Spring and Fall

Most natural,
The soul grows calm and mild,
A little child,
Finding the pull of breath
Better than death . . .
The soul that had believed
And was deceived
Ends by believing more
Than ever before.

Across the top of the clipping, in Eleanor's scrawled hand, was a single notation: "1918."

• • •

In the end, it was yet again Eleanor's inability to forget that proved the stumbling block to her acceptance of her husband's proposal that they live together again as man and wife. Though she still loved him deeply, she was afraid to open herself once more to the devastating hurt she had suffered before.

Nor, after establishing her independence, could she go back to depending on one person for fulfillment and satisfaction. Moreover, she knew that if she stayed at home the lack of productive activity and contacts with new people would be deadly, and she would undoubtedly find herself irritated by the adoring women who surrounded Franklin—Princess Martha, Laura Delano, Margaret Suckley.

When the time came to answer, Eleanor, in characteristic fashion, never mentioned the proposal directly. Instead, she opened the conversation with an impassioned plea for a new war-related assignment that would allow her to move about the country and to travel abroad. She wanted desperately, she said, to be given the chance to visit American troops in England.

It must have been immediately obvious to Roosevelt what his wife was trying to say. With no further discussion, he told her she could travel to England on an extended inspection tour as soon as the proper arrangements were made.

So it happened, in a twist of irony, that the consequence of Franklin and Eleanor's renewed closeness in the summer of 1942 was Franklin's willingness, after months of Eleanor's fruitless pleading, to let her undertake a journey to the war front that would take her thousands of miles away for many weeks. And from Eleanor's excited reaction to the news it was clear that Franklin's attempt to forge a new bond between them had come to a gracious but definite end.

CHAPTER 15

"WE ARE

STRIKING BACK"

"I confide my Missus to the care of you and Mrs. Churchill," the president wrote the prime minister just before Eleanor set off on October 21, 1942, for the inspection trip to England she had longed to take for more than two years. "I know our better halves will hit it off beautifully."

It was twilight when Eleanor arrived at London's cavernous Paddington Station, where a large crowd awaited the special train the prime minister had sent to carry her from the coastal city of Bristol. For days, Eleanor's forthcoming visit had provoked much comment in the London press. "After nine years as [first lady]," the *Evening Standard* observed, "she is more popular than at the beginning of her first term." To residents of London's East End, Eleanor's trip was much anticipated. Impressed by stories of her commitment to the poor, they hoped she would visit them to hear their troubles.

As the first lady stepped from the train, a tall and smiling figure in a long black coat and blue-fox furs, she was met by an official welcoming party which included the king and queen, the duke of Kent, Foreign Minister Anthony Eden, and General Eisenhower, who was in London preparing for the Allied invasion of North Africa, which he had been chosen to lead. "We welcome you with all our hearts," the queen said. As Eleanor drove away in the royal Daimler, the conductor on the train on which she had ridden shook his head in wonderment. "Mrs. Roosevelt never stopped talking and writing for one moment," he said. "I've never seen such energy."

At Buckingham Palace, Eleanor was given an enormous suite specially restored for her visit after a German bombing attack. "We are lost in space, Tommy and I," she wrote Hick that evening, "but we have a nice sitting room with a coal fire and a page takes us hither and yon." The signs of war were everywhere. Before dinner the first night, Eleanor was handed her own ration card and assigned a bed in a shelter; the tub in her bathroom bore a five-inch mark above which the water was not allowed to go, and the heat in the palace was off until the first of November.

Anxious to get out among the people, Eleanor drove with the king and queen on a tour of London. "I was struck by the area of destruction in the City," she recorded in her diary. "Street after street of destruction of small shop buildings, with people living over them." The queen told Eleanor that the wrecked houses they were passing had been very bad in the first place, but Eleanor, revealing once again her capacity to imagine herself in other people's shoes, observed that, "no matter how bad they had been, they were the homes of people." In one crowded section of the city, where only a third of the population was left, she noted sadly that "each empty building speaks of a personal tragedy."

Refreshed after a night's sleep, Eleanor went to the Red Cross Club in London, where hundreds of American soldiers gathered to join in conversation, with shouts of "Hi Eleanor" rising from all parts of the packed room. The morale of the boys was good, she observed; their chief complaints related to the slowness of the mail service from home and the lack of warm woolen socks. With only thin cotton socks, their feet were constantly blistered, and this was one of the reasons, they told her, that they had colds. Eleanor promised to see what she could do. "I know you want heavier socks but don't expect this change too soon," she warned. "You know how the Army hates to change." With this remark, which proved her a "regular," the assembled doughboys gave her a standing ovation.

True to her word, Eleanor approached General Eisenhower the next evening. Eisenhower checked with his quartermasters the following day and discovered there were two and a half million pairs of woolen socks waiting in the warehouses. He promised the first lady they would be distributed at once. "I have already started the various commanders on a check-up to see that no man needs to march without proper footgear," he pledged. Feeling useful at last, Eleanor was overjoyed.

In the days that followed, Eleanor was on the go, visiting army camps and talking with women in every line of work. The previous December, over Churchill's resistance, civilian conscription of women had begun, and as a result the British women, even more than their American counterparts, were doing all manner of jobs that had previously been limited to men: repairing trucks, servicing planes, driving tractors, digging ditches, cutting kale, building ships. "I can feel the exhilaration," Eleanor told her readers. "Many of them were hairdressers, typists or housewives once upon a time. They love their new work." In one factory she visited, 80 percent of the workers were women; in the countryside, a female "land army" had been formed to carry out the work of the farmers who had gone off to war; at the Air Transport Auxiliary, women were ferrying new planes from factories to battle stations. "We have not used women as much as you," Eleanor told the British. This was just the sort of thing, she added, that the president would like to know about.

Everywhere she went, Eleanor made a particular effort to visit the day nurseries that had been set up in factories, government buildings, churches, and community centers. As far as she could learn, the British mothers had been reluctant to use the nurseries at first, but the numbers were increasing steadily. Searching for the human details that she knew her husband relished, she questioned teachers, mothers, and children alike, listening attentively as they spoke.

Mrs. Churchill accompanied Eleanor on part of the tour, but the pace was so strenuous that the prime minister's wife found it impossible to keep up. During a visit to the Women's Voluntary Services, a group engaged in the task of distributing clothing sent from America to victims of the bombings, Mrs. Churchill sat down on a marble staircase and waited as her intrepid companion climbed four flights of stairs to chat with the workers. At one point, an English reporter asked Eleanor whether she ever relaxed, slept late, or forgot her obligations. "Not since I can remember," she said. "Why do you ask?" The reporter smiled. "Because I wish you would [rest] now— because I'm tired out."

When the touring party reached the countryside, Eleanor climbed on a farm wagon which had only bales of hay for seats; when they arrived at Bovington Airport, she insisted on climbing into a B-17. "I saw every inch of it, even squeezed up into the pilot's seat," she remarked. She looked down into the nose, where the bombardier and the navigator crouched "like animals at bay." She looked past the bomb bays, where the ball-turret gunner was stuffed, "his feet on a level with his ears." She peered into the tail, where the tail gunner rested on his knees. "I found I'm very fat for the pilot's seat," she laughingly noted; "it wasn't made to accommodate an old lady well over 50. I wondered once or twice whether I would ever be able to move forward or backward again."

But it was well worth doing, Eleanor said, even if she got a little muddy and untidy, for it let her feel what each boy in a bombing mission did, and with that image in her mind she could better understand what they were thinking and feeling.

Eleanor enjoyed her time with Mrs. Churchill. She "is very attractive, and has a charming personality—young looking for her age," she noted in her diary, but it was hard to know what she really believed, because she never voiced any opinions publicly. "One feels that she has had to assume a role because of being in public life, and that the role is now part of her, but one wonders what she is like underneath."

She spent a night at Chequers, the prime minister's country home, and dined with the Churchills in London on several occasions. She was particularly amused to see the prime minister with his little grandson, Winston, "who is a sweet baby, and exactly like the PM," she noted. "They sat on the floor and played a game and the resemblance was ridiculous." But tensions between her and Churchill inevitably flared when the conversation turned to politics.

One night, at a small dinner party which included Churchill and his wife, Treasury Secretary Henry Morgenthau, Minister of Information Brendan Bracken, and Lady Limerick of the British Red Cross, the prime minister brought up the subject of Spain. Why couldn't we have done something to help the Loyalists, the antifascist faction in the Spanish Civil War? Eleanor asked Churchill, repeating an argument she had often had with her husband. The prime minister replied that the two of them would have been the first to lose their heads if the Loyalists had won. Eleanor replied that she cared not a whit about losing her head, whereupon the prime minister said: "I don't want you to lose your head and neither do I want to lose mine." At this point, Mrs. Churchill leaned across the table and said, "I think perhaps Mrs. Roosevelt is right." His wife's intervention only increased Churchill's agitation. "I have held certain beliefs for sixty years and I'm not going to change now," he growled. With that he got up, an abrupt signal that dinner was over.

Unaccustomed to having women argue with him in public, Churchill did not know what to make of Eleanor Roosevelt. It was still difficult for him to absorb the extent to which she was an independent force, the most famous woman in America, a person whose opinions were sought after and quoted. Nonetheless, he could see that the British people had fallen in love with her. In his cables to Roosevelt, he described her visit as a triumphant success. "Mrs. Roosevelt has been winning golden opinions here from all for her kindness and her unfailing interest in everything we are doing," he wrote. "We are most grateful for the visit and for all the encouragement it is giving to our women workers. I did my best to advise a reduction of her programme and also interspersing it with blank days, but I have not met with success and Mrs. Roosevelt proceeds indefatigably. . . . I only wish you were here yourself."

Determined to see as many soldiers as she could, Eleanor spent long, tiring days traveling to Red Cross clubs and army camps across the country. "Every soldier I see is a friend from home," she noted in her column, displaying her trademark sincere sentiment, "and I want to stop and talk with him whether I know him or not. When I find we really have some point of contact, it gives me a warm feeling around the heart for the rest of the day."

At an army camp in Liverpool, she inspected a regiment of Negro troops;

she visited their sick bay, cook house, and mess, and was pleased to note that they seemed to be doing very well. Before Eleanor left America, she had heard from several sources that racial tensions were rising in English camps because white Southerners "were very indignant" to find out that the Negro soldiers were not looked upon with terror by English girls. "I think we will have to do a little educating among our Southern white men and officers," she had written Henry Stimson. "It is important for them to recognize that in different parts of the world, certain situations differ and have to be treated differently." Fearful that Eleanor would fan the flames of controversy once she got to England, Stimson had gone to see the president shortly before the first lady was scheduled to leave. In confidence, he asked the president to caution his wife against making any public comment about "the differential treatment which Negroes receive in the United Kingdom from what they receive in the U.S." The president promised to pass the word along, and most likely he did; the only thing Eleanor said about Negroes while she was in England was how well the troops seemed to be.

For Eleanor, a special aspect of her trip was the chance it provided to spend time with her son Elliott, who was stationed with his photo-reconnaissance unit at Steeple Morton, not far from Cambridge. Elliott had come to Buckingham Palace the first night his mother arrived, and the two of them had talked by the fire in her sitting room until 2 a.m. She was delighted to see that her son's snap judgments about the British were being revised in the wake of his growing admiration for the way they were taking the war. Elliott also joined his mother at Chequers, and she journeyed to Steeple Morton to meet his fellow soldiers. After years of worrying about her father's namesake, Eleanor liked the man he was becoming. "He has matured," she wrote Hick, "and will be a good citizen I think."

As Eleanor continued her remarkable ramblings through Bath to Birmingham and back to London, she found herself even more of a celebrity abroad than at home. "The First Lady is receiving the greatest ovation ever paid any American touring Britain," a reporter on the London staff of *Newsweek* observed. "Groups loiter about the American Embassy all day long hoping to catch a glimpse of her. There are spontaneous outbursts of cheers and clapping at stations when she unexpectedly appears."

So positive was Eleanor's press that Hitler's propaganda chief, Joseph Goebbels, felt compelled to issue a directive to all German journalists. "The hullabaloo about Eleanor Roosevelt should be left to die down gradually and should not result in Mrs. Roosevelt's journey being popularized or invested with a certain importance." But Goebbels held no power over the British and American press, which followed Eleanor day after day, quoting her remarks and observations as if she were an elected official in her own right. Back in Washington, Hick was thrilled. "I'm simply delighted with the press you are getting," she wrote Eleanor. "I'm awfully happy about it and so proud of you."

The president, too, was delighted by the success of Eleanor's trip. From

Hyde Park, where he had gone for the weekend before the November off-year elections, he cabled Churchill to thank him for helping to make his wife's visit a triumph. "She has had what I would call an almost unanimously favorable press in this country," Roosevelt proudly announced.

• • •

The 1942 off-year elections took place in an atmosphere decidedly unfavorable to the administration. Polls recorded a general dissatisfaction with the conduct of the war at home and abroad.

Recent news from the Far East had been depressing. In August, the navy had chosen the mountainous island of Guadalcanal for its first offensive in the Pacific. Though the marines had made a successful landing, they soon encountered fierce opposition and were still engaged, two months later, in grisly combat with the Japanese. Losses on both sides were sickeningly high. On the Eastern front, after ten weeks of bloody, hand-to-hand fighting in homes, factories, attics, and cellars, the German drive on Stalingrad was still moving forward. Americans, unaware of Roosevelt's plans for the invasion of North Africa, were frustrated by the apparent lack of movement on a second front.

At home, many people had grievances: farmers complained about walking twenty miles to their county rationing board for a few gallons of kerosene; small businessmen found the burden of regulation heavy; Southern whites viewed the rising racial unrest with alarm; housewives failed to see the war-related necessity of many rationed items; union organizers were upset by the ceilings on wages.

Displeasure with the system of rationing was heightened on October 31, when, just three days before the election, OPA Administrator Leon Henderson announced that, in three weeks' time, coffee would be rationed at the rate of one cup a day for each person over fifteen. The announcement sent a major shock through the country, where eighty-three million Americans considered themselves faithful coffee drinkers, consuming an average of three cups per day. Since coffee had first appeared in seventeenth-century America, when New Amsterdam burghers began to drink it at breakfast instead of beer, it had become an integral part of daily life.

The problem, the OPA tried to explain, was the scarcity of ships: the ships that were being used to haul coffee from Central America and Brazil were needed to carry weapons and soldiers abroad. It all made sense, but the loss was immediate and deeply felt. "So far," a woman from New York wrote, this has been "the wartime measure to have affected one the most."

It was thus an irritated public that went to the polls on Tuesday, November 3. With the pundits predicting a Republican sweep in the Congress, the president was "under no illusions," White House aide William Hassett remarked, "as to the outcome of the result." In Hyde Park, a heavy rain fell as Roosevelt entered the white frame town hall, just off Main Street in the village, to cast his vote. In contrast to other years, when he was accompanied by his wife, his mother, and Missy LeHand, this time, Hassett noted, he was all alone. For Missy, still in her sister's house in Somerville, this was the first election in almost two decades in which she was unable to cast her vote along with the president. Wanting him to know she was there in spirit, she had sent a telegram to Hyde Park earlier that morning: "I am fighting for you."

As the president approached the registration desk to begin the familiar routine, the chairman of the election board, J. W. Finch, peered up over his spectacles. "Name, please?" he asked with a straight face. "Roosevelt," the president replied, with a twinkle in his eye; "I think that's what I said last time." Indeed, he had been saying it for nearly forty years at the same place. "Not so big a vote today," the president observed, upon learning that only 174 of his neighbors had voted so far. "No, a little slow, so far," Finch replied.

The light turnout in Hyde Park was repeated in districts everywhere. The vote proved to be the smallest since 1930, totaling only one-half the number of voters who went to the polls in the last presidential year, 1940. The low turnout favored the Republicans, who picked up forty-four seats in the House, nine seats in the Senate, and a number of governorships. Though the Democrats still retained a slim majority in both houses, there were immediate signs, *U.S. News* reported, "that an unofficial coalition was in the making between anti–New Deal Democrats and Republicans to pluck all budding social reforms from future war legislation."

Though Roosevelt was not happy with the results, he was glad the election was over. "Found the President in high spirits," Hassett recorded on Wednesday morning, "not a trace of the post election gloom which, according to his enemies, should encircle him . . . No bitter word toward anyone." Indeed, at his press conference that Friday he made only one reference to the elections, saying he assumed that "the new Congress would be as much in favor of winning the war as the Chief Executive himself."

• • •

The weekend after the election, the president went to Shangri-la, the presidential retreat in the woods of Maryland, about seventy-five miles from Washington. The rustic camp, built by the Civilian Conservation Corps as a summer camp for boys and girls in the thirties and later known as Camp David, had been fitted out for the president's use in the summer of 1942 after he was told that, with a war on, it was no longer advisable for him to cruise the open waters on his presidential yacht. The retreat consisted of six oak cabins connected by a series of dirt paths. The principal cabin, used by the president and his guests, had a combination living and dining room, a kitchen, four bedrooms, two baths, and a screened-in stone porch at the edge of the woods. Roosevelt chose the name Shangri-la to express his appreciation of the reinvigorating effects of the time he was able to spend in the secret paradise, away from the turmoil and confusion of Washington,

D.C. Settled comfortably on his porch, overlooking the valley, the president was able to relax, arranging his stamps, playing solitaire, reading, talking with friends.

This weekend, however, the president was uncharacteristically tense. His face wore a strained and uneasy look; his buoyancy was diminished. The invasion of North Africa was scheduled to begin on Sunday, November 8, and he was worried. "He knew that it was largely because of his insistence that this invasion was taking place," Sam Rosenman observed, "that on the next day many American lives might be lost," and "he was concerned—deeply." He had ordered the risky endeavor over the opposition of his service chiefs. Aware that he was showing his anxiety, he told Grace Tully simply that he was expecting an important message.

Four thousand miles away, stationed in a command post deep in the tunnels under the Rock of Gibraltar, where the blackness was only partially pierced by feeble electric bulbs and the damp air was stagnant, General Eisenhower was having an equally rough time. This was not the operation he would have chosen; never had anyone undertaken a night landing on a hostile coast so far from home base. Yet, as the commander of the invasion, he was responsible for the lives of the seventy thousand Americans who were steaming through the Atlantic on six hundred ships. Among these was the president's son FDR, Jr., a gunnery officer on the destroyer *Mayrant.* Furthermore, since the convoy was under radio silence, there was no way to tell exactly where it was or if it had been spotted by the menacing line of German submarines that stretched the length of the Middle Atlantic.

Zero hour was sunrise, Sunday morning, November 8, which was Saturday night at Shangri-la. The ever-changing plans called for a three-pronged assault against French North Africa, from Algiers in the mid-Mediterranean to Oran and Casablanca on the Atlantic coast of Africa. Only twelve days out of 365 were fit for debarkation at Casablanca and Oran; the rest of the year, the heavy fifteen-foot-high breakers of the Atlantic surf would make it impossible to land, tossing the ships about like matchwood.

Political ambiguities aggravated the military danger. For months, Roosevelt and his advisers had wrestled with alternative ways to convince the French that the invading force was intended to liberate, not conquer America's former ally. If the Vichy French forces in North Africa opposed the landing with their full strength, a great many lives would be lost and there would be little hope of gaining control. Indeed, aware of the importance of securing some sort of acceptance by the French, Roosevelt insisted that the initial attacks be made by an exclusively American ground force. "The operation should be undertaken on the assumption that the French will offer less resistance to us than they will to the British," he had written Churchill. "We agree," Churchill responded. "We have plenty of troops highly trained for landing. If convenient, they can wear your uniform. They will be proud to do so."

The troops that were heading toward North Africa were carrying with them an astonishing array of material. "This is just to let you know," supply chief General Somervell wrote Eisenhower on the eve of the invasion, "that we have been giving everything we have to outfitting your organization, both here and in England. God knows Ike we wish you the best of luck and outstanding success. The country needs one badly."

In this first encounter with the enemy, the army was determined that American boys have the best equipment their country could give them: the new streamlined Sherman tanks, new multiple gun mounts, amphibious tractors, submachine guns, and a revolutionary rocket launcher named "bazooka" which had so impressed the commander of II Corps, General George Patton, when he first saw it tested, that he demanded it be issued to his troops even though there was no time to teach them how to use it. The ground commanders also insisted on providing each soldier with a staggering supply of items designed to ensure maximum comfort. These included extra wool blankets, sun and dust goggles, dust respirators, mosquito bars, head nets, magnifying glasses, black basketball shoes, rubber boats, bed socks, hip boots, stepladders, and bicycles.

The proliferation of materials had made the loading process in the States a nightmare. At Newport News, Virginia, the central clearing point for the ships, thousands of men were needed to sort through the badly marked crates of stuff that arrived from army supply centers across the land. At one point, twenty-five railway cars were needed just to carry the barracks bags of a single regimental combat team. Unschooled in logistics, inexperienced loaders invariably stored the small-arms ammunition and other cargo needed first in the deepest holds of the ships. Heavy equipment that should have gone into bottom stowage arrived later and was put on top instead.

The chaos of the loading process would be duplicated at the other end, when the time came to unload the ships and send the troops ashore. "It was as though some gigantic overhead scoop full of supplies had suddenly emptied its contents," one military observer noted. "Nothing had been stacked. One box was simply dumped on top of another." Everywhere one looked, there were "boxes, crates, ammunition and gasoline drums piled and scattered."

As the hour of the invasion approached, the tension on the ships mounted. Africa had never seemed so dark and mysterious to the ancient sea-rovers, naval historian Admiral Samuel Morison observed, as she seemed that night to these seventy thousand young men, the great majority of whom had been civilians in 1940 with absolutely no experience at sea.

To make matters worse, the men were so burdened by weapons, ammunition, and equipment—some of the barrack bags were reported to weigh as much as 180 pounds—that they could hardly move, much less run to shore. "I realize," one officer wrote, "that the great American public may not like the idea of their sons going to war without a complete wardrobe akin to the one which Gary Cooper might have in Hollywood, but I also know he can't wrestle it around in North Africa." Indeed, several soldiers were drowned in the landing simply because they were unable to regain their footing after being rolled over by a wave. As the rest of the troops struggled through the surf, more and more stuff was jettisoned. By daybreak, the beaches were strewn with water-soaked bags and ruined equipment.

Had the president been aware of the chaos that attended the American landings, his anxiety would have been even greater. As it was, a thousand times over in that long day, with tense and uneasy eyes, he had glanced at his White House phone, waiting for a call to tell him the invasion had begun. Finally, shortly before 9 p.m., Saturday, November 7, the phone rang. Grace Tully took the call and told the president that the War Department was on the line.

As he reached for the phone, Tully vividly remembered years later, his hand was shaking. He listened intently for several minutes without saying a word. Despite all the difficulties, luck had prevailed. The Atlantic surf was unusually calm. The first wave of landings was accompanied by a minimum of loss. "Thank God. Thank God," the president said. "That sounds grand. Congratulations. Casualties are comparatively light—much below your predictions. Thank God." With a broad smile on his face, he put down the phone and turned to his guests. "We have landed in North Africa," he said. "Casualties are below expectations. We are striking back."

Exultant, the president prepared a message to the nation announcing the successful landing of the American troops. This was the news for which so many had been waiting for so long, General Somervell observed. The U.S. had at last taken the offensive on a large scale. "America is on the march. Not a defensive march. Not a part time campaign. Not a small sector. This is the real thing, the biggest of its kind ever attempted." General George Marshall's wife, Katherine, was in Washington Stadium attending a night football game when the president's announcement came over the public-address system. Suddenly Mrs. Marshall understood why her husband had been so preoccupied. The crowd of twenty-five thousand went wild. "Like the waves of an ocean," she wrote, "the cheers of the people rose and fell, then rose again in a long sustained emotional cry. The football players turned somersaults and handsprings down the center of the field; the crowd went wild. . . . We had struck back."

"*This is it.* Those were the words that raced through the mind of the nation at 9 o'clock on the night of Saturday, November 7th," *Newsweek* observed. "The U.S. had at last taken the offensive on a major scale. In a nation where the sting of defeat had gone deeper than most citizens would admit, this was the best of all possible news. From one end of the country to the other there spread a feeling that now the United States was going to show the world—as it had always done before."

"They followed the North African campaign in the newspapers and on the radio," Winston Estes writes in *Homefront.* "Names of places they dared not try to pronounce became familiar to them. They located a map. They examined action photos in the newspapers." The war had entered their homes.

As if the tide were turning everywhere, the news from the British forces in Egypt was equally positive. At El Alamein, with the help of the three hundred Sherman tanks Roosevelt had sent after the fall of Tobruk, the British Eighth Army, under Field Marshal Bernard Montgomery, had finally gained the offensive. Thirty thousand German soldiers had been taken prisoner; Rommel was in full retreat. All over Great Britain, Eleanor noted in her column, church bells pealed to celebrate the victory. "Now, this is not the end," Churchill told his people. "It is not even the beginning of the end. But it is, perhaps, the end of the beginning."

"Jesus Christ," Steve Early remarked as euphoria swept the land. "Why couldn't the Army have done this before the election!"

In fact, the original date for the attack had been sometime in October, the 30th at the latest. "Please make it before Election Day," Roosevelt had pleaded with Marshall, folding his hands in a mock prayer. But when Eisenhower and his commanders decided to postpone the operation until November 8, five days after the election, Roosevelt didn't say a word. This was a decision that rested with Eisenhower, he told friends, not with the Democratic National Committee.

The euphoria in the States was short-lived. The luck that had accompanied the military phase of the landings disappeared when the politics set in. On the night of the landings, Roosevelt had broadcast a message to the French people in North Africa. "We come among you to repulse the cruel invaders who would remove forever your rights of self government. . . . We come among you solely to defeat and rout your enemies. Have faith in our words. We do not want to cause you any harm."

To buttress America's case that this was a liberation rather than an invasion, arrangements had been made by Roosevelt's man in Algiers, Robert Murphy, for General Henri Giraud, the French general who had recently escaped from a German prison camp, to accompany the American troops and take charge. But when Giraud's arrival was delayed, Murphy turned to the former commander-in-chief of the French navy, Admiral Jean-François Darlan, who happened to be in Algiers visiting a sick son. Darlan had collaborated with the Nazis when the Germans invaded France; now, once again, he bowed to superior force and agreed to cooperate with the American authorities. Though the British did not like the idea of negotiating with a representative of Vichy France, Murphy and Eisenhower believed Darlan could be useful in persuading local French forces to join the Allies. In France, however, the Vichy government, under Marshal Henri Pétain, refused to cooperate. "We are attacked," he announced. "We shall defend ourselves; this is the order I am giving." The confusion was compounded when General Charles de Gaulle, speaking from London for the Free French Forces, bitterly denounced Darlan. "The U.S. can pay traitors but not with the honor of France," he proclaimed. "What remains of the honor of France will stay intact in my hands."

The Darlan deal was vigorously denounced in the United States as well, particularly in liberal circles. "Prostitutes are used," Freda Kirchwey wrote in *The Nation*. "They are seldom loved. Even less frequently are they honored." What appeared to Eisenhower and his commanders as a reasonable military expedient to reduce the fighting by the French was now seen as a serious political error, a form of appeasement. Suddenly, Stimson admitted, "the enormous benefits which that deal brought to us in the immediate laying down of the arms of the French were as nothing compared with the sacrifice in dealing with a member of the Vichy government." In Washington, Henry Morgenthau was apoplectic. "Poor Henry was sunk," Stimson observed. "He was almost for giving up the war which he said had lost all interest for him."

Roosevelt was enraged by the mounting tide of criticism, particularly since it came from those who generally supported him. Sam Rosenman later said he had never seen the president so deeply affected by a political attack. "He showed more resentment and more impatience with his critics throughout this period than at any other time I know about. He so sincerely detested Fascism and Nazism that the charges of undue and unnecessary collaboration with some former Fascists in North Africa were painfully distressing." At times he seemed obsessed by his critics, reading aloud every word of every unfavorable column; at times he refused to talk about North Africa at all, taking escapist pleasure in leisurely dinners and long drives in the country with Princess Martha.

Feeling irritable, Roosevelt decided at week's end, November 13, to take the overnight train to Hyde Park. Though he had to be back in Washington early Monday morning, he knew, with characteristic clearness, that sleeping in his old bedroom would soothe him, as it always did. Accompanied by Harry and Louise Hopkins and Princess Martha, he spent thirty-six hours relaxing over breakfast, talking by the fire, and calling on his cousin Laura Delano, who was convalescing from pneumonia. Despite the frosty temperatures in the Hudson Valley that weekend, he found what he was looking for —warmth, security, and peace of mind.

Returning to Washington with a clear head, he agreed to issue a clarifying statement to the press which removed much of the sting of the criticism. "I have accepted General Eisenhower's political arrangements for the time being," he said. "I thoroughly understand and approve the feeling in the United States and Great Britain and among all other United Nations that in view of the history of the past two years no permanent arrangement should be made with Admiral Darlan. The present temporary arrangement . . . is only a temporary expedient justified solely by the stress of battle."

Meanwhile, the news from the war front was excellent. Both Algiers and Oran were in Allied hands. Allied fighters had driven away German and

Italian dive-bombers. At Casablanca, despite fierce fighting, the U.S. forces had secured their beachheads. The great port of Rabat had fallen. The Allies were plunging into Tunisia. By November 14, a week after the invasion had begun, the Axis forces were in full retreat.

The Allied victory in North Africa, army historians contend, represented the triumph of superior military force, of abundant equipment, weapons, and supplies in the hands of the Allied soldiers. The Desert Fox, Erwin Rommel, would have agreed with this assessment. "The bravest men can do nothing without guns, the guns nothing without ammunition," he once said. "The battle is fought and decided by the quartermasters before the shooting begins."

•   •   •

"The news from Africa has given the British people a tremendous lift," Eleanor wrote in her column from England. "Everywhere there was a feeling of: 'now we are fighting together.' It seemed to add to the people's courage and was reflected in group after group. The dockers along the Liverpool docks and streets cheered more lustily. One woman said: 'God Bless Your Men; May this be the beginning of the end for old Hitler.' "

By the final days of Eleanor's trip, the soles of her shoes were completely gone, and the newspaperwomen who had followed her for three weeks looked as though they were "about to die." But the trip was an unqualified success. In London, reporter Chalmers Roberts wrote, "Mrs. Roosevelt has done more to bring a real understanding of the spirit of the United States to the people of Britain than any other single American who has ever visited these islands."

There was much debate about how to send her home. Both Churchill and Ambassador John Winant thought it too risky to send her by a commercial flight along the southern route. Her trip had been so publicized that her plane would present a juicy target to the Germans. As the discussions stalled, Roosevelt finally weighed in, telling Churchill to send her as quickly as possible. He wanted her home.

•   •   •

When Eleanor's plane landed in Washington on November 17, 1942, she saw the Secret Service standing near the waiting cars and, glancing swiftly round, realized, with a tug at her heart, that the president had taken time off to meet her. Her eyes glowed as she stepped from the plane and gave her husband a hug. "I really think Franklin was glad to see me back," she confided in her diary, "and I gave a detailed account of such things as I could tell quickly and answered his questions. Later I think he even read this diary and to my surprise he had also read my columns."

That, after thirty-six years of married life, her husband's simple gesture afforded Eleanor such unconcealed delight, suggests how deeply she still loved him despite the troubles in their marriage. For his part, the president was pleased to have her back, safe and sound and in such high spirits. "I met her at the airport," he cabled Churchill, "and found her well and thrilled by every moment of her visit. My thanks to you and Mrs. Churchill for taking such good care of her."

At noon, Eleanor lunched with Franklin in his office, "which is something I only do on particular occasions," she proudly reported. She gave him the presents she had brought—a shillelagh, a cane from Londonderry, and a tin of Scottish shortbread—and they talked together for more than an hour. That evening, they dined together again, just the two of them, while Eleanor shared with her husband everything she had seen and felt.

Because the war had been brought home to Britain more deeply than it had to the United States, she told her husband, the British people were ahead of us in mobilizing every person to do his part. With women in particular, America was just at the beginning; Eleanor believed there would inevitably be an enormous expansion of the sphere of women's work. The key challenge she saw, after visiting England's day nurseries, was to set up similar programs in America, for "it was useless to expect women to go into factories without making arrangements for care of children."

That Eleanor also shared with her husband her observations on the excellent morale of the Negro troops, who found the prejudice in England much less than in the American South, is suggested by the fact that the president sent a confidential memorandum to Attorney General Francis Biddle that afternoon, asking him to study the constitutional question of universal suffrage. "Would it be possible," he wrote, "for the Attorney General to bring an action against, let us say, the State of Mississippi, to remove the present poll tax restrictions? I understand that these restrictions are such that poor persons are, in many cases, prevented from voting. . . ." Though he cautioned that the issue of race should not be raised, it was clearly a radical suggestion whose implementation twenty-five years later would forever alter the face of Southern political life.

In the days that followed, as Eleanor permitted herself to unwind from her trip, she spent more undistracted time with her husband than she had in months. They dined alone together again in midweek, and on the weekend she traveled with him to Shangri-la. "Quiet day," she recorded, "devoted mostly to reading all the things which had accumulated, from reports to magazines." Surprisingly relaxed, she allowed herself the luxury of spending over an hour and a half having her hair and nails done, something she normally could not stand to do.

It must have been a pleasant interlude for them both, with the president relieved and happy over the course of events in North Africa, and Eleanor jubilant about her trip to England. "It was deeply interesting and I am very glad I went," she wrote her friend Martha Gellhorn. "I did see an enormous amount and I think, with the training which Tommy and I acquired in the past through traipsing around in our own country, we got a great deal of what was underneath as well as what was on top."

But the peripatetic Eleanor was never able to relax for very long; she was home for less than a week when she began traveling again: first to New York overnight, then to Philadelphia to a bond rally for "women in war work," then to Connecticut for a day with the faculty and students at the Connecticut College for Women.

Curiously, years later, when she came to write about her homecoming from England in her autobiography, she mistakenly recalled that the very day she arrived home Franklin had a large dinner for the president of Ecuador. "I should have liked at least one evening to catch up on my family, for I had been away several weeks," she wrote, "but that is a pleasure a public person cannot always count on. Naturally Franklin could make no change in an engagement of this kind which had been arranged weeks before." In fact, the dinner with the president of Ecuador did not take place until a week *after* Eleanor arrived home, and, according to the White House Usher's Diary, Eleanor did not even attend. After taking tea with her husband's foreign visitor, she went off to dine with Joe Lash and then took the overnight train to New York.

In the intervening years, the guilt she may have felt in neglecting her duty as her husband's hostess in favor of a dinner with Joe Lash had been transmuted into anger at officialdom and sorrow for herself. The convoluted memory may also have masked an unwillingness on Eleanor's part to admit that, every time Franklin tried to draw close to her, she invariably moved away.

On Thanksgiving Day, the president and the first lady attended religious services in the East Room. Members of the Cabinet, congressional leaders, and members of the Supreme Court, about two hundred people in all, had been invited for this first-ever service, designed by the president, who personally selected the hymns. Earlier in the week, Eleanor had received a letter from someone asking why the president could not have cut out Thanksgiving entirely this year, adding that there was nothing to be grateful for. "I can think of a thousand things," she countered, "for which I am deeply thankful. I am grateful for the fact that my country is made up of many peoples; that I have an opportunity to show that I really believe that all men are created equal; that our boys whom I love have not fallen; for my husband's strength and for his belief in God."

Though Roosevelt seldom talked about religion, Eleanor was right in recognizing the strength of his belief in God. "His religious faith," Robert Sherwood once observed, "was the strongest, most mysterious force that was in him." Christened an Episcopalian, he had become a warden in the St. James Church in Hyde Park, as his father had before him. Though he did not attend church regularly as president, he drew upon the Bible frequently for inspiration, and greatly enjoyed singing hymns.

For this Thanksgiving service, the president had chosen a few of his favorites: "Faith of our Fathers," "Come, Ye Thankful People Come," and "Battle Hymn of the Republic." The service opened with the president's reading of his Thanksgiving Proclamation, continued with the prayers and lessons from the Book of Common Prayer, and ended with the hymns. It was all well conceived, William Hassett recorded in his diary, "and carried out with dignity and simplicity." The only note of displeasure was voiced by the president later that night. "I selected the hymns, but I couldn't control the singing," he remarked, noting that the Marine Corps band had jazzed up the melodies. "They made a two step out of the Battle Hymn," he noted wryly.

•   •   •

Three days after Thanksgiving, as ordered by the OPA, coffee rationing went into effect. The order followed a week during which all sales were halted to allow the dealers to make the necessary preparations for the new system. Eleanor promptly announced that the limitation to one cup a person per day would be observed in the White House as well, and that the after-dinner demitasse would be dispensed with. "Personally, whether I drink coffee, tea or hot water, it is all the same to me," she told her press conference. But for millions of Americans who, unlike Eleanor, cared passionately about their coffee, November 29 was "a drab and gloomy day."

By the end of November, government regulations extended into almost every aspect of American life. Shortages of iron and steel prohibited the manufacture of a wide range of consumer items, including electric refrigerators, vacuum cleaners, sewing machines, electric ranges, washing machines and ironers, radios and phonographs, lawn mowers, waffle irons, and toasters. The use of stainless steel was prohibited in tableware. Shoe manufacturers were ordered to avoid double soles and overlapping tips; lingerie makers were limited to styles without ruffles, pleating, or full sleeves.

As the level of public irritation increased, someone had to take the blame, and that someone was OPA Administrator Leon Henderson, the man "who had to step on everybody's toes in order to protect everybody from runaway inflation." Henderson, journalist David Brinkley observed, "was not one of the boys. He was never known to have slapped a back at a Rotary Club luncheon. He was merely a brilliant public servant who took nothing for himself." For Democrats, still smarting from the loss of forty-four seats in the by-election, Henderson was the ideal whipping boy. A powerful bloc of legislators threatened to cut off all OPA appropriations until Henderson was replaced. The word went out: Henderson's days were numbered.

To forestall damage to the OPA, Henderson submitted his resignation. "I have determined to cut my connection with government completely," he wrote the president. "Different times require different types of men. I hope I have been suited to the battling formative period. I am decidedly not adjustable to the requirements of the future as it now begins to disclose its outline." After his resignation, OPA official John Kenneth Galbraith noted, Henderson was "never completely happy again. The public interest had been his mistress, his true love, and now he was cut off from that love. Divorced from public concerns, he did not wholly exist."

Liberals were disconsolate. "We have lost one of the bravest and best of the generals that we possessed," *The New Republic* wrote. "If there was one high ranking leader in government who was right on policy all the way through it was Leon Henderson. He was right on the battle for expansion; right on the steel construction program; right in demanding conversion a year before it was accomplished, right in foreseeing, early, the necessity of adequate price and cost control." To I. F. Stone, Henderson's resignation marked "the second phase of the New Deal retreat, as the alliance with big business in May 1940 marked the first."

The struggle for control of the OPA was accompanied by a struggle over manpower that pitted the military, the War Department, and civilian authorities against one another. In mid-October, War Manpower Commission chief Paul McNutt had come to the president with a plea to combine Selective Service and the U.S. Employment Service under his authority. This was the only way, McNutt argued, to allocate the manpower needed by the armed forces and by essential industry in an orderly manner. The president was sympathetic to the idea of combining both military and civilian manpower under the same supervision, but he knew Secretary of War Stimson was adamant against the idea of the combination and against McNutt, the man who would be king. The whole trouble, Stimson believed, was the softheartedness of the president, who he feared "might quite possibly hate so to hurt the feelings of McNutt he would take McNutt's plan."

Stimson's worries were justified. Though the president delayed the inevitable for a while, offering the manpower job to Ickes one day and then taking it back the next, he finally decided not only to keep McNutt but to give him the authority he needed to accomplish his goals. On December 5, he signed an executive order which centralized all manpower decisions, including selective service, in McNutt's hands. In this way, Roosevelt was able to bridge the gap between the military's desire for compulsory national service and his own desire to keep the job market voluntary as long as possible. With this sweeping order, *The New York Times* observed, McNutt was given "more power over men in this country than anyone has ever exercised before in its history. McNutt may now, in effect, say whether a man is to go into the Army or the Navy, the Marine Corps, Coast Guard, shipbuilding or some other plants or to a farm."

Another key decision was made that fall with the establishment of the Controlled Materials Plan, a bold new vertical system of materials distribution, which finally broke the logjam on raw materials. Designed by a former investment banker, Ferdinand Eberstadt, the CMP brought an end to the continuing battles between contractors for scarce materials. It assured the completion of end products by allotting each contractor the supplies he needed of three critical materials—steel, copper, and aluminum—at the time the contract was signed.

• • •

Eleanor was in New York on December 2, 1942, for the Day of Mourning and Prayer, sponsored by Jewish leaders to focus public attention on the desperate situation of the European Jews. In various synagogues throughout the city, special services were held; in factories and stores, Jewish laborers halted production for ten minutes, and several radio stations went silent.

The Allied world had been aware for months that Jews from all over Europe were being rounded up and deported by train to various "labor camps" in the East, but a new and devastating report from a reliable source had just reached the United States. The report, from German refugee Gerhart Riegner, revealed that a plan had been discussed in the Führer's headquarters to deport all the Jews in German-occupied countries to concentration camps in the East, where they would be "at one blow exterminated in order to resolve, once and for all the Jewish question in Europe." Though officials in the State Department questioned the validity of the report, it did explain the mass killings in Russia, the round-ups in Holland and France, the crowded trains heading toward Poland.

The next morning, sensitized to the situation by the Day of Prayer, Eleanor noticed a small item buried in the paper which filled her, she said, "with horror." In Poland, it was reported, more than two-thirds of the Jewish population had been massacred. News of massive killings in Poland had been leaking out for months, but this was the first time that Eleanor had fully absorbed the enormity of the slaughter. At the beginning of the year, there was only one camp, Chelmno, to which Jews were being deported and killed; by the end of the year, a half-dozen more, including Auschwitz, Belzec, Treblinka, Sobibor, and Birkenau, were in full operation. In the space of twelve months, nearly three million Polish Jews had been murdered.

The Riegner report so terrified Jewish leader Rabbi Stephen S. Wise that he asked for a meeting with the president. The meeting, which included Adolph Held of the Jewish Labor Committee and Maurice Wertheimer of the American Jewish Congress, took place at noon on December 8. According to Held's notes, the president received the group hospitably and immediately launched into a story of his own about his plans for postwar Germany. When the president had finished, Wise read aloud a two-page statement put together by a group of Jewish leaders which stressed that "unless action is taken immediately the Jews of Hitler's Europe are doomed." The group asked the president to issue a warning against war crimes. He readily agreed, and asked the Jewish leaders to draft a statement for him. The meeting drew to a close. Roosevelt had talked 80 percent of the time. "We shall do all in our power to be of service to your people in this tragic moment," he said as he bid the group goodbye.

But all in his power was not very much. In early November, Roosevelt had requested a new war-powers bill that would have given him the power to suspend laws that were hampering "the free movement of persons, property and information into and out of the United States." The intent of the legislation was simply to make it easier for Allied military and industrial consultants to come in and out of the United States, but had it passed it might have opened the gates of immigration to Jewish refugees. Once this was made clear, the bill had no chance. The powerful conservative coalition, strengthened immeasurably by the by-elections, crushed it. "The ugly truth," *Newsweek* observed, "is that anti-Semitism was a definite factor in the bitter opposition to the President's request."

"The question of the Jewish persecution in Europe is being given top news priority by the English and the Americans," Goebbels remarked in his diary that same week. "At bottom, however, I believe both the English and the Americans are happy that we are exterminating the Jewish riff raff."

● ● ●

A Gallup poll released on December 8 revealed that Eleanor Roosevelt was probably "the target of more adverse criticism and the object of more praise than any other woman in American history." Few Americans, Gallup found, were neutral in their feelings about this powerful woman who had refused to accept the traditional role of a president's wife. Nearly half the people polled were emphatically positive in their approval, pleased with the fact that "she has a personality of her own and doesn't allow herself just to sit at home and do nothing." Her "social consciousness and her efforts on behalf of the poor" drew particular praise, as did her ability "to take a stand on almost any current problem." With equal fervor, however, about two out of five persons expressed strong disapproval of almost everything about her. "She ought to stay at home, where a wife belongs; she is always getting her nose into the government's business; why the way she acts, you'd think the people elected her president; she interferes in things that are not her affair; she is stirring up racial prejudice." With such strong feelings on both sides, the strangest moment came for one field reporter when an old man scratched his head and said, "Never heard of her."

Yet, beneath her public face, beneath the courage, tenacity, and conviction she showed to the world, there remained a striking vulnerability which revealed itself once again during the Christmas holidays. As she raced from one activity to the next, organizing parties for the White House staff and the soldiers who guarded the president, distributing Christmas presents to the poor, attending the children's party of the Kiwanis Club and the tree-lighting ceremony at the Salvation Army, she admitted to Joe Lash that she had come of late years "to dread, not what I do for those I love, but the mass production side & the formal impersonal things I have to do. I'm always with so many people & always so alone inside. . . ."

Still, she kept to her usual back-breaking schedule, even on Christmas Day, which found her, in between church services and luncheon for fifteen at the White House, motoring to Walter Reed Hospital to see the soldiers who had been wounded in the invasion of North Africa. As she went from bed to bed, she was introduced to a young man whose body was so badly burned he could barely speak. The doctor told her he had been a pianist. She said nothing then, but a few weeks later she wrote the commanding officer of the hospital and asked him to tell the soldier whose hands were burned that, as soon as he was able, if he would like to practice on the White House piano, he should feel free to do so. "This was the beginning of a friendship that was to continue until Mrs. Roosevelt's death," the soldier, Hardie Robbins, later recalled. "I didn't know that I would be in the hospital for seventeen months, but after a year's practice on the White House Steinway, Mrs. Roosevelt invited me to lunch with her and the President."

New Year's Eve in the White House was a far more festive occasion than it had been in 1941. As the U.S. approached its thirteenth month of fighting, the president retained, reporters observed, "the same buoyancy of confidence and determination" as he had at his first inaugural. Though America's first year of war had been strenuous, dangerous, and frustrating, it had ended on a triumphant note with the invasion of North Africa.

"Looking back across the year," I. F. Stone wrote, "the President has much with which to be pleased. The task of mobilizing a fairly prosperous and contented capitalist democracy for war is like trying to drive a team of twenty mules, each stubbornly intent on having its own way. Only by continual compromise with the ornery critters is it possible to move forward at all. Examined closely, by the myopic eye of the perfectionist, Mr. Roosevelt's performance in every sphere has been faulty. Regarded in the perspective of his limited freedom of choice and the temper of the country, which has never really been warlike, the year's achievements have been extraordinary."

"At the end of the first year of her intensified war effort," *The New York Times* boasted, "the United States was turning out more war materiel than any other country in the world. She was producing more than Great Britain, more than Russia, more than Germany with all the resources of Europe at her disposal."

To be sure, there was unhappiness and frustration all around. There were complaints that the army was trying to take over the entire civilian economy. War Production Board head Donald Nelson's decision the previous January to leave procurement in the hands of the military, rather than place it in the hands of a civilian agency, was criticized as a sign of weakness. There were concerns about the president's decision in March 1942 that "pending antitrust suits deemed capable of interfering with war production be dropped and that such suits be avoided as far as possible during the conflict." This action, which brought an end to New Dealer Thurman Arnold's trust-busting division in the Justice Department, was seen by *The New York Times* as "one of the first major indications that the Chief Executive was prepared to subordinate internal social struggles to the prosecution of the war."

And the guardians of small business continued to worry. Despite the passage of the Small Business Act in May 1942, which set up a capital fund of $150 million to finance the conversion of small plants to war work, big business continued to receive the lion's share of military contracts. In 1940, historian John Blum points out, approximately 175,000 companies provided 70 percent of the manufacturing output of the U.S., while one hundred companies produced the remaining 30 percent. By the beginning of 1943, that ratio had been reversed. The hundred large companies formerly holding only 30 percent now held 70 percent of all government contracts.

But with billions of dollars expended on the war effort in 1942, unemployment had virtually ended, and millions of Americans had moved above the poverty line. There was much to celebrate as the year came to an end.

• • •

The New Year's festivities at the White House began with cocktails at seven-thirty, followed by dinner at eight. The Hopkinses, the Morgenthaus, the Sherwoods, and the Rosenmans were there, along with Prince Olav and Princess Martha. Dinner was followed by a private screening of Humphrey Bogart and Ingrid Bergman in *Casablanca.* The film could not have been more appropriate, though few of the guests understood its significance at the time. In ten days, Roosevelt was scheduled to leave for his next secret war conference with Churchill; his destination was Casablanca.

While a mood of good cheer enveloped the White house, Missy LeHand was in a state of despair as she sat alone with her sister in her Somerville house. The first months at home had been difficult. "She would see the news, hear the news, read the news, and it was so hard for her," neighbor Dawn Deslie recalls. "You'd sense the total frustration of someone who'd been at the center of everything and now could not even speak your name." Gradually, Missy had established her own routine. To accommodate her illness, the downstairs den was converted into a bedroom and a full-time nurse was hired. Missy would work with the therapist in the mornings, take rides with friends in the afternoons, and frequently go to the movies at Harvard Square in the evenings.

Still, Missy's heart belonged to the one person who never visited and rarely called. Roosevelt did pen occasional notes to her, but talking with her on the telephone continued to be too painful, wearying, and aching an ordeal. Consumed by his own loss of her working presence, he seemed immune to her incalculably larger hurt. Fate had dealt a nasty turn to both of them, but, whereas Roosevelt had managed to sterilize his memories and suppress his powerful feelings, Missy had only managed to make her memories more vivid and intense.

For hours on end, she would sift through her treasure chest of mementos —the colorful invitations and handwritten notes that served as physical reminders of the glamorous life she had once enjoyed. Over the years, she had kept a signed copy of every major speech the president had delivered. The informal tone of his various signatures revealed the warmth of their relationship. "For Marguerite, who helped to prepare the inaugural," he wrote beside the first inaugural address. "A successful speech though not a gem," he scrawled beside a copy of his Convention Hall speech in Philadelphia in October 1940. "From Who do you think," he teased in sending along another campaign speech that same month. But sorting through mementos of the past must have only reminded Missy of her terrible loss.

"She started crying New Year's Eve about 11:30 and we couldn't stop her," her sister Ann Rochon reported to the president. "And then she had a heart spell and kept calling 'F.D., come, please come. Oh F.D.' It really was the saddest thing I ever hope to see, we were all crying, she was very depressed all through the Holidays and that was the climax. She was expecting you to call Christmas day and when we sat down to dinner her eyes filled with tears and she said 'A Toast to the President's health' and there again in the middle of dinner—another toast to you. She loves your gift and kept saying sweet, lovely, beautiful, I love it. She watches for the Postman every trip.... She worries about you all the time."

In the president's study, a round of champagne was served at midnight. The first toast the president offered was his customary one: "To the United States of America." He then added a new toast, which brought a smile to Eleanor's face: "To the United Nations." It meant, she exulted, that "we really are conscious of this bond between the United Nations," a bond that must be strong enough and permanent enough to keep us together in peace as well as war. Eleanor offered the next toast: "To those members of the family and friends who are in other parts of the world and unable to be with us tonight."

The final toast, coming from a man who found it difficult to say what he was feeling at any given moment, was perhaps the most heartfelt. "To the person who makes it possible for the President to carry on," Roosevelt said, as he gestured gently toward Eleanor, an affectionate smile on his face.

CHAPTER 16

"THE GREATEST MAN
I HAVE EVER KNOWN"

Τhe President was in high spirits in the early days of 1943. At midnight, January 9, he was set to begin the first leg of a seventeen-thousand-mile top-secret journey to Casablanca for a ten-day meeting with Winston Churchill. The trip promised the drama and adventure upon which his health of spirit depended. He would be the first president in history to fly overseas, the first since Abraham Lincoln to visit his troops in an active theater of war.

The security concerns were agonizing. Casablanca was filled with Vichyites and Axis agents; if the Germans discovered the site of the conference, protection could not be guaranteed. Indeed, it was later determined that the Germans did find out, through a coded message in Berlin, that a summit meeting was taking place at Casablanca, but fortunately, because the word "Casablanca" was translated literally as "white house" instead of the Moroccan city, Hitler assumed the meeting was in Washington.

The more the president's aides fretted over the risk he was taking, the more excited Roosevelt became, his enthusiasm like that of a young child escaping the control of his parents. To preserve absolute secrecy, elaborate deceptions were planned at every point. From Washington, the presidential train headed north as if it were taking Roosevelt and Hopkins on a routine trip to Hyde Park. But once it reached Baltimore, it turned around and came back on a different line, heading south to Miami, where a Boeing Clipper stood ready to carry the travelers across the Atlantic to North Africa. From his window, Roosevelt glimpsed the jungle of Dutch Guiana, the vast Amazon River, and the western rim of the Sahara Desert.

Equally merry, Churchill was heading toward Casablanca in a Liberator bomber. Observing the prime minister's high spirits, Lord Moran noted that, whenever he got away from his red dispatch boxes, he put his cares behind him. "It's not only that he loves adventure; he feels, too, at times that he must 'let up' . . . shed for a little the feeling that there are more things to do in the 24 hours than can possibly be squeezed in." Perhaps, Moran suggested, the president also had that feeling. "It's the instinct to escape, to take a long breath. Besides, neither of them, in a way, have ever grown up."

Not even the crude accommodations on the flight managed to dampen Churchill's mood. In the stern of the unheated bomber, two mattresses were stretched side by side, one for the prime minister, the other for Lord Moran. In the middle of the night, Moran awoke with a start to find Churchill crawling down into the well below. He had burned his toe on the red-hot metal connections of an improvised heating arrangement placed at the foot of his mattress. Hours later, Moran awoke again to discover a shivering prime minister on his knees, trying to keep out the draft by putting a blanket against the side of the plane. "The P.M. is at a disadvantage in this kind of travel," Moran wryly noted, "since he never wears anything at night but a silk vest. On his hands and knees, he cut a quaint figure with his big, bare, white bottom."

The site of the conference was the Anfa Hotel, a creamy-white structure shaded by palm trees, overlooking the Atlantic. For weeks, the soldiers of General Patton's Third Battalion had worked to surround the hotel and its environs with two lines of heavy barbed wire. If anyone so much as approached these lines, he risked being shot by hundreds of American infantrymen stationed on the roofs. Heavy anti-aircraft batteries were deployed throughout the area. Every morsel of food and every drop of liquor to be consumed by the president and the prime minister had been tested by medical officers and then placed under heavy guard. Still, Patton remained feverishly nervous about the whole affair. "I hope you'll hurry up and get the hell out of here," he raged at Dr. McIntire the day of the president's arrival. "The Jerries occupied this place for two years and their bombers know how to hit it. They were around ten days ago and it's a cinch they'll be back.''

The president and the prime minister were installed in separate villas fifty yards apart. The president's villa boasted a two-story living room with French windows that looked out on a luscious orange grove, a master bedroom with heavy drapes and a sunken bathtub, and two bedrooms on the second floor: one for Harry Hopkins and the other for Elliott and FDR, Jr., who had been summoned to Casablanca to join their father. The president had also requested the presence of Hopkins' twenty-one-year old son, Robert, who was stationed in Tunisia as a combat photographer. For young Robert, whose parents were divorced when he was seven and who had rarely seen his father while he was growing up, the chance to share daily meals and conversation was a great treat.

Within minutes of the president's arrival, Churchill was at the door, ready for a drink before dinner. As always, the two friends were delighted to see one another. "Father was . . . not a bit tired," Elliott recalled. "He was full of his trip, the things he'd seen." Relief and pleasure were evident in the glow of his eyes and the smile on his face. Here in Casablanca, there was no need to think about Ickes or Stimson or Morgenthau, no need to worry about the nagging concerns of politics.

Through a relaxed, candlelit dinner, the conversation flowed. The talk was of Stalin and the Eastern front. Roosevelt had hoped that Stalin would agree to join the summit, but the Russian leader had cabled that he could not leave his country in the midst of the Battle of Stalingrad. For five months, the German Sixth Army, victors in Belgium and Holland in 1940, had been engaged in savage fighting in and around Stalingrad. In September, Nazi dive-bombers had set fire to large portions of the city, and the German army had rammed its way through the Russian defenses in the northwestern sector. "Stalingrad makes me ashamed," Eleanor had written Hick in October, at the height of the battle, commenting that, in the absence of a second front, the Soviet forces were carrying the brunt of the land fighting against the Germans.

Somehow, the Russians had managed to hang on, however, and in late November, the Red Army had launched a counteroffensive which cut the German army in two, trapping nearly three hundred thousand German soldiers without food, supplies, or ammunition. When Roosevelt and Churchill met in Casablanca, German rations had been reduced to a few ounces of bread a day, and more than ninety thousand German troops had died from starvation. It was now only a matter of days until German Field Marshal Friedrich von Paulus would be forced to surrender his huge German force. "After nearly three and one half years of victories, conquests, advances and the exhilaration of creating fear and uncertainty," British historian Martin Gilbert wrote, "the Germans appeared vulnerable. The inevitability of triumph was gone."

But the price of the Russian victory at Stalingrad was almost incomprehensible. In this single battle, the Russians had lost more than one million men, more than the United States would lose in the entire war. To be sure, American munitions and supplies had played a critical role in the victory. During the last quarter of 1942, the U. S. had sent Stalin 60,000 trucks, 11,000 jeeps, 2 million pairs of boots, 50,000 tons of explosives, 450,000 tons of steel, and 250,000 tons of aviation gas. American vehicles substantially increased the mobility of the Red Army, while American machinery and raw materials helped the Soviet Union maintain its war production despite the losses of great industrial areas to the enemy.

Still, Stalin insisted angrily, the Soviets were enduring a disproportionate loss of life. The time had come for the Allies to bear a larger burden of the fighting. "I feel confident," Stalin wrote Roosevelt on the eve of the Casablanca Conference, "that no time is being wasted, that the promise to open a second front in Europe which you, Mr. President, and Mr. Churchill gave for 1942 or the spring of 1943 at the latest, will be kept."

It was not to be that simple. Again the British chiefs were united in their opposition to a major cross-Channel attack. Instead, they argued in favor of invading Sicily, convinced that victory there would come quickly and easily, hopeful that it might knock Italy out of the war. Once more, General Marshall carried the banner against what he saw as a diversionary campaign in favor of a direct assault before the end of the year on Nazi-occupied Western Europe. But the American chiefs were divided among themselves. Admiral King wanted American forces to keep positive pressure on the Japanese in the Far East, where, after five months of fighting, Japanese resistance at Guadalcanal was finally coming to an end; General Arnold argued for weakening Germany first by heavy bombing from the air.

After four days of intense discussion, Roosevelt opted to go along with the British plan to invade Sicily instead of France in 1943. Though he remained sympathetic to Stalin's request for a major operation to divert German troops from Russia, he concluded that Allied deficiencies in shipping—of cargo boats, tankers, destroyers, and escort vessels—were still too great to allow the cross-Channel attack to proceed. In early 1943, sinkings of merchant ships still exceeded new construction; the United Nations had less tonnage at the end of 1942 than they had at the beginning. The most troublesome shortages were escort vessels and landing craft. Without escort vessels to protect convoys, it was impossible to send American troops to Europe for a second front. "One of the most poignant arguments in favor of invading Sicily," envoy Averell Harriman recalled, "was that the troops to be used were for the most part already in the Mediterranean," obviating the need for ocean transport.

Until the American home front could be geared to peak production in 1943, Roosevelt reasoned, the goals of the war front had to be reduced to intermediate levels. Hopkins was not happy about the decision, preferring to get on with the invasion of France, but both he and Marshall understood that shipping was the major consideration. Beyond Sicily, the two leaders agreed to two offensive operations in the Far East, the seizure of Rabaul, on the island of New Britain, and the invasion of Burma in conjunction with the Chinese.

Now that the major decisions were behind him, Roosevelt left the grounds of his villa for the first time. With General George Patton as his guide, he embarked on a daylong journey to Rabat, some eighty-five miles to the northwest, to visit the troops. Along the way, joined by Averell Harriman, Harry Hopkins, and Hopkins' son Robert, the president enjoyed a picnic lunch with twenty thousand soldiers of General Mark Clark's Fifth Army. After lunch, settled comfortably in an open jeep, he inspected the troops of the Ninth Infantry Division. Robert Hopkins later recalled with pleasure "the faces of the men standing rigidly at attention as they broke into wide grins when they saw who it was inspecting them." One soldier was so excited that he jumped up and down, "like an animated jack-in-the-box, unable to say a word."

To Roosevelt, who roared with laughter when he heard one soldier say, "Gosh—it's the old man himself!" the sight of so many young Americans in good health and high spirits was a tonic for the soul. "Those troops," he told his son Elliott, "they really look as if they're rarin' to go. Tough, and brown and grinning, and . . . ready." Later, he visited Port Lyautey, scene of some of the heaviest fighting during the landings, and placed wreaths on the graves of American and French soldiers.

That night, while the president shared a quiet dinner in his villa with Churchill, FDR, Jr., and Elliott went into town to explore the night life of Casablanca, with its spicy smells and exotic music, its open-air cafés and narrow winding streets, its colorful mixture of fortune-tellers and snake charmers. FDR, Jr., "certainly was in rollicking form," Elliott reported in a letter to his mother, hinting that perhaps too much liquor had been consumed. "I do hope that after this war he can settle down to some kind of work, because if he doesn't I fear that he may waste a brilliant mind like Hall did."

When the boys returned to the villa, the president was still up, anxious to hear all about their evening on the town. "As always," Elliott recorded, "he was envious of our relative freedom, and listened to my story with the greatest gusto."

The president's good mood continued through dinner with the sultan of Morocco the following night. Magnificently dressed in white silk robes, the sultan and his entourage arrived bearing gifts—a gold-painted dagger in a gorgeous teakwood case for the president, and a high golden tiara for the first lady. "One glimpse of the tiara," Elliott laughingly recalled, "and Father gave me a straight-faced sidelong look, and then a solemn wink. The same thought was in both our minds: a picture of Mother presiding over a formal function at the White House with that imposing object perched atop her hairdo."

Seated on the sultan's left, Churchill did not share in the president's good humor. Since Muslim etiquette prevented the drinking of liquor in public, there was no wine served either before or during the meal. This did not set well with the prime minister, who had announced earlier that day, when Hopkins found him drinking a bottle of wine for breakfast, that "he had no intention of giving up alcoholic drink, mild or strong, now or later." Explaining further, he said that "he had a profound distaste on the one hand for skimmed milk, and no deep rooted prejudice about wine," so he had reconciled the conflict in favor of the latter. "He had lived to be 68 years old and was in the best of health, and had found that the advice of doctors, throughout his life, was usually wrong."

Churchill's mood darkened still further as the president led his dinner companions into a discussion of the postwar scene, cheerfully predicting that colonialism would soon be a thing of the past. While the sultan delighted in the prospect of his country's independence, Churchill shifted uneasily in his chair, coughing persistently until the conversation changed. But the mood the president had set had a rhythm of its own, and the conversation soon returned to the forbidden subject of postcolonialism.

In the days that followed, the conferees were preoccupied with the thorny problem of French politics. From the start of the conference, Roosevelt was determined to bring together the warring factions represented by General Henri Giraud, the compromise leader of the French forces in North Africa, and General de Gaulle, the valiant symbol of the French resistance. The president told Churchill that he would produce the bride (Giraud) if Churchill produced the groom (de Gaulle). Giraud's presence was easily arranged, but de Gaulle flatly refused to deal with anyone connected to the Vichy regime. Only when Churchill threatened to stop paying his salary in London did the proud Frenchman agree to come to North Africa.

Yet, once he reached Casablanca, de Gaulle refused to call upon Giraud. Churchill was furious. "Well, just look at him!" Churchill remarked, as de Gaulle stalked down the garden path after a stormy session with British leaders. "His country has given up fighting, he himself is a refugee, and if we have to turn him down he's finished. Look at him! He might be Stalin, with 200 divisions behind his words!"

Finally, Roosevelt decided to intervene, asking de Gaulle to meet him in his villa. "The General was sullen," Mike Reilly noted, "never smiled, and he had that unmistakable attitude of a man toting a large chip on each shoulder. He and the President shook hands, and then everybody left them alone together." Or so it seemed. Behind the drapes, Reilly remained half hidden, his pistol removed from his holster. "I saw before me the President of the United States in a hot argument," the Secret Service chief explained. "The man was six foot three, the President a cripple."

For his part, de Gaulle noticed shadows at the rear of the balcony and saw the curtains moving, but he never said a word, carrying on the conversation as if he and Roosevelt were completely alone. By the end of the session, a breakthrough had been achieved: de Gaulle agreed to sign a memorandum of unity with Giraud. "In human affairs the public must be offered a drama," Roosevelt told de Gaulle. If the news of Casablanca could be accompanied by a joint declaration of the French leaders, even if it concerned only a theoretical agreement stating they both wanted France freed and would consult and collaborate, it would, Roosevelt predicted, "produce the dramatic effect we need."

"Let me handle it," de Gaulle agreed. In his memoirs, the French leader attributes his change of heart to the president's soothing charm. Despite their differences, de Gaulle was convinced that Roosevelt was governed by "the loftiest of ambitions" and that "his intelligence, his knowledge and his audacity gave him the ability . . . to realize them."

The atmosphere chilled the next day, however, when Churchill lost his temper with de Gaulle. "In these days," Lord Moran observed of his boss, "when he is stretched taut, certain people seem to get on his nerves: de Gaulle is one of them." The argument arose just as Giraud was being escorted into the room by Hopkins for a historic handshake with de Gaulle. Reacting quickly, Roosevelt paid no attention to Churchill's diatribe, turning instead to de Gaulle. "Will you at least agree," he said in his kindest manner, "to be photographed beside me and the British Prime Minister along with General Giraud?"

"Of course," de Gaulle replied, knowing full well that serious disputes of substance still remained unresolved. "Will you go so far as to shake General Giraud's hand before the camera?" "I shall do that for you," de Gaulle answered. The picture was snapped, the dramatic moment captured for posterity. In the foreground, a stiff-necked de Gaulle offers his hand to Giraud. In the background is the seated president, his face thrown back in wholehearted enjoyment of the delicious scene.

As the Frenchmen departed, Roosevelt and Churchill remained behind on the lawn to talk with the assembled newsmen. The day was so lovely, with a bright sun and blue skies, and Roosevelt was feeling so gay, that in a spontaneous moment he called for the unconditional surrender of Germany, Italy, and Japan. Churchill was stunned. Though he and Roosevelt had exchanged views on unconditional surrender on several occasions, no final agreement on a text had been reached. Later that evening, Harriman recalled, Churchill was "in high dudgeon. He was offended that Roosevelt should have made such a momentous announcement without prior consultation. . . . I had seen him unhappy with Roosevelt more than once, but this time he was more deeply offended than before. I also had the impression that he feared it might make the Germans fight all the harder."

Roosevelt blithely explained later that getting de Gaulle and Giraud together had been so complicated that it reminded him of Grant and Lee, "and then suddenly the press conference was on, and Winston and I had no time to prepare for it, and the thought popped into my mind that they had called Grant 'Old Unconditional Surrender' and the next thing I knew I had said it."

But the deed was done, and Churchill could not remain angry at Roosevelt for long. With the work of the conference completed, he suggested that he and the president travel together to Marrakesh, the jewel of Morocco, a city which combined a perfect climate, a wealth of ancient monuments, and a unique setting of palm trees against snow-capped mountains.

"Let us spend two days there," Churchill said. "I must be with you when you see the sunset on the snows of the Atlas Mountains." Delighted to stretch his trip a little longer, Roosevelt agreed. The journey by automobile took five hours, with time out for a basket lunch along the way. Driving together along the plain, Roosevelt and Churchill fell into easy conversation, heartily enjoying their last moments of freedom before returning to the burdens that awaited them at home. During the last hour of the journey, the shapes of the mountain peaks began to emerge on the horizon, the palm trees to grow more thickly. At 6 p.m., they reached a spectacular villa, surrounded by a fairyland of fountains and waterfalls, where they were to spend the night.

At the top of the villa stood a sloping tower six stories high with a magnificent view of the snow-capped mountains. It was the view Churchill wanted to share with the president. The steep, winding stairs were too narrow to accommodate Roosevelt's wheelchair, so Mike Reilly and George Fox made a cradle with their hands to carry him step by step to the top, his legs, Moran noted, "dangling like the limbs of a ventriloquist's dummy." At the topmost terrace, the president sat with Churchill for half an hour, gazing at the purple hills, where the light was changing every minute. "It's the most lovely spot in the whole world," the prime minister remarked.

At this moment, Churchill was perhaps at the peak of his wartime power. The conference had ended exactly as he had hoped—with a postponement of the cross-Channel attack and the decision to invade Sicily. Never again, with Stalin's power rising every day, would Churchill enjoy such influence with Roosevelt.

The president's plane was scheduled to leave for the United States the following morning at seven-thirty. Churchill had intended to see Roosevelt off, but after a long evening of food, drink, speeches, and songs, he had trouble getting out of bed. At the last minute, still clad in his red-dragon dressing gown and black velvet slippers, he raced outside to catch the president's car. At the airfield, the photographers begged for a shot. "You simply cannot do this to me," he laughingly remarked, and they obliged, lowering their cameras.

As the president's plane took off, Churchill put his hand on American Vice-Consul Kenneth Pendar's arm. "If anything happened to that man," he said, "I couldn't stand it. He is the truest friend; he has the farthest vision; he is the greatest man I have ever known."

• • •

"Dearest Babs," Franklin wrote Eleanor as he flew back to the States. "All has gone well though I'm a bit tired—too much plane. It affects my head just as ocean cruising affects yours."

Roosevelt hated flying. He vastly preferred the slower pace of ocean travel. "He always used to tell me that clouds were dull," Eleanor explained. "What he loved was the sea all around him, the motion of the waves." Franklin had long tried to convince Eleanor that getting there was half the fun, soliciting her companionship on languid trips by boat and train, but to Eleanor's mind nothing was comparable to flying. Possessed by a deep-rooted horror of wasting time, she always wanted to get where she wanted to go as quickly as possible.

"What do you know!" Franklin excitedly wrote Eleanor as he crossed the northern coast of South America. "Back in the US. Saturday evening and we should get to Washington by 8 p.m. on Sunday [January 31]." Having been away for nearly a month, he seemed eager to see his wife, to tell her all that had happened, to hear her speak, as if the time apart had created a surge of forgotten emotions. Perhaps, on coming home, he indulged himself in the fancy that Eleanor would be there, just as his mother had always been, to welcome him back with warmth, love, and exuberant delight.

But the spell was quickly broken when he arrived in the White House and found a handwritten note from Eleanor: "Welcome home! I can't be here Sunday night as months ago I agreed to open a series of lectures at Cooper Union but I'll be home for dinner Monday night as I don't want you to tell all the story and miss it. . . . I have to be gone again for the day Tuesday but will be back Wednesday a.m. I'm terribly sorry not to be home. I think I will now delay going west til late March. . . . Much love and I am so glad you are back."

That evening, while Eleanor kept her engagement at Cooper Union, the president relaxed in his study with Anna and John, who had arrived in Washington for a winter vacation while he was in Casablanca. The president's animated spirits were so contagious, his stories of the conference so vibrant, that both Anna and John were enthralled. "I'd give my eyeteeth to go along on such a trip," John suddenly announced. "That couldn't be done," the president replied. "And why not?" John ardently persisted. "Why couldn't I?"

"Well," the president countered, "you are not in uniform!" Roosevelt's reply was most likely nothing more than a statement of White House protocol surrounding military conferences, but to young Boettiger, already sensitive about his civilian status, it seemed a personal attack that could not have come at a worst moment.

For months, John had been suffering from bouts of depression, displayed in a sudden ebbing of interest in his work at the *Seattle Post-Intelligencer* and a withdrawal from his wife and family. Anna assumed that she was somehow at fault. "I feared," she later admitted to John, "you were getting tired of something or other about me or in me."

But, unbeknownst to Anna at the time, John's melancholy had deeper roots. Paralyzing doubts about his abilities had surfaced periodically in the course of his marriage, but now, as John entered his fortieth year, they were assuming more powerful proportions than before. Haunted by the knowledge that his position as publisher of the paper was dependent upon his status as the president's son-in-law, John had begun to envision military service as an escape from his depression and pain. The choice was not easy, however, for it meant leaving Anna alone in Seattle to cope with running the paper.

The president's careless comment settled the issue. "I won't say that one remark of his did it," John later admitted, "but it went farther than any or all influences that did make my mind up." The following day, he wrote a letter to his old friend General Eisenhower requesting that he be commissioned in the army and put into service in North Africa.

Anna was crushed. "From the moment you wrote that letter," she wrote, "I began to suffer acutely. I seemed to know all too accurately what it was going to be like when you left." Confused by the rashness of the decision, fearful that his leaving implied a rejection of her, terrified of running the paper on her own, she was nonetheless afraid that if she tried to dissuade him from going he would regret it for the rest of his life and take out his anger on her. "Maybe I was wrong not to have told you all I was thinking and dreading," she later confessed, "but I just couldn't."

Two days later, Eleanor accompanied Anna and John to Union Station, where they boarded a sleeper train to Seattle. "I went to the train and stayed till it pulled out," Eleanor wrote Joe Lash. "Anna seemed to want me." The president was delighted with John's decision to serve, Eleanor went on, but Anna couldn't help feeling resentful. "Happiness is a fragile thing and she fears its shattering. I can't be delighted either. I wish pride compensated fear with me."

"I hated to see you go," Eleanor wrote Anna, "for I know that having John consider going off ends something very close and precious which you two have had. . . . Yet always men have had the urge for adventure and fared forth and the women are always held by 'appendages.' "

• • •

No sooner had the president returned to Washington than his attention was yanked from global strategy to domestic politics. At the War Production Board, a tremendous crisis was brewing. The military had lost faith in the leadership of Donald Nelson, believing him too weak, too nice, and too tolerant. There was merit to the military's claim. Torn between the competing demands of conflicting agencies, Nelson was habitually indecisive. Stimson's diary during this period is filled with recriminations against Nelson's inability to take charge. Returning from a meeting with Nelson, Knox, Ickes,

Navy Undersecretary James Forrestal, and rubber chief William Jeffers, Stimson was irate. "It was a pathetic spectacle. . . . it was like four hungry dogs quarreling over a very inadequate bone—the Army for planes and gas; Navy escort vessels; Ickes octane gas; Jeffers rubber."

In truth, however, the nub of the military's complaint was not directed at Nelson's administrative weaknesses, but at his insistence on civilian control of the production process. The military, geared to think of its own needs first, was forever arguing that too much steel or rubber or manpower was being devoted to civilian activity. Though Nelson listened to the military, he insisted on a balance between civilian and military needs. When newsprint grew short, the army argued for the elimination of comic strips, but Nelson refused. When the army opposed the diversion of scarce labor materials to build housing for war workers in overcrowded cities, Nelson argued that decent housing was essential to maintaining production.

The continued pulling and hauling between military and civilian priorities made for disorderly administration. Stimson was in despair over the "disjointed" conduct of the war. "The President is the poorest administrator I have ever worked under in respect to the orderly procedure and routine of his performance," he confessed to his diary. One evening while Roosevelt was in Casablanca, Stimson unburdened himself to Felix Frankfurter. "He wanted to relieve himself by talking," Frankfurter observed, "for he has had a good many headaches recently"—all of them attributable to bad organization.

Frankfurter told Stimson "he had better make up his mind that orderly procedure is not and never has been the characteristic of this Administration —it has other virtues but not that. . . . he had better reconcile himself to looseness of administration and the inevitable frictions and conflicts resulting therefrom which naturally go against the grain of an orderly, systematic brain like his."

While Roosevelt was in Casablanca, however, the quarrels within the WPB had become so bitter that Congress had stepped into the fray, threatening to replace the strife-torn organization with a new superagency, bringing production, manpower, and supply under one roof. The time had come, Economic Stabilization Director Jimmy Byrnes told Roosevelt, for Nelson to be replaced. First Knudsen had been in trouble, Roosevelt mused, now Nelson. Perhaps businessmen were not as qualified as everyone thought to run complicated government agencies.

There was only one man for the job, Byrnes counseled, one man who would please both the army and the Congress—Bernard Baruch. The decision was not an easy one for Roosevelt; Donald Nelson had been a loyal and devoted chief. But he finally agreed, directing Byrnes to prepare a letter for his signature asking Baruch to become the new chairman of the WPB. Acting with dispatch, for fear that Roosevelt might change his mind, Byrnes drafted the letter immediately and then read it to Baruch later that afternoon.

Baruch was delighted. This was the job he had craved since the war began. He asked only that he have time to check with his doctor the next day, to make sure that, at seventy-three, he was healthy enough to undertake the task. Byrnes was disappointed, fearing the delay would open the door for Roosevelt to back down, which is precisely what Roosevelt did.

Later that night, at supper with Hopkins, Roosevelt began to question his decision. Hopkins told Roosevelt that, by appointing Baruch and giving in to the army, he would look weak. Baruch would emerge the conquering hero, the most powerful man in Washington. Better, Hopkins advised, to let the storm pass and keep Nelson at the post. The president agreed.

This was not the first time Roosevelt had by-passed Baruch. As much as he respected the shrewd financier, Roosevelt did not like him a great deal. "They are too much alike," I. F. Stone keenly observed; "both are charmers. Mr. Roosevelt feels about Baruch as a young married woman does when her mother tries to help her by showing her the right way to handle a maid or a baby. He resented Al Smith's attempt to 'help' him when he first succeeded Smith as Governor and there is reason to believe that he has been irked by Baruch's burning desire to show him how *really* to run a war."

When Baruch arrived at the Oval Office to advise the president of his acceptance, Roosevelt greeted him in his customary genial fashion. "Mr. President, I'm here to report for duty," Baruch said. The salutation went unacknowledged. "It was as though he had not heard me," Baruch recalled. The president then launched into a curious monologue about Middle Eastern politics which lasted until he was called to leave for a Cabinet meeting. "That was the end of it," Baruch later wrote; "neither he nor I ever mentioned the WPB Chairmanship—then or later." The "strange and disagreeable little drama" had come to an end.

• • •

On Friday night, February 5, seeking rest from his strenuous trip and escape from the muddle of Washington, Roosevelt journeyed to Hyde Park for a long weekend, accompanied by Bill Hassett, Pa Watson, and Grace Tully. He slept until ten or eleven each morning, relaxed over leisurely meals, and rummaged through his library. A heavy snowfall had blanketed the lawns and the trees just before his arrival, warming the atmosphere of the Big House. "Most of my time was spent asleep," Roosevelt reported to Anna when he returned to Washington the following Wednesday. "I did as little work as possible—and now I am ready for practically anything."

While Franklin was unwinding at Hyde Park, Eleanor was traveling by train through Connecticut and Massachusetts to Portland, Maine, visiting old friends, naval hospitals and war plants. She left New York on Saturday morning, then spent the day with Esther Lape and Elizabeth Read in Saybrook, Connecticut. Elizabeth was in a miserable state, suffering from cancer and "so far away in her mind" that she could scarcely participate in the conversation. For Eleanor, the only solace came in observing the "constant care and devotion" that Esther generously extended to her lifelong companion. Through most of this "marriage," Elizabeth had subordinated her interests and concerns to Esther's; now Esther was returning that love, dedicating all her energies to her dying friend.

From Connecticut, Eleanor journeyed north to Somerville, Massachusetts. There, on Sunday afternoon, she visited Missy in her home. During the thirties, Eleanor had visited 101 Orchard a number of times. "We got to know Mrs. Roosevelt very well," Missy's next-door neighbor Barbara Dudley recalled, "because, whenever there was a crisis or a big event in the family, she came up to help Missy out. When Missy's mother died, she took over the kitchen. I remember we were imagining that we'd have all kinds of fancy foods, but she made two things only: tomato soup and peanut-butter sandwiches."

Though there was little improvement in Missy's speech, the circulation in her right side was returning. "Where it was just like an icicle," her sister Ann Rochon told Eleanor, "is as warm as the left side now." With three speech lessons a day instead of one, two vigorous massages, and two hours of exercise each morning, there was, Ann reported, "a decided change for the better." What is more, Missy "realizes it and is *so* excited." But, Ann confessed, "Missy worries so terribly about the President."

On reaching Portland at 9 p.m. that Sunday, Eleanor went immediately to the shipyards to talk with women working the graveyard shift. "It was really very dramatic to see the plant at night," Eleanor later wrote, praising the high spirits of the women workers. "Exhibiting her usual energy," the *Portland Press Herald* observed, "Mrs. Roosevelt mounted a platform to speak with several women welders by literally 'walking the plank' which was the only means of ascending the platform erected four feet above the ground." Sitting down beside them, Eleanor asked questions about the nature of their work, the training they had received, how many children they had, how they were being cared for, how the shopping got done.

Now, for the first time, the government was targeting its recruitment ads directly and predominantly at housewives. "The real situation," *Business Week* observed, "is that unless industry draws 2.8 million more [women] away from household or school duties in 1943 . . . production quotas will have to be revised down."

In the ads directed at housewives, the temporary nature of the job was stressed, the idea being that women would come into the factories during the war and then go back home as soon as it was over. "A woman is a substitute," one War Department brochure claimed, "like plastic instead of metal." To ease the transition, the work was presented as similar in kind to the work housewives already knew how to perform. "If you've sewed on buttons, or made buttonholes on a machine," a Labor Department pamphlet urged, "you can learn to do spot welding on airplane parts. If you've done fine embroidery, or made jewelry, you can learn to do assembly on time fuses, radio tubes. If you've used an electric mixer in your kitchen, you can learn to run a drill press. If you've ironed your sheets in an electrical mangle, you can learn to run a blueprint machine. Are you ready?"

The government's vigorous recruitment of women provoked fierce opposition in many quarters. In their lead editorial in April 1943, *Catholic World* argued that "women who maintain jobs outside their homes . . . weaken family life, endanger their own marital happiness, rob themselves of man's protective capabilities, and by consequence decrease the number of children. The principal evil in women's work is that it alienates the life of the wife from the life of the husband and gives marriage as much permanence as the room sharing of two freshmen at boarding school."

Eleanor took a more practical approach. If the country needed married women to work, as it undoubtedly did, then it was the country's responsibility to preserve home life as much as possible by helping to lighten the housekeeping burdens. Back in September, Eleanor had forecast "a very chaotic situation" unless government stepped in with a comprehensive program which included day nurseries and play schools adjacent to the plants, community laundries, family restaurants organized to provide fully prepared takeout foods for working women, and the provision of transportation for children from their homes to their schools.

Eleanor's early fears were realized in 1943, as the absentee rate among women working in war industries soared, creating havoc on production lines. The major cause, the Women's Bureau argued, lay in "women's outside responsibilities—the difficulty they have in carrying on a full-time job in the factory and also keeping up a family, doing the shopping, marketing and all the other things which must be done if you are to carry on both jobs." Attempts at purchasing food at the close of the day were often fruitless, because stocks were exhausted and the store was ready to close. The result was that homemakers working the day shift had to remain away from work in order to secure food for their families. "No matter how intense a woman's interest in her job may be," the War Manpower Commission observed, "her children must be cared for, the work of running the house falls on her and she must have time for shopping."

In her talks with the women at the South Portland Shipbuilding yard, Eleanor called for a wide range of creative solutions—staggering the opening and closing times of the factories, keeping bank and department stores open at night, encouraging butchers to hold back part of their meat supply until 6 p.m., asking war plants to hire personal shoppers for the women, to take their orders in the morning and have the filled grocery bags waiting at the door at the end of the shift.

For two hours, the women in the Portland plant shared the details of their daily lives with the first lady. She asked about their homes and their families as well as their work. "Shyly they came forward to speak to her," one of the workers, Betty Blakeley reported, following her as she journeyed from one job to the next, joining her in the cafeteria for a midnight snack. For her part, Eleanor was pleased to see how "extremely interested" the women were in their work—one woman drove fifty miles a day to reach the shipyard; another endured an eighteen-mile bus ride each way. All of them loved the experience, the camaraderie of the plant, the pride in a job well done. As she left, she told the women that her trip through the yard had made her very proud of them and "the wonderful way they had taken hold, particularly of the hard and dirty jobs always heretofore assigned to men."

The following week, Eleanor flew to Des Moines, Iowa, to visit the headquarters of the Women's Army Auxiliary Corps. Legislation creating the opportunity for women to serve with the army as clerks, cooks, chauffeurs, airplane spotters, telegraphers, secretaries, and telephone operators had been signed by the president the previous May. The response was overwhelming. Before the first day of registration had come to an end, more than thirteen thousand women had applied—an "infinite variety," *Life* reported, including "college girls and career women, shop girls and stenographers, housewives and widows," girls whose fathers were army men, girls whose husbands were flying planes and driving tanks, girls who had never passed the gates of a military post. Ultimately, 350,000 women would serve as members of the Women's Army Corps and the WAVES (Women Accepted for Voluntary Emergency Service in the Navy).

When she arrived at Fort Des Moines, a little before noon, Eleanor toured the mess hall, the kitchen, and the barracks. There were forty women in each barrack. "Fall out" time was 5 a.m., with reveille at 6 and classes from 8 to 5. The training encompassed calisthenics, map reading, poison-gas identification, military courtesy, airplane spotting, current events, and parade formation. "In our spare time," one young recruit, Ruth Thompson Pierce, wrote her mother, "we have chores. Scrubbing floors, washing windows, policing grounds, and picking up papers. My knees are like two balloons from scrubbing floors." At KP, she later recalled, "gruff army men would give us heavy cast-iron pots to lift, hundred-pound sacks of flour to carry. Then they would stand around laughing. But we refused to cry 'uncle.' It was exhausting and exhilarating and I loved it."

Eleanor relished the sight of so many women from so many different backgrounds working together. Though she imagined that "the lack of privacy must seem hard to the older women," with double-decker bunks and two thousand people eating in the cafeteria at the same time, she marveled at the adventurous spirit of this female "army behind the fighting forces." Standing on a barracks porch in icy weather, she reviewed twenty-eight hundred bundled-up officer candidates and then watched another sixteen hundred pass in review in the Coliseum. With WAAC bands playing at both reviews, it was a memorable occasion. "I am sure that if all people in the country could see it," Eleanor wrote in her column the following day, "they would be as enthusiastic and as full of admiration as I am about the training and the women who take it."

Eleanor's desire to spend time with women war workers brought her a few weeks later to the Kaiser Company shipyard in Portland, Oregon, where women made up 60 percent of the work force. There she talked at length with Henry Kaiser and his son Edgar about the most critical problem women war workers faced—the lack of adequate day care.

In the summer of 1942, the president, at Eleanor's urging, had approved the first government-sponsored child-care center under the Community Facilities Act which had passed Congress the previous year. The Lanham Act, as it came to be known, provided local aid to war-impacted communities for schools, hospitals, water and sewers, and recreational facilities. Since the summer, six additional centers had been funded in Connecticut, Texas, and North Carolina, but the total number of children covered was only 105,000 —"a mere drop in the bucket," one reporter noted, at a time when perhaps two million children needed care.

For months, Eleanor had been calling on private industry to recognize that providing a day-care center was as essential as providing a cafeteria. Until the needs of working mothers with young children could be fully met, she argued, there was no possibility of ensuring a stable work force. But Eleanor's message was not easily accepted by a generation of men and women who believed, as the Minneapolis chief of welfare, John O. Louis, proclaimed, that "the child should be cared for by its own mother; and that only in those instances where inadequacies of physical surroundings, or mental and moral environment make it absolutely necessary, the child be placed outside the home."

"The worst mother is better than the best institution," Mayor LaGuardia argued in January 1943, and few officials publicly disagreed. So prevalent was the theory that mothers belonged at home that Frances Perkins, the sole woman in the Roosevelt Cabinet, felt compelled to speak up against government-sponsored day care. "What are you doing," Perkins asked the chief of the Children's Bureau, Katherine Lenroot, "to prevent the spread of the day nursery system which I regard as a most unfortunate reaction to the hysterical propaganda about recruiting women workers."

Undeterred, Eleanor stepped up her campaign for day care. Whether one felt it advisable or not for women to work, the fact remained that women were working: more than three million new women had entered the work force between 1940 and 1942, and three million more were expected to enter before the war was over, bringing the total of female workers to nineteen million. Furthermore, the profile of the female worker was changing. Whereas the majority of women workers had been young and single, now 75 percent were married, 60 percent were over thirty-five, and more than 33 percent had children under fourteen. Without day care, Eleanor argued, there was a real danger of child neglect.

From war centers across the country, disturbing reports were coming in of makeshift, unsatisfactory solutions to the child-care problem. In one family in Chicago, *Fortune* reported in February 1943, "a 9 year old boy gets up in a cold house, rouses and feeds his 4 year old sister, delivers her to kindergarten on his way to school, takes her home and prepares her lunch, then locks her in the house while he returns to school." In another family in Connecticut, *The Saturday Evening Post* reported, "a woman in the grave-yard shift drives her car close to the windows of the place where she is employed and her four children sleep in the automobile." In California, a four-year-old girl is found with a box of matches in her hands. She has been trying to light the gas stove as her mother does. The teenage girl who was supposed to baby-sit for her had not shown up.

"These are not isolated cases," *The Saturday Evening Post* concluded after sending a team of reporters around the country. "You can multiply them and cases like them by the thousands. First let it be understood that this country has long had a serious child care problem never adequately met. Now the industrial upheaval of war is blowing up the child care prob-lem to the proportions of an enormous and thinly stretched balloon."

Believing that child neglect was verging on a national scandal, Eleanor pleaded with Kaiser to create a model child-care center that could serve as a prototype for other wartime industries. Kaiser empathized with Eleanor's concern. More than four thousand of the sixteen thousand women at Swan Island and Oregonship, the two Kaiser shipyards in Portland, were mothers, many with children of preschool age. If a day-care center could be con-structed at the shipyard so that the mothers could bring their children before work and stop in to see them during the day, the level of productivity would undoubtedly rise.

Within weeks of Eleanor's visit, under the leadership of young Edgar Kaiser, plans were under way to construct a spectacular day-care center, complete with the newest play equipment, the most sophisticated teaching devices, a cafeteria staffed by nutritionists, and an infirmary staffed by nurses and doctors. With construction costs covered by the U.S. Maritime Commis-sion and operating costs borne by Kaiser, nothing was spared in the attempt to create a wholesome, happy environment for the children.

The Swan Island Center was built in the shape of a wheel, which enclosed a great inner court protected from outside traffic. The spokes were fifteen playrooms, each with long banks of windows on two sides to ensure proper lighting. "It was as nice a building as one could imagine," the center's director, James Hymes, recalled. "The walls were painted in beautiful pastel shades; the chandeliers had a futuristic look, with the letters of the alphabet and elephants painted on them. It was one of those rare settings where the only obstacles, like time, were not man-imposed."

Outstanding teachers were recruited to staff the center, which was open whenever the shipyard was open—six days a week, fifty-two weeks a year. Mount Holyoke graduate Mary Willett was teaching at an exclusive nursery school on the East Coast when she heard about the new center at the Kaiser shipyards. "I could tell immediately that this was something special," she recalled, "a chance to reach children from all different backgrounds at a very early age. I was thrilled when the telegram came offering me a position at $55 a week. How privileged I was to be part of this great experiment!"

When Miss Willett reached the Swan Island Center, the situation was even better than she hoped. The children, ranging from eighteen months to six years, came from farms in Minnesota, Ohio, and Iowa, from city streets in St. Louis, Los Angeles, and Oakland, from Southern towns and foreign lands. "We had Indian children, Mexican children, and black children," she recalled. "I remember one big black woman whose son, Freddy, was in the program. She was so happy to know that, for the first time in Freddy's life, he was not being Jim Crowed."

The Swan Island Center was a head-start program a quarter of a century ahead of its time. One woman came all the way from Louisiana because she heard the program was great for children. And the experience was unique for the teachers as well. "It was without question the highlight of my whole career," Mary Willett lovingly recalled fifty years later.

In its first year of operation, the Swan Island Center served nearly two thousand children. Opened at first only for day and swing shifts, it soon added cots and bedding supplies to accommodate the graveyard shift, keeping its doors open twenty-four-hours a day. During summers and school vacations, it operated a separate program for children from ages six to twelve. An additional program was created for nonenrolled Swan Island families who needed emergency care just for the day, if their usual arrangement broke down. The total cost for full-time care, including food, was 75 cents per child per day, $1.25 for two. And the center went a step further. At the end of the day, tired workers could pick up, at cost, fully cooked dinners to bring home to their families. For this Eleanor was directly responsible. "She had seen a food-service operation in England," Director James Hymes recalled, "and had told Henry Kaiser about it."

The success of the Swan Island Center stimulated war plants and shipyards across the nation to provide day care. It was estimated that each child-care center serving forty mothers made possible eight thousand productive man hours monthly. Slowly, Eleanor was winning her long struggle to make child care recognized as a national problem that required a collective response. Though the needs of working mothers were never fully met, nearly $50 million would be spent on day care before the war came to an end, $3 million for construction of new centers and $47 million for operating expenses. By the summer of 1945, more than a million and a half children would be in day care.

• • •

When Eleanor returned home from her travels in late February, she found that her husband had been sick in bed for a week with an intestinal grippe. In her absence, Margaret Suckley had taken care of him, sharing tea with him in the late afternoon, sitting by his bedside at night, traveling with him to Hyde Park. It happened that Churchill was also confined to his bed that week, suffering from fever and pneumonia. "Oddly enough," *The New York Times* observed, while the papers were full of war maps showing the tides of battle, "the two most important war graphs of the last fortnight were never published.... They are the temperature charts of the recent sick rooms in the White House and at 10 Downing Street.... It is no exaggeration to say that the doctors' charts were fully as important for the world as any maps in the newspaper."

"I think I picked up sleeping sickness or Gambia fever or some kindred bug in that hell hole of yours called Bathhurst," Roosevelt teased Churchill, referring to the capital of British Gambia, where his plane had refueled en route to Casablanca. "It laid me low—four days in bed—then a lot of sulphadiathole which cured the fever and left me feeling like a wet rag. I was no good after 2 p.m. and after standing it for a week or so, I went to Hyde Park for five days: got full of health in glorious zero weather—came back ... and have been feeling like a fighting cock ever since. Please, please for the sake of the world don't overdo these days. You must remember that it takes about a month of occasional let-ups to get back your full strength. ... Tell Mrs. Churchill that when I was laid up I was a thoroughly model patient and that I hope you will live down the reputation in our Press of having been the 'world's worst patient.' "

•   •   •

As the tenth anniversary of Roosevelt's first inaugural approached, reporters remained astonished by his unruffled demeanor. Amid tumultuous events abroad, turmoil in Congress, and trouble at home, he remained relaxed, good-humored, and self-assured.

The war had cut into many of Franklin's favorite relaxations. The hours before bed that he had used to devote to his stamp collection now went to a study of thick reports about tanks and planes, while the unending pile of work on his desk—four thousand letters a day compared with the four hundred President Hoover received—took away the late-afternoon swims he had so enjoyed in the White House pool.

But still he was able to joke and to laugh. And still he found ways to relax—over cocktails, movies, and cards. At his ritual cocktail hour, the unwritten rule remained that all talk of politics or war must cease. On weekends at Hyde Park, he refused to work until after noon, indulging in long hours of sleep and lazy jaunts through the woods that invariably lifted his spirits.

While Roosevelt continually renewed his energies through relaxation, Adolf Hitler diminished his strength through overwork. "The Fuhrer seems to have aged 15 years during three and a half years of war," Goebbels noted in his diary that same March. "He doesn't get out into the fresh air. He does not relax. He sits in his bunker, fusses and broods." In time, Albert Speer argued, Hitler's tendency to overwork left him "permanently caustic and irritable," unable to absorb fresh impressions, unwilling to listen to criticism.

During the early days of the war, Hitler had taken great pleasure in the ritual of a late-afternoon tea to which, much like Roosevelt's cocktail hour, he invited close associates and friends for relaxed conversation and idle gossip. But as the pressures of war mounted, the hour for tea was steadily pushed back, from four to six to eight to ten. By 1943, Speer noted, Hitler's evening tea did not begin until two o'clock in the morning. While most of Berlin slept, Hitler sat with his aides, recounting tales from his youth or from the early days of struggle. Within this intimate circle, Speer remarked, Hitler's familiar stories "were appreciated as if they had been heard for the first time," but exhaustion took its toll, and no one could "whip up much liveliness or even contribute to the conversation." At the end of the "relaxed" tea, Hitler was more agitated than when it began.

Roosevelt's tenth anniversary in office found Eleanor, in Tommy's judgment, "a bit worn as to patience," still tending to crowd too many engagements into a single day. "Five minutes here and five minutes there are not satisfactory to anyone," Tommy complained in a letter to Esther Lape. But as long as America's boys were dying abroad, Eleanor refused to lighten her load; as long as she was privileged to travel, the least she could do was to visit wounded soldiers in hospitals wherever she went. "I'm completely exhausted after a hospital day," she confessed to Joe Lash, "& I lie awake thinking what we should do in the future for them but one goes on with daily round of life."

Eleanor had promised Lash before he went into the army that she would give up any other engagement if she had a chance to see him. Despite the pressure of an almost inhuman schedule, she kept her promise. No sooner was Lash transferred to weather-forecasting school at Chanute Field than Eleanor journeyed to Urbana, Illinois, to see him.

She arrived at the Hotel Lincoln on Friday night, having reserved room 332 for herself and Tommy and a connecting room for Lash. At 9 p.m., Lash joined Eleanor for dinner in her room. On Saturday, they stayed in the hotel all day long, eating all their meals in their room except for lunch, which they ate in the hotel dining room. Afterward, Lash "stretched out luxuriantly" on the bed for a long nap. "I'm so happy to have been with you," she wrote Joe Lash after she returned to Washington on Sunday. "Separation between people who love each other, makes the reunion always like a new discovery. You forget how much you love certain movements of the hands or the glance in the person's eyes or how nice it is to sit in the same room & look at their back!"

Three weeks later, Eleanor joined Joe Lash again, this time at the Hotel Blackstone in Chicago. Here, too, they stayed in Eleanor's room most of the day. In the afternoon, they went out for a walk; in the evening, Lash was so drowsy that he fell asleep on the bed while Eleanor stroked his forehead. "I loved just sitting near you while you slept . . . ," Eleanor later wrote.

But the pleasures Eleanor derived from her time with Lash were quickly dispelled when she was told by a hotel employee that her room had been bugged. For weeks, it turned out, Lash had been under surveillance by the army's Counter-Intelligence Corps. Mistakenly convinced that he was part of a communist conspiracy, the CIC had been reading his mail and trailing him wherever he went. When the first lady's telegram arrived, inviting him to join her at the Hotel Blackstone, the CIC bugged her room.

Apparently unconcerned about the impropriety of spending two weekends in adjoining rooms with a young serviceman, Eleanor went to see Hopkins as soon as she returned and pleaded with him to find out what was going on. Hopkins took the matter up with General Marshall, who confirmed that Mrs. Roosevelt's room had indeed been bugged. When the president learned that army agents had put his wife under surveillance without presidential authorization, he was furious. Moving quickly to take action against everyone responsible, he ordered an immediate shake-up of the army's intelligence operations, including the disbanding of the CIC. In addition, military orders were drawn up to send Lash overseas, along with his entire group of weather forecasters.

Years later, Lash was still unsure whether the president himself was behind the decision that sent him to the South Pacific. "All the top men who were involved in this affair—the President, Hopkins, Marshall—were preoccupied with decisions that carried the fate of nations and millions of lives," Lash recorded. "They would understandably be impatient with G-2 and its obsession with Eleanor Roosevelt and myself. They may well have decided that, in addition to shaking up G-2, the most expeditious way of getting rid of the Lash problem was to ship me overseas along with a group of fellow student forecasters so it would not seem that I had been singled out for this sanction."

•   •   •

In March, Eleanor's attention was drawn once again to the struggle for equal treatment in the military. On her desk she found an eloquent plea for help from Henry Jones, a Negro sergeant stationed at Carlsbad Army Air Field in New Mexico. Sergeant Jones described the morale-shattering treatment visited upon Negro soldiers as a consequence of segregated facilities. The Negro men of the 349th Aviation Squadron were "loyal Americans," he began, "ready and willing to do their part to preserve Democracy. For the most part the Personnel of this Squadron is made up of young men who were born and lived in the Northern states where they enjoyed to a large degree the advantages of a democracy. However, the fact that we want to do our best for our country and to be valiant soldiers, seems to mean nothing to the Commanding Officer of our Post as indicated by the fact that 'Jim Crowism' is practiced on the very grounds of our camp."

The sergeant's complaint focused on the Negro soldier's unequal access to recreational facilities and transportation—visible symbols of injustice. At the post theater, with a total capacity of over a thousand seats, only 20 seats, in the last row, were provided for Negroes. At the post exchange, where refreshments were served, Negroes did not have the privilege of eating inside the building. On buses to and from camp, the front seats were reserved for white soldiers; Negro soldiers were either crammed into one small row of seats in the rear or passed up altogether and forced to walk.

"We do not ask for special privileges," Jones concluded, speaking for 121 fellow Negro soldiers whose signatures were attached. "All we desire is to have equality; to be free to participate in all activities, means of transportation, privileges and amusements afforded any American soldier."

After reading Jones' letter, Eleanor wrote a long letter to Henry Stimson describing the conditions at Carlsbad and said she would appreciate it very much if he would request an investigation. Unfortunately, the discrimination at Carlsbad was standard practice throughout the country, since the majority of army camps were located in the South and the Southwest, where strict segregation prevailed.

Most army camps boasted a central post theater, where movies were shown, lectures delivered, and concerts performed. In some camps, as Jones described, Negroes were confined to a few seats in the last row. In other camps, a separate, less adequate space was allocated. "They have a show where the colored go," one GI explained, "and you sit on the outside to see the picture. If it rains there isn't any picture." Observing these unequal arrangements, the singer Lena Horne cut short her tour of army posts. German POWs imprisoned in the U.S., she argued, had a better opportunity to hear her than Negro soldiers.

For Negro soldiers, like Henry Jones, who had lived all their lives in the North, subjection to the Jim Crow laws of the South was intolerable. In almost every Southern city or town, Negro soldiers were restricted to a small area of the city where a few restaurants and lounges were crowded together on a single block. If they tried to go elsewhere, restaurants refused to serve them, merchants evicted them, and townspeople shouted at them.

To many Negroes, army historian Ulysses Lee concluded in his study of Negro troops, "the uncertainty of their status was as damaging to morale as the knowledge of definite restrictions." Since the rules varied widely from post to post and from town to town, each recruit had to find his own way through the maze of shaded meanings. Would he be served if he tried to make a purchase at the main post exchange? Was there a special Negro branch? Was he free to enter the gym, the bowling alley, the theater? Was he allowed to subscribe to a Negro newspaper? Which chair should he use in the barber shop, in the dentist's office? "That's the kind of democracy we are fighting for," Private Laurence Burnett pointedly remarked upon discovering that he had to sit in a colored-only chair at the dental clinic. "It is so foolish it makes me laugh most of the time. I can't sit in a dental chair that a white man has sat in or will sit in in the future!"

When Eleanor heard these stories, she felt like weeping. "What a lot we must do to make our war a real victory for democracy," she said, again and again. From her sitting room on the second floor, she fired off passionate missives to General Marshall asking him to investigate the unacceptable situations described by men like Henry Jones. So large was the flow of Eleanor's letters to Marshall that the general was forced to assign one and later two members of his staff to respond.

Finally, on March 10, 1943, the War Department took corrective action. A directive was issued to all service commands forbidding the designation of any recreational facilities, "including theaters and post exchanges," by race. The new directive required the removal of remaining "White" and "Colored only" signs in the designation of facilities, specifying that, if only one facility existed on a camp, arrangements must be made for its equal use by troops of both races. Though the directive did not touch on transportation, perhaps the most deeply felt problem, and though it did not prevent the continued use of separate facilities as long as they were not designated by racial signs (on many posts, blacks still frequented what had been the colored service club, since it was closest to their barracks, only now it was known as Service Club No. 2), it did establish the principle that Negro troops were to be given equal opportunity to use all the existing facilities provided for the welfare and recreation of soldiers. "The fact that anyone could use any facility," army historians observed, "was enough to turn the tide of Negro soldiers' morale upward." It was a beginning wedge in the desegregation of the armed forces.

Eleanor's special advocacy of Negro troops involved her later that same spring in the fortunes of the 99th Pursuit Squadron, the first unit of Negro combat pilots. The flight program at Tuskegee Air Field had been instituted in March 1941 in response to a legal suit filed by a young black pilot, Yancey Williams, who had been denied admission to the all-white Air Corps. Through 1941 and 1942, the program produced nearly a thousand black combat pilots, but by the spring of 1943 not a single one had been sent into combat. "We were undoubtedly the most highly trained squadron in the US," Louis Purnell, a member of the 99th, later wrote; "the Air Corps brass couldn't decide what to do with us so we flew and flew for nearly a whole year simply to maintain our proficiency." Inspectors had declared the 99th ready for deployment in September 1942, but still nothing happened. "The waiting got tiresome," squadron leader Benjamin Davis, Jr., recalled.

In March, Tuskegee Director Frederick Patterson turned to Eleanor for help. "The program of preflight training is going forward," he explained, "but morale is disturbed by the fact that the 99th Pursuit Squadron trained for more than a year is still at Tuskegee and virtually idle." Eleanor sent a copy of Patterson's letter to Stimson with a cover note of her own: "This seems to me a really crucial situation."

The long period of waiting came to an end on the morning of April 15, 1943, when the members of the 99th boarded a ship en route to North Africa. News of the squadron's departure spread quickly through the Negro press, which had been agitating for months "to get our boys overseas like everybody else." It was a "tremendous moment," Benjamin Davis, Jr., recalled. "All the members of the 99th were beginning to understand the significance of an assignment which went far beyond purely military considerations. If a black fighter squadron could get a good account of itself in combat, its success might lead the way to greater opportunities for black people throughout the armed services."

"As we left the shores of the United States," Davis recalled, "we felt as if we were separating ourselves, at least for the moment, from the evils of racial discrimination. Perhaps in combat overseas, we would have more freedom and respect than we had experienced at home."

The Tuskegee airmen would prove to the world, a Defense Department study later noted, that "blacks could fly in combat with the best of the pilots of any nation." In the course of 1,578 missions over North Africa, Italy, and Germany, the 99th Pursuit Squadron would be credited with shooting down 111 airborne craft and destroying 150 on the ground. Winners of a hundred Distinguished Flying Crosses, the 99th was the only escort group that never lost a single bomber to an enemy fighter.

•　•　•

On April 13, 1943, Roosevelt was scheduled to leave for a sixteen-day train trip through the deep South and the Midwest to inspect army bases and training camps. It was almost seven months since his last inspection trip, and the commander-in-chief was anxious to take his own measure of the readiness of the American soldier.

Eleanor had intended to accompany her husband on the trip, but when she learned that Anna, agitated by John's imminent departure to North Africa, was on her way to Washington, she decided to stay with her daughter for several days and then join Franklin on the road later in the week. Anna was still finding it hard to accept John's decision to leave the hard plodding job of publishing the paper to her while he opted for a glamorous assignment abroad. "Men are always little boys, I guess," Eleanor told her daughter. Never had the bond between mother and daughter seemed stronger. "I'll always be on hand when you need me," Eleanor promised.

In Eleanor's absence, Laura Delano and Margaret Suckley once again accompanied the president on his trip. Ross McIntire, Steve Early, Grace Tully, and Basil O'Connor were also on the train, though, from what Tommy could gather, Roosevelt spent all his time with Laura and Margaret, "had two meals every day with them and only once or twice had any of the others on the train at meals." Feeling irritated at Laura Delano, whom she considered "an imperious thing," Tommy failed to understand that on trips like this, when he was out among thousands of people all day long, the president needed to relax, and with Laura and Margaret he could say what he wanted and never worry about the consequences.

As usual, Margaret was in charge of the president's dog, Fala. A favorite with the crowds, Fala was invariably greeted by oohs and aahs whenever he emerged from the train for his limbering-up walks. Laura had also brought along a dog, a five-month-old Irish setter. "She had to get off at every stop," Tommy complained, "find a grass stop and wait for the biological functions which she then discussed in detail with anyone who would listen. One night she was off the train and the secret service did not realize it until the train had started. They threw her on and threw the dog after her and were much annoyed."

The president stopped first at the Parris Island Marine boot camp in South Carolina, where two thousand recruits were massed to render honors and be reviewed. After the official ceremonies, the president was driven to the rifle range, where, in the midst of a howling windstorm, he witnessed an elaborate target practice with Garand rifles.

No longer were American soldiers training with broomsticks and stovepipes; no longer did the army look like "a few nice boys with BB guns." By the spring of 1943, after only three years of mobilization, the American army had expanded from fewer than five hundred thousand to 4.3 million, and the president had authorized a total of 7.5 million by the end of the year. Nothing so large had ever been created in such a short time. "Just imagining it and willing it into existence," historian Geoffrey Perrett has written in his study of the American army in World War II, "was a brilliant, thrilling adventure of the spirit."

Nor were the men soft and overweight, as they had been in September of 1940, when the president first witnessed maneuvers in upstate New York. At Fort Benning, Georgia, the next day, the president was told that the men in training had pulled in their belts an average of four inches while adding an inch to their chests and ten pounds of muscle. Driving through the wooded hilly terrain of Fort Benning, the president saw paratroopers leaping from huge transports in groups of eighty-two and watched with interest as officer candidates ducked and dodged through a field alive with tracer bullets and exploding charges.

"Fort Benning is such an immense post," Roosevelt's naval aide William Rigdon wrote in his report of the trip, "and there was so much of interest happening here today, as to create within one the same feeling he would experience in attending his first 5 ring circus." After visiting the Parachute School, Roosevelt visited the Infantry School, where every phase of the complex training of an infantryman was demonstrated. "Even in the Infantry, the ground arm requiring the least technical training," army historian Robert Palmer notes in his study of the procurement of enlisted personnel, "the private had to understand the use of a dozen weapons. He had to acquire at least an elementary knowledge of many things besides: camouflage and concealment; mine removal and the detection of booby traps; patrolling and map reading; and combat intelligence; recognition of American, Allied and enemy aircraft, armored vehicles, and other equipment; the use and disposal of captured equipment; the processing of prisoners of war; first aid, field sanitation, and maintenance of life and health out of doors over long periods and under conditions of extreme difficulty."

Although these facts were understood by the high command of the armed forces, the combination of voluntary enlistment in the navy and the Marine Corps, and priorities established in 1942 which gave the army air force first call on the army's highest-quality men, had left a disproportionate share of the nation's lowest-quality enlistees—in terms of intelligence and education —in the ground forces. By mid-1943, Lieutenant General Leslie McNair, commanding general of the army ground forces, was so worried about the situation, believing that American soldiers were sustaining avoidable casualties because ground troops "did not represent a fair cross section of the nation's manpower," that the priority of air and ground forces was reversed.

At Fort Oglethorpe, Georgia, the following day, the president inspected three companies of WAAC trainees. Standing in formation along the border of the parade field, trim and neat in their khaki summer uniforms, the women were so excited to see the president that they momentarily forgot their military status and broke ranks to wave. The president smiled broadly and waved back. The next day, he enjoyed a hearty meal at Camp Gruber consisting of salad, chili con carne, macaroni, carrots, French-fried potatoes, rolls, and butter. "I don't get as good a meal as that in the White House," he laughingly remarked, referring, of course, to the infamous Henrietta Nesbitt.

Eleanor joined her husband at their son Elliott's home in Fort Worth, Texas, on the morning of April 19. Though Elliott was overseas, the Roosevelts enjoyed the chance to see their daughter-in-law Ruth and their three grandchildren. "This is a lovely restful home," Eleanor noted in her column that day, though everywhere she looked she was reminded of her absent son, who was stationed in Africa. "How many men there are today whose little children will have to learn to know them after their babyhood is over," she remarked. Photographs, books, saddles, and pictures all spoke of her son's interests, but it might be years before he would be home again.

The next day, the president and the first lady headed to Monterrey, Mexico, for dinner with Mexican President and Mrs. Manuel Avila Camacho. Though the visit was not announced until that afternoon, the streets were lined with thousands of people holding flags, flowers, and children. Ever since the president's Good Neighbor Policy in 1933, which declared America's commitment to equality and cooperation among the American republics and called for an abolition of all artificial barriers to trade, Roosevelt had been a popular figure in Latin America. Driving with Mrs. Avila Camacho, Eleanor proudly carried on a small conversation in Spanish, the result of the Spanish lessons she had begun that winter in Washington. At Corpus Christi, Texas, the following day, the president addressed the body of naval cadets and witnessed an impressive aerial show highlighted by an exhibition of dive-bombing in which seaplanes dived to within fifty feet of the water before releasing their dummy bombs over a small yellow float moored in the bay. At each direct hit, the crowd roared with applause. There was also a large contingent of WAVES at the base, and Eleanor was amused to learn that "some of the officers who had been very much opposed to them were now clamoring for more."

On Easter Sunday, the president stopped at Fort Riley, Kansas, one of the oldest military posts in the nation, dating back to 1852. After lunch at the Cavalry School Club, Roosevelt spoke reassuringly to the troops, contrasting this inspection tour with the last one he had made, seven months earlier. "It seems to me that I see in you that intangible thing," he said, "a very definite improvement." Morale was strikingly higher than it had been before. He could see it by watching the faces of the officers and listening to them talk. He could see it by looking at the tough seasoned bodies of the young recruits. He could see it by driving through the grounds of bustling camps where only dirt and mud had existed a short time before. "The Army has gone through growing pains and today the Army is a grown-up unit." Indeed, so impressed was he by the healthy appearance of the men and women he had seen that he had begun, he admitted, to come around to the idea Eleanor had originally backed, of continuing some form of national service even in peacetime.

On returning to Washington, the president met with the press. "His spirits were higher and he looked fresher," reporters noted. He had seen "a picture of America's resources, physical, industrial, agricultural and spiritual," being summoned to "an all out effort" to win the war. "He had traveled many miles in various kinds of conveyances, had felt sun and wind and rain, had eaten turkey, hot dogs, chili and a seven course Mexican dinner, had made talks and been among crowds. But for him, it was fun; it was one of his favorite ways of relaxing."

•   •   •

In the middle of the president's tour, the White House mail pouch had carried a disturbing letter from Interior Secretary Ickes suggesting that the situation in the Japanese internment camps was rapidly becoming worse. The evacuees, Ickes warned, "who first accepted with philosophical understanding the decision of their Government," were becoming increasingly bitter. "I do not think that we can disregard the unnecessary creating of a hostile group right in our own territory," Ickes wrote.

Troubled by the tone of Ickes' letter, the president asked Eleanor to take a side trip to the Gila River Camp in Arizona before returning to Washington. It was a risky request for Roosevelt to make, knowing as he did the strength of Eleanor's negative feelings about the original order to evacuate. Sending her to check things out would inevitably involve her again in the situation. But there was no one else he trusted as much to bring him back an unvarnished picture of what was going on.

The Gila River Camp, housing twelve thousand people, was one of ten permanent camps built by the War Relocation Authority to house the hundred thousand evacuees. The others included Heart Mountain in Wyoming, Topaz in Utah, Manzanar in California, and Minidoka in Idaho. Set in the middle of the desert, Gila endured temperatures that ranged between 125 degrees in the summer and thirty degrees below in winter. In the summer, one evacuee wrote, "You could not take hold of a doorknob without a handkerchief in hand." On summer nights, the internees all slept out of doors, some between wet sheets, others with wet towels on their heads.

Arriving on April 23, Eleanor was spared the unbearable heat of the summer sun, though she did encounter the swirling dust that left everyone's hair white, mouths gritty, and eyes red. "It chokes you and brings about irritations of the nose and throat," she wrote. For many evacuees, the ever-present dust in the desert camps was enemy number one. "It gets into every pore in the body," one evacuee wrote; "it comes in through every crack in the room of which there are thousands; it comes sifting down from the roof and it gets through your clothes and sticks to your body."

Eleanor was escorted through the camp by Dillon Myer, director of the War Relocation Authority, which oversaw the ten centers. Myer was overwhelmed by Eleanor's energy. She "covered everything in the center of any importance," he wrote, "including all the wards in the hospitals, the schools and all phases of the service activities so that she could report back to the President."

Eleanor came away from her sojourn with increased respect for the ingenuity and endurance of the Japanese Americans. Despite the wind and the dust, the internees had created a productive community. On the land surrounding the camp, they were raising livestock and producing vegetables sufficient to feed the entire camp. A camouflage-net factory was producing far beyond expectations. Within the camp itself, the evacuees had set up their own barber shops, dental offices, newspapers, adult-education courses, movie theaters, and government. In the ten centers as a whole, over 25 percent of the adult population were enrolled in a wide variety of classes, including psychology, English, American history, cabinetmaking, radio repair, auto mechanics, and shorthand, with English and American history the two most popular subjects.

"Everything is spotlessly clean," Eleanor marveled. The people worked on their whitewashed barracks constantly, and "you can see the results of their labors." Handmade screens created a sense of individuality and privacy amid rows of residential blocks that otherwise looked exactly alike. "Sometimes there are little Japanese gardens, sometimes vegetables or flowers bloom. Makeshift porches and shades have been improvised by some out of gunny sacks and bits of wood salvaged from packing cases."

Considerable ingenuity had also been used, Eleanor observed, in planning schools. There were nearly thirty thousand Japanese-American children of school age in the ten centers. Establishing schools for them amid hostile local school authorities had been a major undertaking. Requests to the

University of Arizona for library books and faculty lectures had been regularly rejected. "We are at war," University of Arizona President Alfred Atkinson said, "and *these people* are our enemies." Yet, despite all these problems, a complete school system had been established. In the absence of school buildings, different barracks had been set aside for a nursery school, an elementary school, a high school, and a library. Other barracks, their walls decorated with paper flowers and paintings, had been turned into laundry rooms and recreation centers and mess halls. The food was adequate, Eleanor noted, though the evacuees were in no way being "coddled," as some newspapers charged.

From a superficial point of view, the daily life at Gila seemed bearable. The evacuees had decent shelter, sustenance, and work. But Eleanor had learned from long practice to look below the surface in order to understand the inner life of the institutions she inspected. What was not bearable, she recognized, was the loss of freedom: the barbed-wire fences and the armed guards in sentry towers surrounding the camp; the regulations confining everyone to barracks by nine with lights out by ten; the orders given to the guards to shoot anyone who approached within twenty feet of the fence.

No matter how hard the WRA tried to make the camp look like an ordinary community, it was a penitentiary, imprisoning people who had never been convicted of doing anything wrong. No matter how enthusiastic the teachers, it was impossible to teach the principles of American democracy to citizens and residents whose fundamental rights had been taken away. "To be frank with you," sighed Mrs. Jones, an elementary-school teacher appointed by the WRA, "it embarrasses me to teach them the flag salute. Is our nation indivisible? Does it stand for justice for all? Those questions come up to my mind constantly."

Beyond the loss of liberty, Eleanor recognized, was the breakdown of the traditional family structure. With thousands of people assembled together, parents were unable to exercise the strict control they had once had over their children. "With everyone eating in mess halls," one Gila resident explained, "the family eating pattern was broken up completely. Table manners were forgotten. Conversation was impossible."

In the topsy-turvy world of the camps, the Nisei held the upper hand. "We hold the advantage of numbers," young Charles Kikuchi recorded in his diary, "and the fact we are citizens. Many of the parents who would never let their daughters go to dances before do not object so strenuously now. There can no longer be conflict over types of food served as everybody eats the same thing—with forks. The Nisei as a whole rejoice that they no longer have to attend Japanese language school."

"For the young people, it was an adventure," high-school student Jiro Ishihara observed. "But for the older people it was intolerable. I understood this only much later, when I became a parent myself and realized how hard it must have been for my parents to wake up one day and know that every ritual their life depended upon had been taken away."

"Feel sort of sorry for Pop tonight," Charles Kikuchi wrote shortly after arriving at the camp. "He had his three electric clippers hung on the wall and Tom has built him a barrel chair for the barber seat. It's a bit pathetic when he so tenderly cleans off the clippers after using them. He probably realizes he no longer controls the family group."

The split between the generations had been unwittingly aggravated, Eleanor came to understand, by the War Department's decision on January 28, 1943, to allow the American-born Nisei to enlist in a special unit in the army to be trained for combat. Though the new policy had been enthusiastically embraced by Nisei who rushed to sign up, the despair had deepened on the part of Issei, who were not allowed to volunteer, contributing to the decline in morale Harold Ickes had noted.

Henry Ebihara spoke for many in a poignant letter to Stimson. "I was very happy when I read your announcement that Nisei Americans would be given the chance to volunteer for active combat duty. But at the same time I am sad—sad because under your present laws I am an enemy alien. I am 22 years old, American in thought, American in act, as American as any other citizen. I was born in Japan. My parents brought me to America when I was only two years old. . . . Please give me a chance to serve in the armed forces. How can a democratic nation allow a technicality of birthplace to stand in the way when the nation is fighting to preserve the rights of free men?"

The only answer, Eleanor determined, taking into account all the reasons for the declining morale in the camps, was to relax the exclusion order and allow the Japanese to return to their homes, "to start independent and productive lives again." Dillon Myer agreed. Now that military necessity could no longer be considered a viable rationale, he argued that the time had come to open the doors of the camps.

"To undo mistakes is always harder than not to create them originally," Eleanor observed, "but we seldom have foresight. Therefore we have no choice but to try to correct our past mistakes."

The president listened carefully to Eleanor's report. Though he did not admit that the original decision had been a mistake, he agreed with her that "normal American life is hardly possible under any form of detention" and that "the best hope for the future lies in encouraging the relocation of Japanese Americans throughout the country." But at the same time, he was hearing from Stimson that if he moved too quickly a massive public outcry would result. It was the opinion of the War Department that the recent decline in morale could be traced to the activities of "a vicious, well-organized pro-Japan minority group to be found at each relocation project." The first step, Stimson argued, was to remove these agitators to a separate camp at Tule Lake; then, and only then, could steps be taken to clear the remaining evacuees for release.

The president backed Stimson's decision to segregate the troublemakers, but he promised Eleanor that he would meet with Myer and figure out ways to relax the order so that exit permits could be issued to individual Japanese who had work to do and a place to go. The process was slow and cumbersome, but by the end of 1943, between those who had joined the army and those who had received work permits to leave, nearly one-third of the evacuees had left the camps.

CHAPTER 17

"IT IS BLOOD

ON YOUR HANDS"

By 1943, Washington was pretty much like any other boomtown during the war—its population had nearly doubled since 1940, decent housing was impossible to find, uniforms were everywhere, gasoline was scarce, buses were overcrowded, and living costs were high. Most of the newcomers were women, searching for jobs as typists and clerks in the burgeoning federal bureaucracy, which had spread its offices into every available space, into ugly temporary buildings, old schools, apartments and homes, gymnasiums and skating rinks. They were called GGs, or government girls; they came on buses and trains with their suitcases in their hands, to live in huge dormitories specially erected for them; and with their help, journalist David Brinkley wrote, "the federal government created more records in the four years of war than in its entire previous history."

The 11th of May was a soft spring day in Washington. Couples sauntered along the banks of the Potomac; strollers circled the Reflecting Pond. In weather like this, the president would ordinarily have taken the time to enjoy a leisurely ride through the hills of Virginia, but since Prime Minister Churchill was due to arrive that evening for a two-week visit, Roosevelt was forced to spend the entire day at his desk, cleaning up correspondence.

The one break in the day came at 2:30 p.m., when he received an off-the-record visit from the Russian artist Elizabeth Shoumatoff. Madame Shoumatoff had come to paint a portrait of the president, at the request of Lucy Mercer Rutherfurd. Considering the impact Lucy had had on his marriage, and the promise he had made to Eleanor never to see her again, Roosevelt decided to keep Shoumatoff's visit a private matter.

Shoumatoff had met Lucy Rutherfurd six years before in Aiken, South Carolina, when Lucy's stepdaughter, Alice Rutherfurd, had commissioned her to do a portrait of Lucy. Meeting Lucy for the first time was "quite impressive," Shoumatoff recalled. "Very tall, like the rest of her family, exquisitely lovely and gracious, she impressed you not so much by her striking appearance as by the shining quality in her features, particularly in her smile." An acute observer, Shoumatoff noticed that the clothes Lucy wore made her look older than she was, "as if deliberately diminishing the thirty-years difference between herself and her husband.

Winthrop Rutherfurd was seventy-five years old and in frail health when Shoumatoff first met him. Though she had come to draw a portrait of Lucy, Lucy asked her to paint her husband first. "Winthrop Rutherfurd, in spite of his advanced years," Shoumatoff later recalled, "was one of the handsomest men" she had ever painted, "and certainly the most aristocratic." He looked like "an English peer with his chiseled features, sharp eyes, and a sarcastic expression around his mouth." Curiously, Shoumatoff observed, "there was something about his face that vaguely resembled FDR."

Observing the daily routine in the Rutherfurd household during that first meeting, Shoumatoff was struck by the unflagging attention Lucy gave to her husband. "Everything whirled around him; their life was governed by his invalid regime. She never went out in the evenings and completely devoted her existence to making him happy and comfortable." Through nearly two decades of marriage, Lucy had mothered Winthrop's five children (a sixth had died on the eve of their wedding) and given birth to a daughter of her own, Barbara Rutherfurd. Barbara was fourteen, a student at the fashionable Fermate School for Girls in Aiken, when Shoumatoff first met Lucy. Watching Lucy with her extended family, Shoumatoff remarked that she had "seldom seen a mother more beloved and respected than was Lucy by her step-children."

For the Rutherfurds, as for most residents of the Aiken winter colony, the social season stretched from mid-October until after the Easter holidays. During these months, the calendar was filled with charity balls, bazaars, and sporting events, including the annual hunt breakfast, the point tournament at the Palmetto Golf Club and the thoroughbred races at the Aiken Mile. Through the twenties and thirties, Winthrop and Lucy Rutherfurd were regulars at all these events; the Rutherfurd name frequently appeared in the society pages of the *Aiken Standard & Review*. Since Winthrop's illness, Lucy had led a quieter life, but the comings and goings of the Rutherfurd children were regularly noted in the local paper. There were stories of athletic achievement—all four boys, Winthrop Jr., John, Hugo, and Guy, were outstanding athletes, champion golfers, tennis players, and scull racers—while Alice and Barbara excelled at horseback riding. There were descriptions of social engagements and debutante balls. The sheer variety of activities the children enjoyed was impressive.

Lucy had been so pleased by the first portrait that she asked Shoumatoff to come to their summer estate, in Allamuchy, New Jersey, to paint a second picture of her husband, with his fox terriers. It was in Allamuchy, Shoumatoff recalled, on a moonlit evening as she and Lucy were driving along the woodland roads, that Lucy first talked of Franklin Roosevelt. Shoumatoff had heard rumors that Lucy and Franklin had enjoyed a romance before Lucy was married, but on this occasion Lucy simply talked about his leadership qualities, "his extraordinary ability to work, his dynamic approach to anything he undertook."

It was not until the spring of 1943, when Shoumatoff was back in Aiken for a series of additional portraits, that the conversation returned to Roosevelt. "You should really paint the President," Lucy told her friend. "He has such a remarkable face. There is no painting of him that gives his true expression. I think you could do a wonderful portrait. Would you do a portrait of him if it was arranged?" Delighted and daunted by the challenge, Shoumatoff was stunned when Lucy called the following morning to say she had telephoned Washington and the president would sit for a portrait in two weeks, on May 11. "I did not understand how the whole thing could have been arranged so quickly," she admitted.

The answer lay in the affection Roosevelt still held for the woman he had once loved. If little by little passion had been extinguished by absence, regret smothered by routine, the memories were still there. The man who had disciplined himself nearly a quarter-century ago to give Lucy up must have felt he had a right to indulge the legitimate wishes of an old friend.

The exact shape of Franklin's friendship with Lucy over time is not easy to fix. Through the twenties and thirties, the only evidence that they ever saw one another is the oft-told tale that Lucy attended Roosevelt's first inaugural as his special guest, half concealed in a limousine on the edge of the crowd. The only other recorded contacts through these two decades are a couple of chatty letters Lucy wrote in 1927, the first congratulating Roosevelt on becoming a grandfather with Anna's first child, the second describing a summer holiday in Europe with the children. As long as Winthrop Rutherfurd was healthy and strong, as long as Missy LeHand guarded the gates to the White House, the risks of further association must have seemed tremendous.

The first hint of a personal meeting is contained in the handwritten version of the White House usher diary for Friday, August 1, 1941. In addition to the typed list of official appointments on the president's schedule each day, a handwritten diary was kept which filled in his movements both before and after the scheduled appointments: his trips to the doctor's office, his exercise time in the pool, his sojourns in the map room, his off-the-record guests. At eight-forty that night, the handwritten diary records a visit by a Mrs. Paul Johnson. "Mrs. Johnson," according to Roosevelt's Secret Service agent, William Simmons, was a coded name for Lucy Rutherfurd. Though we cannot say for sure that the Mrs. Johnson who visited the president on the first of August was indeed Lucy Rutherfurd, the fact that she met with him alone and stayed with him until 11 p.m. and then returned for dinner the following evening and did not leave until nearly midnight underscores that she must have been somebody special in Roosevelt's life.

The timing of the first meeting makes sense. Winthrop Rutherfurd had recently suffered a stroke and was a bedridden invalid. Early in his illness, when he was desperately sick, Lucy had contacted Roosevelt for help, perhaps to gain admission to Walter Reed. The friendship had been renewed. During these same months, Lucy's mother had been placed in the Waverly Sanitarium, in Rockville, Maryland, and her only sister, Violetta, had moved to D.C., giving Lucy other reasons to come to Washington. On Roosevelt's side, the timing was also right. Missy was still in the hospital recovering from her stroke, and Eleanor was in Campobello for the final session of her summer leadership institute.

"Mrs. Johnson" returned to Washington three months later, on November 9, accompanied by her daughter (presumably Barbara Rutherfurd). The two women took tea with the president in the late afternoon, and then Mrs. Johnson dined with him alone in his study. Eleanor was in New York at the time. In December, young Barbara visited the White House on her own, to eat dinner with Harry Hopkins and the president in Roosevelt's study. The following spring, Mrs. Johnson showed up twice for dinner, and then, in October, when Eleanor was en route to England, she returned once more, dining with him one day and taking tea with him the next. Nothing specific is known of the conversation they shared. If the infatuation of their earlier days was still alive, it is not likely that either allowed the other to know.

When Shoumatoff arrived at the president's office that day in May 1943, he greeted her with such friendliness that his hand, she later wrote, seemed to stretch across the entire room. "How is Mrs. Rutherfurd? And how is Barbara?" he asked. Throughout the sitting, he was "very cheerful," talking at length about the royal refugees in the U.S. and the recent visit of the Soviet ambassador to the United States, Maxim Litvinov. As Shoumatoff finished her sketch, she commented that his gray suit and blue tie were too drab for a painting. The president laughed and then suggested that he put on his favorite navy-uniform cape. Perfect, the artist replied, and the portrait was completed. A week later, she returned to Aiken and presented the handsome painting to a "delighted" Lucy.

· · ·

Churchill arrived in Washington the evening of May 11, just as the Allied operation in North Africa was coming to a successful conclusion. Two days earlier, the Axis forces in Tunisia had surrendered unconditionally to the Allies.

It had been a long struggle for the Allies, longer than expected. After the first flush of victory in French North Africa, the Allied drive on Tunis had come up against the fierce resistance of reinforced German forces under the leadership of the great "Desert Fox," German General Erwin Rommel. On February 20, at Kasserine Pass, inexperienced American forces had encountered their first blitzkrieg attack by German tanks, artillery, and dive-bombers. Though the Americans fought bravely, they were outmaneuvered by the seasoned German troops: their defense of the pass was ill-conceived, their tanks were under-armed, their equipment was inferior, their training for the removal of mines was inadequate, and their air-ground communications were faulty. The Germans broke through the pass, destroyed a large cache of weapons, and took thousands of American prisoners.

Two weeks after the battle at Kasserine Pass, a telegram addressed to Mrs. Mae Stifle on Corning Street arrived at the Western Union Station in the small town of Red Oak, Iowa, population six thousand. "The Secretary of War desires me to express his deep regret that your son Daniel Stifle . . . is missing in action." Fifteen minutes later, a second telegram arrived, telling Mrs. Stifle that her second son, Frank, was also missing in action. A few minutes later, Mrs. Stifle's daughter, Marie, received word that she had lost her husband, Daniel Wolfe. As the evening wore on, the telegrams kept coming until there were twenty-seven. The Gillespies on Second Street had lost two boys—Charles, twenty-two, and Frank, twenty. Duane Dodd and his cousins, the two Halbert boys, were missing.

The families gathered in the lobby of the Hotel Johnson, next door to the Western Union Station, and tried to make sense of what was happening. Someone recalled seeing something in the papers about a difficult engagement at a place called Kasserine Pass, but it would take weeks for the people of this small town to come to understand that their entire National Guard unit had been destroyed in a single battle. Red Oak had suffered a disproportionate loss, greater than any other town in the United States. Only two years earlier, the members of Company M had marched side by side through the streets on their way to war; now their names were listed side by side on the official casualty list.

Red Oak, Iowa, was the "hometown we dreamed of overseas," one serviceman wrote after the war, "rich and contented, with chicken and blueberry pies on Sundays, for whose sake, some said, we were fighting the war." Looking up the main street, one could see the newly painted store fronts of J. C. Penney and Montgomery Ward, the sandstone structure of the Hudson State Park, and, across the way, the Green Parrot, an ice-cream parlor full of young people. On the road into Red Oak was the Grand Theater, where farmers from surrounding towns brought their children on Saturdays for a double feature. Everyone in this small town knew someone on the list.

By March, the Americans had recovered from their reversal at Kasserine Pass and were pushing forward aggressively. By April, with General Patton in command, American troops had finally joined up with General Montgomery's Eighth Army, having started two thousand miles apart. The Axis forces were driven eastward and trapped in the Tunisian tip, where they surrendered. Nearly a quarter-million Germans and Italians were taken prisoner. The Allied victory in Africa was complete.

The Tunisian victory cast a bright light on the May summit, which became known as the "Trident Conference." Goebbels noted in his diary on the eve of the conference that "the Americans are happy as children to be able for the first time to take German troops into custody. . . . My thoughts often turn to North Africa and to our soldiers. . . . The only comforting thought is the fact that they are falling into the hands of a civilized opponent." For his part, Churchill could not help recalling "the striking change which had taken place in the situation since he had last sat by the President's desk and had heard the news of the fall of Tobruk. He could never forget the manner in which the President had sustained him at that time."

Much had happened in the past year. At Stalingrad, Guadalcanal, El Alamein, and Tunis, the Allies had shown that the Axis powers could be defeated in battle. But, as Martin Gilbert has written, these places "stood on the periphery of the areas under Axis control. The continent of Europe, and the vast island expanses of South East Asia, were still under the military rule of those who had chosen to make war. The Allies, for all their recent triumphs, stood at the edge of immense regions confronted by hugely powerful forces still to be overthrown."

The central issue at the Trident Conference was the timing of the cross-Channel invasion—in particular, what to do with the twenty divisions that would come free when the invasion of Sicily was completed, sometime in August. Once again, the old disagreements emerged. Churchill wanted to use these divisions to invade Italy, postponing still further the cross-Channel invasion; Roosevelt wanted to send them to England to build up the monstrous force that would be needed to invade France in the spring of 1944. In the days ahead, the discussions would become increasingly intense, but first, Roosevelt insisted, it was time to relax with drinks and dinner.

Since Eleanor was en route to New York for a meeting of the Committee for the Care of European Children, the president asked his daughter, Anna, to be his hostess at dinner. Anna had come to Washington earlier in the week to bid farewell to her husband as he sailed overseas to North Africa, and she was thrilled by her father's request. Since her girlhood, she had yearned to be important to her father, to be needed by him. Indeed, the presiding image from her childhood was the memory of her father coming home from work and shutting himself up for hours in a room with cigar-smoking politicians. Forbidden to interrupt or even to peek inside, she could imagine nothing more wonderful than to be invited, as she now was, to take her mother's place in the inner sanctum of her father's political life.

Seated opposite the president, with Hopkins on her left and Churchill on her right, Anna made a striking impression. Her blue eyes shone, her warmth radiated. After dinner, the guests were treated to a preview of an unreleased film, *The Battle of Britain*. It was excellent, Anna told John, "so much so that the PM wept." All in all, Anna enthused, the entire evening was "intensely interesting."

That weekend, the president took Churchill to Shangri-la, along with Eleanor, Anna, Hopkins, and Beaverbrook. As the guests piled into the cars for the two-hour trip to the wooded Maryland retreat, Eleanor insisted that Churchill sit beside Franklin in the back seat while she occupied one of the small front seats. Churchill would have none of this, insisting that Mrs. Roosevelt take her proper place by her husband's side. The conflict of wills went on for three minutes, Churchill recalled, as "the British empire went into action" against the formidable Mrs. Roosevelt. In the end, Eleanor relented, agreeing to sit beside her husband while Churchill sat up front.

As the motorcade approached Frederick, Maryland, Churchill asked if he could see the house of Barbara Frietchie, whose courage in placing a Union flag outside her attic window as the Confederate army marched by inspired John Greenleaf Whittier's poem "Barbara Frietchie." The discussion prompted Roosevelt to quote the famous lines " 'Shoot, if you must, this old gray head, / But spare your country's flag,' she said." When it was clear that this was as far as Roosevelt could go, Churchill chimed in, quoting from memory the entire poem. While his companions were asking themselves how he could do this when he hadn't read the poem for thirty years, Churchill went on to give a brilliant review of the Battle of Gettysburg, along with a lengthy disquisition on Stonewall Jackson and Robert E. Lee.

Eleanor was impressed by Churchill's memory, his wit, and his extensive knowledge. "He is always using quotations & can quote endless poetry," she wrote Lash. She was also impressed by Lord Beaverbrook, who "fell completely for Anna & offered to help her on her paper," yet "none of them," she remarked, with evident pride in her husband's personality, has "the geographic knowledge, nor all around historical knowledge & grasp of the whole picture today which our own raconteur has & he can outtalk them all too which amused Anna & me very much."

On the trip to Shangri-la, the president told Churchill he was looking forward to a few hours with his stamp collection. Later, Churchill sat by his side, watching "with much interest and in silence for perhaps half an hour as he stuck them in, each in its proper place, and so forgot the cares of State." But all too soon, Churchill noted, General Walter Bedell Smith arrived, carrying an urgent message from Eisenhower. "Sadly FDR left his stamp collection and addressed himself to his task."

The evening was great fun, Anna reported to John, though she discovered that "the PM picks his teeth all through dinner and uses snuff liberally. The sneezes which follow the latter practically rock the foundations of the house and he then blows his nose about three times like a fog horn." But the conversation was sparkling, Anna enthused, as Churchill, Roosevelt, and Beaverbrook vied with one another in telling stories. The only unpleasant moment came when Eleanor insisted on telling a story of her own, "which showed all too plainly her dislike for a certain lady [most likely Princess Martha] whom you and I and the boss like!"

In the morning, the president took Churchill fishing in a nearby stream. "He was placed with great care by the side," Churchill recorded, "and sought to entice the nimble and wily fish. I tried for some time myself at other spots. No fish were caught, but he seemed to enjoy it very much, and was in great spirits for the rest of the day."

After the relaxing weekend, the presidential party descended the Alleghenies and returned to Washington, where, Stimson recorded, "a very decided deadlock" arose between the president and the prime minister. "The British are holding back dead from going on with [Operation] Bolero . . . and are trying to divert us off into some more Mediterranean adventures. Fortunately the President seems to be holding out. I talked with Marshall. . . . He seems to be glad to have my backing in the matter because the burden of the whole thing has been falling on him."

The debate went on for days, and the longer it continued, the hotter it became. As the tension mounted, Churchill's mood darkened, shifting from anger to irritation to despair. After one heated session, Lord Moran found him pacing up and down his room, scowling at the floor. "The President is not willing to put pressure on Marshall," Churchill lamented. "He is not in favor of landing in Italy. It is most discouraging. I only crossed the Atlantic for this purpose. I cannot let the matter rest where it is." For his part, Marshall thought Churchill was acting like "a spoiled boy," and Hopkins found him "a little subdued—for Winston that is."

As Churchill got ready to leave, a compromise was achieved: a general resolution was drafted calling on the Allied commander-in-chief "to plan such operations in exploitation of Husky [the Allied invasion of Sicily] as are best calculated to eliminate Italy from the war and to contain the maximum number of German forces." In other words, Roosevelt was willing to consider the possibility of taking action in Italy if and only if he was assured that such action would not detract in any substantial way from the buildup for the cross-Channel attack. This was not the firm commitment to invade Italy that Churchill wanted, but it was a step in the right direction.

Churchill's departure on May 27 brought a collective sigh of relief to the White House staff. As much as everyone revered the prime minister, the president's aide William Hassett observed, he was "a trying guest—drinks like a fish and smokes like a chimney, irregular routine, works nights, sleeps days, turns the clock upside down." Even Franklin, Eleanor observed, who "really likes the PM and believes he can manage him in the end," was utterly exhausted. The morning after Churchill left, Roosevelt took Princess Martha and Harry Hopkins to Hyde Park, where he slept ten hours a day for three days straight until he recovered from Churchill's visit.

• • •

When the president returned to the White House on June 2, he was greeted with the unwelcome news that the nation's coal miners, under the leadership of John L. Lewis, had gone on strike. For months, Lewis had been engaged in a running battle with the War Labor Board to secure an increase of $2 a day for the miners. He had used every weapon in his armory, including the threat to strike, but he had been unable to shake the WLB from its position that any wage increase would violate the "Little Steel" formula promulgated by the president the year before to restrain both wage advances and cost-of-living increases. Under the formula, wage increases were allowed only if necessary to correct serious maladjustments or gross inequities. The ink was scarcely dry on the latest WLB refusal when Lewis and the miners decided to strike.

The effect of the strike—which took five hundred thousand miners off the job and closed more than three thousand mines—was devastating. Without coal to process the iron ore or fire the steel plants, eleven blast furnaces had to be shut down. Steel production faltered. Railroad schedules were cut back for lack of fuel. Production of guns and tanks slowed. The chain of losses reached deep into the national economy.

While Roosevelt considered his options in long meetings with Ickes and Jimmy Byrnes, angry letters poured into the White House from citizens and soldiers at home and abroad. "You must have lace on your pants for allowing John L. Lewis to pull such a stunt," Sophia Carroll wrote from Maryland. "I think you are equally guilty with John L. Lewis for the mess we are in," Esther Morrow wrote. "You babied and petted him until he thinks he is boss also."

Opinion among the GIs was even more damning. Pfc. John Adkins spoke for 90 percent of the soldiers, according to *Stars and Stripes,* when he wrote from North Africa, "While these American boys are over here sweating, bleeding and dying to protect America and even the right to strike, those people back there have the gall to quit their jobs."

"What sort of traitors are those miners?" one marine asked. "I've just come down from the North with a plane load of men who were injured in the Attu fighting. One of them was minus a leg. . . . His entire life is pretty well ruined. Imagine it must be rather bewildering to return from battle . . . to find the defenders of the homefront bargaining for another dollar or two to add to already mountainous wages."

"If I were on the front lines, and a Marine was scared or tired and refused to fight or advance I would have to shoot him," another soldier, John Jaqua, observed. "Unless my sense of values is completely warped, he is doing no more than a laborer who strikes."

As the strike continued, public anger at the miners turned against the labor movement as a whole. Labor spokesmen tried in vain to set the record straight, pointing out that the great majority of labor leaders had kept the no-strike pledge they had given after Pearl Harbor. To be sure, disgruntled employees at various plants had engaged in unauthorized wildcat strikes from time to time. In July 1942, scattered employees at the Detroit diesel-engine division at General Motors, upset because their departments were not included in a pay-raise award, had walked out. A few weeks later, workers at Monroe Auto Equipment brought claims of "speed-up" and walked out when new gears were installed in their machines. Most of these wildcat strikes had been quickly settled, and production had continued with little interruption. But with the country at war, the general public refused to make fine distinctions. By an overwhelming majority, the people believed that strikes should be outlawed.

In the halls of Congress, the protest reached a crescendo. In the second week of June 1943, the House joined the Senate in supporting a bill, the Smith-Connally Act, that imposed drastic penalties and restrictions on any person encouraging a strike in government-owned plants. The bill was a humiliating setback to the entire labor movement. "It is the judgment of the CIO," CIO President Philip Murray wrote Roosevelt, "that this proposed legislation if enacted into law would constitute one of the most serious blows directed against our national war effort and be the equivalent of a major military disaster."

Eleanor told a *New York Times* reporter she was sick at heart about the whole situation. Though she could not condone the stoppage of work in an industry so vital to war production, she knew from her visits to the coal mines in Appalachia that the miners had genuine grievances that badly needed remedying. She had seen the unpainted shanties with muddy yards on muddy streets where the miners lived. She understood the tremendous risks the miners endured—in 1941, 64,764 were killed or injured as a consequence of gas explosions, bad ventilation, defective timbering, and cave-ins. She had witnessed the miners' helpless dependence on high-priced company stores that kept them "in hock" forever by running a tab which was then deducted from their weekly pay checks. "I have seen pay envelopes containing three cents," she said. For all these reasons, she believed that "the settlement of the strike should be brought about in the light of what the miners and their families have lived through for the past ten years. I think they are entitled to some concessions."

Eleanor's opinion was not popular, but the president listened to her words. Despite his fury at John L. Lewis, which led him, in the privacy of the Oval Office, to crack that "he would be glad to resign as President if Lewis committed suicide," he kept a tight rein over his temper in public, allowing the situation to speak for itself. "I understand the devotion of the coal miners to their union," he said, speaking more in sadness than in anger. "Every improvement of the conditions of the coal miners of this country has had my hearty support. And I do not mean to desert them now. But I also do not mean to desert my obligations and responsibilities as President of the U.S. and Commander-in-Chief of the Army and Navy. The first necessity is the resumption of coal mining."

Acting under the cover of his emergency war powers, Roosevelt instructed Ickes to take over the mines in the name of the government. At the same time, he ordered the five hundred thousand miners to return to work, reminding them that they were working for the government "on essential war work and it was their duty no less than that of their sons and brothers in the Armed Forces to fulfill their war duties." Stimson wanted the president to go even further, to tell the miners that they would all be inducted if they refused to go back to work, but for the time being, Roosevelt was hesitant to use induction as a penalty.

While Lewis was deciding how to respond, a telephone call brought one of the striking miners the sad news that his son, who was in the navy, had been killed in the Pacific. "I ain't a traitor," the miner burst out, "damn 'em I ain't a traitor. I'll stay out until hell freezes over. Dickie was fighting for one thing, I'm fighting for another and they ain't so far apart." But on the sixth day of the strike, Lewis ordered his men back to work.

There remained the thorny problem of the Smith-Connally Act, which arrived in the White House pouch for the president's signature in the middle of June. "If I were FDR I wouldn't sign it," Eleanor confided to Joe Lash, "but I'm not enough of a politician to judge the temper of the country." William Hassett agreed. "This is a bad bill, through which, if approved, labor stands to lose its hard won gains."

The War Department argued that the president should sign the legislation. "In spite of imperfections of the bill," Stimson wrote, "it has enough good points on the vital issues of having young men at home perform their duties without discrimination like the soldiers, making it an important moral issue to have the bill passed."

The sentiment of the country was overwhelmingly in favor of the bill. A woman from Sewanee, Tennessee, spoke for many in a stormy letter to the president. "We the people are getting fed up with you and your spineless treatment of labor. . . . I was one of your ardent admirers when you first went into office but now I can hardly wait for the day you go out of office. Between you and your treatment of labor and Mrs. Roosevelt and the niggers, this is one hell of a place."

The president kept the country and the Congress waiting for the maximum time he could—nine and one-half days plus two Sundays—while he pondered his decision. On June 25, at 3:15 p.m., he sent his answer to the Congress: he had decided to veto the bill. "Let there be no misunderstanding of the reasons which prompt me to veto this bill at this time," he began. "I am unalterably opposed to strikes in wartime. I do not hesitate to use the powers of government to prevent them." He clearly understood, he said, that it was the will of the American people "that no war work be interrupted by strike or lockout." But the American people should realize that, for the entire year of 1942, "99.95 percent of the work went forward without strikes, and that only 5 one-hundredths of 1 percent of the work was delayed by strikes. That record has never been equaled in this country. It is as good or better than the record of any of our Allies in wartime."

He conceded that laws are often necessary "to make a very small minority of people live up to the standards that the great majority of the people follow," but he contended that, far from discouraging strikes, the bill's provisions would stimulate labor unrest.

Eleanor was pleased by the president's veto, as was organized labor. "In vetoing the Smith-Connally bill, President Roosevelt has demonstrated once more," CIO President Philip Murray said, "his sound understanding of the nature of the democracy for which we are fighting and the need for full mobilization of the nation for victory." But the euphoria was short-lived. At 3:30, only fifteen minutes after it had received the president's veto message, the Senate overrode the veto fifty-six to twenty-five. As soon as word of the Senate action reached the House, the members immediately laid aside debate on a Commodity Credit Corporation extension and took up the override. Representative Clifton Woodrum set the tone when he called for "action, not tomorrow, not Monday, but today, so that we can send the message to our boys in the foxholes that the American people are behind them." At 5:28 p.m., the House joined the Senate in the override, and the Smith-Connally Act became law.

Stimson considered the congressional override, only the eighth time in ten years that the Congress had enacted a bill into law over Roosevelt's veto, "a bad rebuff and an unnecessary rebuff. . . . His administration really is beginning to shake a little and throughout the country there is evident feeling that he has made a mistake in regard to labor."

In a conversation at Hyde Park the following week, Eleanor asked Franklin if he thought "our lack of leadership and discipline in Congress came about because we'd been in power too long." The president replied reflectively. "Perhaps, we certainly have no control. I think the country has forgotten we ever lived through the 30s."

Unchastened by the congressional slap, Lewis struggled on in defense of the miners. Twice again in the months ahead, he ordered his men on strike. Twice again, the president seized the mines. There was more idleness in 1943 due to strikes in the mining industry than in any other. Finally, an ingenious solution was reached whereby the United Mine Workers shifted their focus from a straight pay raise to "portal to portal pay." For years, the miners had suffered under a system which saw their hourly wage begin only when they reached their place of work deep within the mine. The long ride in a metal cart from the top of the mine to the bottom was not considered work. Through Ickes' intervention, an agreement was reached that allowed the miners to be paid "portal to portal," from the moment they entered the mine to the moment they left. Since extra time did not violate the "Little Steel" formula, the solution was approved by the War Labor Board.

"We were thrilled at the news," coal miner Michael Lilly recalled. "Once you entered the coal mines, you were in danger. It was dark from the moment you went in. Anything could happen on the way down. I was always afraid. Now I knew from the moment I got into the cart at the top of the hill the money was kicking in. That eased everything a great deal."

•   •   •

As Eleanor worked on her column in Hyde Park on Sunday morning, June 20, she was wrapped in gloomy spirits. "The domestic scene," she admitted, referring not only to the coal dispute but to a rash of racial disturbances that had recently broken out, "is anything but encouraging and one would like not to think about it, because it gives one a feeling that, as a whole, we are not really prepared for democracy."

Three weeks earlier, in Mobile, Alabama, a racial incident in the Addsco shipyard had resulted in the loss of ten thousand workers for seven days. "No city in the deep South has felt the war more sharply than Mobile, Alabama," journalist Selden Menefee concluded after a nationwide tour of the United States in the first half of 1943. "Here is an historic town that slept for 230 years, then woke up in two. The population of Mobile's metropolitan area has increased by 60%, from 79,000 in 1940 to an estimated 125,000 in the spring of 1943." Drawn by the magnet of the great shipyards of Mobile, many of the new arrivals were poor whites from the hinterlands. "If these 'poor whites' are full of anti-Negro prejudices, as they are," Menefee observed, "it is because the whiteness of their skins is the one thing that gives them a degree of social status."

The trouble began when a group of skilled Negro welders were upgraded and assigned to work on the same job with white welders. To the white welders, the idea of being forced to work side by side with Negroes was an unacceptable wedge in the time-honored system of segregation. "We realize the fact that they are human beings," Archie Adams wrote in a letter to the *Mobile Register,* but "we don't any more want to work or want our women to work alongside a Negro than you would want to take one into your dining room and sit him down between your wife and mother to eat dinner, or for your wife to invite the cook in for a game of bridge, or take her to the movies."

As the morning shift began, a group of white welders, armed with bricks, clubs, and bars, attacked the Negro welders. "No nigger is goin' to join iron in these yards," one worker shouted. The fighting soon spread to other parts of the yard. Before it ended, eleven Negroes were carried to the hospital. Peace was restored only when the company decided, in a move reluctantly approved by the FEPC, to assign the skilled Negro welders to a separate shipway, where they would not mingle with whites. With vital production heavily curtailed, it seemed the only way to avoid future trouble. But it was clearly a step backward, as Eleanor assuredly understood.

Worse was to come. A few hours after Eleanor finished her cheerless column, while she and Franklin were entertaining Queen Wilhelmina of the Netherlands in the library after dinner, word was received at Hyde Park of bloody rioting in Detroit. The disturbance had begun at Belle Isle, a public park frequented mostly by blacks. By midafternoon, the temperature in Detroit had hit ninety-one and the park was filled to capacity, with a hundred thousand people. As evening approached, the bridge to the mainland was jammed with cars and pedestrians. A few scuffles broke out between whites and blacks. A young white couple was assaulted and robbed of $2 by a group of seven Negroes. Two white girls got into a fight with a Negro girl. One of the white girls knocked the Negro girl down; the Negro girl bloodied the white girl's nose and blackened her eye. A rumor floated that a group of whites had thrown a Negro woman and her baby off the bridge. Shortly after midnight, at a nightclub on Hastings Street, in the heart of "Paradise Valley," the Negro district, a well-dressed Negro carrying a briefcase took the microphone, stopped the music, and announced that fighting was in progress on Belle Isle, that three Negroes had been killed and a Negro woman and her baby drowned. He urged everyone to get guns and cars and join the fight. The rioting spread.

Groups of Negroes came out into the streets, smashing windows, stopping streetcars, stoning whites. Gangs of whites charged into Negro areas, chasing and beating Negroes as they walked down the street. By midnight, four hundred were injured and ten were dead. Later in the morning, a milk driver making his rounds in the Negro district and an Italian doctor answering an emergency call were beaten to death. During the worst hours of the fighting, Governor Harry Kelly of Michigan stubbornly insisted that he could handle the situation with local and state police. Without a request from the governor for federal troops, or certification that state authorities could not control the violence, the president was constitutionally unable to act. It was not until Monday morning, eighteen hours after the rioting had begun, that the governor finally asked for help. The federal troops, thirty-eight hundred strong, arrived at 11 a.m., and by late afternoon peace was restored, but by then death had come to twenty-five Negroes and nine whites, while nearly one thousand were injured.

That night, in Detroit's Receiving Hospital, reporters noted that bleeding Negroes and whites sat side by side, joined by a common bewilderment at the incomprehensible events they had seen. The story was told of a colored woman of light complexion who was beaten to death by colored men who mistook her for a white woman. In another part of the city, white youths had begun to close in on a Negro. Three white sailors stepped in and broke it up. "He's not doing you any harm," one of the sailors said. "Let him alone." "What's it to you?" snapped one of the gang. "Plenty," replied the sailor. "There was a colored guy in our outfit and he saved a couple of lives. Besides you guys are stirring up something that we're trying to stop."

In the days that followed, politicians and reporters sought to understand why the explosion had taken place. To many people in both the North and the South, the answer was clear: Eleanor Roosevelt was "morally responsible" for the riot. "It is blood on your hands, Mrs. Roosevelt," the *Jackson Daily News* declared on June 22. "You have been personally proclaiming and practicing social equality at the White House and wherever you go, Mrs. Roosevelt. What followed is now history." Detroit resident John Lang pointed his finger in the same direction. "It is my belief," he wrote the president, that "Mrs. Roosevelt and Mayor [Edward] Jeffries of Detroit are somewhat guilty of the race riots due to their coddling of negroes."

Eleanor responded with composure. "I suppose when one is being forced to realize that an unwelcome change is coming, one must blame it on someone or something," she replied.

Stimson's initial reaction was to blame "the deliberate effort that has been going on on the part of certain radical leaders of the colored race to use the war for obtaining the ends which they were seeking, and these ends are very difficult because they include race equality to be social as well as economic and military and they are trying to demand that there will be this complete intermixing in the military." But when Stimson saw the pictures in *Life* magazine that showed Negroes being beaten and assaulted by whites, generally young white boys, he told General Somervell he had "come to the conclusion that we have got to do something . . . or there will be real trouble in the tense situation that exists among the two races throughout the country."

The truth was that dozens of causes had coincided to bring about the riots. C. E. Rhetts, special assistant to Attorney General Francis Biddle, spent the first week of July in Detroit, interviewing hundreds of people, including politicians, policemen, FBI agents, labor leaders, civil-rights leaders, and journalists. "Many newspapers and individuals have charged that the enemy fomented this riot," Rhett stated at the beginning of his report. "But though there is no doubt that the riot gave great comfort and some aid to the enemy, no evidence has yet been developed to indicate that he contrived it." On the contrary, Rhett concluded, the riot was the product of the spontaneous combustion of a number of troubling elements.

For one thing, Detroit had grown phenomenally during the previous two years, adding nearly 500,000 people, including 150,000 Negroes, to its population of 2.5 million. As Negroes and whites competed for what little housing, transportation, and recreation was available, the fascist exhortations of radio commentators Father Charles Coughlin and Gerald K. Smith found fertile soil. The Ku Klux Klan took on new life. "The old, subdued, muted, murderous Southern race war," one journalist noted, "was transplanted into a high-speed industrial background." Housing conditions for Negroes, Rhett reported, were "deplorable." Time and again, real-estate investors had blocked any chance for the construction of adequate federal housing, and "the vacillation which characterized the federal government's position in the case of the Sojourner Truth Negro housing project last year did not help."

Trailer camps were everywhere, and with them, as one reporter described it, "a sizable population of delinquent, rootless 'trailer boys'—the cruel, pitiable, negative young savages who are good for riots and fascist putsches." For months, conflicts between whites and blacks in the high school had been on the increase. "Large segments of the negro community hate the police, probably not without reason." All these factors, taken together, created a "highly explosive community."

The riots cast a baleful shadow on the home front, rendering false the image of a united people in time of war. "Like a defective screw in a great machine, though apparently insignificant," Eleanor's friend Pauli Murray warned the president, the problem of race "can literally wreck our national endeavor.... This matter has become a national menace." Civil-rights leaders entreated Roosevelt to address the nation in a fireside chat. "We urge you to go on the radio at the earliest possible moment," Walter White wrote. The only solution to the racial problem, Mary McCleod Bethune observed, is "a straight forward statement and program of action from the President."

For her part, Eleanor believed that the race riots put us "on a par with Nazism which we fight, and makes us tremble for what human beings may do when they no longer think but let themselves be dominated by their worst emotions." In countless memos she had warned her husband about the disgraceful living conditions that accompanied the overcrowded boomtowns. For months, she had worried about rising racial tensions, calling at one point for an interracial conference of Negro and white leaders. Now that the long-anticipated explosion had taken place, she was convinced that the conservative Southern bloc in Congress, which repeatedly refused to better conditions for Negroes, was largely to blame. "Detroit should never have happened," she wrote Trude Pratt, "but when Congress behaves as it does why should others be calmer?"

While Eleanor suffered outwardly, the president reacted calmly, telling reporters at his weekly press conference that he refused to become aroused as long as war production continued at top levels. At one point, a week after the riots, he considered making a nationwide statement about race, but in the end he abandoned the idea. He was convinced, Eleanor told Lash, that "he must not irritate the southern leaders as he feels he needs their votes for essential war bills." Better to wait, he decided, until later in the summer, when he intended to deliver a more general address to the nation on the home front.

The presidential silence on race was not easy for liberals to understand. "Why," *New Republic* writer Thomas Sanction asked, "hasn't Mr. Roosevelt come to us with one of his greatest speeches, speaking to us as Americans, speaking to us as the great mongrel nation . . . why hasn't he come to us and talked to us in the simple and genuine language that Lincoln might have used, why hasn't he come waking memories of the old American dream, of live and let live, of a land where all men are endowed with inalienable rights, of a country where all men are created equal?"

• • •

As the riots faded from the national consciousness, the president turned his attention to the invasion of Sicily, which was scheduled to begin in early July. At the end of his working day, Roosevelt frequently visited the map room to follow the buildup of the Allied landing force. By the first week of July, one-third of the invading force, 160,000 men, with six hundred tanks and two thousand landing craft were assembled in Malta, waiting for the weather to clear so they could make their move. At dawn on July 10, the landings began. Despite the high winds, which blew the paratroopers too far inland, Allied forces successfully fought off both Italian and German troops. The Axis, having lost a quarter of a million troops in Tunisia, had only ten Italian divisions and two German panzer units stationed in Sicily at the time of the invasion. Two weeks later, as the invading forces swept toward Palermo, on the western half of the northern coast, Roosevelt headed to Shangri-la with Robert Sherwood and Sam Rosenman to begin work on a major speech to the nation—his first fireside chat on the war since February.

Between the coal strike and the riots in Mobile and Detroit, national morale was suffering. "The whole world is watching our domestic troubles," reporter Edwin James wrote in *The New York Times.* "Our President has said, and often, that we would show the world that a democracy could be made to work at war as well as any totalitarian state.... Therefore, much depends on how we run our democracy at war. And we are not running it any too well."

In his speech, Roosevelt wanted to make it clear to the American public that the home front and the war front were one and the same; that the factory worker at home was as crucial to the war as the soldier abroad. If the identity between the two fronts could be reinforced, he believed, morale and productivity would go up. What the home front worker needed was neither to be reprimanded nor flattered; he simply needed information about the relationship between his workaday job and the effort to beat the Nazis. Once he had that information, he could be trusted to do his job.

On July 27, the day before his speech, Roosevelt was asked at his press conference what the talk would be about. "It is going to be about the war," Roosevelt quipped, provoking laughter throughout the room. "Abroad or at home, sir?" one reporter asked. "You know, I hoped you would ask that question just that way," Roosevelt replied, then proceeded to deliver an extemporaneous mini-version of his speech. "There are too many people in this country ... who are not mature enough to realize that you can't take a piece of paper and draw a line down the middle of it and put the war abroad on one side and put the home front on the other, because after all it all ties in together. When we send an expedition to Sicily, where does it begin? Well it begins at two places practically; it begins on the farms of this country, and in the mines of this country. And then the next step in getting that army into Sicily is the processing of the food, and the processing of the raw material into steel, then the munitions plants that turn the steel into tanks and planes or the aluminum. . . . And then, a great many million people in this country are engaged in transporting it from the plant, or from the field, or the processing plant to the seaboard. And then it's put on ships that are made in this country . . . and you have to escort and convoy with a lot of other ships. . . . Finally, when they get to the other side, all these men go ashore. . . . But all through this we have to remember that there is just one front, which includes at home as well as abroad. It is all part of the picture of trying to win the war.''

Roosevelt was in high spirits as he sat before the microphones in the Diplomatic Reception Room at 9:25 p.m. on July 28. As the speech was being put into final form, word had come over the radio that Italian dictator Benito Mussolini had been ousted from power. In the wake of the Allied invasion of Sicily, the Grand Fascist Council had convened, and Mussolini had been summoned to a meeting with King Victor Emmanuel of Italy at which he was told he was being relieved of his offices. When Mussolini was leaving the palace, the king had him arrested and asked Marshal Pietro Badoglio to form a new government.

The stunning news from Italy provided the perfect backdrop to the president's argument that the home front and the war front were inexorably tied together. "The first crack in the Axis has come," he began. "The criminal, corrupt Fascist regime in Italy is going to pieces. The pirate philosophy of the Fascists and Nazis cannot stand adversity."

In contrast, he argued, the productivity of the democracies was "almost unbelievable." The logistical war was entering a new phase. The margin of Allied production over the Axis was now estimated to be three to one. The month of July promised a new peak of 4,560 planes, with a total output of eighty-six thousand expected by the end of 1943, nearly double the output for the previous year.

Production of merchant ships was even more impressive. "This year," Roosevelt proudly observed, "we are producing over 19 million tons of merchant shipping and next year our production will be over 21 million tons. For several months, we have been losing fewer ships by sinkings and we have been destroying more and more U-boats. We hope this can continue. But we cannot be sure." As it turned out, the decline in shipping losses during the spring of 1943 would prove to be permanent. The Battle of the Atlantic was finally being won, releasing a flood of American munitions and troops into the major overseas theaters.

Overall, munitions output in 1943 would be 83 percent greater than in 1942, aircraft tonnage 140 percent higher, merchant ships 100 percent higher, and naval ships 75 percent higher. The United States had come a long way since 1940 and 1941, when the army and navy needed all they could get of everything—tanks, bombs, planes, ships, rifles. Now, with important exceptions—steel, landing craft, and escort vessels—stockpiles were sufficiently high to permit cutbacks.

American ingenuity had also filled the critical gap in the rubber supply after Pearl Harbor, when the Far Eastern plantations that had supplied the United States with 90 percent of its rubber were suddenly lost to Japanese conquest. At that moment, one reporter wrote, when production of all synthetic rubber totaled a mere twelve thousand tons a year, one-fiftieth of American's annual prewar needs, "our very national existence was at the mercy of a dwindling stockpile." But by 1943, production of synthetic rubber had turned the corner. Eighty-three percent of the 308,000 tons of new rubber supplies produced in 1943 would come from synthetic rubber. The first tires concocted by chemists from farm alcohol and petroleum had been released to essential civilian drivers. The crisis had passed.

"To a large degree," army historians have concluded, "the improvement in the military situation [in 1943] was a result of the huge outpouring of munitions from American factories and of ships from American yards. These trends coincided with a basic change that was occurring in the military position of the Anglo-American coalition—the regaining of the strategic initiative."

"We are still far from our main objectives in the war," Roosevelt cautioned. But, compared with the previous year, progress was being made. "You have heard it said," he concluded, "that while we are succeeding greatly on the fighting front, we are failing miserably on the homefront. I think this is another of those immaturities—a false slogan easy to state but untrue in the essential facts. . . . Every combat division, every naval task force, every squadron of fighting planes is dependent for its equipment and ammunition and fuel and food, as indeed it is for manpower, dependent on the American people in civilian clothes in the offices and in the factories and on the farms at home . . .

"The plans we have made for the knocking out of Mussolini and his gang have largely succeeded. But we still have to defeat Hitler and Tojo on their own home grounds. No one of us pretends that this will be an easy matter. . . . This will require far greater concentration of our national energy and our ingenuity and our skill. It's not too much to say that we must pour into this war the entire strength and intelligence and will power of the United States."

Novelist Saul Bellow remembers the exhilarating experience of listening to Roosevelt speak. "I can recall walking eastward on the Chicago Midway on a summer evening. The light held after nine o'clock, and the ground was covered with clover, more than a mile of green between Cottage Grove and Stony Island. The blight hadn't yet carried off the elms, and under them drivers had pulled over, parking bumper to bumper, and turned on their radios to hear Roosevelt. They had rolled down the windows and opened the car doors. Everywhere the same voice, its odd Eastern accent, which in anyone else would have irritated Midwesterners. You could follow without missing a single word as you strolled by. You felt joined to these unknown drivers, men and women smoking their cigarettes in silence, not so much considering the President's words as affirming the rightness of his tone and taking assurance from it."

• • •

The weekend after the president's speech, Eleanor entertained labor leader Walter Reuther and his wife at Val-Kill. She talked with the young couple for several hours, spending the afternoon outside in the sun and then moving onto the porch, where, she wrote, they "watched the sun go down in a brilliant red ball of fire." Reuther had a way of talking about industrial democracy that excited Eleanor. It was his dream to change both labor and management from their narrow pressure-group thinking to create a new form of workplace governance that would draw on the strengths of both sides.

As long as the man behind the machine was viewed as "the worker," standing in a class apart from management, the illusion would persist that he had no ideas to contribute to the successful operation of the plant. As long as management appealed to labor with the same techniques used to sell cigarettes and toothpaste, the immense creative reservoir which lay in the minds of millions of laborers would remain untapped. But if labor could be seen as something more than skill and brawn hired by the hour, if the workers could be given a measure of responsibility for generating new ideas, then there was no limit to the productivity of the American economy.

Reuther's idea centered on the notion of continuing the governmental functions of the War Production Board after the war ended, in a new entity to be called the Peace Production Board. The Peace Board would be charged with the responsibility of administering the nation's industrial effort for the benefit of the greatest number of citizens. Its first task, Reuther suggested, would be to oversee the conversion of aircraft factories into factories for prefabricated housing.

"He is much the most interesting labor leader I've met," Eleanor wrote Anna, "and I hope you meet him. He spent two years with a younger brother bicycling around the world and earning their way. He's been to such out of the way places as Baluchistan, worked a year in Russia. Now he's dreaming dreams of the postwar world and you would find him intensely interesting."

It was typical of Eleanor, when she found someone she liked, to wish that Anna could be there, too. With Anna, Eleanor once explained, she had grown to something different from her love for her boys, "to a mature understanding and sympathy, a feeling that we think and feel alike and can visit each other as friends and companions." For her part, Anna had come to trust her mother's love. She knew, her son Johnny later observed, "she had more of her mother than she had earlier in her life and more than anyone else in the family" and she took pleasure in that. "Darling Mum," Anna wrote after they spent a week together in Seattle, "somehow and no matter how long we have been separated, there is a click when we get together and a continuous clicking until we have to part once more."

So it was that Eleanor, knowing that Anna was having a difficult time at the paper with John away, traveled to Seattle in midsummer. In John's absence, the burden of editing the paper and dealing with the continuing machinations of William Randolph Hearst had fallen on Anna's shoulders. No sooner had John left than Hearst had put in place as associate publisher a man named Charles Lindemann, who Anna believed had "a terrific hatred" for the New Deal, did not like her, and was doing everything he could to ensure that she failed.

Though Eleanor's plane reached Seattle long past midnight, Anna was at the airport waiting. "She looks very thin," Eleanor wrote Lash, "but is making a wonderful effort to meet what is almost an intolerable situation." Working with people she neither liked nor trusted was very difficult for her, Eleanor explained, but "if possible she was going to stick it out."

For Anna, as for thousands of other women whose husbands had gone off to war, there were new burdens and new responsibilities. It was a confusing time. Yet mingled with the weight of obligation there was also a sense of exhilaration. During her first week of editing the paper on her own, Anna could honestly say that, despite the intrigue and the challenge, she loved it. "I'm having the time of my life—calling on all the tact I possess," Anna wrote John, "enjoying making my own decisions and attempting to use my bean for all it's worth." The situation had become more difficult since then, but even so, Anna told John, "You'd be amazed at the timid gal you used to know—who was always hearing spooks in the house and depending on you to defend her from all sorts of imaginary dangers! Now I drive myself alone at any and all times of the day and night, through the worst as well as the best parts of town."

With Eleanor, Anna could talk about her feelings—her pride in her new-found independence, her anger at John for leaving, her daily struggles at the paper. "It is the first time since you left that I've had someone to 'blow-off' to and it's been a very relaxing experience," Anna wrote John. For six peaceful days, Eleanor accompanied Anna to the office in the morning and sat by her side in the afternoon as she banged away on her typewriter. In the evenings, they played badminton, went swimming, and then celebrated the close of the day with an "old-fashioned" cocktail.

The more Anna extended herself to find a life of her own, the closer she felt to her mother. No longer seeing her mother with the eyes of a child, she was able to empathize with Eleanor's lifelong attempt to establish an independent identity. For her part, Eleanor was pleased to be needed. "I think having me here relaxed her because she could talk about all sorts of things she had not felt like discussing with others," she told her son-in-law.

At the same time, Eleanor confided to Anna her own worries about Jimmy and Elliott. Jimmy and his second wife, Rommie, had spent a miserable Fourth of July weekend at Hyde Park. Rommie claimed the president kept mentioning Jimmy's first wife, Betsey Cushing, and snubbed her at every opportunity. Elliott had also spent a weekend at home, but the visit was tense. She and he had such different philosophies, Eleanor told Anna, that she had to be careful around him at all time. "I only like being in close quarters with people whom I love very much," she admitted. "I made the discovery long ago that very few people made a great difference to me, but that those few mattered enormously. I live surrounded by people, and my thoughts are always with the few that matter whether they are near or far."

Eleanor's visit to Seattle served to renew both her own and Anna's spirits, but her absence from Washington exacted a toll on her relationship with her husband. Though she talked with him once while he was in Hyde Park for the weekend with Margaret Suckley, the conversation was distant and he seemed evasive about his plans for the rest of the summer. "It was nice talking with you last night," Eleanor wrote the following day, "but I began to wonder if you were planning to leave for parts unknown very soon. Will you call me . . . and tell me what your plans are? Of course I'll come at once to Washington if you are leaving in the near future."

"I guess one of the sad things in life," Eleanor admitted to Joe Lash, "is that rarely do a man and woman fall equally in love with each other and even more rarely do they so live their lives that they continue to be lovers at times and still develop and enjoy the constant companionship of married life."

* * *

The midsummer weeks of 1943 witnessed expanding activity in the American Jewish community in behalf of the European Jews. During the last days of July, an Emergency Conference to Save the Jewish People of Europe was convened at the Hotel Commodore in New York City. Through three sweltering days, fifteen hundred people listened to an impressive group of speakers, including Mayor Fiorello LaGuardia, writers Dorothy Parker and Max Lerner, and former President Herbert Hoover, offer a range of plans for rescue.

Roosevelt's response to a plea for cooperation was a vague, noncommittal message, read at the end of the conference, which spoke of the government's "repeated endeavors" to save the European Jews and promised that "these endeavors will not cease until Nazi power is forever crushed." Yet, far from making repeated endeavors, the government had attempted very little on the rescue front, and the few actions they had taken, such as the two-power American-British Conference on Refugees which had been held in Bermuda the previous spring, had produced little or no results.

Eleanor sent an equally unsatisfactory message to the Emergency Conference, which revealed complete misunderstanding of the situation. Though she was glad "to be of help in any way," she could not figure out, she said, what could be done at the present time. If, however, a program of action could be formulated, she was certain that the American people, "who have been shocked and horrified by the attitude of the Axis powers toward Jewish people will be more than glad to do all they can to alleviate the suffering of these people in Europe and to help them reestablish themselves in other parts of the world if it is possible to evacuate them."

Contrary to Eleanor's assumption, a program of action already existed and was spelled out in detail by the speakers at the conference. The first step, rescue advocates argued, was to form a governmental agency officially charged with rescuing Jews. With this in place, former President Hoover suggested, additional measures could be taken, including Allied protection and support for those Jews who had escaped to neutral countries, pressure on Palestine to absorb more Jews, and preparations for refugee havens in Africa. Beyond these actions, Mayor LaGuardia observed, the U.S. must open its own doors to increased immigration. "Our own government cannot urge other nations to take the initiative before it takes action of its own."

The stumbling block was not ignorance of what should be done but the absence of sustained will and desire on the part of either the government or the people to do anything at all. Despite Eleanor's claim that the American public was "shocked and horrified" about what was going on, the vast majority of ordinary people had only a vague idea of what was happening to the European Jews. Most American newspapers printed very little about the slaughter of the Jews. If mass killings were mentioned, they were generally presented not as the systematic murder of an entire race of people, but as an unfortunate byproduct of the general ravages of war. Nor could most Americans, growing up in a democratic culture, comprehend the unprecedented scale and savagery of Hitler's determination to obliterate the Jews.

Of course, Roosevelt was privy to far greater information than the ordinary citizen. Though neither he nor anyone else in his administration fully understood the extent of what only much later came to be known as the Holocaust, he had read the Riegner report the previous November. He had met that fall with Rabbi Wise and a delegation of Jewish leaders to talk about the slaughter of European Jews. He had spent nearly an hour in July talking with Jan Karski, a leader in the Polish underground who had traveled to London and Washington at great risk to report on the terrible events he had witnessed in Poland. Disguised as a policeman, Karski had seen the insides of the Belzec concentration camp, on the western border of Poland, where thousands of Jews were being gassed. "I am convinced," Karski told Roosevelt, "that there is no exaggeration in the accounts of the plight of the Jews. Our underground authorities are absolutely sure that the Germans are out to exterminate the entire Jewish population of Europe."

Why, then, did Roosevelt fail to provide leadership on this momentous issue? The answer, some suggest, is that he was wholly absorbed in waging a global war and believed that the only solution to the Jewish problem was the final defeat of Hitler and the rooting out of the Nazi system. To the extent that rescue efforts would divert time, attention, and resources from this ultimate goal, thereby lengthening the war, he could not sanction them. Yet, as David Wyman argues in *The Abandonment of the Jews,* "virtually none of the rescue proposals involved enough infringement on the war effort to lengthen the conflict at all or to increase the number of casualties, military or civilian." In fact, when other humanitarian needs were at issue, when refugees in Yugoslavia and Greece were in desperate straits, transportation somehow materialized, the war effort was bent, and the rescue was achieved. Moreover, the rationale that only victory would save the European Jews ignored the chilling question which *The New Republic* asked that summer: "Will any of these Jews survive to celebrate victory?"

The problem lay in the political landscape. Few in Congress showed concern about saving the European Jews. The majority of church leaders were silent on the issue; the intellectual community remained inert. Even the American Jews, who did more than anyone else to publicize the slaughter and press for action, were hampered by a lack of unity. When the Committee for a Jewish Army first proposed the Emergency Conference, rival Jewish leaders and Rabbi Stephen Wise did everything they could to undermine it. Other Jews, like Roosevelt adviser Sam Rosenman, feared that, if too much attention were paid to the plight of the European Jews, American anti-Semitism would increase. Such divisions weakened the pressure on Roosevelt, allowing him to fall back on his rationale that the most important thing he could do to help the Jews was to win the war as quickly as possible.

In mid-August, Peter Bergson, the organizer of the Emergency Conference, met with Eleanor Roosevelt at Hyde Park. Their conversation deepened Eleanor's awareness of the need for action. In her column the next day, she emphasized that the Jews in Europe had suffered as had no other group. "The percentage killed among them," she wrote, "far exceeds the losses among any of the United Nations." Though still admitting that she wasn't sure what could be done to save them, she predicted that "we will be the sufferers if we let great wrongs occur without exerting ourselves to correct them."

CHAPTER 18

"IT WAS A SIGHT
I WILL NEVER FORGET"

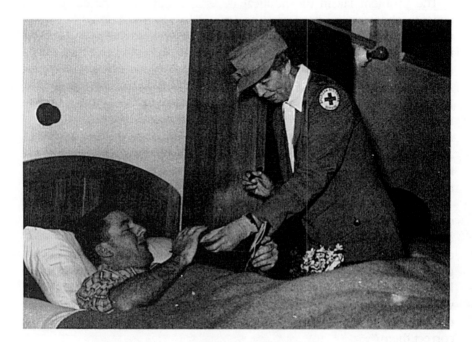

Augustus 1943 was a busy month at Hyde Park. There was activity everywhere, movement all day long. On the 12th, Churchill and his daughter Mary arrived at the president's estate to spend the weekend relaxing on the Hudson before the two leaders set off for a weeklong conference in Quebec. As usual, Churchill's visit caused considerable commotion in the Roosevelt household. The timing of the trip was particularly difficult for Eleanor, who was preparing an even longer trip of her own, to the South Pacific to visit American troops. "These last few days at home are busy for me," she confided in Lash, "& having the Churchills won't make it easier but somehow I'll get off!"

The weekend was filled with picnics on the hilltop, with hamburgers and hot dogs barbecued on the grill and watermelon slices for dessert. Knowing this was the first time Mary Churchill had eaten watermelon, the president laughingly admonished her not to swallow any of the pits lest they grow into watermelons in her stomach. Through the entire meal, Sam Rosenman observed, the prime minister enjoyed himself, his cheerfulness revealing "more eloquently" than the official bulletins "how much better we were doing in the war." The president, too, was in a jovial mood—although, as Rosenman commented, "even during the darkest days of the war he never seemed so worried or so downcast as the Prime Minister."

After lunch, the president and the prime minister sat under the trees, talking, laughing, and telling stories. "You know," Churchill told Eleanor, "one works better when one has a chance to enjoy a little leisure now and then. The old proverb all work and no play makes Jack a dull boy holds good for all of us."

Only the stifling summer heat cut into the pleasure of the weekend. On Friday night, Churchill recorded, it was so hot that he could barely breathe. Unable to sleep, he wandered across the back lawn to the bluff overlooking the Hudson River. There he sat for hours, only returning to the Big House, refreshed and relaxed, after the sun had risen.

At dinner Saturday night, Churchill launched into a discussion of "his hopes that the fraternal relationship between the United States and Great Britain would be perpetuated in peacetime." Eleanor, Averell Harriman recorded, was less than enchanted by this idea. "Mrs. Roosevelt seemed fearful this might be misunderstood by other nations and weaken the United Nations concept." The prime minister took just the opposite tack, arguing that the only hope for the United Nations lay in "the leadership given by the intimacy of the U.S. and Britain in working out misunderstandings with the Russians—and the Chinese too." Listening to the lively conversation, Harriman was impressed by the purity of Eleanor's idealism. Churchill was also impressed. Having grown accustomed by now to her spirited interruptions, he was able to enjoy the byplay. She had "a spirit of steel and a heart of gold," he told Harriman later that night.

The next morning, with Churchill en route to Quebec a day early, Eleanor relished the chance to be alone with her husband. As the time for her departure to the South Pacific drew near, she found herself in a tranquil mood, happy for once to sit still and enjoy the summer day. "Your mother is so pleased with herself," Tommy reported to Anna. "She has lost 25 pounds and looks very slim and young and it has not made her face look drawn."

After a leisurely breakfast, Eleanor joined Franklin in his study as he penned letters to General MacArthur and Admiral Halsey in her behalf. Though both men had already been apprised of the first lady's visit, Eleanor was afraid that undue security concerns would keep her from seeing the troops and the battlefields. In particular, she yearned to visit Guadalcanal, where Joe Lash was stationed. Recognizing how much it meant to her to see young Lash, the president paved the way. "She is especially anxious to see Guadalcanal," he told Admiral Halsey, "and at this moment it looks like a pretty safe place to visit." But of course, he added, "I would not have you let her go to any place which would interfere in any way with current military or naval operations—in other words, the war comes first." This was the best Eleanor could hope for, and she was pleased.

Enjoying her husband's company, Eleanor decided to postpone her departure for New York, where she was supposed to appear on a radio show with Mayor LaGuardia to talk about "Unity at Home—Victory Abroad." Hurried arrangements were made to tape the broadcast from Hyde Park. "I spoke from the library," she later wrote, "with my husband listening which was a curious situation, for I have often sat listening to him but I cannot remember when he sat listening to me. The fact that I could speak from there gave us several more hours in the country together and I was happy not to miss the pleasant, leisurely luncheon out of doors and the good talk, which is one of the rare things we enjoy when only a small company is gathered together."

In the late afternoon, Eleanor left for New York and the president returned to Washington. Since he was leaving for Quebec the following day and she was flying out that night to San Francisco en route to the South Pacific, this was the last time they would see one another for nearly six weeks. "The P[resident] was very sweet to her when she left," Tommy reported to Esther Lape. "She left all her jewelry and instructions as to their disposal in case anything happened. It gave me a queer feeling."

Anna, too, was plagued with worry as Eleanor boarded the unheated army bomber that was to take her to the South Pacific. "Darling, it kinda gives me the creeps to think of you heading off into space. Please don't take any more chances than you have to."

•   •   •

While Eleanor flew west, Roosevelt journeyed north by train, accompanied, as usual, by Harry Hopkins. On Tuesday evening, August 17, a small crowd was gathered in the president's car to celebrate Hopkins' fifty-third birthday. For Hopkins, who was being subjected daily to vicious attacks in the papers, the relaxed celebration was a moment to be cherished. Though controversy had attended Hopkins from the start of his unconventional relationship with the president, the recent spate of criticism had assumed an unusual virulence. In one paper after another, it was charged that the president's closest friend was benefiting in questionable ways from his position of public trust.

One story, told by a Republican congressman on the floor of the House and retold in the papers, held that Lord Beaverbrook had presented Louise Hopkins with a gift of emeralds worth nearly a half-million dollars. Though the story was vehemently denied by Louise Hopkins, who insisted that she did not own even a single emerald, the damage was done. The emerald story was followed by reports of an extravagant dinner for sixty invited guests which Bernard Baruch held at the Hotel Carlton in honor of Harry and Louise. Since the dinner coincided with the publication of an article in

The American magazine in which Hopkins urged the populace to accept rationing as part of the inevitable sacrifice of war, the newspapers took great pleasure in running the dinner menu at the Carlton, complete with caviar and pâté de foie gras, alongside Hopkins' call for sacrifice.

As one attack followed another, Hopkins pondered what to do. The final blow came when the *Chicago Sunday Tribune* published a malicious article which likened him to the Siberian mystic Grigory Rasputin, whose ability to improve the condition of Alexis, the hemophiliac heir to the Russian throne, made him a favorite at the court of Czar Nicholas and Czarina Alexandra. The article featured side-by-side pictures and compared their leering expressions, their clumsy demeanor, and their malevolent influence over their nations. Against the advice of the president, Hopkins decided to sue for libel. "This is a fight in which you would be licked before you could even get started," Roosevelt warned Hopkins. "The whole proceedings would give them a glorious opportunity to pile on smears. . . . What earthly good would it do you to win a verdict and receive damages of one dollar?" Though Hopkins eventually backed down, the hurt remained.

Adding immeasurably to Hopkins' stress that summer was his wife's desire to move out of the White House into a house of their own. Louise was convinced that their lives would never be their own so long as they remained at the president's beck and call in the second-floor suite. Eager to invite her own guests to dinner and to serve her own meals as she thought they should be served, she had begun to look for a house in Georgetown. For Harry, it was a difficult choice, knowing as he did that Roosevelt would not be pleased. But by midsummer, the pressure to move proved irresistible. "Harry and Louise are going to move to their own house," Eleanor reported to Joe Lash, "though P[resident] doesn't like their going."

On the surface, Harry's relationship with the president remained as before, but underneath, the cord of communion was cut. For the president, accustomed to standing at the absolute center of Hopkins' life, his friend's decision to move seemed to suggest an ebbing of affection, a form of abandonment. Though Hopkins postponed the move for five months, a frost descended on their relationship.

When Churchill was at Hyde Park before the trip to Quebec, he had found Hopkins "ailing and fearing he had lost favor with his chief." But in short order "it seemed like old times again," and Churchill delighted in the presence of the straight-speaking Hopkins. So now, as Hopkins relaxed with the president on the train, mixing a round of old-fashioneds to celebrate his birthday, everything appeared for the moment the same as it had always been.

In Quebec on the evening of the 17th, the president and the prime minister stayed in the Citadel, a magnificent fortress that stood above the St. Lawrence River on the heights of Cape Diamond. The aides were quartered in the Château Frontenac, a few miles away, where the official working sessions took place. For five days prior to the arrival of the president and the prime minister, the military experts had been doing preliminary "pick and shovel" work. Now, with both leaders present, the time for decision had come.

The principal business at the Quebec Conference was to decide the date for the cross-Channel attack. Though Churchill was still haunted by his memories of World War I, he knew, Lord Moran claimed, that the time had come to give way. He could delay the decision no longer. As he studied the plans for the invasion, he could not help being impressed by the massive numbers that would be engaged, the tonnage involved. More than once, Moran recalled, he referred to the plan as "majestic."

With the target date set for May 1, 1944, the two leaders turned their attention to the details of the landing—the numbers of landing craft required, the building of synthetic harbors, the extent of shipping necessary. In the midst of these discussions, British Minister of Defense Lord Ismay records a curious conference in Churchill's bathroom. "If a stranger had visited," Ismay wrote, "he might have seen a stocky figure in a dressing gown of many colors, sitting on a stool and surrounded by a number of what our American friends call 'top brass.' While an admiral flapped his hand in the water at one end of the bath in order to simulate a choppy sea, a brigadier stretched a lilo [an inflatable rubber mattress] across the middle to show how it broke up the waves. The stranger would have found it hard to believe that this was the British high command studying the most stupendous and spectacular amphibious operation in the history of the war."

Churchill's apparent change of heart brought relief to Roosevelt and the American high command, but Hopkins feared that the decision was not irrevocable, that Churchill might change his mind again, as he had done the previous year. In a conversation with Moran one morning, Hopkins spoke of Churchill in an uncharacteristically aggressive way. Though Churchill had seemingly thrown in his hand, Hopkins told Moran he was convinced that "Winston's obstinacy, his drawn out struggle to postpone a second front in France has in fact prolonged the war. That if he had been reasonable earlier we might now be in sight of peace." Was Hopkins right? Moran asked himself. "That must remain the riddle of the war."

In the meantime, the news arriving from the Italian front was excellent. On August 17, reports confirmed that, after only thirty-one days of fighting, the island of Sicily was under Allied control. The campaign had succeeded beyond expectations, so much so that Eisenhower was now recommending that the success in Sicily be followed up with an assault on the Italian mainland, beginning September 3. This was, of course, what Churchill had wanted all along, and finally Roosevelt agreed, believing that the plans for Operation Overlord were firmly set.

As the planning for the cross-Channel attack became more detailed, the question of command arose. The president and prime minister had previously agreed that the commander of Overlord should be British, since

Eisenhower had commanded the landings in North Africa. Based on this understanding, Churchill had offered the post to Field Marshal Alan Brooke, chief of the imperial general staff. But now, as the contours of the invasion became clear, Churchill recognized that the Americans would be sending "a very great preponderance" of the troops, five times more than the British. When Roosevelt argued for an American commander on the basis of the numbers, Churchill gracefully agreed. To balance the scale, the Southeast Asian command was established under Lord Louis Mountbatten, with General Joseph W. Stilwell as his deputy.

While in Quebec, the president and the prime minister discussed the atomic bomb. Churchill had agreed the previous year that research and manufacture of the bomb should take place in the United States, but the British felt that the Americans were deliberately keeping them from knowing what was going on. To provide an amicable solution to what was becoming a divisive issue, Roosevelt agreed to sign a joint "tube alloy" memo with Churchill, which ensured full sharing of all the work and promised that no secrets would be withheld on either side. Each nation also promised never to use the bomb against the other and not to use it against a third party without the other's consent.

Stalin provoked the only dark moment at the Quebec Conference. On the sixth afternoon of the summit, a cable arrived from Moscow. "Until now the matter stood as follows," the Russian premier asserted. "The United States and Great Britain made agreements but the Soviet Union received information about the results of the agreements between the two countries just as a passive third observer. I have to tell you that it is impossible to tolerate such situation any longer." Both Roosevelt and Churchill were offended by the tone of the message. "We are both mad," Roosevelt announced as he arrived for dinner that evening. Curiously, Harriman noted, Roosevelt's anger made him gayer than usual; his conversation at dinner sparkled with banter and good cheer. In contrast, Churchill arrived at dinner "with a scowl and never really got out of his ill humor all evening." Stalin, Churchill told Harriman, is "an unnatural man. There will be grave troubles."

When the conference closed on August 25, Churchill followed Roosevelt to Washington for an additional round of talks. As always, Churchill's presence turned the White House upside down, creating havoc for everyone, including Hick, who was forced to vacate her bedroom on the second floor and move upstairs. "I gather she didn't like the third floor," Tommy told Anna. "However, I know your father would have spasms if any of the Churchill party had to go on the third floor and Hick was left on the second. One would think knowing the criticism of Harry's being there that she would take a hint."

"PM's sleeping arrangements have now become quite promiscuous," British Foreign Office Undersecretary Sir Alexander Cadogan noted. "He talks with President till 2 am and consequently spends a large part of day hurling himself violently in and out of bed, bathing at unsuitable moments and rushing up and down the corridors in his dressing gown."

Accustomed by now to Churchill's irregular routine, Roosevelt found refuge at Hyde Park, where he escaped for the weekend while Churchill remained in the White House. But Hopkins had returned from Quebec so exhausted that he had to be admitted to the Naval Hospital for another series of blood transfusions. Although he joked that it was nothing serious, that Quebec and Churchill had simply been "too much for him," he admitted that he was "in pretty bad shape" and remained in the hospital for three weeks.

Before leaving for London, Churchill sent a warm telegram to Eleanor in the South Pacific, telling her that he was sorry she'd been unable to join the presidential party in Quebec but realized that her journey was "of high importance to our common interests and causes."

• • •

In truth, Eleanor was finding her days in the South Pacific grimly depressing. To start, she was traveling without Tommy for the first time in years, having decided that the twenty-thousand-mile trip would be too strenuous for her faithful secretary. But without someone to share the experience, Eleanor was overcome with loneliness. "I feel a hundred years away as though I were moving in a different and totally unattached world," she admitted to Tommy. "I don't like it much."

Everywhere she went that first week, she met with resistance on the part of the top brass, who regarded her trip as a nuisance and insisted on surrounding her with so much protection that she felt cut off from the ordinary soldiers she had come to see. When she landed in New Caledonia and presented Admiral Halsey with the president's letter supporting her desire to go to Guadalcanal, Halsey was blunt: "Guadalcanal is no place for you, Ma'am!" he said. "If you fly to Guadalcanal, I'll have to provide a fighter escort for you, and I haven't got one to spare." Crushed at the thought of having come so far and not being able to see Joe Lash, Eleanor refused to give up, getting Halsey to agree that he would put off his final decision until she returned from New Zealand and Australia.

"In some ways," Eleanor cabled Franklin from Noumea, "I wish I had not come on this trip. I think the trouble I give far outweighs the momentary interest it may give the boys to see me. I do think when I tell them I bring a message from you to them, they like it but anyone else could have done it as well and caused less commotion!"

In a letter to Hick, she revealed her feelings more completely. "I have no zest for travel any more," she admitted. "If it does any good I'll be satisfied. I can't judge at all whether it will accomplish what FDR hoped for or not."

As anxiety crowded in on her, Eleanor stepped up her schedule. On the go from dawn till dusk, virtually without a break, she toured one hospital after another, drove hundreds of miles in an open jeep to talk with soldiers at their camps, gave dozens of speeches to tremendous crowds, pinned her name on the wall maps of Red Cross clubs in every part of Australia and New Zealand, attended large receptions at night, and still managed to write and type a four-hundred-word column every day.

Everywhere she went, wearing the crisp blue-gray summer suit of the Red Cross, Eleanor assured the soldiers she met that they were not forgotten at home. "When I left," she told them, "my husband asked me to give you a message. He said to tell you that every day he goes down to the map room in the White House and notes on the maps where you are and what you are doing. He said to tell you that you have done and are doing a wonderful job. He wants me to give you his deepest admiration and gratitude . . . and now that I have given his message let me add mine. . . ."

"We liked this speech," one soldier said. "Her sincerity permeated every word. I can tell you that after a year of listening to nothing but bassooning top sergeants and officers, it was good to hear a kind lady saying nice things."

Realizing that many of these men would never see their homes and their families again, Eleanor had a hard time concealing her emotions. Every time she grabbed a new hand, one reporter noted, her eyes lit up with a resolute effort to make contact, to project "a genuine impulse of friendship towards the person she is greeting."

Traveling in Queensland, she saw in the distance a convoy of army trucks loaded with troops headed for the battlefront. She insisted that she catch up with them to tell them goodbye and wish them luck. Trudging down the rough road, the *Times* reporter observed, "her shoes dusty and scarred by rocks," she stopped at each truck and spoke to each soldier in full battle dress. "At one point her voice quavered but she quickly recovered and continued on down the line."

Eleanor's indomitable energy staggered the mind of everyone who followed her. "Mrs. Roosevelt literally took New Zealand by storm," wrote Major George Durno, a former newspaperman who had been assigned to her by Air Transport Command. "She did a magnificent job, saying the right thing at the right time and doing 101 little things that endeared her to the people." A friend of Hopkins witnessed an impromptu visit to a Red Cross club with Eleanor leading the way, "followed by a brace of generals and admirals manfully teetering on the edge of collapse." As Eleanor's party swept in, two privates were standing by an electric heater without benefit of trousers. "While management gasped for shame and the entourage gasped for breath, she coolly and graciously chatted with the two boys both paralyzed with amazement and chagrin but thrilled through and through." Everyone in the club was charmed by Eleanor's simplicity and graciousness, Hopkins' friend confirmed, though he himself could not get his mind off the two boys without any pants. "The talk over, Eleanor departed, the management collapsed and the two boys grasped their scorched legs and burst into all sorts of excited exclamation."

As Eleanor's visit continued, Admiral Halsey found himself yielding to her charm, professing total admiration of her dedication and commitment. "When I say that she inspected those hospitals," he reported, "I don't mean that she shook hands with the chief medical officer, glanced into a sun parlor, and left. I mean that she went into every ward, stopped at every bed, and spoke to every patient: What was his name? How did he feel? Was there anything he needed? Could she take a message home for him?" And a promise made was a promise kept. When Sergeant Al Lewis asked her to call his girlfriend, Helen Carl, she would later follow through, provoking the young girl's breathless astonishment on hearing the White House was calling!

Beneath her cheerful exterior, Eleanor found these hospital visits excruciating. Apparently, as soon as she arrived at a hospital or a military base, the word went out that a woman was coming. For reasons of security, it could not be said that this woman was the first lady. Certain that the young men were expecting a beauty queen, Eleanor feared she would be a woeful disappointment. Each time she entered a new ward, she wished she could be changed "in some magic way" from Eleanor Roosevelt, first lady, into "the sweetheart or the wife or sister the men were longing to see." Her anxiety was such that she failed to see what Halsey immediately saw—the joyous impact she made on everyone she met. "Over here," one soldier said, "she was something . . . none of us had seen in over a year, an American mother." Standing beside her, Halsey witnessed the expressions on the faces of the gruesomely wounded boys as she leaned over them, a warm smile on her face. "It was a sight I will never forget."

From Washington, the president cabled Eleanor every few days, letting her know how he was and assuring her that her trip was making "a fine impression" at home, with absolutely "no disagreeable notes." Worried that she was taking on too much, he suggested she cut back a bit. "If I wasn't busy," she replied, "I'd go crazy." When Admiral Jones invited her to spend a relaxing day at his cottage by the sea, she explained that as soon she got home she would rest but she had no right to do so while she was in the war zone.

In her cables to her husband, Eleanor described the spirit of the soldiers, the scourge of malaria, and the stultifying overprotection of the top brass toward her. "I've had so many Generals and Admirals and MPs to protect me that I remind myself of you," she joked.

As her days in Australia wound to a close, Eleanor journeyed to the seaside town of Cairns, where she spent a long evening talking to a group of soldiers. The one thought on the minds of all these boys, she found, was the desire to finish the struggle so they could go "home." Halfway round the world, home had become the goal for which they were all living.

The rich conversations, the soft air, and the sound of the waves breaking against the beach stirred memories of courtship days at Campobello, when she and Franklin walked along the shore, relishing the chance to be alone, sharing their hopes for the future. "How little I ever thought," she mused, "when I wandered on the moonlit beaches on the coast of Maine that I would one day see one in Australia and sit all evening listening to the waves while we talked of America with American men who wanted to know what was going on at home while they fought a war thousands of miles away."

The next day, to her unbounded delight, Eleanor learned that Admiral Halsey had finally agreed she could go to Guadalcanal. A round of official duties was arranged, including a visit to the cemetery where thousands of American soldiers were buried, a tour through several island hospitals, lunch with General Nathan Twining, commanding officer of the Thirteenth Air Force, and dinner with Admiral Halsey. But for Eleanor, the shining moment of the day came at two-thirty in the afternoon, when a note was slipped to her saying that a young man named Joe Lash was waiting for her outside the tent. Ignoring army protocol, she embraced him warmly, an excited smile on her face. They talked for a while and then arranged to meet again in the late afternoon, after her second hospital tour was done. After dinner, Lash came back once more, and they sat on a screened porch and talked until eleven-thirty.

"How I hated to have you leave last night," Eleanor wrote the next morning, and told him that she was reliving every moment they had had together. "When the war is over I hope I never have to be long away from you. It was so wonderful to be with you, the whole trip now seems to me worthwhile. It is bad to be so personal but I care first for those few people I love deeply and then for the rest of the world I fear."

Now that she had covered seventeen islands, New Zealand, and Australia, the time had come to begin her journey home. Admiral Halsey came to say goodbye. "I was ashamed of my original surliness," he admitted later. "She alone had accomplished more good than any other person, or any group of civilians, who had passed through my area."

The Central Solomons campaign was nearly completed by the time Eleanor left, bringing U.S. forces 350 miles nearer Rabaul on the way to the Philippines and, ultimately, to Japan. But, as naval historian Samuel Eliot Morison has observed, the arduous campaign had brought the Americans only one-tenth of the way to Tokyo. If the United States continued hopping from island to island at this pace, it would take almost ten years to reach Japan. It was just at this point, Morison notes, that "leapfrogging" was substituted for "island hopping." Pacific Fleet Commander Admiral Nimitz had provided the first demonstration of the advantages of leapfrogging by skipping inadvertently over Kiska to take Attu. When the Japanese decided to evacuate Kiska a few weeks later, the United States had secured two victories for the price of one. Henceforth, the Combined Chiefs decided, American forces would leapfrog their way to Japan.

As Eleanor settled into her seat for the flight to San Francisco, she thought of all the things she wanted to tell Franklin. Bone-tired but unable to sleep, obsessed with the thought that somehow there must be a way, through fundamental change in the postwar era, to make sense out of all the carnage she had witnessed, she took out her pad and scribbled a series of notes. Her first note took up labor leader Walter Reuther's suggestion about a Peace Production Board. "FDR, should there not be a call on men like those now in the WPB . . . to remain through transition period" to guide the process of converting from war to peace. "FDR, isn't resumption of peacetime industry largely dependent on bank loan policy and possible guarantees by government in same way as was done for conversion to war industry." Other memos urged that legislation providing for jobs and education for veterans should be passed as soon as possible and made known to every American soldier in every part of the world. For, as it was, "men not chief concern anywhere. Officers have too much, men too little."

The president was in Hyde Park with Princess Martha, her children, and Empress Zita of Austria-Hungary when Eleanor reached San Francisco. At a lunch with Martha and Margaret Suckley, Empress Zita suggested that Eleanor would be very tired when she got home. "No," Roosevelt joked, "but she will tire everybody else." His joking aside, Roosevelt was anxious to see his wife. "Hope you come Washington where I arrive Sat. morning or HP if you get to NY early Friday," he cabled her.

Yet, when she called him from the airport in San Francisco, he could not resist teasing her about the extraordinary lengths she had gone to see her friend Joe Lash. "Did you have fun, darling," he asked in a jocular and perhaps slightly jealous tone, "as if she had been on a pleasure jaunt which he had been big-hearted enough to fix up for her." Eleanor was devastated.

The only thing that had kept her going through her long and tiring days was the thought that she was accomplishing what the president had asked her to do. And now he seemed uninterested and unconcerned. As soon as she hung up the phone, she called Anna in Seattle and poured out her disappointments, remarking that "she had never worked harder in her life." Eleanor said she was going to ask her Pacific escort, Major George Durno, to report to the "OM" on the trip, in the hope that he'd tell him how successful it was. "Poor LL," Anna commented to John. ("OM," "Old Man," "Oscar Mann," "LL," and "Lovely Lady" were the codes Anna and John used for the president and the first lady.)

Eleanor arrived back in Washington on September 25. "Pa asked me more questions than I expected," she told Anna, "and actually came over to lunch with me on Saturday [September 25] and spent two hours." In her husband's presence, Eleanor lightened up, telling entertaining stories of her travels, even poking fun at herself. When she first entered the Pacific area, she joked, she overheard an anguished cry. "Oh, no, Eleanor Roosevelt is on the move again." That evening, she continued her tales at a small dinner with the president, Tommy, and Hick. When asked by reporters on Monday if his wife had told him about her trip, Roosevelt laughed. "Yes, she has been talking ever since she got back."

In the days that followed, reporters noted that the first lady seemed exhausted. "They missed her usual warmhearted gusto. Lines of weariness were traced on her face, netting her friendly blue eyes in a delicate web of fatigue. They were eyes that had seen much—perhaps too much." With rest, they assumed, the exhaustion would dissipate. But as September turned to October, her fatigue deepened, accompanied by an escalating sense of anxiety and dread. A paralyzing depression was setting in.

Eleanor's gloom thickened as she found herself subjected to a new round of criticism for her costly "junkets." When Representative Harold Knutsen of Minnesota complained that Eleanor was gallivanting around the world, "while the farmers in my neighborhood can't even get gasoline to work with their farms," dozens of Republicans followed suit. "The outcry in Congress is so great," Eleanor confided in Joe Lash, "that FDR feels I should not use Government transportation or even go on any far trips for awhile."

Imprisoned in the White House, Eleanor moped to the point where her friends became concerned. "[Tommy] is worried about Mrs. Roosevelt," Trude reported to Lash, "and I feel uneasy too. Mrs. R. is strange, often sits and looks absent mindedly into space and then realizes she has not heard a word. . . . Even the President said something after he had in the presence of [Crown Princess of the Netherlands] Juliana tried to get Mrs. R. to invite Juliana to Washington—and only met complete lack of response."

In their letters to each other that fall, Joe and Trude tried to understand what was wrong. Trude attributed Eleanor's depression to "her deep horror at what she saw and the great sadness at the continuing bloodshed and dying." For all her belief in the Allied cause, Eleanor was appalled when she observed firsthand the horror and the ruin which war entails. Nothing in her previous experience had prepared her for the misery she encountered in the hospitals—the mangled bodies, the stomachs ripped by shells, the amputated limbs, the crushed spirits. Only a few photographs of dead American soldiers had appeared in magazines and newspapers since the war began. The bodies shown were always clothed and intact, as if they were sleeping. The Office of War Information, established by Roosevelt in the spring of 1942 to coordinate the dissemination of war information, had so sanitized the war experience that few people on the home front understood what the war was really about.

At home, traveling from one factory to the next, Eleanor had seen the best face of war—the productivity, the camaraderie, the pride of accomplishment. On the assembly line, planes, tanks, and guns stood as shining emblems of American democracy. In the South Pacific, the emblematic quality was gone, and these same planes and tanks assumed their real shape as lethal weapons of destruction. Slowly, Eleanor began to absorb the terrible reality that all that productive genius which her husband's leadership had helped to call forth was directed toward a single, brutal goal—that of killing and maiming the enemy.

For weeks after she returned, Eleanor kept picturing the cemetery in Guadalcanal, "the crosses row on row," the thousands of young men who had died in that faraway place cut off from the world of their family and friends, the poignant way the living troops had countered the anonymity of the dead by hanging their buddies' mess kits on their crosses and carving personal tributes on each one: "A swell pal," "a good guy," "best friends forever."

By the end of 1943, American casualties, though few in number in comparison with the rest of the nations at war, were beginning to mount. The army and army air force counted 117,142 killed, wounded, or missing in action. For the navy and Marine Corps, each engagement carried its own list of casualties: Pearl Harbor, 2,554; fall of the Philippines, 1,383; Battle of Coral Sea, 705; Battle of Midway, 547; Guadalcanal, Tulagi landings, 6,040; Battle of Savo Island, 1,691; Battle of Guadalcanal, 1,460; Sicilian landings, 1,064; Italian landings, 1,688; Battle of the Atlantic, 3,314.

In a letter to FDR, Jr., written shortly after her return, Eleanor admitted that her trip was "emotionally disturbing" and that she was now preoccupied with the thought of bringing the war to a speedy end. "I know and understand your obsession to see the end of this war," young Franklin replied. "But Mummy, we've got to see it through completely this time."

But if Eleanor's eyes had seen too much of war, the roots of her depression were grounded in deeper soil. "I think," Lash wrote Trude, "another and larger part of it has to do with a great inner loneliness." Eleanor's encounter with death and dying had served notice on the life she was leading, the hours wasted in polite conversation, the endless rounds of social obligations. Though she was tied to her husband in a thousand ways and was devoted to Anna and John and to Joe and Trude, she was still the outsider looking in.

• • •

As she had so many times before in her life, Eleanor sought to escape her sadness through unremitting work, through a redoubled effort to ensure that the world that emerged in the postwar era was worthy of the lives that had been lost. "I think the things one dreads sometimes tend to be forgotten as quickly as possible," she wrote, "but this time . . . we must remember the dreadful things and try to see they don't happen again."

In her columns that fall, she spelled out her hopes for the future: legislation to provide education for returning veterans; a governmental agency to deal with the conversion of industry from war to peace; a permanent international organization that could build on the present cooperation between the United Nations; a relief agency to help people all over the world get back on their feet; an interchange of young people among the various nations as a step toward better understanding.

On previous occasions when Eleanor had tried to get her husband to focus on postwar concerns, she had been unable to attract his attention. To the commander-in-chief it seemed presumptuous, even reckless, to ruminate over the challenges of peace while the Axis powers were winning the war. But now, with the turn in the tide, he found himself willing to look toward the future, both at home and abroad.

In the third week of October, Roosevelt asked Congress for early action on a massive program of education and training for returning GIs—an unprecedented program that would later be known as the GI Bill of Rights. The president's message called on the federal government to underwrite the college education of returning veterans for a period of one to four years. "Lack of money should not prevent any veteran of this war from equipping himself for the most useful employment for which his aptitudes and willingness qualify him," Roosevelt said. "I believe this nation is morally obligated to provide this training and education."

In the weeks that followed, Roosevelt called for additional measures to ensure a smooth transition for every returning veteran. He proposed mustering-out pay on a monthly basis to cover the period of time between discharge and the finding of a new job; unemployment insurance if no job could be found; credits toward social security for time in the service; hospitalization and rehabilitation. Taken together, these measures promised American servicemen more support and more opportunity than any other country had ever given its veterans.

Eleanor was pleased. "I'd like to see us pass all legislation for veterans as soon as possible," she told reporters. "It would add to the confidence of the men to have such legislation an accomplished fact."

The president took another forward-looking step that autumn, when he appointed Bernard Baruch to head a newly created unit under War Mobilization Director Jimmy Byrnes to deal with postwar adjustment problems and the conversion of industry from war to peace. The appointment of Baruch was a master stroke. Had anyone else been put in charge of planning the peace, the conservatives on Capitol Hill, who considered the very word "plan" a communist invention, would have had a field day. But so revered was Baruch by Republicans and Democrats alike that all controversy was suppressed. Once again, Eleanor's delight was palpable. "Baruch is still the most comforting person I know," she exulted. Though the structure of the new unit failed to capture the broad-gauged vision of the Peace Production Board proposed by Walter Reuther, it did promise to bring a unified governmental approach to the conversion process.

The autumn of 1943 also witnessed significant progress in planning an international body to organize the peace. In the past, fearful that public debate on the shape of the postwar world would stir up isolationist attacks and undermine the unity necessary to prosecute the war, Roosevelt had vigorously opposed a detailed discussion of how the Allies would organize the peace. His change of heart could be traced to the phenomenal success of Wendell Willkie's book, *One World*. No book in American publishing history had ever sold so fast. Within two months of its publication, sales had reached a million copies. Based on Willkie's travels through Russia, China, and the Middle East, the book was an eloquent plea for international cooperation to preserve the peace. Unless Roosevelt took the lead, Democratic colleagues warned, the Republicans stood poised to capture the postwar issue in the next campaign.

The president found his opening in the Conference of Foreign Ministers' meeting in Moscow that fall. With Roosevelt's encouragement, Secretary Hull engineered a Four Power declaration pledging the United States, Great Britain, the Soviet Union, and China to continued cooperation in a great international organization to be established at the earliest practicable date. Though no details were determined, the assurance of postwar unity provoked rejoicing on the part of the American public.

The president hosted an elaborate ceremony in the East Room in early November to commemorate the signing of an international agreement for a United Nations Relief and Rehabilitation Administration to feed, clothe, and house the world. "The representatives of 44 nations sat around a long table with the President," Eleanor happily observed. "Behind them were their flags. I watched each man go up to represent his country and thought how interesting it was that, before the end of the war, we have the vision this time to realize that there is much work to do and that preparation by the peoples of the United Nations is necessary.... It was impressive and F[ranklin]'s short speech clear and good. I feel in the end something great may have begun today."

• • •

The first week of November 1943 found the president and the first lady at Hyde Park. The weather was clear and invigorating, Eleanor exulted, "with a sky so blue" that the stars at night were shining as brilliantly as they did in the real winter months. Basking in the beauty of the cool autumn days, the president finished his work in the early afternoons to allow time for picnics at Top Cottage, motor rides through the countryside, and dinners at Val-Kill.

"Good news comes in from every battlefront," William Hassett recorded on November 1. In Italy, after a successful landing on the mainland to the north of Reggio on September 3, the Allied forces were slowly working their way north up the instep of the Italian boot. The fighting was tougher than expected. Though the new Italian government had surrendered on the first day of the invasion, Hitler's troops were fighting furiously every step along the way. The battle for Salerno had been, army historians contend, "one of the bitterest battles of the war." But by the end of October, Allied forces had seized both Palermo and Naples and were only ninety miles from Rome. In the South Pacific, the U.S. landings on Bougainville, the next hop toward Rabaul, had begun. And in the Eastern front, the Red Army was moving forward again toward Kiev after having been driven back halfway to the Dnieper by a German counterattack.

But for Roosevelt, the most encouraging news of the day was Stalin's agreement, at long last, to meet the Allied leaders at a summit conference in Teheran at the end of November. The first leg of the journey would take the president to Cairo to meet Generalissimo Chiang Kai-shek. From there, he and Churchill would journey together to Teheran to join the Russian leader.

As soon as Eleanor heard about the meeting with Stalin, she pleaded with Franklin to bring her along. Never once had she been present at a summit conference, though her sons Elliott and FDR, Jr., had been invited to both Argentia and Casablanca. "Mrs. R wanted very much to go," Trude reported to Joe. "But the Boss just put his foot down. Absolutely no women." Besides, he had already asked Elliott, FDR, Jr., and John Boettiger to join him, and that was plenty of company. Eleanor was crushed, not simply by the decision itself but by the insensitivity of her husband's attitude. But, in characteristic fashion, she deflected the argument from her own disappointment to the wisdom of dragging FDR, Jr., off his ship, which was leaving for Gibraltar in several days, to return to the United States for repairs after a torpedo attack. Feeling strongly that it would hurt her son's relationship to his men to leave his ship, she was furious when the president insisted that he needed both boys and that was that. An argument followed. "The OM sat all over her," Anna reported to John, "and hurt her feelings."

When Anna heard about the trip, she, too, begged to go, "not just because of the interest of the occasion itself," she told her mother, "but because he'll be seeing my John." Eleanor urged her to send a special-delivery letter asking if she could go. "I'll read him your desire," she promised, "but I fear all females are out."

"The answer was, of course, no!" Anna reported bitterly to John. In no uncertain terms, Roosevelt told his daughter that, under navy rules, no women were allowed on shipboard, so there was no way she could come. "Pa seems to take for granted that all females should be quite content to 'keep the home fires burning,' and that their efforts outside of this are merely rather amusing and to be aided by a patronizing male world only as a last resort to keep some individually troublesome female momentarily appeased."

In the days that followed, Anna's irritation toward her father deepened. In long phone calls with her mother, she worked herself into a fury at the thought that her brothers would be attending their third conference in two years but her only request had been flatly denied. Mother, Anna told John, "goes along very strongly with me in our feeling that OM is a stinker in his treatment of the female members of his family. She pointed out that even though I couldn't have gone with him in the ship that it would have been perfectly possible for me to fly. Of course the uniform angle (lack of it) is obvious; but a R[ed] C[ross] uniform and mission could have solved that!"

Anna's sense of injustice was compounded by fear that John was suffering an emotional breakdown in North Africa. Though his early letters revealed a genuine excitement about taking part in "the big show," his recent letters were filled with self-pity at not having been given anything important to do, despite the assurances he had been given before he arrived that he was really needed. Suddenly he had decided that he could no longer go it alone, that the only way he could contribute to the war effort was if he and Anna could work together as one, either by her obtaining an assignment abroad or his coming home.

In frenzied letters to both Anna and Eleanor, John pleaded for help to come home. "Tell me darling if you can," John asked Anna, "what made me do this thing? Why should I, with YOU, with US and with real and patriotic responsibilities at home, tear off to what at this stage gives smaller promise of real usefulness. . . . What could I possibly gain to weigh against the job I left vacant on the homefront and the pain I bring to you. Has what I have done to US impaired your love for me in any way? So please my beloved, don't try to banish US from your thoughts."

"Neither of us is giving to the war effort separately what we could give jointly," John wrote Eleanor, "and I fully realize now what a tragic error it was in every way to attempt anything different. . . . If amends can be made I will be ever so grateful. . . . I hope you won't think too badly of me."

The problem, Anna explained to John, was that, though her mother was sympathetic to his desire for a transfer, she did not expect her father would understand. Nor could she think of anyone "among the higher ups in Washington who would give serious help and consideration to anything suggested by me or LL. I believe they would be nice and kind and put us both off, believing we were just two sentimental females—this one hungry to get her mate back."

The only hope, Anna believed, was for the two of them to get together somewhere so she could restore his confidence and bring him back to his senses. Otherwise she feared he might do something stupid in his obsession to come home. That was why the trip to Teheran mattered so much to her, and why her father's peremptory refusal hurt so badly.

As Anna's anxiety about John deepened, her own fragile confidence wavered; her pride and pleasure in her work at the paper vanished. She found herself unable to cope with the increasingly bitter political struggles over editorial policy. Sensing her daughter's pain, Eleanor wrote to her almost every day. "I realize how desperately lonely you must be dearest and it worries me for you." Why not, Eleanor suggested, think of coming east for Christmas? The family was intending to spend the holidays at Hyde Park, and it would be wonderful if Anna could join them.

When Eleanor invited Anna to come east that winter, she had no way of knowing that her daughter's visit would lead to her taking a permanent position in the White House as her father's hostess, a move that would nearly destroy the powerful bond between mother and daughter that had been forged over a period of twenty years.

• • •

At 10:30 p.m. on November 11, 1943, a cold and rainy night in Washington, the president boarded the *Potomac* for the first leg of his journey to Cairo and Teheran. "I just saw Pa off with Admiral Leahy, Admiral Brown, General Watson, Dr. McIntire, Hopkins," Eleanor told Anna. "I hated to see Pa go and yet I think it will do much good." The next morning, the president was transferred to the battleship *Iowa* to begin the long voyage through the heavy seas of the Atlantic.

"Everything is very comfortable and I have with me lots of work and detective stories and we brought a dozen good movies," Roosevelt wrote Eleanor the first day of the trip. "Weather good and warm enough to sit with only a sweater as an extra over an old pair of trousers and a fishing shirt . . . It is a relief to have no newspapers! I am going to start a one page paper. It will pay and print only news that really has some relative importance!"

After nine days at sea, the *Iowa* pulled into the naval base at Oran. There the president was greeted by Elliott, FDR, Jr., and Eisenhower. "The sea voyage had done Father good," Elliott observed; "he looked fit; and he was filled with excited anticipation of the days ahead." As it turned out, only Elliott was going on with his father to Cairo. After a week of agonizing, FDR, Jr., had finally decided that he had best go back with his ship. This was, of course, what Eleanor had wanted him to do all along, and she was glad that he had the sense of responsibility to know what was right. She should never have gotten so worked up, she admitted to Joe Lash, "for things always turn out this way."

For security reasons, Eisenhower recommended a night flight from Tunis to Cairo. The president was disappointed. He had wanted to follow the road the battle had taken from El Alamein. But once the plane was in the air, he was excited at the prospect of seeing the Pyramids. He asked the pilot to circle the banks of the Nile at sunrise so he could have a good view. "He was thrilled by the monuments, the Sphinx and the Nile," Secret Service chief Mike Reilly recorded. As he looked at the Pyramids, he observed that "man's desire to be remembered is colossal."

In Cairo, Anna's husband, John Boettiger, and Hopkins' son Robert joined the presidential party. Churchill had arrived the night before, accompanied by his daughter Sarah; Chiang and his wife were settled in a villa nearby. No women allowed, Roosevelt had told Eleanor. Yet here, in plain view for all the photographers to see, were Sarah Churchill and Madame Chiang. Roosevelt must have realized at once that Eleanor would be furious.

She was. No sooner had the first pictures of the conference appeared than she fired off a sarcastic note to her husband. "I've been amused that Madame Chiang and Sarah Churchill were in the party. I wish you had let me fly out. I'm sure I would have enjoyed Mme Chiang more than you did though all the pictures show her in animated conversation with you and [Chiang] wears a rather puzzled look as Winston chews his cigar."

The Roosevelts had hosted the temperamental Madame Chiang at the White House the previous spring. Though Eleanor had grown to like her, the president had found her difficult. "In a queer way," Eleanor told Anna, "I think the men (including FDR) are afraid of her. She is keen and drives her point and wants to nail them down and they squirm." To the Secret Service and the White House staff, she was an insufferable prima donna with an unfortunate habit of clapping her hands whenever she wanted something.

In asking Chiang Kai-shek to Cairo, Roosevelt was less interested in China's military contribution to the Pacific war than in aligning China to the Allied cause in the years ahead. "This will be very useful 25 to 50 years hence," he said, "even though China cannot contribute much military or naval support for the moment." Though Roosevelt was under no illusions about Chiang's ill-trained, ill-equipped troops, he believed it essential to keep China in the war against Japan and was willing to make a number of promises to ensure that result. The sessions were not easy; Chiang, with his wife interpreting, was stubborn and demanding, making promises one day only to reverse himself the next. The British and the Americans were at odds on several points.

"I'm sorry things only went *pretty* well with Chiang," Eleanor consoled. "I wonder if he, Mme or Winston made trouble. The questions are so delicate that the Sphinx must be a relief. . . . I loved your quip about the Congress and the one page paper."

On Thanksgiving Day, troubles and misgivings were cast aside as the president hosted a dinner for Churchill and his daughter, Hopkins and his son, Elliott and John, Anthony Eden, Lord Moran, and Pa Watson. "Let us make it a family affair," he said as he sat high in his chair, carving two enormous turkeys which he had brought from home. "I had never seen the President more gay," Churchill noted.

After dinner, the president lifted his glass. "Large families are usually more closely united than small ones . . . and so, this year, with the peoples of the United Kingdom in our family, we are a large family, and more united than ever before. I propose a toast to this unity, and may it long continue!"

Never one to be outdone, Churchill, too, lifted his glass. "He started slowly," Robert Hopkins recalled. "His sentence used a very unusual construction. He stopped. He seemed lost. There was a long pause. He can't get out of this, I thought. He's an old man, his faculties are failing. Then suddenly he picked out a word so perfect, so brilliant, that everyone broke into spontaneous applause. It was a tour de force."

After dinner, the army band played music and dancing began. Since Sarah was in great demand as the only woman present, Churchill asked Pa Watson, Roosevelt's big, bluff aide, to dance. Watching the odd couple from the sofa,

Roosevelt roared with laughter. All in all, it was a delightful evening, one that would remain a high point in Churchill's mind for years.

Roosevelt arrived in Teheran eager to meet Stalin face to face. All his life he had prided himself on finding common ground with disparate men; so now he looked forward to the challenge of creating a bond with the forbidding, unapproachable Russian premier. He had scarcely settled into his bedroom at the yellow mansion which housed the Soviet Embassy when word came that the marshal was at the door. "Seeing him for the first time was indeed a shock," Mike Reilly recalled. "Stalin sort of ambled across the room toward Roosevelt, grinning." Though he was short, he had the presence of a large man; his mustard-colored uniform boasted such large epaulets that it looked, Lord Moran observed, "as if the tailor . . . had put a shelf on each shoulder and on it has dumped a lot of gold lace with white stars."

"I am glad to see you. I have tried for a long time to bring this about," the president said, evoking hearty laughter on Stalin's part. For thirty minutes they chatted briefly about things they would later talk about at length. "He seems very confident, very sure of himself," Roosevelt remarked to his son Elliott. But when the pleasantries were finished, Roosevelt still felt he was dealing with a complete stranger. He had no idea as Stalin left whether he'd been able to dissipate any of the distrust that lay like a thick fog between them.

The conference convened that afternoon in the embassy's boardroom, an immense chamber with dark tapestries on the walls, large, heavy chairs, and a round oak table made specially for the occasion so that no one would argue about who should be placed at its head. "It was a thrilling experience to see the Big Three sitting round the same table at last," Lord Ismay wrote.

Roosevelt, State Department aide Charles Bohlen observed, "clearly was the dominating figure at the Conference." Ismay agreed: "He looked the picture of health and was at his best . . . wise, conciliatory and paternal." Churchill, by contrast, was suffering from a miserable cold, a bronchial cough and an intermittent fever, though, as always, Ismay noted, "mind triumphed over matter, and he did his full share of talking." As for Stalin, he seemed at first not to be seeing or hearing what was passing about him; he had the air of a man absorbed in his own reflections, doodling wolfheads on his pad with downcast eyes.

It was, at first, the old story. Though Roosevelt thought that at Quebec he had gained Churchill's absolute commitment to the cross-Channel invasion, the prime minister was once again suggesting a host of peripheral possibilities—including the capture of Rome and inducements to get Turkey to enter the war. But this time, Stalin's presence was the deciding factor. Bluntly opposing Churchill's diversionary tactics, Stalin argued that the capture of Rome was irrelevant and the hope for Turkish entry into the war illusory. "If we are here to discuss military matters," Stalin said, "then Russia is only interested in Overlord."

As Stalin took the offensive for Overlord, his eyes grew keener, his voice deepened. "I thank the Lord Stalin was there," Stimson later wrote, after reading the minutes of the conference. "In my opinion, he saved the day. He brushed away the diversionary attempts of the PM with a vigor which rejoiced my soul."

As he watched the balance swing against him, Churchill's mood became somber. Unable to purge himself of his abiding fear that catastrophe would accompany a direct assault on the Continent, he told Lord Moran that he believed "man might destroy man and wipe out civilization," Europe would be left desolate, and he would be held responsible.

His only hope, Churchill believed, was to see Roosevelt alone and to win him back. As soon as the first plenary session was over, Churchill asked Roosevelt if they could lunch together. It seemed a simple request, considering the vast number of lunches these two men had shared, from elegant meals at Casablanca to hot dogs at Hyde Park. But Roosevelt firmly declined the invitation; he feared that Stalin's suspicions would be aroused if he and Churchill were seen alone, conferring in a language the Russians couldn't understand.

Having come to Teheran to accommodate Stalin, Roosevelt was determined to do everything he could to make a personal connection with the Russian leader. The task was proving more difficult than he had imagined. "I had done everything he asked me to do," Roosevelt remarked. "I had stayed at his Embassy, gone to his dinners, been introduced to his ministers and generals. He was correct, stiff, solemn, not smiling, nothing human to get hold of. I felt pretty discouraged."

Finally, Roosevelt conjured a way to break the ice. " 'I hope you won't be sore at me for what I am going to do,' " he warned Churchill as they reassembled at the plenary session. As soon as they sat down, Roosevelt began talking privately with Stalin. "I didn't say anything that I hadn't said before, but it appeared quite chummy and confidential. . . .

"Then I said, lifting my hand up to cover a whisper . . . , 'Winston is cranky this morning, he got up on the wrong side of the bed.'

"A vague smile passed over Stalin's eyes, and I decided I was on the right track. . . . I began to tease Churchill about his Britishness, about John Bull, about his cigars, about his habits. It began to register with Stalin. Winston got red and scowled, and the more he did so, the more Stalin smiled. Finally Stalin broke out into a deep, hearty guffaw, and for the first time in three days I saw light."

Suddenly Roosevelt and Stalin had become a twosome, with Churchill, rather than the marshal, the third man out. "From that time on," Roosevelt exulted, "our relations were personal. . . ."

After a while, Stalin, too joined in the fun of teasing the prime minister. Churchill later claimed that he didn't resent the teasing in the slightest, but it couldn't have been easy, and he may have felt envious as he watched Roosevelt turn his considerable charm toward Joseph Stalin.

More important, Churchill must have realized that, as long as Roosevelt and Stalin stuck together on Overlord, there was nothing he could do to stop the invasion. Bowing to reality, he lent his voice to a unanimous agreement that Overlord would be launched on the first of May. The three-some also agreed, over Churchill's initial objection, to a supporting attack in the south of France. And Stalin promised that, once Germany was defeated, Russia would join the war against Japan.

When these decisions had been reached, the tension snapped. On November 30, Roosevelt and Stalin joined Churchill in a jubilant celebration of the prime minister's sixty-ninth birthday. "There were toasts and more toasts," Hap Arnold recalled. "One speech followed another. Churchill extolled the President, glorified Stalin, then the U.S." Roosevelt toasted the valor of the Red Army. As each toast was made, "Stalin went around the table and clicked glasses with all the military men." Finally, Stalin rose to speak.

"I want to tell you, from the Russian point of view, what the President and the United States have done to win the war. The most important things in this war are machines. The United States has proven that it can turn out from 8,000 to 10,000 airplanes per month. Russia can only turn out, at most, 3,000 a month. England turns out 3,000 to 3,500. . . . The United States, therefore, is the country of machines. Without the use of these machines, through Lend-Lease, we would lose the war."

This was the first time the Soviet government had ever publicly thanked the United States for lend-lease. Except for sporadic releases in the Russian press about the arrival of particular items, the people of Russia had never been officially informed about the relationship between the vast American shipments that were coming into Russia every week and the phenomenal success of the Red Army in rolling back the Germans.

At the time of the Teheran Conference, American factories were supplying the Soviet Union with fully two-thirds of their motor vehicles and one-half of their planes; the United States had sent Russia over five thousand fighter planes in 1943 alone, more than to any other theater of war. American rails were enabling the Russians to rebuild their railroad lines; American communication equipment was making possible the control of military movements; American tires and American oil were keeping Russian trucks moving and planes flying. American explosives were being used in the manufacture of bombs and shells in Russian factories; American seeds were being planted in reconquered farmlands that had been devastated in the fighting. At the same time, American industry was supplying thirteen million Soviet soldiers with their winter boots, their uniforms, and their blankets. And for the larder of the Red Army, the United States was sending millions of tons of foodstuff, including wheat, flour, meat, eggs, and milk.

It was an astonishing story: every week, hundreds of thousands of tons of supplies were being loaded onto freight trains and transferred to one group of ships, which plied their way through the icy waters of the Arctic Ocean to Murmansk and Archangel, while another fleet sailed halfway round the world across the Pacific to Siberia, and a third traveled through the Persian Gulf to the port of Basra. For more than two years, American ships had been sailing the hazardous waters of both the Atlantic and the Pacific to bring their precious cargo to the Russian troops. More than 12 percent of the American convoys had been lost in 1942, with a heavy loss of life. But only now was Stalin willing to express the gratitude of his nation.

Midnight came and went, and the toasts continued. Finally, at 2 a.m., Roosevelt asked for the privilege of the last word. "We have differing customs and philosophies and ways of life," he said. "But we have proved here at Tehran that the varying ideals of our nations can come together in a harmonious whole, moving unitedly for the common good of ourselves and of the world."

The conference drew to a close the following day with a wide-ranging discussion of postwar concerns, including the need for an international body to keep the peace, the fate of the Baltic States, the borders of Poland, and the dismemberment of Germany. At one point, in an exercise that would have infuriated Eleanor had she been there, the three men huddled around a large map of Central Europe blandly drawing new borders for Poland.

The next morning, believing that the conference had been "an important milestone in the program of human affairs," Roosevelt departed for Cairo, where he continued his talks with Churchill. Though everybody was tired, one crucial decision remained. The time had come to choose the commander for the Allied invasion. Roosevelt was leaning toward George Marshall; in a letter earlier in the year to General John J. Pershing, commander of American Expeditionary Forces in World War I, Roosevelt said that, although he considered Marshall the most important figure among the Combined Chiefs, and would hate to lose him, he thought it only fair to give him a chance in the field. "I want George to be the Pershing of the Second World War and he cannot be that if we keep him here."

But, the nearer the decision drew, the more Roosevelt worried about losing Marshall's presence from the Joint Chiefs. Everything had worked so well for so long; to break it up now seemed too risky. Better, he reasoned, to keep Marshall in Washington and give Eisenhower the job. Unable to face Marshall directly, Roosevelt sent Hopkins to feel him out. When Marshall gamely replied that he would go along wholeheartedly with whatever decision the president made, the die was cast. "Well, Ike," Roosevelt jovially announced when they met in Tunis, "you are going to command Overlord."

"Homeward bound," Roosevelt cabled Eleanor on December 9. "I am now on a 12 hour plane trip which I hate. But on the whole it has been a real success. . . . Lots to tell you about and lots and lots of love."

•   •   •

Tanned by the sun of North Africa, the president returned to the White House in a positive frame of mind. His spirits were raised still further when he found his entire Cabinet, the congressional leaders, and the White House

DRAFT No. 1   December 7, 1941.

PROPOSED MESSAGE TO THE CONGRESS

Yesterday, December 7, 1941, a date which will live in ~~world history~~ *infamy*

the United States of America was ~~simultaneously~~ *suddenly* and deliberately attacked

by naval and air forces of the Empire of Japan ~~without warning~~.

The United States was at the moment at peace with that nation and was

still in ~~continuing the~~ conversation with its Government and its Emperor looking

toward the maintenance of peace in the Pacific. Indeed, one hour after

Japanese air squadrons had commenced bombing in ~~Hawaii and the Philippines~~ *Oahu*

the Japanese Ambassador to the United States and his colleague delivered

to the Secretary of State a formal reply to a ~~former~~ *recent American* message. ~~from the~~

~~Secretary.~~ *While* This reply ~~contained a statement~~ *stated it seemed useless* that diplomatic negotiations

~~must be considered at an end, it~~ *it* contained no threat ~~neither~~ hint *or war or* of ~~an~~

armed attack.

It will be recorded that the distance ~~of Hawaii, the especially~~ of

Hawaii from Japan make it obvious that the attack ~~was~~ *was* deliberately

or even weeks planned many days ago. During the intervening time the Japanese Govern-

ment has deliberately sought to deceive the United States by false

statements and expressions of hope for continued peace.

1

Shortly before 5 p.m. on Sunday night, December 7, 1941, the president called his secretary, Grace Tully, to his study and began dictating the message he wanted to give to Congress the following day. He signed the declaration of war, which both chambers decisively approved with only one dissenting vote, the same day. (1)

2

3

In September 1942, the president and first lady undertook a two-week inspection tour of factories and army camps. The first stop was the Chrysler tank arsenal, the largest arsenal in the world devoted completely to the production of military tanks. In the car with Franklin and Eleanor to the far right is Donald Nelson, War Production Board chief (2). Later that afternoon, at Ford's Willow Run bomber factory, the president spoke with two midgets working high up on the tail section of a bomber where persons of normal height were unable to fit (3). The first shift enters the North American Aviation plant in Inglewood, California (4).

As more and more married women entered the work force, the president, at Eleanor's urging, approved the first government sponsored day-care center. Before the war's end, nearly $50 million was spent on day care. Here Eleanor visits a group of children at a center in Greensboro, North Carolina (5).

5

For the first time in the history of many companies, women worked on the assembly line as riveters, welders, blueprint readers, and inspectors. "If I were of a debutante age," Eleanor said, "I would go into a factory—any factory where I could learn a skill and be useful." At the Douglas aircraft plant in Los Angeles, California, women made up nearly 60 percent of the work force (6,7).

6

7

Under Henry Kaiser's leadership, the average time to deliver a ship was cut from 355 days in 1940 to 194 days in 1941 to 69 days in early 1942. At top, the president's daughter, Anna, receives a gift from a Kaiser official after christening a merchant ship, the SS *Joseph Teal*, in 1942 (8). Construction of the ship is shown below (9).

9

10

11

The miracle of shipbuilding allowed weapons and supplies to reach Europe and Asia. Lend-lease, Churchill once said, was the "most unsordid act in the history of any nation." The boxes of gunpowder above represent the tiniest fraction of the millions of tons of weapons and supplies shipped to Britain and Russia during the war (10). In 1943, American troops began pouring into Europe. Roosevelt inspects U.S. troops with General Eisenhower in Sicily.

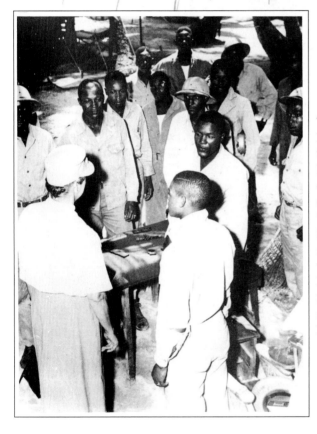

12

Though Admiral William Halsey was initially opposed to Eleanor's visit to the South Pacific in 1943, he ended up expressing admiration for her dedication and commitment. "It was a sight I will never forget," he said after watching her lean over gruesomely wounded soldiers at the base hospital, a warm smile on her face (12). Below, she addresses Negro troops at Penrhyn Island (13).

13

The accustomed rhythms of daily life were disrupted in every factory, business, and home by the institutions of rationing and price control. The motion picture industry contributes to the war bond drive with a premiere (14). A woman presents her ration book to the grocer in order to buy sugar (15).

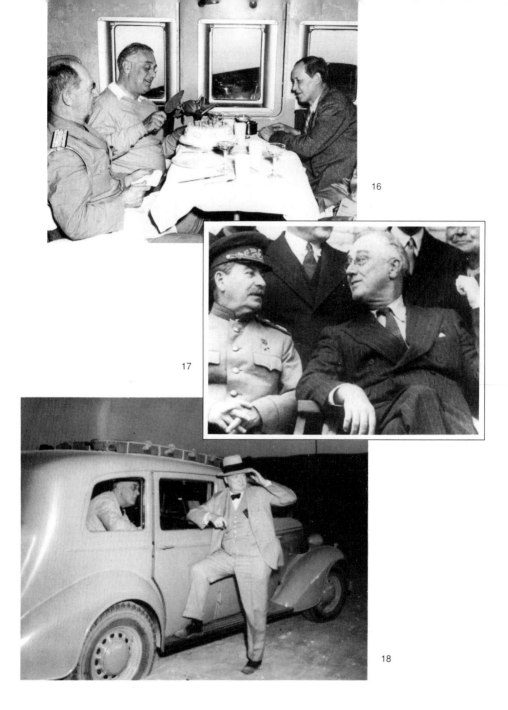

Nineteen forty-three was the year of conferences. Roosevelt cele-
brates his sixty-first birthday with Harry Hopkins and Admiral
William Leahy as he returns from his meeting with Churchill at
Casablanca (16). Roosevelt talks with Russian Premier Joseph Stalin
at the Teheran Conference, where Stalin publicly thanked the U.S.
for lend-lease for the first time (17). Roosevelt and Churchill view
the Pyramids in Egypt on their way to Teheran, Iran (18).

The second Quebec Conference in 1944, Lord Ismay observed, "was more like the reunion of a happy family" on holiday "than the gathering of sedate Allied leaders for an important conference." Mrs. Churchill is seated between Roosevelt and Churchill; Eleanor talks to Canadian Prime Minister Mackenzie King (19). Returning from the Yalta Conference, Roosevelt talks to Ambassador to England John Winant, while Secretary of State Edward Stettinius confers with Harry Hopkins (20).

20

21

22

Despite widespread worries about Roosevelt's health, the 1944 campaign proved, as one reporter said, that "the old master still had it." By 10 p.m. on election night, the trend was clear: the people of the U.S. had returned FDR to the White House for a fourth term. In these pictures, Roosevelt, adhering to ritual, receives his Hyde Park neighbors on the terrace of his home, as Eleanor and Anna stand behind him (21, 22).

23

24

"The days flowed peacefully by," Margaret Suckley recalled of the president's last trip to Warm Springs. In the mornings, he would work on his papers at the table before the fireplace (23). In the afternoons, he would work on the terrace with Grace Tully (24).

25   26

Unable to accompany her father to Warm Springs in April 1945, Anna made arrangements for Lucy Mercer Rutherfurd to visit him the second week of his stay. Lucy is shown here with FDR in pictures taken the day before Roosevelt died (25, 26). On April 12, 1945, Roosevelt was sitting for a portrait by Elizabeth Shoumatoff (27) when he suddenly said, "I have a terrific pain in the back of my head," and slumped forward. He never regained consciousness.

27

28

The president's coffin was carried by train from Warm Springs to Washington to Hyde Park, where he is buried in the green hedged garden of his boyhood home. Anna and Eleanor are pictured here at the end of the service. Elliott, in uniform, is partly hidden on the right (28). The riderless horse behind the cortege is the traditional symbol of the fallen leader (29).

29

30

After Roosevelt died, Eleanor found unexpected comfort in the president's dog. Fala accompanied Eleanor on her walks through the woods at Val-Kill, sat beside her chair in the living room, and greeted her at the door when she came home (30).

staff on hand in the Diplomatic Reception Room to welcome him home. "He was in his traveling linen suit," Stimson recorded, "looked very well, and greeted all of us with very great cheeriness and good humor and kindness. He was at his best. Republicans were mixed with Democrats and they all seemed very glad to have him back safe and sound."

The president's good humor did not extend to his wife and daughter. Knowing they were still angry with him for not taking them along on his fabulous trip, he was withdrawn, ill at ease, uncommunicative. "OM was very cool to me that first day," Anna wrote John, "never mentioned you except to answer my questions by saying that you were well." For her part, Eleanor was determined, in recompense for not being invited, to find out everything that had happened at the conference. That evening, to the president's first dinner home in more than three weeks, she invited Trude Pratt and Franklin's old friend Harry Hooker to join Anna and FDR, Jr. "Tonight," she pledged, "we shall ply him with questions."

The dinner that night, Anna reported to John, was "a complete fiasco," as Eleanor "proceeded to push, push, push at OM to relate his experiences," though FDR "wanted to sit leisurely over cocktails and dinner and tell his story in his own way." Instead, "LL rushed him through cocktails and kept hammering at him until his annoyance was so obvious, Frankie and I were wild, could do nothing about it."

Finally, to appease his wife, the president began telling the story of the conference, revealing in rich detail anecdotes about Stalin and Churchill. So intimate, even indiscreet, were these disclosures that Anna felt compelled to interrupt, putting her hand on her father's arm. If any of the stories were to leak from this room, she warned, looking at Mr. Hooker and Mrs. Pratt, "it would be dynamite and could be used by the 'opposition' to ruin all of your most important plans. OM answered 'you're quite right' but LL did not appreciate my crack!"

"Honestly," Anna admitted to John, "LL uses such poor judgment at times. Tommy and I have had long talks about our sweet and wonderful LL's indiscretions in repeating things to such people as Trude. Also Tommy has good evidence that LL's letters to Joe are opened sometimes and that LL is not always discreet in these letters. By that I mean that Tommy worries that LL might repeat to Joe what OM told that night at dinner. It's all kinda tough, because LL is so damn sweet and unselfish, so lovely and sensitive."

Still, Eleanor refused to give up. When the dinner guests departed, she tried to get more out of the president by following him to his room. Her efforts proved fruitless. It was nearly midnight, he had had a long day, and he was exhausted.

The next morning, Anna joined her father for breakfast in his room. Knowing how uncomfortable Eleanor had made him the night before with her relentless quest for details about the conference, Anna deliberately confined her conversation to good-natured gossip about family and friends —the sort of talk FDR loved.

"I finally managed to break the ice," Anna proudly reported to John, with "a good old chin-fest." During their frolicsome talk, Anna provided her father with juicy details about the "sex peregrinations" of her two brothers Elliott and FDR, Jr. Apparently Elliott was involved in a passionate romance with the actress Faye Emerson, and FDR, Jr., had developed a terrific crush on Kay Summersby, General Eisenhower's beautiful young driver.

As it happened, the president had met Miss Summersby in Algiers when he stopped to see Eisenhower. He had sat only one place away from her at dinner one night, and had shared a picnic lunch with her and Eisenhower the following day. An experienced observer of human nature, Roosevelt had come to the conclusion, he confided in Anna, that this attractive young British woman was sleeping with General Eisenhower! Delighting in the intimacy of their conversation, Anna then recalled that Frankie, in the throes of his own passion for the same woman, had remarked that, as beautiful as she was, "the things she had been through [divorce and death of her subsequent fiancé] had made her a bit of a psychopathic case."

Anna's "chin-fest" with her father continued until nearly 10 a.m., when he had to get ready for a meeting with the vice-president and congressional leaders. As he dressed, he was in great spirits. There was nothing he enjoyed more than exchanging gossip. Yet, with Missy gone, the opportunities for lazy, relaxed conversations had greatly diminished. It was good to have Anna home. For her part, Anna was euphoric. "Ever since my talk with OM about Elliott and other things," she exulted to John, "he and I have been on very good terms—closer, I think, than usual."

Roosevelt's chumminess with his daughter coincided with his loss of Harry Hopkins. On December 21, Hopkins finally moved out of the White House into his new home, a charming town house in Georgetown, at 33rd and N. For Harry and Louise, who had felt for months that Eleanor resented their being at the White House, the move was long overdue. "It is the first time I have had Christmas in my own house for years," Hopkins wrote his youngest son, Stephen, who was a marine in the South Pacific, "and Louie made it the pleasantest that I think I ever had in my life."

But for Roosevelt, Harry's departure was distressing. For nearly three and a half years, ever since May 10, 1940, when the phony war was brought to an abrupt end by Germany's invasion of Western Europe, Hopkins had been his constant companion. Night after night, hearing steps by his study door, Roosevelt had looked up to find Hopkins, an intelligent, amused expression on his face. With Missy gone, no one knew better than Hopkins when Roosevelt needed to relax and when he needed to work. Ever ready with a joke, he knew how to hit the exact line between playfulness and seriousness. Now, though he would still occupy a critical position in the administration, the relationship would not be the same.

As when Missy got sick, Roosevelt no doubt tried to tell himself that everything would be all right, that other friends would take Harry's place. And it was true, to a degree. Coincident with Harry's departure, Margaret

Suckley appeared more frequently at the White House, joining the president almost daily for tea or dinner. But, as much as Roosevelt enjoyed talking with her about his papers and his plans for his library, she never grew as close to him as Missy or Harry had been. That space, left open for a while, was only filled when Anna came to live in the White House the following month.

Christmas found the president at Hyde Park with Eleanor, Anna, FDR, Jr., and Johnny. It was the first Christmas the Roosevelts had spent at Hyde Park since 1932, and the first time the children had been back to the old house since Sara died. "I am sure it will seem very strange to them, as it does to practically everyone," Eleanor wrote. "My mother-in-law lived for so many years in the house, that she really seemed a part of it. Her personality seems to go right on living there."

For Anna, it was a wonderful week. Despite the galaxy of MPs and Secret Service men, she still "loved the old place," the thick woods she had wandered through as a girl, "the gently rolling countryside," the traditional reading of Dickens, and the warmth of the carolers. "There's been no snow," she told John, "but it's been cold, clear and dry with all ponds, waterfalls and streams frozen over." Relaxing with her father, she shared breakfast with him in the mornings, sat beside him in his study in the afternoons, and joined him for cocktails at night. It was the beginning of a new intimacy in their relationship.

Indeed, so comfortable did Anna feel with her father at Christmas that she broached the sensitive subject of accompanying him the next time he took an overseas trip. He readily agreed that if she secured a Red Cross uniform and then flew to meet his navy ship it would work. What is more, he said, the "no women on ships" was merely one of many navy rules, "all of which he was responsible for and which he could break if he so wished." This was just what Anna wanted to hear.

• • •

Roosevelt returned to Washington two days after Christmas, and held a casual press conference on December 28. At the end, he let it be known that he wished the press would no longer use the term "New Deal" to describe his administration, for the times had changed and there was no longer a need for the New Deal.

When asked why the slogan was no longer appropriate, he presented a long allegory. "How did the New Deal come into existence?" he asked. "It was because in 1932 there was an awfully sick patient called the United States of America. He was suffering from a grave internal disorder—he was awfully sick—he had all kinds of internal troubles. And they sent for a doctor."

Old Dr. New Deal prescribed a number of remedies—the Federal Deposit Insurance Corporation (FDIC) to guarantee bank deposits; the Home Owners Loan Corporation (HOLC) to save homes from foreclosures; the

Securities and Exchange Commission (SEC) to provide truth in the sale of securities; minimum wages and maximum hours; abolition of child labor; unemployment insurance, social security, and the Wagner Act to protect labor; and the work-relief programs, the PWA, the WPA, the CCC, and the NYA. It was a long, slow process, Roosevelt admitted; "it took several years before those ills, that illness of ten years ago, were remedied.

"But two years ago," the president continued, after [the sick patient] had become pretty well, he had a very bad accident.... Two years ago on the 7th of December, he got into a pretty bad smash-up—broke his hip, broke his leg in two or three places, broke a wrist and an arm. Some people didn't even think he would live, for a while.

" 'Old Doc New Deal' didn't know anything about broken legs and arms," the president said. "He knew a great deal about internal medicine but nothing about this new kind of trouble. So he got his partner, who was an orthopedic surgeon, 'Dr. Win the War,' to take care of this fellow. And the result is that the patient is back on his feet. He has given up his crutches. He has begun to strike back—on the offensive."

In substituting Dr. Win the War for Dr. New Deal, Roosevelt did not intend to diminish the past accomplishments of the New Deal. Indeed, it was of great historic significance that, despite all the changes the war had brought, it had not called into question the basic institutional reforms identified with the New Deal—such as minimum wage, social security, labor protection, market regulation. He was simply saying that, when the times change and the problems change, the slogans should also change.

Reporters agreed. "The New Deal slogan has outlived its vote-getting usefulness at home, " *U.S. News* pointed out. "The things it stood for in the depression-ridden 30s do not attract votes in the war boom 40s. [Today] there are far more jobs than workers. Farm controls have been thrown away. The urge is to grow more food, not less. The effort is to hold wages down, not raise them; to check rising prices, not spur them on. Many of the Government controls now are called irksome.... As a vote-catcher, [the New Deal] has no more allure than a 1932 glamour girl who did not watch her diet."

With full employment, the work programs of the old New Deal were no longer needed. The CCC was the first to go, felled by the hands of Congress. The end of the CCC was followed by the demise of the WPA, which was given "an honorable discharge" by the president himself. The NYA, already reduced to a skeletal training program for young people about to enter war industries, was next.

"The war has finally accomplished most of what the New Deal set out to do," columnist Raymond Clapper wrote in 1943. "The war has given every workman a job at high wages, removed him from dependence on charity, and through rationing has leveled off the upper crust until the rich man cannot buy any more of many things than the poor man. The common man, in other words, is getting a better break through the war than the New Deal was able to give them."

For Eleanor and her liberal friends, the demolition of the old agencies was difficult to watch. Though she realized that much of their work had become unnecessary under changed conditions, she believed that many of the old activities were even more useful in wartime than they had been during the Depression—housing, recreational facilities, maternity care, day care, public health. To Eleanor's mind, the New Deal was more than a description of old programs; it was a rhapsodic label for a way of life representing a national commitment to social justice and to the bettering of life for the underprivileged. And that commitment, Eleanor argued, was every bit as important in 1943 as it had been a decade before.

No one, Eleanor insisted in reply to a question at her own press conference, has laid the New Deal "away in lavender." On the contrary, "the future is going to require not only interest in the needs of our citizens but the needs of the world."

CHAPTER 19

"I WANT TO

SLEEP AND SLEEP"

Old Doc New Deal was not dead and buried after all. Confounding critics and supporters alike, the president brought the old doctor back for a triumphant encore in the State of the Union message on January 11, 1944.

Roosevelt began the speech as Dr. Win the War, warning his countrymen against overconfidence, reminding them of the distance that still separated American troops from their objectives in Berlin and Tokyo. "If ever there was a time to subordinate individual or group selfishness to the national good, that time is now," he said, looking ahead to the cross-Channel invasion certain to produce casualty lists in America that dwarfed every engagement that had gone before.

"The overwhelming majority of our people have met the demands of this war with magnificent courage and understanding. They have accepted inconveniences; they have accepted hardships; they have accepted tragic sacrifices. However, while the majority goes on about its great work without complaint, a noisy minority maintains an uproar of demands for special favors for special groups. There are pests who swarm through the lobbies of the Congress and the cocktail bars of Washington, representing these special groups as opposed to the basic interests of the nation as a whole.

They have come to look at the war principally as a chance to make profits for themselves."

To counter these special interests and to concentrate the country's energies and resources on winning the war, the president recommended a series of stringent measures: a tax increase, both to produce revenue and keep inflation down; a renegotiation of war contracts to prevent exorbitant profits; a cost-of-food law; a stabilization statute; and a national-service law. Though he had resisted the pressure to conscript civilians for three years, he had now come to believe that a national-service law would assure that the right number of workers went to the right places at the right times. It would alleviate current labor shortages in copper mines, in ball-bearing plants, in the forge industry, and in factories making B-29s. He understood the burden civilian conscription placed on labor and would not recommend a national-service law, he said, unless the other laws were also passed to keep down the cost of living, share the burdens of taxation, and prevent undue profits.

As Roosevelt reached the climax of his speech, he cast aside Dr. Win the War and became Dr. New Deal once more. "It is our duty now to begin to lay plans . . . for the winning of a lasting peace. . . . We cannot be content, no matter how high the general standard of living may be, if some fraction of our people—whether it be one-half or one-third or one-tenth—is ill-fed, ill-housed and insecure. This Republic had its beginning under the protection of certain inalienable political rights—among them rights of free speech, free press, free worship, trial by jury, freedom from unreasonable searches and seizures. They were our rights to life and liberty.

"As our nation has grown in size and stature, however—as our industrial economy expanded—these political rights proved inadequate to assure us equality in the pursuit of happiness. We have come to a clear realization of the fact that true individual freedom cannot exist without economic security and independence. 'Necessitous men are not free men.' People who are hungry and out of a job are the stuff of which dictatorships are made."

In the modern era, Roosevelt argued, a second Bill of Rights was needed to provide a new basis of security and prosperity for every American regardless of race, color, or creed. That economic Bill of Rights must include: the right to a useful and remunerative job; to earnings sufficient for adequate food and clothing and recreation; to decent housing; to adequate medical care; to protection from the economic fears of old age and unemployment; to a good education.

All these rights were implicit in the programs of the New Deal. But never before had Roosevelt stated them in so comprehensive a manner. Nor had he ever been so explicit in linking together the negative liberty from government achieved in the old Bill of Rights to the positive liberty through government to be achieved in the new Bill of Rights. "For decades," political scientist James MacGregor Burns has written, "the fatal and false dichotomy —liberty against security, freedom against equality—had deranged American social thought and crippled the nation's capacity to subdue depression and poverty. Now Roosevelt was asserting that individual political liberty and collective welfare were not only compatible, but they were mutually fortifying."

Roosevelt's speech thrilled liberals—including Eleanor, who listened to it on a small barracks radio as she visited with a group of WAVES at American University. Still excited the following morning, she reread the message in its entirety, certain that her husband would now turn his vital energies to the building of the new America that would make all the sacrifices of war worthwhile.

It was not to be that simple, of course. By insisting that all his proposals were linked, that national service would not work without a tax increase or reduction of excess profits, Roosevelt left himself hostage to the conservative coalition in the Congress, which was in no mood to hear his plea for higher taxes. Convinced that the administration was using the war to legitimize a redistribution of income, the Congress substituted its own revenue bill, which reduced the administration's proposal to a fleshless skeleton. It canceled the automatic 1-percent increase in the social-security tax, which was to be levied on both wage and salary earners and on employer payrolls; it granted relief from existing taxes; it exempted the lumber industry and natural-gas pipelines from the excess-profits tax. Indeed, so replete was the bill with loopholes for special interests that it raised only $2 billion in revenue, in contrast to the president's call for $10.5 billion.

After much thought, Roosevelt decided to veto the bill, even though he realized he was jeopardizing his program, including national service. "It has been suggested by some," he explained in his veto message on February 22, "that I should give approval to this bill on the ground that having asked Congress for a loaf of bread to take care of this war for the sake of this and succeeding generations, I should be content with a small piece of crust." But this bill, Roosevelt charged, in an uncharacteristic display of bitterness, provides "relief not for the needy but for the greedy." His decision made, Roosevelt set off that evening for Hyde Park. He was "in the best of spirits," William Hassett recorded. To have said exactly what he felt seemed to afford him unfeigned pleasure.

The next afternoon, Hassett chronicled, "hell broke out in the Senate." Majority Leader Alben Barkley, who had faithfully carried the president's banner on Capitol Hill for seven years, stood before his colleagues and formally broke with the president, announcing that he would resign as leader. Speaking before a hushed audience, Barkley accused the president of delivering "a calculated and deliberate assault upon the legislative integrity of every Member of Congress. Other members of Congress may do as they please; but, as for me, I do not propose to take this unjustifiable assault lying down. . . . If the Congress of the United States has any self-respect yet left, it will override the veto of the President and enact this bill into law, his objections to the contrary notwithstanding." When Barkley finished, he received a thunderous ovation; "practically every senator stood on his feet and clapped," Vice-President Wallace recorded, making it clear that the president's veto would not be sustained.

Word of Barkley's angry speech reached the president in his study at Hyde Park, where he was examining old family papers with Margaret Suckley. He appeared at first to be unconcerned, predicting that the storm would blow over in a few days. "Alben must be suffering from shell shock," he suggested, attributing the outburst to the fact that Barkley was tired and Mrs. Barkley was ill. When Eleanor spoke to the president from Washington later that afternoon, she found him "quite calm over it." For her part, Eleanor questioned the use of the phrase "not for the needy but for the greedy." Such phrases are "tempting," she told a friend, "but I'm not sure of their wisdom."

Later that night, however, in response to an impassioned call from Jimmy Byrnes, Roosevelt agreed to send a conciliatory note to Barkley, saying that he had never intended to attack the integrity of the Congress, that their differences on the tax issue did not in any way affect his confidence in Barkley's leadership, and that he hoped, if Barkley did resign, he would immediately be re-elected. The president's letter set the stage for the events that followed. On February 25, 1944, amid sustained applause, Barkley resigned and was unanimously re-elected. Then, by large margins in both houses, the Congress overrode the president's veto.

At Hyde Park, where he was joined by Eleanor and Anna for the weekend, the president remained serene. "Still no word of bitterness or recrimination," Hassett noted. On Saturday afternoon, in the midst of a snowstorm, he inspected his tree plantings, observing wryly that the passage of the flawed tax bill over his veto had saved him $3,000 in taxes on his income from his lumbering operations. The next morning, he took great delight at the sight of his grandchildren sledding down the big hill behind the house.

The president's equanimity in the face of his congressional defeat can be traced to his awareness that, despite the loopholes in the present bill, the administration's wartime taxation had generally assumed a just and redistributive character. Year after year, against the wishes of the conservative coalition to substitute a regressive sales tax for stepped increases in the personal and corporate income tax, the administration had prevailed both in securing rising rates and in adding millions of new taxpayers to the rolls. The Treasury was able to finance about 44 percent of the total war expenditures of $304 billion through taxation. The rest was secured through war bonds and borrowing. The debt rose from 43 percent of the GNP in 1940 to 127 percent in 1946.

A transformation had also been effected in the method of collecting taxes. Before the war, individuals were always a year behind in their tax payments, since they were called upon to pay taxes in quarterly installments on the income they had earned the previous year. The system had functioned well enough when rates were low and few people paid taxes, but when millions of people, unfamiliar with preparing tax forms, became taxpayers for the first time, change was inevitable. It took the form of "Pay as You Go," a system that withheld taxes from paychecks before the employee even saw the money, allowing everyone to start the new year free from debt. This was "a revolution in American public finance," journalist David Brinkley has written. Since people were paying taxes with money they had never seen, their resistance to the idea of taxation lessened.

So, while everyone else's nerves became jittery, Roosevelt kept his dispute with Congress in perspective. Remaining at Hyde Park for a full week after the great explosion, he managed, Hassett recorded, to confound his enemies by sleeping ten hours a night, though they "supposed he was lying awake nights worrying about their machinations."

While Roosevelt was in Hyde Park that last week of February, the Eighth Air Force, in Europe, was enjoying what later came to be called "the Big Week," seven days of unparalleled success during which thirty-eight hundred bombers dropped nearly ten thousand tons of bombs, which damaged or destroyed more than 70 percent of the German war plants involved in aircraft production. The tonnage dropped in this single week was equal to the total bomb tonnage dropped by the Eighth Air Force in its entire first year of operation. In contrast to "Black October," 1943, when American losses were so devastating, amounting to more than half of the sorties, that pilots had come to accept as a fact that "you would be shot down eventually . . . that it is impossible to complete a full tour of duty," the Big Week pilots enjoyed the critical advantage of new and improved escort planes. These new planes, P-47 Thunderbolt "Jugs," were equipped with droppable fuel tanks that allowed them to fly much faster and farther than ever before.

Though German industry would show remarkable recuperative powers after the bombing of Big Week, the German air force had been permanently damaged. Over six hundred German fighters had been downed, and nearly a thousand German pilots and crewmen had been killed or wounded. "This was a turning point in the air war against Germany," Churchill later wrote. "From now onwards the U.S. 8th Air Force was able to bomb targets in Germany by day with high accuracy and ever increasing freedom." The back of the Luftwaffe had been broken.

• • •

Returning from Hyde Park on the first of March, Roosevelt found to his great delight that Anna had moved from the guest quarters on the third floor to the spacious Lincoln Suite on the second floor, where Harry Hopkins had lived for three and a half years. The move signaled Anna's commitment to stay with her father for the duration of the war, to serve as the hostess of the White House in her mother's absence, to provide the warm, relaxed companionship he had missed since Missy was taken ill.

Neither father nor daughter had imagined this outcome when Anna first arrived for the Christmas holidays. She had originally intended to return to

Seattle in early January, but as the time for her departure approached, she found that her father did not want her to go. In the four weeks she had been at the White House, he had come to rely on her.

"With no preliminary talks or discussions," Anna recalled years later in a published article, "I found myself trying to take over little chores that I felt would relieve Father of some of the pressure under which he was constantly working." Conquering the old fears and insecurities that had previously diminished her personality in her father's presence, she entertained guests at the cocktail hour, arranged the seating at the dinner table, made suggestions on speeches and saw people her father was too busy to see.

"Father could relax more easily with Anna than with Mother," Elliott observed. "He could enjoy his drink without feeling guilty. Though Mother had gotten to the point where she would think she was relaxing, she was always working."

Blessed with a radiant smile and a ribald sense of humor, Anna took pleasure in the same silly hair-down jokes that her father relished. When she and her father were together, the valets recalled, laughter would ring out. "She could tell a great story," her son Johnny Boettiger said; "she loved gossip and when she laughed, it was a real laugh; she threw her head back and let the laugh out."

And she was beautiful, tall and blonde with long, shapely legs, blue eyes, and healthy skin. Eleanor's friend Justine Polier recalled being with the president in his study one morning when Anna came in. "She walked in in her riding boots after a ride. His whole face lighted up; the world's problems stopped for a few minutes. He just adored her."

What would she think, he inquired as she was preparing to leave, about quitting her job at the *Post-Intelligencer* and coming to work for him? For Anna, the timing of the request was perfect. After months of effort, John Boettiger had finally succeeded in securing a transfer from North Africa to the Pentagon. Working in the White House would allow her not only to be with her father on a daily basis, but to be with her husband as well. Yes, Anna agreed, she would love to move into the White House and help him, "but not until I have talked with mother."

Anna's caution was well advised, knowing as she did from conversations with Tommy that her mother had invariably clashed with every woman who had presumed to fill her role as mistress of the White House—with Jimmy's first wife, Betsey Cushing, and with Missy LeHand and Louise Hopkins. "Louise would arrange dinner parties, and seat the table," Anna was told. "Mother would be home. This would annoy the pants off her." This was not ordinary jealousy at work; the threat Eleanor perceived was to her position, not her marriage. Though she cherished her independence and her freedom to travel she did not want anyone taking over her position as mistress of the White House.

Eleanor was very frank with her daughter. If Anna came to stay, "it would be wonderful," Eleanor said. "She personally would love it," but she did not want to go through with her daughter what she had gone through with Louise Hopkins and others in the White House.

Just recently, an awkward situation had developed when, without telling Eleanor, Grace Tully and Franklin had invited Missy to spend the second week of March at the White House. When Eleanor discovered this, she wrote to Missy canceling the invitation. "I was away last week when Grace and Franklin arranged for you to come down on the 7th of March. I am terribly sorry that they did not realize that I want to be here when you come. Therefore, as I have to go on this Caribbean trip, it will be necessary for you to postpone your trip. I am very sorry that they did not consult me before making plans but it is hard to get everyone together."

Though Eleanor's insistence on being home during Missy's visit reflected a valid desire to make sure that Missy was well taken care of while she was there, the postponement was devastating to Missy, coming as it did on the heels of learning that all her things had been removed from her third-floor bedroom and stored in the East Wing attic. "I know that you will realize," Eleanor had written, "that in order to keep your belongings from being harmed by nurses and children and casual guests I have had them temporarily put where they are safe."

Though Eleanor suggested an alternative date in April, Missy refused to reconsider. "I hope you understand," Missy's sister Ann Rochon wrote Eleanor, "that we did everything we possibly could to make her go to Washington this month but she simply wouldn't allow us to talk about it. We felt the change would do her so much good and of course she always considered it home."

When Anna assured her mother that she understood the ground rules, Eleanor embraced her daughter's decision to move to Washington. In February, Anna put her home in Seattle on the rental market. Her first weeks in the White House proved delightful for everyone, including Eleanor. Whenever Eleanor had to travel, she was glad to know, she admitted, there would be "young life in the White House as it makes it a more cheerful place to anyone who happens to stay there." And when she was home, Eleanor took pleasure in Anna's vibrant personality, which "brought to all her contacts a gaiety and buoyance that made everybody feel just a little happier because she was around."

Though Anna was never given an official title or salary, her assignments, she joked, grew "like Topsy, because I was there all the time and it was easy for Father to tell someone to 'ask Anna to do that' or to look over at me and say, 'Sis, you handle that.' " When it became clear to her that she couldn't write fast enough to take accurate notes on all the things her father asked her to do, she taught herself shorthand at night, when the day's work was done. "It was immaterial to me whether my job was helping to plan the 1944 campaign, pouring tea for General de Gaulle or filling Father's empty cigarette case."

"It was an ideal match for both of them," Anna's son Johnny Boettiger observed, "a perfect fit, hand in glove." For the little girl who still adored her father, there was endless pleasure in the observation that he enjoyed her beauty, her laugh, her pretty dress. For the awkward adolescent who had been so worried about making mistakes in front of her father that she fled from the library one day in tears when an armful of books he had handed her slipped from her grasp, there was the chance to deal with him now from a position of strength and confidence, to take pride in the mastery of a job well done. "She is really in finer health and spirits," her husband reported to Jimmy Roosevelt, "than at any time since the war began."

"Anna's day at the White House begins at 6:45 a.m.," *Time* reported in a glowing portrait of the president's daughter later that spring. She took breakfast with her husband and her five-year-old son, Johnny, in the Lincoln Suite; then Major Boettiger went off to the Pentagon while Johnny headed for kindergarten, accompanied by a Secret Service man. For the rest of the day, until 4 p.m., she was at her father's side, "until Johnny comes marching home," at which point she broke off from work for a quick game of Ping-Pong with him or a swim in the White House pool. Then back to the oval study to work, while Johnny, dressed in a little khaki uniform and cap, strolled the White House grounds, a toy wagon under his arm, pursuing his ambition to become a White House guard. An early supper for Johnny was followed by cocktails and dinner with her father. "The President's daughter will preside over social engagements and welcome visitors of state any time Eleanor Roosevelt is off on a trip," *Time* concluded, "but she has made it plain that she will not be [officially] considered an assistant hostess. She has reiterated . . . instructions to the State Department's protocol office: at White House guest dinners, 'Put me anywhere, I'm not official.'"

•　•　•

The more time Anna spent with her father in the spring of 1944, the more conscious she became of the darkening hollows under his eyes, the loss of color in his face, the soft cough that accompanied him day and night. To her observant eye, his strength seemed to be failing him; he was abnormally tired even in the morning hours; he complained of frequent headaches and had trouble sleeping at night. Sitting beside him in the movies, she noticed for the first time that his mouth hung open for long periods; joining him at his cocktail hour, she saw the convulsive shake of his hand as he tried to light his cigarette; once, as he was signing his name to a letter, he blanked out halfway through, leaving a long illegible scrawl. At first, Anna attributed her father's troubles to the prolonged bout of influenza he had suffered during the winter, but when spring came and he failed to bounce back, she began to worry.

That same spring, Grace Tully noted with alarm that her boss was nodding more frequently over his mail, even dozing off during dictation. "He would grin in slight embarrassment as he caught himself," she recalled, and though she saw "no diminution of clarity or sparkle," she worried nonetheless. In mid-March, former NYA Administrator Aubrey Williams dined with the president in the White House and was "shocked" at how "tired and worn" he looked. Even the ever-faithful Hassett admitted on March 24, "President not looking so well.... This latest cold has taken lots out of him. Every morning in response to inquiry as to how he felt a characteristic reply has been rotten or like hell."

Anna confided her concerns about her father's health to her mother, but Eleanor refused to acknowledge that anything was seriously wrong. "I don't think Mother saw it," Anna told writer Bernard Asbell years later. "She wasn't looking for him to be any different."

If Eleanor failed to see in her husband the alarming changes Anna saw, it was in part because she was hundreds of miles away from him much of the time. In February, she made two extended trips to New York, one to Clarksburg, West Virginia, and one to Pittsburgh. In March, she was in the Caribbean from the 4th to the 28th, inspecting bases and visiting soldiers. And even when she was home, she was so busy—testifying against the deplorable conditions of Negro housing in Washington, D.C.; speaking out against discrimination in the armed forces; calling for the inclusion of women at the peace table—that she had no time simply to sit with her husband and relax.

Even if she had seen her husband more often, it is not clear that Eleanor would have understood what was happening to him. She simply wasn't "interested in physiology," Anna insisted, "that was all there was to it. She seemed to be cerebrating one hundred percent, *all* the time." Having shared so completely in her husband's triumph over polio, "she still believed," as her grandson Johnny Boettiger put it, that "iron will and courage could conquer any illness. Though she was an unusually compassionate woman, she was never patient with illness—her own or anyone else's. This made it hard for her and hard for others."

Reluctant to admit even to herself that Franklin was really sick, Eleanor ascribed his fatigue to psychological factors. For one thing, the spring had brought the disturbing news that Elliott's second marriage, to Ruth Googins, was falling apart. Though Ruth had initially agreed to wait until the war was over to file for divorce, the agreement had broken down, and by the end of March the papers had been filed. "I think the constant tension must tell," Eleanor confided in Joe Lash, "and though [Franklin] has said nothing I think he's been upset by Elliott and Ruth."

Beyond the family problems, there remained in Roosevelt, Eleanor believed, an unspoken anxiety about the forthcoming invasion. "The President hasn't been well," she told her readers in "My Day," "but I think it is probably as much the weariness that assails everyone who grasps the full meaning of war as it is a physical ailment."

Something more than internal stress was at work, however; by the last week of March, Roosevelt's health was deteriorating so steadily that he canceled all appointments and confined himself to his bedroom, taking all his meals on a bed tray with Anna at his side. As always, Roosevelt worked to keep up appearances, summoning his energy to be pleasant. "He is cheerful in spirit," Hassett noted on a day when his temperature reached 104 degrees, "always good natured, none of the ill temper that sick folks are entitled to display."

Though Roosevelt's good spirits fooled reporters and visitors, Anna, who was with him most of his waking hours, could not ignore the discernible signs of trouble. There were too many times in the course of the day when she could see that "the blood was not pumping the way it should through one hundred percent of the body."

After comparing notes with Grace Tully, Anna took it upon herself to summon Dr. Ross McIntire to her quarters to discuss her father's health. A stiff man who zealously guarded his authority as the president's personal physician, McIntire submitted reluctantly to Anna's cross-examination. What was happening to her father? Anna wanted to know. Clearly, something was very wrong. Not to worry, McIntire said. He was recovering from a combination of influenza and bronchitis. A week or two in the sun and he would be his old carefree self again.

McIntire's response did not sit well with Anna. Knowing that McIntire was not a general internist but, rather, an ear-nose-and-throat man chosen to treat her father's chronic sinus condition, Anna feared that his narrow focus had blinded him to larger concerns. "I didn't think," Anna later confessed, that he "really knew what he was talking about." Pushing further, Anna asked if he ever took her father's blood pressure. "When I think it necessary," McIntire replied.

Softening her tone, Anna told McIntire that she was worried. She, too, had seen her father bounce back from many illnesses, but this time he seemed to be losing the struggle. His body seemed to be breaking down little by little. Could McIntire please send the president to the hospital for a thorough checkup? And would he promise not to tell her father that she had suggested it?

• • •

McIntire grudgingly acceded to Anna's request, arranging a checkup for the afternoon of March 28, 1944, at Bethesda Naval Hospital. Anna accompanied her father in the car as the cavalcade headed up Wisconsin Avenue. When they reached the hospital grounds, Roosevelt pointed through the trees to a tall, elegant building. "I designed that one," he told Anna joyfully, fancying a greater contribution to the building than he had really made. Loving architecture as he did, Roosevelt had occasionally submitted drawings for certain public buildings, but there his participation usually stopped. This was probably just as well, for he had a tendency to overlook critical items in his plans, such as closet space and bathrooms.

At the door of the hospital, Anna smiled and waved goodbye. Her mother was returning that same afternoon from her Caribbean tour, and Anna had promised to meet her at the airport. As the president rolled down the corridor in his wheelchair, he waved cheerfully to the patients and the members of the staff who had gathered round to see him. There was nothing in his demeanor to indicate the disturbing symptoms that had brought him to the hospital.

Inside the medical suite, Dr. Howard Bruenn, a young cardiologist, waited anxiously for his famous patient. Bruenn had been told only that the president was not recovering well from a bout of influenza and bronchitis, that a more thorough checkup was needed. "It was a warm day," Bruenn recalled years later, "and I was perspiring a lot. I felt I had a big weight on my shoulders." Having never met the president before, Bruenn had requested from McIntire earlier that day the results of previous heart and chest exams. McIntire wasn't sure he could find them, but when Bruenn pressed him, arguing that without previous results there was no way to make comparisons, McIntire promised to look carefully and send them by messenger if they were found.

The records had not yet arrived as the president was lifted onto the examining table, leaving Bruenn with no comprehension of the patient's history. "I suspected something was terribly wrong as soon as I looked at him," Bruenn recalled. "His face was pallid and there was a bluish discoloration of his skin, lips and nail beds. When the hemoglobin is fully oxygenated, it is red. When it is impaired, it has a bluish tint. The bluish color meant the tissues were not being supplied with adequate oxygen."

At first glance, Bruenn also observed that Roosevelt was having difficulty breathing. The mere act of moving from one side to the other caused considerable breathlessness. Working quickly and methodically, the young doctor put his hands on the president's chest and listened to the sounds of his heart. "It was worse than I feared," he recalled.

The examination revealed that the apex of the heart was much farther to the left than it should have been, suggesting a grossly enlarged heart. If the heart is under increased blood pressure, as Roosevelt's apparently was, one of the first things it does is to increase its size. Bruenn asked his patient to take a deep breath and hold it as long as he could. Roosevelt expelled it after only thirty-five seconds. In the president's lungs, Bruenn heard rales, an abnormal rattling or bubbling sound indicating a dangerous buildup of fluid.

In the midst of the exam, the medical records finally arrived. Bruenn covered the president and excused himself for a moment. Reading swiftly, he noted that high blood pressure had been detected as far back as 1941 (188/105mm). Why McIntire had not called in a heart man earlier was incomprehensible to Bruenn. In the interim, much damage had been done. Roosevelt, Bruenn concluded, was suffering from congestive heart failure. His damaged heart was no longer able to pump effectively. Left untreated, Roosevelt was unlikely to survive for more than a year. And in 1944, the therapy for hypertension was limited.

Bruenn never said a word to Roosevelt of the dark thoughts that were filling his mind. McIntire had instructed him not to volunteer any information to the president. Nor did Roosevelt ask a single question about what Bruenn was finding. On the contrary, throughout the entire exam, Roosevelt chatted genially about a range of topics totally unrelated to his health, and when the exam was finished, he smiled his famous smile and extended his hand. "Thanks, Doc," he said, and then he was gone.

Yet, at some level, Roosevelt must have felt relief in knowing that someone other than he was worrying about what was going on. Though he could not bring himself to ask the questions aloud, he must have harbored terrible fears and frustrations as he found himself unable to sleep at night and too tired to work during the day. At least now something would be done.

At his regular press conference later that afternoon, Roosevelt was asked about his health. Smiling broadly, he said that he had been suffering from bronchitis for the last three weeks but otherwise was fine. He then coughed and patted his chest to demonstrate how it affected him. Asked if he was alarmed by his condition, the president said he'd been told only one of 48,500 cases of bronchitis might develop into pneumonia, so he thought he had a rather slim chance. So effective was Roosevelt's upbeat performance that reporters concluded that his bronchitis had been whipped and that he was feeling fine. "Not only were the President's color and voice better," *The New York Times* observed, "but his spirits were good, too."

When Roosevelt returned to his study after the press conference, Eleanor and Anna were there. Eleanor was in high spirits. Her Caribbean trip had been an unqualified success; her meetings with the soldiers had gone well, and her press coverage had been triumphant. There was much to tell her husband, but first she had a present for him, a souvenir to add to his collection of ships. It was a little model of a jangada, a raftlike native boat used by the fishermen at Recife, Brazil. Pleased with his gift but too tired to talk, now that he no longer needed to perform, Roosevelt retired to his bedroom at seven-thirty.

Dr. Bruenn reported his alarming findings to Dr. McIntire the following day, along with a memorandum of recommendations, including complete bedrest for seven weeks with nursing care, avoidance of tension, digitalis, a change in diet to restrict salt and to lower calories, and the use of an elevated Gatch bed to relieve breathlessness at night. "McIntire was appalled at my suggestions," Bruenn recalled. "The president can't take time off to go to bed," McIntire insisted. "You can't simply say to him, Do this or do that. This is the president of the United States!"

To shore up his position, McIntire called in a team of consultants, including Dr. John Harper, Bruenn's commanding officer at Bethesda, Dr. James Paullin of Atlanta, and Dr. Frank Lahey of Boston. They were shown the

X-rays, electrocardiogram, and other laboratory data, and Bruenn was asked to present his recommendations. The seniors disagreed emphatically with Bruenn's diagnosis; after all, someone said, McIntire had been examining the president for years; it was simply impossible to imagine that Roosevelt had become this gravely ill overnight. As for Bruenn's drastic recommendations, the only one that they supported was the installation of a Gatch bed, which allowed the head to be elevated.

"I was only a lieutenant commander," Bruenn said. "McIntire was an admiral. Harper was my boss. But I knew I was right, so I held my ground." Finally, McIntire agreed to let Paullin and Lahey examine the president later that afternoon; discussions would resume the following day.

After seeing the president, Dr. Paullin announced that he now agreed with Bruenn's diagnosis and would approve a cautious program of digitalization to tone up the heart muscle and strengthen it. "Digitalis was a miracle drug," Bruenn observed later. In 1944, however, it was difficult to calibrate the amount of the digitalis leaf that would produce a therapeutic versus a toxic effect. "The risk," Bruenn admitted, "was that overdosage could lead to nausea, loss of appetite, and further damage to the heart."

Dr. Lahey apparently came away from the exam with a different set of concerns, centered on the president's gastrointestinal tract. It is not clear exactly what worried Lahey, but Dr. Harry Goldsmith of Massachusetts, who has plumbed the question of Roosevelt's health for more than a decade, believes that Lahey may have found an inoperable malignant tumor in Roosevelt's stomach. The cancer may have started, Goldsmith suggests, in a mole over the president's left eye, or in a wen that had been removed from the back of his head earlier in the year and then metastasized to his stomach.

However valid Lahey's line of inquiry may have been, the discussion quickly returned to the president's heart. The doctors finally agreed on a scaled-down version of Bruenn's original recommendations: digitalis would be administered in low doses; a low-fat diet would be instituted; callers would be held to a minimum at lunch and dinner; and the president would be asked to cut his consumption of cigarettes from twenty to ten per day and to limit himself to one and a half cocktails a day. The secret conference was adjourned.

It is not clear how much the president was told of his underlying condition. Though Bruenn was brought in to see the president on a regular basis, he remained under strict orders from McIntire to reveal nothing to Roosevelt. Bruenn assumed that McIntire was talking to the president, but McIntire declared later that he deliberately did not tell Roosevelt what the diagnosis was. It was an extraordinary act of presumption on McIntire's part, depriving Roosevelt of the right to know what was happening to his life.

Shortly after Bruenn's diagnosis, Roosevelt confessed to Eleanor that he was worried. "He suspects the doctors don't know what is the matter," Eleanor admitted to Joe Lash. At one point, suffering pain in his rectal area, he feared there might be a growth. But then the pain subsided and he relaxed. Curiously, during all this time he never once asked his doctors what they knew; day after day, he took his green digitalis pills without asking what they were or why he was taking them; day after day, he had his blood pressure read without asking what it was.

The conspiracy of silence extended to the public. On April 4, 1944, one week after the disconcerting checkup, McIntire blithely assured the press that nothing was wrong, that the president was simply suffering from a case of bronchitis. The results of the checkup were excellent, he claimed. "When we got through we decided that for a man of 62 we had very little to argue about, with the exception that we have had to combat flu plus respiratory complications." McIntire went on to say that all the president needed now was "some sunshine and more exercise."

The digitalis worked. X-rays of Roosevelt's chest taken two weeks after the treatment revealed a significant decrease in the size of the heart and a notable clearing of the lungs. His coughing had stopped, his color was good, his blood chemistries were normal, and he was sleeping soundly at night.

• • •

Although the president was improving, the doctors decided that he needed a period of rest away from the White House, where work inevitably pushed its way into his living quarters, into his upstairs study, even into his bedroom. When Bernard Baruch heard that the president was looking for a place to rest, he offered Hobcaw, his roomy brick mansion situated on a knoll overlooking the Waccamaw River in South Carolina.

Roosevelt, accompanied by Drs. Bruenn and McIntire, Pa Watson, and Admiral Leahy, arrived at the Baruch plantation on Easter Sunday, April 9. In the days before his arrival, the Secret Service had been hard at work building wooden ramps for the front and back staircases, a railing in the fishing pier, and a canvas chute that could, in case of fire, allow the president to slide from his bedroom to the ground.

It was the perfect hideaway. The three press-association reporters who had accompanied the president kept their distance from the mansion, standing by in the Prince Georges Hotel eight miles away just in case something happened. "The Secret Service impressed on us repeatedly to 'stay out of the old man's way,'" Merriman Smith recalled. Though just about every living soul in Georgetown knew "He" was there, Smith laughingly observed, all three reporters went along with the game, giving Roosevelt free rein to do as he pleased day in and day out.

"I want to sleep and sleep," Roosevelt said when he first arrived, "twelve hours a night." In the quiet of Baruch's graceful mansion, surrounded by twenty-three thousand acres of fields, woods, and streams, the president got his wish. He awakened at nine-thirty in the morning and went to bed at nine-thirty at night. In the mornings, he read the papers and worked on his correspondence; on sunny afternoons, he fished from the pier or trolled in the bay; on rainy days, he drove around the estate, stopping to see the elaborate gardens, the deer, and the wild boar. Cocktails were usually served at six, with dinner at seven.

During the second week of Roosevelt's vacation, the mail pouch carried an executive order for the president's signature, directing the secretary of commerce to take possession of the Chicago offices of the mammoth mail-order firm Montgomery-Ward. Since April 12, a strike had been in progress, provoked by the company's failure to comply with the WLB's directive to hold fair elections. The case was a complex one, provoking fiery disagreement within the administration. Stimson argued that, since Montgomery-Ward was not doing war business, the army had no right to stick its nose into the labor situation and extend presidential power far wider than he was sure it ought to be extended. Attorney General Francis Biddle disagreed: since 75 percent of Montgomery-Ward's customers were farmers, and since farmers were engaged in producing food vital to the country's war operations, the army had a responsibility to take over the company.

It is not clear how much Roosevelt focused on the issue, but in the end he sided with Biddle and signed the order sending in the troops. The decision backfired. As steel-helmeted soldiers, bearing guns with bayonets fixed, surrounded the Chicago headquarters, Montgomery's chairman, Sewell Avery, refused to leave his eighth-floor office. There was a moment of hesitation, following which Biddle ordered the soldiers to remove him. Two soldiers locked their hands together to form a seat beneath Mr. Avery; two others steadied him by the shoulders. He struggled slightly and then was lifted bodily into the elevator and onto the street.

The photograph of Mr. Avery being carried from the building—voted by news photographers the best photo of the year—prompted a wave of criticism against Roosevelt. "There is no warrant in the Smith-Connally Act or in the President's wartime powers for this seizure," the *Washington Post* editorialized. "It was the manner in which the troops were used," Walter Lippmann observed, "which has made the affair so notorious." This "great howl" was just what Stimson had feared. In his diary, he lamented the action and predicted "it would be used by [Roosevelt's] enemies as corroborating fear of his seeking autocratic power."

With this single exception, Dr. Bruenn recalled, "the whole period was very pleasant. . . . The president thrived on the simple routine. I had never known anyone so full of charm. At lunch and dinner alike, he animated the conversation, telling wonderful stories, reminiscing with Baruch, talking of current events, pulling everyone in. He was a master raconteur. There was no question about it."

While Roosevelt was at Hobcaw, Anna flew to Seattle to pack up her belongings and get their house ready for occupancy. "Beloved of mine," John wrote her from the White House. "Life is just a mess without you. In some ways I wonder if it is wise for me to confess to you that the whole world—except only you—is like warm flat beer to me and you are excitement and joy and life itself."

"Anna has arranged to bring the children East," Eleanor wrote Franklin from Hyde Park on April 21, "and we will have to open the big house from about the middle of June on. Couldn't you arrange to go up and stay a month at a time and only come back for 2–3 days a month? It would be heavenly for us all." She went on to say she wanted to buy a few things to make the servants' rooms more livable and promised she wouldn't spend much. "May I?" she asked. "Also, if I made a diagram of mama's room so everything could be put back in place could I arrange it as a sitting room with a day bed in case someone had to sleep there?"

The following week, Eleanor and Anna, along with Prime Minister and Mrs. John Curtin of Australia and Costa Rican President Teodoro Picado flew to Hobcaw for lunch with the president. Though there was little time for private conversation, Eleanor noticed with satisfaction that Franklin's color was better and his spirits were high. "I came home feeling that it was the very best move Franklin could have made." The sunshine was working wonders, she decided, predicting that he would return from Hobcaw "in better condition than when he left."

Anna was less sanguine about her father's condition, having talked with Dr. Bruenn after lunch about the long-term effects of coronary disease and the necessity to change her father's White House routine radically. Bruenn also impressed upon Anna the importance of altering Roosevelt's diet—something Eleanor apparently did not understand, for no sooner had she returned to Washington than she sent a bunch of steaks in the mail pouch, hoping the president would enjoy them.

Eleanor's delight in her husband's relaxing days with Baruch would more than likely have been diminished had she known that, on the morning of April 28, at the president's invitation, Lucy Mercer Rutherfurd was heading toward Hobcaw from Aiken, 140 miles away.

A month earlier, at Ridgeley Hall in Aiken, Lucy's ailing husband, Winthrop Rutherfurd, had died, leaving Lucy a widow at the age of fifty-two. Survived by two daughters and four sons, Winthrop was buried at his family's estate in Allamuchy, New Jersey. For Lucy, whose life had revolved around her husband for more than twenty years, it was not an easy time. There were complicated estate problems to solve, worries over the children, and difficult decisions to make. And, for the first time, she was alone.

Lucy arrived shortly before noon, accompanied by her stepdaughter and her stepson's wife. In spite of all she had been through the previous month, she retained her beauty and her charm. She could still reach Roosevelt in a way that no one else could. Lucy's presence at the luncheon that day was officially recorded in a seating chart that remains among the president's papers. This time, perhaps because Mr. Rutherfurd was no longer alive, she is openly listed as Lucy Rutherfurd rather than Mrs. Paul Johnson. The diagram of the table shows that Roosevelt was seated at one end, Baruch at the other, Lucy to the president's right. Other guests included Admiral Leahy and Dr. McIntire, Captain Robert Duncan, and Dr. Bruenn. Years later, Baruch vividly remembered the occasion, in part because he had to give up several of his precious war-ration tickets so that Lucy could make the long drive.

For Roosevelt, Lucy's presence must have provided a delightful tonic, reminding him of his younger self, before his paralysis, before the illness that was now overwhelming him. In Lucy's company he could re-establish continuity with his youth, bringing back in his mind the healthy body in which he had once lived. If his future was disappearing, at least he could relive the happy moments of his past.

During lunch, word came that Navy Secretary Frank Knox had died of a heart attack at the age of seventy. The self-imposed unrelenting pace that marked the life of the energetic Knox had finally taken its toll. Eleanor was in the White House, having lunch with Mrs. Kermit Roosevelt, widow of Teddy Roosevelt's son, when the news came. Assuming that her husband would cut his vacation short and come to Washington for the funeral, she postponed by a week an impending trip to New York, including a half-dozen speaking engagements, so she could be at home when her husband returned.

As it happened, Roosevelt did not return for the funeral, electing to remain in Hobcaw an extra week. Though his health had improved markedly during his stay, he suffered a setback later that afternoon that kept him in bed for several days. Shortly after his lunch with Lucy, he experienced acute abdominal pain, slight nausea, and a throbbing sensation all through his body. Dr. Bruenn tentatively diagnosed gallstones and made arrangements for X-rays as soon as they returned to Washington.

In the meantime, a hypodermic injection of codeine allowed Roosevelt to meet the press at eight that evening to discuss Knox's death. Though Merriman Smith noticed that the color of the president's skin was not particularly healthy, he "seemed in such good spirits" that the reporter thought little of it. When Roosevelt talked of Knox, he revealed little emotion. "That may have been the Roosevelt breeding," Smith observed, "because I've been told people of superior breeding never let their emotions come to the surface publicly." Knox was the first of Roosevelt's wartime Cabinet to die, though four other Cabinet members were in their seventies—Stimson at seventy-six, Hull at seventy-two, and Jones and Ickes at seventy.

Roosevelt explained to reporters that the doctors were keeping him in South Carolina a little longer, "lest his recovery from a bad coughing winter be interrupted." Once the discussion of Knox was out of the way, Smith noted, Roosevelt "chatted gaily," about fishing. He asked the three reporters how they were getting along and, upon hearing that they had to pay $12.50 for a bottle of poor rye at the Prince Georges Hotel, he ordered Pa Watson to serve a round of Baruch's bourbon at once, "lest the reporters feel poorly on their return to the city."

In Washington, Eleanor was disappointed to hear that Franklin had delayed his return until May 7. "You will come home just as I leave which is sad," she wrote, explaining that, because she had switched her appointments around the previous week, she now had to be in New York from the 5th to the 12th. "I hate to be away when you come back!"

It helped, however, to know that Anna would be there, able to take her mother's place in welcoming the president home. Just before Eleanor left, Anna celebrated her thirty-eighth birthday. "Nothing I could give you dear could ever tell you how much I love you," Eleanor wrote in a note accompanying her gifts, "but I hope you and John know what a joy it is to have you near and how much I cherish all our pleasant happy times."

• • •

Roosevelt's return to the White House on Sunday morning, May 7, marked the end of the most complete vacation he had had during his eleven years in the presidency. "I had a really grand time at Bernie's," Roosevelt wrote Hopkins, who was convalescing from an operation at White Sulphur Springs, West Virginia, "slept 12 hours out of 24, sat in the sun, never lost my temper, and decided to let the world go hang."

It had been a rough five months for the president's old friend. In January, Hopkins had entered the hospital with a recurrence of his old intestinal troubles. In February, en route to Florida to recuperate, he had received word from Roosevelt that his eighteen-year-old Marine Corps son, Stephen, had been killed in the Marshall Islands. Then, after his abdominal surgery at the Mayo Clinic in March, he had developed jaundice. Finally, at White Sulphur Springs, he seemed to be getting better.

"It is grand to get the reports of how well you are getting on," Roosevelt wrote, "and I have had a mighty nice letter from [Dr. Andrew] Rivers—couched mostly in medical terms, which, however, I have had translated!

"The main things I get from it are two. First, that it is a good thing to connect up the plumbing and put your sewerage system into operating condition. The second is (and this comes from others in authority) that you have got to lead not the life of an invalid but the life of common or garden sense. I, too, over one hundred years older than you are, have come to the same realization and I have cut my drinks down to one and a half cocktails per evening and nothing else—not one complimentary highball or night cap. Also, I have cut my cigarettes down from twenty or thirty a day to five or six a day. Luckily they still taste rotten but it can be done. The main gist of this is to plead with you to stay away until the middle of June at the earliest. I don't want you back until then. If you do come back before then you will be extremely unpopular in Washington, with the exception of [*Washington Times Herald* Publisher] Cissy Patterson who wants to kill you off as soon as possible—just as she does me. . . ."

"We can all be glad," *The New York Times* editorialized the day after the president returned, that "he has had a chance to enjoy a month of rest and relaxation from the almost overwhelming burdens which his office forces him to carry. He earned every hour of it." Writing in a similar vein, *New*

York Times correspondent Anne O'Hare McCormick remarked that the vacation was "good news for the American people," since Roosevelt would need "all the strength, serenity and fortitude of spirit he could muster" to face the climactic days ahead when Allied armies began pouring into Europe for a fight to the finish.

Hassett found the president "brown as a berry, radiant and happy, insisting he has had a complete rest." But Anna was still worried. Though his color was good and his spirits were high, she could see that he was not his old self. "Anna was afraid," Dr. Bruenn recalled, "that her father would fall back into his old habits now that he was back in the White House. She had read up on cardiovascular disease and she understood how important rest and diet were. She was a great help to me. She became his protector. It was Anna who enforced the new regime."

In the weeks that followed, Anna was by her father's side from the moment he awakened until he went to bed at night, making sure that his workload was kept to six hours a day. "You would find many changes here," Ickes wrote Missy on May 23. "He makes only a few appointments a day—not enough in fact for us to transmit important business—and then goes back to house where he usually lunches alone with Anna. He is supposed to go to bed at 9:30 at night but Anna told me she has difficulty in persuading him to do that. . . . Then he goes away for weekends."

A sampling of the usher diaries for May reveals meetings with Cabinet and congressional leaders in the mornings, lunch with Anna and sometimes Margaret Suckley under the magnolia tree on the southern grounds at 1:30 or 2 p.m., additional meetings in the afternoons, followed by a drive in the countryside or a swim in the pool, cocktails and dinner with Anna and John, bed by 10 or 10:30.

For a man who could not be alone, who relished people as his major source of relaxation, Anna's company was vital. For a while, Princess Martha had been able to take up where Missy and Harry had left off, providing Roosevelt with lively companionship and good cheer. But as Roosevelt's health weakened, his meetings with Martha diminished. Though he continued to see her occasionally during the spring and summer of 1944, their "romance" faded. "With people like Martha," Anna's son Johnny Boettiger speculated, "his performance always had to be on. Surely, it was second nature to him and he loved it, but as his energy decreased, their sparkling conversation left him somewhat depleted. With Anna, who loved to tell stories almost as much as he did, he could sit back and let himself be."

Anna's continuing presence in the White House freed Eleanor to do what she wanted, and "what she wanted," Johnny Boettiger observed, "was to be out on her own. She had an opportunity to develop her character and to enjoy a range of experiences few women had." For Eleanor, being on the road and meeting new people was life itself. "I am always waiting for the day to appear when I shall put on my lace cap and sit by the fire," Eleanor once wrote. "But when I am with a number of young people I become so interested I put off that day a little longer."

Returning home from her trips, Eleanor observed the growing bond between Franklin and Anna with mixed emotions. It was hard for Eleanor to accept that Anna now knew things she did not. In a conversation one day with Eleanor about political possibilities in 1944 and what Roosevelt might think about them, Trude Pratt was struck by Eleanor's wistful comment: "Anna is the only one who would know about that."

The tensions multiplied as the weeks went by. "Anna tried to be as protective as she could with her father's health," Dr. Bruenn observed, "but Eleanor was a different kind of person, more driven, more insistent. She couldn't accept that he was really sick or that he needed to cut down his activities, especially if they related to her concerns. I would sit with the family telling everyone how important it was not to annoy him or upset him at the dinner table but she couldn't stop herself."

Of course, Eleanor drove Franklin no harder than she drove herself; there were just too many things to accomplish, and at some level, even if she couldn't admit it openly, she must have worried that time was running out for both of them. The condition of black Americans remained closest to her heart. It seemed that, the more criticism she received about her advocacy of blacks, the more committed she became. In February, she had attended the opening of the first non–Jim Crow servicemen's canteen in Washington, D.C. When a picture of her appeared in the papers surrounded by a group of white and Negro servicemen and their dates, a bitter controversy flared. "How can anyone," Representative Charles McKenzie of Louisiana argued on the floor of the House, "be a party to encouraging white girls into the arms of Negro soldiers at a canteen dance while singing 'Let Me Call You Sweetheart?' "

"I know, of course, you are bidding for negro votes for your good husband," an "outraged" woman wrote Eleanor, "but isn't it rather a costly price to pay? . . . Would you have enjoyed seeing your daughter Anna being hugged by those negroes. . . . You are the most dangerous woman in America today and may I beg you to stop and think before you are guilty of such a thing again."

Though Eleanor did not doubt her husband's ultimate commitment to racial equality, she believed constant reminders were essential to counter the rising pressures from the conservative coalition in Congress. Her commitment to women required equal vigilance. When she came home from her Caribbean tour, she was upset to find that only men were being sent to an international conference in London on education. She got one woman added at the last moment, but that was not good enough. "Women should be represented in every international conference," she insisted.

When the president was strong and healthy, he had enjoyed and even invited Eleanor's advocacy. "She pushed him terrifically, this I know," Anna admitted. "But you can't ask somebody to be your eyes and ears and then not . . ." Grace Tully recalls a tense moment when Eleanor was cross-examining Franklin at a dinner party. "Mother, can't you see you are giving Father indigestion?" Anna pleaded.

"She couldn't see why," Anna recalled, "at a moment when he was relaxing—I remember one day when we were having cocktails. . . . A fair number of people were in the room, an informal group. . . . I was mixing the cocktails. Mother always came in at the end so she would only have to have one cocktail—that was her concession. She would wolf it—she never took it slowly. She came in and sat down across the desk from Father. And she had a sheaf of papers this high and she said, 'Now, Franklin, I want to talk to you about this.' I have permanently blocked out of my mind what it was she wanted to bring up. I just remember, like lightning, that I thought, 'Oh God, he's going to blow.' And sure enough, he blew his top. He took every single speck of that whole pile of papers, threw them across the desk at me and said, 'Sis, you handle these tomorrow morning.' I almost went through the floor. She got up. She was the most controlled person in the world. And she just stood there a half second and said, 'I'm sorry.' Then she took her glass and walked toward somebody else and started talking. And he picked up his glass and started a story. And that was the end of it.

"Intuitively I understood that here was a man plagued with God knows how many problems and right now he had twenty minutes to have two cocktails—in very small glasses—because dinner was served at a certain hour. They called you and out you went. He wanted to tell stories and relax and enjoy himself—period. I don't think Mother had the slightest realization."

Earlier in the spring, almost as if she were anticipating this terrible moment, Anna had written to John, "I pray I don't get caught in the crossfire between those two." Over the years, Anna had come to understand the pain her mother had endured from being placed in an emotional triangle with her mother-in-law, competing with the older woman for the love of the same man. And she knew about her father's affair with Lucy Mercer. The last thing Anna wanted was to create a situation that would recapitulate her mother's earlier dilemma. But so deep was Anna's pleasure in playing the role of caretaker to her father that there was no way she could give it up, even if it jeopardized her relationship with her mother.

CHAPTER 20

"SUSPENDED IN SPACE"

Through the last days of May and the early days of June, Eleanor observed, everyone seemed to live "suspended in space, waiting for the invasion, dreading it and yet wishing it could begin successfully." In the hush of the moment, Roosevelt tried to maintain a pretense of normal activity, but his secretary Grace Tully noticed that "every movement of his face and hands reflected the tightly contained state of his nerves."

He had done all he could to make sure that the young soldiers who crossed the Channel would have the greatest possible chance of success. From factories in Michigan, Illinois, Indiana, and New York had come the overwhelming majority of the vehicles—the trucks, tanks, armored cars, jeeps, ambulances—that were now carrying the men and supplies to the embarkation posts in southern England. From assembly plants in Ohio, Oregon, and California had come the bombers and the fighter planes that would provide life-sustaining air cover for the invading force. And from shipyards on both coasts had come the largest fleet ever assembled—900 warships in all, including 9 battleships, 23 heavy cruisers, 104 destroyers, and, perhaps most important, from Andrew Higgins in New Orleans had come the landing craft needed to carry the troops onto the beaches. Indeed, so much time had the Allied high command spent worrying about landing craft that Eisenhower once said that, "when he is buried, his coffin should be in the shape of a landing craft, as they are practically killing him with worry."

Yet, with the target date now only days away, there was little either Roosevelt or Eisenhower could do except sit back and wait. "The nearer H hour approached," army historian Gordon Harrison explained in the official army history of the cross-Channel attack, "the more heavily and exclusively the responsibility for the invasion settled on the lower commanders." For the few—Roosevelt, Churchill, Eisenhower, Marshall, Montgomery, and Brooke —would now be substituted the many, "as the battlefield so long seen as a single conceptual problem, becomes a confused and disparate fact—a maze of unrelated orchards and strange roads, hedgerows, villages, streams and woods, each temporarily bounding for the soldier the whole horizon of the war."

Once the order to "go" was given, the chief burden of the fighting would reside with the individual soldier; the advance of each unit would depend in large measure on his courage and skill, on his willingness to jump from the landing craft into water which was sometimes up to his neck, or higher; to wade through the bloodstained waves onto the beach, amid bloated bodies and bullets; and then to walk or crawl up the hill where the vaunted German army was waiting with rifles, mortars, and machine guns. Months of training and experience on other fronts in North Africa or Italy had brought each soldier to this point, but in the hearts of many, fighter pilot and military historian William Emerson admitted, "there was a question of whether we could make it against the big leagues. Till then we'd been fooling around the periphery. Now we were going into the center of things. Beneath the bravado, there was an undercurrent of concern, even fear."

Eisenhower determined that only four days in June provided the combination of conditions necessary for the assault—a late-rising moon for the paratroopers, and, shortly after dawn, a low tide. The invasion was set for Monday, June 5, a month later than originally planned.

Roosevelt had intended to fly to England in early June so that he could be close to Churchill and Eisenhower as the invasion began. When his health prevented the trip, Churchill was sorely disappointed. Even at this late date, the prime minister was still anxious about the whole operation, still oppressed by "the dangers and disasters that could flow from Overlord if the landings should fail." If only Roosevelt were there; then at least some of the tension might be eased. "Our friendship is my greatest stand-by amid the ever-increasing complications of this exacting war," Churchill wrote Roosevelt on June 4, as he journeyed south to be near Eisenhower and the troops. "How I wish you were here."

For his part, Roosevelt decided to spend the weekend in Charlottesville, Virginia, at the home of his military aide Pa Watson. In the quiet of Watson's elegant estate, Roosevelt hoped to prepare a speech to the nation to be delivered once the invasion began. Eleanor was invited to join her husband, but she elected to stay in Washington instead, knowing perhaps that her own anxiety would only contribute to his. For weeks, Eleanor had been unable to sleep through the night. "I feel as though a sword were hanging over my head," she had written in mid-May, "dreading its fall and yet knowing it must fall to end the war."

Several months earlier, Eleanor had received a haunting letter from a woman whose favorite nephew had just been killed while serving in the navy. "It is too bad that you and your husband have not been punished by some deadly disease," the distraught woman wrote. "Maybe though you and your husband will have to look into the faces of the dead corpses of your four sons. . . . God always punishes the wicked in some way." Eleanor published the letter in her column, along with a simple reply. "Neither my husband nor I brought on this war," she wrote, but "I quite understood her bitterness." Now that the target date was drawing near, Eleanor could not free herself from monstrous thoughts of the battlefield, of the dead and the wounded. "Soon the invasion will be upon us," she wrote on June 3; "I dread it."

What is more, Eleanor had no confidence that she could help her husband on this critical speech. The Office of War Information had asked her to prepare a radio speech of her own to be used after the invasion began, but she had declined. It was supposed to be addressed to the mothers of the U.S.A., and she couldn't think of what she wanted to say, she explained to Joe Lash. "I only know I don't want to say any of the things they suggested!"

In Eleanor's absence, Anna and John accompanied Roosevelt to Charlottesville, where the three of them worked together on a draft of the president's speech. Years later, Anna recalled with pleasure the role she and John had played in suggesting that the speech be in the form of a prayer instead of a regular speech. "We all started making our contributions. Father would take a little from all of us and then write it as his own."

That same Saturday, June 3, Eisenhower met with his meteorologists in the Library of Southwick House at Naval Headquarters in Portsmouth. The news was not good. A marked deterioration had taken place in the good conditions originally predicted for June 5. Now Captain J. M. Stagg, senior meteorologist for Supreme Headquarters Allied Expeditionary Force, was saying that June 5 would be overcast and stormy, with high winds and visibility so low that the air force could not be used. And the weather pattern was so unpredictable that forecasting more than a day in advance was highly undependable. With great reluctance, Eisenhower decided to postpone the operation for twenty-four hours.

News of the postponement threw Churchill into "an agony of uncertainty." If the bad conditions continued for another day, Overlord could not be launched for at least another two weeks. Unable to endure the tension, he decided to return to London. In Charlottesville, Roosevelt remained calm, though he, too, elected to return to his nation's capital. In Eleanor's judgment, her husband was better able to meet the tension than many of the others, "because he'd learned from polio that if there was nothing you could do about a situation, then you'd better try to put it out of your mind and go on with your work at hand."

On Sunday night, June 4, Eisenhower met again with his meteorologists. This time Captain Stagg reported a slight improvement in the weather; the rain front was expected to clear in three hours, and the clearing would last until Tuesday morning; later that Tuesday, however, considerable cloudiness was expected to develop. Eisenhower recognized that these conditions were far from ideal but "the question," he said, was "just how long you can hang this operation on the end of a limb and let it hang there." At nine forty-five that night, Eisenhower announced his decision. "O.K., let's go." The invasion would be launched at dawn on the 6th of June. "I don't like it, but there it is," he said. "I don't see how we can possibly do anything else."

On the eve of D-day, a nervous Churchill went to his map room to follow the movement of the convoys as they headed toward the coast of France. "Do you realize," he said to his wife, Clementine, who had joined him before she went to bed, "that by the time you wake up in the morning twenty thousand men may have been killed?"

That same night, Roosevelt went on the air to salute the fall of Rome. "The first of the Axis capitals is now in our hands," Roosevelt said. "One up and two to go!" The Allied struggle to capture Rome had been long and costly, with heavy loss of life. In January, the Germans had pinned down more than 150,000 Allied soldiers to a bridgehead at Anzio on the Tyrrhenian Sea, preventing them from linking up with the main Allied force to the south. It took more than four months of fighting for the Allies finally to break out from Anzio on May 23 and link up with the Allied forces advancing on Rome. Things moved swiftly after that, leading to the capture of Rome in a matter of days. "How magnificently your troops have fought," Churchill telegraphed.

Though Roosevelt knew that thousands of American soldiers were crossing the Channel as he delivered his address, he never tipped his hat, concentrating his remarks on Italy. Shortly after the speech, the president went to bed.

As the clock tolled midnight in Washington, the first waves of young Americans were plunging into the surf. Few had slept the night before, war correspondent Ernie Pyle reported, and many had thrown up their breakfasts, as the invasion turned "from a vague anticipatory dread into a horrible reality." Some, loaded down with gas masks, grenades, TNT, satchel charges, and rifle ammunition, sixty-eight pounds in all, drowned when they first jumped into the water; others were hit by bullets and killed or wounded as they waded in to shore; still others were struck as they scrambled across the beach. Some of the beaches proved easier than others. Omaha was the worst. One infantry company at Omaha lost a quarter of its men in the first forty-five minutes. "I don't know why I'm alive at all," one survivor said. "It was really awful. For hours there on the beach the shells were so close they were throwing mud and rocks all over you. It was so bad that you didn't care whether you got hit or not."

But by 3 a.m., Washington time, when General Marshall called the White House to speak to the president, most of the troops were moving forward, making their way onto the beaches and up the hills. Eleanor was still awake when the call came. Franklin had told her the invasion news before she went to bed, and she became so wrought up she could not sleep. "To be nearly sixty and still rebel at uncertainty is ridiculous isn't it," she chided herself. The White House operator called Eleanor first, knowing she was still up, and asked her to awaken the president. Eleanor entered her husband's room. "He sat up in bed and put on his sweater, and from then on he was on the telephone. . . ."

The official announcement of the invasion came at 3:32 a.m. along with a reading of Eisenhower's order of the day: "Soldiers, sailors and airmen of the Allied Expeditionary Force! You are about to embark upon the great crusade, toward which we have striven these many months. . . . Much has happened since the Nazi triumph of 40–41. . . . Our homefronts have given us an overwhelming superiority in weapons and munitions of war, and placed at our disposal great reserves of trained fighting men. The tide has turned! I have full confidence in your courage, devotion to duty and skill in battle. We will accept nothing less than full victory!"

At 4 a.m., Roosevelt told the White House operator to call every member of the White House staff and ask them all to report to duty at once. One by one the calls were made; only Harry Hopkins, still convalescing in the army hospital in White Sulphur Springs, was excluded from the list. More than anyone else on the staff, Hopkins had deserved to be there that day to share the news of the great invasion he had long supported. Alone in his hospital room, he told his biographer Robert Sherwood, he thought about all the production problems that had challenged the United States in 1939 and 1940, of how the various bottlenecks had been broken and the desperate shortages of strategic materials converted into surpluses. If ever there was a country unprepared for the war, it was the U.S. in 1940. And yet now, only four years later, the United States was clearly the most productive, most powerful country on the face of the earth.

As the news of the invasion reached the American people in the early hours of June 6, church bells tolled, school bells rang, factories sounded their whistles, fog horns blasted. "It is the most exciting moment in our lives," Mayor LaGuardia told reporters. Sporting events were canceled. Retail stores closed. People streamed into the streets. "Outwardly they appeared to be celebrating a victory," *Homefront* author Winston Estes observed, "but underneath all that raucous, uncontrolled excitement, lay a cold fear and a grim anxiety which gnawed at their insides."

"The impulse to pray was overwhelming," historian Stephen Ambrose wrote. People jammed the pews of churches and synagogues in cities and towns throughout the land to sit in silence and pray. "We have come to the hour for which we were born," *The New York Times* editorialized the next day. "We go forth to meet the supreme test of our arms and our souls, the test of the maturity of our faith in ourselves and in mankind."

Roosevelt met with his congressional leaders at 9:50 a.m. and his military leaders at 11:30. The official news was still fragmentary, but by midafternoon, as he lunched with Anna under the magnolia tree, it was clear that the landings had gone pretty well, better than anyone had hoped. Though casualties were high—some sixty-six hundred were recorded that first day alone—they were fewer than expected. The main event of the day was the president's regular press conference at 4 p.m., which drew 180 men and women packed in a solid mass.

"The President was happy and confident," I. F. Stone recorded. "Our faces must have shown what most of us felt as we came in. For he began, after an extraordinary pause of several minutes in which no questions were asked and we all stood silent, by saying that the correspondents had the same look on their faces that people all over the country must have and that he thought this a very happy conference."

"I have just sat in on a great moment in history," a young reporter wrote his mother later that day. "The President sat back in his great green chair calm and smiling, dressed in a snow white shirt with the initials FDR on the left sleeve in blue and a dark blue dotted bow tie. In his hand he held the inevitable long cigarette holder and when he held the cigarette in his mouth it was cocked at the angle they say he always has it when he is pleased with the world."

Still, Roosevelt warned the press against overconfidence. "You just don't land on a beach and walk through—if you land successfully without breaking your leg—walk through to Berlin. And the quicker this country understands it the better."

Later that evening, Roosevelt went on the air to deliver the simple prayer he had prepared in Charlottesville, "a far cry," Rosenman noted, "from the kind of speech Hitler would have made if *his* troops were landing on the beaches of England." The general tone of his voice reflected concentrated, quiet intensity, perfectly matching the mood of the country. He prayed first for "our sons, pride of our Nation. . . . Give strength to their arms, stoutness to their hearts, steadfastness in their faith." He then prayed for the people at home, for strong hearts "to wait out the long travail, to bear sorrows that may come. . . . Give us Faith in Thee," he concluded: "faith in our sons; faith in each other; faith in our united crusade."

As Eleanor listened to her husband, she noted with pleasure that he looked very well and seemed himself again, full of plans for the future. At one moment, he talked of going to England as soon as Hitler was ready to surrender; the next moment, he spoke of Honolulu and the Aleutians. For her part, she had no sense of excitement whatsoever: "All emotion is drained away."

The "hedgerow battles" that followed in the days after the landings were characterized by savage fighting, slow movement, and few geographic gains. Tangled hedges and bushes were ubiquitous in the bocage country surrounding Normandy; everywhere one looked, they boxed in fields and orchards of varying sizes and shapes. "Each hedgerow," army historian Gordon Harrison notes, "was a potential earthwork into which the defenders cut often-elaborate foxholes, trenches, and individual firing pits. The dense bushes atop the hedgerows provided ample concealment for rifle and machine gun positions, which could subject the attacker to devastating hidden fire from three sides. . . . Each field thus became a separate battlefield."

But if the infantry was temporarily splintered by the dense terrain, Allied air and naval power was practically unopposed. From the larger perspective, the overwhelming weight of Allied arms gradually wore down the defenders. "I cannot say enough for the Navy," Corporal William Preston wrote his father, "for the way they brought us in, for the firepower they brought to bear on the beach. Whenever any of us fired a burst of tracer at a target, the destroyers, standing in so close they were almost ashore, fired a shot immediately after us, each time hitting what we were firing at on the nose." And all this time, Preston marveled, while twenty thousand Allied planes formed a protective umbrella in the sky, "not a single German plane" could be seen. "Nobody doubted now," Hap Arnold recorded, "the meaning of the damage reports, photographs, figures and percentages of the great air attack on the Luftwaffe in the five great days of February."

Three weeks after D-day, one million men had been put ashore, along with an astonishing supply of 171,532 vehicles and 566,000 tons of supplies. "As far as you could see in every direction the ocean was infested with ships," Ernie Pyle observed, but when you walked along the beach, a grimmer picture emerged. "The wreckage was vast and startling." Men were floating in the water, lying on the beach; nearly nine thousand were dead. "There were trucks tipped half over and swamped . . . tanks that had only just made the beach before being knocked out . . . jeeps that had burned to a dull gray . . . boats stacked on top of each other. On the beach lay expended sufficient men and mechanism for a small war. They were gone forever now."

"And yet, we could afford it," Pyle marveled. "We could afford it because we were on, we had our toehold, and behind us there were such enormous replacements for this wreckage on the beach that you could hardly conceive of the sum total. Men and equipment were flowing from England in such a gigantic stream that it made the waste on the beachhead seem like nothing at all, really nothing at all."

Standing amid the wreckage, looking out to sea at the immense armada of ships still waiting to unload, Pyle noticed a group of German prisoners. "They stood staring almost as if in a trance. They didn't say a word to each other. They didn't need to. The expression on their faces was something forever unforgettable. In it was the final, horrified acceptance of their doom."

• • •

Comforted by the news from France, Roosevelt journeyed to Hyde Park for seven days in the middle of June. "Much kidding about his destination," Hassett recorded, "even mentioned possibility of taking me into Catskills for a drinking party." A "Swiss family Robinson" caravan left the Bureau of Engraving terminal at 10 p.m. on a warm Thursday night: Franklin and Eleanor; Martha and Olav and their three children; Tommy, Tully, and White House operator Louise Hackmeister.

"I've unpacked a little and have some photos where I can enjoy them," Eleanor wrote Joe Lash the next morning from her desk in Sara's old bedroom, which she had finally taken over, "but really living here is hard for me—I've made Mama's room pleasant and I can work in it and not feel her presence . . . but over here there is no getting away from the bigness of the house and the multitudes of people. Franklin has a diet. The Crown Princess another and running the house is no joke!" Never from choice would she live in this house, Eleanor had confessed several weeks earlier, for her heart was in the cottage, "but suddenly Franklin is more dependent."

Following the simple routine he treasured so greatly at Hyde Park, the president worked in his library in the mornings, organized picnics along the river in the afternoons, took tea at Laura Delano's, and went to bed early. By the time he returned to Washington, he looked, Hassett recorded, "in the pink of condition."

The morning he returned, June 22, 1944, the president hosted a public ceremony in the Oval Office to celebrate his signing of the GI Bill of Rights. This extraordinary bill, which carried out in full the visionary recommendations Roosevelt had made the previous year, had passed the Senate by a vote of fifty to zero and the House by 387 to zero. Acknowledging the intense gratitude the country felt toward the men and women who had given up months and years of their lives in service to their country, the GI Bill was designed to provide the returning veteran with a chance to command the status, education, and training he could have enjoyed if he had not served in the military.

"There is one great fear in the heart of any serviceman," Eleanor observed in her column, quoting a letter from a young soldier overseas, "and it is not that he will be killed or maimed but that when he is finally allowed to go home and piece together what he can of life, he will be made to feel he has been a sucker for the sacrifice he has made."

The GI Bill responded to that fear by providing special opportunities for veterans: it backed them in their efforts to buy a home or get into business by guaranteeing loans up to $2,000; it authorized those who were unable to find a job to receive $20 a week for fifty-two weeks; it provided construction of additional hospital facilities, and, most far-reachingly, it provided $500 a year for college tuition plus a monthly payment of $75 for living expenses.

In 1940, when the average worker earned less than $1,000 a year and when tuition, room, and board ranged from $453 at state colleges to $979 at private universities, a college education was the preserve of the privileged few. By providing an allowance of what amounted to $1,400 a year, the GI Bill would carry more than two million veterans into colleges and graduate schools at a total cost of $14 billion. In the late forties, veterans would constitute almost 50 percent of the male students in all institutions of higher learning. To accommodate the new students, colleges and universities would vastly expand their physical plants. Scores of new urban campuses would be created. Moreover, under the same provision, another three million veterans would receive educational training below college, and two million would receive on-the-job training. Through this single piece of legislation, the educational horizons of an entire generation would be lifted.

Exceeding all expectations, the GIs would do exceptionally well at school. A *Fortune* survey of the class of '49, 70 percent of whom were veterans, concluded it was "the best... the most mature... the most responsible, the most self disciplined group of college students in history." Despite overcrowding in housing and the classroom, they were determined to make the most of this extraordinary opportunity. "We were men, not kids," veteran Chesterfield Smith observed, "and we had the maturity to recognize we had to go get what we wanted and not wait for things to happen to us."

"Almost everything important that happened to me later came from attending college," veteran Larry Montrell would write. "I don't know what I would have been if it hadn't been for that." Returning soldier Dan Condren agreed. "I doubt if I would have moved away from the Texas Panhandle. It set a whole new standard of improved education for a large number of people."

A smiling Roosevelt used ten pens to sign the historic legislation, handing the first to Representative Edith Nourse Rogers of Massachusetts, a strong proponent of veterans' rights and benefits. This bill, Roosevelt pledged, "gives emphatic notice to the men and women in our armed forces that the American people do not intend to let them down."

• • •

The American people were far less generous toward the first wave of Japanese Americans who had been given permission to leave the internment camps in the West to work in other parts of the country. In Great Meadows, New Jersey, where a critical shortage of farm labor existed, a farmer by the name of Edward Kowalick had hired a Japanese American named George Yamamoto. Kowalick was delighted with his new employee; the young Japanese American's suggestions saved hours of work in the greenhouse. But once the townspeople of Great Meadows became aware of Yamamoto's presence, trouble began. A mass meeting was called; the following day, a small shed on the farm was burned and a sign reading "One Mile to Little

Tokyo" was placed on the road leading to Kowalick's farm. After two weeks of tension, Kowalick finally agreed to dismiss Yamamoto; the neighbors celebrated by throwing Kowalick a surprise party.

Similar tensions were generated elsewhere. In Chicago, Eleanor learned of another "deplorable incident." A meat packer had employed a half-dozen Japanese Americans to work in his meat plant. The hiring was done in cooperation with the War Relocation Authority. Things went fine until an army colonel came into the plant and ordered the meat packer to get rid of the six workers. The meat packer resisted, but the colonel insisted, and the men were discharged.

At the same time, the number of Japanese Americans serving in the U.S. Army continued to grow, reaching thirty-three thousand. "I've never had more whole-hearted, serious-minded cooperation from army troops," Lieutenant Colonel Farrant Turner said of the all-Japanese 100th Infantry Battalion, which fought with great distinction in Italy and France. The 442nd Regimental Combat Team, which also fought in Italy and France, was known as the "Christmas tree regiment," because it became the most decorated unit in the entire army. In seven major campaigns, the combined 100th and 442nd suffered 9,486 casualties and won 18,143 medals for valor, including almost ten thousand Purple Hearts. In addition, more than sixteen thousand Nisei served in military intelligence in the Pacific, translating captured documents.

At Topaz, Manzanar, Poston, Heart Mountain, and other relocation camps, the parents of fallen heroes accepted the extraordinary honors on behalf of their sons. The color guard turned out as the medals of the dead were pinned on their mothers' blouses. The familiar sadness of the ceremony was multiplied by its setting: a tawdry tar-paper barrack surrounded by strips of barbed wire which denied the parents of the honored soldiers the very freedom for which their sons had died.

The only answer to this hideous situation, Eleanor had long argued, was to close the camps and begin a massive program of education, reminding every American of his commitment to democracy. Harold Ickes agreed with Eleanor. Now that military necessity could no longer be used to justify the incarceration, "the continued retention of these innocent people," he told the president in June, "would be a blot upon the history of this country."

Roosevelt listened to them both, but he refused to be pushed. "The more I think of this problem of suddenly ending the orders excluding Japanese Americans from the West Coast, the more I think it would be a mistake to do anything drastic or sudden," he wrote Edward Stettinius on June 12. (Stettinius was serving as the acting secretary of state in place of the ailing Cordell Hull.) "I think the whole problem for the sake of internal quiet should be handled gradually, i.e., I am thinking of two methods: a) seeing with great discretion, how many Japanese families would be acceptable to public opinion in definite localities on the West Coast, b) seeking to extend greatly the distribution of other families in many parts of the U.S. . . . Dissemination and distribution constitute a great method of avoiding public outcry."

There was some merit to Roosevelt's idea of distribution, but by deciding to wait until after the election to rescind the exclusion order, he bears responsibility for extending what was already one of America's darkest hours.

• • •

An even darker chapter in the history of the world was being written that summer as Hitler, facing defeat in his conventional war against the Allies, redoubled his efforts to exterminate the Jews. In this phase of the Final Solution, more than one million additional Jews were being rounded up from Western and Central Europe and transported by train to Hitler's "vast kingdom" of secret death camps—Auschwitz, Dachau, Birkenau, Treblinka, Belzec, Chelmno—where nearly two million Jews had already been killed.

In May, the UP reported that three hundred thousand Hungarian Jews were being taken from the Hungarian countryside to Auschwitz and Birkenau. In desperation, rescue advocates pleaded with Washington to bomb the railway lines from Hungary to Auschwitz in order "to slow down or stop the deportations."

The request was forwarded to the newly created War Refugee Board, which the president, under strong pressure from Henry Morgenthau, had finally agreed to establish in January 1944. The goal of the board was "to develop positive, new American programs to aid the victims of Nazism while pressing the Allies and neutrals to take forceful diplomatic action in their behalf." If only it had been set up earlier, War Refugee Board Director John Pehle wistfully noted years later, "things might have been different. Finally there was a place where rescue advocates could go; finally there was a claimant agency mandated to aid the victims of Nazism."

In the early days of spring, the WRB had succeeded in getting Roosevelt to issue his strongest statement yet on the issue, accusing Germany of "the wholesale systematic murder of the Jews" and promising the world that Germany's crimes, "the blackest crimes in all history," would not go unpunished by the Allies. In May, Pehle had scored another victory when Roosevelt agreed to establish an emergency shelter for Jewish refugees in an abandoned army camp in Oswego, New York. Both actions, however, as Pehle freely admits, came far too late to make much difference. If America had lent its prestige to the idea of sanctuaries for refugees in 1939–40, when Hitler was still willing to let the Jews go, perhaps other countries would have followed suit. But once extermination replaced emigration, the only hope for rescue lay in military action aimed at stopping the killing process itself.

The request for Allied bombing of the rail lines ended up on the desk of John McCloy, Stimson's assistant secretary. Though McCloy was not an anti-

Semite like Breckinridge Long, he shared some of the stereotypes and prejudices against Jews held by many men of his generation and social milieu,
including a suspicion of any information coming from Jewish sources. His
answer to the request was a definite no. "The War Department is of the
opinion," he wrote, "that the suggested air operation is impracticable," for
it would require "diversion of considerable air support" essential for other
operations and was of such "doubtful efficacy" that it made no sense.

Pehle refused to give up. The following week, he forwarded another
request to McCloy, this time suggesting that the concentration camps themselves should be bombed, so that "in the resultant confusion some of the
unfortunate people might be able to escape and hide." Though a large
number of inmates would inevitably be killed in such an operation, any
action was better than none for a people who were already doomed. What
was more, Pehle argued, "if the elaborate murder installations were destroyed, it seems clear the Germans could not reconstruct them for some
time."

Once again, McCloy delivered a negative response, arguing that the camps
were "beyond the maximum range" of Allied dive-bombers and fighter
planes stationed in the U.K., France, and Italy. "The positive solution to this
problem," he insisted, repeating the old refrain, "is the earliest possible
victory over Germany."

McCloy's argument that the targets were beyond the reach of Allied
bombers was not technically true. In fact, long-range American bombers
stationed in Italy had flown over Auschwitz several times that spring in
search of the I. G. Farben petrochemical plant which was close by. Jan
Karski and Elie Wiesel were later given a chance to see some of the aerial
reconnaissance photos that were taken on those flights. "It was the saddest
thing," Karski recalled. "With a magnifying glass we could actually read the
names and numbers of the Hungarian Jews standing on line waiting to be
gassed. Yet McCloy claimed the target was too far away."

•   •   •

Having rallied his energies for D-day, Roosevelt succumbed to exhaustion
and melancholy in the weeks that followed. Though he seemed his old self
when he appeared in public, his confident smile still masking vulnerability,
it was increasingly obvious to those closest to him that his characteristic
ebullience had diminished. For this man who adored good food, good
liquor, and good conversation, the Spartan regime the doctors had ordered
had erased much of the joy of daily life.

And, despite the new diet and the new schedule, he was still suffering
from frequent headaches and chronic fatigue, his body no longer able to
supply the stamina he needed to get through his appointments. Eleanor
confided in Anna that one day he had unexpectedly cried out: "I cannot live
out a normal life span. I can't even walk across the room to get my circulation going."

To the members of the White House staff, he seemed curiously withdrawn. Though both politicians and the public expected him to head the Democratic ticket for the fourth time when the party convened in July, he showed no interest whatsoever in the nominating process. His mind seemed preoccupied with intimations of death.

Sam Rosenman recounted a troubling conversation in the Oval Office that summer when the president suddenly turned to him and said that, if the country wanted to build a small memorial to him after he died, he would like it to be situated "in the small park triangle where Constitution and Pennsylvania Avenue cross facing east." Grace Tully recalled an equally disturbing moment, when, in the midst of dictating a letter, the president abruptly switched the subject. "I told Margaret," he mused, "that if anything ever happened to me she is to get Fala. I'm quite sure that Eleanor will be too busy to look after him and he's devoted to Margaret."

Anna tried to cheer her father with light conversation and amusing stories. With Eleanor settled in Hyde Park for the summer, Anna lunched with her father every day under the magnolia tree, joined him at the pool in the afternoon, and dined with him in his bedroom at night. On the one hand, he remained as she had known him as a child, good-natured and uncomplaining. Though he would acknowledge from time to time that he was tired, "it wasn't a complaint," Anna recalled, "it was a statement of fact."

Yet she could not help seeing that he was in fact depressed, and that there was no one with whom he could share his feelings. Though she tried to break his impenetrable façade, the patterns of a lifetime held: the father who had smiled and joked as he was being carried off to the hospital with infantile paralysis was still unable to let his guard down in front of his daughter. Late at night, when she returned to her bedroom suite with John, she railed against "the legacy of self-containment" that had encouraged her father all his life to deny feeling helpless or weak, leaving him forever mistrustful of intimacy.

It was during this period, at some point in late June or early July, that Roosevelt approached his daughter with a whispered request. "What would you think," he is said to have asked, not giving her time to say anything in reply, "about our inviting an old friend of mine to a few dinners at the White House. This would have to be arranged when your mother is away and I would have to depend on you to make the arrangements."

Anna knew at once that the old friend was Lucy Mercer Rutherfurd. And she knew with certainty that her mother would be destroyed if she ever found out. Though the affair had taken place almost three decades earlier, Franklin had promised Eleanor that he would never see Lucy again. "It was almost like a trap in time," Trude Lash later observed. "He couldn't tell Eleanor that he wanted to see Lucy because it was stuck somewhere in the past."

Anna's first reaction was one of anger toward her father for plunging her into an extremely awkward situation. "It was a terrible decision to have to make in a hurry," she later said. Anna had long taken her mother's side in this dispute, sympathizing keenly with the trauma her mother had suffered when she discovered Lucy's letters.

At the same time, Anna knew that her father's strength was failing and she understood how important it would be for him to enjoy some evenings that were, as she put it, "light-hearted and gay, affording a few hours of much needed relaxation." If seeing Lucy again provided the inspiration he needed to assuage his loneliness and buoy his spirits, then who was she to sit in judgment? After all, she herself had fallen in love with her second husband before she was divorced from her first. At thirty-eight years of age, no longer regarding her father from the vantage point of a child, she was learning to accept his weaknesses and enjoy his strengths. If he wasn't perfect, neither was she. "While they were my parents," she later said, "nevertheless they had reached an age where they were certainly entitled to lead their own private lives without having me, of all people, or any of their children say, 'You shouldn't do this' or 'You shouldn't see this person or the other person.' "

Still, it was intolerable to imagine the hurt her mother would experience if she found out. But, as long as the dinners were classified as private engagements not included in the official guest lists, there was no reason to believe that Eleanor would know. "Standards were different in those days," reporter Bob Donovan recalled. "I'm sure there were some reporters, friends of the White House, who knew about Lucy. But none of them ever thought about exposing the situation. The newspaper business in those days was not so damn serious as it is today; it was a hell of a lot more fun. We didn't think we were angels; we knew all the things we were doing; so to point our hand at someone else wouldn't seem sporting!"

Weighing these factors together, Anna told her father she would do as he asked. She would make sure that Lucy came in the back door—the Southwest Gate, across from the Executive Office Building. She would make it understood that the guest list that night was not to be given out. She would, in short, conspire with her father, hoping that her mother would not find out.

Anna arranged for Lucy to visit over the weekend of July 7. It was the first of what would amount to more than a dozen secret meetings between the two old friends over the next nine months. The original plan called for Roosevelt to take Lucy away from Washington to Shangri-la, his mountain hideaway, but with General de Gaulle still in Washington after two days of meetings, the president decided to stay in the White House.

The talks between President Roosevelt and General de Gaulle were intended to ease the tensions between the United States and the French Committee of National Liberation before Allied troops began moving forward into the French interior. Roosevelt wanted to ensure that American soldiers would receive maximum cooperation from the French underground once they finally broke away from the hedgerow country and began advancing toward Paris. But he had resisted giving official recognition to de Gaulle for months, on the grounds the choice should be French, the choice of forty million people, not something foisted on France by an outside power.

The leader of the Free French arrived at the White House on Thursday afternoon, July 6. "He stepped from the automobile," Hassett recorded, "with an air of arrogance bordering on downright insolence, his Cyrano de Bergerac nose high in the air." Roosevelt was waiting at the door, "all smiles and cordiality." There followed a round of official meetings and ceremonies, highlighted by a state dinner on Friday at which the president toasted the health of America's "friend" General de Gaulle and spoke movingly of the common effort to remove every German boot from France, "once and for all."

At eight forty-five that evening, Lucy, having made arrangements to stay with a friend in Georgetown for the weekend, arrived at the White House. It had been a long day for the president, beginning with a press conference that morning at which he announced his decision to recognize the French Committee of National Liberation as the *de facto* authority in France, followed by a luncheon for thirty-six in the State Dining Room at one and a Cabinet meeting at two, but the president remained with his old friend until after eleven.

The final meeting with de Gaulle was completed by noon on Saturday, after which Roosevelt lunched with Anna. Sitting under the grand magnolia tree which had been planted during Andrew Jackson's days in the White House and still boasted huge branches, lemon-scented blossoms, and glossy leaves, Anna agreed to join her father that evening for dinner with Lucy.

At 6:20 p.m. on Saturday, the president called for his car and asked to be driven to 2238 Q Street in Georgetown to call on Mrs. Rutherfurd. After he picked her up at the door, they drove together through the streets of Washington as they had done so many years before. Arriving at the White House, he brought her to his study, where Anna and John were waiting to join them for cocktails and dinner. If Roosevelt experienced a moment of awkwardness when he introduced his favorite child to the woman whose love had nearly destroyed his marriage, he undoubtedly covered it up.

To Roosevelt's delight, the two women liked each other. Anna was immediately impressed by Lucy's "innate dignity and poise which commanded respect." She found Lucy "most attractive and stately" but "warm and friendly" at the same time. For her part, Lucy understood immediately why this beautiful young woman with unbounded vitality, warmth, and humor meant so much to her father.

Anna had not seen Lucy for nearly three decades, but she remembered her clearly. She recalled as a child "feeling happy" whenever Lucy was working in the house. "I liked her warm and friendly manner and smile," Anna later wrote in an unpublished article. For her part, Lucy understood how important it was to Roosevelt that the two of them get along. "Anna is a dear fine person," Roosevelt had written Lucy earlier; "I wish so much that you knew her."

The president's butler, Alonzo Fields, served dinner. "You could sense that this was a special evening," he later recalled. "You could feel that this was someone warm who cared a great deal about him. From then on, every time Lucy came, the president would have no one else but me serve them."

There was much to talk about that night. Across the ocean, London was reeling from a terrifying barrage of Germany's newest weapon, the V-1 flying bomb, a pilotless rocket-powered craft launched from giant concrete bunkers in German-occupied territory in northern France. The V-1 carried more than twelve thousand pounds of high explosives and fell indiscriminately on people and buildings alike. In two weeks, nearly three thousand people had been killed and over ten thousand wounded. Had the V-1 and its even more formidable successor, the V-2 liquid-fuel rocket, been developed earlier in the war, the balance of power might have been fatally tilted against the Allies. But by July 1944, the Allies were moving forward in every sector of the war.

In Normandy, the last German strongholds in Cherbourg had surrendered. On the Eastern front, the Red Army had begun a powerful new offensive that found its troops surging westward into Poland. More than 130,000 Germans had been killed in the last week of June, and sixty-six thousand taken prisoner. And in the Southwest Pacific, after a series of assaults, Allied troops were advancing rapidly along the coast of New Guinea.

Beyond world events, there were memories to share: silly stories Roosevelt loved to tell and retell, "all the ridiculous things," Lucy later wrote, he liked "to say—and do—and enjoy." Years later, Anna's son Johnny Boettiger could easily understand why Anna and Lucy got along so well, and why this meant so much to the president. "The three of them had a capacity for loving humor, for having fun. It wasn't a tight, ironic sense of humor. It was a silly humor that didn't respect the boundaries they all imagined Eleanor would impose."

It was after midnight when Roosevelt retired, but he awakened early the next morning so he could take Lucy on a day trip to Shangri-la. Were Lucy and Roosevelt lovers at this point? It is impossible to know, though, given the state of Roosevelt's health, doubt remains. Still, even if they did not share the same bed, it is reasonable to imagine that there was a pleasing sexuality in their friendship.

Yet, of all the pleasures Lucy gave, perhaps the most important was her willingness and ability to talk to Roosevelt about what was happening to his health. Having nursed her husband through illness for seven years, she must have been highly attuned to the fear and frustration of being inside a body that was breaking down. If Roosevelt was able to talk at all about his fears, about what it was like to be in pain, about the prospect of death, it would have been with Lucy. With everyone else, he had to summon up his energies to be cheerful. But with Lucy, it is possible that he was able to drop his act, to admit his fears and demonstrate his anger.

•   •   •

While Roosevelt was enjoying the company of Lucy Rutherfurd, Eleanor was in Hyde Park celebrating a noteworthy advance against segregation in the South. That Saturday, July 8, 1944, the War Department issued an order to all commanding generals directing that all "buses, trucks or other transportation owned and operated either by the government or by government instrumentality will be available to all military personnel regardless of race. Restricting personnel to certain sections of such transportation because of race will not be permitted either on or off a post camp, or station, regardless of local civilian custom."

The War Department directive spoke squarely to the primary source of racial tension in the South. Restricted by law to a few seats at the back of the bus, Negro soldiers were often relegated to stand at the bus stop for hours as overcrowded buses passed them by. Where separate buses were provided for Negroes and whites, the "colored" buses usually ran on less frequent schedules, forcing Negro soldiers to watch as dozens of "white" buses containing empty seats drove past.

There were scores of incidents. In Savannah, Georgia, forty-three miles from Camp Stewart, the Greyhound bus terminal had separate ticket windows for whites and coloreds. One employee handled both windows; he regularly made the colored GIs wait until all the whites were taken care of, even if the colored GIs had arrived first. It could take up to twelve hours for the Negro soldier to buy a ticket. Yet, if he was late getting back to camp, he was considered AWOL and issued a service penalty.

In Louisiana, a group of nine Negro GIs boarded a train for transfer from the hospital at Camp Claiborne to the hospital at Fort Huachuca in Arizona. The train was delayed for twelve hours. "The only place that would serve us was the lunch room at the station," one of the nine reported. "But we couldn't eat where the white people were eating. To do that would contaminate the very air of the place, so we had to go to the kitchen. That was bad enough but that's not all. About 11:30 that same morning, about two dozen German prisoners of war came to the lunchroom with two guards. They entered the large room, sat at the table. Then meals were served them. They smoked and had a swell time. As we stood on the outside and saw what was going on, we could scarcely believe our own eyes. There they sat: eating, talking, laughing, smoking. They were enemies of our country, people sworn to destroy all the so-called democratic governments of the world. . . . What are we fighting for?"

Resentments multiplied. In Beaumont, Texas, Charles Rico, a black private, was ordered off a bus because he took a vacant seat in a section reserved for whites. After he left the bus, he was beaten by a white policeman and shot twice through the shoulder and the arm. In Mobile, Alabama, where bus drivers were authorized to carry firearms to enforce local laws and customs, Private Henry Williams, a black soldier, was shot and killed when he walked to the wrong section of the bus. In Montgomery, Alabama, a black nurse, Lieutenant Norma Greene, boarded a bus after a shopping tour in preparation for overseas duty. When she refused to get out of the bus after the driver told her it was a "white" bus, she was so badly beaten that her nose was broken and her eyes were blackened.

"[Negroes] have been instructed to regard themselves as soldiers," warned Truman Gibson, civilian aide to the Secretary of War. "They are not conditioned to withstand the shock of attitudes" to which they are subjected day in and day out. One black corporal, insulted by a conductor, threw a "colored only" sign out the window. He was immediately arrested and carried back to camp as a common criminal. "Honey, I am so hurt inside," he wrote his girlfriend, "so much that I don't really know what to do. . . . Just think I may have to fight some day, but honey what will I be fighting for, surely not the rotten conditions we have to bear down here."

For months, Eleanor had been pushing the War Department to do something about the public-transit situation. Responding to innumerable letters from black soldiers, she had barraged the War Department with questions and comments. She understood, she wrote John McCloy, that, if the bus was privately owned, there was nothing the army could do about it. But if it was an army bus, then it was unconscionable to allow segregation to stand. "These colored boys lie side by side in the hospitals in the southwest Pacific with the white boys and somehow it is hard for me to believe that they should not be treated on an equal basis."

Though the directive of July 8, 1944, covered only government-owned or -operated buses, liberals hailed it as "an important step forward in the fight to abolish discrimination," and the Negro press treated it as a great victory. "Extra! Extra!" the *Baltimore Afro-American* headlined: "US Army Bans Jim Crow." "Here It Is!" the *Pittsburgh Courier* enthused, publishing the full text of the order.

Among Southern whites, not surprisingly, the order provoked a fiery protest. Governor Chauncey Sparks of Alabama warned the White House that its malicious action threatened to break down "the essential principle of race relations in the South." As a consequence, Southern politicians would find it extremely difficult "to hold the south within its traditional democratic allegiance in the years to come."

Once again, Eleanor Roosevelt became the target of Southern criticism. A new round of rumors spread, stories of "Eleanor Tuesdays," days when Negro women supposedly went out into the streets en masse with the goal of knocking Southern white women to the ground. There is no evidence that such days actually existed, but so widespread were the rumors that many white women in the South were afraid to go out of their houses on Tuesdays.

Despite the hysterical overtones of the Southern protest, the War Department refused, this time, to back away from its assertion that all soldiers should be treated alike. "This knowledge," army historians observed, "raised morale higher in many units than the construction of the most elaborate service club." Never, Howard University Dean William Hastie assured John McCloy, "have I seen so much enthusiasm and goodwill generated by a particular bit of official action. . . . I think it means more to the Negro soldier than you can possibly realize."

•　•　•

Dramatic changes in the navy that summer gave Eleanor further cause for satisfaction. Under James Forrestal, the boyish-looking financier who had succeeded Frank Knox as secretary on May 11, 1944, the navy was taking unprecedented strides toward racial equality. Within weeks of becoming secretary, Forrestal had instituted a series of experiments designed to bring an end to the navy's dismal record in the use of Negro personnel.

The first change was reflected in a memo to the president on May 20. "Up to the present time," Forrestal observed, though the navy had opened its general service ranks to Negroes in 1942, "the majority of Negroes have been employed in the Shore Establishment," performing the arduous, prosaic work involved in handling ammunition and loading ships. To many Negroes, it seemed that they had simply "swapped the waiter's apron for the stevedore's grappling hook." Looking at the situation, Forrestal concluded that precious energy, money, and morale were being wasted by the navy's insistence on separating Negroes and whites. The time had come "to expand the use of Negro personnel by assigning them to general sea duty."

Forrestal's proposal, which Roosevelt readily approved, called for Negroes to make up 10 percent of the crews of twenty-five large auxiliary ships. To the surprise of many, who had to revise their established notions and prejudices about the Negro's proper place, the experiment worked remarkably well. Official navy records indicate that colored personnel were being "successfully absorbed in the ships' companies." The experiment was then extended to smaller vessels, where, against even higher odds, black and white crew members managed, with a minimum of fuss, to work, eat, and sleep together in extremely close quarters.

Forrestal's innovations came none too soon, for, that July, a bloody tragedy at the ammunition depot at Port Chicago in northern California provided unmistakable evidence of the bankruptcy of the navy's old segregation policy. On the night of July 17, more than six hundred men, mostly black, were hard at work loading tons of ammunition, high explosives, and incendiary bombs into the holds of the S.S. *Bryan*. Shortly after 10 p.m., a deafening explosion erupted. The *Bryan* was sundered in pieces, everyone on the pier was instantly killed, the naval base was left in ruins, and the town of Port Chicago was damaged. Two hundred and two blacks were killed, and another 233 injured. "This single stunning disaster," sociologist Robert Allen observed, "accounted for more than 15 percent of all black naval casualties during the war. It was the worst homefront disaster of World War II."

The loss of so many black sailors at once focused public attention on the injustice of racial discrimination in the navy, motivating Forrestal to press even more strongly for equality of treatment for blacks. In the weeks that followed, he moved in several directions at once: assigning white work units to Port Chicago and other ammo depots; stating that he no longer considered practical the establishment of separate facilities and quotas for Negroes who qualified for advanced training; appointing more Negroes to the navy's V-12 program; insisting on Negro admittance to the Naval Academy; and issuing a far-reaching "Guide to Command of Negro Naval Personnel." In this guide, which *Commonweal* regarded as "an outstanding document in the field of race relations," the navy stated for the first time that it accepted "no theories of racial differences in inborn ability, but expects that every man wearing its uniform be trained and used in accord with his maximum individual capacity determined on the basis of individual performance."

The Negro press and liberal spokesmen were exultant, observing that change in the navy was now coming faster and further than anyone had thought possible. "This improvement" was all the more spectacular, *Commonweal* observed, "in that at the beginning of the war the Navy's race policy was considered worse than the Army's."

To Eleanor, the policy changes in both the army and the navy afforded profound gratification. Indeed, had she been given the choice between supplying the relaxation for her husband that Lucy was providing, or summoning her powers to effect a change in the lives of Negro Americans, she would undoubtedly have chosen the latter. After two decades of social activism, Eleanor's commitment to the underdog had become such an integral part of her makeup that it is impossible to imagine her without a cause to fight.

• • •

On Tuesday morning, July 11, five days before the opening of the Democratic convention in Chicago, Roosevelt finally let it be known that he would accept his party's nomination for a fourth term. At his regular press conference, he read aloud a letter he had written to Bob Hannegan, chairman of the Democratic National Committee. In the letter, in a reversal of the famous statement General William Sherman had made when he renounced plans to run for office, he pledged that if the convention nominated him for the presidency he would accept, and that if the people, the ultimate authority, commanded him to serve he would have "as little right to withdraw as the soldier has to leave his post in the line."

"All that is within me cries out to go back to my home on the Hudson River," he went on, "but the future existence of the nation and the future existence of our chosen form of government are at stake."

While the president was making his momentous announcement, Eleanor was in Dayton, Ohio, preparing for a luncheon talk to a group of three hundred WACs at Wright Field. Approached by reporters, she said her husband's decision was news to her. "The President doesn't discuss these things with me. Many people think he does but most often the first I know of some decision is when I see it in the papers."

Eleanor viewed Franklin's candidacy with mixed emotions. On the one hand, she believed her husband's victory was essential for "the good of the country." The thought of the Republican nominee, Governor Thomas Dewey, as president worried her deeply. "Dewey seems to me more and more to show no understanding of the job at home or abroad," she wrote James. And though she realized that her husband had tended to tire more easily in recent months, she was convinced, she told James, that "if elected, he'll do his job well. I feel sure and I think he can be kept well to do it." On the other hand, the thought of another four years of White House life was almost more than she could bear. "I am very conscious of age and the short time in which I have to live as I like," she admitted to Joe Lash, "and I know that it is such selfish thinking that no one has a right to even let it be in one's mind."

There was no such ambivalence on Capitol Hill. When the news reached the Democratic senators, reporter Allen Drury observed, "it was as though the sun had burst from the clouds and glory surrounded the world. Relief, and I mean relief, was written on every face. The meal ticket was still the meal ticket and all was well with the party."

In accepting the nomination in advance of the convention's decision on the vice-presidency, Roosevelt had discarded the club he might have used to drive the convention into naming the running mate he himself wanted. The choice of the vice-president would be left up to the delegates.

"I am just not going through a convention like 1940 again," he explained, recalling the lengths he had gone to ensure the re-election of Wallace. "It will split the party wide open and it is already split enough between North and South, it may kill our chances for election this fall and if it does it will prolong the war and knock into a cocked hat all the plans we've been making for the future."

The president's apparent indifference to the choice of a running mate worried his aides. "He just doesn't give a damn," Pa Watson observed. Had Roosevelt been in good health, his lack of concern about his potential successor would have been understandable. But since he at least suspected that he was unlikely to live out a full term, it remains incomprehensible.

In truth, Roosevelt's mind that summer was moving in a different direction; his dream was to join hands with Republican Wendell Willkie in the creation of a new liberal party that would combine the liberal elements of the Democratic Party, minus the reactionary elements in the South, with the liberal elements of the Republican Party. Since Willkie had been defeated at the Republican convention by the conservative wing of his party, Roosevelt hoped he would be receptive to the idea. "We ought to have two real parties," Roosevelt told his aide Sam Rosenman, "one liberal and the other conservative. As it is now each party is split by dissenters."

To sound Willkie out, Roosevelt dispatched Rosenman to meet with him in New York in early July. "The meeting obviously had to be a complete secret," Rosenman later recalled, "so I had lunch served in a private suite in the St. Regis Hotel." Indeed, Willkie was so anxious lest anyone find out that he stepped into the bedroom of the suite when lunch arrived so the waiter would not recognize him.

Willkie was instantly drawn to the idea. "You tell the President that I'm ready to devote almost full time to this," he said. "A sound liberal government in the U.S. is absolutely essential to continued co-operation with the other nations of the world." Willkie went on to say he would be glad to meet with Roosevelt to discuss the plan more fully but "he was convinced that the meeting should not take place until after the election."

Roosevelt was so pleased with Willkie's positive response that he couldn't wait. On July 13, he dictated a letter asking Willkie to join him as soon as possible for an off-the-record meeting either in the White House or at Hyde Park, "just as you think best." Unfortunately, news of the letter leaked out, causing great embarrassment to both Willkie and Roosevelt. Now there was no choice, Willkie insisted, but to wait until after the election. (Roosevelt's dream of creating a liberal party would never be realized. In the fall, while Willkie was in the hospital for a minor ailment, he had a massive heart attack and died.)

Meanwhile, Roosevelt was up to his usual games, making each person who came to see him feel that he was the one the president wanted. "He said I was his choice," Henry Wallace recorded in his diary after a meeting on July 10, and at lunch later that week, "He drew me close and turned on his full smile and a very hearty hand clasp, saying, 'I hope it will be the same team.' " Yet, at Shangri-la two weeks earlier, Roosevelt had assured Jimmy Byrnes that *he* was the president's choice for vice-president. "You are the best qualified man in the whole outfit," Roosevelt told Byrnes; "if you stay in you are sure to win."

The plot thickened on July 11, when Roosevelt met with the political bosses—DNC Chair Robert Hannegan, Frank Walker, and Ed Flynn—to discuss the vice-presidency. Over dinner and drinks, with everyone in shirt-sleeves because of the oppressive heat, the full list of candidates was examined. Wallace was rejected out of hand. He was too intellectual, too liberal, too idealistic, too impractical, the bosses claimed. If he were nominated, he would cost the ticket from one to three million votes. Byrnes was just as quickly undone; as a lapsed Catholic and a Southerner with segregationist views, he would alienate Catholics and Negroes. Barkley was a good man, but he was too old.

Roosevelt proposed Supreme Court Justice William O. Douglas. Before Roosevelt appointed him to the Court in 1939, Douglas had been a professor of law at Yale and the chairman of the Securities and Exchange Commission, where he led the fight to bring public utilities under federal regulation. He was young and energetic, the president said, and, what was more, he played an interesting game of poker. Despite Roosevelt's obvious enthusiasm for Douglas, no one else picked up the idea. The talk turned then to Senator Harry Truman. He was a good Democrat, he was from the Midwest, his record on labor was good, and, as Flynn observed, "he had never made any 'racial' remarks." Concerned about Truman's age, which no one could pinpoint (he was sixty), Roosevelt sent for the *Congressional Directory* to check his date of birth. But by the time the *Directory* arrived, the conversation had drifted to other subjects. As the meeting broke up, Roosevelt turned to Hannegan and said, "Bob, I think you and everyone else here want Truman."

Pleased with the turn of events, Hannegan asked Roosevelt to put something in writing. Using a pencil, Roosevelt scribbled an unofficial one-line note on the back of an envelope. "Bob, I think Truman is the right man." It was more than Hannegan had hoped to achieve, but, given Roosevelt's propensity for telling each person what he wanted to hear, it was not enough. A day or so later, Roosevelt was again urging both Wallace and Byrnes to run. The decision was still up in the air.

• • •

In the midst of all the confusion, the president set out for California in his private railroad car, the Ferdinand Magellan, on the first leg of a monthlong journey that would ultimately take him to Hawaii for a discussion of Pacific strategy. Boarding the train in Hyde Park, accompanied by Eleanor and Tommy, Pa Watson and Sam Rosenman, Grace Tully and Dr. Bruenn, he ordered the engineers to move slowly so he would not arrive in San Diego until the convention had completed its balloting for the presidential nomination.

Politics could not be avoided altogether, however. When the train reached Chicago, Bob Hannegan came aboard. The president was just finishing lunch with Eleanor and Sam Rosenman. "We excused ourselves," Rosenman recalled, "and left Hannegan alone with the President for about an hour." The convention was convulsed in bloody turmoil, the DNC chair said; unless the president made his wishes known, there was no telling what would happen. Though still reluctant to "dictate" to the convention after his experience in 1940, Roosevelt agreed to sign a letter which said in essence that he would be very glad to run with either Bill Douglas or Harry Truman, since either one "would bring real strength to the ticket."

At the last minute, Hannegan came running back to Grace Tully. "Grace, the President wants you to retype this letter and to switch the names so it will read 'Harry Truman and Bill Douglas.'"

"The reason for the switch was obvious," Tully later observed. "By naming Truman first it was plainly implied by the letter that he was the preferred choice. By that narrow margin and rather casual action did one man rather than another, perhaps one policy rather than another, eventually arrive at the head of the American government in April of 45."

Since the trip was an official secret, there were no scheduled stops, no crowds to address, no questions to answer. Yet, as the armor-plated train slowly wended its way through the steel mills of Indiana and the cornfields of Oklahoma, rumors began to spread. At various stations along the way, the familiar face of Mrs. Roosevelt was seen; on numerous platforms, the president's little dog, Fala, was spotted taking a stretch. These sightings soon dispelled any questions: the president's train was passing through!

"The trip out was slow and peaceful," Tommy reported to Esther Lape. "We did little work, read and played gin-rummy." For Roosevelt, the leisurely pace of the trip was ideal. For him, the train was a small human community, a society of friends whose conversation was all he needed for stimulation.

This was the first occasion in a long while on which Roosevelt and his wife had spent so much relaxing time together. "The slow speed was a good thing for us both," Franklin later wrote her.

The unbroken hours allowed Franklin to share with Eleanor his hopes for the future, evoking a picture of the happiness that would be theirs once the presidency was over. He wanted to take her on a trip around the world, he said. He talked of buying land in the Sahara Desert and of demonstrating to the Arabs the miracles that could be accomplished through irrigation, electrification, and reforestation. "I think it would be fun," he said, "to go and live in the desert for two or three years and see what we could do." He went over all the details of that faraway period—imagining the trip on a slow freighter that would allow them to take in all the sights along the way.

Engrossed as Eleanor must have been in the charm of the conversation, she still felt the need to protect herself, to preserve the physical and emotional space that had grown between them. She could not let him continue without interrupting him, without reminding him that she had hated long sea voyages ever since she was a child. Undeterred, Franklin went on to suggest a happy compromise. If Eleanor preferred, she could travel instead by air, swooping down to meet his freighter at all the locations they wished to visit and explore!

Whereas Franklin would have lingered on the train for several additional weeks, Eleanor couldn't wait to escape. "Mrs. R was impatient at the slow speed and the waste of time," Tommy observed. Work refused to leave her mind, even for these few summer days. "I don't know that I'm being very useful on the trip as there is nothing to do," she wrote Trude Pratt. "FDR sleeps, eats, works and all I do is sit through long meals which are sometimes interesting and sometimes very dull." If Roosevelt sensed his wife's discomfort, it must have been frustrating for him to realize that she alone was immune to his charms. He could regale everyone else with his sparkling conversation, but his wife was bored!

More than likely, Roosevelt remained oblivious to Eleanor's distress.

Though he liked to think he was savoring her presence, he spent almost no time with her alone. "I don't know why we went," Tommy complained, no doubt echoing Eleanor's sentiments, "as there were many cronies on the train so the President would not have been lonesome." Once again, the possibility of real togetherness was opened and closed before either partner fully understood what was going on.

• • •

When the train reached San Diego on July 20, 1944, Franklin and Eleanor were joined by their son Jimmy and John's wife, Anne Clark, who had moved with their children to California when her husband was transferred to the Pacific. Lunch was served at Anne's house in Coronado, and Jimmy hosted a family dinner. After dinner, Eleanor and Tommy left for Los Angeles, where a plane was waiting to carry them back to Washington.

The next morning, while the convention readied itself for the presidential balloting, Roosevelt was scheduled to review an amphibious-landing exercise in Oceanside, California. Just before he was about to leave, he turned "suddenly white," Jimmy recalled; "his face took on an agonized look."

"Jimmy, I don't know if I can make it," he said. "I have horrible pains." Jimmy was so frightened he wanted to call the doctor, but Roosevelt resisted. It was just stomach pains, he insisted, indigestion from eating too fast and not being able to exercise. He'd be all right in a few minutes if only Jimmy would help him out of his berth and let him stretch out flat on the floor for a while. "So for perhaps ten minutes," Jimmy wrote, "Father lay on the floor of the railroad car, his eyes closed, his face drawn, his powerful torso occasionally convulsed as the waves of pain stabbed him. Never in all my life had I felt so alone with him—and so helpless."

Gradually, his body stopped shaking and the color returned to his face. "Help me up now, Jimmy," he said. "I feel better." Minutes later, he was seated in an open car, heading to the amphibious-training base to witness the Fifth Marine's practice invasion—a colossal exercise involving five thousand Marines and three thousand naval personnel. Situated atop a high bluff overlooking the beach below, he watched the smooth unloading of men and equipment from dozens of landing craft of the type recently used in the landings on Guam.

During the afternoon, he received word from the convention chairman, Samuel D. Jackson, that he had been officially nominated for a fourth term as president. Later that night, speaking from the observation car of his train, he delivered his acceptance speech. "What is the job before us in 1944?" he asked. "First, to win the war—to win the war fast, to win it overpoweringly. Second, to form worldwide international organizations . . . And third, to build an economy for our returning veterans and for all Americans—which will provide employment and provide decent standards of living."

It was not a memorable speech, but the immense crowd filling the Chicago stadium loved it. As the familiar voice came booming through the amplifiers, forty thousand people cheered. Their captain would see them through after all.

Afterward, with Jimmy by his side, a relaxed Roosevelt posed at the table, rereading portions of the speech so a pool of photographers could take pictures. Since there were no processing facilities in San Diego, all the film was flown up to Los Angeles, where the AP agreed to process it and transmit prints to everyone. At the AP, a young editor named Dick Strobel took the film out of the hypo fixing agent and exposed it to light. "There were several negatives to choose from," Strobel later recalled. "In one his mouth was closed; in the other it was open. I chose the one with the open mouth, since it was more obvious that he was talking. I went into my office to write the caption while the darkroom technicians processed the print."

When the picture came out, the photographer, George Skaddings, was appalled. "Hey, you better look at this," he told Strobel. The open mouth made Roosevelt look terrible: his eyes were glassy, his face was haggard, his expression weary. By then, however, it was close to 11 p.m., or 2 a.m. on the East Coast. The papers were yelling for the picture. Strobel decided he couldn't wait any longer to print another negative. "I made the judgment to go with what we had."

The next day, Strobel recalled, "all hell broke loose," as every anti-Roosevelt paper blew the picture up and displayed it prominently. In Washington, the president's press secretary, Steve Early, was furious, and called Skaddings on the carpet. "It's not my fault," Skaddings insisted. "I just shot the picture. Some idiot in L.A. picked it." Early kicked Skaddings off the tour, but the damage was done. The unfortunate photo, which Rosenman insisted bore no resemblance to the man he watched deliver the speech that night, provided Republicans with precisely the ammunition they needed to bolster their argument: the old man was no longer physically capable of being president.

Nominations for the vice-presidency began the next afternoon. Wallace took an early lead, but by the end of the second ballot Truman had emerged the clear-cut victor. Back in Hyde Park, Eleanor was "sick about the whole business." A fervent Wallace supporter, she "had hoped until the last," she wrote Esther Lape, "that Mr. Wallace might have strength enough." It was "bad politics" not to stick to Wallace, as well as "disloyal." Nonetheless, she was much more satisfied with Senator Truman than she would have been with Byrnes or any of the other conservatives who were being considered. Though she did not know Truman, "from all I hear," she wrote, "he is a good man."

•   •   •

At midnight that Friday, July 21, following a zigzag course in a darkened cruiser, Roosevelt sailed westward from San Diego for Pearl Harbor. "Off in a few minutes," he wrote Eleanor, but suggested he might have to hurry back earlier if the German revolt against Hitler got worse. The day before, a group of German officers led by Lieutenant Colonel Klaus von Stauffenberg had tried to assassinate Hitler. At the last minute, however, the briefcase holding the bomb had been inadvertently pushed to the far side of the room, and Hitler had survived the blast. Roosevelt's trip to Hawaii would go forward as planned.

"Yesterday a.m. Jimmy and I had a grand view of the landing operation at Camp Pendleton," he told Eleanor, "and then I got the collywobbles and stayed in the train in the p.m. It was grand having you come out with me."

A tremendous crowd was gathered at the pier when the president's cruiser pulled in. As far as the eye could see, men in whites were standing at attention at the rails of dozens of navy ships. A rousing cheer went up as the gangplank was lowered to receive Admiral Nimitz and some fifty high-ranking officials. Greeting everyone on the deck of the *Baltimore,* Roosevelt observed that one person was noticeably absent—General Douglas MacArthur. When asked where the general was, Nimitz retreated into an embarrassed silence. MacArthur's plane from Brisbane had landed an hour earlier, but the general had insisted on going to his quarters first to drop off his bag and take a bath. The welcoming ceremony was just about to break up when a shrieking siren was heard, indicating MacArthur's arrival. Stepping out from his limo, wearing his leather flying jacket, MacArthur acknowledged the tumultuous applause and raced up the gangplank.

That evening, the president invited both Nimitz and MacArthur to join him for dinner at the elegant beach estate which had been made available to him during his stay. After dinner, the strategic talks began. Seated before a huge wall map of the Pacific, the president reviewed America's situation, using a bamboo pointer to indicate the islands where battles were still being fought.

For six weeks, the American navy had been engaged in a bitter struggle with the Japanese for the control of Saipan, Guam, and Tinian, three of the Mariana Islands. The battle for Saipan had been particularly bloody—more than fourteen thousand marines had been killed—but on July 9, the island had been secured. Two weeks later, both Guam and Tinian had been captured. These were major victories: with the Marianas under control, the mighty B-29s, the largest aircraft ever produced, would finally have the bases from which they could bomb Japan.

Roosevelt's interest in bombing Japan had never diminished, despite the overwhelming difficulties involved. For years he had followed the B-29 through its production and teething problems, never losing faith in General Arnold's quest for a larger, heavier, and more powerful version of the B-17. "The B-29 was a great gamble," military historian William Emerson observed. "General Arnold had committed $3 billion to its production before a single prototype had even been flown. This was more than the Manhattan Project. But Roosevelt backed him all the way, convinced that a superbomber was the only way to get at Japan offensively."

In mid-June, the first B-29s had taken off from eastern China: their target, the iron- and steelworks at Yawata on Kyushu Island. Though the raid produced little material damage, the boost to American morale was enormous. And now, with the capture of the Marianas, they could launch many more direct raids against Japan.

The question was: where to go from here? Admiral Nimitz proposed a direct assault on Formosa and the Chinese coast, bypassing the Philippines and all the small islands along the way. MacArthur disagreed, pressing for the liberation of the Philippines and the bypassing of Formosa. America, he argued, had a moral responsibility to avenge the crushing defeat of 1942, to liberate the Filipinos and to free the American prisoners of war. If Roosevelt chose to bypass the Philippines, MacArthur warned, "I dare to say that the American people would be so aroused that they would register most complete resentment against you in the polls."

"In such a situation," James MacGregor Burns has observed, "Roosevelt was at his best, skillfully placating both the Admiral and the General, steering the discussion away from absolutes, narrowing the differences." In the end, Roosevelt sided with MacArthur, pledging that America would not bypass the Philippines. "As soon as I get back," he promised the flamboyant general, "I will push on that plan [for liberating the Philippines] for I am convinced that as a whole it is logical and can be done." As a matter of fact, Roosevelt went on, he wished he and MacArthur could swap places, though "I have a hunch that you would make more of a go as President than I would as General in retaking the Philippines."

When the strategy sessions were completed, the president traveled around Oahu, inspecting shipyards, hospitals, training grounds, and airfields. "At one of the hospitals," Rosenman reported, "the President did something which affected us all very deeply. He asked a secret service man to wheel him slowly through all the wards that were occupied by veterans who had lost one or more arms and legs. He insisted on going past each individual bed. He wanted to display himself and his useless legs to those boys who would have to face the same bitterness."

Roosevelt generally allowed himself to be seen in public in only two situations—either standing with his braces locked, or seated in an open car. But here, in the presence of so many young amputees, he was willing to reveal his vulnerability, to let them see that he was as crippled as they. "With a cheering smile to each of them," Rosenman observed, "and a pleasant word at the bedside of a score or more, this man who had risen from a bed of helplessness ultimately to become President of the United States and leader of the free world was living proof of what the human spirit could do."

There was one other occasion when Roosevelt had allowed a group of strangers to witness his infirmity, according to Anna Faith Jones. The occasion was the dedication of a new building at Howard University in 1936. Before the ceremony began, Jones' father, Howard's president, Mordecai Johnson, had asked Roosevelt to allow the students to see that he was crippled. They had been so crippled themselves, Johnson pleaded, if the president let them see him as he was, they could say to themselves, If he can do this, we can do anything. Roosevelt agreed. He let himself be lifted from the car and set down in full public view, and then he proceeded to walk slowly and painfully to the podium.

Rosenman claimed he had never seen the president with tears in his eyes, but that afternoon in Oahu, as he was wheeled out of the hospital, "he was close to them." Later that day, Roosevelt reboarded the *Baltimore* for the final leg of his long journey—a visit to the troops at Adak, a treeless island located off the western coast of Alaska.

"THE OLD MASTER

STILL HAD IT"

On Sunday evening, July 30, 1944, while Roosevelt was cruising the Pacific en route to Alaska, Missy Le-Hand was in the movie theater at Harvard Square with her sister Ann Rochon and her friend Maydell Ramsey. A double feature was playing that night: *The Man from Down Under,* starring Charles Laughton as a World War I veteran who smuggles two orphans back into Australia, and *Rationing,* a light comedy about a small-town storekeeper frustrated by wartime restrictions.

The accompanying newsreel featured images of Roosevelt's acceptance speech, delivered from his railroad car at San Diego. As the story was told to Missy's friend Barbara Curtis, "Missy was shocked at the way he looked and the way his voice sounded." Having not seen his picture for several months, she was unaware of all the weight he had lost, unprepared for the haggard look on his face. Until this moment, she had still envisioned him as the vigorous, well-built man she had last seen the previous spring.

It was raining at 11 p.m., when Missy returned to her Orchard Street home. In her bedroom, she began agitatedly leafing through old pictures, almost as if she were trying to conjure up a substitute image for the one that was now in her mind. In her collection of photos she had a handsome shot of Roosevelt in a striped bathing suit, a charming picture of the two of them sitting together on the porch at Warm Springs, a group shot at a picnic. Suddenly her left arm, which had not moved since her stroke three years earlier, began to move up and down. It seemed for a moment as if she might finally recover her faculties.

But the reprieve was short-lived. Sometime after midnight, Ann heard strange noises coming from her sister's room. Looking in, she saw Missy tremble violently and then slump over. An ambulance was called, and at 2 a.m. Missy was taken to Chelsea Naval Hospital.

There doctors determined that she had suffered a cerebral embolism. Death came seven hours later, shortly after 9 a.m. The death certificate listed auricular fibrillation and rheumatic heart disease as contributing factors to the fatal embolism. She was forty-six years old.

Eleanor was in Hyde Park when the news reached her. She immediately sent a telegram to Missy's sister, offering to come to Boston to be with the family during the funeral. "I am sure that for her, after her long illness, death will be a release," Eleanor wrote in her column. "But those who loved her . . . will feel her loss deeply. She was a member of our family for a good many years."

Roosevelt received the sad news by means of a radiogram to his ship from William Hassett and Steve Early. "Regret to inform you that Miss LeHand died in the Naval Hospital at Chelsea at 9:05 today. . . . Admiral Sheldon [of the Bureau of Medicine and Surgery] said she had attended theater last evening and that the change for the worse was unexpected. . . . Have notified Mrs. Roosevelt and Miss Tully. Await instructions."

A second radiogram followed a few hours later, letting the president know that Mrs. Roosevelt would attend the funeral and that his absence had been carefully explained to Missy's family. "I'm glad F is away," Eleanor confided to Lash, "for he would have felt he had to come and these journeys are always depressing."

A statement was drafted in the White House and issued in the president's name. "Memories of more than a score of years of devoted service enhance the sense of personal loss which Miss LeHand's passing brings. Faithful and painstaking, with a charm of manner inspired by tact and kindness of heart, she was utterly selfless in her devotion to duty."

"Missy's death," Arthur Krock noted in *The New York Times,* "severs a shining link between these grim times and the exciting days when the New Deal and the administration were young. Her influence upon the President was very great and constructive as was Mr. Howe's. Many of the friendliest observers of Mr. Roosevelt since he took office have, after these intimate counselors left the White House, attributed certain acts and words of his that evoked widespread criticism to the loss of their devoted and wise services." Writing in a similar vein, Harold Ickes observed that Missy's disability "constituted the greatest loss that the President has suffered since his inauguration."

Letters of condolence poured into the White House, revealing the extraordinary impact Missy had on all those who had come to know her. "What the devil can a fellow say," Roosevelt's old friend Ralph Cropley wrote, "who was as close to Missy as I was in those days when Missy, Louis Howe and I put up the fight to instill in that head of yours the desire to live? Outside of Eleanor, no one knows more than I what sacrifices Missy made for you. She was one of the grandest persons who ever lived."

"I know how profoundly affected you are by Missy's death," journalist Herbert Swope wrote the president. "I, too, loved Missy. She was a rare person in her loyalty, in her intelligence, her courage and her principles."

Some twelve hundred persons attended the funeral mass at St. John's Church in North Cambridge. Hundreds more stood outside as the president's wife, wearing a blue suit and a black straw hat, arrived to join the LeHand family in the second row. The mourners included James Farley, Former Boston Police Commissioner Joseph Timilty, and Joseph Kennedy. Bishop Richard J. Cushing read the prayers, and the body was lowered into a grave at Mount Auburn Cemetery.

To family and friends in the working-class community of Somerville, Massachusetts, Missy was a celebrity. "She was a real role model in our whole family's history," Missy's grand-niece Jane Scarborough observed. "Her life had glamour, excitement, independence, and mystery. I remember when Elliott Roosevelt's book came out implying a romance between the president and Missy, I asked my aunt [Marguerite Collins] what she thought. 'It would be nice to have some spicy past in our family,' she replied with a smile, 'but I simply don't know.'"

Since her sister Ann's divorce, Missy had supported her two nieces, Barbara and Marguerite. It was Missy who took care of their education and bought their clothes for school. "There was an air of magic about Missy," neighbor Barbara Dudley recalled. "She had the most beautiful jewelry, which Ambassador Bullitt had given her. When I was young, I loved to go into her room with my friends and peek in her bureau drawers. She had magnificent underwear from Paris and sweet-smelling perfume. We'd try everything on and then put it all back into the drawers in exactly the same order, so she'd never know."

In her will, Missy divided her belongings between her two nieces. To Marguerite she gave her mink coat, wristwatch with diamonds, small diamond ring, and, perhaps her most precious possession, the small hanging bookcase that President Roosevelt had made for her. To Barbara went her ermine cape, gold watch, and amethyst earrings given to her by Mr. and Mrs. Roosevelt.

The rest of her things—photographs, appointment books, signed drafts of the president's inaugurals and fireside chats—were packed in an old brown suitcase and kept in her sister's closet. The suitcase ended up in Connecticut, in the attic of Barbara's daughter, Jane Scarborough. Years later, Scarborough dimly remembered seeing what must have been the hanging bookcase that Roosevelt made for Missy. "It was in my brother's attic. We often wondered if there were a story behind it. But no one in our generation had any idea what it was. It was so ugly. I think in the end it went off in a garage sale. I wish I had realized what it meant to Missy."

"You and I lost a very dear friend," Grace Tully would later sympathize with Roosevelt. "And he was about to cry," she recalled, "and so was I, and he said, 'Yes, poor Missy.' But he never liked to talk about those things. . . . He didn't want to show any emotion."

Missy's death took its toll on him. While he rallied to greet the troops at Adak on August 3, he suffered an attack of angina a week later while standing on the deck of his ship delivering a speech to ten thousand navy-yard workers in Bremerton, Washington. This was the first time in months he had used his braces. Because of all the weight he had lost, they no longer fitted him properly, so that he had difficulty keeping his balance. A sharp wind began to blow. The heavy rocking of the ship compelled him to grasp the lectern with both hands, making it hard to turn the pages of his speech. As he struggled to keep his place, his voice faltered.

Ten minutes into the talk, he experienced an oppressive sensation in his chest which radiated to both shoulders. The constricting pain lasted nearly fifteen minutes, but he managed, sweating profusely, to continue talking, keeping himself upright by gripping the edge of the lectern. When he finished, he returned to the captain's quarters and collapsed in a chair. Dr. Bruenn cleared everyone out, including Anna, who had flown to the West Coast earlier that evening to join her father for the remainder of his trip. Dr. Bruenn took an electrocardiogram and a white blood count. Though no permanent damage was found, the attack was sufficiently frightening to Roosevelt that he agreed to rest completely during the trip home.

• • •

The week the president returned to Washington provided a defining moment in the young life of the Fair Employment Practices Commission. In its first three years of operation, hampered by administrative shuffling, lack of funds, limited power, cumbersome bureaucratic machinery, and continuing congressional attacks, the FEPC had failed to realize the bright hopes of its founders. Lacking the power of enforcement, the agency succeeded, historian John Blum writes, "only when black workers were courageous enough to file complaints and corporate offenders decent or embarrassed enough to comply." In too many situations, it surrendered to pressure. Three times, for instance, hearings on discrimination in the railroad industry were postponed as powerful interests—big business, the railroads, organized labor unions, and the Southern bloc—were brought to bear.

On August 1, 1944, when ten thousand mass-transit employees in Philadelphia went out on strike to protest the upgrading of eight Negro employees to motormen, the FEPC was confronted with "the supreme test" of its history. The Philadelphia Transit Company had always resisted employing Negroes as conductors and operators. The five hundred Negroes who worked in the company were confined to laboring and custodial jobs. After Roosevelt issued Executive Order 8802, on discrimination, in 1941, a group of Negro employees requested the opportunity to compete for platform and clerical positions. They were told that nothing could be done because the company union had a contract specifying that "customs bearing on the employer-employee relationship" could not be changed without the agreement of both sides.

The FEPC had notified both the company and the union in the fall of 1943 that they were violating the president's executive order. Conferences were held and a directive was issued ordering the company to hire and upgrade Negroes. This was the first time the FEPC had ordered an entire city transit system to offer equal opportunity. But both the company and the union refused to honor the directive. The impasse remained until the spring of 1944, when a new union, pledging nondiscrimination, defeated the old company union in elections to represent the transit workers.

Deciding that the time was ripe for bold action, the FEPC pressed the company to comply with the president's executive order. Under duress, the company announced a new round of qualifying examinations, open to anyone, for the position of motorman. William Barber, a young Negro who had started with the transit system as a laborer and worked his way up to welder, was one of fifty who took the exam. "The exam was a written test, math plus some general questions," Barber recalled. "Eight of us passed. I got a ninety-eight, one of the highest scores. I was pretty proud of that, since several of the people taking it had a college education, while I hadn't finished high school."

As August 1, his first day on the new job, approached, William Barber was excited. "I felt like a pioneer as I went out to catch the trolley to the carbarn. I knew it was a big thing. But when I get to the corner there are no trolleys anywhere. Everyone was milling around, wondering what was going on. So I go back home, put on the radio, and hear that the whole system—everything, all the trolleys, buses, and subways—is on strike on account of me and my friends' starting our training as operators."

The night before, as it happened, the old union, sensing a golden chance to regain its former positions, had called a mass meeting to protest the hiring of Negroes. Three thousand workers cheered lustily when union leader Frank Carney shouted: "We don't want Negroes and we won't work with Negroes. This is a white man's job. Put the Negroes back where they belong—back on the roadway." Workers cheered again when John Smith, a training instructor, announced that he would quit his job rather than instruct a Negro trainee.

Handbills distributed to the crowd argued that seniority would be destroyed if Negroes were allowed to be upgraded. "Your buddies are in the Army fighting and dying to protect the life of you and your family and you are too yellow to protect their jobs until they return. Call a strike and refuse to teach the Negroes. The public is with you." Other handbills bore a fabricated message from Franklin to Eleanor. "You kiss the Negroes and I'll kiss the Jews and we'll stay in the White House as long as we choose."

By the end of the emotional meeting, the decision was made to call a strike. It began at 4 a.m. that Tuesday, August 1. By 6 a.m., all streetcars and buses had been stopped, leaving William Barber and thousands of work-bound Philadelphians stranded on street corners. By 10 a.m., the city's subway and elevated lines were paralyzed. "There was one motorman who was late in hearing about the strike," a reporter for *PM* noted; "his was the only car which rattled merrily around the loop at 23rd and Hunting Park. Four cars full of strikers bore down upon it, chased the passengers out and drove the trolley down to the carbarn."

Along every street, long columns of workers could be seen walking or trying to thumb rides with the few cars that were still on the road. The Philadelphia Navy Yard, employer of nearly forty-five thousand workers, developed an emergency transportation system for its employees. But for most of the city's nine hundred thousand war workers, there was no way to get to work. Production of critical war materials, including radar, heavy artillery, heavy ammunition, and incendiary bombs, was halted.

On the third day of the strike, with the fourth-largest war-production center virtually paralyzed, President Roosevelt took decisive action. He issued an executive order authorizing the secretary of war "to take possession and assume control of the transportation systems of Philadelphia Transportation Company." The order called upon the army to operate the streetcars and subways "on the basis of conditions that prevailed before the strike"; in other words, the army was to be guided by the nondiscriminatory policies laid down by the FEPC. In contrast to the situation that had developed during the Addsco strike in Mobile, Alabama, the previous year, where the government seemed to condone the practice of segregation, this time both the president and the FEPC acted to uphold equal opportunity.

Events moved quickly after that. The citizens of Philadelphia turned against the strikers. "In whatever degree the PTC walkout is based upon race prejudice, it is wholly indefensible and thoroughly un-American," the *Philadelphia Inquirer* editorialized. "It represents nothing but insult and injury to millions of Philadelphians." On Saturday morning, August 5, the strike leaders were arrested for violating the Smith-Connally Act. Hours later, five thousand soldiers moved into the city. And at five that evening, an ultimatum was broadcast to all the strikers: unless they returned to work by Sunday at midnight, they would lose their jobs, receive no unemployment, and fall subject to the draft. "The war cannot wait," Major General Philip Hayes declared, "while the employees of this company make up their minds whether they will come back to work or not."

Roosevelt's strong-arm tactics worked. Faced with the choice of work or war, the strikers hurried back to work. By Monday evening, all the bus lines, streetcars, subways, and elevated trains were running at full capacity. The transit strike made headlines across the country, provoking a new round of protest in the South. "In the case of Philadelphia," the *South Carolina Post* wrote, "the trouble can be traced directly back to the FEPC through its arbitrary and inept policies." The *Savannah News* pinned the blame directly on "Mrs. Eleanor Roosevelt's persistent efforts to force social equality on the American people."

The training of the eight Negroes went forward. "The first runs were tough," William Barber recalled. "People spit at me. I almost lost my temper, but I said, No, I'll just take it. I'm setting an example. And gradually things settled down. I remember one day a woman with a bad attitude came in. I called her stop and she missed it. She started screaming at me. 'Look, lady,' I said. 'If you don't leave in one minute, one or the other of us is going to be meeting our maker very soon.' With that, everyone on the bus burst into cheers and the lady shut up."

Negro newspapers were exultant at the turn of events. "The impossible has happened," the *Pittsburgh Courier* declared, "history has been made! Negro Americans are operating Philadelphia Transit Company Trolley Cars on regular passenger runs in various sections of the city." The *Courier* observed that surveys showed that 52 percent of the citizens of the city were in favor of Negroes' operating trolley cars if they were qualified. Over time, the integration of Negro workers into the transit force proved so satisfactory and was so well received by the public that the company opened up additional opportunities for Negro motormen. Philadelphia was the crowning achievement of the FEPC.

More progress followed. By the end of the war, the number of black workers in manufacturing had increased by six hundred thousand, to a total of two million, while those enrolled in unions had risen by seven hundred thousand. The percentage of Negroes employed in war production had risen from 2.5 percent to nearly 10 percent. More important, Negroes had made significant breakthroughs in access to more highly skilled positions as foremen, craftsmen, and operatives. "These changes," observed Robert Weaver, a Negro authority on employment and housing, represented "more industrial and occupational diversification for negroes than had occurred in the 75 preceding years."

Significant increases were also reported in the number of Negroes in government service. In 1938, despite the large Negro population in Washington, D.C., Negroes represented only 8.4 percent of all federal employees; by 1944, their percentage had grown to 19, the number rising from sixty thousand to two hundred thousand. In 1938, nine out of ten Negroes in federal service were custodians; in 1944, the percentage who were custodians had dropped to 40.

"With more and better employment opportunities," Jacqueline Jones wrote in *Labor of Love, Labor of Sorrow,* "black men gained a new measure of self-respect, which, in turn, affected family relationships." One young woman said her father felt "proud and happy" when he went from selling junk and cleaning cesspools to a carpenter's job at a nearby military base.

To be sure, economic necessity, in the form of the growing labor shortage during the war, played as great a role as the FEPC in forcing companies to open their doors to Negroes. But, as Louis Ruchames concluded in his study of Executive Order 8802, the FEPC "brought hope and confidence" into the lives of Negroes. "The government of the United States was now doing something to help them, and in defending that government, and the country it represented, they were defending their own destiny and future."

• • •

On August 20, Roosevelt escaped for the weekend to Hyde Park. There was "a decided nip in the air," Hassett observed, "a reminder of waning summer." The days had more early fall than late summer in them; darkness came sooner; and, Eleanor wistfully noted as she walked through the woods, the first autumn colors were beginning to show in the trees. "I am afraid before long the summer days will come to an end," she wrote in her column, "and all of us will feel that we have to return to our routine occupations."

The Big House was filled with visitors when Roosevelt arrived. "Too many," Hassett observed, "all ages, sexes and previous conditions of servitude—hardly relaxing for a tired man." Assorted children and grandchildren were there, along with Henry Kaiser and his wife, Sam Rosenman, Trude Pratt, and two veterans who had lost their legs overseas. Feeding this multitude was not an easy chore, Hassett noted, made harder by the fact that neither the president nor Tommy was allowed to eat what everyone else was eating. "Mrs. Roosevelt never noticed I didn't eat anything," Tommy complained to Esther Lape. "She is very impatient with the President because he has to stick to a diet."

It was Eleanor's good fortune, but also her undoing in her relations with ailing family and friends, to enjoy excellent health. Not once during the preceding four years had illness forced her to stay in bed, she rarely contracted colds, she almost never suffered from indigestion, and she once boasted that she had never had a headache. "She feels if she ignores anything that is wrong with anyone, it won't exist," Tommy observed.

But even Eleanor could not will away her husband's declining health. "Pa complains of feeling tired and I think he looks older," she admitted to Anna. "I can't help worrying about his heart." To Lash she expressed similar worries about "whatever he had last spring," but in the end, she concluded, as long as "he still feels his experience and equipment will help him do a better job than [Republican nominee Thomas Dewey]," he would go forward.

Eleanor remained at Hyde Park when the president returned to Washington the morning of the 23rd. At noon, as word of the liberation of Paris reached the White House, Roosevelt met with Stimson. "This is a great day," Stimson observed. Parisians came out into the streets by the tens of thousands to welcome their liberators with flags, flowers, and wine. The triumphant news buoyed Roosevelt's spirits. "He was in better physical form than I expected," Stimson noted, "and was very warm and cordial."

Later that same day, Roosevelt was wheeled to the South Portico, where Anna and Lucy Rutherfurd were waiting for him, along with Lucy's daughter, Barbara, and her stepson John. Tea and biscuits were served for a relaxing hour.

A week later, Roosevelt managed to see Lucy again, this time at Tranquility Farms, her summer estate in northern New Jersey. En route to Hyde Park for the Labor Day weekend, Roosevelt had his train rerouted from his traditional B & O route to the Pa-Leigh route, which allowed him to stop at Allamuchy. The unexpected stop took some of the passengers by surprise. Sara's old cook, Mary Campbell, was greatly concerned, Hassett noted, "when we laid over in New Jersey and she expected to wake in Highland," but no one, not even the three press reporters, who hardly looked up from their card-playing when told the train would be delayed for a few hours, sought to find out where the president was going.

Lucy later told her friend Elizabeth Shoumatoff about the pleasure of seeing Roosevelt in her own home, with its mountain lake, deer park, and thousands of acres of land. Prior to the visit, the house was in an uproar, as servants cleaned the rugs and polished the tables. "You'd think the president was coming," one of Lucy's employees commented. "He is," Lucy proudly announced. Lucy had a special phone installed to receive foreign calls, and she listened as Roosevelt talked with Churchill. Churchill was recovering from a bout of pneumonia. He was feeling better, he told Roosevelt that day, and was confident he could get away for their seventh summit conference, planned for Quebec the following week. "I hope you will pardon a further transgression of the Teheran scale," Churchill went on, alluding to the problems he had caused at Teheran by bringing his daughter after Roosevelt had told Eleanor and Anna no women were allowed. "I am planning to bring Mrs. Churchill with me," he said. "Perfectly delighted that Clemmie will be with you," Roosevelt replied. "Eleanor will go with me."

Roosevelt's visit with Lucy lasted only a couple of hours; he returned to the train in time for a late-afternoon arrival at Highland Station. But he had enjoyed his stopover so much that he asked the Secret Service later that night if the Allamuchy run could be used every now and then as an alternate route to Hyde Park. After careful study, the Secret Service concluded it was satisfied with the safety of the new route even though this required going over the Hell's Gate Bridge in New York. Delighted, Roosevelt smiled and said "he didn't believe the bridge would be blown up during his transit."

Eleanor was waiting at the station when her husband arrived. She had prepared a special dinner for the two of them at Val-Kill, away from the bustle of the Big House. In her cottage, without the ghost of her mother-in-law hovering around, she could relax, share a drink with her husband in the dusk, and listen to the familiar sounds of a country evening.

• • •

A week later, Franklin and Eleanor journeyed to Quebec, arriving at Wolfe's Cove twenty minutes earlier than the prime minister. Roosevelt had made sure to arrive first, so that he could be on the platform, along with the American chiefs of staff, to welcome his old friend. "I'm glad to see you," the president boomed as the prime minister, carrying a cane, stepped from the train. "Look," Roosevelt said, waving a hand toward his wife, "Eleanor's here"; by that time, Mrs. Churchill had spied Mrs. Roosevelt and shouted, "Hello there."

The exuberant scene, Lord Ismay observed, "was more like the reunion of a happy family starting on a holiday than the gathering of sedate Allied war leaders for an important conference. . . . To see them together, whether at work or play, was a joy." Eleanor enjoyed the scene as well. "There is something boyish about the PM," she noted, as she watched him with her husband. "Perhaps that is what makes him such a wonderful war leader."

At lunch, Eleanor recalled, a spirited conversation evolved, during which Churchill twitted her about their differences of opinion on various subjects, most notably Franco's Spain. In her column written later that day, Eleanor delighted in the notion that she had reached a point in life where she could disagree with people on certain things and still remain friends. "I assured him I had not changed, and neither had he, but we like each other nonetheless." But, in the days that followed, Churchill insisted on bringing up Spain at every meal. "He talks picturesquely, but I'm tempted to say stupidly at times," Eleanor confided to Joe Lash. At one point, he became "very much upset," asserting that he had never said what she was quoting him as saying, but she refused to pull back, calling on the Morgenthaus, who had been present when he spoke, to back her up.

"I think he likes me," Eleanor wrote Esther Lape, "but I also think that he feels women should be seen and not heard on any subject of public interest." In keeping with Churchill's attitudes—and, indeed, with the prevailing opinion of the day—the women were not allowed to join the men at any of the official sessions of the conference. "The ladies' duties are all social," Eleanor complained to Elinor Morgenthau. "It seems like such a waste of time." Though the hours she spent with Mrs. Churchill were pleasurable— they went shopping together one morning, and one afternoon took a trip into the countryside, where they sipped tea on a rug in a lovely field—she was unable, she wrote, to grow intimate quickly. It would all be insufferable, she told Elinor, "except for the meals with a few people when PM and F are entertaining."

The first plenary session opened on Wednesday, September 13. "Optimism was at its height," army historians record. Allied forces had entered Belgium and Luxembourg and had seized a series of bridges over river and canal lines in Holland. It was believed that the German armies in the west had been so "decisively weakened by the battles since D-day" that they would collapse if momentum could be sustained. The major topic of discussion was how to prevent another war with Germany. Everyone agreed that the German army should be destroyed and the Nazi leaders severely punished, but Treasury Secretary Henry Morgenthau had in recent weeks devised a far more drastic plan that called for turning Germany into an agricultural nation by obliterating the industrial resources of the Ruhr. Though Stimson was "utterly opposed to the destruction of such a great gift of nature," Roosevelt had invited Morgenthau to Quebec to explain his proposal to Churchill.

"I had barely got underway," Morgenthau later recalled, "before low mutters and baleful looks" indicated the prime minister's strong opposition. "After I finished my piece he turned loose on me the full flood of his rhetoric, sarcasm and violence. He looked on . . . the Treasury plan, he said, as he would on chaining himself to a dead German. . . . I have never had such a verbal lashing in my life."

"I'm all for disarming Germany," Churchill said, "but we ought not to prevent her living decently. There are bonds between the working classes of all countries and the English people will not stand for the policy you are advocating. I agree with Burke. You cannot indict a whole nation."

The president sat by, saying very little, waiting for the tempest to pass. It did. The next day, after being told by Privy Councillor Lord Cherwell that the Treasury Plan would save Britain from bankruptcy by eliminating Germany as a competitor, Churchill opened his mind to Morgenthau's ideas. "After all, the future of my people is at stake," Churchill said, "and when I have to choose between my people and the German people, I am going to choose my people."

After further discussion, both Churchill and Roosevelt agreed to sign an extraordinary memo which called for "converting Germany into a country primarily agricultural and pastoral in its character" by "eliminating the war making industries in the Ruhr and the Saar." Morgenthau was thrilled. Invited to join the president for drinks in Roosevelt's suite at the Citadel, he noted, "We haven't had a talk like this since almost going back to the time when he was governor." It was, Morgenthau recalled, "the high spot of my whole career in Government."

But Morgenthau's euphoria was short-lived. When news of the draconian plan leaked to the press, a loud outcry arose within Roosevelt's Cabinet, and the idea quietly died. "I never heard my husband say that he had changed his attitude on this plan," Eleanor later wrote. "I think the repercussions brought about by the press stories made him feel it was wise to abandon [it] at that time. . . ."

The conference turned next to Pacific strategy. Churchill opened the discussion by declaring that Britain now stood ready and willing to send its main fleet to join in the struggle against Japan. Though Admiral King was initially opposed to the idea, not wishing, in the last stages of the war, to surrender America's exclusive jurisdiction over the area, Roosevelt accepted

Churchill's offer without hesitation, welcoming the British fleet "whenever and wherever possible." American plans for the final blow against Japan envisaged an invasion of the Japanese homeland sometime in 1945, after Germany's defeat.

For the after-dinner entertainment that evening, Roosevelt chose *Woodrow Wilson,* a motion-picture biography on the rise and fall of the twenty-eighth president. The film followed in detail Wilson's harsh descent into illness, incapacitation, rejection, and death. It was a curious selection for Roosevelt to make, coming at a time when he was beset with worries about both his own health and his fate at the hands of the electorate. Only hours earlier, Roosevelt had talked with Canadian Prime Minister MacKenzie King about his chances for re-election in November, and King could see that he was really concerned. Churchill was so restless during the film that he walked out halfway through. He was worried enough about his friend; he did not need a historical reminder of presidential illness. Indeed, so concerned was Churchill with Roosevelt's appearance at Quebec that he went to see Dr. McIntire. McIntire, as usual, assured Churchill that Roosevelt was fine. "With all my heart I hope so," Churchill replied. "We cannot have anything happen to that man." When the film ended, sometime after midnight, Roosevelt seemed depressed, Dr. Bruenn noted, and his blood pressure was elevated to 240/130.

When the conference was over, Churchill accompanied Roosevelt to Hyde Park for two days before returning to England. On arriving at the Big House, the prime minister was delighted to learn that Harry Hopkins, who had not been present at Quebec, was coming to lunch. Hopkins' absence from the conference had troubled both Churchill and Mrs. Churchill. "He seems to have quite dropped out of the picture," Mrs. Churchill had written her daughter from Quebec. "I found it sad and rather embarrassing. We cannot quite make out whether Harry's old place in the President's confidence is vacant, or whether Admiral [William] Leahy is gradually moulding into it."

Churchill later recalled a curious incident at lunch. Hopkins arrived a few minutes late, and the president "did not even greet him." Later that afternoon, Hopkins explained to Churchill his altered position. His marriage, his decision to move from the White House, and his own ill-health had induced a decline in the president's favor. "You must know I am not what I was," Hopkins admitted to Churchill. "He had tried to do too much at once," Churchill later said. "Even his fullness of spirit broke under his variegated activities."

"There was no open breach between them," Hopkins' biographer Robert Sherwood observed, "simply an admission that [Hopkins] was no longer physically fit to share the burdens of responsibility for the big decisions of the war." But Hopkins had made remarkable comebacks before, and in the months ahead, he would rally his energies once more to re-establish himself as Roosevelt's chief adviser.

Mrs. Churchill thoroughly enjoyed her days at Hyde Park, the picnics on the lawn, the good talk, the leisurely walks through the woods. This was the first time that she had met Anna. "She is a wonderful combination of yourself and the President," she wrote Eleanor. "She charmed Winston and me with her gay and vivacious personality."

If Mrs. Churchill flourished in the simple routine of Hyde Park, Eleanor was glad when the visit was over. "My time slips away," she lamented to Joe Lash, explaining that she felt like "a glorified housekeeper" with a household that changed every hour. "These are the days when the resentment at the tyranny of people and things grows on me until if I were not a well-disciplined person I would go out and howl like a dog! The Churchills and party came at 11, Harry Hopkins at 12, the Duke of Windsor at 12:15. After lunch I dashed to the cottage and did one column, returned at 3:30, changed all the orders given at 12:30 and walked with Mrs. Churchill for an hour and a half ending up at Franklin's cottage for tea, worked again 5–7:15, dashed home and had Henry and Elinor and [neighbors from Staatsburg] the Lytle Hulls for dinner. Now the mail is done and my spirit is calm and I can enjoy writing to you."

During Churchill's last night at Hyde Park, the conversation turned to the subject of the atomic bomb. The scientists at Los Alamos were now predicting that a bomb, equivalent to thirty thousand tons of TNT, would almost certainly be ready by August 1945. Admiral Leahy, who was present at the conversation, had little confidence in the whole project. He feared that Roosevelt had assumed too great a risk in allocating such huge sums of money to a mere experiment. But the president and the prime minister were hopeful that the bomb "might perhaps, after mature consideration be used against the Japanese, who should be warned that the bombardment will be repeated until they surrender."

Churchill also asked for assurance at this time that nothing would be said to the Russians about the bomb. In earlier conversations, Roosevelt had expressed the feeling that, since the Russians would find out about it sooner or later, they should at least be advised, as a gesture of friendship to an ally, that a bomb was in the making. But Churchill was adamant, and Roosevelt finally agreed in writing that the matter should continue to be regarded as of "the utmost secrecy."

The long days with Churchill were taxing on Roosevelt. "The President under a heavy strain ever since he went to Quebec," Hassett noted, "continuous talking—sat up with Churchill until 1 o'clock this morning. Fortunately part of the strain is eliminated by departure of the Prime Minister tonight." Soon after the Churchills' departure at about 7 p.m., Roosevelt went to bed, leaving word that he wanted "to sleep right through the morning."

• • •

By late September, when the president returned to Washington, Democratic leaders were filled with anxiety. The Republican challenger, Thomas E. Dewey, was running an efficient campaign. The steady barrage of Republican criticism—suggesting that the government was in the hands of tired old men who were destroying free enterprise, coddling labor, regimenting agriculture, and saddling the country with high taxes and dangerous debt—was achieving its desired effect. Dewey was rising in popularity, while Roosevelt was rapidly losing ground.

The president had to prove to the electorate that he possessed the strength and resilience to rise to the Republican challenge. He began by announcing that he would go out on the stump for a series of speeches; his campaign would officially open on the evening of September 23 with an address to the Teamsters Union at the Statler Hotel in Washington, D.C. The announcement was greeted with relief by Democrats, but apprehension soon set in. Was the president up to the task?

There was reason to worry. Roosevelt did not look good. His loss of weight made him seem much older than his sixty-two years. His color was bad. He had not given a major speech since his appearance at Bremerton, when he had suffered the angina attack in the middle of his delivery. Since then, continuing weight loss and lack of exercise had reduced the already frail muscles in his legs and hips to flab, making it almost impossible for him to maneuver on his braces. Within the White House, the consensus was that the president should no longer even try to walk. But Roosevelt refused to give in. On the eve of his Teamsters speech, he called Dr. McIntire into his bedroom. A few minutes later, when Sam Rosenman came into the room with the latest draft of the speech, he found the president "with his braces on walking up and down, leaning on the arm of Dr. McIntire." In spite of the overwhelming volume of work facing him, Rosenman sadly noted, "he was literally trying to learn to walk again!"

Though Roosevelt eventually did manage to regain sufficient use of his legs to allow him to stand up and speak for short periods from the rear platform of his train, he reluctantly agreed to deliver his Teamsters speech from a sitting position. Having worked over the speech through dozens of drafts, he was afraid to let anything interfere with his concentration and delivery.

In the banquet hall that night were gathered all the leading Democrats in Washington, along with the leadership of the International Brotherhood of Teamsters, Chauffeurs and Warehousemen. As the president was introduced, a worried Anna, seated ten yards from the dais at a table filled with family and friends, turned to Rosenman. "Do you think Pa will put it over?" she whispered. "It's the kind of speech which depends almost entirely on delivery, no matter how good the writing—if the delivery isn't just right, it'll be an awful flop." Rosenman told her there was "no doubt in the world he'll get it over fine," covering his own anxiety with a reassuring tone.

The President began smoothly with a joking reference to his advancing age. "Well, here we are together again—after four years—and what years they have been. You know, I am actually four years older, which is a fact that seems to annoy some people. In fact, in the mathematical field there are millions of Americans who are more than eleven years older than when we started in to clear up the mess that was dumped in our laps in 1933."

Roosevelt proceeded, with a voice that purred softly and then struck hard, to ridicule Republicans for trying to pass themselves off every four years as friends of labor after attacking labor for three years and six months. "The whole purpose of Republican oratory these days seems to be to switch labels. The object is to persuade the American people that the Democratic Party was responsible for the 1929 crash and the depression, and that the Republican Party was responsible for all social progress under the New Deal."

"Now," he said, drawing out his words, "imitation may be the sincerest form of flattery—but I am afraid that in this case it is the most obvious common or garden variety of fraud." Indeed, he went on, when he first heard the Republicans blaming the Democrats for the Depression, he rubbed his eyes and recalled an old adage: " 'Never speak of rope in the house of a man who has been hanged.' In the same way, if I were a Republican leader speaking to a mixed audience, the last word in the whole dictionary that I think I would use is that word 'depression.' "

The audience loved it. They howled, clapped, and cheered. One teamster was so excited, Merriman Smith wrote, that he beat the silver tray with a soup ladle, while his colleague at a neighboring table smashed glasses with a wine bottle. At the family table, Anna's smile brightened, and she began to relax. "The Old Master still had it," the reporter from *Time* observed. "He was like a veteran virtuoso playing a piece he has loved for years, who fingers his way through it with a delicate fire, a perfection of timing and tone, and an assurance that no young player, no matter how gifted, can equal. The President was playing what he loves to play—politics."

Then came the climax of the speech, in which he pitted his dog, Fala, against the entire Republican establishment. "These Republican leaders have not been content with attacks on me, or my wife, or on my sons," Roosevelt said in a mock-serious tone. "No, not content with that, they now include my little dog, Fala. Well, of course, I don't resent attacks, and my family doesn't resent attacks, but Fala does resent them. You know, Fala is Scotch, and being a Scottie, as soon as he learned that the Republican fiction writers in Congress and out had concocted a story that I had left him behind on the Aleutian Islands and had sent a destroyer back to find him—at a cost to the taxpayers of two or three, or eight or twenty million dollars—his Scotch soul was furious. He has not been the same dog since. I am accustomed to hearing malicious falsehoods about myself . . . but I think I have a right to resent, to object to libelous statements about my dog."

The audience went wild, laughing and cheering and calling for more. And the laughter carried beyond the banquet hall; it reverberated in living rooms and kitchens throughout the country, where people were listening to the speech on their radios. The Fala bit was so funny, one reporter observed, that "even the stoniest of Republican faces cracked a smile." In closing, the president outlined the tasks ahead: finishing the war as speedily as possible; setting up international machinery to assure that the peace, once established, would not be broken again; reconverting the economy from the purposes of war to the purposes of peace.

As the familiar voice said good night, the audience was on its feet, shouting and applauding. "There were tears in the eyes of many," Rosenman observed, "including his daughter Anna."

"The 1944 campaign was on," *Time* reported, "and Franklin Roosevelt had got off to a flying start.... The Champ had swung a full roundhouse blow. And it was plain to the newsmen on the Dewey Special that the challenger had been hit hard—as plain as when a boxer drops his gloves and his eyes glaze."

With his triumphant speech behind him, Roosevelt boarded the overnight train for Hyde Park, where he joined Eleanor and Princess Martha for three days in the crisp country air.

• • •

Still, all indications pointed to a close race, with the president's health a major concern. It was rumored that Roosevelt had suffered a stroke, that he had had a major heart attack, that he had undergone a secret operation for cancer, that he was forced to carry a male nurse around with him for the purpose of emptying his bladder two or three times a day. "Let's not be squeamish," the *New York Sun* declared, "six presidents have died in office." The only counterattack, Roosevelt decided, was to go before as many people as possible so they could make up their own minds about his vigor and health.

The president began his tour in New York City on Saturday, October 21. The plan called for him to drive in an open Packard through four of the five boroughs—Brooklyn, Queens, the Bronx, and Manhattan. If the expected crowds materialized, he could easily see three million people in the course of the day. In theory, the plan was excellent, but the weather refused to cooperate. When the president's train reached Brooklyn at 7 a.m., a cold rain was falling, the tail end of a hurricane. The rain flooded the streets, dashed against the buildings, and beat down on the heads of the sidewalk crowds.

Dr. McIntire pleaded with the president to close the Packard's canvas top, but Roosevelt was adamant. The people had come to see that he was still alive and well, and he was determined to give them what they wanted. Taking off his navy cape, he positioned himself in the rear seat of the car, grinning and waving at enormous crowds whose ardor had not been in any way diminished by the dismal weather. The rain drenched his gray suit, splattered his glasses, and ran down his cheeks, but the president never stopped smiling and the crowds went wild. At Ebbets Field, he received a thunderous ovation as he hoisted himself to a standing position and hobbled toward a lectern positioned behind second base. He had rooted for the

Dodgers for years, he said, flashing his best smile. His radiance in the midst of the storm, Hassett noted, seemed undeniable proof that he was physically up to the job.

He was thoroughly soaked by the time his talk was finished, but he laughingly confided to Anna that Dr. McIntire had arranged to bring the car into a Coast Guard motor pool, where he was able to make a complete change of clothes without leaving the car. The green Packard continued through Queens to the Bronx, then went on to Harlem, Broadway, and the garment workers' district. Huge crowds continued to line the streets; at every stop, hundreds of thousands of people were standing in the pouring rain to catch a glimpse of their president.

In midafternoon, the cavalcade pulled up to Eleanor's apartment at 29 Washington Square, where there was a second complete change of clothes for Roosevelt, a late lunch, and a short rest. Though Eleanor had purchased the apartment more than two years earlier, this was the first time Roosevelt had seen it. As she showed her husband around the tall-ceilinged, gracefully decorated rooms, Eleanor asked if he had noticed that there were no steps leading into the apartment. He nodded happily. Everything had been arranged for his comfort, she noted. There were two rooms connected by a bathroom which could be shut off from the rest of the apartment just in case he ever wanted to stay. Franklin said he liked it very much.

In the library, overlooking Washington Square, drinks were served. Dr. McIntire prescribed a glass of bourbon to warm the president up. Roosevelt gulped it down and asked for a second, and then a third. "It was the only occasion," Grace Tully later recalled, "on which I knew him to have more than a couple of drinks." The bourbon did the trick; after lunch, the president retired to the bedroom for a restful nap.

It is interesting to imagine what Roosevelt might have thought as he looked about the cheerful apartment, observing a part of his wife's life he had not seen before. Did his eyes travel about the rooms, conjuring images of Eleanor with her friends, serving dinner, sipping coffee after a night out at the theater? On her dresser, she kept a few framed pictures: one of the two of them when they were young, one of Anna and John, one of Joe Lash. For two decades, Eleanor had enjoyed an independent life apart from his, and now, for a few moments, he was a witness to that life.

After resting for an hour, the president took a hot bath and dressed for dinner. Mixing a round of cocktails before he left, he seemed almost giddy as he was helped into his car and driven to the Waldorf-Astoria, where two thousand members of the Foreign Policy Association were waiting in the grand ballroom to hear him speak.

The text of the speech was designed to focus on the new postwar organization, but the president was so relaxed at the dais that he began to ad-lib. Spotting Eleanor at a table just below him, he was reminded of a story she had told him in 1933 about a trip she had made to a fourth-grade history class. On the wall, he told the crowd, she had seen "a map of the world with a great big white spot on it—no name—no information. And the teacher told her that it was blank, with no name, because the school wouldn't let him say anything about that big blank space. Oh, there were one hundred eighty to two hundred million people in that space which was called Soviet Russia. And there were a lot of children, and they were told that the teacher was forbidden by the school board even to put the name of that blank space on the map." How much had changed since that time, he noted, now that the Americans and the Russians were fighting together against a common enemy.

Listening from a table in the back of the room, Grace Tully wondered if the president would ever get to the prepared text. Sam Rosenman and Robert Sherwood, who had worked on the speech, were wondering the same thing. But the president was, as always, a pro. Returning to the text, he took up the most important question relating to the new world organization, the question that had destroyed the League of Nations. In an emergency, would it have the authority to commit the United States to the use of armed force without waiting for the Congress to act? The president's answer was an emphatic yes.

"Peace, like war," he said, "can succeed only where there is a will to enforce it, and where there is available power to enforce it. The Council of the United Nations [the name Roosevelt had conceived the first time Churchill visited him in Washington had stuck] must have the power to act quickly and decisively to keep the peace by force, if necessary. A policeman would not be a very effective policeman if, when he saw a felon break into a house, he had to go to the Town Hall and call a town meeting to issue a warrant before the felon could be arrested. So to my simple mind it is clear that, if the world organization is to have any reality at all, our American representative must be endowed in advance by the people themselves, by constitutional means through their representatives in the Congress, with authority to act."

As the president ended his speech, he was given a standing ovation; cheers were still ringing in his ears when he was escorted to a waiting elevator to go to the basement, where, on New York Central tracks, his presidential train was waiting to take him to Hyde Park.

The next morning, Hassett reported, the president was elated to discover that he had "no trace of a cold—not even a sniffle after his exposure in New York." Though two of the three pool reporters and several hardy Secret Service men were fighting bad colds, he was none the worse for the wear. Indeed, far from hurting the president, Eleanor observed, the rainy campaign trip had done him good. "Not for a long time had he been in contact with the crowds, meeting with a lot of people and getting an impression of how they feel," she said. It seemed almost as if Roosevelt had absorbed some of the strength and vitality of the many people who wanted so much to see their president that they were willing to stand in a drenching rain for more than four hours. "Their enthusiasm for him and his feeling of being at one with them," Eleanor observed, "seemed to give him an amount of exhilaration and energy and strength that nothing else did."

Roosevelt's high spirits carried him through the rest of the campaign. At the end of October, he journeyed through seven states in three days, delivering major speeches in Philadelphia and Chicago. Once again he was subjected to rain and icy winds, but once again he emerged, in Hassett's words, "brisk as a bee, brimming with health and spirits."

In the meantime, Eleanor observed, "the news from the Pacific is so startling that one holds one's breath." On October 18, American troops had shelled Japanese defenses on the island of Leyte, the first step in the dramatic battle to regain the Philippines. In contrast to the situation two years earlier, when the invasion of North Africa was launched too late to help the president in the midterm elections, this time Roosevelt was lucky. Two weeks before the elections, the nation awoke to banner headlines announcing that General MacArthur had landed in the Philippines; his famous pledge that he would return had been redeemed. "There were extremely light losses," Roosevelt told his press conference that morning. "The enemy was caught strategically unaware."

Two days before the election, Roosevelt traveled to Boston, where he was scheduled to speak at Fenway Park. The trip evoked in speechwriter Robert Sherwood "painful memories" of the trip four years previously, when Roosevelt promised American mothers that their boys would never be sent into a foreign war. Sherwood asked Roosevelt if he would make a reference to that speech, emphasizing that, once the Japanese had attacked Pearl Harbor, the war was no longer a foreign war. Roosevelt readily agreed. He referred to his 1940 pledge and then added: "I am sure that any real American would have chosen, as this Government did, to fight when our own soil was made the object of a sneak attack. As for myself, under the same circumstances, I would choose to do the same thing—again and again and again." With the repetition of the phrase, the crowd applauded loudly.

On election eve, in Hyde Park, with Anna instead of Missy by his side, Roosevelt assumed his usual place at the dining table, tabulating results. Eleanor was in the living room. She "swirled around among the guests," Merriman Smith noted, "seeing that everybody had cider and doughnuts." It was an odd group, Smith observed, watching Margaret Suckley, Laura Delano, and Marion Dickerman, "arty old ladies in tweed, or evening gowns of two decades before."

By 10 p.m., the trend was clear: the people of the United States had returned Franklin Delano Roosevelt to the White House for a fourth term. Though the election was closer than it had been in 1940, Roosevelt had garnered 53.5 percent of the popular vote and 432 electoral votes, to 46 percent and 99 electoral votes for Dewey. Dewey had carried the Midwest, the mountain states, and the New England states of Maine and Vermont, but Roosevelt had kept the support of the various groups that had supported him in previous elections—labor, Catholics, Jews, Negroes, soldiers.

At midnight, adhering to ritual, the president was wheeled out on his porch to greet the torchlight parade of villagers. Standing by her father's side, Anna gently pulled his old navy cape around his shoulders. The president smiled broadly and waved to his neighbors. "It looks like I'll be coming up from Washington again for another four years," he said. In the big spruce tree to the left of the terrace, he spotted a group of young boys. Seeing them reminded him, he said, of the days when he was young and "sought sanctuary from discipline in the friendly branches of that very tree."

After the neighbors left, Eleanor invited the shivering newsmen and photographers into the house for cider, as everyone waited for a message from the Republican challenger. It was 3:16 a.m., Hassett noted, before "the graceless Dewey" officially broadcast his concession, but he sent no message to the victor. "I still think he is a son of a bitch," Roosevelt remarked as he headed off to bed.

In other years, the Roosevelt boys would have been present on election eve, enjoying the moment with their father, but, like millions of other American families that November, the Roosevelts were scattered, with John and FDR, Jr., in the Pacific, Elliott in Europe, and Jimmy in Hawaii. "Word has just come in that Dewey has conceded," John wrote from an unnamed lagoon somewhere in the South Pacific. "I really missed not being with you at Hyde Park to watch the returns come in as we did four years ago. . . . I hope that at this time four years hence we can all be together again and that this show will be over."

CHAPTER 22

"SO DARNED BUSY"

The postelection period was one of confusion and drift for Eleanor, who felt herself tugged in opposing directions. On one side, she was intensely aware, as her friends reminded her, that she commanded more power and respect than any other woman in the United States. Millions of people, Joe Lash insisted, had voted for her as well as the president, conferring on her a conspicuous position of leadership even though her name had not appeared on the ballot. The challenge, Esther Lape advised, with so much opportunity to accomplish so many things, was to take time to think out the best ways to exercise "the tremendously increased powers that are so peculiarly now yours."

Yet, even as she contemplated new ways to use her remarkable position, Eleanor was plagued by guilt and pulled by the more traditional side of her nature. "Maybe I'd do the most useful job if I just became a 'good wife' and waited on FDR," she wrote to Esther Lape a week after the election. "Anna has been doing all of it that Margaret Suckley does not do but she can't go on doing it.

"If I did I'd lose value in some ways because I'd no longer have outside contacts. I'd hate it but I'd soon get accustomed to it. It is funny how hard it is to be honest with yourself and not be swayed by your own wishes, isn't it."

She found it difficult to make a decision, she admitted to Lape. Though she acknowledged her responsibilities to her husband, she felt "inadequate," fearing there was no longer "any fundamental love to draw on, just respect and affection" and "little or no surface friction." At times, she confessed, she felt "a great weariness and sense of futility in life but a lifelong discipline in a sense of obligation and a healthy interest in people" kept her going, and she guessed that was "plenty to go on for one's aging years!"

The agitation the sixty-year-old Eleanor felt in not knowing what to do was echoed in the hearts of the millions of American women for whom the war had been a major turning point, creating new expectations, new adjustments, new problems. Responding to their country's call, women had poured into jobs previously held by men, performing beyond everyone's expectations as truck drivers, lathe operators, welders, riveters, and stevedores.

At the peak of wartime employment, over nineteen million women were employed, constituting one-third of the civilian labor force. Since five million of the total were new workers, the nature of the female labor force had been transformed. Whereas before the war the bulk consisted of widows, unmarried women, and young wives with no children, now married women with children constituted nearly one-half of the female working population. Not surprisingly, the war industries showed the largest gains: between 1940 and 1944, women's employment in war-related work had risen 460 percent, while female membership in unions had quadrupled.

When these women were asked if they enjoyed working more than staying at home, an astounding 79 percent said yes; of this total, 70 percent were married with children. For some, the best part of work was the sociability of the workplace versus the isolation of domestic responsibilities. For others, the best part was the financial independence, the freedom from having to ask their husbands if they could buy a new dress or clothes for the kids, the knowledge that they were contributing to the family's economic welfare. Still others relished the mastery of new skills, the sense of industry, the pleasure of a job well done. "At the end of the day I always felt I'd accomplished something," welder Lola Weixel recalled. "It was good—there was a product, there was something to be seen."

But now, as the war was winding down, the country was beset with worries. What would happen to women after the war? What would the men find when they came home? Would wives be glad to give up their jobs and return to being homemakers, or would they continue working?

In the summer of 1944, the War Department published a pamphlet entitled *Do You Want Your Wife to Work After the War?* Designed as one of a series of GI pamphlets which officers could use to provoke discussions and forums, the pamphlet tried to impress on its readers that women's roles were changing, but the dominant voices were those that spoke against women's working.

"There are two things I want to be sure of after the war," one soldier in the South Pacific was quoted as saying. "I want my wife waiting for me and I want my job waiting for me. I don't want to find my wife busy with a job that some returning soldier needs and I don't want to find that some other man's wife has my job."

"Where I come from," another soldier wrote, "we don't send our wives to work. If I can't make enough money to support a wife I don't expect to get married. My mother had plenty to do right around the house. . . . I'm for the good old-fashioned way."

As demobilization loomed on the horizon, the image of women as comrades-in-arms was replaced by the image of women as competitors for men. And with this shift came a shift in public opinion. Enthusiastic admiration for Rosie the Riveter was replaced by the prevailing idea that "Women ought to be delighted to give up any job and return to their proper sphere —the kitchen." All of a sudden, in every medium of popular culture, women were barraged with propaganda on the value of domesticity.

Magazines that had once given prominent display to products such as Heinz soup and GE cleaners, which allowed women to fly through their chores at home so they could rush to their work in the factory, now featured menus that took a full day to prepare. Numerous articles appeared linking juvenile delinquency to the absence of a mother at home. Pictures of young children smoking cigarettes were printed as warnings to working mothers. Stories of women such as Liz Eck, a brilliant concert soprano, who was giving up her career because it threatened her marriage, were displayed prominently. Mrs. Eck planned to concentrate on being a wife and mother, she said, because "it's the only lasting happiness a woman can have."

Ignoring poll after poll that suggested that the majority of women wanted to continue working, the women's magazines focused almost exclusively on those women who were ready to quit. "My position is to go," Mrs. Cliff Ferguson was quoted in the June 1944 issue of *Ladies' Home Journal,* "unless of course my man comes back wounded. He wants me home and I want to be there. And we want kids."

"Am I planning to stop work after the war? I'll say I am," Mrs. Irma Stewart told the *Journal.* "It will be grand to get back to normal living again." Camilla Taylor expressed similar sentiments in *Women's Home Companion.* "I really believe I'll do better by my children and husband when I stay home. Anyhow, housework is infinitely more satisfactory than office work. You can't tell me that any job is as worthwhile as creating a home."

Movies and plays followed suit. *Soldier's Wife* was a successful play on Broadway which Eleanor went to see in the fall of 1944. It centered, Eleanor told her readers, on the wife of a GI who "found herself an authoress overnight, but decided that her marriage meant more to her than all the possibilities temptingly held out to her." Perhaps it was meant simply as entertainment, Eleanor wrote, "perhaps no real lesson was intended, but it certainly carries one."

Through her columns and her speeches, Eleanor tried to present a more rounded view of women's work, reminding her audience that different women worked for different reasons. To be sure, the women who were working solely for patriotic reasons would "gladly relinquish their jobs the day war comes to an end," as would women who planned to raise a family as soon as their husbands returned. But, Eleanor predicted, since millions of women were working out of economic necessity, "a good proportion" would undoubtedly remain in the labor market.

The nation could not afford, Eleanor warned, to return to an economy of scarcity in which women and minorities were denied the right to work. "To give anyone who wants to work a chance to work," she said, "it is necessary to envisage a future in which you produce to a maximum and sell to the rest of the world." What the women workers needed, she argued, was the courage to ask for their rights with a loud voice, demanding equal pay for equal work, an expansion of day care, and a proper share in postwar planning. "Women are fully as capable as men," she asserted. "Men and women were meant to work together."

Labor leader Walter Reuther wholly agreed with these sentiments. Speaking to UAW delegates at the first national women's conference in Detroit, he argued that "industry must not be allowed to settle the employment problem by chaining women to kitchen sinks." The solution would come only through planning now for reconversion. He called for the creation of an overall production board, representing labor, management, and government, to work toward peacetime employment and toward meeting the country's needs in housing, transportation, and durable consumer goods. "We must start planning immediately," he urged; "sixty million jobs will not create themselves."

But even as Reuther was speaking, women were losing their jobs with unseemly haste; their layoff rate was 75 percent higher than for men. In some factories, supervisors made a practice of harassing women into leaving —placing them on the midnight shift, reassigning them to undesirable jobs, transferring them to new locations, and closing down day-care centers. In other factories, all pretense was abandoned, as gleeful supervisors handed quit slips to every woman on the line, willingly subjecting themselves to ridicule as cartoonists satirized management's abrupt about-face in its attitudes toward women. In one cartoon, a supervisor is depicted handing a termination notice to a distressed-looking woman. "Now that War is nearly over," he tells her, "so sorry, have suddenly remembered you are incapable of working in factory."

•   •   •

By the eleventh month of 1944, the layoffs were affecting men as well as women. War production had reached its peak in November of 1943 and was beginning to move downward. At Brewster Aeronautical in Long Island, New York, 13,500 workers had been thrown out of work on three days' notice when the navy suddenly terminated the company's fighter-plane contract.

The navy had no problem with the quality of Brewster's work; on the contrary, the Brewster workers, like the overwhelming majority of their fellow workers, had done their job faster and better than anyone had anticipated. Indeed, so well had the arsenal of democracy lived up to its name that the unimaginable had happened: the country was now making more munitions than were needed to win the war.

The time had come, War Production Board chief Donald Nelson argued, for reconversion to begin, for the government to design measures to ensure a smooth transition to a peacetime economy. As a first step, Nelson proposed to lift restrictions on the use of aluminum, magnesium, and other materials no longer needed for war production, so that small companies whose war work was done could begin building schools, hospitals, railroad equipment, and appliances needed in the civilian economy. Eleanor Roosevelt wholly agreed with this line of thinking. We must begin now, she wrote in her column, to work out the methods "whereby every worker will be assured of a job when his war work comes to an end."

Creating structured programs for workers laid off from defense plants would alleviate the pressures that were leading to chaos in some factories as workers who were still needed to produce wartime goods were anxiously reconverting themselves, moving by the thousands into lower-paying non-war jobs, hoping to get a jump start on the future before the war came to an end.

But the military refused even to think about reconversion, fearing that if civilian production were allowed to expand, if refrigerators, dishwashers, and automobiles suddenly became available, the populace would think the crisis had passed and would begin to relax, opening the way "for dangerous leakages of materials and manpower." Convinced that the war demanded undivided attention until the job was done, the War Department argued that continuing restrictions on the production of civilian goods was the only means of combating complacency. "Many people seem to believe that this is the time for the seventh-inning stretch," supply chief General Brehon Somervell said, "and while they're stretching, the Nazis are digging in."

To bolster their point of view, the military argued that critical shortages of supplies still remained, despite the astonishing success of the overall production effort. Undersecretary of War Robert Patterson held a press conference with a group of soldiers just returning from France, where intense fighting was still going on. The GIs told stories of infantry units forced into battle without enough shells and grenades, of campaigns stalled and lives lost because of the strict rationing of ammunition. "It's tough to see your buddies get killed and not be able to stop it," one GI said.

These dramatic stories created a "misperception of the problem," Senator James Mead of New York argued, speaking as the new chairman of the Truman Committee on National Defense. "Insufficient production in the United States has not been the cause of shortages of weapons and ammunition at the front. Any shortage has been due, up to now, solely to transportation problems overseas." Donald Nelson agreed. For the military to focus on production shortages instead of on the difficulties of supplying a far-flung army was "one of the most dangerous bits of double talk."

But as historian Bruce Catton has observed, "neither facts nor logic made any impression." The military was not open to argument. Its position was utterly simple: there must be no interference whatsoever with the war effort.

The military found a natural ally in big business, who feared that speedy reconversion would confer advantage on small companies, which, because they were not essential cogs in the war machine, could more easily make the shift to civilian production. What was at stake in the reconversion battle was nothing less than the future of the American economy. The industrial giants were determined to dominate postwar production just as they were dominating production for the war. If small businesses and independent producers were allowed to get a head start in the race for peacetime markets, the established industrial order—in which fewer than one hundred large corporations were producing more than two-thirds of all the goods and services—would be overthrown.

As chairman of the Smaller War Plants Corporation, Maury Maverick put up a valiant fight for small business. Small business needed a head start, Maverick argued, to compensate for the overwhelming preference given to big business in the granting of wartime contracts. Much of the opposition to reconversion, he declared, "was motivated by nothing more lofty than a desire to save the postwar business opportunities for the big manufacturers." But every attempt he made to secure peacetime work for small business or to move forward on reconversion was stymied by the developing military-industrial alliance.

"You know what they're doing to me," Maverick complained, referring to the big-business interests. "They started on the roof, then they took rubber hoses and beat me, on top of the roof, and then they threw me down that chute—you know—and then they threw me down the steps to the third floor, and they kicked me, on that escalator, and I got a leg cut off and both of my ears. . . . I just came out with my life."

Eleanor found herself on Maury Maverick's side, believing that small business must be protected. Her heart ached for every individual thrown out of work by the cutbacks in war production. In conversations and correspondence with Walter Reuther, she explored the idea of creating a pool of machine tools which could be moved around to different factories, allowing war production and civilian production to move forward at the same time.

Roosevelt listened to his wife, but in the debate between Donald Nelson and labor leaders on one side and James Byrnes and the military on the other, he came down on the side of the military, agreeing with Byrnes that the country should not be asked to do two things at once, to pursue an all-out war-production effort while simultaneously releasing materials and facilities for civilian production. Better to risk unemployment in selected areas then to divide the nation's attention at a time when casualties on both fronts were mounting.

The argument over reconversion came to be known as "the war within a war." The fight between the military and the civilian elements, Nelson believed, was one of the most severe fights the government ever witnessed. Byrnes strenuously urged that Roosevelt remove Nelson from his post as war-production chief and replace him with someone sympathetic to the military's point of view. Roosevelt agreed that something had to be done, but, in characteristic fashion, he refused to face the issue head on, electing instead to send Nelson on a special mission to China to determine how China's industrial potential could be strengthened for more effective use against the Japanese. It was a graceful exit but an exit nonetheless, making room for the triumph of the military-industrial interests.

• • •

Late in the afternoon on November 27, after a busy day of engagements, Roosevelt boarded the train for Warm Springs, Georgia, for a three-week vacation at the Little White House. This was his first extended visit to Warm Springs since Pearl Harbor, and he was eagerly looking forward to his traditional Thanksgiving meal with the polio patients.

Eleanor had elected to stay in Washington. Since Laura and Margaret were accompanying Roosevelt, she told Hick, "I don't have to go." She planned instead to celebrate Thanksgiving in Lexington, Virginia, with Joe and Trude Lash. Lash had returned from the South Pacific in October and had married Trude in early November in a simple ceremony in New York City, which Eleanor attended. Their marriage must not have been easy for Eleanor, however close she had grown to Trude. Once again, she was the outsider looking in, wishing the couple well, but knowing that her special relationship with the intense young sergeant would never be the same. "You and Joe were very sweet to let me share your evening after the wedding," Eleanor wrote Trude the next day, "and I am very grateful and love you both very much."

Eleanor's plans for Thanksgiving did not materialize. Shortly before she was ready to leave, she received a letter from Joe telling her he feared her presence would jeopardize his chances for admission to Officers Candidate School. "Mrs. Roosevelt's feelings were hurt as you know they can be," Tommy explained to Esther Lape. "Trude was smart enough to sense this and so they wrote an appeasing letter," in which they begged forgiveness, reinvited her, and admitted that what they had done in disinviting her was wrong, "that no one should weigh love against expediency."

"But the weighing was already done," Tommy shrewdly observed, "and nothing would make ER go now. These brilliant people don't seem to be able to understand ER. If the whole thing had been put on the basis of wanting her no matter the cost, she wouldn't have gone."

"A new LL crisis," Anna confided in John, "brought on by Joe and his gal. It may blow over but for the present it makes for the usual tenseness."

Longing for company, Eleanor filled her calendar with engagements. In the forty-eight hours after her husband left, she met with two Yugoslavians who presented her with a report on the terrible conditions existing among the civilian population in Yugoslavia; hosted a small luncheon for the widow of Presidential Appointments Secretary Marvin McIntyre, who had died in December 1943; entertained a group of veterans from the Naval Hospital; brought the biographer Catherine Drinker Bowen to tea; met with twenty-three students from American University; had cocktails with Hick; dined with nine guests on the South Portico; hosted an evening with British war correspondent William Courtney; and paid a late-night call to Elinor Morgenthau, who was alone for the evening. On returning to the White House at ten-thirty, she worked on her mail until well after midnight, and then began a letter to Trude.

"I am very depressed tonight," she admitted. "Elliott called me from Beverly Hills to say he was going to be married on Saturday. He says he has known the girl, Faye Emerson, by name some time. He told me when here, however, he did not mean to marry til he was home, had a job etc. and I fear it is just another of his quick actions because of loneliness. I've certainly not succeeded in giving my children much sense of backing. I called FDR and told him and he took it calmly. . . . I have a curious kind of numb and dread feeling."

At Warm Springs, Roosevelt saw only a handful of visitors during his entire stay. In the mornings, he slept late, read, and attended to his mail; in the afternoons, he sunned himself on the terrace behind his house, swam in the pool, and rambled about the countryside in his '38 Ford; in the evenings, he sat beside the fieldstone fireplace in his living room, talking with Laura, Margaret, and a few local friends.

Roosevelt loved Warm Springs: the rugged terrain, the climate, the rustic cottage he had designed, "a little house," he once wrote, "flush with the ground in front but in back out over the ravine a porch as high as the prow of the ship. Wonderful for sunsets. A home for all the time I'll spend here."

Many times in the course of his presidency, Franklin had drawn solace from the "little house," but perhaps never more so than on this extended trip. The day after he arrived, Lucy Rutherfurd appeared. Taking up residence in the guest cottage, to the left of the main house, she was an ideal companion, joining Roosevelt on his afternoon drives, sitting by his side on the porch, talking over meals, reading by the fire.

Perhaps, for a few moments, Roosevelt knew the happiness of belonging to someone, of being together, of completing a circuit of emotion. In his fitted auto he drove with Lucy for hours, maneuvering the dusty roads with skill, delighting in the spectacular views, the hills of stately oaks and pines, the fields dotted with mountain laurel and wild azaleas. At times he would slip away from his cottage without the Secret Service, relishing the freedom of the open road.

On Saturday morning, December 2, Roosevelt finished his mail earlier than usual. At noon, he and Lucy drove off together to his favorite picnic retreat, Dowdell's Knob, overlooking the Pine Mountain Valley. The peaceful afternoon long remained in Lucy's mind. "You know," she told Anna months later, "your father drove me in his little Ford up to . . . Dowdell's Knob, and I had the most fascinating hour I've ever had. He just sat there and told me of some of what he regarded as the real problems facing the world now. I just couldn't get over thinking of what I was listening to, and then he would stop and say, 'You see that knoll over there? That's where I did this-or-that,' or 'You see that bunch of trees?' Or whatever it was. He would interrupt himself, you know. And we just sat there and looked."

"As Lucy said all this to me," Anna recalled, "I realized Mother was not capable of giving him this—just listening. And of course, this is why I was able to fill in for a year and a half, because I could listen."

While Franklin was with Lucy, Eleanor was embroiled in a policy struggle in Washington. Before leaving for Warm Springs, Roosevelt had appointed Edward Stettinius to replace the retiring Cordell Hull as secretary of state. Stettinius had asked for and been given authority to appoint his own assistant secretaries. When the appointments were announced, Eleanor was very upset to find that Stettinius had surrounded himself with conservatives, including James Dunn, a wealthy croquet-playing diplomat who had allied himself with General Franco in Spain, and Will Clayton, a former member of the Liberty League and the biggest cotton broker in the world.

After an unsatisfactory phone conversation with Franklin about the situation, Eleanor sat down on the night of December 4 and wrote a long, irritated letter to her husband: "I realize very well that I do not know the reasons why certain things may be necessary. . . . It does, however, make me rather nervous for you to say that you do not care what Jimmy Dunne [*sic*] thinks because he will do what you tell him to do and that for three years you have carried the State Department and you expect to go on doing it. I am quite sure that Jimmy Dunne is clever enough to tell you that he will do what you want and to allow his subordinates to accomplish things which will get by and which will pretty well come up in the long time results to what he actually wants to do.

"The reason I feel we cannot trust Dunne is that we know he backed Franco and his regime in Spain. We know that now he is arguing Mr. [John] Winant and the War Department in favor of using German industrialists to rehabilitate Germany because he belongs to the group which Will Clayton represents, plus others, who believe we must have business going in Germany for the sake of business here.

"I suppose I should trust blindly when I can't know and be neither worried or scared and yet I am both and when Harry Hopkins tells me he is for Clayton etc. I'm even more worried. I hate to irritate you and I won't speak of any of this again but I wouldn't feel honest if I didn't tell you now."

But, of course, she did speak of it again, waiting only twenty-four hours to let him know that she was still very unhappy about the State Department. "Now if Clayton brings down [First National Bank of New York President] Leon Fraser," she sarcastically remarked, "it will be perfect!" Before she closed, however, she noted that she was sending along the first page of a glowing letter she had received about the president's leadership, "one of many which has come breathing faith and admiration and since I am such a pest I thought this might compensate a little!"

The following day, she pressured him on Yugoslavia. Her conversation with the two young Yugoslavians had convinced her that something had to be done to alleviate the desperate situation in that ravaged land, where communist leader Tito's partisans were putting up a brave fight against the German army. She placed a call to Warm Springs. Dr. Bruenn, who had begged Eleanor time and again not to upset her husband, was in the living room when the call came. "She insisted that the president order troops and supplies to the partisans in Yugoslavia, forgetting what I'd said about not pushing him. He kept telling her it was impossible because there were no lines of communication and the Germans were occupying that part. But she kept pushing. He got more and more upset, as did I. She had tunnel vision. Anything interesting to her was paramount."

Italy was next. She was glad, she told her husband, that the United States was officially protesting Churchill's veto of the antifascist Count Carlo Sforza as foreign minister in the new Italian Cabinet, "but," she went on, "are we going to use any real pressure on Winston? I am afraid words will not have much effect."

Beyond dealing with the pressures from his wife, Roosevelt was bombarded with appeals from various members of his Cabinet anxious about their status in the postelection period. At seventy-seven, Stimson feared that the president might want a younger man to finish up with. He hated to be in the position where he might be dragged on beyond the time when the president really wanted him. Through Hopkins, Roosevelt let Stimson know that just the opposite was true: now that Hull was gone, Stimson was the only man of commanding stature in the Cabinet. The president wanted him to go on giving his advice and help as he had always given it.

Burdened with similar worries, Harold Ickes had sent Roosevelt a letter of resignation, hoping for reassurance that his services were still needed. Recognizing what Ickes wanted, Roosevelt penned a flattering letter from Warm Springs, teasing the old curmudgeon that if he said anything more about resigning he would find a Marine Guard from Quantico dogging his footsteps day and night. "Of course I want you to go along at the Old Stand where you have been for 12 years," Roosevelt wrote. "We must see this thing together."

"Your letter," Ickes gratefully replied, "makes me feel all fluttery. To have you write about me as you did is like an accolade to my spirit. No one can be so generous as you and from no one else would what you wrote mean so much."

Despite these intrusions, Roosevelt profited greatly from his days at Warm Springs. Dr. Bruenn was visibly pleased at the improvement in the president's appearance. The color in his skin was normal, and his spirits were high.

Eleanor talked with her husband shortly before he left Warm Springs. She was very sorry, she said, but she could not be in Washington to meet him when he returned. Her aunt Tissie (Elizabeth Hall) had died, and she had to go to New York for the funeral. "He sounds as though his three weeks in Warm Springs, Georgia had given him much enjoyment," she told her readers, "as well as time to think over the world and its affairs. Even if you are always at the end of a telephone wire, and if dispatches and pouches continue to come, still the change of scenery and the concerns of a different community . . . do something to one's mind and spirit."

•   •   •

On returning home, Roosevelt was greeted by the appalling news that on December 16 the Germans had caught the Allies by surprise with a massive counteroffensive in the Ardennes. Designed to drive the Allies back through Belgium to Antwerp on the North Sea, the daring German move, which became known as the Battle of the Bulge, dispelled Allied hopes for an early end to the war.

Hitler had been at work for months building up the kind of strike force that had served him so brilliantly early in the war. By mid-December, he had amassed more than 2,500 tanks, posted in 10 panzer divisions; in all, 250,000 German soldiers were facing a scant 80,000 Allied troops.

Hitler's audacious plan had been revealed to the German military only four days before the offensive began, when a dozen German generals and field commanders were gathered in a bus in the middle of the night, driven aimlessly around the countryside to make them lose their bearings, and set down at the entrance to an underground bunker which turned out to be the Führer's headquarters. There, from Hitler himself, "hunched in his chair," William Shirer wrote, "his hands trembling, his left arm subject to a violent twitching which he did his best to conceal," they learned for the first time of the mighty offensive intended to recapture the initiative for the Germans.

For ten days, with a thick mist rendering Allied operations in the air virtually impossible, the Germans drove forward, outnumbering and outgunning the unprepared American troops. At the Schnee Eifel in southeastern Belgium, nearly nine thousand Americans were forced to surrender, marking the second-largest single mass surrender in American history (Bataan was the first). For those who had imagined that Germany was essentially defeated, this was a bitter and depressing period.

Through the worst days, Roosevelt remained calm. He followed the course of the attack on the wall charts in his map room, watching somberly as the red pins, signaling German forces, multiplied, forcing the green pins, signaling the United States, into a full retreat. Yet not once, Marshall marveled, did he seek to interfere in any way with Eisenhower's command; not once did he force the Joint Chiefs to explain how this disaster had been possible. He had relied on these men through the entire war, and he would continue to rely on them now. "In great stress," Marshall declared, "Roosevelt was a strong man."

Roosevelt's steadiness in the midst of the crisis kindled gratitude in Stimson as well. "He has been extremely considerate," Stimson recorded in his diary. "He has really exercised great restraint, for the anxiety on his part must have been very heavy."

Eleanor was not as stalwart as her husband. She found the bad news from Europe difficult to absorb. "I cannot help thinking," she wrote, "of the weariness and disappointment of the men who have taken these miles of enemy territory and are now being driven back. Setbacks like these must be expected, but it makes one's heart ache to think of the gloom and disappointment among our soldiers and the news of individual losses, which will come increasingly often knocking at our doors."

By Christmas Eve, the worst of the German attack was over. With the clearing of the fog, the air superiority of the Allies was finally brought into play, and the battle began to turn. In less than a week's time, in what General James Gavin has called "an amazing performance," General George Patton, Third Army commander, was able to move his entire army the fifty miles from the Saar River to Bastogne, positioning himself to attack the Germans from the south. By the middle of January, a month after the beginning of the offensive, the German forces were back to where they had started; the Bulge had been erased.

German losses were shocking—120,000 men killed, wounded, or missing, plus a loss of 1,600 planes, 600 tanks, and 6,000 vehicles. American casualties were also brutal, with 19,000 killed and 48,000 wounded. But the Americans could replenish their infantry and their supplies, whereas the Germans could not. Hitler's wild gamble would cost him greatly; defeat in the West was now inevitable.

•　•　•

At the height of the Battle of the Bulge, with the army desperate for replacements, a dramatic call went out to all Negro units in the European theater. Representing a major break with traditional army policy, which kept blacks segregated in their own, predominantly service divisions, the call invited Negro soldiers to volunteer as infantrymen and fight side by side with white troops in the front lines. Negro volunteers were promised a six-week training period and then, for the first time, assignment "without regard to color or race to the units where assistance is most needed." Those who answered the call would have "the opportunity of fighting shoulder to shoulder to bring about victory."

The response to the army's appeal was phenomenal. Within a matter of weeks, more than four thousand Negro soldiers had volunteered. Currently serving as truck drivers, construction engineers, stevedores, and longshore-men, the Negro soldiers recognized they were being presented with an opportunity to affirm their competence and courage on the battlefield and to prove that whites and blacks could work together. In one engineering outfit consisting of 186 men, 171 volunteered for combat. "We've been giving a lot of sweat," one Negro ordnance man said. Now the time had come "to mix some blood" with the sweat.

For many volunteers, the chance to move from service units to combat units was the answer to their dreams. Though Negro service troops had played a critical role building bridges, constructing airports, driving trucks filled with food, clothing, and medical supplies through mud, snow, and sleet, Negroes resented seeing such a large percentage of their men (over 90 percent) assigned to the rear lines. "It is hard to identify one's self with fighting a war," one Negro soldier said, "when all one does is dig ditches and lay concrete."

For months, civil-rights leaders and the black press had been protesting the War Department's failure to use Negro soldiers in a combat capacity. Only three Negro divisions had been established, and of these only one, the 92nd, fighting with the Fifth Army in Italy, had seen extensive action on the battlefield. The 93rd had been sent to the South Pacific in 1943, but had participated in few engagements; the Second Cavalry had reached North Africa in early 1944 only to be broken up into service units. "My brother is now serving in the 2d cavalry division," Mrs. Francis Lewis wrote FDR when the conversion took place. He was "trained for a year approximately for combat duty," but now his division has been transformed into a labor unit. Please, she begged, "give our colored soldiers the opportunity to take their rightful place in this democracy."

"It is hard to decide which is more cruel," Lucille Milner observed in *The New Republic,* "this new pattern of murdering the ambition, the skills, the high potential contributions of the gifted Negro or the old pattern of physical brutality."

When asked to justify its position, the War Department had consistently fallen back on the poor records of Negro combat troops in World War I and the inability of the Negroes, as Stimson put it in a statement that became known as the "Negro is too dumb to fight" policy, "to master efficiently the techniques of modern warfare."

"It so happens," Stimson went on, "that a relatively large percentage of Negroes inducted in the Army have fallen within the lower educational classifications," so low that training proved impossible. According to a recent study, Stimson argued, 20 percent of Negroes and 74 percent of whites were rated in grades 1, 2, and 3 (considered the most rapid learners) by army classification tests; whereas 80 percent of Negroes and 26 percent of whites fell into grades 4 and 5 (considered the slowest learners).

No one could argue with Stimson's facts; what he failed to mention was the direct relationship between level of schooling and performance on the test. In the 1940s, almost 75 percent of the Negro registrants came from the poorest regions of the country, the Southern and border states, where educational and economic opportunities were so limited that four out of five Negroes had not completed the fourth grade. Indeed, the performance of whites from these same areas was almost as poor as blacks. Nationwide, of course, whites fared much better, with 41 percent of the white registrants having graduated from high school, compared with only 17 percent of the blacks. These differences in schooling proved to be major determinants of success on the classification tests.

Stimson's statement raised a passionate outcry in the black community. "The consensus," NAACP official Roy Wilkins wrote Roosevelt, was that Mr. Stimson had "offered gratuitous insult" to all Negro soldiers, miserably reflecting "upon the ability and patriotism of Negro citizens generally." What did the Negro soldier think about Mr. Stimson's blanket statement? *The Crisis* asked. "He considers it a vicious attack upon his manhood." But now, in the wake of the Battle of the Bulge, Negro soldiers were finally to be given a chance.

The first twenty-five hundred volunteers assembled in Noynes, France, in early January to begin a six-week course in tactics and weapons. The training was rigorous. When the six weeks were up, officers arrived to take the soldiers to their new assignments. Only then did the Negro soldiers learn that a change had been effected: instead of being integrated on an individual basis, they were to be formed into platoons and then sent into white combat units. Though disappointed by the change, the Negro volunteers remained enthusiastic about their adventure. "They were used to broken promises," Jean Byers shrewdly observed in her study of the Negro soldier, "and were anxious to prove their capabilities."

Within the mixed divisions, blacks and whites ate, slept, and played ball together; they used the same bathrooms and the same showers; they were given a chance to know and respect each other. As they fought their way together across Germany, prejudices would break down.

When told about the plan for integrated platoons, 64 percent of the whites were skeptical. Three months later, 77 percent said their attitudes had become highly favorable. "When I heard about it," a platoon sergeant from South Carolina admitted, "I said I'd be damned if I'd wear the same patch they did. After that first day when we saw how they fought I changed my mind. They're just like any of the other boys to us."

At one point, in the midst of heavy fighting, a black platoon was so decimated that a white squad had to be added to it. "You might think that wouldn't work," the company commander said, "but it did. The white squad didn't want to leave the platoon. I've never seen anything like it."

Treated with equality, the Negro platoons fared brilliantly. "They are aggressive as fighters," one white lieutenant said. "The only trouble is getting them to stop. They just keep pushing."

"I am mighty proud of these men," Lieutenant Robert Trager announced. "I have seen them in action that other soldiers wouldn't go through. I can say truthfully they are the best platoon I have ever led barring none."

Though Negroes were returned to their former segregated units after the Battle of the Bulge was over, the excellent performance of the integrated platoons demonstrated once again the waste and impracticality of segregation. Under the pressure of events, traditional attitudes were slowly shifting. Startling changes had occurred in a short period of time.

• • •

The Christmas holidays found the Roosevelt family together at Hyde Park. Anna and John were there, along with Sistie, Buzz, and Johnny; Ethel DuPont, FDR, Jr.'s wife, had come with their three children; and Elliott had arrived with his new wife, Faye Emerson. She is "pretty, quiet and hard," Eleanor told Hick, "but I don't think she is more than a passing house guest."

On Christmas Eve, Roosevelt sat in his customary place to the right of the fire for his annual reading of *A Christmas Carol.* In the corner of the book-lined library, surrounded by huge piles of presents, the candlelit tree glistened. At Roosevelt's feet, grandchildren of varying ages were sprawled on the rug, listening with noisy delight as the consummate old actor concocted different voices for each character, from the nervous pitch of Bob Cratchit to the bullying tone of Ebenezer Scrooge. "Next year," Eleanor said quietly when the reading was done, "we'll *all* be home again."

On Christmas Day, Elliott accompanied his father on a long drive around the estate to inspect the tree cuttings. Later that night, father and son sat together by the fire in the president's bedroom, talking. "Father spoke to me about Mother in terms I had never heard him use before," Elliott recalled. "You know, he said, 'I think that Mother and I might be able to get together now and do things together, take some trips maybe, learn to know each other again.' He talked at length of his appreciation of her as a person, her strength of character, her value to him. 'I only wish she wasn't so darned busy,' he said. 'I could have her with me much more if she didn't have so many other engagements.' "

After nearly forty years of marriage, Roosevelt still retained an intense admiration for his unusual wife, who, despite her stubbornness, her eccentricities, her moodiness, and her lack of understanding of him, remained, he told Elliott, "the most extraordinarily interesting woman" he had ever known. Thinking back to the polio attack that had nearly ended his life, he could not help remembering how steadfast she had been, how vigorously she had raised her voice against his mother in behalf of a full recovery. And surely their life together since then had been full, dramatic, and memorable.

The next day, Elliott took it upon himself to tell his mother what his father had said. "I was delighted when Mother expressed the same desire, that the day would soon come when their intimidating workloads could be rearranged to give them more time together."

"I hope this will come to pass," Eleanor said, her lips parting in a smile.

CHAPTER 23

"IT IS GOOD

TO BE HOME"

A s the year 1945 dawned, Roosevelt's health preoccupied his family and friends. On days when his eyes looked bright or his color seemed good or his spirits were high, his colleagues convinced themselves that their beloved chief would see the war to its end after all. "President in gleeful mood," Hassett exulted on January 11, detailing the teasing way in which Roosevelt had characterized the entrance he and Pa Watson had made into the bedroom that morning: "said we tripped in like fashion mannequins and, sitting there in bed, gave an imitation." A few days earlier, Budget Director Harold Smith recorded his own delight in finding that the president was looking "very well" and seemed in good form.

There were other days, however, when his lips were blue and his hands shook, when his mind was unable to focus and his best attempts to rally his energies collapsed in exhaustion. After a Cabinet meeting on January 19, Frances Perkins had an anguished sense of the president's enormous fatigue. "He had the pallor, the deep gray color of a man who had long been ill," she observed. "He looked like an invalid who had been allowed to see guests for the first time and the guests had stayed too long."

Sometimes, Perkins recalled, Roosevelt could go in a matter of hours "from looking pretty well to looking very badly," almost as if the spring of his remarkable vitality had suddenly snapped. His eyes would assume a glassy look, his jaw would slacken, and his mouth would droop. His fatigue at that point was apparently so deep that he was not even aware that he had lost control of the muscles in his face.

There was a story told on Capitol Hill that winter of two senators, Wyoming's Joseph O'Mahoney and Connecticut's Frank Maloney, who came to see the president on successive half-hours. Both were old friends of Roosevelt's, both had been to the Oval Office dozens of times. When O'Mahoney emerged at the end of the first half-hour, Maloney was anxious to know how the president seemed. "He was absolutely terrific," O'Mahoney said. "He told some wonderful stories, he talked about what a pain in the ass a certain person was; he was funny; he was charming; it was just like old times." Reassured by this excellent report, Maloney went in and sat down. Roosevelt looked up but said nothing, his eyes fixed in a strange stare. After a few moments of silence, Maloney realized that Roosevelt had absolutely no idea who his visitor was. A pious Catholic, Maloney crossed himself and ran to get Pa Watson, fearing the president had suffered a stroke. "Don't worry," Watson said. "He'll come out of it. He always does." By the time Maloney returned to the Oval Office, Roosevelt had pulled himself together. Smiling broadly, he greeted Maloney warmly and launched into a spirited conversation.

So the days passed, some good, some bad, as Roosevelt moved toward an unprecedented fourth term.

• • •

On the morning of inauguration day, January 20, 1945, the family quarters of the White House echoed with the sounds of children racing through the corridors, anxious to play outside in the newly fallen snow. Roosevelt had insisted that every grandchild—a baker's dozen in all, ranging in age from two to eighteen—attend the ceremony. He wanted the family all together, Eleanor later recalled, "realizing full well this would certainly be his last inauguration, perhaps even having a premonition that he would not be with us very long. . . ."

The White House "bulged at the corners," Eleanor recalled, with every bedroom, dressing room, and maid's room on both the second and third floors occupied. In order to find space for two grandchildren and their nurse who arrived at the last minute, Eleanor had to give up her own bedroom suite and sleep in the maid's quarters on the third floor. "I was not too comfortable, nor, I fear, too sweet about it," she admitted, but she was determined to honor her husband's request.

Roosevelt had also asked that his eldest son, Jimmy, on whose arm he had leaned through three inaugurations, be granted temporary duty in Washington so that he could be present at this fourth ceremony. Jimmy later recalled standing beside his father that morning as Roosevelt gazed out the window across the snow-covered lawn, watching the children coast down the hill and then race to the top again. Though the gentle slope of the White House lawn could hardly compare with the sledding hill at Hyde Park, Roosevelt delighted in watching his grandchildren enjoy the same simple pleasures he had enjoyed as a child.

Turning his attention to the morning papers, Roosevelt's eye was drawn to the headline story in *The New York Times*: "Housekeeper Rejects Roosevelt's Menu Choice for Luncheon." The story detailed the battle between the president and Mrs. Nesbitt over the president's desire to serve chicken à la king at his inaugural luncheon for two thousand guests. "We aren't going to have that because it's hot and you can't keep it hot for all those people," Mrs. Nesbitt flatly stated, suggesting that her word in this case was law, no matter what her boss desired. She would serve chicken salad instead, along with unbuttered rolls, coffee, and unfrosted cake.

In the weeks before the election, Roosevelt had joked with Anna and Grace Tully that the main reason he wanted to be elected to a fourth term was to be in a position to fire Mrs. Nesbitt! Yet the election had come and gone and the humorless Nesbitt remained at her post, still insisting that her only duty was to produce "plain food plainly prepared," regardless of the president's special desires. If the coffee she sent on the breakfast tray tasted bitter, then he could make his own with a percolator beside his bed. If he had a special craving for the big white asparagus that came in large cans, then his secretaries could search around and find it! As long as Henrietta Nesbitt retained the title of chief housekeeper, she and she alone was in charge.

For his fourth inaugural, Roosevelt dispensed with the traditional ceremony on the Capitol steps, as well as the marching bands, fancy floats, and hundreds of thousands of guests. "Who is there here to parade?" he replied when reporters asked whether there was going to be one. In keeping with the gravity of the moment, he prepared a five-minute speech to be delivered from the South Porch of the White House in front of the smallest inaugural crowd in generations. "Dog catchers have taken office with more pomp and ceremony," Secret Service chief Mike Reilly noted.

"The day was bitterly cold," General Marshall's wife, Katherine, recalled. "The President was pale and drawn, his hands trembled constantly, his voice appeared weak." Yet his message was strong. Grasping the edge of the lectern, he spoke quietly and poignantly of the catastrophic war that was putting America through a supreme test, "a test of our courage, of our resolve, of our wisdom, of our essential democracy. If we meet that test— successfully and honorably—we shall perform a service of historic importance which men and women and children will honor throughout all time."

After the ceremony, the luncheon began. With two thousand guests it was the largest luncheon ever held during Roosevelt's twelve years in the White House. Resting for a moment with Jimmy in the Green Room before facing the throng, Roosevelt was seized by a pain in his chest. "He was thoroughly chilled," Jimmy recalled, "and the same type of pain, though somewhat less acute, that had bothered him in San Diego was stabbing him again. He gripped my arm and said, 'Jimmy, I can't take this unless you get me a stiff drink. You'd better make it straight.' I brought him a tumbler half full of whiskey which he drank as if it was medicine. Then he went to the reception."

As always, the president made a determined effort to remain cheerful in the company of his guests. But he was tired and distracted, and it showed. Mrs. Woodrow Wilson was among the visitors that day; as she looked at the president, she was overcome with anxiety. "Oh, Mrs. Perkins," she cried when she saw the secretary of labor in the corridor, "did you get a good look at the President? Oh, it frightened me. He looks exactly as my husband looked when he went into his decline."

After making a short appearance at the public luncheon, the president retreated to the Red Room, where he relaxed with Princess Martha and a few friends, leaving Eleanor to circulate among the guests. All went smoothly except for one thing: the chickens Mrs. Nesbitt had bought for the chicken salad weren't frozen properly, leaving only a small amount of usable chicken for a salad that was supposed to feed two thousand people. The problem did not go unnoticed. At a party later that night, the toastmaster, George Jessel, began his remarks: "Mrs. Roosevelt, I wish to ask you seriously how it is humanly possible to make chicken salad with so much celery and so little chicken." Eleanor answered candidly, "I do not know, Mr. Jessup [*sic*]. I had a hard time finding any chicken myself." Eleanor's lighthearted response brought the house down.

• • •

Two days after his inauguration, Roosevelt embarked on a strenuous journey to meet Churchill and Stalin at Yalta, a Soviet port on the Black Sea. The secret meeting was intended to review the immediate military situation and to reach agreement on the structure of the postwar world.

The White House buzzed with rumors, if Lillian Parks' memory is to be trusted, that Eleanor "would finally be going with the President on something important"; the maids speculated that, with the sea air and the romance of the high seas, the president and first lady would become intimate once again.

The rumors proved false. Though Eleanor had humbled herself to ask the president if she could go with him on the trip, he had invited Anna instead, making a choice that came out of his own feelings, his need for someone to take care of him, to sit by his side, to preserve his strength—all the things his wife could not do. "If you go," he rationalized to Eleanor, "they will all feel they have to make a great fuss, but if Anna goes it will be simpler," especially since Churchill and Harriman were both bringing their daughters.

"You know," Pa Watson explained to Frances Perkins, who thought it odd that Anna was going instead of Eleanor or one of the boys, "Anna can do things with her father and with other people that the boys can't. They can't manage him. Anna can handle him. She can tell him, 'You mustn't see people.' 'You mustn't do that. It tires you out. You'll be no good tomorrow.' And she can also handle the other people."

For her part, Anna was so thrilled at the chance to meet Stalin and serve as her father's confidante that she refused to acknowledge that she was hurting her mother. Realizing that if her mother went she could not go, she hungrily accepted the rationale that daughters would be simpler than wives. "I wanted desperately to go," she admitted later, "so I just fell in with this, just blocked it out for my own purposes very selfishly."

Eleanor made a valiant effort to rise above her hurt and go about her business, but it was impossible to ignore the bustle of preparations when everyone else seemed to be going—Jimmy Byrnes, Pa Watson, Harry Hopkins, Admiral Leahy, even Ed Flynn, the boss of the Bronx. "I am tired and very depressed tonight," she admitted to Joe Lash the day before the president left. "The next years seem impossible to live through."

The presidential party boarded the U.S.S. *Quincy* in Newport News, Virginia, the morning of the 23rd. Anna later recalled sitting alone with her father on the deck that morning as the ship steamed past the coastline of Virginia. Feeling relaxed and happy, Roosevelt discoursed at length on the various birds that inhabited the Virginia shores. Then, suddenly, he told Anna to look at a particular spot on the shoreline. "Over there," he said casually and without a trace of self-consciousness, "is where Lucy grew up."

"Ocean voyage is certainly the life of Reilly," Anna reported to John that first day, as the great warship cruised the Atlantic in weather that would remain calm the entire week. The gentle roll helped the president sleep until ten or eleven in the morning; at twelve, he lunched with Anna and his male cronies; in the afternoons, he lounged on the deck, enjoying the warm sunshine, sorting his stamps, and reading quietly by himself; at five, cocktails were served on the deck, followed by dinner and a movie. "Oh darling," an exultant Anna wrote John, trying as always to shore him up, "I'm so grateful to you for letting me come—because I know that you would have been of so much more real value."

On the seventh day at sea, January 30, Roosevelt celebrated his sixty-third birthday. He had forgotten the date, he claimed, until a surprise package from Lucy Rutherfurd and Margaret Suckley arrived with his breakfast tray. It contained "a lot of little gadgets," he delighted in telling Anna, including a pocket comb, a room thermometer, and a cigarette lighter that could be used in the wind; they were whimsical gifts, but they signaled affection and intimate knowledge on the part of the givers, and that made him feel good.

That evening, Anna added a surprise of her own, a festive party with five cakes, three of the same size representing the first three terms, then a huge cake representing the fourth term, and finally a tiny cake with a large question mark representing a possible fifth term. She had also engineered the perfect present—a handsome map showing the route to Yalta along with a little message from everyone accompanying him and a brass ashtray fashioned from the case of a five-inch shell that had been fired by the *Quincy* during her first combat engagement at D-day. "Anna made the dinner a gala occasion," Jimmy Byrnes recalled, noting that Roosevelt seemed happy and gay even though he looked tired and worn. "Our birthday dinner," Anna told John, "was a great success. [Roosevelt] won all the money at poker, and seemed to enjoy all our little jokes."

Twenty-five hundred miles away, Eleanor was working on her husband's behalf, making the rounds of the annual birthday balls held to benefit the March of Dimes in its fight against polio. Starting early in the morning with the making of a newsreel, she hosted the traditional birthday luncheon for movie stars in the East Room, met with the trustees of the National Foundation for Infantile Paralysis, toured five balls, returned to the White House to read the president's message of appreciation to the nation, journeyed to the State Department to cut the cake at midnight, and then resumed her tour of the balls until 1 a.m.

Throughout the long day, Eleanor remained, as always, gracious and outgoing, but it was not hard to see her loneliness under the public persona. In the midst of her public duties, she tried to send a personal birthday telegraph to her husband, but the ship was under radio silence because two German submarines had been reported nearby. As it happened, the only communication he received from her that day was an irritated letter she had written four days earlier about the battle that had broken out in Congress over Roosevelt's nomination of Henry Wallace to succeed Jesse Jones as secretary of commerce.

She was sorry she had to bother him about this, she had written, but if he refused to put his prestige behind Wallace, the conservatives would have their way and it would look as if he had nominated Wallace simply to have him beaten. "Of course Jones has behaved horribly," she insisted, "but I guess he's the kind of dog you should have ousted the day after election and given him the reasons."

Tired and sick, anxious about Yalta, Roosevelt did not need to hear this from his wife on his birthday. Though he rarely chose to reveal to anyone the full extent of what he was thinking or feeling, he spoke openly to Anna about his frustrations with Eleanor. It's "a very sad situation," Anna told John: "the only times he has mentioned her to me on this trip have been times when he's griped about her attitudes toward things he's done or people he likes."

As the *Quincy* was steaming east into the Mediterranean, Churchill was flying south to the island of Malta, where he and Roosevelt were scheduled to meet before going to Yalta. The journey began badly, Lord Moran reported: the prime minister was running a temperature and feeling generally out of sorts. Huddled in his greatcoat against the seat of the plane, he looked, his daughter Sarah observed, "like a poor hot pink baby about to cry!" It was a restless night for all; when Churchill awoke the next morning, he was "in the doldrums," turned his face against the wall, and called for Clemmie, who was thousands of miles away.

The war had taken its toll on both partners of the Grand Alliance. Roosevelt's decline was more dramatic, but some of Churchill's vaunted vitality had also been sapped. "It is not the flesh only that is weaker," Moran lamented. "Martin [Churchill's private secretary] tells me that his work has deteriorated a lot in the last few months; and that he has become very wordy, irritating his colleagues in the Cabinet by his verbosity." For four years, Moran noted, Churchill had kept his own counsel, "sharing his secret thoughts with no man." Whereas the president had Harry Hopkins, "someone in whom he could confide," Churchill had no one to whom he could open his heart and unburden his soul. And now, Moran believed, he was paying the price for his long isolation.

Harry Hopkins, meanwhile, was also in bad shape. He had traveled to London for talks with Churchill, then to Paris to confer with de Gaulle, and then to Naples to join Stettinius. "He was so weak," Stettinius recalled, "that it was remarkable that he could be as active as he was. He fought his way through difficult and trying conferences on coffee, cigarettes, an amazingly small amount of food, paregoric and sheer fortitude." On the flight from Italy to Yalta, he was so sick that he lay collapsed in a cot the entire ride.

When the *Quincy* pulled into the Grand Harbor at Valetta, Malta, Churchill came aboard. The president was sitting on the deck waiting for his old friend. Sarah Churchill, who had not seen Roosevelt since Teheran, was shocked at "the terrible change in him," as were most of the members of the British party. But Churchill saw what he wanted to see—the smile, the jaunty cigarette holder, the cloth cap. He wrote Clemmie that night, "my friend has arrived in the best of health and spirits. Everything going well!"

Over the course of the day, Sarah felt better about Roosevelt, her attention drawn from his physical condition to his mental outlook, to his "bright charm" and his "brave expansive heart." Churchill was also struck by the president's high spirits and his friendly manner. "He must have noticed the candle by my bed when we were at the White House," Churchill told Moran, "because there was a small lighted candle at the luncheon table by my place to light my cigar."

That evening, Roosevelt and Churchill dined together on the *Quincy*. At ten-thirty, Anna gently but firmly broke up the party so that her father could rest before his midnight flight to Russia. Minutes later, as Anna was frantically packing, Hopkins and his son Robert arrived at her cabin. "Harry demanded a drink," Anna wrote in her diary, "so I gave him my one bottle. A few minutes after they had left I went to get the bottle and it was gone. Stettinius had confided to me earlier that Hopkins has a return of his dysentery, has been drinking far too much."

When Roosevelt arrived at Luga Airport in Malta, some twenty transport planes were waiting to carry the British and American delegations, totaling nearly seven hundred persons, to the Crimea. The flight was long and cold.

Churchill was standing on the airfield in Saki when the president exited from his plane. Together they inspected the guards of honor, the president sitting in an open jeep, Moran noted, while the prime minister walked beside him, "as in her old age an Indian attendant accompanied Queen Victoria's phaeton."

The drive from the Saki airfield to Yalta was eighty miles. Anna placed herself beside the president "so that he could sleep as much as he wanted and would not have to 'make' conversation." During the drive, Harriman pulled up beside the president's car and told Anna that in about forty-five minutes they would reach a house along the road where Foreign Commissar Vyacheslav Molotov was waiting with vodka, wines, caviar, fish, bread, and butter. With Roosevelt's concurrence, the decision was made not to stop; the drive to Yalta was long and hard enough as it was. The same invitation was issued to Churchill, Anna noted, and that "tough old bird accepted with alacrity." Though Churchill had already eaten lunch in his car, he could see how disappointed the Russians were at the Americans' failure to stop, so he fell on the food and showed by his appetite his appreciation of Molotov's magnificent refreshments. Relaxed and fortified, he returned to his car and proceeded to recite Byron's "Childe Harold" to Sarah for the remainder of the journey to Yalta.

• • •

The Conference was held in Lividia Palace, the former summer home of Czar Nicholas. Situated more than 150 feet above the Black Sea, the fifty-room palace included a main building with two wings, each one built around a separate courtyard, and a turreted tower with Moorish arches. Roosevelt was installed in the czar's bedroom in the left wing; Anna found herself in the opposite wing, "a block and a half away." General Marshall and Admiral King were given suites on the second floor, where the czarina and her five children had lived, while the remaining members of the delegation, including Hopkins, Leahy, Watson, Byrnes, and Harriman, were scattered in various sections of the palace.

The first session of the conference was held on February 4 in the grand ballroom, a rectangular room with arched windows and a huge fireplace. Stalin invited Roosevelt to sit in the presider's chair, closest to the fireplace, while he and Churchill took seats on opposite sides of the round table. With Roosevelt were Hopkins, Leahy, Stettinius, and Bohlen; with Churchill were Anthony Eden, Undersecretary to the Foreign Office Sir Alexander Cadogan, Secretary to the Cabinet Sir Edward Bridges, and British Ambassador Sir Archibald Clark Kerr. With Stalin were Foreign Commissar Molotov, Ambassador to the United States Andrei Gromyko, Soviet Deputy Foreign Minister Andrei Vyshinsky, and Soviet diplomat Ivan Maisky.

The discussion opened with a review of the military situation. For the first time, Stettinius noted, the Russian generals talked from maps, mentioning exactly where their troops were at the moment and making a complete disclosure of their plans for the future. On the Eastern front, Soviet troops had enveloped Budapest, taken Warsaw, driven the Nazis out of Yugoslavia, penetrated Austria and Czechoslovakia, and conquered East Prussia, and were now poised at the Oder River, less than fifty miles from Berlin. On the Western front, General Marshall reported that the Allies had completely recovered from the Battle of the Bulge, had expelled all German forces from Belgium, and were now entering Germany east of St. Vith. Six of the capital cities captured by the Germans in 1939 and 1940 were now liberated: Paris, Brussels, Warsaw, Belgrade, Budapest, and Athens. The war in Europe was slowly coming to an end. When the presentations of the generals were completed, the Big Three agreed to complete collaboration on all future military operations. "This is the first time such a thing has ever been done," Stettinius marveled.

While the first session was going on, Anna was "sitting on tacks." Her father was hosting the formal dinner that evening, and no definite list of invitees had been made up. Harriman kept assuring her "it was quite customary to do things this way," but Anna worried that certain people's feeling would be hurt. Her worries were realized when Dr. Bruenn told her Jimmy Byrnes was having a tantrum and she had better go to his room at once.

"Fire was shooting from his eyes," Anna recorded in her diary that night. He was furious that he had not been invited to the formal session: "Harry H. had been at the Conference—why hadn't he?" And now, Anna wrote, "he was asking me the only favor he would ever ask me in his life: to go and tell FDR that he would not attend the dinner." Knowing that her father would be upset, Anna argued and cajoled for twenty minutes. Many times she was tempted to say, "Okay, who cares anyhow if you do or don't get to the dinner," but she realized that if Byrnes did not go there would be thirteen at the table, "which I knew would give superstitious FDR ten fits. Finally won my argument on the stupid basis of superstition."

The dinner was a success. Stalin, Roosevelt, and Churchill were all in good humor, and the conversation was relaxed and personal. No subject of importance came up until the last half-hour, when the discussion turned to the rights and responsibilities of big powers versus small powers. "Stalin made it quite plain," Bohlen recorded, "he felt the three great powers which had borne the brunt of the war . . . should have the unanimous right to preserve the peace. Said it was ridiculous to believe Albania would have an equal vote with three powers who won war. He would never agree to have any action of any of the great powers submitted to judgment of small powers."

Both Roosevelt and Churchill recognized in Stalin's thought an undercurrent of antagonism to the concept of the United Nations, but little more was said at the moment, and the dinner ended on a pleasant note. "FDR seemed happy about both the Conference and the dinner," Anna wrote. "FDR says Jimmy [Byrnes] made a fine toast. This amused me as J. had told me very firmly that if he went to the dinner as a favor to me, he would not open his mouth!"

"Life is quickly assuming a definite pattern," Anna noted. In the mornings, while the president ate breakfast, worked on his pouch, and dictated responses to America's domestic problems, Anna made the rounds of Harry's room, Steve Early's room, and anyone else she ran into, "to pick up information on the day's plans, what meetings are scheduled outside the big conference, gossip on meetings, etc."

After making her morning rounds, she went into her father's room "to get his version of events and fill him in with any gossip" she had picked up that might be "amusing or interesting" to him. Her talks with Harry, for instance, revealed that Harriman's daughter Kathleen and FDR, Jr., had had a heavy romance two years earlier, and that Hopkins used to carry letters between them.

The plenary sessions convened after lunch and lasted for four or five hours. When he returned to his suite, Roosevelt typically enjoyed a quick rubdown and then dressed for dinner, with people rushing in and out of his study, sometimes at ten-minute intervals. The formal dinners, complete with buckets of Caucasian champagne and thirty or forty standing toasts, were generally lengthy affairs, making sleep a precious commodity.

"Just between you and me," Anna explained to John, "we are having to watch OM very carefully from physical standpoint. He gets all wound up. Seems to thoroughly enjoy it all but wants too many people around and then won't go to bed early enough. The result is he doesn't sleep well. Ross and Bruenn are both worried because of the old ticker trouble."

Dr. McIntire had been telling her for months that everything was going to be all right; that, as long as her father got sufficient rest, he could live a productive life for years to come. But now, at Yalta, Anna had the chance to talk at length with Dr. Bruenn, who gave her a more honest assessment. "I have found out through Bruenn who won't let me tell Ross I know," Anna confided in John, "that this ticker situation is far more serious than I ever knew. And the biggest difficulty in handling the situation here is that we can of course tell no one of the ticker troubles. (Better tear off and destroy this paragraph.)"

"I am using all the ingenuity and tact I can muster to try to separate the wheat from the chaff," she went on, "to keep the unnecessary people out of OM's room and to steer the necessary ones in at the best times. This involves trying my best to keep abreast as much as possible of what is actually taking place at the Conference so I will know who should and should not see the OM."

Harry Hopkins, Anna soon discovered, was in the best position to know what was really going on. Though he was so sick that he spent most of the conference in his bedroom, venturing out only to attend the plenary sessions, his room was a center of activity, with members of all three delegations stopping by to seek his advice. "I wish Harry was in better fettle," Lord Moran recorded in his diary. "He knows the President's moods like a wife watching the domestic climate. He will sit patiently for hours, blinking like a cat, waiting for the right moment to put in his point and if it never comes . . . he is content to leave it to another time."

It was Hopkins who persuaded Roosevelt to side with Churchill instead of Stalin on the issue of giving France a significant role in the occupation of Germany. Though France was a country without an army (Stalin's argument), Churchill was thinking of the future, when the American troops had gone home and Britain was left to contain the might of Russia. At that moment, a strong France would be critical to the overall stability of Europe. Giving France a zone of occupation was thus an important first step. Once Roosevelt was brought to agree with Churchill on this, Stalin was forced to go along.

• • •

Each of the Big Three leaders had different priorities at Yalta. Roosevelt was primarily concerned with reaching an accord on the new international organization and bringing Russia into the war against Japan as quickly as possible. The Joint Chiefs had told Roosevelt it was worth almost any price to secure the Red Army's military assistance in the Far East, where the invasion of Japan was expected to cost a million American casualties. Churchill wanted above all to maintain the British Empire and to keep Europe from being dominated by one power (thus his stance on France). Stalin had little interest in such abstractions; his mind was sharply focused on the borders of Poland, on reparations from Germany, and on various pieces of real estate in the Far East.

At meetings held the previous September with Britain and Russia at the Dumbarton Oaks estate in Washington, D.C., to discuss the framework of a postwar security organization, the United States had outlined a world organization of two houses: a large Assembly and a small Security Council consisting of seven members, four of them permanent—the U.S., Russia, Great Britain, and China. In cases that involved the sending of United Nations forces to trouble spots or mediating international disputes, any one of the Big Four could exercise a veto. However, if one of the Big Four were involved, that country could discuss the problem but could not vote on it. When the Dumbarton Oaks Conference ended, two key issues remained unresolved: the Soviet Union was refusing to go along with the voting procedures in the Security Council, and was insisting on sixteen seats in the Assembly for the sixteen Soviet republics.

At Yalta, Stalin dramatically shifted. He accepted Roosevelt's voting proposals for the Security Council and said he would now be satisfied with two or three extra seats in the Assembly for the republics that had suffered the most during the war—the Ukraine, White Russia, and Lithuania. Churchill was pleased. As long as each member of the Commonwealth had a separate vote, he had no trouble granting Stalin's request for a few extra votes for the Soviet republics.

The issue was not so easy for Roosevelt; firmly committed to the principle of one vote for each member of the Assembly, he found the idea of any extra votes at all abhorrent. Yet, if he refused to compromise with Stalin after the Russian leader had come so far, then the whole structure of the United Nations would be in jeopardy. After struggling for several days, Roosevelt endorsed Stalin's proposal on the condition that, if the United States needed to add two extra votes of its own to satisfy Congress, it could do so.

The Polish problem was to take up more time and generate more heat than any other issue at Yalta, though in many ways, as Averell Harriman observed, "events were in the saddle," and the fate of Poland had already been decided before the subject was even taken up. With Stalin's troops occupying the entire country and a communist regime firmly in place in Warsaw, "it would have taken," Harriman argued, "a great deal more leverage than Roosevelt and Churchill in fact possessed, or could reasonably be expected to apply, in order to alter the situation fundamentally."

Roosevelt was willing to be flexible about Poland's borders—the Soviet plan basically called for the westward movement of the entire country, compensating Russia at Germany's expense—as long as the government itself was free, independent, and strong. "The most important matter," Roosevelt argued in his opening presentation, "is that of a permanent government for Poland...a government which would represent all five major parties." Churchill agreed: "I am more interested in the question of Poland's sovereign independence and freedom than in particular frontier lines. I want the Poles to have a home in Europe and to be free to live their own lives there. This is what we went to war against Germany for—that Poland should be free and sovereign."

Now it was Stalin's turn. "The Prime Minister has said that for Great Britain the question of Poland is a question of honor. For Russia it is not only a question of honor but of security." For more than a century, Poland had been the traditional invasion route to Russia; Napoleon had come that way, Hitler had come that way, and the Soviet Union was determined that this would never happen again. Indeed, Stalin threatened, he would continue the war as long as necessary in order to ensure a friendly government in Poland. This was, he concluded, "a matter of life and death for the Soviet State."

Realizing that without a settlement on Poland the Big Three would break up, Roosevelt did what he could in the days that followed to extract concessions from Stalin. He got Stalin to agree that the communist government in Warsaw should be "reorganized on a broader democratic basis" to include the leaders of the exile government in London, and that "free and unfettered elections" would be held soon, perhaps within a month. On paper it looked good, but the critical matter of supervising the elections to ensure that they were truly free remained obscure.

As it was written, the formula was "so elastic," Admiral Leahy complained to Roosevelt, "that the Russians can stretch it all the way from Yalta to Washington without even technically breaking it."

"I know, Bill," Roosevelt wearily replied, "I know it. But it's the best I can do for Poland at this time."

In the end, Roosevelt biographer James MacGregor Burns concludes, Roosevelt's position on Poland resulted not, as many have since charged, from "naïvete, ignorance, illness or perfidy, but from his acceptance of the facts: Russia occupied Poland. Russia distrusted its Western allies. Russia had a million men who could fight Japan. Russia could sabotage the new peace organization. And Russia was absolutely determined about Poland and always had been."

The Polish issue settled, Roosevelt turned back to his original goal: securing Russian help in the war against Japan. The costly invasions of Iwo Jima and Okinawa were about to begin. The American military chiefs believed that the war against Japan would continue at least eighteen months after Germany's surrender. The first test of the atomic bomb was not to take place for another five months. The United States needed Russia's help. It could mean the savings of tens of thousands of American lives.

With all this in mind, Roosevelt negotiated a secret agreement with Stalin in which Stalin pledged to enter the war against Japan within two to three months of Germany's surrender. In return, Roosevelt agreed to legitimize Russian claims in the Far East, including the recovery of southern Sakhalin from Japan, the annexation of Japan's Kurile Islands, the lease of Port Arthur as a naval base, the right to use the international port at Dairen, and a joint share with the Chinese in control over the Manchurian railroads.

High spirits were evident on the part of all three leaders on February 8, when it was Stalin's turn to host the formal dinner. Held at Yusupov Palace, Stalin's sumptuous dinner lasted until 2 a.m., with forty-five standing toasts. Stalin toasted Churchill as "the bravest governmental figure in the world," the courageous leader of a great nation that had stood alone "when the rest of Europe was falling flat on its face before Hitler." In reply, Churchill toasted Stalin as "the mighty leader of a mighty country that had taken the full shock of the German war machine" and broken its back. Stalin then saluted Roosevelt as "the man with the broadest conception of national interest; even though his country was not directly endangered, he had forged the instruments which led to the mobilization of the world against Hitler."

•   •   •

"We have wound up the Conference, successfully, I think," Roosevelt happily reported to Eleanor as the presidential party left Yalta. "I am a bit exhausted but really all right. It has been grand hearing from you."

Roosevelt's long absence had been hard on Eleanor. Though she had passed the first week pleasantly enough at her apartment in New York, she seemed at loose ends in Washington, feeling far removed from the center of action, waiting every day for mail from her husband and daughter. "LL was really so happy to get a letter from you," John reported to Anna. "She has had so little word. . . . That is somewhat tragic." Anna and John wrote faithfully to one another almost every day—"What a lonesome barn this is," John told Anna the day after she left; "only one night and I am dying"—but Eleanor heard from Franklin only twice.

Matters were not improved when Roosevelt asked Lieutenant A. L. Conrad, a White House courier who had returned early from Yalta, to bring Eleanor a bouquet of flowers. "Lt. Conrad came to lunch," Eleanor reported to Franklin, "and brought the orchids which he said you told him to get me. Many thanks dear but I rather doubt his truth since you wouldn't order orchids [orchids were tremendously expensive at that time of year] and so I suggest you don't forget to pay him!"

But personal hurts seemed secondary, Eleanor conceded, against the momentous events at Yalta. When the official communiqué from the conference came over the wires, Eleanor was pleased to hear that full agreement had been reached on the structure of the new United Nations. This to her was the most important issue at Yalta. "All the world looks smiling!" she told Franklin. "You must be very well satisfied and your diplomatic abilities must have been colossal. I think having the first United Nations meeting in San Francisco is a stroke of genius."

The mood of the American delegation as they boarded the *Quincy* on Great Bitter Lake was one of "supreme exultation" as telegrams of praise flooded in from around the world. Though parts of the protocol remained secret, the published communiqué met the enthusiastic response of opinion leaders everywhere. The fact that agreement was reached on so many subjects, ranging from the United Nations to German reparations to the role of France and the frontiers of Poland, seemed extraordinary. William Shirer labeled the agreements "a landmark in human history"; the *New York Times* editorialized that they seemed "to justify or surpass most of the high hopes placed on this fateful meeting."

"We really believed in our hearts," Hopkins later recalled, "that this was the dawn of the new day we had all been praying for and talking about for so many years."

But as the *Quincy* proceeded westward to Algiers, clouds seemed to settle over the ship. Hopkins was by now so desperately ill that he was unable to leave his cabin. The thought of the nine-day voyage across the Atlantic in rough seas filled him with dread, and he decided to leave the ship at Algiers, rest at Marrakesh for a few days, and then fly back to Washington.

Roosevelt was angered by Hopkins' decision to leave. "Why did Harry have to get sick on me," he muttered, his voice trailing off. He was counting on Hopkins to help with the report on the Yalta Conference, which he had promised to deliver to Congress as soon as he returned. Though Sam Rosenman was scheduled to come aboard and help with the speech, no one but Hopkins knew the full story of what had gone on and what could be revealed.

"The president was good and mad," Harry's son Robert recalled, "so much so that he didn't actually say goodbye when he left. Dad had always rallied before, the president reasoned. Why couldn't he rally now? Besides, the best road to recovery was to keep your spirits up, and the best way to do that was to stay together."

Weary himself, the president was unable to see that Hopkins, who had always been there beside him, loving him and fighting for him, had simply reached the limit of his endurance. All that Roosevelt could see was that Hopkins was leaving him, as Missy had left him before, and Louis Howe before that. Perhaps, if Roosevelt had been able to explain any of those feelings to Hopkins, Hopkins might have stayed on the ship. But the sad truth is that nothing was said, and the two old friends parted with a frosty farewell that proved to be their last.

Two days later, Roosevelt's military aide, the bluff and genial Pa Watson, suffered a cerebral hemorrhage aboard the *Quincy* and died. "One moment he was breathing and the next his pulse had stopped," Anna recorded in her diary. McIntire and Bruenn broke the news to Roosevelt in his cabin while Anna waited and worried outside. "He was very, very upset," Bruenn recalled. "I shall miss him almost more than I can express," Roosevelt said.

"Many in Washington considered Watson merely a jovial companion to the President," Sam Rosenman observed. "He was much more. Like Missy, he had an uncanny instinct for distinguishing between the fake and the genuine in human beings and human conduct. . . . The President had seen many of his friends die; but in his weakened and tired condition, the death of Watson seemed to have a more depressing effect on him than the death of any of the others."

For days, the president remained in his cabin, withdrawn, quiet, and preoccupied, refusing to work with Rosenman. "It was a sorry ship," Rosenman recalled. It was not until February 26, the day before the *Quincy* was scheduled to land at Newport News, that Roosevelt finally agreed to go over the minutes of the meetings and begin working on the speech. It was "none too soon," Rosenman remarked.

Knowing of Watson's death and Hopkins' illness, Eleanor was nervous as she waited for her husband to come home, fearing that he would be in worse shape than when he left. Yet, to her surprise, when he landed in Washington, he seemed unaccountably well and, in spite of the sorrow, retained some of the exhilaration of the trip, "leading you to forget" for a moment, she said, how tired he was.

"Look at the communiqué from the Crimea," he told Eleanor, "the path it charts! From Yalta to Moscow, to San Francisco and Mexico City, to London and Washington and Paris! Not to forget it mentions Berlin! It's been a global war, and we've already started making it a global peace."

• • •

In the years to come, the rosy assessments that surrounded the initial publication of the Yalta protocol would give way to severe criticism as the Yalta Conference came to be seen by many as a symbol of failure in foreign policy, a series of surrenders to Russia that led inexorably to the Cold War and the loss of Eastern Europe to the communists. Critics, profiting by their knowledge of later events not known to the participants at the time, have focused most of the blame on Roosevelt, a "sick man at Yalta," unfit for the job of negotiating with Stalin.

What is the truth of these claims? It must be agreed at the outset that Roosevelt *was* a sick man at Yalta. It was obvious to anyone who saw him that his strength was waning. "To a doctor's eye," Lord Moran wrote, stunned at the change in the president since Quebec, "he has all the symptoms of hardening of the arteries of the brain in an advanced stage so that I give him only a few months to live." Averell Harriman, who had not seen the president since November, was equally taken aback. "The signs of deterioration seemed to me unmistakable," Harriman later admitted.

Still, the question remains: did Roosevelt's physical condition impair his judgment? There is no simple answer. The Americans who worked with him most closely at the conference—Stettinius, Leahy, Harriman, and Byrnes—are unanimous in their belief that Roosevelt was in full possession of his faculties at all times. Admittedly, Harriman observed, the long conference tired him. "Nevertheless he had blocked out definite objectives which he had clearly in his mind and he carried on the negotiations to this end with his usual skill and perception." Admiral Leahy agreed. "It was my feeling," Leahy later concluded, "that Roosevelt conducted the Crimean Conference with great skill and that his personality had dominated the discussions."

Even Anthony Eden, who was disheartened when he first saw Roosevelt at Malta, later acknowledged that Roosevelt's ill-health did not seem to alter his judgment. To Eden's surprise, Roosevelt not only kept up with Churchill in the round of conferences, but also found time to conduct a whole separate enterprise—negotiations with Stalin over the Far East.

Certainly, if Roosevelt had been in better health, he might have held out longer on a number of detailed points—he might have insisted on stronger safeguards with regard to Poland, he might have kept more ambiguous his commitments to Russia in the Far East, he might have fought harder against the two extra Assembly seats—but in the end, there is no evidence that fine points of language would have made a great deal of difference in the course of events. "If Stalin was determined to have his way," Averell Harriman concluded years later, "he was bound to bend or break the agreements even if they'd been sewn up more tightly." Unless, of course, the people of the United States were willing to go to war with Russia over Poland or Latvia or Lithuania, which Harriman seriously doubted they were.

• • •

At noon on March 1, 1945, Roosevelt went up to the Capitol to address a joint session of Congress. The chamber was filled to overflowing with everyone anxiously awaiting the president's report on the Yalta Conference. In time-honored fashion, the doorkeeper announced the members of the Supreme Court, the members of the Cabinet, and finally the president of the United States. A hush went over the great chamber as the door opened to reveal the president seated in his wheelchair. In all the times the president had addressed the Congress, this was the first time he had ever allowed himself to come down the aisle in his wheelchair. Always before, either supported by the arm of a colleague or leaning on crutches, he had "walked" to the well.

And now, also for the first time, instead of standing behind the lectern in a position above the well, he seated himself in a soft chair in front of a small table on the floor below the dais. "I hope you will pardon me for the unusual posture of sitting down during the presentation of what I want to say," he began, "but I know that you will realize that it makes it a lot easier for me in not having to carry about ten pounds of steel around on the bottom of my legs; and also because I have just completed a fourteen thousand mile trip."

The applause at this point was sustained. Seated in the front row, Frances Perkins found herself close to tears. "It was the first reference he had ever made to his incapacity, to his impediment, and he did it in the most charming way. I remember choking up to realize that he was actually saying, 'You see, I'm a crippled man.' He had never said it before and it was one of the things that nobody ever said to him or even mentioned in his presence. It wasn't done. It couldn't be done. He had to bring himself to full humility to say it before Congress."

For twelve years, Roosevelt had engaged in what writer Hugh Gallagher has felicitously called "a splendid deception." The public had no idea that their president could stand only for short periods of time, that he could walk only when pushed along by the momentum of another person, that he had to be carried up and down steps and helped into bed at night by his valet. Eleanor's young friend Jane Plakias remembered her shock when she first realized the extent of Roosevelt's paralysis. "I was at a picnic at Val-Kill. I saw a car drive up and two big Secret Service agents lifted Roosevelt out of the backseat and carried him into his wheelchair. It never occurred to me he couldn't walk. I never got over that."

There was an unspoken code of honor on the part of the White House photographers that the president was never to be photographed looking crippled. In twelve years, not a single picture was ever printed of the president in his wheelchair. No newsreel had ever captured him being lifted into or out of his car. When he was shown in public, he appeared either standing behind a podium, seated in an ordinary chair, or leaning on the arm of a colleague. If, as occasionally happened, one of the members of the press corps sought to violate the code by sneaking a picture of the president looking helpless, one of the older photographers would "accidentally" block the shot or gently knock the camera to the ground. But such incidents were rare; by and large, the "veil of silence" about the extent of Roosevelt's handicap was accepted by everyone—Roosevelt, the press, and the American people.

But now the energy required to sustain the deception was no longer there. The effect on the listeners was electric. Even though the speech itself was too long and rambling, the reaction to it was overwhelmingly favorable. Freed from the burden of his braces, Roosevelt delivered an intimate, chatty address that sounded, Eleanor noted, as if he were in his private study talking to a small group of friends.

For years, Roosevelt's handicap had been regarded as a badge of courage by those who had worked closely with him, witnessing the extraordinary effort he had to make every day to overcome his physical affliction. And now, for a brief moment, the entire chamber was allowed to see what Roosevelt's colleagues had always seen. But rather than lessening their regard for him, as Roosevelt had always feared it might, this glimpse of Roosevelt's vulnerability only magnified the power and charm of his personality.

"First of all," Roosevelt said, opening the formal part of his speech, "I want to say, it is good to be home." He then went on to discuss the work of the conference, the plans to bring defeat to Germany with the greatest possible speed, the design for the new United Nations. "This time," he insisted, as he outlined the plans for the April 25 meeting in San Francisco, "we are not making the mistake of waiting until the end of the war to set up the machinery of peace. This time, as we fight together to win the war finally we work together to keep it from happening again."

In preparing his address, Sam Rosenman later conceded, Roosevelt made "one of his major mistakes in public relations." He chose, unwisely, to keep secret for the time being that part of the Yalta agreement that granted the Soviet Union three votes in the Assembly. By deciding not to take the American people into his confidence, explaining to them how insignificant a concession this really was, Roosevelt opened himself to sharp attack when the news eventually leaked. Perhaps if Harry Hopkins had been able to work on the speech the mistake would not have been made, but Hopkins was in such terrible condition by the time his plane landed that he was forced to go straight to the Mayo Clinic in Minnesota.

Nevertheless, the speech that day was a great success, and the president, Perkins thought, looked "really well." He had a slight sunburn, which gave his skin color and vitality; his eyes were bright and his voice was strong.

• • •

Roosevelt, of course, was not well. When Canadian Prime Minister MacKenzie King visited the White House in mid-March, he was left with the distinct impression that the president was failing. "He looked much older," King observed, and "I noticed in looking at his eyes very closely that one eye had a clear direct look" while the other one was "not quite on the square."

Nonetheless, after a long talk with Roosevelt on the first evening of his visit, King was reassured. The president and the Canadian prime minister "talked steadily from 8:30 until twenty past 11," when King looked at the clock. "The President said he was not tired; was enjoying the talk." He spoke of Churchill and Stalin, of Yalta and the United Nations. And "on the whole," King concluded, "I found more strength in him than I had expected. In fact, I felt less concerned than I had at the beginning."

It was the conversation at lunch the next day that disturbed King. Word for word, Roosevelt repeated two long stories about Jimmy Byrnes' converting to Catholicism and Winston Churchill's swimming in the ocean that he had told King the night before. King noticed that Mrs. Roosevelt and Anna "seemed a little embarrassed," but nothing was said.

King was not alone in his worries. "I saw the President today," former OPA chief Leon Henderson recorded in his diary a few days later. "And I'm scared." After leaving the government, Henderson had gone into private business, and had not seen the president since 1942. "It wasn't only his appearance as an old man. . . . It wasn't just his preoccupation with other affairs. It was the whole atmosphere of incredibility. . . . It was agonizing to me to see his plain difficulty in conversation. He wandered from topic to topic. I had a horrible vision that he might grow weaker and weaker, that his enemies would trample him underfoot as they did Woodrow Wilson."

The following week, speechwriter Robert Sherwood emerged from a weekly meeting with Roosevelt feeling "profoundly depressed." Never before, Sherwood noted, had he seen the president so unnaturally quiet and even querulous. Never had he found himself "in the strange position of carrying on most of the conversation with him." The only time the president perked up, Sherwood observed, was during lunch on the sun porch, when, "under the sparkling influence of his daughter Anna," he almost seemed to be his old self.

The five-week trip to Yalta had brought Roosevelt closer to Anna than ever before, and the old man reveled in the warmth of his daughter's love. For her part, Anna had returned from Yalta full of self-possession. She had handled her responsibilities extremely well, and her father could not have asked for a better companion. And she had enjoyed herself thoroughly. "The other meetings have all been tiddlywinks compared with this one," her husband, John, happily pointed out. "So you can say fiddlesticks to your brothers."

Though Anna was never given an office in the West Wing (she worked at a desk in her bedroom), never had an official title, and never took a salary, unlike her brother Jimmy, who got $10,000 a year for assisting his father, there was no question, *Life* magazine reported that spring, that Washington considered her the one to call to get through to the Big Boss. First Louis

Howe had controlled access to the throne, later it was Missy, and still later Harry Hopkins. "But for weeks now," *Life* reporter John Chamberlain observed, "the rumor mongers have been busy whispering a new secret: control of access has passed to Anna Roosevelt Boettiger, the long-legged, energetic and handsome eldest child," the "free-speaking, free-cursing" daughter of President Roosevelt. "Anna," Jim Farley once remarked, "has the most political savvy of all the Roosevelt children."

"For purposes of public consumption," Chamberlain concluded, "she may continue to pose as someone simply living in the White House in prolonged transit from and to a newspaper job. But no matter what the White House press agents may say, it is a fair bet that Missy LeHand's shoes have at last found a permanent occupant. Daddy's girl has her work cut out for her, running Daddy."

• • •

A great deal of work had piled up while Roosevelt was at Yalta. On the domestic front, the president's first priority was passage of the National Service Act, which he had once again called upon Congress to enact in his State of the Union speech on January 6, 1945. Having come to believe that a total mobilization of all the country's human resources was needed to bring a speedy end to the war, Roosevelt was now convinced that the "work or fight" bill was essential.

The House had passed the national-service bill in February, but it was stuck in the upper chamber, where a majority of senators bridled at the thought of any further extension of controls over individuals. The Senate delay infuriated Roosevelt. "He seemed to feel," Budget Director Harold Smith reported on March 12, "he did not want to send anything more to the Congress until it had disposed of the manpower issue. . . . He felt [Congress] was kicking the manpower situation around and said that in almost every battle of the war if there had been just a little more in the way of men and materials the result could have been a little more decisively on our side."

But Roosevelt's disappointments at home that spring were more than balanced by victories abroad. In Germany, the Third Army was advancing rapidly toward the Rhine. "Don't tell anyone," General Patton telephoned General Omar Bradley, commander of the Twelfth Army Group, on the morning of March 23, "but I'm across. I sneaked a division over last night. But there are so few Krauts around here, they don't know it yet." And in the Pacific, the Battle of Iwo Jima, begun on February 19, 1945, was finally won. Halfway between Tokyo and the U.S. base on Saipan in the Marianas, the island of Iwo Jima was critical to the United States as a base from which heavily loaded B-29s could bomb Japan. To make Iwo Jima theirs, the U.S. Marines had stormed what was probably the most heavily defended spot per acre of ground in the world. Battling through caves and dugouts forty feet deep, the marines had absorbed terrible losses—more than six thousand were killed and fifteen thousand wounded, representing the greatest number of casualties in a single encounter of the Pacific war to date. But with the taking of Iwo Jima, a great victory was achieved, for American planes could now begin to bomb Japan with their full weight.

Still, the specter of Japan's zeal made it clear that the war in the Pacific would be even longer and bloodier than anyone had projected. Only two hundred of the 20,700 Japanese troops on Iwo's garrison remained alive at the end of the battle; so humiliating was the thought of capture that hundreds, perhaps thousands, committed suicide, some by leaping into the Suribachi volcano.

As reports of the Iwo Jima fighting reached Washington, Stimson met with Roosevelt to discuss the A-bomb project. Apparently several people at the State Department, including Jimmy Dunn, had become alarmed about rumors that the director of the Office of Scientific Research and Development, Vannevar Bush, and Harvard President James Conant had, at extravagant cost, sold the president a lemon. Stimson wanted to assure the president that substantial progress was indeed being made, that "practically every physicist of standing," including four Nobel Prize winners, was engaged on the project. Indeed, "the bomb was expected to be ready for testing in mid summer," Stimson promised, in plenty of time to have a major impact on the Pacific war.

Stimson went on to explain the opposing schools of thought regarding the bomb's use and future control. Though there was no question that America was developing the weapon in order to use it, the question remained: Could a demonstration of the bomb precede the military drop, "with subsequent notice to Japan that [it] would be used against the Japanese mainland unless surrender was forthcoming"?

In a conversation with economist Alexander Sachs the previous December, Roosevelt purportedly agreed with Sachs that the first step should be a nonmilitary demonstration before a team of international scientists. The next step would be a warning, outlining exactly where and when the bomb would be dropped, so civilians could escape. In a similar conversation with Vannevar Bush, Roosevelt questioned whether the bomb should actually be dropped on the Japanese or used simply as a threat. But either option remained premature until the bomb was ready.

Nor was any decision reached with regard to future control, after the war. General Leslie Groves, head of the Manhattan Project, and the military were on one side, wanting the project to remain solely in America's hands; Bush and Conant were on the other, favoring international control and free access to laboratories around the world. Whichever way the president went, Stimson argued, his policy must be in place before the bomb was ready for use. Roosevelt agreed, but nothing more was said. Feeling good about this wide-ranging conversation, Stimson left, never imagining that this was the last time he would see his boss.

• • •

In the middle of March, Lucy Rutherfurd came to Washington for a week. She stayed in Georgetown with her sister, Violetta, and her brother-in-law, William Marbury. The timing of the visit, arranged most likely with Anna's help, coincided with a three-day trip Eleanor was taking to North Carolina to speak to the legislative assembly in Raleigh and attend a conference on "Education in the Mountains" in Montreat, North Carolina.

In preparation for Lucy's arrival on Monday afternoon, March 12, Roosevelt approved a long list of visitors in the morning, including U.S. Ambassador to China Patrick Hurley, Secretary of State Edward Stettinius, U.S. Ambassador to Brazil Adolf Berle, and Budget Director Harold Smith. Smith told the president he looked well but seemed to have lost some weight. "Do you think so?" the president asked, with a look that suggested to Smith that he might be a bit sensitive about the subject.

If Roosevelt was concerned about his appearance for Lucy's sake, his worries were quickly dispelled that afternoon, when he motored to pick her up, for Lucy thought he looked more handsome than ever. While everyone else lamented his extreme thinness, Lucy told her friend Madame Shoumatoff that there was "something about his face that shows the way he looked when he was young," the way he looked when she first fell in love with him. "Having lost so much weight," Lucy said, "his features, always handsome, are more definitely chiseled."

Secret Service agents later recalled riding behind the president's car as he and Lucy headed off for a leisurely drive through the Virginia countryside before returning to the White House for dinner. Seated together in the back seat, sealed by a glass partition from the chauffeur, the two old friends enjoyed a few moments of privacy. For Roosevelt, Hick once observed, motoring was not only a favorite form of recreation, it was almost a necessity, for he had so few ways of getting a change of scene. Watching his excitement as he readied himself to leave on a drive, one visitor recalled that "he was like a little boy going to the circus."

Anna and John joined Lucy and the president for dinner that night in his study. "Never was there anything clandestine about these occasions," Anna later insisted. "On the contrary, they were occasions which I welcomed for my father because they were light-hearted and gay, affording a few hours of much needed relaxation for a loved father and world leader in a time of crisis."

Yet, if nothing underhanded was intended, the fact remained that Lucy's visits were kept strictly secret from Eleanor. "I doubt that father felt he was doing anything wrong in seeing Lucy," Jimmy observed, "but I certainly can understand his keeping it a secret because he believed mother would take it badly and would be hurt."

Lucy came to dinner again the following night, along with Anna, John, and MacKenzie King. King made no specific reference to Lucy in his diary that night, saying only that the dinner that evening was "strictly a family affair," which he "greatly enjoyed." As King got up to leave at nine-thirty,

Roosevelt said that, if there was any way he could help in the prime minister's upcoming election, he would gladly do so. Warmly shaking King's hand, Roosevelt invited him to return any time to the White House, Warm Springs, or Hyde Park. Lucy remained with the president in the study another hour and then Roosevelt went to bed.

The next day, after a busy round of appointments, Roosevelt was wheeled into the sun parlor for lunch with Lucy and Anna. Anna later recalled welcoming these rare, relaxed meals "because I felt the pressure of the war, with constant decisions to be made, must be relegated to the background occasionally." Lucy was "a wonderful person," Anna said, and "I was grateful to her." At seven-thirty that night, Lucy returned, to enjoy a three-hour dinner alone with the president.

When Eleanor came back to the White House on Thursday morning, Lucy's visits stopped. On Saturday, Eleanor and Franklin celebrated their fortieth wedding anniversary at a small family luncheon with Anna, Franklin's old friend and law partner Harry Hooker, and the Morgenthaus. If Anna felt in any way self-conscious about her curious role as go-between for her father and Lucy, she gave no evidence to anyone, remaining open and warm with both her parents. Hassett noted the "complete contrast in the position of the principals to the scene forty years ago when the bride was given away by her 'Uncle Ted,' " who, "in the very hey day of his popularity, stole the whole picture."

That evening, Franklin and Eleanor celebrated again with a small formal dinner in the State Dining Room. The guests included Crown Princess Juliana of Holland; the Dutch ambassador, Alexander Loudon, and his wife, Elizabeth; Assistant Secretary of State Nelson Rockefeller; and Anna and John. The dinner was followed by a movie, *The Suspect,* an Edwardian murder mystery about a man driven to kill his nagging wife. The party dispersed sometime after midnight. "Thus," Hassett observed, "another milestone is passed in the career of an extraordinary man and wife."

Eleanor remained in town until Monday morning, when she left on a four-day trip that would take her to New York and then to Greensboro, North Carolina, to attend a seminar on "The Returning Black Serviceman" at Bennett College and to meet with twenty-five hundred young women at the women's college of the state university. These were just the kind of gatherings Eleanor relished. "This world of young people, especially of young women," she wrote in her column, "is a very exciting world, for in their hands lies so much of the promise of this nation."

With Eleanor away, Roosevelt acted once more, writer Jim Bishop observed, "like a boy on vacation from school." He and Lucy took a long drive together through the countryside on Monday afternoon, dined with Anna and John on Tuesday, and were served tea together in the study on Wednesday. At the Gridiron dinner the following night, just after Lucy's weeklong visit had come to an end, reporter Allen Drury, who had been saddened at first to see how old the president looked, found a definite spark of the old FDR as Roosevelt passed by, "the head going up with a toss, the smile breaking out, the hand uplifted and waving in the old familiar way."

• • •

When Eleanor returned from North Carolina, she was saddened to discover that Hick had packed up her things and moved back to Long Island. Hick had been suffering for several months from diabetes, and the stress of her position at the Democratic National Committee was draining her limited energy. Under doctor's orders, she had quit her job and made arrangements to leave Washington for good.

Before leaving, Hick had penned a long farewell note to Eleanor. "The goodbyes have all been said," Hick wrote, "and presently I shall be on the way out of Washington with two orchids pinned to my shoulder. . . . With you as an example, I tried awfully hard to do a good job, and most of the time, I think I honestly did give the Women's division the best that was in me. But many times I was irritable and impatient and intolerant. One of the qualities I loved most in you is your tolerance. . . .

"I wish I had the words to tell you how grateful I am for your many kindnesses these past four years. It did two wonderful things—kept me near you and made it possible for me to hang on to my house, which is infinitely precious to me. I shall miss you. Yet I shall feel that you are near. After all these years, we could never drift very far apart. You are a very wonderful friend, my dear." Though Hick's love for Eleanor had not turned into a lasting romance, as Hick had originally hoped, their friendship had remained constant.

Now the curious double life Hick had led while she lived in the White House could be brought to an end. Fearing that the politicians she worked with at the Democratic National Committee would expect her to produce favors for them if they realized she was actually staying at the White House, she had pretended she was living at the Mayflower Hotel. If someone escorted her home from a party, she would say goodbye in the lobby, walk toward the elevators, wait until her escort had departed, and then take a cab to the White House. Her closest friends, including Judge Marion Harron and a few of her former female colleagues, knew of her residence, but never once did a single reporter mention Hick's living arrangements in a story. Her secret was protected.

For Eleanor, Hick's continuing friendship had been invaluable. Never would Eleanor forget that it was Hick who had originally suggested to her that her nightly letters to her friends could be transformed into a newspaper column. Now Eleanor's syndicated column was a daily fixture, appearing six times a week in hundreds of papers in cities and towns throughout the country. Indeed, that same March, as Hick was leaving Washington, the syndicate asked Eleanor to sign up for another five years, until December

1950. She was especially pleased by the length of the contract. Since it carried her two years past the 1948 election, she would finally, she believed, be able to write without the constraints of being first lady.

But if Eleanor's career had been helped by friendship with Hick, Hick's career had suffered. By giving up her identity as a newspaperwoman, Hick later acknowledged, she had paid a terrible price. She was particularly reminded of her loss, she said, when Madame Chiang was at the White House. Eleanor had invited Hick to attend Chiang's joint press conference with the president in the Oval Office. Hick was anxious to meet Chiang but felt compelled to decline the invitation. "The office would be packed," Hick wrote. "Probably not all of the working people could get inside. I could imagine some of my former colleagues muttering, 'What's she doing, taking up room in there. She's no longer a reporter.'"

Yet, even though Hick had surrendered to her passion, she had not lost her pride. Years later, when Eleanor completed the second installment of her autobiography, she sent Hick a draft of the pages covering the first inauguration, including a description of the interview she had given Hick on inaugural day. At the end of the inaugural paragraph, Eleanor had commented: "Later I came to realize that in the White House one must not play favorites." Thinking it sounded as if she had gotten the chance to cover Eleanor Roosevelt just because she was "a nice tame pet reporter," Hick dashed off a letter to Tommy.

"Tommy, I didn't get that story because I was anybody's pet reporter.... In those days (pardon an old lady her conceit) I was somebody in my own right. I was just about the top gal reporter in the country. Forgive me but I was good, I knew it.... I got the story because I earned it.... Maybe I'm being silly. But I just can't let the high spot of my newspaper career—the only thing in my whole life I'm really proud of—fizzle out like a wet firecracker, as though I was a nice tame little girl who was somebody's pet until she learned that she didn't play favorites!"

Eleanor changed the paragraph to read: "Soon after the inaugural ceremonies Lorena Hickok, to whom I had promised an interview, came up to my sitting room. Both my husband and Louis Howe had agreed to the interview because she was the outstanding woman reporter for the Associated Press and they both had known her and recognized her ability in New York."

"EVERYBODY
IS CRYING"

On Saturday night, March 24, 1945, after dinner with Crown Princess Martha and Crown Prince Olav, Franklin and Eleanor took the overnight train to Hyde Park, where the president planned to relax, get a lot of sleep, and do a few things at the library. "Hope he responds to good air and quiet," Hassett noted the morning after their arrival.

"Everything is just beginning to grow," Eleanor observed happily. The sight of budding trees and young flowers poking through the ground combined to produce a sense of serenity and a feeling of renewal. On Sunday afternoon, Franklin spoke with Eleanor of something that had long been in his mind. He wanted her to travel with him on April 20 to San Francisco for the opening session of the United Nations, and then, sometime in late May or early June, he wanted her to accompany him to London, Holland, and the front.

They would travel by ship to Southampton and then by train to Buckingham Palace, where they would stay with the king and queen for several days. He owed a return visit to the royal family, he said, and this seemed to be the best time. Then he would like to drive with the king through the streets of London, give an address before the houses of Parliament, and spend time with Churchill at Chequers. He had already told Churchill of his plans, and the prime minister was enthusiastic.

Roosevelt, Churchill predicted, "is going to get from the British people the greatest reception ever accorded to any human being since Lord Nelson made his triumphant return to London. . . . It will come genuinely and spontaneously from the hearts of the British people; they all love him for what he has done to save them from destruction by the Huns; they love him also for what he has done to relieve their fear that the horrors they have been through for five years might come upon them again in increased fury."

After London, they would visit men on the battlefields, call on Queen Wilhelmina in Holland, stay at the Hague, and end up in Paris. So excited was Roosevelt at the thought of the trip that he had been unable to keep it a secret. He had brought it up in recent conversations with MacKenzie King and Frances Perkins and seemed as happy as he had been in months. "I have long wanted to do it," he said to Perkins. "I want to see the British people myself. Eleanor's visit in wartime was a great success. I mean a success for her and for me so that we understood more about their problems. . . . I told Eleanor to order her clothes and get some fine things so that she will make a really handsome appearance."

When Perkins protested that a trip to Europe would be too dangerous, that the Germans would be out to get him, Roosevelt put his hand over his mouth and whispered, "The war in Europe will be over by the end of May." It comforted Perkins, she said later, to know that Roosevelt realized this. "I've always remembered it."

Eleanor listened eagerly to Franklin's plans. When her husband was like this, brimful of ideas, flushed, and triumphant, there was no one like him. Perhaps, in the closeness of the moment, she, too, began imagining the trip in all its splendid detail, erasing the painful knowledge, made even more vivid in recent days, of Franklin's considerable decline.

For the first time, Eleanor sadly noted that weekend, Franklin no longer wanted to drive his own car. He let her drive, which he had never done before, and he let her mix the cocktails, something that would have been inconceivable only a few months earlier. Nor, she observed, was he able to enjoy her usual way of arguing with him on a matter of public policy. In the midst of a heated discussion on peacetime conscription, she "suddenly realized he was upset," that he "was no longer the calm and imperturbable person" who had always goaded her on to vehement arguments. "It was just another indication of the change which we were all so unwilling to acknowledge.''

Yet here he was talking with such enthusiasm about plans for the future that she, too, began to believe all these trips would come to pass. Beyond San Francisco and London, he still had dreams of taking her around the world with him, and of spending a couple of years in the Middle East to help bring parts of the desert to life with reforestation, irrigation, proper farming, and conservation.

When Eleanor laughingly suggested that he might like ''to enjoy life for a few years without responsibility,'' without taking on ''new and perplexing problems,'' he turned to her and with very characteristic emphasis said, ''No, I like to be where things are growing.'' His comment reminded her of something he had said years before, when they first visited the Grand Canyon. She thought it ''the most beautiful and majestic sight'' she had ever seen, but he disagreed. ''No, it looks dead,'' he said. ''I like my green trees at Hyde Park better. They are alive and growing.''

''That sense of continuing growth and development was always keenly present with him,'' Eleanor observed. ''He never liked to dwell on the past, always wanted to go forward.'' So now, though she worried about signs of ebbing strength, she took heart in his crazy plans to help straighten out the Middle East and Asia. ''Does that sound tired to you?'' she said to a friend who had commented on his sunken appearance. ''I'm all ready to sit back. He's still looking forward to more work.''

While the president was at Hyde Park, relations with Stalin reached a point of crisis. Roosevelt had been trying for weeks to put the best light on the deteriorating situation in Poland, where, in spite of Stalin's solemn agreements at Yalta, the communist regime in Warsaw was refusing to broaden its base or hold free elections. Churchill had been urging Roosevelt to intervene, warning that if forceful action were not taken soon their hopes for democracy in Poland would vanish. Roosevelt had been slow to respond, fearing that a direct confrontation with Stalin on Poland would defeat his larger dream for the United Nations.

But as continuing reports, each more disturbing than the last, filtered in from Harriman and Stettinius, Roosevelt finally agreed with Churchill that the time had come to address Stalin directly. ''I cannot conceal from you,'' Roosevelt cabled Stalin on March 29, ''the concern with which I view the developments of mutual interest since our fruitful meetings at Yalta. . . . I must make it quite plain to you that any solution which would result in a thinly disguised continuance of the present Warsaw regime would be unacceptable and would cause the people of the United States to regard the Yalta agreements as having failed.''

Though Stalin evaded the issue in an unsatisfactory reply, Churchill was much relieved to know that he and Roosevelt were now acting in concert. ''Our friendship,'' he assured the president, ''is the rock on which I build for the future so long as I am one of the builders. I always think of those tremendous days when you devised Lend-Lease, when we met at Argentia, when you decided, with my heartfelt agreement, to launch the invasion of Africa and when you comforted me for the loss of Tobruk by giving me the 300 Shermans of subsequent Alamein fame. I remember the part our personal relations have played in the advance of the world cause now nearing its first military goal."

•   •   •

When the president returned from Hyde Park the morning of March 29, Grace Tully was saddened to see that his four-day weekend "had failed to erase any of the fatigue from his face." He looked drawn and gray, and the shadows under his eyes seemed to have darkened. "Did you get any rest at Hyde Park?" Tully asked. "Yes, child, but not nearly enough. I shall be glad to get down south."

At four that afternoon, Roosevelt was scheduled to leave for Warm Springs for a two-week rest, accompanied by Laura, Margaret, Tully, and Bruenn. He had packed his "usual leisure time paraphernalia," Tully recalled, "his stamp collection, catalogue and equipment," and was looking forward to the trip. Anna had planned to go, too, but at the last minute her six-year-old son, Johnny, had come down with a serious gland infection and had to be hospitalized at Walter Reed, where he was being administered daily doses of penicillin, a radical new drug still in a stage of experimental use.

Unable to accompany her father, Anna made arrangements for Lucy Rutherfurd to come to Warm Springs the second week of his stay. Knowing this, Franklin gently dissuaded Eleanor from coming. "He was very amusing about it," Eleanor recalled years later. "He loved going to Warm Springs but he said to me that he felt that there were certain things I had to do, and I'd better wait and come down later. He would take two people whom he enjoyed having with him, Margaret Suckley and Laura Delano, and he said, in an amusing way, that he did not have to make any effort with either of them."

The train pulled into the tiny station at Warm Springs at 2 p.m. "The President was the worst looking man I ever saw who was still alive," the station agent recalled. Mike Reilly, too, had an inkling that something was wrong when he went to transfer the president into a car. Normally the process was "pretty simple, despite his 180 pounds and his complete inability to use his legs. He depended entirely upon his hands and arms and shoulders. Usually he'd turn his back to the auto and one of the Detail would lift him. He'd reach backward until his hands had secured a firm grip on each side of the car door, and then he'd actually surge out of your arms into the car and onto the jump seat." But on this day, it took every bit of Reilly's strength to make the transfer, for the president was "absolutely dead weight."

But Reilly took heart in the knowledge that "Warm Springs had saved his life once" and could do so again. "I always felt he looked upon it as a miraculous source of strength and health," Reilly noted. So, when Roosevelt headed toward the Little White House, "it wasn't just a matter of our hoping the trip would help the Boss, we just naturally assumed it would."

By the end of a week in the warm Georgia sun, the old magic seemed to be working. "The days flowed peacefully by," Margaret Suckley recalled, "with FDR getting slowly but steadily more rested. His appetite, too, improved from day to day and his spirits rose as he felt less tired." During the mornings, he would work on his papers and give dictation; after lunch, a nap and a drive through the rolling countryside, where the peach trees were covered with fruit.

On Thursday, April 5, Sergio Osmeña, the president of the Philippines came for lunch. After Osmeña left, Roosevelt held a leisurely press conference in his living room. "He was in fine form," Suckley noted, "and looked so much better than a week ago that we almost forgot he was still not his old self. He looked as though he had put on some weight, and his face looked fuller and much less tired."

"It was a beautiful, tranquil afternoon," Merriman Smith noted; "the President was in a friendly and easy mood." While Fala waddled from one person to the next, sniffing trouser cuffs and wagging his tail, Roosevelt told reporters that he and Osmeña had discussed the war in the Pacific and the not-too-distant day of complete Philippine independence. The relaxed interview was just about over when a reporter abruptly shifted ground, asking Roosevelt to comment on a news leak that Russia was going to get three votes in the United Nations General Assembly.

"That," Roosevelt said, with a roaring laugh, "is not even subtle." But, in the genial atmosphere of his living room, Roosevelt went on to explain how the controversial three-vote situation had come about. "As a matter of fact, the plea for votes was done in a very quiet way. Stalin said to me—and this is the essence of it—'You know, there are two parts of Russia that have been completely devastated. . . . One is the Ukraine, and the other is White Russia. In these sections, millions have been killed, and we think it would be very heartening—would help build them up—if we could get them a vote in the Assembly.' It is not really of any great importance. It is an investigatory body only." With this, Roosevelt drew the conference to an end and went for a nap.

While Franklin was away, Eleanor had much to keep her busy, between her usual rounds of beneficent activities and her commitments to her friends. On the weekend of April 6, she and Tommy went to Hyde Park to begin the process of opening up the Big House for the summer. Franklin called her there that Saturday night but, as she explained in a long, chatty letter the next day, she had been half asleep when he called, having put in a long day unpacking barrels, rearranging china, and clearing off shelves. She ached from the unwonted exercise, she told him, though it had been fun.

"I forgot to tell you," she went on, "that Elinor Morgenthau had a serious heart attack at Daytona, Florida and Henry has been terribly worried. I think Elinor can't stand the war strain and trying not to show it has had an effect on her circulation. . . . I haven't felt sleepy tonight so I've written James, Elliott, and Frankie, Elinor, Rommie and Sisty and now I must go to bed as we leave in the morning and go up to New Hampshire tomorrow night and I'll be in Washington Wed. eve."

"Much love to you dear," she concluded. "I'm so glad you are gaining. You sounded cheerful for the first time last night and I hope you'll weigh 170 lbs when you return."

Unbeknownst to Eleanor, Franklin's good cheer that Saturday night was likely prompted by the knowledge that Lucy Rutherfurd was coming to see him on Monday. Phone logs at the FDR Library reveal that Roosevelt called Lucy in Aiken almost every day while he was at Warm Springs. She was planning to drive to Warm Springs on Monday, April 9, with her painter friend, Elizabeth Shoumatoff. Roosevelt told her he would meet their car in Macon at 4 p.m. The roads were tricky, however, and the two women lost their way, arriving quite late. "Nothing in sight," Shoumatoff observed, no presidential cars, no limousines. "Nobody loves us," Lucy joked, "nobody cares for us." Continuing on toward Warm Springs, they noticed a crowd gathered in front of a corner drugstore in the small village of Greenville. Franklin Roosevelt was sitting in an open car with Margaret Suckley and Fala, drinking a Coca-Cola. Shoumatoff was struck at once by "the expression of joy on FDR's face upon seeing Lucy," and by Lucy's relief in knowing that Roosevelt had not forgotten her after all.

Dinner that night, Shoumatoff recalled, found Roosevelt "full of jokes," basking in the admiration of four women (Margaret and Laura had been invited to join Lucy and her friend). Shoumatoff's eye was drawn to Laura's exotic looks, her bright-blue hair, her striking dinner pajamas, and her "profile as beautiful as a cameo," but Roosevelt, she noted, seemed constantly to address himself to Lucy, in a wide-ranging conversation that moved from Churchill to Stalin to food.

The next morning, while Roosevelt sat on the sun porch working on his papers, Shoumatoff began preliminary sketches for a portrait which Lucy wanted to give to her daughter, Barbara. Even as Shoumatoff sketched, Roosevelt continued joking with Lucy. Watching the affectionate rapport between them, Shoumatoff's photographer, Harold Robbins, whom she had brought along to help her with her work, thought they were like "happy kids enjoying golden days as if there would be no end to them."

In the afternoon, Roosevelt took the four women for a long drive in his open coupe. Along the way, he encountered Merriman Smith riding a horse which he had hired for the afternoon at the village drugstore. "As I reined in the horse," Smith recalled, "Roosevelt bowed majestically to me. His voice was wonderful and resonant. It sounded like the Roosevelt of old. In tones that must have been audible a block away, FDR hailed me with 'Heigh-Ho, Silver!' "

After dinner, Roosevelt gave Lucy a photograph taken when the two of them had first met, when he was assistant secretary of the navy. As Shoumatoff looked at the picture of the handsome young Roosevelt and then at Lucy's "beautiful, slightly flushed face," she felt happy for them. "The quiet and beauty of the place," she later wrote, "the privacy of the surroundings, seemed almost created for the new blossoming of those old memories."

The following day, April 11, Roosevelt was in high spirits as he worked on a draft of his Jefferson Day speech. "I remember so clearly seeing him writing and writing," Suckley recalled years later, "a little bent over the table, Miss Tully waiting by his side, pencil in hand. . . . Then, when he had finished, I remember distinctly how he came into the room from the porch, a look of great satisfaction on his face, and said, 'Well, I've written much of that speech in my own hand.'"

It was "a good speech," Hassett recorded, fueled, as most of Roosevelt's speeches were, by a striking combination of optimism and belief in the American people. "The only thing we have to fear is fear itself," Roosevelt had said in his famous first inaugural; and now, in the peroration of the last speech he would write, he returned to the same theme. "The only limit to our realization of tomorrow," he wrote, "will be our doubts of today. Let us move forward with strong and active faith."

That evening, Henry Morgenthau, in transit to Washington from Florida, joined Roosevelt and the four women for cocktails and dinner. "I was terribly shocked when I saw him," Morgenthau recorded in his diary. "I found he had aged terrifically and looked very haggard. His hands shook so that he started to knock over the glasses. I had to hold each glass as he poured out the cocktail. . . . I have never seen him have so much difficulty transferring himself from his wheelchair to a regular chair, and I was in agony watching him."

After two cocktails, Roosevelt seemed to improve. He was in good spirits when he called Anna in Washington to check on Johnny's progress. "He was full of this wonderful barbecue that was coming off the next day," Anna recalled. "The only bad thing about it," he told her, was that he knew ahead of time that he was going to overeat, but he intended to "thoroughly enjoy it."

The conversation at supper was lively and agreeable, though Shoumatoff detected "an encompassing tension" which she attributed to Morgenthau's presence. As soon as the outsider left, "the atmosphere resumed its former easy and pleasant manner." With Roosevelt settled comfortably in an armchair by the fireplace, Shoumatoff volunteered to tell her favorite ghost story about the black-pearl necklace of Catherine the Great. "Upon finishing my story," Shoumatoff recalled, "another was about to be told when Dr. Bruenn and his assistant arrived. The President, like a little boy, asked to stay up longer, but finally consented to retire, telling me he would be ready for my painting the next morning."

"The sky was clear" in Warm Springs on April 12, 1945, Suckley recalled, "with the promise of a hot day." At noon, the president was sitting in his living room with Lucy, Laura, and Margaret while Shoumatoff stood at her easel, painting. Shoumatoff was struck by his "exceptionally good color"; Suckley, too, thought he looked "surprisingly well, and very fine in a double breasted gray suit and crimson tie."

The mail was heavy; a stack of letters and documents awaited the president's signature. Hassett took each paper as it was signed and spread it on a chair for the ink to dry. "Well," Roosevelt teased, "are you through with your laundry yet? Is it all dry?" Among the documents was a letter prepared for the president's signature by the State Department. "A typical State Department letter," Roosevelt laughingly observed. "It says nothing at all." His spirits remained high as he came to a bill just passed by Congress which extended the life of the Commodity Credit Corporation. "There," he boasted to the women as he signed his name with a flourish, "there is where I make a law."

At that moment, Lizzie McDuffie, the president's maid, was walking to the guest cottage to make the beds. Looking through the living-room window, she saw Roosevelt sitting in his chair, laughing and smiling at Lucy. "The last I remember," Lizzie said later, "he was looking into the smiling face of a beautiful woman."

At one o'clock, the butler came in to set the table for lunch. Roosevelt glanced at his watch and said, "We've got just fifteen minutes more." Then, suddenly, Shoumatoff recalled, "he raised his right hand and passed it over his forehead several times in a strange jerky way." Then his head went forward. Thinking he was looking for something, Suckley went over to him and asked if he had dropped his cigarette. "He looked at me," Suckley recalled, "his forehead furrowed with pain, and tried to smile. He put his left hand up to the back of his head and said, 'I have a terrific pain in the back of my head.' And then he collapsed."

Suckley reached for the telephone and asked the operator to find Dr. Bruenn and send him over at once. In the meantime, the president's valet, Arthur Prettyman, and the butler carried the unconscious president into the bedroom. When Dr. Bruenn arrived, he could tell at once that the president had suffered a cerebral hemorrhage. "It was a bolt out of the blue," Bruenn later observed. "A good deal of his brain had been damaged."

Lucy and the other women were still standing in the living room. "The confusion was so great," Shoumatoff recalled. "Nobody seemed to know whether they were coming or going."

"We must pack up and go," Lucy whispered to Shoumatoff. "The family is arriving by plane and the rooms must be vacant. We must get to Aiken before dark." In a few moments, Shoumatoff recalled, she and Lucy were back in the guest cottage, hurriedly tossing their things into suitcases. It was about two-thirty when they left.

In the bedroom, Bruenn did what he could, "which wasn't much," he admitted. He notified Dr. McIntire, who placed an emergency call to Atlanta to Dr. James Paullin, who had been part of the team that examined Roosevelt at Bethesda Naval Hospital the previous year. Bruenn took off the president's clothes and put on his pajamas. By the time Grace Tully reached the house, there were terrible sounds of tortured breathing coming from the bedroom. "All you could hear was breathing," Lizzie McDuffie recalled. "It was kind of like—deep, steady, long gasps."

Tully dropped her head to pray while Hassett went into the bedroom. "His eyes were closed," Hassett recorded, "mouth open—the awful breathing . . . But the Greek nose and the noble forehead were grand as ever. . . . I knew that I should not see him again."

Shortly before three-thirty, Roosevelt's breathing stopped. Dr. Bruenn was on the bed giving him artificial respiration when Dr. Paullin arrived. "We put a shot of adrenaline into his heart," Bruenn recalled—"sometimes that starts the heart up again—nothing worked. And that was it." The president was dead.

• • •

Hassett called the White House to break the news to Press Secretary Steve Early. The two men agreed to say nothing more until Eleanor was told. Dr. McIntire had called her an hour earlier to tell her that Roosevelt had fainted. The doctor was "not alarmed," Eleanor recalled, but suggested she prepare to go to Warm Springs that evening. Should she cancel her speaking engagement at four that afternoon? Eleanor asked. No, McIntire insisted, it would cause great comment if she canceled and then at the last minute flew to Warm Springs.

Arriving at the Sulgrave Club promptly at 4 p.m., Eleanor took a seat between Mrs. Woodrow Wilson and Mrs. Allen Dougherty, chairman of the charity event. Dressed in a soft red suit which one reporter described as "unusually smart," Eleanor delivered a short talk and then returned to the head table to listen as the celebrated pianist Miss Evelyn Tyner played. In the middle of the piece, Eleanor was told she was wanted on the telephone. The message gave her "a quick start," one of the ladies seated nearby later recalled.

Quietly excusing herself, Eleanor went to the phone. Steve Early was on the line. He was "very much upset," Eleanor recalled, and he "asked me to come home at once. I did not even ask why. I knew down in the heart that something dreadful had happened. Nevertheless the amenities had to be observed, so I went back to the party. . . ."

Resuming her place at the head table, Eleanor waited until Miss Tyner's piano piece was completed, joined in the applause, and then rose to say, "Now I'm called back to the White House and I want to apologize for leaving before this delightful concert is finished." The audience gave her a standing ovation and she left the room.

"I got into the car and sat with clenched hands all the way to the White House. In my heart I knew what had happened, but one does not actually formulate these terrible thoughts until they are spoken. I went to my sitting room and Steve Early and Dr. McIntire came to tell me the news."

Anna was at Bethesda Naval Hospital with Johnny when she heard. She had been told by Dr. McIntire earlier in the afternoon that her father had collapsed, but since there was nothing she could do she had returned to the hospital. "I hadn't been there more than about twenty minutes," she recalled, "when the head of the Naval Center Hospital, in Bethesda, came and only said one sentence, 'Mrs. Boettiger, my car's waiting to take you to the White House.' And he'd been told, too, obviously. And that is the way it was done."

When she got back to the White House, Anna went to her mother's sitting room. Eleanor had already changed into a black dress, sent for the vice-president, and cabled her four sons, all in active service. "He did his job to the end," she wrote, "as he would want you to do." In the midst of indescribable confusion, she had the presence of mind to call the hospital in Daytona Beach where Elinor Morgenthau lay ill to ask that the radio be removed from her room lest Elinor hear the news and suffer a setback.

At five-thirty, Vice-President Harry Truman arrived at the White House, not knowing why he had been asked to come. He was ushered into the first lady's sitting room where Eleanor was waiting with Anna, John and Steve Early. Eleanor stepped forward to greet him, placing her arm gently on his shoulder. "Harry," she said, "the President is dead." For a moment Truman was unable to speak. Then, at last, he found his voice to ask if there was anything he could do for her.

In reply, Eleanor said: "Is there anything we can do for you? For you are the one in trouble now." She told Truman she was planning to fly to Warm Springs that night and wondered if it was still proper for her to use a government plane. Truman assured her that it was. Minutes later, Stettinius came to the doorway. With tears streaming down his face, he discussed the plans to assemble the Cabinet and swear in the new president.

By 7 p.m., nearly all the members of the Cabinet were gathered in the Cabinet Room, along with Chief Justice Harlan Stone. "It was a very somber group," Stimson recorded, as he looked at the faces of Morgenthau, Biddle, Ickes, Perkins, and Stettinius. "For with all his idiosyncrasies our Chief was a very kindly and friendly man and his humor and pleasantry had always been the life of the Cabinet meetings. I think every one of us felt keenly the loss of a real personal friend. I know I did. I have never concealed the fact that I regarded his administrative procedures as disorderly, but his foreign policy was always founded on great foresight and keenness of vision, and at this period of great confusion of ideas in this country, the loss of his leadership will be most serious."

Minutes after the swearing in, Eleanor left for Warm Springs. When she appeared at the front portico of the White House, she talked for a few minutes with Anna, who was staying behind to coordinate plans for the funeral service. Heading toward the car, she leaned over to recognize the clustered group of ushers, doormen, and women reporters who stood there. "A trooper to the last," reporter Bess Furman marveled. Then she kissed Anna goodbye and "strode with her usual determined gait to the waiting limo. Silent and alone, she went to her husband."

Harry Hopkins was still at St. Mary's Hospital in Rochester, Minnesota, when he heard the news. Frail as he was, he made plans to fly immediately to Washington. Then, from his hospital bed, he began calling his friends, feeling a desperate need to talk about Roosevelt. "You and I have got something great we can take with us the rest of our lives," he told Robert Sherwood. "It's a great realization because we know it's true what so many people believed about him and what made them love him. The President never let them down. That's what you and I can remember."

"Oh, we all know he could be exasperating," Hopkins went on, "and he could seem to be temporizing and delaying and he'd get us all worked up when we thought he was making too many concessions to expediency. But all of that was in the little things, the unimportant things—and he knew exactly how little and how unimportant they really were. But in the big things—all the things that were of real, permanent importance—he never let the people down."

It was after midnight in London when Churchill heard that Roosevelt was dead. "I felt as if I had been struck a physical blow," Churchill recalled. "My relations with this shining personality had played so large a part in the long, terrible years we had worked together. Now they had come to an end, and I was overpowered by a sense of deep and irreparable loss."

In Moscow, Ambassador Harriman learned of Roosevelt's death at about 3 a.m. local time. He drove to the Kremlin to tell Stalin. The Russian leader appeared "deeply distressed," Harriman recorded, holding the envoy's hand for nearly thirty seconds before asking him to sit and talk. Stalin then questioned Harriman closely about the circumstances of Roosevelt's death and sent a message to the State Department asking that an autopsy be performed to determine if Roosevelt had been poisoned.

As word spread from city to town within the United States, ordinary people, politicians and reporters struggled to come to terms with Roosevelt's death. For the millions who adored him and for those who despised him, an America without Roosevelt seemed almost inconceivable. He was in his thirteenth year as president when he died. Those who had just reached the legal voting age of twenty-one in time for this fourth election had been only nine years old when he took the oath of office for the first time. Schoolgirl Anne Relph remembered riding her bicycle back to the playground after hearing that Roosevelt had died, "and feeling, as a child, that this was going to be the end of the world, because he was the only president I'd ever known. I was almost not aware that there could be another president. He had always been THE PRESIDENT, in capital letters."

Correspondent I. F. Stone was at the *PM* newspaper office in New York when a copy boy ran out of the wire room with a piece of United Press copy confirming the president's death. "That first flash," Stone recalled, "seemed incredible; like something in a nightmare, for down under the horror was the comfortable feeling that you would wake to find it all a dream. The Romans must have felt this way when word came that Caesar Augustus was dead." Journalist Studs Terkel heard the news while he was having drinks in the Stevens Hotel. "Everybody left. I'm walking south on Michigan Boulevard, and I can't stop crying. Everybody is crying." Reporter Jack Altschul was in his office at *Newsday,* "God, there were people in the office who were professed Republicans and may have come from stockbroking families who have never forgiven Roosevelt . . . but I can remember going with some of the guys to the bar where we used to hang out after we put out the new edition, and the guys were crying."

"I am too shocked to talk," Senate Majority Leader Alben Barkley told reporters. "It is one of the worst tragedies that ever happened." Mr. Republican, Senator Robert Taft agreed. "The President's death," he said, "removed the greatest figure of our time at the very climax of his career, and shocks the world to which his words and actions were more important than those of any other man. He dies a hero of the war, for he literally worked himself to death in the service of the American people." And Alf Landon, Republican presidential nominee in 1936 said, "it is tragic he could not have lived to see the fruition of his greatest undertaking."

Even the normally staid *New York Times* was extravagant in its editorial praise. "Men will thank God on their knees a hundred years from now, that Franklin D. Roosevelt was in the White House. . . . It was his hand, more than that of any other single man, that built the great coalition of the United Nations. . . . It was his leadership which inspired free men in every part of the world to fight with greater hope and courage. Gone, now, is this talent and skill. . . . Gone is the fresh and spontaneous interest which this man took, as naturally as he breathed air, in the troubles and the hardships and the disappointments and the hopes of little men and humble people."

• • •

Churchill once said that to encounter Franklin Roosevelt, with all his buoyant sparkle, his iridescent personality, and his inner élan was like opening your first bottle of champagne. Roosevelt genuinely liked people, he enjoyed taking responsibility, and he adored being president. Alone among our modern presidents, he had "no conception of the office to live up to," political scientist Richard Neustadt noted, "he was it. His image of the office was himself-in-office." He did not have the time or the inclination for a melancholy contemplation of the "burdens" of the presidency. "Wouldn't you be President if you could?" he once naïvely asked a friend. "Wouldn't anybody?"

Whether sorting his stamp collection with Missy LeHand at his side, inspecting the troops in the company of his wife, probing the latest Hollywood gossip with Harry Hopkins, enjoying the company of a stylish woman, co-opting a potential rival, delivering a fireside chat, charming a disgruntled Cabinet officer, exchanging repartee with reporters or confidences with Churchill, Roosevelt's ebullience permeated every aspect of his leadership. "Under Roosevelt," historian William Leuchtenburg observed, "the White House became the focus of all government—the fountainhead of ideas, the initiator of action, the representative of the national interest. He took an office which had lost much of its prestige and power in the previous twelve years and gave it an importance which went well beyond what even Theodore Roosevelt and Woodrow Wilson had done. [He] re-created the modern Presidency."

"He was one of the few statesmen in the twentieth century, or any century," the British philosopher Isaiah Berlin wrote, "who seemed to have no fear of the future." Though the United States was miserably unprepared for war in the spring of 1940, Roosevelt never doubted that the American home front would eventually win the war, that the uncoerced energies of a free people could overcome the most efficient totalitarian regime. To his mind, there was no danger too great, no challenge too profound to yield to the combined efforts of the American people. He would provide the framework, the opportunity, and the inspiration, and the people would do the rest.

It was fashionable during the war to decry the chaos and confusion in Washington, the mushrooming bureaucracies with overlapping jurisdictions and inconsistent mandates. Yet it seems, with the luxury of hindsight, that no other form of organization could have produced the triumphs and transformations of Roosevelt's America. Indeed, it was not an organization at all. There was no master plan, no neat division of responsibilities, no precise allocation of burdens. The conduct of the nation during the war mirrored the temperament, the strengths, and the frailties of a single man. A lesser man, a man of smaller ego, would have sought greater control, more rigid lines of responsibility and authority. But Roosevelt never felt that he or his leadership was threatened by multiplicity and confusion. He could try everything; he could move in different directions at the same time; he could let the horses run, never doubting his ability to rein them in should they threaten to become uncontrollable. As long as the home front was big at the base, as long as the great majority of the American people were involved in the production effort, he could afford to let things be confused at the top.

His critics were certain that he would straitjacket the free-enterprise system once the war began. To this day, Franklin Roosevelt remains the symbol of big government and the controlled economy. Yet, under Roosevelt's wartime leadership, the government entered into a close partnership with private enterprise, enabling business to realize its full potential for the first time in many years. Despite the wide variety of government controls, private producers freely negotiated their contracts with the government, and no one was told where to move or where to work. Business was exempted from antitrust laws, allowed to write off the full cost of investments, given the financial and material resources to fulfill contracts, and guaranteed a substantial profit. The leader who had once proclaimed his intention to master the forces of organized money had become their greatest benefactor.

But even as he reached out to business during the war years, Roosevelt insisted on preserving the social gains of the previous decade. His partnership with business was not forged at the expense of American labor. On the contrary, the American workingman during the war enjoyed full employment, generous earnings, new fringe benefits, and a progressive tax code. Union membership expanded by more than six million. In less than half a decade, the Depression, which Roosevelt had fought so vigorously but with limited success, had been ended. Fueling this advance of business and labor was the material reality of an extraordinary, seemingly limitless, flow of weapons and vehicles far in excess of those Roosevelt predictions which had been scorned as "visionary" by economists and businessmen alike. Though Roosevelt had not lived to see the end of the war, his goal of making America "the arsenal of democracy" was abundantly fulfilled before he died. Between 1940 and 1945, the United States contributed nearly three hundred thousand warplanes to the Allied cause. American factories produced more than two million trucks, 107,351 tanks, 87,620 warships, 5,475 cargo ships, over twenty million rifles, machine guns, and pistols, and forty-four billion rounds of ammunition. "There is little doubt," army historians conclude, "that America's outpouring of war materiel rather than an Allied preponderance of manpower was the dominant factor in winning the war."

"The figures are all so astronomical that they cease to mean very much," historian Bruce Catton wrote. "Say that we performed the equivalent of building two Panama Canals every month with a fat surplus to boot; that's an understatement, it still doesn't begin to express it all, the total is simply beyond the compass of one's understanding. Here was displayed a strength greater even than cocky Americans in the old days of unlimited self-confidence had supposed; strength to which nothing—literally nothing, in the physical sense—was any longer impossible."

Roosevelt's success in mobilizing the nation to this extraordinary level of collective performance rested on his uncanny sensitivity to his followers, his ability to appraise public feeling and to lead the people one step at a time. More than any previous president, he studied public opinion: he read a variety of newspapers; he analyzed polls; he traveled the country when he could and dispatched his wife when he could not; he brought in people of clashing temperaments to secure different points of view; he probed visitors at dinner; he tried out his ideas on reporters. But more than diligence was involved. Like any great artist, Roosevelt relied on his own intuition to fit the smallest details and the most disparate impressions into a coherent pattern. He was able to sense what the people were thinking and feeling.

'Above all, he possessed a magnificent sense of timing. He understood when to invoke the prestige of the presidency and when to hold it in reserve, when to move forward and when to pull back. "I am like a cat," he once said. "I make a quick stroke and then I relax." He was committed to the

Allied cause from the start of the war, but he understood that he had to bring an isolationist people along little by little, through a combination of decisions, speeches, and events.

He let the reaction to the Nazi invasion of Western Europe build before he addressed the joint session of Congress on May 16, 1940. He let a citizens' group take the lead on the draft in the summer of 1940 while he focused on making the destroyer deal with Britain. Then, when it looked as though the draft would be defeated, he delivered a strong endorsement that carried the bill through. He sat quietly for days on the *Tuscaloosa* after receiving Churchill's urgent plea for help with Britain's financial crisis until he suddenly emerged with the idea of "lending" Britain weapons to be paid back in kind after the war. Then, perfectly sensing just how far the public was willing to go at that moment, he successfully sold the idea of lend-lease to the Congress and the country as America's best alternative to war. He resisted strong pressure to convoy ships in the spring of 1941, believing that convoys would bring America into the war before the American people were ready. Yet, once again perfectly sensing the state of public feeling—in which the growing commitment to the Allied cause was undercut by the fear of sending American boys abroad—he dramatized the grim situation on the seas by declaring an "unlimited emergency," which made it seem that he was moving further than he really was. Determined not to carry a divided country into war, he waited for events to unify the nation. The wisdom of this assessment was confirmed when the extension of the draft passed the House by only a single vote in August 1941. It would take the Japanese attack on Pearl Harbor to shatter isolationism once and for all and create the unified support necessary to win the war.

Roosevelt's sense of timing was also manifest in his actions as commander-in-chief. Once again, he knew when to invoke his powers and when to hold them in reserve. He picked a first-class military team—Marshall, King, Arnold, Leahy—and gave them wide latitude to run the war. Never once, Stimson admiringly remarked, did Roosevelt overturn his commanders' decisions for personal or political motives. Though the Democrats would have been greatly strengthened in the 1942 elections if the invasion of North Africa had occurred a few days earlier, he did not interfere with Eisenhower's decision to begin the landing six days after the election. Through the worst days of the war—the weeks after Pearl Harbor, the early days at Guadalcanal, the Battle of the Bulge—he remained calm and imperturbable, earning the deep respect of every single one of his commanders.

Yet, at critical junctures, he had the courage to force action over the protest of his military advisers, and almost all of these actions had a salutary effect on the war. In 1940, he insisted on giving all aid to Britain short of war, though his military chiefs warned him that he was jeopardizing America's own security in so doing. He brought Russia under the lend-lease umbrella at a time when his military advisers believed Russia had almost no chance of holding out. He encouraged the Doolittle raid on Japan, which inadvertently led to great success at Midway. He personally made the hotly debated decision to invade North Africa, and later granted MacArthur permission to recapture the Philippines. It was Roosevelt who gambled on the production of the B-29 superbomber, decided to spend $2 billion on an experimental atomic bomb, and demanded that the Allies commit themselves to a postwar structure before the war was over.

To be sure, there were errors in Roosevelt's wartime leadership. A precious year was lost in 1940–41, when the mobilization process was not pushed hard enough, when, as Washington lawyer Joe Rauh noted, "the arsenal of democracy was more democracy than arsenal." Indeed, had it not been for the period of borrowed time provided by the heroic resistance of the British and the Russians, the United States might not have been able to overcome the head start of the Axis in time to influence the course of the war. And once the mobilization got under way, he failed to protect small business against the military's tendency to lavish its contracts on the nation's industrial giants. It was during the war years that the links were forged that would lead to the rise of the "military-industrial complex" in postwar America.

One must also concede the failures of vision that led to the forcible relocation of the Japanese Americans, and the lack of a more decisive response to the extermination of the European Jews. Totally focused on winning the war, Roosevelt mistakenly accepted the specious argument that incarceration of the Japanese Americans was a military necessity. In so doing, he deprived tens of thousands of men, women, and children of Japanese descent of their civil liberties, and trampled on values he himself cherished.

Sorting out Roosevelt's actions and inactions with respect to the European Jews is more complicated. He believed that winning the war was the best means of rescuing the Jews. And there was merit to his belief. By the time the news of the systematic murder of the Jews reached the West in mid-1942, it was too late to mount a massive rescue effort short of winning the war as quickly as possible. But Roosevelt's intensity of focus blinded him to a series of smaller steps that could have been taken—the War Refugee Board could have been established earlier and given more authority; the United States could have applied more pressure on Germany to release the Jews and more pressure on neutral countries to take them in; the United States Air Force could have bombed the train tracks and the concentration camps. "None of these proposals guaranteed results," holocaust scholar David Wyman admits. "But all deserved serious consideration. . . . Even if few or no lives had been saved, the moral obligation would have been fulfilled."

But in the end, Roosevelt's strengths far outweighed his weaknesses. Despite confusions and conflicts, clashing interests and disparate goals, the American people were successfully combined in an unparalleled national enterprise. Indeed, at times, it seemed as if Roosevelt alone understood the complex and shifting relationship between the nation's effort at home and its struggle across the globe. "More than any other man," historian Eric

Larrabee concludes in his study of Roosevelt's wartime leadership, "he ran the war, and ran it well enough to deserve the gratitude of his countrymen then and since, and of those from whom he lifted the yoke of the Axis tyrannies. His conduct as Commander in Chief . . . bears the mark of greatness."

•   •   •

It was nearly midnight by the time Eleanor reached Warm Springs. She was, everyone commented, calm and composed when she arrived. When she walked into the living room, she embraced her two cousins and Miss Tully. Then she sat down on the sofa and asked each of them to tell her exactly what had happened. Tully recounted her own schedule that day; she had been dressing for lunch when she first heard the president was sick and had been in the living room when he died. Eleanor listened quietly and then turned to Margaret, who described sitting on the sofa crocheting when the president slumped forward in his chair.

Then Laura began to speak, telling Eleanor some brutal truths: Franklin had been sitting for a portrait when he collapsed. The painter was a friend of Lucy Rutherfurd's. Mrs. Rutherfurd was there as well, sitting in the alcove by the windows. The two women had been staying in the guest cottage as Franklin's guests for the past three days.

"It was a malicious thing to do," Eleanor's niece Eleanor Wotkyns later suggested, "but very fitting for her. She was a small, petty woman, jealous all her life of Eleanor's great success. Though she thought herself every bit as smart as Eleanor, she hadn't done a thing in her life except raise red setters and let her chauffeur drive her to dog shows all over the country. This was an act of revenge."

Laura's explanation was that "Eleanor would have found out anyway." Too many people knew the president had been sitting for a portrait when his cerebral hemorrhage struck. Too many people knew that Lucy was there. Still, Laura must have understood how devastating the news would be to Eleanor. Henceforth, thoughts of her husband's final days would be inextricably linked in her mind with thoughts of Lucy Mercer Rutherfurd.

When Laura finished speaking, Eleanor walked into the bedroom to see her husband's body. She closed the door behind her and remained inside —alone with her husband—for more than five minutes. When she emerged from the bedroom, Tully recalled, her eyes were dry and her face was composed. She sat down on the sofa again and questioned Laura further. Had Franklin seen Lucy at other times in recent years? Yes, Laura replied. Lucy had dined at the White House a number of times. Had anyone else been present? Yes, she and Margaret and . . . Anna. Indeed, Anna was the one who had arranged Lucy's visits.

Eleanor gave no visible sign then or in the days to come of the pain she must have felt on hearing these words. "At a time like that, you don't really feel your own feelings," she explained later. "When you're in a position of being caught in a pageant, you become part of a world outside yourself and you act almost like an automaton. You recede as a person. You build a facade for everyone to see and you live separately inside the facade. Something comes to protect you. I was well prepared for it. My grandmother brought me up to prepare for it, in a social way. I was never permitted as a child to say that I had a headache. I was trained to put personal things in the background."

Then Eleanor returned to the bedroom to select the clothes for her husband's burial—a double-breasted blue business suit flecked with gray, a soft white shirt, and a dark-blue-and-white four-in-hand tie. The president's valet finished dressing the body. He tenderly parted the hair and combed it back. Eleanor nodded her approval, and the body was brought into the living room and placed in a casket. "Oh, he was handsome," Lizzie McDuffie exclaimed. "You wouldn't have thought he had a day's illness."

The next morning, thousands of villagers were gathered at the little railroad station in Warm Springs to say goodbye to their president. They stood in clusters, heads bowed, openly weeping, as a military guard of honor lifted the bronze coffin into the rear car of the presidential train. A special cradle had been erected so the casket could be seen through the window as the train moved slowly eight hundred miles north toward the nation's capital. Hundreds of thousands of people lined the tracks along the way. "They came from the fields and the farms," INS reporter Robert Nixon wrote, "from hamlets and crossroads: and in the cities they thronged by the thousands to stare in humble reverence and awe."

"Men stood with their arms around the shoulders of their wives and mothers," Merriman Smith noted. "Men and women openly wept. Church choirs gathered at the trackside and sang Rock of Ages and Abide with Me." As the train made its way through Georgia's valleys and hills, Smith noticed four Negro women in a cotton field working on a spring planting. They were "kneeling near the edge of the field. Their hands were clasped together in prayerful supplication."

Several times during the long trip, various members of the president's staff walked through the train to the lounge car where Eleanor was seated. Was there anything they could do to help? they wanted to know. Each time, Eleanor thanked them but said there was nothing she needed.

As night fell, the rest of the train was dimmed so the president's catafalque could be seen for miles. "I lay in my berth all night with the window shade up," Eleanor recalled, "looking out at the countryside he had loved and watching the faces of the people at stations, and even at the crossroads, who came to pay their last tribute all through the night."

In the early morning, Eleanor sent for Grace Tully. "Did Franklin ever give you any instructions about his burial?" she asked. "She had difficulty saying that," Tully recalled. "Her eyes welled and her voice broke. It was only momentary. It was the only time during the whole ordeal I ever saw her almost lose her control." Tully recalled for Eleanor a conversation she had had with the president a year before. He had asked to be buried in the green-hedged garden of his ancestral home. He had also placed a memo outlining his wishes in his bedroom safe, asking for a plain white monument containing no carving or decoration, only the dates of his birth and his death. He wanted the monument to be placed on the grave from east to west. He hoped "my dear wife will on her death be buried there also."

Tully went on to recount other requests the president had made, including that Fala be given to Margaret Suckley. He assumed that Mrs. Roosevelt would be too busy to look after him. Unable to hide her disappointment, Eleanor hurried on to the next subject—she needed Tully's help, she said, in drafting a form letter to acknowledge the thousands of condolence messages.

The funeral train crossed the Potomac River and pulled into Union Station. Thousands stood in silence as Anna, Elliott, and Elliott's wife entered the rear car. (FDR, Jr., and John were in the midst of battle and unable to leave their ships; Jimmy was still en route from San Diego.) President Truman and the Cabinet were there, along with General Marshall, Admiral King, and members of Congress. As two military bands played and army bombers thundered overhead, the funeral procession moved down Constitution Avenue to 18th Street, to Pennsylvania Avenue, and finally to the White House.

Never, Truman later wrote, would he forget the sight of so many people in grief. "The streets," recalled General Marshall's wife, Katherine, "were lined on both sides with troops. In back of them could be seen the faces of the crowds. At each intersection the crowds extended down the side streets as far as you could see. Complete silence spread like a pall over the city, broken only by the funeral dirge and the sobs of the people."

The White House was in a state of confusion when the cavalcade arrived at the South Portico. Reporters were jamming the lobby, and the staff members were standing around in tears. The coffin was lifted from the caisson and carried up the front stairs. Eleanor alighted first. She walked slowly by herself into the mansion, her face composed. Whenever she was in trouble, Hick later observed, "she would walk unusually erect with her head held high. She was walking very erect that day."

The coffin was wheeled down a long red carpet to the East Room, where an honor guard was waiting to watch over the body until the funeral service at four that afternoon. "Can you dispense with the Honor Guard for a few moments and have the casket opened?" Eleanor asked White House usher J. B. West. "I would like to have a few moments alone with my husband."

"Please don't let anybody come in," Eleanor instructed as West and two other ushers guarded the doors. "Mrs. Roosevelt stood at the casket," West recalled, "gazing down into her husband's face. Then she took a gold ring from her finger and tenderly placed it on the President's hand. She straightened, eyes dry, and she left the room. The coffin was never opened again."

Now the time had come to confront Anna. Returning to the family quarters, Eleanor asked her daughter to come into her sitting room. Her face was "as stern as it could get when she was angry," Anna recalled. She demanded to know why she had never been told about Mrs. Rutherfurd. Was it true that Mrs. Rutherfurd had been at the White House and that Anna had made the arrangements? Yes, Anna nodded, explaining that one evening, when she was taking notes from her father on things he wanted done, he had mentioned to her that he would like to invite his old friend Mrs. Rutherfurd to dinner. Would she object? he had asked her. She hadn't known how to respond at first, Anna said, but in the end, when she thought of all the burdens her father was facing and of his declining health, she decided it was not up to her to deny him. "It was all above board," she assured her mother. "There were always people around."

"Mother was so upset about everything and now so upset with me," Anna later recalled. Indeed, so intense was the confrontation that Anna feared her mother would never be able to forgive her, and that their close relationship would no longer be the same.

"Mother was angry with Anna," Jimmy acknowledged, "but what was Anna to do? Should she have refused Father what he wanted? She was not in a position to do so even had she wanted to. Accepting the confidence of Father, should she have betrayed him by running to report to Mother every move he made? A child caught between two parents can only pursue as honorable a course as possible. Anna could no more serve as Mother's spy than she could as Father's spy on Mother."

Yet Anna's son Curtis understood some of what Eleanor must have been feeling. "He was her husband," Curtis said. "She was his wife. He was president. She was first lady. And now Anna had walked into the picture and made it possible for Lucy to return to the president's life. It must have seemed an unforgivable act."

•   •   •

The East Room was filled with flowers at 4 p.m. as the simple service began. Mrs. Roosevelt and the Roosevelt family sat in the front row, across the aisle from President Truman, Mrs. Truman, and their daughter, Margaret. Behind the president's family sat Cabinet members, Supreme Court justices, labor leaders, agency heads, politicians, and diplomats from all the countries of the United Nations, including British Foreign Minister Anthony Eden and Russian Ambassador to the U.S. Andrei Gromyko. "It was the final roll call of the Roosevelt era," reporter Bess Furman noted.

At Eleanor's request, the ceremony began with "Faith of Our Fathers," a hymn the president loved, and closed with the celebrated lines of Roosevelt's first inaugural: "The only thing we have to fear is fear itself." Throughout the service, Eleanor remained dry-eyed, her calmness in sharp contrast to the sobs of those around her. Harry Hopkins, *Time* reported, "stood almost fainting beside his chair, white as death and racked with sobs."

"After everyone left," Secret Service agent Milton Lipson recalled, "Mrs. Roosevelt took a last look at all the flowers and asked us if we'd arrange to have them all taken to a mental hospital. Then, seeing us teary-eyed, she added, 'Oh, of course, if any of you want a souvenir, please help yourself.' I still have my pressed flower."

Later that evening, the funeral train headed north toward Hyde Park, curving along the east bank of the Hudson, the route Roosevelt had taken so many times. "I'll never forget that train trip," Anna recalled. "As usual, the Secret Service had assigned staterooms and berths to each individual. I've never known who assigned it to me but I was given Father's stateroom. All night I sat on the foot of that berth and watched the people who had come to see the train pass by. There were little children, fathers, grandparents. They were there at 11 at night, at 2 in the morning, at 4—at all hours during that long night."

The president's coffin was lifted from the train at the riverfront and placed in a caisson, which was brought up the steep hill by six black-draped horses. Directly behind it walked a hooded horse, its saddle empty, its stirrups reversed—the traditional symbol of the fallen leader. As the cortege made its way up the hill, past the ice pond and the open field, the music started getting louder and louder, with cannons booming until the caisson stopped outside the hedge where a large assembly waited: President Truman and the Cabinet, General Marshall and Admiral King, James Farley and Edward Flynn, congressmen and senators, family and friends.

The four hedge walls of the rectangular garden were lined with West Point cadets in scarlet capes as the president's body was carried to the grave. "The funeral was very beautiful," Trude Lash wrote Joe. "The day was gloriously snappy, very sunny and blue, white lilacs were in bloom," and "the birds were singing."

The president's seventy-eight-year-old pastor, the Reverend George Anthony, recited the familiar lines: "We commit his body to the ground, earth to earth, dust to dust." The West Point cadets raised their rifles and fired three volleys. After each volley, Trude noted, Fala barked, a child whimpered, and then it was over.

As the crowd dispersed, Eleanor remained in the garden. She stood quietly, her head bowed, watching the workmen as they shoveled soil onto her husband's grave. Then, silent and alone, she walked away.

As Eleanor left, Moses Smith, an old tenant farmer on the estate, picked up a bucket and walked over to water a row of young maples. "He wanted me to plant these trees," he said. "I planted them for him. He'll never see them now."

CHAPTER 25

"A NEW
COUNTRY IS
BEING BORN"

Eleanor returned to the White House immediately after the funeral to begin the task of packing up the family furniture and all the personal possessions that had accumulated over a period of twelve years. She had promised the Trumans she would be out by Friday night, and she intended to keep her word. Monday morning, Henrietta Nesbitt came into Mrs. Roosevelt's bedroom. "She had all her clothes out of wardrobes and over chairs, and was sorting them," Nesbitt recalled. "I was thinking she'd never make it, with all there was to do, but at the same time I knew she would." The next morning, Jimmy Byrnes found her in the president's bedroom, packing books and personal belongings. She saved the president's study, crammed with pictures, models of ships, Currier and Ives prints, and tiny souvenirs from all over the world for last. "My husband was a collector with a great interest in history," she explained to her readers, "so there were many things to go over." Eventually a thousand boxes would be sealed, filling twenty army trucks. She was "a bit keyed up," she admitted to Joe Lash, "because there is so much to do and to think about." Her eyes were tired, one reporter noted, and she was pale, but she worked without pause.

In the midst of the packing, Eleanor took Bess and Margaret Truman on a tour of the White House. "In the years I have been here I have taken many people through," Eleanor wrote in her column that day. "I always have a pride in the beauty of the rooms, their proportions, the woodwork and the historically interesting furnishings which remain the same no matter what individuals may live here. It was good to find Mrs. Truman appreciative of the things that I have loved."

In private, Bess and Margaret Truman were appalled at what they saw: walls streaked with dust and faded along the outlines of all the pictures that had been taken down, shabby furniture badly in need of upholstering, threadbare carpets that hadn't been cleaned in years, draperies that were actually rotting. Eleanor had been so busy that she had not paid much attention to the physical condition of the mansion, leaving untouched a $50,000 congressional allocation for upkeep and repair. "Mrs. Roosevelt was more concerned about people being swept under the national rug due to injustice than she was about someone finding dirt under the White House rug," White House butler Alonzo Fields explained. "The White House upstairs is a mess," Margaret Truman wrote. "I was so depressed." White House usher J. B. West confirmed Margaret Truman's impression. "It was like a ghost house," he recalled. "What little was left in the White House gave it the appearance of an abandoned hotel."

While talking with Mrs. Truman, Eleanor suggested that she hold a press conference that week. Eleanor promised to sit by her side and introduce her to the women reporters. "Do you think I ought to do that?" a worried Bess Truman queried Frances Perkins. "It terrifies me. I don't even think of public affairs."

"No, Mrs. Truman," Perkins replied. "I don't think you ought to feel the slightest obligation to do it. Mrs. Roosevelt is an unusual person. She enjoys it. There certainly isn't anything the press has a right to ask you."

Eleanor Roosevelt was more than "an unusual person"; she was unique. She had seized the power inherent in the position of first lady, to become, in the words of a contemporary reporter, "a Cabinet Minister without portfolio," an influential advocate for social reform. In her efforts to reach a mass audience, she had become the first president's wife to hold regular press conferences, to write a syndicated daily column, to deliver sponsored radio broadcasts, to enter the lecture circuit. She had broken precedent time and again—when she spoke before the Democratic National Convention in 1940, traveled overseas to visit American troops in England and the South Pacific, and journeyed twice to Capitol Hill to testify before congressional committees on the plight of migrant workers and the conditions of life in the District of Columbia. No first lady before had ever become such a public figure. Her breadth of activities created new expectations against which her successors would be measured.

• • •

On her last full day in the White House, Eleanor invited all the members of the Women's Press Corps to a farewell tea in the State Dining Room. She stood at the door shaking each hand warmly as fifty-seven newswomen filed in. "Traces of grief" were etched on her pale features, one reporter noted, "her black costume relieved only by a pearl necklace and the small fleur-de-lis pin."

The newswomen had brought their notebooks. She lifted her hand. It was shaking uncontrollably. "This is a social thing," she said, "not a press conference. If you want to say Mrs. Roosevelt said this or that in conversation, that is your privilege but I do not want to be quoted directly." She talked in a low voice, twisting her tortoiseshell glasses in her hand, telling reporters how much she had enjoyed the press conferences over the years. The experiment begun twelve years earlier had, she believed, been a good thing. Her insistence on having only female reporters at her press conferences had forced newspapers to hire women and enhanced the careers of dozens of women reporters. She now told them that her apartment in New York and her cottage at Hyde Park were all she wanted to take care of. The Big House, she hoped, if the children agreed, would be turned over to the nation.

"Nearly all that I can do is done," Eleanor wrote Hick later that day. "The upstairs looks desolate and I will be glad to leave tomorrow. It is empty and without purpose to be here now." With everything gone that makes a home, she wrote Lash, she couldn't wait to leave. "I never did like to be where I no longer belonged. I am weary and yet I cannot rest. When do you think that will cease?"

Before falling asleep that night in the White House, Eleanor looked out her bedroom window for the last time. "I have always looked out at the Washington monument the last thing at night," she confided to her readers, "and the little red light at the top of it has twinkled at me in friendly fashion."

The next morning, Eleanor had her last breakfast on the sun porch and said goodbye to the office staff and the house staff. "We were all in tears," Mrs. Nesbitt recalled. "There is always a certain emotional strain about the last time for anything," Eleanor wrote in her column. "When you have lived twelve years in a house, even though you have always known that it belonged to the nation, you grow fond of the house itself and fonder still of all the people connected with your life in that house." She rode down in the old cage elevator that morning, she admitted, "with a feeling of melancholy and I suppose something of uncertainty because I was saying goodbye to an unforgettable era" and, from that day forward, "I would be on my own."

As she walked out the door, Eleanor waved to onlooking journalists and "without a backward glance," according to a *Newsweek* reporter, headed for Union Station, where a train was waiting to take her to New York. "Her departure," the *Boston Evening American* noted, "signified the end of an era for a generation which has never known any President but Franklin Delano Roosevelt or any First Lady but Mrs. Roosevelt."

When she reached her Washington Square apartment, Eleanor was exhausted. A cluster of reporters was waiting at the door. She had nothing to tell them. "The story," she said simply, "is over."

• • •

But the story was not over. Indeed, for Eleanor, whose strength of will was never more apparent than in the spring of 1945, a new chapter was beginning. She had passed through difficult days—absorbing not only the death of her husband but the discovery that Lucy Rutherfurd was with him when he died. Yet, as she doggedly resumed her labors—writing her daily column, traveling, and beginning to answer the hundreds of thousands of letters that were sent to the White House after the president's death—she gradually moved toward reconciliation with her husband's memory.

She had fought him on so many issues for so many years, pressuring him when her pressure was neither wanted nor welcome, that the full import of her husband's meaning to the nation had been hidden from her. But now, wherever she went, people—porters at the station, taxi drivers, doormen, elevator men, passengers on the train, riders in the subway—told her how personally bereaved they felt, how much they had loved him, how much they missed him. "I am realizing day by day," she wrote in her column, "how much my husband meant to young people in Washington, to veterans in the service hospitals, to men and women."

"It has warmed my heart," she told her readers, "to discover how many people would stop and speak to me as they left the train, often murmuring only: We loved your husband." On the subway in New York, a man, visibly controlling his emotion, came up to her and said: " 'He was like a friend who came and talked to us every now and then.' These spontaneous outbursts of affection for my husband from casual people whom I have never seen before, are spoken so sincerely that I often wish my husband could hear them himself."

She was stunned, she wrote her aunt Maude Gray as the United Nations Conference opened in San Francisco in late April, by the "upsurge of love" on the part of so many people, and by their realization of how much they had depended on him. "One feels in the San Francisco Conference that a strong hand is missing," she went on. "I am sad that he could not see the end of his long work which he carried so magnificently."

Eleanor confessed to her friends she had not realized until after he was gone how much she, too, had depended on her husband. "I find that mentally I counted so much on Franklin," she wrote Joe Lash, "I feel a bit bereft." The readjustment to being alone, she said, without someone else at the center of her life, was harder than she would have imagined. She was only now beginning to realize, she told Elinor Morgenthau, who was recovering from her heart attack, how much she had relied on "Franklin's greater wisdom," and it left her "without much sense of backing." Moreover, she observed, "I think we had all come to think of him as able to carry the world's problems and now we must carry them ourselves."

Eleanor had decided, even before the funeral train from Warm Springs reached Washington, that if the children agreed, which they eventually did, she would turn the Big House over to the government and make Val-Kill her permanent home. By the fall, the Big House had to be emptied of everything the family wanted—a task requiring hours of sorting and packing. In the midst of her labors, Eleanor took unexpected comfort in Fala's return to the Roosevelt household. Shortly after the funeral, Jimmy Roosevelt had written Margaret Suckley and asked her to send Fala back. "In talking to my sister and brother, we all feel very disappointed that Fala is not staying with Mother," Jimmy wrote. Fala was "part of the family," and it would make Mother "very happy to have him back." Suckley agreed, and Fala came to live at Val-Kill. Soon he and Eleanor became inseparable. Fala accompanied her on her walks through the woods, sat beside her chair in the living room, and greeted her at the door when she came home. "No one was as vociferously pleased to see me as Fala," she noted proudly after a trip to New York. Still, Fala missed the president. When General Eisenhower came to Hyde Park to lay a wreath on Roosevelt's grave, Fala heard the sirens of the motorcade and thought his master was returning. "His legs straightened out" and "his ears pricked up," Eleanor noted; he was hoping to see his master coming down the drive.

•   •   •

As the war in Europe came to a close, Eleanor was saddened anew that Franklin had not lived to see the triumphant end result of his wearying labors. On April 30, 1945, as the Red Army advanced on Berlin, Adolf Hitler hastily married his mistress, Eva Braun, and then committed suicide with her in his underground bunker. A week later, a newly assembled German government surrendered unconditionally. When Eleanor heard Truman, Churchill, and Stalin proclaim the surrender of Germany on the radio on May 8, she could almost hear her husband's voice making the announcement. "V-E Day was a curious day," she confessed to Maude Gray. "It was sad Franklin couldn't have announced it. I felt no desire to celebrate."

"I cannot help but think today of that little garden in Hyde Park where Franklin Roosevelt lies," Harry Hopkins told reporters the same day. "No man in the world contributed more to victory and freedom, and I believe that the free people of the earth will forever bless his name."

Churchill, too, thought of his friend on V-E Day as the bells pealed throughout England and all of London came out into the streets, laughing, cheering, dancing, singing. "It was without any doubt Churchill's day," *New Yorker* correspondent Molly Panter-Downes observed. He was greeted everywhere he went with a roaring enthusiasm that "exceeded by double" anything anyone remembered. But even as he celebrated what he called the greatest day in the long history of England, Churchill's thoughts turned to Roosevelt and to "the valiant and magnanimous deeds of the USA" under his magnificent leadership. These extraordinary deeds, Churchill predicted, "would forever stir the hearts of Britons in all quarters of the world in which they dwell."

Ten weeks later, Churchill was unceremoniously swept out of office when the Labour Party triumphed in the British elections. Having gone to bed on election night believing he had won, he awoke just before dawn "with a sharp stab of almost physical pain"; a subconscious conviction that he was beaten "broke forth and dominated" his mind, he said, only to be confirmed later that day. The news that he had lost was difficult for Churchill to absorb. "It's no use pretending I'm not hard hit," he told Lord Moran. "It would have been better to have been killed in an aeroplane or to have died like Roosevelt."

Now it was Eleanor's turn to recall what Churchill meant to her husband, to the British, and to the Americans. "His place in the hearts of the people of Great Britain is safe for all time," she wrote. "No one in the British empire —nor in the United States—who heard his brave words after Dunkirk will ever feel anything but the deepest respect and gratitude and affection for Churchill, the man and the war leader."

A week after the British elections came the news that an atomic bomb had been dropped on Hiroshima. Eleanor had first learned about the secret weapon in July 1943, when a young physicist working on the project came to see her in her Washington Square apartment. The young man, Irving Lowen, was worried that Germany was pulling ahead of the United States in the search for an atomic weapon. He begged Eleanor to impress upon the president the need to proceed as quickly as possible. The president agreed to see Lowen at Eleanor's urging, but when the young scientist breached security a second time by returning to see Eleanor, he was transferred out of the Manhattan Project.

Eleanor did not question the decision to drop the bomb, believing that it would bring the war to a speedier end, but she "could not help feeling a little sad," she wrote, "when the news came that we had to use our second atomic bomb." She had hoped that "after the first bomb, which was followed by Russia's declaration of war and their prompt entry into Manchuria, the Japanese would decide to accept unconditional surrender and the loss of life could come to an end." It was not until August 15, six days later, that Japan finally surrendered.

The most destructive war in history had come to an end. The best estimates put the number of deaths at an unimaginable 50 million people. The Soviet Union lost 13 million combatants and 7 million civilians. The Germans calculated losses of 3.6 million civilians and 3.2 million soldiers. The Japanese estimated 2 million civilian and 1 million military deaths. Six million Jews had been killed. The number of British and commonwealth deaths is calculated at 484,482. With 291,557 battle deaths and 113,842 nonhostile deaths from accident and disease, the United States suffered the fewest casualties among the major nations.

When the word was flashed on August 15 that the war was over, Eleanor found herself "filled with very curious sensations." Though she was thrilled "to be in a world where peace has come," she had no desire to join the happy throngs on the streets. Recalling the way the people had celebrated when the last war ended, she felt that this time "the weight of suffering which has engulfed the world during so many years could not so quickly be wiped out." Moreover, she admitted to her daughter, "I miss Pa's voice and the words he would have spoken."

• • •

"Now that the war is over," war worker Mary Smith lamented, "I've lost my job—for no other reason apparently except that I am a woman." The bomb was dropped, Frankie Cooper recalled, and a few days later the foreman gathered all the women in the shipyard together. He told them that the first troop ship was coming home from the Pacific and he asked them to take off their welders' caps, let their hair down, and go down to the dock to meet the soldiers. "We were thrilled. We all waved," Cooper said. The next day, all the women were laid off. "It was a shock." At the Kaiser day-care center in Portland, Oregon, schoolteacher Mary Willett experienced a similar jolt. Though her center had cared for two thousand children at its peak and had received national attention for its excellent work, it was permanently closed down and all the teachers were dismissed just two weeks after the war was over.

In her columns that fall, Eleanor tried in vain to stem the tide. She argued on principle that everyone who wanted to work had a right to be productive. She asked industry to face the fact that many women were obliged to work to support their families and that "it was essential they be treated in this respect on a par with the men." She railed against the closing of the child-care centers as a shortsighted response to a fundamental social need. "Many thought they were purely a war emergency measure," she wrote in September. "A few of us had an inkling that perhaps they were a need which was constantly with us, but one that we had neglected to face in the past." She had received a number of letters from women, she reported, appealing to her to help keep the child-care centers open. Some of the women who wrote had husbands who were killed in the war. Others had husbands who were crippled or wounded. For these women, work was the only means of supporting their family. "My whole life and that of my two children," Mrs. Dorothy Thibault wrote, "depends on my working eight hours each day. My little girl is 4 and the boy is 2 and one-half. The care and training they have received in this childcare center is the best possible thing that could have happened to them."

Despite all these problems—despite the layoffs, the insufficient child care, and the postwar elevation of domestic virtues into an ideology—millions of women would refuse to abandon the workplace. Though female jobs in manufacturing fell sharply after the war, the rate of female employment as a whole began climbing steadily upward again in 1947, soon surpassing the wartime peak. "My husband would have been happy if I went back to the kind of girl I was when he married me," Frankie Cooper recalled, "and that was a little homebody there on the farm, in the kitchen. I wasn't that person anymore. . . . I tried it for a couple, three years, but it just didn't work out. . . . I did all the things—churned butter, visited the neighbors, I became president of the PTA—I did all the things, but I wasn't satisfied. I just had that restlessness. . . . I wanted to go back to work."

As women's expectations shifted, divorces multiplied. In 1946, the United States would experience the highest divorce rate in the world, thirty-one divorces for every hundred marriages. Shirley Hackett had supported herself while her husband was away and had become accustomed to an independent life. But the moment her husband returned, she was expected to revert to the role of housewife. When her husband found her writing checks to pay the bills, he asked, "Why do you want to do that? I'm back!" When he saw her changing a tire on the car, he treated her as if she were "insane" to think that she could do such a thing. Troubles developed in the marriage.

War wife Dellie Hahne had a similar experience. "My husband did not care for my independence," she recalled. "He had left a shrinking violet and come home to a very strong oak tree." The marriage lasted only a few years. "I think the seeds of my liberation and many other women's started with the war," she observed. The first intimation Hahne had of the changes that were taking place came when she was invited to a friend's house for Sunday dinner and heard the mother and grandmother talk about which drill would bite into a piece of metal at the factory. "My God, this was Sunday dinner in Middle America and to hear, instead of a discussion of the church service, a conversation about how to sharpen tools—it was a marvelous thing. I remember thinking that these women would never again be the same."

Throughout the war, Eleanor had talked unceasingly about her hopes for the next generation of women, but even she could not have foreseen the myriad ways in which the experiences of women war workers would affect the lives and prospects of their daughters. "Mothers that worked during the war . . . I think they have a less conservative outlook than if they had stayed in the home," Frankie Cooper said. "They traveled . . . met different kinds of people, they listened to different kinds of ideas, they went home with a completely different outlook on life. I think that this rubbed off on their children. You see, the boys that went overseas had their war stories, and the women that were in war work had theirs. And daughters and sons listened to these."

In a *Senior Scholastic* poll of thirty-three thousand girl students taken in 1946, 88 percent wanted a career in addition to homemaking, and only 4 percent chose homemaking exclusively. The war had proved to millions of women, Frankie Cooper observed, that they could do things they'd thought they couldn't, and now they were telling their daughters: "You can do anything you want to. You can be anybody you want to. And you can go anywhere you want to."

The war had made possible, social historian William Chafe has written, what no amount of agitation could achieve. "The content of women's lives had changed, and an important new area of potential activity had opened up to them. Work had proved liberating and once a new consciousness had been formed, there was no going back."

•   •   •

From the beginning of the war, Eleanor had insisted that the struggle abroad would not be worth winning unless democracy were renewed at home. All along, Franklin had assured her that the mobilization process would be an agent of change, that once the dormant energies of democracy were unleashed, the country would be transformed.

Eleanor had been unable to share in her husband's optimism; she had worried constantly about what America would look like after the fighting stopped, whether the liberal and humane values which had animated the New Deal were being sacrificed to the necessities of war. But in the fall of 1945, as she began traveling around the country again, she realized that the nation had taken even greater strides toward social justice during the war than it had during the New Deal. Indeed, the Roosevelt years had witnessed the most profound social revolution in the country since the Civil War—nothing less than the creation of modern America.

The small-town America, where people clung to their roots, immobilized within their ethnic and income class, had passed into history. Over fifteen million Americans had left their home towns to work in war plants and shipyards and were living in a different state or county from the place of their birth. Twelve million more had entered the armed forces and been flung out over the turbulent globe. More than 20 percent of the entire population had taken part in the great migration. They had moved from the farm to the factory, from the South to the North, from the East to the exploding states of the Western rim. And there would be no return. The habit of mobility, which would prove both liberating and fragmenting, had become ingrained. America had become irrevocably an urban nation.

The war had been both a catalyst of unity and a disrupter of community ties. More than ever, citizens sought their identity not through ethnic bonds, but as Americans. Flagmakers fell months behind in their orders. There was a sharp decline in foreign-language radio broadcasts, and many foreign-language publications went bankrupt. Men and women hastened to become American citizens—almost two million aliens became naturalized during the six years preceding and following the war. Yet this new national identity also threatened the smaller units within which Americans had located themselves, both physically and psychologically. It would prove difficult—perhaps impossible—to re-establish the once-secure ties of neighborhood and community.

No segment of American society had been left untouched. More than seventeen million new jobs had been created, industrial production had gone up 100 percent, corporate profits doubled, and the GNP had jumped from $100 billion to $215 billion. The war had radically changed the shape of the American economy, exerting a profound impact on the everyday lives and expectations of people in all parts of the country. In 1940, only 7.8 million Americans out of 132 million made enough money to pay taxes; in 1945, that figure had risen to nearly 50 million in a population of 140 million. The wartime economy allowed millions of Americans who had been on relief to get back on their feet and start over again. Miners had enjoyed steady employment for the first time in twenty years. Automobile workers had doubled their incomes and expanded their skills. Black sharecroppers had left the rural South for the cities of the North, where, despite terrible racial tensions and a hard destiny, they would find a more abundant life than the one they had left behind.

The society of a few haves and a multitude of have-nots had been transformed. Because of the greatest—indeed, the only—redistribution of income downward in the nation's history, a middle-class country had emerged. Half of the American people—those at the lower end of the compensation scale—had doubled their income, while those in the top 20 percent had risen by little more than 50 percent. Those in the bottom half of earners had seen their share of the country's income increase by 16 percent, while those at the top had lost 6 percent. As a result, social historian Geoffrey Perrett observed, "barriers to social and economic equality which had stood for decades were either much reduced or entirely overthrown."

The foundation of postwar progress had been constructed. When the war ended, pent-up demand—desire matched with money—would fuel a postwar boom. And wartime policies would ensure that business had the capital to meet this demand. They had enjoyed large profits and a tax code which enabled industry to carry forward the paper losses from accelerated depreciation to offset taxes. Thus, industry had a large cushion of capital. They had won a new respect from the government and the electorate. They had benefited from a multitude of technological advances and, even more important, had discovered the intimate relation between technology, research, and growth which, a half-century later, is still a dominating characteristic of the modern economy. The fears of a return to depression—which so preoccupied the political leaders who followed Roosevelt—would never be justified.

The American economy had not merely been revitalized, it had been altered. The old laissez-faire ideal—buyers and sellers conducting transactions in an untrammeled market—was gone forever. The feared socialist order would not materialize. Instead, a new economic order would come into being, one that economists would call "a mixed economy." No longer would government be viewed as merely a bystander and an occasional referee, intervening only in times of crisis. Instead, the government would assume responsibility for continued growth and for fairness in the distribution of wealth. Big government—modern government—was here to stay.

The new responsibilities of government amounted to nothing less than a new relationship between the people and those whom they chose for service, a new understanding, a revised social contract, one framed within the democratic limits of the original understanding, but drastically changed in content.

It may well be true that a social revolution is not possible without war or violent internal upheaval. These provide a unity of purpose and an opportunity for change that are rarely present in more tranquil times. But as the history of other countries and America's own experience after World War I illustrates, war and revolution are no guarantee of positive social change. That depends on the time, the nation, and the exercise of leadership. In providing that leadership, Franklin Roosevelt emerges as the towering public figure of the twentieth century.

•　•　•

Eleanor Roosevelt added a vital dimension of her own to the achievements of wartime America. At a time when her husband was preoccupied with winning the war, she remained an uncompromising voice in behalf of justice in the allocation of wartime gains. Though the logic of Roosevelt's mobilization program in 1940 dictated a policy of accommodation with anti–New Deal business interests, Eleanor strove with considerable effect not only to maintain the fundamental goals of the New Deal but to further social advance. Many joined her in this effort—civil rights leaders, labor leaders, liberal spokesmen. But her voice in the highest councils of decision was always influential and often decisive.

Eleanor Roosevelt's stand on civil rights, her insistence that America could not fight racism abroad while tolerating it at home, remains one of the affirming moments in the history of the home front during the war. Though she was naïve about many aspects of the racial problem, she was far ahead of the president and the times in her understanding that separate but equal facilities were not enough, that the fact of segregation itself impaired the lives of the Negro population.

She had insisted, against the advice of the White House staff, that the president meet with Negro leaders to discuss what could be done about discrimination and segregation in the armed forces. Progress was slow and incomplete, but these meetings, along with Eleanor's continuing intervention, eventually led to broadened opportunities for Negroes in both the army and the navy. Between 1940 and 1945, the Negro military force had increased in size from 5,000 to 920,000 and the number of Negro officers had grown from 5 to over 7,000. Moreover, whereas almost every Negro soldier in 1940 was confined to a service unit, by war's close Negroes held responsible jobs in almost every branch of the army as artillerymen, tankmen, infantrymen, pilots, paratroopers, doctors, and more. "The Negro was no longer regarded as an Army auxiliary," Jean Byers concluded in her study of the Negro in World War II. "He had at last attained the status of a soldier."

The changes in the navy during the war were even more spectacular. Though the navy still had not succeeded in using every Negro "in accordance with his maximum capacity," since half the Negro sailors still remained in the stewards' branch, great strides had been taken. "The Navy of 1945," Byers concluded, "was hardly recognizable as the Navy of 1941." At the start of the war, the navy considered it unthinkable to allow Negroes to enter its organization on an equal footing with white men; Negro sailors could enlist only if willing to serve as mess men. By 1945, hundreds of Negroes were serving in all manner of posts, as machinists and metalsmiths, radiomen and electricians. In 1941, the navy adhered to a rigid policy of racial segregation; in 1945, the navy officially declared that the integration of black and white sailors was "both possible and desirable." In sum, "the Negro was considered a servant by the Navy in 1941; in 1945, the Negro was acknowledged as a sailor."

More than anyone else in the White House, Eleanor was responsible, through her relentless pressure of War Department officials, for the issuance of the two directives that forbade the designation of recreational areas by race and made government-owned and -operated buses available to every soldier regardless of race. By the end of the war, only one major step was needed to ensure true equality for Negro soldiers, and that step would come in 1948, when President Truman issued Executive Order 9981, ending segregation in the armed forces.

Through her travels and her close ties with Negro leaders, Eleanor made Franklin more aware of the new spirit of militancy that was developing within the Negro community in reaction to continuing discrimination in employment. She played an instrumental role in the negotiations surrounding the threatened March on Washington which led to the creation of the FEPC, the first presidential action on civil rights since the Civil War. She provided access for Negro leaders and ordinary Negro citizens. American Airlines President C. R. Smith recalled that, when he came to the White House one night, "the place was running over with blacks." Smith said to Eleanor: "Looks like we're entertaining most of the blacks in the country tonight." She said: " 'Well, C.R., you must remember that the President is their President also.' " Such moments were all part of a bigger victory— making the federal government more relevant and more responsive to Negro Americans.

Though civil rights remained the great unfinished business of American democracy at the end of the war, Eleanor could take much satisfaction in knowing that the war had been a turning point in the struggle, a watershed experience in which the seeds of the protest movements of the succeeding decades were sown. Looking back on the 1940s, historian Carey McWilliams observed that "more has happened in the field of race relations in this country; more interest has been aroused; more has been said and written; more proposed and accomplished than in the entire span of years from the end of the Civil War to 1940." These years, historian Richard Dalfiume confirms, constitute "the forgotten years of the Negro revolution."

Eleanor was also far ahead of her time in championing the movement of women into the factories. Through her speeches and her columns, she provided a powerful counterweight to the negative attitudes that prevailed in the early years of the war against women working outside the home. She played a central role in securing government funds for day-care centers and in getting local cities and towns to provide after-school programs, takeout foods, and community laundries. If there had been no Eleanor Roosevelt, women would still have gone to work, but the conditions under which they worked would have been far less conducive to the preservation of home life, and their resulting productivity would have been substantially lower.

Eleanor's influence can also be seen in the generally supportive position Roosevelt adopted toward labor during the war despite the rising frustration and anger of Congress and the public against unions and strikes. Her constant reminder that labor should not bear the brunt of sacrifice as the country converted to a war footing, served to counter the powerful voices of the businessmen who flooded into Washington during the war. And her insistence on the importance of planning for the postwar period played an important role in Roosevelt's call for the GI Bill of Rights.

She also had her own share of failures. Her misguided appointments and actions at the Office of Civilian Defense brought about the congressional outburst which blunted her voice and forced her resignation. Her call for tolerance toward the Japanese Americans was lost in the tide of hysteria that followed Pearl Harbor. Her attempts to bring more refugees into the United States met with limited success. Her call for the protection of small business went unheeded. Her hopes for using the defense emergency as a lever for replacing the slums were never realized.

Unsympathetic observers referred to her as "Lady Bountiful," "The Busybody," "The Meddler," and "The Gab." It was said that she was not a systematic thinker, that she had no ability to focus or to set priorities, that her chatty columns qualified as journalism only through her position, that she was the victim of her generous impulses, intervening in behalf of any person in trouble, whether the complaints were justified or not. "Oh, my God, here's another one," officials at the War Department and the State Department would lament when yet another missive from Mrs. Roosevelt would reach them.

Even Eleanor's most ardent admirers in the Roosevelt inner circle admitted that she pushed her husband too hard at the end of the day, when he was tired and needed to relax. "She would come in after he'd been wrestling with major problems all day long and insist that he find a job for some unemployed actor in New York," Anna's daughter, Eleanor Seagraves, recalled. And if he refused to do something she asked, she would come back again and again until it reached the point where he had to tell his aides to keep her away. If he would not meet somebody she thought he should meet, she would simply invite the person to dinner without telling anyone and seat the person next to the president. "I think he let her get away with stuff he wouldn't have," White House aide Jonathan Daniels said, "if he hadn't had that sense of guilt."

It was said jokingly in Washington during the war years that Roosevelt had a nightly prayer: "Dear God, please make Eleanor a little tired." But in the end, he often came around to her way of thinking. Labor adviser Anna Rosenberg had been one of those who criticized Eleanor's unceasing pressure on the president, but years later she changed her mind. "I remember him saying, 'We're not going to do that now. Tell Eleanor to keep away; I don't want to hear about that anymore.' And then 2–3 weeks later he would say, 'Do you remember that thing Eleanor brought up? Better look into it, maybe there's something to it—I heard something to indicate that maybe she's right.' I'm not sure she would have had the opportunity to bring things to his attention unless she pressured him—I mean he was so involved and in retrospect it was never anything for herself.... He would never have become the kind of President he was without her."

They made an extraordinary team. She was more earnest, less devious, less patient, less fun, more uncompromisingly moral; he possessed the more trustworthy political talent, the more finely tuned sense of timing, the better feel for the citizenry, the smarter understanding of how to get things done. She could travel the country when he could not; she could speak her mind without the constraints of public office. She was the agitator; he was the politician. But they were linked by indissoluble bonds and they drew strength from each other. "The truth of the matter is that a deep and unshakeable affection and tenderness existed between them," Jimmy Roosevelt said.

On the walls of the president's study hung a charming portrait of Eleanor painted when she was young. "You know, I've always liked that portrait," Franklin told Frances Perkins. "It's a beautiful portrait, don't you think so? ... You know the hair's just right, isn't it? Lovely hair! Eleanor has lovely hair, don't you think so?" As Perkins listened, she was struck by the "light in his eye," which to her mind signaled "the light of affection." White House aide Isador Lubin also witnessed frequent moments of affection, when the president would kid Eleanor about something in a light way and would "give her a whack on the fanny."

The fact that "certain parts of their marriage were not as happy as one would have hoped," Anna later said, did not mean that Eleanor didn't love Franklin. "She did love Father. There wasn't any doubt." Eleanor's close friend Esther Lape agreed. "I don't think she ever stopped loving him. That was why he always had the ability to hurt her."

"He might have been happier with a wife who was completely uncritical,"

Eleanor observed in her memoirs. "That I was never able to be, and he had to find it in other people. Nevertheless, I think I sometimes acted as a spur, even though the spurring was not always wanted or welcome. I was one of those who served his purposes."

"She had indeed served his purposes," historian Lois Scharf wrote, "but he had also served hers. He furnished the stage upon which her incomparable abilities and human qualities could gain the widest audience and respect. Few Presidents and no other First Ladies have ever used the platform to such effect. In less obvious ways he was her spur as much as she was his." Together they mobilized existing forces "to create a far different political and social landscape than the one that had existed when they entered the White House."

Though years would pass before the full extent of these changes were understood, Eleanor was convinced in the fall of 1945 that "a new country is being born." It seemed to her, she told her son Jimmy, that "a giant transference of energy" had taken place between the president and the people. "In the early days, before Pearl Harbor," she said, "Franklin was healthy and strong and committed to the Allied cause while the country was sick and weak and isolationist. But gradually, as the president animated his countrymen to the dangers abroad, the country grew stronger and stronger while he grew weaker and weaker, until in the end he was dead and the country had emerged more powerful and more productive than ever before."

It was a romanticized view of her husband's leadership, ignoring the many fierce arguments they had had during the war regarding his decision to intern the Japanese Americans, his failure to do more to help the Jews of Europe, his surrender to big business on military contracts, his caution on civil rights. She had brooded over his shortcomings while he was alive, but now she could idealize him as she had idealized her father, and grasp the elements of his greatness—his supreme confidence, his contagious faith, his sense of timing, his political skills. Beneath all, there had been, she could now see, a fundamental commitment to humane and democratic values, a steadiness of purpose, a determination to win the war as fast as possible, a vision of the principles on which the peace would be based, a dedication to better the life of the average American.

"As I look back over the years," she wrote, "I think that I am most grateful for the fact that my husband earned and deserved the love and respect of his countrymen. He cared greatly about his fellow man and they returned his concern with a full measure of affection."

• • •

As Eleanor began to realize the magnitude of her husband's legacy, she also came to terms with Lucy's return to Franklin's life and with Anna's role in making her visits possible. While she was going through her husband's belongings at Hyde Park, she came upon a little watercolor of Franklin that Lucy's friend Madame Shoumatoff had painted. She instructed Margaret Suckley to send the painting on to Lucy.

"Thank you so very much," Lucy wrote Eleanor; "you must know that it will be treasured always. I have wanted to write you for a long time to tell you that I had seen Franklin and of his great kindness about my husband when he was desperately ill in Washington, and of how helpful he was too, to his boys—and that I hoped very much that I might see you again. . . . I think of your sorrow—you—whom I have always felt to be the most blessed and privileged of women must now feel immeasurable grief and pain and they must be almost unbearable. . . . As always, Affectionately, Lucy Rutherfurd."

Later that week, Anna telephoned Lucy. She had not spoken to Lucy since her father's death, but now, perhaps knowing from Margaret Suckley what Eleanor had done, she felt free to call. "Your telephoning the other night meant so much to me," Lucy wrote Anna. "I did not know that it was in me just now to be so glad to hear the sound of any voice—and to hear you laugh—was beyond words wonderful."

> *I had not written before for many reasons—but you were constantly in my thoughts & with very loving and heart torn sympathy & I was following every step of the way. This blow must be crushing to you—to all of you—but I know that you meant more to your Father than any one and that makes it closer & harder to bear. It must be an endless comfort to you that you were able to be with him so much this past year. Every second of the day you must be conscious of the void and emptiness, where there has always been—all through your life—the strength of his beloved presence—so filled with loving understanding, so ready to guide and to help. I love to think of his very great pride in you. . . . He told me so often & with such feeling of all that you had meant of joy & comfort on the trip to Yalta. He said you had been so extraordinary & what a difference it made to have you. He told me of your charm & your tact—& of how everyone loved you. He told how capable you were & how you forgot nothing & of the little typewritten chits he would find at his place at the beginning or end of the day—reminding him of all the little or big things that he was to do. I hope he told you these things—but sometimes one doesn't. In any case you must have known—words were not needed between you. I have been reading over some very old letters of his— and in one he says: "Anna is a dear fine person—I wish so much that you knew her"—Well, now we do know one another—and it is a great joy to me & I think he was happy this past year that it was so. . . . And through it all one hears his ringing laugh & one thinks of all the ridiculous things he used to say—& do—& enjoy. The picture of him sitting waiting for you that night with the Rabbi's cap on his extraordinarily beautiful head is still vivid.*
>
> *Forgive me for writing of things which you know so much better than I— & which are sacred—& should not ever be touched on by a stranger. I somehow cannot feel myself to be that, & I feel strongly that you understand.*

My love to your husband—and to you—Anna darling, because you are his child & because you are yourself.
I am very devotedly & with heartbroken sympathy

Lucy Rutherfurd

Anna kept Lucy's letter in her bedside table for the rest of her life, "showing it," her son Johnny recalled, "only on a few occasions, in privacy, to those for whom she had a special trust and care and to whom she wished to convey something of herself for which she had no words of her own. Perhaps no one other than Lucy could have confirmed the father-love she so treasured, first and to the end, and the depth of her loss." At the same time, Anna's daughter, Sistie, speculated, Lucy's precious letter may have lessened the guilt Anna felt toward her mother. "Perhaps, by revealing what a fine person Lucy was, a person of such innate dignity and poise, the letter justified the quiet arrangements Anna had made to bring Lucy and her father together."

A strain between mother and daughter lasted through the summer and into the fall. The return to Seattle in June had not been easy for Anna and John. A disagreement with publisher William Randolph Hearst led to their severance from the *Post-Intelligencer,* and John was having trouble figuring out what to do. His self-esteem was at a low ebb. For almost a quarter of a century, he wrote Eleanor, he had had "a flood of work" constantly ahead of him, but now he had no specific responsibilities and "he was running scared." The death of FDR marked the end of an era for John, his son, Johnny, observed, the end of an inspired time in which he had lived in the protective shadow of his father-in-law's position. His old feelings of inferiority now returned, creating serious tensions in his marriage.

When Anna came east in mid-October, she was worried about her husband and anxious about the future. Walking with her mother through the Big House, she was close to tears. It was the last time she would ever see the house as she had known it as a child. The government was about to take it over and begin the process of turning it into a museum. "I think it is very hard for her," Eleanor confided in Hick. Later that night, when the conversation turned to John, Anna broke down. Her tears released the remaining tension between mother and daughter, just as Eleanor's tears had released the strain between them two decades earlier, when Anna was an adolescent.

Eleanor assured Anna that all was forgiven between them. She had come to the realization that her daughter had never meant to hurt her, but was only trying to provide a measure of relaxation for her weary father. What is more, she had come to forgive Franklin as well. "All human beings have failings," she later observed, "all human beings have needs and temptations and stresses. Men and women who live together through long years get to know one another's failings; but they also come to know what is worthy of respect and admiration in those they live with and in themselves."

• • •

For the rest of her life, her son Elliott observed, Eleanor "chose to remember only the lovely times they had shared, never the estrangement and pain." She loved to quote word for word the things they had told one another. She kept up the traditions he had established for the family—including the picnic on the Fourth of July and the reading of Dickens at Christmas. Maureen Corr, Eleanor's secretary during the forties and fifties, remembers her "constantly talking about what Franklin did or what Franklin said or . . . how Franklin thought about this or that. And every time she mentioned his name you could hear the emotion in her voice and see the glow in her eyes."

In early December 1945, President Truman telephoned Eleanor in her Washington Square apartment. The first meeting of the United Nations General Assembly was scheduled to open in January in London. Would she be willing to serve as a member of the American delegation? Oh no, she said, she could not possibly do it. She had no experience or background in foreign affairs. Truman refused to be put off. He urged her to think about it for a while and assured her he had no doubt whatsoever about her capabilities. Eleanor debated her decision for days. She considered the United Nations to be the greatest of her husband's legacies, and she longed for the job, but was terrified of failure. Finally, conquering what she called her "fear and trembling," she accepted the position, setting forth on a new journey into the field of universal human rights that would make her "the most admired person in the world"—and an important figure in American public life for nearly two more decades.

In these first months on her own, Eleanor derived constant comfort from a little verse sent to her by a friend. "They are not dead who live in lives they leave behind. In those whom they have blessed they live a life again." These simple lines, she wrote, inspired her to make the rest of her life worthy of her husband's memory. As long as she continued to fight for his ideals, he would continue to live.

AFTERWORD

Harry Hopkins resigned from the government after Roosevelt died. "The time has come," he wrote President Truman, "when I must take a rest." In September 1945, at a White House ceremony, he was awarded the Distinguished Service Medal for what Truman called his exceptional ability in welding the Allies together in World War II. Four months later, in January 1946, Hopkins died. He was fifty-five. "A strong, bright, fierce flame has burned out a frail body," Churchill said on hearing the news.

Lucy Mercer Rutherfurd continued to divide her time between her estates in Aiken, South Carolina, and Allamuchy, New Jersey. In June 1945, she told her friend Elizabeth Shoumatoff that she had burned all of Roosevelt's letters. Three years later, Lucy was diagnosed with leukemia. She died in July 1948, at the age of fifty-seven, and was buried beside her husband at Tranquility Farms in Allamuchy.

Malvina Thompson continued to work for Mrs. Roosevelt until 1953, when she died in a New York hospital from a brain hemorrhage. She was sixty-one.

Crown Princess Martha returned with her husband to Norway after it was liberated in May 1945. In June, King Haakon and the royal family were officially welcomed home with a triumphant celebration. In 1954, Martha died of a liver ailment at the age of fifty-three. The crown prince never remarried. He became king when his father died in 1957, and ruled until his death in 1991. His son, Harald, is now king of Norway.

Winston Churchill settled unhappily into his postwar role as leader of the parliamentary opposition, occupying his days with the writing of his monumental history of World War II. In 1951, the Conservatives were returned to power and Churchill became prime minister a second time. He remained in power until 1955, when ill-health forced his resignation. He suffered a massive stroke in early January 1965 and died two weeks later, at the age of ninety. He was the first commoner to be accorded a state funeral since the duke of Wellington more than a century earlier.

Lorena Hickok eventually moved to a little cottage in Hyde Park, where she remained until her death in 1968, at the age of seventy-five. In her will, she requested that her ashes be scattered among the trees along the Hudson. The funeral home, unaware of her request, placed them on a shelf along with other unclaimed items, where they remained for years, until her sister, Ruby, honored her request.

Joe Lash remained friendly with Eleanor until the end of her life. After Eleanor's death, the Roosevelt children authorized him to write her biography based on her private papers. Published when Lash was sixty-one, the book won the Pulitzer Prize. Lash died in 1987 at the age of seventy-seven.

Anna and John Boettiger bought a newspaper in Phoenix, Arizona, in 1946. When the newspaper failed, John became increasingly depressed. In 1949, he and Anna were divorced. The following year, John committed suicide by jumping from the window of a New York hotel. Two years later, Anna married Dr. James Halsted, a clinical professor of medicine at Albany Medical College. Anna died of cancer in 1975, at the age of sixty-nine.

John Roosevelt died in 1981 of heart failure at New York Hospital. He was sixty-five. The only one of the Roosevelt boys who never ran for elective office, he was a businessman and an investment banker. In 1952, he became a Republican. He was married twice.

FDR, Jr., died of cancer in 1988, on his seventy-fourth birthday. He served three terms in Congress from the Upper West Side of Manhattan. He ran twice for governor of New York, losing the first race to Averell Harriman, the second to Nelson Rockefeller. In 1960, he campaigned for John Kennedy and was appointed undersecretary of commerce. He was married five times.

Elliott Roosevelt died of congestive heart failure in 1990, at the age of eighty. He authored fourteen books, including three biographical works on his family, and a series of mystery novels which cast Eleanor as a detective. In 1962, he moved to Miami Beach, where he served as mayor. He was married five times.

James Roosevelt died in 1991, at the age of eighty-three, of complications from a stroke. In 1950, he won the Democratic nomination for governor of California, but was defeated by Earl Warren. He was elected to Congress four years later from the 26th district in California. He remained in the

House for six terms. In 1972, he played a prominent role in Democrats for Nixon. He was married four times.

Eleanor Roosevelt remained an important political figure until her death in 1962, at the age of seventy-seven. She was a leading force behind the United Nations' Declaration of Human Rights adopted in 1948, a vigorous advocate for the establishment of a Jewish state in Israel, a prominent actor in New York politics, a supporter of Adlai Stevenson, and a founding member of Americans for Democratic Action. During her last years, she was often called "the greatest woman in the world." Mourners at her funeral included President and Mrs. Kennedy, Vice-President Johnson, former Presidents Truman and Eisenhower, Chief Justice Earl Warren, Adlai Stevenson, Frances Perkins, James Farley, Sam Rosenman, and Francis Biddle. She was buried next to her husband in the rose garden at the Hyde Park estate. A plain white marble monument marks the grave. As President Roosevelt wished, it contains no decoration and no inscription except the following:

FRANKLIN DELANO ROOSEVELT

1882–1945

ANNA ELEANOR ROOSEVELT

1884–1962

A NOTE ON SOURCES

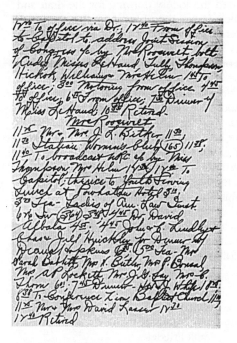

This book relies predominantly upon a multitude of primary materials: manuscript collections, memoranda, private letters, diaries, memoirs, office files, oral histories, pamphlets, newspapers, periodicals, personal interviews. The White House Usher Diaries proved an especially invaluable guide at the start of the project. These day-by-day, even minute-by-minute chronologies reveal when the president and the first lady awakened, who joined them for meals and meetings, how much time was spent with each visitor, where they went during the day, when they went to bed at night. With these daily chronologies as my base, I searched for personal diaries, letters, oral histories, and memoirs of the people who were with Franklin and Eleanor Roosevelt at particular moments of interest. Eleanor's daily columns also proved essential. Though they ramble from one topic to the next, and often were limited to an account of her daily activities, they do give us an insight into contemporaneous concerns and perceptions.

I treasure the details that emerged from these primary sources: an interview with the president's daughter-in-law revealed the nightly ritual Roosevelt followed as he tried to fall asleep in the middle of the war; a talk with the White House butler produced the unforgettable image of Winston Churchill standing in his long under-wear, demanding ninety-year-old brandy in his White House suite every night; an oral history provided the telling description of how the president's face would light up when his daughter, Anna, walked into the room; a diary entry revealed the dramatic scene when the president's mother wheeled him away from the dinner table in order to end an unpleasant discussion with Eleanor; letters to the president asking him to muzzle his wife, chain her up or, at the very least, make her stay at home with her knitting, revealed the depth of animosity felt by some toward her unusual independence.

Some of my favorite details came from the press reports of the time: the woman's scream from the audience as she witnessed the lottery drawing for the draft and realized that her son held the first number drawn; the observation that the president's nervousness before his press conferences resembled that of an opera singer about to go on stage; the likening of Harry Hopkins' weary look to that of "an ill-fed horse at the end of a hard day," the run on maps when Roosevelt announced that he wanted people listening to his fireside chat to follow along with a map spread before them; the sweat dripping from Wendell Willkie's forehead as he delivered his acceptance speech; the trembling of Roosevelt's hands as he stood before a Joint Session of Congress; the image of dozens of laborers working around the clock to stuff huge chunks of ice into the primitive air-conditioning in the president's train; the spontaneous remark when a worker at the Chrysler tank arsenal realized the man in the visitor's car was President Roosevelt—"By God, if it ain't old Frank."

Details such as these can only emerge from research. To remedy gaps in knowledge by fabricating details, even those which may seem inconsequential, is to shift from nonfiction to fiction and is a betrayal of the historian's trust.

Though my story took place more than a half century ago, I was able to talk with scores of people who knew the Roosevelts and the members of their extended family personally. A list of my interviews follows.

INTERVIEWS

Winthrop Aldrich
Bernard Asbell
Carl Ally
Toinette Bachelder
William Barber
Mildred Barker
Roberta Barrows
Eleanor Bartman
Betty Bishop
John Boettiger, Jr.
Dr. Howard Bruenn
Dorothy Butturf
Maureen Corr
Barbara Mueller Curtis
Egbert Curtis
Dawn Deslie
Robert Donovan
Betty Dooley
Jim D'Orta
Dorothy Dow
Barbara Dudley
Virginia Durr
Meg Egeberg
George Elsey
William Emerson
Creekmore Fath
Lewis Feuer

Alonzo Fields
Fran Fremont-Smith
Frank Friedel
Larry Fuchs
John Kenneth Galbraith
David Ginsburg
Rosemary Goepper
Arthur Goldschmidt
Edna Gurewitsch
Kate Roosevelt Haddad
Diana Hopkins Halsted
Elinor Hendrik
Robert Hopkins
James Hymes, Jr.
Jiro Ishihara
Tama Ishihara
Barbara Jacques
Eliot Janeway
Frances Kaplan
Jan Karski
Mary Keyserling
Mary Gaston Kramer
Trude Lash
Michael Lilly
Milton Lipson
Mayris Chaney Martin
Sara McClendon

Henry Morgenthau III
Louise Morley
Kathleen Harriman Mortimer
Robert Nathan
Verne Newton
Thomas P. O'Neill
John Pehle
Ruth Thompson Peirce
Esther Peterson
Jane Plakias
Joyce Ralph
Joseph Rauh
Curtis Roosevelt
Eleanor Wotkyns Roosevelt
Elliott Roosevelt
James Roosevelt

James Roosevelt, Jr.
Jane Scarborough
Eleanor Seagraves
Virginia Shipp
David Smith
Grace Stang
Richard Strobel
Margaret Suckley
Mark Talisman
Walter Trohan
Mary Veeder
Betsey Roosevelt Whitney
Elizabeth Wickenden
Billy Wilder
Mary Willett
Page Huidekoper Wilson

NOTES

ABBREVIATIONS USED IN NOTES

AB	Anna Boettiger*
AH	Anna Halsted*
ER	Eleanor Roosevelt
FDR	Franklin Delano Roosevelt
HH	Harry Hopkins
JL	Joseph Lash
LH	Lorena Hickok
MLH	Missy LeHand
SDR	Sara Delano Roosevelt
WC	Winston Churchill
WW	Walter White

AM	*Atlantic Monthly*
BEA	*Boston Evening American*
BG	*Boston Globe*
CB	*Current Biography*
CR	*Congressional Record*
LHJ	*Ladies' Home Journal*
MD	"My Day" (Eleanor Roosevelt's column)
NR	*New Republic*
NYHT	*New York Herald Tribune*
NYT	*New York Times*
OH	Oral History
PC	*Pittsburgh Courier*
SEP	*Saturday Evening Post*
TIMS	*This Is My Story* by Eleanor Roosevelt
TIR	*This I Remember* by Eleanor Roosevelt
TP	*Times Picayune,* New Orleans, Louisiana
WP	*Washington Post*

FDRL	Franklin D. Roosevelt Library
OF	Office File, Franklin D. Roosevelt Papers
PPF	President's Personal File, Franklin D. Roosevelt Papers
PSF	President's Secretary's File, Franklin D. Roosevelt Papers

PREFACE

9 living arrangements at the White House: William Seale, *The President's House: A History* (1986), vol. II, pp. 926–28.

10 he could truly see . . . : George Martin, *Madame Secretary: Frances Perkins* (1976), p. 435.

11 "the most influential woman . . .": Joan Hoff-Wilson and Marjorie Lightman, eds., *Without Precedent: The Life and Career of Eleanor Roosevelt* (1984), p. 11.

11 "this is no ordinary time . . .": *WP*, July 19, 1940, p. 1.

---

* Anna Roosevelt was married to John Boettiger during the war years. She married James Halsted in 1952.

CHAPTER ONE: "The Decisive Hour Has Come"

13 On nights filled with tension: interview with Betsey Whitney.
14 John Cudahy call: *WP*, May 10, 1940, p. 1.
14 German planes in the air: Jay Pierpont Moffat, *The Moffat Papers* (1956), p. 307.
14 "Pa" Watson: *NYT*, July 23, 1939, sect. VI, p. 6.
14 Stunned Belgians: *WP*, May 10, 1940, p. 1.
14 A thirteen-year-old: *Time*, May 20, 1940, p. 18.
14 Bombs were also falling: *Newsweek*, May 20, 1940, p. 18.
14 freeze all assets: *WP*, May 10, 1940, pp. 1, 3.
15 had received "proof": *NYT*, May 10, 1940, p. 1.
15 "The decisive hour . . .": *Time*, May 20, 1940, p. 22.
15 "in times of crisis . . .": Adolf Berle quoted in Moffat, *Papers*, p. 307.
15 Irvin McDuffie: obituary, *NYT*, Jan. 31, 1946, p. 28.
15 "he couldn't help . . .": ER interview, Graff Papers, FDRL.
15 straightened his legs: Hugh Gregory Gallagher, *FDR's Splendid Deception* (1985), p. 163.
15 Description of bedroom: *Collier's*, Sept. 14, 1946, pp. 96–97.
15 Eleanor basket: *NYT*, July 5, 1936, sect. IV, p. 7.
15 "Like every room . . .": Arthur M. Schlesinger, Jr., *The Age of Roosevelt*, vol. II, *The Coming of the New Deal* (1958), p. 511.
16 his aunt Laura: Geoffrey C. Ward, *Before the Trumpet* (1985), pp. 117–18.
16 "We assured him . . .": James Roosevelt, *My Parents: A Differing View* (1976), p. 81.
16 "very active . . .": AH, *OH*, Columbia University.
16 "a wonderful playmate . . .": AH interview, Graff Papers, FDRL.
16 "the handsomest . . .": interview with James Roosevelt.
16 "trial by fire": Joseph P. Lash, *Eleanor and Franklin* (1971), p. 267.
16 "There had been a plowing . . .": *Collier's*, Aug. 24, 1946, p. 12.
17 "his vital links . . .": Arthur M. Schlesinger, Jr., *The Age of Roosevelt*, vol. I, *The Crisis of the Old Order* (1957), p. 407.
17 "Anyone who has gone . . .": Lash, *Eleanor and Franklin*, p. 424.
17 "He was smiling . . .": interview with Eliot Janeway.
17 FDR's morning routine: *New Yorker*, June 16, 1934, pp. 24–25.
18 ER's visit to the city: *MD*, May 9–11, 1940.
18 honored by *The Nation*: *NYT*, May 2, 1940, p. 18.
18 "distinguished service . . .": *Nation*, May 18, 1940, p. 623.
18 "What is an institution? . . .": ibid.
18 "My dear, I don't care . . .": *NYT*, May 2, 1940, p. 18.
19 "It never seems . . .": *MD*, May 3, 1940.
19 "I will do my best . . .": *NYT*, May 2, 1940, p. 18.
19 "Mrs. Roosevelt's incessant . . .": *Fortune*, May 1940, p. 160.
19 Lucy Mercer: Bernard Asbell, *The FDR Memoirs* (1973), pp. 228–33.
19 "the bottom dropped . . .": Joseph P. Lash, *Love, Eleanor* (1982), p. 66.
19 Story of SDR and divorce: ibid., pp. 66–71; James Roosevelt, *My Parents*, pp. 99–102; AH, unpublished article, box 84, Halsted Papers, FDRL.
20 "an ordeal to be borne": Asbell, *FDR Memoirs*, p. 222.
20 "an exaggerated idea . . .": Geoffrey C. Ward, *A First-Class Temperament* (1989), p. 17.
20 "There's no doubt . . .": Raymond Moley, *The First New Deal* (1966), pp. 273–75.
20 "When Missy gave . . .": Lillian Rogers Parks, *The Roosevelts: A Family in Turmoil* (1981), p. 177.
20 "she had a certain class . . .": Asbell, *FDR Memoirs*, p. 247.
21 "The first thing . . .": *NYT*, June 10, 1934, sect. VI, p. 9.
21 "Albany was the hardest . . .": *SEP*, Jan. 8, 1938, p. 60.
21 "In terms of companionship . . .": interview with Eliot Janeway.
22 poked his head: *SEP*, Jan. 8, 1938, p. 60.
22 George Marshall: *Time*, July 29, 1940, pp. 30–33.
22 "Don't you think so . . .": Leonard Mosley, *Marshall: A Hero for Our Times* (1982), pp. 121–22.

22 pre–World War II army: R. Elberton Smith, *The Army and Economic Mobilization* (1959), pp. 24–35, 119–26.

22 "It's a terrible thing . . .": Samuel I. Rosenman, *Working with Roosevelt* (1952), p. 167.

23 136 divisions: Erwin Rommel, *The Rommel Papers* (1953), p. 3.

23 U.S. merely five divisions: memo, Col. J. H. Burns, Ordnance Dept. Executive, to Assist. Sec. of War, May 10, 1940, Morgenthau Papers, FDRL.

23 almost no munitions industry: Charles J. Hitch, *America's Economic Strength* (1941), p. 67.

23 Marshall trying to get Woodring: Richard M. Ketchum, *The Borrowed Years, 1938–1941* (1989), pp. 537–38.

23 "His real weakness . . .": ER interview, Graff Papers, FDRL.

24 "If I were you . . .": *SEP,* June 5, 1948, p. 90.

24 Louis Johnson: Ketchum, *Borrowed Years,* pp. 537–38.

24 Marshall found it incomprehensible: Forrest C. Pogue, *George C. Marshall: Ordeal and Hope, 1939–1942* (1966), vol. II, p. 23.

24 "I'm sorry . . .": ibid., pp. 93–94.

24 "I think he knew exactly . . .": James Rowe, *OH,* FDRL.

24 "I never heard him call . . .": Robert Cutler, *No Time for Rest* (1966), p. 223.

24 "Informal conversation . . .": ibid., p. 224.

25 Cudahy wired: *Time,* May 20, 1940, p. 25.

25 "tangible evidence . . .": Joseph P. Kennedy to Treasury Dept., May 10, 1940, Morgenthau Papers, FDRL.

25 "After the World War . . .": Military Establishment Appropriations Bill, statement of Gen. Marshall, April 30, 1940, p. 30.

25 ". . . a little drawn eyed . . .": *NYHT,* May 11, 1940, p. 19.

25 "Glancing around the room . . .": *NYT,* Feb. 1, 1942, sect. VI, p. 7.

26 "Like an opera singer . . ."; "all-in": ibid.

26 "the best newspaperman . . .": Betty Houchin Winfield, *FDR and the News Media* (1990), p. 1.

26 On press conferences: John Gunther, *Roosevelt in Retrospect* (1950), pp. 134–39; Samuel I. and Dorothy Rosenman, *Presidential Style* (1976), pp. 330–39.

26 bachelor correspondent: Charles Hurd, *When the New Deal Was Young and Gay* (1965), p. 241.

26 "By the brilliant but simple trick . . .": Schlesinger, *Coming of the New Deal,* p. 566.

26 "History will like to say . . .": *NYHT,* May 11, 1940, p. 19.

26 "Good morning . . .": press-conference typescript, collection of speeches, FDRL.

27 "partly in consideration . . .": *NYHT,* May 11, 1940, p. 19.

27 Choate School: *Choate Catalogue,* 1934–1936, p. 33.

27 Malvina Thompson: Lash, *Eleanor and Franklin,* p. 315; Minnewa Bell, *OH,* FDRL.

27 "good Vermont granite . . .": biographical facts on M. Thompson, LH Papers, FDRL.

27 "who makes life . . .": *NYT,* April 13, 1953, p. 27.

27 ER and Tommy traveled: *Life,* Feb. 4, 1940, p. 70.

27 "will o' the wisp": Elliott Roosevelt and James Brough, *A Rendezvous with Destiny* (1975), p. 71.

28 "It was the best education . . ." . . . "One time . . .": Alfred Steinberg, *Mrs. R* (1958), p. 162.

28 "She saw many things . . .": Frances Perkins interview, Graff Papers, FDRL.

28 "Watch the people's . . .": Steinberg, *Mrs. R,* p. 209.

28 "did not know what . . .": ibid.

29 ER in Puerto Rico: Ruby Black, *ER* (1940), p. 296.

29 "I realized that . . .": *NYT,* April 22, 1937, p. 24.

29 "Mrs. Roosevelt Spends Night . . .": William Leuchtenburg, *Franklin D. Roosevelt and the New Deal* (1963), p. 192.

29 "There is something . . .": *MD,* May 11 and 13, 1940.

29 Near the Chapel: *Choate Catalogue,* p. 35.

29 "I wonder that the time . . .": *MD,* May 9, 1940.

30 Talking with her young friend: Lash, *Eleanor and Franklin,* p. 608; *NYHT,* May 27, 1940, p. 8.

30 Her deepest fear: Lash Diary, May 10, 1940, Lash Papers, FDRL.

30 "How to preserve . . .": *NYT,* May 11, 1940, p. 23.
30 president opened: Gunther, *Roosevelt in Retrospect,* pp. 131–34.
30 Cordell Hull: *CB,* 1940, pp. 412–15.
30 Belgian gold reserves: memo for Treasury from Butterworth, May 10, 1940, Morgenthau Papers, FDRL.
31 Morgenthau had been huddled: memos of May 10, 1940, activities in Morgenthau Papers, FDRL.
31 "as though she had . . .": *CB,* 1940, p. 645.
31 HH: *CB,* 1941, pp. 405–6.
31 HH in and out of hospitals: interview with Robert Hopkins.
31 "He was to all intents . . .": Robert E. Sherwood, *Roosevelt and Hopkins* (1948), p. 10.
31 "an ill-fed horse . . .": *CB,* 1941, p. 406.
31 "a very sad dog": from "Harry Hopkins: At FDR's Side," documentary written by Verne Newton, FDRL. Hereafter cited HH documentary, FDRL.
31 "you wouldn't think . . .": *WP,* Oct. 31, 1943, p. 2.
31 "to galvanize . . .": Marquis Childs, *I Write from Washington* (1942), p. 170.
32 "only a five or six months . . .": Harold L. Ickes, *The Secret Diaries of Harold L. Ickes,* vol. III, *The Lowering Clouds, 1939–1941* (1954), p. 175.
32 90 percent of America's supply: *Time,* May 20, 1940, p. 73.
32 Reconstruction Finance: Ickes, *Secret Diaries,* vol. III, p. 175.
32 word came from London: ibid., p. 176.
32 "I welcome it, indeed . . .": Richard Collier, *1940: The World in Flames* (1979), p. 74.
32 Attlee's blunt reply: ibid., p. 76.
33 "Looking backward . . .": *NYT Magazine,* Sept. 14, 1941, p. 5.
33 "Churchill was the best . . .": Ickes, *Secret Diaries,* vol. III, p. 175.
33 the two leaders had come to admire: *Churchill & Roosevelt: The Complete Correspondence* (1984), vol. I, p. 6.
33 "I shall at all times . . .": ibid., p. 89.
33 second-floor study: William Seale, *The President's House,* vol. II (1986), p. 989; Rexford G. Tugwell, *The Democratic Roosevelt* (1957), p. 301.
34 "invariably got that lived-in . . .": Frances Perkins, *The Roosevelt I Knew* (1946), p. 66.
34 The president mixed the drinks: Rosenman, *Working with Roosevelt,* pp. 150–51.
34 FDR's storytelling: ibid., p. 152.
34 John Taber story: *Time,* May 20, 1940, p. 19.
34 "I didn't realize . . .": interview with Toi Bachelder.
35 "he would not be surprised . . .": Ickes Diary, p. 3248, Library of Congress.
35 "Vic and I arriving . . .": HH to MLH, May 22, 1939, HH Papers, FDRL.
35 "the real purpose . . .": HH to MLH, Aug. 31, 1939, HH Papers, FDRL.
35 "There is no one here . . .": Sherwood, *Roosevelt and Hopkins,* pp. 114–15.
35 "Even the most ardent . . .": *Newsweek,* Aug. 12, 1944, p. 16.
35 "should have been off . . .": Fulton Oursler, *Behold This Dreamer!* (1964), pp. 424–25.
35 "Gosh, it will be good . . .": MLH to FDR, Dec. 1936, PPF 3737, FDRL.
36 "She was working away . . .": interview with Margaret Suckley.
36 "In a funny way . . .": AB to LH, Dec. 2, 1935, LH Papers, FDRL.
36 "Work had become . . .": interview with Eleanor Wotkyns.
36 "She could be . . .": interview with Curtis Dall Roosevelt, son of Anna Roosevelt and Curtis Dall.
36 "If only Mother . . .": interview with Elliott Roosevelt.
37 "Stay for dinner . . .": HH documentary, FDRL; David E. Lilienthal, *The Journal of David E. Lilienthal,* vol. 1 (1964), pp. 169–70.
37 "There was a temperamental . . .": Perkins quoted in Louis W. Koenig, *The Invisible Presidency* (1960), p. 317.
37 "feminine sensitivity": Sherwood, *Roosevelt and Hopkins,* p. 2.
37 borrowed a pair of pajamas: *New Yorker,* Aug. 7, 1941, p. 26.
37 "It was Harry . . .": Sherwood, *Roosevelt and Hopkins,* p. 173.
37 Helen Douglas story: interview with Billy Wilder.
37 "We come here tonight . . .": text of speech, *NYT,* May 11, 1940, p. 1.
38 British troops were pouring: *WP,* May 11, 1940, p. 1.

38   "a profound sense...": Winston S. Churchill, *The Second World War,* vol. I, *The Gathering Storm* (1948), p. 601.
38   "The day was unforgettable...": Helen Gahagan Douglas, *OH, FDRL.*
39   "OK, Helen...": interview with Billy Wilder.
39   she felt terribly left out: interview with Elliott Roosevelt.
39   "All her life...": interview with Eleanor Wotkyns.

CHAPTER TWO: "A Few Nice Boys with BB Guns"

40   Here, on the...: Neil MacNeil, *Forge of Democracy: The House of Representatives* (1963), p. 132.
40   In the Congress in 1940: *NYT,* Jan. 7, 1940, sect. VI, p. 3.
41   The president's arrival: *WP,* May 17, 1940, p. 4; *NYT,* May 17, 1940, p. 10.
41   "walls of sand...": Cordell Hull, *The Memoirs of Cordell Hull,* vol. II (1948), p. 769.
41   Absent were both: *NYT,* May 17, 1940, pp. 1, 10; *Charlotte Observer,* May 17, 1940, p. 2.
41   failed to put on glasses: *Time,* May 27, 1940, p. 17.
42   "I trust you realize...": WC to FDR, May 15, 1940, *Churchill & Roosevelt: The Complete Correspondence* (1984), vol. I, p. 37.
42   "The great knife...": quoted in Carl Degler, *Out of Our Past* (1959), p. 383.
42   employment and tax statistics: *Historical Statistics of the United States Colonial Times to 1957* (1961), pp. 67–73, 713–15.
42   Thirty-one percent: Richard Polenberg, *One Nation Divisible* (1980), p. 19.
43   small-town nation: ibid., p. 17.
43   "Class membership...": ibid., p. 16.
43   "It is hard to think...": William Leuchtenburg in Harvard Sitkoff, *Fifty Years Later: The New Deal Evaluated* (1985), p. 230.
44   "These are ominous days...": transcript of speech, collection of speeches, FDRL.
45   "the President's big round number...": Irving Holley, Jr., *Buying Aircraft* (1964), p. 228.
45   "like an utterly impossible...": Edward R. Stettinius, Jr., *Lend-Lease* (1944), pp. 12–13.
45   In times of crisis: Grant McConnell, *The Modern Presidency* (1976), p. 4.
45   "believed that with enough...": *AM,* Sept. 1949, p. 43.
45   "So passionate a faith...": ibid., p. 39.
46   In his imagination: interview with James Roosevelt.
46   "There's something...": Perkins, *OH,* Columbia University.
46   "His most outstanding...": W. M. Kiplinger, *Washington Is Like That* (1942), p. 14.
46   "those who hear it...": Samuel I. and Dorothy Rosenman, *Presidential Style* (1976), p. 321.
46   "his capacity to inspire...": *Collier's,* Sept. 12, 1946, p. 102.
46   "the new President...": *Collier's,* March 11, 1933, p. 8.
46   "the renewal of the courage...": Rosenman and Rosenman, *Presidential Style,* p. 323.
47   "the President is right": *Time,* May 27, 1940, p. 21.
47   "a four alarm fire...": *Newsweek,* May 27, 1940, p. 35.
47   "was quickly succeeded...": *Time,* May 27, 1940, p. 22.
47   "tragically late": ibid., p. 21.
47   "the failure of the New Deal...": *NYT,* May 17, 1940, p. 10.
47   "a defense hysteria...": *Vital Speeches,* vol. 6, pp. 485–86.
47   response to Lindbergh speech: *NYT,* May 21, 1940, p. 12.
48   "During the present...": *CR,* 76th Cong., 3rd sess., May 13, 1940, p. 5947; May 15, 1940, p. 6163.
48   "If I should die tomorrow...": Ted Morgan, *FDR: A Biography* (1985), p. 523.
48   "but when he did get angry...": ER interview, Graff Papers, FDRL.
48   "When I read Lindbergh's speech...": Henry Stimson to FDR, May 21, 1940, PSF 106, FDRL.
48   ER told a newspaper reporter: *NYT,* May 21, 1940, p. 12.
48   congressional appropriations: Mark S. Watson, *Chief of Staff* (1950), pp. 166–69.
49   "on russet roads...": *Time,* May 21, 1940, p. 18.
49   biggest peacetime maneuver: *NYT,* April 28, 1940, p. 19.

49 Blues were heading: *NYT,* May 7, 1940, p. 8; *TP,* April 27, 1940, p. 4.
49 games were intended: *TP,* April 28, 1940, p. 1; *NYT,* April 28, 1940, p. 19.
49 supplies: *Newsweek,* May 13, 1940, p. 29.
49 announcement of games: *TP,* April 14, 1940, sect. II, p. 6.
49 men, women, and children: *TP,* May 10, 1940, p. 1.
49 discrete exercises: ibid.
49 "Consider the task . . .": *TP,* April 14, 1940, sect. II, p. 6.
50 "drilling bright tunnels . . .": *TP,* May 10, 1940, pp. 1, 3.
50 squadron of Red bombers: *NYHT,* May 10, 1940, p. 7.
50 Two days later: *TP,* May 14, 1940, p. 23.
50 maneuver accidents: *TP,* May 5, 1940, p. 1; May 13, 1940, p. 29; May 15, 1940, p. 27; May 18, 1940, p. 7.
50 By week's end: *TP,* May 19, 1940, p. 15.
50 army bombers crashed: *NYT,* June 18, 1940, p. 3.
50 lack of equipment was cited: *TP,* May 25, 1940, p. 3; *NYT,* May 26, 1940, p. 2.
50 Germans' form of attack: Senator Lodge in *CR,* 76th Cong., 3rd sess., May 27, 1940, p. 6876.
50 "the greatest . . .": *TP,* May 23, 1940, p. 3.
51 General Short admitted: *NYT,* May 26, 1940, p. 2.
51 "Too frequently . . .": *Army and Navy Journal,* June 1, 1940, p. 962.
51 "It is a mistake . . .": *Cavalry Journal,* Jan.–Feb. 1940, p. 35.
51 "one finger of the fan-like . . .": *CR,* May 27, 1940, p. 6877.
51 As townspeople watched: *TP,* May 16, 1940, p. 18.
51 "They were hit . . .": *CR,* May 15, 1940, p. 6135.
51 "road-bound": *NYT,* May 26, 1940, p. 2.
52 "the noise of ten robots . . .": *NYT,* Sept. 8, 1940, sect. VII, p. 26.
52 "The gravity of this situation . . .": *CR,* p. 6877.
52 a secret meeting took place: Christopher R. Gabel, "1940 Maneuvers: Prelude to Mobilization," Ohio State University, given to author by Dr. Gabel.
52 "Overnight, the pleasant doings . . .": *Time,* May 27, 1940, p. 19.
52 "The fact remains . . .": ibid.
53 "What smoldered beneath . . .": ibid., p. 21.
53 "There were evidently . . .": George Martin, *Madame Secretary* (1976), p. 435.
53 "that man . . ."; Howland Spencer: William Leuchtenburg, *Franklin D. Roosevelt and the New Deal* (1963), p. 176.
53 ill-will crystallized: ibid., p. 147.
54 "of organized . . .": Franklin D. Roosevelt, *Public Papers and Addresses of Franklin D. Roosevelt, 1940* (1941), pp. 568–69.
54 "as certain as night follows day . . .": *Journal of Economic History,* Winter 1953, p. 69.
54 "It was a political necessity . . .": I. F. Stone, *Business as Usual* (1941), p. 126.
54 NDAC: *WP,* May 29, 1940, pp. 1, 2; *NYT,* May 29, 1940, pp. 1, 15.
54 William Knudsen: *CB,* 1940, pp. 464–65.
55 "To many a citizen . . .": *Time,* Dec. 23, 1940, p. 14.
55 "I am most happy . . .": Norman Beasley, *Knudsen* (1947), p. 246.
55 Edward Stettinius: *CB,* 1940, pp. 761–62.
55 "now the captains . . .": Constance McLaughlin Green, *Washington* (1963), p. 467.
55 "In the field of national defense . . .": *Journal of Economic History,* Winter 1953, p. 74.
55 "a little something . . .": *NR,* June 24, 1940, p. 264.
55 Sidney Hillman: *CB,* 1940, pp. 386–88.
55 Leon Henderson: ibid., pp. 377–79.
56 "If you are going . . .": Stimson Diary, Aug. 26, 1940, Yale University.
56 suppose that: Bruce Catton, *The War Lords of Washington* (1969), p. 121.
56 "The conflict was enduring . . .": John Kenneth Galbraith, *A Life in Our Times* (1981), pp. 108–9.
56 "At times . . .": interview with John K. Galbraith.
56 "In private life . . .": quoted in *Army and Navy Journal,* Nov. 2, 1940, p. 226.
56 "the cry . . ."; "let democratic processes . . .": *NR,* Sept. 30, 1940, p. 446.

57 "Who is my boss?...": Smith conference notes, May 30, 1940, Harold Smith Papers, FDRL.

57 "So long as...": Stone, *Business as Usual,* p. 129.

57 "I think people...": Franklin D. Roosevelt, *Public Papers and Addresses, 1940,* pp. 241–50.

57 "an uneasy one...": Catton, *War Lords,* p. 25.

57 fireside chats: Russell D. Buhite and David W. Levy, eds., *FDR's Fireside Chats* (1992), p. xv.

57 "a few people...": Betty Houchin Winfield, *FDR and the News Media* (1990), p. 104.

58 "You felt he was talking...": ibid.

58 "he looked for words...": Rosenman and Rosenman, *Presidential Style,* p. 92.

58 a dozen drafts: ibid., p. 11.

58 "there was a last minute dash...": Grace Tully, *F.D.R., My Boss* (1949), p. 100.

58 "There was no levity...": Rosenman and Rosenman, *Presidential Style,* p. 196.

58 "The President was worried...": ibid.

58 "He was conscious...": Frances Perkins, *The Roosevelt I Knew* (1946), p. 72.

58 "My friends...": *NYT,* May 27, 1940, p. 12.

59 "cost plus fixed fee": R. Elberton Smith, *The Army and Economic Mobilization* (1959), pp. 280–302; see also Gerald White, *Billions for Defense* (1980).

60 "One can't be sure...": Joseph P. Lash, *Eleanor Roosevelt: A Friend's Memoir* (1964), p. 67.

60 "glad [the president]...": Lash Diary, May 27, 1940, Lash Papers, FDRL.

CHAPTER THREE: "Back to the Hudson"

61 rearmament versus aid to Allies: Mark S. Watson, *Chief of Staff* (1950), ch. 10 generally.

61 "the War Department...": ibid., p. 303.

61 "if we had to fight...": Cordell Hull, *The Memoirs of Cordell Hull,* vol. II (1948), p. 766.

61 "If Great Britain goes down...": Maurice Matloff and Edwin Snell, *Strategic Planning for Coalition Warfare, 1941–1942* (1953), p. 13.

62 "And if I should...": Harold L. Ickes, *The Secret Diaries of Harold L. Ickes,* vol. III, *The Lowering Clouds, 1939–1941* (1954), p. 200.

62 "one airplane sent...": *CR,* 76th Cong., 3rd sess., p. 3588.

62 "At this moment...": William C. Bullitt, *For the President, Personal and Secret* (1972) p. 416.

62 "The Paris police...": ibid., p. 434.

62 "This may be the last...": ibid., pp. 440–41.

62 "the whole root and core...": Arthur Bryant, *The Turn of the Tide* (1957), p. 5.

62 May 24, St. Eloi Church: Norman Gelb, *Dunkirk* (1989), p. 128.

62 Hitler's first great mistake: Martin Gilbert, *The Second World War* (1989), p. 73.

62 "miracle of Dunkirk": Robert Leckie, *Delivered from Evil: The Saga of World War II* (1987), p. 171.

62 From Harwich and Margate: Hanson W. Baldwin, *The Crucial Years, 1939–1941* (1976), pp. 39–41.

63 nearly 340,000 men escaped: Winston S. Churchill, *The Second World War,* vol. II, *Their Finest Hour* (1949), p. 115.

63 "We shall go on...": Winston S. Churchill, *Great War Speeches* (1957), p. 25.

63 "So hypnotic...": *AM,* Sept. 1949, p. 41.

63 opinion poll: Richard M. Ketchum, *The Borrowed Years, 1938–1941* (1989), p. 354.

63 "must not blind us...": Churchill, *Speeches,* p. 23.

63 chaos of the retreat: General Sir William Edmund Ironside, *Time Unguarded* (1962), p. 354; Gilbert, *Second World War,* p. 86.

63 Left in ruins: Gelb, *Dunkirk,* p. 233.

64 "Over a distance...": *NYHT,* June 7, 1940, p. 3.

64 Britain's best troops: Edward R. Stettinius, Jr., *Lend-Lease* (1944), p. 24.

64 "all the first fruits...": Churchill, *Finest Hour,* p. 125.

64 only 600,000 rifles: Gilbert, *Second World War,* p. 261.

64 "Never has a nation...": Churchill, *Finest Hour,* p. 128.

64 "most secret" letter, FDR's response: letter of May 15, 1940, *Churchill & Roosevelt: The Complete Correspondence* (1984), vol. I, p. 37.

64 FDR directed his military chiefs: John Morton Blum, *From the Morgenthau Diaries* (1965), vol. II, pp. 149–50.

64 violently disagreed: Matloff and Snell, *Strategic Planning*, pp. 14–15.

65 "I regret to tell you . . .": Blum, *Morgenthau Diaries*, vol. II, p. 151.

65 "We have a school . . .": Watson, *Chief of Staff*, p. 307.

65 ". . . seriously prejudicial . . .": Marshall to Woody, June 18, 1940, George Catlett Marshall, *The Papers of George Catlett Marshall*, vol. II (1981), p. 247.

65 "It would take two years . . .": Watson, *Chief of Staff*, p. 311.

65 ". . . found to be short . . .": Matloff and Snell, *Strategic Planning*, p. 17.

65 "to absolutely disapprove . . .": Watson, *Chief of Staff*, p. 304.

65 ". . . dangerous adventurism": *NYT,* June 21, 1940, p. 6.

65 "in a towering rage . . .": Charles Edison to FDR, June 14, 1940, PSF 189, FDRL.

65 "I say it is too risky . . .": *CR,* 76th Cong., 3rd sess., June 21, 1940, pp. 8783–84.

66 "All of Mr. Roosevelt's . . .": *NR,* July 1, 1940, p. 11.

66 Marshall reluctantly agreed: Watson, *Chief of Staff*, pp. 309–10.

66 "It was the only time . . .": Marshall, *Papers*, p. 262.

66 "I am delighted . . .": Philip Goodhart, *Fifty Good Ships That Saved the World* (1965) p. 60.

66 Since the equipment was scattered: ibid., p. 61.

66 Working night and day: Stettinius, *Lend-Lease*, p. 27.

66 "Go ahead and load": Goodhart, *Fifty Good Ships*, p. 62.

66 All through that night; worth over $300 million: H. Duncan Hall, *North American Supply* (1955), p. 138; Goodhart, *Fifty Good Ships*, p. 60.

67 "For weeks . . .": Stettinius, *Lend-Lease*, pp. 28–29.

67 FDR, Jr., was graduating: *BEA,* June 10, 1940, p. 12.

67 news reached the White House: *Time,* June 17, 1940, p. 13.

68 "If your conscience . . .": Stimson Diary, Dec. 29, 1940, Henry L. Stimson Papers, Manuscripts and Archives, Yale University Library. Hereafter cited Stimson Diary, Yale University.

68 "grave and pale . . .": *Time,* June 17, 1940, p. 13.

68 "a deep growl . . .": Churchill, *Finest Hour,* p. 116.

68 "We will extend . . .": *NYHT,* June 10, 1940, p. 13.

68 "We all listened to you . . .": June 11, 1940, cable, *Churchill & Roosevelt Correspondence,* vol. I, p. 43.

68 "determined faith . . .": Stetson Conn and Byron Fairchild, *The Western Hemisphere* (1960), p. 36.

69 While he appreciated: Richard Leighton and Robert Coakley, *Global Logistics and Strategy, 1940–1943* (1955), p. 30.

69 "full of the elan": Adolf A. Berle, *Navigating the Rapids, 1918–1971* (1973), p. 322.

69 "Though I mildly suggested . . .": *MD,* June 12, 1940.

69 "It was a fighting speech . . .": *Time,* June 17, 1940, p. 13.

69 "rose to the occasion . . .": quoted in Ketchum, *Borrowed Years,* p. 358.

69 German troops entered Paris: Gilbert, *Second World War,* p. 94.

69 Parisians awakened: Noel Barber, *The Week France Fell* (1976), pp. 157–66.

70 A week later: *Time,* July 1, 1940, pp. 20–25; Robert Payne, *The Life and Death of Adolf Hitler* (1973), p. 390.

70 Marshall and Stark were convinced: Leighton and Coakley, *Global Logistics,* pp. 19–21.

70 "one of his most decisive . . .": Eric Larrabee, *Commander in Chief* (1987), p. 47.

70 "to keep that Japanese dog . . .": *Churchill & Roosevelt Correspondence,* vol. I, p. 38.

71 fired Secretary Woodring: *NYT,* June 21, 1940, p. 1.

71 "When the President did decide . . .": John Gunther, *Roosevelt in Retrospect* (1950), p. 42.

71 president would make good: Bernard M. Baruch, *Baruch: The Public Years* (1960), p. 277; *Time,* Oct. 19, 1939, p. 16.

71 coalition Cabinet: Geoffrey Perrett, *Days of Sadness, Years of Triumph* (1973), p. 42.

71 Henry Stimson: *CB,* 1940, pp. 766–67.

71 "Even if I had had . . .": Ickes, *Secret Diaries,* vol. III, p. 214.

71 Frank Knox: *CB,* 1940, pp. 461–62.
71 "a truce between the New Deal...": Bruce Catton, *The War Lords of Washington* (1969), pp. 23–24.
71 both men had expressed; "double cross": *NYT,* June 12, 1940, pp. 1, 4; *NR,* July 1, 1940, p. 4.
72 "Abroad, these nominations...": *WP* quoted in *Army and Navy Journal,* June 29, 1940, p. 1058.
72 For six hours before: Charles Hurd, *When the New Deal Was Young and Gay* (1965), pp. 255–63.
72 Hitler's visit to Paris: Payne, *Life and Death of Hitler,* pp. 390–91; Albert Speer, *Inside the Third Reich* (1970), pp. 171–72.
72 "There, you see...": Speer, *Third Reich,* p. 171.
`73 "... the dream of my life...": ibid., p. 172.
73 "In the past...": ibid.
73 "delightfully cool and brilliant": *NYHT,* June 24, 1940, p. 4.
73 Springwood: *American Heritage,* April 1987; Clara and Hardy Steeholm, *The House at Hyde Park* (1950), pp. 123–24.
73 Description of SDR: *LHJ,* April 1934, p. 13; *NYT,* Sept. 8, 1941, p. 1; Kleeman notes, Kleeman Papers, FDRL; *Literary Digest ,* Feb. 24, 1934, p. 13.
73 "The weather was...": *NYHT,* June 24, 1940, p. 4.
73 "Of course not...": interview with Margaret Suckley.
74 a tray of cocktails: *TIR,* p. 195.
74 "Shrieks of laughter...": Martha Gellhorn, *OH,* FDRL.
74 "My mother...": *TIR,* p. 196.
74 "Perhaps I have lived...": James Roosevelt, *My Parents: A Differing View* (1976), p. 31.
74 "and realize a little...": SDR to FDR, May 21, 1940, box 10, Roosevelt Family Papers Donated by the Children, FDRL.
74 "Nothing ever seemed...": Eleanor Roosevelt, *On My Own* (1958), p. 23.
74 On FDR activities during June 21 weekend: *Poughkeepsie Eagle News,* June 21, 1940, p. 11; June 22, 1940, p. 18; *NYHT,* June 22, 1940, pp. 7, 16; June 23, 1940, p. 18; June 24, 1940, p. 4; *NYT,* June 24, 1940, p. 12.
74 "All that is in me...": Joseph P. Lash, *Eleanor and Franklin* (1971), p. 116.
75 On Sara Delano and Algonac: Geoffrey C. Ward, *Before the Trumpet* (1985), ch. 2; Rita Halle Kleeman, *Gracious Lady* (1935).
75 "all traces of sadness...": Ward, *Trumpet,* p. 85.
75 "pain-killing can itself...": John R. Boettiger, Jr., *A Love in Shadow* (1978), p. 29.
75 "If there remained in Franklin...": ibid.
75 On James Roosevelt: Ward, *Trumpet,* ch. 1.
76 "No moment of Franklin's day...": ibid., pp. 125–26.
76 "... with a curious little...": Sara Delano Roosevelt, *My Boy Franklin* (1933), pp. 4–5.
76 "of his own accord...": ibid.
76 FDR and his father: Kenneth S. Davis, *FDR: The Beckoning of Destiny, 1882–1928* (1971), pp. 70–71.
76 "nice child...": Ward, *Trumpet,* p. 145.
76 relationships with children: ibid., pp. 139–42.
77 "It never occurred to me...": Sara Delano Roosevelt, *My Boy,* pp. 17–18.
77 "We never were strict...": ibid., p. 33.
77 one consequence: Alice Miller, *The Drama of the Gifted Child* (1981), p. 15.
77 Accompanying Mr. James: Ward, *Trumpet,* p. 122.
77 story of steel rod: Geoffrey C. Ward, *A First-Class Temperament* (1989), p. 607.
78 "By the warmth...": Samuel I. Rosenman, *Working with Roosevelt* (1952), p. 24.
78 "Perhaps in the long run...": *SEP,* Sept. 16, 1939, p. 95.
78 "We dusted his birds...": SDR's diary quoted in Ward, *Trumpet,* p. 177.
78 "They knew things...": Bess Furman, *Washington By-Line* (1949), p. 272.
78 "They didn't like him...": Ward, *Trumpet,* p. 203.
78 "Almost overnight...": Sara Delano Roosevelt, *My Boy,* p. 35.
78 FDR at Harvard: Ward, *Temperament,* pp. 258–62.
79 "She was an indulgent mother...": Ward, *Trumpet,* p. 245.
79 "The effort to become...": Ward, *Temperament,* flap copy.

79 "I know what pain . . .": Franklin D. Roosevelt, *FDR: His Personal Letters,* vol. I (1947), p. 518.

79 "The journey is over . . .": Lash, *Eleanor and Franklin,* pp. 128–29.

80 "Don't let her feel . . .": ibid., p. 130.

80 "I have more respect . . .": ibid., p. 136.

80 "You are mighty lucky . . .": ibid., p. 137.

80 "Reasonable it is to assume . . .": *LHJ,* April 1934, p. 12.

80 "I think probably the thing . . .": ER interview, Graff Papers, FDRL.

CHAPTER FOUR: "Living Here Is Very Oppressive"

81 "The President was enormously . . .": Frances Perkins, *The Roosevelt I Knew* (1946), pp. 69–70.

81 "All that she . . .": interview with Curtis Roosevelt.

82 "Living here is . . .": ER to AB, June 4, 1940, Bernard Asbell, *Mother and Daughter* (1988), p. 118.

82 ER had worked for the Red Cross: *TIMS,* pp. 254–55.

82 "I loved it . . .": Joseph P. Lash, *Love, Eleanor* (1982), p. 67.

82 ". . . I knew no one . . .": *TIMS,* p. 262.

82 *Potomac* offered escape: John Gunther, *Roosevelt in Retrospect* (1950), pp. 89–90.

83 "cries of terror": Joseph P. Lash, *Eleanor and Franklin* (1971), p. 29; see also *TIMS,* p. 7.

83 Norman Davis: *CB,* 1940, pp. 227–29.

83 ER's proposal for Davis: Lash Diary, May 27, 1940, Lash Papers, FDRL.

83 Red Cross in spring of 1940: Foster Rhea Dulles, *The American Red Cross* (1950), p. 346.

83 "the imminence . . .": Lash Diary, May 27, 1940, Lash Papers, FDRL.

84 "You don't want to go . . .": *NYT,* May 27, 1940, p. 1.

84 "been asleep"; "I think occasionally . . .": *NYHT,* May 27, 1940, p. 8.

84 "war hysteria": ibid.

84 "take us right into . . ."; "defend the American dollar . . .": *NYT,* May 27, 1940, p. 13.

84 "Poor Mrs. Roosevelt . . .": *NYT,* May 28, 1940, p. 22.

84 "was to demonstrate . . .": Lash Diary, May 27, 1940, Lash Papers, FDRL.

84 "I really think . . .": Tommy to AB, June 17, 1940, box 75, Halsted Papers, FDRL.

85 "anything that makes . . .": *MD,* May 21, 1940.

85 Arthurdale: *SEP,* Aug. 4, 1934, pp. 5–7, 61–65; Lash, *Eleanor and Franklin,* ch. 37, pp. 393–417.

85 "Deeply disillusioned . . .": Lash Diary, May 27, 1940, Lash Papers, FDRL.

86 City College: Lash Diary, May 10, 1940, Lash Papers, FDRL.

86 "God Bless You": Lash Diary, June 1, 1940, Lash Papers, FDRL.

86 "the anxiety which hangs . . .": *MD,* May 20, 1940.

86 At dinner with FDR and HH: Lash Diary, June 3, 1940, Lash Papers, FDRL.

86 "terribly guilty": ibid.

87 "Both Harry Hopkins . . .": interview with Elizabeth Wickendon.

87 HH's leadership of WPA: Robert E. Sherwood, *Roosevelt and Hopkins* (1948), pp. 67–71, 75–76.

87 "people don't eat . . .": ibid., p. 52.

87 "If I deserve . . .": HH documentary, FDRL.

87 "is one of the few . . .": *MD,* Aug. 22, 1938.

87 If Eleanor loved: interview with Eleanor Wotkyns.

88 "Around the White House . . .": Lillian Rogers Parks, *The Roosevelts: A Family in Turmoil* (1981), pp. 74–75.

88 "In the days before . . .": interview with Eliot Janeway.

88 "It was strange . . .": interview with Elliott Roosevelt.

88 "his New Deal . . .": Sherwood, *Roosevelt and Hopkins,* p. 11.

88 "The war news . . .": HH to ER, Aug. 31, 1939, HH Papers, FDRL.

88 "a total friendship": Perkins, *OH,* Columbia University.

88 HH's bedroom: Sherwood, *Roosevelt and Hopkins,* pp. 203–4.

89 "ordinary fooling . . .": Perkins, *OH,* Columbia University.

89 "Harry and Missy . . .": Tommy to AB, June 17, 1940, box 75, Halsted Papers, FDRL.

89 "It had begun to cause . . .": Perkins, *OH,* Columbia University.

89 "One day . . .": Tommy to AB, April 1940, box 75, Halsted Papers, FDRL.

90 "could not live . . .": Kenneth S. Davis, *Invincible Summer* (1974), pp. 107–8.

90 "He looked at me quizzically . . .": *TIR,* p. 76.

90 "My zest in life . . .": Lash, *Love, Eleanor,* p. 159.

90 "The times of depression . . . ": Lesley Hazelton, *The Right to Feel Bad* (1984), p. 123.

91 "Within a few months . . .": Davis, *Invincible Summer,* p. 110.

91 Elliott Roosevelt: Lash, *Eleanor and Franklin,* pp. 1–13; David McCullough, *Mornings on Horseback* (1981), pp. 76–79; Edmund Morris, *The Rise of Theodore Roosevelt* (1979).

91 "Yesterday during my Latin . . .": Lash, *Eleanor and Franklin,* p. 7.

91 "Teedee is a much quicker . . .": McCullough, *Mornings,* p. 145.

91 courted Anna Hall: ibid., pp. 248–50. On Anna Roosevelt, see Lash, *Eleanor and Franklin,* pp. 14–20.

91 Robert Browning: Lash, *Eleanor and Franklin,* p. 23.

91 "dressed in some blue gray . . .": Geoffrey C. Ward, *Before the Trumpet* (1986), p. 265.

92 "one of the most . . .": *TIMS,* p. 1.

92 "grateful to be allowed . . .": ibid., p. 13.

92 "dominated my life . . .": ibid., p. 6.

92 "With my father . . .": ibid.

92 When he was drinking: Ward, *Trumpet,* p. 275; Morris, *Rise of Theodore Roosevelt,* pp. 429–30.

92 Knickerbocker Club episode: Lash, *Eleanor and Franklin,* pp. 51–52.

92 "stood first in his heart": *TIMS,* p. 9.

92 "a shy solemn child . . .": ibid., pp. 5–6.

92 "as a child senses . . .": ibid., p. 11.

93 "I acquired a strange . . .": ibid., p. 16.

93 "I would sit . . .": ibid., p. 13.

93 "a curious barrier": ibid., p. 17.

93 "Little Ellie . . .": ibid., pp. 17–18.

93 "a blue eyed . . .": Lash, *Eleanor and Franklin,* p. 33.

93 "A child stood . . .": ibid., p. 729.

93 "My darling little . . .": ibid., p. 42.

94 "I was always longing . . .": *TIMS,* p. 32.

94 "I can remember standing . . .": ibid., p. 19.

94 "Death meant . . .": ibid.

94 "he held out his arms . . .": *TIMS,* pp. 20–21.

94 "subconsciously I must have . . .": ibid., pp. 29–30.

95 "We must remember . . .": Lash, *Eleanor and Franklin,* p. 49.

95 "My aunts told me . . .": *TIMS,* p. 34.

95 "It was her father . . .": Lash, *Eleanor and Franklin,* p. 3.

95 "We do not have to . . ."; "The things always to remember . . .": *American Heritage,* Nov. 1984, p. 18.

95 used to hide books: Alfred Steinberg, *Mrs. R* (1958), p. 32.

95 boarding school in London: *TIMS,* pp. 54–88.

96 "a new life": ibid., p. 65.

96 "started me . . .": Eleanor Roosevelt and Helen Ferris, *Your Teens and Mine* (1961), p. 44.

96 "happiest . . .": Lash, *Eleanor and Franklin,* p. 87.

96 "always wanted to discuss . . .": Michael Teague, *Mrs. L: Conversations with Alice Roosevelt Longworth* (1981), p. 155.

96 Rivington Street settlement: *TIMS,* p. 108; Lash, *Eleanor and Franklin,* pp. 98–99.

96 "tremendously interested . . .": *TIMS,* p. 27.

96 "My God . . .": Eleanor Roosevelt and Ferris, *Your Teens and Mine,* p. 181.

97 "Though I only wrote . . .": Lash, *Eleanor and Franklin,* p. 110.

97 "It is impossible . . .": ibid., p. 109.

97 "When he told me . . .": Eleanor Roosevelt and Ferris, *Your Teens,* pp. 181–82.

97 "I was thinking . . .": Lash, *Eleanor and Franklin,* p. 110.

97   Eleanor burned them: ibid., p. 101.
97   "I am the happiest man...": Franklin D. Roosevelt, *FDR: His Personal Letters,* vol. I (1947), p. 518.
97   "For ten years...": *TIMS,* p. 163.
97   "He had always been...": Geoffrey C. Ward, *A First-Class Temperament* (1989), p. 12.
98   "The polio was very...": John R. Boettiger, Jr., *A Love in Shadow* (1978), p. 90.
98   "were joined...": Rexford G. Tugwell, *The Democratic Roosevelt* (1957), p. 529.
98   "I hated to see you go...": Lash, *Eleanor and Franklin,* p. 345.
99   ER brought together representatives: David S. Wyman, *Paper Walls* (1985), p. 18.
99   June 20 meeting: *NYT,* June 21, 1940, pp. 1, 3.
99   "You know, darling...": Lash Diary, June 25, 1940, Lash Papers, FDRL.
99   "It was kind...": Lash, *Eleanor and Franklin,* p. 635.
99   "I think men are worse...": ER to AB, June 26, 1940, Asbell, *Mother and Daughter,* p. 119.
99   "finding homes...": *MD,* July 13, 1940.
100   "The children are not...": *NYT,* July 7, 1940, p. 5.
100   "an enormous psychosis...": Breckinridge Long, *The War Diaries of Breckinridge Long* (1966), p. 108.
100   On Long: Henry L. Feingold, *The Politics of Rescue* (1970), pp. 131–35.
101   "upon a showing...": Wyman, *Paper Walls,* pp. 119–21.
101   "I think your mother...": Tommy to AB, July 12, 1940, box 75, Halsted Papers, FDRL.
101   "The English cannot spare...": Harold L. Ickes, *The Secret Diaries of Harold L. Ickes,* vol. III, *The Lowering Clouds, 1939–1941* (1954), p. 239.
101   "The very surest way...": Long, *War Diaries,* p. 119.
101   Estimates show: Wyman, *Paper Walls,* pp. 169, 211.
102   "The long pathetic...": ibid., p. 39.
102   the *St. Louis:* Arthur Morse, *While Six Million Died* (1983), pp. 270–88.
102   "The Jew party...": Ward, *Temperament,* p. 252.
102   "In the dim distant...": ibid., p. 254.
102   Roper polls: Daniel Yankelovich, "German Behavior, American Attitudes," talk given in May 1988 at a conference at Harvard on the Holocaust and the Media, sponsored by the Anti-Defamation League, the Harvard Divinity School, the Nieman Foundation, and WCVB-TV, Boston.
102   brought to ER's attention: Lash, *Eleanor and Franklin,* p. 636.
103   president had been hearing tales: Wyman, *Paper Walls,* pp. 188–91; Feingold, *Politics of Rescue,* pp. 128–31.
103   "the treacherous use...": *NYT,* May 17, 1940, p. 10.
103   "today's threat...": Franklin D. Roosevelt, *Public Papers and Addresses of Franklin D. Roosevelt, 1940* (1941), p. 238.
103   "He was somewhat...": Lash Diary, June 25, 1940, Lash Papers, FDRL.
104   "the list could be...": Lash, *Eleanor and Franklin,* p. 636.
104   "she had this sense...": interview with Trude Lash.
104   PAC: Wyman, *Paper Walls,* pp. 138–48; ER to Welles, Oct. 1, 1940, OF 3186, FDRL.
104   "I know it is due...": Lash, *Eleanor and Franklin,* p. 636.
104   "We all know...": J. Buttinger to ER, Nov. 15, 1940, OF 3816, FDRL.

CHAPTER FIVE: "No Ordinary Time"

106   "Franklin always smiled...": *TIR,* p. 213.
106   "really meant to develop...": Perkins, *OH,* Columbia University.
107   "Perhaps it wasn't...": ibid.
107   "This is a..." *U.S. News,* July 12, 1940, p. 24.
107   "No President...": ibid.
107   "George, I am chained...": Ted Morgan, *FDR: A Biography* (1985), p. 520.
107   FDR had signed contract: ibid., p. 527.
107   "The role of elder...": *TIR,* p. 212.
108   Top Cottage: *NYT Magazine,* Aug. 24, 1941, p. 231; Geoffrey C. Ward, *A First-Class Temperament* (1989), p. 741.
108   "Every time he came...": interview with Margaret Suckley.

108 "If times were normal . . .": *U.S. News,* July 12, 1940, p. 24.
108 "a speeding car . . .": ibid.
108 "I think my husband . . .": ER interview, Graff Papers, FDRL.
108 "Now, whether . . .": ibid.
108 ". . . When you are in the center . . .": *TIR,* p. 214.
109 "It was a position . . .": Lash Diary, July 18, 1940, Lash Papers, FDRL.
109 "one never knows . . .": Lash Diary, July 15, 1940, Lash Papers, FDRL.
109 "the President might have . . .": Lash Diary, Feb. 5, 1940, Lash Papers, FDRL.
109 "They all in their serene . . .": Joseph P. Lash, *Love, Eleanor* (1982), p. 74.
109 "Will the President seek . . .": *NYT,* Nov. 4, 1939, p. 18.
109 "When you have been . . .": *NYT,* Nov. 6, 1939, p. 11.
109 "would not look forward . . .": ER to Isabella Greenway, Aug. 20, 1940, ER Papers, FDRL.
109 "there was no end . . .": Lash Diary, Feb. 3, 1940, Lash Papers, FDRL.
109 9,211 tea guests: Joseph P. Lash, *Eleanor and Franklin* (1971), p. 613.
109 "take on a job . . .": Lash Diary, July 17, 1940, Lash Papers, FDRL.
110 "At the present moment . . .": ER to Isabella Greenway, Aug. 20, 1940, ER Papers, FDRL.
110 Meeting with Farley: James A. Farley, *Jim Farley's Story: The Roosevelt Years* (1948), pp. 246–52, unless otherwise indicated.
112 "Mrs. Roosevelt, what is the President . . .": Roland Redmond, *OH,* FDRL.
112 Huey Long story: *NYT,* Sept. 8, 1941, p. 10.
112 FDR's study at Hyde Park: *NYT Magazine,* Aug. 24, 1941, p. 23.
112 "Everything right within reach": *Collier's,* Sept. 14, 1946, p. 96.
113 Hopkins to Chicago: Robert E. Sherwood, *Roosevelt and Hopkins* (1948), pp. 176–77.
114 "There was a great deal . . .": Perkins, *OH,* Columbia University.
114 "as deserted as a church . . .": Farley, *Jim Farley's Story,* p. 260.
114 ". . . dead cats and overripe tomatoes . . .": Marquis Childs, *I Write from Washington* (1942), p. 194.
114 "There was bitterness . . .": Edward J. Flynn, *You're the Boss* (1962), p. 156.
114 "If Harry Hopkins . . .": *Newsweek,* July 22, 1940, p. 15.
114 "He threw one leg . . .": Farley, *Jim Farley's Story,* p. 263.
114 "Be that as it may . . .": ibid.
115 "One would never . . .": Samuel I. Rosenman, *Working with Roosevelt* (1952), p. 208.
115 "Top Cottage was . . .": interview with Egbert Curtis.
116 "There were days . . .": Bernard Asbell, *The FDR Memoirs* (1973), p. 241.
116 "I tried fishing . . .": *TIMS,* pp. 345–46.
116 Missy clearly the "wife": Asbell, *FDR Memoirs,* p. 249.
116 Missy and FDR to Warm Springs: ibid., p. 237.
116 "Warm Springs was not much . . .": interview with Egbert Curtis.
116 "We didn't like . . .": Theo Lippman, Jr., *The Squire of Warm Springs* (1977), p. 91.
116 "I can still remember . . .": interview with Egbert Curtis.
117 "So ended . . .": Elliott Roosevelt and James Brough, *An Untold Story: The Roosevelts of Hyde Park* (1973), p. 230.
117 "heart action . . .": Asbell, *FDR Memoirs,* p. 252.
117 "a little crack-up"; "a nervous breakdown": ibid.
117 "I had a most enjoyable . . .": Bernard LeHand to FDR, July 10, 1927, box 21, Roosevelt Family Papers Donated by the Children, FDRL.
117 "Except for a few intervals . . .": interview with Egbert Curtis.
118 "Don't you dare . . .": Ward, *Temperament,* p. 792.
118 "He was in there . . .": Asbell, *FDR Memoirs,* p. 253.
118 "My mother-in-law thought . . .": *TIMS,* p. 336.
118 "I hated the arguments . . .": James Roosevelt, *My Parents: A Differing View* (1976), p. 78.
118 "*the* big issue": AH interview, Bernard Asbell. Transcript given to author by Professor Asbell.
118 "Father sympathized . . .": James Roosevelt, *My Parents,* p. 78.
119 "Marguerite LeHand . . .": *Newsweek,* Aug. 12, 1933, p. 15.
119 "If she thought . . .": Rosenman, *OH,* Columbia University.
119 "We loved Missy . . .": Lillian Rogers Parks, *The Roosevelts: A Family in Turmoil* (1981), p. 177.
119 "She always did it . . .": interview with Margaret Suckley.

119 "Without making a point . . .": interview with Barbara Curtis.
120 "Missy could be . . .": Parks, *Family in Turmoil,* p. 184.
120 "Missy was an operator . . .": interview with Eliot Janeway.
120 "She was one of the few . . .": Rosenman, *OH,* Columbia University.
120 "By this time the bleachers . . .": Rosenman, *Working with Roosevelt,* p. 113.
120 "For some reason . . .": interview with Curtis Roosevelt.
120 "Missy alleviated . . .": interview with Elliott Roosevelt.
120 "This is where Missy . . .": Asbell, *FDR Memoirs,* p. 255.
120 "Dearest ER . . .": MLH to ER, n.d., box 21, Roosevelt Papers Donated by the Children, FDRL.
120 ER resolutely refused: Eleanor Roosevelt, *My Days* (1938), p. 220.
121 "it would have been . . .": James Roosevelt, *My Parents,* p. 104.
121 "Everyone in the closely knit . . .": Elliott Roosevelt and Brough, *Untold Story,* p. 196.
121 "I suppose father had a romance . . .": James Roosevelt, *My Parents,* p. 104.
121 "From FDR to MAL . . .": Asbell, *FDR Memoirs,* p. 262.
121 "I think by 1940 . . .": interview with Egbert Curtis.
122 "the most delightful . . .": *MD,* July 18, 1940.
122 "as close a relationship . . .": AH, review of Joseph P. Lash, *Eleanor Roosevelt, A Friend's Memoir,* box 36, Halsted Papers, FDRL.
122 "It was a confusing time . . .": interview with Lewis Feuer.
122 "It is funny how quickly . . .": Lash, *Love, Eleanor,* p. 323.
123 "Joe was pretty vulnerable . . .": interview with Lewis Feuer.
123 "Perhaps . . . my miseries . . .": AH, review of Joseph P. Lash, *Eleanor Roosevelt: A Friend's Memoir,* box 36, Halsted Papers, FDRL.
123 "There wasn't a lampshade . . .": tour guide, Val-Kill, Hyde Park, New York.
123 Eleanor led Joe outside: Lash Diary, July 15, 1940, Lash Papers, FDRL.
123 talked till midnight: Lash Diary, July 16, 1940, Lash Papers, FDRL.
124 "She was entranced . . .": interview with Lewis Feuer.
124 "I'd like you to feel . . .": Lash, *Love, Eleanor,* p. 315.
124 "She personifies . . .": Lash Diary, March 24, 1940, Lash Papers, FDRL.
124 "At times there is . . .": Lash Diary, April 22, 1940, Lash Papers, FDRL.
124 "Nonsense . . .": Lash Diary, July 17, 1940, Lash Papers, FDRL.
124 "strangely subdued": *NYT,* July 16, 1940, p. 1.
125 "The President could have had . . .": quoted in Francis Biddle, *In Brief Authority* (1962), p. 142.
125 "This convention is bleeding . . .": Herbert S. Parmet and Marie B. Hecht, *Never Again* (1968), p. 185.
125 "acting out his curious . . .": James MacGregor Burns, *Roosevelt: The Lion and the Fox* (1956), p. 426.
125 "I have never seen . . .": Rosenman, *Working with Roosevelt,* p. 210.
125 ER listening to FDR's statement: Lash Diary, July 16, 1940, Lash Papers, FDRL.
125 Barkley oratory: *Chicago Daily Tribune,* July 17, 1940, p. 2.
125 "And now, my friends . . .": *NYT,* July 17, 1940, p. 1.
126 delegates' response to statement: Burns, *The Lion and the Fox,* pp. 427–28; Farley, *Jim Farley's Story,* pp. 280–81.
126 "leather-lunged . . .": Burns, *The Lion and the Fox,* p. 428.
126 Massachusetts banner seized: Parmet and Hecht, *Never Again,* p. 186.
126 demonstration raged: *NYT,* July 17, 1940, p. 3; *Chicago Daily Tribune,* July 17, 1940, p. 3.
126 "even obvious things . . .": Lash Diary, July 16, 1940, Lash Papers, FDRL.
126 "The President . . .": Perkins, *OH,* Columbia University.
127 "Absolutely no . . .": ibid.
127 "How would it be . . .": *Collier's,* Sept. 7, 1946, p. 25.
127 "Call her up . . .": Perkins, *OH,* Columbia University.
127 "Things look black here . . .": *TIR,* p. 214.
127 "comforted if she thought . . .": Lash Diary, July 16, 1940, Lash Papers, FDRL.
127 ". . . extremely dangerous . . .": Tommy to LH, July 25, 1940, LH Papers, FDRL.
127 "For someone like me . . .": Joseph P. Lash, *Eleanor Roosevelt: A Friend's Memoir* (1964), p. 129.

127 "... 'petticoat government' ...": Lash Diary, July 17, 1940, Lash Papers, FDRL.
127 "Well, would you like ...": ER interview, Graff Papers, FDRL.
127 "Harry Hopkins has been ...": *TIR*, pp. 214–15.
128 "overcome with emotion": Lash Diary, July 17, 1940, Lash Papers, FDRL.
128 "Thanks, Jim ...": Farley, *Jim Farley's Story*, p. 283.
128 "Never had the delegates ...": *WP*, July 18, 1940, p. 1.
128 ER sang along: Lash Diary, July 17, 1940, Lash Papers, FDRL.
128 "felt as though it were ...": *TIR*, p. 215.
128 "general satisfaction ...": Rosenman, *Working with Roosevelt*, p. 212.
129 "The party longs ...": Perkins, *OH*, Columbia University.
129 "Well, damn it ...": Grace Tully, *F.D.R., My Boss* (1949), p. 239.
129 "I suppose all the ...": Rosenman, *Working with Roosevelt*, p. 213.
129 convention out of control: *WP*, July 19, 1940, p. 1.
129 "He not only wants ...": Perkins, *OH*, Columbia University.
129 "quite concerned ...": Rosenman, *Working with Roosevelt*, p. 215.
129 ER arrival: *NYT*, July 19, 1940, pp. 1, 5.
129 Farley confided: Farley, *Jim Farley's Story*, p. 299.
129 "which was just ...": Perkins, *OH*, Columbia University.
130 convention rose to its feet: *NYT*, July 19, 1940, p. 4.
130 "The rebel yells ...": ibid.
130 "It was agony ...": Perkins, *OH*, Columbia University.
130 "Poor Mrs. Wallace ...": ibid.
130 "The noise in the room ...": ER interview, Graff Papers, FDRL.
130 "meeting ground ...": J. William T. Youngs, *Eleanor Roosevelt: A Public and Private Life* (1985), pp. 99–100.
131 scene in president's study: Parmet and Hecht, *Never Again*, p. 194; Burns, *The Lion and the Fox*, p. 429.
131 "As the fight got ...": Rosenman, *Working with Roosevelt*, p. 215.
131 "Put that in shape ...": Ross McIntire, *White House Physician* (1946), p. 125.
131 "hamlike paw ...": ibid.
131 "until the Democratic party ...": Rosenman, *Working with Roosevelt*, p. 216.
132 "Sam, give ...": ibid., p. 217.
132 "Fine, I'm glad ...": ibid., p. 216.
132 "Pa, I hope ...": ibid., p. 217.
132 "Pa Watson was almost ...": ibid.
132 "Oh, she *can't* go ...": ER interview, Graff Papers, FDRL.
133 ER quietly rose: *U.S. News*, July 26, 1940, p. 9.
133 "Nobody could appreciate ...": *WP*, July 19, 1940, p. 1.
133 "No man who is ...": *NYT*, July 19, 1940, pp. 1, 5.
133 Genuine applause: Lash, *Eleanor and Franklin*, p. 623.
133 "above the petty ...": ibid., p. 624.
134 "weary and bedraggled ...": Rosenman, *Working with Roosevelt*, p. 219.
134 Missy was in tears: ibid.
134 FDR's acceptance speech: *WP*, July 19, 1940, pp. 1, 6.
134 "painful humbuggery ...": Hedley Donovan, *Roosevelt to Reagan* (1985), pp. 20–21.
134 ER on platform: *Chicago Daily Tribune*, July 19, 1940, p. 1.
135 " 'Her speech was ...": *TIR*, p. 218.
135 "You young things ...": Lash Diary, July 19, 1940, Lash Papers, FDRL.
135 "it had all been a dream ...": *TIR*, p. 218.
135 "What a schedule ...": Lash Diary, July 19, 1940, Lash Papers, FDRL.
135 "swamped with wires ...": Tommy to LH, July 25, 1940, LH Papers, FDRL.
135 "Your speech practically finished ...": AB to ER, July 19, 1940, Bernard Asbell, *Mother and Daughter* (1988), p. 121.
135 "Mrs. Roosevelt *saved* ...": AB to ER, July 22, 1940, box 59, Halsted Papers, FDRL.
135 "he is sulking ...": Tommy to LH, July 25, 1940, Halsted Papers, FDRL.
135 "Jim, I'm going to ...": Farley, *Jim Farley's Story*, p. 317.
136 "Gosh. It seems hard ...": Tommy to LH, July 25, 1940, LH Papers, FDRL.
136 "was much like ...": *MD*, July 20, 1940.
136 "... truly a magnificent person ...": Tommy to LH, July 25, 1940, LH Papers, FDRL.

CHAPTER SIX: "I Am a Juggler"

137 "I am a juggler...": Ted Morgan, *FDR: A Biography* (1985), p. 550.
138 life in the capital that summer: *NYT Magazine,* July 28, 1940, p. 10.
138 "I shudder for the future...": J. Garry Clifford and Samuel R. Spenser, Jr., *The First Peacetime Draft* (1986), p. 175.
138 electric fans bothered him: Samuel I. Rosenman, *Working with Roosevelt* (1952), p. 204.
138 On July 16, Hitler: William L. Shirer, *The Rise and Fall of the Third Reich* (1981), p. 753; Martin Gilbert, *The Second World War* (1989), pp. 107–14.
138 "Mr. President...": *Churchill & Roosevelt: The Complete Correspondence* (1984), vol. I, p. 57.
138 "the survival of the British...": William M. Goldsmith, *The Growth of Presidential Power,* vol. III, *Triumph and Reappraisal* (1974), p. 1754.
139 "in all probability...": ibid.
139 "It would have been too encouraging...": Rosenman, *Working with Roosevelt,* p. 225.
139 black-veiled matrons: Clifford and Spenser, *Peacetime Draft,* p. 175.
139 "...conscription might die...": *NYHT,* April 3, 1940, p. 13.
139 "The President has taken...": Stimson Diary, Aug. 1, 1940, Yale University.
139 Stimson's cold sweat: Jay Pierpont Moffat, *The Moffat Papers* (1956), p. 327.
140 press conference: Franklin D. Roosevelt, *Public Papers and Address of Franklin D. Roosevelt, 1940* (1941), pp. 317–21.
140 "It may very easily...": FDR to L. B. Sheley, Aug. 26, quoted in Clifford and Spenser, *Peacetime Draft,* p. 204.
140 "To tie it up...": *MD,* July 11, 1940.
140 ER a dreamer: Lash Diary, Sept. 18, 1940, Lash Papers, FDRL.
140 "The way it was written...": May Craig to ER, Aug. 6, 1940, "The Papers of Eleanor Roosevelt, 1933–1945," Susan Wars and William H. Chafe, eds., University Publications of America, 1986. Hereafter cited ER Microfilm Collection, FDRL.
140 "I am not bucking...": ER to May Craig, Aug. 8, 1940, ER Microfilm Collection, FDRL.
140 "is simply a question...": *MD,* Aug. 6, 1940.
140 "stupid beyond belief...": *NYT,* Sept. 17, 1940, p. 25.
141 "We are all sorry to see...": ibid.
141 "a dozen timid...": Clifford and Spenser, *Peacetime Draft,* p. 192.
141 "What Wendell Willkie thinks...": ibid.
141 "like nothing a Republican...": *WP,* June 28, 1940, p. 1.
141 On Willkie: *NYT Magazine,* June 28, 1940, p. 6.
142 "Nothing so extraordinary...": Harold L. Ickes, *The Secret Diaries of Harold L. Ickes,* vol. III, *The Lowering Clouds, 1939–1941* (1954), p. 221.
142 "a momentous conference...": Stimson Diary, Aug. 13, 1940, Yale University.
142 Acheson had: *NYT,* Aug. 11, 1940, p. 18.
142 Jackson on constitutional authority: Jackson to FDR, Aug. 27, 1940, *Public Papers and Addresses, 1940,* pp. 394–405.
142 cabled WC the good news: *Churchill & Roosevelt Correspondence,* vol. I, pp. 58–60.
143 "steal half the show": Clifford and Spenser, *Peacetime Draft,* p. 200.
143 FDR arrived in Ogdensburg: *NYT,* Aug. 17, 1940, p. 3; Aug. 18, 1940, p. 2.
143 "girls in their prettiest...": *NYT,* Aug. 18, 1940, p. 3.
143 "The weather was beautiful...": Stimson Diary, Aug. 17, 1940, Yale University.
143 drilling with broomsticks: *NYT,* Aug. 18, 1940, p. 3.
143 "They haven't got the bodies...": *TP,* Aug. 20, 1940, p. 7.
143 never fired a gun: *NYT,* Aug. 7, 1940, p. 3.
143 falling to the ground: *NYT,* Aug. 18, 1940, p. 3.
144 "The voluntary system...": *NYT,* Aug. 23, 1940, p. 9.
144 "Let us not...": *NYT,* Aug. 8, 1940, p. 3.
144 "The men themselves...": Clifford and Spenser, *Peacetime Draft,* p. 204.
144 "the radio in the President's car...": *NYT,* Aug. 18, 1940, p. 2.
144 Willkie's reception in Elwood: *NYHT,* Aug. 18, 1940, pp. 1, 29; *NYT,* Aug. 18, 1940, p. 35; Clifford and Spenser, *Peacetime Draft,* p. 194; Steve Neal, *Dark Horse: A Biography of Wendell Willkie* (1984), pp. 133–35.
144 "Today we meet...": *NYT,* Aug. 18, 1940, p. 33.

145 "He has a good voice . . .": *MD,* Aug. 20, 1940.
145 "It was a brave speech . . .": column from Aug. 21, 1940, paper unidentified, ER Microfilm Collection, FDRL.
145 Starling had train moved: *Time,* Aug. 26, 1940, pp. 11–12.
146 "He talked at random . . .": Moffat, *Moffat Papers,* p. 325.
146 "Willkie is lost": ibid.
146 "able and courageous . . .": ibid., p. 327.
146 "had originally felt . . .": J. W. Pickergill, ed., *The Mackenzie King Record,* vol. I, *1939–1944* (1960), p. 131.
146 "Almost with tears . . .": ibid.
146 "a place of terror . . .": Richard Collier, *1940: The World in Flames* (1979), p. 210.
146 "perhaps today would mark . . .": Moffat, *Moffat Papers,* p. 327.
146 ". . . bargain or sale . . .": *Churchill & Roosevelt Correspondence,* vol. I, pp. 63–64.
147 "Congress is going . . .": Grace Tully, *F.D.R., My Boss* (1949), p. 244.
147 yellowish tint; "brooding about something . . .": David E. Lilienthal, *The Journal of David E. Lilienthal,* vol. 1 (1964), p. 207.
147 "twenty odd jammed in . . .": *Time,* Sept. 16, 1940, p. 11.
147 "the most important event . . .": ibid.
147 "It is all over . . .": Franklin D. Roosevelt, *Public Papers and Addresses, 1940,* p. 379.
147 "massive,-grey-headed . . .": *Time,* Sept. 16, 1940, p. 11.
148 "the most dictatorial . . .": James MacGregor Burns, *Roosevelt: The Lion and the Fox* (1956), p. 441.
148 "Note well the word . . .": reprinted in *NYT,* Sept. 4, 1940, p. 13.
148 "If Mr. Roosevelt can . . .": Clifford and Spenser, *Peacetime Draft,* p. 213.
148 "a decidedly unneutral act . . .": Winston S. Churchill, *The Second World War,* vol. II, *Their Finest Hour* (1949), p. 358.
148 "Let it roll on . . .": ibid., p. 362.
148 "their four tunnels raking . . .": *BG,* Sept. 4, 1940, p. 1.
148 "by the long arm . . .": Churchill, *Finest Hour,* p. 368.
148 "There were coffee makers . . .": Philip Goodhart, *Fifty Good Ships That Saved the World* (1965), pp. 194–95.
149 "We haven't had . . .": excerpts reprinted in *WP,* Sept. 4, 1940, p. 4.
149 "The President's . . .": ibid.
149 "exactly as a princess . . .": Bess Furman, *Washington By-Line* (1949), p. 288.
149 On Martha and family: Patricia C. Bjaaland, *The Norwegian Royal Family* (1986), pp. 22–41.
149 "I cannot accept . . .": Shirer, *Rise and Fall,* p. 705.
150 "It left the door . . .": *NYT,* April 29, 1939, p. 1.
150 royal couple spent weekend: ibid., p. 9.
150 Martha's escape to the U.S.: *Time,* Sept. 3, 1940, p. 28; *Newsweek,* Sept. 9, 1940, p. 19.
150 "brave words": *MD,* Aug. 30, 1940.
150 "Martha would sit . . .": interview with Trude Lash.
150 "Nothing is more pleasing . . .": James Roosevelt, *My Parents: A Differing View* (1976), p. 17.
150 "at his sparkling best . . .": James Roosevelt and Sidney Schalett, *Affectionately, F.D.R.* (1959), p. 22.
151 "adoringly . . .": Joseph P. Lash, *Love, Eleanor* (1982), p. 399.
151 "She was a lot of fun . . .": interview with Eleanor Seagraves.
151 "It became a kind . . .": interview with Henry Morgenthau III.
151 "but the big bonfire . . .": *MD,* Sept. 9, 1940.
151 "Mrs. Roosevelt loved . . .": interview with Henry Morgenthau III.
151 bombers over London: Shirer, *Rise and Fall,* p. 780; *London Times,* Sept. 9, 1940, p. 4; *Newsweek,* Sept. 16, 1940, pp. 22–23.
151 "The London that we knew . . .": Ben Robertson, *I Saw England* (1941), p. 121.
151 Goering had decided: Shirer, *Rise and Fall,* pp. 774–80.
151 "A few more weeks . . .": ibid., p. 777.
152 "no longer such things . . .": Molly Panter-Downes, *London War Notes, 1939–1945* (1971), pp. 98–99.
152 "The amazing part . . .": ibid.

152 "human character can stand...": Robertson, *I Saw England,* p. 130.
152 "vast smoky pall": *Newsweek,* Sept. 16, 1940, p. 23.
152 "We are on the brink...": *NYT,* Sept. 8, 1940, p. 8.
152 Empress Zita: *NYT,* July 21, 1940, p. 25.
153 "Sara was known...": interview with Egbert Curtis.
153 Martha in Rose Suite: Victoria Henrietta Nesbitt, *White House Diary* (1948), pp. 253–54.
153 "...a special character...": interview with Milton Lipson.
153 "I don't think...": Martha to FDR, Aug. 6, 1941, box 21, Roosevelt Family Papers Donated by the Children, FDRL.
153 "There was no question...": interview with James Roosevelt.
153 "the president's girlfriend": interview with Roberta Barrows.
153 "Early tried every way...": interview with Walter Trohan.
154 "Martha and her lady-in-waiting...": *MD,* Sept. 26, 1940.
154 "there was always a Martha...": Lash, *Love, Eleanor,* p. 399.
154 "I can't imagine...": interview with Betsey Whitney.
154 flirting was the one thing: interview with Eleanor Wotkyns.
154 Missy was distraught...: interview with James Roosevelt.
154 "Absolutely not...": interview with Barbara Curtis.
154 "Missy had me put...": Lash, *Love, Eleanor,* p. 118.
155 William Bullitt: *CB,* 1942, pp. 122–25.
155 "He used to telephone her...": interview with Barbara Curtis.
155 "the one real romance...": James Roosevelt, *My Parents,* p. 107.
155 "...Bullitt used Missy...": interview with Henry Morgenthau III.
155 "I was very much amused...": John Morton Blum, *From the Morgenthau Diaries,* vol. I, *Years of Crisis, 1928–1938* (1959), p. 134
155 "I don't know why...": James Roosevelt, *My Parents,* p. 107.
155 "I remember that she...": interview with Roberta Barrows.
155 "Nearer my age than father's...": James Roosevelt, *My Parents,* p. 106.
156 Anna admitted: interview with James Roosevelt.
156 "Are you always so agreeable?...": Lash Diary, June 4, 1940, Lash Papers, FDRL.
156 In mid-July: John Morton Blum, *From the Morgenthau Diaries,* vol. II, (1965), p. 290.
156 "delay in enacting...": Stimson Diary, Aug. 2, 1940, Yale University.
156 "no such harsh...": I. F. Stone, *The War Years, 1939–1945* (1988), p. 17.
156 "a lousy bill": Blum, *Morgenthau Diaries,* vol. II, p. 293.
156 "the very kinds of...": ibid., p. 295.
157 "a grave...": ibid., p. 296.
157 "This is abandoning...": Ickes, *Secret Diaries,* vol. III, pp. 210, 295–96.
157 "there was no clearcut...": Lash Diary, Aug. 1, 1940, Lash Papers, FDRL.
157 "draft such capital...": *MD,* Aug. 6, 1940.
157 "I, for one, am glad...": *MD,* Aug. 30, 1940.
157 "...should the government...": *Newsweek,* Aug. 19, 1940, p. 38.
158 "There are a great...": Stimson Diary, Aug. 26, 1940, Yale University.
158 "I regret to say...": Ickes, *Secret Diaries,* vol. III, p. 295.
158 "I want a tax bill...": Blum, *Morgenthau Diaries,* vol. II, p. 292.
158 "Leave the President alone...": Lash Diary, Aug. 5, 1940, Lash Papers, FDRL.
158 "a liability into...": R. Elberton Smith, *The Army and Economic Mobilization* (1959), p. 475.
159 A study: ibid., p. 413.
159 "We had to take industrial...": ibid., p. 414.
159 Story of poker game: interview with Verne Newton.

CHAPTER SEVEN: "I Can't Do Anything About Her"

161 A. Philip Randolph: *CB,* 1940, pp. 671–73.
162 Mary McCleod Bethune: *CB,* 1942, pp. 79–81.
162 Walter White: ibid., pp. 888–90.
162 "by his being a colored man": ibid., p. 888.
162 "I quite understand...": Joseph P. Lash, *Eleanor and Franklin* (1971), p. 522.
162 darkies: ibid.

162 "began to resemble . . .": Harvard Sitkoff, *A New Deal for Blacks,* vol. 1 (1978), p. 60.
162 Under the AAA, NRA: Arthur M. Schlesinger, Jr., *The Age of Roosevelt,* vol. III, *The Politics of Upheaval* (1960), p. 431.
162 "Is it true . . .": ER to HH, July 16, 1935, HH Papers, FDRL.
163 to sign executive order: Sitkoff, *New Deal,* vol. 1, p. 69.
163 Negroes share in New Deal: ibid., pp. 70–74.
163 "For the first time . . .": ibid., p. 83.
163 ER in 1938 in Alabama: ibid., p. 64.
163 ER in 1939 and Marian Anderson: Lash, *Eleanor and Franklin,* p. 525.
163 "Blacks in the thirties . . .": Nancy J. Weiss, *Farewell to the Party of Lincoln* (1983), p. 157.
163 "I did not choose . . .": Walter White, *A Man Called White* (1948), pp. 179–80.
164 "They were afraid . . .": *TIR,* p. 164.
164 "Frankly, some of his messages . . .": Early to Tommy, Aug. 5, 1935, Lash, *Eleanor and Franklin,* p. 518.
164 "If I were colored . . .": ibid., p. 519.
164 "If you have any influence . . .": Meldra Barber to MLH, June 4, 1940, PPF 3737, FDRL.
164 "The South is sick and tired . . .": *CR,* 76th Cong., 3rd sess., Jan. 8, 1940, p. 130.
164 "No, certainly not . . .": Frank Freidel, *Franklin D. Roosevelt: A Rendezvous with Destiny* (1990), p. 246.
164 ER represented the more generous: Schlesinger, *Politics of Upheaval,* p. 435.
164 photos of ER entertaining blacks: Sitkoff, *New Deal,* p. 95.
164 "I'm not for the Democrats . . .": Weiss, *Party of Lincoln,* p. 292.
165 "When you start . . .": ibid., p. 211.
165 Negroes to recruiting stations and figures in services: Jean Byers, "A Study of the Negro in Military Service," War Department Study, June 1947, p. 67, given to the author by Jean Byers Sampson.
165 "forget our special grievances . . .": W. E. B. Du Bois in Richard Polenberg, *War and Society: The United States, 1941–1945* (1972), p. 100.
165 ". . . everyone is excited . . .": Henry Davis to ER, Sept. 9, 1940, forwarded by Tommy to Sec. Stimson on Sept. 19, OF 93, FDRL.
166 Negro high-school teacher; "There is no place . . .": *SEP,* Dec. 14, 1940, p. 61.
166 "Hell, if you said . . .": *PC,* July 13, 1940, p. 3.
166 strictly mess men: Byers, "Negro in Military Service," p. 213.
166 mess men's duties: *PC,* Dec. 28, 1940, pp. 1, 4.
166 drawn into the navy: *PC,* Oct. 5, 1940, p. 1.
166 "Our main reason . . .": ibid., p. 4.
166 "I am still 100 percent . . .": *PC,* Dec. 28, 1940, p. 4.
167 "Since other mess attendants . . .": *PC,* Dec. 7, 1940, p. 4.
167 "I understand the plight . . .": *PC,* Nov. 9, 1940, p. 4.
167 new conscription law: Ulysses G. Lee, *The Employment of Negro Troops* (1966), pp. 69–75.
167 "In the selection . . .": ibid., p. 74.
167 "no man shall be inducted . . .": ibid.
167 "faith, cooperation and energy": *New York Age,* Sept. 21, 1940, p. 1.
167 "There is a growing feeling . . .": ER to FDR, n.d., PSF 177, FDRL.
168 "She has already spoken . . .": Early to Watson, Sept. 19, 1940, OF 2538, FDRL.
168 FDR's meeting with leaders: entire conversation is from *BG,* Jan. 24, 1982, p. A15; *American Heritage,* Feb.–March 1982, p. 24. These articles reveal the contents of tape-recorded conversations at the White House in 1940.
169 "for critical experiments . . .": George Catlett Marshall, *The Papers of George Catlett Marshall,* vol. II (1981), p. 376.
169 ". . . to satisfy the Negro . . .": Stimson Diary, Sept. 27, 1940, Yale University.
169 "In the process of evolution . . .": report, "Employment of Negro Man Power in War," Nov. 1925, FDRL.
170 "Soldiers who were asked . . .": Polenberg, *War and Society,* p. 123.
170 "We did not want to violate . . .": WW to ER, Oct. 4, 1940, ER Microfilm Collection, FDRL.
170 "The policy of . . .": Lee, *Negro Troops,* p. 76.
171 Early gave false impression: press release, Oct. 9, 1940, OF 93, FDRL.

171 "a stab in the back . . .": NAACP release, Oct. 11, 1940, OF 93, FDRL.
171 "none is more shameful . . .": *Crisis,* Dec. 1940, p. 375.
171 "I am sorry . . .": WW to ER, Oct. 12, 1940, ER Microfilm Collection, FDRL.
171 "no fixed policy . . .": FDR statement, OF 93, FDRL.
171 "Rest assured . . .": FDR to WW, Oct. 25, 1940, OF 93, FDRL.
171 "We are inexpressibly shocked . . .": *Crisis,* Nov. 1940, p. 356.
171 "The Negro situation . . .": Jim Rowe to FDR, Oct. 31, 1940, OF 93, FDRL.
171 "Never before . . .": *PC,* Oct. 19, 1940, p. 1.
171 "It looks as though . . .": Will Alexander, *OH,* FDRL.
172 Davis and Hastie: Lee, *Negro Troops,* pp. 79–81.
172 "the Negroes are taking advantage . . .": Stimson Diary, Oct. 22, 1940, Yale University.
172 ". . . a colored Admiral": Stimson Diary, Oct. 25, 1940, Yale University.
172 "Are you crazy . . .": A. P. Allen to FDR, Oct. 25, 1940, OF 93, FDRL.
172 "It is incomprehensible . . .": Mr. and Mrs. Alexander Kirk, Oct. 25, 1940, OF 93, FDRL.
172 "in the fight for equitable . . .": *PC,* Nov. 2, 1940, p. 1.
172 ". . . to insure a square deal . . .": WW to FDR, Nov. 4, 1940, OF 93, FDRL.
172 "the basic fact of segregation . . .": Lash, *Eleanor and Franklin,* p. 532.
173 PAC had submitted 567 names: David S. Wyman, *Paper Walls* (1985), p. 143.
173 only fifteen visas issued: Henry L. Feingold, *The Politics of Rescue* (1970), p. 141.
173 "a singleness of purpose . . .": ibid., p. 136.
173 "We can delay . . .": ibid., p. 173.
173 "Mr. McDonald is so wrought up . . .": ER to FDR, Sept. 28, 1940, OF 3186, FDRL.
173 "Please tell me . . .": FDR to Welles, Oct. 2, 1940, OF 3186, FDRL.
173 "I found that he was . . .": Breckinridge Long, *The War Diaries of Breckinridge Long* (1966), pp. 134–35.
174 "pull any sob stuff": Wyman, *Paper Walls,* p. 147.
174 "Something does seem wrong . . .": ER to FDR, Oct. 10; reply, Oct. 16, 1940; both in OF 3186, FDRL.
174 S.S. *Quanza: NYT,* Aug. 21, 1940, p. 5.
174 "Impossible . . .": Stella K. Hersham, *A Woman of Quality* (1970), p. 40.
174 "Complete despair . . .": quoted in ibid., p. 40.
174 "I remonstrated violently . . .": quoted in Feingold, *Politics of Rescue,* p. 144.
174 "When he told me . . .": Marlin to George Warren, Sept. 27, 1940, OF 3186, FDRL.
174 "Mrs. Roosevelt . . .": Hersham, *A Woman of Quality,* p. 41.
175 "The department does not refuse . . .": *Nation,* Dec. 28, 1940, p. 649.
175 "It looks again . . .": Joseph Buttinger to ER, Nov. 15, 1940, OF 3186, FDRL.
175 "all Jews . . .": this letter attached to ibid.
175 "FDR, Can't something be done?": ER to FDR, Nov. 27, 1940, OF 3186, FDRL.
175 "The President's overriding concern . . .": Justine Polier, *OH,* FDRL.
175 "Franklin, you *know* . . .": ibid.
176 "True, the Nazis . . .": Wyman, *Paper Walls,* p. 35.
176 "her deepest regret . . .": interview with James Roosevelt.
176 Willkie campaign in thirty states: *Time,* Nov. 4, 1940, p. 12.
176 FDR telescoped three "inspections": *NYT,* Oct. 1, 1940, p. 1.
176 unprecedented quantities of land: R. Elberton Smith, *The Army and Economic Mobilization* (1959), p. 441.
177 "said to be . . .": *NYT,* Oct. 1, 1940, p. 14.
177 Glenn Martin plant: *Fortune,* Dec. 1939, pp. 73–76.
177 unemployment rolls: Kenneth S. Davis, *FDR: Into the Storm, 1937–1940* (1991), p. 613.
177 "The main point . . .": FDR to John Boettiger, Oct. 1, 1940, box 7, Halsted Papers, FDRL.
177 the president journeyed to Midwest: *NYT,* Oct. 11, 1940, p. 1; Oct. 13, 1940, p. 1.
177 "one knifing through the air . . .": *NYT,* Oct. 13, 1940, p. 22.
177 Schools dismissed: *Time,* Oct. 21, 1940, p. 15.
177 "I have come here today . . .": *NYT,* Oct. 11, 1940, p. 11.
177 Jimmy: *NYT,* April 23, 1939, p. 3; Ted Morgan, *FDR: A Biography* (1985), pp. 462–66.
178 FDR, Jr.: *NYT,* April 23, 1939, p. 3.
178 "golden boy": interview with Trude Lash.
178 Elliott: Morgan, *FDR,* pp. 458–61.
178 "Elliott was the most like . . .": Minnewa Ball, *OH,* FDRL.

178 John: Morgan, *FDR,* pp. 455–57.
178 worked under a pseudonym: John Gunther, *Roosevelt in Retrospect* (1950), p. 198.
178 "None of them really lived . . .": Abram Sacher, *OH, FDRL.*
178 "She didn't know . . .": interview with Curtis Roosevelt.
178 "I don't seem to be able . . .": Joseph P. Lash, *Love, Eleanor* (1982), p. 159.
179 "She felt that the guilt . . .": Elliott Roosevelt and James Brough, *A Rendezvous with Destiny* (1975), p. 67.
179 "she was so unsure . . .": Lash Diary, Aug. 1, 1940, Lash Papers, FDRL.
179 "I was not allowed . . .": John R. Boettiger, Jr., *A Love in Shadow* (1978), p. 45.
179 "At a visceral level . . .": interview with Curtis Roosevelt.
179 "she determined . . .": Lash, *Love, Eleanor,* p. 56.
179 "your mother only bore you . . .": interview with James Roosevelt.
179 "It did not come naturally . . .": Lash, *Love, Eleanor,* p. 57.
179 "Franklin loved . . .": ER interview, Graff Papers, FDRL.
179 "I was the disciplinarian . . .": ibid.
180 "very unpredictable . . .": James Halsted in Bernard Asbell, *Mother and Daughter* (1988), p. 9.
180 "the most unexpected spots . . .": AH, "What Does It Feel Like to Be the Offspring of Famous Parents?," manuscript, n.d., box 84, Halsted Papers, FDRL.
180 "traumatic": AB interview, Graff Papers, FDRL.
180 "did not realize that Anna . . .": Eleanor Roosevelt and Helen Ferris, *Your Teens and Mine* (1961), p.71.
180 "It never occurred to me . . .": *TIMS,* p. 338.
180 "This outburst of mine . . .": Eleanor Roosevelt and Ferris, *Your Teens and Mine,* p. 70.
181 "I felt very strongly . . .": AH, *OH,* Columbia University.
181 "I was mad . . .": Asbell, *Mother and Daughter,* p. 40.
181 "Emotionally . . . ": AH, *OH,* Columbia University.
181 "Eleanor saw in John . . .": interview with Curtis Roosevelt.
181 "I love Anna so dearly . . .": Asbell, *Mother and Daughter,* p. 68.
181 "The Northwest welcomed . . .": *SEP,* July 8, 1939, p. 25.
181 "jovial manner . . .": ibid.
182 "as slim and boyish . . .": *NYT,* April 23, 1939, p. 21.
182 "Perhaps I needed . . .": Lash, *Love, Eleanor,* p. 232.
182 "I begin to feel . . .": *MD,* Oct. 18, 1940.
182 "I supposed that is why . . .": Lash, *Love, Eleanor,* p. 200.
182 "you can count on . . .": *NYT,* Oct. 25, 1940, p. 1.
182 "wide crack in a dam . . .": Davis, *FDR: Into the Storm,* p. 614.
182 "Dearest Franklin . . .": ER to FDR, Oct. 11, 1940, box 16, Roosevelt Family Papers Donated by the Children, FDRL.
183 "I painted her a pretty dark . . .": Harold L. Ickes, *The Secret Diaries of Harold L. Ickes,* vol. III, *The Lowering Clouds, 1939–1941* (1954), p. 351.
183 "I will not pretend . . .": Robert E. Sherwood, *Roosevelt and Hopkins* (1948), p. 186.
183 Lewis speech: *WP,* Oct. 26, 1940, p. 5.
184 "sad and low . . .": Matthew and Hannah Josephson, *Sidney Hillman: Statesman of American Labor* (1952), p. 488.
184 "John never can forget . . .": notes attached to letter, Charles Michelson to Steve Early, Sept. 29, 1940, PSF 194, FDRL.
184 MLH served as hostess: Bernard Asbell, *The FDR Memoirs* (1973), p. 245.
184 "We take the liberty . . .": Amalgamated to FDR, Oct. 26, 1940, OF 2546, FDRL.
184 "Paducah labor is for you . . .": Oct. 26, 1940, OF 2546, FDRL.
184 "Don't let Lewis' speech . . .": Local #6082 to FDR, Oct. 26, 1940, OF 2546, FDRL.
184 "John L. Lewis has kicked . . .": Alex Tunis to FDR, Oct. 25, 1940, OF 2546, FDRL.
184 "You are the only President . . .": Mrs. Grim to FDR, n.d., OF 2546, FDRL.
185 "Old age pensions . . .": Mrs. L. M. Feirer to FDR, Oct. 26, 1940, OF 2546, FDRL.
185 "I am an old campaigner . . .": Samuel I. Rosenman, *Working with Roosevelt* (1952), p. 238.
185 "Great Britain would never . . .": *NYT,* Oct. 29, 1940, pp. 1, 12.
185 "The way of the man . . .": *BG,* Oct. 31, 1940, p. 1.

185 "I have just come...": David E. Lilienthal, *The Journal of David E. Lilienthal,* vol. 1, (1964), p. 223.
185 Early kicking Sloan: *Time,* Nov. 11, 1940, pp. 17–18.
186 "Negroes...": Weiss, *Farewell,* pp. 280–81.
186 "I am a Democrat...": *NYT,* Nov. 1, 1940, p. 20.
186 "any old-time politician...": Rosenman, *Working with Roosevelt,* p. 241.
186 "...a very bitter campaign...": Stimson Diary, Oct. 29, 1940, Yale University.
186 "The first number...": *NYT,* Oct. 30, 1940, p. 1.
186 Mrs. Mildred Bell gasped: *WP,* Oct. 30, 1940, pp. 1, 2.
187 Michael Thomson: *Cleveland Press,* Oct. 30, 1940, p. 1.
187 Jack Clardy: *Charlotte Observer,* Oct. 30, 1940, p. 1.
187 James Cody; "This is the first...": *NYT,* Oct. 30, 1940, p. 1.
187 "As I listened...": ER to JL, Oct. 30, 1940, Lash Papers, FDRL.
187 "Very simply and honestly...": *NYT,* Oct. 31, 1940, p. 14.
187 "It's not necessary...": Rosenman, *Working with Roosevelt,* p. 242.
188 "Today...": *MD,* Nov. 2, 1940.
188 "extraordinarily jovial": *NYT,* Nov. 6, 1940, p. 2.
188 "What name please?...": *WP,* Nov. 6, 1940, p. 2.
188 "would do all the things...": Lash Diary, Nov. 5, 1940, Lash Papers, FDRL.
188 buffet supper: *NYT,* Nov. 6, 1940, pp. 1, 2.
188 FDR on election night: Grace Tully, *F.D.R., My Boss* (1949), p. 240; Lash Diary, Nov. 5, 1940, Lash Papers, FDRL; *NYT,* Nov. 6, 1940, pp. 1, 2.
188 "Mike, I don't want...": Michael F. Reilly, *Reilly of the White House* (1947), p. 66.
189 "It looks all right...": James MacGregor Burns, *Roosevelt: The Soldier of Freedom* (1970), p. 4.
189 "a little jig...": *NYT,* Nov. 6, 1940, p. 2.
189 "We want Eleanor...": ibid.

CHAPTER EIGHT: "Arsenal of Democracy"

190 "Just how does the President think?...": Eric Larrabee, *Commander in Chief* (1987), p. 644.
191 "a question here...": Perkins, *OH,* Columbia University.
191 "All of you use...": John Morton Blum, *From the Morgenthau Diaries,* vol. II, *Years of Urgency, 1938–1941* (1965), p. 202.
191 "The more I sleep...": *U.S. News,* Nov. 29, 1940, p. 20.
191 "Hope you have...": ER to FDR, Dec. 2, 1940, box 16, Roosevelt Family Papers Donated by the Children, FDRL.
191 "made of scraps...": *MD,* Dec. 3, 1940, box 16, Roosevelt Family Papers Donated by the Children, FDRL.
191 "give impetus to...": *NYT,* Dec. 17, 1940, p. 20.
191 "In every place...": Tommy to AB, Nov. 18, 1940, box 75, Halsted Papers, FDRL.
192 At Guantanamo Bay, etc.: Robert E. Sherwood, *Roosevelt and Hopkins* (1948), pp. 222–23.
192 "I think of you...": ER to FDR, Dec. 4, 1940, box 16, Roosevelt Family Papers Donated by the Children, FDRL.
192 death of Lothian: Richard M. Ketchum, *The Borrowed Years, 1938–1941* (1989), p. 572.
192 "My dear Mr. President...": *Churchill & Roosevelt: The Complete Correspondence* (1984), vol. I, pp. 102–9.
193 "I didn't know...": Sherwood, *Roosevelt and Hopkins,* p. 224.
193 "Nobody that I know of...": ibid.
193 a "flash of almost clairvoyant...": George Martin, *Madame Secretary: Frances Perkins* (1976), p. 435.
193 "very much like chasing...": Stimson Diary, Dec. 18, 1940, Yale University.
194 "Well, let me...": text of speech, Franklin D. Roosevelt, *Public Papers and Addresses of Franklin D. Roosevelt, 1940* (1941), pp. 604–15; also *NYT,* Dec. 18, 1940, pp. 1, 10; *WP,* Dec. 18, 1940, pp. 1, 2.
194 "was really based...": Perkins, *OH,* Columbia University.
194 America First Committee: Wayne S. Cole, *America First* (1953), p. 14.

195 "really enjoyed working . . .": Sherwood, *Roosevelt and Hopkins,* p. 226.
195 "No man can tame . . .": Franklin D. Roosevelt, *Public Papers and Addresses, 1940,* p. 638.
195 "unholy alliance . . .": ibid., p. 639.
195 "the great arsenal . . .": ibid., p. 643.
195 recent Gallup poll: George Gallup, *The Gallup Polls: Public Opinion, 1935–1971,* vol. 1, *1937–1948* (1972), p. 255.
195 "I call for this . . .": Franklin D. Roosevelt, *Public Papers and Addresses, 1940,* p. 644.
195 large part of old city destroyed: *London Times,* Dec. 30, 1940, p. 2.
196 "The havoc was comparable . . .": *NYT,* Dec. 31, 1940, p. 1.
196 "London has nothing . . .": Joseph Goebbels, *The Goebbels Diaries, 1939–1941* (1983), p. 222.
196 "When I visited . . .": WC to FDR, Dec. 31, 1940, *Churchill & Roosevelt Correspondence,* vol. I, p. 123.
196 Walter Reuther: *Business Week,* Jan. 17, 1942, p. 60.
196 "slow and costly . . .": Walter Reuther, "A Program for Utilization of the Auto Industry for Mass Production of Defense Plants," attached to letter, Philip Murray to FDR, Dec. 20, 1940, OF 4234, FDRL.
196 "Conventional methods . . .": ibid.
196 "We propose . . .": ibid.
196 "the most important . . .": quoted in I. F. Stone, *Business as Usual* (1941), p. 238.
196 "the first great . . .": ibid.
196 "It is well . . .": FDR to William Knudsen, Dec. 31, 1940, OF 4234, FDRL.
197 Cadillac plant: *Time,* Dec. 30, 1940, pp. 13–14.
197 "Mr. Knudsen . . .": John Barnard, *Walter Reuther and the Rise of the Auto Workers* (1983), p. 78.
197 "The fear . . .": Stone, *Business as Usual,* p. 235.
197 "labor had grown . . .": Bruce Catton, *The War Lords of Washington* (1969), pp. 91–92.
197 "There is only . . .": Morgenthau quoted in Barnard, *Walter Reuther,* p. 78.
197 Christmas holidays at the White House: White House Usher Diaries, FDRL; *MD,* Dec. 20–27, 1940.
198 ER shopping: *NYT,* Nov. 29, 1940, p. 18.
198 "He was just bursting . . .": Victoria Henrietta Nesbitt, *White House Diary* (1948), p. 257.
198 On Mrs. Nesbitt: Elliott Roosevelt and James Brough, *A Rendezvous with Destiny* (1975), p. 47; William Seale, *The President's House,* vol. II (1986), p. 929.
198 "plain foods . . .": Grace Tully, *F.D.R., My Boss* (1949), p. 115.
199 "Fluffy": Seale, *President's House,* vol. II, p. 966.
199 "always handsome . . .": Elliott Roosevelt and James Brough, *An Untold Story* (1973), p. 297.
199 "Fix it anyhow . . .": Lillian Rogers Parks, *The Roosevelts: A Family in Turmoil* (1981), p. 170.
199 "My God! . . .": Tully, *F.D.R.,* p. 116.
199 "Do you remember . . . ": FDR to ER, April 29, 1942, box 75, Halsted Papers, FDRL.
199 ultimatum: Nesbitt, *White House Diary,* p. 279.
199 ER's scrambling eggs: Elliott Roosevelt and Brough, *Rendezvous with Destiny,* p. 48.
200 "to put it mildly . . .": John Gunther, *Roosevelt in Retrospect* (1950), p. 92.
200 ER did not consider: *TIR,* p. 118.
200 Fala became FDR's friend: Tully, *F.D.R.,* p. 129.
200 "Not even one crumb . . .": interview with Margaret Suckley.
200 "In years to come . . .": William K. Klingaman, *1941* (1988), pp. 30–31.
200 economy at home: Donald Rogers, *Since You Went Away* (1973), pp. 13–28.
200 "an orgy of spending . . .": *NYT,* Dec. 25, 1940, p. 1.
200 "Here life is not . . .": *WP,* Dec. 25, 1940, p. 1.
201 "Here is something . . .": *MD,* Jan. 1 and 2, 1941.
201 "Eleanor was forever . . .": interview with Trude Lash.
201 "he had an idea . . .": Samuel I. Rosenman, *Working with Roosevelt* (1952), p. 263.
201 ER and guests in FDR's box: *NYT,* Jan. 7, 1941, p. 5.
201 Text of speech: *NYT,* Jan. 7, 1941, p. 4.
202 "It looked to me . . .": *MD,* Jan. 6, 1941.

202 "presents a new concept . . .": *NYT,* Jan. 9, 1941, p. 19.
202 "the Roosevelts apparently . . .": *NYT,* Jan. 11, 1941, p. 3.
202 "intensifying and exhilarating . . .": *SEP,* Sept. 16, 1939, pp. 96, 98.
202 reporters noted: *NYT,* Jan. 19, 1941, sect. VI, p. 3.
203 "One of the grand things . . .": *WP,* Jan. 19, 1941, p. 2.
203 "Serious but not . . ."; " . . . after nearly . . .": *NYT,* Jan. 19, 1941, sect. VI, p. 3.
203 "part of his nature . . .": Joseph P. Lash, *Eleanor and Franklin* (1971), p. 344.
203 "The President talked . . .": Perkins interview, Graff Papers, FDRL.
203 "Frankfurter said . . .": Stimson Diary, Jan. 4, 1941, Yale University.
204 "He seems to want . . .": David E. Lilienthal, *The Journal of David E. Lilienthal,* vol. 1 (1964), p. 169.
204 "Each imagines . . .": Lash Diary, March 20, 1941, Lash Papers, FDRL.
204 "He had more serenity . . .": quoted in Arthur Schlesinger, Jr., *The Crisis of the Old Order, 1919–1931* (1956), p. 407.
204 "Bright-eyed . . .": *WP,* Jan. 21, 1941, p. 1.
204 Pegler called her: Tamara Hareven, *Eleanor Roosevelt: An American Conscience* (1968), pp. 273–74.
204 "and tend to her . . .": J. William T. Youngs, *Eleanor Roosevelt: A Personal and Private Life* (1985), p. 198.
204 "Instead of tearing . . .": Hareven, *Eleanor Roosevelt,* p. 271.
205 "We don't want . . ."; "If I could be worried . . .": *NYT,* Oct. 26, 1940, p. 9.
205 "She is the President's . . .": *U.S. News,* Dec. 20, 1940, pp. 9–10.
205 "The nearer I draw . . .": *MD,* Jan. 10, 1941.
205 "It was wonderful . . . ": *MD,* Jan. 12, 1941.
205 "I always have been . . .": *WP,* Jan. 21, 1941, p. 3.
205 ER raised troubling question: Lash Diary, Jan. 16, 1941, Lash Papers, FDRL.
206 "I think we are going . . .": *NYT,* Jan. 26, 1941, p. 1.
206 On Palmer: Lash Diary, Jan. 16, 1941, Lash Papers, FDRL; *Time,* Feb. 3, 1941, p. 59; *PM,* Jan. 19, 1941, p. 9; March 26, 1941, p. 9.
206 "arose from . . .": *PM,* Jan. 19, 1941, p. 9.
206 "in the long run . . .": *Time,* Feb. 3, 1941, p. 59.
206 Palmer had been under: *PM,* Jan. 19, 1941, p. 9; March 26, 1941, p. 9.
206 "Would he be sensitive . . .": Lash Diary, Jan. 16, 1941, Lash Papers, FDRL.
206 "My mother-in-law . . .": Eleanor Roosevelt, *Tomorrow Is Now* (1963), pp. 64–65.
207 SDR invited: ibid.
207 Elizabeth Read and Esther Lape: Joseph P. Lash, *Love, Eleanor* (1982), pp. 78–82; Blanche Wiesen Cook, *Eleanor Roosevelt,* vol. I, *1884–1933* (1992), pp. 288–301.
207 Nancy Cook and Marion Dickerman: Lash, *Love, Eleanor,* pp. 82–85.
207 "Boston marriage": ibid., p. 82.
208 "If I had to go out . . .": Eleanor Roosevelt and Lorena Hickok, *Ladies of Courage* (1954), p. 262.
208 "She loved it . . .": Lash, *Eleanor and Franklin,* p. 307.
208 "squaws" and "she-men": Cook, *Eleanor Roosevelt,* vol. I, p. 302.
208 "My generation . . .": Rita Halle Kleeman, *Gracious Lady: The Life of Sara Delano Roosevelt* (1935), p. 291.
208 "My mother-in-law . . .": Geoffrey C. Ward, *A First-Class Temperament* (1989), p. 564.
209 "My Missus and . . .": quoted in Kenneth S. Davis, *Invincible Summer* (1974), p. 35.
209 "The peace of it . . .": Ward, *Temperament,* p. 740.
209 "Can you tell me *why* . . .": ibid.
209 Gallup poll: *U.S. News,* Jan. 31, 1941, p. 17.
209 Nineteen members of family: *WP,* Jan. 20, 1941, p. 2.
210 "There are men . . .": *WP,* Jan. 21, 1941, p. 2.
210 "A nation, like a person . . .": ibid., p. 3.
210 "the government . . .": Richard Leighton and Robert Coakley, *Global Logistics and Strategy, 1940–1943* (1955), p. 77.
210 "to carry on . . .": Senator Taft quoted in Charles A. Beard, *President Roosevelt and the Coming of the War, 1941* (1948), p. 67.
210 "The lend-lease . . .": David Lawrence, *Diary of a Washington Correspondent* (1942), p. 92.

210 On Kennedy: Michael Beschloss, *Kennedy and Roosevelt* (1980), pp. 238–41.
211 "Somehow or other . . .": John Boettiger to Joseph P. Kennedy, Jan. 31, 1941, Boettiger Papers, FDRL.
211 "if my statements . . .": Kennedy to Boettiger, Feb. 10, 1941, Boettiger Papers, FDRL.
211 "It is, I think . . .": FDR to Boettiger, Feb. 1941, Boettiger Papers, FDRL.
212 "another step away . . .": Ketchum, *Borrowed Years,* p. 578.
212 "sick and shrunken . . .": Sherwood, *Roosevelt and Hopkins,* p. 234.
212 her shock: interview transcript from HH documentary, FDRL.
212 "Mr. Churchill . . .": ibid.
212 "And from this hour . . .": Winston S. Churchill, *The Second World War,* vol. III, *The Grand Alliance* (1950), p. 21.
212 "I suppose you wish . . .": Lord Moran, *Churchill—the Struggle for Survival, 1940–1965* (1966), p. 6.
213 HH asked WC: Sherwood, *Roosevelt and Hopkins,* pp. 253–55.
213 "In the last war . . .": Winston S. Churchill, *Great War Speeches* (1957), pp. 93–105.
213 "the madmen . . .": *NYT,* Feb. 12, 1941, pp. 1, 6.
214 "He was elected . . .": ibid., p. 1.
214 "thankful beyond words": *MD,* Feb. 11, 1941.
214 "the most unsordid act . . .": *NYT,* March 13, 1941, p. 1.
214 "Thank God! . . .": Molly Panter-Downes, *London War Notes, 1939–1945* (1971), p. 137.
214 "one of the most massive . . .": interview transcript from HH documentary, FDRL.
214 "The blind side . . .": Harold L. Ickes, *The Secret Diaries of Harold L. Ickes,* vol. III, *The Lowering Clouds, 1939–1941* (1954), p. 480.
214 "I am just worried . . .": Blum, *Morgenthau Diaries,* vol. II, p. 232.
214 "The more I think . . .": Stimson Diary, March 5, 1941, Yale University.
215 "Upon his return . . .": *SEP,* April 26, 1941, p. 73.
215 "It tore Eleanor's . . .": Martha Gellhorn interview, OH, FDRL.
215 "Yes, the decisions . . .": James MacGregor Burns, *Roosevelt: The Soldier of Freedom* (1970), p. 49.
215 "the Führer finally . . .": Goebbels, *Goebbels Diaries, 1939–1941,* p. 240.

CHAPTER NINE: "Business As Usual"

216 "This house is . . .": Victoria Henrietta Nesbitt, *White House Diary* (1948), p. 261.
216 Fort Bragg: *Fortune,* May 1941, p. 162.
217 labor force of 28,500: *NYT,* Feb. 16, 1941, p. 31.
217 "extraordinarily interesting . . .": *MD,* March 31, 1941.
217 at any number of spots: *Fortune,* May 1941, pp. 58, 62.
217 "We're building . . ."; "the worst malaria . . .": *U.S. News,* Aug. 29, 1941, p. 28.
217 most rudimentary facilities: Ulysses G. Lee, *The Employment of Negro Troops* (1966), p. 43.
217 "If our plans . . .": *U.S. News,* Aug. 29, 1941, p. 28.
218 "But to the new . . .": Lee Kennett, *GI* (1987), p. 42.
218 "curved streets . . .": ibid., p. 43.
218 "they were the best run . . .": Geoffrey Perrett, *There's a War to Be Won* (1991), p. 36.
218 "sitting on the top . . .": *NYT,* March 23, 1941, sect. IV, p. 7.
218 "that wave . . .": Edwin Martin to FDR, March 21, 1942, OF 93, FDRL.
218 "Fala stood . . .": *MD,* March 31, 1941.
218 "You do have . . .": *NYT,* April 2, 1941, p. 14.
219 LH moved to Washington: Doris Faber, *The Life of Lorena Hickock* (1980), pp. 278–79.
219 "I never knew . . .": LH unpublished manuscript, box 1, LH Papers, FDRL.
219 "But that was not . . .": ibid.
220 "You'd better watch out . . .": Faber, *Lorena Hickok,* p. 94.
220 "There must have been . . .": ibid., p. 16.
220 "I am *not* unhappy . . .": Joseph P. Lash, *Love, Eleanor* (1982), pp. 254–55.
221 "Every woman wants . . .": Joseph P. Lash, *A World of Love: Eleanor Roosevelt and Her Friends, 1943–1962* (1984), p. 116.
221 " . . . I want to put . . .": ER to LH, March 7, 1933, box 1, LH Papers, FDRL.
221 "I felt a little . . .": ER to LH, March 5, 1933, box 1, LH Papers, FDRL.

221 "Oh! how good . . .": ER to LH, March 6, 1933, box 1, LH Papers, FDRL.
221 "The nicest time . . .": ER to LH, March 11, 1933, box 1, LH Papers, FDRL.
221 "Funny how even . . .": LH to ER, Dec. 5, 1933, box 1, LH Papers, FDRL.
221 "While they seem . . .": interview with William Emerson.
221 "Eleanor had so many . . .": interview with Trude Lash.
222 women routinely used: Carroll Smith-Rosenberg, ch. 14 in Nancy F. Cott and Elizabeth H. Pleck, *A Heritage of Her Own* (1979).
222 "You taught me more . . .": Lash, *Love, Eleanor,* p. 211.
222 "A reporter should never . . .": ibid., p. 133.
223 "Unwittingly . . .": interview with Eleanor Seagraves.
223 "No question that Hick . . .": conversation with Anna Seagraves, Eleanor Seagraves' daughter.
223 "I should work . . .": Lash, *Love, Eleanor,* p. 161.
223 " . . . you will be disappointed . . .": ibid., p. 208.
223 "I'd rather go alone . . .": ibid., p. 181.
223 "cry from the heart . . .": Faber, *Lorena Hickok,* p. 180.
223 "I went to sleep . . .": ibid., p. 156.
223 "I know you have . . .": Lash, *Love, Eleanor,* p. 223.
223 "You think some . . .": ibid., p. 240.
223 "I could shake you . . .": ibid., p. 229.
224 "shouted and stalked . . .": Faber, *Lorena Hickok,* p. 177.
224 "I hope you are having . . .": ibid., p. 174.
224 "Of course you should have . . .": Lash, *Love, Eleanor,* p. 218.
224 " . . . if I didn't love you . . .": Faber, *Lorena Hickok,* p. 266.
224 "Of course dear . . .": Lash, *Love, Eleanor,* p. 254.
224 "I'd never have believed . . .": ibid., pp. 277–78.
224 "You are wrong about Louis . . .": ibid., p. 278.
225 Accepting ER's invitation: LH unpublished manuscript, box 1, LH Papers, FDRL.
225 "A more discouraging . . .": *U.S. News,* April 11, 1941, p. 20.
225 strike statistics: Rosa Swafford, *Wartime Record of Strikes and Lockouts, 1940–1945* (1946), p. vii.
225 "Some friends of labor . . .": Raymond Clapper, *Watching the World* (1944), p. 218.
225 War Department's use of statistics: Byron Fairchild and Jonathan Grossman, *The Army and Industrial Mobilization* (1959), p. 60.
226 "All these men . . .": Lash Diary, Feb. 16, 1941, Lash Papers, FDRL.
226 "I cannot escape . . .": *MD,* Dec. 9, 1940.
226 River Rouge plant: *Life,* Aug. 19, 1940, pp. 37–39.
226 "the last unconquered citadel . . .": *Newsweek,* April 14, 1941, p. 35.
227 Ford contracts: *WP,* Nov. 7, 1940, p. 1; *NYT,* Nov. 30, 1940, p. 9.
227 "union enemy . . .": Fairchild and Grossman, *Mobilization,* p. 39.
227 "Ford is the country's . . .": *Nation,* Dec. 14, 1940, p. 595.
227 "a bad thing . . .": *NYT,* Dec. 29, 1940, p. 12.
227 "to let bygone issues . . .": Stimson Diary, Jan. 1, 1941, Yale University.
227 War Department pressed to reject bid: *NYT,* Feb. 6, 1941, p. 11.
227 "Best news . . .": *Nation,* Feb. 8, 1941, p. 147.
227 Supreme Court decision: *Business Week,* Feb. 14, 1941, p. 14.
227 Description of strike: *Detroit News,* April 2, 1941, p. 1; *NYT,* April 3, 1941, pp. 1, 18.
228 "more Negroes . . .": Mary Bethune to ER, April 4, 1941, ER Microfilm Collection, FDRL.
228 "It will be a bitter . . .": *PC,* April 12, 1941, p. 4.
228 "watching and waiting . . .": *NYT,* April 4, 1941, p. 14.
228 "With the help . . ."; "I am convinced . . .": *Detroit News,* April 13, 1941, p. 1.
229 White journeyed: *Detroit News,* April 9, 1941, p. 1.
229 "dimmed the power . . .": Peter Collier and Robert Horowitz, *The Fords* (1987), p. 170.
229 Rolls-Royce: ibid., p. 178.
229 Edsel humiliated by turnabout: Norman Beasley, *Knudsen* (1947), p. 261.
229 "Mr. Ford gave . . .": Robert Lacey, *Ford* (1986), p. 376.
229 votes counted: Charles Sorenson and William Samuelson, *My Forty Years with Ford* (1956), p. 268.
229 "It was a measure . . .": Lacey, *Ford,* p. 377.

230 "It was perhaps . . .": Sorenson and Samuelson, *Forty Years,* p. 260.
230 "treason" penalties: *NYT,* April 2, 1941, p. 1.
230 "perfect nonsense . . .": ibid., p. 14; also *BEA,* April 12, 1941, p. 3.
230 ER's press conference: *NYT,* April 8, 1941, p. 19.
230 "The infamous hand . . .": *Time,* June 16, 1941, p. 15.
231 "Franklin Roosevelt . . .": ibid.
231 with help of federal troops: *NYT,* June 10, 1941, p. 10.
231 "The armed forces . . .": *Time,* June 16, 1941, p. 15.
231 "Washington rarely . . .": David Lawrence, *Diary of a Washington Correspondent* (1942), p. 144.
231 "What has not yet . . .": ibid., p. 141.
231 "It took Hitler . . .": *Fortune,* July 1941, p. 68.
231 "gobbling an intolerable share . . .": *Business Week,* April 26, 1941, p. 19.
232 Packard, Willys, Chevrolet: *Business Week,* Jan. 18, 1941, p. 56.
232 "You can't have 500 . . .": *Fortune,* July 1941, p. 68.
232 "We cannot fight a war . . .": *Nation,* May 3, 1941, p. 519.
232 "The entire industry . . .": Beasley, *Knudsen,* p. 313.
232 "The problem is to turn . . .": *Nation,* May 3, 1941, p. 519.
232 "I am afraid . . .": Stimson Diary, May 29, 1941, Yale University.
232 "to begin thinking . . .": *NYT,* Feb. 18, 1941, p. 1.
232 "cheerfully forego . . .": [James Rowe] to FDR, July 22, 1941, Henderson Papers, FDRL.
233 "The President has . . .": Eric Larrabee, *Commander in Chief* (1987), p. 63.
233 Yugoslavia: Martin Gilbert, *The Second World War* (1989), p. 170.
233 British ships being sunk: Robert Dallek, *Franklin D. Roosevelt and American Foreign Policy, 1932–1945* (1981), p. 260.
233 "to forcibly stop . . .": Stimson Diary, Dec. 19, 1941, Yale University.
233 waiting for him to cross: James MacGregor Burns, *Roosevelt: The Soldier of Freedom* (1970), p. 91.
234 41 percent, 50 percent: Dallek, *Roosevelt and Foreign Policy,* p. 261.
234 "one could not . . .": *U.S. News,* May 2, 1941, p. 22.
234 "which is the cutest . . .": FDR, Jr., to AB, April 2, 1941, box 68, Halsted Papers, FDRL.
234 "the U.S.A. . . .": Joseph Goebbels, *The Goebbels Diaries, 1939–1941* (1983), p. 336.
234 "He reassured me . . .": Stimson Diary, April 22, 1941, Yale University.
234 "I am worried . . .": Stimson Diary, May 23, 1941, Yale University.
234 "Knudsen simply is . . .": Harold L. Ickes, *The Secret Diaries of Harold L. Ickes,* vol. III, *The Lowering Clouds, 1939–1941* (1954), p. 509.
235 "He still has the country . . .": ibid., p. 511.
235 "I turn to Missy . . .": ibid., pp. 487–88.
235 "FDR looked as bad . . .": *Time,* May 19, 1941, p. 16.
235 "My heart sank . . .": *MD,* April 25, 1941.
236 "What he's suffering . . . ": Robert E. Sherwood, *Roosevelt and Hopkins* (1948), p. 293.
236 "waiting to be pushed . . .": John Morton Blum, *From the Morgenthau Diaries,* vol. II (1965), p. 254.
236 "a compact with . . .": Larrabee, *Commander in Chief,* p. 42.
236 May percentages: George Gallup, *The Gallup Polls: Public Opinion, 1935–1971,* vol. I, *1937–1948* (1972), pp. 278–80.
236 "Missy was . . .": interview with Eliot Janeway.
236 "Since defense is now . . .": Lash Diary, April 20, 1941, Lash Papers, FDRL.
237 "probably the most crucial . . .": *NYT,* May 12, 1941, p. 15.
237 "There is no one . . .": *MD,* May 11, 1941.
237 "Isn't she amazing?": Bernard Asbell, *Mother and Daughter* (1988), p. 132.
237 "on the way . . .": ibid.
237 everything not newly planted: *MD,* May 10, 1941.
237 "very tired . . .": Asbell, *Mother and Daughter,* p. 131.
237 "The situation with Harry . . .": ibid.
237 "Franklin is much better . . .": ER to Esther Lape, May 23, 1941, ER Microfilm Collection, FDRL.
238 Preparation of speech: Sherwood, *Roosevelt and Hopkins,* pp. 279–80.
238 "If I may say so . . .": Samuel I. Rosenman, *Working with Roosevelt* (1952), p. 279.

238 "There's only a small . . .": ibid., p. 284.
238 "For almost an hour . . .": *NYT,* June 2, 1941, p. 1.
238 Text of speech: *NYT,* May 28, 1941, p. 2.
239 "The atmosphere . . .": *MD,* May 27, 1941.
239 "like an oncoming wave . . .": ibid.
239 ER asked HH to join FDR: Sherwood, *Roosevelt and Hopkins,* p. 298.
240 "would have been difficult . . .": Rosenman, *Working with Roosevelt,* p. 288.
240 "They're 95 percent favorable . . .": Sherwood, *Roosevelt and Hopkins,* p. 298.
240 Stimson was pleased: Stimson Diary, May 27, 1941, Yale University.
240 "We listened to father's . . .": AB to ER, May 29, 1941, box 59, Halsted Papers, FDRL.
240 Listener polls: *NYT,* June 1, 1941, sect. IX, p. 10.
240 "demagogic and aggressive": Goebbels, *Goebbels Diaries, 1939–1941,* p. 240.

CHAPTER TEN: "A Great Hour to Live"

241 "she may have begun . . .": interview with Curtis Roosevelt.
241 "Missy was not as relaxing . . .": interview with Elliott Roosevelt.
241 "sit and simper . . .": interview with Trude Pratt.
242 "when to approach FDR . . .": *SEP,* Jan. 8, 1938, p. 9.
242 "Some of the people . . .": *TIR,* pp. 169–70.
242 "The president would work . . .": interview with Barbara Curtis.
242 "She said quietly . . .": interview with Egbert Curtis.
242 On June 4, 1941: Lillian Rogers Parks, *The Roosevelts: A Family in Turmoil* (1981), p. 186.
242 Missy arose: Grace Tully, *F.D.R., My Boss* (1949), p. 246.
242 "It was very secret . . .": interview with Toi Bachelder.
243 "She's gotten up . . .": Parks, *Family in Turmoil,* pp. 186–87.
243 "Missy loved . . .": ibid.
243 "It's sad . . .": ibid., p. 187.
243 ". . . She's been taking opiates . . .": Bernard Asbell, *Mother and Daughter* (1988), p. 132.
243 "change of life": ibid., p. 133.
243 "Too many women . . .": *Good Housekeeping,* July 1943, p. 30.
243 "The letters told . . .": Bernard Asbell, *The FDR Memoirs* (1973), p. 403.
244 "Missy has been worse . . .": Asbell, *Mother and Daughter,* p. 133.
244 "licks the joints . . .": *Hygeia,* April 1942, p. 270.
244 "I was distressed . . .": AB to MLH, n.d., box 36, Halsted Papers, FDRL.
244 "My dear Missy . . .": SDR to MLH, Aug. 3, 1941, box 10, Roosevelt Family Papers Donated by the Children, FDRL.
245 "The strange thing . . .": interview with Elliott Roosevelt.
245 "Roosevelt had absolutely . . .": interview with Eliot Janeway.
245 "As I sat . . .": Ickes Diary, July 12, 1941, Library of Congress.
245 "No words will ever . . .": FDR to Dr. Harper, Aug. 27, 1941, PPF 3737, FDRL.
246 "The case has been . . .": Dr. Winfred Overholser to FDR, Aug. 28, 1941, PPF 3737, FDRL.
246 "the children . . .": interview with James Roosevelt.
246 Roosevelt's will: copy of last will and testament of Franklin D. Roosevelt, dated Nov. 12, 1941, FDRL.
246 "I owed her . . .": James Roosevelt, *My Parents,* p. 108.
246 "Negroes will be considered . . .": Richard Polenberg, *War and Society: The United States, 1941–1945* (1972), p. 114.
247 "We have not had . . .": The Annals of the American Academy of Political and Social Sciences, Sept. 1942, p. 74.
247 "It is not the policy . . .": *Fortune,* March 1941, p. 163.
247 "Negroes who are experienced . . .": *PC,* Sept. 28, 1940, p. 3.
247 "What happens . . .": *New York Post,* March 6, 1941, n.p.
247 "shunted from pillar . . .": *Chicago Defender,* June 12, 1943, p. 1.
247 "Only power . . .": Jervis Anderson, *A. Philip Randolph* (1973), p. 248.
247 "we ought to get . . .": Murray Kempton, *Part of Our Time* (1965), p. 250.
248 "I think the first . . .": ibid.
248 "the voiceless and helpless . . .": *Chicago Defender,* June 12, 1943, p. 1.

248   "Be not dismayed . . ." "Call to Negro Americans," July 1, 1941, OF 93, FDRL.
248   "crying for their . . .": Kempton, *Part of Our Time*, p. 251.
248   "Let the Negro . . .": Anderson, *A. Philip Randolph*, p. 251.
248   "The pressures of matters . . .": Watson to WW, April 8, 1941, OF 93, FDRL.
249   ER at Virginia College: *PC,* April 12, 1941, p. 3.
249   ". . . when there would be . . .": *NYT,* June 8, 1941, p. 41.
249   "Mrs. Roosevelt's coming . . .": Joseph Albright to Steve Early, June 8, 1941, OF 93, FDRL.
249   Naval Academy refused: Harvard Committee for Democracy and Education to FDR, April 11, 1941, OF 93, FDRL.
249   "To order taking Negroes . . .": FDR to Knudsen, May 25, 1941, OF 93, FDRL.
249   "I have talked with Mr. Hillman . . .": Knudsen to FDR, May 28, 1941, OF 391, FDRL.
250   "I have talked with the President . . .": ER to A. P. Randolph, June 10, 1941, ER Microfilm Collection, FDRL.
250   "I am submitting . . .": *PC,* June 21, 1941, p. 4.
250   "gripped their heart . . .": Randolph to Knudsen, June 3, 1941, OF 391, FDRL.
250   "When I got . . .": John Salmond, *A Southern Rebel* (1983), p. 194.
250   "Get the missus . . .": Joseph P. Lash, *Eleanor and Franklin* (1971), p. 534.
250   "Mrs. Roosevelt . . .": Kempton, *Our Time,* p. 251; Walter White, *A Man Called White* (1948), p. 193.
251   "except the President's . . .": Watson to FDR, June 14, 1941, OF 93, FDRL.
251   "Mr. President, time . . .": Anderson, *Randolph,* p. 256.
251   ". . . What would happen . . .": *Chicago Defender,* June 28, 1941, p. 2.
251   "I'm sorry Mr. President . . .": Anderson, *Randolph,* pp. 256–57.
251   "A tall courtly . . .": Roy Wilkins, *Standing Fast* (1982), p. 180.
251   "Gentlemen, it is clear . . .": Anderson, *Randolph,* p. 258.
252   "one of those . . .": Stimson Diary, June 18, 1941, Yale University.
252   "more can be done . . ."; "It was not enough . . .": quoted in *PC,* June 28, 1941, p. 4.
252   "As Coy was . . .": interview with Joe Rauh.
252   "Who is this guy . . .": Anderson, *Randolph,* p. 259.
252   "We've got every piece . . .": interview with Joe Rauh.
252   "one of the greatest . . .": ibid.
252   "to provide for the full . . .": press release, OF 93, FDRL.
252   "The President has just . . .": Randolph to ER, June 24, 1941, ER Microfilm Collection, FDRL.
253   "the Negro people . . .": Randolph to ER, June 23, 1941, ER Microfilm Collection, FDRL.
253   "very glad that the march . . .": ER to Randolph, June 26, 1941, ER Microfilm Collection, FDRL.
253   "as the most significant . . ."; "a great step forward": Louis Ruchames, *Race, Jobs and Politics* (1953), p. 22.
253   "Never before . . .": *Chicago Defender,* June 25, 1941, p. 2.
253   "Now the guns . . .": Joseph Goebbels, *The Goebbels Diaries, 1939–1941* (1983), p. 424.
253   ". . . new territory in Europe . . .": William L. Shirer, *The Rise and Fall of the Third Reich* (1981), p. 796.
253   "The novelty . . .": Alan Bullock, *Hitler* (1962), p. 651.
254   "We have only . . .": ibid., p. 652.
254   "Since I struggled . . .": Shirer, *Rise and Fall,* p. 851.
254   "Everything is well . . .": Goebbels, *Goebbels Diaries, 1939–1941,* p. 423.
254   "War is mainly . . .": Winston S. Churchill, *The Second World War,* vol. III, *The Grand Alliance* (1950), p. 316.
254   Russians killed: Martin Gilbert, *The Second World War* (1989), p. 218.
254   "Tell the B.B.C. . . .": Churchill, *Grand Alliance,* p. 331.
255   "The Prime Minister's compliments . . .": Martin Gilbert, *Winston S. Churchill,* vol. VI, *'Finest Hour': 1939–1941* (1983), p. 1119.
255   "I have only one . . .": Churchill, *Grand Alliance,* p. 331.
255   "No one has been . . .": ibid., pp. 331–33.
255   "Perhaps he was not . . .": Harold L. Ickes, *The Secret Diaries of Harold L. Ickes,* vol. III, *The Lowering Clouds, 1939–1941* (1954), p. 549.
255   precious and . . .": quoted in William Langer and Everett Gleason, *Undeclared War* (1953), pp. 537–38.

255 "a case of . . ." . . . "no one who would save . . .": Langer and Gleason, *Undeclared War,* pp. 542–43.

256 "tools of British . . .": Robert E. Sherwood, *Roosevelt and Hopkins* (1948), p. 303.

256 Michael Quill: James Loeb, *OH, FDRL.*

256 "Will it be good . . ." . . . "He said he thought . . .": Lash Diary, June 23, 1941, Lash Papers, FDRL.

256 "Of course we are . . .": *NYT,* June 25, 1941, p. 7.

257 HH's double mission: Sherwood, *Roosevelt and Hopkins,* p. 308.

257 "Tell him, tell him . . .": Averell Harriman and Elie Abel, *Special Envoy to Churchill and Stalin, 1941–1946* (1975), p. 73.

257 "No man could forget . . .": Sherwood, *Roosevelt and Hopkins,* p. 344.

257 "Not once did . . .": ibid., p. 343.

257 "There was little . . .": Charles E. Bohlen, *Witness to History, 1929–1969* (1973), pp. 357–58.

258 HH cabled FDR: Sherwood, *Roosevelt and Hopkins,* pp. 333–34.

258 "The country is awake . . .": *Life,* July 7, 1941, p. 17.

259 "educational phase": *Fortune,* April 1941, p. 36.

259 To be sure: ibid.

259 ALCOA: *NR,* Jan. 27, 1941, p. 104.

259 "the battered citadel . . .": I. F. Stone, *The War Years, 1939–1945* (1988), p. 154.

259 "There never was a monopoly . . .": interview with Arthur Goldschmidt.

259 "As soon as Roosevelt . . .": ibid.

260 "When the story . . .": *Time,* July 7, 1941, p. 10.

260 five thousand dishpans: *Woman's Home Companion,* Nov. 1941, p. 120.

260 "Many a good dessert . . .": *NYT,* July 22, 1941, pp. 1, 21.

260 "He laughed over this . . .": David E. Lilienthal, *The Journal of David E. Lilienthal,* vol. 1 (1964), p. 404.

261 "I am sick and tired . . ."; "thoroughly miserable": John Morton Blum, *From the Morgenthau Diaries,* vol. II (1965), p. 264.

261 "one of the most . . .": Ickes, *Secret Diaries,* vol. III, p. 592.

261 "Get the planes off . . .": Blum, *Morgenthau Diaries,* vol. II, p. 264.

261 "highly unfair . . .": Stimson Diary, Aug. 1, 1941, Yale University.

261 "All of these . . .": Stimson Diary, Aug. 4, 1941, Yale University.

261 "In the first place . . .": quoted in Ed Cray, *General of the Army: George C. Marshall, Soldier and Statesman* (1990), p. 198.

261 "we must get 'em . . ."; "hoity-toity humor . . .": Stimson Diary, Aug. 1, 1941, Yale University.

262 "very much on the ball . . .": Ickes, *Secret Diaries,* vol. III, p. 592.

262 "we ought to come . . .": ibid., p. 595.

262 "We have done . . .": *NR,* April 15, 1946, p. 546.

262 "Our own Army . . .": ibid., p. 547.

262 long list of supplies: ibid.

262 "My husband . . .": *TIR,* p. 224.

262 "There was nothing . . .": Ross McIntire, *White House Physician* (1946), p. 130.

262 "I hope to be gone . . .": FDR to SDR, Aug. 3, 1941, PPF 8, FDRL.

263 "I hope this map . . .": Martha to FDR, n.d., box 21, Roosevelt Family Papers Donated by the Children, FDRL.

263 On the morning of the 4th: McIntire, *Physician,* p. 130.

263 "They came back . . .": Perkins, *OH,* Columbia University.

263 On the decks of the *Augusta:* Henry H. Arnold, *Global Mission* (1949), p. 248.

263 "Churchill probably never . . .": W. H. Thompson, *Assignment: Churchill* (1955), p. 224.

263 "We are just off . . .": *Churchill & Roosevelt: The Complete Correspondence* (1984), vol. I, p. 226.

264 ". . . last filament of the spider's web . . .": Sherwood, *Roosevelt and Hopkins,* pp. 347–49.

264 "You'd have thought . . .": ibid., p. 351.

264 "the longest way . . .": *NYT Magazine,* Sept. 14, 1941, p. 5.

264 "I suppose you could say . . .": Sherwood, *Roosevelt and Hopkins,* p. 236.

265 "Around us were numerous . . .": Thompson, *Assignment,* pp. 231–32.
265 "the wrong war . . .": James MacGregor Burns, *Roosevelt: The Soldier of Freedom* (1970), p. 150.
265 "It's marvelous . . .": Blum, *Morgenthau Diaries,* vol. II, p. 375.
265 "It is terribly important . . .": ibid.
265 "The Japanese . . .": ibid.
266 "to slip the noose . . .": Robert Dallek, *Franklin D. Roosevelt and American Foreign Policy, 1932–1945* (1981), p. 274.
266 "would be compelled . . .": Churchill, *Grand Alliance,* p. 390.
266 "would wage war . . .": Gilbert, *Churchill,* vol. VI, p. 1168.
266 "the final . . .": Churchill, *Grand Alliance,* p. 393.
267 "One got the impression . . .": Theodore Wilson, *The First Summit* (1969), p. 109.
267 "The same language . . .": H. V. Morton, *Atlantic Meeting* (1943), p. 114.
267 "If nothing else . . .": Elliott Roosevelt, *As He Saw It* (1946), p. 33.
267 "Every word seemed to stir . . .": Churchill, *Grand Alliance,* p. 384.
267 "to court disaster": *NYT,* July 16, 1941, p. 1.
267 "reaching the point . . .": Forrest C. Pogue, *George C. Marshall: Ordeal and Hope, 1939–1942* (1966), vol. II, p. 147.
267 "the battle . . .": ibid.
268 "As far as the men . . .": *Life,* Aug. 18, 1941, p. 17.
268 "OHIO": ibid.
268 "The absence . . .": Stimson to FDR, Aug. 15, 1941, PPF 20, FDRL.
268 "Mindful of the next . . .": Pogue, *Ordeal and Hope,* p. 152.
268 "On this vote . . .": Alfred Steinberg, *Sam Rayburn* (1975), p. 171.
268 "a decidedly . . .": HH draft article, HH Papers, FDRL.
268 "The Americans . . .": Sherwood, *Roosevelt and Hopkins,* p. 367.

CHAPTER ELEVEN: "A Completely Changed World"

270 suffered a stroke in June: Lash Diary, June 4, 1941, Lash Papers, FDRL.
270 "I should not be . . .": Bernard Asbell, *Mother and Daughter* (1988), p. 134.
270 "peace of mind": FDR to SDR, July 23, 1941, box 10, Roosevelt Family Papers Donated by the Children, FDRL.
270 "Of course, you are right . . .": SDR to FDR, July 23, 1941, box 10, Roosevelt Family Papers Donated by the Children, FDRL.
271 SDR insisted on walking: James Roosevelt and Sidney Schalett, *Affectionately, F.D.R.* (1959), p. 316.
271 ER's sudden premonition: *NYT,* Sept. 9, 1941, p. 8.
271 "A telegram has . . .": Fred Delano to FDR, Sept. 27, 1941, PPF 8, FDRL.
271 SDR dressing up: Geoffrey C. Ward, *A First-Class Temperament* (1989), p. 3.
271 cigarette butts: Michael F. Reilly, *Reilly of the White House* (1947), p. 82.
271 "a mother should . . .": Frances Perkins, *The Roosevelt I Knew* (1946), p. 67.
271 "Although we are now . . .": Rita Kleeman, "Compilation of Material for an Article About Mrs. James Roosevelt," Kleeman Papers, FDRL.
271 "I lie on my bed . . .": SDR to FDR, Aug. 1, 1941, box 10, Roosevelt Family Papers Donated by the Children, FDRL.
272 could see them in her mind's eye: SDR to Monroe Robinson, Aug. 6, 1941, PPF 8, FDRL.
272 "Now that he is back . . .": Rita Halle Kleeman, *Gracious Lady: The Life of Sara Delano Roosevelt* (1935), p. 233.
272 Details of FDR-SDR last meeting: Ward, *Temperament,* pp. 5–6.
272 "The President went out . . .": Reilly, *Reilly,* p. 84.
272 "shut himself off . . .": *NYT,* Sept. 9, 1941, p. 8.
272 "I am so weary . . .": ER to LH, Sept. 7, 1941, LH Papers, FDRL.
273 "of course attending . . .": Joseph P. Lash, *Love, Eleanor* (1982), p. 355.
273 "The endless details . . .": ibid.
273 "The funeral was nice . . .": Asbell, *Mother and Daughter,* p. 136.
273 "He never looked toward . . .": *WP,* Sept. 10, 1941, p. 1.
273 "I think Franklin . . .": Lash, *Love, Eleanor,* pp. 360–61.

273 "Don't you think ...": James Roosevelt, *My Parents: A Differing View* (1976), p. 31.
273 "You promised me ...": SDR to FDR, July 14, 1941, box 10, Roosevelt Family Papers Donated by the Children, FDRL.
273 to wear his rubbers: ER interview, Graff Papers, FDRL.
273 "Mama, will you please ...": interview with Betsey Whitney.
273 Sara simply announced: John Gunther, *Roosevelt in Retrospect* (1950), p. 165.
273 "At first sight ...": Sara Delano Roosevelt, *My Boy Franklin* (1933), p. 42.
274 sorting through ...: Grace Tully, *F.D.R., My Boss* (1949), p. 105.
274 "No one on his staff ...": Ward, *Temperament*, p. 9.
274 "all the lines ...": *MD,* Sept. 8, 1941.
274 "I kept being appalled ...": Asbell, *Mother and Daughter,* p. 136.
274 "I had so much insecurity ...": Lash Diary, Aug. 1, 1940, Lash Papers, FDRL.
274 "I did not quite know ...": *TIMS,* p. 162.
275 "she could make it ...": Joseph P. Lash, *Eleanor and Franklin* (1971), p. 303.
275 "If you'd just run a comb ...": Ward, *Temperament,* p. 175.
275 "What happened would never ...": AH interview with Bernard Asbell.
275 "I looked at ...": Lash, *Love, Eleanor,* p. 356.
275 "She thought ...": *MD,* Sept. 9, 1941.
275 "Mother went to father ...": James Roosevelt, *My Parents,* p. 113.
275 "Can I have ...": FDR to ER, Oct. 7, 1941, box 16, Roosevelt Family Papers Donated by the Children, FDRL.
275 "Do be an angel ...": FDR to ER, Oct. 8, 1941, box 16, Roosevelt Family Papers Donated by the Children, FDRL.
275 "a rare treat ...": Victoria Henrietta Nesbitt, *White House Diary* (1948), p. 268.
276 "Pa sprang on me ...": Asbell, *Mother and Daughter,* p. 137.
276 FDR waited until AB came east: Lash Diary, Oct. 23, 1941, Lash Papers, FDRL.
276 "Hyde Park is now ...": Lillian Rogers Parks, *The Roosevelts: A Family in Turmoil* (1981), p. 241.
276 "as they told him ...": Joseph P. Lash, *Eleanor and Franklin* (1971), p. 643.
276 she took a bottle of gin: interview with Willliam Emerson.
277 When Hall drank: Eleanor Wotkyns, *OH,* FDRL.
277 "The level of noise ...": interview with Curtis Roosevelt.
277 "had a penchant ...": Elliott Roosevelt and James Brough, *A Rendezvous with Destiny* (1975), p. 93.
277 "There was nothing ...": Eleanor Wotkyns, *OH,* FDRL.
277 "This watching Hall ...": Asbell, *Mother and Daughter,* p. 137.
277 "fired first upon ...": *NYT,* Sept. 12, 1941, p. 1.
277 *Greer* had deliberately stalked: Robert Dallek, *Franklin D. Roosevelt and American Foreign Policy* (1981), p. 287.
278 "No matter what ...": *NYT,* Sept. 12, 1941, p. 4.
278 "It was the firmest ...": Stimson Diary, Sept. 11, 1941, Yale University.
278 "shoot on sight" policy: *NYT,* Oct. 19, 1941, p. 5.
278 "Sentiment on Capitol Hill ...": David Lawrence, *Diary of a Washington Correspondent* (1942), p. 206.
278 "Roosevelt's deviousness ...": Dallek, *Roosevelt and Foreign Policy,* p. 289.
278 "suddenly gone ...": William Hassett to FDR, Sept. 21, 1941, box 19, Roosevelt Family Papers Donated by the Children, FDRL.
279 ghastly noises: interview with William Emerson.
279 "My idea of hell ...": Lash, *Love, Eleanor,* p. 357.
279 "The President returned ...": Tommy to AB, Sept. 24, 1941, box 75, Halsted Papers, FDRL.
279 " 'Hall has died' ...": James Roosevelt, *My Parents,* p. 113.
279 "My mother-in-law ...": ER to Martha Gellhorn, Oct. 1, 1941, ER Microfilm Collection, FDRL.
279 "the terrible waste ...": Tommy to AB, Sept. 24, 1941, box 75, Halsted Papers, FDRL.
279 ER dug out old photos: Joseph P. Lash, *A World of Love: Eleanor Roosevelt and Her Friends, 1943–1962* (1984), p. xviii.
279 "The loss of someone ...": *TIR,* p. 230.
280 "no government agency ...": *NYT,* Aug. 26, 1941, p. 5.

280 "There are 135,000,000 . . .": Lash, *Eleanor and Franklin*, p. 642.
280 "I'm worried . . .": Lash, *Love, Eleanor*, p. 355.
280 "I honestly think . . .": Tommy to AB, Sept. 24, 1941, box 75, Halsted Papers, FDRL.
280 "If I feel depressed . . .": *LHJ*, Oct. 1944, p. 43.
281 ER attire on September 29: *WP*, Sept. 30, 1941, p. 10.
281 "You are Mrs. Roosevelt . . .": *MD*, Sept. 29, 1941.
281 ER outlined three goals: *NYT*, Sept. 30, 1941, p. 28.
281 "I am ridiculously busy": ER to Martha Gellhorn, Nov. 10, 1941, ER Microfilm Collection, FDRL.
281 "He was glad . . .": Anna Rosenberg Hoffman, *OH*, FDRL.
281 "What's this I hear? . . .": *TIR*, p. 231.
281 "There is an advantage . . .": Lash Diary, Oct. 5, 1941, Lash Papers, FDRL.
282 "We all had . . .": ibid.
282 *Pink Star:* Franklin D. Roosevelt, *Public Papers and Addresses of Franklin D. Roosevelt, 1940* (1941), p. 399.
282 *Kearney: NYT*, Oct. 8, 1941, p. 1.
282 *Reuben James:* Richard M. Ketchum, *The Borrowed Years, 1938–1941* (1989), p. 605.
282 "I think the Navy . . .": Stimson Diary, Oct. 23, 1941, Yale University.
282 only 30 percent: *NYT*, Oct. 1, 1941, p. 8.
283 majority of 72 percent: *NYT*, Oct. 9, 1941, p. 5.
283 "If we continue . . .": *WP*, Sept. 7, 1941, p. 1.
283 "American war vessels . . .": *NYT*, Oct. 18, 1941, p. 9.
283 Senate finally agreed: *NYT*, Nov. 8, 1941, p. 1.
283 "He had no more tricks . . .": Robert E. Sherwood, *Roosevelt and Hopkins* (1948), p. 383.
283 FDR had agreed to a policy: Dallek, *Roosevelt and Foreign Policy*, pp. 273–75.
283 Tojo replaced Konoye: ibid., p. 303.
284 "very discouraged and cynical . . .": Perkins, *OH*, Columbia University.
284 "Just as you move . . .": HH to MLH, Nov. 12, 1941, HH Papers, FDRL.
285 "so quick and full . . .": interview with Virginia Shipp.
285 FDR's trip was postponed: *NYT*, Nov. 21, 1941, p. 13.
285 "I must say . . .": FDR, Jr., to ER, Nov. 26, 1941, box 57, Halsted Papers, FDRL.
285 "I tell you frankly . . .": Joel Seidman, *American Labor: From Defense to Reconversion* (1953), p. 66.
285 "We felt a weight . . .": *MD*, Nov. 23, 1941.
286 "fairly blew up . . .": Stimson Diary, Nov. 26, 1941, Yale University.
286 "a very tense, long day . . .": Stimson Diary, Nov. 27, 1941, Yale University.
286 "If the current negotiations . . .": Stark to FDR, Nov. 27, 1941, PSF 80, FDRL.
286 FDR instructed Hull: Stimson Diary, Nov. 28, 1941, Yale University.
286 "very sorry that he . . .": ibid.
286 train reached Newman: *NYT*, Nov. 30, 1941, p. 34.
286 "had a few drinks . . .": A. Merriman Smith, *Thank You, Mr. President* (1946), p. 107.
286 "You had to have . . .": Bernard Asbell, *The FDR Memoirs* (1973), p. 400.
287 "endure the ordeal . . .": ibid.
287 "the Far East picture . . .": Tully, *F.D.R.*, p. 249.
287 "for the honor and pride . . .": Cordell Hull, *The Memoirs of Cordell Hull*, vol. II (1948), pp. 1089–90.
287 "nearly in tears . . .": Tully, *F.D.R.*, p. 251.
287 "That means . . .": *NYT*, Dec. 2, 1941, p. 27.
287 "the blood rush up . . ." . . . "Don't let it . . .": Perkins, *OH*, Columbia University.
287 "We've got our sources . . .": ibid.
288 December 6: Forrest C. Pogue, *George C. Marshall: Ordeal and Hope, 1939–1942* (1966), vol. II, pp. 224–27.
288 December 7: ibid., pp. 226–29.
288 "The Japanese are . . .": ibid., p. 229.
288 189 Japanese planes: Vice Admiral Homer N. Wallin, *Pearl Harbor—Why, How: Fleet Salvage and Final Appraisal* (1968), p. 88.
288 "snugly side by side . . .": Harold L. Ickes, *Secret Diaries of Harold L. Ickes*, vol. III, *The Lowering Clouds, 1939–1941* (1954), p. 661.
289 Knox relayed the news: Sherwood, *Roosevelt and Hopkins*, p. 431.

289 "Mr. President . . .": *American Heritage,* Nov. 1989, p. 54.
289 "All the secretaries . . .": *MD,* Dec. 7, 1941.
289 ER returned to work: *TIR,* p. 233.
289 "the news of the war . . .": Asbell, *Mother and Daughter,* p. 139.
289 "deadly calm . . .": ER interview Graff Papers, FDRL.
289 "each report more . . .": ibid.
289 "he was completely . . .": ibid.
289 "had never had . . .": *American Heritage,* Nov. 1989, p. 60.
289 "I never wanted . . ."; "We haven't . . .": ER interview, Graff Papers, FDRL.
290 "Hi, Old Man . . .": interview with James Roosevelt.
290 "Within the first hour . . .": Tully, *F.D.R.,* p. 255.
290 remarkable conversation: interview with Alonzo Fields.
290 "No American who lived . . .": Marquis Childs, *I Write from Washington* (1942), p. 241.
290 ". . . It's quite true. . . .": Winston S. Churchill, *The Second World War,* vol. III, *The Grand Alliance* (1950), p. 538.
290 "To have the United . . .": ibid., p. 539.
291 "He was alone . . .": Tully, *F.D.R.,* p. 256.
291 "Yesterday comma . . .": ibid., p. 256.
291 "She leaned over . . .": *PM,* Dec. 8, 1941, "Amidst Crowded Days" diary in clippings of Mrs. Franklin D. Roosevelt, compiled, edited and executed by A. Cypen Lubitsh, 1943, box 3201, ER Papers. Hereafter cited Scrapbook, ER Papers, FDRL.
291 "For months now . . .": ibid.
291 "The Japanese . . .": ibid.
291 "Chinese, not Japanese, please . . .": *Life,* Dec. 22, 1941, pp. 81–82.
292 "It was very . . ."; "I'm thankful . . .": Perkins, *OH,* Columbia University.
292 "The effect on the Congressmen . . .": Stimson Diary, Dec. 7, 1941, Yale University.
292 "How did it . . ."; "How did they catch . . .": *American Heritage,* Nov. 1989, p. 86.
293 "I don't know, Tom . . .": Francis Biddle, *In Brief Authority* (1962), p. 206.
293 "was how we should . . .": Stimson Diary, Nov. 25, 1941, Yale University.
293 "Neither Army or Navy . . .": Frank Knox, "Report by the Secretary of the Navy to the President," Dec. 14, 1941, PSF 80, FDRL.
293 "The anti-aircraft . . .": interview with William Emerson.
294 "We are operating . . .": Wallin, *Pearl Harbor,* p. 45.
294 "The damage was . . .": Ross McIntire, *White House Physician* (1946), p. 137.
294 "Missy telephoned . . .": Asbell, *FDR Memoirs,* p. 401.
294 "that the indecision . . .": Stimson Diary, Dec. 7, 1941, Yale University.
294 "You know . . .": Perkins, *OH,* Columbia University.
294 "Monday was almost . . .": Childs, *I Write,* p. 242.
295 "the unprovoked . . .": *NYT,* Dec. 9, 1941, p. 1.
295 Rankin: ibid.
295 "American soil . . .": ibid.
295 "he would support . . .": *NYT,* Dec. 8. 1941, p. 6.
295 "no strikes . . .": George Martin, *Madame Secretary: Frances Perkins* (1976), p. 451.
295 "Labor's response . . .": Hillman to FDR, Dec. 12, 1941, OF 4076, FDRL.
295 ER to West Coast: *TIR,* p. 236.
295 "Hell, this isn't . . .": *Los Angeles Times,* Dec. 10, 1941, p. D.
296 "looking for all the world . . .": *TIR,* p. 236.
296 "I am not here to give . . .": *Los Angeles Times,* Dec. 10, 1941, p. D.
296 ". . . to cooperate with . . .": *Los Angeles Times,* Dec. 9, 1941, p. 2.
296 "Rumors were everywhere . . .": interview with Jiro Isihara.
296 "Let's be honest . . .": *NYT,* Dec. 15, 1941, p. 9.
296 "We know there are . . .": *MD,* Dec. 15, 1941.
297 "When she starts bemoaning . . .": Tamara Hareven, *Eleanor Roosevelt: An American Conscience* (1968), p. 167.
297 "I think almost . . ." *Washington Star,* Dec. 17, 1942, Scrapbook, ER Papers, FDRL.
297 "He was all alone . . .": Samuel I. Rosenman, *Working with Roosevelt* (1952), p. 312.
297 "Was it possible . . .": James MacGregor Burns, *Roosevelt: The Soldier of Freedom* (1970), p. 171.

297   Hitler's speech: text in William L. Shirer, *The Rise and Fall of the Third Reich* (1960), pp. 897–900.
298   "a state of war . . .": *New York Times,* Dec. 9, 1941, p. 1.
298   "It seems like . . .": ER to LH, Dec. 11, 1941, LH Papers, FDRL.
298   "No more Congressional . . ."; "gloomy in winter . . .": LH manuscript, LH Papers, FDRL.
298   "with not a little annoyance": William Seale, *The White House: The History of an American Idea* (1992), p. 228.
298   "One of the Secret Service . . .": interview with Milton Lipson.
299   "Henry, I will not . . .": *TIR,* p. 237.
299   "Mrs. Roosevelt is very . . .": Tommy to Esther Lape, Dec. 16, 1941, box 6, Esther Lape Papers, FDRL.

CHAPTER TWELVE: "Two Little Boys Playing Soldier"

300   "You should have . . .": interview with Alonzo Fields.
300   "It had not occurred . . .": *MD,* Dec. 22, 1941.
301   "he was like a child . . .": Lord Moran, *Churchill—The Struggle for Survival, 1940–1965* (1966), p. 11.
301   "It was night time . . .": W. H. Thompson, *Assignment: Churchill* (1955), p. 246.
301   "Even in the half-light . . .": Moran, *Churchill,* p. 11.
301   "The President was . . .": Mrs. Charles Hamlin, "Memories," FDRL; also in *NR,* suppl., April 1946.
301   "It must have been . . ."; "I have a toast . . .": ibid.
302   "At ten o'clock . . .": *TIR,* p. 242.
302   WC was installed: William Seale, *The President's House* (1986), p. 974; Robert E. Sherwood, *Roosevelt and Hopkins* (1948), p. 442.
302   "Now, Fields . . .": interview with Alonzo Fields.
302   "I'll be back . . .": ER interview, Graff Papers, FDRL.
303   "There is no question . . .": ibid.
303   "Mother would just fume . . .": interview with Elliott Roosevelt.
303   "that she worried . . .": Lillian Roger Parks, *The Roosevelts: A Family in Turmoil* (1981), p. 99.
303   "There was a wild burst . . .": *NYT,* Dec. 24, 1941, p. 4.
303   In the course of the Arcadia Conference: Martin Gilbert, *Winston S. Churchill,* vol. VII, *Road to Victory: 1941–1945* (1986), pp. 35–36.
303   "The news around . . .": Stimson Diary, Dec. 25, 1941, Yale University.
303   sweeping through Malaya: Sherwood, *Roosevelt and Hopkins,* p. 453.
304   end of December: Elena Skrjabina, *Siege and Survival* (1971), p. 28.
304   "When you leave . . .": ibid., p. 30.
304   "He was always a gay . . .": ibid., p. 51.
304   one million would die; counterattack: James MacGregor Burns, *Roosevelt: Soldier of Freedom* (1970), pp. 187–88; Martin Gilbert, *The Second World War* (1989), p. 284.
305   "a hell of a row": quoted in Moran, *Churchill,* p. 21.
305   "Our people are very . . .": ibid., p. 24.
305   "We live here as . . .": Winston S. Churchill, *The Second World War,* vol. III, *The Grand Alliance* (1950), p. 608.
305   Christmas Eve: Seale, *President's House,* p. 974; *NYT,* Dec. 25, 1941, pp. 1, 12; *WP,* Dec. 25, 1941, pp. 1, 5.
305   "old and good friend": *NYT,* Dec. 25, 1941, p. 12.
305   "Let the children . . .": *WP,* Dec. 25, 1941, pp. 1, 5.
306   "Her voice did not . . .": Lash Diary, Dec. 26, 1941, Lash Papers, FDRL.
306   for Fala: *Washington Star,* Dec. 26, 1941, Scrapbook, ER Papers, FDRL.
306   "She could never get . . ."; "it kept him . . .": Lash Diary, Jan. 1, 1942, Lash Papers, FDRL.
306   "He was really incapable . . .": Fulton Oursler, *Behold This Dreamer!* (1964), pp. 424–25.
307   "I guess I'm usually . . .": MLH to FDR, n.d., PPF 3737, FDRL.
307   "I don't know what . . .": Bernard Asbell, *The FDR Memoirs* (1973), p. 402.
307   "Missy and I . . .": Ann Rochon to ER, Jan. 1, 1942, PPF 3737, FDRL.
307   "Xmas was a very sad day . . .": Bernard Asbell, *Mother and Daughter* (1988), p. 141.

307 "jolly and care free...": Moran, *Churchill,* p. 15.
308 "He just wasn't having...": John Morton Blum, *From the Morgenthau Diaries,* vol. III (1967), p. 122.
308 "a tremendous occasion...": Moran, *Churchill,* p. 15.
308 "it was difficult...": ibid.
308 WC's methods: Sherwood, *Roosevelt and Hopkins,* p. 261.
308 "for sustained...": *AM,* Sept. 1949, p. 41.
308 "wastes little time...": Moran, *Churchill,* p. 13.
308 "does not reflect...": *AM,* Sept. 1949, p. 40.
309 "Churchill is always...": Thompson, *Assignment,* p. 253.
309 "Do you realize...": Moran, *Churchill,* p. 16.
309 "I cannot help reflecting...": text of speech, *NYT,* Dec. 27, 1941, p. 4.
309 "the first sound...": David E. Lilienthal, *The Journal of David E. Lilienthal,* vol. 1 (1964), p. 418.
309 "They had witnessed...": *WP,* Dec. 27, 1941, pp. 1, 3.
310 "I hit the target...": Moran, *Churchill,* p. 17.
310 "It was a tragic...": Hamlin, "Memories," FDRL.
310 "everyone completely...": *MD,* Dec. 26, 1941.
310 "She saw in Churchill...": interview with Curtis Roosevelt.
310 "Nobody enjoyed the war...": Martha Gellhorn, *OH,* FDRL.
310 "The walls were covered...": interview with George Elsey.
311 "They looked like...": interview with James Roosevelt.
311 motored to Mount Vernon: *NYT,* Jan. 2, 1941, p. 1.
311 "After the war..."..."You know Winston...": Justine Polier, *OH,* FDRL.
312 "batted an eyelash": Samuel I. Rosenman, *Working with Roosevelt* (1952), p. 320.
312 "Churchill wasn't very fond...": interview with Elliott Roosevelt.
312 "The Prime Minister...": Lash Diary, Jan. 1, 1942, Lash Papers, FDRL.
312 "I like Mr. Churchill...": Asbell, *Mother and Daughter,* p. 141.
312 best story was told: Sherwood, *Roosevelt and Hopkins,* p. 442.
312 "Bathtubs were a contrivance...": Joseph P. Lash, *Roosevelt and Churchill, 1939–1941* (1976), p. 15.
312 "The Prime Minister...": Sherwood, *Roosevelt and Hopkins,* p. 442.
312 declaration signed: *NYT,* Jan. 3, 1942, pp. 1, 4.
312 "It was as quiet...": Hamlin, "Memories."
312 "President ought to do!...": Lash, *Roosevelt and Churchill,* pp. 19–20.
313 "You would have been...": Sherwood, *Roosevelt and Hopkins,* p. 478.
313 "His lips are...": Moran, *Churchill,* p. 13.
313 "It is fun...": ibid., p. 27.
313 "We must raise...": *NYT,* Jan. 7, 1942, p. 5.
313 "The figures reached...": *U.S. News,* Jan. 10, 1942, p. 15.
313 "Oh—the production people...": Sherwood, *Roosevelt and Hopkins,* p. 474.
313 "who never met...": Bruce Catton, *The War Lords of Washington* (1948), p. 84.
314 "These figures...": *NYT,* Jan. 7, 1942, p. 5.
314 complete ban: *NYT,* Jan. 2, 1942, p. 1.
314 rationing cars and trucks: *NYT,* Jan. 16, 1942, p. 14.
314 Leon Henderson said: *NYT,* Jan. 3, 1942, p. 1.
314 "In the dealers'...": *Time,* Jan. 12, 1942, p. 61.
314 "Mr. Knudsen looked...": Alfred Steinberg, *Mrs. R* (1958), p. 279.
314 "I said nothing...": *MD,* Jan. 14, 1942.
315 Donald Nelson: W. M. Kiplinger, *Washington Is Like That* (1942), pp. 37–38.
315 "final" decisions: *Life,* Jan. 26, 1942, p. 29.
315 "Look here...": Norman Beasley, *Knudsen* (1947), p. 341.
315 "I have never seen...": Jesse H. Jones, *Fifty Billion Dollars* (1951), p. 272.
315 By the end of the luncheon: Beasley, *Knudsen,* pp. 342–43.
315 "For more than a year...": Winston M. Estes, *Homefront* (1976), p. 45.
316 Emergency Price Control Bill: *NYT,* Jan. 31, 1942, pp. 1, 26.
316 ER's promises on use of sugar: *NYT,* Jan. 27, 1942, p. 18.
316 run on sugar: *NYT,* Feb. 10, 1942, p. 13.
316 "It never crossed...": *NYT,* Jan. 27, 1942, p. 18.

316 "It is perfectly . . .": *MD*, Jan. 20, 1942.
317 ship sinkings: *U.S. News*, Feb. 27, 1942, p. 15.
317 "We are in a war . . .": *Fortune*, May 1942, p. 68.
317 "We've got to have . . .": Dwight D. Eisenhower, *Crusade in Europe* (1948), p. 22.
317 "He was standing . . .": Moran, *Churchill*, p. 35.
317 "The news came . . .": *MD*, Feb. 16, 1942.
317 "Perhaps it is good . . .": ibid.
317 "calm and serene . . .": William D. Hassett, *Off the Record with F.D.R.* (1958), p. 22.
317 "neither time . . .": *NYT*, Jan. 25, 1942, sect. VI, pp. 3, 24.
318 "I realize . . .": Frederick C. Lane, *Ships for Victory* (1951), p. 144.
318 "fourth in tonnage . . .": *Fortune*, May 1942, pp. 65, 68.
318 "It gives you . . .": ibid., p. 170.
318 Henry Kaiser: *CB*, 1942, pp. 431–35.
318 delivery time cut: *Time*, May 25, 1942, p. 82.
318 Liberty Ship: John Bunker, *Liberty Ships* (1972), p.7.
319 "No one is as good . . .": quoted in Rosenman, *Working with Roosevelt*, p. 5.
319 "I'm going to speak . . .": *NYT*, Feb. 24, 1942, pp. 1, 4.
319 "The map business . . .": *NYT*, Feb. 21, 1942, p. 8.
319 sixty-one million at radios: *NYT*, Feb. 25, 1942, p. 4.
319 "Selfish men . . ." . . . ". . . tell that to the Marines!": *NYT*, Feb. 24, 1942, p. 4.
320 "even more effective . . .": Rosenman, *Working with Roosevelt*, p. 329.
320 "one of the greatest . . .": *NYT*, Feb. 24, 1942, p. 5.
320 "Sometimes I wish . . .": FDR to R. Leffingwell, March 16, 1942, Franklin D. Roosevelt, *FDR: His Personal Letters* (1947), pp. 1298–99.
320 "No one understood . . .": Eric Larrabee, *Commander in Chief* (1987), p. 11.
321 "the worst single . . .": Burns, *Soldier of Freedom*, p. 216.
321 "Two Japs with Maps . . .": Roger Daniels, *Concentration Camps USA* (1970), p. 32.
321 "the very fact that . . .": Carey McWilliams, *Prejudice: Japanese Americans* (1944), p. 109.
321 "mad dogs, yellow vermin . . .": Daniels, *Concentration Camps USA*, p. 31.
321 "California was given . . .": quoted in John Armor and Peter Wright, *Manzanar* (1988), p. 29.
321 "These people . . ."; "Originally . . .": ER, typescript, "For Colliers—Japanese Relocation Camps," attached to packet of information provided by Dillion Meyer to ER, letter stamped May 13, 1943, box 881, ER Papers, FDRL.
321 40 percent of the total: Richard Lingeman, *Don't You Know There's a War On?* (1970), p. 337.
321 "We might as well . . .": Peter Irons, *Justice at War* (1983), pp. 39–40.
322 Issei, Nisei: Francis Biddle, *In Brief Authority* (1962), p. 213.
322 California political establishment: ibid., p. 226.
322 as reasonable and as humane: William Manchester, *The Glory and the Dream* (1975), p. 299.
322 "the burdens . . ."; "I do not think . . .": Biddle, *Authority*, p. 219.
322 "We are having . . .": Charles Kikuchi, *Kikuchi Diary* (1973), p. 49.
322 "there was a lack . . .": Mine Okubo, *Citizen 13660* (1966), p. 36.
323 "Can this be . . ."; "The senselessness . . .": *NR*, June 15, 1942, pp. 822–23.
323 "I could not help . . .": *TIR*, p. 231.
323 "prevented him . . .": ibid.
324 "I can't take . . .": Anna Rosenberg Hoffman, *OH*, FDRL.
324 "I am brought . . .": FDR to La Guardia, Dec. 18, 1941, PSF 12, FDRL.
324 "I rise today to utter . . .": *CR*, 77th Cong., 2nd sess., Feb. 6, 1942, p. 1097.
324 "The work of OCD . . .": *Liberty*, April 7, 1942, Scrapbook, ER Papers, FDRL.
325 "the storm that burst . . .": Marquis Childs, *I Write from Washington* (1942), p. 262.
325 "parasites and leeches . . .": Mrs. A. E. Curtenius to ER, Feb. 11, 1942, box 953, ER Papers, FDRL.
325 "I am not in the least . . .": ER to Paul Kellogg, Feb. 10, 1942, ER Microfilm Collection, FDRL.
325 "in these troubled . . .": Mrs. Ethel Jamison to ER, Feb. 8, 1942, ER Microfilm Collection, FDRL.
325 "instruction in physical . . .": *NYT*, Feb. 7, 1942, Scrapbook, ER Papers, FDRL.

325 "I still believe in . . .": ER to Flo Kerr, Feb. 18, 1942, ER Microfilm Collection, FDRL.

326 Clark Foreman: *Nation,* Feb. 21, 1942, p. 213.

326 none of $300 million for slum clearance: *NR,* Dec. 29, 1941, p. 887.

326 white workers overcrowded: ibid., p. 886.

326 population of Detroit: Walter White, "What Caused the Detroit Riots," unpublished manuscript, p. 1, OF 93, FDRL.

326 migrated from farmlands: *NYT,* July 5, 1943, p. 9.

327 sleeping in boxcars: *NR,* Dec. 29, 1941, p. 886.

327 five thousand a month: *NYT,* Aug. 9, 1942, sect. IV, p. 10.

327 ". . . be released unless . . .": *Nation,* Feb. 21, 1942, p. 213.

327 "Surely you would not . . .": Mrs. Diggs to ER, Jan. 18, 1942, box 850, ER Papers, FDRL.

327 "After a conference . . .": Palmer to ER, Jan. 30, 1942, box 846, ER Papers, FDRL.

327 On February 28: *Detroit News,* March 1, 1942, p. 15; *NYT,* March 1, 1942, p. 40.

327 "Many dead and wounded": *Detroit News,* March 8, 1942, p. 10.

327 On April 29: *NYT,* April 30, 1942, p. 8.

328 ER's attention to Foreman: ER to FDR, April 30, 1942, box 16, Roosevelt Family Papers Donated by the Children, FDRL.

328 "What can we do . . .": FDR to McIntyre, June 26, 1942; reply, July 13, mentioned that McNutt had promised a job; both in OF 4947, FDRL.

328 "Such a commission . . .": FDR to Edwin Embree, March 16, 1942, box 4, OF 93e, FDRL.

328 "The nation cannot . . .": *Washington Star,* Jan. 9, 1942, Scrapbook, ER Papers, FDRL.

328 "are probably the most . . .": R. J. Divine to ER, Jan. 21, 1942, box 1638, ER Papers, FDRL.

328 "I am not . . .": ER to R. J. Divine, Jan. 29, 1942, box 1638, ER Papers, FDRL.

328 "the enlistment . . .": Dennis Nelson, draft ch., "Negro in the Navy," p. 3, OF 93, FDRL.

328 "in view of . . ."; "there had been no . . .": ibid., p. 4.

328 "I think that with all . . .": FDR to Knox, Jan. 9, 1942, box 11, PSF, FDRL.

329 "that members of the colored . . .": Chairman, General Board, to Sec. of Navy, Feb. 3, 1942, box 11, PSF, FDRL.

329 "Officers of the U.S. Navy . . .": FDR to Sec. of Navy, Feb. 9, 1942, box 11, PSF, FDRL.

329 Dorie Miller's exploits: *Texas History,* March 1977, pp. 10–13.

329 "an unidentified Negro . . .": *NYT,* Dec. 21, 1942, p. 5; *NYT,* Feb. 8, 1942, p. 35.

329 Miller's name finally released: *NYT,* March 13, 1942, p. 3; *PC,* March 14, 1942, p. 1.

330 "the greatest honor . . .": *PC,* March 21, 1942, p. 1.

330 second report to Knox: Chairman, General Board, to Sec. of Navy, March 20, 1942, box 11, PSF, FDRL.

330 "a forward step": *PC,* April 8, 1942, p. 1.

330 ". . . historic barrier": *NYT,* April 8, 1942, p. 11.

330 "I look for an acceleration . . .": FDR to Fraternal Council of Negro Churches, Mar. 16, 1942, OF 93, FDRL.

330 "For the government to terminate . . .": Richard Polenberg, *War and Society: The United States, 1941–1945* (1972), p. 117.

330 "of trying to turn . . .": *NYT,* July 2, 1942, p. 44.

330 "a bunch of snoopers . . .": Roi Ottley, *New World A-Coming* (1943), p. 302.

331 "Anyone who hears . . .": Polenberg, *War and Society,* p. 109.

331 "Don't you think . . .": Jessie Lupo to ER, Sept. 2, 1942, OF 93, FDRL.

331 "I've come to one . . .": *MD,* March 10, 1942.

332 "This drive to . . .": *New York Daily News,* May 6, 1942, Scrapbook, ER Papers, FDRL.

332 "If Mrs. Roosevelt's . . .": *New York World Telegram,* March 14, 1942, Scrapbook, ER Papers, FDRL.

332 When FDR was asked: *NYT,* March 14, 1942, p. 8.

332 more than seven million: Lingeman, *Don't You Know,* pp. 67–68.

332 greatest shift: ibid., p. 69.

332 "It wouldn't take . . .": ibid., p. 71.

332 "was the real gold rush . . .": ibid., p. 69.

333 agricultural depression broken: ibid., p. 67.

333 "by and large . . ."; "and despite . . .": Harold Vatter, *The U.S. Economy in World War II* (1985), p. 129.

333 "Before the war . . .": quoted in ibid., p. 129.

CHAPTER THIRTEEN: "What Can We Do to Help?"

334   MLH's right leg had improved: Ross McIntire to FDR, June 1, 1942, PPF 3737, FDRL.
335   MLH was depressed: Lillian Rogers Parks, *The Roosevelts: A Family in Turmoil* (1981), p. 188.
335   "I wanted her to feel . . .": Bernard Asbell, *The FDR Memoirs* (1973), p. 403.
335   Missy eluded her nurse: interview with James Roosevelt.
335   "She felt there was . . .": Asbell, *FDR Memoirs,* p. 403.
336   tried to set herself on fire: Parks, *Family in Turmoil,* p. 188.
336   "extraordinarily beneficent role . . .": Felix Frankfurter, *From the Diaries of Felix Frankfurter* (1975), p. 162.
336   "one of the very . . .": ibid.
336   "Knowing how deeply . . .": William D. Hassett, *Off the Record with F.D.R.* (1958), p. 34.
336   "Many human emotions . . .": *MD,* April 14, 1942.
336   ER's new apartment: *NYT,* April 5, 1942, p. 19.
337   "When I am in New York . . .": *NYT,* April 16, 1942, p. 16.
337   "At last I am settled . . .": Joseph P. Lash, *Love, Eleanor* (1982), p. 389.
337   "Just a week from tonight . . .": ibid., pp. 381–82.
337   "With you I have . . .": ibid., p. 378.
337   "It was a curious . . .": interview with Lewis Feuer.
337   "I want to be able . . ."; ". . . know that . . .": ER to JL, May 2, 1942, Lash Papers, FDRL.
337   "so it would be always . . .": ER to JL, April 22, 1942, Lash Papers, FDRL.
337   "Wouldn't it be fun . . .": ER to JL, April 18, 1942, Lash Papers, FDRL.
338   "Your telegram came . . .": ER to JL, May 2, 1942, Lash Papers, FDRL.
338   Trude Pratt: Lash, *Love, Eleanor,* pp. 206–7.
338   "Of one thing . . .": ibid., pp. 383–84.
338   "Our friend Hick . . .": Tommy to Esther Lape, Joseph P. Lash, *A World of Love: Eleanor Roosevelt and Her Friends, 1943–1962* (1984), p. xxi.
338   "if she was out . . .": LH manuscript, LH Papers, FDRL; Doris Faber, *The Life of Lorena Hickok* (1980), p. 283.
339   LH and Marion Harron: Faber, *Lorena Hickok,* pp. 290–91.
339   ER experienced: interview with James Roosevelt.
339   second wartime fireside chat: text in *NYT,* April 29, 1942, pp. 1, 14.
340   "General Maximum Price Regulation": John Kenneth Galbraith, *A Life in Our Times* (1981), p. 165.
340   "As we sit here . . .": *NYT,* April 29, 1942, p. 14.
340   "The men operating . . .": Eric Larrabee, *Commander in Chief* (1987), p. 6.
340   Plans for Doolittle raid: Henry H. Arnold, *Global Mission* (1949), pp. 298–99.
340   Details of raid: Duane Schultz, *The Doolittle Raid* (1988), pp. 145–55.
341   Within an hour: ibid., p. 300.
341   ". . . base in Shangri-la": Hassett, *Off the Record,* p. 41.
341   first good news: Robert E. Sherwood, *Roosevelt and Hopkins* (1948), p. 542.
341   "I hope my two boys . . .": Mrs. T. J. Dykema to FDR, May 19, 1942, OF 5510, FDRL.
341   "Give us more . . .": James Jordon to FDR, May 19, 1942, OF 5510, FDRL.
341   ". . . a very good . . .": Stimson Diary, April 18, 1942, Yale University.
341   Midway: James MacGregor Burns, *Roosevelt: The Soldier of Freedom* (1970), pp. 225–26; Admiral J. J. Clarke, *Carrier Admiral* (1967), p. 94; Samuel Eliot Morison, *History of United States Naval Operations in World War II,* vol. IV (1960), p. 80.
342   "the first decisive . . .": Admiral King, 1st Official Report, March 1, 1944, p. 525.
342   "With broken heart . . .": Burns, *Soldier of Freedom,* p. 227.
342   "We've got to go . . .": Forrest C. Pogue, *George C. Marshall: Ordeal and Hope, 1939–1942* (1966), vol. II, p. 304.
342   "the hardness of heart . . .": Stimson Diary, May 27, 1942, Yale University.
342   "his cigarette-holder gesture . . .": Pogue, *Marshall,* vol. II, p. 306.
342   ". . . under 24-hour guard . . .": ibid.
343   "Oh how glad I am . . .": George McJimsey, *Harry Hopkins* (1987), pp. 247–48.
343   "What Harry and George . . .": *Churchill & Roosevelt: The Complete Correspondence* (1984), vol. I, p. 441.

343 "It was not like him . . .": J. W. Pickergill, ed., *The Mackenzie King Record*, vol. I, *1939–1944* (1960), p. 38.

343 Louis Johnson trying: Sherwood, *Roosevelt and Hopkins*, pp. 524–25.

343 "Anything like . . .": *Churchill & Roosevelt Correspondence*, vol. I, p. 449.

344 "an owlish, wise look . . .": Alonzo Fields, *My 21 Years in the White House* (1961), p. 100.

344 "Stone Ass": Thomas Parrish, *Roosevelt and Marshall* (1989), p. 276.

344 "head-down in their desire . . .": Charles E. Bohlen, *Witness to History, 1929–1969* (1973), p. 128.

344 "at the present time . . .": FDR to Joint Chiefs, May 6, 1942, box 106, PSF, FDRL.

344 "The fact that the Russians . . .": Bohlen, *Witness*, p. 127.

344 "developments were clear . . .": Averell Harriman and Elie Abel, *Special Envoy to Churchill and Stalin, 1941–1946* (1975), p. 137.

344 "an open, warm . . .": Lash, *Love, Eleanor*, p. 394.

344 Memorial Day parade: *MD*, May 30, 1942.

345 "American boys . . .": *New York Daily News*, May 6, 1942, Scrapbook, ER Papers, FDRL.

345 "to go round . . ."; "he could not help but think . . .": Harriman and Abel, *Special Envoy*, p. 143.

345 "The President was on . . .": Winston S. Churchill, *The Second World War*, vol. IV, *The Hinge of Fate* (1950), p. 338.

345 "I confess that when . . .": ibid.

345 "I can't help . . .": Stimson Diary, June 20 and 21, 1942, Yale University.

346 "He surely is an informal . . .": Hassett, *Off the Record*, p. 67.

346 "We knew what efforts . . .": Churchill, *Hinge of Fate*, p. 341.

346 "Research in the realm . . .": Joseph Goebbels, *The Goebbels Diaries, 1942–1943* (1948), p. 140.

347 "Alex, what you are . . .": Richard Rhodes, *The Making of the Atomic Bomb* (1986), p. 314.

347 By 1945, more than 120,000: Paul S. Boyer, et al., *The Enduring Vision* (1993), p. 909.

347 groundbreaking discoveries: Richard Lingeman, *Don't You Know There's a War On?* (1970), p. 128.

347 "There was something . . .": Hastings Ismay, *The Memoirs of General Lord Ismay* (1960), p. 256.

347 "It was a bitter . . .": Martin Gilbert, *Winston S. Churchill*, vol. VII, *Road to Victory: 1941–1945* (1986), p. 128.

347 "Defeat is one thing . . .": Churchill, *Hinge of Fate*, p. 343.

347 "What can we do . . .": ibid.

348 "To neither of those men . . .": *TIR*, p. 252.

348 "one of the heaviest blows . . .": Churchill, *Hinge of Fate*, p. 343.

348 "What matters is that . . .": Lord Moran, *Churchill—The Struggle for Survival, 1940–1965* (1966), p. 41.

348 "I am sure myself that . . .": *Churchill & Roosevelt Correspondence*, vol. I, p. 520.

348 "secret baby": Stimson Diary, June 21, 1942, Yale University.

349 "we now had only weeks . . .": Dwight D. Eisenhower, *Crusade in Europe* (1948), p. 72.

349 "the blackest day . . .": Captain Harry Butcher, *My Three Years with Eisenhower* (1946), p. 29.

349 "A lot of these guys . . .": FDR, Jr., to ER, May 13, 1942, ER Papers, FDRL.

349 "We failed to see . . .": Larrabee, *Commander in Chief*, p. 9.

349 HH confided: Sherwood, *Roosevelt and Hopkins*, p. 593.

349 "In smart sets . . .": *Time*, July 13, 1942, p. 14.

349 "Looking better . . .": Hassett, *Off the Record*, p. 57.

349 "He's gained ten pounds . . .": Bernard Asbell, *Mother and Daughter* (1988), p. 144.

349 "Harry head over heels . . .": Hassett, *Off the Record*, p. 80.

350 "to happiness of HH . . .": ibid., p. 91.

350 "It is going to be . . .": HH to MLH, July 28, 1942, HH Papers, FDRL.

350 "I'm worried about Harry's . . .": Lash, *Love, Eleanor*, p. 400.

350 "I imagine . . .": Lash, *World of Love*, p. xxiv.

350 "She did everything . . .": Diana Hopkins, *OH*, FDRL.

351 "Mrs. R and Louise . . .": interview with Diana Hopkins Halsted.

351 "Hopkins is equally . . .": *Time,* July 13, 1942, p. 14.
351 "of Negro toil . . .": *NR,* July 13, 1942, p. 46.
351 "I relize [sic] . . .": Odell Waller to ER, June 8, 1942, PSF 143, FDRL.
352 "a wholly personal . . .": FDR to Darden, June 15, 1942, PSF 143, FDRL.
352 "Dearest Babs . . .": FDR to ER, June 16, 1942, PSF 143, FDRL.
352 "It's a grand . . .": ibid. ER wrote note on memo and returned it to FDR.
352 ER tried all day: Parks, *Family in Turmoil,* p. 175.
352 "would not take 'No' . . .": Ted Morgan, *FDR* (1985), p. 572.
353 "I felt that she would not . . .": Joseph P. Lash, *Eleanor and Franklin* (1971), p. 671.
353 "Mr. Randolph . . .": Pauli Murray, *OH,* FDRL.
353 "Have you ever thought . . .": *Nation,* July 13, 1942, p. 32.
353 "Waller's debt . . .": *Richmond Times-Dispatch,* July 3, 1942, p. 6.
353 "We lost the fight . . .": *NR,* July 13, 1942, p. 46.
353 "I cannot understand . . .": Armand Kreeger to ER, Aug. 6, 1942, box 1638, ER Papers, FDRL.
353 "I am very much . . .": Winnie Downing to ER, July 5, 1942, box 1638, ER Papers, FDRL.
353 "I wonder if it ever . . .": ER to Pauli Murray, Aug. 3, 1942, Pauli Murray Papers, FDRL.
354 "And this just removed . . .": Pauli Murray, *OH,* FDRL.
354 "She must've . . .": interview with Diana Hopkins Halsted.
354 "It's the first time . . .": Lash interview with Esther Lape, Lash Papers, FDRL.
354 "A very nice affair . . .": Hassett, *Off the Record,* p. 95.
354 "Harry trembled . . .": ibid.
354 "After Harry married . . .": interview with Diana Hopkins Halsted.
354 work for Norway: Wilhelm Morgenstierne, in *Märtha Norges Kronprincesse 1929–1954* (n.d.), pp. 70–71, courtesy of Neils Justensen, Norwegian Embassy. Translated for the author by Toril Lampert.
355 "No sooner would Louise . . .": interview with Diana Hopkins Halsted.
355 "Then they'd . . .": Diana Hopkins Halsted, *OH,* FDRL.
355 "Victory" suit: John Morton Blum, *V Was for Victory* (1976), p. 94.
355 "women grow their own . . ." . . . "proper support . . .": *Hygeia,* Aug. 1942, pp. 582, 622.
355 "Certainly Uncle Sam . . .": ibid., p. 624; see also *Business Week,* Sept. 19, 1942, pp. 57–59.
356 ration books: Cabell Phillips, *The 1940s* (1975), pp. 86–87.
356 yellow dye, corn syrup: Lingeman, *Don't You Know,* pp. 244–45; *U.S. News,* Feb. 20, 1942, p. 16.
356 black markets: Blum, *V Was for Victory,* pp. 96–97; *Time,* Dec. 21, 1942, p. 95.
356 "curious independence . . .": Marquis Childs, *I Write from Washington* (1942), p. 299.
356 order forbidding new tires: *NYT,* Dec. 22, 1942, p. 1.
356 certificate program: Galbraith, *Life in Our Times,* p. 155.
356 "Roosevelt was outraged . . .": ibid.
357 rationing of gasoline: *NYT,* April 23, 1942, pp. 1, 16.
357 "The very men to whom . . .": Raymond Clapper, *Watching the World* (1944), p. 199.
357 "I want to talk to you . . .": *Time,* June 22, 1942, p. 16.
358 "Today I am mailing . . .": Mrs. Kirkland to FDR, June 13, 1942, OF 150, FDRL.
358 "On December 7th . . .": Benjamin Cohen to FDR, July 1, 1942, OF 150, FDRL.
358 hundred thousand rubber bands: Samuel Werner and Esther Fisher to FDR, June 27, 1942, OF 150, FDRL.
358 "Mr. Facts": *NYT,* Aug. 16, 1942, sect. VII, p. 5.
358 "The nation waits . . .": ibid.
358 "Gas rationing . . .": Rubber Survey Committee Report, Sept. 10, 1942, p. 6, OF 150, FDRL.
358 "The Baruch report . . .": *NR,* Sept. 21, 1942, p. 336.
358 ". . . grow by its own criticism": *Fortune,* Nov. 1942, p. 227.
358 Effects of gas rationing: *Time,* May 25, 1942, p. 16.
359 "a meteor burst . . .": Lewis Gannet, "Books," in Jack Goodman, ed., *While You Were Gone* (1946), pp. 447–63.
359 "You cannot expect . . .": *NYT,* Sept. 8, 1942, pp. 1, 15.
359 "placed a pistol . . .": *NYT,* Oct. 3, 1942, p. 1.
359 FDR appointed Byrnes: *NYT,* Oct. 4, 1942, p. 1; Nov. 18, 1942, sect. VII, p. 5.

CHAPTER FOURTEEN: "By God, If It Ain't Old Frank!"

361 made it clear to ER: interview with James Roosevelt.
361 "You're the only . . .": Geoffrey C. Ward, *A First-Class Temperament* (1989), p. 629n.
361 "They were just very good . . .": interview with Eleanor Seagraves.
361 "She was the only person . . .": ibid.
361 "flirted like mad": interview with Eleanor Wotkyns.
361 "It was quite . . .": interview with Curtis Roosevelt.
362 Margaret Suckley: interviews with Winthrop Aldrich, Eleanor Seagraves, Curtis Roosevelt, and Eleanor Wotkyns.
362 Daisy in charge of papers: interview with Margaret Suckley.
362 "Evidently the P[resident] . . .": Joseph P. Lash, *A World of Love: Eleanor Roosevelt and Her Friends, 1943–1962* (1984), p. 3.
362 "She had a compulsion . . ": interview with Curtis Roosevelt.
362 "I just don't know . . .": interview with Eleanor Wotkyns.
362 "swing-and-duck rivalry . . .": *Collier's,* July 11, 1942, p. 110.
362 "Ford is making . . .": ibid.
363 Chrysler tank arsenal: *Machinery,* Dec. 1941, p. 107; "Our Nation at War: Log of the President's Inspection Trip," p. 2, box 61, OF 200, FDRL.
363 "By God if it ain't . . .": A. Merriman Smith, *Thank You, Mr. President* (1946), p. 50.
363 M-4 Sherman tank: *NYT,* May 26, 1942, p. 18.
363 "A good drive! . . .": *NYT,* Oct. 2, 1942, p. 15.
363 tank production in U.S. and Germany: Harry Thomson and Lidas Mayo, *The Ordnance Department: Procurement and Supply* (1960), pp. 239, 255.
363 "the most enormous room . . .": Robert Lacey, *Ford: The Man and the Machine* (1986), p. 391.
363 "It is a promise . . .": ibid., p. 393.
363 Only one bomber: "Our Nation at War," p. 3.
363 Ford in far corner: ibid., p. 394.
364 Spotting two midgets: Ford's News Bureau, press release, Sept. 18, 1942, OF 200, FDRL.
364 women working on assembly line: "Summary of Willow Run Bomber Plant," April 30, 1942, p. 4, OF 200, FDRL; *NYT,* July 11, 1942, p. 16.
364 "I feel quite certain . . .": *NYT,* Feb. 16, 1941, p. 22.
364 "The present number . . .": "Policy on Women," *Manual of Operations: War Manpower Commission,* Oct. 17, 1942, Record Group 86, Woman's Bureau, National Archives, Washington, D.C.
364 "Finally valued by others . . .": Sherna Berger Gluck, *Rosie the Riveter Revisited* (1987), p. xiv.
364 "the woman behind . . .": ibid., p. 11.
365 "Actually what attracted . . .": ibid., p. 135.
365 "I'm pretty old . . .": *BEA,* April 16, 1942, p. 5.
365 "every bit of preparation . . .": *Pensacola Journal,* Feb. 2, 1942, Scrapbook, ER Papers, FDRL.
365 "no woman with dependent children . . .": Chester Gregory, *Women in Defense Work During World War II* (1974), p. 19.
365 "You cannot expect . . .": Lacey, *Ford,* p. 393.
365 "if success is measured . . .": Irving Holley, Jr., *Buying Aircraft* (1964), p. 527.
365 Great Lakes: "Historical Information about the U.S. Naval Training Station, Great Lakes," OF 200, FDRL.
366 "It was a luxury . . .": Dennis D. Nelson, *The Integration of the Negro into the Navy* (1951), p. 29.
366 "Brehon, that was grand!": "Our Nation at War," p. 14.
366 shortage of copper and brass: R. Elberton Smith, *The Army and Economic Mobilization* (1959), p. 28; Constance McLaughlin Green, Harry C. Thomson, and Peter C. Root, *The Ordnance Department: Planning Munitions for War* (1955), p. 488.
366 "Life on the train . . .": A. Merriman Smith, *Thank You,* p. 53.
367 "The Flying Fortress": "Our Nation at War," p. 24.
367 "joint Army-Navy E": *NYT,* Aug. 11, 1942, p. 10.
367 "This was an airplane . . .": Martin Cardin, *Flying Forts* (1968), p. 3.

367 "To me the Flying Fortress . . .": ibid., p. 5.
367 "My mother was horrified . . .": Inez Sauer interview, University of Southern California Collection.
367 Anna christened the U.S.S. *Teal: NYT,* Sept. 24, 1942, p. 1.
367 remembering the lessons: AB to Hall Babbitt, Publicity Director, Nov. 3, 1942, box 68, Halsted Papers, FDRL.
368 "When we finished . . .": Lyn Childs in "Rosie the Riveter," PBS Documentary.
368 ". . . With the help of God . . .": "Our Nation at War," pp. 27–28.
368 "Just look at those . . .": *NYT,* Jan. 24, 1943, sect. VII, p. 30.
368 "He can mentally visualize . . .": ibid., p. 30.
368 cut into four pieces: ibid., p. 3.
368 "Your father missed you . . .": Daisy Suckley to AB, Oct. 15, 1942, box 74, Halsted Papers, FDRL.
368 "It was almost . . .": AB to Daisy Suckley, Oct. 23, 1942, box 74, Halsted Papers, FDRL.
368 Douglas Aircraft: *Douglas View,* Sept. 1942, pp. 13–14; *NYT,* June 26, 1942, p. 17.
368 "the lipsticks . . .": *SEP,* May 30, 1942, p. 30.
368 "The factory's no place . . .": Inez Sauer interview, University of Southern California Collection.
369 "Look at Tarzan! . . .": *Aviation,* June 1942, pp. 249–50.
369 Consolidated, B-24: *NYT,* March 16, 1942, p. 1.
369 "doing a swell job . . .": *NYT,* Oct. 15, 1942, p. 25.
369 "I never did anything . . .": *SEP,* May 30, 1942, p. 31.
369 "I'll deny it to the end . . .": quoted in *American Women at War: By 7 Newspaper Women* (1942), p. 13.
369 "I hardly saw a man . . .": *MD,* Oct. 8, 1942.
369 "FDR seemed happy . . .": ER to Lash, Sept. 29, 1942, Lash Papers, FDRL.
369 "Had it not been . . .": Sybil Lewis interview, University of Southern California Collection.
370 not "so much . . .": ibid.
370 "I still don't . . .": *Social Forces,* Oct. 1942, p. 79.
370 "It don't make . . .": ibid.
370 Hudson Naval Ordnance shutdown: *NYT,* June 3, 1942, p. 16.
370 "You can't expect . . .": *Social Forces,* Oct. 1942, p. 81.
370 "At first I thought . . .": ibid.
370 "Alice, I said good night . . .": ibid., p. 80.
370 "Eleanor Clubs": FBI report, OF 93, FDRL.
371 "All the Negroes": ibid.
371 "It was but logical . . .": ibid.
371 "Instead of forming . . .": *LHJ,* Oct. 1942, p. 23.
371 "I think he was really . . .": interview with James Roosevelt.
372 Brass: Erna Risch, *The Quartermaster Corps* (1953), p. 63.
372 silk: ibid., p. 70.
372 1.6 million to 5.4 million: Kent R. Greenfield, Robert R. Palmer, and Bell I. Wiley, *The Organization of Ground Combat Troops* (1947), pp. 209–11.
372 "no appearance of strain . . .": *NYT,* Oct. 2, 1942, p. 1.
372 "the American people . . .": Russell D. Buhite and David W. Levy, eds., *FDR's Fireside Chats* (1992), pp. 240–48.
373 She recognized . . . : interview with James Roosevelt.
373 "She bothered him . . .": Anna Rosenberg, *OH,* FDRL.
373 "You couldn't find . . .": AH interview, Lash Papers, FDRL.
374 "She was a few years . . .": *TIMS,* p. 130.
374 "If I had it to do over . . .": Eleanor Roosevelt and Helen Ferris, *Your Teens and Mine* (1961), p. 186.
374 "I think I must have spoiled . . .": *TIMS,* p. 180.
374 "I know what a delight . . .": Joseph P. Lash, *Eleanor and Franklin* (1971), p. 182.
374 "young and immature . . .": Ward, *Temperament,* p. 415.
375 "easily the most beautiful . . .": ibid., p. 359.
375 "She was gay . . .": Elliott Roosevelt and James Brough, *An Untold Story: The Roosevelts of Hyde Park* (1973), p. 73.
375 "same brand . . .": ibid., p. 82.

375 drawn to one another: Elizabeth Shoumatoff, *FDR's Unfinished Portrait* (1990), p. 16.
375 "Lucy was a wonderful . . .": AH interview, Bernard Asbell. Transcript given to author by Prof. Asbell.
376 "Of course he was in love . . .": quoted in *NYT,* Aug. 13, 1966, p. 23.
376 "I saw you 20 . . .": Lash, *Eleanor and Franklin,* pp. 225–26.
376 "You were a goosy girl . . .": ibid., p. 223.
376 Winthrop Rutherfurd: *NYT,* March 21, 1944, p. 19.
377 "Did you know . . .": Lash, *Eleanor and Franklin,* p. 227.
377 "Up to the time . . .": Joseph P. Lash, *Love, Eleanor* (1982), p. 70.
377 "he emerged tougher . . .": quoted in Lois Schraf, *ER: First Lady of American Liberalism* (1987), p. 56.
377 "I have the memory . . .": Kenneth S. Davis, *Invincible Summer* (1974), p. 93.
377 "Psyche" by Virginia Moore: as quoted in Lash, *Eleanor and Franklin,* p. 245.
378 if she stayed . . . When the time . . . : interview with James Roosevelt.

CHAPTER FIFTEEN: "We Are Striking Back"

379 "I confide my Missus . . .": FDR to WC, Oct. 19, 1942, box 12, Roosevelt Family Papers Donated by the Children, FDRL.
379 "After nine years . . .": as reprinted in *NYT,* Oct. 21, 1942, p. 4.
379 "We welcome you . . .": *BEA,* Oct. 24, 1942, p. 3.
380 enormous suite: *Newsweek,* Nov. 2, 1942, p. 48.
380 "We are lost . . .": ER to LH, Oct. 23, 1942, LH Papers, FDRL.
380 ration card and bed in shelter: *Newsweek,* Nov. 2, 1942, p. 8.
380 "I was struck . . .": ER diary of trip to Great Britain, Oct. 24, 1942, box 2962, ER Papers, FDRL.
380 "Hi Eleanor . . .": *BEA,* Oct. 26, 1942, p. 14.
380 "I have already . . .": Joseph P. Lash, *Eleanor and Franklin* (1971), p. 662.
381 "I can feel . . .": *MD,* Nov. 7, 1942.
381 "We have not used . . .": *BEA,* Oct. 26, 1942, p. 3.
381 Mrs. Churchill sat down: *NYT,* Oct. 29, 1942, p. 25.
381 "Not since I can remember . . .": *NYT,* Oct. 31, 1942, p. 8.
381 "I saw every inch . . .": ER diary of trip, Oct. 29, 1942, box 2962, ER Papers, FDRL.
381 "like animals at bay . . .": Martin Cardin, *Flying Forts* (1968), p. 148.
381 "I found I'm very fat . . .": *NYT,* Oct. 30, 1942, p. 6.
381 She "is very attractive . . .": ER diary of trip, Oct. 30, 1942, box 2962, ER Papers, FDRL.
382 "who is a sweet . . .": ER diary of trip, Oct. 25, 1942, box 2962, ER Papers, FDRL.
382 "I don't want . . .": ER diary of trip, Oct. 27, 1942, box 2962, ER Papers, FDRL.
382 ". . . winning golden opinions . . .": *Churchill & Roosevelt: The Complete Correspondence* (1984), vol. I, p. 655.
382 "Every soldier I see . . .": *MD,* Nov. 5, 1942.
383 "were very indignant . . .": ER to Stimson, Sept. 22, 1942, box 851, ER Papers, FDRL.
383 "the differential treatment . . .": Stimson Diary, Oct. 2, 1942, Yale University.
383 Elliot; "he has matured . . .": ER to LH, Nov. 5, 1942, LH Papers, FDRL.
383 "The First Lady is . . .": *Newsweek,* Nov. 9, 1942, p. 45.
383 "The hullabaloo . . .": Willi A. Boelcki, ed., *Secret Conferences of Dr. Joseph Goebbels* (1970), p. 291.
383 "I'm simply delighted . . .": LH to ER, Oct. 26, 1942, LH Papers, FDRL.
384 "She has had . . .": *Churchill & Roosevelt Correspondence,* vol. I, p. 656.
384 people had grievances: John Morton Blum, *V Was for Victory* (1976), p. 231.
384 Henderson announced: *NYT,* Nov. 1, 1942, sect. IV, p. 12.
384 eighty-three million coffee drinkers: *NYT,* Nov. 29, 1942, sect. IV, p. 8.
384 ". . . the wartime measure . . .": ibid., p. 9.
384 "under no illusions . . .": William D. Hassett, *Off the Record with F.D.R.* (1958), p. 132.
385 "I am fighting for you": MLH to FDR, Nov. 4, 1942, PPF 3737, FDRL.
385 "Name, please? . . .": *NYT,* Nov. 4, 1942, p. 5; Hassett, *Off the Record,* p. 133.
385 light turnout: Herbert Nicholas, ed., *Washington Despatches, 1941–45* (1981), p. 11; *NYT,* Nov. 7, 1942, p. 30.
385 "that an unofficial . . .": *U.S. News,* Nov. 13, 1942, p. 17.

385 "Found the President . . .": Hassett, *Off the Record,* p. 135.
385 "the new Congress . . .": *NYT,* Nov. 7, 1942, p. 30.
385 Shangri-la: Samuel I. Rosenman, *Working with Roosevelt* (1952), pp. 349–50.
386 "He knew that it was largely . . .": ibid., p. 363.
386 showing his anxiety: Grace Tully, *F.D.R., My Boss* (1949), p. 264.
386 Eisenhower having rough time: Dwight D. Eisenhower, *Crusader in Europe* (1948), pp. 96–97.
386 Zero hour: Stimson Diary, Nov. 7, 1942, Yale University.
386 "The operation should be . . .": *Churchill & Roosevelt Correspondence,* vol. I, p. 583.
386 "We agree . . .": ibid., p. 591.
387 "This is just to let . . .": Richard Leighton and Robert Coakley, *Global Logistics and Strategy, 1940–1943* (1955), p. 445.
387 best equipment: ibid., pp. 440–41.
387 "It was as though . . .": ibid., p. 449.
387 never seemed so dark: Samuel Eliot Morison, *The History of United States Naval Operations in World War II,* vol. II, *Operations in North African Waters* (1947), p. 54.
387 "I realize . . .": Leighton and Coakley, *Global Logistics,* p. 452.
388 "Thank God . . .": Tully, *F.D.R.,* p. 264.
388 "America is on the march . . .": quoted in News Bulletins, Nov. 11, 1942, PSF, FDRL.
388 "Like the waves . . .": Katherine Tupper Marshall, *Together* (1946), p. 140.
388 "*This is it* . . .": *Newsweek,* Nov. 16, 1942, p. 17.
388 "They followed the North African . . .": Winston M. Estes, *Homefront* (1976), p. 129.
389 "Now this is not . . .": Robert E. Sherwood, *Roosevelt and Hopkins* (1948), p. 656.
389 "Jesus Christ . . .": James MacGregor Burns, *Roosevelt: The Soldier of Freedom* (1970), p. 291.
389 "Please make it . . .": Forrest C. Pogue, *George C. Marshall: Ordeal and Hope, 1939–1942* (1966), vol. II, p. 402.
389 "This was a decision . . .": Burns, *The Soldier of Freedom,* p. 290.
389 "We come among you . . .": Rosenman, *Working with Roosevelt,* p. 364.
389 "We are attacked . . .": Pétain quoted in News Bulletin, Nov. 8, 1942, PSF, FDRL.
389 "The U.S. can pay . . .": Charles de Gaulle, *The Complete War Memoirs* (1964), p. 134.
390 "Prostitutes are used . . .": *Nation,* Nov. 21, 1942, pp. 529–30.
390 "the enormous benefits . . .": Stimson Diary, Nov. 16, 1942, Yale University.
390 "He showed more resentment . . .": Rosenman, *Working with Roosevelt,* p. 363.
390 "I have accepted . . .": Sherwood, *Roosevelt and Hopkins,* p. 653.
391 the triumph of superior . . . : George Howe, *Northwest Africa: Seizing the Initiative in the West* (1957), pp. 669–77.
391 "The bravest men . . .": Erwin Rommel, *The Rommel Papers* (1953), p. 328.
391 "The news from Africa . . .": *MD,* Nov. 8, 1942.
391 "about to die": ER diary of trip, Nov. 11, 1942, box 2962, ER Papers, FDRL.
391 "Mrs. Roosevelt has done more . . .": Lash, *Eleanor and Franklin,* p. 668.
391 "I really think . . .": ER diary of trip, Nov. 17, 1942, box 2962, ER Papers, FDRL.
392 "I met her at the airport . . .": *Churchill & Roosevelt Correspondence,* vol. II, p. 7.
392 "which is something . . .": *MD,* Nov. 17, 1942.
392 gave him the presents: *Newsweek,* Nov. 30, 1942, p. 38.
392 "it was useless to expect . . .": *NYT,* Nov. 18, 1942, p. 27.
392 "Would it be possible . . .": FDR to Biddle, Nov. 17, 1942, PSF 76, FDRL.
392 "Quiet day . . .": *MD,* Nov. 21, 1942.
392 "It was deeply interesting . . .": ER to M. Gellhorn, Dec. 1, 1942, ER Microfilm Collection, FDRL.
393 "I should have liked . . .": *TIR,* p. 278.
393 Thanksgiving Day service: Hassett, *Off the Record,* p. 142.
393 "I can think of a thousand . . .": *MD,* Nov. 23, 1942.
393 "His religious faith . . .": Sherwood, *Roosevelt and Hopkins,* p. 9.
394 "and carried out . . .": Hassett, *Off the Record,* p. 141.
394 "Personally, whether I . . .": *NYT,* Nov. 24, 1942, p. 1.
394 "a drab and gloomy day": *NYT,* Nov. 29, 1942, sect. VII, p. 8.
394 "who had to step . . .": I. F. Stone, *The War Years, 1939–1945* (1988), p. 142.
394 "was not one of the boys . . .": David Brinkley, *Washington Goes to War* (1988), p. 133.

394 "I have determined...": Henderson to FDR, Dec. 15, 1942, PSF 151, FDRL.
394 "never completely happy...": John Kenneth Galbraith, *A Life in Our Times* (1981), p. 179.
395 "We have lost...": *NR,* Dec. 28, 1942, p. 847.
395 "the second phase...": Stone, *War Years,* p. 144.
395 McNutt had come: Smith conference notes, Dec. 4, 1942, Harold Smith Papers, FDRL.
395 "might quite possibly hate so...": Stimson Diary, Nov. 7, 1942, Yale University.
395 December 5 executive order: *NYT,* Dec. 5, 1942, p. 1.
395 "more power over men...": *NYT,* Dec. 6, 1942, p. 1.
395 CMP: Blum, *V Was for Victory,* pp. 122–23.
396 Day of Mourning and Prayer: David S. Wyman, *The Abandonment of the Jews: America and the Holocaust, 1941–1945* (1984), p. 71.
396 Riegner report: ibid., pp. 44–45.
396 "at one blow...": Martin Gilbert, *The Second World War* (1989), p. 351.
396 "with horror": *MD,* Dec. 5, 1942.
396 Wise asked for meeting: Arthur D. Morse, *While Six Million Died* (1983), pp. 26–28.
396 "unless action is taken...": Wyman, *Abandonment,* p. 72.
396 "We shall do...": ibid., p. 73.
397 "the free movement...": *NYT,* Nov. 3, 1942, p. 1.
397 "The ugly truth...": *Newsweek,* quoted in Wyman, *Abandonment,* p. 57.
397 "The question of the Jewish...": Boelcki, ed., *Secret Conferences,* p. 240.
397 "the target of more adverse...": *NYT,* Dec. 19, 1942, p. 23.
397 "to dread, not what...": Joseph P. Lash, *Love, Eleanor* (1982), p. 417.
398 "This was the beginning...": *California Pioneer Teacher,* p. 6, Hardie Robbins Papers, FDRL.
398 "Looking back across...": Stone, *War Years,* p. 134.
398 "At the end...": *NYT,* Nov. 15, 1942, p. 3.
398 "pending anti-trust suits...": *NYT,* March 29, 1942, p. 1.
398 "one of the first major...": ibid.
399 approximately 175,000 companies: Blum, *V for Victory,* p. 123.
399 New Year's festivities: Rosenman, *Working with Roosevelt,* pp. 364–65.
399 "She would see the news...": interview with Dawn Deslie.
399 mementos: in the possession of Jane Scarborough.
400 "She started crying...": Ann Rochon to Mr. Pres., Dec. 31, 1942, PPF 3737, FDRL.
400 "To the United..."; "To the person who makes...": Rosenman, *Working with Roosevelt,* p. 364.

CHAPTER SIXTEEN: "The Greatest Man I Have Ever Known"

401 first to fly overseas: ER interview, Graff Papers, FDRL.
401 first since Lincoln: *NYT,* Jan. 27, 1943, p. 6.
402 heading south to Miami: Grace Tully, *F.D.R., My Boss* (1949), p. 208.
402 "It's not only that...": Lord Moran, *Churchill—The Struggle for Survival, 1940–1965* (1966), pp. 86–87.
402 "The P.M. is at a disadvantage...": ibid., p. 86.
402 Description of security: "Log of the Trip of the President to the Casablanca Conference," p. 522, OF 200, FDRL; *NYT,* Jan. 27, 1943, p. 6; Michael F. Reilly, *Reilly of the White House* (1947), p. 149.
402 "I hope you'll hurry...": Ross McIntire, *White House Physician* (1946), p. 149.
403 The president's villa: Elliott Roosevelt, *As He Saw It* (1946), pp. 65–66.
403 "Father was ... not a bit tired...": ibid., p. 64.
403 "Stalingrad makes me ashamed...": ER to LH, Oct. 1, 1942, LH Papers, FDRL.
403 "After nearly three...": Martin Gilbert, *The Second World War* (1989), p. 399.
404 60,000 trucks: Robert H. Jones, *The Roads to Russia* (1969), appendix; "14th Report to Congress on Lend-Lease Operations for the Period Ending Dec. 31, 1943," FDRL.
404 "I feel confident...": James MacGregor Burns, *Roosevelt: The Soldier of Freedom* (1970), p. 315.
404 "One of the most poignant...": Averell Harriman and Elie Abel, *Special Envoy to Churchill and Stalin, 1941–1946* (1975), p. 183.

405 "the faces of the men . . .": *Life,* March 8, 1943, p. 51.

405 "Gosh—it's . . ."; "Those troops . . .": Elliott Roosevelt, *As He Saw It,* pp. 106–7.

405 "certainly was in rollicking form . . .": Elliott to ER, Feb. 28, 1943, box 57, Halsted Papers, FDRL.

405 "As always . . .": Elliott Roosevelt, *As He Saw It,* p. 94.

405 "One glimpse of the tiara . . .": ibid., p. 110.

406 "he had no intention . . .": Robert E. Sherwood, *Roosevelt and Hopkins* (1948), p. 688.

406 sultan delighted: Elliot Roosevelt, *As He Saw It,* pp. 110–12.

406 the bride, the groom: Sherwood, *Roosevelt and Hopkins,* p. 680.

406 "Well, just look at him! . . .": Moran, *Churchill,* p. 88.

406 "The General was sullen . . .": Reilly, *Reilly,* p. 157.

406 de Gaulle noticed shadows: Charles de Gaulle, *The Complete War Memoirs* (1964), p. 390.

407 "In human affairs . . .": ibid., pp. 389–92.

407 "In these days . . .": Moran, *Churchill,* p. 87.

407 "Will you at least . . ." . . . "I shall do that . . .": de Gaulle, *War Memoirs,* p. 399.

407 "in high dudgeon . . .": Harriman and Abel, *Special Envoy,* pp. 188–89.

407 "and then suddenly . . .": ibid., p. 188.

408 "Let us spend two days . . .": Winston S. Churchill, *The Second World War,* vol. IV, *The Hinge of Fate* (1950), p. 621.

408 made a cradle: McIntire, *White House Physician,* p. 155.

408 "dangling like the limbs . . ."; ". . . most lovely spot . . .": Moran, *Churchill,* p. 90.

408 "You simply cannot . . ."; "If anything happened . . .": Eric Larabee, *Commander in Chief* (1987), p. 39.

409 "Dearest Babs . . .": Burns, *The Soldier of Freedom,* p. 324.

409 "He always used to tell me . . .": ER interview, Graff Papers, FDRL.

409 "What do you know! . . .": FDR to ER, Jan. 29, 1943, box 12, Roosevelt Family Papers Donated by the Children, FDRL.

409 "Welcome home! . . .": ER to FDR, Jan. 28, 1943, box 16, Roosevelt Family Papers Donated by the Children, FDRL.

409 "I'd give my eyeteeth . . .": John R. Boettiger, Jr., *A Love in Shadow* (1978), p. 238.

410 "I feared you were getting tired . . .": ibid.

410 "I won't say . . .": Bernard Asbell, *Mother and Daughter* (1988), p. 154.

410 "From the moment . . .": ibid.

410 "I went to the train . . .": ER to JL, Feb. 3, 1943, Lash Papers, FDRL.

410 "I hated to see you go . . .": Asbell, *Mother and Daughter,* p. 154.

411 "It was a pathetic . . .": Stimson Diary, Jan. 9, 1943, Yale University.

411 "The President is the poorest . . .": Stimson Diary, March 28, 1943, Yale University.

411 "He wanted to relieve . . .": Felix Frankfurter, *From the Diaries of Felix Frankfurter* (1975), p. 168.

411 Byrnes told FDR: James F. Byrnes, *Speaking Frankly* (1947), pp. 171–73.

412 HH told FDR: Sherwood, *Roosevelt and Hopkins,* pp. 699–700.

412 "They are too much alike . . .": I. F. Stone, *The War Years, 1939–1945* (1988), p. 151.

412 "Mr. President, I'm here . . .": Bernard M. Baruch, *Baruch: The Public Years* (1960), pp. 317–18.

412 "Most of my time . . .": FDR to AB, Feb. 10, 1943, box 62, Halsted Papers, FDRL.

412 "so far away in her mind . . .": Joseph P. Lash, *A World of Love: Eleanor Roosevelt and Her Friends, 1943–1962* (1984), p. 100.

413 "We got to know Mrs. Roosevelt . . .": interview with Barbara Dudley.

413 "Where it was just . . .": Ann Rochon to ER, May 14, 1943, box 1731, ER Papers, FDRL.

413 "It was really very dramatic . . .": *MD,* Feb. 7, 1943.

413 "Exhibiting her usual . . .": *Portland Press Herald,* Feb. 8, 1943, p. 1.

413 "The real situation . . .": *Business Week,* Jan. 9, 1943, p. 72.

413 "A woman is a substitute . . .": Paul Boyer et al., *The Enduring Vision* (1993), p. 914.

413 "If you've sewed on buttons . . .": leaflet, U.S. Department of Labor and Women's Bureau, April 1943, Division of Research, Record Group 86, Women's Bureau, National Archives, Washington, D.C.

414 "women who maintain jobs . . .": *Catholic World,* April 3, 1943, pp. 482–86.

414 "a very chaotic situation . . .": *NYT,* Sept. 2, 1942, p. 12.

414 "women's outside responsibilities...": *NYT*, March 6, 1943, p. 10.
414 "No matter how intense...": War Manpower Commission, "The Employment of Women: Facing Facts in the Utilization of Manpower," June 1943, Division of Research, Record Group 86, Women's Bureau, National Archives, Washington, D.C.
414 called for wide variety: *NYT*, Sept. 2, 1942, p. 12; *Portland Press Herald*, Feb. 8, 1943, p. 2.
414 "Shyly they came forward...": *Portland Press Herald*, Feb. 9, 1943, p. 2.
415 "infinite variety...": *Life*, June 8, 1942, pp. 26–27.
415 ER toured: *MD*, Feb. 14, 1943.
415 "In our spare time...": interview with Ruth Thompson Pierce.
415 "the lack of privacy...": *MD*, Feb. 14, 1943.
415 reviewed twenty-eight hundred: *NYT*, Feb. 15, 1943, p. 1.
415 "I am sure that if...": *MD*, Feb. 14, 1943.
415 Lanham Act: *NYT*, Sept. 1, 1942, p. 15.
416 "a mere drop in the bucket": *SEP*, Oct. 10, 1942, p. 106.
416 "the child should be...": *Public Welfare*, May 1943, p. 141.
416 "The worst mother...": *NYT*, Jan. 26, 1943, p. 16.
416 "What are you doing...": Perkins to Katherine Lenroot, June 26, 1942, Children's Bureau 1942; records of the Department of Labor, Record Group 174, National Archives, Washington, D.C.
416 Statistics on female employment: Boyer, *The Enduring Vision*, p. 913.
416 "a 9 year old boy...": *Fortune*, Feb. 1943, p. 224.
417 "a woman in the graveyard shift...": *SEP*, Oct. 10, 1942, p. 20.
417 "These are not isolated cases...": ibid.
417 women at Portland shipyards: *NYT Magazine*, Nov. 7, 1943, p. 20.
417 plans under way: ibid.
417 "It was as nice...": interview with James Hymes.
417 "I could tell immediately...": interview with Mary Willett.
418 "We had Indian children...": ibid.
418 "It was without question...": ibid.
418 In its first year: pamphlet, *One Year Anniversary*, n.d., loaned to author by Mary Willett.
418 "She had seen a food-service...": interview with James Hymes.
418 nearly $50 million: Margaret O'Brien Steinfels, *Who's Minding the Children? The History and Politics of Day Care in America* (1973), p. 67.
419 "Oddly enough...": *NYT*, March 6, 1943, p. 9.
419 "I think I picked...": *Churchill & Roosevelt: The Complete Correspondence* (1984), vol. II, pp. 156–57.
419 "The Führer seems...": Joseph Goebbels, *The Goebbels Diaries, 1942–1943* (1948), p. 266.
419 "permanently caustic...": Albert Speer, *Inside the Third Reich* (1970), p. 294.
420 "were appreciated as if...": ibid., pp. 296–97.
420 "a bit worn as to patience...": Tommy to Esther Lape, April 6, 1943, box 6, Esther Lape Papers, FDRL.
420 "I'm completely exhausted...": Joseph P. Lash, *Love, Eleanor* (1982), p. 457.
420 "stretched out luxuriantly...": ibid., pp. 441–42.
420 "I loved just sitting...": ibid., p. 449.
421 room had been bugged: ibid., pp. 489–91.
421 "All of the top men...": ibid., p. 490.
421 "loyal Americans...": Henry Jones to ER, Feb. 3, 1943, attached to ER to Stimson, March 8, 1943, ER Microfilm Collection, FDRL.
422 ER wrote to Stimson: ibid.
422 "They have a show...": Philip McGuire, *Taps for a Jim Crow Army* (1983), p. 13.
422 Lena Horne cut tour: Ulysses G. Lee, *The Employment of Negro Troops* (1966), p. 307.
422 "the uncertainty...": ibid., p. 30.
422 "That's the kind of democracy...": memo to Director of Intelligence, Morale Report on 493rd Port Battalion, June 17, 1943, Record Group, p. 107, National Archives, Washington, D.C.
422 "What a lot we must do...": *MD*, July 28, 1943.
423 general forced to assign: Larrabee, *Commander in Chief*, p. 104.
423 "including theaters...": Lee, *Negro Troops*, p. 308.

423 "The fact that anyone . . .": ibid., p. 400.

423 "We were undoubtedly . . .": *Air and Space,* Oct.–Nov. 1989, p. 35.

423 "The waiting got tiresome": Benjamin O. Davis, Jr., *Autobiography* (1992), p. 90.

423 "The program of preflight . . ."; "This seems to me . . .": ER to Stimson, April 10, 1943, box 890, ER Papers, FDRL.

424 "tremendous moment . . .": Davis, *Autobiography,* p. 93.

424 "As we left the shores . . .": ibid., p. 94.

424 "blacks could fly . . .": *Black Americans in Defense of Our Nation,* Washington, D.C.: Department of Defense (1990), p. 64.

424 1,578 missions: *Air and Space,* Oct.–Nov. 1989, p. 38.

424 "the hard plodding . . .": ER to FDR, April 1, 1943, box 16, Roosevelt Family Papers Donated by the Children, FDRL.

424 "Men are always little boys . . .": Asbell, *Mother and Daughter,* p. 158.

424 "had two meals every day . . .": Lash, *World of Love,* p. 3.

425 "She had to get off . . .": ibid.

425 army had expanded: Kent R. Greenfield, Robert R. Palmer, and Bell I. Wiley, *The Organization of Ground Combat Troops* (1987), pp. 212–17.

425 "Just imagining it . . .": Geoffrey Perrett, *There's a War to Be Won* (1991), p. xxvi.

425 "Fort Benning is such . . .": "Log of the President's Inspection Trip," April 15, 1943, OF 200, FDRL.

425 "Even in the Infantry . . .": Robert R. Palmer, Bell I. Wiley, and William Keast, *The Procurement and Training of Ground Combat Forces* (1948), p. 2.

426 "did not represent . . .": ibid., p. 4.

426 "I don't get as good . . .": "Log," April 18, 1943.

426 "This is a lovely . . .": *MD,* April 19, 1943.

426 headed to Mexico: *NYT,* April 22, 1943, p. 1.

427 "some of the officers . . .": "Log," April 21, 1943.

427 "It seems to me . . .": "Log," April 25, 1943.

427 "The Army has gone . . .": ibid.

427 "His spirits were higher . . .": *NYT,* April 25, 1943, p. 8; *U.S. News,* April 30, 1943, p. 31.

427 "who first accepted . . .": Ickes to FDR, April 13, 1943, Harold Ickes Papers, Library of Congress, Washington, D.C.

428 camps built by War Relocation Authority: Carey McWilliams, *Prejudice: Japanese Americans* (1944), p. 156.

428 "You could not take hold . . .": Audrie Girdner and Anne Loftis, *The Great Betrayal* (1969), p. 212.

428 "It chokes you . . .": ER, "Japanese Relocation Camps," unpublished manuscript written for *Collier's,* attached to letter, Dillion Myer to ER, May 13, 1943, box 881, ER Papers, FDRL.

428 "It gets into every pore . . .": letter received by evacuee in Granada from another evacuee in Topaz, Feb. 12, 1943, attached to Dillion Myer to ER, May 13, 1943, box 881, ER Papers, FDRL.

428 "covered everything . . .": Dillion Myer, "Autobiography," *OH,* University of California at Berkeley.

428 "Everything is spotlessly clean . . .": *MD,* April 23, 1943.

428 "Sometimes there are little . . .": ibid.

429 "We are at war . . .": McWilliams, *Prejudice,* p. 160.

429 "coddled": ER, "Japanese Relocation Camps."

429 "To be frank with you . . .": McWilliams, *Prejudice,* p. 212.

429 "With everyone eating . . .": interview with Jiro Ishihara.

429 "We hold the advantage . . .": Charles Kikuchi, *The Kikuchi Diary* (1973), p. 81.

429 "For the young people . . .": interview with Jiro Ishihara.

430 "Feel sort of sorry for Pop . . .": Kikuchi, *Diary,* p. 61.

430 "I was very happy . . .": Henry Ebihara to Stimson, Feb. 4, 1943, attached to letter, Dillion Myer to ER, May 13, 1943, box 881, ER Papers, FDRL.

430 "to start independent . . .": ER, "Japanese Relocation Camps."

430 "To undo mistakes . . .": ibid.

430 "normal American life . . .": FDR to Ickes, April 24, 1943, Harold Ickes Papers, Library of Congress, Washington, D.C.

430 "a vicious, well-organized...": Stimson to Myer, May 10, 1943, attached to Dillion Myer to ER, May 13, 1943, box 881, ER Papers, FDRL.

CHAPTER SEVENTEEN: "It Is Blood on Your Hands"

432 Washington in 1943: Selden Menefee, *Assignment USA* (1943), pp. 36–40.
432 "the federal government...": David Brinkley, *Washington Goes to War* (1988), p. 111.
433 visit from Shoumatoff: Elizabeth Shoumatoff, *FDR's Unfinished Portrait* (1990), pp. 80–81.
433 "quite impressive...": ibid., p. 75.
433 "Winthrop Rutherfurd...": ibid.
433 "Everything whirled..."; "seldom seen...": ibid., pp. 76–77.
433 comings and goings of Rutherfurd children: *Aiken Standard & Review,* society page for various issues, 1939–45.
434 "his extraordinary...": Shoumatoff, *FDR's Portrait,* p. 79
434 "You should really paint..."; "I did not understand...": ibid., p. 80.
434 Lucy at inauguration: Elliott Roosevelt and James Brough, *An Untold Story: The Roosevelts of Hyde Park* (1973), p. 282.
434 letters of 1927: Lucy to FDR, April 16 and July 2, 1927, box 21, Roosevelt Family Papers Donated by the Children, FDRL.
435 "Mrs. Johnson": the Usher Diary recorded the dates and times of Mrs. Johnson's visits. Bernard Asbell discovered this information when interviewing William D. Simmons, a Secret Service man. See Bernard Asbell, *The FDR Memoirs* (1973), p. 411.
435 "How is Mrs. Rutherfurd?...": Shoumatoff, *FDR's Portrait,* p. 82.
436 Kasserine Pass: George Howe, *Northwest Africa* (1957), ch. XXII, pp. 438–58.
436 Red Oak: *Life,* May 3, 1943, p. 26.
436 "The Secretary of War...": *SEP,* Aug. 17, 1946, pp. 15, 71.
436 "hometown we dreamed of...": ibid., p. 14.
437 "the Americans are happy...": Joseph Goebbels, *The Goebbels Diaries, 1942–1943* (1948), pp. 372, 376.
437 "the striking change...": Winston S. Churchill, *The Second World War,* vol. IV, *The Hinge of Fate* (1950), p. 706. Churchill is quoting from a summary of the agreed-upon Anglo-American record of the meeting.
437 "stood on the periphery...": Martin Gilbert, *The Second World War* (1989), p. 401.
437 AB hostess at dinner: AB to John Boettiger, May 15, 1943, box 5, Boettiger Papers, FDRL.
438 "the British empire...": Churchill, *Hinge of Fate,* pp. 710–11.
438 " 'Shoot, if you must...' ": Robert E. Sherwood, *Roosevelt and Hopkins* (1948), p. 729.
438 "He is always using...": Joseph P. Lash, *Love, Eleanor* (1982), p. 508.
438 "with much interest..."; "Sadly FDR left...": Churchill, *Hinge of Fate,* p. 712.
438 "the PM picks his teeth...": AB to John Boettiger, May 15, 1943, box 5, Boettiger Papers, FDRL.
439 "He was placed...": Churchill, *Hinge of Fate,* p. 713.
439 "a very decided deadlock...": Stimson Diary, May 16, 1943, Yale University.
439 "The President is not willing...": Lord Moran, *Churchill—The Struggle for Survival, 1940–1965* (1966), p. 104.
439 "a spoiled boy": Stimson Diary, May 25, 1943, Yale University.
439 "to plan such operations...": Hastings Ismay, *The Memoirs of General Lord Ismay* (1960), p. 298.
439 "a trying guest...": William D. Hassett, *Off the Record with F.D.R.* (1958), p. 169.
439 "really likes the PM...": Joseph P. Lash, *A World of Love: Eleanor Roosevelt and Her Friends, 1943–1962* (1984), p. 11.
440 effect of the strike: *NYT,* May 1, 1944, p. 1.
440 "You must have lace...": Sophia Carroll to FDR, April 28, 1943, OF 290 #2, FDRL.
440 "I think you are equally guilty...": Esther Morrow to FDR, n.d. [April 1943], OF 290 #2, FDRL.
440 "While these American boys...": Robert Meyer, Jr., *The Stars and Stripes: Story of World War II* (1960), p. 60.
440 "What sort of traitors...": "A fighting man" to FDR, June 1, 1943, Harold Ickes Papers, Library of Congress, Washington, D.C.

440 "If I were on the front lines . . .": John Jaqua to Ernest Jaqua, May 23, 1943; Ernest Jaqua sent a copy of his son's letter to HH, June 1, 1943, HH Papers, FDRL.

441 unauthorized wildcat strikes: Rosa Swafford, *Wartime Record of Strikes and Lockouts, 1940–1945* (1946), pp. 16–17.

441 "It is the judgment . . .": Philip Murray to FDR, June 15, 1943, OF 497b, FDRL.

441 "I have seen pay envelopes . . .": *NYT,* May 9, 1943, p. 6.

441 "he would be glad to resign . . .": Smith conference notes, June 3, 1943, Harold Smith Papers, FDRL.

441 "I understand the devotion . . .": *NYT,* May 3, 1943, p. 4.

442 "on essential war work . . .": *NYT,* June 4, 1943, p. 1.

442 FDR hesitant to use induction: Stimson Diary, June 9, 1943, Yale University.

442 "I ain't a traitor . . .": Rochelle Chadakoff, ed., *Eleanor Roosevelt's My Day* (1989), vol. 1, p. 293.

442 "If I were FDR . . .": Lash, *World of Love,* p. 24.

442 "This is a bad bill . . .": Hassett, *Off the Record,* p. 180.

442 "In spite of imperfections . . .": Stimson Diary, June 25, 1943, Yale University.

442 "We the people . . . ": Mrs. Cravens to FDR, June 26, 1943, OF 407b, FDRL.

442 "Let there be no . . .": text of speech, *NYT,* June 26, 1943, pp. 1, 3.

443 "In vetoing the Smith-Connally . . ."; "action, not tomorrow . . .": ibid., p. 4.

443 "a bad rebuff . . .": Stimson Diary, June 25, 1943, Yale University.

443 "our lack of leadership . . ."; "Perhaps . . .": Lash, *World of Love,* p. 34.

443 More idleness in 1943 in mining: Swafford, *Wartime Record,* p. 33.

443 "portal to portal pay": *Monthly Labor Review,* Dec. 1943, p. 115; see also T. H. Watkins, *Righteous Pilgrim* (1990), pp. 753–59.

444 "We were thrilled . . .": interview with Michael Lilly.

444 "The domestic scene . . .": *MD,* June 20, 1943.

444 "No city in the deep South . . ."; "If these 'poor whites' . . .": Menefee, *Assignment USA,* pp. 51, 56.

444 "We realize . . .": *Mobile Register,* June 3, 1943, p. 8.

444 "No nigger is goin' . . .": Menefee, *Assignment USA,* p. 155.

444 separate shipway: *Mobile Register,* June 8, 1943, pp. 1, 7.

445 rioting in Detroit: Robert Shogan and Tom Craig, *The Detroit Race Riots* (1964); see also accounts in *Detroit Free Press.*

445 "He's not doing . . .": *Detroit Free Press,* June 22, 1943, pp. 1, 2, 8.

446 "It is blood . . .": *Michigan History,* Fall 1969, p. 198.

446 "It is my belief . . .": Lang to FDR, July 29, 1943, OF 93c, FDRL.

446 "I suppose when one . . .": ER to Josephus Daniels, July 23, 1943, ER Microfilm Collection, FDRL. Daniels had sent her a copy of his editorial denouncing criticisms.

446 "the deliberate effort . . .": Stimson Diary, June 24, 1943, Yale University.

446 "come to the conclusion . . .": Stimson Diary, July 5, 1943, Yale University.

446 "Many newspapers and individuals . . .": C. E. Rhett to Biddle, June 12, 1943, OF 93c, FDRL.

446 "The old, subdued, muted . . .": *NR,* July 5, 1943, p. 9.

446 ". . . the vacillation . . .": C. E. Rhett to Biddle, June 12, 1943, OF 93c, FDRL.

447 "a sizable population . . .": *NR,* July 5, 1943, p. 10.

447 "Large segments . . .": C. E. Rhett to Biddle, July 12, 1943, OF 93c, FDRL.

447 "highly explosive . . .": ibid.

447 "Like a defective screw . . .": Pauli Murray to FDR, June 18, 1943, OF 93c, FDRL.

447 "We urge you . . .": WW to FDR, June 21, 1943, OF 93c, FDRL.

447 "a straight forward statement . . .": Bethune to FDR, June 22, 1943, OF 93c, FDRL.

447 "on a par with Nazism . . .": *MD,* July 13, 1943.

447 "Detroit should never . . .": Lash, *World of Love,* p. 32.

447 "he must not irritate . . .": ibid., p. 38.

447 "Why hasn't Mr. Roosevelt . . .": *NR,* July 5, 1943, p. 12.

448 first week in July: Gilbert, *Second World War,* p. 442.

448 "The whole world . . .": *NYT,* June 27, 1943, sect. IV, p. 3.

448 "It is going to be about the war . . .": *NYT,* July 28, 1943, p. 9; Franklin D. Roosevelt, *Public Papers and Addresses of Franklin Delano Roosevelt, 1943* (1950), p. 324.

449 "The first crack in the Axis . . .": text of speech, *NYT,* July 29, 1943, p. 4.

450 "our very national existence . . .": *AM,* Oct. 1943, p. 72.
450 "To a large degree . . .": Richard Leighton and Robert Coakley, *Global Logistics and Strategy, 1940–1943* (1955), p. 601.
450 "We are still far . . .": *NYT,* July 29, 1943, p. 4.
450 "I can recall . . .": Saul Bellow, *It All Adds Up: From the Dim Past to the Uncertain Future* (1994), pp. 28–29.
451 "watched the sun go down . . .": *MD,* Aug. 1, 1943.
451 "He is much the most interesting . . .": Bernard Asbell, *Mother and Daughter* (1988), p. 163.
451 "to a mature understanding . . .": Lash, *Love, Eleanor,* p. 378.
451 "Darling Mum . . .": Asbell, *Mother and Daughter,* p. 150.
452 "a terrific hatred": AB to John Boettiger, June 26, 1943, box 5, Boettiger Papers, FDRL.
452 "She looks very thin . . .": Lash, *World of Love,* p. 41.
452 "I'm having the time . . .": AB to John Boettiger, May 28, 1943, box 5, Boettiger Papers, FDRL.
452 "You'd be amazed at the timid . . .": AB to John Boettiger, Aug. 1, 1943, box 5, Boettiger Papers, FDRL.
452 "It is the first time . . .": AB to John Boettiger, July 16, 1943, box 5, Boettiger Papers, FDRL.
452 "I think having me here . . .": ER to John Boettiger, July 18, 1943, box 26, Boettiger Papers, FDRL.
453 "I only like being . . .": Lash, *World of Love,* p. 43.
453 "It was nice . . .": ER to FDR, July 18, 1943, box 16, Roosevelt Family Papers Donated by the Children, FDRL.
453 "I guess one of the sad things . . .": Lash, *World of Love,* p. 104.
453 "repeated endeavors . . .": *NYT,* July 26, 1943, p. 19.
453 "to be of help . . .": David S. Wyman, *The Abandonment of the Jews: America and the Holocaust, 1941–1945* (1984), p. 145.
454 "Our own government . . .": *NYT,* July 26, 1943, p. 19.
454 "I am convinced . . .": Jan Ciechanowski, *Defeat in Victory* (1947), p. 182.
454 "virtually none of . . .": Wyman, *Abandonment,* p. 337.
455 "Will any of these Jews . . .": quoted in ibid., p. 150.
455 "The percentage killed . . .": *MD,* Aug. 12, 1943.

CHAPTER EIGHTEEN: "It Was a Sight I Will Never Forget"

456 "These last few days . . .": Joseph P. Lash, *A World of Love: Eleanor Roosevelt and Her Friends, 1943–1962* (1984), p. 54.
457 "more eloquently . . .": Samuel I. Rosenman, *Working with Roosevelt* (1952), pp. 387–88.
457 "You know . . .": *MD,* Aug. 16, 1943.
457 "fraternal . . .": Averell Harriman and Elie Abel, *Special Envoy to Churchill and Stalin, 1941–1946* (1975), p. 222.
457 "Mrs. Roosevelt . . .": ibid.
457 "Your mother is so pleased . . .": Tommy to AB, Aug. 11, 1943, box 75, Halsted Papers, FDRL.
457 "She is especially anxious . . .": Franklin D. Roosevelt, *Public Papers and Addresses, 1943* (1950), p. 1439.
458 "I spoke from the library . . .": *MD,* Aug. 15, 1943.
458 "The P[resident] was very sweet . . .": Lash, *World of Love,* p. 55.
458 "Darling, it kinda gives me . . .": AB to John Boettiger, Aug. 11, 1943, box 5, Boettiger Papers, FDRL.
458 gift of emeralds: Robert E. Sherwood, *Roosevelt and Hopkins* (1948), p. 614.
458 denied by Louise: *NYT,* Jan. 8, 1943, p. 6.
458 extravagant dinner: Sherwood, *Roosevelt and Hopkins,* p. 698.
458 publication of article: ibid.
459 final blow: ibid., p. 750.
459 "This is a fight . . .": ibid., p. 698.
459 Eager to invite: Tommy to AB, Sept. 2, 1943, box 75, Halsted Papers, FDRL.
459 "Harry and Louise . . .": Lash, *World of Love,* p. 54.

459 "ailing and fearing . . . ": James MacGregor Burns, *Roosevelt: The Soldier of Freedom* (1970), p. 392.

459 "it seemed like . . .": ibid.

460 "pick and shovel": *NYT,* Aug. 18, 1943, p. 1.

460 haunted by memories, "majestic": Lord Moran, *Churchill—The Struggle for Survival, 1940–1965* (1966), p. 116.

460 "If a stranger had visited . . .": Hastings Ismay, *The Memoirs of General Lord Ismay* (1960), p. 309.

460 "Winston's obstinacy . . .": Moran, *Churchill,* p. 117.

461 "a very great preponderance": Winston S. Churchill, *The Second World War,* vol. V, *Closing the Ring* (1951), p. 76.

461 discussed the atomic bomb: Martin Gilbert, *Winston S. Churchill,* vol. vii, *Road to Victory: 1941–1945* (1986), pp. 470–71.

461 "Until now . . .": Harriman and Abel, *Special Envoy,* p. 225.

461 "We are both mad . . .": ibid., p. 226.

461 "I gather she didn't like . . .": Tommy to AB, Sept. 2, 1943, box 75, Halsted Papers, FDRL.

461 "PM's sleeping arrangements . . .": Sir Alexander Cadogan, *The Diaries of Sir Alexander Cadogan, O.M. 1938–1945* (1972), p. 559.

462 "too much for him . . .": George McJimsey, *Harry Hopkins* (1987), p. 295.

462 "of high importance . . .": ER to FDR, Sept. 6, 1943, box 16, Roosevelt Family Papers Donated by the Children, FDRL.

462 "I feel a hundred . . .": Lash, *World of Love,* p. 62.

462 "Guadalcanal is no place . . .": Joseph P. Lash, *Eleanor and Franklin* (1971), p. 684.

462 "In some ways . . .": Lash, *World of Love,* p. 60.

462 "I have no zest . . .": ibid.

463 "When I left": *NYT,* Aug. 28, 1943, p. 13.

463 "We liked this speech . . .": ibid.

463 "a genuine impulse . . .": J. William T. Youngs, *Eleanor Roosevelt: A Personal and Public Life* (1985), p. 9.

463 "her shoes dusty and scarred . . .": *NYT,* Sept. 13, 1943, p. 21.

463 "Mrs. Roosevelt literally . . .": Lash, *World of Love,* pp. 62–63.

463 "followed by a brace . . .": copy of letter received by Florence Kerr attached to HH to ER, Oct. 19, 1943, box 214, HH Papers, FDRL.

464 "When I say that . . .": Lash, *Eleanor and Franklin,* p. 685.

464 "in some magic way . . .": *TIR,* p. 298.

464 "Over here . . .": *NYT,* Sept. 6, 1943, p. 19.

464 "It was a sight . . .": Lash, *Eleanor and Franklin,* p. 685.

464 "a fine impression . . .": FDR to ER, Aug. 30, 1943, box 12, Roosevelt Family Papers Donated by the Children, FDRL.

464 "If I wasn't busy . . .": as repeated in ER to Tommy, Sept. 18, 1943, Malvina Thompson Papers, FDRL.

464 "I've had so many . . .": ER to FDR, Sept. 15, 1943, box 16, Roosevelt Family Papers Donated by the Children, FDRL.

465 "How little I ever thought . . .": *MD,* Sept. 12, 1943.

465 "How I hated . . .": Lash, *World of Love,* p. 71.

465 "I was ahamed . . .": Lash, *Eleanor and Franklin,* p. 691.

465 "leapfrogging" substituted: Samuel Eliot Morison, *The Two-Ocean War* (1963), p. 282.

466 "FDR, should there . . .": ER notes, Sept. 22, 1943, box 12, Roosevelt Family Papers Donated by the Children, FDRL.

466 "No, but she will . . .": William D. Hassett, *Off the Record with F.D.R.* (1958), p. 200.

466 "Hope you come . . .": FDR to ER, Sept. 21, 1943, box 12, Roosevelt Family Papers Donated by the Children, FDRL.

466 "Did you have fun . . . ": repeated by AB in AB to John Boettiger, Nov. 11, 1943, box 6, Boettiger Papers, FDRL.

466 "she had never . . .": AB to John Boettiger, Sept. 22, 1943, box 6, Boettiger Papers, FDRL.

466 "Pa asked me . . .": Bernard Asbell, *Mother and Daughter* (1988), p. 169.

466 "Oh, no, Eleanor . . .": *NYT,* Aug. 30, 1943, p. 8.

467 "Yes, she has been . . .": *NYT,* Sept. 29, 1943, p. 23.

467 "They missed her usual . . .": *Time,* Oct. 4, 1943, p. 25.

467 "while the farmers . . .": *NYT,* Oct. 17, 1943, p. 28.
467 "The outcry in Congress . . .": Lash, *World of Love,* p. 84.
467 "[Tommy] is worried . . .": ibid., p. 81.
467 "her deep horror . . .": ibid.
467 "the crosses row on row . . . ": *MD,* Sept. 17, 1943.
467 American casualties: figures provided by the Army History Center and Navy History Center, Washington, D.C.
467 "emotionally . . ."; "I know and understand . . .": FDR, Jr., to ER, Oct. 21, 1943, box 26, Boettiger Papers, FDRL.
468 "I think another . . .": Lash, *World of Love,* p. 81.
468 "I think the things . . .": *NYT,* Aug. 28, 1943, p. 3.
469 "Lack of money . . .": Theodore Mosch, *The G.I. Bill* (1975), p. 32.
469 "I'd like to see . . .": *NYT,* Dec. 18, 1943, p. 12.
469 "Baruch is still . . .": ER to John Boettiger, Dec. 8, 1943, box 6, Boettiger Papers, FDRL.
470 *One World:* Jack Goodman, ed., *While You Were Gone* (1946), p. 452–53.
470 "The representatives of 44 nations . . .": *MD,* Nov. 9, 1943.
470 "with a sky so blue . . . ": ibid.
470 "Good news comes . . .": Hassett, *Off the Record,* p. 218.
470 "one of the bitterest . . .": Robert Coakley and Richard Leighton, *Global Logistics and Strategy, 1943–1945* (1989), p. 192.
470 "Mrs. R wanted very much . . .": Lash, *World of Love,* p. 93.
470 "The OM sat all over her . . .": AB to John Boettiger, Dec. 6, 1943, box 6, Boettiger Papers, FDRL.
471 "not just because of . . .": AB to ER, Nov. 11, 1943, box 57, Halsted Papers, FDRL.
471 "I'll read him your desire . . .": ER to AB, Nov. 6, 1943, box 57, Halsted Papers, FDRL.
471 "The answer was . . .": AB to John Boettiger, Nov. 11, 1943, box 6, Boettiger Papers, FDRL.
471 ". . . Pa seems to take . . .": AB to John Boettiger, Nov. 11, 1943, box 6, Boettiger Papers, FDRL.
471 "goes along very strongly . . .": AB to John Boettiger, Dec. 11, 1943, box 6, Boettiger Papers, FDRL.
472 "Tell me darling . . .": John Boettiger to AB, May 29, 1943, box 5, Boettiger Papers, FDRL.
472 "Neither of us is giving . . .": Asbell, *Mother and Daughter,* p. 165.
472 "among the higher ups . . .": AB to John Boettiger, Sept. 18, 1943, box 5, Boettiger Papers, FDRL.
472 "I realize how desperately lonely . . .": ER to AB, Oct. 10, 1943, box 57, Halsted Papers, FDRL.
473 "I just saw Pa . . .": ER to AB, Nov. 11, 1943, box 57, Halsted Papers, FDRL.
473 "Everything is very comfortable . . .": FDR to ER, Nov. 18, 1943, box 12, Roosevelt Family Papers Donated by the Children, FDRL.
473 "The sea voyage . . .": Elliott Roosevelt, *As He Saw It* (1946), p. 133.
473 "for things always . . .": Lash, *World of Love,* p. 96.
473 "He was thrilled . . .": Michael F. Reilly, *Reilly of the White House* (1947), p. 170.
473 "I've been amused . . .": Lash, *World of Love,* p. 96.
474 "In a queer way . . .": Asbell, *Mother and Daughter,* p. 156.
474 clapping her hands: Lash, *World of Love,* pp. 1–2.
474 "This will be very useful . . .": Frank Freidel, *Franklin D. Roosevelt: A Rendezvous with Destiny* (1990), p. 478.
474 "I'm sorry things only went . . .": ER to FDR, Dec. 5, 1943, box 12, Roosevelt Family Papers Donated by the Children, FDRL.
474 "Let us make it . . .": Churchill, *Closing the Ring,* p. 300.
474 "Large families . . .": Elliott Roosevelt, *As He Saw It,* p. 16.
474 "He started slowly . . .": interview with Robert Hopkins.
474 WC asked Pa Watson: Churchill, *Closing the Ring,* p. 301.
475 "Seeing him . . .": Reilly, *Reilly,* p. 179.
475 "as if the tailor . . .": Moran, *Churchill,* p. 146.
475 "I am glad to see . . .": Charles E. Bohlen, *Witness to History, 1929–1969* (1973), p. 144.
475 "He seems very confident . . .": Elliott Roosevelt, *As He Saw It,* p. 176.
475 "It was a thrilling experience . . .": Ismay, *Memoirs,* p. 337.
475 "clearly was the dominating . . . ": Bohlen, *Witness,* p. 142.

475   "He looked the picture . . .": Ismay, *Memoirs,* p. 338.
475   doodling wolfheads: Bohlen, *Witness,* p. 151.
475   "If we are here . . .": Moran, *Churchill,* p. 147.
476   "I thank the Lord . . .": Stimson Diary, Dec. 5, 1943, Yale University.
476   "man might destroy . . . ": Moran, *Churchill,* p. 151.
476   to see FDR alone: ibid., p. 146.
476   "I had done . . ." . . . "A vague smile . . .": Frances Perkins, *The Roosevelt I Knew* (1946), pp. 83–84.
476   "From that time on . . .": ibid., pp. 84–85.
477   "There were toasts . . .": Henry H. Arnold, *Global Mission* (1949), p. 498.
477   "I want to tell you . . .": *Foreign Relations of the United States: The Conferences at Cairo and Teheran, 1943* (1961), p. 469.
477   American factories were supplying: Fourteenth Report on Lend-Lease for period ending December 31, 1943, pp. 30–33, FDRL.
477   every week: ibid.
478   "We have differing customs . . .": Burns, *Soldier of Freedom,* p. 411.
478   huddled around a map: ibid., pp. 412–13.
478   "an important milestone . . .": *NYT,* Dec. 7, 1943, p. 6.
478   "I want George . . .": Sherwood, *Roosevelt and Hopkins,*p. 760.
478   "Well, Ike . . .": Dwight D. Eisenhower, *Crusade in Europe* (1948), p. 207.
478   "Homeward bound . . .": Lash, *World of Love,* p. 98.
479   "He was in his traveling . . .": Stimson Diary, Dec. 17, 1943, Yale University.
479   "OM was very cool . . .": AB to John Boettiger, Dec. 19, 1943, box 6, Boettiger Papers, FDRL.
479   "Tonight . . .": *MD,* Dec. 17, 1943.
479   "a complete fiasco . . ." . . . "the things she had been through . . .": AB to John Boettiger, Dec. 19, 1943, box 6, Boettiger Papers, FDRL.
480   "I finally managed . . .": ibid.
480   "Ever since my talk . . .": AB to John Boettiger, Dec. 27, 1943, box 6, Boettiger Papers, FDRL.
480   "It is the first time . . .": Henry H. Adams, *Harry Hopkins* (1977), p. 351.
481   first Christmas at Hyde Park since 1932: *NYT,* Dec. 26, 1943, p. 5.
481   "I am sure it will seem . . .": *MD,* Dec. 20, 1943.
481   "loved the old place . . .": AB to John Boettiger, Dec. 27, 1943, box 6, Boettiger Papers, FDRL.
481   "no women on ships . . .": ibid.
481   "How did the New Deal . . .": text of speech, *NYT,* Dec. 29, 1943, p. 8.
482   "The New Deal slogan . . .": *U.S. News,* Jan. 7, 1944, pp. 26–27.
482   "an honorable discharge": *NYT,* Dec. 5, 1943, pp. 1, 32.
482   "The war has finally . . .": Raymond Clapper, *Watching the World* (1944), p. 131.
483   "away in lavender": Lash, *Eleanor and Franklin,* p. 696.
483   "the future . . .": *U.S. News,* Jan. 14, 1943, p. 24.

CHAPTER NINETEEN: "I Want to Sleep and Sleep"

484   "If ever there was a time . . .": text of speech, *NYT,* Jan. 12, 1944, p. 12.
485   ". . . the fatal and false . . .": James MacGregor Burns, *Roosevelt: The Soldier of Freedom* (1970), p. 426.
486   ER who listened: *MD,* Jan. 11, 1944.
486   "It has been . . . relief not for the needy . . .": *NYT,* Feb. 23, 1944, p. 14.
486   "in the best . . ."; "hell broke . . .": William D. Hassett, *Off the Record with F.D.R.* (1958), p. 235.
486   "a calculated and deliberate . . .": *NYT,* Feb. 24, 1944, p. 12.
487   "practically every senator . . .": Henry A. Wallace, *The Price of Vision* (1973), p. 302.
487   "Alben must be . . .": Hassett, *Off the Record,* p. 235.
487   Barkley was tired: Burns, *Soldier of Freedom,* p. 426.
487   "quite calm . . ."; "but I'm not sure . . .": Joseph P. Lash, *A World of Love* (1984), pp. 112–13.
487   call from Jimmy Byrnes: James F. Byrnes, *Speaking Frankly* (1947), pp. 211–12.

487   "Still no word . . .": Hassett, *Off the Record,* p. 237.
487   The Treasury was able: Harold G. Vatter, *The U.S. Economy in World War II* (1985), pp. 104–5.
488   "a revolution in American . . .": David Brinkley, *Washington Goes to War* (1988), p. 218.
488   "supposed he was lying . . .": Hassett, *Off the Record,* p. 238.
488   "the Big Week": Martin Cardin, *Flying Forts* (1968), p. 444; interview with William Emerson.
488   "you would be shot down . . .": Michael Sherry, *The Rise of American Air Power* (1987), p. 157.
488   "This was a turning point . . .": Winston S. Churchill, *The Second World War,* vol. V, *Closing the Ring* (1951), p. 462.
489   "With no preliminary . . .": John R. Boettiger, Jr., *A Love in Shadow* (1978), p. 253.
489   "Father could relax . . .": interview with Elliott Roosevelt.
489   "She could tell . . .": interview with John Boettiger, Jr.
489   "She walked in . . .": Justine Polier, *OH,* FDRL.
489   "but not until . . .": Joseph P. Lash, *Eleanor and Franklin* (1971), p. 699.
489   "Louise would arrange . . .": Bernard Asbell, *Mother and Daughter* (1988), p. 99.
489   "it would be wonderful . . .": Lash, *Eleanor and Franklin,* p. 699.
490   "I was away last week . . .": ER to MLH, Feb. 18, 1944, box 87, ER Papers, FDRL.
490   "I know that you . . .": ibid.
490   "I hope you understand . . .": Ann Rochon to ER, n.d., box 1731, ER Papers, FDRL.
490   "young life in the White House . . .": *MD,* March 4, 1944.
490   "brought to all her contacts . . .": *TIR,* p. 319.
490   "like Topsy . . .": Asbell, *Mother and Daughter,* pp. 175–76.
490   "It was immaterial . . .": ibid., p. 176.
491   "It was an ideal . . .": interview with John Boettiger, Jr.
491   fled from the library: *The Woman,* May 1949, pp. 8, 9.
491   "She is really in finer . . .": John Boettiger to Jimmy Roosevelt, Aug. 15, 1944, box 26, Boettiger Papers, FDRL.
491   "Anna's day at the White House . . .": *Time,* May 29, 1944, p. 18.
491   "He would grin . . .": Grace Tully, *F.D.R., My Boss* (1949), p. 274.
492   ". . . tired and worn": *NYT,* March 26, 1944, p. 35.
492   "President not looking so well . . .": Hassett, *Off the Record,* p. 239.
492   "I don't think mother . . .": Asbell, *Mother and Daughter,* p. 177.
492   "interested in physiology . . .": ibid.
492   "she still believed . . .": interview with John Boettiger, Jr.
492   "I think the constant tension . . .": Lash, *World of Love,* p. 115.
492   "The President . . .": *MD,* April 6, 1944.
493   "He is cheerful in spirit . . .": Hassett, *Off the Record,* p. 240.
493   "the blood was not pumping . . .": Asbell, *Mother and Daughter,* p. 177.
493   comparing notes with Grace: Tully, *F.D.R.,* p. 274.
493   "I didn't think . . .": Asbell, *Mother and Daughter,* p. 177.
493   "I designed that one": Jim Bishop, *FDR's Last Year* (1974), p. 3.
494   "It was a warm day . . .": interview with Howard Bruenn.
494   "I suspected something . . .": ibid.
494   "It was worse . . .": ibid.
494   examination revealed: *Annals of Internal Medicine,* April 1970, pp. 580–81; hereafter cited as Bruenn, "Clinical Notes."
495   "Thanks, Doc": Bishop, *Last Year,* p. 6.
495   "Not only were . . .": *NYT,* March 29, 1944, p. 1.
495   little model: *NYT,* March 31, 1944, p. 38.
495   "McIntire was appalled . . .": interview with Howard Bruenn.
496   "I was only a lieutenant commander . . .": ibid.
496   "Digitalis was a miracle drug . . .": ibid.
496   Goldsmith suggests: *Surgery, Gynecology & Obstetrics,* Dec. 1975, pp. 899–903.
496   "He suspects the doctors . . .": Lash, *World of Love,* p. 118.
497   "When we got through . . .": *NYT,* April 5, 1944, p. 1.
497   Hobcaw: Bernard M. Baruch, *Baruch: The Public Years* (1960), pp. 335–37.

497 "The Secret Service...": A. Merriman Smith, *Thank You, Mr. President* (1946), p. 139.

497 "I want to sleep and sleep...": Bishop, *Last Year,* p. 25.

498 Montgomery Ward strike: *NYT,* April 13, 1944, p. 1.

498 Stimson argued: Stimson Diary, May 4, 1944, Yale University.

498 Biddle disagreed: Francis Biddle, *In Brief Authority* (1962), pp. 315–16.

498 Sewell Avery refused: *NYT,* April 27, 1944, pp. 1, 14; Aaron Levenstein, *Labor Today and Tomorrow* (1945), pp. 1, 2.

498 "There is no warrant...": "Comments on the Montgomery Ward Case," May 11, 1944, box 3, OF 4451, FDRL.

498 "It was the manner...": ibid.

498 "great howl": Stimson Diary, May 4, 1944, Yale University.

498 "Beloved of mine...": John Boettiger to AB, April 10, 1944, box 6, Boettiger Papers, FDRL.

499 "Anna has arranged...": ER to FDR, April 21, 1944, box 16, Roosevelt Family Papers Donated by the Children, FDRL.

499 "I came home...": *TIR,* p. 328.

499 "in better condition...": *NYT,* April 13, 1944, p. 8.

499 Winthrop Rutherfurd: obituary, *Aiken Standard,* March 24, 1944, p. 4; *NYT,* May 21, 1944, p. 17.

499 Baruch vividly remembered: Bernard Asbell, *The FDR Memoirs* (1973), p. 412.

500 acute abdominal pain: Bruenn, "Clinical Notes," p. 548.

500 "seemed in such good spirits...": Smith, *Thank You,* pp. 140–41.

500 "lest his recovery...": ibid., p. 141.

500 "You will come home...": ER to FDR, April 29, 1944, box 16, Roosevelt Family Papers Donated by the Children, FDRL.

501 "Nothing I could give...": ER to AB, May 1, 1944, box 57, Halsted Papers, FDRL.

501 "I had a really grand time...": FDR to HH, May 18, 1944, HH Papers, FDRL.

501 Stephen killed: *NYT,* Feb. 13, 1944, p. 1.

501 "It is grand to get..."; "The main things...": FDR to HH, May 18, 1944, HH Papers, FDRL.

501 "We can all be glad...": *NYT,* May 8, 1944, p. 18.

502 "good news...": ibid.

502 "brown as a berry...": Hassett, *Off the Record,* p. 241.

502 "Anna was afraid...": interview with Howard Bruenn.

502 "You would find...": Ickes to MLH, May 23, 1944, Harold Ickes Papers, Library of Congress, Washington, D.C.

502 "With people like Martha...": interview with John Boettiger, Jr.

502 "what she wanted...": ibid.

502 "I am always waiting...": *MD,* April 18, 1944.

503 "Anna is the only one...": Lash, *Eleanor and Franklin,* p. 700.

503 "Anna tried to be...": interview with Howard Bruenn.

503 "How can anyone...": Margery Truiz to FDR, Feb. 16, 1944, with excerpts from newspaper article, OF 93, FDRL.

503 "I know, of course...": "Outraged" to ER, Feb. 28, 1944.

503 "Women should be represented...": *NYT,* March 31, 1944, p. 38.

503 "She pushed him terrifically...": Asbell, *Mother and Daughter,* p. 176.

504 "Mother can't you see...": Tully, *F.D.R.,* p. 110.

504 "She couldn't see...": Asbell, *Mother and Daughter,* p. 177.

504 "I pray I don't...": AB to John Boettiger, April 7, 1944, box 6, Boettiger Papers, FDRL.

CHAPTER TWENTY: "Suspended in Space"

505 "suspended in space...": ER to FDR, May 2, 1944, box 16, Roosevelt Family Papers Donated by the Children, FDRL.

505 "every movement...": Grace Tully, *F.D.R., My Boss* (1949), p. 265.

505 900 warships: Max Hastings, *Overlord: D-Day and the Battle for Normandy* (1984), p. 80.

506 "when he is buried...": Harry C. Butcher, *My Three Years with Eisenhower* (1946), p. 275.

506 "The nearer H hour..."; "as the battlefields...": Gordon Harrison, *Cross-Channel Attack* (1989), p. 274.

506 order to "go": ibid., p. 284.

506 "there was a question...": interview with William Emerson.

506 "the dangers and disasters..": Averell Harriman and Elie Abel, *Special Envoy to Churchill and Stalin, 1941–1946* (1975), p. 311.

506 "Our friendship...": *Churchill & Roosevelt: The Complete Correspondence* (1984), vol. III, p. 162.

506 "How I wish...": ibid., p. 186.

507 "I feel as though...": ER to Doris Fleeson, May 15, 1944, ER Microfilm Collection, FDRL.

507 "It is too bad...": *MD,* Jan. 6, 1944.

507 "Soon the invasion...": ER to Esther Lape, June 3, 1944, Lape Papers, FDRL.

507 "I only know...": Joseph P. Lash, *A World of Love: Eleanor Roosevelt and Her Friends, 1943–1962* (1984), p. 124.

507 "We all started...": AH interview, Graff Papers, FDRL.

507 Eisenhower met: Stephen E. Ambrose, *The Supreme Commander: The War Years of General Dwight D. Eisenhower* (1970) p. 415.

507 "an agony...": Hastings Ismay, *The Memoirs of General Lord Ismay* (1960), p. 357.

507 "because he'd learned...": ER interview, Graff Papers, FDRL.

508 "the question...": Harriman and Abel, *Special Envoy,* p. 274.

508 "Do you realize...": Martin Gilbert, *Winston S. Churchill,* vol. VII, *Road to Victory, 1941–1945* (1986), p. 794.

508 "The first of the Axis...": Franklin D. Roosevelt, *Public Papers and Addresses of Franklin D. Roosevelt, 1944,* (1950), p. 147.

508 "How magnificently...": *Churchill & Roosevelt Correspondence,* vol. III, p. 163.

508 "from a vague...": Ernie Pyle, *Brave Men* (1944), p. 356.

508 "I don't know why...": ibid., pp. 364–65.

509 "To be nearly sixty...": Lash, *World of Love,* p. 124.

509 "He sat up in bed...": ER interview, Graff Papers, FDRL.

509 "Soldiers, sailors and airmen...": Robert Meyer, Jr., *The Stars and Stripes* (1960), p. 234.

509 HH thought about production problems: Robert E. Sherwood, *Roosevelt and Hopkins,* (1948), p. 807.

509 "...the most exciting moment...": Stephen E. Ambrose, *D-Day* (1994), p. 494.

509 "Outwardly they appeared...": Winston M. Estes, *Homefront* (1976), p. 257.

509 "The impulse to pray...": Ambrose, *D-Day,* p. 495.

510 "We have come...": quoted in ibid., p. 494.

510 "The President was happy...": I. F. Stone, *The War Years, 1939–1945* (1988), p. 236.

510 "I have just sat in...": letter from "The B." to "Mom," June 6, 1944, Reminiscences by Contemporaries, FDRL.

510 "You just don't land...": Franklin D. Roosevelt, *Public Papers and Addresses, 1944,* p. 159.

510 "a far cry...": Samuel I. Rosenman, *Working with Roosevelt* (1952), p. 433.

510 "our sons, pride...": press release, June 6, 1944, attached to "The B." to "Mom," June 6, 1944, Reminiscences by Contemporaries, FDRL.

510 "All emotion...": *MD,* June 6, 1944.

511 "Each hedgerow..."; "I cannot say enough...": Harrison, *Cross-Channel Attack,* p. 284.

511 "I cannot say...": quoted in Annette Tapert, ed., *Lines of Battle: Letters from American Servicemen, 1941–1945* (1987), pp. 160–61.

511 "Nobody doubted now...": Henry H. Arnold, quoted in "The War Reports of General of the Army George Marshall, General of the Army H. H. Arnold, Fleet Admiral Ernest J. King." N.Y.: J.B. Lippincott Co. (1947), p. 67.

511 "As far as you could...": Pyle, *Brave Men,* p. 358.

511 "There were trucks..." ... "They stood staring...": ibid., pp. 367–69.

512 "Much kidding...": William D. Hassett, *Off the Record with F.D.R.* (1958), p. 252.

512 "I've unpacked a little...": Lash, *World of Love,* p. 118.

512 "in the pink...": Hassett, *Off the Record,* p. 254.

512 GI Bill of Rights: Theodore Mosch, *The GI Bill* (1975), p. 40.

512 "There is one great fear . . .": *MD,* June 25, 1944.
513 "the best . . . the most mature . . .": Harold G. Vatter, *The U.S. Economy in World War II* (1985), pp. 137–38.
513 We were men . . .": Joseph C. Goulden, *The Best Years* (1976), p. 67.
513 "Almost everything important . . .": quoted in Mark Jonathan Harris, Franklin D. Mitchell, and Steven J. Schechter, *The Homefront* (1984), p. 221.
513 "I doubt if . . .": quoted in ibid., p. 221.
513 "gives emphatic notice . . .": James MacGregor Burns, *Roosevelt: The Soldier of Freedom* (1970), p. 509.
513 Edward Kowalick: memo, newspaper clippings, April 1–23, 1944, Harry Alpert to Philleo Nash, PSF 4245g, FDRL.
514 "deplorable incident": Wilbur La Roe, Jr., to ER, May 27, 1944, attached to Sec. to ER to John McCloy, June 1, 1944, box 919, ER Papers, FDRL.
514 "I've never had more . . .": *NYT,* Feb. 2, 1943, p. 17.
514 "Christmas tree regiment": John Armor and Peter Wright, *Manzanar* (1988), p. 149.
514 seven major campaigns: ibid., p. 148.
514 "the continued retention . . .": Kai Bird, *The Chairman, John McCloy* (1992), p. 171.
514 "The more I think . . .": quoted in Allan R. Bosworth, *America's Concentration Camps* (1967), p. 209.
515 "to slow down . . .": Bird, *Chairman,* p. 211.
515 "to develop positive . . .": Arthur D. Morse, *While Six Million Died* (1983), p. 314.
515 "finally there was . . .": interview with John Pehle.
515 "the wholesale . . .": Morse, *Six Million Died,* p. 337.
516 "The War Department . . .": ibid., p. 358.
516 "in the resultant . . .": Bird, *Chairman,* p. 216.
516 "if the elaborate murder . . .": Morse, *Six Million Died,* pp. 359–60.
516 "beyond the maximum range . . .": Bird, *Chairman,* p. 221.
516 "It was the saddest . . .": interview with Jan Karski.
516 "I cannot live out . . .": Jim Bishop, *FDR's Last Year* (1974), p. 8.
517 "in the small park . . ."; "I told Margaret . . .": ibid., p. 70.
517 "it wasn't a complaint . . .": *The Woman,* May 1949, p. 10
517 "the legacy . . .": interview with John Boettiger, Jr.
517 "What would you think . . .": interview with James Roosevelt.
517 "It was almost . . .": interview with Trude Lash.
517 "It was a terrible decision . . .": AH, *OH,* Columbia University.
518 "light-hearted and gay . . .": AB typescript on Lucy and FDR, box 84, Halsted Papers, FDRL; Hereafter cited as AB on Lucy.
518 "While they were my parents . . .": AH, *OH,* Columbia University.
518 "Standards were different . . .": interview with Robert Donovan.
518 Anna told . . .: AH, *OH,* Columbia University.
519 "He stepped . . .": Hassett, *Off the Record,* p. 259.
519 "all smiles . . .": Charles de Gaulle, *The Complete War Memoirs* (1964), p. 571.
519 America's "friend": Franklin D. Roosevelt, *Public Papers and Addresses, 1944,* pp. 194–96.
519 "innate dignity . . .": AB on Lucy, box 84, Halsted Papers, FDRL.
519 "feeling happy"; "I liked her . . .": ibid.
520 "Anna is a dear fine . . .": Bernard Asbell, *Mother and Daughter* (1988), p. 188.
520 "You could sense . . .": interview with Alonzo Fields.
520 More than 130,000 Germans: Martin Gilbert, *The Second World War* (1989), p. 549.
520 "all the ridiculous things . . .": Asbell, *Mother and Daughter,* p. 188.
520 "The three of them . . .": interview with John Boettiger, Jr.
521 "buses, trucks . . .": Ulysses G. Lee, *The Employment of Negro Troops* (1966), p. 397.
521 separate buses: ibid., p. 322.
521 Camp Stewart: Jean Byers, "A Study of the Negro in Military Service," War Department Study, June 1947, p. 64.
521 "The only place . . .": ibid., p. 68.
521 Charles Rico: *PC,* Aug. 22, 1942, p. 1.
522 Henry Williams: Truman Gibson to Secretary of War, Nov. 17, 1942, Record Group 107, National Archives, Washington, D.C.
522 Norma Greene: ibid.

522   "[Negroes] have been . . .": Truman Gilson to Assistant Secretary of War, May 14, 1943, Record Group 107, National Archives, Washington, D.C.

522   "Honey, I am so hurt . . .": Morale Report of 494th Port Battalion, June 1, 1943, Record Group 107, National Archives, Washington, D.C.

522   "These colored boys . . .": ER to John McCloy, Sept. 29, 1943, ER Microfilm Collection, FDRL.

522   "an important step . . .": *PC,* Sept. 9, 1944, p. 1.

522   "Extra! Extra! . . .": Lee, *Employment of Negro Troops,* p. 398.

522   "the essential principle . . .": *PC,* Sept. 2, 1944, p. 1.

522   "to hold the south . . .": Daniels to Hassett, Aug. 29, 1944, box 7, OF 93b, FDRL.

523   "This knowledge raised . . .": Lee, *Employment of Negro Troops,* p. 400.

523   "have I seen so much . . .": Hastie to McCloy, Sept. 5, 1944, Record Group 107, National Archives, Washington, D.C.

523   "Up to the present . . .": Forrestal to FDR, May 20, 1944, box 84, PSF, FDRL.

523   "swapped the waiter's apron . . .": *Common Ground,* Winter 1947, p. 63.

523   "to expand the use . . .": Forrestal to FDR, May 20, 1944, box 84, PSF, FDRL.

523   "successfully absorbed . . .": Lee Nichols, *Breakthrough on the Color Front* (1954), p. 60.

523   "This single stunning . . .": Robert L. Allen, *The Port Chicago Mutiny* (1989), p. 64.

524   "an outstanding . . .": *Commonweal,* Sept. 21, 1945, pp. 546–48.

524   "This improvement . . .": ibid., p. 546.

524   "as little right . . .": *U.S. News,* July 21, 1944, p. 27.

524   "All that is within . . .": ibid.

525   "The President doesn't . . .": *NYT,* July 12, 1944, p. 12.

525   "the good of the country": Lash, *World of Love,* p. 129.

525   "Dewey seems . . .": James Roosevelt and Sidney Schalett, *Affectionately, F.D.R.* (1959), p. 353.

525   "I am very conscious . . .": Lash, *World of Love,* p. 130.

525   "it was as though . . .": David McCullough, *Truman* (1992), p. 299.

525   "I am just not going . . .": Rosenman, *Working with Roosevelt,* p. 439.

525   "He just doesn't . . .": Sherwood, *Roosevelt and Hopkins,* p. 820.

525   "We ought to have . . .": Rosenman, *Working with Roosevelt,* p. 463.

526   "The meeting obviously . . .": ibid., p. 464.

526   "You tell the President . . .": ibid., p. 466.

526   "just as you . . .": ibid., p. 468.

526   "He said I was . . .": John Morton Blum, *The Price of Vision: The Diary of Henry A. Wallace, 1942–1946* (1993), p. 362.

526   "He drew me . . .": ibid., p. 367.

526   "You are the best . . .": quoted in McCullough, *Truman,* p. 303.

526   would cost the ticket: Rosenman, *Working with Roosevelt,* pp. 444–45.

527   "he had never . . .": Edward J. Flynn, *You're the Boss* (1962), p. 181.

527   "Bob, I think you . . .": Ted Morgan, *FDR: A Biography* (1985), p. 728.

527   "Bob, I think Truman . . .": McCullough, *Truman,* p. 301.

527   "We excused ourselves . . .": Rosenman, *Working with Roosevelt,* p. 449.

527   "Grace, the President . . ."; "The reason for the switch . . .": Tully, *F.D.R.,* p. 276.

528   "The trip out . . .": Tommy to Esther Lape, July 24, 1944, box 6, Esther Lape Papers, FDRL.

528   "The slow speed . . .": FDR to ER, July 21, 1944, box 12, Roosevelt Family Papers Donated by the Children, FDRL.

528   "I think it would be fun . . .": James Roosevelt and Schalett, *Affectionately, F.D.R.,* p. 348.

528   "Mrs. R was impatient . . ": Tommy to Esther Lape, July 24, 1944, box 6, Esther Lape Papers, FDRL.

528   "I don't know that . . .": Lash, *World of Love,* p. 129.

529   "I don't know why . . .": Tommy to Esther Lape, July 24, 1944, box 6, Esther Lape Papers, FDRL.

529   "suddenly white . . ." . . . "So for perhaps . . .": James Roosevelt and Schalett, *Affectionately, F.D.R.,* pp. 351–52.

529   "Help me up . . .": James Roosevelt, *My Parents: A Differing View* (1976), p. 279.

529   "What is the job . . .": Franklin D. Roosevelt, *Public Papers and Addresses, 1944,* p. 204.

530 "There were several negatives...": interview with Dick Strobel; see also Rosenman, *Working with Roosevelt,* p. 453.
530 "Hey, you better...": interview with Dick Strobel.
530 "I made the judgment...": ibid.
530 "all hell broke loose...": ibid.
530 "It's not my fault...": ibid.
530 "sick about the whole business...": Lash, *World of Love,* p. 132.
530 "had hoped until the last...": ER to Esther Lape, July 29, 1944, box 5, Esther Lape Papers, FDRL.
530 "From all I hear...": ibid.
530 "Off in a few minutes": FDR to ER, July 21, 1944, box 12, Roosevelt Family Papers Donated by the Children, FDRL.
531 "Yesterday a.m....": ibid.
531 noticeably absent: Rosenman, *Working with Roosevelt,* p. 456.
531 leather flying: William Manchester, *American Caesar* (1978), p. 365.
531 "The B-29 was a great...": interview with William Emerson.
532 "I dare to say...": Manchester, *American Caesar,* p. 369.
532 "In such a situation...": Burns, *Soldier of Freedom,* pp. 488–89.
532 "As soon as I...": D. Clayton James, *The Years of MacArthur,* vol. II (1975), p. 535.
532 "At one of the hospitals...": Rosenman, *Working with Roosevelt,* p. 458.
532 "With a cheering smile...": ibid.
532 one other occasion: interview with Anna Faith Jones.
533 "he was close to them": Rosenman, *Working with Roosevelt,* p. 459.

CHAPTER TWENTY-ONE: "The Old Master Still Had It"

534 MLH at movies: *Yankee Magazine,* June 1977, p. 174.
534 "Missy was shocked...": Bernard Asbell, *The FDR Memoirs* (1973), p. 404.
534 collection of photos: interview with Jane Scarborough.
535 telegram to Missy's sister: ER to Ann Rochon, July 31, 1944, PPF 3737, FDRL.
535 "I am sure that for her...": *MD,* July 31, 1944.
535 "Regret to inform...": memo from Hassett and Early to FDR, July 31, 1944, PPF 3737, FDRL.
535 "I'm glad F...": Joseph P. Lash, *A World of Love: Eleanor Roosevelt and Her Friends, 1943–1962* (1984), p. 133.
535 "Memories of more than a score...": *NYT,* Aug. 1, 1944, p. 15.
535 "Missy's death...": ibid., p. 14.
535 "constituted the greatest...": T. H. Watkins, *Righteous Pilgrim* (1990), p. 807.
535 "What the devil...": Ralph Cropley to FDR, Aug. 1, 1944, PPF 3737, FDRL.
536 "I know how profoundly...": Herbert Swope to FDR, Aug. 1, 1944, PPF 3737, FDRL.
536 funeral mass at St. John's: *BEA,* Aug. 2, 1944, p. 4.
536 "She was a real...": interview with Jane Scarborough.
536 "There was an air...": interview with Barbara Dudley.
536 In her will: copy in PPF 3737, FDRL.
536 "It was in my brother's...": interview with Jane Scarborough.
537 "You and I lost...": Asbell, *FDR Memoirs,* p. 404.
537 speech in Bremerton: Samuel I. Rosenman, *Working with Roosevelt* (1952), pp. 461–62.
537 FDR collapsed in a chair: Bruenn, "Clinical Notes," p. 586; Elliott Roosevelt and James Brough, *A Rendezvous with Destiny: The Roosevelts of the White House* (1975), p. 378.
537 "only when black workers...": John Morton Blum, *V Was for Victory* (1976), p. 196.
537 Philadelphia transit strike: Louis Ruchames, *Race, Jobs and Politics: The FEPC* (1953), p. 105.
538 "customs bearing...": ibid.
538 "The exam was..."; I felt like a pioneer...": interview with William Barber.
538 "We don't want Negroes...": AP dispatch, Aug. 2, 1944, 3:24 p.m., box 8, OF 4245G, FDRL.
538 "Your buddies are in...": Ruchames, *Race, Jobs and Politics,* p. 109.
539 "You kiss the Negroes...": ibid., p. 117.
539 "There was one motorman...": *PM,* Aug. 2, 1944, p. 10.

539 nearly forty-five thousand: *BEA*, Aug. 1, 1944, p. 3.

539 "to take possession...": executive order, Aug. 3, 1944, quoted in *NYT*, Aug. 4, 1944, pp. 1, 8.

539 "on the basis of conditions...": *NYT*, Aug. 4, 1944, pp. 1, 18.

539 "In whatever degree...": *Philadelphia Inquirer*, Aug. 1, 1944, p. 12.

539 "The war cannot wait...": *NYT*, Aug. 6, 1944, p. 1.

540 protest in the South: News Items, Aug. 19, 1944, box 8, OF 4245G, FDRL.

540 "The first runs...": interview with William Barber.

540 "The impossible has...": *PC*, Aug. 19, 1942, p. 1.

540 By the end of the war: Harold G. Vatter, *The U.S. Economy in World War II* (1985), p. 127; Richard Polenberg, ed., *America at War* (1972), p. 107.

540 "These changes...": Vatter, *U.S. Economy*, p. 134.

540 Negroes in government: Robert H. Ziegler, *American Workers, American Unions, 1920–1985* (1986), p. 82.

540 "With more and better...": Jacqueline Jones, *Labor of Love, Labor of Sorrow* (1985), p. 254.

541 "brought hope and confidence...": Ruchames, *Race, Jobs and Politics*, p. 159.

541 "a decided nip...": William D. Hassett, *Off the Record with F.D.R.* (1958), p. 266.

541 "I am afraid before long...": *MD*, Aug. 24, 1944.

541 "Too many...": Hassett, *Off the Record*, p. 267.

541 "Mrs. Roosevelt never noticed...": Tommy to Esther Lape, July 24, 1944, box 6, Esther Lape Papers, FDRL.

541 never had a headache: Rex Tugwell, *OH*, FDRL.

541 "She feels...": Tommy to Esther Lape, box 6, Esther Lape Papers, FDRL.

541 "Pa complains...": ER to AB, Aug. 24, 1944, box 57, Halsted Papers, FDRL.

541 "whatever he had...": Lash, *World of Love*, p. 135.

541 "This is a great day...": Stimson Diary, Aug. 23, 1944, Yale University.

542 managed to see Lucy again: Jonathan Daniels, *Washington Quadrille* (1968), p. 289.

542 "...to wake in Highland": Hassett pages from original diary for Sept. 1, 1944, Hassett Papers, FDRL.

542 "You'd think the president...": interview with Grace Stang.

542 "I hope you will pardon...": *Churchill & Roosevelt: The Complete Correspondence*, (1984), vol. III, p. 305.

542 "Perfectly delighted...": ibid.

542 "he didn't believe...": Hassett, *Off the Record*, p. 269.

543 "I'm glad to see you...": *NYT*, Sept. 12, 1944, p. 56.

543 "was more like the reunion...": Hastings Ismay, *The Memoirs of General Lord Ismay* (1960), p. 372.

543 "There is something...": *MD*, Sept. 11, 1944.

543 "I assured him...": ibid.

543 "He talks picturesquely...": Lash, *World of Love*, p. 140.

543 "I think he likes me...": ER to Esther Lape, Sept. 22, 1944, box 5, Esther Lape Papers, FDRL.

543 "The ladies' duties...": Lash, *World of Love*, p. 137.

543 "except for the meals...": ibid.

543 "Optimism was...": Robert Coakley and Richard Leighton, *Global Logistics and Strategy, 1943–1945* (1968), p. 534.

544 "utterly opposed...": Stimson Diary, Sept. 6, 1944, Yale University.

544 "I had barely got...": John Morton Blum, *From the Morgenthau Diaries* (1967), vol. III, p. 369.

544 "I'm all for disarming...": Lord Moran, *Churchill—The Struggle for Survival, 1940–1965* (1960), p. 190.

544 "After all, the future...": Blum, *From the Morgenthau Diaries*, vol. III, p. 371.

544 "converting Germany into...": ibid., p. 372.

544 "We haven't had a talk...": ibid.

544 "the high spot...": ibid., p. 373.

544 "I never heard...": *TIR*, p. 334.

545 "whenever and wherever possible": James MacGregor Burns, *Roosevelt: The Soldier of Freedom* (1970), p. 519.

545 WC restless during film: Martin Gilbert, *Winston S. Churchill,* vol. VII, *Road to Victory, 1941–1945* (1986), p. 964.
545 "With all my heart . . .": Jim Bishop, *FDR's Last Year* (1974), p. 143.
545 FDR seemed depressed: ibid., p. 139.
545 "He seems to have . . .": Gilbert, *Churchill,* vol. VII, p. 969.
545 "did not even greet him": Winston S. Churchill, *The Second World War,* vol. VI, *Triumph and Tragedy* (1953), p. 142.
545 "You must know . . .": ibid.
545 ". . . no open breach . . .": Robert E. Sherwood, *Roosevelt and Hopkins* (1948), p. 814.
546 "She is a wonderful combination . . .": *Churchill & Roosevelt Correspondence,* vol. III, p. 332.
546 "My time slips away . . .": Lash, *World of Love,* p. 139.
546 bomb ready by August 1945: Gilbert, *Churchill,* vol. VII, p. 969.
546 "might perhaps . . .": ibid., p. 970.
546 "the utmost secrecy": ibid.
546 "The President under . . .": Hassett, *Off the Record,* p. 272.
547 "with his braces . . .": Rosenman, *Working with Roosevelt,* p. 474.
547 In the banquet hall: *Time,* Oct. 2, 1944, p. 21.
547 "Do you think Pa . . .": Rosenman, *Working with Roosevelt,* p. 478.
547 "Well, here we are . . .": Franklin D. Roosevelt, *Public Papers and Addresses of Franklin D. Roosevelt, 1944* (1950), p. 284.
548 "The whole purpose . . ."; "Now, imitation may be . . .": ibid., p. 285.
548 One teamster was so excited: A. Merriman Smith, *Thank you, Mr. President* (1946), p. 155.
548 "The Old Master . . .": *Time,* Oct. 2, 1944, p. 21.
548 "These Republican leaders . . .": Franklin D. Roosevelt, *Public Papers and Addresses, 1944,* p. 290.
548 "even the stoniest . . .": *Time,* Oct. 2, 1944, p. 22.
548 In closing: Franklin D. Roosevelt, *Public Papers and Addresses, 1944,* p. 291.
549 "There were tears . . .": Rosenman, *Working with Roosevelt,* p. 478.
549 "The 1944 campaign . . .": *Time,* Oct. 2, 1944, p. 22.
549 "Let's not be squeamish . . .": quoted in Jim Bishop, *FDR's Last Year* (1974), p. 157.
549 train reached Brooklyn: Hassett, *Off the Record,* p. 278.
549 Dr. McIntire pleaded: Ross McIntire, *White House Physician* (1946), p. 207.
549 He had rooted for the Dodgers: Hassett, *Off the Record,* p. 279.
550 complete change of clothes: *The Woman,* May 1949, p. 112.
550 first time FDR had seen it: Hassett, *Off the Record,* p. 279.
550 FDR at ER's apartment: *TIR,* p. 337.
550 "It was the only occasion . . .": Grace Tully, *F.D.R., My Boss* (1949), p. 282.
550 "a map of the world . . .": Franklin D. Roosevelt, *Public Papers and Addresses, 1944,* p. 344.
551 Tully wondered: Tully, *F.D.R.,* p. 282.
551 "Peace, like war . . .": Franklin D. Roosevelt, *Public Papers and Addresses, 1944,* p. 350.
551 "no trace . . .": Hassett, *Off the Record,* p. 282.
551 "Not for a long time . . .": *NYT,* Oct. 25, 1944, p. 23.
551 "Their enthusiasm for him . . .": ER interview, Graff Papers, FDRL.
552 "brisk as a bee . . .": Hassett, *Off the Record,* p. 287.
552 "the news from the Pacific . . .": *MD,* Oct. 15, 1944.
552 "There were extremely light . . .": Frank Freidel, *Franklin D. Roosevelt: A Rendezvous with Destiny* (1990), p. 563.
552 "painful memories": Sherwood, *Roosevelt and Hopkins,* p. 829.
552 "I am sure . . . ": ibid., pp. 829–30.
552 "swirled around among . . .": Smith, *Thank You,* p. 159.
552 election results: Harold Gosnell, *Champion Campaigner* (1952), pp. 211–12.
553 "It looks like . . .": Franklin D. Roosevelt, *Public Papers and Addresses, 1944,* p. 414.
553 "sought sanctuary . . .": Hassett, *Off the Record,* p. 294.
553 "the graceless Dewey"; ". . . son of a bitch": ibid.
553 "Word has just come . . .": John Roosevelt to FDR, Nov. 8, 1944, box 20, Roosevelt Family Papers Donated by the Children, FDRL.

CHAPTER TWENTY-TWO: "So Darned Busy"

554 Millions of people: Joseph P. Lash, *A World of Love: Eleanor Roosevelt and Her Friends, 1943–1962* (1984), p. 146.
554 "the tremendously increased...": ibid., p. 149.
554 "Maybe I'd do...": ibid., p. 150.
554 "If I did I'd lose...": ibid.
555 "inadequate"... "great weariness...": ibid.
555 one-third of civilian labor force: Richard Polenberg, ed., *America at War* (1972), p. 131.
555 79 percent said yes: *LHJ*, June 1944, p. 23.
555 "At the end...": Ruth Milkman, *The Dynamics of Gender at Work* (1987), p. 103.
555 "There are two things...": *War Department Educational Manual* (1944), p. 1, Record, Group 56, National Archives, Washington, D.C.
556 "Where I come from...": ibid., p. 23.
556 "Women ought to be delighted...": Frieda Miller, "Women's Conference on War and Postwar Adjustments of Women Workers," Dec. 1–5, 1944, Record Group 86, National Archives, Washington, D.C.
556 "it's the only lasting...": George Q. Flynn, *The Mess in Washington* (1979), p. 182.
556 "My position is to go...": *LHJ*, June 1944, p. 22.
556 "Am I planning...": ibid., p. 23.
556 "I really believe...": *Women's Home Companion*, July 1944, p. 24.
556 "found herself an authoress...": *MD*, Oct. 20, 1944.
557 "gladly relinquish...": *NYT*, April 25, 1944, p. 20.
557 "a good proportion": *NYT*, April 24, 1944, p. 15.
557 "To give anyone who wants...": *NYT*, April 25, 1944.
557 "Women are fully as capable...": *NYT*, Oct. 12, 1944, p. 42.
557 "industry must not...": *NYT*, Dec. 10, 1944, p. 42.
557 layoff rate 75 percent higher: Flynn, *Mess in Washington*, p. 181.
557 "Now that War...": Milkman, *The Dynamics of Gender at Work*, p. 141.
557 Brewster Aeronautical: Walter Reuther to ER, July 11, 1944, ER Microfilm Collection, FDRL; *NYT*, May 21, 1944, p. 35.
558 "whereby every worker...": *MD*, Sept. 20, 1944.
558 "for dangerous leakages...": Bruce Catton, *The War Lords of Washington* (1969), p. 231.
558 "Many people seem...": Byron Fairchild and Jonathan Grossman, *The Army and Industrial Manpower* (1959), p. 80.
558 "It's tough to see...": Catton, *War Lords*, pp. 267–68.
558 "... Insufficient production...": ibid., p. 268.
559 "one of the most...": Donald M. Nelson, *Arsenal of Democracy* (1946), p. 409.
559 "neither facts nor logic...": Catton, *War Lords*, p. 232.
559 "was motivated by...": ibid., p. 253.
559 "You know what they're doing...": ibid, p. 290.
560 "the war within a war": Nelson, *Arsenal of Democracy*, p. 43.
560 Nelson on mission to China: ibid., pp. 412–13.
560 "I don't have to go": Lash, *World of Love*, p. 151.
560 "You and Joe...": ibid., p. 147.
560 "Mrs. Roosevelt's feelings...": ibid., pp. 154–55.
560 "But the weighing...": ibid.
561 "A new LL crisis...": AB to John Boettiger, Nov. 24, 1944, box 6, Boettiger Papers, FDRL.
561 "I am very depressed...": Lash, *World of Love*, p. 157.
561 At Warm Springs: Theo Lippman, Jr., *The Squire of Warm Springs* (1977), pp. 15–17.
561 "a little house...": ibid., p. 199.
561 Lucy in guest cottage: Lippman, Jr., *Squire*, p. 15.
562 "You know...": Bernard Asbell, *The FDR Memoirs* (1973), p. 413.
562 "... Mother was not capable...": ibid.
562 "I realize very well...": ER to FDR, Dec. 4, 1944, box 16, Roosevelt Family Papers Donated by the Children, FDRL.
562 "The reason I feel...": ibid.

563 "Now if Clayton . . .": ER to FDR, Dec 5, 1944, box 16, Roosevelt Family Papers Donated by the Children, FDRL.

563 "She insisted . . .": interview with Howard Bruenn.

563 ". . . any real pressure on Winston? . . .": ER to FDR, Dec. 6, 1944, box 16, Roosevelt Family Papers Donated by the Children, FDRL.

563 FDR let Stimson know: Stimson Diary, Dec. 12, 1944, Yale University; Robert E. Sherwood, *Roosevelt and Hopkins* (1948), p. 835.

563 "Of course I want you . . .": FDR to Ickes, Dec. 9, 1944, box 75, PSF, FDRL.

564 "Your letter makes me . . .": Ickes to FDR, Dec. 13, 1944, box 75, PSF, FDRL.

564 visibly pleased: interview with Howard Bruenn.

564 Her aunt Tissie: ER to FDR, Dec. 18, 1944, box 16, Roosevelt Family Papers Donated by the Children, FDRL.

564 "sounds as though . . .": *MD,* Dec. 19, 1944.

564 December 16: Martin Gilbert, *The Second World War* (1989), p. 618.

564 "hunched in his chair . . .": William L. Shirer, *The Rise and Fall of the Third Reich* (1960), p. 1091.

565 "In great stress . . .": Forrest C. Pogue, *George C. Marshall: Organizer of Victory, 1943–1945* (1973), p. 486.

565 "He has been extremely . . .": Stimson Diary, Dec. 31, 1944, Yale University.

565 "I cannot help thinking . . .": *MD,* Dec. 20, 1944.

565 "an amazing performance": Eric Larrabee, *Commander in Chief* (1987), p. 488.

565 casualties: Shirer, *Rise and Fall,* pp. 1095–96.

565 "without regard to color . . .": Ulysses G. Lee, *The Employment of Negro Troops* (1966), p. 689.

566 four thousand volunteered: ibid., p. 693.

566 "We've been giving . . .": Jean Byers, "A Study of the Negro in Military Service," War Department Study, June 1947, p. 165.

566 "It is hard . . .": ibid., p. 89.

566 "My brother is now . . .": Mrs. Lewis to FDR, March 15, 1944, box 6, OF 93, FDRL.

566 "It is hard to decide . . .": *NR,* March 13, 1944, p. 342.

566 "Negro is too dumb to fight": *PC,* March 18, 1944, p. 1.

566 "to master . . ."; "It so happens . . .": Stimson to Congressman Fish, Feb. 19, 1944, *CR,* p. 2007.

567 In the 1940s: Byers, "Negro in Military Service," pp. 16–19.

567 "The consensus . . .": Roy Wilkins to FDR, March 9, 1944, box 6, OF 93, FDRL.

567 "He considers it . . .": *Crisis,* Sept. 1944, p. 290.

567 First volunteers: Byers, "Negro in Military Service," p. 165.

567 "They were used . . .": ibid., p. 167.

567 "When I heard about it . . .": ibid., p. 174.

567 "You might think . . .": ibid., p. 175.

568 "They are aggressive . . .": ibid., p. 170.

568 "I am mighty proud . . .": ibid.

568 "pretty, quiet and hard . . .": Lash, *World of Love,* p. 161.

568 "Next year . . .": Elliott Roosevelt and James Brough, *A Rendezvous with Destiny: The Roosevelts in the White House* (1975), p. 391.

568 "Father spoke . . .": Elliott Roosevelt and James Brough, *An Untold Story: The Roosevelts of Hyde Park* (1973), p. 307.

568 "the most extraordinarily . . .": interview with Elliott Roosevelt.

569 "I was delighted . . ."; "I hope . . .": Elliott Roosevelt and Brough, *Untold Story,* p. 308.

CHAPTER TWENTY-THREE: "It Is Good to Be Home"

570 "President in gleeful . . .": William D. Hassett, *Off the Record with F.D.R.* (1958), p. 309.

570 "very well": Smith conference notes, Jan. 1, 1945, Harold Smith Papers, FDRL.

570 "He had the pallor . . .": quoted in *Collier's,* Sept. 21, 1946, pp. 102–3.

570 "from looking pretty well . . .": Perkins, *OH,* Columbia University.

571 story of two senators: interview with Eliot Janeway.

571 "realizing full well . . .": *TIR,* p. 339; see also ER interview, Graff Papers, FDRL.

571   "bulged at the corners . . .": *TIR,* p. 339.
571   Jimmy later recalled: interview with James Roosevelt.
572   "Housekeeper Rejects . . .": *NYT,* Jan. 20, 1945, p. 1.
572   "We aren't going to have . . .": ibid.
572   joked with AB and Grace: Grace Tully, *F.D.R., My Boss* (1949), p. 115.
572   "plain food . . .": ibid.
572   "Who is there here . . .": Samuel I. Rosenman, *Working with Roosevelt* (1952), p. 516.
572   "Dog catchers have . . .": Michael F. Reilly, *Reilly of the White House* (1947), p. 516.
572   "The day was bitterly cold . . .": Katherine Marshall, *Together* (1946), p. 232.
572   "a test of courage . . .": Franklin D. Roosevelt, *Public Papers and Addresses of Franklin D. Roosevelt, 1945* (1950), p. 523.
572   two thousand guests, largest luncheon: Bess Furman, *Washington By-Line* (1949), p. 312; *NYT,* Jan. 21, 1945, p. 3.
572   "He was thoroughly chilled . . .": James Roosevelt and Sidney Schalett, *Affectionately, F.D.R.* (1959), p. 355.
573   "Oh, Mrs. Perkins . . .": Perkins, *OH,* Columbia University.
573   chickens Mrs. Nesbitt had bought: Victoria Henrietta Nesbitt, *White House Diary* (1948), p. 300.
573   "Mrs. Roosevelt, I wish to ask . . .": Katherine Marshall, *Together,* p. 232.
573   "would finally be going . . .": Lillian Rogers Parks, *The Roosevelts: A Family in Turmoil* (1981), p. 261.
573   "If you go . . .": *TIR,* p. 339.
573   ". . . Anna can do things . . .": Perkins, *OH,* Columbia University.
574   "I wanted desperately . . .": Bernard Asbell, *Mother and Daughter* (1988), pp. 181–82.
574   "I am tired and very depressed . . .": Joseph P. Lash, *A World of Love: Eleanor Roosevelt and Her Friends, 1943–1962* (1984), p. 164.
574   "Over there . . .": Asbell, *Mother and Daughter,* p. 187.
574   "Ocean voyage is . . .": AB to John Boettiger, Jan. 27, 1945, box 6, Boettiger Papers, FDRL.
574   "Oh darling . . .": ibid.
574   "a lot of little gadgets": AB to John Boettiger, Jan. 30, 1945, box 6, Boettiger Papers, FDRL.
574   five cakes: ibid.
575   brass ashtray: *Foreign Relations of the United States: The Conferences at Malta and Yalta, 1945* (1955).
575   "Anna made the dinner . . .": James F. Byrnes, *Speaking Frankly* (1947), p. 22.
575   "Our birthday dinner . . .": AB to John Boettiger, Jan. 31, 1945, box 6, Boettiger Papers, FDRL.
575   radio silence: AB notes on Yalta, Feb. 1, 1945, box 84, Halsted Papers, FDRL.
575   "Of course Jones . . .": Lash, *World of Love,* p. 165.
575   "a very sad situation . . .": AB to John Boettiger, Feb. 6, 1945, box 6, Boettiger Papers, FDRL.
575   WC running a temperature: Lord Moran, *Churchill—The Struggle for Survival, 1940–1965* (1966), p. 232.
575   "like a poor hot pink . . .": Martin Gilbert, *Winston S. Churchill,* vol. VII, *Road to Victory* (1986), p. 1163.
576   "in the doldrums": Moran, *Churchill,* p. 233.
576   "It is not the flesh . . .": ibid., p. 232.
576   "sharing his secret . . ."; "someone in whom . . .": ibid., p. 174.
576   "He was so weak . . .": Edward Stettinius, *Roosevelt and the Russians* (1949), p. 57.
576   "the terrible change in him": Sarah Churchill, *A Thread in the Tapestry* (1967), p. 76.
576   "my friend has arrived . . .": Gilbert, *Churchill,* vol. VII, p. 1167.
576   "bright charm . . .": Sarah Churchill, *Thread in Tapestry,* p. 76.
576   "He must have noticed . . .": Moran, *Churchill.* p. 234.
576   "Harry demanded a drink . . .": AB notes on Yalta, Feb. 2, 1945, box 84, Halsted Papers, FDRL.
577   "as in her old age . . .": Moran, *Churchill,* p. 234.
577   "so that he could sleep . . .": AB notes on Yalta, Feb. 3, 1945, box 84, Halsted Papers, FDRL.
577   "tough old bird . . .": ibid.

577 Relaxed and fortified: Sarah Churchill, *Thread in Tapestry*, p. 78.
577 Lividia Palace: Stettinius, *Roosevelt and the Russians*, pp. 81–82.
577 "a block and a half away": AB notes on Yalta, Feb. 3, 1945, box 84, Halsted Papers, FDRL.
577 Russian generals talked from maps: Stettinius, *Roosevelt and the Russians*, p. 239.
578 "This is the first time . . .": ibid., p. 240.
578 "sitting on tacks . . .": AB notes on Yalta, Feb. 4, 1945, box 84, Halsted Papers, FDRL.
578 "Fire was shooting . . .": ibid.
578 "Stalin made it . . .": Charles Bohlen, minutes, Tripartite Dinner Meeting, 8:30 p.m., William Rigdon Papers, FDRL.
578 "FDR seemed happy . . .": AB notes, Feb. 4, 1945, box 84, Halsted Papers, FDRL.
579 "Life is quickly . . .": AB notes, Feb. 5, 1945, box 84, Halsted Papers, FDRL.
579 "to get his version . . .": ibid.
579 "Just between you and me . . ."; "I have found out through Bruenn . . .": AB to John Boettiger, Feb. 6, 1945, box 6, Boettiger Papers, FDRL.
579 "I am using . . .": ibid.
580 "I wish Harry . . .": Moran, *Churchill*, p. 241.
580 HH persuaded FDR: Robert E. Sherwood, *Roosevelt and Hopkins* (1948), p. 859.
580 Dumbarton Oaks: ibid., p. 854.
581 issue not so easy for FDR: ibid., pp. 855–57.
581 "events were in the saddle": "it would have taken . . .": Averell Harriman and Elie Abel, *Special Envoy to Churchill and Stalin, 1941–1946* (1975), p. 405.
581 "The most important matter . . .": James MacGregor Burns, *Roosevelt: The Soldier of Freedom* (1970), p. 570.
581 "The Prime Minister . . .": ibid.
581 "reorganized on a broader . . .": ibid., p. 572.
582 "so elastic . . .": William Leahy, *I Was There* (1950), pp. 315–16.
582 "I know, Bill . . .": ibid.
582 "naïvete, ignorance . . .": Burns, *Soldier of Freedom*, p. 572.
582 FDR negotiated secret agreement: Stettinius, *Roosevelt and the Russians*, p. 255.
582 forty-five standing toasts: Bohlen, minutes, Tripartite Dinner, William Rigdon Papers, FDRL.
582 "We have wound up . . .": Lash, *World of Love*, p. 168.
583 "LL was really so happy . . .": John Boettiger to AB, Feb. 11, 1945, box 6, Boettiger Papers, FDRL.
583 "What a lonesome barn . . .": John Boettiger to AB, Jan. 23, 1945, box 6, Boettiger Papers, FDRL.
583 "Lt. Conrad came to lunch . . .": Lash, *World of Love*, p. 167.
583 "All the world looks smiling! . . . ": ibid., p. 168.
583 mood of "supreme exultation": Sherwood, *Roosevelt and Hopkins*, p. 869.
583 "a landmark . . ."; "to justify or surpass . . .": quoted in Ross McIntire, *White House Physician* (1946), p. 221.
583 "We really believed . . .": Sherwood, *Roosevelt and Hopkins*, p. 870.
583 "Why did Harry . . ."; "The president was good and mad . . .": interview with Robert Hopkins.
584 "One moment he was breathing . . .": AB notes on Yalta, Feb. 20, 1945, box 84, Halsted Papers, FDRL.
584 "He was very, very . . ."; "I shall miss him . . .": interview with Howard Bruenn.
584 "Many in Washington . . .": Rosenman, *Roosevelt and Hopkins*, p. 524.
584 "It was a sorry ship . . ."; "none too soon": ibid., p. 527.
584 "leading you to forget": ER interview, Graff Papers, FDRL.
584 "Look at the communiqué . . .": Elliott Roosevelt, *As He Saw It* (1946), p. 246.
585 "To a doctor's eye . . .": Moran, *Churchill*, p. 242.
585 "The signs of deterioration . . .": Harriman and Abel, *Special Envoy*, p. 389.
585 "Nevertheless he had blocked . . .": ibid.
585 "It was my feeling . . .": Leahy, *I Was There*, p. 321.
585 Eden later acknowledged: Anthony Eden, *The Memoirs of Anthony Eden, Earl of Avon: The Reckoning* (1965), p. 594.
585 "If Stalin was determined . . .": Harriman and Abel, *Special Envoy*, p. 389.
586 first time FDR wheeled down aisle: Perkins, *OH*, Columbia University.

586 "I hope you will pardon me . . .": Rosenman, *Working with Roosevelt,* p. 527.

586 "It was the first . . .": Perkins, *OH,* Columbia University.

587 "accidentally . . .": Hugh Gregory Gallagher, *FDR's Splendid Deception* (1985), pp. 94, 96.

587 Roosevelt delivered: *MD,* March 1, 1945.

587 "First of all . . .": Rosenman, *Roosevelt and Hopkins,* p. 536.

587 "one of his major mistakes . . .": ibid., p. 537.

587 looked "really well": Perkins, *OH,* Columbia University.

588 "He looked much older . . ." . . . ". . . more strength in him . . .": J. W. Pickergill and D. F. Foster, eds., *The Mackenzie King Record,* vol. II, *1944–1945* (1968), p. 325.

588 "seemed a little embarrassed": ibid., p. 329.

588 "I saw the President . . .": Leon Henderson diary, March 13, 1945, Henderson Papers, FDRL.

588 "profoundly depressed . . .": Sherwood, *Roosevelt and Hopkins,* p. 880.

588 "The other meetings . . .": John Boettiger to AB, Feb. 15, 1945, box 6, Boettiger Papers, FDRL.

589 "But for weeks now . . .": *Life,* March 5, 1945, p. 96.

589 "Anna has . . .": quoted in ibid., p. 100.

589 "For purposes of public consumption . . .": ibid., p. 108.

589 "He seemed to feel . . .": Smith conference notes, March 12, 1945, Harold Smith Papers, FDRL.

589 "Don't tell anyone . . .": Omar Bradley and Clay Blair, *A General's Life* (1983), pp. 521–22.

589 more than 6,000 . . . : Robert Meyer, Jr. *The Stars and Stripes: Story of World War II* (1960), pp. 376–78.

590 Only two hundred: Samuel Elliot Morison, *The Two-Ocean War* (1963), p. 524.

590 "practically every physicist of standing . . .": Stimson Diary, March 15, 1945, Yale University.

590 "with subsequent notice . . .": Peter Wyden, *Day One: Before Hiroshima and After* (1984), p. 126.

590 Stimson argued: Stimson Diary, March 15, 1945, Yale University.

591 "Do you think so?": Smith conference notes, March 12, 1945, Harold Smith Papers, FDRL.

591 "something about his face . . .": Elizabeth Shoumatoff, *FDR's Unfinished Portrait* (1990), p. 98.

591 Hick once observed: LH unpublished manuscript, box 1, LH Papers, FDRL.

591 "he was like a little boy . . .": Mrs. Kermit Roosevelt quoted in ibid.

591 "Never was there anything . . .": AH on Lucy.

591 "I doubt that father felt . . .": James Roosevelt, *My Parents* (1976), p. 103.

591 "strictly a family affair . . .": Pickergill and Foster, eds., *Mackenzie King Record,* p. 334.

592 "because I felt the pressure . . .": AB draft letter to the editor concerning column "FDR Romance," n.d., box 84, Halsted Papers, FDRL.

592 "wonderful person . . .": AB to Margaret Suckley, Oct. 28, 1948, box 74, Halsted Papers, FDRL.

592 "I was grateful to her . . .": AB draft letter to the editor concerning column "FDR Romance," n.d., box 84, Halsted Papers, FDRL.

592 "the complete contrast . . .": Hassett, *Off the Record,* pp. 323–24.

592 "Thus another milestone . . .": ibid.

592 "This world of young people . . .": *MD,* March 21, 1945.

592 "like a boy on vacation . . .": Jim Bishop, *FDR's Last Year* (1974), p. 485.

593 "the head going . . .": quoted in ibid., p. 520.

593 LH quit her job: Doris Faber, *The Life of Lorena Hickok* (1980), p. 300.

593 "The goodbyes . . .": ibid., pp. 300–301.

593 LH had pretended: LH unpublished manuscript, box 1, LH Papers, FDRL.

594 "the office would be packed . . .": ibid.

594 "Later I came to realize . . .": LH to Tommy, July 23, 1949, LH Papers, FDRL.

594 "Soon after the inaugural ceremonies . . .": *TIR,* p. 78.

CHAPTER TWENTY-FOUR: "Everybody Is Crying"

595 "Hope he responds...": William D. Hassett, *Off the Record with F.D.R.* (1958), p. 326.
595 "Everything is just...": Joseph P. Lash, *A World of Love: Eleanor Roosevelt and Her Friends, 1943–1962* (1984), p. 177.
595 He wanted her to travel: ibid., p. 174; J. W. Pickergill and D. F. Foster, eds., *Mackenzie King Record*, vol. II, *1944–1945* (1968), p. 328.
596 "is going to get...": quoted in Samuel I. Rosenman, *Working with Roosevelt* (1952), p. 546.
596 "I have long wanted..."; "The war in Europe...": *Collier's*, Sept. 21, 1946, p. 103.
596 "suddenly realized...": *TIR*, p. 343.
597 "to enjoy life..." ... "No, I like...": *MD*, April 20, 1945.
597 "the most beautiful..." ..."That sense...": ibid.,
597 "No, it looks dead...": ibid.
597 "He never liked...": ibid.
597 "Does that sound...": Joseph P. Lash, *Eleanor and Franklin* (1971), p. 719.
597 "I cannot conceal...": *Churchill & Roosevelt: The Complete Correspondence* (1984), vol. III, pp. 595–96.
597 "Our friendship...": ibid., p. 574.
598 "had failed to erase...": Grace Tully, *F.D.R., My Boss* (1949), p. 356.
598 "Did you get any rest...": ibid.
598 "usual leisure time...": ibid., p. 358.
598 "He was very amusing...": ER interview, Graff Papers, FDRL.
598 "The President was the worst...": Bernard Asbell, *When F.D.R. Died* (1961), p. 14.
598 "pretty simple, despite...": Michael F. Reilly, *Reilly of the White House* (1947), pp. 226–27.
598 "Warm Springs had saved..."; "it wasn't just a matter...": ibid.
599 "The days flowed...": Margaret Suckley, *OH*, FDRL.
599 "He was in fine form...": ibid.
599 "It was a beautiful...": A. Merriman Smith, *Thank You, Mr. President* (1946), p. 184.
599 "That is not even subtle": ibid., p. 185.
599 "As a matter of fact...": Asbell, *When F.D.R. Died*, p. 28.
599 "I forgot to tell you..."; "Much love...": Lash, *World of Love*, pp. 181–82.
600 "Nothing in sight..."; "Nobody loves us...": Shoumatoff, *FDR's Unfinished Portrait* (1990), p. 100.
600 "full of jokes...": ibid.
600 "profile as beautiful...": ibid., pp. 102–3.
600 "happy kids enjoying...": Lillian Rogers Parks, *The Roosevelts: A Family in Turmoil* (1981), p. 262.
600 "As I reined in...": A. Merriman Smith, *Thank You*, p. 186.
601 "beautiful, slightly flushed face...": Shoumatoff, *FDR's Portrait*, p. 108.
601 "I remember so clearly...": Margaret Suckley, *OH*, FDRL.
601 "a good speech": Hassett, *Off the Record*, p. 333.
601 "The only limit...": James MacGregor Burns, *Roosevelt: The Soldier of Freedom* (1970), p. 597.
601 "I was terribly shocked...": John Morton Blum, *From the Morgenthau Diaries*, vol. III (1967), p. 416.
601 "He was full of this...": AH interview, Graff Papers, FDRL.
601 "an encompassing tension...": Shoumatoff, *FDR's Portrait*, p. 114.
601 "The sky was clear...": Margaret Suckley, *OH*, FDRL.
602 "exceptionally good color": Shoumatoff, *FDR's Portrait*, p. 115.
602 "surprisingly well...": Margaret Suckley, *OH*, FDRL.
602 "...through with your laundry...": Parks, *Family in Turmoil*, p. 263.
602 "A typical State Department letter...": Asbell, When *F.D.R. Died*, p. 33.
602 "...there is where I make a law": Hassett, *Off the Record*, p. 334.
602 "The last I remember...": Asbell, *When F.D.R. Died*, p. 36.
602 "We've got..."; "he raised his right hand...": Shoumatoff, *FDR's Portrait*, p. 117.
602 "He looked at me...": Margaret Suckley, *OH*, FDRL.
602 "It was a bolt...": *Navy Medicine*, March–April 1990, p. 13.

602   "The confusion..." ..."We must pack up and go...": Shoumatoff, *FDR's Portrait,*
       pp. 118–19.
602   "which wasn't much": *Navy Medicine,* March–April 1990, p. 13.
603   tortured breathing: Tully, *F.D.R.,* p. 362.
603   "All you could hear...": Asbell, *When F.D.R. Died,* p. 45.
603   "His eyes were closed...": Hassett, *Off the Record,* p. 335.
603   "We put a shot...": *Navy Medicine,* March–April 1990, p. 13.
603   "not alarmed": *TIR,* p. 343.
603   "unusually smart": Asbell, *When F.D.R. Died,* p. 50.
603   "a quick start": ibid., p. 51.
603   "very much upset...": *TIR,* p. 344.
603   "Now I'm called back...": Asbell, *When F.D.R. Died,* p. 51.
603   "I got into the car...": *TIR,* p. 344.
604   "I hadn't been there...": AH interview, Bernard Asbell.
604   "He did his job...": *NYT,* April 13, 1945, p. 3.
604   presence of mind to call: *Newsweek,* April 23, 1945, p. 40.
604   "Harry, the President is dead...": David McCullough, *Truman* (1992), p. 342.
604   "Is there anything...": ibid.
604   ER told Truman she was planning: ibid.
604   "It was a very somber group...": Stimson Diary, April 12, 1945, Yale University.
605   "A trooper to the last": Bess Furman, *Washington By-Line* (1949), p. 314.
605   "strode with her usual...": *Time,* April 23, 1945, p. 18.
605   "You and I have...": Robert E. Sherwood, *Roosevelt and Hopkins* (1948), p. 880.
605   "Oh, we all know...": ibid., pp. 880–81.
605   "I felt as if...": Winston S. Churchill, *The Second World War,* vol. VI, *Triumph and
       Tragedy* (1953), p. 412.
605   "deeply distressed": Averell Harriman and Elie Abel, *Special Envoy to Churchill and
       Stalin, 1941–1946* (1975), p. 440.
605   "and feeling as...": Roy Hooper, *Americans Remember the Home Front* (1992, abridged
       ed.), p. 228.
606   "That first flash...": I. F. Stone, *The War Years, 1939–1945* (1988), p. 273.
606   "Everybody left...": Hooper, *Americans Remember,* p. 229.
606   "God, there were...": ibid., p. 227.
606   "I am too shocked...": Asbell, *When F.D.R. Died,* p. 117.
606   "The President's death...": ibid., p. 117.
606   "it is tragic...": *BEA,* April 14, 1945, p. 4.
606   "Men will thank God...": *NYT,* April 13, 1945, p. 18.
606   WC said like opening champagne: John Gunther, *Roosevelt in Retrospect* (1950), p. 18.
606   "no conception of the office...": Richard E. Neustadt, *Presidential Power and the Mod-
       ern Presidency* (1990), p. 136.
606   "Wouldn't you be...": Gunther, *Roosevelt in Retrospect,* p. 49.
607   "Under Roosevelt...": William Leuchtenburg, *Franklin D. Roosevelt and the New Deal*
       (1963), p. 327.
607   "He was one of the few...": Isaiah Berlin, *Personal Impressions* (1981), p. 26.
608   contributed nearly: compiled from charts in R. Elberton Smith, *The Army and Economic
       Mobilization* (1959), pp. 9–27; also Geoffrey Perrett, *Days of Sadness, Years of Triumph*
       (1973), p. 399.
608   "There is little doubt...": Smith, *The Army and Economic Mobilization,* p. 706.
608   "The figures are all...": Bruce Catton, *The War Lords of Washington* (1969), p. 306.
608   "I am like a cat...": James MacGregor Burns, *Leadership* (1978), p. 281.
609   Never once: Stimson Diary, April 14, 1945, Yale University.
609   action over the protest: Eric Larrabee, *Commander in Chief* (1987), p. 15.
609   "the arsenal...": interview with Joe Rauh.
610   "None of these proposals...": David S. Wyman, *The Abandonment of the Jews: America
       and the Holocaust, 1941–1945* (1984), p. 335.
610   "More than any...": Larrabee, *Commander in Chief,* p. 644
611   calm and composed; Tully recounted her schedule: Tully, *F.D.R.,* p. 366.
611   Laura began to speak: Bernard Asbell, *Mother and Daughter* (1988), p. 186.
611   "It was a malicious thing...": interview with Eleanor Wotkyns.

611 "Eleanor would have . . .": Jim Bishop, *FDR's Last Year* (1974), p. 635.
611 alone with her husband; eyes dry: Tully, *F.D.R.*, p. 366.
611 Had Franklin seen Lucy: Asbell, *Mother and Daughter*, p. 186.
611 "At a time like that . . .": Asbell, *When F.D.R. Died*, p. 155.
612 valet tenderly parted the hair: Bishop, *Last Year*, p. 621.
612 "Oh, he was handsome . . .": Asbell, *When F.D.R. Died*, p. 130.
612 "They came from the fields . . .": *BEA*, April 15, 1945, p. 5.
612 "Men stood with their arms . . .": A. Merriman Smith, *Thank You*, pp. 193–94.
612 "I lay in my berth . . .": *TIR*, p. 345.
612 "Did Franklin ever . . .": Asbell, *When F.D.R. Died*, p. 153.
613 "my dear wife will . . .": Tully, *F.D.R.*, p. 367.
613 Truman later wrote: McCullough, *Truman*, p. 357.
613 "The streets were lined . . .": Katherine Marshall, *Together* (1946), p. 244.
613 White House in state of confusion: Victoria Henrietta Nesbitt, *White House Diary* (1948), p. 309.
613 "she would walk . . .": LH interview, Graff Papers, FDRL.
613 "Can you dispense . . ." . . ."Mrs. Roosevelt stood . . .": J. B. West, *Upstairs at the White House* (1973), p. 56.
614 "as stern as it could get . . .": AB notes attached to letter to JL, Jan. 28, 1972, box 36, Halsted Papers, FDRL.
614 "Mother was so upset . . .": ibid.
614 "Mother was angry with Anna . . .": Asbell, *Mother and Daughter*, p. 186.
614 "He was her husband . . .": interview with Curtis Roosevelt.
614 "It was the final roll call . . .": Furman, *Washington By-Line*, p. 313.
614 "stood almost fainting . . .": *Time*, April 23, 1945. p. 19.
614 "After everyone left . . .": interview with Milton Lipson.
615 "I'll never forget . . .": John R. Boettiger, Jr., *A Love in Shadow* (1978), p. 261.
615 "The funeral was . . .": Lash, *World of Love*, p. 184.
615 watching the workmen: *Time*, April 23, 1945, p. 20.
615 "He wanted me to plant . . .": *BEA*, April 14, 1945, p. 7.

CHAPTER TWENTY-FIVE: "A New Country Is Being Born"

616 "She had all . . .": Victoria Henrietta Nesbitt, *White House Diary* (1948), p. 311.
616 "My husband . . .": *MD*, April 18, 1945.
616 "a bit keyed up . . .": Joseph P. Lash, *A World of Love: Eleanor Roosevelt and Her Friends, 1943–1962* (1984), p. 188.
616 eyes were tired: *Newsweek*, April 30, 1945, p. 24.
616 "In the years . . .": *MD*, April 16, 1945.
617 "Mrs. Roosevelt . . .": interview with Alonzo Fields.
617 "The White House upstairs . . .": David McCullough, *Truman* (1992), p. 373.
617 ". . . like a ghost house . . .": J. B. West, *Upstairs at the White House* (1973), p. 58.
617 "Do you think . . .": Perkins, *OH*, FDRL.
617 "a Cabinet Minister . . .": quoted in Joan Hoff-Wilson and Marjorie Lightman, eds., *Without Precedent: The Life and Career of Eleanor Roosevelt* (1984), p. 11.
618 "Traces of grief . . .": *Newsweek*, April 30, 1945, p. 44.
618 "This is a . . .": ibid., p. 24.
618 "Nearly all that . . .": Lash, *World of Love*, p. 189.
618 "I never did . . .": ibid.
618 "I have always . . .": *MD*, April 20, 1945.
618 "We were all in tears": Nesbitt, *White House Diary*, p. 313.
618 ". . . When you have . . .": *MD*, April 20, 1945.
618 ". . . feeling of melancholy . . .": Eleanor Roosevelt, *On My Own* (1958), p. 1.
618 "without a backward glance": *Newsweek*, April 30, 1945, p. 44.
618 "Her departure . . .": *BEA*, April 20, 1945, p. 5.
619 "The story is over": *Newsweek*, April 30, 1945, p. 44.
619 "I am realizing . . .": *MD*, April 21, 1945.
619 "It has warmed . . .": *MD*, Sept. 9, 1945.
619 " 'He was like . . .' ": *MD*, Nov. 9, 1945.

619 "upsurge of love...": Lash, *World of Love,* p. 191.
619 "I find that...": ibid., p. 188.
619 "Franklin's greater wisdom...": ibid., p. 186.
619 "I think we had...": ibid., p. 190.
620 ER had decided: Eleanor Roosevelt, *On My Own,* p. 4.
620 "In talking...": Joseph P. Lash, *Eleanor: The Years Alone* (1972), p. 23.
620 "No one was...": *MD,* June 9, 1945.
620 "His legs straightened out...": J. William T. Youngs, *Eleanor Roosevelt: A Personal and Public Life* (1985), p. 205.
620 "V-E Day was...": Lash, *World of Love,* p. 191.
620 "I cannot help...": *NYT,* May 9, 1945, p. 18.
620 "It was without...": *The New Yorker Book of War Pieces* (1947), p. 474.
620 "the valiant and...": Winston S. Churchill, *The Second World War,* vol. VI, *The Grand Alliance* (1953), p. 376.
621 "with a sharp stab...": ibid., p. 583.
621 "It's no use pretending...": Lord Moran, *Churchill—The Struggle for Survival, 1940–1965* (1966), p. 310.
621 "His place...": *MD,* July 29, 1945.
621 ER had first learned: Joseph P. Lash, *Eleanor and Franklin* (1971), pp. 704–7.
621 "could not help...": *MD,* Aug. 10, 1945.
621 number of deaths: Martin Gilbert, *The Second World War* (1989), p. 746.
621 U.S. suffered the fewest: information obtained from the Naval Historical Center and the Army Historical Center, Washington, D.C.
622 "filled with very...": David Emblidge, ed., *Eleanor Roosevelt's "My Day,"* vol. II, *The Post-War Years, Her Acclaimed Columns, 1945–1952* (1990), p. 28.
622 "to be in a world...": Lash, *World of Love,* p. 202.
622 "the weight of suffering...": Emblidge, ed., *Eleanor Roosevelt's "My Day,"* p. 28.
622 "I miss Pa's voice...": ER to AB, Aug. 14, 1945, box 76, Halsted Papers, FDRL.
622 Now that the war...: *Independent Woman,* Oct. 1945, p. 274.
622 "We were thrilled...": Frankie Cooper interview, University of Southern California Collection.
622 Though her center: interview with Mary Willett.
622 "it was essential...": *MD,* Sept. 7, 1945.
622 "Many thought they...": ibid.
622 "My whole life...": *Detroit Free Press,* June 14, 1945, Reuther Library.
623 "My husband would...": Frankie Cooper interview, University of Southern California.
623 In 1946: Joseph C. Goulden, *The Best Years, 1945–1950* (1976), p. 41.
623 "Why do you want...": Mark Jonathan Harris, Franklin D. Mitchell, and Steven J. Schechter, *The Homefront: America During World War II* (1984), p. 231.
623 "My husband did not care...": ibid., p. 230.
623 "My God, this was...": ibid.
623 "Mothers that worked...": Frankie Cooper interview, University of Southern California.
623 *Senior Scholastic* poll: William H. Chafe, *The American Woman: Her Changing Social, Economic and Political Role, 1920–1970* (1972), p. 179.
623 "You can do...": Frankie Cooper interview, University of Southern California.
624 "The content of women's lives...": Chafe, *American Woman,* p. 195.
624 Over fifteen million: Richard Polenberg, ed., *America at War* (1972), p. 124.
624 more than seventeen million: Polenberg, ed., *America at War,* p. 26.
625 GNP: Goulden, *The Best Year,* p. 92.
625 "barriers to social...": Geoffrey Perrett, *Days of Sadness, Years of Triumph: The American People, 1939–1945* (1973), p. 11.
626 between 1940 and 1945: Jean Byers, "A Study of the Negro in Military Service," War Department Study, June 1947, pp. 41, 49.
626 "The Negro was no longer...": ibid., p. 50.
627 "in accordance with...": ibid., p. 237.
627 "The Navy of 1945...": ibid.
627 "both possible...": ibid., p. 238.
627 "the Negro was considered...": ibid.
627 "the place was running...": C. R. Smith, *OH,* FDRL.

627 "more has happened...": Carey McWilliams, *Brothers Under the Skin* (1943), p. 4.

628 "the forgotten years...": *Journal of American History*, June 1968, p. 90.

628 "Oh, my God": Anna Rosenberg Hoffman, *OH, FDRL.*

628 "She would come in...": interview with Eleanor Seagraves.

629 "I think he let her...": Jonathan Daniels, *OH, FDRL.*

629 "Dear God,...": Jean Gould and Lorena Hickok, *Walter Reuther: Labor's Rugged Individualist* (1972), p. 345.

629 "I remember him...": Anna Rosenberg Hoffman, *OH, FDRL.*

629 "The truth of the matter...": James Roosevelt and Sidney Schalett, *Affectionately, F.D.R.* (1959), p. 313.

629 "You know, I've always...": Perkins interview, Graff Papers, FDRL.

629 "give her a whack...": James Halstead, *OH, FDRL.*

629 "certain parts...": AH, *OH,* Columbia University.

629 "She did love...": AH interview, Graff Papers, FDRL.

629 "I don't think...": Esther Lape interview, Lash Papers, FDRL.

629 "He might have been...": *TIR,* p. 349.

630 "She had indeed...": Lois Scharf, *ER: First Lady of American Liberalism* (1987), p. 140.

630 "a new country...": interview with James Roosevelt.

630 "a giant transference...": ibid.

630 "In the early days...": ibid.

630 "As I look back...": *MD,* Nov. 25, 1945.

631 "Thank you...": Lucy Rutherfurd to ER, May 2, 1945, ER Papers, FDRL.

631 "Your telephoning...": Lucy Rutherfurd to AB, May 9, 1945, box 70, Halsted Papers, FDRL.

632 "showing it only on...": John R. Boettiger, Jr., *A Love in Shadow,* p. 261.

632 "Perhaps, by revealing...": interview with John Boettiger, Jr.

632 "a flood of work...": Bernard Asbell, *Mother and Daughter* (1988), p. 191.

632 end of an era: Boettiger, Jr., *Love in Shadow,* p. 263.

632 "I think it is...": Lash, *World of Love,* p. 205.

632 "all human beings...": *TIR,* p. 349.

633 "chose to remember...": Elliott Roosevelt and James Brough, *Mother R* (1977), p. 83.

633 "constantly talking...": Maureen Corr, *OH, FDRL.*

633 Truman telephoned ER: Elliott Roosevelt and Brough, *Mother R,* pp. 68–69.

633 "fear and trembling": ibid., p. 69.

633 "the most admired...": Garry Wills, *Certain Trumpets: The Call of Leaders* (1994), p. 62.

633 "They are not dead...": *MD,* April 25, 1945.

BIBLIOGRAPHY

Manuscripts and Personal Papers

MANUSCRIPT COLLECTIONS CONSULTED AT THE FRANKLIN D. ROOSEVELT LIBRARY
Boettiger, John
Coy, Wayne
Halsted, Anna Roosevelt
Hassett, William D.
Henderson, Leon
Hickok, Lorena
Hopkins, Harry
Kleeman, Rite Halle
Lape, Esther
Lash, Joseph P.
Morgenthau, Henry, Jr.
Rigdon, William
Roosevelt, Anna Eleanor
Roosevelt, Franklin D.
   Collection of Speeches
   Papers Pertaining to Family, Business, and Personal Affairs
   Office File
   President's Personal File
   President's Secretary's File
Roosevelt, James
Roosevelt Family: Papers Donated by the Children
Smith, Harold
Suckley, Margaret

HENRY L. STIMSON PAPERS, MANUSCRIPTS AND ARCHIVES, YALE UNIVERSITY LIBRARY

Oral History Transcripts

ELEANOR ROOSEVELT ORAL HISTORY TRANSCRIPTS, FRANKLIN D. ROOSEVELT LIBRARY
Bell, Minnewa
Corr, Maureen
Daniels, Jonathan
Douglas, Helen Gahagan
Halsted, Diana Hopkins
Halsted, James
Hight, Mr. and Mrs. John
Hirschhorn, Joan Morgenthau
Hoffman, Anna Rosenberg
Lash, Trude
Morgenthau, Henry, II
Murray, Pauli
Polier, Justine
Redmond, Roland

Roosevelt, Elliott
Roosevelt, Elliott, Jr.
Roosevelt, James
Rowe, James
Tugwell, Rexford
Wotkyns, Eleanor

ROBERT D. GRAFF INTERVIEWS, FRANKLIN D. ROOSEVELT LIBRARY
Halsted, Anna Roosevelt
Perkins, Frances
Roosevelt, Eleanor

COLUMBIA UNIVERSITY ORAL HISTORY TRANSCRIPTS
Halsted, Anna Roosevelt
Perkins, Frances
Rosenman, Samuel I.

BOOKS

Acheson, Dean. *Present at the Creation.* New York: Norton, 1969.
Adamic, Louis. *Dinner at the White House.* New York: Harper, 1948.
Adams, Henry H. *Harry Hopkins: A Biography.* New York: Putnam, 1977.
Alinsky, Saul. *John L. Lewis: An Unauthorized Biography.* New York: Putnam, 1949.
Ambrose, Stephen E. *The Supreme Commander: The War Years of General Dwight D. Eisen-
    hower.* Garden City, N.Y.: Doubleday, 1970.
———. *D-Day: The Climactic Battle of World War II.* New York: Simon & Schuster, 1994.
American Women at War, by 7 Newspaper Women. New York: National Association of Manu-
    facturers, 1942.
Anderson, Jervis. *A. Philip Randolph: A Biographical Portrait.* New York: Harcourt Brace
    Jovanovich, 1973.
Armor, John, and Peter Wright. *Manzanar.* New York: Times Books, 1988.
Arnold, Henry H. *Global Mission.* New York: Harper, 1949.
Asbell, Bernard. *When F.D.R. Died.* New York: Holt, Rinehart & Winston, 1961.
———. *The FDR Memoirs.* Garden City, N.Y.: Doubleday, 1973.
———. *Mother and Daughter: The Letters of Eleanor and Anna Roosevelt.* New York: Fromm,
    1988.
Baldwin, Hanson W. *The Crucial Years, 1939–1941.* New York: Harper & Row, 1976.
Barber, Noel. *The Week France Fell.* New York: Stein & Day, 1976.
Barnard, John. *Walter Reuther and the Rise of the Auto Workers.* Boston: Little, Brown, 1983.
Baruch, Bernard M. *Baruch: The Public Years.* New York: Holt, Rinehart & Winston, 1960.
Beard, Charles A. *President Roosevelt and the Coming of the War, 1941.* New Haven, Conn.:
    Yale University Press, 1948.
Beasley, Maurine H. *Eleanor Roosevelt and the Media: A Public Quest for Self-Fulfillment.*
    Chicago: University of Illinois Press, 1987.
Beasley, Norman. *Knudsen: A Biography.* New York: McGraw-Hill, 1947.
Bellow, Saul. *It All Adds Up: From the Dim Past to the Uncertain Future.* New York: Viking,
    1994.
Berle, Adolf A. *Navigating the Rapids, 1918–1971: From the Papers of Adolf A. Berle.* Edited
    by Beatrice Bishop Berle and Travis Beal Jacobs. New York: Harcourt Brace Jovanovich,
    1973.
Berlin, Isaiah. *Personal Impressions.* Edited by Henry Handy. New York: Viking, 1981.
———. *Washington Despatches 1941–45: Weekly Political Reports from the British Embassy.*
    Edited by H. G. Nicholas. Chicago: University of Chicago Press, 1981.
Beschloss, Michael. *Kennedy and Roosevelt: The Uneasy Alliance.* New York: Norton, 1980.
Biddle, Francis. *In Brief Authority.* Garden City, N.Y.: Doubleday, 1948.
Bird, Kai. *The Chairman, John McCloy: The Making of the American Establishment.* New York:
    Simon & Schuster, 1992.
Bishop, Jim. *FDR's Last Year.* New York: William Morrow, 1974.
Bjaaland, Patricia C. *The Norwegian Royal Family.* Tano, 1986.

Black, Ruby. *ER*. New York: Duell, Sloane & Pearce, 1940.

Blum, John Morton. *From the Morganthau Diaries*. Boston: Houghton Mifflin. Vol. I, *Years of Crisis, 1928–1938*, 1959. Vol. II, *Years of Urgency, 1938–1941*, 1965. Vol. III, *Years of War, 1941–1945*, 1967.

———. *V Was for Victory: Politics and American Culture During World War II*. New York: Harcourt Brace Jovanovich, 1976.

Boelcki, Willi A., ed. *Secret Conferences of Dr. Joseph Goebbels: The Nazi Propaganda War, 1939–1943*. New York: E. P. Dutton, 1970.

Boettiger, John R., Jr. *A Love in Shadow*. New York: Norton, 1978.

Bohlen, Charles E. *Witness to History, 1929–1969*. New York: Norton, 1973.

Bosworth, Allen R. *America's Concentration Camps*. New York: Norton, 1967.

Boyer, Paul, Clark Clifford, Jr., Joseph Kett, Neal Salisbury, Harvard Sitkoff, and Nancy Woolch. *The Enduring Vision: A History of the American People*. Lexington, Mass.: D. C. Heath, 1993.

Bradley, Omar, and Clay Blair. *A General's Life*. New York: Simon & Schuster, 1983.

Brinkley, David. *Washington Goes to War*. New York: Knopf, 1988.

Bruenn, Howard J. "Clinical Notes on the Illness and Death of President Franklin D. Roosevelt." *Annals of Internal Medicine*, vol. 72 (April 1970).

Bryant, Arthur. *The Turn of the Tide: A History of the War Years Based on the Diaries of Field-Marshall Lord Alanbrooke*. Garden City, N.Y.: Doubleday, 1957.

Buhite, Russell D., and David W. Levy, eds. *FDR's Fireside Chats*. Norman, Okla.: University of Oklahoma Press, 1992.

Bullitt, William C. *For the President, Personal and Secret: Correspondence Between Franklin D. Roosevelt and William C. Bullitt*. Edited by Orville H. Bullitt. Boston: Houghton Mifflin, 1972.

Bullock, Alan. *Hitler: A Study in Tyranny*. New York: Harper & Row, 1962.

Bunker, John. *Liberty Ships: Ugly Ducklings of World War II*. Annapolis, Md.: Naval Institute Press, 1972.

Burns, James MacGregor. *Roosevelt: The Lion and the Fox*. New York: Harcourt, Brace, 1956.

———. *Roosevelt: The Soldier of Freedom*. New York: Harcourt Brace Jovanovich, 1970.

———. *Leadership*. New York: Harper & Row, 1978.

Butcher, Harry C. *My Three Years with Eisenhower: The Personal Diary of Captain Harry C. Butcher, USNR, Naval Aide to General Eisenhower, 1942 to 1945*. New York: Simon & Schuster, 1946.

Byrnes, James F. *Speaking Frankly*. New York: Harper, 1947.

Cadogan, Sir Alexander. *The Diaries of Sir Alexander Cadogan, O.M., 1938–1945*. Edited by David Dilks. New York: Putnam, 1972.

Cardin, Martin. *Flying Forts*. New York: Meredith Press, 1968.

Catton, Bruce. *The War Lords of Washington*. New York: Greenwood Press, 1969.

Chadakoff, Rochelle, ed. *Eleanor Roosevelt's My Day*. Vol. I, *Her Acclaimed Columns, 1936–1945*. New York: Pharos Books, 1989.

Chafe, William H. *The American Woman: Her Changing Social, Economic and Political Role, 1920–1970*. New York: Oxford University Press, 1972.

Childs, Marquis. *I Write from Washington*. New York: Harper, 1942.

Churchill, Sarah. *A Thread in the Tapestry*. New York: Dodd, Mead, 1967.

Churchill, Winston S. *The Second World War*. Boston: Houghton Mifflin, vol. I, *The Gathering Storm*, 1948. Vol. II, *Their Finest Hour*, 1949. Vol. III, *The Grand Alliance*, 1950. Vol. IV, *The Hinge of Fate*, 1950. Vol. V, *Closing the Ring*, 1951. Vol. VI, *Triumph and Tragedy*, 1953.

———. *Great War Speeches*. New York: Corgi Books, 1957.

Ciechanowski, Jan. *Defeat in Victory*. Garden City, N.Y.: Doubleday, 1947.

Clapper, Raymond. *Watching the World*. New York: McGraw-Hill, 1944.

Clarke, Admiral J. J., with Clark G. Reynolds. *Carrier Admiral*. New York: David McKay, 1967.

Clifford, J. Garry, and Samuel R. Spenser, Jr. *The First Peacetime Draft*. Lawrence, Kan.: University Press of Kansas, 1986.

Coakley, Robert, and Richard Leighton. *Global Logistics and Strategy, 1943–1945*. Washington, D.C.: Center for Military History, 1989.

Cole, Wayne S. *America First: The Battle Against Intervention, 1940–1941*. Madison, Wisc.: University of Wisconsin Press, 1953.

Collier, Peter, and Robert Horowitz. *The Fords: An American Epic.* New York: Summit Books, 1987.

Collier, Richard. *1940: The World in Flames.* New York: Penguin, 1979.

Conn, Stetson, and Byron Fairchild. *The Western Hemisphere: The Framework of Hemispheric Defense.* Washington, D.C.: Office of the Chief of Military History, 1960.

Cook, Blanche Wiesen. *Eleanor Roosevelt.* Vol. I, *1884–1933.* New York: Viking Penguin, 1992.

Cott, Nancy F., and Elizabeth H. Pleck. *A Heritage of Her Own: Towards a New Social History of American Women.* New York: Simon & Schuster, 1979.

Cray, Ed. *General of the Army: George C. Marshall, Soldier and Statesman.* New York: Norton, 1990.

Cutler, Robert. *No Time for Rest.* Boston: Little, Brown, 1966.

Dallek, Robert. *Franklin D. Roosevelt and American Foreign Policy, 1932–1945.* New York: Oxford University Press, 1981.

Daniels, Jonathan. *Washington Quadrille: The Dance Beside the Documents.* Garden City, N.Y.: Doubleday, 1968.

Daniels, Roger. *Concentration Camps USA: Japanese-Americans and World War II.* New York: Holt, Rinehart and Winston, 1970.

Davis, Benjamin O., Jr. *Benjamin O. Davis, Jr., American: An Autobiography.* New York: Plume, 1992.

Davis, Kenneth S. *FDR: The Beckoning of Destiny, 1882–1928.* New York: Putnam, 1971.

———. *Invincible Summer: An Intimate Portrait of the Roosevelts, Based on the Recollections of Marion Dickerman.* New York: Atheneum, 1974.

———. *FDR: Into the Storm, 1937–1940.* New York: Random House, 1993.

Degler, Carl. *Out of the Past: The Forces That Shaped Modern America.* New York: Harper, 1959.

Donovan, Hedley. *Roosevelt to Reagan: A Reporter's Encounter with Nine Presidents.* New York: Harper & Row, 1985.

Dulles, Foster Rhea. *The American Red Cross: A History.* New York: Harper, 1950.

Eden, Anthony. *The Memoirs of Anthony Eden, Earl of Avon: The Reckoning.* Boston: Houghton Mifflin, 1965.

Eisenhower, Dwight D. *Crusade in Europe.* Garden City, N.Y.: Doubleday, 1948.

Emblidge, David, ed. *Eleanor Roosevelt's My Day.* Vol. II, *The Post-War Years. Her Acclaimed Columns, 1945–1952.* New York: Pharos Books, 1990.

Estes, Winston M. *Homefront.* New York: Avon, 1976.

Faber, Doris. *The Life of Lorena Hickok: E.R.'s Friend.* New York: Morrow, 1980.

Fairchild, Byron, and Jonathan Grossman. *The Army and Industrial Mobilization.* Washington, D.C.: Office of the Chief of Military History, 1959.

Farley, James A. *Jim Farley's Story: The Roosevelt Years.* New York: McGraw-Hill, 1948.

Feingold, Henry L. *The Politics of Rescue: The Roosevelt Administration and the Holocaust, 1938–1945.* New Brunswick, N.J.: Rutgers University Press, 1970.

Fields, Alonzo. *My 21 Years in the White House.* New York: Coward-McCann, 1961.

Flynn, Edward J. *You're the Boss.* New York: Collier Books, 1962.

Flynn, George Q. *The Mess in Washington.* Westport, Conn.: Greenwood Press, 1979.

Foreign Relations of the United States. The Conferences at Cairo and Teheran, 1943. Washington, D.C.: U.S. Government Printing Office, 1961.

Foreign Relations of the United States. The Conferences at Malta and Yalta, 1945. Washington, D.C.: U.S. Government Printing Office, 1955.

Foreign Relations of the United States. The Conferences at Washington and Quebec, 1943. Washington, D.C.: U.S. Government Printing Office, 1970.

Foreign Relations of the United States. The Conferences at Washington, 1941–42, and Casablanca, 1943. Washington, D.C.: U.S. Government Printing Office, 1968.

Frankfurter, Felix. *From the Diaries of Felix Frankfurter.* Edited by Joseph P. Lash. New York: Norton, 1975.

Freidel, Frank. *Franklin D. Roosevelt: A Rendezvous with Destiny.* Boston: Little, Brown, 1990.

Furman, Bess. *Washington By-Line.* New York: Knopf, 1949.

Galbraith, John Kenneth. *A Life in Our Times.* Boston: Houghton Mifflin, 1981.

Gallagher, Hugh Gregory. *FDR's Splendid Deception.* New York: Dodd, Mead, 1985.

Gallup, George. *The Gallup Polls: Public Opinion, 1935–1971*. New York: Random House, 1972. Vol. I, *1937–1948*.

Gaulle, Charles de. *The Complete War Memoirs*. New York: Simon & Schuster, 1964.

Gelb, Norman. *Dunkirk: The Complete Story of the First Step in the Defeat of Hitler*. New York: Morrow, 1989.

Gilbert, James. *Another Chance: Postwar America, 1945–1948*. Philadelphia: Temple University Press, 1981.

Gilbert, Martin. *Winston S. Churchill*. Boston: Houghton Mifflin. Vol. VI, *"Finest Hour": 1939–1941*, 1983. Vol. VII, *Road to Victory: 1941–1945*, 1986.

———. *The Second World War: A Complete History*. New York: Henry Holt, 1989.

Girdner, Audrie, and Anne Loftis. *The Great Betrayal: The Evacuation of the Japanese-Americans During World War II*. New York: Macmillan, 1969.

Gluck, Sherna Berger. *Rosie the Riveter Revisited: Women, the War, and Social Change*. Boston: Twayne, 1987.

Goebbels, Joseph. *The Goebbels Diaries, 1942–1943*. Edited by Louis Lochner. Garden City, N.Y.: Doubleday, 1948.

———. *The Goebbels Diaries, 1939–1941*. Edited by Fred Taylor. New York: Putnam, 1983.

Goldsmith, William M. *The Growth of Presidential Power*. Vol. III, *Triumph and Reappraisal*. New York: Chelsea House, 1974.

Goodhart, Philip. *Fifty Good Ships That Saved the World: The Foundations of the Anglo-American Alliance*. Garden City, N.Y.: Doubleday, 1965.

Goodman, Jack, ed. *While You Were Gone: A Report of Wartime Life in the US*. New York: Simon & Schuster, 1946.

Gosnell, Harold. *Champion Campaigner: Franklin D. Roosevelt*. New York: Macmillan, 1952.

Gould, Jean, and Lorena Hickok. *Walter Reuther: Labor's Rugged Individualist*. New York: Dodd, Mead and Co., 1972.

Gould, Joseph C. *The Best Years*. New York: Atheneum, 1976.

Green, Constance McLaughlin. *Washington: Capital City, 1879–1950*. Princeton, N.J.: Princeton University Press, 1963.

———, Harry C. Thomson, and Peter C. Root. *The Ordnance Department: Planning Munitions for War*. Washington, D.C.: Office of the Chief of Military History, 1955.

Greenfield, Kent R., Robert R. Palmer, and Bell I. Wiley. *The Organization of Ground Combat Troops*. Washington, D.C.: Office of the Chief of Military History, 1947.

Gregory, Chester. *Women in Defense Work During World War II: An Analysis of the Labor Problem*. Jericho, N.Y.: Exposition Press, 1974.

Gunther, John. *Roosevelt in Retrospect*. New York: Harper, 1950.

Hall, H. Duncan. *North American Supply*. London: Her Majesty's Stationery Office & Longmans, Green & Co., 1955.

Hareven, Tamara. *Eleanor Roosevelt: An American Conscience*. Chicago: Quadrangle, 1968.

Harriman, Averell, and Elie Abel. *Special Envoy to Churchill and Stalin, 1941–1946*. New York: Random House, 1975.

Harris, Mark Jonathan, Franklin D. Mitchell, and Steven J. Schechter. *The Homefront: America During World War II*. New York: Putnam, 1984.

Harrison, Gordon. *Cross-Channel Attack*. Washington, D.C.: Center for Military History, 1989.

Hassett, William D. *Off the Record with F.D.R.* New Brunswick, N.J.: Rutgers University Press, 1958.

Hastings, Max. *Overlord: D-Day and the Battle for Normandy*. New York: Simon & Schuster, 1984.

Hazelton, Lesley. *The Right to Feel Bad: Coming to Terms with Normal Depression*. New York: Ballantine Books, 1985.

Hershan, Stella K. *A Woman of Quality*. New York: Crown, 1970.

Hitch, Charles J. *America's Economic Strength*. New York: Oxford University Press, 1941.

Hoff-Wilson, Joan, and Marjorie Lightman, eds. *Without Precedent: The Life and Career of Eleanor Roosevelt*. Bloomington, Ind.: Indiana University Press, 1984.

Holley, Irving, Jr. *Buying Aircraft: Materiel Procurement for the Armed Forces*. Washington, D.C.: Office of the Chief of Military History, 1964.

Hoopes, Roy. *Americans Remember the Home Front: An Oral Narrative of the World War II Years in America*. Abridged edition. New York: Berkley Books, 1992.

Howe, George. *Northwest Africa: Seizing the Initiative in the West*. Washington, D.C.: Office of the Chief of Military History, 1957.

Hull, Cordell. *The Memoirs of Cordell Hull*. Vol. II. New York: Macmillan, 1948.

Hurd, Charles. *When the New Deal Was Young and Gay: FDR and His Circle*. New York: Hawthorn Books, 1965.

Ickes, Harold L. *The Secret Diaries of Harold L. Ickes*. Vol. III, *The Lowering Clouds, 1939–1941*. New York: Simon & Schuster, 1954.

Irons, Peter. *Justice at War: The Story of the Japanese American Internment Cases*. New York: Oxford University Press, 1983.

Ironside, General Sir William Edmund. *Time Unguarded: The Ironside Diaries, 1937–1940*. New York: David McKay, 1962.

Ismay, Hastings. *The Memoirs of General Lord Ismay*. New York: Viking, 1960.

James, D. Clayton. *The Years of MacArthur*. Vol. II. Boston: Houghton Mifflin, 1975.

Janeway, Eliot. *The Struggle for Survival*. New Haven, Conn.: Yale University Press, 1951.

Jones, Jacqueline. *Labor of Love, Labor of Sorrow: Black Women, Work, and the Family from Slavery to the Present*. New York: Basic Books, 1985.

Jones, Jesse H., with Edward Angly. *Fifty Billion Dollars: My Thirteen Years with the RFC*. New York: Macmillan, 1951.

Jones, Robert H. *The Roads to Russia: United States Lend-Lease to the Soviet Union*. Norman, Okla.: University of Oklahoma Press, 1969.

Josephson, Matthew, and Hannah Josephson. *Sidney Hillman: Statesman of American Labor*. Garden City, N.Y.: Doubleday, 1952.

Kearney, James R. *Anna Eleanor Roosevelt: The Evolution of a Reformer*. Boston: Houghton Mifflin, 1968.

Kempton, Murray. *Part of Our Time*. New York: Simon & Schuster, 1965.

Kennett, Lee. *G.I.: The American Soldier in World War II*. New York: Charles Scribner's Sons, 1987.

Ketchum, Richard M. *The Borrowed Years, 1938–1941: America on the Way to War*. New York: Random House, 1989.

Kikuchi, Charles. *Kikuchi Diary: Chronicle from an American Concentration Camp*. Urbana, Ill.: University of Illinois Press, 1973.

Kimball, Warren, ed. *Churchill & Roosevelt: The Complete Correspondence*. 3 vols. Princeton, N.J.: Princeton University Press, 1984.

Kiplinger, W. M. *Washington Is Like That*. New York: Harper, 1942.

Kleeman, Rita Halle. *Gracious Lady: The Life of Sara Delano Roosevelt*. New York: Appleton-Century, 1935.

Klingaman, William K. *1941*. New York: Harper & Row, 1988.

Koenig, Louis W. *The Invisible Presidency*. New York: Rinehart, 1960.

Lacey, Robert. *Ford: The Man and the Machine*. Boston: Little, Brown, 1986.

Lane, Frederick C. *Ships for Victory: A History of Shipbuilding Under the US Maritime Commission in World War II*. Baltimore: Johns Hopkins University Press, 1951.

Langer, William L., and Everett S. Gleason. *Undeclared War: 1939–1940*. New York: Harper & Row, 1952–53.

Larrabee, Eric. *Commander in Chief: Franklin Delano Roosevelt, His Lieutenants, and Their War*. New York: Harper & Row, 1987.

Lash, Joseph P. *Eleanor Roosevelt: A Friend's Memoir*. Garden City, N.Y.: Doubleday, 1964.

———. *Eleanor and Franklin: The Story of Their Relationship*. New York: Norton, 1971.

———. *Eleanor: The Years Alone*. New York: Norton, 1972.

———. *Roosevelt and Churchill, 1939–1941: The Partnership That Saved the West*. New York: Norton, 1976.

———. *Love, Eleanor: Eleanor Roosevelt and Her Friends*. Garden City, N.Y.: Doubleday, 1982.

———. *A World of Love: Eleanor Roosevelt and Her Friends, 1943–1962*. Garden City, N.Y.: Doubleday, 1984.

Lawrence, David. *Diary of a Washington Correspondent*. New York: H. C. Kinsey, 1942.

Leahy, William. *I Was There*. New York: McGraw-Hill, 1950.

Leckie, Robert. *Delivered from Evil: The Saga of World War II*. New York: Harper & Row, 1987.

Lee, Ulysses G. *The Employment of Negro Troops: US Army and World War II*. Washington, D.C.: Office of the Chief of Military History, 1966.

Leighton, Richard, and Robert Coakley. *Global Logistics and Strategy, 1940–1943.* Washington, D.C.: Office of the Chief of Military History, 1955.

Leuchtenburg, William. *Franklin D. Roosevelt and the New Deal.* New York: Harper & Row, 1963.

———. *In the Shadow of FDR: From Harry Truman to Ronald Reagan.* Ithaca, N.Y.: Cornell University Press, 1983.

Levenstein, Aaron. *Labor Today and Tomorrow.* New York: Knopf, 1945.

Lilienthal, David E. *The Journals of David E. Lilienthal.* Vol. 1, *The TVA Years.* New York: Harper & Row, 1964.

Lingeman, Richard R. *Don't You Know There's a War On? The American Home Front 1941–1945.* New York: G. P. Putnam's Sons, 1970.

Lippman, Theo, Jr. *The Squire of Warm Springs: FDR in Georgia, 1924–1945.* Chicago: Playboy Press, 1977.

Long, Breckinridge. *The War Diaries of Breckinridge Long: Selections from the Years 1939–1944.* Edited by Fred L. Israel. Lincoln, Neb.: University of Nebraska Press, 1966.

MacNeil, Neil. *Forge of Democracy: The House of Representatives.* New York: David McKay, 1963.

Manchester, William. *American Caesar: Douglas MacArthur, 1880–1964.* Boston: Little, Brown, 1978.

Marshall, George Catlett. *The Papers of George Catlett Marshall.* Vol. II, *"We Can't Delay," July 1, 1939–Dec. 6, 1941.* Edited by Larry Bland. Baltimore: Johns Hopkins University Press, 1981.

Marshall, Katherine Tupper. *Together: Annals of an Army Wife.* New York: Tupper & Love, 1946.

Martin, George. *Madame Secretary: Frances Perkins.* Boston: Houghton Mifflin, 1976.

Matloff, Maurice. *Strategic Planning for Coalition Warfare, 1943–45.* Washington, D.C.: Office of the Chief of Military History, 1959.

——— and Edwin M. Snell. *Strategic Planning for Coalition Warfare, 1941–1942.* Washington, D.C.: Office of the Chief of Military History, 1953.

McConnell, Grant. *The Modern Presidency.* New York: St. Martin's, 1976. Second Edition.

McCullough, David. *Mornings on Horseback.* New York: Simon & Schuster, 1981.

———. *Truman.* New York: Simon & Schuster, 1992.

McGuire, Philip. *Taps for a Jim Crow Army.* Santa Barbara, Calif.: ABC-Clio, 1983.

McIntire, Ross. *White House Physician.* New York: Putnam, 1946.

McJimsey, George. *Harry Hopkins: Ally of the Poor and Defender of Democracy.* Cambridge, Mass.: Harvard University Press, 1987.

McWilliams, Carey. *Brothers Under the Skin.* Boston: Little, Brown, 1943.

———. *Prejudice: Japanese Americans, Symbol of Racial Intolerance.* Boston: Little, Brown, 1944.

Menefee, Selden. *Assignment U.S.A.* New York: Reynal & Hitchcock, 1943.

Meyer, Robert, Jr. *The Stars and Stripes: Story of World War II.* New York: David McKay, 1960.

Milkman, Ruth. *The Dynamics of Gender at Work: Job Discrimination by Sex During World War II.* Chicago: University of Illinois Press, 1987.

Miller, Alice. *The Drama of the Gifted Child.* Translated by Ruth Ward. New York: Basic Books, 1981.

Moffat, Jay Pierpont. *The Moffat Papers.* Edited by Nancy H. Hooker. Cambridge, Mass.: Harvard University Press, 1956.

Moley, Raymond. *The First New Deal.* New York: Harcourt, Brace and World, 1966.

Moran, Lord. *Churchill—The Struggle for Survival, 1940–1965: Taken from the Diaries of Lord Moran.* Boston: Houghton Mifflin, 1966.

Morgan, Ted. *FDR: A Biography.* New York: Simon & Schuster, 1985.

Morison, Samuel Eliot. *The History of United States Naval Operations in World War II.* Boston: Little, Brown. Vol. II, *Operations in North African Waters, October 1942–June 1943,* 1947. Vol. IV, *Coral Sea, Midway and Submarine Action, May 1942–Aug. 1942,* 1960.

———. *The Two-Ocean War: A Short History of the United States Navy in the Second World War.* Boston: Little, Brown, 1963.

Morris, Edmund. *The Rise of Theodore Roosevelt.* New York: Coward, McCann & Geoghegan, 1979.

Morse, Arthur D. *While Six Million Died: A Chronicle of American Apathy*. Woodstock, N.Y.: Overlook Press, 1983.

Morton, H. V. *Atlantic Meeting*. New York: Dodd, Mead, 1943.

Mosch, Theodore R. *The G.I. Bill: A Breakthrough in Educational and Social Policy in the United States*. New York: Exposition Press, 1975.

Moscow, Warren. *Roosevelt and Willkie*. Englewood Cliffs, N.J.: Prentice-Hall, 1968.

Mosley, Leonard. *Marshall: A Hero for Our Times*. New York: Hearst Books, 1982.

Neal, Steve. *Dark Horse: A Biography of Wendell Willkie*. Garden City, N.Y.: Doubleday, 1984.

Nelson, Dennis D. *The Integration of the Negro into the Navy*. New York: Farrar, Straus and Young, 1951.

Nelson, Donald M. *Arsenal of Democracy*. New York: Harcourt, Brace, 1946.

Nesbitt, Victoria Henrietta. *White House Diary*. Garden City, N.Y.: Doubleday, 1948.

Neustadt, Richard E. *Presidential Power and the Modern Presidency: The Politics of Leadership from Roosevelt to Reagan*. New York: Free Press (Macmillan), 1990.

The New Yorker *Book of War Pieces, London, 1939, to Hiroshima, 1945*. New York: Schocken Books, 1947.

Nichols, Lee. *Breakthrough on the Color Front*. New York: Random House, 1954.

Okubo, Mine. *Citizen 13660*. New York: Columbia University Press, 1966.

Ottley, Roi. *New World A-Coming*. Boston: Houghton Mifflin, 1943.

Oursler, Fulton. *Behold This Dreamer!* Boston: Little, Brown, 1964.

Panter-Downes, Molly. *London War Notes, 1939–1945*. New York: Farrar, Straus & Giroux, 1971.

Parks, Lillian Rogers, with Francis Spatz Leighton. *The Roosevelts: A Family in Turmoil*. Englewood, N.J.: Fleet, 1981.

Parmet, Herbert S., and Marie B. Hecht. *Never Again: A President Runs for a Third Term—Roosevelt versus Willkie, 1940*. New York: Macmillan, 1968.

Parrish, Thomas. *Roosevelt and Marshall: Partners in Politics and War*. New York: Morrow, 1989.

Payne, Robert. *The Life and Death of Adolf Hitler*. New York: Praeger, 1973.

Perkins, Frances. *The Roosevelt I Knew*. New York: Viking, 1946.

Perrett, Geoffrey. *Days of Sadness, Years of Triumph: The American People, 1939–1945*. New York: Coward, Cabell & Geoghegan, 1973.

———. *There's a War to Be Won: The United States Army in World War II*. New York: Random House, 1991.

Phillips, Cabell. *The 1940s: Decade of Triumph and Trouble*. New York: Macmillan, 1975.

Pickergill, J. W., ed. *The Mackenzie King Record*. Vol. I, *1939–1944*. Chicago: University of Chicago Press, 1960.

Pickergill, J. W., and D. F. Foster, eds. *The Mackenzie King Record*. Vol. II, *1944–1945*. Toronto: University of Toronto Press, 1968.

Pogue, Forrest C. *George C. Marshall: Ordeal and Hope, 1939–1942*. Vol. II. New York: Viking, 1966.

Polenberg, Richard. *War and Society: The United States, 1941–1945*. Philadelphia: Lippincott, 1972.

———. *One Nation Divisible: Class, Race and Ethnicity in the US since 1938*. New York: Viking, 1980.

———, ed. *America at War: Homefront, 1941–1945*. Englewood Cliffs, N.J.: Prentice-Hall, 1968.

Pyle, Ernie. *Brave Men*. New York: Henry Holt & Co., 1944.

Reilly, Michael F. *Reilly of the White House*. New York: Simon & Schuster, 1947.

Rhodes, Richard. *The Making of the Atomic Bomb*. New York: Simon & Schuster, 1986.

Risch, Erna. *Quartermaster Corps: Organization, Supply and Service*. Vol. 1. Washington, D.C.: Office of the Chief of Military History, 1953.

Robertson, Ben. *I Saw England*. New York: Knopf, 1941.

Rogers, Donald, *Since You Went Away*. New Rochelle, N.Y.: Arlington House, 1973.

Rommel, Erwin. *The Rommel Papers*. Edited by Liddell Hart and Basil Henry. New York: Harcourt, Brace, 1953.

Roosevelt, Eleanor. *This Is My Story*. New York: Harper, 1937.

———. *My Days*. New York: Dodge Publishing Co., 1938.

———. *This I Remember.* New York: Harper & Brothers, 1949.

———. *It Seems to Me.* New York: Norton & Co., 1954.

———. *On My Own.* New York: Curtis Publishing Co., 1958.

———. *Tomorrow Is Now.* New York: Harper, 1963.

——— and Helen Ferris. *Your Teens and Mine.* Garden City, N.Y.: Doubleday, 1961.

——— and Lorena Hickok. *Ladies of Courage.* New York: Putnam, 1954.

Roosevelt, Elliott. *As He Saw It.* New York: Duell, Sloane & Pearce, 1946.

———. *A Rendezvous with Destiny: The Roosevelts of the White House.* New York: Putnam, 1975.

———. *Mrs. R: Eleanor Roosevelt's Untold Story.* New York: Putnam, 1977.

——— and James Brough. *An Untold Story: The Roosevelts of Hyde Park.* New York: Putnam, 1973.

Roosevelt, Franklin D. *FDR: His Personal Letters.* Vol. I, *The Early Years.* Edited by Elliott Roosevelt. New York: Duell, Sloane & Pearce, 1947.

———. *Public Papers and Addresses of Franklin D. Roosevelt.* Edited by Samuel I. Rosenman. 1937–1940, 4 vols. New York: Macmillan, 1941. 1941–1945, 4 vols. New York: Harper, 1950.

Roosevelt, James, with Bill Libby. *My Parents: A Differing View.* Chicago: Playboy Press, 1976.

——— and Sidney Schalett. *Affectionately, F.D.R.: A Son's Story of a Lonely Man.* New York: Harcourt, Brace, 1959.

Roosevelt, Sara Delano. *My Boy Franklin.* As told to Isabel Leighton and Gabrielle Forbush. New York: Long & Smith, 1933.

Rosenman, Samuel I. *Working with Roosevelt.* New York: Harper, 1952.

——— and Dorothy Rosenman. *Presidential Style: Some Giants and a Pygmy in the White House.* New York: Harper & Row, 1976.

Ruchames, Louis. *Race, Jobs and Politics: The FEPC.* New York: Columbia University Press, 1953.

Salmond, John. *A Southern Rebel: The Life and Times of Aubrey Willis Williams.* Chapel Hill, N.C.: University of North Carolina Press, 1983.

Scarf, Maggie. *Intimate Partners: Patterns in Love and Marriage.* New York: Ballantine Books, 1987.

Scharf, Lois. *ER: First Lady of American Liberalism.* Boston: Twayne Publishers, 1987.

Schlesinger, Arthur M., Jr. *The Age of Roosevelt.* Boston: Houghton Mifflin. Vol. I, *The Crisis of the Old Order, 1919–1933,* 1957. Vol. II, *The Coming of the New Deal,* 1958. Vol. III, *The Politics of Upheaval,* 1960.

Schultz, Duane. *The Doolittle Raid.* New York: St. Martin's, 1988.

Seale, William. *The President's House: A History.* 2 vols. Washington, D.C.: National Geographic Society, 1986.

———. *The White House: The History of an American Idea.* Washington, D.C.: The American Institute of Architects Press, 1992.

Seidman, Joel. *American Labor: From Defense to Reconversion.* Chicago: University of Chicago Press, 1953.

Sherry, Michael. *The Rise of American Air Power: The Creation of Armageddon.* New Haven, Conn.: Yale University Press, 1987.

Sherwood, Robert E. *Roosevelt and Hopkins: An Intimate History.* New York: Harper, 1948.

Shirer, William L. *The Rise and Fall of the Third Reich: A History of Nazi Germany.* New York: Touchstone, 1981.

Shogan, Robert, and Tom Craig. *The Detroit Race Riots.* Philadelphia: Chilton Books, 1964.

Shoumatoff, Elizabeth. *FDR's Unfinished Portrait.* Pittsburgh, Pa.: University of Pittsburgh Press, 1990.

Sitkoff, Harvard. *A New Deal for Blacks: The Emergence of Civil Rights as a National Issue.* New York: Oxford University Press, 1978.

———, ed. *Fifty Years Later: The New Deal Evaluated.* New York: Oxford University Press, 1978.

Skrjabina, Elena. *Siege and Survival: The Odyssey of a Leningrader.* Carbondale, Ill.: Southern Illinois University Press, 1971.

Smith, A Merriman. *Thank You, Mr. President: A White House Notebook.* New York: Harper, 1946.

Smith, R. Elberton. *The Army and Economic Mobilization*. Washington, D.C.: Center for Military History, 1959.

Sorenson, Charles, and William Samuelson. *My Forty Years with Ford*. New York: Norton, 1956.

Speer, Albert. *Inside the Third Reich: Memoirs*. New York: Macmillan, 1970.

Steeholm, Clara, and Hardy Steeholm. *The House at Hyde Park*. New York: Viking, 1950.

Steinberg, Alfred. *Mrs. R*. New York: Putnam, 1958.

——. *Sam Rayburn: A Biography*. New York: Hawthorn Books, 1975.

Steinfels, Margaret O'Brien. *Who's Minding the Children? The History and Politics of Day Care in America*. New York: Simon & Schuster, 1973.

Stettinius, Edward R. *Lend-Lease: Weapon for Victory*. New York: Macmillan, 1944.

——. *Roosevelt and the Russians: The Yalta Conference*. Garden City, N.Y.: Doubleday, 1949.

——. *The Diaries of Edward R. Stettinius Jr., 1943–1946*. Edited by Thomas M. Campell and George C. Herring. New York: New Viewpoints, 1975.

Stone, I. F. *Business as Usual: The First Year of Defense*. New York: Modern Age, 1941.

——. *The War Years, 1939–1945*. Boston: Little, Brown, 1988.

Swafford, Rosa L. *Wartime Record of Strikes and Lockouts, 1940–1945*. Washington, D.C.: U.S. Department of Labor, 1946.

Tapert, Annette, ed. *Lines of Battle: Letters from American Servicemen, 1941–1945*. New York: Pocket Books, 1987.

Teague, Michael. *Mrs. L: Conversations with Alice Roosevelt Longworth*. Garden City, N.Y.: Doubleday, 1981.

Thompson, W. H. *Assignment: Churchill*. New York: Farrar, Straus & Young, 1955.

Thomson, Harry, and Lidas Mayo. *The Ordnance Department: Procurement and Supply*. Washington, D.C.: Office of the Chief of Military History, 1960.

Tugwell, Rexford G. *The Democratic Roosevelt: A Biography of Franklin D. Roosevelt*. Garden City, N.Y.: Doubleday, 1957.

Tully, Grace. *F.D.R., My Boss*. New York: Charles Scribner's Sons, 1949.

Vatter, Harold G. *The U.S. Economy in World War II*. New York: Columbia University Press, 1985.

Walker, Turnley. *Roosevelt and the Warm Springs Story*. New York: Wyn, 1953.

Wallace, Henry A. *The Price of Vision: The Diary of Henry A. Wallace, 1942–1946*. Edited by John Morton Blum. Boston: Houghton Mifflin, 1973.

Wallin, Vice Admiral Homer N. *Pearl Harbor—Why, How: Fleet Salvage and Final Appraisal*. Washington, D.C.: Naval History Division, 1968.

Ward, Geoffrey C. *Before the Trumpet: Young Franklin Roosevelt, 1882–1905*. New York: Perennial Library, 1986.

——. *A First-Class Temperament: The Emergence of Franklin Roosevelt*. New York, Harper & Row, 1989.

Watkins, T. H. *Righteous Pilgrim: The Life and Times of Harold L. Ickes, 1874–1952*. New York: Henry Holt, 1990.

Watson, Mark S. *Chief of Staff: Prewar Plans and Preparations*. Washington, D.C.: Office of the Chief of Military History, 1950.

Weiss, Nancy J. *Farewell to the Party of Lincoln: Black Politics in the Age of FDR*. Princeton, N.J.: Princeton University Press, 1983.

Welles, Sumner. *The Time for Decision*. New York: Harper, 1944.

West, J. B., with Mary Lynn Kotz. *Upstairs at the White House: My Life with the First Ladies*. New York: Coward, McCann & Geoghegan, 1973.

White, Gerald. *Billions for Defense: Government Financing by the Defense Plant Corporation During World War II*. University, Ala.: University of Alabama Press, 1980.

White, Walter. *A Man Called White*. New York: Viking, 1948.

Wilkins, Roy. *Standing Fast: The Autobiography of Roy Wilkins*. New York: Viking, 1982.

Wills, Garry. *Certain Trumpets: The Call of Leaders*. New York: Simon & Schuster, 1994.

Wilson, Theodore. *The First Summit: Roosevelt and Churchill at Placentia Bay, 1941*. Boston: Houghton Mifflin, 1969.

Winfield, Betty Houchin. *FDR and the News Media*. Chicago: University of Illinois Press, 1990.

Wyden, Peter. *Day One: Before Hiroshima and After*. New York: Simon & Schuster, 1984.

Wyman, David S. *The Abandonment of the Jews: America and the Holocaust, 1941–1945*. New York: Pantheon, 1984.

——. *Paper Walls: America and the Refugee Crisis, 1938–1941*. New York: Pantheon, 1985.

Youngs, J. William T. *Eleanor Roosevelt: A Personal and Public Life*. Boston: Little, Brown, 1985.

Ziegler, Robert H. *American Workers, American Unions, 1920–1985*. Baltimore: Johns Hopkins University Press, 1986.

ACKNOWLEDGMENTS

This book would not have been possible without the research help of Linda Vandegrift, my friend and colleague, who labored with me every day from the very start of the project six years ago. Her diligence in digging through archives, her love of detail, and her passion for the subject accompanied me every step along the way. This book is, in many ways, her creation as well as mine.

I wish to acknowledge at the outset my debt to the extraordinary circle of Roosevelt scholars whose histories and biographies educated and inspired me. Their books, listed in the bibliography and acknowledged in my endnotes, provided a foundation for this study. At the Franklin D. Roosevelt Library in Hyde Park, New York, where so much of my research was done, I owe a special thanks to the former director, Dr. William Emerson. His enthusiasm for the idea of studying Roosevelt's leadership of the home front was decisive for me in the early, unfocused months, and as the years went by, he became a mentor and friend, always willing to share so generously his vast knowledge and experience. I am grateful to the entire staff of the Roosevelt library, including its present director, my friend, Verne Newton, Ray Teichman, Bob Parks, Mark Renovitch, Paul McLaughlin, John Ferris, Nancy Snedeker, and Karen Burtis.

I am also grateful to the scores of people I interviewed over the years who gave of their time and their memories without asking anything in return. Several members of the Roosevelt family were especially helpful, including James and Elliott Roosevelt, who are no longer alive, Eleanor Seagraves, and Curtis Roosevelt. Particular thanks to Trude Lash, Henry Morgenthau, Robert Hopkins, Eleanor Seagraves, and Harold Ickes for permission to quote from various letters and papers. Grateful acknowledgement is also made to the University of Southern California for permission to publish excerpts of oral histories of Dan Condren, Frankie Cooper, Shirley Hackett, Dellie Hahn, Sybil Lewis, Larry Mantrell, and Inez Sauer. The University of Southern California retains exclusive ownership of all copyrights to the interviews. I am also grateful to Columbia University for permission to quote from the oral histories of Frances Perkins and Samuel Rosenman and to Yale University for permission to quote from Henry Stimson's Papers. I want to thank Jeanine Derr for conducting research in the National Archives in Washington, Andrew Blankstein for searching through old newspapers at the Library of Congress, and Lulie Haddad for researching the oral histories at Columbia University.

A number of friends and colleagues sustained me in various ways over the long course of this book, including Alfred Checchi, Phyllis Grann, Arnold Hiatt, Michael Rothschild, and Janna Malamud Smith. And I owe a special debt to my agent, Sterling Lord, who was there when I needed him, as he has always been.

At Simon and Schuster, I owe thanks to Lydia Buechler, Terry Zaroff, Frank and Eve Metz, Victoria Meyer, and Elizabeth Stein. In the course of the last six months, as all the pieces of the book were being put together, I relied on Liz Stein for so many things, talking to her nearly every day, that I can hardly imagine doing a book without her warmth, humor, and support. From beginning to end, I was fortunate once again to have Alice Mayhew as my editor. At every stage of the writing, I benefited greatly from her critical intelligence and her broad, penetrating knowledge. She seems to understand intuitively when to leave a writer alone and when to intervene, when to offer criticism and when to simply encourage. She is, as every one of her authors knows, the best there is.

My husband, Richard Goodwin, has been at my side through all my writing life. This book would not be what it is without him. He shared in the shaping of the story, helped me to articulate the larger themes and spent weeks of his time editing the final manuscript. He is my best friend and my most loving and constructive critic.

INDEX

PHOTO CREDITS

Doris Kearns Goodwin is the author of the critically acclaimed and bestselling *Team of Rivals: The Political Genius of Abraham Lincoln*, in part the basis for Steven Spielberg's major motion picture, *Lincoln*. She was awarded the Pulitzer Prize in history for *No Ordinary Time: Franklin & Eleanor Roosevelt: The Home Front in World War II* and is also the author of the bestsellers *Wait Till Next Year*, *The Fitzgeralds and the Kennedys*, and *Lyndon Johnson and the American Dream*. She lives in Concord, Massachusetts, with her husband, Richard N. Goodwin.

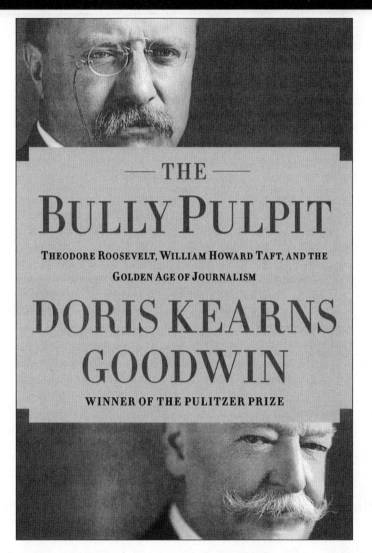

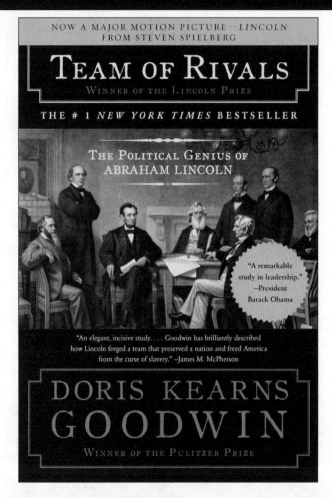